The Southern Textile Basketball Tournament

The Southern Textile Basketball Tournament

A History, 1921–1997

by
Mac C. Kirkpatrick *and*
Thomas K. Perry

McFarland & Company, Inc., Publishers
Jefferson, North Carolina, and London

The present work is a reprint of the illustrated case bound edition of The Southern Textile Basketball Tournament: A History, 1921–1997, *first published in 1997 by McFarland.*

LIBRARY OF CONGRESS CATALOGUING-IN-PUBLICATION DATA

Kirkpatrick, Mac C., 1960–
    The Southern Textile Basketball Tournament : a history, 1921–1997 / by Mac C. Kirkpatrick and Thomas K. Perry.
       p.   cm.
    Includes bibliographical references and index.

    ISBN 0-7864-2446-X (softcover : 50# alkaline paper) ∞

    1. Southern Textile Basketball Tournament — History.
2. Southern Textile Basketball Tournament — Registers.
3. Basketball — Tournaments — South Carolina — History.
I. Perry, Thomas K., 1952–   . II. Title.
GV885.49.S58K57   2005
796.323'63'0975727 — dc21
                                                97-24656

British Library cataloguing data are available

©1997 Mac C. Kirkpatrick and Thomas K. Perry. All rights reserved

No part of this book, specifically including the index, may be reproduced or transmitted in any form or by any means, electronic or mechanical, including photocopying or recording, or by any information storage and retrieval system, without permission in writing from the publisher.

On the cover: (clockwise from top) Winnsboro Mill (Winnsboro, South Carolina) vs. Ware Shoals Mill (Ware Shoals, South Carolina), late 1940s (*courtesy Sheryl Gaddy*); 1957 Southern Textile Basketball Tournament program cover (*courtesy STAA*); Early 1950s action involving Winnsboro Mill (Winnsboro, South Carolina) team (*courtesy Sheryl Gaddy*); 1961 Southern Textile Basketball Tournament program cover (*courtesy STAA*).

Manufactured in the United States of America

McFarland & Company, Inc., Publishers
  Box 611, Jefferson, North Carolina 28640
    www.mcfarlandpub.com

To the exceptional men and women who made
the Southern Textile Basketball Tournament
an event of class, character, and dignity

Acknowledgments

When such a project as this one draws to a close, there is an odd mixture of euphoria and emptiness. For two years, microfilm, tournament programs, phone calls, and interviews were our constant companions, and from them emerged this story of the Southern Textile Basketball Tournament. It comprises a portion of that unique cotton mill heritage of South Carolina, though in later years the STBT grew far beyond the courts of the local mill villages.

Friends gave unselfishly of their time and technical support. Don Roper, Ted Pittman, and Warren Rollins shared their vast expertise of tournament history. Bill Cunningham could always help navigate the most maddening of computer glitches, and listened patiently as countless ideas were discussed, reshaped, and either found their way into the book or were tossed aside. Jesse Scott, professor of history at Newberry College, guided students Jason Stansel and Heath Taylor in an independent study which furthered this research.

To the folks who wrote letters, talked with us on the phone, and agreed to interviews: Thank you for sharing the memories. Those special moments are the foundations of this endeavor.

Most of all, Wanda Amick (Mac's special lady) and Donna Perry (Tom's wife) were proofreaders extraordinaire who helped to keep everything in perspective during the difficult times. Your patience and encouragement made it all possible, and your love made it worthwhile. And to Meghan (Tom's daughter): Daddy can go ride bikes now.

Mac C. Kirkpatrick
Thomas K. Perry
Spring 1997

Table of Contents

Acknowledgments vii
Preface 1

The 1920s 3
The 1930s 14
The 1940s 22
The 1950s 32
The 1960s 48
The 1970s 68
The 1980s 82
The 1990s 92

Endnotes 99
Appendices
1   Southern Textile Basketball Tournament Rosters 103
2   All Southern (All Tournament) Selections 345
3   War-Time Tournament Rosters 370
4   War-Time All Tournament Selections 373
5   Southern Textile Athletic Association Hall of Fame 374
6   Southern Textile Basketball Tournament Timeline 377
7   Player Profiles 385
Bibliography 405
Index 407

Preface

If textile league baseball research constituted a treasure hunt, then gathering information on the Southern Textile Basketball Tournament can be likened to exploring a vast natural resource. The tournament is, of course, still in operation, though it has long pursued a more egalitarian course than pure mill hill hoops.

It started with Dr. L.P. Hollis' trip to Springfield, Massachusetts, where he met the inventor of the game, Dr. James Naismith. The face of sports in the South would be forever changed. This new game, with its quirky rules and funny uniforms, became much more than a midwinter preparation for baseball. It was taken to heart by the mill village people, who cheered for, fought for, and swore loyalty to their heroes of the hardwood.

The Southern Textile Basketball Tournament found a permanent home in Greenville, the self-proclaimed "Textile Capital of the World," and each generation of players produced memorable achievements. Paul "Smokey" Barbare, Lucille Foster Thomas and Bert Hill starred in the early years. Then came Earl Wooten, Ward Williams, Ellerbe "Big Daddy" Neal, and Eckie Jordan. Sue Vickers, Billy Cunningham, Pete Maravich, Doug Moe, Mickey Davis and Henry Logan added luster in the '50s and '60s. Tree Rollins, Larry Nance, Dwight Durante, and Mel and Al Daniel continued to adorn the heritage. There was an orderly succession rather than a usurping of the spotlight. Instead of jealousy and comparisons, there was a knowledge by the players that they had shared in something remarkable. The appendices of this book, created from tournament programs and Greenville *News* microfilm, are dedicated to all who played in this "Greatest Basketball Show on Earth."

This is not to say the tournament skirted its share of rough times. Dwindling crowds have long been a problem, and there have been years when teams showed little interest in participating. With the passing of time, even Greenville has shown a reluctance to acknowledge its textile roots, choosing to disavow the mill hill heritage as it moved forward and became a truly international city.

So where do we go from here? The old tournament has moved from Textile Hall to Memorial Auditorium, and now resides at Eastside High School. But renewed emphasis on youth teams hearkens back to the idea of L.P. Hollis and the other founding fathers, who believed that such a gathering should foster goodwill, teamwork, and achievement. Continuation of the industrial competition offers a certain pride of ownership when new divisional champions are crowned each year.

What began as "linthead" recreation grew and was embraced by thousands of players, coaches and fans who, throughout the years, created their own special memories. For each of you, we hope this book evokes the very best of those times.

The 1920s

The good doctor's game was *the* topic of conversation on the campus of Springfield (Mass.) College that autumn in 1905. Created as an indoor sport to bridge the cold winter months between football and baseball, Dr. James A. Naismith's brainchild was a wonderful mixture of sprints, jumps and endurance. His *Original Rules of Play* had come forth on January 15, 1892, to govern this new game, basketball.

1. The ball may be thrown in any direction with one or both hands.
2. The ball may be batted in any direction with one or both hands (never with the fist).
3. A player cannot run with the ball. The player must throw it from the spot on which he catches it, allowance to be made for a man who catches the ball when running at a good speed if he tries to stop.
4. The ball must be held in or between the hands. The arms or body must not be used for holding it.
5. No shouldering, holding, pushing, tripping, or striking in any way the person of an opponent shall be allowed: the first infringement of this rule by any player should count as a foul: the second shall disqualify him until the next goal is made, or, if there was evidence to injure the person, for the whole game, no substitutes allowed.
6. A foul is striking at the ball with the fist, violation of Rule Four, Five, and such as decided in Rule Six.
7. If either side makes three consecutive fouls, it shall count a goal for the opponents (consecutive means without the opponents in the meantime making a foul).
8. A goal shall be made when the ball is thrown or batted from the grounds into the basket and stays there, providing those defending the goal do not touch or disturb the goal. If the ball rests on the edge and the opponent moves the basket, it shall count as a goal.
9. When the ball goes out of bounds, it shall be thrown onto the field of play by the person first touching it. In case of a dispute, the umpire shall throw it straight onto the field. The thrower-in is allowed five seconds; if he holds it any longer, it shall go to the opponent. If any side persists in delaying the game, the umpire shall call a foul on that side.
10. The umpire shall be judge of the men and shall note the fouls and notify the referee when three consecutive fouls have been made. He shall have the power to disqualify men according to Rule Six.
11. The referee shall be judge of the ball and shall decide when the ball is in play, in bounds, to which side it belongs, and shall keep time. He shall decide when a goal has been made, and keep account of the goals with any other duties that are usually performed by a referee.
12. The time shall be two fifteen minute

halves, with five minutes' rest in between.

13. The side making the most goals in that time shall be declared the winner. In the case of a draw, the game may, by argument of the captains, be continued until another goal is made.[1]

In the ensuing 13 years, those original rules had been changed and reshaped to accommodate an ever accelerating pace in a game growing in both acceptance and appeal.

On campus that autumn was a recent graduate of the University of South Carolina. Lawrence Peter Hollis, upon completing his studies, had gone to Monaghan Mill in Greenville, South Carolina, to become secretary of the YMCA. Mill management, however, deemed him too young to begin such a job, and packed him off to Springfield for extra course work. His presence there forever changed the face of athletics in the South.

"I listened to Dr. Naismith, bought his book and read it, stopped in New York on my way home and purchased a basketball, and carried my prize possessions back to Greenville," said Hollis.[2] Basketball had come to Dixieland, and Monaghan organized the area's first team. Some of their games may have been played in the old P & N Warehouse, but soon the mill management authorized the construction of a gymnasium. The coach was Dr. Steele, a philosophy professor and basketball coach at Furman University who offered his services on the condition that the college be able to use the court. The arrangement was met with acceptance by both parties.[3]

Dr. Hollis remembered that those first games were between the Greens and Golds. "We got some cotton cloth and made green uniforms for one team and gold for the other. Osborn Hunnicutt was the leader of the Greens, and Doc Cobb was captain of the Golds."[4]

This indoor game was greeted with enthusiasm by the athletes of the mill village, and it was a welcomed lead-in to the ever popular baseball season. Walt Barbare, former shortstop with the Pittsburgh Pirates who played and coached in the Southern Textile Basketball Tournament, remembered how nonstandardized the game could be. "We went over to Anderson and the goals had been put on poles much higher than the regulation ten feet. They had the only goal of the game."[5]

John L. Harrison, coach at Woodside Mill (Greenville), remembered those early years, filled with adventure when a road trip had to be undertaken.

"I'll never forget a trip we made to New Holland Mill in Gainesville, Georgia. It's about a hundred and ten miles, and we left here about ten A.M. in an old seven passenger Chandler automobile. Back then, we didn't have any modern roads, and those old red clay roads in Georgia were really something. We wore out two sets of tire chains, one coming and one going! We made it to Lula, about 20 miles from Gainesville, and that was when we really hit the mud. Took us about four hours to make it into Gainesville from there, and it was seven P.M. The game started an hour later, and everyone was worn down from pushing and lifting that old Chandler car. The worst part of all, though, was that we lost the game."[6]

One of Harrison's players, Martin "Cat" Henson, talked of a trip in a northerly direction to play the Charlotte (N.C.) YMCA team, a contest filled with trials and tribulations of its own.

"In the first half we stayed right with them and made a real game of it. But when we came out for the second half, we could not stand up. The floor was so slippery, but for some reason the Charlotte team didn't have any trouble at all, and we couldn't figure out what had happened. We suspected they put what we called 'slick-um' on the floor, but no matter what we tried, whether resin or gasoline on the bottoms of our shoes, it didn't keep us from falling every time we went to make a move. We lost that one, too."[7]

Sometimes when the visiting teams came calling, they did so only when a guaranteed amount of money was settled upon.

Woodside had challenged a Spartanburg team to a game, but a $100 guarantee was a sticking point in negotiations. Coach Harrison was able to get the price to $60, yet he still had to pay the $75 rental fee for Textile Hall—a lot of money in the early years of the 20th century. "We sold shares to the workers at the mill, lost the game, and came out two dollars in the hole after we paid our bills for the evening," he remembered.[8]

For all the out-of-town adventures, though, it was the head-to-head competition among the Greenville mill teams which fostered the most excitement. "Cat" Henson recalled one of those heated battles with crosstown rival Monaghan.

"We were playing over there one night, and one of their boys was tripped accidentally. We were told by the referee it had better not happen again. Later, one of us was pushed or fell into one of their players, and things got kind of rough for awhile. It was bad enough that after the game the ref locked himself in the athletic office and didn't come out until everyone had left!"[9]

With such competition, both local and out-of-state, drawing more and more interest from the rabid fans at the respective mill villages, it was only a matter of time before a way would be found to declare a real champion in this new sport of basketball. And 1921 seemed as good a year as any to start.

The first meeting to form the Southern Textile Basketball Tournament was attended by Dr. L.P. Hollis, W.M. Grier, G.L. Doggett, H.R. McCartney (all living in or around Greenville), W.V. Martin and F.R. Corwin (from Spartanburg), and J.L. Gourley (from Greer). Their mission was simple: to fulfill the need for a wholesome sporting event, and to develop the competitive talents and capabilities of young athletes in the mill communities.[10] There was a framed motto hanging in Dr. Hollis' office concisely stating this aim:

> No printed page, no spoken plea,
> May teach young hearts what men should be.
> Not all the books on all the shelves,
> But what the Teachers are themselves.[11]

On February 25, 1921, the teams gathered at old Textile Hall on West Washington Street. The building was designed for trade shows, certainly *not* for basketball, since the undersized court was on the building's second floor. Streetcars ran in front, and Franklin, Chandler, Maxwell, Paige and Hupmobile autos lined the streets. It was a great day, and the games began in earnest. "It wasn't that everyone deliberately got rough; we just played for keeps on every play. There wasn't any soft job or easy money to be handed out then. We played for the love of the game," said "Cat" Henson.[12]

Piedmont's G.L. Doggett remembered buying a touring car, and assigning his son Carlisle the task of driving the team back and forth to Greenville. Liz Morman of Monaghan Mill scored the historical first field goal in the Southern Textile Basketball Tournament against Schoolfield Mill.[13]

Friday night's banquet was given extensive coverage in the February 26, 1921, edition of the Greenville *News*. Tournament president W.V. Martin voiced his desire that such an association would forever eliminate from textile sports the elements of professionalism, and urged all teams to pledge never to pay another player. (Textile league baseball regularly employed the practice of paying players for their particular skills, a tradition that would never be totally absent from its younger sister.)

W.M. Grier, toastmaster for the occasion, read to the audience congratulatory messages received through a local "radio station" made possible by the technical wizardry of Robert S. Huntington. The first was signed by Warren G. Harding, president of the United States. Other speeches followed, in *quick* succession, by W.D. Gordon, G.N. Douglas, Milton G. Smith, A.H. Cottingham, Marjorie Potwin and F.R. Corwin. All excelled in economy of language since they were limited to 90 seconds each, a rule steadfastly enforced by Moss Penn (secretary of the Junior Chamber of Commerce), dressed as a traffic cop complete with whistle and a stop-go sign. The

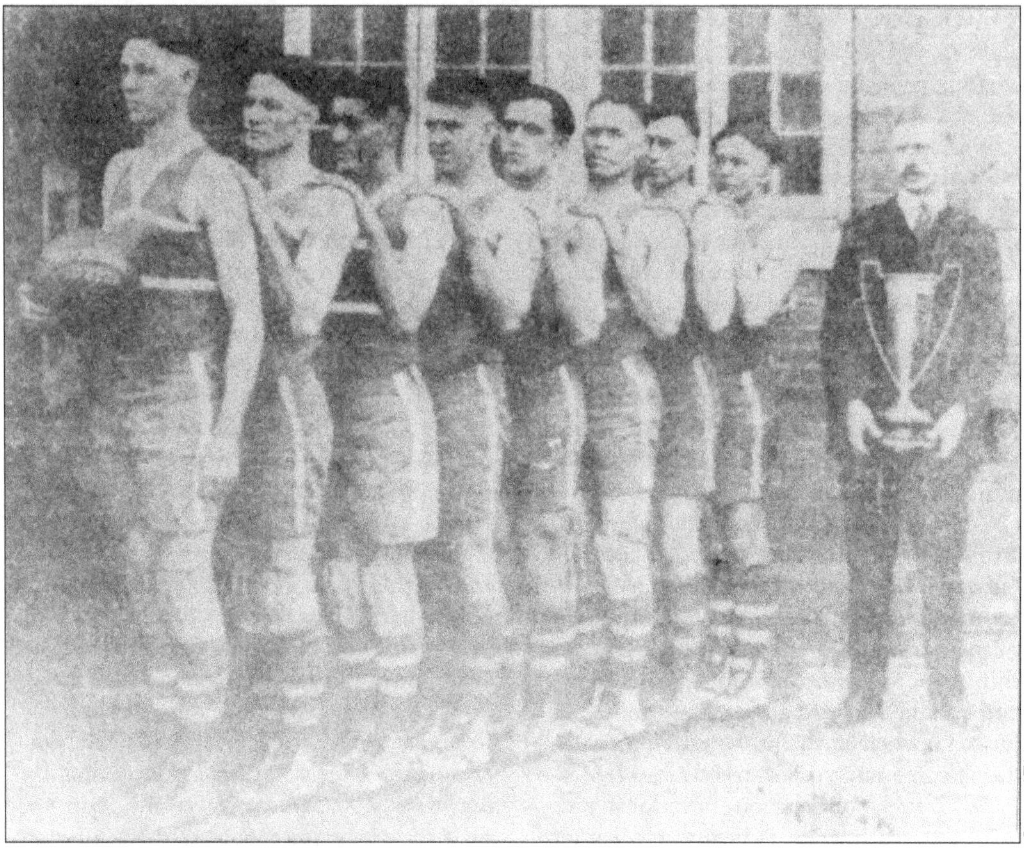

Courtesy STAA

Courtesy STAA

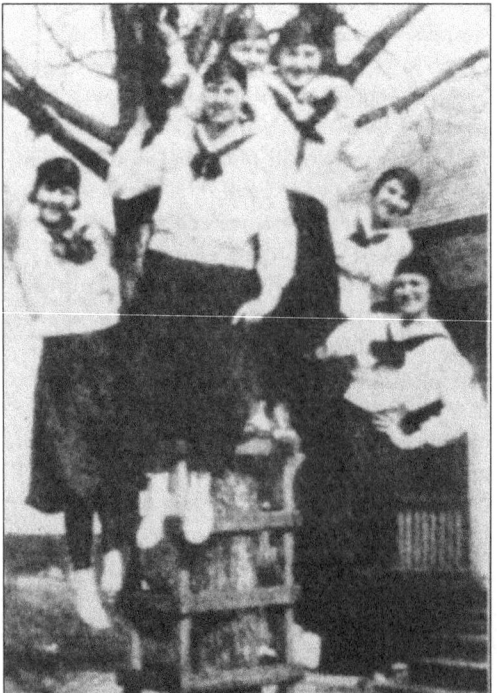

Above: **1921 Woodside Mill (Greenville, S.C.), Class A men's champions: (*l–r*) Winnie Hinson, Martin Hinson, Luther Durham, Jess Buchanan, Andy Baker, Herman Porter, Bill Porter, Walter Greer, and Walter McAbee (coach).**
Left: **1921 Monaghan Mill (Greenville, S.C.), Class A women's champions: (*l–r*) Essie Nolan, Lois Hudgens, Carolyn Barton, Minnie Heath, Inez Reid, and Fannie Center.**

common theme of the evening was to encourage both the highest levels of clean sportsmanship for all textile mill villages and to promote fellowship among all the teams. Particularly lauded that evening were members of the team from Judson Mill, who earlier that day agreed to defer a game's scheduled starting time when they could have demanded a forfeit. Finally, Professor Hugh T. Shockley, a referee from Spartanburg, South Carolina, praised all teams for their conduct that day, and urged them never to stoop to lesser ethical behavior.

A later tournament program (1937) reported that the Class B lads from Greer won their first game 72–10, though no opponent was listed. In their next game against Apalache Mill, they were leading 15–11 with nine minutes left when their last substitute fouled out and four players were left to finish. Apalache won 21–20 as Peck Leatherwood scored 17 points on free throws, invoking the rule that allowed one player to take all foul shots for the team.

Morning and afternoon games were held on "Championship Saturday," punctuated by quite a spectacle. A parade of players, led by Grand Marshall Holmes B. Springs, wound its way from Textile Hall, down to the post office, and back to the Ottaray Hotel. As the final games came to a close, it was truly a hometown celebration: Woodside defeated Schoolfield 26–15 for the Class A men's championship, the Monaghan Scouts defeated Apalache 22–16 for the Class B men's crown, and the Monaghan A team defeated that mill's B team 47–15 for the women's title. "The idea," recounted Dr. Hollis, "was to have our own textile teams in a tournament the same as the colleges were doing."[14] It was quite a beginning.

"Scoop" Latimer, sports editor of the Greenville *News*, was fond of saying that "the best basketball of all is played in Textile Hall." Superb players began to grace the side-by-side courts in the venerable structure, etching their moments of glory in the foundation of the tournament. Woodside's Martin "Cat" Henson and his coach, John L. Harrison, Monaghan's Walt Barbare and Lucille Foster Thomas, Greer Mill's Jimmy Green, and Victor Mill's Fred "Footsie" Hooper were pioneers in the early development of the game.

There were more teams for the 1922 edition, enough that the tournament moved its opening round to Thursday, though gate receipts were not enough to defray expenses. A deficit of $351 was incurred. A special Pullman car brought 47 players and many more fans from Schoolfield Mill to their accommodations at the Hotel Imperial, and they even had designated "song and

1922 Monaghan Mill (Greenville, S.C.), Class A women's champions: (*sitting, l–r*) Geneva Henderson, Tyler Barton, Oveida Henderson; (*standing, l–r*) Beatrice Sheppard, Buna Glasco, Essie Nolan, and Teen Smoak (coach).

cheer leaders": Daisy Smith for the women and George M. Douglas for the men.[15]

Interestingly, during the opening round, Furman and The Citadel played while the tournament teams were dining. And certainly the textile athletes earned their meal. Woodside Mill defeated Schoolfield 39–36 in the Class B men's division, outlasting the Virginia lads in triple overtime (each extra period was five minutes). However, it was the initial women's game that astounded fans and produced the most lopsided score in Southern Textile Basketball Tournament history, as Monaghan defeated Apalache 98–2. The score at half was 64–0. Oveida Henderson had 50 points and Minnie Heath 48 to account for the winner's total, and McCarter scored the loser's only basket with less than two minutes to play. They followed up the Apalache Massacre by blowing away the Schoolfield women 62–13 to claim their second straight championship. The Monaghan women's teams would go on to dominate early tournament play, winning titles in 1921–1923, 1925, 1929 and 1931.

When Pacific Mill of Columbia, South Carolina, made it to the Class A men's final (eventually beating Schoolfield 30–21 for the title), General Superintendent W.P. Hamrick wired the team that all overseers and employees who owned autos would load them up with rooters and drive to Greenville for the championship game. They got to see their boys take home the trophy, a full-sized basketball of polished metal, and establish themselves as a juggernaut which swept to Class A titles in 1922, 1924, and 1925.

There were enough entries in 1923 to generate gate receipts sufficient to pay all expenses and liquidate at least a portion of the debt. And to complement the basketball games, both a volleyball tournament (won by Schoolfield) and a checker competition (W.V. Winck of Piedmont took home the silver cup) were added.

What did fans behold in Textile Hall during tournament time? For the first time a cafeteria was operated and meals could be obtained at any hour, a sure advantage to going outside in the cold to rustle up something to eat. They could join in rousing songs containing the name of their favorite clubs, and since bands representing the local mills held center stage during intermissions, there was never a shortage of music. Several hundred people always gathered tightly about the ropes that cordoned off the courts, urging their favorites on.

And of course, there was always one more good basketball story someone had to share. Walt Barbare held court and described a game with a good City View team from Greenville that journeyed up the road to Travelers Rest for a game. The locals surprised the City View lads, who had been overconfident and started its second team, and it was a close game to the wire.

"The scorekeeper, a Travelers Rest fan, did not use a scorebook, but took a knife and whittled a notch in a stick each time a team scored. The game ended eighteen to seventeen in City View's favor, but the whittling scorer pointed to a Travelers Rest player and said, 'That man right there shot a goal and I forgot to give him a notch.' So he cut another one, and the home team was declared a nineteen to eighteen winner." [16]

The following year a free throw contest was added in place of the volleyball and checkers. Bunting (from New Holland Mill) and Nettie Forrest (from Judson Mill) won the men's and women's competition, respectively, each winning a medal.

"Bunting was really something," remarked Jess Buchanan, a veteran of Woodside's 1921 Class A men's champions. "He was tough to handle, and was the first showman ever to come through here. He was the first player I can remember using the one-hand push shot, he could dribble with either hand, and he could pass the ball behind his back. I later heard he was from the University of Alabama." [17]

There were rumblings of poor attendance (local residents were chastised by visitors for taking so little interest in the festivities), enough for the Pacific Mill team of Columbia (S.C.) to bid to host the tournament by offering use of *two* gymnasiums and a $450 bonus. Charlotte (N.C.) also extended a bid. That same Pacific team claimed its second Class A men's championship, a 25–24 win over Woodside Mill before 4,000 fans, including 200 faithful followers brought to the game by a special train.

The first Class A men's All-Southern team was selected in 1924, and those honored were Walter Henson (Woodside Mill), Hubert Nolin (Monaghan Mill), Bunting (New Holland Mill), Arthur Bedenbaugh (Pacific Mill), and Jim Oeland (Converse Mill). Women were not to be recognized as All-Southern performers for another four years.

And the gentlemen of the press were always available to give their views on the events, as did this nameless writer: "Throngs came and went to Textile Hall yesterday, while myriads of athletes besported themselves in the first day's play of the fourth annual Southern Textile Basketball Tournament. As each game was played new stars came from among the many to shine brilliantly before the admiring fans. Some of those in the throngs, who sat and watched the ball pass hither and yon with incredible swiftness, were cheering their favorites. To some it must have been a pang of sorrow to see their teams go down in defeat, while some on the other side cheered lustily for their team to go up one more step toward the coveted reward that will be settled in the form of a championship." [18] It may have been unclear who won, but the words did sound impressive.

As the Southern Textile Basketball Tournament continued to gain prestige, its comparison to college basketball followed naturally. "Scoop" Latimer explored this in one of his columns. "The colleges of the country have long appreciated the fact that a winning team in any line of athletics is not only a good advertisement for the institution, but it is a most laudable way in which college loyalty may be created. Does not this apply as well to industrial plants which seek to make their employees feel pride in their work? Petty personal prejudice is overcome, differences are set aside in the support of the team, and all are enthusiastic in the outcome of the games and the interest of their teams." [19]

With 56 teams in 1925, it became necessary to use facilities other than Textile Hall to manage the schedule, so the Parker High School gymnasium sported some Thursday and Friday action. The women's games that year boasted lopsided scores, like Highland Park's 71–11 win over Woodside Mill, and Monaghan's win over Lonsdale Mill (Seneca, S.C.), 53–6. Monaghan's 29–27 win over Highland Park in the semifinals, thanks to C.V. Henderson's last-second shot, proved to be the most exciting portion of the competition. Three thousand fans crowded the Hall to see Pacific Mill of Columbia capture its third Class A men's championship in four years, a 41–25 walk over Judson.

There was still a huge push to steer away from professionalism in the game. Southern Textile Athletic Association president W.M. Grier cited the problem with textile league baseball's practice of paying players. "The boys for whom the sport was begun and who were to receive the benefit were put on the bench, and men who did not work in the mill but loafed much of the week did the playing on Saturday and received good money for it.... Those who conceived the idea of this tournament thought it would be best to start athletics on a purely amateur basis." [20] Saxon Mill president John A. Law echoed Grier's sentiments, noting that the real value of athletics was in the development of community spirit and in the training of community leaders. The more athletics remained strictly amateur, the greater the benefit to the community. [21] Taking both men at their word, officers of the Southern Textile Athletic Association (the governing body of the tournament) voted during its annual meeting to regulate "paid" amateurs, ruling ineligible players who received money for their athletic abilities the previous three years.

In these growing years of the tournament, there would be conflict over this

1921 Piedmont Mill (Piedmont, S.C.) team.

point of professionalism, and no one had to wait very long for it to surface. The eligibility of Paul Barbare of Lyman Mill's Class A men's team was revoked in 1926, but he was reinstated upon submission of affidavits from Pelzer Mill that said he had not received pay for playing baseball there in 1923. Dunean Mill's Dave Sanders lost, then regained, his Class A eligibility after proving he indeed had been on the mill payroll the required three months. In the semifinals against Apalache Mill, Sanders scored 20 points to lead his team to a 38–31 win, so his presence was not insignificant.

Blood also boiled as one defending champion, evidently due to disqualified or ineligible players, was not permitted to compete. There was a major protest made by A.J. Wallace, on behalf of the Pacific Mill Class A men's team, in a letter to Southern Textile Athletic Association president L.P. Hollis.

"We note through the Greenville press that many players who were ruled ineligible have been reinstated and are participating in the games. We are further advised that all restrictions were today lifted and all players who were previously disqualified are permitted to play. We presume that since our exclusion the rules were modified so that these players might participate. This, of course, only aggravated our belief that Pacific was greatly discriminated against which ultimately resulted in absolute exclusion. Since the Pacific team was not permitted the privilege of participating in the tournament, we of course are prompted to contest the title which the Association will confer upon the winner, to wit: Southern Textile Champion. We do this as we feel that the tournament this year is not representative sufficiently to cover the field. We will not concede a championship until we have been defeated and put out of the way."[22] There is no record of an answer from the STAA to this protest, but it would be a decade before any Pacific Mill team traveled north to participate again.

Most of the 1926 tournament focused on play in the women's division, given a rousing opening day start when Piedmont bested Monaghan's defending champions 29–17 in Class A action. Thousands of fans, band music and exciting play kept Textile

Hall in an uproar, but attention was also focused on the new style of uniforms—bloomers and silk sweaters—that gave the ladies more freedom of movement than the old dress and leggings. When Leakesville Mill defeated Piedmont 36–34 in a Class A semifinal game, another innovation was noted. "Wearing mannish trunks instead of bloomers, the playing of Leakesville was speeded up by the new style of playing uniform."[23] The North Carolina women defeated Judson 35–33 for the championship, but the excitement proved too much for Burham, their star guard. She fainted near the end of the game and was carried from the court, but reentered the fray during the overtime period.

Along with the Draper Mill women's team, Leakesville was commended for their class and determination, praise not limited only to their hardcourt performances. The players from both teams paid expenses out of their own pockets just to be able to participate in the tournament. That was the true amateur spirit the founders sought.

At least one mill was very proud of its women's program. The 1927 edition of American Spinning's Class B team, nicknamed the "Dimpled Darlings," brought home the first championship in *any* sport in more than 20 years. And they did it in a most extraordinary manner, finishing the year with a 17–0 mark. One local sportswriter lauded their efforts, though he seemed more transfixed by their looks than their athletic skills.

If the tournament had been a beauty show as well as a basketball carnival, the Darlings would have won first prize for pulchritude. Prettier girls are not to be found in an Atlantic City bathing contest, and the beauty of the "dimpled dolls" is the kind that won't rub off. They have found that exercise in athletics is better for the complexion than rouge or lipstick.

Miss Lena Donald was the coach who, for health reasons, stepped down. Coach Bridwell assumed the duties and finished off a perfect season. Miss Trussell, who in her first year as a member added great strength to the team, was the center brilliantly

1921 Piedmont Mill (Piedmont, S.C.) team.

surrounded by a cluster of gems in the championship victory (she scored 23 points in an opening round 40–6 win over Woodside). She played with the fire and dash and precision that characterized her work in other games, and loomed as one of the best girl forwards in the whole tournament.... The team played as a unit, and there was honor for all in bringing championship glory to the American Spinning Company.[24]

An additional division, Class AA men's, was added in 1928 (and lasted only that year), and was an early forerunner of the Open Division which would emerge in the late 1950s. Oddly, the one memory associated with the AA was that in the consolation finals on Saturday, Piedmont won by forfeit when Lonsdale Mill (Seneca, S.C.) walked off the court to protest an official's ruling. It was the first time such an act had occurred in tournament play. This was also the first year an All-Southern women's team was recognized, and included Silvers (Beacon Mill); Lucille Foster (Monaghan Mill); Madge Doggett (Piedmont Mill); Carlie Penley (Beacon Mill); Thelma Boiter (Piedmont Mill); and Katherine Shope (Beacon Mill).

The highlight performance was in the opening round of the men's Class A action, when Calloway Mill defeated Pelzer 63–30. Clarence Higgenbotham, whose 38 points paced the winners, was "the scoring weapon that gashed to shreds the loose disjointed defense Pelzer attempted to offer. The man-to-man defense of the losers failed to fathom the alternating passing and dribbling attack of the visitors, who were maneuvering the ball to the goal zones for well-timed and amply directed shots."[25] The receipts for that year were the best ever, easily surmised by the 3,000 fans who viewed the final day's action, but there were also reflections of a simpler time. The team from Clinchfield Mill forfeited to Judson Mill and returned home with a teammate who had a death in the family.

The last year of the decade, and the ninth for the tournament, was a time to contemplate what had been accomplished. W.M. Grier of Woodside Mill, president of the Southern Textile Athletic Association, cited six goals which had been achieved:

1. The standardization of basketball in textile communities.
2. A recognition (of mill workers) by other classes.
3. A development of plant pride.
4. An appreciation of team play, in work and sport.
5. A recognition of authority.
6. The value of coordinated effort.[26]

Much like textile league baseball, tournament basketball (and indeed all textile sports and recreation) served in part as a productivity tool, fostering community and workplace pride, and drawing all of village life tightly together, with the mill at the center.

"Let us mention another result," continued Grier. "Each team has changed its method of playing. Players have come to realize that it is teamwork that counts in the end, and they have coordinated this effort on the basketball court and in their daily tasks. They realize to become efficient they must know their job, and must be able to get along with their associates and know how to accomplish the best results by working with them."[27]

There were other changes and innovations which impacted the flavor of the tournament. No special referees were used for women's games. For quite a while, Miss Frances Major (basketball coach at Anderson Girls' High) handled this, but the regular officials (all men) called all the games. It was interesting that in the women's consolation final, the rules were bent by the arbiters. Beacon Mill blasted American Spinning 50–20, and they did so while using only five players (omitting a guard), rather than the six for women's basketball at the time. They won behind extraordinarily balanced scoring as Katherine Shope (18), Willie McMahon (16) and Pauline Penley (16) totaled all the points.

It was a sign of the tournament in particular, and basketball in general, that the results of the opening day's competition were telegraphed to station WLW in Chicago (a Crosley Broadcasting Station) and broadcast worldwide, putting textile basketball before millions of people. Local writers kept the home folks entertained with their heroic and incredibly wordy prose. "The last day of competition finds the ranks thinned down to a few war-torn and weary but outstanding aggregations which are ready to gird on their trappings and plunge into the final battles that are to decide the championship of the Southern Textile Athletic Association."[28]

The Roaring Twenties sputtered to a close in the grip of the Great Depression, and most of the textile communities felt the results of the hard times. But the tournament, brainchild of far-thinking leaders, was not allowed to die. It would move, sometimes by fits and starts, but always forward, and mature in the dynamic years of the 1930s.

The 1930s

The Depression grew worse in the 1930s, and businesses suffered. Most of the cotton mills were on short time and were fighting to survive. Citizens of the mill village did their best to make ends meet — planting a garden, keeping a few chickens and a cow on small parcels of land provided by the company. The threat of labor strife grew as the movement to organize workers spread to the Carolinas. It was not the best of times to promote a sporting event founded upon the qualities of teamwork and fair play, but that is exactly what the Southern Textile Basketball Tournament continued to do.

Words from the 1930 tournament program underscored this effort. "To gauge the importance of this tournament would be a well nigh impossible undertaking. It is the prime event of the year athletically and socially in the lives of hundreds of our boys and girls. Here they play the game they love under the most favorable conditions and the best referees it is possible to procure. Here they meet old friends and make new ones."[1]

For 500 athletes, it was a chance to forget the hard times, the shortages of work and food, the worry and wondering. When the games began, and the sound of leather on hardwood echoed off the walls, and the smells of sweat and liniment floated through the locker rooms, it only mattered that there was basketball to be played.

Action was hard and fast, and fans did not have to wait very long for the first big upset. The women's division provided the excitement as Orr Mill's Class A team defeated the powerhouse Monaghan team 20–12. One sportswriter extolled the Anderson women: "The guarding of the Orr girls was nothing less than miraculous. They seemed to be drawn to the ball as if by a magnet and made life unbearable for the Monaghan forwards. To the Misses Smith, Jolley and McKinley more than to any others goes the honors of causing this big upset."[2]

It was not a tournament for the faint of heart, and fans were on the increase. Scores were now broadcast twice a day over the Charlotte (N.C.) radio stations, offering complete coverage for the basketball faithful in that locale. Friday's action was characterized by blowouts, beginning with the Monaghan Class A women's 54–9 crushing of American Spinning, exacting revenge for their upset loss to Orr. American Spinning's Class B men held on to some portion of homestead honor in the consolation semifinals, beating Simpsonville 56–29 as Edgar Harbin equaled the entire output of the losers. In the B men's championship bracket, Spartan Mill devastated Winnsboro 75–25 as Ralph Steading (28 points) and Albert Bullington (20) paced the winners.

The Orr Mill ladies offered a second improbable sequence of events in their march toward the championship. Trailing Beacon Mill by three points with just seconds to play, Orr forward Virginia Kinnett put up a shot (which went in), was fouled, and proceeded to sink the charity toss. Orr then scored two baskets in overtime for a 26–22 win. Not even the music of the Piedmont Band, "offering several popular selections that would make our grandmas do the old time jig,"[3] could soothe the frazzled nerves of players and fans.

Sometimes it did not even take frenzied action to unsettle the competitors. Adjoining courts were a problem, and players were frequently confused when the whistle from the other court sounded. The suggestion was offered to have referees use whistles with different tones for each game.

Despite the deepening economic woes, interest in the tournament continued to grow. One local sportswriter, Carl Weimer, called attention to those undergoing the real hardships. "Players undergo a real sacrifice to participate," he said. "They are not paid, thus losing their wages. Out-of-town organizations have their expenses paid but not their salaries while away from work."[4]

With the scorekeepers perched on their stands, much like a tennis umpire, and with the courts now chained rather than roped off, the 1931 edition of the tournament roared to life. Mayor A.G. Mann welcomed the players to Greenville at halftime of the first Thursday evening game. In the men's Class B semifinals, Dunean and Converse mills battled to a tie in regulation, and did the same during a five minute overtime. The scorer then discovered an error (his lofty perch did not preclude mistakes), which put Dunean ahead by one point. Converse loudly protested their opponents' being awarded the game. Southern Textile Athletic Association officers conferred, and then ordered the game to be replayed later that evening. Undaunted, Dunean blew away the Spartanburg team 56–27.

It was competition in the Class A men's division that captivated the local writers. Carl Weimer commented on Lonsdale Mill's semifinal win over Monaghan Mill by noting that "the Heaths and all of the others fit together like a Cadillac engine. Their defense was as tight as a Scotchman during a panic."[5] Not to be outdone, Eual Thornton offered Homeric prose to pay tribute to Avondale Mill when that team edged Lonsdale Mill for the championship Saturday evening. "Taps were tattooed on the 11th Southern Textile Basketball Tournament last night, but the echoes aroused the entire Alexander City AL citizenry from their night's slumber, as the Avondale cage quint realized its dream by sweeping from behind like a destructive tornado in the final seconds to overcome Lonsdale's one tally lead and grasp the huge trophy 29–28.

"The huge mass of humanity that had put in its appearance for the complete surprise was quickly to divide their opinions and before the initial hooker had been chalked up Avondale had plenty of adopted spectators to share in their victory. Even the taciturn removed all obstacles and joined in the tremor."[6]

The rules to govern tournament play had undergone as many changes as the game itself, and by 1932 it was necessary to publish a standardized listing. Again, heading the top of the list was the prohibition against any form of professionalism.

1. No player shall be allowed to play in the tournament who is under contract to a professional team.
2. Each player must have been a full-time employee of the plant he represents for at least three months prior to the tournament.
3. Any player who represented another in the previous tournament must have been employed for nine consecutive months by the plant they represent.
4. School children who derive their livelihood from the plant they represent shall be allowed to play in the tournament.
5. A player may be registered and play in Class C until he has passed his 19th birthday.
6. Any player who has been registered in Class C for two tournaments must move to a higher classification.
7. No player shall be allowed to play in a lower classification than the highest classification in which he has played.

8. Members of a cup-winning Class B or C team are automatically moved to the next higher classification.
9. Any player found to be ineligible will be barred from the tournament as soon as the fact is known, but games in which he has played cannot be contested.
10. Conduct unbecoming a gentleman, during a game or in connection with his entrance into the tournament, will automatically bar him from this and all future tournaments.
11. All girls' games shall be played on two-division courts.
12. Each girls' team shall be allowed to use not more than two school teachers who must be continuously employed by their mill school.
13. All rules set forth as governing the tournament apply to both boys' and girls' teams.
14. Any dispute arising over playing rules, time and scoring will be settled by three referees appointed by teams involved and one by the president of the Association.[7]

There were other changes much more unpleasant than additions, deletions and emendations of rules. The Southern Textile Athletic Association bank account was with People's State Bank, which closed during the year. Desperate to save money, tournament officials eliminated the free throw contest, the formal Friday night banquet, and trophies for runner-up teams. But the basketball was good, as shown by Lonsdale's 22–16 win in the Class A men's finals over Winnsboro (who owned regular season victories over Newberry College and Wofford College). The winners finished the year undefeated, the losers at 30–9.

It was a lighthearted story, though, which claimed the year's most valuable memory award. Walter Bozeman, All-Southern forward with Avondale Mill, was having lunch in a local restaurant when Piedmont Mill guard James Picklesimer walked in. "Pick" struck up a conversation with Bozeman (who did not recognize his fellow competitor), asking who Avondale played.

1932 Pelzer Mill (Pelzer, S.C.), Class A Women's Champions.

"A team by the name of Piedmont," he said.

"They won't give you much trouble, will they?" Picklesimer asked innocently.

"I imagine we could beat them with one hand tied behind our backs," responded Bozeman.

It was coincidence that the man assigned to guard Bozeman was Picklesimer, who kidded his taller opponent about putting one hand behind his back and taking a few shots. Bozeman managed only three points as Piedmont won 39–25.[8]

The year 1933 turned out to be a busy one. Sixty-one teams came to play (50 from South Carolina, 3 from Alabama, 8 from North Carolina), totaling 750 players. This necessitated playing 34 games from 9:00 A.M. to closing on Thursday, yet 2,000 fans braved the long hours. Courts other than those at Textile Hall were used, with several games being played at St. Mary's School. There was the addition of the 110 pound tournament (the weight limit) for younger boys, and six teams signed up to christen the new division. Ralph Harbin, later a textile baseball great, was one of the players, as was R. Putman of Dunean Mill, "a 70 pound substitute forward, [who] gave the crowd lots to laugh about with his dribbling and handling of the ball."[9] It must have helped, as his team copped the first championship.

Enthusiasm from sportswriters was certainly not a problem, proven by an excerpt from Dave Tillinghast's "Echoes of Sports": "This notable event that brings thrills as well as pangs to the hearts of the younger generation as well as the older in the textile communities of North and South Carolina and Alabama is the grand finale for basketball in textile circles and is looked forward with as great interest by the boys and girls who do the playing as the World Series by pastimers in the major leagues. It is a grand finish."[10]

Two other items added a distinct flavor to the tournament. First, the Southern Textile Athletic Association was granted a charter by the South Carolina secretary of state, making it a not-for-profit organization, a move which helped to ease the financial burdens during these troubled times. Secondly, on Friday evening, February 24, the players were guests at a dance held at the Poinsett Hotel, and it was widely attended and enjoyed by all.

Coaches outside the textile communities soon offered words of praise for what they observed. Jack Reames, coach of the undefeated Parker High School Golden Tornadoes of 1933, offered his opinions.

I have followed the Southern Textile carnival for years. I have seen the entry list grow constantly. More important and vital than that, I have seen the quality of basketball stepped up year by year until now these textile teams are employing the latest and best in modern basketball play....

I am afraid the public does not properly appreciate what these boys are accomplishing or the handicap under which they play. Many of them do a full day's work before donning the togs for a hard game at night. Weeks before the tournament they spend three or four nights a week either drilling and getting into condition or else playing rival teams — forgetting a hard day's work that has gone before....

Basketball is all extra and yet they come to this hall and give and take with as good grace as any college or high school team in the land would.

And I would especially praise sportsmanship here. The teams in this hall display the highest regard for the rules, the decisions of the officials, and for each other. Their conduct as participants is without reproach.[11]

The game was getting good enough to bewitch the young and entice them away from that other sacred sports tradition of the mill villages — baseball. Pete Fowler, a former major league pitcher with the St. Louis Cardinals and a fine textile player for many years in the Spartanburg area, attended the 1933 festivities with his son, Pete Jr. "That boy of mine doesn't care for baseball much, but he eats basketball alive."[12]

Nobody was standing still, either, and the easing of the poor economic times of the 1930s allowed for the pursuit of the bigger and better. "Scoop" Latimer noted the "echoes of humming cotton mills, a refreshing refrain of better times in the industrial south, resounded in a prosperous paean throated by a record-breaking crowd of spectators (approximately 3000) and players (more than 70 teams) at the opening of the 14th annual Southern Textile Basketball Tournament."[13] There were so many scheduled games that the tournament started a day earlier, on Wednesday, February 14, 1934.

"Dixie's Own World Series" would involve many more fans in 1934, as three radio broadcasts, made by local personality Jimmie Thompson, aired at noon, 2:00 P.M. and 9:30 P.M. A press box and radio booth were installed in the center of the balcony, overlooking both courts at Textile Hall. It was a good place to see C. Couch set the men's individual scoring record with 30 points in Friday's Class B consolation semifinals, as Woodside Mill pounded Anderson Mill 49–29.

For the women, *The Official Women's Basketball Guide* (1934) became the game's governing document. The tournament's executive committee adopted the "center throw," rather than the center jump after every basket, as the means for putting the ball in play. The big change, though, was in the social calendar. For the first time a queen of the Southern Textile Basketball Tournament would be selected from among the 200 women players, and voted upon by all the participants.

The annual dance was held at Textile Hall from 10:30 P.M. Friday to 1:00 A.M. Saturday, with music provided by Fitzgerald's University Club Orchestra. Only the players could attend (they were tagged for identification) but spectators were permitted in the balcony for an admission price of $1. With much fanfare, Christine Garrett, "demure, starry-eyed little forward" from Piedmont Mill was crowned the Queen of the Tournament. Her attendants were Susan Keys from American Enka and Etrulia Johnson from Dunean Mill. The three were decked out in fashions provided by Stewart's, the leading Greenville women's apparel shop of the day.[14] It was a bit of the Cinderella story, and for a few hours the citizens of the mill village saw the fairy tale come true.

From "Dixie's Own World Series," the tournament became "The Greatest Athletic Meet in the World" in 1935, and secured its first corporate backing: Coca Cola sponsored the broadcast of the games over radio station WFBC at 2:00 P.M. and 9:30 P.M. It was a massive gathering, with 92 teams, 5 divisions and 1,500 players. Three thousand fans sat through opening-round games on February 20, at three different locations: Textile Hall, St. Mary's School, and Greenville High School. With much fine tuning done in the tournament the last few years, it was time to sit back and watch some good basketball. It was also a sign of the times when the following appeared in the year's program: "The Association is not responsible for lost articles, injuries or damages. If your team dresses in the Hall, you must make the necessary arrangements to have property watched, or check same at the official check room on the ground floor."

When Dunean Mill's Class A men defeated Avondale Mill 45–44 in the opening round, Willie Riddle intercepted a pass in the last few seconds and dribbled the length of the floor to lay the ball in just before the final buzzer. It was the most important two of the 23 points for this gentleman with the nickname "Dummy." In a less-than-gentle time, the designation was specific: Willie was deaf, but he overcame the disability to become a perennial All-Southern choice. Another legendary performer, Bert Hill, starred for Poe's Class A men, pouring in 38 in a 64–30 rout of Joanna Mill in the consolation bracket, and following that up with a 42-point performance to lead Poe over American Enka, 78–36. Textile baseball players George Blackwell (Southern Bleachery), Manning Bagwell (Drayton Mill), Jean Belue

Top: 1935 Russell Manufacturing (Alexander City, Ala.), Class B Men's Champions.
Bottom: 1936 American Enka (Enka, N.C.), Class A Women's Champions: *(l–r)* Susie Simmons, Lois Allen, Betty Osborne, Blanche Medford, Mary Byrd, Eloise Glass, Mary Clarke, Mildred Crownover, Doris Penland, Jessie Mills, Mertis Prince, Elizabeth Holcombe.

(Chiquola Mill), and Woodrow Abernathy (Inman Mill) did a little double duty for their respective employers. John H. Garraux doubled as tournament president and Judson Mill coach.

For the finals on February 23, Textile Hall was reconfigured to one court, with extra bleachers extending to the balcony on one side and to the stage on the other. There was seating for 6,000, and the crowd that night totaled 5,000. Dunean's Class A men won the title by defeating Victor Mill 33–30, but the women's Class A battle commanded as much attention. Though losing to American Enka 32–14, the Stanly Mill team redefined the parameters of determination. These ladies fielded a team only two weeks prior to the tournament and managed to play five games in that time, yet they had *no* indoor court. Determination was also a trait closely associated with Wilma Whitlock, Drayton Mill's center, as she competed against Renfrew Bleachery in the Class B women's finals. With the thought of losing too much to bear, "she gave every ounce of energy in the furious fray and collapsed in the fourth quarter. Play was stopped and first aid given... Resounding applause greeted her return..."[15] Her efforts could not stave off a 29–15 loss.

The 1936 Southern Textile Basketball Tournament boasted staggering attendance figures February 19–22, as reported by the Greenville *News*: 2,000; 2,500; 3,500; and 6,000. It was big enough to persuade Governor Olin D. Johnston to present trophies to the champions and consolation winners, cajole Pacific Mill of Columbia back into the fold after a decade's absence (over a dispute regarding ineligible players), pick up another sponsor (Verner Springs Water Company), and provide a tournament physician and trained nurse for any medical emergencies.

There were times when certain teams garnered most of the accolades, and 1937 was just the year for women's Class A Lanett Mill and men's Class A Southern Bleachery. The Alabama team "is composed of married women, most with families. Louise Belcher Wood is the mother of two, works in the plant, keeps house, and in ten games was the team's leading scorer at 23 points per game."[16] She certainly lived up to star billing, scoring 34 in the March 2 win over Dunean, bucketing an astounding 62 points March 3 as Lanett blasted Winnsboro 83–18, and scoring 30 in a 42–37 loss to Judson in the March 4 consolation finals.

Coach Lyles Alley, later coach and athletic director at Furman University, assembled a stellar array of talent for his Southern Bleachery squad: Charles Brooks (Clemson University), Herbert Wall (Clemson), James Gay (University of South Carolina), L.S. Meisenheimer (Furman University), Clarence Rushing (Mississippi State University), Bud Hendley (Wofford College), Bert Hill (Duke University), Charles Suddeth (Greer High), Howard Maness (Greer High), and Ben Burnett (Greer High). They were brought together for the single purpose of winning the Class A championship, which they did. They also won the Corn Trophy, presented by the Corn Products Company to the Class A team scoring the highest number of points in the tournament; later, it was given to the winning team, who could take permanent possession with three consecutive championships. With such illustrious company, U.S. Senator Ellison Durant "Cotton" Smith, oldest member in that august body, felt right at home presenting trophies to the champions and runners-up.

By the time the 18th annual tournament rolled around in 1938, it was time to acknowledge the deeds of the bona fide old-timers. For the first time, a composite listing of all All-Southern performers from 1926 forward was presented, as was a list of championship teams for those years. John H. Garraux, who according to "Scoop" Latimer was to the textile tournament what P.T. Barnum was to another "Greatest Show on Earth," said, "As the referee's whistle sounds off the first game, we hope that it will be a signal to release a flood of good cheer which will radiate the spirit of true friendship among every team entered in the tournament; that every game will be a contribution to further elevate the high standard of sportsmanship which permeates the tournament, instilling into the mind of the public a higher regard for the spirit and skill of the game.... The tournament belongs to the people of the great textile industry in the southern states. It is yours, for you have made it what it is today."[17]

Latimer paid particular honors to another veteran personality. "True southern hospitality, as warm as country fried chicken at a Methodist parsonage, is offered by the venerable host, G.L. Doggett of Piedmont. He has the glad hand for everybody and his smile radiates cheer and good fellowship. The grand old man makes winners out of losers with his comforting words to the less fortunate teams. No matter how badly a group is beaten the player doesn't leave the hall crestfallen and dejected, not after 'Pappy Doggett' has bestowed his gentle pat-on-the-back."[18]

The tournament may have taken a glance back, but the game moved ahead full tilt in 1938. It was the year when the center jump (jump ball after every basket) was eliminated, and higher scores accompanied the accelerated action. With new bleachers installed, the old hall braced for the fans packing in to watch the "fast break game." And come they did: 4,000 on March 2, 5,000 for the March 3 semi-finals, and 6,000 for the March 4 championships. The Class B women of Lanett Mill wasted little time amazing the fans, destroying Monaghan 69–7 as their fine center Lucille Wood scored 30. But for all the potential action set forth by the new men's rule, Southern Bleachery's Class C men "froze" the ball in the last several minutes to preserve a 32–29 win over Peerless Woolen Mill and claim the title.

Those men with ties to textile league baseball were present as player and spectator. "Chick" Galloway, Presbyterian College coach; Walt Barbare, pioneer in basketball competition at Monaghan and former major league shortstop; and Ford Garrison, former major leaguer reminisced about old times. Three other active players used basketball to keep in shape during the winter months before reporting to the New York Yankees' farm clubs. Denny Smith of the Greer Mill Class A team would soon leave for the Class A Binghamton (N.Y.) club, and Ralph Harbin of the Woodside Mill Class B squad would move on to Butler, Pennsylvania. Tom "Toady" Smith would follow them north after completing his duties as coach of the Southern Worsted's Class A women's team.

The tournament was still touted as strictly amateur, purely democratic, promoted for and by the people of the textile industry, with the only profit being goodwill and a better understanding of the mill folk's common problems.[19] It seemed as if nothing could slow its growing popularity unless, of course, it was one's loyalty to the old alma mater. In the 1939 games, Southern Bleachery's Class B men had to forfeit to Judson Mill in the opening round, since most of the team played with Taylors High, and the school just happened to be competing in the state tournament in Columbia.

Despite the rumblings of war in Europe, the decade was ending on a high note for the Southern Textile Basketball Tournament. But the 1940s would prove to be a lot more difficult to navigate.

The 1940s

This is one tournament that has weathered storms and depressions. It has enjoyed consistent growth and attained the prestige and prominence that until now no other basketball event can equal it in the number of participants. Also the caliber of play is superior to that seen in the aggregate of a hundred games and no other tourney offers richer rewards in such a brilliant array of medals and trophies.

"Scoop" Latimer
(Greenville *News*, Wednesday, March 5, 1941)

It was a new decade slowly leaving behind the Depression years. Outlooks were brighter, and places like Czechoslovakia and Iwo Jima, Normandy and Pearl Harbor, Auschwitz and Bataan were far-off spots on the map with little meaning. The 21st running of the Big Show opened in a festive Textile Hall decked out in a red and white color scheme, and good basketball was the rule. Joe Anders started with the Brandon Mill C men's team in 1938, and then went on up to Class B and A divisions. He recalled being courtside from 9:00 A.M. until 11:00 P.M. "Once a player, always a player, and I didn't want to miss one minute of action."[1]

Class B meant "bang" in 1940 as Brandon Mill crushed Mills Mill 90–21 on March 6, with the whole starting five reaching double figures: Buck Friar (22), Ray Wynn (21), Thackston (15), Cox (12), and Morrow (10). Dixie Mercerizing almost matched that victory margin, pounding Converse Mill 74–10 behind the trio of Myrtle Dooley (21), Opal Outlaw (20) and Jackie Marlowe (20).

The Tennessee women did not stop until they claimed the division championship, pounding Lonsdale Mill 48–7 in semifinal action, and outdistancing Grey Hosiery (Hendersonville, N.C.) 39–30 in the finals. Lupton City celebrated twice as the Class A men, the Dixie Aces, squeaked by Peerless Woolen Mill 34–33 in an overtime semifinal game, and swept by Southern Bleachery in the finals to share the highest laurels with the women's team. Six thousand fans were on hand to applaud their efforts, and William P. Jacobs, president of Presbyterian College and secretary of the South Carolina Cotton Manufacturer's Association, presented the trophies at the closing ceremonies.

Famous, and soon-to-be-famous, names continued to ease into the lineups of the mills: Ford Garrison (Boston Red Sox), Union Bleachery's C men; Marvin Rackley (Brooklyn Dodgers), Oconee Mill's Class C

men; Bill Voiselle (New York Giants), Ninety Six Mill's Class B men; Art Fowler (Cincinnati Reds), Converse Mill's Class B men; and George Blackwell (local sports legend), Southern Bleachery's Class A Men. All found basketball a dandy way to get in shape for the upcoming baseball season. Kathlyn Kelley Owens, a high school student who made the 1936 Olympic team as a high jumper, was a standout for Lonsdale Mill's Class B women, and in the 1941 consolation finals her 20 points secured a 29–11 win over Judson Mill. Peerless Woolen Mill boasted seven-foot center Reba Wyatt, the tourney's first "big man."

Walter Davis picked up his basketball skills at Woodside Mill's YMCA in the mid–1930s, played midget ball and wound up on the Class B team. "I used to love watching Earl Wooten on offense for Pelzer, and Willie Riddle on defense for Dunean, they were both so good. The tournament affected my life profoundly. I learned teamwork, the value of competition, a desire to

Top: 1940 Southern Textile Basketball Tournament program cover.
Bottom: 1940 Dunean Mill (Greenville, S.C.) Class A Men's Champions.

24 The Southern Textile Basketball Tournament   *The 1940s*

Top: 1940 Dixie Mercerizing (Lupton City, Tenn.), Class B Women's Champions: *(l–r)* Pepper Martin, Ina Cox, Edna Wagner, Jackie Henderson, Myrtle Dooley, Juanita Walker, Opal Outlaw, Marie Martin, Virginia Parris, Helen Waddell, Ruby Caver.
Bottom: 1941 Pacific Mill (Columbia, S.C.), Class B Men's Champions: *(front row, l–r)* J.D. Pitman (coach), B.E. Davis, Ed Herbert, Shorty McQuarters, Dewey Pursley, Allen Martin; *(back row, l–r)* Lewis White (coach), Archie Pearson, James Darby, Ace Herbert, Bill Simpson, Doyle Jaco (mgr).

win, and I made lifelong friends. Those were the days I truly thought would never end."[2]

Hinkie McCurry, a homegrown product of Orr Mill, took much the same path, moving from midget ball and on to Class B. "I enjoyed getting to know all the different people and playing with and against the likes of Earl Wooten, Fred Whitten, Johnny Ashmore, Sammy Meeks and Fred Morrison. You had to love being in the middle of the competition with those guys."[3]

The prose of "Scoop" Latimer could also call particular attention to deserving players, as in 1941 to Chatham Manufacturing's Anne Lineback. In leading her team to a 33–22 win over American Enka in the finals of the Class A women's division, the "lithe and lilting forward" was "darting hither and anon like a sprite, eluding Enka's guard to move in firing range for two hair raising shots from difficult angles. By now the Elkin elf seemed to be waving a magic wand over the championship goal as her team assumed a commanding lead."[4] From the famous to the sophisticated — the triple pass from the Z formation was the play used by Dixie Mercerizing to assure their Class A men's championship win over Southern Bleachery, 38–33 on March 8 — to the mundane (the Mills Mill teams had no gym in which to practice, so they honed their skills with perpetual road games), the tournament reflected everything the game had to offer.

The 1942 edition was highlighted by balanced scoring attacks from several teams. In setting the tournament scoring record up to that time, the Class A Dunean men routed Ninety Six in the opening round on March 5, 102–46, behind the production of Fred Parks (25), Fred Cox (24) and Bob Donnan (21). But with turnabout being fair play, they in turn were blasted 71–29 a day later by Southern Bleachery. May-McEwen-Kaiser Mill offered its own formula for victory in the opening day of the Class B men's action, blowing past Lockhart Mill 71–30 as Burwell (19), Roach (18), Reiber (16) and Walker (15) starred. Hanes Hosiery popped Piedmont 88–45 in the Class A men's consolation semifinals on Friday, led by Coot Greer (26), Gardner (21), and Hugh Hampton (21). Glory, though, was reserved for the Dixie Mercerizing Class A men, whose 54–35 win over McCrary Hosiery Mill gave them their third straight championship and permanent possession of the Corn Trophy.

There was balance, too, in the attendance figures, as fans sought respite from war news which bode little good for the Allies. Three thousand came for each of the first two rounds, 4,500 for the semis and 4,000 for the finals. Because of the war, 1942 would be the last Southern Textile Basketball Tournament until 1946, but even the global conflict could not shut down the game in the cotton mill capital of the world.

The new kid on the block, the Greater Greenville Basketball Tournament, drew 27 teams in 1943, composed mainly of high school players and service representatives who were described in the local press as "young and old, tall and short, protruding of mid-section, gray of head, all enthusiastic of visage."[5] The varsity of Parker High found itself split among several of the entries: Mickey Ellis and Billy Wakefield to Woodside's B team; Calvin Morrow to Brandon's Class B entry; Effie Evington to Union Bleachery's B's; and Bill Moody to the B boys of Monaghan.

Games were held at Dunean Mill and Parker High gyms, and the Parker band was the sole provider of courtside tunes. The war-time tournament also drew some big-name veterans into action, like Dunean's Willie Riddle and Willie Wilbanks, Woodside Mill's Speedy Couch, Southern Bleachery's Palmer McAvoy, and Pelzer's Earl Wooten (playing with Mills Mill). There was a noticeable absence of the women's division that year.

Crowds were smaller, with 250 on opening day and 650 for the semifinals, and fans saw teams like the 70th Service Squadron, the 25th Service Group, and the 349th Service Squadron supplanting the familiar mill

1942 Chatham Mfg. (Elkin, N.C.), Class A Women's Champions.

teams. The soldier boys, though, did not fare well against the lintheads. With gas rationing in effect, trolley cars provided the best transportation to and from the gyms. The basketball continued to prove interesting.

Veteran Willie Riddle's 15 points led Dunean's Class A men over the 70th Service Squadron 39–29 in opening round play on February 24. Dunean's B team was victorious over Poe Mill, 46–17, as future great Bob Stowe scored 11. Action on February 25 found another legend-in-the-making, Effie Evington, popping in 18 as the Class B Union Bleachery squad outclassed St. Albans High School 45–27.

Woodside's B men edged Dunean 38–37 in the February 26 championship as "the score bounced around like popcorn on a hot skillet."[6] The Class A finals provided a rousing end to the new tournament, thanks to a magnificent defensive performance by veteran Willie Wilbanks. Playing for Dunean against Mills Mill, he had the task of guarding Mr. Offense himself, Earl Wooten. "He hated to see me coming," Wilbanks noted.[7] That night, he was on Wooten like glue, going all out all over the court. During a timeout toward the end of the game, Willie went for a drink of water and collapsed near the bench. "My wife thought I was dead, but all that happened was I swallowed my gum. I was back in the game in two minutes."[8] Wilbanks' modesty hides the fact that he played himself to near exhaustion while holding the incomparable Wooten to only six points. Despite his efforts, Mills Mill prevailed 48–45 and claimed the title.

In the Class A consolation, Monaghan defeated the 349th Service Squadron 57–45 as Bomar Keller (20), Raymond Christopher (14), and Johnny Blackston (13) led the way; Mississippi Hinton's 22 led the soldiers.

The tournament changed its name in 1944 to the Piedmont Area Basketball Tournament (the name stuck in 1945 as well). Longtime textile sports figure Clarence "Doodle" Thomas was president, and he was able to persuade both Meadors Manufacturing Company (awards for the All-Star selections) and local sportsman Waddy Anderson (trophies) to donate the championship hardware. Four divisions — midget boys (115-pound weight limit), Class B and

A men, and women — translated into a 57-game slate, and March 17's second-round action held enough highlights to thrill even die-hard fans.

In Class B action, Welford-Lyman-Tucapau High School upset heavily-favored Woodside 33–27, and Union Bleachery walloped Camperdown 57–24 as Effie Evington had 19 tallies. For the women, Drayton's "Dimpled Darlings" defeated Asheville Victory's junior team 41–15 behind Wilma Whitlock's 23 points, and Mills Mill defeated Anderson Mill 21–20 in double overtime. Class A men's action produced high scoring individual performances, as Floyd Owens' 30 led Dunean past Ninety Six Mill 60–22, and Earl Wooten's 42 moved Pelzer past Woodside 70–40.

By the time the finals rolled around, Dunean positioned itself for championship conquests in all four divisions, winning two. The mill captured the midget boy's and the Class A men's divisions, but the latter was a real struggle. Trailing Monaghan 25–18 at the half, the Dynamos turned up the defensive heat and held the Eagles scoreless in the final frame, walking off with a 30–25 win. The Class B men lost to Beacon Mill 28–24 in overtime, and the women gave Asheville Victory a run before falling by a 31–28 score.

For Thomas Perry, the 1944 tourney proved to be his one appearance, "and the source of my only regret as a textile athlete, since I've always wished I'd played in more." Born and raised at Gluck Mill, where "basketball was the only game in town in the winter months" he was recruited by crosstown Anderson Mill to play Class C ball. That year, watching Earl Wooten display his offensive fireworks for Pelzer's Class A men, was just wonderful. "But I was more profoundly touched when I saw Willie Riddle, a deaf mute, work his magic for Dunean. Knowing how hard he worked, making himself good enough to become an All-Southern selection time and again, has been an inspiration to me. I learned to be competitive and aggressive without animosity, and discovered that dedication and hard work were the two components for success. Pretty good lessons, don't you think?"[9]

The last of the war-time tournaments packed a basketful of thrills as well. In the second round on February 22, ageless Willie Riddle scored 27 to lead Dunean's Class A men over Lonsdale Mill, 68–25. Brandon's Class B men definitely had the good luck charm of the year to secure the services of both Effie Evington and Bob Stowe, and the efforts of the two produced a championship. In the February 23 semifinals Evington had 21 and Stowe 14 as the Braves popped Judson 40–24, and in the finals Stowe had 18 and Evington 16 to pace the team past Woodside, 47–23. Fifteen hundred saw that championship game on February 24, and then stuck around for more thrills. Eckie Jordan's late field goal led the Pelzer women past defending champions Gradegg, 23–21, certainly not the last time the name of that rising star would be mentioned in tournament history. Drayton Mill laid claim to the Class A men's crown, besting Dunean 38–35, led by 6'6" center Salmans and his nine points. The court action may not have been as intense from 1943 to 1945 as in prior tournaments, but the skills of the participants, and the entertainment they gave to a war-weary populace, could not be underestimated. They provided good, solid basketball for their fans, and made possible the smooth resumption of the Southern Textile Basketball Tournament's "friendly hostilities" in the postwar years.

Within a few months, V-E and V-J days followed the close of the 1945 Piedmont Area tournament, and the next winter the 23rd annual "traditional" festivities came on the scene as if the war had been but an interruption to be overcome. Fifty-eight teams and 625 players bore witness to its ongoing popularity, as did the new ticket prices: 60 cents general admission, 30 cents for school children and servicemen in uniform, and a whopping $1.30 for reserved seats for the finals.

The war years had knit families closely together in the mill villages, and this carried over onto the team rosters. "It wasn't in the tournament," Thomas Perry remembers, "but one night during the season the whole starting five for Gluck Mill were Perrys, me and four of my brothers. Guess we made the official scorer's job a difficult one that evening! But there were five of us overseas at the same time during the war, so it was nice to have at least one night that brought us all back together."[10] And Pelzer's Class A women's entry for 1946 boasted three sets of sisters: Leoda Jordan Turpin and Eckie Jordan, Mildred Houston Jordan and Allene Houston, and Jean and Roberta Fowler.

When the action started in 1946, prolific scorers and firecracker finishes became the talk of the town. Fred Whitten's 30 points led Orr Mill over Lonsdale 65–37 in the opening Class B men's round February 26. A day later, Dunean's Class A men sported the talents of Ward Williams (28) and Carl Green (23) in a 71–47 thumping of the Thrilling Threads of American Enka. That same day, in a Class A consolation matchup, Ninety Six edged Mills Mill 56–54 on a half-court buzzer-beater. The shooter's name was omitted from the game summary, though Lewis Drummond did receive credit for leading the winners with 20 points.

The Class B Anderson Mill men, The Whiz Kids, won that division championship 44–43 over Woodside Mill, behind the spirited leadership of brothers Jimmy and Ezra Embler. For Chafer Honea, another member of the team, it became his favorite tournament memory. "I recalled trudging up the steps to the gym above the company store over at the mill, dutifully following my older sister who played on the women's team there. During practice, guess it was hard to conduct business downstairs. The old building was destroyed by a tornado in 1936, but when we won that championship in '46, I thought of all the hard practices, coaches who pushed us, teammates and opponents I'd come to know and respect,

1946 Dunean Mill (Greenville, S.C.), Class B Women's Champions: *(front row, l–r)* Laura Pepper, Patti Brown, Betty Lollis, Ruth McDonald; *(back row, l–r)* Dorothy Wood, Peggy Wood, Sadie Elliott, Donnan, Margaret Putman, Ward Williams (coach).

and realized I had been taught what sportsmanship was all about. Basketball did more than just keep me out of trouble, it made a better person out of me. I don't think anyone in my shoes could have any regrets about playing in the tournament."[11]

Increasing interest continued in 1947 as more than 800 players were involved in the week-long frenzy. There was certainly no shortage of celebrities either. Virgil Stallcup played with the Ware Shoals Class B men, and Cincinnati Reds teammate Sammy Meeks joined Orr Mill's B contingent. O'dell "Red" Barbery (Washington Senators) joined Stallcup at Ware Shoals. Viola Thompson and Elizabeth Mahon, participants in the All-American Girls Professional Baseball League, played for Orr Mill and Brandon Mill, respectively. Cedric Loftis, All Southern Conference with Duke, and Donald Anderson, All Southern Conference with the University of North Carolina, were teammates at Hanes Hosiery. Hoyt Hambright, former McCrary Hosiery Mill standout and now athletic director at Rex Mill in Gastonia, North Carolina, played football at the University of South Carolina and was recipient of the Jacobs Blocking Trophy. Bill Moody of Dunean Mill and Joe Anders of Brandon Mill, both Greenville Spinners, were permitted to report late to the Brooklyn Dodgers' rookie camp in Pensacola, Florida, due to their participation in the tournament. Oconee Mill's Marvin Rackley came home from the Dodgers' stay in Havana, Cuba, to get into action with the Class C team. Art Fowler (Cincinnati Reds) again put aside his pitching talents to give Clifton Mills' Class B men a lift. Rhoten Shetley, Furman University graduate and athletic director at Watts Mill in Laurens, intended to retire from pro *football*'s Brooklyn Dodgers that year.

Another legend in the making, Punchy Howard, began play with the Piedmont Mill midget team in the late 1930s, and moved on up to the big teams there from 1945 to 1952 before finishing with Victor Mill in 1953–'54. "There was one game with Peerless Woolen Mill in Georgia that sticks in my mind, not because of the score or anything, but it was so darn cold that the clock froze up! And heck, we played right on as if nothing was wrong. You know, the roughest players were those like Ward Williams and 'Tex' Ritter who came down from Indiana; not dirty, just real competitive. And for all the fun I had in textile basketball, it was a baseball memory that I cherish most. When Joe Anders and I were teammates with the Spinners in Greenville, we took a three-game tour of Cuba one year, and Fidel Castro was one of the pitchers. That probably qualified as my brush with fame."[12]

The spectators — 4,000 each the first two days with several hundred turned away for the finals on February 29 — witnessed the greatest start-to-finish tournament performance as Earl Wooten put on a scoring clinic. He had 47 on February 26 as Pelzer's Class A men blitzed Oconee Mill 76–55; came back with 41 February 27 in a 73–54 win over Southern Bleachery; and scored 21 in a 53–47 loss to Hanes Hosiery on February 28. His 109 points gave him a per game average of 36.3, good enough to be named Most Valuable Player in his division, and his efforts were applauded by the more than 20,000 fans in attendance that week. Another highlight captured the same gutty performance shown by Wooten. In quarterfinal action Thursday, Monaghan Mill's Class B men upset pre-tournament favorite Woodside Mill 51–50, despite having to finish the game with only four players. With a roster of six, two men went by the wayside with fouls, but the remaining four held on for an overtime victory.

Walter S. Montgomery, president of Spartan Mill, presented trophies and awards to teams and individuals, and the ceremony was praised for its simplicity. The overflow crowd applauded all the tributes to the recipients, but their loudest hurrahs were reserved for the MVP announcements: Class A Men — Earl Wooten, Pelzer Mill; Class A Women — Doris Shugart, Chatham Manufacturing; Class B Men — Bill Moody, Dunean Mill; Class B Women — Nealy

Late 1940s. Winnsboro Mill (Winnsboro, S.C.) vs. Ware Shoals Mill (Ware Shoals, S.C.).

Hall, Judson Mill; and Class C Men — Don Cox, Dunean Mill. Just like the postwar economy, everything pointed to bigger and better as the tournament moved ahead.

"Scoop" Latimer always had the words to describe the arrival of the annual event. "Surging crowds, thrilling games, teeming excitement, and a thousand other things crowded the opening of the 25th annual [1948] Southern Textile Basketball Tournament in Greenville yesterday as favorites won all twenty two inaugural contests and set the stage for the five day Silver Anniversary carnival."[13] When the Class A men from Dunean garnered an opening round 81–46 win over Union Bleachery, "all players were pouring high voltage into electric play."[14] Latimer christened tournament legend Earl Wooten "The Man of Magic."

The anniversary issue impacted both the veterans and newcomers. G.L. Doggett of Piedmont, who was so instrumental in helping to create the tournament, had seen his four sons play in it, and this year watched his grandchildren participate. Harry Clark, who recently was hired as supervisor of athletics and recreation at Judson Mill, and who had played football, basketball and baseball while alternately attending Duke and Wake Forest universities, commented that the March Madness was the greatest thing he ever saw.

"Playing ball in the late 1940s was just plain fun," remembers Wade Burton, a Southern Baptist minister who started with pick-up games at the Lonsdale Mill YMCA and played from 1946 to 1948 with the Ware Shoals Mill team. "My favorite part of the game was the beauty and skill of set shots; I still don't like to see folks dunk a ball. And I think we had a youthful enthusiasm so lacking in present-day sports."[15]

Enthusiasm, however, was not lacking in the 1948 games. From opening round action on March 2, when the Class B men of Pacolet Mill rode Bobby Brown's 33-point performance to a 66–46 defeat of Glen Lowery Mill, to the March 6 championships, there was action galore. When Hanes Hosiery defeated Peerless Woolen Mill 56–47 in the semifinals of the Class A men's division, Latimer got back into the act, describing the victor's Hilliard Nance as "fast and elusive, a ubiquitous rabbit hopping around to make uncanny shots or play an almost invincible guarding game..."[16] The Hanes team captured permanent possession of the Corn Trophy after defeating Chatham Manufacturing 63–47 for their third straight championship. The scenario was precisely reversed in the Class A women's final when Hanes, despite fielding basically the same strong team that went to the 1947 National Amateur Athletic Association Women's Tournament quarterfinals, came up short and lost to the Blanketeers 37–31.

The decade's final extravaganza was filled with turmoil, great performances and big crowds, all ingredients for an interesting few days. It was a surprise to everyone that Hanes Hosiery's Class A men, defending champions and permanent possessors of the Corn Trophy for three consecutive titles, chose not to participate. They passed up the Southern Textile Basketball Tournament in favor of the AAU National Tournament. Another perennial power in that same division, Chatham Manufacturing, withdrew. Coach Don Brock said that three starters were out with injuries and a fourth had quit the team to go into business for himself, so there were only six eligible players. But he cited another side to their withdrawal, noting "that players and plant officials talked about the large crowds in recent years, and felt that winning teams in the tournament divisions should receive a cut of gate receipts to offset expenses."[17]

The action on the court, though, was as fast and furious as ever. Margaret Ballenger of Victor Mill's Class B women was knocked unconscious in March 2's 27–26 win over Woodside Mill, and spent the evening at Greenville General Hospital. With the absence of two Class A powerhouses, Pelzer and Peerless Woolen mills more than took up the slack.

Crowds poured in until "a fireman's hook and ladder outfit were the essentials for getting a bare glimpse of last night's tickling tussles in the Class A men's division ... as some 4000 basketball-crazed fans jammed their way into gigantic Textile Hall."[18] Peerless played teams from Montgomery, Alabama; Nashville, Tennessee; Knoxville, Tennessee; and Newport, Tennessee, all members of the Southern Professional Basketball League, to tune up for tournament action. Nothing, however, prepared them for Earl Wooten. Now christened "The Atomic Bomb," the little guy weaved and darted for 40 points as Pelzer bested Monaghan 93–72 in the semifinals on March 4, and popped the nets for 38 in the 80–61 championship win over Peerless before 5,000 screaming fans.

Stan Hilley, who played with Ware Shoal Mill's Class C men in the late 1940s, remembered how the tournament crowded out everything else. "It was just understood that the high school team would be the mill's C team. With two high school and two C games a week, it didn't leave much time to study. I was in awe of the tournament, and would hitchhike from Ware Shoals to Greenville to see it. Over the years, I realized how special it was."[19]

The postwar tournaments carried forth the successful tradition, but many changes awaited. There was another war looming, and Hilley spoke for many when he commented, "My only regret was not being able to stay home and play more, but the Korean War didn't give a lot of us much of a choice!"[20] Before the fabulous '50s were through, the very foundations of the tournament would be shaken.

The 1950s

I was surprised to find that so many young players, developed in the tournament, have gone on to make names for themselves in college.
  Press Maravich, Clemson University Basketball Coach
  (Greenville *News*, March 15, 1958)

In a decade of great changes, the 1950 tournament began with a comfortable familiarity. Professional baseball players made it a point to participate and gain a bit of off-season conditioning. Sammy Meeks, of the Orr Mill B team, was granted a special six-day delay in reporting to the Cincinnati Reds' spring training camp in Tampa, Florida, for that reason. Earl Wooten continued his annual high scoring onslaught, attested by his 43-point performance against Monaghan Mill on March 2. Nonetheless, Monaghan held on for a 77–70 win, relegating the Earl of Pelzer and his teammates to a spot in the Class A men's consolation bracket.

Prolific scoring was the rule across all divisions. Wooten's performances did not disappoint, as he scored 40 and led Pelzer over Anderson Mill 86–77 in the semifinals, and then notched 34 in a 74–42 win over Lyman Mill in the consolation finals. Just to show off, he was one-for-three in the last two minutes on shots five paces beyond the half-court line. Dorothy Nimmons popped in 28 points, easily outdistancing the opposing team as Piedmont Mill crushed Brandon 78–16 in Class B women's action on March 2, and Effie Evington had 33 to lead the Class B Union Bleachery men's team over Russell Manufacturing, 65–56. Dave Houston upheld the honor of the Class C men, as his 31 eased Oconee Mill past Greer Mill, 51–50.

At tournament's end, the awards ceremony featured James F. Byrnes, a former secretary of state under Franklin D. Roosevelt who was given a huge ovation by the crowd of 5,000. Fox Movietone was on hand to film the festivities and provide newsreels for distribution to theaters across the country. A tribute was paid by Southern Textile Athletic Association president Horace Whitmire to founding father Dr. L.P. Hollis. "The officers and Executive Committee wish to express their deep and sincere appreciation of Dr. Hollis' fine contribution to the welfare of textile communities in Greenville and throughout the south."[1]

Beauty pageant winners and beastly finishes were orders of the day for the 1951 tournament, and both were furnished by the Class B women's division. Fredda Acker, a former Mrs. America, had an excellent season with Anderson Mill. In the consolation finals, Glen Lowery Mill defeated Calhoun Falls Mill, 34–32, or so it seemed.

After both teams had left the floor, a scoring error was discovered and the game was actually a tie. First an overtime period was ordered, but it was then decided to declare duplicate champions, for the first and last time in Southern Textile Basketball Tournament history.

Deran Walters, whose playing days spanned the whole decade, and whose teammate was Ellerbe "Big Daddy" Neal at American Enka, remembered the recruiting wars. "I attended Wake Forest University from 1945 to 1948 the only way I could have, on a basketball scholarship. The mills, though, recruited *much* tougher than the colleges did, and that's why there was so much keen competition. Heck, I remember Hanes Hosiery having four starters from the University of North Carolina team for three years running. My best memories are of the battles under the boards with Dunean's Ward Williams, and it was fun to watch players with the skills of Pelzer's Earl Wooten, Dunean's Bob Stowe, Tex Ritter and Larry Ashley, and Piedmont's Ernie

Courtesy STAA

Top: 1951 Southern Textile Basketball Tournament program cover.
Bottom: Early 1950s action involving Winnsboro Mill (Winnsboro, S.C.) team.

Early 1950s action involving Winnsboro Mill (Winnsboro, S.C.) team.

Chambers. Competition? The tournament was that from start to finish."[2]

There seemed a bit of the spirit of Halloween hanging over the 1952 tournament, when about the only predictable occurrence was the undefeated Appleton Mill's women marching to the Class B title. Hurley Badders, reporting for the Greenville *News*, offered his comments on Judson's 56–54 win March 5 over Firestone Textile Inc. in Class B men's action. "The victory was secure only after the 'Roy Riegels of basketball' paved the way. Riegels was the historic football player who ran the wrong way in the Rose Bowl, and, also, Firestone claims a man that scored the wrong goal. E.T. Green, captain of the North Carolina quintet, apparently had his tongue over his eye tooth and couldn't see what he was saying, or doing, for the cage ace dipped in the two points that spelled victory for Judson."[3] Excelsior Mill also forfeited to Dunean in Class B men's action on the same day, because not enough players could be obtained to field a team.

The Class A men's consolation bracket fared no better than their B counterparts. American Enka did not bother to stay around after its opening-day loss, and forfeited the March 7 game to Slater. The Piedmont men lost a tough 62–60 decision to Peerless Woolen Mill, as they were forced to play the last four minutes with only four men on the floor.

In the Class A championship division, one high scoring affair March 5 was won by Dunean over Piedmont, 107–90, as the Dynamos were led by Larry Ashley (26) and Tex Ritter (25); Ernie Chambers had 31 for the losers. This relatively benign contest set the stage for a remarkable final. Before 4,500 screaming fans, Pelzer led Dunean 81–80, and with scant seconds left on the clock, defensive standout Dave Putman stole the ball. Putman was probably the least likely Dynamo on the court to shoot the ball, but with two ticks left and his teammates begging him "Shoot! Shoot!" he launched a two-hand set shot that swished just as the horn sounded. It was said that Earl Wooten was so disgusted after the game that he drove all night and straight into spring training and baseball season. Nobody asked Gerald Becker how he felt

The 1950s — The Southern Textile Basketball Tournament

Top: 1953 Monaghan Mill (Greenville, S.C.), Class A Men's Champions: *(front, l–r)* Roy Skinner, Fig Newton, James Gowan, Ken Pittman; *(back, l–r)* Effie Evington, Brice Kirkpatrick, Warren Mullinax, Harold Burns.
Bottom: 1953 Appleton Mill (Anderson, S.C.), Class B Women's Champions: *(front, l–r)* Lewis Acker (coach), Fredda Acker, Barbara Sanders, Joyce Spears, Bobbie Martin, Joyce Sheridan; *(back, l–r)* Annie Allen, Sue Greenway, Doris Hiott, Jo Billings, Opal Spears, Edna Rhodes.

after scoring 35 in a losing cause. In this game, it was also noted that Ward Williams of Dunean dunked one of his shots, a seldom-used maneuver in the tournament, even by men who could execute it.

To top off this most unusual year, seven Class A men were chosen All-Southern, the first time it had been other than the customary five. Then there was a discussion by the executive committee that "outsiders"—persons not affiliated with the textile plants they represented—should be declared ineligible. This, of course, would have banned the popular college athletes from playing in the tournament, and fan interest would have dwindled. Fortunately, all of the madness subsided at the close of action Saturday.

The wisdom of allowing the mills to use players other than those who worked on site was borne out the next year. Leading his Class B Lyman teammates over Liberty, 80–67, in the opening round was "Jumping" Joe Smith, who popped in 32. Smith was the leading scorer for the University of South Carolina throughout the season. Brice Kirkpatrick, a standout freshman at Furman University, had 34 as the Class A men from Monaghan Mill blew away Chicopee 104–77. Two future major league baseball players, Billy O'Dell and Don Dillard, played with Liberty Mill's Class B and Southern Bleachery's Class C men, respectively.

The use of these "outsiders" enhanced the competition for the mill hill boys like Allan Moore. "My career ran the gamut, beginning with midget ball and playing in all the men's classifications, including the Open Division, for Greer Mill. It was an honor to play against Earl Wooten—my pick for all-time best offensive player—and Tex Ritter—all-time best defensive player. When I started, all the mills had teams for the whole year, so fans followed their favorites through both regular season and tournament play. Eventually, teams would be assembled for postseason play only, and there would be little interest or fan support.

"In the 1940s and 1950s, the Southern Textile Basketball Tournament was something I looked forward to from the start of the season. It brought everyone on the mill village closer together and made for many good memories. The tournament was such a great time, and certainly no one regrets being a part of it." [4]

The 1954 tournament was a time for remembering families and cultivating legends. John Emery, former All-Southern player with mill teams at Piedmont, Victor and Pelzer mills, had three children participating in the tournament: daughter Arnelle (Piedmont B women), son Carroll (Piedmont C men), and son Douglas (Piedmont midgets). The Foster brothers—Fred, Charles, Dewey, Harry and Roy—shared past glories when they ran the court for the Brandon Braves. For good measure, South Carolina Lt. Gov. George Bell Timmerman was on hand to present awards and trophies, and soak up the family lore.

Columnist Jim Anderson augmented the legend of Earl Wooten by sharing a tall tale in the sports pages of the Greenville *News*. "When Earl was a teenager, he killed birds with rocks thrown righthanded. Zinn Beck, a scout for the Chattanooga Lookouts baseball team, was on a hunting trip in the area, and took the opportunity to meet the boy wonder. After watching a rock throwing exhibition, the veteran exclaimed, 'Son, you'll be the greatest righthanded pitcher in history!'

'But Mr. Beck,' Wooten answered, 'I'm lefthanded. I throw right to keep from tearing up the birds.'"[5] There was just no stopping Wooten, either on or off the court.

The men's Class A and B championship games offered the spectators all they could have wanted. Pelzer defeated Dunean 99–93 to take the honors in the A bracket, building a 60–37 halftime advantage and barely holding on. High scorers for the winners were Earl Wooten (39) and Neild Gordon (25), while Dunean was led by Tex Ritter (30) and Big Jim Slaughter (26). Pelzer, in fact, boasted two future college coaches: Gordon, who would guide programs at

Newberry and Winthrop colleges, and Bobby Roberts, who would head the program at Clemson University. The B trophy was claimed by Union Bleachery in a 70–55 win over Beacon Mill. With the victory they became one of the few teams in tournament history to win successive titles in different classes, having won the C division in 1953.

For Slater Mill's Alton White, the post-season competition was like waiting for Christmas. "I started over at Woodside Mill, shooting at an honest-to-goodness basket because we didn't have an iron rim! Then we moved to Slater, where I played midget, C and B ball, and there are two special memories that stick with me. First, I played both high school and midget ball at a hundred and fifteen pounds, and remember running alongside the school bus down White Horse Road in a *heavy* sweatsuit to make that weight limit. Second was when Slater won the B men's championship in 1953.

"Playing basketball kept me off the streets, because that was the only other place I had to go. And the Southern Textile Basketball Tournament was the best thing that ever happened to us mill kids. Oh, they have better players now than when we were there, but overall it has lost a lot because the mills don't participate wholeheartedly anymore."[6]

Bob Seawright remembers the fun of being a teenager in 1954 and going from the small mill town of Ware Shoals to the big city of Greenville. "Willie Wilbanks, the mill's athletic director, would get the high school players together for the tournament. We'd have games at Dunean or maybe Woodside, and then move on to Textile Hall.

"Playing two games on the same day was pretty demanding, but the guys would always have plenty of energy left to run around Greenville before heading back to Ware Shoals."[7]

If nothing else, the 1955 tournament offered a rollercoaster ride of emotions that kept 12,000 folks quite interested for four days. Two former powerhouses in the Class A men's division, Chatham Manufacturing and Dixie Mercerizing, neglected to send teams, complaining that the recruiting and use of "outsiders" increased the cost of participation to remain competitive. Two scoring stars, Dunean's Jim Slaughter and American Enka's Ellerbe "Big Daddy" Neal, were prevented from playing. The executive committee said that any player who received money or other forms of compensation for playing basketball, or who had signed a professional contract for the 1954-55 season, would be ruled ineligible. Evidence was presented that both men had played professionally early in the 1954 campaign with the Washington Bullets.

There were swift ends to exciting games due to a unique tournament rule — the first basket scored in double overtime would decide the winner. Pelzer and Calhoun Falls fought to a 70-all tie at the end of regula-

1955 Southern Textile Basketball Tournament program cover.

tion in March 2's Class B action, and held together at 75-all after the first overtime period. On the opening tip of the second extra period, Pelzer's Bill Thomason grabbed the ball and drove in for the winning layup, making history of the battle. Some games did not require special rules to churn up excitement. Glen Lowery's Class C men pulled a March 3 upset, racing by Mills Mill 68–53 as future University of South Carolina baseball coach June Raines scored 22.

Nothing that year compared with the women's team from Her Majesty, led by Dolly Woods, Sara Wooten and Charlotte Saxon of Mauldin High School. In Friday night's semifinals, they defeated Lonsdale Mill 42–37, the first loss for the Seneca team after 59 straight wins. Woods scored 26 points and was given a singular honor: She was called the ladies' answer to Earl Wooten because of her scoring and ball handling.

Wooten, of course, was his usual self, getting 37 in a semifinal 99–79 win over American Enka on March 4, then pocketing 40 with a series of hooks and drive-in shots as Pelzer repeated as Class A men's champions with an 83–78 win over Monaghan. His former teammate, Neild Gordon, led Monaghan with 32 points (of which 30 were scored in the first half).

There was a reminder, too, of how swiftly time had passed. Dr. L.P. Hollis was one of two surviving members of the "Magnificent Seven" who started the Southern Textile Basketball Tournament. He and representative Charles Varner, a player in the first competition in 1921, were chosen to present the team and individual awards. They were given an ovation that echoed in the night and faded only as the lights dimmed.

A big change ushered in the 1956 competition, one that the founding fathers of the tournament had not foreseen. The

1955 Pelzer Mill (Pelzer, S.C.) Class A Men's Champions: *(front row, l–r)* Randy Whaley, Frank Felts, Bill Scott; *(back row, l–r)* Earl Wooten (coach), Bobby Roberts, Pete Harris, Tom Scott.

Open Division, so named because it was open to all industrial teams, replaced the Class A men's division. The little town of Pelzer certainly felt the reverberations of the change. The mill team had won the Class A men's championship four of the past seven years, and would be competing for the Corn Trophy, awarded only to teams who could amass three consecutive titles in that division. With the change they did not bother to field a team, and players like Randy Whaley and Bobby Roberts moved on to Monaghan. Most devastating, though, was the loss of prolific scorer Earl Wooten to archrival Piedmont. The "Magic Man" would never again wear the uniform of the Pelzer Bears.

Six teams inaugurated the new division, with Paty Lumber Company of Johnson City, Tennessee, becoming the first ever nontextile related company to participate. The timbermen came to Greenville well staffed: captain John Seward was a two time All Southern Conference performer with Duke University; Jimmy Seward was a standout at East Tennessee State University; and Joe Treadway gave steady performances for four years with the University of Tennessee. Paty eventually lost to Greer in semifinal action March 2, and did not remain for the March 3 consolation finals. "Unable to play in Saturday's game. Regret but unavoidable. Many thanks for your hospitality,"[8] read the telegram from John Seward to tournament president Willie Wilbanks. Monaghan then received the consolation trophy.

Two thousand fans watched opening-round action as Wooten scored 45 (21 on free throws) to lead Piedmont over Monaghan, 83–74. A new classification, perhaps, but the same old story as far as Wooten was concerned. In the semis, Dunean was led by Jim Slaughter's 28 points and walloped Piedmont 93–69, despite Wooten's 37. That set the stage for one of the greatest finals ever played in the tournament, as Dunean bested American Enka 119–105; at the half, the score was 63–61. Tex Ritter's 36 led the winners and helped overcome a 49-point performance by Enka's "Big Daddy" Neal.

Oddly, at the Southern Textile Athletic Association meeting on March 3, it was decided to end the Open trial and reinstate the Class A men's division, and to mandate that "A" players derive their livelihood from the plant they represented, or receive half their support from parents employed at that plant.[9] But what had been put in motion could not be stopped, and in a few short years the "Open" would be the highlight show of the tournament.

Bringing the rest of the action into perspective, president Willie Wilbanks offered an observation on the Class C men. "The boys playing out there today are much better basketball players than the 'C's of 1929 when I started. Now they all have the experience of biddy, midget and high school teams. It's just better basketball."[10] With high schools there was always the possibility of a conflict between state championship and textile championship, and this year the Southern Textile Basketball Tournament lost three teams to the pull of old alma mater. The women's teams from Easley Mill and Her Majesty, and Glen Lowery's C men all declined to participate. But the action in 1957 remained fast and furious.

In C action, Jerry Garner's 33 points led Pelzer over Apalache Mill 56–31 on February 28, but the next night Pelzer was routed 104–47 by Belton's balanced scoring of Furman Bannister (24), J.L. Lowe (23) and Doug Broome (22). For the Class B men, Camperdown popped LaFrance Mill 84–59 as North Greenville Junior College starter Buddy Davidson had 34 for the winners, and Simpsonville ran by Union Bleachery 78–50 as Jack Long (30) and Gary Henderson (29) led the way. In the women's division, it was Roberta Bowman's time to shine. Her 32 points on March 2 helped Liberty Mill topple Greer 59–32 in the consolation semifinals, and she followed that up with 38 in a 53–40 consolation finals win over Judson Mill. With 94 points in three games, no one questioned this sharpshooter's ability.

There was a bit of the old to perfectly frame the 33rd edition of the games. A veteran of many tournaments, former Parker High School athletic director Jack Reames recalled a game years before when he was a timekeeper. "There was no electric clock then, so I held a stop watch on the game. One team led by about seventeen points at the half, but the other guys began to make impossible shots in the second half, and the first thing you know they were trailing by only five. I looked at the watch, and there was two minutes, forty-eight seconds to play. Then it was a tie score, and it was one and then the other ahead. You know what? I became a spectator! Like everyone else, I was interested in who would make the next goal. The team that had the first-half lead was trailing by two points when I suddenly remembered I was the timekeeper. The game had gone about a minute-and-a-half over.

"I grabbed for the gun, and at the same time the trailing team took a shot. The ball swished through the net to tie the score as the gun sounded. In the overtime, the team that led nearly all the way eked out the win. But until this year it was a secret!"[11]

Top: 1956 Hanes Hosiery Mill (Winston-Salem, N.C.) Class A Women's Champions: *(front row, l–r)* Cynthia Bowers, Maude Fulp, Phyllis Snipes, Ulala Mitchell, Rosa Nichols; *(back row, l–r)* Eckie Jordan (coach), Bonnie Hobson, Louise Sink, Pearl Gaither, Wanda Harrelson. *Bottom:* 1956 Southern Textile Basketball Tournament program cover.

A 41-year-old veteran truly caught the fancy of the crowds. Though his Calhoun Falls Clippers lost to Pelzer Mill 78–46 in the opening round of Class B men's action, Ford Waldrop was the story of the game. He had played with Piedmont Mill's C men in 1929, and nearly two decades later he came off the bench to score five points. The next night his Clippers were bumped from the tournament as Victor Mill edged out a 60–54 win, but the magic was there one last time. Waldrop tallied 26, and left the floor a true champion.

Style was "in" in 1957. The squad from Russell Manufacturing sported new uniforms and new colors every year — not surprising since the company was in the business of making uniforms. For this year it was red, white and blue for the well-dressed player's entire ensemble — jacket, T-shirt and uniforms. In their new silk threads, the B men raced by Judson Mill 87–54 on opening day with five players scoring in double figures.

Familiar faces were in evidence everywhere. Chick Galloway held court in the stands and remembered playing basketball at Presbyterian College in the days before his trek to the American League with Connie Mack and the Philadelphia Athletics. "A game against Newberry College was played on an outdoor court and barrel staves were used for goals. No nets, just two wobbly hoops."[12]

Grady Wallace, a University of South Carolina product who would play in the Open Division on a regular basis in a couple of years, was a hot topic of conversation since being named a second team Associated Press All-American, joining the company of future NBA legend Elgin Baylor. Wallace, in fact, had just scored 41 against Duke University to raise his season average to 31.4 points per game — best in the nation.

Warmest regards, though, were held for Dunean Mill veteran Willie Riddle. The Amateur Athletic Union had recently named him to the Hall of Fame for deaf players, but his disability in no way hin-

1957 Southern Textile Basketball Tournament program cover.

dered him from competing with the best players the region had to offer. Though he had several good years and was a multiple recipient of All-Southern honors, his finest hour may have been in 1935 when he led Dunean's Class A men to victories over Avondale Mill (45–40), Chatham Manufacturing (41–40), Judson Mill (28–27), and Victor Mill (33–30) for the championship. He was unanimous All-Southern. It was said he always saved his best for tournament play, and no one dared argue the point.

Class A action returned, and 2,500 fans jammed the old Hall for the semifinals, watching two stars on a championship collision course. American Enka swept by Dunean 79–65 as 6'11" Ellerbe "Big Daddy" Neal had 30, and Piedmont rode Earl Wooten's 40-point performance to an 88–69 win over Monaghan. The crowd doubled for the action March 9 as Enka won a thriller, 96–89. Wooten scored a basket early in the second half to pass the 1,000 point mark for tournament games, and play was stopped so he could be presented with the ball. For Wooten and his teammates, it was the worst possible thing that could have happened. Though Wooten scored 50 for the evening, momentum shifted to Enka and Ron Rogers. Overshadowed for most of the tournament, this Little All-American poured in 41 to lead the Tarheel players to the win; Neal added 27.

The March 9 competition was interesting for two other reasons. In the Class A men's consolation, Dunean forfeited to Greer Mill, an unlikely action by one of the most fiercely competitive teams in tournament history. But with injuries to Ward Williams and Bob Stowe, there were just not enough men left to put a team on the floor. The B men's consolation finals offered a happier story for the citizens of Greenville as Judson Mill bested Joanna 78–64 behind Doyle Sellers' 45 points.

At the close of the action, the Southern Textile Athletic Association's Executive Committee made a decision which would forever change the tournament started exclusively to promote competition among the mill communities. From now on, it was open to *all* industrial teams in the South, increasing both the number of teams and its prestige. The times were changing, and the region was no longer a one-industry monopoly.

The next year was the celebration of the tournament's 35th anniversary, summed up in a ditty appearing on the sports pages of the Greenville *News*. It was ascribed to no author, but perhaps was the work of sports editor Jim Anderson.

> Say! Is it the 35th they play?
> The 35th Textile Tourney today?
> Former stars cannot be here.
> These greats of yesteryear.
> Heath, Barbare, Berry, Hill.
> Hampton, Cabiness and Dill.
> Many more ... and lovely Janes:
> The Dixie Aces and Red Flames.
> Now it's time for more tootin'
> With Neal, Huey, and Earl Wooten.[13]

Everyone wanted to talk about the past and present greats of the sport. Multiple winners of All-Southern honors in Class A (and later, Open) action was a hot topic of conversation, and fans cited Paul "Smokey" Barbare as the first three-time winner, 1925–27 with Judson Mill. Fletcher Heath matched him, but with *three* different teams: Victor Mill (1928), Lonsdale Mill (1931) and Monaghan Mill (1933). Esco "Spec" Leopard pulled a trey from 1930–32 with Lonsdale, and Connie Mac Berry matched him in 1933–34 with Monaghan Mill and in 1939 with Southern Bleachery. Harry Anderson, from 1940–42 with Dixie Mercerizing, and Gerald Becker with Pelzer in 1949, 1951–52, rounded out the three-time winners.

John Emery was remembered as the first four-time recipient, in 1934 with Pelzer and in 1936–38 with Piedmont. Effie Evington, with Monaghan Mill in 1951–54, was a more recent four-time honoree. Bob

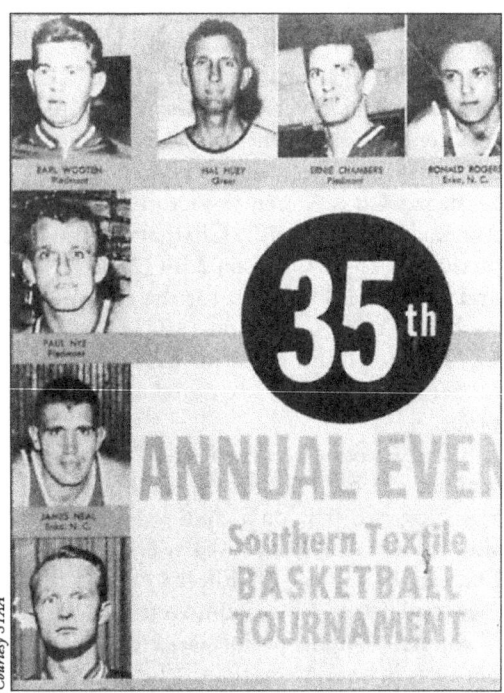

1958 Southern Textile Basketball Tournament program cover.

Stowe garnered five acknowledgments while playing with Dunean (1947–48, 1952, 1954–55). Six-time winners included Bert Hill, Duke University star, with Poe Mill in 1935 and then 1937–41 with Southern Bleachery; Hugh Hampton with Hanes Hosiery (1941–42, 1946–48, 1952); and Ward Williams with Dunean (1946, 1950–53, 1956). No one, though, topped Earl Wooten, who received the honor an unprecedented 12 times (eight with Pelzer and four with Piedmont).

Johnny Hunter, a baseball scout with the New York Giants, opened a two-sport front, remembering Greenville as a hotbed of diamond talent. He praised Fletcher Heath, Fred McAbee, George Blackwell, "Rags" Suddeth, Hob Lee, Ted Cabiness and Bill Broome as fine players. Switching to basketball, he repeated Cabiness and Heath, then added Bert Hill, Harry Anderson, Connie Mac Berry, Earl Wooten, John Emery, Scoop Putman, Hugh Hampton and Ward Williams, recommending them all for special accolades.[14]

There was even room to praise a "zebra." J. Dolen Hedrick officiated this 300th game in the 35th annual tournament. As a player, he finished up in 1939, playing with Adams-Millis when they won the Class B men's championship; he began his officiating career in 1940. A Southern Conference referee as well, he was ahead of his time in seeking a 30-second shot clock. "Of course, that was never needed in the Southern Textile Basketball Tournament," he noted. "No textile team ever waited that long to shoot."[15]

Observers were not shy about citing the talents of the present-day players alongside their predecessors. Bill Barbary, a Clemson University football standout the year before, joined Southern Bleachery's B men. Annie Tribble played with Poinsett Lumber and found her way to Clemson as the women's head basketball coach. And Monaghan's Morris "Fig" Newton was on leave from his army assignment at Camp Polk (La.) to participate in the games.

The Southern Textile Basketball Tournament's enormous influence on college basketball in the state was finally recognized. Victor Mill sent Wayne Fowler and Buddy Davidson to North Greenville Junior College, and Wayne Godfrey to Spartanburg Junior College and then on to the University of South Carolina. Liberty Mill groomed Fred Powers for four years at Wofford College and Bobby Roberts for two at Furman. Monaghan scooted Gene Seay first to North Greenville and then to Clemson, and Effie Evington to Furman for four great years.

No one, though, benefited like North Greenville. In addition to Fowler, Davidson and Seay, their 1957-58 team had deep textile roots that fed a very successful 31–2 campaign and a third straight trip to the National Junior College Tournament in Hutchinson, Kansas. All-American Pistol Pete Carlisle (Anderson Mill's B men), Dag Wilson (Piedmont Mill's Open entry), Mickey Long (Dunean Mill's C men), and Joe Hiott (Piedmont Mill's B men) were four of the five starters. Substitutes included Ronnie McCallister and Mickey Flynn (Greer Mill's C men).

Of course, no one could ever overlook the strong family ties. Courtney Heath, a 1930s star for Brandon Mill, was proud of son Buddy (Easley Mill's B men) and daughter Patsy Rackley (Easley Mill's women's squad). His former teammates Charles Foster and Whitey McDonald cheered sons Charles Jr. and Michael, respectively both carrying on the tradition with Brandon's C men. Jess Buchanan, a member of Woodside Mill's 1921 B men champions, proudly watched son John with the Brandon B men.

"Frog" Stansell learned the game at Gluck Mill watching textile games as a boy. He then played Class C and B ball there and at Anderson Mill. "I was fortunate to play with Gluck the year we beat a very good Dunean team in the B consolation bracket," he remembered, "but the tournament was more than just wins and losses. Playing in that setting taught me discipline, self control, the importance of teamwork, and the necessity of physical fitness, things that still affect my life in a positive manner. My only regret is that age caught up with me and I could not play any longer, but when your last competitive game is at age forty-six, those regrets are small, indeed."[16]

Others were becoming more concerned with what the tournament may have lost. Long-time Dunean player and coach Ward Williams saw more and more mill kids using their sports skills to get to college, but the available talent pool for teams was greatly diminished. Even one of the founding fathers, Dr. L.P. Hollis, worried that teams were placing too much emphasis on winning rather than enjoying the fellowship and competition, traits on which the tournament was founded.[17]

For many of the mill village schoolkids, it was reading, writing, arithmetic and hardwood action. The gym at Woodside Mill played host to many of the early-round games, and it was not uncommon to see three or four classes from the school spend their recess time as spectators. The children brought their enthusiasm with them as they pulled hard for their favorite teams and even made up some cheers as they went along. Others involved in the action were not as fortunate. In the Class C semifinals on March 14, 1958, the Belton Mill men were forced to forfeit to Pelzer, and the reason was most unique: Team members were unable to get permission to be excused from classes in order to go to the basketball tournament. Often there was a glowing example of how well the kids paid attention in school. On March 13, Pelzer's women upset the unbeaten Liberty Mill team, 40–39, on Barbara Harris' 40-foot set shot with ten seconds left. Most of the Pelzer team had been coached by Bobby Roberts at Palmetto High School *before* he moved on to Liberty.

Second-round action heated up to a boil and set the tone for one of the most competitive five days any fan could have hoped for. Beacon Mill upset the top-ranked Lonsdale Mill ladies of Seneca, 40–35, in a rough and tumble affair. Lonsdale's Beverly Dooley went out with a broken collarbone and teammate Ruth McDaniel collapsed due to a nervous disorder. In Russell Manufacturing's 76–71 win over Greer's B men, one of Greer's outstanding players, Butch Miller, scored 12 points before suffering a head injury late in the first half; he did not return to the game. A different kind of rough and tumble emerged when Joanna beat Brandon 53–47 in Class B men's action. A spectator started a fight that carried over onto the floor, and it was said to be the first untoward incident in the 35 years of tournament play. The B men's consolation was pure on-court excitement, as Fiberglas defeated Mills Mill 63–57 in triple overtime.

The semifinals offered some fine performances and more than a few heroics for the 3,000 spectators. When Dunean edged Union Bleachery in Class C men's competition, Earl Whittington scored only two points, but they came with five seconds left to provide the winning margin. Gerald Grayson hit two free throws with 20 seconds left as the Class B men from Russell Manufacturing defeated defending champion Courtaulds, 86–85. Jimmy Holden's 41 points (30 in the first half) helped move Monaghan's Class B men into the finals with an 88–68 win over Lonsdale Mill. Harriett Kitchen did not allow the ladies to be overlooked as she popped in 32 to lead her Liberty team past Fiberglas, 55–34, in the consolation semis. For the Class A men from Enka, though, consolation was just not good enough. "Big Daddy" Neal's 32 points (and he sat out much of the last half with four personal fouls) could not stave off Monaghan's 88–70 upset win, putting the North Carolina team in the loser's bracket. Enka immediately forfeited all of its remaining games and returned home.

The next night 3,500 fans watched as Piedmont swept to the Class A men's title, pummeling Monaghan, 90–67. All starters were in double figures: Earl Wooten (26), Mack Isner (21), Ernie Chambers (17), Paul Nye (15), and Jim Slaughter (11). Slater upset Russell Manufacturing 87–75 in overtime for the Class B men's champi-

1959 Southern Textile Basketball Tournament program cover.
Piedmont Mill's 1958 Class A Champions.

onship; James Wilson had 13, but 8 came in the extra period to ice the win.

The decade's last year brought on the ultimate change, as the tournament moved from Textile Hall to Memorial Auditorium. The cramped courts, seats with obstructed views, and often inadequate heating were exchanged for spacious playing areas and improved physical facilities. The voices remembering the purpose of the Southern Textile Basketball Tournament were being drowned out by advocates of progress, so the words of Hubert Nolin seemed especially important. An All-Southern performer in 1924-25, and later a prominent attorney in Greenville, he noted that "the tournament has been one of the finest things ever for textile athletics. It was a wonderful thing from the start, particularly when each community had such rivalry. Good sportsmanship resulted and friends were made for life."[18]

Sam Patton, coach of American Enka, chose to follow the original premise of the Southern Textile Basketball Tournament and play employees of the company in the team's quest for the Open Division title, rather than recruiting players especially for the games. Like Nolin's words, it seemed a quaint anachronism. More to the tune of these modern times was the return of the Open Division, which replaced the Class A men's section for 1959. With the possibility of big-time college players participating, excitement about the tournament abounded. Nolin's idea of community rivalry was dealt a blow by a growing trend away from competing in regular season textile league basketball. When the Class C Monaghan men upset Woodside Mill

56–54 for the championship, they did so with a team brought together solely to play in the March gathering. "Showtime" was encroaching—basketballs in team colors were used in pre-game warmups, and Woodside (red, black and white), Liberty (white and black) and Maness Sporting Goods (orange and white) offered a little technicolor variety.

If nothing else, the new surroundings of Memorial Auditorium energized the scoring parade, and no one had to wait long to see it. The opening games on March 11 spotlighted the Open Division as Piedmont blitzed Pelzer 111–73 behind Dayton University All-American Jack Sallee's 31 points; Jerry Garner had 25 for the losers. Columbia's Pacific Terrifics blew away Ware Shoals in Class C men's action, 86–27, as Vic Jordan equaled the losers' output. And Wunda Weve popped Saco-Lowell 41–27 in the women's division as Pat Murphy's 33 points were more than enough to assure the win.

The March 12 action offered exciting battles in two women's contests. Lonsdale Mill outdistanced Wunda Weve 57–43 behind the dual barrage of Winona Foster (30) and Brenda Addis (25), and Pat Murphy had another good outing with 25 to pace the Weavers. Jackson Mill slipped by Carolina Plating 41–39, led by Shelby Pryor's 29 points, and Carolyn Clayton kept Carolina close with her 25 points. Much like Monaghan Class C men's champs, the Jackson ladies were organized shortly before the tournament, with the nucleus drawn from Crescent High School's state championship team. To round out the

1959 Piedmont Mill (Piedmont, S.C.) Open Division Men's Champions: *(front row, l–r)* Doug Hoffman, Tommy Kearns, Earl Wooten (coach), Paul Nye, Jim Lewis; *(back row, l–r)* Don Roper, Jack Salee, Mack Isner, Ernie Chambers, Jim Slaughter.

March 12 excitement, Greer Mill came from 20 points down to edge Ware Shoals 56–54 in the B men's consolation bracket.

The semifinals on March 13 featured even hotter action. Winona Foster's 30 led Lonsdale past Joanna 58–39 in women's action, and Piedmont waltzed by Texize 101–84 in the Open Division as University of North Carolina All-American Tommy Kearns poured in 40. The night, though, belonged to Vince Yockel, a Clemson University product playing for the B men of Piedmont Mill. His 54 points powered Piedmont past Monsanto (of Pensacola, Fla.) 90–70, and he fouled out with four minutes remaining. Ex–Auburn University captain Jim Diamond offered a fine 24-point performance for the Floridians.

The finals on March 14 were pure icing. Winona Foster's 33 lifted Lonsdale over Slater 51–39 for the women's championship and left the star only one point shy of Roberta Bowman's 94 point total in 1956. The ladies' consolation bracket was equally compelling when Bobbie Burns lit up the night with 38 (tying Bowman's 3-year-old record) to lead Anderson Mill over Ware Shoals 55–47. The men matched the women game for game, first as Vince Yockel's 33 gave Piedmont an 88–71 Class B championship over Greer Mill. Open Division winner Piedmont Mill rode Jack Sallee's 32-point spree to edge Monaghan 91–84; Furman University alumni Tom Conard (28) and Dick Wright (23) led a valiant effort by the underdogs.

Some may have mourned the passing of old Textile Hall to close out the '50s, but no one could argue that the new facility had not offered quite an inauguration.

The 1960s

Having an Open Class makes the rest of the tournament possible.
  Earl Wooten
  (Greenville *News*, Saturday, March 12, 1960)

Old Man Winter engineered a freeze in 1960 clearly superior to any ball control slowdown the tournament had ever seen. Major snowstorms hit the Greenville area March 9 and 11, playing havoc with everything from game schedules to dining and sleeping arrangements. Memorial Auditorium was literally home to the tournament, as 150 cots for men and 50 for women were set up to accommodate the stranded teams. The two groups were, of course, as far removed as possible from one another, and immovable screens were placed between the men and women. Concession stands were kept open, offering a menu of sandwiches and soft drinks.[1]

Keeping to any kind of a schedule was something akin to a nightmare. The Newberry All Stars were unable to make it to the tournament at all, and forfeited their Open Division game to Dixie Ford of Greenville. Adventure stories abounded as teams struggled to arrive. Newry Mill players arrived four hours late as team members helped push 15 cars out of the way to clear a path to Memorial Auditorium. The Monsanto team (of Pensacola, Fla.) tried to make the trip in the company plane, but was grounded in Atlanta and forced to take a train into Greenville. Lonsdale Mill team members arrived by train at the Southern Depot, but could not find transportation to the auditorium until a Railway Express truck driver offered a ride.[2] It had to be the first instance of an express delivery of a whole team.

Even as the games were played, the weather was still a factor. In the Open Division, Dillard's Sporting Goods blew away Carolina Plating 122–66, breaking the record of 119 set by Dunean Mill's Class A Men in 1956, and equaled earlier on March 9 by Russell Manufacturing's B men in a 119–64 walloping of Union Bleachery. Dillard's had only four players make it to the game, and were allowed to select a fifth man from the audience. Bobby Fleming had played with the Anderson Mill B men in 1956, and it was fitting that he hit the free throw which broke the record with 32 seconds left in the game, and then added a jumper with two seconds to go for the final margin.

A second Open Division game March 10 was a 122–87 Monaghan win over Speed Queen of Chattanooga, Tennessee, tying Dillard's Sporting Goods' "long standing" (one day) scoring record. The winners placed six in double figures: Gene Seay (34), Buddy McCall (20), Jack League (17),

1960 recipients of the Harold R. Turner Sportsmanship Trophy: *(l–r)* **Mrs. Harold R. Turner, Jim Diamond (winner), Jo Dawkins (winner), Brown Mahon.**

Jim Whitfield (15), Fig Newton (12) and Dick Tyler (16). In defense of Speed Queen, however, it took the team ten hours to traverse the snow-covered roads between Chattanooga and Greenville, and they arrived at 5:00 A.M. on game day. Four players were left stranded near Cartersville, Georgia, when their car slid off the road, though fortunately no injuries occurred.[3]

The spirit of the 1960 tournament was captured by the B men from Poinsett Mill, who played the whole regular season without a win. They were to play Fiberglas on March 9, but the game was postponed when the Anderson team could not get to Greenville. Rescheduled for 9:00 A.M. the next day, the same thing happened, and Fiberglas offered to forfeit. Poinsett refused, to a man agreeing, "We want to play." Eleven A.M. was the start of Fiberglas's one sided victory, 81–35, placing four in double figures: Leroy Parnell (22), Jerry Parnell (20), Larry Lowe (19), and Jimmy Smith (12). Poinsett gutted it out and played a 1:30 P.M. game against Greer the same day, losing for the final time that year, 57–53. But they won the hearts of the fans and must have made old L.P. Hollis proud.[4]

The weather may have been frightful, but inside Memorial Auditorium it was all toasty, with more high-scoring performances the rule rather than the exception. In women's action on March 10, Sue Vickers scored 32 to lead Slater past Joanna 63–37, and in the men's C division, Dickie Dietz led Stone Manufacturing over Slater Mill, 37–33. Dietz was not far removed from starting his successful major league baseball career.

Open competition finished off the March 10 games. In the consolation bracket, LaFrance Mill moved past Carolina Plating

110–83 behind Ed Brinkley's 30 points; there were 51 personal and three technical fouls called in this rough and tumble affair. The Stevens Rockets team (composed of the Greer, Victor and Apalache plants) bombed Dixie Ford 100–49 behind the University of South Carolina trio of Mike Callahan (30), Walt Hudson (18) and Bob Frantz (15).

The Rockets kept up their winning ways March 11, upsetting the defending champion Piedmont Rangers 75–52, and the five starters went all the way, each one registering double figures: Mike Callahan (24), Jimmy Herring (15), Willard Fowler (13), Leon Gravley (12), and Bob Frantz (11). Sue Vickers kept up a torrid pace, getting 39 in Slater's 56–37 win over the ladies from Poinsett Lumber. This left her 23 points shy of Roberta Bowman's 1956 record of 94 total tournament points.

Legendary Clemson University football coach Frank Howard presented the trophies and awards after the completion of March 11's games, and the bashful baron had to respect the competition he witnessed. The Sue Vickers onslaught continued as she claimed the scoring record with a 30-point performance, leading Slater past Lonsdale Mill 54–37; Brenda Addis put on a show of her own, scoring all but seven of Lonsdale's points. And in the Class B men's finals, Dunean blitzed Monaghan, 82–64, as Presbyterian College's Mickey Long (22), North Greenville Junior College's Ricky Duncan (20), and Ronnie Russell (19) led the way. Even in the winter wonderland, it was a hot start to a new decade.

The customary gathering of old timers was no different in 1961, but some of them admitted they were not all that keen about

1961 Cannon Mill (Central, S.C.) Class C Men's Champions: *(front, l–r)* Tommy McNeil, Ronnie Maravich, Jimmy Sutherland, Johnny Chapman; *(back, l–r)* Frank Cox, Tommy Risher, Walter Cox, Pete Maravich, Pete Carlisle (coach).

1961 recipients of the Harold R. Turner Sportsmanship Trophy: *(l–r)* Mrs. Harold R. Turner, Steve Brown (winner), Sue Vickers (winner).

competition in the days of yore. "Things sure have changed. Look at the difference in the facilities and the caliber of play out there as compared to when we first started this thing," noted June Campbell, a Monaghan Mill player in 1921. "Play was so rough in those days we had to wear long pants, and they were equipped with knee pads. And I mean they were *well* padded. The floors were so rough you didn't have any skin left on your knees the way we got tossed around. It was almost like first and ten in football. We just played rough."[5]

Teammate Fred "Peck" Ellis echoed the sentiments by insisting, "*Don't* take me back to the good old days. We once had a referee with a white moustache, and he smoked cigars. All he would do was toss the ball up for center jump and get out of the way. There were only two fouls — slugging and tripping — but he never called anything."[6]

Rounding out the Monaghan trio of 1921 was Walt Barbare. "The only foul was something you did behind a man's back. You could do anything to his face." He even admitted to bending the rules a bit. "I wasn't supposed to play that year because the rule then forbade a professional athlete from competing in the Southern Textile Basketball Tournament, and I was a shortstop for the Boston Braves. But I went in as a substitute, and we lost 27 to 25 or something like that. Tournament official L.P. Hollis said he was glad of the loss as there was no need of disciplinary action on his part!"[7]

Old-timers and spectators were in for a steady diet of fast action. The 1961 tournament tacked on an extra day, and the March 7 games offered a bit of name recognition. When Monaghan coasted by Wyandotte Mill 118–69 in the Open Division, they were led by ex–North Carolina State sparkplug Dick Tyler (39), Gene Seay (20), Daddy Neal (18), Jack League (14), and Fig Newton (11). And brothers Ronnie (22) and

Pete (18) Maravich, sons of Clemson University coach Press, led the Class C Cannon Mill men by Piedmont, 89–64. Certainly, the tone for the 1961 tournament was set: balanced scoring would rule the day.

Two thousand fans watched the high scoring action March 8, especially the Piedmont Mill Open Division entry setting yet another single-game scoring record, this one a 124–88 win over Lonsdale Mill. Dillard's Sporting Goods blew past Pelzer 110–59 in the same division, led by John Adcock of Young Harris College (31), Bryan Pinson of Furman University (27), Ed Krajack of Clemson (25), and Tony McEntyre of Furman (12). The Class C Greer men had an easy time in a 97–42 pasting of Liberty Mill, placing six in double figures: T.J. Ingle (21), Wayne Gambrell (19), Jim Wall (16), Steve Gambrell (11), Bob Barton (14), and George Coan (10). In women's action, Lonsdale wasted little time in outdistancing Carolina Plating 55–12, setting a course to meet the powerhouse Slater Mill team in the finals. Brenda Addis (21) and Beverly Dooley (20) led the potent attack.

The tournament received an added boost when Tom Chilton, the nation's second-leading scorer (32.1 ppg) from East Tennessee State, joined the Open Division's Chattanooga VFW team on March 9.[8] His rebounding was the talk of the town after their 118–88 win over Slater, but his 27 points was bettered by teammates Joe Gardner from the University of Miami (45) and Clyde Eads from Florida State (31). In B men's action, Dunean edged Lyman 75–72 in a contest where balance outdid stellar individuality. Jimmy Chapman (22), Earl Whittington (15), Leon McWhite (14) and Ronnie Cross (13) led Dunean, while Leon Eubanks of Lyman took scoring honors with 34.

The March 10 semifinals proved to be a maker of memories for the 3,000 in attendance. Even with Tom Chilton's 25 points, Chattanooga VFW could not survive its Open Division battle with Monaghan, losing 118–82 as Gene Seay (30) and Daddy Neal (24) led the way for the Eagles. The game was halted for ten minutes midway through the opening half due to a power failure, the first time anyone was accused of "lighting the scoreboard down." Piedmont's Open victory over Dillard's Sporting Goods, 83–63, was made easier by the fact that the losers finished the game shorthanded. When Ed Krajack fouled out with more than nine minutes to play, four men were left, and Dillard's eventually wound up with only three on the floor. Dunean's B men had no such reason when they blew a seven-point lead with three minutes left (and a three-point lead with 22 seconds to go), finally losing to Greer 73–69 in overtime. In that extra period, Steve Brown scored all six points for the winners on free throws. The Slater women offered by far the finest display of basketball, dropping Greer 82–41 behind double-digit scoring of Pat Murphy (29), Sue Vickers (19), Judy Hodgens (11), Linda Brown (10), and Joan Knight (10).

Miss South Carolina, Sandra Browning, was on hand to present the championship hardware after the competition ended March 11 before 4,000 fans. The Southern Textile Athletic Association also began its Hall of Fame, and the two charter members were past presidents Clarence Thomas and Dr. L.P. Hollis.[9] Slater's women were the only defending champions to repeat, beating back Lonsdale Mill in a hard-fought 62–50 win as Sue Vickers poured in 37 to lead the way. The C men from Slater did not fare as well, falling 75–72 to Cannon Mill as the Maravich brothers (32 for Ronnie and 18 for "Pistol Pete") were too strong. Scoring posed no problem in the Open Division finals, where Piedmont bested Monaghan 94–77. In fact, five from each team scored in double figures: for Piedmont, Vince Yockel (25), Pete Carlisle (21), Dag Wilson (13), Rex Frederick (12), and Earl Maxwell (12); for Monaghan, Daddy Neal (22), Fig Newton (16), Gene Seay (13), Dick Tyler (12), and Jimmy Holden (10).

The tournament was a popular gathering place for college coaches, and Erskine's Red

Myers and Clemson's Bobby Roberts took in the 1962 clashes to pick up talent for their programs. Coach Myers had to be doubly proud on opening day (March 5) when Pelzer's B squad edged Davis Mechanical 102–96 in double overtime; his own Michael Jordan poured in 42 for the winners. Upsets were the rule in early C men's action. Woodside ran by Slater 66–54 even though the losers were composed of the Slater-Marietta High School team, recent Class B state champions. Neighboring Monaghan repeated the deal, edging regular-season champions Lonsdale Mill, 48–44. Excitement carried on into March 6, when Berkeley's B men came from five down in the last 75 seconds to squeak by Homelite, 82–81, on Tip Massey's shot at the buzzer; Norman Greene had 42 for Berkeley, Steve Dacus 33 for Homelite.

Fans witnessed a bit of history in March 7's action when the Slater women crushed Dunean, 80–12. Sue Vickers had 53 points, shattering her old record of 39, and left little doubt of her dominance in tournament play. Slater's C men could have used a few of those points as their favored status did little good. They were knocked out of the action after being upset for the second straight game, this time a 61–51 victim of Easley. Mackie Nichols' 34 led the winners.

The Open Division kicked into high gear on March 8, as Piedmont buried Dillard's Sporting Goods 111–83 behind the scoring of Don Carver (29), Vince Yockel (27), Gene Seay (16), Bob Benson (14), and Dag Wilson (10). Todd-Moore did much the

1961 Southern Textile Basketball Tournament program cover.
Dunean Mill's 1960 Class B Champions.

Top: 1962 Southern Textile Basketball Tournament program cover.
Bottom: 1963 Southern Textile Basketball Tournament program cover.

same to Chattanooga VFW, 115–87, thanks to the University of South Carolina combination of Grady Wallace (32), Mike Callahan (26), and Art Whisnant (24). The C men continued as a most inhospitable place for favorites, and this time defending champion Cannon Mill was blasted by Pelzer, 90–64. It was a rough game (Pelzer lost Sam Rogers with a broken arm seven minutes before the end of the first half), and the winners capitalized at the free-throw line, hitting 36 of 42.

This tournament, though, belonged to Sue Vickers. With 36 points in a 76–44 semifinal win over Carolina Plating on March 9, and 25 more in the championship March 10 as Slater defeated Simpsonville 55–44, she proved herself one of the fairest, fiercest competitors in the games' history. While the women of Slater took the title path as expected, Class A Apalache surprised everyone in a 74–66 win over Pelzer, as all five starters scored in double figures: Jimmy Herring (20), Steve Gambrell (16), Don Lister (16), June Raines (14), and Wayne Gambrell (10). Governor Fritz Hollings was in distinguished company when he presented the trophies and awards to champions such as these.

Talent still glittered in 1963, enough that Press Maravich (North Carolina State University), Lyles Alley (Furman University) and Bill Connell (Wingate College) joined the frequent fan duo of Red Myers and Bobby Roberts at courtside for a scout's dream. For Maravich, an added bonus on opening day (March 4) was watching son Pete (25 points) and teammate Jim Sutherland (32) lead Cannon Mill's C men past Piedmont, 96–60. Mickey Davis spiced up the women's action, popping in 26 to key Murrell Brothers Sand past Sangamo, 58–38. She scored 27 two nights later, but that total could not stop Monsanto (Pensacola, Fla.) from upsetting the Sanders, 52–38.

The semifinal action March 8 offered a veritable feast for the fans. In Open competition, Stanly Mill crushed Dillard's Sporting Goods, 118–63, behind sharpshooters Tom Burton (25), Dick Whitis (23) and Jim Wiles (20). In the Class A men's bracket, Pelzer edged Slater 87–86 on Jimmy Coble's jumper with four seconds left, the most spectacular of his 22 points; he was joined in the scoring by Don Helms (21), Cooper (21), Doug Harris (16), and James Thomason (11). The Class B men's consolation offered an interesting twist. Teammates at North Greenville Junior College, Mac Lemmons and Wendell Lee went separate ways for the tournament; Lemmons' 34 led Steel Heddle past Lee (31 points) and his Stone Manufacturing teammates, 83–67.

Four thousand fans came back for more

March 9, and the championship clashes did not disappoint. Old rivals Piedmont and Pelzer met for the Class A men's laurels, with the Rangers edging the Pelzerites 101–94. Larry "Choppy" Patterson led the victory march with 49, and he was supported by 22 from Earl Wooten, who was named All-Southern for the twelfth and final time. The familiar Slater women won their fourth straight title, riding Sue Vickers' 37-point performance to a 54–49 win over Poinsett Lumber.

The 1963 tournament, though, showcased Glen Lowery's Dorothy Dubose, not exactly a recognized name at the start of the yearly court battles. Though her team lost to Bahan 34–32 in March 6 action, she scored 20, hitting 16-of-19 from the foul line. The next night, she had 29 in a 45–24 win over Saco-Lowell. And in the consolation finals on March 9, a 34–31 heartbreak at the hands of Carolina Plating, she hit 17 more from the charity stripe to break her two-day-old record.

For Herman Evatt, the tournament was a chance to see many of the great players perform. With Pelzer's Class B team and Fiber Industries' A men from 1962–72, he was afforded a good seat from which to observe the abilities of Earl Wooten, Doug Moe, Lenny Rosenbluth, Billy Cunningham, Grady Wallace and Pete Maravich. "It was a good way to learn, watching those guys. All of them were such fantastic athletes."[10]

Fans in attendance March 10 for the opening action of the 1964 tournament saw a bit of innovation from the Open Division Murrell Brothers Sand team. They defeated

1963 Slater Mill (Slater, S.C.) Class A Women's Champions: *(sitting, l–r)* Judy Clark, Diane Smith, Joan Kirby, Priscilla Hunt, Doris Capps; *(standing, l–r)* Ann Thornton, Peggy Chumley, Sue Vickers, Leila Harvin, Arlene Wood, Margaret Wright (coach).

the Williamston All Stars 88–62 by using a two-platoon system, insuring a fresh team on the floor at all times. First it would be Gerald Glur (Furman), Leroy Peacock (Furman), Don Mahaffey (Clemson), Gary Burnisky (Clemson), and Jim Brennan (Clemson). Then would come Don Frye (Furman), Charlie Jennings (Furman), Nick Milasnovich (Clemson), Mike Bohanak (Clemson), and Bill Wade (Furman). That same day, the Class B Conso men upset top-seeded Saco-Lowell 82–80, rallying from 13 down in the first half. Led by Ralph Brown's 39, including a one-and-one with four seconds left to seal the win, they gave notice of the excitement yet to come.

Quarterfinal action March 12 produced a classic in the A division. It was not that Piedmont defeated Lyman 92–82; neither was it the stellar performances of Lyman's Steve Brown (38 points) or Piedmont's Vince Yockel (33 points). There were 25 fouls called on each team, both scored 22 points from the charity stripe, and Leon Gravley, former player and now referee, called so many fouls that his whistle tooted out. Calling one of the many infractions, his whistle offered only silence, so he calmly stopped the game, proceeded to the scorer's table and picked up another one to finish out the game. Gravley looked sheepishly over to Southern Textile Athletic Association president Ward Williams, himself a former All-Southern performer, and said simply, "It just wouldn't blow."[11]

Another former referee, Willie Bishop, could sympathize with Gravley's busy night. "We used to start the tournament in the 1940s at nine A.M. I would call several games during the morning, change into a uniform and play with Southern Bleachery

1964 Southern Textile Basketball Tournament program cover.
Lyman Mills 1963 Class B Champions.

1965 Southern Textile Basketball Tournament program cover.
Monsanto (Greenwood) 1964 Class A Champions.

in the afternoon, and then call games again at night. I'd wind up officiating seven games in all. Sometimes there would be a few minutes to rest on a cot I'd set up in the locker room."[12]

The March 14 finals offered all the customary thrills. Murrell Brothers Sand captured the Open crown, outdistancing Mikro 112–95 in overtime. Nine points down with three minutes left, the Sanders tied it up, then ripped off 11 straight in the extra period to cap a run of 28 points in five minutes. Murrell was led by Nick Milasnovich (28 points), Mikro by Doug Moe (28 points). In Class A men's action, it was a different setting but the same result as Monsanto (Greenwood) edged Piedmont 83–78 for the championship, their sixth win in seven games against the Rangers that season. The winners placed five in double figures: Don Carver (20), Herb Edmonds (17), Pete Carlisle (17), Garrett Nation (16), and Jim Diamond (13). Piedmont was paced by Vince Yockel's 31.

Union Bleachery's B men celebrated big time in their 66–58 win over Anderson Hosiery, their first B championship in a decade. Mike Fair of Monaghan's C men hit a last-second shot in the second overtime for a 47–45 win over Saco-Lowell. He had missed the final shot both in regulation and in the first overtime, but his teammates' confidence in him paid off in championship form. And in the biggest upset in recent memory, Singer's women edged Slater 43–42 as Linda Linn's 18 points led an inspired team effort and denied Slater a fifth straight title.

The Open division competition reached new heights in 1965 as some of the region's most celebrated players joined the teams, and they got right down to business. On March 10, Mikro of Charlotte, led by the

University of North Carolina tandem of Doug Moe (27) and Billy Cunningham (23), and Wofford College's George Lyons (23), moved past Washington Mill, 98–85. Murrell Brothers Sand defeated Hanes Hosiery 104–86 as Bob McCullough of Benedict College had 26, and it was said that "he wowed folks with behind-the-back passes and twisting lay-ups."[13] North Carolina State's Cliff Dwyer scored 23 for the losers. In other opening-day action, the Class A Lyman men ran past Slater Mill 92–79, despite Leroy Peacock's 39. His game high total could not best the Lyman trio of Wayne Greene (26), Steve Brown (24), and Clarence Russell (20). The defending women's champions, Singer of Anderson, blasted Pelzer 50–18 as Claudia Garrett's 19 outdistanced the loser's total. Vickie Chapman accounted for all but three of Pelzer's points.

The Greenville Old Pros heated up the action again March 11, crushing Peerless Community Center 153–103 to shatter the old single-game scoring record by 29 points; the Pros poured in 68 field goals, and most of the points were accounted for by Davidson College teammates Don Davidson (38) and Fred Hetzel (36).

A bit more glitter was added when the Southern Textile Athletic Association Hall of Fame added Bert Hill, All-Southern with Poe Mill (1935) and Southern Bleachery (1937-39), and later a star at Duke University, and Mrs. Clarence Thomas, who as Lucille Foster of Monaghan Mill was one of the first great players in the women's division.

The semifinals of March 12 offered perhaps the most heralded individual matchup in tournament history when Mikro and the Greenville Old Pros met in the Open Divi-

1965 Slater Mill (Slater, S.C.) Class A Women's Champions: *(kneeling, l-r)* Peggy Chumley, Toni Sellars, Susan Chumley, Linda Weaver, Mickey Davis; *(standing, l-r)* Margaret Wright (coach), Doris Capps, Nadene Jeflords, Mae Hill, Leila Harvin, Ouida Williams, Sandy Burgess.

sion. The Charlotte team had Billy Cunningham, All-American at the University of North Carolina and Atlantic Coast Conference Player of the Year. The Sandlappers countered with Fred Hetzel, All-American at Davidson College and Southern Conference Player of the Year. With Cunningham scoring 39 (25 in the first half) and getting help from teammates Doug Moe (21) and Jesse Branson (21), Mikro pounded out a 112–78 win. Hetzel did have 20, but the Old Pros were led by Don Davidson's 25.

"It was a terrific tournament with lots of great competition," noted Doug Moe, "and I can remember beating Fred Hetzel and his Davidson College teammates in the Open Division semifinals. But they were only one of a number of good teams to be playing that year."

Mikro sported the likes of Moe, former UNC stalwart and the coach at Elon College; Billy Cunningham, UNC All-American; Jim Huddock, UNC alumnus and first team captain for coach Dean Smith; Robert Sorrell, a fine player and one of the first African Americans to play in the Southern Textile Basketball Tournament; and Elon College teammates Jesse Branson and Bill Morningstar.

"One memory, though, means more to me than the championship we won that year," added Moe. "I was good friends with Press Maravich, and watching his son Pete participate in Class C ball as a twelve-year-old was really something. It was pretty easy to predict greatness for that young man."[14]

There was also controversy. In the men's B division, Anderson Hosiery had defeated Liberty Mill 77–60 on March 11, but used ineligible players to do it. When this breach of rules was discovered, Liberty was awarded a victory and made the most of it, defeating Lyman 75–68 to reach the finals.

The championship round on March 13 offered two gems. Mikro took the Open crown with a 96–84 win over Murrell Brothers Sand, and they were led by Elon College's Jesse Branson (30), Billy Cunningham (23) and Doug Moe (21).

"I got here courtesy of Moe," laughs Cunningham. "He was assistant coach at Elon then, but we had known each other in high school in Brooklyn, New York. Doug graduated a couple of years ahead of me, going to the University of North Carolina, and I followed him down South. So tagging along to Greenville probably wasn't all that unusual.

"I had a good time during the tournament, meeting folks and competing against some great players. That semifinal game against the Old Pros, when they played up the battle between Fred Hetzel and me, was a great game to be involved in. You know, even after thirty years, Moe, Huddock and I still talk on the telephone a couple of times a week. Heck, I wouldn't take anything for the memories we made there in 1965."[15]

No one, though, matched the intensity of the women's finals as Slater blew past the defending champions of Singer, 67–52. Mickey Davis scored 42, 17 of which came in the final seven minutes to ice the win.

Jerry Parris offered a unique perspective on the tournament in the mid–1960s. "I wasn't very good at playing, so I started refereeing at age twelve. And I started calling high school games when I was a junior, barely seventeen. Then I made it to the original March Madness, the Southern Textile Basketball Tournament, and being here was the most fun part of the year for me.

"My most special memory came several years later when David Lawrence of Shelby, North Carolina, broke Earl Wooten's single tournament scoring record in 1992. Can you believe it," he said, "I was selected to call three of his team's games that week? What impressed me more than anything was his sportsmanship; he was the consummate gentleman. That last night he needed fifty points for the record, and he wound up with sixty-three. A great defensive player, Lawrence also made several superb blocks, too. It was an honor being part of his history-making tournament, and it has remained my distinct privilege to be associated with this fine event over the years."[16]

Top: 1966 Southern Textile Basketball Tournament program cover. Mikeo's 1965 Open Division Champions.
Bottom: 1966 Sunshine Cleaners (Columbia, S.C.) Open Division Men's Champions: *(front row, l–r)* Bill Simpson, John Shroeder, Grady Wallace (coach); *(back row, l–r)* Don Whitehead, Jimmy Collins, Henry Logan, Terry Lucansky.

1967 Southern Textile Basketball Tournament program cover.
Monsanto's (Greenwood) 1966 Class A Champions.

The Open and Women's divisions may have been a showcase of college talent for the fans' enjoyment, but the men's Class C bracket was an opportunity for college coaches to scout the best high school talent for their programs. The players were also allowed a comfort zone, since many of the sponsors often kept entire teams intact. Witness the 1966 representations: Saco-Lowell (Daniel High, Clemson, S.C.); Simpsonville Mill (Hillcrest High, Simpsonville, S.C.); Microtron (Greer High, Greer, S.C., and Byrnes High, Spartanburg, S.C.); Poe Hardware (Greenville High, Greenville, S.C.); Dill's Warehouse (J.L. Mann High, Greenville, S.C.); Piedmont Mill (Wren High, Piedmont, S.C.); and Maxon Shirt Co. (Wade Hampton High, Greenville, S.C.).[17]

In the games of March 17, 1966, Woodside edged the favored Simpsonville squad 62–61, but chose a most unusual strategy. Jack Anderson took the last shot with Woodside trailing by one, had the shot blocked but recovered and put the ball back up and in with three seconds left for the winning bucket. Balanced scoring was the key in Salem Garment's pounding of Union Bleachery, 76–34, with four in double figures: David Byers (20), John Dillard (19), C.E. Ellenburg (12), and Randy Talley (11).

Things were already off to a rocking start two days earlier, thanks to competition in the women's division. Singer defeated Bigelow-Sanford 53–28 as a pair of Carolyns — Brown and Garrett — each scored 20 for the winners. Piedmont's Linda Porter had 21 in a 49–35 breeze over Oconee Gas. The ladies, unlike the men, dealt with a pretty drastic rule change, eliminating the roving guard and forward from tournament play. "We're not used to this rule," noted

Mickey Davis, formerly of Ware Shoals and now with the Atlanta Tomboys. "We play the Amateur Athletic Union rules during the year, *with* a roving forward and guard. This makes for a faster game, with four players from each team on one side of the court."[18] But that change did not seem to slow them down as the tournament progressed. The next day, Davis's Tomboys routed Poe Hardware 74–30, led by Edwina Bryan (33) and Vivian Maslen (28). They topped that a day later, besting the old scoring record by three in an 83–48 pounding of Piedmont as Maslen (35) and Mickey D (22) shared the honors.

With the emergence of African American players at predominantly white universities in the wake of the civil rights movement of the 1960s, the Southern Textile Basketball Tournament was blessed with the presence of one of the nation's finest athletes, Henry Logan. One of the first black players at a major college (Western Carolina University), Logan was an integral part of Sunshine Cleaners' push to the Open Division title. Paired with former University of South Carolina All-American Grady Wallace, the awesome combination wasted little time in showing how hard they would be to stop. Against Washington Mill (Winston-Salem, N.C.) in their opening game on March 17, Logan and Wallace each scored 27 in a 114–94 win. In the semifinals on March 18, Logan took charge, firing in 42 in an 88–81 triumph over defending champion Mikro of Charlotte. They steamrolled on through the championship game with the Greenville Old Pros the next evening, winning 90–82. Both Logan and Wallace were elected to the All-Southern team.

The Class A and B men offered the fans a few more thrills. In the B consolation, Gluck Mill defeated Parker Mill 82–78 in overtime. Down three with less than a minute to play, the Anderson, South Carolina, team used a pressing defense to turn the tide. Gluck was led by Ethan Embler (29), Boyd Sanders (21) and Gary Whitlock (20); Don Lewis led Parker with 30. In the March 19 finals, Monsanto (Greenwood, S.C.) defeated Monsanto (Pensacola, Fla.) 72–69 for their third straight Class A title and permanent possession of the Corn Trophy. There was certainly no love lost between the sister plants, as 46 fouls were called.

Strong teams converged on Greenville for the 1967 campaign, best exemplified by the Saco-Lowell men in the Class B division — they were undefeated (20–0) and averaged 94 points per game during the regular season while holding opponents to 65. Controlling these hardwood wars would be an equally talented group of officials, most of them former players like Fred Snoddy, Ralph Bridgeman, Arnold Campbell, Harold Fuller, and Leon Gravley (all from Greer); Boyce Howard, Jr. (Taylors); Jimmy Smith (Mauldin); and Don Dean and Whitey Kendall (both from Greenville). Kendall commanded awesome respect as the supervisor of officials, and his credentials included Atlantic Coast Conference and Southeastern Conference tours of duty, and a Gator Bowl Tournament for good measure.[19] And college coaches Frank Selvy (Furman) Neild Gordon (Newberry), and Lefty Driesell (Davidson) were looking carefully over the talent to augment their respective programs.

The strong Class B contingent wasted little time getting the city rocking. In action March 7, Doug Bagwell scored 45 as Sangamo bested Union Bleachery, 85–56. Saco-Lowell won their 21st straight, a 91–57 cakewalk over Martin Manufacturing as five men scored in double figures: Jimmy Wilson (20), Stanley Wilson (19), Jimmy Campbell (13), Joe Garrett (13), and Tommy Krieg (12). Pratt-Read defeated Bigelow-Sanford 80–72 in double overtime, led by Ronnie Hughes' 30 points; he hit 11 straight free throws in the extra periods to seal the win.

March 8 was an active day at Memorial Auditorium. Guthrie Motors started the Open Division action, popping Perkins Auto 102–92 as Clemson's Gary Helms had 31; R.D. Carson topped the losers with 35.

The men's defending Class A champions, Monsanto of Greenwood, edged Lyman 98–93 in a game where 70 fouls were called and 67 points were scored from the free throw line. B action featured blowout specials: Monaghan swamped Bigelow-Sanford 84–39; Lyman belted Piedmont 93–30 (they led 57–15 at the half); Monsanto (Pensacola, Fla.) crushed LTV ElectroSystems 73–33; and Pelzer popped Pratt-Read 87–40, employing a devastating fast break. Not to be outdone, the Belton Class C men ran away from Appleton 124–44 as Lanny Taylor's point total matched that of the whole Anderson team. To top off the day, 6'7" Ricky Snipes signed with Lefty Driesell's Davidson College, then trotted out to score 22 and lead Poe Hardware C's over John Perkins Industries, 74–43.[20]

Next day's action featured some wonderful individual performances across all divisions. Belton ran away from Metro-Atlantic 116–73 in Class C action, and posted an incredible 240 points for two games; Lanny Taylor (32), Jack Ross (25), and John Campbell (23) led the way. In a B men's games, Lyman ousted Monsanto (Pensacola, Fla.) behind the scoring tandem of Fred Coan (39) and Rick Dunagin (38). For the women, Fiber Industries relied on Ann Dobson's 23 points to edge Sangamo, 41–38 in triple overtime. The Open Division offered two gems. Mikro beat Schottland's 101–68 as Jesse Branson (34) and Dwight Durante (23) topped all scorers. Branson, an Elon product, had played one year with the Philadelphia 76ers; Durante, a Catawba College standout, would soon get a crack at stardom with the Harlem Globetrotters.[21] Hinton's All Stars edged Washington Mill 99–98 as Jerry Smith (All Southern Conference and honorable mention All-American) popped in 43; Jay Beal's 41 was a solid performance for the losers.

Semifinal highlights produced both the routine and the unusual. There were no surprises when the Class B Saco-Lowell men moved past Lyman 70–60 to run their record to 23–0. Nor was it earth-shattering when Pelzer edged Sangamo 62–60 in the

1967 Monsanto (Greenwood, S.C.) Class A Men's Champions: *(front row, l-r)* Jim Brown, Ray Lark, Johnny Taylor, Bill Wilson; *(back row, l-r)* Lee Smtih (mgr), Jerry Gordon, Don Carver, Joe Martin, Garrett Nation, Jim Diamond (coach).

**1968 Southern Textile Basketball Tournament program cover.
IMMS 1967 Women's Champions.**

same division, putting two men on scoring ace Danny Bagwell. Though he scored 27, the strategy worked just well enough. What proved extraordinary was Slater's huge upset of the Belton juggernaut in Class C men's action. Four men in double figures — Johnny Dillard (26), Bill Darby (20), Ronnie Cobb (19) and Lewis Talley (18) — overcame exceptional scoring outbursts from Belton's Lanny Taylor (35) and John Campbell (30).

Deserving winners emerged from the March 11 battles. Gary Helms' 30 led Guthrie Motors to the Open Division championship, 71–63, over Mikro. Monsanto (Greenwood) won its fourth consecutive Class A championship with an 84–69 romp past Homelite. Saco-Lowell capped a perfect season by taking the Class B men's title over Pelzer, 84–61. But the night belonged to Patsy Neal, whose 41 points led IMMS past Slater, 63–58; a deadly shooter, she was 19-of-20 from the free throw line.

The 1968 tournament opened with controversy, which placed it in step with that tumultuous year of national violence. Longtime player Grady Wallace, former University of South Carolina All-American, was making his final appearance in the Dribble Derby, but not in the way he envisioned. What exactly happened is unclear, but Wallace's task of putting together a team for Columbia's Sunshine Cleaners composed of Gamecock team members did not occur. Instead, it took coach Frank McGuire's involvement to resolve this political battle. Skip Harlicka, Jack Thompson, Frank Stoddard, Gary Gregor and Lynn Burkholder formed the nucleus for Hunt Machinery, and Wallace and Sunshine Cleaners were the odd fellows out. Grady made his way to Spartanburg's Spaulding Fibers, part of a still formidable collection of competitors like Bobby Lewis (small college All-American at South Carolina State), Art Whisnant (former Atlantic Coast Conference Player of the Year at the University of South Carolina) and Dick Wright (former Furman University star). The old guy was happily positioned for one last effort.[22]

Others, like Saco-Lowell and Sangamo, made it a tournament to remember in a more positive way, distributing 4,000 tickets and inviting the Greer and Byrnes High School bands to play. The crowds witnessed blowouts on opening day March 13, especially in the Class C men's tilts, all involving Piedmont Mill teams. Poe Hardware, composed of Greenville High School players, crushed Piedmont #1, 94–48; Monaghan blew away Piedmont #2, 95–44; and Metro-Atlantic walloped Piedmont #3, 74–27. The Piedmont women's team fared little better in second-round action. Sangamo blew past #2, 48–13, as Carolyn Pharr scored 38 (20 in the first half). IMMS, led by Patsy Neal's 19 points (including one basket and three foul shots in the final minute), defeated #1, 40–35. Neal was a former All-American and current teacher and tennis coach at Brevard Junior College who commuted to Greenville for the tournament.

Jerry Sims remembers those days. "I started playing when I was nine years old. Willie Wilbanks came to Ware Shoals and started a community foundation which sponsored athletic programs for all the kids on the mill village. I wound up playing in both Class C and B competitions with Ware Shoals Mill. Two memories stand out for me, and they're at opposite ends of the spectrum. Once in the tournament, I stole

1969 Southern Textile Basketball Tournament program cover.
Russell Manufacturing's 1968 Class A Champions.

the ball and scored the winning points against Pelzer with fourteen seconds to go. But against Dunean, I missed a free throw with no time on the clock that would have won the game, and then we lost in overtime. The lessons were good ones, though. We learned to be competitive and to strive to do our best."[23]

The March 15 quarterfinals provided a mass of humanity in action. Guthrie Motors cruised past Hinton's All Stars in Open Division action, 94–76, despite 33 points by ex–Furman guard Jerry Smith; Clemson alumnus Gary Helms had 31 for the winners. Monsanto (Pensacola, Fla.), Class A men's favorites who arrived in Greenville courtesy of a chartered plane, crushed PPG Industries, 99–53. Leading scorer Don Gates (a season average of 38.5 ppg) had 31, and was joined by Don Livingston (19), Dennis Wilson (11), Gerald Grant (11), and Ken Blanton (10) in double figures. Some of the Class B men's excitement took place off the court as Fiber Industries protested March 14's 67–61 loss, maintaining Sangamo's use of an ineligible player. The protest was upheld, and Fiber made the most of it, beating Bigelow-Sanford, 64–57. In other B action, Colin Mintz stole the ball and scored with five seconds left in overtime as Madison Throwing Company edged Gluck Mill, 76–74. Jim Yates was brilliant in defeat, scoring 40.

Overtime was the story of the day with the Class C men. First, Poe Hardware slipped by Slater, 64–62, as Sammy Eskew's 40-footer tied the score for Poe with 11 seconds left. Teammate Mike Jones, who did not score in regulation, had four in the extra period to lead the win. Ross Tire beat Singer, 71–63, as David Morrow poured in 31, including six in overtime. The steady performance of Patsy Neal was the highlight in women's action, and IMMS rode her 34-point performance to a 52–44 win over Dunean.

The March 16 semifinals offered fine individual and team efforts, beginning with two Open Division games. Guthrie Motors defeated Hunt Machinery, 91–81, as Erskine College sophomore Mike Jenkins led the way with 31, and even the late addition of Western Carolina University's All-American, Henry Logan, could not stave off defeat for the Columbia, South Carolina, team. Mikro edged K.G. Carpet 96–88 behind the strong play of Dwight Durante (30 points, 20 in the first half) and Jackie Wilson (32 points, 23 in the second half). Defending Class A champion Monsanto (Greenwood, S.C.) was outdistanced by Saco-Lowell, 76–55, as the winners executed an effective fast break. In Class B men's action, Fiber Industries marched on to the finals with a 52–40 win over Lyman Mill, still making the most of their upheld protest on opening day.

There were upsets and vindications March 17 as the tournament drew to a close. Excitement reigned in the women's contest when Slater upset defending champions IMMS, 52–50, as Sharon Morgan's basket with four seconds left bested a fine 31-point performance by the loser's Patsy Neal. The frenzied finish was duplicated in the Open Division when Mikro edged Guthrie Motors 74–72 in overtime for the title. Mikro led 52–43 in the first half before Guthrie converted a five-point play. Willie Pegram scored on a goaltending call, cashed in on the technical foul toss when coach Mike Ross protested the call a bit too much, and then hit the jumper on the inbounds pass. It was close the rest of the way until, with four seconds left, Pegram's two free throws gave Guthrie a 66–64 lead, but North Carolina State's Eddie Biedenbach hit Lee Davis's with a perfect 80-foot inbounds pass, and Davis's last-second jumper found nothing but net.[24] Mikro then finished out the win in the extra period.

Russell Manufacturing finally won its first Class A title, outrunning Saco-Lowell 102–93 behind the fine 43-point performance of Jimmy Childers. Poe Hardware ended three years of frustration by taking the Class C men's honors from Monaghan, 64–62, when Willie Rogers hit the winning basket with eight seconds left. The clan of champions was completed when Madison Throwing Company, a pick-up team from the industrial plants in this North Carolina town, defeated Fiber Industries 77–61 for the Class B men's crown.

The 46th edition (1969) became a spotlight for the women's division. IMMS sported a 55–1 tournament record (their only setback being a 52–50 loss to Slater in the 1968 finals), and to prove a point they moved through the season undefeated, averaging 80 points per game, while giving up only 36. The March 11 opening round saw the defending champions from Slater fall before the youthful Ware Shoals Mill team 49–40; most of the victor's players were from Ware Shoals High's 2A state champions. Wunda Weve then edged Sangamo, 41–39, as Reba Lowe (who averaged 38 points per game during the year) led the way with 21. There was nothing close or unexpected about the quarterfinals on March 13 when IMMS blasted Piedmont #1, 67–16, as Patsy Neal (25) and Carolyn Pharr (24) provided the spark. K.G. Carpet then beat Monaghan 59–33 behind Jean McDowell's 32. IMMS, though, exited March 14's semifinals in their first loss of the season, 58–44, to a spirited Ware Shoals team. K.G. Carpet halted the youngsters in the finals, winning 58–46 as Vivian Maslen scored all of K.G's fourth-quarter points (15), and their last 17 in a row.

To their credit, the men played hard and offered a good many thrills of their own. Pelzer's Class C win over Monaghan on March 11, 54–53, was decided with two seconds to go on Jerry Riddle's jumper. The next day, K.G. Carpet began a run at the Open championship by downing Inman & Associates, 117–93, with an awesome display of balanced scoring from Doug Alexander (27), Chuck Alexander (24), Allen Johnson (23), and James Brown (22). In March 13's Class A quarterfinals Monsanto (Pensacola, Fla.) placed six in double figures—John Taylor (20), Don Gates (18), Jerry Secrist (18), Ron Ellison (16), Holly (14), and Eddie Carter (12)—as they romped to a 121–52 win over Kendall. Dewayne Montgomery of Phillips Fibers provided fireworks in the Class B competition, scoring 32 in a win over Monaghan on March 11, and 35 in a 96–42 pasting of Bigelow-Sanford on March 13. The best game March 14 was K.G. Carpet's 84–76 win over Guthrie Motors in Open action. The "Lonesome Five," as K.G.'s starters were known because they usually started and finished the game, were led by former Oglethorpe College star Doug Alexander with 40 points, while backcourt mate Allen Johnson of the University of Georgia added 28.

On March 15, Atlanta's Rug Men beat Mikro 87–79 for the Open title, led again by the tandem of Allen Johnson (26) and Doug Alexander (23). Mikro, led during the competition by Dwight Durante, scoring champion of the Carolina Conference and hailing from Catawba College, played without its star. He was in Chicago talking with the Harlem Globetrotters about a career. The Cinderella story starred the Class A men of Dunean, coming from behind to upset Monsanto (Pensacola, Fla.) 78–76, as veteran Skeeter Hammett had 34. They competed during the regular season in the Class B division, but moved up a notch and kept the magic throughout the tournament.

The festivities finished up the decade of the 1960s in high class fashion, due primarily to the inclusion of African American players and their solid performances. Robert Sorrell, Henry Logan and Dwight Durante led the way and many followed, improving the caliber of play in the Southern Textile Basketball Tournament, especially in the Open competition, which kept the big show moving through a turbulent era.

The 1970s

Living up to Harry Foster's words ("This is the biggest tournament of its kind in the world, which is the way it should be since Greenville is the textile center of the world"—Greenville *News,* March 10, 1970) seemed a tall order, but with 64 teams and 1,000 players in the 1970 tournament, fans could count on a good effort. Some of the 1970 squads brought hefty reputations: Russell Manufacturing's Class A men were 28–1, averaging an amazing 131 points per game while holding opponents to 80; Lyman's Class B men were 22–1, losing only to a Class A team. Some came to play good basketball but have a good time as well; the Homestead Terrace women's team carried the illustrious nickname Bo-nat's Frauleins, assuring that no fan could ever forget them.

Open Division action cranked everything up on March 10, as Guthrie Motors, made up mostly of former Clemson players, cruised by Transit Homes 109–95 with the help of Butch Zatezalo's 30. Ark Polk, All-League in the Ohio Valley Conference while playing with Western Kentucky, burned through 33 to lead Texize past General Fireproofing, 109–84. Texize, in fact, garnered the "All Everything" label, as *seven* of their roster players received all conference honors while in college. In a stellar C men's game March 11, Monaghan's team concept overwhelmed Jackson Mill, 89–74. An awesome fast break spawned a trio of scorers—Ken Harbin (24), Gary Pittman (21), and Donald Davis (20)—and team defense did not allow any Jackson player to reach double figures.

In the Open quarterfinals on March 12, Kenro won an offensive shootout over Tolbert's, 136–116, its fast break hitting warp speed in the last five minutes. Six men went double digits for the winners: Allen Johnson (29), Pat Moriarity (28), Doug Alexander (20), Mike Dahl (20), Larry Barnett (19), and Ernie Crain (12). Mel Gibson, small college All-American at Western Carolina University, had 38 for Tolbert's. Emma Howard's free throw in the second overtime (the first was scoreless) moved Texize past Westvaco, 31–30, in women's action.

There was double overtime nailbiting topping off the March 13 semifinal battles. Skeeter Hammett and Jimmy Riddle each had two free throws in the second extra period to lead Dunean's Class A men past Monaghan, 76–71; Hammett had 31 to take game honors. In Open play, Butch Zatezalo hit a 16-foot jumper with three seconds left to give Guthrie Motors a 120–118 win over defending champions Kenro. The game itself was a pendulum of emotions. Gary Helms stole an inbounds pass with one second left and hit a sweeping baseline hook to knot the score for Guthrie at 104. He then hit a 20-foot jumper with 12 seconds left in the first overtime to put the Motor boys ahead 114–112, only to see Kenro's Ernie Crain return the favor with only three seconds to go. Zatezalo (34) and Helms (31) led Guthrie, while Mike Dahl (38) paced

1970 Southern Textile Basketball Tournament program cover.
Dunean Mill's 1970 Class A Champions.

Kenro. Billy Ware scored only one point for his Parker Mill Class B team, but it was with eight seconds left for a 66–65 win over Clark-Schwebel.

The finals on March 14 were no less intriguing. The consolation game for the Class C men was decided only when Ronnie Cureton hit a free throw with no time remaining on the clock as Jackson Mill edged Poe Hardware, 60–59. Poe, down four with 11 seconds to go, scored five points on a three-point play and lay up. Cureton then hit a charity toss with five seconds to go, and scored his winning point after he was fouled going for a rebound. In the Open title game, Guthrie Motors could not contain Texize, winding up on the short end of a 95–81 score. One of their starters, Butch Zatezalo, "was called out of town unexpectedly," and without his playmaking and scoring skills, the Williamston team was at a disadvantage.

Southern Textile Athletic Association president Harry Foster offered a quote at the close of the 1970 games, not as optimistic as he was a few days earlier. "The Open division suffered a bit this year. Guys like Billy Cunningham and Fred Hetzel, both who were here a couple of years ago, weren't so concerned with money. They just wanted to play some basketball. But now the players are more interested in 'How much do I get?'"[1]

High scoring individual performances would make for a lot of spectator fun in 1971, from start to finish. On opening day (March 10), Doug Lowe's 33 powered Crown-Metro's C men past Southern Filters, 90–37; Charles Breazeale's 30 led General Electric past Dunean in B men's action,

1971 Southern Textile Basketball Tournament program cover.
Texize's 1970 Open Division Champions

66–51; and Steve Burnette's 37 moved the A men of Fiber Industries past LTV ElectroSystems, 89–62.

Point output poured over into the March 11 games, and the names became a bit more familiar to the crowds. In the Open Division, Southern Bank beat Carolina Engineers, 121–100, as Furman assistant Wayne Kruer and Virginia Tech alumnus Lloyd King each scored 30; Larry Taylor, a University of Georgia product, had 46 in a losing cause. Texize matched that with a win of their own, 87–63 over the S.C. All Stars, as Haywood Hill's 36 topped All Stars John Roche (35) and Bobby Cremins (18). Charles Breazeale scored another 30, but his General Electric mates fell in a B men's division tilt, 78–64, as Terry Smith's 33 paced Easley Mill to the win.

Quarterfinal action on March 12 included a 116–107 Kenro win over Electric Services in Open play, as Oglethorpe College's Doug Alexander scored 34 to pace the winners, and Mike Salerni matched that total for the Electricians. Mike Adams' 34 led Rohm-Haas over Taylors Mill, 89–75, while Steve Moore had 32 in a losing cause. The B men's division certainly offered the most exciting game of the day when Easley Mill edged Conso 68–66 despite trailing 36–23 at the half; Terry Smith, who finished with 31, led Easley to the win.

Southern Bank's Lloyd King kept up his scoring blitz in the semifinals March 13 with a 40-point effort against Kenro, but the Atlanta team still took the Open win, 107–99, as Guilford College's Pat Moriarity (29) and Doug Alexander (27) proved to be a formidable tandem. Doug Lowe matched his opening day total of 33 to move Crown-Metro over Southern Industrial Mechanical 90–76 in C men's action. Edwina Bryan's 23 paced Kenro over Slater 51–40 in women's play. Defense was the story,

Top: 1971 Russell Manufacturing (Alexander City, Ala.) Class A Men's Champions.
Bottom: 1972 Southern Textile Basketball Tournament program cover. Texize's 1971 Women's Champions.

though, as no Slater player reached double figures.

Championship Saturday (March 14) was a clean-up day for Texize. The women avenged their previous year's loss in the finals with a 45–28 whipping of Kenro (they had a 28–8 halftime lead); Marty Vaughn (17), Judy Murray (11) and Patsy Neal (10) paced the winners. The men captured a second straight Open title, the first team ever to accomplish the double, beating Kenro 102–89 as Middle Tennessee State's Booker Brown scored 30 and Erskine's Skip Goley chipped in 24 to pace the win. Russell Manufacturing put on a clinic in balanced scoring to take the A men's title, 97–72 over Lyman, as six players scored in double figures: Dewey Sanders (26), Owen Butts (15), L.M. Hunter (14), Mike Hearn (13), Wayne Rape (13), and Arthur Hicks (10). Poe Hardware's C men rode Marion Miller's jumper with six seconds left to a 74–73 win over Crown-Metro.

The 1972 edition offered games spiced with the interesting, and no one had to wait very long for things to start rolling. A March 29 Open Division contest saw Transit Homes edge Mikro 82–80, though Danny Dixon's jumper at the buzzer seemed to tie the score. Officials ruled that Mikro player-coach Mike Ross (a student of Al McGuire at Belmont Abbey College) was fouled before the shot. On the line after time expired, Ross' first effort missed. John Thornton, honorable mention All-American at South Carolina State, kept the Charlotte team close with his 36-point effort, which featured his remarkable driving ability.

The defending women's champions, Texize, wasted little time in establishing their intent to repeat, crushing Jackson Mill, 70–22. They were 19–0 during the regular season, and all six starters averaged in double figures: Marty Vaughn (26.0), Reba Lowe (19.2), Judy Murray (16.9), Patsy Neal (15.0), Debbie Rogers (12.0), and Emma Howard (10.0).

Comeback victories flavored the action on March 30. Fiber Industries extended a precarious 26–22 halftime advantage to a 79–51 win over Sally Mill in B men's action, thanks to the 36 points from O'Louis McCullough. The Saco-Lowell women were more remarkable, coming back from a 20–5 deficit to edge Slater 47–45, tying the score and finally pulling ahead in the last seconds of the game.

Transit Homes won another Open Division tilt March 31, 115–89 over the Atlanta Satellites, as Vanderbilt University's Tom Arnholt had 46 for the winners. It was a team put together especially for the tournament, and the players had a difficult time remembering each other's names. Arnholt, in fact, would not be available for the finals against Texize since he had already committed to the Kentucky-Tennessee interstate game. Coach Ruppert Elliott explained his philosophy. "We decided that this year, if we had a team, it would be competitive. So I called college coaches from all around and learned who their seniors were, and then, with the help of the coaches, weed them out and decide which guys I wanted. And we got some real good ones."[2] Atlanta coach James Haines formulated some ideas of his own as the game ended. "Our players all work, and we didn't get out of here 'til late last night, went back to Atlanta, worked today, and drove back up here to play tonight. It made a difference. We'll be back up here next year, and we'll be right."[3]

Ware Shoals Mill's B men provided thrills galore in their win over Tele. Sec. Down 44–24 at the half, they staged a magnificent rally and came away with a 78–71 victory. The men from Pelzer #2 slipped by Home Real Estate 65–63 in a Class C nail-biter. The Realtors had the ball out of bounds with three seconds left and the score tied, but when Barry Isom broke to get clear, he charged into Pelzer's Charles Lesley. Lesley calmly went to the line and sank both free throws for the win.

Pelzer, in fact, carried that momentum into the April 2 finals, running past Crown-Metro 85–73 for the C men's title. O'Louis McCullough topped off a great tournament as his 37 points led Fiber Industries past Ware Shoals 88–85 and to the B men's trophy. Russell Manufacturing won its third straight Class A title, and permanent possession of the Corn Trophy, by blasting Rohm-Haas, 94–61. For the second straight year, the Texize contingent swept to two championships. Marty Vaughn's 23 points led to a 71–62 win over Lyman for the women, and the men captured their third Open crown, beating Transit Homes, 96–86.

With 76 teams from five states kicking off the 1973 games, Dr. L.P. Hollis, now 90, said, "We had no idea when we started the tournament that it would attract the attention it did. We had the old Textile Hall to play in, and we had two courts, and it was just great. The tournament has been a wonderful spirit builder and a fine thing for athletics in this area."[4]

Rohm-Haas and Russell Manufacturing wasted little time in setting the stage for a rematch of the previous year's Class A men's championship battle. Rohm-Haas crushed E-Systems 104–36 (after leading 61–23 at the half) with the talent of five double digit scorers: Bernard Richardson (23), Ken Hoffman (18), Cleo Dawson (14), Charles Carlisle (12), and James Kelly (10). The next day (March 21) Russell overpowered Daniel Construction 113–86 behind the balanced scoring of Arthur Hicks and Owen Butts, each with 23; Steve Brown had 32 in a losing cause. In early Open Division action on March 21, the S.C. All Stars edged Kenro 96–91, but some of Frank McGuire's best — Bobby Carver (25), Rick Aydlett (23), Skip Harlicka (16), Billy Walsh (10), and Bobby Cremins (9) — had to scrap hard for the win and overcome Doug Alexander's 30-point effort for the Georgia team.

The favorites continued their winning ways in the March 22 quarterfinals. Transit Homes outlasted Decorative Components 113–104 in Open action as Tom Arnholt's 44 paced the winners. In the Class A men's division, Rohm-Haas used devastating full court pressure to run away from Monaghan, 91–61. Russell Manufacturing held off Fiber Industries, 97–95, as the two teams combined for 12 points in the last minute of play. Fiber's Joel Williams took scoring honors with his 35-point effort.

For the women, Appleton Mill defeated Kenro 55–48 as Jamie Lee (14), Vicki Burton (12), and Brenda Paulk (12) led the way. At Anderson Junior College, these ladies were runners-up in the National Junior College tournament in Michigan. Sporting a 21–5 record, they were coached by Annie Tribble, and sometimes answered to the name of "Tribble's Trotters."[5]

The March 24 finals offered both familiarity and change. The men of Russell Manufacturing won their fourth straight Class A title, 81–73 over Rohm-Haas, behind the scoring of Jerry Sanders (22), Arthur Hicks (20), Mike Hearn (15), and Owen Butts (11). For the first time in three years, no Texize team claimed a title. The Ware Shoals Mill women upset the defending champions in the March 23 semifinals, but could not sustain their momentum and fell to Appleton 34–19 in the championship. Transit Homes avenged their 1972 Open Division loss to Texize with a 115–101 win in the finals. Vanderbilt's Tom Arnholt had 37 points (he was 14-of-14 from the free throw line), and Newberry College's Clyde Agnew scored ten straight early in the second half to ignite Transit's push to victory.

It took an international event to derail a tradition in 1974. Russell Manufacturing of Alexander City, Alabama, had won the last four Class A men's championships, and the Arab oil embargo did what no competition on the court was able to do — bring the streak to an end. Coach Vercho Carter said, "Our company didn't feel it was fair to let the boys use their own gas. You couldn't buy but two dollars' worth at a time, and we felt we would need all the gas that the company might get under rationing."[6] Eighty-six other teams, though, came to town for the action.

Games fluctuated between nail-biters and blowouts. In women's action on March 26, Cindy Hanenburger converted a three point play with 30 seconds to go, and Blackwell & Son Real Estate nosed out Pelzer Mill, 35–34. Spartan Leasing then

1973 Southern Textile Basketball Tournament program cover.

destroyed Fiber Industries, 60–4 (the score at the half was 34–2). On March 27, Marty Vaughn's 29 led Slater Mill to a 66–16 shellacking of Brookline Carpets. It took all of Johnny White's 30 points to move Saco-Lowell past Slater 65–64 in a Class B men's game; 20 came in the second half and brought the winners back from a nine-point deficit.

Pittman's Textile Machinery was an Open Division team constructed from two old adversaries, Newberry and Presbyterian colleges. They defeated Piedmont Sheet Metal on March 28, 95–63, behind Clyde Agnew's 28 points; Agnew was the unofficial state scoring champion that year. In the March 29 semifinals, Pittman's edged Young-Love Fabrics 97–91, this time with Presbyterian's George Hester (31 points) leading the way. Hester's college teammate, Steve Crowe, scored 33 for the losers. Pittman's was on a collision course with defending champions Transit Homes in the finals. Led by Tom Arnholt's 35, Transit whacked Castings Inc. 120–97 on March 28. In March 30's title game, Pittman's held an 11-point lead at the half, but Transit rallied to tie the score, force overtime, and eventually take the game, 116–112. Lee Fowler's 38 led the winners, while Agnew's 30 paced Pittman's.

In 1974, it was the road to the women's title which offered big-time excitement. Texize, the pre-tournament favorite, was in reality the national championship team from Anderson Junior College, but somebody must have forgotten to tell the Slater Mill ladies. Composed mainly of Easley and Travelers Rest high school players, and adding veterans Marty Vaughn and Regina Gilstrap (Baptist College), they outdid themselves by winning 48–46 in the semifinals. Slater scored the last eight points of the game in the final 90 seconds. Gilstrap fed Jan Rampey for a layup with five seconds left for the winning basket. Ware Shoals Mill also engineered a semifinal upset with a 42–34 win over Spartan Leasing, a team drawn primarily from the University of South Carolina women's team and the state's AIAW title holder. It was almost anticlimactic when Slater bested Ware Shoals, 41–29, for the championship.

Rohm-Haas used the oil embargo, and Russell Manufacturing's resulting absence, to end two years of finals frustration, outdistancing Lyman Mill 87–77 for their first Class A men's title. Bernard Richardson led the winners with 39 points.

The margins of victory were certainly slimmer in 1975 than in recent years, though stellar individual performances were still to be found. Ashworth Brothers' narrow 66–65 double overtime win over Bigelow-Sanford on March 26 set the tone, and not just for Class B men's action. Sangamo Electric's A men took the floor later that day, and pounded out a workmanlike 104–89 victory over Lyman. A trio of 20-plus performers — Robert Davis (28), Robert Cannon (24) and Doug Bagwell (22) — paced Sangamo, overcoming the efforts of Lyman's Charlie Robinson (31) and Sammy Moody (23). In Open action a

Top: 1975 Southern Textile Basketball Tournament program cover. Cryovac's 1974 Class B Champions.
Bottom: 1976 Southern Textile Basketball Tournament program cover. Appleton Mill's 1975 Womens' Champions.

day later, the Jackson Five edged Green Creek Ruritan, 99–98, as Ron Del Ray's free throw in overtime was the difference. Sam Goodwin (32) and former Atlanta Hawk Gary Gregor (19) led the winners.

The Open quarterfinals of March 28 offered a relative breather. Fleet Supply, drawing most of its members from Wake Forest University, popped Drummond Oil 120–112 as four starters had more than 20 points: Willie Griffin (24), Mike Parrish (23), Eddie Payne (22) and Charlie Davis (21); Shaft McMinns had 31 for Drummond. It was back to the norm in another Open tilt, when Defender Chemical eased past Glur Real Estate 85–83 on the strength of two charity tosses by Jo Jo Bethea in the final seconds. And in C men's action, Ronald White's 22 points (with a three-point play in the last seconds) enabled Dunean Cafe to top Fred Fraley Tru Ride, 60–58.

The rest of the tournament offered more of the close games, beginning with Pittman's Textile Machinery's 77–76 win over the Jackson Five in Open action. Marion Miller had 31 to pace Pittman's, including an amazing 25-foot bank shot at the buzzer in overtime for the win. Jackson, led by Gary Gregor and Skip Harlicka, led 55–40 well into the second half, but fell victim to Pittman's switch from zone to man-to-man defense. Slater, the defending women's champions, had an uphill battle to beat Hampton Industries, 65–62, and top scorer Janice Lee (32 points). The defending Class A men's champions, Rohm-Haas, did not fare as well, falling 75–73 to Daniel Construction as Steve Brown's two free throws with six seconds left capped a come-from-behind victory.

Daniel completed its sweep to the Class A title the next night, beating Norwich Pharmacal 84–77 as David Dobson had 33 (complementing his 30-point performance the day before). Tommy Rutledge led Norwich with 33. Defender Chemical took the Open crown by downing Pittman's Textile Machinery 97–87 and overcoming a fine 41-point onslaught by Newberry College's Clyde Agnew. Pelzer's 94–72 win, and a fourth straight Class C men's title, was the only breather of the day, and fans cheered the victor's Nathaniel Walker's 43-point effort.

The action in 1976 was driven by the Open Division from start to finish. Clemson's Jeff Reisinger nailed two free throws with 12 seconds left and TMR Inc. edged Drummond Oil 95–93 in a March 24 game. University of South Carolina's Alex English scored 27 to lead Lexington County Recreation to a 111–83 defeat of Young-Love Fabrics, and oddly it would be his one appearance in the tournament. Committed to another tournament, English missed Lexington's 92–86 win March 26 over A & M Mobile Homes, and their 93–82 win over Non-Fluid Oil in the finals on March 28. They finished 36–1 for the season.

Names familiar to area hoop fans peppered the lineups. Dunean Cafe blew past Ross Tire 79–55 in March 24's C men's opening round, thanks to 37 points by Ronald White. The next day the Slater women put five in double figures — Marty Vaughn (16), Vivian Humphries (14), Jan Rampey (12), Jenny Lyerly (10), and Regina Gilstrap (10) — to crush Brookline Carpets, 65–36. Pittman's Textile Machinery, featuring several players from the Newberry College team that advanced to the quarterfinals of the NAIA national tournament, moved to a 106–95 Open Division win over Daniel Construction. Clyde Agnew, the all-time leading scorer at the college, had 21. Rounding out the March 25 action, David Dobson's free throw with five seconds left in the second overtime gave the Daniel Construction Class A men an 82–81 win over Singer of Pickens.

Quarterfinal action featured two more Open tilts. TMR Inc. defeated Arnold Palmer Cadillac 97–80, with a defense that held George Adams, former San Diego Conquistador of the American Basketball Association, to six points. Non-Fluid Oil ran away from Able Supply, 105–85, as Middle Tennessee State University teammates Tim Sisneros (37) and Jimmy Powell (23) took scoring honors. The semifinals of

March 27 featured three tremendous performances: Doug Bagwell's 31 moved Sangamo Electric past Sirrine 77–67 in Class A men's action; Terry Smith's 30 ignited the Class B Alice Manufacturing men past Dunean 98–81; and Ronald White's 30 put Dunean Cafe past Carotell 74–64 and into the men's Class C finals.

Title day offered a diverse fare. Pelzer Mill won its fifth straight Class C title, 67–55 over Dunean Cafe. The B men's final was close all the way, decided with three seconds left when Alice Manufacturing's Johnny White hit the last two of his 34 for a 77–75 win over Renfrew Bleachery. That excitement, though, would give way to one of the most bitter controversies ever to engulf the tournament, and it occurred in the Class A title game.

Sangamo Electric had taken an 89–84 overtime win over Brookline Carpets, but a protest was then filed with the executive committee of the Southern Textile Athletic Association. Brookline coach Phil Clark discovered late in the fourth quarter that a Sangamo starter, playing under an assumed name, had participated in junior college competition. Rules for that year specified that a Class A player must be a full-time employee of the business the team represented. Clark contacted the Greenville *News*, which had arranged for individual photos of the players that year. A local broadcaster matched that shot and a college photo of the man in question. The protest was upheld. It was the only time in tournament history when a team won (or lost) a championship under protest.[7]

Future stars dotted the hardwood as the 1977 edition got underway. While George Adams had already tasted professional glory in the American Basketball Association and now lent his considerable talents to Chick-Fil-A in the Open division, there was a

1976 Brookline Carpets (Greenville, S.C.) Class A Men's Champions.

quintet playing with the Class C men who would earn accolades in both college and pro sports. Larry Nance (Clemson University and the National Basketball Association) joined PBM of Anderson; Zam Fredrick (University of South Carolina, NBA) was a member of the Pelzer #1 team; Willie Scott (USC, National Football League) played with Non-Fluid Oil; Horace Wyatt (Clemson, NBA) and Terry Kinard (Clemson, NFL) joined American Can. For the second year in a row, a Class A men's controversy commanded the limelight. Golden Strip Motors defeated Alice Manufacturing 100–91, but was forced to forfeit when it was discovered they had used an ineligible player. A fine 31-point performance by Golden Strip's Ken Harbin was nullified.

On March 23, Non-Fluid Oil began its pursuit of the Open Division crown by blasting D & L Advertising, 105–70, as Wayne "Tree" Rollins scored 25. Rollins, at 7'1", was joined by 6'10" Wayne Croft and 6'8" David Brown on a formidable front line. Rollins anchored the middle for some fine Clemson squads in the 1970s, and like many of his teammates, traveled the road to Greenville after the ACC season ended.

"The Southern Textile Basketball Tournament was well organized, and made up of some of the most intense competitors I'd run across. Since it was structured and well officiated, we didn't have to worry so much about getting hurt, which could easily happen if you opted for playground ball during the off-season to keep in shape.

"You always remember the competition the most," he says, "though it may not have been quite comparable to the ACC. But those guys played hard, and worked hard in a very compressed time frame to mold themselves into a team. And oddly enough, I remember the crowds we played in front of—pretty good numbers with lots of enthusiasm. I enjoyed my time there in the tournament."[8]

In women's action, Laurens Glass defeated American Auto Parts 53–39 behind the scoring of Sheila Foster (23) and Judy Stroud (17). Foster was obviously successful as head coach at Boiling Springs High, where Stroud was one of her starters. Alice Manufacturing took advantage of their protest win and bested the Class A men from Singer (Pickens) 90–88, led by Terry Smith's 37-point effort. In the men's Class B wars, Appleton fought uphill all the way. Down by nine to Carolina Material Handling at the half, they tied the game with 11 seconds left, and finally won in overtime, 105–103. Joe Geer scored 47 for the winners, all but ten after intermission.

The games of March 24 offered two great contests. Diane Limbaugh's 34 led Discount Fence to a 98–26 pasting of Pelzer, and Brookline Carpets' defending Class A men's champions squeaked by Monaghan 99–96, sparked by Nixon Allen (30) and Wilbert Robinson (26).

The semifinals offered up a tasty variety for the fans. "Tree" Rollins, who usually dunked for his points, used a deadly ten-foot fadeaway jumper to score 32 and move Non-Fluid Oil by Daniel Construction, 95–88. Diane Limbaugh had another solid effort, bagging 22 as Discount Fence popped Brown's Woodworks, 62–43. Athletic Attic used James Clark's 41-point masterpiece to edge Hoechst Celanese 77–71 in Class A men's action. Slater defeated Parke-Davis 100–86 in a Class B men's classic shootout. James Williams (31), McBruce Young (30) and Joe Hill (24) led the winners, but the game's scoring honors went to Parke-Davis's Leonard White, with 41. Neely's upset defending champion Pelzer Mill, 78–65, in the Class C men's game. Jimmy Foster led the winners with 32, and Zam Fredrick's 22 topped the Pelzer effort.

Though Darrell Floyd's Sandwich Shop barely escaped the semi-finals, a 57–56 squeaker over Laurens Glass, they wasted little time in crushing Discount Fence 78–46 in the March 26 women's finals, riding a 24–7 run in the second half to an impressive victory. Athletic Attic took the A men's honors with a 107–103 double overtime win over defending champion Brookline Carpets, as James Clark, with 46 (his second

1977 Non-Fluid Oil (Greenville, S.C.) Open Division Men's Champions: *(front, l–r)* Jim Phillips (coach), Jo Jo Bethea, John Franklin, Stan Elrod, Eddie Payne, Bruce Harmon, Jerry Compton (coach); *(back row, l–r)* Clyde Agnew, Dave Brown, Tree Rollins, Wayne Croft, John Cottingham.

straight 40-plus performance), and Donald Davis, with 30, led the winners. Even with that impressive front line, it was guard Jo Jo Bethea's driving layup with 17 seconds left that led Non-Fluid Oil to the Open title, 84–82 over Chick-Fil-A.

Forfeits always seemed to be lurking as the last half of the decade progressed, and 1978 was no exception. On opening day (March 20), the Class C Jiffie Jonnie men were awarded a 2–0 win because Dogwood Hills Manufacturing was guilty of using an ineligible player. But as usual, there was something good to overcome the disappointment, and this time the Class A men's division provided the cure. Greenville Valve, behind the 46-point performance of Presbyterian College standout Steve Crowe, slipped by Pelzer, 67–62. The Anderson County players were paced by a not-too-shabby 38-point spree by Ronnie Cureton. By the middle rounds, many players were getting into the scoring act, and it had a distinct local flavor.

The March 21 action featured Darrell Floyd's 42–39 victory over American Auto in the women's division. Kim Basinger, a University of Texas standout from Easley, scored 14 for the winners. In Open Division play, Furman's Bruce Grimm had 42 points to pace D & L Advertising to a 110–104 win over Brevard. In a Wednesday Class A men's battle, Taylors Mill moved past Singer of Pickens in a high scoring affair, 104–101, with each team boasting a stellar performer. Lee Smith's 37 paced the Taylors team, and Garland Dukes had 44 for the Singer squad. In another Class A gem on March 23, Slater Mill defeated Cryovac, 70–66, behind the 41 points of McBruce Young.

There were old-timers present who could put things in perspective, no matter how frenzied the atmosphere. Hubert Nolin, a member of the Monaghan Mill Class A men's champions in 1923, and still a fan more than half a century later, spoke of those days. "The tournament was the greatest thing that ever happened to boys in the industrial area. There was great competition and great support from the community. It was an honor to play for a mill team."[9]

Pelzer claimed two titles on Championship Saturday. The women pounded out a 76–56 win over Slater. Former University of Tennessee All-American and Olympian Trish Roberts (20 points) and college teammate Sybil Blalock (17) provided the firepower. The C men swept past Neely's, 89–76, their fifth title in six years. In the B finals, Slater slipped by Michelin Gold, 69–67, on Preston Smith's two free throws with 13 seconds to go. His quote, explaining his team's slow start, was as much on target as his winning shots. "A lot of us work on the third shift, and it took us awhile to get loosened up."[10]

The decade's closing tournament commenced on a somber note. Dr. L.P. Hollis, the driving force behind the founding of the competition, had recently died, and the 1979 Southern Textile Basketball Tournament was dedicated to his memory. The battles were as fierce as ever, witnessed by the Keyboards' 115–100 win over Daniel Construction in a March 21 Open Division contest, and a whopping 59 fouls were called. Former University of South Carolina forward Mike Greiner scored 39 before fouling out, and he got plenty of offensive support from Fred Melson (26) and Howard White (23).

That same day, Darrell Floyd's pounded Athletic Attic 63–30, led by Clemson's Debra Buford (14) and Newberry College's Barbara Langford (10). Sponsor Floyd was a local legend, an Associated Press All-American at Furman in 1955 and 1956 (and the nation's leading scorer). He also coached the team, which included daughters Nancy, Diane and Libby. But it was another of his players who embodied the true spirit of the tournament.

Only seven months before, at midnight on August 25, Kathy Wilson was hit by a car while crossing the street to her dormitory at Clemson. Her injuries, a skull frac-

1978 Pelzer Mill (Pelzer, S.C.) Class A Women's Champions: *(front row, l–r)* Sister Green, Sybil Blalock, Pearl Moore, Lisa Garrett; *(back row, l–r)* Doots Wright (coach), Tammy Boggs, Neet Cooper, Trish Roberts, Susan Fuller, Sadie Sellers, B.J. Bell, Bill Hopkins (coach).

ture behind the left ear and a severe concussion, sent her into critical care at Greenville Memorial for three days. Such a tragedy would have ended the career of many athletes, but less than a month later she was shooting baskets and jogging. Wilson did not miss a single game, averaging six points and five rebounds per contest, and then she packed up and came over for the textile tournament.[11]

Non-Fluid Oil continued its impressive play evident in the last few years, and came with a team drawn from several area colleges. When they defeated the Keyboards 117–103 on March 23, Clemson's Chubby Wells (24) and Greg Coles (23) led the way, and they were joined in double figures by Winthrop's Ronnie Creamer (14), Clemson's Derrick Johnson (13), Newberry's Bobby Griffin (12), and University of South Carolina–Spartanburg's Lucius Pitts (13). On March 25 they bested Chick-Fil-A 102–100 for the championship, thanks to a Pitts jumper with four seconds to go. Pitts (30), Johnson (24), and Wells (22) starred for the Oilers. It was nearly identical to the 1978 finals, and provided Non-Fluid with its third straight Open title.

If nothing else, the 1970s witnessed the high water mark of Open Division play. Big name players gave great performances, but it was in front of fewer and fewer fans. Teams may have been company sponsored, but few used enough home grown talent to stir any community (or organizational) pride. From the mill sponsored team (with mill village support), to company sponsored teams (with corporate support), the Southern Textile Basketball Tournament was poised to take another historical turn to assure its survival.

The 1980s

One last change, one odd twist, brought the old tournament full circle. Big crowds and media coverage from the late 1940s through the 1970s had faded, and rather than being an event for the fans, it had become a fellowship shared among the players. That was the motivation L.P. Hollis had when he and the other founders brought the Southern Textile Basketball Tournament into being some 60 years before.

J.L. Gourley, now 95, was honored as the lone survivor of the original seven. His career began in 1912 at the YMCA of Monaghan Mill (Kannapolis, N.C.), and detoured to South Carolina in 1919 when he became secretary of the "Y" at Victor Mill in Greer. "The tournament was strictly for the folks who worked in the mill, and the original intent was to provide recreation for the textile workers," he remembered. "Whoever could get to the tournament with a team was welcomed to enter."[1]

In front of ever dwindling crowds, the 1980 edition brought forth solid competition from all divisions. Vivian Humphries started the action with a bang, scoring 32 to lead Hanna–Sides to a 76–75 double overtime win over Byrd's on March 19. The Open Division's Tri Dips moved past Sam Wyche Sports World 118–106, with four players scoring 20 or more points: Anthony Brown (24), Tommy Mack (22), James Sanders (22), and Melvin Jones (20). Alice Manufacturing rode the hot hand of Terry Smith to back-to-back Class A wins; his 32 against 3M on March 19 helped secure a 75–72 win, and his 36 on March 20 moved his club past Michelin in overtime, 84–83. But there was a sour note lurking in the Class B men's semifinals.

Greenville County Recreation seemingly defeated Cryovac-Simpsonville 86–71 on March 21. Simpsonville filed a protest, alleging first that one Greenville starter was playing under an assumed name, and second, that he had participated in Class A competition the year before. Both points were proven, and since Southern Textile Athletic Association rules disallowed moving down into another classification, the protest was upheld and Greenville County Recreation was eliminated from action. Fortunately, a strong championship round would soon rid the tournament of the bad aftertaste.

Pelzer's strong C men's team won their sixth title in the past seven years, 85–81 over Dalton's Furniture. Down 65–51 after three periods, Dalton's trailed by only four with 35 seconds left, but could get no closer. Singer-Pickens edged Dunean for the Class A men's title, 77–73. Dunean kept fouling to get the ball back, and Singer kept making free throws, but it took Marty Hopkins' jumper with 15 seconds left to end the seesaw battle. Chick-Fil-A blew past Non-Fluid Oil 106–88 in Open competition with a Furman-dominated lineup of Al Daniel (25 points), Ronald White (18), Clyde Mayes (18), and Jonathan

Moore (14). Sparser crowds were treated to excellent hoop action as the tournament's new decade kicked off.

Competition heated right up for the 1981 games. On March 17, Pete's Market, with a powerful array of high school stars, barely squeaked by Southeastern Products' Class C men, 48–47, and it was a frenzied finish. Jeff Sumner's field goal brought his team to within one in the closing seconds, and

Top: 1980 Southern Textile Basketball Tournament program cover. Michelin's 1979 Class B Champions.
Bottom: 1981 Southern Textile Basketball Tournament program cover. Chick-Fil-A's 1980 Open Division Champions.

Southeastern called a time-out. However, they had none left, and the result was a technical foul. Then, committing a dead-ball foul on the inbounds pass and two lane violations for not lining up correctly for the free throws, they presented Pete's with five charity tosses, and every one missed the mark. Southeastern grabbed the last miss with one second showing, but could not get off a shot.

The Pelzer women, on the other hand, blew away the Piney Mountain Tappettes 84–27 the same day, and provided excitement by setting new records of 37 field goals and 84 points, topping the Atlanta Tomboys' 15-year-old record. Francis Marion College's Angie Jones (31 points) and Anderson Junior College's Sadie Sellers (29 points) paced the winners.

The March 19 highlight was reminiscent of the Pete's Market win, as the Class B men of the U.S. Post Office defeated the Law Enforcement Center, 95–88. Through four overtimes, 76 fouls were called and five players from each team exited. The Deputies, led by Paul Guy's 35 before he fouled out, survived the last two minutes of the third overtime with four players, and all of the fourth with three (and two of them had four fouls). Officials explained the game would continue even if just one player remained, which would have made an inbounds pass an interesting thing to watch.

Players whose names would become quite familiar, both in college and in the pros over the next few years, made their presence known in the tournament. Chick-Fil-A's C men boasted of Tyrone Corbin and Xavier McDaniel, while the Open squad claimed Zam Fredrick and Larry Nance. Fredrick had 27 in the semifinals, a 117–88 win over Jet Rest, going 12-for-20 from the floor. It became a time to remember, though, for Clemson recruit Joe Ward.

Playing with Fast Fare, Ward scored 37 in an 86–69 Class C semifinal win over Chick-Fil-A on March 20, and bettered that in the finals the next evening. He poured in 41 (17 in the fourth quarter), including the winning 22-foot bank shot with two seconds left as his team edged Dalton's Furniture, 75–74. "I could have jumped right out of the gym!" he said.[2] Dunean defeated Alice Manufacturing 88–75 for the Class A men's title, and averaged 92 points in tournament games, but it was clearly young Ward's moment.

A deep loss was felt in 1982 with the passing of Ken Pittman, former player and officer. Over the objections of Dr. Hollis, he favored the concept of Open Division competition. Though this created a tradition of revolving rosters, since teams were able to add players until opening day (and several teams might list the same player in hopes of recruiting him), Pittman correctly perceived that college stars would attract the crowds and keep the dribble derby going. He was also aware that the Class C men attracted college coaches from around the area. Furman assistant coach Terry Shelton agreed that the youngsters were displacing the Open teams and becoming the tournament's focal point, and as if to prove the point, at least eight players from the 1982 Class C teams signed with NCAA Division I schools.[3]

The March 22 games offered a great start to the competition. From A & C Warehouse's 70–21 rout of Orders Tile in a B men's battle, to Clayton Rhodes' fine performance (35 points) in leading Alice Manufacturing past George Coleman Ford 72–69 in the same division, to Steve Crowe (38 points) and Robin Ellenburg (30 points) teaming up to push the Class A Greenville Valve men past Black's Mechanical 77–71, the tone was set for some excellent basketball to follow.

A mid-week frenzy featured Bahan's 75–58 pounding of the defending Class A men's champions from Dunean, paced by Ronald White's 46 points, a continuation of his scoring spree begun on March 22 (24 points) and March 23 (31 points). In women's action, Pittman's Textile Machinery won over Sam Chapman Karate, 80–59. Brantley Southers and Marsie McAlister, freshman teammates at the University of South Carolina, scored 31 and 24,

1982 Chick-Fil-A (Greenville, S.C.), Open Division Men's Champions: *(front row, l–r)* Terry Shelton (coach), J. Holland, Mel Daniel, W. Hanks, Dale Crow; *(back row, l–r)* Jim Ball, W. Gibson, Horace Wyatt, K. Laws, Reggie Small, Al Daniel, M. Doyle, Chubby Wells, Doodles.

respectively. In Class B clashes, Paul Gash had 30 to lead PPG over Spartan Foods 83–78, and Southeastern Products' solid team performance overcame Clayton Rhodes' 40-point effort in an 80–66 defeat of Alice Manufacturing.

When title time rolled around on March 27, Chick-Fil-A moved to the head of the class. They defeated the Sonics of Abbeville 89–77 for their third consecutive Open Division championship, though most of the excitement occurred in the March 26 semifinals when Mel Daniel of Furman scored the final two of his 27 points with 17 seconds left in a 100–99 squeaker over Washington City. Their C men, led by William Mills (21 points, 7 rebounds, 3 assists, 2 steals, 5 dunks), then defeated Dalton's Furniture 81–72 in a hard fought game. Ware Shoals Mill brought home the Class A laurels, 75–72 over Bahan, as they overcame a magnificent effort by Ronald White to capture that win. White scored 35 for a total of 161 points in four games, breaking Jim Charles' record of 153 in 1977.

In a fitting close, the women from Pittman's Textile Machinery edged Non-Fluid Oil 70–60, honoring the memory of Ken Pittman. Clemson's Jenny Lyerly, playing in her tenth tournament, had 14 for the winners.

Old-timers commented that Chick-Fil-A's broad based recruiting was reminiscent of the tournament's glory years, when the mills hired employees solely for their basketball ability. With three consecutive Open titles, there was no arguing with success. Add to this the rule that Class A and B players must be full-time employees of the business they represented, and 1983 must have seemed an anachronism.

Unlike earlier years, though, these games were close all the way. Emb-Tex, by sagging three defenders around him, found a way to "stop" 1982 scoring champion Ronald White (33 points) and preserve an 89–78 win over Bahan in Class A men's action March 23. A bit later, it took a fine 32-point effort from Allen University's Kenny Holmes to move the Sonics past Bow-Tie Grand 96–92 in Open action.

In Class B action the next day, Professional Medical Products lost to George Coleman Ford, 53–52, but a protest was lodged by the losers, alleging that the Coleman team had used a player not on its original roster. This was upheld by the executive committee, and the team from Greenwood advanced after all.[4]

Three-time Open champion Chick-Fil-A was pushed to the limit in March 25's semifinals, but finally defeated Black Diamond 110–103 in overtime with extraordinary fire power. Brothers and former Furman standouts Al (22 points) and Mel (21 points) Daniel led the win; former Ohio State player and current Furman assistant coach Jim Cleamons added 10. Black Diamond's Ray Smith had 35. Chick-Fil-A had an even more difficult time in the finals, but emerged with an 88–82 win over Goin' Jesse's and their fourth straight Open title. The same trio of Mel Daniel (29), Al Daniel (15) and Jim Cleamons (15) paved the way to the win.

Chem-Size won the women's title with a 63–57 (or 2–0, depending upon one's point of view) win over Pittman's Textile Machinery. With three seconds left, Chem-Size's Debra Buford drove to the basket and collided with Pittman's Sheila Hodge. Buford was on the floor for 24 minutes as medical attention was administered. Pittman's forfeited rather than wait for play to resume and prolong an inevitable defeat, so either score would seem appropriate for the record book.

The 1984 games offered comebacks, close calls and blow-outs. The A men from Pelzer #1 got things off to a great start on March 27, coming back from 21 points down in the last seven minutes against Saco-Lowell, forcing an overtime, and finally winning 55–54 when Ronnie Cureton banged in a 35-footer at the buzzer. For the last few years, fans could always count on Ronald White for stellar performances, and he did not disappoint; his 39 points (27 in the second half) led Bahan's Class A men past American Hardware, 88–64. Lisa Washington of Anderson Junior College netted 25 and moved Bennett Oil past C. Dan Joyner 65–58 in women's action. Beth Couture of Erskine College sustained the excitement for the ladies on March 26. Her two free throws with eight seconds left enabled Gilstrap Real Estate to edge Pelzer 68–67, and even then they barely escaped when Mary Ellenburg's 13-footer rimmed out as the buzzer sounded. The 3M Class B men had the unusual distinction of winning two games in one day, defeating Avco Lycoming 73–70 in the morning and edging Cryovac 68–66 in the afternoon.

Action on March 27 featured high scoring Open tilts as the tournament geared up. Vince Perone's outdueled Rug Doctor 124–116 as Furman's George Singleton (29) and Clemson's Chubby Wells (27) paced the winners. Wofford College's Mike Howard popped in 38 for the Rugmen. Black Diamond then ran past the Sonics 117–100, using former NBA Seattle Supersonic Ron Smith and his 32-point performance to secure the win. Henry Holmes' 38 led the Sonics. But as in years past, there always had to be a downer. Carper Real Estate had defeated Pelzer #2 in Class C men's action, but had used two players from Laurinburg (N.C.) Institute. Since the rules stated that no prep players could participate in C games, a forfeit was ordered. Pelzer, getting ready for a consolation game with Dunean, was bumped up into the winners bracket, and Dunean was awarded a consolation bracket forfeit.

There was plenty of action to go around in the finals on March 29. With 11 seconds to go, Industrial Packaging led Alford Real Estate by five points in the Class C battle, but after a Mike Garrison jumper and a Kevin Fowler steal and basket (he was also fouled), the score stood 71–70. Fowler's free throw, however, refused to fall, and IP barely escaped with the win. The B men from George Coleman Ford experienced a similar fate, watching a 17-point halftime lead evaporate as Greenwood Mill came back behind the inspired play of Steve Conway (22 points). Coleman did, though, hold on for a 50–47 victory. The women from Bennett Oil went nine minutes without scoring, and watched a nine-point lead turn to a two-point deficit before methodically pounding out a 53–39 win over Gilstrap Real Estate. Singer of Anderson rode Charles Dacus's three free throws in the last 17 seconds (and 20 points for the game) to a 70–67 Class A men's championship clincher over Monaghan. The Open title game was anything but close as Black Diamond opened up a 23–6 lead and cruised past Hobart, 114–93.

If the focus on Class C action was considered a youth movement, then the 1985 tournament took it a step further. The feature this year was the championship games of the junior division, showcasing players under age 14.[5] For folks like Ted Pittman, whose father Ken had nursed the games through lean years by promoting the Open Division, giving the Southern Textile Basketball Tournament back to the kids would be the only way it would continue to survive.

"My involvement with the tournament literally began the night I was born," Pittman chuckled. Ken, then player-coach of Monaghan's strong Class A team, was notified of the impending birth of his son, and left for the hospital to be with his wife, Connie. After delivery, and making sure that all was well with mother and child, he returned to Textile Hall and scored 35 to lead Monaghan over Liberty, 91–76.

"Heck, Dad even got my brother Gary and I out of school one day each year to come and watch the games. It was that important to him to keep this textile tradition alive, and he wanted to keep our family a part of it all." Ted spent five years with teams in the youth divisions, four years with Class C men's teams, and two in the Class A bracket. He and Gary also played at Newberry College from 1977 to 1980 for Neild Gordon, another tournament veteran.

"College coaches came to look at high school guys, yes, but we were not making money," Ted remembered. "In fact, the first five years I served on the executive committee, we operated in the red, but when we gave this back to the kids, things began to improve. In 1985 we had sixteen youth teams, growing to seventy-seven in the next ten years, and hey, they view this as their postseason reward. There's some corporate sponsorship now, and I think much of that is because the young people of the community are benefiting directly from the textile tournament.

"We now make a profit," he says, "but we maintain the integrity of the competi-

1984 Southern Textile Basketball Tournament program cover.
Pelzer Mill's 1934 Class A Womens' Champions.

tion at all levels. Everyone here enjoys being associated with this event because we believe it still means something to the city of Greenville and its people."[6]

There were still violations which required rulings to maintain that integrity Pittman discussed. Two Class C men's teams, B.J. Music and Home Plate Restaurant, were forced to withdraw because the players were unable to produce their birth certificates. As in years past, though, other performers were around to pick up the slack.

Steve Crowe, of the Class A Greenville Valve team, scored 34 as his team bested Parker Mill 82–79 on March 19. His stellar work was matched by Stephanie Garner as she popped in 22, leading Bennett Oil past Pest Control 81–59 in women's action. The next day, the Central Savannah River Area All Stars annihilated Brady's Barber Shop 109–45 in Class C men's action, placing six in double figures: Rodney Jets (26), James Jackson (18), D.J. Harrison (16), Anthony Rice (13), David Dickerson (10), and James Munlyn (10).

Above all else, 1985 qualified as the "David Drummond Show" when he poured through 160 points in four games, leading his Class B Avco Lycoming team to the divisional title. He scored 42 in an 85–63 blitz March 19 over Reliance Electric, and bettered that with 54 as Avco defeated Givens Youth Center, 87–74. In the March 22 semifinals, his 40 points paved the way to a 69–53 win over U.S. Post Office. And 24 more (22 in the first half) against Southern Bank in the finals resulted in a 77–65 victory.

The Open title that year was claimed by Southeastern Electric in a 93–89 squeaker over Black Diamond, as University of South Carolina–Spartanburg's Scott Little (35) and Furman's Mel Daniel (15) paced the win. The Class A men from Michelin trailed at the half, but rallied for a 63–52 title win over PPG. The balanced scoring of Joel Henderson (14), John Furmanski (14), Rodney Sullivan (11), Nixon Allen (10), and Dave Mahoney (10) proved too much for the Shelby team to overcome. Pearl Moore's 22 points led Bennett Oil to the women's title, a 50–30 walk past Gilstrap Real Estate. The Class C trophy went to the Central Savannah River Area All Stars as they edged Chick-Fil-A, 82–79. They were led by D.J. Harrison (25), David Dickerson (12), David Holloway (12) and James Munlyn (12), while Chick-Fil-A was paced by Chris Duncan (21) and Kelsey Weems (20).

There was something different, even worrisome, pervading the 1986 tournament. Individual stars still came to play, as Pearl Moore returned with Four Star Sports after having led the nation in scoring that year while at Francis Marion College. But there was an innocent observation by veteran Frank Norris which shed light on what was wrong. A former Class B player from 1931 to 1941, and having attended every tournament since 1931, his wisdom was respected.

"Back then, there were leagues that went on, so the mills knew which players would be on their teams. The rivalries were really great. It seemed like there was a fight almost every game."[7] Southern Textile Athletic Association officials understood what Norris was saying, and how the lack of community support for teams had almost vanished.

Secretary Fred Byrd noted that "when textile plants stopped their recreation programs, things stopped in the tournament. Textile people used to follow their teams, and now most of them don't even know their plants have a team."[8]

Treasurer Phil Harley, of course, talked dollars and cents. "They used to pay people to play ball — they were given good jobs at the plant just to play ball. Now some teams have to pay their way into the tournament, because the plants don't even pick up the hundred dollar entry fee."[9]

"If something isn't done to help attendance," noted president Jyles Phillips, "I'd venture to say this tournament won't last two years, or maybe three at the most. We lost money last year and will this year. We've already considered moving to another site." Phillips also understood the effects of a broader economic question. "We may be losing a part of the heritage of Greenville County. But they [the textile industry] are in one of the greatest struggles they've ever been in because of imports. And with all of their cuts to be competitive, well, playing basketball just doesn't make cloth."[10]

But the pessimism could not hold down the competition, and real gems were to be found. Carper Real Estate's C men mixed two state champions to form their squad, Hart County (Ga.) High School and Rutherfordton-Spindale Central (N.C.) High School, but still were outduelled by Chick-Fil-A 76–73 in semifinal action. In the second C tilt, Corporate Benefits defeated defending champions Central Savannah River Area All Stars, 82–68. Despite a severe height disadvantage (CSRA boasted 6'11" James Munlyn from South Aiken High and 6'10" Stanley Roberts from Lower Richland High), the Benefits were aptly led by 6'7" Bennett Jackson of Blenheim High.

Open action was just as entertaining and unpredictable. Bridges' Lounge defeated Brown's Bombers 125–120 in triple overtime, and the losers proved themselves extraordinary competitors in this semifinal game. They lost four men on fouls yet nearly won the game with three men on the floor; they missed a free throw in the final seconds of the second overtime. Clemson's Chubby Wells poured in 42 for Brown's. The V.A. Jets were not shorthanded and crushed Bridges' Lounge in the final, 102–72, behind the play of William Irick (27) and Roger Carr (23). V.A. was a true powerhouse, going 62–3 for the year and 216–7 over the previous three seasons.

A degree of sadness draped the 1987 games. The program was dedicated to Harry Foster, who had recently passed away. A player, coach, and officer from executive committee to president, he was a proponent of the Open Division concept, which in 1959 forever changed the Southern Textile Basketball Tournament. Fans and players also mourned the death of Willie Wilbanks, long time player and athletic director, associated with the tournament since 1927. It was also decided to hold a combined reunion of the old baseball and basketball players on March 27, where teammates and competitors could remember the very best of the old guard.

The old guard met and remembered while the new guard played on. In action March 25, Greenwood Mill edged Lowenstein 96–94 in Open play behind the 39 points of Wiley Adams, an NAIA All-American from Presbyterian College. The next evening, however, his 35 could not outdistance the tandem of Clemson University's Anthony Jenkins (29) and Marc Campbell (25), and prevent a 104–100 loss to Olympic Gym. Olympic carried their momentum into March 27's semifinals, running past Dick Brooks Honda, 101–90, as Clemson alumni Larry Middleton (32), Murray Jarman (17) and Marc Campbell (17) led the way. Their title dreams, though, fell a step short.

In a stunning upset, Snyder's Auto rallied from a 64–43 halftime deficit to defeat Olympic 102–100 and take the Open crown. They pressed all over the floor during the second half, while Central Wesleyan's Raymond Lawson (28) and Furman's Mel Daniel (24) heated up the scoring. "I felt like I had something to prove tonight," Lawson said. "I wanted to win the respect of my opponents."[11]

The C title clash was a bit more sedate as Chick-Fil-A easily defeated Alford Real Estate, 81–62. The winners, coached by Eau Claire High's George Glymph, drew most of its players from the Columbia area, such as Barry Manning and Joe Rhett (Eau Claire), and Tracy Garrick and William Goodwin (Lower Richland). But even the close games and the area high school stars were not enough to draw the crowds. More people came for the reunion than saw the action in the finals, but those who ran the tournament still knew it offered good basketball, and pushed to preserve it.

A new twist came the next year, when some of Saturday's championship games were taped and televised Sunday, April 3, on WAXA-TV, Channel 40 in Anderson. And players were bringing more and more skills to the tournament, often more than the athletic variety. For the Class A men of St. Francis Hospital, both Dr. James McNaughton and Dr. Mike Kelly were on the roster. The power performances for this year, though, were found in the women's division, especially with Gould's Surveyors.

For one game, they featured Miriam Walker of Claflin College, the NAIA women's national player of the year. On March 30, she had 27 in a 96–47 pasting of Chick-Fil-A, and teammate Cheryl Nix of Clemson had 23. Oddly, Walker would not play in another tournament game. That same day, Foothills Real Estate ran past C. Dan Joyner's, 65–49, as Erskine College's Beth Couture had 22 for the winners. Joyner's was led by the University of South Carolina's Marsi McAlister-Kenyon's 27 points. When both teams won the semifinal tilts on April 1 (Foothills bombed Four Star Sports 75–58, and Gould's blew away Haynesworth Mill 78–31), the stage was set for a whale of a finale. No one left disappointed as the Surveyors claimed a 63–59 win. Couture had another fine game, leading Foothills with 22 points, but she was no match for the total team effort of Gould's, whose 237 points in three games easily broke the record of 212 set by the Atlanta Tomboys in 1966.

The gentlemen were hard pressed to match that caliber of play, but they gave some fine efforts in the attempt. In Open competition, both finalists used stellar team performances to overcome an opponent's individual effort. Snyder's Auto edged Poinsett Grocery 103–100 despite 30 points by the Grocer's Terry Stewart, a University of South Carolina–Spartanburg product. Dillard's Sporting Goods edged the Sonics 89–87, though Richard Ramey had 34 for the losers. Dillard's bested Snyder's in April 2's finals for the title. In C men's action, Chick-Fil-A defeated Dillard's 85–77 for the championship as Bruce Evans had 30 (21 in the second half). Everick Sullivan, who had ten for the winners, arrived only one hour before game time, having played a Friday all star game in Louisville, Kentucky. For Chick-Fil-A, this title business was getting to be old hat, as they racked up their eighth various division championship in the '80s.

Southern Textile Athletic Association president Fred McAbee kept things focused as he offered his philosophy on the tournament. "It's changed," he noted, "from a spectator sport to a player participation, and for lots of reasons. The tournament started going downhill when the textile plants sold the houses on the mill villages. They lost that sense of community.

"Mill teams were replaced as the feature attraction, first by the Open division, and more recently by the Class C men as interest peaked in the recruiting of high school players.

"Kids are going to be the salvation of the Southern Textile Basketball Tournament, and we had forty-eight entered in the junior division this year. If we can create a program for them, supervise it, and give them something to do to keep them out of trouble, then we ought to do it. That's the reason to keep it going."[12]

For 1989, it was "Hot Dogs and Hoops," a Thursday/Friday special when $3 paid for admission, a hot dog and a soft drink. And there was a little taste of the past, as Ruppert Elliott and Charles Roddy—both past presidents, players, coaches and officials—were inducted into the Southern Textile Athletic Association Hall of Fame. But again it was sparse crowds that watched the tournament move toward some impressive games in Saturday's finals.

Jimmy's Disco grounded the Charleston Flyers 109–93 for the Open title behind the Central Wesleyan foursome of John Perry (29), Raymond Lawson (21), Ed Young (14), and J.W. Miller (13). The Flyers' Mike Gillison scored 41, including nine three-pointers, but his stellar performance was just not enough. Michelin's Class A men outdistanced PPG 75–59, riding Clayton Rhodes' 28 points to its second consecutive title.

1989 Southern Textile Basketball Tournament program cover.
Monaghan Mill's 1921 Class A Champions.

For the B men, Shedd's edged Digital 63–59 as four starters hit double figures: Kell Brownlee (15), Dion King (11), Joe Abercrombie (11), and "Root Beer" Johnson (10). In C action, Chick-Fil-A defeated Carper Real Estate 87–76 for its fifth title in eight years. The Boston Beanery women moved past Comfort Inn 86–78 behind the play of Toni Edwards (28) and Jackie Moore (21).

The number of teams participating dwindled to 50 in 1990 (there was no women's division at all). Long-time associate Charles Roddy pointed to economics, saying, "I believe it's due to plant closings. Some industries are having hard times." He also noticed something missing in the competition. "The Open Division is down a little bit. Guys that played before won't play now. They're concerned they'll get hurt."[13] One thing was certain: The grand old tournament was forever changed, yet it possessed a remarkable urge to survive.

The 1990s

Fewer teams, fewer sponsors, fewer fans — that accurately describes the Southern Textile Basketball Tournament in 1990. For the first time since 1943, there were no women's teams competing. Even the staunchest supporters of this textile tradition had to ask themselves what reasons there were to attend.

Nathaniel Jones, a referee for more than 30 years, offered one answer: "The players are still going to carry on the way they did in the past, because there is a lot of pride when you play in the tournament."[1]

Pride could be manifested either in an individual blaze of glory or in methodical teamwork, and the B men offered examples of both on the tournament's opening day of 1990. Jeffrey Harper poured in 38 to lead St. Francis Hospital past Wangner Systems 75–56, and Shaw Properties used the points from four starters — McCullough (25), Young (22), Nance (14) and Shaw (14) — to defeat CRS Sirrine by a nearly identical score, 75–54.

Balanced scoring ruled the second round on March 27, starting with the popular C men's division as Dunean routed Miller Oil 73–37 behind Tron Brock (21), Adrian Barton (14), Cedric Brockman (12) and Lamont Jones (10). The Greenville Fire Department's A team went one better, as Dempsey Cohen (26), R. Sitton (14), V.L. Means (12), B. Hyatt (10) and Ken Sterling (10) led an 82–77 win over Saco-Lowell. Steve Crowe's 30, moving Greenville Valve past Digital 62–58 in B men's action, was the stellar individual effort of the day.

Overlooked until the third round on March 28, the Open Division erupted with a flurry of team scoring that did not let up until Championship Saturday was over. The Charleston Flyers edged Z Control 113–106 behind the quintet of Lowe (26), Jordan (24), Mike Gillison (22), Miller (15) and D. Thomas (11). Z Control had six in double figures but still lost the game. The Sixers blew Top Gun from the competition with a 116–101 win, led by Hill (32), James Brown (26), Barry Kincaid (19), Arthur Snipe (18), and Haskins (11); John Perry's 35 paced Top Gun.

The Flyers continued their scoring onslaught with a 120–109 win over the V.A. Jets as Keith Freyer (36) and Mike Gillison (35) formed an impressive duo. The Charleston entry could not sustain the pace in the title game, however, as Poinsett Grocery used the same balanced strategy to fashion a 131–98 blowout. Carl Smith (30), Jimmy Brown (27), Todd Gambrell (19), Roy Wright (18), Moody (14) and Eric Marable (11) led the way. As usual, all attention was focused on the high school talent as Chick-Fil-A claimed the C division championship with a 90–86 win over Carper Real Estate. Their exploits were given a big writeup in the Sunday *News*, while all other title games were mentioned only by a boxscore.

"When we were kids, we would ride the

bus and then walk down to West Washington Street to old Textile Hall, and we'd bring our sandwiches," tournament official Fred McAbee reminisced as the 1991 games got underway. "Nobody had money, so we'd bring our lunch, watch ball games that day, and go home at night when it was all over with."[2] Now, except for an occasional family member, old-timer, or college coach, hardly anyone bothered to come at all.

The 50-team junior tournament was held two weeks prior; that plus the $100 fee paid by the teams to enter the big show generated just about all the available revenue. A slam dunk contest was added to try and spark more interest, but it was left to a near empty auditorium to bear witness to this 68th edition.

The Open Division offered everything that the few spectators could have hoped for. On March 26, Barry Kincaid's 50 moved the Sharkheads past Excalibur 124–107. The Sixers blew away Over the Hill 95–46 with six in double figures — Hill (24), Shaw (21), McKinley (19), Mack (10), Jeter (10), and Young (10). Kincaid's individual effort was bested two days later by the University of Massachusetts' Carl Smith, whose 14 three-pointers (10 in the first half) made for a 52-point outburst and a 128–98 Poinsett Grocery victory over the Sixers. That same day the Sharkheads disarmed Top Gun 120–117 behind scorers Roger Carr (31), Barry Kincaid (29), Martin (24), and Freeman (21); the ever-present John Perry paced the Gunners with 32.

But this was just a warm-up to what the college coaches and recruiters had come to see — the high school players in the Class C men's division, especially the Beach Ball All Stars. Six-eight Michael Blassingame (Seneca), 6'6" Chuck Robinson (James Island), 6'7" Desi McQueen (Bennettsville), and 6'11" twins Simeon and Sammy Haley (Myrtle Beach) made them the overwhelming favorites to take the trophy.

In the March 29 semifinals, Kent Stallard's buzzer-beating three-pointer moved his 8 O'Clock Supers into overtime with the Stars. The Supers finally lost 99–94, but it took six of the Beach players in double figures to finish them off: McQueen (19), Blassingame (17), Ricky Daniels (14), Robinson (13), Wendell Brown (13), and Jermaine Scott (12). In the other semifinal, Marcus Parson's trey tied things up between his Carolina Upstate team and Metro, but Metro prevailed 99–97 on Kevin Benson's tip in at the overtime buzzer. Carolina was led by Brady Ledford's 34, but he could not hold off Metro's sextet of Kevin Irby (21), Kenny Jackson (20), Nick Griffin (15), Tarrance Albert (10), Vincent Lynch (10) and Benson (10). Beach Ball then knocked off Metro on March 30 for the title.

The big names dominated the 1992 tournament. Southeastern Products' Open Division entry included Furman University's David Stamey, David Brown and Bruce Evans, and the University of South Carolina's Barry Manning and Jo Jo English. They made good on the notoriety, beating the Sharkheads 111–102 on March 19, with Stamey (28), Brown (25), English (23) and Evans (20) contributing strong performances. Southeastern topped off its run for the trophy by knocking off S&M Sports 106–98 March 21 as all the "fab five" hit for double figures: Stamey (28), Manning (19), English (19), Evans (16), and Brown (11).

Larry Carper put his Class C men's team together by inviting players based on recommendations from recruiting specialists and college assistant coaches. He asked for players whose schools were on spring break during tournament week, and never saw his team until they gathered for the first time. But after 15 years of effort, Carper Real Estate took home its first championship. With the exception of a close 66–61 win over Palmetto Expo on March 18, everything else was a blowout on the way to the title. They moved past Washington City the next day, 83–71, and then smashed perennial power Chick-Fil-A 64–38 behind the play of Anthony Jackson (18), Derrick Hammonds (15) and Anton Hatchett (13). An 88–61 win over Metro on March 21 was again secured on the broad shoulders of Hatchett (27) and Jackson (22).

Things got cooking early on March 17 when the C men of Chick-Fil-A had seven in double figures to scratch LYF-TFM, 87–39: Shoomond Williams (15), Eldrick Leamon (15), Sidney Moore (11), Michael Hamilton (10), Jeff Maness (10), Ralph Roundtree (10) and Ricky Robertson (10). Cleve Cox popped in 31 to lead his Class B Vernon Heating & Air to a 100–54 rout of 3M. But no one approached the heights set by David Lawrence, whose record-setting 63-point performance (50 in the first half) led S&M Sports over the Lynch Mob in a torrid 143–132 affair.

Cox and Lawrence sustained their remarkable performances throughout the tournament. Cox had another 31 on March 18, in an 86–55 win over Mt. Vernon Mill; 51 (third highest effort in Class B history) as Vernon edged Fiberweb 87–83 on March 19; a mere 21 in a semifinal 82–63 win over Greenville Valve; and 34 in a 92–84 loss to American Federal in the championship. He scored 137 points in his four games, an average of 34.2.

Lawrence may not have matched his 63-point opening game performance, but he had some impressive stints left. A 58-point spree March 18 moved S&M to a 123–111 victory over Steak & Waffle; 46 more played a big part in a 120–113 upset of defending champion Poinsett Grocery. Southeastern Products managed to limit him to a mere 37 in the championship game, and like Cox his magnificent individual effort fell just short. However, Lawrence's 204 total points and his 51.0 per game average were tournament records.

The women's division matched the men's stride for stride all through the week. Jenny Lyerly popped in 22 to lead R&G past St. Francis Hospital 56–43 on March 18, a solid start to showcase the ladies of the court. TKO rode the efforts of Sherry Davis (18), Annette Alston (13), Brenda Cain (11) and Lisa Diaz (11) to a 63–38 run over Skocdopole a day later, but the semifinals of March 20 offered perhaps the best overall team performances of the last ten years. Triple Play outdistanced R&G 77–60, as ten players reached double figures, led by Sherry Oldevak (18), Melinda Hall (17), Michelle Bryant (13), Rosalyn Jennings (12) and Natalie Kleckley (10). R&G was led by Tracy Rucker (13), Jenny Lyerly (11), Dawn Raab (10), Carla Gambrell (10) and Catina Freeman (10). Triple Play claimed the title when they edged TKO 77–74 on March 21. Melinda Hall, whose day job was girl's coach at J.L. Mann High, led the champions with 22.

A few notable achievements rounded out a fine week of basketball. Alice Manufacturing upset four-time defending champion Michelin 79–67 in March 19's Class A men's action, and when they defeated Greenville Fire Department 56–48 on March 21, it was their first championship since 1978. An old crowd favorite, Clayton Rhodes, did not allow his Michelin teammates to sink into self-pity, and his 36 on March 21 moved them past Michelin-Spartanburg 72–58 and a claim to the consolation title. For sheer participation, no one did it like Southeastern Products and Dice & Associates in the Class C men's battle on March 19. Southeastern won 95–75, using 13 players, and Dice was not far behind with 11. That pretty well summed up the 1992 tournament — a good time was had by all.

Whatever the magic, it did not move from the old year to the new, and edition number 70 again focused on the Class C men. The top prospect was Mauldin High's Kevin Garnett, who played both in the 16 and Under and C divisions. He scored 23 on March 15 to lead Plan Home Health Care to a 64–48 win over Western Carolina AAU for the 16 and Under title, and though he played solid ball for that organization's C entry — he had 16 the following day in an 89–65 rout of Carver Builders — he did not play a major role in the division championship hunt.

Chad Davis was another player stirring college recruiters into a frenzy. The McDonald's High School All-American from Chattanooga, Tennessee, scored 24 in March 16's round to move Metro II past

Dice & Associates 79–70, but like Garnett was not around when the title games were being decided. That excitement belonged to the team members of Carper Real Estate, who erased a seven point deficit in the last three minutes to take a second straight crown, 78–69 over Metro I. Carper was paced by Jeff McInnis (17), Glen Young (16), Earl McPherson (15), Tavaris Johnson (14), and Maktor Ndiaye (10). Dice & Associates recovered from the loss to Davis' team in the opening round and captured the consolation hardware with a 90–71 walk over Southeastern Freight. They were also led by five stellar performers: Erik Rothwell (24), Kenisey Adair (16), Jamie Kelly (15), Tommy Johnston (14) and Matthew Rollins (13).

There was still some honor to be claimed by the "old gentlemen" of the Open Division. John Perry's 16 points would have seemed unimportant in Sincerely Yours' 98–56 semifinal win over the Dream Team, except that he became the all-time leading scorer in the division. His 350 points moved him past Clemson's Chubby Wells. The Dream Team had earlier beaten a good S&M Sports squad, 122–109, using four 20-point performances—from Harvey Macobson (26), Dewayne Long (26), Tyshawn Staggs (24), and George Adams (23)—to outduel S&M's David Lawrence (38) and Charlie Herbert (31). Southeastern Products' major college players led a 108–78 blowout of the Orangemen in semifinal action; Furman's David Stamey (22), the University of South Carolina's Barry Manning (19), Chris Leso (12), Joe Rhett (12), and the University of Georgia's Shawn Golden (13) powered the win.

In the women's division, M. Vick edged NCR 56–50 with Pearl Moore (16), Elnora Jones (12), Monique Pompili (11) and Jolette Law (12) scoring all but five of the points. Vick claimed the championship a day later. Taking notes, R&G used the same balanced attack to claim a 63–21 consolation bracket win over Greenville City Recreation behind the strong play of Catina Freeman (22), Jennifer Cox (16), Lee Haley (11) and Karen Neely (10).

The men relied more on individual effort. Cleve Cox's 36 led Palmetto Expo over St. Francis Hospital 81–56 in a B consolation win on March 19, and Dempsey Cohen's 35 enabled Greenville Fire Department to claim the A title on March 20, 85–76 over Alice Manufacturing.

Furman assistant Jimmy Gaffney relished the thought of scouting the talented 1994 high school stars. "This class is known throughout the country. Close to twenty of these kids will play some form of Division I basketball."[3] The University of South Carolina's Eddie Fogler, East Tennessee State's Alan LeForce and Furman's Joe Cantalfio looked on as Poinsett Grocery crushed Brown's Bombers 100–65 with a display of balanced power as eight players hit double figures: Titus Shelton (15), Shane McCravy (13), Jermaine Gaines (12), Reccus Nix (11), Patrick Garner (11), Stan Simmons (11), Geoff Bentzel (10) and Erik Rothwell (10). As talented as Poinsett was, Southeastern Products was the showcase team.

"This is a lot of fun for me," said Chester High School's Will Gallman. "I don't have three or four guys around me like I did during the season, and it's a chance to do my thing." And with Kevin Garnett, Derrick Drummond, Hagen Rouse and Damous Anderson around? "Those guys make it easy to play. There's no pressure."[4]

Southeastern wasted little time establishing its supremacy, blowing away the Sonics 82–43 on March 22, and two days later polishing off Sterling, 85–37. The title was theirs after an 88–76 win over Upperstate I on March 26. Gallman, already committed to Eddie Fogler and the University of South Carolina though only a junior, had 34, and Garnett, two years away from being an NBA sensation, had 21 points, 25 rebounds and four blocked shots.

There were uncharacteristic embarrassments, like a number of forfeits playing havoc with scheduling and with the integrity of the tournament. AMP-AKZO and St. Francis Hospital (Class B men), Greenville Valve (Class B men, this one involving an unnamed protest), and Michelin-Spartanburg (Class A men) all found reasons not to show.

A more troubling incident marred the men's Open Division title game and Southeastern Products' quest for a third straight championship. Carolina Magic had finally tied the game at 71, only to see Southeastern tack on the next 15 points. USC's Barry Manning, late of the Continental Basketball League, racked up 33 for game honors, but the contest was stopped with 6:45 left and Carolina down 94–81. A Magic player was called for a charge and made an obscene gesture at a referee, and after a short meeting the officials declared the game over.

Amid all this, there were other games worth remembering. The Class B Southeastern Freight men stopped Aneda Clock #1 81–48 on March 23 behind the scoring of Travis Butler (20), Seth Wylie (19), Robert Pickel (18), Mike Adams (10) and Charles Butler (10). Mel Daniel's fine 32-point gem a day later led American Federal past Alice Manufacturing in Class A action. Michelle Bryant's 25 led Triple Play to the women's title, 65–62 over T-shirts Plus, though Lisa Diaz's 26 took game-high honors in a losing cause.

Two long-standing men's classifications, classes A and B, merged to become the Closed Division in 1995, still based on the premise that players were employees of the companies they represented. Individual efforts broke on top from day one. Clayton Rhodes' 30 led Michelin US-1 over the Enterprise All Stars 82–69; Steve Smith's 31 could not prevent his Greenville Valve team from coming up short, 69–68, to the YMCA; and Nissan's John Shell poured in 33 in an 81–75 victory over Cryovac I. The March 22 special was Southeastern Freight's 81–66 walk over the City of Greenville behind Charles Butler's 33. A day later, brothers Wayne (32) and Todd (26) Wray led PPG to a 97–75 rout of the Clinton Horsemen. Todd Wray pulled the trigger one more time in the semifinals March 24, scoring 31 as PPG blew past Fiberweb, 77–61.

From opening day, there was a definite collision course for the favorites in both the Open and C men's divisions. When Barry Kincaid and Kevin Burroughs each scored 32 in a 112–91 Sharkheads win over S&M Sports on March 20, and Fat Friday's matched that win a day later, routing the USCS Club 105–82 behind the solid play of Ricky Jones (27), Adrian Barton (18), Devin Gray (15), Thomas Gray (12), and David Young (10); no one doubted who would be involved in the Open's clash of champions. The March 24 semifinals were more of the same. Kincaid's 54 (with eight three-pointers) powered a Sharkhead 119–109 win over S&R Auto, and Devin Gray's 32 led to Fat Friday's narrow 118–112 decision over Showtime. The final game was close all the way, and Fat Friday's prevailed 96–92 as David Young (29) and Devin Gray (22) paced the victory; Roger Carr's 38 for the Sharkheads took game honors.

Ditto for the C men, as Southeastern Products (105–66 over UCBA) and Carper Real Estate (96–71 over Western Carolina V) seized March 22 wins and stormed all the way into the March 25 finals. Though Carper had three popping in more than 20—James Hunter (27), Seco Camero (22) and Rob Turner (20)—they could not overcome the balance of the five starters in double figures for Southeastern Products. Derrick Drummond (24), Shawn Ellis (19), Will Gallman (16), Chris McGowens (14) and Damous Anderson (10) secured a hard-fought 97–93 championship win.

The women's division offered excellent performances as well. Carolyn Brown's 33 was what Sissy's Furniture needed to edge T-shirts Plus 63–61 on March 23. Sportsman Shop's Kelli Garrett was brilliant during the March 24 semifinals against Triple Play, but her 28 points could not stave off a 61–53 loss brought on by the triple threat of Sherry Oldevak (20), Shandy Bryan (15) and Michelle Gregoire (14).

Another major change awaited in 1996. It had been announced that Memorial Auditorium would be torn down to make room for a Bi-Lo Center, and for the first time since 1959 the Southern Textile Basketball Tournament would have to search for a new home. All the questions about the future of "The Greatest Basketball Show on Earth" arose once more even as the games started.

It was still the place to be, according to Greenville High School coach and athletic director Bill Johnson. "It has been great for the young women and young men of South Carolina," he said on March 21, 1996. "If they want to try to continue their basketball, this is the place to be. This gives college coaches an opportunity to come and get a second look at a player they may have overlooked."[5] The solid performances in both Class C women and men bore out the truth of his statement.

On the same day Johnson expounded upon the tournament's significance to high school players, Krystal Scott popped in 22 to lead her Upstate Lady Sonics past Marquee, 56–44. She had 17 more in the title game March 23, and was joined by Crishina Hill (12) and Maya Grady (10) in a 48–44 win over Roll Tech; Shorelle Harrison's 21 led the Tech team. Marquee, paced by Rachel Jones' 20, roared past R&G 66–24 for the consolation prize earlier that day.

Poinsett Grocery's C men whipped the SC Bulls 88–75 on March 21, led by Yahnik Martin (27) and Quincy Haywood (21). Martin continued his scoring in March 23's title game with 26, matching Travis Smith (24), an outstanding guard for Dick James, almost bucket for bucket. But it was Smith and his team who fashioned a 75–69 win over Martin and Poinsett. In the consolation bracket, Curt Small's 32 paced Carper Real Estate over Upperstate, 80–67.

There was no mystery in making a case for fine play in the Open Division. The Represent team outdistanced UNV 110–98 in play March 19, led by Turbo Moore's 40 points, but it was a scorer's paradise as six from each team managed double figures. N. Gardner (16), W. Coleman (11), A. Smith (10), Staley (10) and Wakefield (10) joined Moore for the winners; Henry Bailey (22), Chris Brashier (15), Zack Dowling (12), Dondray Burton (12), Houston (11) and Scott Patterson (11) lit it up for UNV.

The women were showcased in both title games on March 23. WCCP edged King Valley 78–69 for the A championship as Michelle Gregoire (15), Renee Williams (14) and Melinda Campbell (14) led the way. The consolation battle was even closer with Low Country finally slipping by the Lady Hornets, 70–67. The fab four of Maria Williams (22), Kelli Garrett (12), Joy Clifford (10) and Brenda Washington (10) accounted for all but six of the winner's total.

After a months-long search for a new home, and perhaps new lifeblood, the 1997 tournament opened at the Eastside High School gym with the younger generation ready to set sparks flying on the court. Tradition did not play nearly as major a role anymore, as statistician Randy LaFoy attests. "Not only do they not remember Earl Wooten, they don't even remember John Wooden."[6]

With the move to a smaller facility, and with the elimination of the men's Open Division, there was less mention than usual about the games. The Greenville *News* only carried results on March 28 and 29, and no coverage at all was offered for Championship Saturday.

The finest competition proved to rest within the men's Closed Division, as Parker Mill and the YMCA moved deliberately toward a showdown. Joey Brooks popped in 29 on March 27 as Parker ran by Cryovac 81–66, and Tim Moody had an astounding 60 as the YMCA edged the City of Greenville, 90–82. Moody's point total — he would average 40.3 points in his four starts — broke Bob Stowe's Class A-Closed Division single game record of 55, which had stood since 1955. Moody scored 42 more the next day as his team took a 73–71 squeaker from MCP, and Tim Young's 26 nudged Parker past AMP-AKZO, 69–62. The finals were all a fan could hope for, a 75–74 burner as Young (24) and Brooks (24) led Parker past YMCA and Moody (29).

The high school kids kicked it in gear to impress the college coaches. The SC Bulls Class C men edged the Upstate Seniors 88–

86, following the leadership of Kenyatta Campbell (19), Lamont Speaks (17), Joe Hamilton (16), and Rhdala Sojo (14). Derrick Burton (24), Keith Stringer (21) and Carlos Copeland (20) gave superb performances, but their efforts fell just short. The ladies from the Upstate Sonics displayed the same kind of teamwork in the March 29 consolation finals, running by Berea, 64–46. Krystal Scott (14), Eboni Littlejohn (13), Crishina Hill (12), and Heather Crowe (10) proved too much for Terri Rucker (23) and her team.

The Southern Textile Basketball Tournament is no longer a commanding presence in the city of Greenville. March comes and goes, and the games elicit little response from the citizens. Multiple pages of basketball glory in the Greenville *News* are reduced to brief mentions, boxscores, and an occasional feature article on days gone by.

Still, it does not die, and that can be attributed to the wisdom of men like Fred McAbee and Ted Pittman. "Give it back to the kids," they urged, and following that simple directive gives new life to this textile tradition.

Created for the mill village people, the tournament moved on and became, first, a showcase for the best college talent in the southeast; then, a haven for college recruiters and coaches looking to strengthen their programs with solid high school talent; and finally, a place for the young people to learn all that a great game has to teach.

Some discussion has already begun on moving the tournament one last time, perhaps to Furman University, and that would be a fitting gesture, a final brush stroke to this rich portrait. Since it was L.P. Hollis who offered the use of the Monaghan Mill gym to Dr. Steele and the college in exchange for Steele's services as coach of the mill kids, now it is Furman offering a home to Dr. Hollis's brainchild.

The seven men who so long ago set in motion the Southern Textile Basketball Tournament would surely be proud today that it has returned to its roots, providing recreation for the people of the community and honoring all who have ever played.

Endnotes

The 1920s

1. From the 1986 Southern Textile Basketball Tournament program.
2. The Greenville *News*, March 21, 1985.
3. The Greenville *News*, March 12, 1959.
4. *Ibid*.
5. The Greenville *News*, March 7, 1957.
6. *Ibid*.
7. *Ibid*.
8. *Ibid*.
9. *Ibid*.
10. From the 1969 Southern Textile Basketball Tournament program.
11. From the 1979 Southern Textile Basketball Tournament program.
12. The Greenville *News*, March 6, 1957.
13. The Greenville *News*, March 1, 1950.
14. The Greenville *News*, March 12, 1959.
15. The Greenville *News*, February 16, 1922.
16. The Greenville *News*, March 7, 1957.
17. The Greenville *News*, March 6, 1957.
18. The Greenville *News*, February 15, 1924.
19. The Greenville *News*, February 19, 1925.
20. *Ibid*.
21. *Ibid*.
22. The Greenville *News*, February 14, 1926.
23. The Greenville *News*, February 13, 1926.
24. The Greenville *News*, February 13, 1927.
25. The Greenville *News*, February 17, 1928.
26. From the 1929 Southern Textile Basketball Tournament program.
27. *Ibid*.
28. The Greenville *News*, February 16, 1929.

The 1930s

1. From the 1930 Southern Textile Basketball Tournament Program.
2. The Greenville *News*, February 14, 1930.
3. The Greenville *News*, February 16, 1930.
4. The Greenville *News*, February 19, 1931.
5. The Greenville *News*, February 21, 1931.
6. The Greenville *News*, February 22, 1931.
7. From the 1932 Southern Textile Basketball Tournament program.
8. The Greenville *News*, February 27, 1932.
9. The Greenville *News*, February 26, 1933.
10. The Greenville *News*, February 23, 1933.
11. The Greenville *News*, March 26, 1933.
12. The Greenville *News*, February 24, 1933.
13. The Greenville *News*, February 15, 1934.
14. The Greenville *News*, February 17 and 18, 1934.
15. The Greenville *News*, February 24, 1935.
16. The Greenville *News*, March 2, 1937.
17. The Greenville *News*, March 3, 1938.
18. The Greenville *News*, March 5, 1938.
19. From the 1934 Southern Textile Basketball Tournament program.

The 1940s

1. Interview with Joe Anders, March 1995.
2. Interview with Walter Davis, March 1995.

3. Interview with Hinkie McCurry, June 1995.
4. The Greenville *News*, March 9, 1941.
5. The Greenville *News*, February 24, 1943.
6. The Greenville *News*, February 26, 1943.
7. The Greenville *News*, March 29, 1974.
8. *Ibid*.
9. Interview with Thomas Perry, June 1995.
10. Interview with Thomas Perry, June 1995.
11. Interview with Chafer Honea, May 1995.
12. Interview with "Punchy" Howard, March 1995.
13. The Greenville *News*, March 3, 1948.
14. *Ibid*.
15. Interview with Wade Burton, April 1995.
16. The Greenville *News*, March 6, 1948.
17. The Greenville *News*, March 4, 1949.
18. The Greenville *News*, March 4, 1949.
19. Interview with Stan Hilley, April 1995.
20. *Ibid*.

The 1950s

1. From the 1950 Southern Textile Basketball Tournament program.
2. Interview with Deran Walters, March 1995.
3. The Greenville *News*, March 6, 1952.
4. Interview with Allan Moore, March 1995.
5. The Greenville *News*, March 4, 1954.
6. Interview with Alton White, March 1995.
7. Interview with Bob Seawright, February 1995.
8. The Greenville *News*, March 3, 1956.
9. The Greenville *News*, March 4, 1956.
10. The Greenville *News*, March 1, 1956.
11. The Greenville *News*, March 3, 1956.
12. The Greenville *News*, March 7, 1957.
13. The Greenville *News*, March 12, 1958.
14. The Greenville *News*, March 14, 1958.
15. *Ibid*.
16. Interview with "Frog" Stansell, April 1995.
17. The Greenville *News*, March 13, 1958.
18. The Greenville *News*, March 11, 1959.

The 1960s

1. The Greenville *News*, March 10, 1960.
2. *Ibid*.
3. The Greenville *News*, March 11, 1960.
4. *Ibid*.
5. The Greenville *News*, March 8, 1961.
6. The Greenville *News*, March 9, 1961.
7. *Ibid*.
8. The Greenville *News*, March 10, 1961.
9. From the 1962 Southern Textile Basketball Tournament program.
10. Interview with Herman Evatt, March 1995.
11. The Greenville *News*, March 14, 1964.
12. *Ibid*.
13. The Greenville *News*, March 11, 1965.
14. Interview with Doug Moe, April 1996.
15. Interview with Billy Cunningham, April 1996.
16. Interview with Jerry Parris, March 1995.
17. The Greenville *News*, March 12, 1966.
18. The Greenville *News*, March 17, 1966.
19. The Greenville *News*, March 7, 1967.
20. The Greenville *News*, March 9, 1967.
21. The Greenville *News*, March 10, 1967.
22. The Greenville *News*, March 15, 1968.
23. Interview with Jerry Sims, April 1995.
24. The Greenville *News*, March 17, 1968.

The 1970s

1. The Greenville *News*, March 15, 1970.
2. The Greenville *News*, March 31, 1972.
3. *Ibid*.
4. The Greenville *News*, March 20, 1973.
5. The Greenville *News*, March 25, 1973.
6. The Greenville *News*, March 27, 1974.
7. The Greenville *News*, March 28, 1976.
8. Interview with Wayne "Tree" Rollins, June, 1996.
9. The Greenville *News*, March 24, 1978.
10. The Greenville *News*, March 26, 1978.
11. The Greenville *News*, March 21, 1979.

The 1980s

1. The Greenville News, March 23, 1980.
2. The Greenville *News*, March 22, 1981.
3. The Greenville *News*, March 21, 1982.
4. The Greenville *News*, March 25, 1983.
5. The Greenville *News*, March 19, 1985.

6. Interview with Ted Pittman, March 1995.
7. The Greenville *News*, March 30, 1986.
8. *Ibid*.
9. *Ibid*.
10. *Ibid*.
11. The Greenville *News*, March 29, 1987.
12. The Greenville *News*, April 3, 1988.
13. The Greenville *News*, March 25, 1990.

The 1990s

1. The Greenville *News*, February 7, 1997.
2. The Greenville *News*, March 27, 1991.
3. The Greenville *News*, March 26, 1994.
4. The Greenville *News*, March 25, 1994.
5. The Greenville *News*, March 21, 1996.
6. Interview with Randy LaFoy, April 1997.

Appendix 1

Southern Textile Basketball Tournament Rosters

This appendix must be considered the definitive record of the teams of the Southern Textile Basketball Tournament. It includes the officers, coaches, players, and champions in all divisions of the tournament. Many mills have had more than one owner over the years, and have had various name changes. Lonsdale Mill (Seneca, S.C.), for example, has also been known as Seneca Mill and Utica-Mohawk. In every case of multiple names, the authors have used the one considered most familiar and recognizable. Included below are the names of every person either participating in, or scheduled to participate in, this "Greatest Basketball Show on Earth."

1921

Officers: W.V. Martin (Spartanburg, S.C.), President; L.P. Hollis (Greenville, S.C.), 1st Vice-President; F.C. Bragg (Spartanburg, S.C.), 2nd Vice-President; H.R. McCartney (Greenville, S.C.), 3rd Vice-President; J.L. Gourley (Greer, S.C.), Secretary; A.E. Marwick (Rock Hill, S.C.), Treasurer.

Class A Men

Woodside Mill A (Greenville, S.C.), champions: John Harrison (coach), Walter McAbee (coach), Winnie Henson, Martin Henson, Luther Durham, Jess Buchanan, Andy Baker, Herman Porter, Bill Porter, Walter Greer, John Freeman.

Schoolfield Mill (Danville, Va.), runners-up: Robert Mahaffey, Harper, C. Mahaffey, Dewey Copus, Brooks, Orliss Nichols, Fogleman.

Monaghan Mill (Greenville, S.C.): Howard McCarthy (coach), Walt Barbare, Liz Morman, Peck Ellis, Henry Henson, Cline Henson, Harley Heath, Roy McElrath, Earl Kelly, Gus Barbare, Elmer Compton.

Victor Mill (Greer, S.C.): Fred "Footsie" Hooper.

Other Teams: Piedmont Mill (Piedmont, S.C.); **Blue Jackets** (N/A); **Woodside Mill B** (Greenville, S.C.); **Glen Lowery Mill** (Whitmire, S.C.); **Pacific Mill** (Columbia, S.C.); **Judson Mill** (Greenville, S.C.); **Monaghan P.R.A.** (Greenville, S.C.).

Class B Men

Monaghan Mill (Greenville, S.C.), champions: Walt Barbare (coach), Adger Campbell, Jim Barbare, June Campbell, Ralph Barton, Roy McElrath, Charlie Orr, Paul Barbare, Ralph Barton, Howard McCartney, Hubert Nolin, W. Glasgow, J. Brown.

Apalache Mill (Greer, S.C.), runners-up: R. Tillotson, G. Mason, C. Tillotson, Peck Leatherwood, E. Manley.

Greer Mill (Greer, S.C.): Jimmy Green.
Other Teams: **Textile Industrial Institute** (Spartanburg, S.C.); **Rock Hill Bleachery** (Rock Hill, S.C.); **Woodside Mill** (Greenville, S.C.); **Whitney Mill** (Spartanburg, S.C.); **Wallace Mill** (Union, S.C.); **Lonsdale Mill** (Seneca, S.C.); **Saxon Mill** (Spartanburg, S.C.); **Drayton Mill** (Spartanburg, S.C.); **Victor Mill** (Greer, S.C.); **Ottaray Mill** (Union, S.C.).

CLASS A WOMEN

Monaghan Mill A (Greenville, S.C.), champions: Essie Nolan, Lois Hudgens, Carolyn Barton, Minnie Heath, Inez Reid, Fannie Center, J. Center, Davenport, Henderson.

Monaghan Mill B (Greenville, S.C.), runners-up: Long, O. Henderson, Shepard, G. Henderson, Ballenger, Ashmore.

Other Teams: **Judson Mill** (Greenville, S.C.); **American Spinning** (Greenville, S.C.); **Glen Lowery Mill** (Whitmire, S.C.); **Piedmont Mill A** (Piedmont, S.C.); **Piedmont Mill B** (Piedmont, S.C.); **Victor Mill** (Greer, S.C.).

1922

Officers: W.V. Martin (Spartanburg, S.C.), President; L.P. Hollis (Greenville, S.C.), 1st Vice-President; H.R. McCartney (Greenville, S.C.), 2nd Vice-President; F.R. Corwin (Greenville, S.C.), 3rd Vice-President; J.L. Gourley (Greer, S.C.), Secretary; W.M. Grier (Greenville, S.C.), Treasurer.

CLASS A MEN

Pacific Mill (Columbia, S.C.), champions: Wallace, Martin, Ingram, Taylor, Bedenbaugh.

Schoolfield Mill (Danville, Va.), runners-up: G.C. Suttles (coach), Robert Mahaffey, John Hager, W.C. Mahaffey, Dewey Copus, Estelle Nichols, R.H. Goodman, Orliss Nichols, Paul Barton.

Ware Shoals Mill (Ware Shoals, S.C.), consolation winners: Moseley, Dorn, Gambrell, Whitman, Collins, Cook, Chalmers.

Victor Mill (Greer, S.C.): Brooks, Hooper, Herrin, Brady, Wood, R. Brady.

Highland Park Mill (Charlotte, N.C.): Marsh, Thomas, Jones, Belk, Hudson, Hunt.

New Holland Mill (Gainesville, Ga.): W.C. Stallworth (coach), W.B. Peterson, E.S. Alley, R.C. Allen, C.C. Miller, E.H. Ashley, Hub Kenney, S. Forrester, George Cobber.

Woodside Mill (Greenville, S.C.): Walter Henson, M. Henson, Herman Porter, Buchanan, C. Porter, Benson.

Monaghan Mill (Greenville, S.C.): Walt Barbare, Ellis, Martin Henson, W. Henson, Norman, Charlie Orr, Heath.

CLASS B MEN

Greer Mill (Greer, S.C.), champions: Brewton, Bragg, Hardin, Taylor, Westmoreland, Belcher, Milledge Brannon, Grier, Fred Center, F. Jones, C. Jones, Jimmy Green, Smiley Smith, Clarence Miller, Sanford Hood, Putnam, Bill Glasco.

Victor Mill (Greer, S.C.), runners-up: E. Campbell, H. Wilson, L. Pruitt, F. Hudson, E. Smith, R. Norman, R. Campbell, H. Hudson.

Schoolfield Mill (Danville, Va.), consolation winners: Clifford Mahaffey, Chester Lemons, Walter Murray, Howard Hopper, Guerrant Fray, J.C. Sweatt, Yates Nicholls, Lee Hudson, W.L. Furr.

Wallace Mill (Union, S.C.): Haile, Mason, Viley, Lawson, Coleman.

Pelzer Mill (Pelzer, S.C.): Kay, E. Westmoreland, J. Westmoreland, Fennell, Davenport, Rogers.

Mills Mill (Greenville, S.C.): Putnam, Young, Davis, Ballew, Smith.

Apalache Mill (Greer, S.C.): Manley, Mason, Stevenson, Amos, Tillotson, Smith.

Judson Mill (Greenville, S.C.): J. McClure, Sanders, Landreth, Powell, Mullinax, R. McClure.

Monaghan Mill (Greenville, S.C.): A. Campbell, J. Campbell, Cartee, Glasco, Wiggins, Christopher, Johnson, Heath, Olson.

Woodside Mill (Greenville, S.C.): Carter, Grier, Clippard, Stevens, Baker, Smith, Whitten.

Lonsdale Mill (Seneca, S.C.): Winkler, Corbett, Moore, Haynes, Suttles.

Saxon Mill (Spartanburg, S.C.): Bishop, Champion, Sparks, Mitchell, Corn, Lowe.

Dunean Mill (Greenville, S.C.): Franks, Floyd, Badger, Ray, Badger.

Piedmont Mill (Piedmont, S.C.): Mock, Smith, N. Anderson, Pickleseimer, L. Anderson.

Ottaray Mill (Union, S.C.): Powell, Cordell, Eads, Turner, Howard.

CLASS A WOMEN

Monaghan Mill (Greenville, S.C.), champions: Geneva Henderson, Tyler Barton, Oveida

Henderson, Beatrice Sheppard, Buna Glasco, Essie Nolan, Center, "Teen" Smoak (coach).

Schoolfield Mill (Danville, Va.), runners-up: Maude Flippin (coach), Reva Nelson, Mattie Davis, Ruth Pryor, Annie McKenzie, Ruth Hall, Mrs. Bob Mahaffey, Mary Copeland, Myrtle Scare, Sallie Jones, Beulah Safriet, Elva Sutphin.

Judson Mill (Greenville, S.C.), consolation winners: Forrest, Hodge, R. Gosnell, Estes, M. Gosnell, McDonald, Thompson.

Saxon Mill (Spartanburg, S.C.): Jenkins, Neill, Foster, Foster, Suttles, Leonard, Hays.

Greer Mill (Greer, S.C.): C. Carmen, Brown, Harmon, Henson, D. Carmen, Bragg, Campbell, Greenway.

Victor Mill (Greer, S.C.): Norman, Littlefield, Terry, Westmoreland, Pitts, L. Jones, R. Jones, Brady.

Schoolfield Mill B (Danville, Va.): Elvie McCain, Irene Fields, Ruby Hardiman, Eleanor McCullough, Belle Copeland, Jeannette McCain, Minnie Hungate, Ruby Few, Alma Cook, Pearl Hall, Carrie Garner, Hattie Parker.

Lonsdale Mill (Seneca, S.C.): Thompson, Martin, King, Nichols, Miller, Thomas.

American Spinning (Greenville, S.C.): E. Miller, Bayne, Owens, A. Miller, Brady, Hale.

Piedmont Mill (Piedmont, S.C.): Elvie Osteen, Pickleseimer, Wilson, Wilson, Elsie Osteen, Duncan.

Apalache Mill (Greer, S.C.): McCarter, Hawkins, Tucker, Leopard, Stevenson, McCarter.

---1923---

Class A Men

Monaghan Mill (Greenville, S.C.), champions: Walt Barbare (coach), Noland, Barbare, P. Barbare, Barton, Henson, McElrath.

Woodside Mill (Greenville, S.C.), runners-up: Buchanan, Porter, W. Henson, Durham, G.N. Henson.

Highland Park Mill (Charlotte, N.C.), consolation winners:

New Holland Mill (Gainesville, Ga.): Bunting.

Other Teams: **Pacific Mill** (Columbia, S.C.); **Victor Mill** (Greer, S.C.); **Schoolfield Mill** (Danville, Va.); **Dunean Mill** (Greenville, S.C.); **Judson Mill** (Greenville, S.C.); **Proximity Mill** (Greensboro, N.C.).

Class B Men

Pacific Mill (Columbia, S.C.), champions.
Piedmont Mill (Piedmont, S.C.), runners-up.
Schoolfield Mill (Danville, Va.), consolation winners.

Other Teams: **Calloway Mill** (LaGrange, Ga.); **Judson Mill** (Greenville, S.C.); **Victor Mill** (Greer, S.C.); **Whitney Mill** (Spartanburg, S.C.); **Monaghan Mill** (Greenville, S.C.); **Greer Mill** (Greer, S.C.); **Glen Lowery Mill** (Whitmire, S.C.); **Pelzer Mill** (Pelzer, S.C.); **Ottaray Mill** (Union, S.C.); **Saxon Mill** (Spartanburg, S.C.); **Woodside Mill** (Greenville, S.C.); **Apalache Mill** (Greer, S.C.); **Rock Hill Bleachery** (Rock Hill, S.C.); **Wallace Mill** (Union, S.C.); **Tryon Mill** (Tryon, N.C.).

Class C Men

Piedmont Mill (Piedmont, S.C.), champions.
Victor Mill (Greer, S.C.), runners-up.
Greer Mill (Greer, S.C.), consolation winners.

Other Teams: **Walhalla Mill** (Walhalla, S.C.); **Lonsdale Mill** (Seneca, S.C.); **Woodside Mill** (Greenville, S.C.); **Monaghan Mill** (Greenville, S.C.); **Judson Mill** (Greenville, S.C.).

Class A Women

Monaghan Mill (Greenville, S.C.), champions: Krulein Smoak (coach), Beatrice Brown, Minnie Heath, O. Henderson, V. Henderson, Mary Hendrix, Essie Batson, McKey, M. Childress, E. Noland, Oveido Owens, Viola Austin.

Schoolfield Mill (Danville, Va.), runners-up: M. Davis, R. Nelson, T. Eaton, E. Copeland, M. Copeland, Cannady.

Class B Women

Highland Park Mill (Charlotte, N.C.), champions.

Glen Lowery Mill (Whitmire, S.C.), runners-up.

Judson Mill (Greenville, S.C.), consolation winners: Nettie Forrest.

Other Teams: ; **Schoolfield Mill** (Danville, Va.); **Monaghan Mill** (Greenville, S.C.); **Greer Mill** (Greer, S.C.); **Chesnee Mill** (Chesnee, S.C.); **Wallace Mill** (Union, S.C.); **American Spinning** (Greenville, S.C.); **Lonsdale Mill** (Seneca, S.C.); **Walhalla Mill** (Walhalla, S.C.); **Piedmont Mill** (Piedmont, S.C.); **Whitney Mill** (Spartanburg, S.C.).

---1924---

Officers: L.P. Hollis (Greenville, S.C.), President; Charles Boling (Columbia, S.C.), 1st

Vice President; Brown Mahon (Greenville, S.C.), 2nd Vice President; G.C. Suttles (Danville, Va.), 3rd Vice President; J.W. Stribbling (Greenville, S.C.), Secretary; W.M. Grier (Greenville, S.C.), Treasurer.

Class A Men
Pacific Mill (Columbia, S.C.), champions: Knox, Wallace, Hilliard, Arthur Bedenbaugh, Martin.
Woodside Mill (Greenville, S.C.), runners-up: Buchanan, Walter Henson, Shorty Smith, Porter, M. Henson.
New Holland Mill (Gainesville, Ga.), consolation winners: Bunting.
Monaghan Mill (Greenville, S.C.): Hubert Nolin.
Spray Mill (Spray, N.C.): Koontz, C.E. Clark.
Converse Mill (Spartanburg, S.C.): Jim Oeland.
Draper Mill (Draper, N.C.): Carl Brooks (coach).
Other Teams: **Lanett Mill** (Lanett, Ala.); **Victor Mill** (Greer, S.C.); **Highland Park Mill** (Charlotte, N.C.); **Dunean Mill** (Greenville, S.C.).

Class B Men
Pelzer Mill (Pelzer, S.C.), champions.
Chesnee Mill (Chesnee, S.C.), runners-up.
Clover Mill (Clover, S.C.), consolation winners.
Other Teams: **Glen Lowery Mill** (Whitmire, S.C.); **Woodside Mill** (Greenville, S.C.); **American Spinning** (Greenville, S.C.); **Apalache Mill** (Greer, S.C.); **Saxon Mill** (Spartanburg, S.C.); **Piedmont Mill** (Piedmont, S.C.); **Dunean Mill** (Greenville, S.C.); **Abbeville Mill** (Abbeville, S.C.); **Spartan Mill** (Spartanburg, S.C.); **Greer Mill** (Greer, S.C.); **Judson Mill** (Greenville, S.C.); **Whitney Mill** (Spartanburg, S.C.); **Schoolfield Mill** (Danville, Va.); **Monaghan Mill** (Greenville, S.C.); **Ottaray Mill** (Union, S.C.); **Piedmont Scouts** (Piedmont, S.C.); **Pacific Mill** (Columbia, S.C.).

Class C Men
Schoolfield Mill (Danville, Va.), champions.
Monaghan Mill (Greenville, S.C.), runners-up.
Greer Mill (Greer, S.C.), consolation winners.
Other Teams: **Victor Mill** (Greer, S.C.); **Judson Mill** (Greenville, S.C.); **Pelzer Mill** (Pelzer, S.C.); **Lonsdale Mill** (Seneca, S.C.); **Woodside Mill** (Greenville, S.C.).

Class A Women
Judson Mill (Greenville, S.C.): Nettie Forrest.
Leakesville Mill (Leakesville, N.C.): Clark.
Highland Park Mill (Charlotte, N.C.), champions.
Monaghan Mill (Greenville, S.C.), runners-up.
Schoolfield Mill (Danville, Va.), consolation winners
Other Teams: **American Spinning** (Greenville, S.C.).

Class B Women
Teams: Schoolfield Mill (Danville, Va.), champions; Lonsdale Mill (Seneca, S.C.), runners-up; Woodside Mill (Greenville, S.C.).

1925

Officers: W.M. Grier (Greenville, S.C.), President; G.W. Belk (Pelzer, S.C.), 1st Vice President; H.R. McCartney (Greenville, S.C.), 2nd Vice President; V.O. Duncan (Piedmont, S.C.), Treasurer; Charles Boling (Columbia, S.C.), Secretary; Mrs. J.L. Harrison (Greenville), Girls' Hostess.

Class A Men
Pacific Mill (Columbia, S.C.), champions: Bob Ingram, Wallace, Henson, Arthur Bedenbaugh, Buddy Martin, Knox, Shealy, Ransom.
Judson Mill (Greenville, S.C.), runners-up: Louis Barbare, Parker, Paul Barbare, McClure, Carlisle Chandler, D. Trammell, Franks.
New Holland Mill (Gainesville, Ga.), consolation winners: Rhett Turnipseed (coach), Harrison, Allen, Peterson, F. Colbert, Whitley, Waldrop, G. Colbert.
Monaghan Mill (Greenville, S.C.): Herbert Nolin, Thomas, Crane, McElrath, Coleman, Wiggins.
Dunean Mill (Greenville, S.C.): Dave Sanders, Gus Barbare, J. Henson, Heath, H. Henson, McClure.
Manchester Mill (Manchester, Ga.): Mahaffey, Gladden, Bowie, Conway, Griffin, Long, Hunt.
Converse Mill (Spartanburg, S.C.): G. West, Calvert, Jim Oeland, Pete Fowler, Knight, H. West, Colbert, Kallgher, Flowers.
Spray Mill (Spray, N.C.): Clark, Robinson, Adkins, Kasey, Merriman.

Victor Mill (Greer, S.C.): Wilson, Mason, Herring, Campbell, Brady, Bradley.
Other Teams: Lyman Mill (Lyman, S.C.); Apalache Mill (Greer, S.C.).

CLASS B MEN

Piedmont Mill (Piedmont, S.C.), champions: Beasley, D. Smith, Clark, Webb, J.Smith, Trammell, Anderson, Kelly, E. Smith.
Pelzer Mill (Pelzer, S.C.), runners-up: W. Westmoreland, Sargent, J. Westmoreland, Holliday, Haney, Kay.
Glen Lowery Mill (Whitmire, S.C.), consolation winners: Cudd, Ross, Puckett, Hill, Reid, Campbell, Bostic, Padgett, Reel, Matthew.
Pacific Mill (Columbia, S.C.): Franklin, A. Scott, White, Smith, Byars, W. Scott, Walker, Cooper.
Whitney Mill (Spartanburg, S.C.): Moore, Allen, Huskey, Gossett, Sibley, McAllister.
Dunean Mill (Greenville, S.C.): Huff, Hughes, Blackwell, Allen, Wood, McCauley, Bridges, Christopher.
Apalache Mill (Greer, S.C.): Glenn, Leopard, Smith, Leatherwood, Weathers, Ivester.
Abbeville Mill (Abbeville, S.C.): Wilson, Blanchette, Dudley, Langley, Herndon, Stalnaker.
Monarch Mill (Union, S.C.): Crocker, Cabiness, Nichols, Mathew, Shirley, Shettle, Arthur.
Monaghan Mill (Greenville, S.C.): A. Campbell, J. Campbell, Carter, Childress, Heath, N. Childress, Wiggins, Anderson, Williams, N. Campbell.
Woodside Mill (Greenville, S.C.): Brookshire, Pendleton, McLand, Bower, Baker, Smith.
Saxon Mill (Spartanburg, S.C.): Champion, Bishop, Robinson, Ballenger, Corn, Smith, Elledge.
Spartan Mill (Spartanburg, S.C.): E. Henderson, Timmons, Mooneyham, Allen, Henderson, Pettit.
Judson Mill (Greenville, S.C.): Wyatt, Mahon, Moreland, McClure, Owens, Lawson, Ashemore, Chandler, Powell, Mabrey.
Greer Mill (Greer, S.C.): M. Jones, F. Jones, Mode, Glass, Hood, Miller, Bragg.
Clover Mill (Clover, S.C.): Maxwell, Vaslandughan, Gettys, Harvey, Crawford, Hague, Clinton, Beangbarg.
Lonsdale Mill (Seneca, S.C.): Hardin, Padgett, McMillan, Mason, McClellan, Lee.
Clinchfield Mill (Marion, N.C.): C. Copeland, Copeland, Sprinkle, Sanders, Miller.

Ottaray Mill (Union, S.C.): Hanna, Garner, S. Howell, F. Howell, Turner, Pearson.
Other Teams: **Southern Bleachery** (Taylors, S.C.); **Highland Park Mill** (Charlotte, N.C.).

CLASS C MEN

Piedmont Mill (Piedmont, S.C.), champions: Ayers, J. Gilreath, Bishop, G. Gilreath, McAbee, Pickleseimer.
Pacific Mill (Columbia, S.C.), runners-up: Culclasure, Barkfield, Franklin, Briggs, Hendrix, Mayers.
Greer Mill (Greer, S.C.), consolation winners: Green, Wilson, Miller, Barbery, Westmoreland.
American Spinning (Greenville, S.C.): Bridwell, Peace, Harbin, Moore, Nealey.
Other Teams: **Southern Bleachery** (Taylors, S.C.); **Saxon Mill** (Spartanburg, S.C.); **Woodside Mill** (Greenville, S.C.); **Judson Mill** (Greenville, S.C.); **Walhalla Mill** (Walhalla, S.C.); **Victor Mill** (Greer, S.C.); **Highland Park Mill** (Charlotte, N.C.); **Pelzer Mill** (Pelzer, S.C.); **Monaghan Mill** (Greenville, S.C.); **Abbeville Mill** (Abbeville, S.C.).

CLASS A WOMEN

Monaghan Mill (Greenville, S.C.), champions: C.V. Henderson, O. Henderson, McMahan, Mosley, Painter, Jones, Childress.
Leakesville Mill (Leakesville, N.C.), runners-up: E. Hill, Clark, Robinson, Hall, Barbare, Simpson, Edwards, Barham, Hill.
Dunean Mill (Greenville, S.C.): Turner, Chandler, Leatherwood, Presley, Roddy, Pickens.
Highland Park Mill (Charlotte, N.C.): Estridge, Carson, Brown, Wilson, Kistler, Rouse.
Lyman Mill (Lyman, S.C.): Brown, Parker, Fallis, Melton, Harmon, Humphries.
Other Teams: **American Spinning** (Greenville, S.C.); **Walhalla Mill** (Walhalla, S.C.); **Woodside Mill** (Greenville, S.C.); **Lonsdale Mill** (Seneca, S.C.).

CLASS B WOMEN

Whitney Mill (Spartanburg, S.C.), champions: Huskey, Greer, Goforth, Wolfe, Reed, Smith, Belchefmorte.
Saxon Mill (Spartanburg, S.C.), runners-up: Wood, Lovelace, Waddell, Suttles, Gault, Foster.
Pacific Mill (Columbia, S.C.): Hughes, Annie Gunter, Bradleham, McEntyre, Ella Kirby, B. Hughes. Varn, Brice.

Other Teams: **Victor Mill** (Greer, S.C.); **Greer Mill** (Greer, S.C.).

CLASS C WOMEN
Woodside Mill (Greenville, S.C.), champions: E. McCall, S. Bowen, P. Bowen, Chandler, Clippard, Barnette.
Lonsdale Mill (Seneca, S.C.), runners-up: Addis, Padgett, C.L. Thompson, W. Thompson, Holcombe, Nichols, Gambrell.
Other Teams: **Judson Mill** (Greenville, S.C.).

—————— 1926 ——————

Officers: L.P. Hollis (Greenville, S.C.), President; H.C. Stalworth (Gainesville, Ga.), 1st Vice President; J.L. Woodward (Greer, S.C.), 2nd Vice President; Harley Heath (Pelzer, S.C.), 3rd Vice President; C.V. Verner (Piedmont, S.C.), Treasurer; L.A. Ramey (Spartanburg, S.C.), Secretary; Mrs. J.L Harrison (Greenville, S.C.), Girls' Hostess.

CLASS A MEN
Lyman Mill (Lyman, S.C.), champions: Jim Wood (coach), Walt Barbare (coach), Roy Norman, Zero Lindsay, Britt Bryson, Ed Tillinghast, Paul Barbare, Lawrence Pruitt, D.K. Smith, Johnnie Smith, E. Pruitt.
Dunean Mill (Greenville, S.C.), runners-up: McClure, H. Henson, J. Henson, Wood, Mullinax, Glenn, Dave Sanders, Merman, Turner, Robertson.
Spartan Mill (Spartanburg, S.C.), consolation winners: Timmons, C.B. Mooneyham, Fowler, Henderson, Allen, Lancaster.
New Holland Mill (Gainesville, Ga.): Rhett Turnipseed (coach), Waldrop, Webb, Canup, Colbert, J. Waldrop, Wilson, Holsey.
Woodside Mill (Greenville, S.C.): McLeod, Clippard, Buchanan, Baker, Bowen, Brookshire.
Piedmont Mill (Piedmont, S.C.): Britt Bryson, Johnny Beasley, Smith, Trammell, Pickleseimer, Anderson.
Judson Mill (Greenville, S.C.): Parker, Gus Barbare, Tidwell, McClure, Hall, Moreland, Louis Barbare.
Victor Mill (Greer, S.C.): Mason, Hutchinson, Herrin, G. Horton, G. Hudson, Pruitt, Frady, Wilson.
Converse Mill (Spartanburg, S.C.): H. Calvert, West, C. Calvert, Fowler, Oeland, Quinn, R. Calvert.
Apalache Mill (Greer, S.C.): Leopard, Weathers, Smith, R. Leatherwood, Stevenson, Hawkins.
Whitney Mill (Spartanburg, S.C.): McAllister, Moore, Huskey, Allen, Sibley, Gossett.

CLASS B MEN
Monaghan Mill (Greenville, S.C.), champions.
Lonsdale Mill (Seneca, S.C.), runners-up.
Pelzer Mill (Pelzer, S.C.), consolation winners: Sorgens, F. Westmoreland, Welbourn, Holliday, Letterfield.
Dunean Mill (Greenville, S.C.): Greer, Huff, Davis, Turner, Bedingfield.
Judson Mill (Greenville, S.C.): Trammell, Kay, Cook, Blackwell, Harvell, Lavender.
Other Teams: **Clinchfield Mill** (Marion, N.C.); **Lyman Mill** (Lyman, S.C.); **Greer Mill** (Greer, S.C.); **Piedmont Mill** (Piedmont, S.C.); **Monarch Mill** (Union, S.C.); **American Spinning** (Greenville, S.C.).

CLASS C MEN
Monaghan Mill (Greenville, S.C.), champions: Henson, Galloway, Johnson, Kelly, Crenshaw.
Saxon Mill (Spartanburg, S.C.), runners-up: Fisher, Hill, Martin, Champion, Lovelace, Robertson, Corn.
Piedmont Mill (Piedmont, S.C.), consolation winners:
Walhalla Mill (Walhalla, S.C.): Beattie, Hunt, Burdett, Lester, Garrett.
Dunean Mill (Greenville, S.C.): Robertson, Bedingfield, Turner, Roddy, Few, Reed, Walker, Lybrand.
Other Teams: **Greer Mill** (Greer, S.C.); **Draper Mill** (Draper, N.C.); **Southern Bleachery** (Taylors, S.C.); **Pacific Mill** (Columbia, S.C.); **Victor Mill** (Greer, S.C.); **American Spinning** (Greenville, S.C.); **Woodside Mill** (Greenville, S.C.); **Pelzer Mill** (Pelzer, S.C.); **Simpsonville Mill** (Simpsonville, S.C.).

CLASS A WOMEN
Leakesville Mill (Leakesville, N.C.), champions: I. Clark, L. Landreth, E. Hill, L. Hill, E. Barham, M. Simpson, Moon, Barron, Moore.
Judson Mill (Greenville, S.C.), runners-up: Barbare, V. Henderson, Gibson, Henderson, Estes, Cobb, E. Henson.
Lyman Mill (Lyman, S.C.), consolation winners: Norman, Parker, Fallis, Melton, Humphries, Harmon, Brown,

Southern Textile Basketball Tournament Rosters Appendix 1   109

Monaghan Mill (Greenville, S.C.): Long, Heath, McMahon, J. Carter, Mitchell, Clary, Huff, Madden, Bendall, Brown, Parker.
Piedmont Mill (Piedmont, S.C.): C. Osteen, League, Shirley, E. Osteen, R. Pack, S. Osteen, Clifford.

CLASS B WOMEN
Piedmont Mill (Piedmont, S.C.), champions: Boiter, Wench, Doggett, Wakefield, Clifford, Campbell, Huff, Campbell, Howard.
Whitney Mill (Spartanburg, S.C.), runners-up: Huskey, Williams, Goforth, Greer, Smith, Greer, Wolfe, Reid, Reid.
Draper Mill (Draper, N.C.), consolation winners: Purdy, Lindsay, Foster, Hamrick, Hendley, Purdy, Bolton.
Lonsdale Mill (Seneca, S.C.): Garrett, Saunders, Thompson, Padgett, Smith, Hughes.
Simpsonville Mill (Simpsonville, S.C.): M. Cox, L. Calvert, M. Goodenough, Rogers, Thackston, R. Goodenough, C. Calvert.
Victor Mill (Greer, S.C.): Williams, Waters, Wilson, Stroud, Brady, Smith, Moses, Miller.
American Spinning (Greenville, S.C.): Fowler, Miller, Tate, Williams, Brown, Miller.
Lyman Mill (Lyman, S.C.): L. Starnes, Stoney, Myers, Gray, West, Holland, Hicks.
Dunean Mill (Greenville, S.C.): Roddy, Alexander, Ballard, Sanders, Worrel, Alexander.
Other Teams: **Greer Mill** (Greer, S.C.).

―――――― 1927 ――――――

Officers: L.P. Hollis (Greenville, S.C.), President.

CLASS A MEN
Lyman Mill (Lyman, S.C.), champions: Walt Barbare (coach), Lindsay, Tillinghast, Paul Barbare, Pruitt, D.K. Smith, J.Smith, Norman.
Victor Mill (Greer, S.C.), runners-up: Hubert Herrin, Dick Wilson, Mason, Horton, Few, Simmons, Hutchinson.
Pelzer Mill (Pelzer, S.C.), consolation winners: Sargent, W. Westmoreland, J. Westmoreland, Satterfield, Kay, Rogers.
Spartan Mill (Spartanburg, S.C.): E. Henderson, Mooneyham, Fowler, Allen, H. Henderson.
Piedmont Mill (Piedmont, S.C.): Johnny Beasley, W. Anderson, L. Anderson, McAbee, Clyde Gilreath, Quinn, Grover, J. Gilreath, Pack.
Greer Mill (Greer, S.C.): Bragg, Jones, Belcher, Brannon, Westmoreland, Burnett.
Lonsdale Mill (Seneca, S.C.): Hardin, Morgan, McClellan, Lee, Pruitte, McMillan.
Judson Mill (Greenville, S.C.): Mahon, Moreland, L. Barbare, Mullinax, Hall, Trammell.
Apalache Mill (Greer, S.C.): Manley, E. Weathers, Smith, G. Leatherwood, Stevenson, G. Weathers, Glenn.
New Holland Mill (Gainesville, Ga.): Webb, Harrison, Waldrop, Colbert, Wilson, E. Wilson, Strickland.
Manchester Mill (Manchester, Ga.): Beasley, H. Hancock, G. Long, H. Allen, G. Conway, W. Griffith, Bowie, Sledge, Slidel.
Huntsville Mfg. (Huntsville, Ala.): Champion, Snipes, Brazier, Jones, Howard, Bragg.
Woodside Mill (Greenville, S.C.): Smith, Porter, McLeod, Baker, Buchanan, Brookshire, Bowen.

CLASS B MEN
Calloway Mill (LaGrange, Ga.), champions: M. Lester, Higgenbotham, Spence, Simpson, Lesley, H. Lester, Estes, Anderson.
Lyman Mill (Lyman, S.C.), runners-up: Pettigrew, Thackston, Reid, Lackey, Eubanks, Godfrey, Lille, Wingo.
Woodside Mill (Greenville, S.C.), consolation winners: J. Ellenburg, Herbert, L. Ellenburg, VeHorn, Ramey, Stephens, Boggs, Bowen.
Ware Shoals Mill (Ware Shoals, S.C.): Wright, Fletcher, Graham, Robertson, Howard, Workman, L. Verner, Workman, Clark.
Greer Mill (Greer, S.C.): F. Green, Westmoreland, Wilson, Pressley, Barbare.
Dunean Mill (Greenville, S.C.): Greer, Jones, Turner, Davis, Blackwell, Bedingfield, Roddy, Ballenger.
Saxon Mill (Spartanburg, S.C.): Watkins, Fisher, Gault, Lovelace, Eldridge, Horn, Robertson, Walden, Lonedeu, Robinson.
Monaghan Mill (Greenville, S.C.): Heath, Galloway, Johnson, Kelly, Brezeale, Ballenger, Hudgens.
Draper Mill (Draper, N.C.): Turner, Gauldin, Cobbs, Hemrick, Creasey.
Judson Mill (Greenville, S.C.): Kay, Chandler, Scarborough, Cook, Hodge, Ivester.
Other Team: **Ottaray Mill** (Union, S.C.).

Class C Men

Monaghan Mill (Greenville, S.C.), champions: Stephenson, Henson, Ballenger, Reid, Curry, King, Simmons, Mull.
Union Bleachery (Greenville, S.C.), runners-up: Floyd, B. Belcher, Taylor, Cooper, Brooks, Ivey.
Camperdown Mill (Greenville, S.C.), consolation winners: McDowell, F. Huff, Gosnell, Breazeale, Norris, R. Huff.
Glen Lowery Mill (Whitmire, S.C.): Ross, Puckett, Gregory, Eakins, Brooks, Ramsey, Cabiness, Smith.
Lyman Mill (Lyman, S.C.): Brown, Reid, Pettigrew, Eubanks, Holland, C. Reid, Connor, Fallis.
Victor Mill (Greer, S.C.): Tipton, L.C. Pearson, J. Pearson, Lowe, Smith, Smith, Poole, Anderson, Hewitt, Few.
American Spinning (Greenville, S.C.): Bridwell, McNeely, Duncan, Porter, Major, Quinn, Burnett, Burns.
Simpsonville Mill (Simpsonville, S.C.): Lynn, Porter, Walters, Johnson, Barbare, Godfrey, Jameson, Lynch.
Woodside Mill (Greenville, S.C.): Pollard, Paxton, Burton, Canup, Hardin, Foster, Coggins.
Pelzer Mill (Pelzer, S.C.): Pryor, Wilson, Jenkins, Sargent, Davis, Pridmore, Dickard, Roberts.
Walhalla Mill (Walhalla, S.C.): Hunt, Beattie, Leister, Sanders, Williams, Lillian, Williams, Lee, Glasby.
Piedmont Mill (Piedmont, S.C.): Ayers, Evans, Pack, Brown, Herd, Allen, Porter.
Other Teams: **Caroleen Mill** (Caroleen, N.C.).

Class A Women

Lyman Mill (Lyman, S.C.), champions: Norman, Trammell, Fallis, Melton, Bernie, Neal, Parker, Grey, Pruitt, Bruce, Veal.
Leakesville Mill (Leakesville, N.C.), runners-up: I. Clark, Moore, Landreth, E. Hill, C. Hill, Tullouch, Gilmore, Brooks.
Monaghan Mill (Greenville, S.C.), consolation winners: Major (coach), Buff, Hudgens, Langston, M. Reid, Long, Brown, B. Reid, L. Reid, Grant.
Dunean Mill (Greenville, S.C.): Jones, Sanders, Martin, McAlister, Worrell, Pressley, Worrell.
Other Teams: **Judson Mill** (Greenville, S.C.); **Piedmont Mill** (Piedmont, S.C.).

Class B Women

American Spinning (Greenville, S.C.), champions: Bridwell (coach), Miller, Trussell, Nix, Fowler, Williams, Neely, E. Miller, Coleman.
Lonsdale Mill (Seneca, S.C.), runners-up: Padgett, R. Watson, Pruitt, Hudgens, Thompson, C. Watson, Hughes, Pridson.
Draper Mill (Draper, N.C.), consolation winners: L. Purdy, Sparks, Hamrick, Bolick, Hundley, Williams, Smith, Lindsay, E. Purdy.
Apalache Mill (Greer, S.C.): Tapp, Leatherwood, L.E. Ashemore, Sumner, Stevenson, Manly, Lunny.
Woodside Mill (Greenville, S.C.): Bowen, Reeves, Hamrick, Chandler, Edwards, Ward, Peterson, Tucker, M. Reeves, Brown.
Walhalla Mill (Walhalla, S.C.): McCall, Elliott, McCall, Smith, Sanders, Leister.

1928

Officers: John G. Grier (Greenville, S.C.), President; J.D. Brown (Greenville, S.C.), Vice-President; G.C. Suttles (Spartanburg, S.C.), Vice-President; J.W. Wood (Lyman, S.C.), Vice-President; C.V. Verner (Piedmont, S.C.), Treasurer; Leonard Howard (Greenville, S.C.), Secretary; Harry B. Jones (Greenville, S.C.), Commissioner.

Class AA Men

Lyman Mill (Lyman, S.C.), champions: J.W. Wood (coach), Fred Emerson, Britt Bryson, Lawrence Pruitt, Edward Tillinghast, John Lindsay, D.K. Smith, Johnie Smith, Ray Norman.
Victor Mill (Greer, S.C.), runners-up: J.L. Gourley (coach), Lloyd Horton, Harley Heath, Hubert Mason, Dick Wilson, Hubert Herrin, W. Hutchinson, Courtney Heath, Fletcher Heath.
Piedmont Mill (Piedmont, S.C.), consolation winners: J.M. Terry (coach), Clarence Beasley, J.Q. Trammell, Clyde Gilreath, Dave Sanders, Walter Anderson, Dennis Picklesimer, Jack Gilreath, Charlie Brown.
Lonsdale Mill (Seneca, S.C.): Will Morgan (coach), George Weathers, Eddie Weathers, Marvin Stevenson, Albert Page, Roy Leatherwood, Esco Leopard, Roy Stevenson, J.F. Mason, Padgett.

Southern Textile Basketball Tournament Rosters   Appendix 1   111

CLASS A MEN

Calloway Mill (LaGrange, Ga.), champions: Clarence Higgenbotham, M. LeSter, Irwin Spence, Glen Simpson, Kersey, Estes, Copeland, Lester.

New Holland Mill (Gainesville, Ga.), runners-up: Rhett Turnipseed (coach), Dills, J. Waldrop, Spencer, Colbert, Wilson, D. Waldrop, Cleveland, Pilgrim.

Pelzer Mill (Pelzer, S.C.), consolation winners: Westmoreland, Sargent, McGraw, Jenkins, Dickert, Rogers.

Greer Mill (Greer, S.C.): Bragg, Greene, Hardin, P. Westmoreland, Barbare, J. Westmoreland, Brannon.

Lyman Mill (Lyman, S.C.): Thackston, Pettigru, McMakin, Lecky, Eubanks, E. Eubanks, D. Waldrop.

Judson Mill (Greenville, S.C.): Ansel Kay, Moreland, C. Tidwell, Scarborough, Hall.

CLASS B MEN

Lanett Mill (Lanett, Ala.), champions: Bozeman, Rhodes, Lewis, Leverette, Gay, King, Porter, Brewster, Roach.

Monaghan Mill (Greenville, S.C.), runners-up: Ballenger, Stevens, Reed, Walls, Henson, Mull.

Woodside Mill (Greenville, S.C.), consolation winners: C.S. Smith (coach), Otto Herbert, Eugene Harbin, Willard Bowen, John Ellenburg, D.T. Vehorn, T.C. Hunt, Matt Stephens, Fred Ellenburg.

Walhalla Mill (Walhalla, S.C.): Rochester, Sanders, Morse, Leister, Williams, Smith, Elliott.

Riverdale Mill (Riverdale, Ala.): Fred Hunt (coach), George Goggans, Jack Harris, Orlando Johnson, Homer Bradfield, John Harris, Delma Fullerton, Roy Ray, Wilbert Brown.

American Spinning (Greenville, S.C.): J.D. Bridwell (coach), James McNeely, Herman Duncan, Edgar Major, Raleigh Peace, Ray Boggs, Robert Bridwell, Clinton Cooper, Velt Nix, Price.

Piedmont Mill (Piedmont, S.C.): George McCall (coach), Elmer Herd, Paul Clark, Clarence Allen, Seth Pack, Floyd Porter, Willie Bolden, Clyde Evans, Jerome Grover, Bolton.

Draper Mill (Draper, N.C.): Turner, Holland, H. Gauldin, Combs, Francis Medford, Gosnell, Francis, S. Gauldin.

Ware Shoals Mill (Ware Shoals, S.C.): B. Werner, Clatworthy, Graham, L. Werner, Robertson, Wright.

CLASS C MEN

Victor Mill (Greer, S.C.), champions: Dill, Lowe, Few, Beason, Hewitt.

Draper Mill (Draper, N.C.), runners-up: Hawkes, McBride, Gordon, Logan, Merriman, Franks, Breazeale, Stoltz, Gardner, Grogan.

Dunean Mill (Greenville, S.C.), consolation winners: Galloway, Bogan, Harvell, L.D. Davis, McDaniel, L.C. Davis, Franks.

Judson Mill (Greenville, S.C.): Carter Newman (coach), Carter Newman Jr., Nathan Wilson, Fred Tumblin, Lillius Tidwell, Willie Tallant, James Nichols, Harold Bolt, Ty Cobb, Chandler.

Pelzer Mill (Pelzer, S.C.): Pryor, Sargent, Wilson, Roberts, Moore, Netter, Davenport.

American Spinning (Greenville, S.C.): Quinn, N. Smith, Crawford, Neely, Cooper, Boggs, Wilbanks, C. Smith.

Simpsonville Mill (Simpsonville, S.C.): Godfrey, Bridges, Porter, Barbery, Jameson.

Mills Mill (Greenville, S.C.): Sisk, Sexton, Few, Fulbright, Massey, Davis, Kask.

Camperdown Mill (Greenville, S.C.): John McDowell, R. Huff, Gosnell, Breazeale, Norris, Few.

Calloway Mill (LaGrange, Ga.): R. Reese, Mitchell, R. Smith, F. Smith, Higgenbotham, Sellars, Harris, E. Reese, Collars, Hackenback.

Spartan Mill (Spartanburg, S.C.): F. Mooneyham, Gregory, Ballentine, Dodd, Roland, Smith, Shippey.

Woodside Mill (Greenville, S.C.): Couch, Foster, Osborne, Byers, Burton, Hawkins, Paxon, Coggins.

Apalache Mill (Greer, S.C.): M. Glenn, Crain, Rector, Millwood, Jackson, McCarter.

Monaghan Mill (Greenville, S.C.): Simmons, Morehead, Stewart, Bagwell, Fleming, Stewart.

Greer Mill (Greer, S.C.): Barton, Pruitt, C. Hemphill, B. Hemphill, Westmoreland, Cox, Greene.

CLASS A WOMEN

Beacon Mill (Swannanoa, N.C.), champions: Yates (coach), Willie McMahon, Silvers, Katherine Shope, Carlie Penley, Pauline Penley, Gibbs, Todd, Ladd.

Piedmont Mill (Piedmont, S.C.), runners-up: Mrs. S.B. Wilson (coach), Kate Huff,

Thelma Boiter, Madge Doggett, Ruth Shirley, Kathleen Clifford, Minnie Pack, Sarah Doggett, Dorothy Clifford, Elva Osteen, Mary McCall.
Lonsdale Mill (Seneca, S.C.), consolation winners: Padgett, Leatherwood, Blair, R. Watson, Thompson, Hughes, Stevens.
Victor Mill (Greer, S.C.): Heath, Moss, F. Wilson, R. Compton, White, Compton, Waters.
Lyman Mill (Lyman, S.C.): Emma Major (coach), Grace Norman, Lydina Pruitt, Cleo Alexander, Mary Greene, Camelia Smith, Trannie Melton, Agnes Gray, Elizabeth Parker, Edna Trammell.
American Spinning (Greenville, S.C.): Bratton Williams (coach), Ethel Miller, Ruby Nix, Viney Miller, Florence Trussell, Janette Porter, Susan Williams, Flora Coleman, Lou Fowler, Janette Neely.
Monaghan Mill (Greenville, S.C.): Kathryn Long (coach), Inez Neely, Lucille Foster, Virginia Langston, Dovie Hudgens, Elsie Case, Louise McKeown, Inez Brown, Lucille Buff, Buena McIntyre, McGowan.
Greer Mill (Greer, S.C.): Hemphill, Gowan, Kelly, Taylor, R. Brewton, Stroud, Skinner, Flynn, E. Brewton.

──────── 1929 ────────

Officers: Harry B. Jones (Greenville, S.C.), President; J.D. Brown (Greenville, S.C.), Vice-President; G.C. Suttles (Spartanburg, S.C.), Vice-President; John H. Garraux (Greenville, S.C.), Vice-President; C.V. Verner (Piedmont, S.C.), Treasurer; Leonard Howard (Greenville, S.C.), Secretary; Mrs. Dee Campbell (Piedmont, S.C.), Girl's Teams Hostess; Paul Troutman (Ware Shoals, S.C.), Boy's Teams Host.

CLASS A MEN

Lanett Mill (Lanett, Ala.), champions: Walt Bozeman, Vance, Lewis, Gay, Brewster, McDenny, Felton Leverette.
Pelzer Mill (Pelzer, S.C.), runners-up: M.B. Tucker (coach), James Sargent, James Westmoreland, W.J. Westmoreland, Jack Jenkins, J.C. Satterfield, Herbert McGraw, Emil Wilson, Jesse Rogers.
Monaghan Mill (Greenville, S.C.), consolation winners: Breazeale, Henson, Hudgens, Coleman, Stephens, H. Ballenger, Walls.
Judson Mill (Greenville, S.C.): Moreland, Nichols, Tidwell, Hall, Scarborough, Blackwell.
New Holland Mill (Gainesville, Ga.): Carl Stallworth (coach), Ward Dills, George Colbert, Loy Spencer, Ralph Cleveland, Marvin Wood, J.E. Strickland, Elmo Wilson, John Waldrep.
Greer Mill (Greer, S.C.): Bragg, Jones, Hardin, Westmoreland, Brannon, Green, Belcher.
Piedmont Mill (Piedmont, S.C.): J.M. Terry (coach), Walter Anderson, Leroy Anderson, Clyde Gilreath, Johnnie Beasley, Charlie Brown, Fred Pack, Clifton Gilreath, Dennis Picklesimer.
Woodside Mill (Greenville, S.C.): Herman Porter (coach), Thomas Herbert, Clyde Smith, Fred Ellenburg, John Ellenburg, Andrew Baker, Jack Bowen, Walter Greer.

CLASS B MEN

Avondale Mill (Alexander City, Ala.), champions: Keith, Smith, Odell Roberts, McCullough, W. Peters, Edwin Price, O. Peters, Ingram.
Monaghan Mill (Greenville, S.C.), runners-up: Hugh Anderson (coach), William Simmons, Wideman Durham, Daniel Bagwell, Amous Galloway, Thomas Reid, Ben Mull, H.R. Flemings.
Walhalla Mill (Walhalla, S.C.), consolation winners: Sanders, Beatty, Williams, Smith, Elliott, Gilliard, Seigler, Bailey.
American Spinning (Greenville, S.C.): Duncan, Boggs, Crawford, Major, Mauldin, Quinn, Porter.
Pelzer Mill (Pelzer, S.C.): C.B. Jordan (coach), C.C. Moore, Joe Hadden, Bill Sargent, Carl Pryor, Francis Bass, Walter Moore, Ray Davenport, Eugene Roberts.
Chicopee Mill (Gainesville, Ga.): Waters, Fletcher, Pace, Bone, Richards, Strickland.
Greer Mill (Greer, S.C.): Pruitt, Barton, Cox, Green, Taylor, Hemphill, Hill.
Camperdown Mill (Greenville, S.C.): Norris, McDowell, Gosnell, Breazeale, Crawford, Huff, Hill.
Piedmont Mill (Piedmont, S.C.): Charlie Allen (coach), Jerome Grover, Elmer Herd, Seth Pack, Clarence Allen, Clyde Evans, Willie Bolden, Walter Madden, Baldwin.
Beacon Mill (Swannanoa, N.C.): Morgan, Connelly, Bugg, M. King, Alexander, Galloway, Owenby, Burnette.

Southern Textile Basketball Tournament Rosters Appendix 1   113

Saxon Mill (Spartanburg, S.C.): Wylie Bourne (coach), Paul Gault, Frank Watkins, Everett Jackson, Clyde Hill, Hix Lovelace, Charlie Byrd, Boyce Williams, Gabe Hill Jr.

Victor Mill (Greer, S.C.): F.H. Harper (coach), George Beason, Leon Dill, James Poole, L.C. Pearson, Ralph Lowe, Chester Henderson, Linder Duncan, Willard Heath.

Columbus Mill (Columbus, Ga.): E. Rogers, Brown, Floyd, R. Rogers, Harris, Pratt, Riddle, Clark.

Abbeville Mill (Abbeville, S.C.): Wilson, Stalnaker, Dudley, Blanchett, Bell, Walker, Godfrey.

Woodside Mill (Greenville, S.C.): Couch, Holcombe, Osborne, Hardin, Byers, Stephens, Bowen.

Simpsonville Mill (Simpsonville, S.C.): R. Bridges, R. Godfrey, Childers, Barbery, Porter, Abbott.

Ware Shoals Mill (Ware Shoals, S.C.): Paul Troutman (coach), L. Werner, Wright, Martin, Fletcher, B. Werner, Gresham, Collins, Galloway, Graham.

CLASS C MEN

Dunean Mill (Greenville, S.C.), champions: Frank Floyd (coach), L.C. Davis, Scoop Putman, Whitey McDonald, L.D. Davis, Chadwick, Odell Putman, Dendy Barnes.

American Spinning (Greenville, S.C.), runners-up.

Berkeley Mill (Balfour, N.C.), consolation winners: Heaton, Capps, Sanders, Hammond, Greene.

Southern Bleachery (Taylors, S.C.): Keeler, Wilson, Jim Gay, Jackson, Bridgeman.

Monaghan Mill (Greenville, S.C.): Foster, Reed, Ross, Moore, Odam, Allison, Jolly, W. Moore.

Greer Mill (Greer, S.C.): Burton, Woodward, Bradshaw, C. Hemphill, Westmoreland, Belcher.

Other Teams: **Spartan Mill** (Spartanburg, S.C.); **Glenwood Mill** (Easley, S.C.); **Apalache Mill** (Greer, S.C.); **Mills Mill** (Greenville, S.C.); **Woodside Mill** (Greenville, S.C.); **Judson Mill** (Greenville, S.C.).

CLASS A WOMEN

Monaghan Mill (Greenville, S.C.), champions: Fred Ellis (coach), Dovie Hudgens, Lucille Buff, Virginia Langston, Inez Brown, Elsie Case, Louise McKown, Oveida Henderson, E.L. Henderson, Lucille Foster, Katherine Long.

Piedmont Mill (Piedmont, S.C.), runners-up: Mrs. Dee Campbell (coach), Dorothy Clifford, Elvie Osteen, Sarah Doggett, Ruth Shirley, Annie Pinson, Mattie Lois, Evelyn Bowen, Lillian Grover, Mary McCall, Thelma Boiter, Lucille Scott.

Beacon Mill (Swannanoa, N.C.), consolation winners: James Bonham (coach), Pauline Penley, Willie McMahon, Carlie Penley, Lillian Gibbs, Reavelle Penley, Roselle Allen, Nellie Bartlett, Katherine Shope, Edna Shope.

American Spinning (Greenville, S.C.): Horace Carter (coach), Ruby Nix, Viney Miller, Clara Bryant, Jessie Carter, Mary Cantrell, Grace Childs, Ethel Miller, Florence Hopkins, Lou Miller, Bessie Carter.

CLASS B WOMEN

Orr Mill (Anderson, S.C.), champions: Virginia Kinnett, Sara Kinnett, Cooper, Morris, Smith, Jolly, McKinley, Bevill.

Monaghan Mill (Greenville, S.C.), runners-up: Brown, Breazeale, Langston, Breazeale, Sheppard, Gregory, Powers, Darnell, Burgess.

Dunean Mill (Greenville, S.C.), consolation winners: Turner, Taylor, Hughes, Blackwell, Gwinn, M. Turner, Owens, Osteen, Greene, Cobb.

Lanett Mill (Lanett, Ala.): Mitchell, Raye, Toney, Raye, Brand, Webb, Looser, Roach, Smith, McLure.

―――――― 1930 ――――――

Officers: Harry B. Jones (Greenville, S.C.), President; J.D. Brown (Greenville, S.C.), Vice President; G.C. Suttles (Canton, N.C.), Vice President; Leonard Howard (Greenville, S.C.), Vice President; C.V. Verner (Piedmont, S.C.), Treasurer; John H. Garraux (Greenville, S.C.), Secretary; W.M. Grier (Greenville, S.C.), Advisory Council Chairman; Mrs. Dee Campbell (Piedmont, S.C.), Womens' Hostess; Paul Troutman (Ware Shoals, S.C.), Men's Host.

CLASS A MEN

Lonsdale Mill (Seneca, S.C.), champions: C.M. Padgett (coach), Esco Leopard, Willard Heath, Eddie Weathers, Courtney Heath, Roy Stevenson, Marvin Stevenson, Willie Morgan, Roy Leatherwood.

Piedmont Mill (Piedmont, S.C.), runners-up: Ralph Bowie (coach), Johnnie Beasley,

Clarence Allen, Seth Pack, James Picklesimer, Elmer Herd, Jerome Grover, William Bolden, Clyde Evans.

Monaghan Mill (Greenville, S.C.), consolation winners: Hugh Anderson (coach), Edward Ballenger, Linnell Brazie, Lee Coleman, Wideman Durham, Jesse Hudgens, Millwood Stephens, Clyde Walls, Thornwell Henson.

New Holland Mill (Gainesville, Ga.): W.C. Stallworth (coach), John Waldrop, Ward Dill, Loy Spencer, George Colbert, Roy Wilson, Robert Strickland, Marvin Wood, Ralph Cleveland, Dewey Pilgrim.

Avondale Mill (Alexander City, Ala.): Charles Smith (coach), Homer Ingram, Lewin Smith, Odel Roberts, Edwin Price, Omrin Peters, Emmett Keith, Jasper McCullough, Roscoe Slagle.

Woodside Mill (Greenville, S.C.): W.M. Grier (coach), Hughey Smith, John Holcombe, Ellenburg, D.T. Vehorn, Herbert, Carlton Couch, Harold Osborne, Lester Burton, Harmon Williams.

Class B Men

Victor Mill (Greer, S.C.), champions: C.M. Campbell (coach), Leon Dill, Virgil Tipton, Willie Hutchinson, Ralph Lowe, George Beason, Elford Campbell, Linder Duncan, Pearson, Frank Hewett.

Spartan Mill (Spartanburg, S.C.), runners-up: B.G. Pirkle (coach), Carl Mooneyham, Ralph Steading, Guy Sanders, Ralph Dodd, Paul Gregory, William Walters, Albert Bullington.

Beacon Mill (Swannanoa, N.C.), consolation winners: N.A. Long (coach), E.K. Mann, Dwight Morgan, Lowe Bugg, Roy Alexander, T.E. Bagley, Marion King, Vesta Calloway, Boyd Owenby.

American Spinning (Greenville, S.C.): Velt Nix (coach), Edward Duncan, Clarence Cooper, John Mauldin, Robert Burns, Hubert Crawford, Glenn, Dewey Quinn, Wallace Dean, Edgar Harbin.

Monaghan Mill (Greenville, S.C.): Clyde Johnson (coach), Robert Ellison, Amos Galloway, Walter Wooten, Daniel Bagwell, William Simmons, Thomas Henderson, Dennis Elder, Fred Curry.

Orr Mill (Anderson, S.C.): Troy Kirby (coach), Lee Whitten, Clarence McLesky, Porter Stamps, David Price, Harry Stamps, J.C. Buchanan, Lelious Smith, Willie Cary.

Leakesville Mill (Leakesville, N.C.): J.K. McConnell (coach), Francis Barban, Homer Hall, Collins, Clyde Carter, James Burnett, Barbour, Beverly Warren, John Galimore, Arthur Whitehead, Samuel Freeman.

Glenwood Mill (Easley, S.C.): J.L. Alexander (coach), J.D. Loftis, Wales Owens, C.P. Mullinax, J.L. Alexander, Buford Spearman, Preston Rice, F.L. Owens.

Dunean Mill (Greenville, S.C.): Harry Orr (coach), L.C. Davis, Wilton Putnam, Willie Riddle, Lewis Davis, Homer Kelly, Lewis McDonald, Homer Dendy, Felix Chadwick.

Pelzer Mill (Pelzer, S.C.): Mack Bannister (coach), Roy Kay, Joe Hedden, Charles Westmoreland, James Davis, Randolph Roberts, Roy Davenport.

Southern Worsted (Greenville, S.C.): H.L. Harrison (coach), Clyde Smith, Fred Knox, N.A. Collins, Colvin Sanders, James Long, Sam Simpson, Dewitt Williamson, John Wall.

Chicopee Mill (Gainesville, Ga.): J.W. Brown (coach), James Fletcher, Ralph Smith, Robert Waters, Walter Richards, Wallace Nix, Roy Pace, Laws, William Chastain, Ralph Bone.

Apalache Mill (Greer, S.C.): D.R. Bogan (coach), Victor Mooney, Raymond Bryant, Vincent Glenn, Earl Belue, Walter McCarter, Mark Rector, Marvin Glenn, Lethca Campbell.

Simpsonville Mill (Simpsonville, S.C.): E.M. Goodenough (coach), Eugene Barbery, Carl Bunton, Frank Smith, Lloyd Childers, Leonard Barbery, Herman Bunton, Robert Bridges, Odell Lynch.

Winnsboro Mill (Winnsboro, S.C.): J.C. Otis (coach), Leonard Culclasure, H. Culclasure, Ingram, Frank Garrick, J.C. Otis, Coley Spigner, Ralph Sentelle, John Durden, Clyde Surratt.

Class C Men

Southern Bleachery (Taylors, S.C.), champions: Fred Coleman (coach), Herman Keeler, James Gay, James Langston, Woodrow Wilson, William Jackson, Hubert Robinson, Barbare, Lindsay Meisenheimer, Ernest Floyd.

American Spinning (Greenville, S.C.), runners-up: Walter Richardson (coach), Ralph Morgan, Woodrow Fowler, Roy Bridwell, H.P. Wilbanks, Jack Roberts, Connie Morris, Harry Davis, Nathan Wilson.

Judson Mill (Greenville, S.C.), consolation winners: Lewis Foster (coach), J.D. McAlister,

Will Vickery, Bill Grahl, Ott Evans, Doyle Ballew, Broadwell, James Duffie, J.W. James.

Pelzer Mill (Pelzer, S.C.): Alfred Gosnell (coach), George Alverson, David Roberts, Clarence Emery, Bill Jordan, Herman Jordan, Roy Williams, Frank Woods, B.F. Ross.

Dunean Mill (Greenville, S.C.): Leo Norris (coach), Fred Floyd, William Suttles, Marvin Turner, Coley McAlister, Paul Bogan, O. Suttles, Edward Simmons, Paul Shook.

Berkeley Mill (Balfour, N.C.): W.E. Heaton (coach), Melvin Brevard, Joseph Capps, Mont Parker, Beamon Hammond, Carl Hammond, Case, Donald Parker, Horace Peeler, George Heaton.

Monaghan Mill (Greenville, S.C.): Clyde Walls (coach), Flynn Glasco, Jack Mull, Etworth Nolan, Hubert Ross, Harrison Waldrop, Wallace Foster, Ralph Campbell, Chester Keller.

Greer Mill (Greer, S.C.): Clarence Flynn (coach), John Brewton, Ben Burnett, John Belcher, Landrum Woodward, Fred Chandler, Charlie Taylor, Woodrow Hanvey, E.P. Wilson, Hamby.

Victor Mill (Greer, S.C.): Herbert Green (coach), James Suddeth, Howard Maness, Herbert Wall, Alvin Waters, Thomas Tipton, Charles Suddeth, Broadus Cabaness, James Deshields.

Union Bleachery (Greenville, S.C.): H.C. Harrison (coach), James Ivey, Hilliard Bradley, James Willis, Frank Robertson, William Bishop, Buzzie Mullinax, Fred Jewell, Charles Ivey.

Woodside Mill (Greenville, S.C.): Otto Herbert (coach), Harry Meares, Truman Herbert, Dewey Burton, Andrew Ramey, Leonard Canup, Charles Couch, Ralph Wooten, Dewey Bowen.

Simpsonville Mill (Simpsonville, S.C.): T.E. Kay (coach), Sam Bunton, Alvin Medlock, Edwin Coker, Carl Hamby, Tollie Suddeth, Dewitt Gaillard, Henry Giles, Harold Bagwell.

Southern Worsted (Greenville, S.C.): M.R. Snipes (coach), Roy Hogg, Arad Ertzberger, Montague Simpson, Roy Williamson, Wiliam Holloway, James Loftis, Haskell Dill, Walter Fisher.

Brandon Mill (Greenville, S.C.): Paul Byers (coach), Fred Foster, Charles Foster, Mann, Roy Huff, Roy Foster, James Howard, Douglas Lee, Charles Mahon, Charles Williams.

Piedmont Mill (Piedmont, S.C.): Leroy Anderson (coach), Leonard Gilreath, Curtis Terry, Palmer Howard, Roy Garrett, Roy Corbin, Charlie Powell, William Buckheister, Cliff Garrison.

Mills Mill (Greenville, S.C.): J.B. McCall (coach), Clarence Porter, James Abbott, Lewis Abbott, Eugene McAlister, Wayman Henry, Buford Thompson, Payton Smith, Thomas Putnam.

Lonsdale Mill (Seneca, S.C.): Harley Heath (coach), Frank Gaillard, Dewey Stevenson, Charles Watson, Marvin Leatherwood, Lasco Allsep, Baker, George Martin, Coley Garrett, Cecil Padgett.

CLASS A WOMEN

Orr Mill (Anderson, S.C.), champions: D.C. Jolley (coach), Virginia Kennett, Sarah Kinnett, Kathleen Cooper, Sara Smith, Frances Jolly, Jewel McKinley, Nadine Morris, Peggy Lyons, Thelma Barton, Hattie Bevill.

Piedmont Mill (Piedmont, S.C.), runners-up: Ralph Bowie (coach), Osteen, Thelma Boiter, Dorothy Clifford, Minnie Pack, Ruby Doggette, Ruth Shirley, Lillian Grover, Lucille Doggette, Christine Garrett, Evelyn Bryson, Bertie Bryson.

Monaghan Mill (Greenville, S.C.), consolation winners: Fred Ellis (coach), Lucille Foster, Lucille Buff, Oveida Henderson, V. Langston, Sue Langston, Inez Brown, Mamie Sheppard, Hudgens, Vera Allison, Katherine Worthy.

Dunean Mill (Greenville, S.C.): Madge Turner, Smith, Nally, Gwinn, Martin, Blackwell, Green, Johnson.

Beacon Mill (Swannanoa, N.C.): Willie McMahan, P. Penley, Mann, R. Penley, Gibbs, C. Penley, Allen, Penley, Patton, B. Penley.

American Spinning (Greenville, S.C.): V. Miller, Coleman, Nix, Childs, Cooper, C. Miller, Carnes.

CLASS B WOMEN

Pelzer Mill (Pelzer, S.C.), champions: E.W. Edwards (coach), Sara Kelly, Sarah Jordan, Catherine Hackney, Geneva Garrett, Hazel Harris, Agnes Caldwell, Minter Simmons, Venice Dickson, Mackey, Nell Woods.

Ware Shoals Mill (Ware Shoals, S.C.), runners-up: Aubrey Hill (coach), Juanita Barnes, Nora Robinson, Annie Langley, Mattie Copeland, Sara Freeman, Dora Robinson, Georgia Martin, Nancy Drake, Eleanor Highsmith.

Anderson Mill (Anderson, S.C.), consolation winners: Eleanor Cathcart (coach), Frances Burriss, Helen Cooper, Clara Parkman, Mabel Connor, Grace Richardson, Lois Gray, Clark, Ada Carter, Grant, Lena Honea, Vera Scott.

Greer Mill (Greer, S.C.): W.O. Glasco (coach), Elizabeth Jones, Beulah Brewton, Helen Stroud, Gillette Wright, Frances Jones, Ruth Brewton, Clara Burnett, Marie Woodward, Agnes Hemphill.

Winnsboro Mill (Winnsboro, S.C.): Jessie Douglas (coach), Ruby Brannon, Bondell Legrand, Styles, Ollie McDonald, Hazel Williamson, Mabel Hudson, Ruby Floyd, Bertie Spires, Mae Dove, Eunice Edenfield, Edna Branham.

Woodside Mill (Greenville, S.C.): W.M. Grier (coach), Anne Tucker, Sue Bowen, Edna Miller, Pearl Hendrix, Alma Patterson, Lucy Bridges, Mary McConnell, Helen Thompson, Gladys Patterson.

1931

Officers: Charles Verner (Piedmont, S.C.), President; Jesse Brown (Greenville, S.C.), Vice-President; B.J. Pirkle (Spartanburg, S.C.), Vice-President; J.D. Brown (Gainesville, Ga.), Vice-President; Leonard Howard (Greenville, S.C.), Treasurer; John Garraux (Greenville, S.C.), Secretary; W.M. Grier (Greenville, S.C.), Director-Free Throw Contest; Mrs. J.L. Harrison (Fountain Inn, S.C.), Girls' Teams Hostess; G.L. Doggett (Piedmont, S.C.), Boys' Teams Host.

CLASS A MEN

Avondale Mill (Alexander City, Ala.), champions: Charles Smith (coach), Roscoe Slagle, Troy Holly, Emmett Keith, Walt Bozeman, John Turner, Omrie Peters, Edwin Price, Odell Roberts, Lewin Smith.

Lonsdale Mill (Seneca, S.C.), runners-up: Joe Mason (coach), Esco Leopard, Fletcher Heath, William Pruitt, Courtney Heath, Marvin Stevenson, Willard Heath, Eddie Weathers, Roy Garner, Chick Heath.

Piedmont Mill (Piedmont, S.C.), consolation winners: Ralph W. Bowie (coach), Leroy Anderson, Clarence Allen, Willie Bolden, Clyde Evans, Seth Pack, Elmer Herd, Jerome Grover, James Bishop.

Ware Shoals Mill (Ware Shoals, S.C.): H.E. Newbury (coach), Walter Martin, Bill Werner, Lewis Werner, Grier Wright, Talmadge Watt, Eddie Head, Harry Stalnaker, J.A. White Jr.

Chicopee Mill (Gainesville, Ga.): J.W. Brown (coach), John Laws, Robert Waters, Thomas Paris, Ralph Smith, James Fletcher, Roy Pace, Robert Lee, Paul Bell.

Monaghan Mill (Greenville, S.C.): Clyde Johnson (coach), Thornwell Henson, Jessie Hudgens, Daniel Bagwell, Lewis Elder, Milward Stephens, George Ballenger, Coleman.

Lyman Mill (Lyman, S.C.): D.N. Murph (coach), Albert DeLoach, D.K. Smith, Lawrence Pruitt, J.E. Sargent, Boyce West, Clyde Gilreath, J.W. McMakin, Elliott Eubanks, Bryson.

Walhalla Mill (Walhalla, S.C.): A.S. Campbell (coach), Ray Williams, Harold Williams, Roy Smith, Bert Elliott, Wilmer Sanders, Adger Campbell, Aldrich Rochester, Sigles.

CLASS B MEN

Dunean Mill (Greenville, S.C.), champions: Leonard Howard (coach), Woodrow Barnes, Emmery Jones, William Riddle, Homer Dendy, Lewis D. Davis, William Roddy, Louis C. Davis, Carroll Owens.

Spartan Mill (Spartanburg, S.C.), runners-up: B.J. Pirkle (coach), Albert Bullington, Ralph Dodd, Carl Mooneyham, Paul Gregory, R.E. Steading, W.J. Walters, G.L. Sanders, Troy Taylor.

Southern Bleachery (Taylors, S.C.), consolation winners: Fred H. Coleman (coach), Carl Hughes, Ethel Wilson, James Gay, William Gosnell, John Coker, William Belcher, John Langston, Luther Owens, Keeler, Jackson.

Union Bleachery (Greenville, S.C.): H.C. Harrison (coach), Charles Brooks, Hilard Bradley, James Willis, Frank Robertson, James Ivey, Ernest Marshbanks, Buzzie Mullinax, Sam Knight, Guy Hawkins, Jewell.

Abbeville Mill (Abbeville, S.C.): Fred Carroll (coach), William Blanchett, Leroy Wilson, George Walker, Royce Blum, James Blanchett, Leslie Wilson, Aaron McCurry, Rayford Carroll.

American Spinning (Greenville, S.C.): Edgar Harbin (coach), Woodrow Fowler, Clarence Cooper, Harry Davis, J.M. Porter, Harold Wilbanks, Jack Roberts, Ralph Morgan, Lee Burns.

Glen Lowery Mill (Whitmire, S.C.): J.L. Wertz (coach), Mark Conner, Jesse James, Fred

Grant, Irby Rains, Troy Ward, Fred Prather, William Darby.

Draper Mill (Draper, N.C.): E.W. Mooney (coach), Sanford Haymore, Ferman Holland, T.H. Hamrick, Coy McBride, Audery Grogan, Fred Stultz, Alvis Turner, Clarence Combs.

Leakesville Mill (Leakesville, N.C.): Earl Moore (coach), Clyde Carter, Homer Hall, Howard Barham, W. Latcher, Edwin Tenny, Leslie Collins, Clifton Barham, Webster.

Converse Mill (Spartanburg, S.C.): Charley Holland, Yonnie Green, Grady Parris, Walter Quinn, Chalmers Wooten, Roy Evington, Bishop, Brown.

Glenwood Mill (Easley, S.C.): J.L. Alexander (coach), Buford Spearman, Furman Owens, Wales Owens, Paul Mullinax, Roy Holliday, J.D. Loftis, Lee Alexander, Preston Wright, Rice.

Mills Mill (Greenville, S.C.): Walt Barbare (coach), Clarence Porter, James Abbott, Joyce Massey, Eugene McAlister, Waymon Henry, Lewis Abbott, Fred Sisk, James Revis.

Orr Mill (Anderson, S.C.): C.T. Cooper (coach), Lee Whitten, David Price, Porter Stamps, Harry Stamps, John Bevill, Clarence Buchanan, Ralph Thackston, Ralph McClain.

Riverdale Mill (Riverdale, Ala.): C.J. Williams (coach), John Fullerton, John Harris, Walter Lloyd, Leon Sands, Thomas Milner, Samuel Brown, Elmo McGinty, Leroy Brown.

Southern Worsted (Greenville, S.C.): C.L. Maxwell (coach), James Long, O'dell Holloway, Montague Simpson, S.L. Simpson, J.P. Walls, James Loftis, Fred Marshall, Sam Knox, Hogg.

Winnsboro Mill (Winnsboro, S.C.): Henry Huff (coach), Coley Spigner, Virgil McSwain, Leonard Culclasure, James Otis, Joseph Dean, William Huff, Ernest Dreher, James Herndon, H. Culclasure.

CLASS C MEN

Victor Mill (Greer, S.C.), champions: C.M. Campbell (coach), Ted Cabiness, Howard Maness, J.L. Suddeth, C.T. Suddeth, Alvin Waters, Jack Tipton, Wilton Pruitte, Charles Elmore.

Pelzer Mill (Pelzer, S.C.), runners-up: Dutch Vaughn (coach), David Roberts, David Hughes, Tobie Williams, George Alberson, Clarence Emery, Frank Wood, William Jordan, Herman Jordan.

Piedmont Mill (Piedmont, S.C.), consolation winners: Jack Gilreath (coach), Curtis Terry, Harry Waldrop, Roy Garrett, Jewel Smith, Palmer Howard, Leonard Gilreath, Ford Waldrop, Alton Patterson.

Dunean Mill (Greenville, S.C.): C.W. Christopher (coach), James B. Perry, Fred Floyd, William J. Suttles, Paul J. Bogan, Ollie M. Suttles, John R. Beddingfield, William L. Landers, William O. Smith.

Anderson Mill (Anderson, S.C.): W.J. Ligon (coach), Carlton Williams, Harry Burris, Glenn Smith, Green Mahaffey, T.S. Frederick, Clinton Cole, William Gunter.

Brandon Mill (Greenville, S.C.): Guy A. Whitener (coach), Arledge Lee, Charles Foster, Edwin Beeks, Clyde Ross, James Carnes, Ray Hood, Roy Huff, Howard.

Judson Mill (Greenville, S.C.): John Garraux (coach), J.D. McAlister, Paul Moreland, Frank McDaniel, Doris Broadwell, J.W. James, William McGraw, John Hazel, Otis Evans.

Lonsdale Mill (Seneca, S.C.): Harley Heath (coach), Ralph Padgett, Cecil Padgett, Franklin Gilliard, Dewey Stevenson, George Martin, Martin Leatherwood, William Alsep, C.D. Padgett.

Monaghan Mill (Greenville, S.C.): Hugh Anderson (coach), Harrison Waldrop, Hubert Ross, William Keller, Ethworth Nolin, Walter Reid, Clint Ballew, Joseph Ross, Jack Mull.

Lyman Mill (Lyman, S.C.): D.N. Murph (coach), Byrd Alexander, Runty Pettigrew, Harry West, Oscar Walker, Meggs Odell, Slim Stewart, Lefty Morgan, Tipton Turner.

Walhalla Mill (Walhalla, S.C.): A.S. Campbell (coach), Jack Hunnicutt, M.C. Williams, Gene Alexander, William Leister, Charlie Kilpatrick, Irby Mauldin, Gilliard.

CLASS A WOMEN

Monaghan Mill (Greenville, S.C.), champions: Hubert Nolin (coach), Lucille Foster, Inez Brown, Myrtice Skelton, Ruth Darnell, Eunice Burgess, Sue Langston, Myrtice Gunter, Virginia Langston, Oveida Henderson.

Pelzer Mill (Pelzer, S.C.), runners-up: E.W. Edwards (coach), Margaret Kelly, Sarah Kelly, Lou Cook, Catherine Hackney, Sara Jordan, Hazel Harris, Venice Dickson, Elsie Jenkins, Avis Dickson.

Orr Mill (Anderson, S.C.), consolation winners: R.M. Smith (coach), Elizabeth Smith, Kathleen Cooper, Sarah Kinnett, Gladys Kinnett, Frances Jolly, Hattie Bevill, Callie Hooper, Nadine Morris, Inez Buchanan, Edna Lundkovsky.

American Spinning (Greenville, S.C.): D.W. Quinn (coach), Edna Cooper, Selma Carnes, Viney Miller, Ethel Miller, Ruby Nix, Inez Neely, Helen Burns, Louise Doggett, Eva Doggett, Lou Miller.

Dunean Mill (Greenville, S.C.): Wayne McDaniel (coach), Madge Turner, Vera Blackwell, Mary Smith, Agnes Jones, Helen Owens, Vera McAlister, Margaret Whitfield, Agnes Sorgee, Blanche Nesbett, Etrulia Johnson, Putnam.

Lyman Mill (Lyman, S.C.): W.F. Howard (coach), Trannie Melton, Addie Stephens, Jessie Thorne, Helen Howard, Dorothy Reid, Ann Starnes, Louise Pruitte, Ruth Stroud, Virginia Crowe, Gladys West, Pettigrew.

Piedmont Mill (Piedmont, S.C.): Ralph Bowie (coach), Minnie Pack, Mary McCall, Ruth Shirley, Elvie Osteen, Christine Garrett, Kathleen Clifford, Thelma Boiter, Dorothy Clifford, Daisy Osteen, Lillian Grover.

Class B Women

American Enka (Enka, N.C.), champions: Louise Agee (coach), Betty Parker, Mary Duckett, Jenny Cathey, Agnes Brown, Mattie Radcliffe, Ruth Boone, Charlotte Smith, Althea Crawford, Audrey Robinson, Nora Roberts.

Ware Shoals Mill (Ware Shoals, S.C.), runners-up: Evelyn Jones (coach), Lucille Barnes, Helen Clark, Mary Freeman, Sara Freeman, Dora Robinson, Elizabeth Jones, Mattie Copeland, Georgia Martin, Nancy Drake, Eleanor Waldrop.

Glen Lowery Mill (Whitmire, S.C.), consolation winners: Felie Williams (coach), Hazel Kohn, Thelma Puckett, Nannie Simms, Agnes Campbell, Rosa Shirley, Mamie Ray, Betty Douglas, Sara Stone, Shady Huckaby, Louise Campbell, Duffie, Spires.

Anderson Mill (Anderson, S.C.): Ellenor Cathcart (coach), Grace Richardson, Lene Honea, Lucille Lee, Vera Scott, Othella Keaton, Nannie Gray, Mable Conner, Ada Carter, Clara Parkman.

Abbeville Mill (Abbeville, S.C.): Fred Carroll (coach), Sybil Campbell, Agnes Warren, Frances Blum, Edna Clark, Edna Bond, Rosa Campbell, Emma Argo, Edna Bradberry, Margie New, Agnes James.

Brandon Mill (Greenville, S.C.): Claude Lee (coach), Edna Timmons, Katherine Mahon, Maude Doyle, Alva Smith, Dorothy Fortune, Rosa Allison, Eleanor Owens, Sybil Gossett, Lois Childers.

Winnsboro Mill (Winnsboro, S.C.): Henry Huff (coach), Clara Walsh, Mabel Hudson, Grace Gorman, Bertie Spires, Marjorie Hammond, Grace Duffie, Robbie Sandifer, Annie Herrin, Ruby Shirley, Eunice Edinfeld, Byron.

---1932---

Officers: Charles Verner (Piedmont, S.C.), President; J.D. Brown (Greenville, S.C.), Vice-President; Harry B. Jones (Greenville, S.C.), Vice-President; J.W. Brown (Gainesville Ga.), Vice-President; Lawrence Smith (Greenville, S.C.), Vice-President; John H. Garraux (Greenville, S.C.), Secretary; Leonard Howard (Greenville, S.C.), Treasurer; Mrs. J.L. Harrison (Fountain In, S.C.), Girls' Hostess; G.L. Doggett (Piedmont, S.C.), Boy's Host.

Class A Men

Lonsdale Mill (Seneca, S.C.), champions: J.F. Mason (coach), Esco Leopard, Eddie Weathers, James Richardson, Marvin Stevenson, Frank Gilliard, William Pruitt, Marvin Leatherwood, Coke Watson.

Winnsboro Mill (Winnsboro, S.C.), runners-up: Henry Huff (coach), Ebin Reid, R. Culclasure, Sam Fayonsky, Ladd Maxwell, James Herndon, Ed Maxwell, M. Maxwell.

Victor Mill (Greer, S.C.), consolation winners: Leon Dill, Wilson, Frye, Hutchinson, Beason, Hewitt, Duncan, Horton.

Dunean Mill (Greenville, S.C.): Putnam, Dendy, Ellenburg, Kelly, McDonald, J. Campbell, A. Campbell, Bozeman, Chadwick.

Chicopee Mill (Gainesville, Ga.): J.W. Brown (coach), Harold Smith, John Lawes, Ellis Tanner, Paul Bell, Clyde Deaton, Robert Waters, Fred Tanner, Ralph Smith, Aaron Moore, Ralph Smith.

Piedmont Mill (Piedmont, S.C.): Gomer Thompson (coach), R.W. Bowie (coach), Clarence Beasley, Willie Bolden, James Picklesimer, Fred Pack, James Bishop, Charles Brown, Walter Grover, Clyde Evans, Seth Pack, Clarence Allen.

Avondale Mill (Alexander City, Ala.): Walter Bozeman, Slagle, Roberts, Price, Peters, Champion, Holly, Turner, Keith, Heath.

Draper Mill (Draper, N.C.): Hawks, Stultz,

Southern Textile Basketball Tournament Rosters

Dewey McBride, Furman Holland, Hamrick, Turner, Haymore, Murphy.

Orr Mill (Anderson, S.C.): Lee Whitten, Stamps, Roberts, Price, Bevills, Buchanan, Thackston.

Monaghan Mill (Greenville, S.C.): Coleman, Stephens, Ballenger, Bagwell, Hudgens, Henderson, Elder, Herrin.

Spartan Mill (Spartanburg, S.C.): B. Mooneyham, Carl Mooneyham, Ted Crain, Dodd, Gregory, Steadings, Taylor.

Walhalla Mill (Walhalla, S.C.): Gilliard, Rochester, Smith, Alexander, Leister, Elliott, Williams, Robertson.

Renfrew Bleachery (Travelers Rest, S.C.): Coker, Osborne, Hunt, Hawkins, Barbare, R. Foster, C. Foster.

CLASS B MEN

Judson Mill (Greenville, S.C.), champions: Bolt, Rogers, Frank McDaniel, Tallant, J.W. James, McAlister, Tumblin, King, Broadwell, Weldon Rogers.

Southern Bleachery (Taylors, S.C.), runners-up: Keeler, Jim Gay, Wilson, Owens, Bishop, Meisenheimer, Jackson, Belcher, Herbert Walls, Langston.

Southern Worsted (Greenville, S.C.), consolation winners: J.E. Loftis (coach), O'dell Holloway, James DeShields, Thomas Fowler, Fred Knox, Curtis Maxwell, Roy Hogg, DeWitt Williamson, Montague Simpson, Grady Simpson, George Long.

American Spinning (Greenville, S.C.): Fowler, Quinn, Morgan, Wilbanks, Cooper, Nix, NcNeely.

Glen Lowery Mill (Whitmire, S.C.): S.J. Bostic (coach), Walter Gosnell, Fred Prather, Mark Connor, Troy Ward, Jessie James, Theodore Black, William Yarborough, Colby Grant.

Joanna Mill (Joanna, S.C.): A.B. Galloway Jr. (coach), Eugene Abrams, W.J. Abrams, Harry Barrett, Truman Godfrey, Roland Godfrey, Fred Ross, Vernon Ross, Charlie Girk, Lumas Pickett, Bruce Galloway.

Anderson Mill (Anderson, S.C.): Ripley, Williams, English, Spearman, Nixon, Cole, Gunter, Kelly, Smith, Carter.

Collins & Aikman (Roxboro, N.C.): Gentry, Strum, Day, Mauney, C. Wilburn, G. Walker, A. Walker, E. Wilburn, Jones.

Union Bleachery (Greenville, S.C.): Brooks, Berry, Marshbanks, Robinson, J.D. Ivey, Hawkins, Waldrop, Knight.

Proximity Mill (Greensboro, N.C.): Baynes, Noah, Deaton, Walker, Garner, McLean.

Mills Mill (Greenville, S.C.): Porter, A. Abbott, Massey, B. McCallister, Henry, L. Abbott, W. McCallister.

CLASS C MEN

Pelzer Mill (Pelzer, S.C.), champions: Harley Heath (coach), Geddens Roche (coach), David Hughes, Fred Ross, Herman Jordan, William Jordan, Clarence Emery, George Alverson, Roy Brown, B.F. Ross, Joe Jenkins, Raymond Geddings.

Piedmont Mill (Piedmont, S.C.), runners-up: Jack Gilreath (coach), Roy Garrett, Joesph Patterson, Curtis Terry, Harry Waldrop, Jewell Smith, Ford Waldrop, Leroy Hunnicutt, Clifton Garrison, Palmer Howard, Madden, H. Garrett, Underwood.

Lyman Mill (Lyman, S.C.), consolation winners: Alexander, Reeves, West, Morgan, Turner, Odell, Pettigrew, Reames, Hill, Bowen.

Judson Mill (Greenville, S.C.): James Hall (coach), Arthur Cobb, Bill McGraw, James Trammell, Paul Moreland, Harry Trammell, John Hazel, Clyde Cobb, B.L. Hughes, Leonard Hill, William Williams, Cornelius Rayburn.

Union Bleachery (Greenville, S.C.): Hawkins, Robertson, Bishop, Brooks, Starkey, Nelson, F. Waldrop, W. Bishop, Hester, G. Howard.

Marion Mfg. (Marion, N.C.): Rose, Settlemyre, Smith, Pennington, Broome, Elmore, Stamey, T. Clayton, W. Clayton.

Orr Mill (Anderson, S.C.): Ashworth, Buchanan, Attaway, Thompson, Barnes, Cleveland, Lyons, Ellison.

Spartan Mill (Spartanburg, S.C.): Cothran, Candler, Ross, Cannon, Lands, Burnett, Taylor.

Lonsdale Mill (Seneca, S.C.): Martin, Garrett, Padgett, Alsept, Rackley, Whitt, Ledford.

Monaghan Mill (Greenville, S.C.): Wallace Foster, Ballew, Langston, Waldrop, Hughes, Campbell, Reid, Hughes, Ross.

Dunean Mill (Greenville, S.C.): Huggins, Floyd, Suttles, Turner, Beddingfield, Bogan, Stroud, Landers.

Woodside Mill (Greenville, S.C.): Couch, Mears, Canup, Clippard, Herbert, Bowen, Hill.

Class A Women

Pelzer Mill (Pelzer, S.C.), champions: Sarah Jordan, S. Kelly, Hackney, H. Kelly, A. Dickson, Cook, Frances Hammond, Jenkins.

Monaghan Mill (Greenville, S.C.), runners-up: Lucille Thomas, Henderson, S. Langston, V. Brown, Inez Brown, Virginia Langston, E. Brown.

American Enka (Enka, N.C.), consolation winners: E. Morgan, Helen Shuford, Willie Justus, Agnes Parker, Faye Herron, Charlotte Justus, Boone, Ratcliffe, B. Parker.

Anderson Mill (Anderson, S.C.): Fine, Burriss, Eleanor Cathcart, Carter, Scott, Richardson, Keaton, Keith.

American Spinning (Greenville, S.C.): L. Miller, E. Cooper, V. Miller, Nix, F. Ward, M. Ward, Hale.

Other Teams: **Lyman Mill** (Lyman, S.C.).

Class B Women

Glen Lowery Mill (Whitmire, S.C.), champions: Hazel Kohn, Huckaby, Billie Douglas, Cole, M. Ray, Shirley, Pruitt, H. Ray, Campbell.

American Enka (Enka, N.C.), runners-up: Keys, Fite, Roberts, Hyatt, Medford, Rozell O'Kelly, Lander, Phillips.

Spartan Mill (Spartanburg, S.C.), consolation winners: Biershenk, Lois Dobbins, Wilma Whitlock, Dora Jackson, Sara Bryson, Beulah Jackson, Starnes, Lancaster.

Kenneth Mill (Walhalla, S.C.): Harden, V. Sanders, E. Williams, Y. Sanders, L. Duncan, M. Williams, Lee, D. Sanders, McCall.

Southern Worsted (Greenville, S.C.): Hill, Knox, West, Fleming, Davis, Long, Brown.

Winnsboro Mill (Winnsboro, S.C.): Moss, Stephenson, Gibson, Duffie, Ramsey, Gartman.

Other Teams: **Marion Mfg.** (Marion, N.C.).

1933

Officers: Jesse D. Brown (Greenville, S.C.), President; Charles Smith (Alexander City, Ala.), Vice-President; Harry B. Jones (Greenville, S.C.), Vice-President; Lawrence Y. Smith (Greenville, S.C.), Vice-President; John H. Garraux (Greenville, S.C.), Secretary; Charles V. Verner (Piedmont, S.C.), Treasurer; Elinor Cathcart (Anderson, S.C.), Womens' Hostess; G.L. Doggett (Piedmont, S.C.), Mens' Host; W.M. Grier (Greenville, S.C.), Director 110 Pound Tournament.

Class A Men

Monaghan Mill (Greenville, S.C.), champions: Arthur McMinn (coach), Lee Coleman (coach), Paul Brazie, Daniel Bagwell, Linnell Brazie, Connie Mack Berry, William Coleman, Nick Elder, William Stephens, Willard Heath, Jesse Hudgens, Fletcher Heath.

Victor Mill (Greer, S.C.), runners-up: S.V. Wilson (coach), Alvin Waters, Charles Suddeth Jr., Howard Maness, Charles Horton, Porter Frye, Willie Hutchinson, George Beason, Markham Ballenger, Wilton Pruitt, James Suddeth, Cabiness.

Judson Mill (Greenville, S.C.), consolation winner: John H. Garraux (coach), Ansel Kay, Harold Bolt, Weldon Rogers, J.D. McAlister, Fred Tumblin, Frank McDaniel, Willie Tallant, J.W. James, James Hall, Doris Broadwell.

Piedmont Mill (Piedmont, S.C.): Gomer Thompson (coach), Clyde Evans, Charlie Brown, Jerome Grover, James Pickelsimer, Clarence Beasley, Clarence Allen, Seth Pack, Fred Pack, William Bolden.

Glen Lowery Mill (Whitmire, S.C.): L.J. Bostic (coach), Mark Connor, Troy Ward, Walter Gosnell, Theodore Black, Fred Prather, Everett Mize, Jessie James, Fred Grant.

Southern Bleachery (Taylors, S.C.): W.F. Davis (coach), Fred Coleman (coach), Woodrow Wilson, Herman Keeler, L.S. Misenheimer, John Langston, Hubert Robinson, Luther Owens, Herbert Wall, Carl Hughes, James Gay, Wells.

Mills Mill (Greenville, S.C.): J.P. Friar (coach), Bill Lynch (coach), Eugene McAlister, Clarence Porter, Henry Wright, Albert Moon, Lewis Abbott, James Abbott, William McAlister, Joel Prewitt, Cal McCauley, Alfred Coggins, Massey.

Avondale Mill (Alexander City, Ala.): Charles Smith (coach), Roscoe Slagle, Emmett Keith, Edwin Price, Kelly Champion, Troy Holly, Raymond Waldrop, John Turner, Willis Slagle.

Lyman Mill (Lyman, S.C.): D.N. Murph (coach), Lawrence Pruitt, Joe Gibson, J.W. McMakin, James Sargent, Albert DeLoach, Paul Barbare, Wideman Durham, James Hart, Furman.

Renfrew Bleachery (Travelers Rest, S.C.): Chester Eddy (coach), Fred Bishop (coach), Harold Osborne, Fred Knox, Claude Hawkins, Roy Foster, Vaughn Smith, Linder Duncan, Beverly Southerland, Paul Hunt.

Winnsboro Mill (Winnsboro, S.C.): Bill Wells (coach), Marvin Stevenson, Edward Maxwell, Eben Reid, Raymond Culclasure, James Herndon, Coley Spigner, Jim Rice.

Ware Shoals Mill (Ware Shoals, S.C.): H.E. Newbury (coach), James Head, Walter Martin, James Lollis, Grier Wright, William Werner, James McNinch, Lewis Werner, Melvin Tate, Dwight McNinch.

American Spinning (Greenville, S.C.): Dewey Quinn (coach), Edgar Harbin, Edgar Major, Edgar Duncan, Ralph Morgan, John Mauldin, Woodrow Fowler, Ray Boggs, Clyde Hayes, Clarence Cooper.

Dunean Mill (Greenville, S.C.): Leonard Howard (coach), Clarence Thomas, Winfred Kelly, William Riddle, Homer Dendy, Grayson Roddy, Carol Owens, Wilton Putman, Sam Turner, Lewis McDonald, Sam Ranich.

Walhalla Mill (Walhalla, S.C.): Louis Elliott (coach), J.A. Gilliard, J.A. Rochester, M.C. Williams, Roy Smith, R.F. Williams, E.B. Morse, E.T. Alexander, S.P. Wells, W.H. Williams.

CLASS B MEN

Erlanger Mill (Lexington, N.C.), champions: Childress, Link, Everhart, Essex, Sowers, Bell, Richey.

Converse Mill (Spartanburg, S.C.), runners-up: W.A. Nicholson (coach), Charles Holland, Yonnie Green, Jesse Bishop, Chalmers Wooten, B.A. Brown, Ted Quinn, W.A. Quinn, Roy Evington.

Lyman Mill (Lyman, S.C.), consolation winners: D.N. Murph (coach), James O'Dell, Roy Garrett, William Simpson, Charles Reeves, Lefty Morgan, Runnie Pettigrew, Harry West, Charles Alexander, Ralph Campbell.

American Enka (Enka, N.C.): Marshall Meadows (coach), Andy Brandell Jr., Clyde Merrill, Vincent Cooper, Homer Johnson, Edward McDowell, Richard Allen, Owen Ingram, Troy Miller, O. Morgan, G. Morgan, Barrett.

Proximity Mill (Greensboro, N.C.): F.C. Garner (coach), Jesse Costner (coach), Archie Baynes, Lawrence Edwards, Clarence Hobbs, Howard Noah, Howard Maness, Monroe Deaton, William Walker, Corliss Garner, Gunthrus McLean, Howard Boone.

Pelzer Mill (Pelzer, S.C.): C.C. Roberts (coach), Harley Heath (coach), John Emery, David Hughes, Joe Jenkins, George Alverson, Herman Jordan, Bill Brown, Charles Westmoreland, Fred Ross, Bill Jordan.

Camperdown Mill (Greenville, S.C.): Waters Huff (coach), John McDowell, Ralph Huff, Frank Childers, Ernest Norris, Haskel Gosnell, James Cohn, Alvin Cohn, Ben Landreth, Gilmer Huff, Walter Breazeale.

Simpsonville Mill (Simpsonville, S.C.): D.L. Goodenough (coach), Harold Bagwell, Carl Bunton, Jack Thackston, Harmen Williams, Dewitt Gilliard, Leonard Barbare, Harold Coker, William Coker, Bryan Rodgers, Bob Bridges.

Anderson Mill (Anderson, S.C.): McDuffie Irwin (coach), George Weathers (coach), J.B. Spearman, Carl Ripley, Glenn Smith, William Gunter, Obie James, Clinton Cole, Frank Wray, Leason Heaton, Carlton Williams, J.B. Kelly.

Gossett Mill (Anderson, S.C.): J.C. Moreland (coach), Courtney Heath (coach), Claude Hendrix, James Smith, Kenneth Ables, Roy Hurt, Robert Fortner, Albert Lee, Delvin Smith, Buck Bearden, Ervin Sexton, Paul Summey.

Southern Worsted (Greenville, S.C.): James Loftis (coach), Charles Curry, Thad Raines, Haskell Dill, Charles Hogg, Sam Smith, Grady Simpson, Gideon Long, James DeShields, Hewie Simpson, Luther Alexander.

Spindale Mill (Spindale, N.C.): Earle Yelton (coach), Joe Watson, Gerald Lipscomb, Woodrow Freeman, Wayne Harris, Thomas Dorsey, Howard McDonald, Robert Edwards, Leslie Tanner, Turner.

Elizabeth James Mill (Marion, N.C.): R.L. James (coach), Lois Clayton, Walter Lawing, Lee Anderson, Max Willis, Robert James, D.H. Long, Ray Quinn, Clyde Hensley, Roy Hensley, Mark Miller.

Monaghan Mill (Greenville, S.C.): Amos Galloway (coach), Wallace Foster, Etworth Nolan, Clint Ballew, Hubert Ross, Henry Langston, Hayman Reid, Claud Johnson, Harrison Waldrop.

CLASS C MEN

Piedmont Mill (Piedmont, S.C.), champions: Jack Gilreath (coach), Walter Madden, Alton Patterson, J.W. Rampey, Curtis Terry, Clayton Boiters, Harry Waldrop, Ford Waldrop, Houston Calvert, Dewey Collins, Leroy Hunnicutt, Underwood, Jack Ashworth,

Victor Mill (Greer, S.C.), runners-up:

Herbert Greer (coach), Herbert Wood, Donald Jackson, Robert Brown, Theron Beamon, Felton Suddeth, Grady Burnett, Virgil Pruitt, Ernest Poole, Sidney Dobson, R.D. Burnett, Jackson.

Avondale Mill (Alexander City, Ala.), consolation winners: Charles Smith (coach), Ralph Holly, Ralph Davis, Lois Watwood, Willie Brooks, Brinton Pair, Floyd Blankenship, Robert Ingram, Fred Boos.

Brandon Mill (Greenville, S.C.): R.R. Hood (coach), Fred Cox, Robert Freeman, William Lanford, Jimmy Lusk, Harry Mears, James Lee, Bubba Huff, Pete Huff, James Carnes Jr., William Attaway.

Lonsdale Mill (Seneca, S.C.): A.H. Padgett (coach), J.F. Mason (coach), C.D. Padgett, Lasco Alsep, Plumer Rackley, Coley Garrett, Ralph McDonald, Clarence Gilliard, George Morgan, George Martin, Rufus Trantham, Frank Morgan.

Mills Mill (Greenville, S.C.): Thomas Ingle (coach), Joyce Massey (coach), Frank Norris, Lewis Chandler, Carl Henry, Homer Shuttleworth, Henry Tollison, Paul Campbell, Clarence Bridges, Stanley Ball, Daniel Grey, John Ballew, Hawkins, Richey.

Spartan Mill #1 (Spartanburg, S.C.): L.T. Cothran (coach), J.L. Massebeau (coach), Stanley Lancaster, George Biershank, Douglas Cannon, Paul Burnett, J.R. Lands, Elmer Clubb, Foster Chandler, W.G. Cothran.

Spartan Mill #2 (Spartanburg, S.C.): W.E. Cothran (coach), Russell Lands (coach), Clinton Smith, Ernest Foster, Charles Lands, Worth Gault, Ralph Gibbs, Wylie O'Shields, Edwin Burnett, Robert York, Greer.

Woodside Mill (Greenville, S.C.): D.T. Vehorn (coach), Otto Herbert (coach), Leonard Canup, Dewey Bowen, Andrew Ramey, Truman Herbert, Charles Couch, J.W. Hill, Cecil Clippard, Bud Hodge.

Pelzer Mill (Pelzer, S.C.): Horace Smith (coach), Harley Heath (coach), Edward Dickard, Tobie Williams, Clip Crymes, Bill Sanders, J.W. Jordan, Horace Davenport, Ellis Geddings, Snake Galloway, Harold Pryor, Ralph Cannon.

Judson Mill (Greenville, S.C.): Lester Wood (coach), Paul Moreland, Clyde Cobb, Arthur Cobb, Harry Trammell, Homer Compton, James Trammell, Leland Estes, Leonard Hill, Russell Chapman, William McGraw.

Greer Mill (Greer, S.C.): John Brewton, Woodrow Harvey, Charlie Taylor, Sanford Giles, Fred Jones, Ben Burnette, R.L. Poole, Roy Johnson, Tom Lee, Harold Forrester.

Marion Mfg. (Marion, N.C.): J.L. Gourley (coach), T.C. Clayton, Robert Broome, James Settlemyre, Keith Smith, Howard Ingle, Robert Burgin, Cecil Mask, Charles Hall, John Byrd, Verle Wood.

Monaghan Mill (Greenville, S.C.): Thomas Reid (coach), Carl Nolan, Aaron Powers, John Ward, Ralph Snelson, Gene Ross, Jack Mull, Gordon Barnett, George Campbell, Charles Hughes, Julius Bradshaw.

Union Bleachery (Greenville, S.C.): Charles Brooks (coach), Clinton Hester, Edgeworth Pace, Barney Hawkins, William Nelson, James Brown, William Bishop Jr., Ray Starkey, Cecil Brooks, Columbus Jones, Wilson Dobbins.

American Spinning (Greenville, S.C.): Charles Smith (coach), A.B. Davis, G.W. Friddle, Coley Major, Woodrow Wilson, George Spake, Grady Pike, William Nix, Willie Wilbanks, Frank Cooper, Fred Trammell.

CLASS A WOMEN

Lyman Mill (Lyman, S.C.), champions: W.F. Howard (coach), Sarah McMakin, Louise Pruitt, Mary Todd, Dorothy Reid, Virginia Starnes, Lillian Corn, Dessie Pettigru, Gena Bright, Nina Barry, Christine Smart, Gladys West, Jessie Thorne.

American Enka (Enka, N.C.), runners-up: Louise Agee (coach), Helen Shuford, Bettie Parker, Mattie Ratcliff, Charlotte Justus, Ruth Boone, Willie Justus, Mary Byrd, Susie Keys, Jessie Hyatt, Howard.

Glen Lowery Mill (Whitmire, S.C.), consolation winners: L.J. Bostic (coach), Betty Douglas, Ophelia Williams, Cornelia Spratt, Shady Huckaby, Mamie Ray, Helen Black, Agnes Campbell, Willie Pruitt, Lola Puckett, Elaine Tobias, Doris Davis, Ruth Ray, Bright.

Dunean Mill (Greenville, S.C.): Lucille Thomas (coach), Runette Simpson, Maude Gwinn, Madge Gosnell, Gladys Worrell, Etrulia Johnson, Vera Blackwell, Evelyn Putman, Georgia Floyd, Margaret Whitfield, Mary Smith.

Pelzer Mill (Pelzer, S.C.): A.C. Gosnell (coach), Harley Heath (coach), Sarah Jordan, Sarah Kelly, Avis Dickson, Kitty Hackney, Geneva Garrett, Helen Kelly, Virginia Dickson, Lilly Holliday, Mildred Kelly, Bill Terry.

Piedmont Mill (Piedmont, S.C.): Mrs. M.B.

Southern Textile Basketball Tournament Rosters   Appendix 1

King (coach), Minnie Pack, Thelma Bowie, Frances Pack, Rachel Staples, Dorothy Clifford, Ruth Shirley, Eva Lancaster, Pauline Hollingsworth, Ruby Doggett, Christine Garrett.

Anderson Mill (Anderson, S.C.): Irwin McDuffie (coach), George Weathers (coach), Clyde Elrod, Blanche Sanders, Grace Richardson, Ella McAuley, Robbie Bailey, Bertie Hines, Jewell Dunn, Lena Honea, Helen Cooper, Ada Carter, Alma Burriss, McCall, House, Floyd.

Monaghan Mill (Greenville, S.C.): Thornwell Henson (coach), Winnie Herrin, Ola Davis, Oveida Henderson, Eunice Herrin, Clara Smith, Inez Brown, Vivian Brown, Lucille Buff, Sue Langston, Essie Brown, Pearline Smith, B. Langston.

American Spinning (Greenville, S.C.): Velt Nix (coach), Ruby Nix, Frances Ward, Florence Hopkins, Mourn Ward, Lucille Hale, Ethel Miller, Edna Cooper, Etta Herd, Rosa Allison, Fay Nix, Gladys Smith.

CLASS B WOMEN

Winnsboro Mill (Winnsboro, S.C.), champions: M.V. Wells (coach), Winnie Stevenson, Grace Gartman, Hazel Williamson, Lois Ramsey, Bobbie Sandifer, Willie Summers, Blanche Ramsey, Cora Moss, Thelma Collins, Margaret Lindsay, Ruby Floyd.

Stanly Mill (Oakboro, N.C.), runners-up: Venie Murphy (coach), Alzelene Johnston, Grace Garrison, Virginia Hovis, Velda Garrison, Annie Bradshaw, Kathryn Homsley, Maude Hovis, Gertie Hovis.

Southern Worsted (Greenville, S.C.), consolation winners: Charles Cathcart (coach), Mattie Rollins (coach), Argyle Hogg, Earline Davis, Thalia Hawkins, Daisy Wynn, Rose Maxwell, Bartie Brown, Earline Gosnell, Gladys Hogg, Sarah West, Russell Long, Virginia Montgomery, Florence Cathcart.

Brandon Mill (Greenville, S.C.): R.R. Hood (coach), F.B. Smith (coach), Catherine Masters, Myrtle Smith, Dorothy Fortune, Lois Childress, Villa M. Porshea, Annette Tannery, Ruenette Sheppard, Elizabeth Mahon, Nancy Mahon, Eunice Eades, Ruth Smith, Olfria Smith.

Kenneth Mill (Walhalla, S.C.): A.C. Rouda (coach), Roy Smith (coach), Mae Sanders, Ruth Elliott, Hazel Sanders, Inez Duncan, Frances Harden, Mildred Williams, Elva Epps, Dorothy Sanders, Ruby Garrett, Sarah Gillespie.

American Enka (Enka, N.C.): Louise Agee (coach), Rozelle O'Kelly, Minnie Fite, Margie Roberts, Alma Bowen, Crystal Medford, Jennie Cagle, Frederica Ingle, Mildred Crownover, Genevieve Byrd.

Piedmont Mill (Piedmont, S.C.): S.R. Wilson (coach), Rachel Jenkins, Louise Pack, Catherine Mulligan, Mary Osteen, Claudia Flemming, Inez Goldsmith, Reba Hollingsworth, Elizabeth Pickelsimer, Nancy Norris, Mary Burriss, Lois Burriss, Bowen, Davis.

1934

Officers: Jesse D. Brown (Greenville, S.C.), President; Harley Heath (Pelzer, S.C.), Vice-President; F.C. Garner (Greensboro, N.C.), Vice-President; Harry B. Jones (Greenville, S.C.), Vice-President; Charles S. Smith (Alexander City, Ala.), Vice-President; O.S. Scarborough (Winnsboro, S.C.), Vice-President; John H. Garraux (Greenville, S.C.), Secretary; C.V. Verner (Piedmont, S.C.), Treasurer; Lucille Thomas (Greenville, S.C.), Girls' Hostess; G.L. Doggett (Piedmont, S.C.), Boys' Host; W.M. Grier (Greenville, S.C.), Director 110 Pound Tournament; Dean Bishop (Greenville, S.C.), Secretary 110 Pound Tournament.

CLASS A MEN

Monaghan Mill (Greenville, S.C.), champions: Lee Coleman (coach), Connie Mac Berry, Nick Elder, Bud Stephens, Dan Bagwell, Wilson Wakefield, Harry Herrin, Clyde Hudgens, Hardin.

Winnsboro Mill (Winnsboro, S.C.), runners-up: Porter Frye (coach), Bill Wells (coach), T.S. Shealy, Marvin Stevenson, Jack Ohlsen, Coley Speigner, Ray Wilson, Ed Maxwell, Jimmie Herndon, Bradford South.

Proximity Mill (Greensboro, N.C.), consolation winners: Edwards, Brasher, Deaton, William Walker, Murphy, Boone, Baynes, Garner.

Spindale Mill (Spindale, N.C.): Freeman, Harris, Edwards, Lipscomb, L. Davis, C. Davis, Landrum, McDonald, Yelton, L.D. Davis.

Judson Mill (Greenville, S.C.): McAlister, Kay, McDaniel, Broadwell, Hall, James, Rogers, Tumblin, Nichols, Barbare.

Piedmont Mill (Piedmont, S.C.): L.G.

Thompson (coach), Clyde Gilreath, Clarence Allen, Fred Pack, Willie Bolden, Johnny Beasley, Jerome Grover, Seth Pack, Everette King, Charlie Brown, Leron Anderson.
  Walhalla Mill (Walhalla, S.C.): L.B. Elliott (coach), M.C. Williams, W.W. Gilliard, L.R. Smith, E.T. Alexander, C.R. Gilliard, J.A. Gilliard, E.B. Morse, Julian Mills.
  Pelzer Mill (Pelzer, S.C.): Clarence Emery, I. Jenkins, Rochester, Pickelsimer, Jordan, P. Jenkins, John Emery.
  Erlanger Mill (Lexington, N.C.): Childress, Link, Young, Essick, Leonard, Seyles, Bell, Crowell.
  Manchester Mill (Manchester, Ga.): Meadors, Stewart, Hurst, Byard, Calloway, Thompson, Bowie, Allen, Bradley.
  Beacon Mill (Swannanoa, N.C.): Buchanan, Vallencourt, Buggs, Bagley, Winslow, Morgan, King, Moore.
  Lyman Mill (Lyman, S.C.): Gibson, Campbell, Jay McMakin, Durham, Jim Hart, McElveen, DeLoach, Hill.
  Dunean Mill (Greenville, S.C.): Willie Riddle, Thomas, Owens, Kelly, Jenkins, McDonald.
  Lonsdale Mill (Seneca, S.C.): Leopard, Weathers, Pruitt, Heath, Gilliard, Leatherwood, Watson.
  Southern Bleachery (Taylors, S.C.): Keeler, Duncan, Langston, Maness, Chapman, Suddeth, Gay.
  Victor Mill (Greer, S.C.): Cabiness, Horton, Suddeth, Alvin Waters, Hutchinson, Hewitt, Lipton.
  Ware Shoals Mill (Ware Shoals, S.C.): Lollis, Wright, Tate, McNinch, Lewis, Werner, Watt, Eleazer, Martin, Sanders.
  Renfrew Bleachery (Travelers Rest, S.C.): F. Knox, Coleman, Hunt, Hawkins, Foster, Hopkins, DeShields, Jones.
  Mills Mill (Greenville, S.C.): Abbott, Porter, Massey, McAlister, L. Abbott, Coggins, Ingle.
  Calloway Mill (LaGrange, Ga.): Smith, Michell, Copeland, Kersey, Burdette, Yates, Conner.
  Glen Lowery Mill (Whitmire, S.C.): Ward, Black, Connor, Prather, Cheatham, Branks, Raines, Grant.
  Sylacauga Mill (Sylacauga, Ala.): Ingram, Clark, Hammond, Stanton, Pearson, Nivens, Pearson, McCarthy, Gordon, Johnson, Hickman.

Class B Men

Lyman Mill (Lyman, S.C.), champions: Alexander, Reeves, West, R. Pettigrew, Garrett, Morgan, Reid, C. Pettigrew.
  Piedmont Mill (Piedmont, S.C.), runners-up: Jack Gilreath (coach), James Terry, Harry Waldrop, Walter Madden, Lee Hunnicutt, S.C. Hawkins, Clayton Boiter, Alton Patterson, J.W. Rampey, Ford Waldrop, Jerry Underwood, Mann.
  Woodside Mill (Greenville, S.C.), consolation winners: C. Couch, Hill, J. Couch, Canup, Lee, Ramey, S. Couch.
  Stark Mill (Hogansville, Ga.): Bond, Copeland, Trussel, Lester, Bussey, Barton, Hamer, Armstrong, Lunsford, Barter.
  Joanna Mill (Joanna, S.C.): O.M. Templeton (coach), Fred Ross, Tom Gastley, Charlie Girk, Grady Spires, Gerald Morse, Bruce Galloway, Gene Abrams, Lumas Puckett, Red Walker, Jack Hunnicutt, Bass, Byers.
  Sayles Biltmore Bleachery (Biltmore, N.C.): J.T. Hollingsworth (coach), Owen Roberts, Luther King, George Davis, John Cook, Carroll Lance, J.C. Melton, Earnest Cook, Richard Harrison, Waverly Ingle, F. Cook.
  Southern Worsted (Greenville, S.C.): Hogg, Pollard, Curry, C. Pollard, Long Byrd, Bowie Crain.
  Monaghan Mill (Greenville, S.C.): Carl Nolin, Foster, Langston, E. Nolan, Waldrop, Ballew, Ross, Reid, Powers.
  Gossett Mill (Anderson, S.C.): Hendrix, Lee, V. Smith, Sexton, Moore, Bobo, D. Smith, Phillips.
  Inman Mill (Inman, S.C.): Parriss, Duncan, Jenkins, Rogers, Vaughn, Burns, Martin, Pack, Correll.
  Anderson Mill (Anderson, S.C.): Ray, Cason, Heaton, Kelly, Vandiver, Smith, Cole, Pettigru, Spearman.
  Avondale Mill (Alexander City, Ala.): Bishop, Coker, Martin, Harris, Payne, Boose, Ingram, Holley.
  Marion Mfg. (Marion, N.C.): Bull, Lawrence, Burgin, Hall, Davis, Walker, Lewis, Biggerstaff.
  American Enka (Enka, N.C.): Morgan, Fincannon, Allen, Cooper, Johnson, Merrill, Miller, Chandler, Merritt.
  Bacon Mill (Lenoir City, Tenn.): Baskett, Thomas, Littleton, Connor, Babb, Monger, Derieux, V. Thomas.

Southern Textile Basketball Tournament Rosters Appendix 1 125

Lynchburg Mill (Lynchburg, Va.): Sweeney, Miller, St. Clair, Dowdy, Stewart, Garner, Stevens, Dejosrett, Sinkley.
Erwin Mill (Erwin, Tenn.): Taylor, Sewell, Parker, Stephenson, Byrd, Woodworth, Few, Bost, Few, House.
Sycamore Mill (Sycamore, Ala.): Blankenship, Sims, McCullars, King, Thurman, Franklin, Robertson, Cox.
Caroleen Mill (Caroleen, N.C.): Metcalf, Dobbins, Willis, Neal, Hawkins, Harris, Head.

CLASS C MEN

Judson Mill (Greenville, S.C.), champions: Moreland, Chapman, Sterling, Cobb, Eates, Christopher, Anthony.
Chicopee Mill (Gainseville, Ga.), runners-up: Miller, Moore, Evans, McDaniel, Paul Smith, Waters.
Dunean Mill (Greenville, S.C.), consolation winners: Gosnell, Huggins, Donnan, Stroud, Garren, Putnam, Cox, Whitworth, Turner.
Chiquola Mill (Honea Path, S.C.): Ivester, Ferguson, Carr, Keasler, Simmons, Werner, Thompson, Dorn.
Brandon Mill (Greenville, S.C.): Huff, Meares, Carnes, McDonald, Freeman, Townsend, Thackston, Whitmire, Campbell, Edens.
Greer Mill (Greer, S.C.): Taylor, Giles, Penland, Brewton, Burnette, Smith, Lee, Forrester, Poole.
Poe Mill (Greenville, S.C.): Whitted, L. Lister, Waldrop, Evans, Grastie, B. Lister.
Lonsdale Mill (Seneca, S.C.): Gilliard, Allsep, Whitt, Rackley, Garrett, Morgan, Padgett.
Spartan Mill (Spartanburg, S.C.): Biershank, Cothran, Gibbes, Cannon, Burnett, Lands, Chandler, Yord, Smith, Eledge.
Victor Mill (Greer, S.C.): G. Burnett, Dobson, Poole, R. Burnett, Pruitt, Meyer, Jackson, Brown, Wilson.
Southern Bleachery (Taylors, S.C.): C. Bryant, R. Bryant, Smith, Hawkins, Reardon, Bridgeman, Taylor, Hughes, Bridges, Ross.
Mills Mill (Greenville, S.C.): Abbott, Hawkins, Richey, Shuttleworth, Chandler, Toby, Capps, Cothran, Bridges, Henry, Norris.
American Spinning (Greenville, S.C.): Willie Wilbanks, Nix, Davis, Wilson, Cooper, Sparks.

CLASS A WOMEN

Pelzer Mill (Pelzer, S.C.), champions: Harley Heath (coach), Kitty Frick, Sarah Jordan, Avis Dickson, Virginia Dickson, Helen Kelly, Willie Terry, Lucia Holliday, Eva Saylors, Lillie Ballard, Minter S. Whitt.
Lyman Mill (Lyman, S.C.), runners-up: Dessie Pettigrew, Nina Barry, Dot Reid, Bright, Pruitt, Thorne, Hannah, Carne, Connor.
Dunean Mill (Greenville, S.C.), consolation winners: Thomas, Greene, Mary Smith, Gwynne, Whitfield, Blackwell, Etrulia Johnson, Hardin, Taylor.
Glen Lowery Mill (Whitmire, S.C.): Suber, Pruitt, Huckaby, Campbell, Ray, Black, Hester, Coggins, Willlingham, Douglas.
American Enka (Enka, N.C.): Mary Byrd, Susan Keys, Morgan, Osborne, Ratcliff, Hyatt, Roberts, O'Kelly, Fite.
Piedmont Mill (Piedmont, S.C.): Ruth Evatt (coach), Louise Pack, Thelma Bowie, Nellie Bowen, Dorothy Clifford, Rachel Jenkins, Minnie Pack, Claudia Fleming, Ruth Shirley, Frances Pack, Reba Hollingsworth, Christine Garrett.
Winnsboro Mill (Winnsboro, S.C.): Cora Moss, Bobbie Sandifer, Hazel Williamson, Lois Ramsey, Winnie Stevens, Estelle Gibson, Willie Summers, Sallie Gibson, Cletise Collins, Maude Hilburn.
Orr Mill (Anderson, S.C.): Sanders, Lundkovsky, O'Barr, Jolley, Smith, Newman, Jackson.
Southern Worsted (Greenville, S.C.): Long, Davis, West, Gosnell, Montgomery, Sanders, Jackson, Brown, Coggins.
Beacon Mill (Swannanoa, N.C.): Dodson, McMahan, Lewis, Sterlin, R. Penley, King, Jones, B. Penley, Dodson.

CLASS B WOMEN

Stanly Mill (Oakboro, N.C.), champions: Black, Johnson, Withers, G. Garrison, V. Garrison, Morris, Abernathy, Murphy, Porter, Hall, Sherrill.
American Enka (Enka, N.C.), runners-up: Hawkins, Holcombe, Brown, Medford, Crownover, Prince, Byrd, Line, Williams.
Renfrew Bleachery (Travelers Rest, S.C.), consolation winners: MacWilliams, E. Coleman, L. Lockaby, Cunningham, E. Lockaby, Henderson, M. Hunt, Edwards.
Brandon Mill (Greenville, S.C.): Gunter,

Masters, Mahon, Porshea, Gambrell, Kay, Tannery, Edwards.

Monaghan Mill (Greenville, S.C.): Ellis, Smith, Garwood, Summers, Suddeth, Case, Hill, Bishop, Anderson.

Marion Mfg. (Marion, N.C.): Lucille Flack (coach), Fender, Epley, Epps, Alice Barnes, Rogers, Fisher, Black, Hall, Glenn, Grace Proctor.

Poe Mill (Greenville, S.C.): Patterson, Pruitt, Heston, Huggins, Summer, Scott, Dudley, Osteen.

Judson Mill (Greenville, S.C.): Owens, Tallant, J. Cobb, Dempsey, Ward, L. Cobb, Wedd.

1935

Officers: John H. Garraux (Greenville, S.C.), President; Harley Heath (Pelzer, S.C.), Vice-President; Harry B. Jones (Greenville, S.C.), Vice-President; F.C. Garner (Greensboro, N.C.), Vice-President; O.S. Scarborough (Winnsboro, S.C.), Vice-President; J.B. Doar (Greenville, S.C.), Vice-President; J.F. Mason (Seneca, S.C.), Vice-President; Jesse D. Brown (Greenville, S.C.), Secretary; C.V. Verner (Piedmont, S.C.), Treasurer; Lucille Thomas (Greenville, S.C.), Girls' Hostess; G.L. Doggett (Greenville, S.C.), Boys' Host; Jimmie Thompson (Greenville, S.C.), Publicity Director.

CLASS A MEN

Dunean Mill (Greenville, S.C.), champions: Leonard Howard (coach), Clarence Thomas (coach), Sam Turner, Ralph Stroud, Willie Riddle, Winfred Kelly, Robert Donnan, Paul Barbare, Fred Ellenburg, Gary Benton.

Victor Mill (Greer, S.C.), runners-up: S.V. Wilson (coach), Charles Horne, Howard Maness, William Hewitt, Tillman English, William Waters, Wilton Pruitt, Charles Suddeth, Hubert Herrin, Ted Cabiness, William Hutchinson.

Poe Mill (Greenville, S.C.), consolation winners: Dick Wilson (coach), Bert Hill, G.K. King, Leon Dill, Earl Price, George Alverson, Leonard Barbare, Robert Stafford, William Kermode, J.L. Hadaway, G.W. Wright (mgr).

Monaghan Mill (Greenville, S.C.): A.J. McMinn (coach), Clyde Hudgens (coach), Woodrow Wakefield, Ralph Campbell, Lewis Elder, Wallace Foster, Harrison Waldrop, Daniel Bagwell, Eugene Randolph, Milwood Stephens, William Leister, Roberts, Chapman.

Lyman Mill (Lyman, S.C.): Buddy Sims (coach), Y.L. Senn (coach), Charles Reeves, Harry West, Durham Wideman, Roy Garrett, James McElveen, Halley Wilson, Rube Morgan, Runnie Pettigrew, Byrd Alexander, D.K. Smith.

Calloway Mill YMCA (LaGrange, Ga.): J.D. Tolbert (coach), Metz Cannon, James Mitchell, O.T. Kersey, Albert Conyers, Clarence Higgenbotham, James Brown, Curtis Bryant, Palmer Sheperd, Frank White, Nathaniel Slaughter Jr.

Southern Bleachery (Taylors, S.C.): A.W. Meisenheimer (coach), Marshall Wilson (coach), Joe Hendrix, George Blackwell, James Wilson, J.T. Langston, Ralph Coker, Estell Keeler, Charles Horton, James Gay, Carl Hughes, Lindsay Meisenheimer.

American Enka (Enka, N.C.): Andy Brandol (coach), Vincent Cooper, Clyde Merrill, Owen Morgan, Ray Norman, Troy Miller, Homer Johnson, Arthur Fincannon, Earle.

Pelzer Mill (Pelzer, S.C.): John Emery, J.E. Pickelseimer, Joe Jenkins, J.A. Rochester, Herman Jordan, David Hughes, Jack Jenkins, Gary Helms, Fred Ross.

Judson Mill (Greenville, S.C.): John Garraux (coach), J.W. James (coach), Frank McDaniel, Russell Chapman, Charles Cobb, Jack Sterling, Doris Broadwell, Paul Moreland, J.D. McAlister, R.P. Patillo, J.W. James, Dan Matthews.

Avondale Mill (Alexander City, Ala.): Charles Smith (coach), Phillip Avery, Bill Evans, David Long, Troy Holley, Lester Smith, Wilbur Payne, John Turner, Odell Roberts, Bruce Harris, Fred Boss, Collins.

Erlanger Mill (Lexington, N.C.): J.L. Blaylock (coach), J.J. Moon (coach), Carl Everhart, Henry Essick, Jacob Sowers, William Bell, James Link, Baster Young, Jack Childers, George Mauney, George Beeker, Lowns.

Glen Lowery Mill (Whitmire, S.C.): Archie Cheatham (coach), Jimmie James, Ted Black, Fred Grant, Troy Ward, Clarence Erskine, Clyde Brank, Fred Prather.

Walhalla Mill (Walhalla, S.C.): L.B. Elliott (coach), J.W. Mills, T.E. Alexander, L.R. Smith, C.W. Garrett, J.A. Gilliard, C.R. Gilliard, K.C. Hunt, W.M. Sanders, W.L. Sanders.

Manchester Mill YMCA (Manchester, Ga.):

Southern Textile Basketball Tournament Rosters Appendix 1 127

T.P. Barclay (coach), Walker Hilton, Fred Stewart, William Callaway, T.R. Byard, Wilson Casper, Jerry Canup, Merril Hurst, Robert Malcolm, James Meadors.

Chatham Mfg. (Elkin, N.C.): Hoyt Hambright (coach), Edd Maxwell, Abb Crater, Pete McBride, Charles Munday, Kermit Mackle, Harvey Stockton, Huber Mounce, Tat Davis, Charles Gough.

Winnsboro Mill (Winnsboro, S.C.): Jack Ohlsen (coach), Jimmie Herndon, Porter Frye, John Gunter, Thomas Shealy, Marvin Stevenson, Johnny Herndon, M.V. Wells, Coley Spigner, Peg Baker, Shirley.

Joanna Mill (Joanna, S.C.): A.B. Galloway Jr. (coach), Bruce Galloway, Fred Ross, Lumas Puckett, Eugene Abrams, Grady Spires, Charlie Girk, Thomas Gastley, Jack Hunnicutt.

Sylacauga Mill (Sylacauga, Ala.): C.C. Daly (coach), Grover Parker, James Persons, Robert King, Wilbourn Downs, Otha Nevins, Benjamin Haynes, Homer Ingram, Harold McCarty, William Stanton Jr., Leon Hammond, Noynes.

Ware Shoals Mill (Ware Shoals, S.C.): George Hughes (coach), Harry Eleazer, George Lewis, Charles Strickland, John Bedingfield, Barron McNinch, Melvin Tate, William Wright, James Lollis, Joseph Moore.

CLASS B MEN

Russell Manufacturing (Alexander City, Ala.), champions: S.R. Crew (coach), Vercho Carter (coach), Bruce McEachern, Floyd Blankenship, Paul Austin, Barto Hughes, Thomas Duke, Douglas Woody, J.C. Clements, Allen Clark Jr., Russell Turner, Ralph McGinty, Hubbles, Miller.

Brandon Mill (Greenville, S.C.), runners-up: Horace Whitmire (coach), Courtenay Heath (coach), Henry Bland, Arthur Carnes Jr., A.L. Estes, Fred Foster, Frank Freeman, Roy Huff, Ralph Kay, Dennis Loftis, Henry Smith, Ralph McDonald.

Drayton Mill (Spartanburg, S.C.), consolation winners: Ted Crain (coach), Leonard Hill, E.J. Johnson, S.W. Ray, Shuford Finley, James Paschal, L.E. Owens, Ray Lancaster, James Hughes, Ramon Kelly, Manning Bagwell.

Spartan Mill (Spartanburg, S.C.): L.T. Cothran (coach), W.G. Cothran, Robert York, George Biershank, Foster Chandler, Ralph Gibbs, Clinton Smith, J.R. Lands, Elmer Clubb, Douglass Cannon, Horace Sitton, Burdett.

Tryon Mill (Tryon, Ga.): J.C. Woods, Carl Ragland, Wilson Bigger, Howard Williams, Harold Yancy, James Williams, Ralph Hardeman, Clinton Norman.

Piedmont Mill (Piedmont, S.C.): Jack Gilreath (coach), R.W. Bowie (coach), Harry Waldrop, John Rampey, Leroy Hunnicutt, Roy Corbin, Clayton Boiter, James Terry, Ford Waldrop, Alton Patterson, Tom Pack.

Belton Mill (Belton, S.C.): J.B. Mitchell (coach), Carlton Nelson, Aubrey Shockley, George Stalcup, David Haynie, James Warnock, Floyd Cummings, William Sargent, Ira Thompson, James Nelson, Robert Hancock.

Chicopee Mill (Gainesville, Ga.): J.W. Brown (coach), T.H. Paris (coach), Royce Ramey, William Hatfield, Clifford Watter, Alfred Gunthrope, Joseph Smith, June Boggs, Aaron Moore, Dean Evans, John McDaniel, Carlton Mills.

Woodside Mill (Fountain Inn, S.C.): J.A. Mims (coach), E.P. Childress, Oscar Hallams, C.E. Godfrey, Wilton Shaver, J.W. McCall, Lloyd Childress, Arvin Weaver, James Stewart, George Parson, P.L. Woods.

Brandon Mill (Woodruff, S.C.): C.M. Padgett (coach), E.L. Leopard (coach), C.D. Padgett, Harold Taylor, Leroy Taylor, Edward Sanders, Harry Christopher, Edward Padgett, Frank Nabors, J.C. Fleming, F.L. Summey, Sam Williams, Clifford.

Stark Mill (Hogansville, Ga.): E.W. Roberts (coach), W.C. Hayes (coach), Carl Frazier, Lewis Hamer, John Copeland, William Barton, Rufus Bond, Horace Denny, James Lester, James Lunsford, Ervell Bussey, Martin.

Bacon Mill (Lenoir City, Tenn.): R.H. Babb (coach), Virgil Thomas, Cecil Thomas, Henry Foster, Homer Littleton, Raymond Derieux, R.H. Baskette, Raymond Clark, Gene Connor, Leland Monger, Denny.

Greer Mill (Greer, S.C.): Taylor, D. Smith, Giles, Burnett, Brewton, E. Smith.

Columbus Mill (Columbus, Ga.): Charlie Carmack, Harry Morgan, Harold Granberry, Pete Davis, Elmer Riddle, Woodfin Combs, E.G. Hubbard Jr., Charles Adams.

Pilot Mill (Valdese, N.C.): Lenoir Lowdermilk (coach), Edwin Flack, Laird Jacob, B.E. Scharaboro, Donald Campbell, Louis Vinay, Alex Vinay, John Bonner, John Garrou, Clyde Berry, Jean Dalmas Jr.

Collins & Aikman (Roxboro, N.C.): B.B.

Mangrum (coach), B.B. Knight (coach), Archie Walker, Sam Oliver Jr., Claude Wilborn, Emmett Wilborn, Enos Slaughter, Tommie Crowder, Carlton Slaughter, Ransome Frederick, Lester James, Jack Craven.

Sycamore Mill (Sycamore, Ala.): Homer White (coach), Herman Duke, Glenn Williams, William Cabe, Horace Barnes, Jack Blankenship, John King, John Roberson, Clyde Franklin, Woodrow Thurman, James Roberts.

Chiquola Mill (Honea Path, S.C.): Ollie Anderson (coach), Temp Thompson, Dwight McNinch, James Ivester, Melvin Carr, George Anderson Jr., Jap Simmons, Clifford Keasler, Clifton Dorn, Jean Belue.

Erwin Mill (Erwin, Tenn.): Oscar Simpson Jr. (coach), Gilbert Woodworth, Ernest Sewell, Walter Parker, Chester Taylor, Edwin Bost, William Few, Edgar Geddie, Edward Byrd, Lewis Stephenson, Thomas Ralph.

Anderson Mill (Anderson, S.C.): D.R. Simpson (coach), Harold Richardson, B.E. Kelly, Frank Ray, Norton Cole, William Gunter, A.M. Smith, Odell Spearman, Hugh Wofford, Frank Stovall, Leason Heaton, Sewell.

Slater Mill (Slater, S.C.): F.B. Pinson (coach), Furman Pinson, Clarence Wright, James Oglesby, Ralph Ellis, Cole Vaughn, Bill Lynch, Raymond Parnell, John McMakin, Price.

American Enka (Enka, N.C.): Andy Brandl (coach), Harold Gudger, Fred Allen, Wollner Gaston, William Condor, Coke Candler, Eugene Reece, Hubert Ray, Bryce Wright, Meld, Reed, Canton.

Poe Mill (Greenville, S.C.): Grady Holtzclaw (coach), Edward James, E.J. Whitehead, H.L. Vaughn, Louie Leaster, John Ferguson, J.B. Doar Jr., Fred Williams, Norman Roland, J.E. Hudgens.

Union Bleachery (Greenville, S.C.): Ralph Belcher (coach), Charles Brooks (coach), Cecil Brooks, Charles Brooks, Roy Robertson, Bruce Brown, William Nelson, William Dobbins, W.A. Bishop Jr., Hilliard Bradley, Hugh Lester, Allison.

Simpsonville Mill (Simpsonville, S.C.): Eugene Barbery (coach), Dewitt Gilliard, Jack Thackston, Harold Bagwell, James Hamby, William Coker, Robert Barbary, Truman Godfrey, Twyman Brashier, Arthur Waters, Harold Coker, Hammett.

Woodside Mill (Greenville, S.C.): A.H. Pollard (coach), J.W. Hill, Kenneth Clontz, Reuben Ramsey, Andrew Ramey, Leonard Canup, Charles Couch, Harry Mears, Truman Herbert, James Tucker, Dacus Stewart.

Appleton Mill (Anderson, S.C.): Alex Skelton (coach), Austin Elrod, Zamie Bowman, Roy Hall, Claud Spake, Clinton Cason, A.A. McClellan, Rodney Floyd, Sidney Bailey, Frank Moore, L.C. Bryant.

Victor Mill (Greer, S.C.): Milledge Brannon (coach), James Green (coach), Ben Burnett, Sanford Giles, Baxter Hemphill, C.M. Hemphill Jr., Leslie Brewton, Fred Smith, Edward Smith, Dennis Smith, Harold Forrester, Creighton Taylor.

Inman Mill (Inman, S.C.): L.B. Sheehan, John Bonham, Paul Rogers, Elijah Walker, Hayes Clark, Leonard Correll, Eulan Martin, Woodrow Abernathy, Lewis Howell, Earl Vaughn.

CLASS C MEN

Piedmont Mill (Piedmont, S.C.), champions: Seth Pack (coach), Bill Bolden (coach), Robert Traynham, Walter League, Fred Clifford, Joe Looney, Sloan Terry, J.D. Hunnicutt, Veldee Cooper, Harry Bishop, Charles Kimbo, Charles Poole.

Pelzer Mill (Pelzer, S.C.), runners-up: William Harris, David Jenkins, General Dickard, Willie Crymes, Horace Davenport, Ralph Cannon, J.W. Jordan, Galloway.

Judson Mill (Greenville, S.C.), consolation winners: James Duffie (coach), J.D. McAlister (coach), Harley Chapman, Mays Williams, Clyde Cobb, Leonard Kelly, Harold Compton, Homer Compton Jr., Ernest Driscoll, Ralph Lewis, James Forest, James Trammell.

Mills Mill (Greenville, S.C.): Thomas Pittman (coach), Grady Revis (coach), Harold Abbott, James Cothran, Frank Norris, Homer Shuttlesworth, H.Y. Simmons, John Hawkins, Fred Bridges, R.C. Toby, Charles Smith, James McCall Jr.

Greer Mill (Greer, S.C.): C.W. Flynn (coach), Raymond Smith, R.F. Roper, Fred Hemphill, Broughton Jones, Gresham Westmoreland, Leroy Walls, Roy Taylor, Carroll Belcher, Lewis Hemphill, Lewis Johnson, Walker.

Orr Mill (Anderson, S.C.): D.C. Jolly (coach), Joe Ashworth, Henry Buchanan, John Frith, George Jolly, Harry Davis, Baxter Gunnells, C.T. Cooper Jr., Robert Buchanan, William Hattaway, Jack Smith.

Brandon Mill (Greenville, S.C.): J.M. Bolt (coach), Humpie Lee (coach), Larry Campbell, Dewey Foster, Pete Huff, James Townsend, Howard Thackston, James Thomas, Tommie Whitmire, Milton Whitmire, Barney Fowler.

Dunean Mill (Greenville, S.C.): F.H. Hooper (coach), Charles Bragg, Thomas Turner, James Roddy, Roy Owens, James Gosnell, Carl Cox, Paul Case, Robert Cooper.

Glen Lowery Mill (Whitmire, S.C.): C.H. Brooks (coach), Grady Cabiness (coach), Eddie Franks, Carl Hester, Harry Summers, Charles Franks, F.L. Layton, Marion King, Richard Kohn, Curtis Watkins, Earl Prince, Ansel Bailey.

Monaghan Mill (Greenville, S.C.): Clyde Walls (coach), Thornwell Henson (coach), Ralph Snelson, Harmon Coleman, Lewis Coleman, Aaron Powers, C.D. Hughes, George Campbell, Eugene Ross, James Keller, Leroy Davis, Jack Gantt, Griffin.

Woodside Mill (Greenville, S.C.): Dewey Bowen (coach), Kenneth Bell, Buddy Hodge, Charles Freeman, James Payne, Frank Hines, J.H. Grice, Winston Herbert, Ralph Harbin, Fred Bomar, Harold McConnell.

Lyman Mill (Lyman, S.C.): Ligon Pettigrew (coach), Marshall Miller (coach), Alexander Milford, Russell Sheriff, Bockey Hilliard, Charles Mullinax, Loran Smart, Clayton Adams, Howard Aughtry, Winfred Humphries, Judson Sloan, Claude Cheek.

American Spinning (Greenville, S.C.): Gene Trammell (coach), Woodrow Fowler (coach), Homer Cooper Jr., George Spake, Thomas Trammell, Jackson Nix, Jack Putman, David McNeely, Jack Fowler, John Hollingsworth, Arvel Davis, Woodrow Wilson, Knox.

Victor Mill (Greer, S.C.): S.V. Wilson (coach), William Thornton, Don Jackson, Grady Burnett, Horace Myers, Robert Brown, Virgil Pruitt, Milton Maness, Richard Burnett, Wilburn Wilson, Ernest Poole.

Southern Bleachery (Taylors, S.C.): Walter Meisenheimer (coach), Lyles Alley (coach), Artie Barton, Charles Worley, Alvin Broadnox, Thomas Carr, Robert Edwards, Thomas Goodlett, Cloto Bridgeman, Barton Meisenheimer, Harold Forrest, Joseph Owens.

American Enka (Enka, N.C.): Andy Brandl (coach), J.C. Gibbs, Carl Brooks, Dennie Parris, Robert Scharff, Charles Lance, Garland Rogers, Homer Smith, Tarvis, Ray.

Poe Mill (Greenville, S.C.): Vernon Allen (coach), Paul Kinnett, Garvin Garrett, Lewis Grastie, William Allen, James Rogers, Joe Brown, Davis Scott, Marion Dudley, Robert Lister, Alvin Lancaster.

Lonsdale Mill (Seneca, S.C.): Clyde Davis (coach), W.T. Pruitt (coach), Clarence Gilliard, J.I. Crooks, Ralph James, George Morgan, Andrew Bell, Marvin Ledford, Hoyt Gibson, Delmar Chandler, Ulysses McDonald, McDaniel, Jones.

CLASS A WOMEN

American Enka (Enka, N.C.), champions: Louise Agee (coach), Lois Allen, Mary Byrd, Mary Clark, Minnie Fite, Terrell Hollifield, Susie Keys, Blanche Medford, Edith Morgan, Rozelle O'Kelly, Betty Osborne, Myrtis Prince, Agnes Parker, Allen, Robertson.

Stanly Mill (Oakboro, N.C.), runners-up: Venie Murphy (coach), Sarah Black, Grace Garrison, Velda Garrison, Virginia Hovis, Alzelene Johnson, Helen Withers, Ferol Norris, Gertie Hovis, Bessie Sherrill, Ralphine Johnson.

Lyman Mill (Lyman, S.C.), consolation winners: W.F. Howard (coach), W.O. Glasco (coach), Sarah McMakin, Gene Bright, Jewell Lawrence, Nina Barry, Azlee Hannon, Ann Mitchell, Louise Pruitt, Dorothy Cox, Mary Woodward, Sally Beach, Lena Pettigrew, Dessie Cannon.

Southern Worsted (Greenville, S.C.): C.S. Cathcart (coach), Roy Waldrop (coach), Sarah West, Evelyn Jones, Lottie Jackson, Baryie Jackson, Dorothy Sanders, Doris West, Florence Cathcart, Myrtle Davis, Russell Long, Argyl Hogg, Gladys Hogg, Thalia Hawkins, Brown.

American Spinning (Greenville, S.C.): H.L. Carter (coach), Hoyt Carter (coach), Ruby Nix, Nellie Miller, Frances Ward, Agnes Fowler, Frances Nix, Vina Miller, Sarah Nix, Ethel Miller, Lucille Fowler, Pearl Carter, Mary Neill, Moraine Lewis, Mooney.

Pelzer Mill (Pelzer, S.C.): Mrs. Harley Heath (coach), Lucia Holliday, Avis Dickson, Sarah Bass, Eva Saylors, Kathryn Ramey, Helen Kelly, Virginia Dickson, Sarah Jordan, Bill Terry, Ballard, Holliday.

Dunean Mill (Greenville, S.C.): C.H. Thackston (coach), Mary Smith, Mable Foster, Lula Case, Thelma Owens, Evelyn Putnam, Mary Wright, Mary Watson, Mildred Carpenter, Helen Johnson, Vera Blackwell.

Glen Lowery Mill (Whitmire, S.C.): Betty Douglas (coach), Willie Pruitt, Ruth Coggins, Mamie Ray, Hazel Suber, Agnes Campbell, Shady Huckaby, Rosa Hester, Helen Black, Sarah Dallas, Rosa Crow, Ruth Ray.

Class B Women

Renfrew Bleachery (Travelers Rest, S.C.), champions: Chester Eddy (coach), Thomas Nicholas (coach), Lena Foster, Sarah Ferguson, Lucille Runion, Linda Dunkin, Ruth McWilliams, Helen Hendricks, Reba Gantt, Fay Henderson, Eloise Lockaby, Edna Coleman, Madeline Hunt.

Drayton Mill (Spartanburg, S.C.), runners-up: Mrs. L.R. Corbin (coach), Mary Bobo, Margaret Smith, Wilma Whitlock, Ozie Duckett, Pauline Smith, Ruby Adams, Nina Smith, Ruth Bobo, Aubrey Cleveland, Bunice Owens, Blanche Osborne, Beulah Jackson.

Marion Mfg. (Marion, N.C.), consolation winners: J.L. Gourley (coach), Lucille Flack, Lucille Barnes, Alice Barnes, Gladys Hall, Vernie Epps, Annie Fisher, Margaret Gourley, Marjorie Rogers, Florence Epley, Grace Proctor.

Greer Mill (Greer, S.C.): C.O. Burnett (coach), Beulah Brewton, Pauline Brewton, Eleanor Giles, Eva Hemphill, Annie Woodward, Annie Wright, Nora Marcus, Tamar Durham, Etta Wright, Frances Hemphill, Mavoureen Giles.

Union Bleachery (Greenville, S.C.): H.C. Harrison (coach), Ophelia Brooks, Virginia Gibson, Frances Harrison, Clinton Hester, Ellen Johns, Hattie Johns, Nellie Phillips, Beulah Robertson, Katherine Turner, Evelyn Youngblood, Audrey Epps, Mildred Harrison, Cecil Brooks.

Victor Mill (Greer, S.C.): Frances Finley (coach), Emma Cook, Mildred Finley, Nellie Hughes, Anita Thornton, Grace Tipton, Sarah Tucker, Lee Turner, Fannie Vaughn, Augusta Waters, Maggie Wilson, Irene Miller, Agnes Mayfield, Wharton.

Mollohon Mill (Newberry, S.C.): J.C. Kilgore (coach), Mary Day, Lola Gowan, Mary Suit, Eva Reeves, Lois Willis, Ruby Burton, Hilliard Jackson, Paul Stribble, Melzie Martin, Dorothy Longshore.

Aiken Mill (Bath, S.C.): Mrs. W.F. Lipford (coach), Lillian Sizemore, Sallie West, Mamie Williams, Cleda Beard, Gladys Bandy, Lena Friar, Kathleen McElhaney, Dorothy Bridges, Dorothy Strong, Lucille Cunningham.

Slater Mill (Slater, S.C.): F.B. Pinson (coach), Viola Willis, Olean Babb, Dorothy Rogers, Iva Springfield, Aileen Springfield, Willie Southerlin, Ruth Goodwin, Eunice Allen, Lillian Wood.

Poe Mill (Greenville, S.C.): Paul Kinnett (coach), Marie Davis (coach), Hazel Scott, Evelyn Dill, Frances Hudgens, Ellen Patterson, Virginia Block, Vera Williams, Margaret Roberson, Willie Burrell, Ruby Heaton, Frances Summer, Lula Prewett, Louise McDowell.

American Enka (Enka, N.C.): Louise Agee (coach), Pauline Brown, Mildred Crownover, Hazel Davis, Elizabeth Holcombe, Frederica Ingle, Virginia Lamb, Eretha Maney, Doris Penland, Lillian Wilkie, Prince.

Simpsonville Mill (Simpsonville, S.C.): G.P. Garrett (coach), Mary White (coach), Boots Devall, Louise Cannady, Louise Calvert, Inez Haney, Helen Waldrop, Helen Brashier, Minnie Cox, Willie Stephens, Ruth McKay, H. Calvert, Thackston.

Brandon Mill (Greenville, S.C.): Arthur Carnes (coach), Kascenia Aiken, Mildred Barnett, Evelyn Baker, Margaret Baker, Irene Foster, Gaynelle Heath, Nancy Kay, Ruth Loftis, Katherine Masters, Elizabeth Mahon, Eva McCall, Villa Porshea.

Judson Mill (Greenville, S.C.): R.R. Pridmore (coach), Janett Cobb, Ganell Owens, Elizabeth Owens, Ruby Ward, Frances Holland, Sarah Cordell, Margaret Allen, Judith Bishop, Vera Blakely, Theora Broadwell, Clara Gosnell, Mildred Hembree, Ward.

Monaghan Mill (Greenville, S.C.): Fred Ellis (coach), Ruth Ellis, Ruth Powers, Evelyn Bishop, Margaret Summers, Georgia Ross, Louise Anderson, Hazel Sanders, Jewell Jones, Udine Murray, Rose Gantt, Retha Huggins, Louise Suddeth.

Inman Mill (Inman, S.C.): Lillian McHam, Myrtle McHam, Clara Emory, Louise Walker, Marie Bryson, Annie Fisher, Jessie Johnson, Cora Fox, Helen Fennell, Jewel Lewis, Jennie Lewis, Josephine Carter.

---1936---

Officers: John H. Garraux (Greenville, S.C.), President; Harley E. Heath (Pelzer, S.C.), Vice-President; O.S. Scarborough (Winnsboro, S.C.), Vice-President; C.V. Verner

Southern Textile Basketball Tournament Rosters Appendix 1 131

(Peidmont, S.C.), Vice-President; J.B. Doar (Greenville, S.C.), Vice-President; J.F. Mason (Seneca, S.C.), Vice-President; Jesse D. Brown (Greenville, S.C.), Secretary; C.L. Eddy (Renfrew, S.C.), Treasurer; Lucille Thomas (Greenville, S.C.), Girls' Hostess; Louise Agee (Enka, N.C.), Ass't Girls' Hostess; G.L. Doggett (Greenville, S.C.), Boys' Host; Jimmie Thompson (Greenville, S.C.), Publicity Director.

CLASS A MEN

Chatham Mfg. (Elkin, N.C.), champions: Hoyt Hambright (coach), Ab Crater, Clarence Davis, Kermit Mackie, Don Campbell, Heber Mounce, Ed Maxwell, Pete McBride, Fred Hambright, Delos Jones, Scott Fitzgerald, Morrell, Corky Cornelius.

Piedmont Mill (Piedmont, S.C.), runners-up: Leroy Anderson (coach), J.M. Terry (coach), John Emery, Seth Pack, Tom Pack, Alton Patterson, J.W. Rampey, Curtis Terry, Ford Waldrop, Harry Waldrop, Roy Corbin.

Proximity Mill (Greensboro, N.C.), consolation winners: W.J. Pennington (coach), Ellis Brasher, Lawrence Murphy, Lawrence Edwards, Henry Coe, Roe Deaton, Howard Boone, William Walker, Corliss Garner, Archie Baynes, Carlyle Davis, Herndon.

Erwin Mill (Erwin, Tenn.): Oscar Simpson Jr. (coach), Fred Parker, Alton Stephenson, Edwin Bost, William Aiken, Chester Taylor, William Hickle, Ralph Erwin, Ernest Sewell, Edward Byrd, Walter Parker, Findler.

Brandon Mill (Woodruff, S.C.): C.M. Padgett (coach), Esco Leopard, C.D. Padgett, Harold Taylor, J.C. Flemming, George Blackwell, Leroy Taylor, Eugene Teague, F.D. Sumner, Austin Littlejohn, Dennis Loftis.

American Enka (Enka, N.C.): S.G. Morse (coach), Fred Allen, Coke Chandler, Bill Conder, Vincent Cooper, Wallner Gaston, Louis Goslin, Harold Gudger, Troy Miller, Owen Morgan, Herman Perritts.

Pelzer Mill (Pelzer, S.C.): H.P. Suddeth (coach), David Hughes, Joe Jenkins, James Picklesimer, Fred Ross, Clarence Allen, Ed Dickard, Willie Crymes, Herman Jordan, Guines, Dickinson, Dixon.

Dixie Mercerizing (Lupton City, Tenn.): A.L. Johnston (coach), Melvin Seals, Carl Phillips, Lester Smith, Tyrus Coppinger, Emmett Harris, T.L. Pierce, Dave Telford, Bill Evans.

Judson Mill (Greenville, S.C.): John H. Garraux (coach), Sam Moreland (coach), Dan A. Matthews, Russell Chapman, Frank McDaniel, Doris Broadwell, James Hall, Clarence Rushing, J.W. James, R.P. Patillo, Marshall DeFoor, M.W. Rogers, Hill.

Woodside Mill (Greenville, S.C.): A.E. Wilson (coach), Otto Herbert (coach), Carlton Couch, Charles Couch, J.W. Hill, James Tucker, Leonard Canup, Truman Herbert, J.D. Justice, Woodrow Eskew, Dewey Bowen, Andrew Ramey, Hall.

Monaghan Mill (Greenville, S.C.): A.J. McMinn (coach), Clyde Hudgens (coach), Jessie Hudgens, Marchant Cottingham, Ralph Campbell, Fletcher Heath, Harrison Waldrop, Milwood Stephens, Daniel Bagwell, Wallace Foster, Lewis Elder.

Monaghan Mill "Night Owls" (Greenville, S.C.): Harry Herron, Harry Daurenheim, Theodore Henderson, Ammons Galloway, Ralph Snelson, Thornwell Henson, Carl Nolin, Lee Coleman, Clyde Christopher, R.E. Roberts.

Ware Shoals Mill (Ware Shoals, S.C.): Charles Strickland, Melvin Tate, Grier Wright, Ray Wilson, George Mabry, John Beddingfield, Woodrow Sanders, Barron McNinch, John Culbertson, James Lollis.

Dunean Mill (Greenville, S.C.): Leonard Howard (coach), Carroll Owens, William Riddle, James Suddeth, Lewis McDonald, Robert Donnon, Clarence Thomas, Jackson Bell, Ralph Stroud, Fred Ellenburg.

Brandon Mill (Greenville, S.C.): J.M. Bolt (coach), Bert Martin (coach), Henry Bland, James Carnes, Leland Estes, Fred Foster, Charles Foster, Roy Foster, Courtenay Heath, Ralph McDonald, Ralph Morgan, Henry Smith.

Walhalla Mill (Walhalla, S.C.): William Leister (coach), Ray Smith, Johnny Gilliard, Gene Alexander, Coley Garrett, Williard Mills, J.B. Elliott, Clarence Morton, Raymond Gilliard, Winfred Littleton, Gannett.

Victor Mill (Greer, S.C.): S.V. Wilson (coach), Broadus Cabiness, Grady Burnett, Richard Burnett, Tillman English, Wilton Pruitt, Willie Hutchinson, William Waters, Hubert Herrin, Lloyd Horton, Virgil Pruitt.

Winnsboro Mill (Winnsboro, S.C.): Harry Sargent, Eben Reid, Marvin Stephenson, Reggie Baker, Melvin Wells, Johnny Herndon, Leonard Culclasure, Porter Frye, Bill Wells, Culclasure.

Joanna Mill (Joanna, S.C.): Galloway, Ross, Gastley, Moore, Abrams, Hunnicutt, Spires, Charlie Girk.

Southern Bleachery (Taylors, S.C.): Suddeth, Gay, Keeler, Adair, Swails, Lancaster, Maness, Hughes, Wall.

Class B Men

Judson Mill (Greenville, S.C.), champions: Tap Pack (coach), Lad Maxwell (coach), James Trammell, Arley Chapman, Harley Chapman, Paul Moreland, Ray Casey, Leonard Kelly, James Forrest, Ernest Driskell, Gordon Rayburn, William Tidwell.

Chicopee Mill (Gainesville, Ga.), runners-up: J.W. Brown (coach), Tom Paris (coach), Ralph Smith, Newton Boleman, Carlton Miller, June Boggs, Dean Evans, Paul Smith, Hugh Boleman, Aaron Moore, Young Sailors, John McDaniels.

New Holland Mill (Gainesville, Ga.), consolation winners: Rhett Turnipseed (coach), Bonnell Jarrard, James Patterson, Jack Jenkins, Selma Maddox, David Strickland, Felix Forrester, James Wilson, T.J. Chapman, Winton Coker.

Cramerton Mill (Cramerton, N.C.): R.W. Dyer (coach), Z.V. Brindle, R.R. Leeper, L.B. Keeter, W.W. Stowe, V.L. Reece, S.W. Keeter, J.A. Reece, S.R. Brindle.

Dunean Mill (Greenville, S.C.): F.H. Hooper (coach), Roy Owens, James Gosnell, Paul Case, Thomas Turner, Charles Bragg, Fred Floyd, Robert Cooper, Carl Cox, William Suggs.

Fairfax Mill (Fairfax, Ala.): Sam Mason (coach), Allen Reeves, Ralph McGinty, Walker Dixon, Julian Dixon, Richmond Pearson, Earl Gresham, Lester McCormick, James Yarborough, James Barnes, Money.

Greer Mill (Greer, S.C.): James Greene (coach), C.M. Hemphill Sr. (coach), Claudius Hemphill Jr., William Smith, Charlie Taylor, Sanford Giles, James Barton, John Belcher, John Brewton, Lenhardt Roper, Ben Burnett.

Lonsdale Mill (Seneca, S.C.): W.C. Pruitt (coach), J.F. Mason (coach), J.A. Bell, U.K. McDonald, George Morgan, Rufus Trantham, Ernest Dooley, Charlie Owens, Ralph James, Lasco Alsep, Clyde Davis, Hoyt Gibson, Troutman.

Inman Mill (Inman, S.C.): E.G. Ammons (coach), S.B. Smith (coach), Pete Raymond, James Corell, Thomas Rogers, Woodrow Abernathy, George Clark, Walter Dotherow, Elijah Walker, Hubert Cashion, John Bonham, James Shehan.

Equinox Mill (Anderson, S.C.): J.M. McAlister (coach), Bill Webb, William Lyles Jr., Frank Cole, Negrous Kelley, Thomas Ray, Clay Allen, R.L. Vickery, Willie Webb.

Columbus Mill (Columbus, Ga.): A.D. Reeves (coach), Charles Carmack, Harry Morgan, Harold Granberry, Robert Harrison, James Matthews, Elmer Riddle, Woodfin Combs, Charles Adams, Dan Voight.

Sayles Biltmore Bleachery (Biltmore, N.C.): W.D. Wright (coach), Fletcher Brown, William Ford, James Riley, Carroll Lance, George Davis Jr., John Cooke, Owen Roberts, Kenneth Bartlette, Richard Garrison, Luther King, Owens.

Pilot Mill (Valdese, N.C.): Clarence Rhoney, Paul Flack, Claude Owens, Alexander Vinay, Louis Vinay, John Bounous, Harlin Murray, Lenoir Lowdermilk, Laird Jacob, Howard Pruette, Ebony.

Chiquola Mill (Honea Path, S.C.): James Huskey, Clifton Dorn, Clifford Keasler, Ollie Anderson, James Ivester, Dwight McNinch, James Thompson, Frank Greer, George Scott, David Carr, Thrift.

American Spinning (Greenville, S.C.): C.A. Bowers (coach), Edgar Major (coach), Ford Garrison, Melvin Roberts, Beauford Davis Jr., Robert Nix, George Spake, Lester Lewis, Woodrow Putman, Jack Fowler, Homer Cooper, Sidney Wilson.

Drayton Mill (Spartanburg, S.C.): Ted Crain (coach), Mud Owens (coach), L.E. Owens, E.L. Johnson, Raymond Kelly, Leonard Hill, Suford Finley, James Hughes, George Hughes, E.L. Davis, Paul Burnett, J.C. Matthews.

Pacific Mill (Columbia, S.C.): D. Pursley, Gordon, Cooper, R. Pursley, Briggs, Darby, Porter, McWhorter.

Appleton Mill (Anderson, S.C.): Alex Skelton (coach), Claude Spake, Fred Powell Jr., William Cason, Roy Hall, M.A. Pruitt, Hugh White, L.E. Smith, Robert Church, Bill Hendrix, D.R. McAllister.

Brandon Mill (Greenville, S.C.): Fred Mahon (coach), W.L. Foster (coach), Frank Freeman, Ralph Dickert, Clyde Batson, R.L. Gambrell, Paul Hollingsworth, Charlie Johnson, Buford McCarson, John Smith, Robert Sheppard, Charles Rogers.

Southern Textile Basketball Tournament Rosters   **Appendix 1**   133

Woodside Mill (Fountain Inn, S.C.): John Harrison (coach), James McCall, Wilton Shaver, James Stewart, James Moore, Henry Giles, Clarence Godfrey, Ervin Weaver, Arvin Weaver, P.L. Woods, Paul Evatt.

Marion Mfg. (Marion, N.C.): Terry Moon (coach), T.R. Whetstine (coach), John Jolly, Charles Hall, Verl Wood, Robert Burgin, James Brooks, John Hunt, J.W. Davis, Millard Hall, Roger Flack, James Lawrence.

Spartan Mill (Spartanburg, S.C.): Biershenk, Cothran, Chandler, Gibbs, Cannon, Sands, Lawless, Smith.

Piedmont Mill (Piedmont, S.C.): Jack Gilreath (coach), Joe Looney, Robert Traynham, Charles Poole, Fred Clifford, J.D. Hunnicutt, Lee, Sam League.

Southern Bleachery (Taylors, S.C.): Smith, Harley, Bridgeman, Brownlee, Owens, Bryant, Edwards, Bridgeman, Goodlette.

CLASS C MEN

Pelzer Mill (Pelzer, S.C.), champions: Alfred Gosnell (coach), J.W. Jordan, R.M. Cannon, M.M. McCall, H.M. Davenport, E.D. Galloway, L.W. Woodcock, W.G. Harris, W.M. Floyd, L.T. Harris.

Victor Mill (Greer, S.C.), runners-up: H.L. Greer (coach), Thomas Tipton (coach), William Thornton, Donald Jackson, Conway Myers, Wilburn Wilson, Troy Brown, Lloyd Campbell, Milton Maness, Buddie Bennett, Eugene Lowe.

Orr Mill (Anderson, S.C.), consolation winners: D.C. Jolly (coach), Troy Kirby (coach), Henry Buchanan, Harry Davis, Baxter Gunnells, George Jolly, Charles Buchanan, Claude Turner, Willard Ashworth, James Hawkins, Hugh Wofford.

Spindale Mill (Spindale, N.C.): Rollins, Morris, Yelton, Cline, Yelton, Hamrick, Grayson, Felton, Hampton, Heffner, Templeton, Hill.

Dunean Mill (Greenville, S.C.): C.M. Campbell (coach), Paul Putman, William Johnson, Karry Landers, Tommy Roddy Jr., James Sheppard, Frank Lynn, Minor Christopher, William Putnam, Carl Holland, Robert Snoddy.

Equinox Mill (Anderson, S.C.): J.B. Spearman (coach), Tyle Vickory (coach), Clarence Boyles, Donnie Irby, Hubert Vickery, Lusco Goodson, Randolph Gibbs, James Meredith, Odell Scarborough, J.D. Smith, Cecil McCully, Roy McCully.

Woodside Mill (Greenville, S.C.): R.N. Ramsey (coach), Eugene Campbell (coach), John Hardin, Joe Whitmire, Ray Herbert, James Pitts, Fred Bomar, John Harbin, John Hines, Roy Reeves, Charles Freeman, Kenneth Bell.

Camperdown Mill (Greenville, S.C.): J.H. McDowell (coach), Jamie Dill, Fred Johnson, Charles Whitaker, Louie McDowell, William Landreth, James Bruce, Dennis Whitaker, Benjamin Landreth, George Mattox Jr., James Goodwin.

Belton Mill (Belton, S.C.): Ira Thompson (coach), Ray Snipes (coach), Thomas Cheatham, J.C. McAlister, James Deanhardt, Marvin Shaw, John Cummings, Sherman Carlton, Walter Nelson, J.T. King, Fred Stalcup, Hugh Moore.

Judson Mill (Greenville, S.C.): John Garraux (coach), John Trammell (coach), J.D. McAlister (coach), J.B. Adams, Ossie Sheck, Harold Compton, Robert Junkin, Nathan DeFoor, Clyde Cobb, Mays Williams, Paul Hazel, Dock Treadway, Narlan Duncan.

Anderson Mill (Anderson, S.C.): Barney Smith (coach), Marvin Cargill, William Embler, Claude Reeves, Alvin Patterson, George Long, John Stastney Jr., L.T. Embler, James Craft, Otis Buchanan, Oscar Snyder.

Simpsonville Mill (Simpsonville, S.C.): D.L. Goodenough (coach), A.J. Barbare, R.E. McKay, Wilton Coker, Robert Thackstone, Lee Bagwell, Larry Coker, Willie Cox, Earl Brashier, Charles Brashier, Willie Hinton, Gary, Peden, Young, Cothran.

Brandon Mill (Greenville, S.C.): J.A. Carnes (coach), Ralph Kay (coach), Barney Fowler, Andrew Kay, Earl Bawlin, Dewey Foster, Bobbie Fortune, James Thomas, Howard Thackston, Larry Campbell, J.W. Townsend, B.H. Huff.

Poe Mill (Greenville, S.C.): Jim McDowell (coach), Lewis Lister (coach), Jack Williams, James Rogers, David Scott, Paul Kennedy Jr., Lewis Grastie, James Mundy, Robert Lister, Woodrow Davis, Warren Heaton, D.J. Brown, McCullum.

Union Bleachery (Greenville, S.C.): Clyde Harrison (coach), Charles Brooks (coach), Ansel Bridwell, Roy Brooks, McClure Epps, Walker Dilworth, William Harrison, Tom Robertson, Harold Green, Clarence Green, Woodrow Taylor, James Starkey.

Piedmont Mill (Piedmont, S.C.): Leonard

Waldrop (coach), S.C. Hawkins (coach), Fred Collins, Charles Bass, George Buckheister, Billie Wilson, Larry Walker, Frank Grover, Jamie McCall, Ralph Clark, A.C. Taylor, Howard Humphries.

Monaghan Mill (Greenville, S.C.): J.W. Ross (coach), Phillip Stewart, Jack Gantt, Clayton Langston, Charles Glascoe, Joe Bagwell Jr., Leroy Davis, Franklin Griffith, Willie Ross, Maxwell Coleman, Allen Keller, Garrett.

Inman Mill (Inman, S.C.): Eugene Davis (coach), J.C. Davis (coach), James Bagwell, Norman Jenkins, Durward Mason, Arthur Jackson, Robert Moore, Dennis Gray, Thomas Miller, William Rogers, Ralph Ramsey.

Greer Mill (Greer, S.C.): C.W. Flynn (coach), Gresham Westmoreland, Broughton Jones, Roy Taylor, Carroll Belcher, Lewis Hemphill, Jack Lee, Fred Hemphill, Dewey Moore, Raymond Smith, Leo Bishop.

Mills Mill (Greenville, S.C.): Ansel Abbott (coach), Tom Ingle (coach), Harold Abbott, Wilburn Trammell, James Hawkins, Frank Norris, Albert Osborne, James Bridges, R.D. Cothran, Ansel McCallister, James McCall Jr., Homer Shutteworth.

Winnsboro Mill (Winnsboro, S.C.): Marvin Stevenson (coach), W.L. Collins, Russell Collins, Bryce Wages, Herbert Hoover, Charlie Mixon, Albert Molner, George Osborne, J.B. Enloe.

Class A Women

American Enka (Enka, N.C.), champions: Louise Agee (coach), Lois Allen, Mary Byrd, Mary Clarke, Mildred Crownover, Eloise Glass, Elizabeth Holcombe, Susie Keys, Blanche Medford, Jessie Mills, Betty Osborne, Doris Penland, Mertis Prince, Slaps, Susie Simmons.

Pelzer Mill (Pelzer, S.C.), runners-up: R.R. Hood (coach), Harley Heath (coach), Sarah Jordan, Avis Jordan, Leoda Jordan, Helen Kelly, Virginia Dickson, Lucia Holliday, Eva Saylors, Blanch Littlefield, Inez Dickson, Emma Coker, Flora Addison.

Lyman Mill (Lyman, S.C.), consolation winners: Lyles Alley (coach), Mary Woodward, Ann Cobb, Jackie Starnes, Virginia Harley, Nina Barry, Louise Smith, Doris Smith, Jewel Lawrence, Sally Beach, May West, Azalea Hannon, Sarah McMakin, Harley.

Dunean Mill (Greenville, S.C.): Mrs. Lucille Thomas (coach), Josie Barr, Lula Case, Olive Tinsley, Mable Foster, Catherine Stafford, Vera Blackwell, Helen Johnson, Mary Smith, Mildred Carpenter, Evelyn Putnam, Geraldine Owens, Margaret Donnan.

Renfrew Bleachery (Travelers Rest, S.C.): C.L. Eddy (coach), Margaret McKinney, Grace Werner, Rheba Gantt, Edna Brown, Lena Foster, Ruth McWilliams, Fay Henderson, Lois Tollison, Madeline Hunt.

Stanly Mill (Oakboro, N.C.): Sara Black, Venie Murphy, Helen Withers, Alzelene Johnson, Virginia Hovis, Helen Garrison, Valda Garrison, Rita Garrison, Ruth McKelvey, Bessie Sherrill, Feral Morris, Addie Felton.

Class B Women

Drayton Mill (Spartanburg, S.C.), champions: L.R. Corbin (coach), Bill Whitlock (coach), Floreine Switzer, Audrey Cleveland, Marguerite Hudgens, Pauline Smith, Geneva Jarrett, Ruby Adams, Ruth Bobo, Mary Bobo, Beulah Splawn, Cornelia Harley, Katherine Harley, Mary Whitlock.

Judson Mill (Greenville, S.C.), runners-up: Mrs. Robert Pridmore (coach), Red Pridmore (coach), Elizabeth Owings, Jannett Cobb, Ruth Barr, Ruby Ward, Evelyn Ashmore, Frances Von Holland, Sarah Cordell, Margaret Allen, Odett Rhymer, Dorothy Dover, Dorothy Wood.

Slater Mill (Slater, S.C.), consolation winners: F.B. Pinson Jr. (coach), Elizabeth Babb, Mary Wood, Frances Ellis, Aileen Springfield, Ivah Springfield, Minnie Southerland, Glynda Hill, Ruth Goodwin, Lila Wood, Viola Willis.

Union Bleachery (Greenville, S.C.): M.F. Evatt (coach), Harold Thompson (coach), Frances Harrison, Katherine Turner, Beulah Robertson, Irene Ivey, Ophelia Brooks, Audrey Epps, Elizabeth Johns, Annie Evington, Mary Robertson, Nellie Phillips, Mary Ivey, Eppley.

Monaghan Mill (Greenville, S.C.): Edith Henson (coach), Inez Brown (coach), Mildred Bishop, Virginia Suddeth, Frances Blackstone, Mary Foster, Margaret Summers, Georgia Ross, Rose Gantt, Hazel Sanders, Euddine Murray, Sybil Sheppard, Frances Anderson.

Marion Mfg. (Marion, N.C.): Mrs. Terry Moore (coach), Jack Jolly (coach), Lucille Flack, Gladys Hall, Vernie Epps, Alice Barnes, Grace Moore, Margie Rogers, Juanita Moody, Mary L. Barnes, Maude Hennessee, Florence Eppley, Pearl Eppley.

Pilot Mill (Valdese, N.C.): F.L. Jacobs (coach), Addie McCloud, Adeline Perron, Stella

Sinclair, Willie Bradshaw, Ruby Bowman, Vergie Wright, Margie Rudisill, Anna Rhoney, Mary Cline, Mary Pons, Essa Hood.

Poe Mill (Greenville, S.C.): Paul Kinnett (coach), Maria Davis (coach), Frances Sumner, Elva McCallum, Mary Hudgens, Willie Burell, Ellen Patterson, Louise McDowell, Hazel Scott, Ruby Heaton, Lula Pruitt, Ida Rader, Avinell McCollum, Eva Black.

Inman Mill (Inman, S.C.): Mrs. E.G. Ammons (coach), N.G. Hardie (coach), Ruby Jenkins, Helen Smith, Josephine Cartee, Marie Bryson, Ruby Lewis, Wilmer Walker, Clara Emery, Helen Fennell, Annie Fisher, Ruth Waldrop, Elsie Smith, Margaret Rodgers.

Brandon Mill (Greenville, S.C.): Villa Porshea (coach), Mrs. W.R. Foster (coach), Agnes Edwards, Grace Bright, Myrtle Lee, Eva McCall, Mary Loftis, Clara Loftis, Elizabeth Martin, Evelyn Baker, Margaret Baker, Gaynelle Heath, Irene Foster, Janell Gambrell.

Chatham Mfg. (Elkin, N.C.): Claudia Austin (coach), Frances Rothrock, Madia Swain, Lila Swain, Grace Mosencup, Melba Poole, Linda Fisher, Mildred Poole, Lillian Myers, Hixie Ashe, Madie Austin, Margaret Taylor, E. Swain.

1937

Officers: Harley Heath (Pelzer, S.C.), President; Horace Whitmire (Greenville, S.C.), Vice President; Leonard Howard (Greenville, S.C.), Vice President; O.S. Scarborough (Winnsboro, S.C.), Vice President; Joe Lyons, Anderson, S.C., Vice President; C.V. Verner (Piedmont, S.C.), Vice President; John H. Garraux (Greenville, S.C.), Secretary; C.L. Eddy (Renfrew, S.C.), Treasurer; Louise Agee (Enka, N.C.), Assistant Girls' Hostess; G.L. Doggett (Piedmont, S.C.), Boys' Host; Jimmie Thompson (Greenville, S.C.), Publicity Director.

CLASS A MEN

Southern Bleachery (Taylors, S.C.), champions: Lyles Alley (coach), L.S. Meisenheimer, James Gay, Clarence Rushing, Charles Brooks, Ben Burnett, Alvis Hendley, Charles Suddeth, Bert Hill, Herbert Wall, Howard Maness, Wilson, Barbery, Nau.

Spartan Mill (Spartanburg, S.C.), runners-up: L.T. Cothran (coach), J.H. Calvert (coach), Douglass Cannon, Ralph Dodd, C.B. Mooneyham, C.E. Trammell, J.H. Calvert, George Biershank, Bud Kinard, Dennie Hendrix, A.B. Posey.

Judson Mill (Greenville, S.C.), consolation winners: John Garraux (coach), Frank McDaniel, James Trammell, Paul Moreland, J.D. McAlister, Leonard Kelly, James Hall, Charles Cobb, Harold Compton, J.W. James, Bill Tidwell.

Woodside Mill (Greenville, S.C.): Domer Reeves (coach), Carlton Couch, Otto Herbert, Leonard Canup, Charles Couch, C.E. Heath, Truman Herbert, J.D. Justus, James Tucker, Andrew Ramey, Lloyd Hendricks.

Walhalla Mill (Walhalla, S.C.): Lee Smith, Louie Elliot, Coley Garrett, John Smith, Johnny Gaillard, Willard Mills, Raymond Gaillard, Winfred Littlejohn, Sanders.

Victor Mill (Greer, S.C.): S.V. Wilson (coach), William Thornton (coach), Wilton Pruitt, Grady Burnett, William Arledge, Alvin Waters, Richard Burnett, Donald Jackson, Willie Hutchinson, Troy Brown, Markham Ballenger, Troy Westmoreland.

Drayton Mill (Spartanburg, S.C.): Ted Crain (coach), Walter Crain, I.W. Owens, E.L. Johnson, Manning Bagwell, Ralph Gibbs, J.D. Morgan, R. Stallings, Leland Estes, Joe Durham, Harry Smith.

American Enka (Enka, N.C.): Andy Brandl (coach), Robert LeRoy (coach), Owen Morgan, Vincent Cooper, Carl McCain, Charles Munday, Fred Allen, Coke Candler, Harold Gudger, Mitchell Gaddy, Wollner Gaston, Louis Gosselin.

Brandon Mill (Greenville, S.C.): J.A. Carnes Sr.(coach), S.G. Bagwell (coach), J.A. Carnes Jr., Alvin Jenkins, Ralph McDonald, Ralph Morgan, Henry Thackston, Floyd Smith, James Townsend, Roy Foster, Charles Foster, Henry Bland, C. Foster.

Dixie Mercerizing (Lupton City, Tenn.): Harry Anderson (coach), Melvin Seals, Carl Phillips, Eddie Lewis, James Dean, William Millsaps, Everett Martin, Emmett Harris, Charles Cox.

Greer Mill (Greer, S.C.): L.C. Taylor (coach), Woodrow Hanvey, Clarence Flynn, Landrum Taylor, Sanford Giles, Lenhardt Roper, Charles Taylor, Thomas Smith, Dennis Smith, John Bruton, Harold Forrester, G.L. Belcher.

Brandon Mill (Woodruff, S.C.): C.M. Padgett (coach), C.D. Padgett, John Fleming,

George Blackwell, Dennis Loftis, Robert Barbery, LeRoy Taylor, Howard Taylor, Dan Kirby, Edward Padgett, Eugene Teague.

Chicopee Mill (Gainesville, Ga.): J.W. Brown (coach), J.A. Neighbors (coach), Aaron Moore, Arthur Hudgens, Newton Boleman, Edward Doss, Ralph J. Smith, Hayne DeLong, June Boggs, Levis Clarke, Ralph E. Smith, Boleman.

Monaghan Mill (Greenville, S.C.): Lee Coleman (coach), Sam Moreland (coach), Dan Bagwell, Harry Davernheim, Nick Elder, Wallace Foster, J.C. Hudgens, Bud Stephens, Harrison Waldrop, W.W. Wakefield, Harry Herring.

Equinox Mill (Anderson, S.C.): Allen Parnell (coach), Reese Allen, Frank Ray, Clenton Cole, R.L. Vickery, Clay Moore, Glenn Smith, George Harper, Bill Webb, William F. Webb, Clint Cason, Hendrix.

Dunean Mill (Greenville, S.C.): Ronald Donnan (coach), C.H. Thomas (coach), Lewis McDonald, Robert Donnan, William Riddle, Paul Case, Ralph Stroud, Clarence Thomas, Fred Floyd.

Columbus Mill (Columbus, Ga.): A.D. Reeves (coach), Harry Morgan, Bryan Harrison, Jack Able, Fred Hurston, Elmer Riddle, Carval Hubbard, Charlie Carmack, W.F. Richardson Jr., Woodfin Combs, Oscar Noble, Pete Davis.

Monaghan Mill Owls (Greenville, S.C.): C.F. Stensell (coach), A.J. McMinn (coach), Theodore Henderson, Ralph Snelson, Amos Galloway, Emil Langston, Hannon Reid, Woodrow Mattox, Ed Ballenger, Ralph Campbell, Wideman Durham, Lewis Cook.

Lyman Mill (Lyman, S.C.): D.N. Murph (coach), Ted Cabiness, Roy Garrett, Paul Edwards, James McElveen, Buddy Simms, Byrd Alexander, Runnie Pettigrew, Harry West, J.W. McMakin, Patterson.

Inman Mill (Inman, S.C.): E.G. Ammons (coach), Guy Emory (coach), Harold Vaniewsky, Paul Rogers, Sidney Vaniewsky, Howard Steadman, Virgil Abernathy, George Clark, Walter Dotherow, Robert Shehan, Leonard Correll, Preston Fisher.

Pelzer Mill (Pelzer, S.C.): R.R. Hood (coach), C.C. Roberts (coach), Ralph Cannon, Bill Jordan, Horace Davenport, Willie Crymes, Fred Ross, Curtis Walker, Clarence Allen, Manly McCall, David Galloway, Buck Harris.

Glen Lowery Mill (Whitmire, S.C.): R.E. Beck (coach), Teddy Black, Troy Ward, Richard Kohn, E.L. Layton, Clyde Branks, P.E. Tarte Jr., Fred Prather, Fred Grant, Ansel Bailey, Summey, Cabiness.

Piedmont Mill (Piedmont, S.C.): Harry Waldrop (coach), Leroy Anderson (coach), Ford Waldrop, J.D. Hunnicutt, John Emery, Edgar Patterson, Curtis Terry, Robert Traynham, Charles Poole, John Rampey, Jerry Underwood, Walter League.

Lonsdale Mill (Seneca, S.C.): J.F. Mason (coach), Eddie Weathers, Frank Galliard, George Morgan, Ralph James, Wilton Shaver, W.T. Pruitt, Lasco Alsep, Harold Burroughs, Ulysses McDonald, Clyde Davis.

Class B Men

Peerless Woolen Mill (Rossville, Ga.), champions: Paul Ellis (coach), Mike O'Neal, Clinton Norman, Phil Thach, Jack Bailey, Fred Carter, William Cordell, Sam Millsaps, Arthur Brown, Kenneth Farmer, Bennett, Osteen, Rogers.

Fairfax Mill (Fairfax, Ala.), runners-up: Sam Mason (coach), Ralph McGinty, Chester Jersey, Lester McCormick, George McGinty, Horace Denny, James Waldrop, James Barnes, Edge.

Winnsboro Mill (Winnsboro, S.C.), consolation winners: R.M. Frew (coach), Homer Sargent Jr., W.L. Collins, A.M. Troyano, C.F. Cline Jr., Charles Mixon, Ed Ward, Oscar Collins, Bill Barfield, Gary Brunnemer, Mason, Musfield.

Abbeville Mill (Abbeville, S.C.): T.J. Kelly (coach), O.B. Duffie (coach), Ralph Simpson, Charles Timmons, Leslie Wilson, Ralph Wilson, N.B. New, Russell Sammeth Jr., Rayford Carroll, C.B. Williams, William McCurry, Rufus Powell.

Draper Mill (Draper, N.C.): Frank Stein (coach), Lawson Talbott, Clyde Powell, Edward Gerringer, Carl Powell, William East, Harold Squire, Thomas Murphy, Oaklet Burnett, James Marlowe, Doris Shropshire.

Dunean Mill (Greenville, S.C.): Paul Bogan (coach), Hoyl Snoddy (coach), Clarence Odell, William Reese, Arthur Riddle, Robert Cooper, C.T. Bullock, Tommy Plumley, Roy Owens, Otis Putman.

Martha Mill (Thomaston, Ga.): W.M. Gunter (coach), John Lawhorn, Louis Mitchell, E.S. Scott, Evans Morgan, Clarence Ard, William DeVaughn, Erving Mitchell, Louis

Southern Textile Basketball Tournament Rosters Appendix 1 137

Matthews, Tuck Bethel, Raymond Winover, Earls.

New Holland Mill (Gainesville, Ga.): R.R. Turnipseed (coach), T.J. Chapman, David Strickland, James Wilson, Roy Jenkins, Sylvester Jones, Bonnell Jarrard, Selma Maddox, Felix Forrester, Winton Coker, Randolph Chapman.

McEwen Mill (Burlington, N.C.): Ralph Berryhill (coach), John Lloyd, Arlie Hahn, Stephen Collins, William Slaughter, Joseph Cox, Thomas Frazier, Raymond Simmons, Louis Johnson, Dewey Melton.

Brandon Mill (Greenville, S.C.): Ralph Kay (coach), Fred Foster (coach), Jesse Ross, James Thomas, Larry Campbell, John Smith, Fred Cox, Pete Huff, James Dickard, Dewey Foster, Bobbie Fortune, Roy Hawkins.

Erlanger Mill (Lexington, N.C.): J.J. Moon (coach), J.C. Childers (coach), Conrad Madison, Raymond Crowell, Roy Bell, Fred Crowell, R.H. Shoaf, Sam Jenkins, Dennis Talbert, Claude Johnson, Howard McGinn, Howard Phillips.

American Spinning (Greenville, S.C.): Edgar Harbin (coach), J.M. Trammell (coach), Frank Cooper, George Deanhardt, Ford Garrison, Hoot Major, Jack Putman, Claud Crawford, Arvil Davis, J.H. Hollingsworth, George Spake, Weaver Hunter.

Union Bleachery (Greenville, S.C.): Q.M. Rhodes (coach), James Ivey (coach), Roy Robertson, B.C. Hawkins, Ray Starkey, Cecil Brooks, Barrett Aycock, William Nelson, John Floyd, Jack Dilworth, William Force, William Bishop.

Lyman Mill (Lyman, S.C.): J.P. Edwards (coach), Frank Mullinax, James Cobb, Claude Cheek, Floyd English, Winfred Humphries, Howard Aughtrey, Clayton Adams.

Woodside Mill (Greenville, S.C.): Cleveland Collins (coach), R.N. Ramsey, Woodrow Lee, Fred Pitts, Clyde Hodge, Clifton Collins, Dacus Stewart (coach), Winston Herbert, Frank Hines, Robert Byers, J.H. Grice, Everett Waldrop.

Mills Mill (Greenville, S.C.): J.A. Coggins (coach), Thomas Ingle (coach), Charles Abbott, Harry Smith, A.C. Capps, Albert Henry, E.F. McAlister, Carl Henry, James Bridges, James Hawkins, Thomas Abbott, M.E. Clark.

Piedmont Mill (Piedmont, S.C.): Leonard Waldrop (coach), J.R. Shirley (coach), A.C. Taylor, Fred Collins, Joe Looney, George Buckheister, O.V. Lee, Fred Clifford, Jamie McCall, Sloan Terry, Frank Grover, B.F. Evans.

Slater Mill (Slater, S.C.): W.C. Lynch (coach), James Oglesby (coach), R.E. Ellison, Arthur Garrett, Frank Julian, Furman Pinson, Colie Vaughn, Ralph Ellis, Lonzo Hart, Aaron Powers, Clarence Wright, Hembree.

Spray Mill (Spray, N.C.): J.K. McConnell (coach), Bethel Washburn, John Gallimore, Clyde Carter, Audrey Grogan, Eldridge Lovell, William Royster, Carlyle Barksdale, D.C. Williams, Payton Jefferies, Latcher Webster, Simmons, H. Carter.

Threads Inc. (Gastonia, N.C.): J. Witten (coach), James Morgan, Raymond Buckner, John Koppen, James Black, John Moore, R. Wilson, Nick Kerhulas, John Leary, Frank Melton, Clyde Cloniger.

Other Teams: **Judson Mill** (Greenville, S.C.); **Equinox Mill** (Anderson, S.C.); **Anderson Mill** (Anderson, S.C.); **Ninety Six Mill** (Ninety Six, S.C.).

CLASS C MEN

Woodside Mill (Greenville, S.C.), champions: Bud Hodge (coach), Dewey Bowen (coach), John Hardin, Monroe Ramsey, Charles Freeman, Joe Whitmire, H.E. McConnell, Charles Payne, Ralph Harbin, Fred Bomar, Douglas Smith, Andrew Manley.

Judson Mill (Greenville, S.C.), runners-up: John Harbin, John Hall, Harold Ledford, David Greer, Ralph Williams, Knarlan Duncan, J.B. Durham, Carven Landreth, Paul Hazel, Lewis Case Jr.

Greer Mill (Greer, S.C.), consolation winners: James Greene (coach), M.L. Brannon (coach), Furman Taylor, Jack Lee, Roy Taylor, Carroll Belcher, Dewey Moore, Edwin Redmon, James Burnett, Fred Hemphill, Raymond Smith, Charles Jones.

Ninety Six Mill (Ninety Six, S.C.): L.H. McNeil (coach), Howard McAbee (coach), Alvin Drummond, Harold Ivester, Buna Wells, Luke Woods, Calvin Drummond, Bill Voiselle.

Camperdown Mill (Greenville, S.C.): J.W. McDowell (coach), Charlie Penland (coach), James Dill, Dennis Whitaker, W.A. Dickens Jr., Walter Goodwin, George Mattox Jr., William Landreth, Charles Whitaker, Fred Johnson, Melvin Gunter, Lottie McDowell.

Victor Mill (Greer, S.C.): B.J. Nix (coach), Conway Meyers (coach), Walter Godfrey, Dewey Painter, Buddie Bennett, Junior Pruitt,

Fred Wilkins, Lewis Rodgers, Lloyd Horton, Wilburn Wilson, William Meyers, S.V. Wilson Jr., Campbell.

Converse Mill (Spartanburg, S.C.): H.B. Davis (coach), Charles Wooten, Pete Fowler, Sebo Green, Roy Reid, Voyle Massey, James Mason, Grady Henderson, Richard Evans, Paul Mathis, Hugh Lark.

Pelzer Mill (Pelzer, S.C.): A.B. Benton (coach), George Ray (coach), Liston Woodcock, Wyatt Garrett, Charles Crawford, Telford Harris, Cyrel Haney, J.P. Floyd, C.B. Crymes, Jack Coker, Roy Vehorn.

Union Bleachery (Greenville, S.C.): Robert Price (coach), Clarence Greene, Charles Epps, Roy Brooks, William Harrison, Joe Robertson, Walker Dilworth, McClure Epps, Harold Greene, Ansel Bridwell, W.M. Burns.

Peerless Woolen Mill (Rossville, Ga.): Walter Lauter (coach), Carl Crosslin, J.M. Blake, Bill French, Shelby Akers, Courborn Raider, Fred Moody, Ernest Carson, Tyrus Arnold, Robert Green, Clifford Gilreath.

American Spinning (Greenville, S.C.): Buster Morton (coach), Thurman Morgan Jr., Alfred Belt, Willard Bagwell, Bill Morgan, James Reid, James McCullough, Hillard Hainey, Lewis Gosnell, Wesley Gilstrap.

Inman Mill (Inman, S.C.): Paul Ballew (coach), Elijah Walker (coach), Percival Cashion, Norman Jenkins, C.W. Abernathy, Wesley Jackson, Ralph Ramsey, Frank Miller, Robert Martin, Edward Culbreth, Hugh Rogers, Dennis Gray.

Joanna Mill (Joanna, S.C.): A.B. Galloway Jr. (coach), Rhett Abrams, James Simpson, Clisby Templeton, Tillman Morse, Olga Hair, James Brown, Crawford Starnes, Rudolph Prater, Cecil Farmer.

Mills Mill (Greenville, S.C.): R.R. Brock (coach), J.B. McCall (coach), William Henry, J.B. Osborne, Dewey Lowery, Claude Chapman, Edgar Trammell, Ansel McAlister, Charles Pearson, W.G. Suttlesworth, R.D. Smith, Lester Ball.

Anderson Mill (Anderson, S.C.): Barney Smith (coach), Clint Cole (coach), William Embler, Carter Gaines, James Cobb, Otis Buchanan, George Long, Oscar Snyder Jr., Stephen Cason, Alvin Patterson, Richard Hammonds, Howard Smith.

Slater Mill (Slater, S.C.): Doots Wright (coach), J.H. Oglesby (coach), William Clark, Marion Douglas, William Ivester, James McMakin, Harold Taylor, Fayte Cody, Robert Ellis, Clarence Mars, Gilbert Rogers, Leslie Wood, Dudley.

Orr Mill (Anderson, S.C.): D.C. Jolly (coach), Troy Kirby (coach), Albert Seymour, James Hawkins, Arnold Brown, J.T. Perrin, Robert Lyons, C.W. Blackwell Jr., Mackay Gunnells, Ray Perry, Henry Buchanan.

Monaghan Mill (Greenville, S.C.): J.W. Ross (coach), T.W. Henson (coach), Franklin Griffith, Allen Keller, C.H. Langston, Phillip Stewart, James Keller, Alriage Oglesby, Fred Bagwell, Andrew Gantt, Thomas Stevens, Carlos Thompson, J. Miller.

Ware Shoals Mill (Ware Shoals, S.C.): Lawrence Weir (coach), B.U. White (coach), Cary Futch, Horace Thompson, Henry Simpson, Deck Gray, Jerome Davis, Wesley Shaver, Dwight McNinch, Adger Culbertson.

Spartan Mill (Spartanburg, S.C.): L.T. Cothran (coach), C.R. Smith (coach), James Burwell, Garland O'Shields, J.F. Smith Jr., Elmer Johnson, Ralph Lands, Dick Condry, Cecil Lands, Johnnie Burch, C.R. Smith, Lloyd Crowe.

Dunean Mill (Greenville, S.C.): Fred Hooper (coach), C.M. Campbell (coach), Bruce Mosley, M.L. Christopher, Thomas Roddy, William Gilmore, Carl Holland, William Johnson, Robert Snoddy, Raymond Putman, Paul Putman, William Putman.

Poe Mill (Greenville, S.C.): Paul Kennett (coach), George Alverson (coach), Joe Westmoreland, George Dudley, Bill Williams, Roy Rogers, Everette Pittman, David Scott, Bill Wilson Jr., Robert Lester, Carlos Grastie, Woodrow Davis, Lewis Grastie.

Equinox Mill (Anderson, S.C.): J.B. Spearman (coach), Ralph Parnell (coach), Ralph Gibbs, Clarence Voyles, James Meredith, Hubert Vickery, Fred Harbin, Odell Scarborough, J.D. Smith, James Simpson, Luiaco Goodson, Furman Johnson.

CLASS A WOMEN

American Enka (Enka, N.C.), champions: Louise Agee (coach), Lois Allen, Beulah Brown, Mary Byrd, Mary Clarke, Mildred Crownover, Geneva Burnett, Blanche Medford, Jessie Mills, Betty Osborne, Mertis Prince, Jennie Robertson, Nell Summer.

Chatham Mfg. (Elkin, N.C.), runners-up: Claudia Austin (coach), A.R. Plaster (coach), Melba Poole, Addie Biddix, Cleo Dunn, Lena

Smith, Elsie Gatewood, Lelia Swain, Mildred Poole, Linda McIlwee, Alene Matthews, Kathryn Whitner, Hattie Robbins.

Judson Mill (Greenville, S.C.), consolation winners: Ellen Switzer (coach), Janett Cobb, Lille Westmoreland, Louise Calvert, Ruth Barr, Janie Duncan, Elizabeth Owings, Ruby Ward, Louise Cobb, Velva Owens, Ethel Trammell, Willie Mae Garrett.

Lanett Mill (Lanett, Ala.): Fred Ballenger (coach), Agnes Wood, Florie Lovelace, Virginia Edwards, Louise Wood, Mary Jenkins, Matilee Smith, Rosa Looser, Mary Rainey, Cornell Webb, Lula Looser, Ruth Reed, Laura Looser, Allen.

Stanly Mill (Oakboro, N.C.): Venie Murphy (coach), Betty Abernatty, Sarah Black, Bessie Sherrill, Rita Garrison, Grace Garrison, Alzelene Johnson, Helen Withers, Dorothy Clemmer, Willards.

Inman Mill (Inman, S.C.): Mrs. E.G. Ammons (coach), Margaret Rodgers (coach), Margie Emory, Clara Emory, Ruth Collins, Ruth Rogers, Annie West, Louise Lewis, Wilma Walker, Mildred Jenkins, Annie Fisher, Ruth Waldrop, Marie Bryson, Josephine Cartee.

Drayton Mill (Spartanburg, S.C.): L.R. Corbin (coach), Ruth Bobo, Cornelia Harley, Ruby Adams, Kathryn Harley, Tamar Durham, Mary Bobo, Florence Switzer, Wilma Whitlock, Rachel Durham, Beulah Splawn, Nell Jackson, Pauline Smith.

McEwen Mill (Burlington, N.C.): Pauline Blanchard, Paittie McAdams, Thelma Combs, Margaret Long, Ruth James, Kathleen Jones, Gertrude Faucette, Annie Blanchard, Betty Beale, Obera Jones, Polly Gentry, Louise Pender.

Pelzer Mill (Pelzer, S.C.): A.C. Gosnell (coach), M.M. Taylor (coach), Sarah Jordan, Leoda Jordan, Inez Dickson, Bertha Whitt, Beatrice Crymes, Emma Davenport, Imagene Hanvy, Eva Saylors, Kitty Frick, Lucia Holliday, V. Dickson, Erick.

Glen Lowery Mill (Whitmire, S.C.): Aliene Pearce (coach), Thelma Puckett, Shady Huckabee, Agnes Bailey, Ruth Coggins, Doris Hembree, Helen Black, Corrie McKain, Lena Evans, Louise Horton, Iva Black.

Lyman Mill (Lyman, S.C.): W.F. Howard (coach), Mary Woodward, Gena Bright, Louise Smith, Azalia Hannon, Ann Cobb, Virginia Harley, Nina Barry.

Winnsboro Mill (Winnsboro, S.C.): R.M. Frew (coach), Mary Waters, Myrtis Sturky, Willie Summer, Mildred Hackle, Margaret Walsh, Bernice Branham, Lois Collins, Dorothy Howell, Velma Baggatt, Virginia Coker, Margaret McFie, Ruby Sargent.

Dunean Mill (Greenville, S.C.): Mrs. Clarence Thomas (coach), Mrs. F.L. Hooper (coach), Margaret Donnan, Mildred Carpenter, Lula Case, Olive Tinsley, Josie Barr, Annette Smith, Mary Smith, Vera Blackwell, Evelyn Putnam, Mabel Foster, Myrtie Mason, Violet Bowman.

Calhoun Falls Mill (Calhoun Falls, S.C.): B.K. Sharp (coach), Sarah Jordan, M.M. Harrison, Tabitha Thomas, Nena Martin, Esma Harrison, Fannie Davis, Ruby Wilhite, Marion Lander, Edna Jones, Inez Jones, Edna Chastain, Lane.

Pilot Mill (Valdese, N.C.): Lenoir Lowdermilk (coach), Virgie Wright, Adeline Perron, Addie McClure, Willie Bradshaw, Margie Rudisell, Stella Sinclair, Juanita Elliot, Anniebelle Rhoney, Margie Hildebrand, Ruth Gossage, Juanita Lowdermilk, Mary Cline.

1938

Officers: Harley Heath (Pelzer, S.C.), President; Horace Whitmire (Greenville, S.C.), Vice-President; Leonard Howard (Greenville, S.C.), Vice President; O.S. Scarborough (Winnsboro, S.C.), Vice President; Ted Crain (Spartanburg, S.C.), Vice President; John H. Garraux (Greenville, S.C.), Secretary; C.L. Eddy (Renfrew S.C.), Treasurer; Louise Agee (Enka, S.C.), Assistant Girls' Hostess; G.L. Doggett (Piedmont, S.C.), Boy's Host.

CLASS A MEN

Southern Bleachery (Taylors, S.C.), champions: Lyles Alley (coach), Herbert Wall, Ray Wilson, Ben Burnett, Charles Suddeth Jr., Charles Nau, Charles Barbary, Bert Hill, L.S. Meisenheimer, Alvis Hendley Jr., Howard Maness.

Piedmont Mill (Piedmont, S.C.), runners-up: J.M. Terry (coach), Leroy Anderson (coach), John Emery, James Terry, Harry Waldrop, J.D. Hunnicutt, Charles Poole, Robert Traynum, Ford Waldrop, Pat Patterson, John Rampey, Tom Pack, Clarence Emery.

Winnsboro Mill (Winnsboro, S.C.), consolation winners: H.M. Frew (coach), Ed Ward, Homer Sargent, T.L. Shealy, Marvin Stephenson, W.L. Collins, Bob Smith, Charlie Mixon, Gary Brunnemer, C.F. Cline, M.V. Wells.

Pelzer Mill (Pelzer, S.C.): H.G. Smith (coach), Willie Crymes, J.W. Jordan, Ralph Cannon, Dan Kirby, Horace Davenport, Fred Ross, Paul Byars, Earl Byars, Curtis Walker, M.D. Helms.

Chicopee Mill (Gainesville, Ga.): J.A. Neighbors (coach), Ralph Smith, Joe Smith, Lewis Clark, Junius Boggs, Hayne DeLong, Charles Strickland, Hugh Dorsey, Robert Abercrombie, Arthur Hudgens.

American Enka (Enka, N.C.): Andy Brandl (coach), Sam Patton, Owen Morgan, Bob Stafford, Vincent Cooper, Charles Munday, Fred Allen, Russell Allen, Carl McCain, Holly Hipps, Wollner Gaston.

Greer Mill (Greer, S.C.): H.H. Burgin (coach), C.W. Flynn (coach), Paul Moreland, Sanford Giles, Leslie Bruton, Charlie Taylor, Lenhardt Roper, Thomas Smith, Landrum Taylor, Dennis Smith, Woodrow Harvey.

Columbus Mill (Columbus, Ga.): A.D. Reeves (coach), Carval Hubbard, Charlie Carmack, John Goodwin, W.F. Richardson Jr., A.B. Brown Jr., Pete Davis, Elmer Riddle, Woodfin Combs, Bryan Harrison, Fred Hurston, Julius Martin.

Dunean Mill (Greenville, S.C.): Clarence Thomas (coach), Oscar Cox, Otis Putnam, Paul Case, Earl Cooper, Ralph Stroud, Willie Riddle, Clarence Odell, Robert Donnan, Samuel Turner, Roy Owens.

Brandon Mill (Woodruff, S.C.): C.M. Padgett (coach), Dennis Loftis, Edward Padgett, C.D. Padgett, Harold Taylor, Leroy Taylor, Lewis Keesler, Thomas Gastly, Charles Blanton, J.C. Flemming, Travis Wall.

Judson Mill (Greenville, S.C.): James Hall (coach), James Trammell, Henry Bland, Leonard Kelly, Mays Williams, Charles Cobb, J.W. James, Fountain Williams, Ossie Sheck, W.T. Tidwell.

Glen Lowery Mill (Whitmire, S.C.): William Bryce (coach), Harry Summers, Ansel Bailey, Fred Prather, Clyde Brank, Ted Black, Y.L. Puckett, Richard Kohn.

Peerless Woolen Mill (Rossville, Ga.): Paul Ellis (coach), Phil Thack, Dick Osteen, William Cordell, Fred Carter, Clint Norman, Kenneth Farmer, Sam Milsaps, Ted Rogers.

Walhalla Mill (Walhalla, S.C.): Lee Smith (coach), Johnnie Galliard, Coley Garrett, John Smith, William Robinson, Lewis Sanders, Harold Williams, Wilmer Sanders, Winfred Littleton, Louie Elliott, Rochester.

Drayton Mill (Spartanburg, S.C.): L.R. Corbin (coach), J.D. Morgan, Bus Huffstetler, Roy Durham, Boyd McCraw Jr., John Lacey Jr., Joe Durham, Elbert Johnson, Manning Bagwell, Ralph Gibbs, Edward Kirby Jr.

McCrary Hosiery Mill (Asheboro, N.C.): Paul Cheek (coach), Stuart Flythe, Neil Cockerham, Carlos Halleman, Paul Roy, Henry Essick, Ernest Swing, William Wright, Lawrence Edwards, Wilbur Rogers.

Monaghan Mill (Greenville, S.C.): C.F. Stancell (coach), S.R. Moreland (coach), Wideman Durham, William Stephens, Harry Herring, Jesse Hudgens, Wallace Foster, Fletcher Heath, Daniel Bagwell, Thomas Henderson, Nich Elder, M.C. Cottingham.

CLASS B MEN

Union Bleachery (Greenville, S.C.), champions: Charles Brooks (coach), Cecil Brooks (coach), W.A. Bishop, Roy Brooks, Walker Dillworth, Jack Dillworth, Ansel Bridwell, Howard Holt, B.C. Hawkins, Harold Green, Vladimir Melnikoffe, Belcher, Epps, Turner, Harrison.

Mills Mill (Greenville, S.C.), runners-up: Tom Ingle (coach), James Hawkins (coach), James Trammell, William Shuttleworth, Charles Porter, Frankie Norris, Albert Osborne, James Bridges, Cecil Hawkins, Frank Saxton, Harold Abbott, A.C. Capp.

Southern Bleachery (Taylors, S.C.), consolation winners: Sherman Bridgeman (coach), Clysses Bridgeman (coach), Harold Forrest, William McCain Jr., Clarence Smith, Edward Smith, Robert Barbare, George Brownlee Jr., Artie Barton, James Jones, Clato Bridgeman, Wilburn Asbury.

Piedmont Mill (Piedmont, S.C.): Steve Pack (coach), Leroy Hunnicutt (coach), George Buckheister, Ray Darnell, Veldee Cooper, Frank Grover, Fred Collins, Sloan Terry, Cliff Clark, Gomer Evans, Fred Clifford, Eddie Dill, Graves.

Abbeville Mill (Abbeville, S.C.): A.D. Simpson (coach), Ralph Wilson, Charles Williams, Ralph Simpson, Preston Able, James Blanchett, Miller New, William Crews, Leslie Wilson, Sterling Hall, James McDonald.

Poinsett Mill (Greenville, S.C.): James

Southern Textile Basketball Tournament Rosters Appendix 1 141

Townsend (coach), Milton Freeman (coach), Elbert Lavender, Paul Fair, Robert Hodge, James Millwood, Johnnie Freeman, Monroe Millwood, Marion Butler Jr., James Alexander, Arthur Bridwell, Townsend.

Southern Worsted (Greenville, S.C.): James Loftis (coach), Thomas Fowler, Thomas McCauley, John Vess, William Vess Jr., James Simpson, Eli Williamson, Robert Flynn, Bobo Long, Thomas Smith Jr.

Woodside Mill (Greenville, S.C.): Dewey Bowen (coach), Cleveland Collins (coach), Ralph Harbin, Monroe Ramsey, Fred Bomar, Maxwell Hardin, Fred Pitts, Frank Hines, Harold McConnell, Charles Freeman, Andrew Manley, R.N. Ramsey, M. Massey.

Converse Mill (Spartanburg, S.C.): H.B. Davis (coach), George Fowler, Charles Reid, Voyle Massey, Vance Powers, Theron Evans, William Croxdale, Sephas Green, Hugh Lark, Hugh Howard, James Quinn.

Brandon Mill (Greenville, S.C.): L.P. Loftis (coach), Ralph McDonald (coach), Robert Gambrell, Jesse Ross, Luther McBee, Dewey Foster, Larry Campbell, B.H. Ruff, Walter Sayers, Harold Fowler, Earl Bowlin, James Thomas.

Southern Franklin Processing (Greenville, S.C.): L.A. Burgess (coach), Edwin Briggs, Jeremiah McNeely, Jonas McNeely, James Watson, James Trammell, Clyde Lollis Jr., Hilliard Jones, Thomas Rice, Arthur Moody, Marion Butler Jr.

Pacific Mill (Columbia, S.C.): L.A. White (coach), William Gordon, Oliver Gordon, James Gordon, Francis Jennings, Joseph Bertram, Herbert Knox, Clarence Pursley, Homer Sturkie, Albert McQuarters, Oliver Darby.

CLASS C MEN

Southern Bleachery (Taylors, S.C.), champions: Lyles Alley (coach), Ernest Bridgeman, Hilliard Bridgeman, Waymon Edwards, Warren Trammell, Willie Bishop, James Epting, Bernice Bowers, Thomas Batson, Jimmie Bull, Lloyd Edwards, Long, Hammett, McNamara, Nichols, Forrest.

Peerless Woolen Mill (Rossville, Ga.), runners-up: Walter Lauter (coach), Ty Arnold, Ernest Carson, Orville Boren, William French, Fred Mandy, Roger Bennett, Jennings Green, William Crow, Carl Crosslen, Burlin Green, Coulbourne Raider.

Pelzer Mill (Pelzer, S.C.), consolation winners: C.C. Roberts (coach), J.P. Floyd, Jack Coker, Telford Harris, William Harris, Harold Ross, Luther Autry, Charles Crawford, Cryal Haney, Truman Gains, Garvin Pridmore.

Spartan Mill (Spartanburg, S.C.): L.T. Cothran (coach), C.R. Smith (coach), Lester Eledge, Lewis Mahaffey, Robert White, John Earnhart, Garland O'Shields, Dick Condrey, Walter Lands, Ralph Lands, Lewis Burch, James Smith.

Lonsdale Mill (Seneca, S.C.): J.F. Mason (coach), Clyde Davis (coach), Frank Whitt, Joe James, Ostell Shirley, Harley James, Garnett Latham, Horace Gaillard, Ross Morgan, Joe Mattison, Ralph Maxie, James Black.

Joanna Mill (Joanna, S.C.): R.P. Gowan (coach), D.E. Abrams (coach), Morton Hamm, Algie Abrams, Olga Hair, Cecil Farmer, Putman Morse, Rudolph Prater, Vernon Rowe, Clisby Templeton, Ralph Prater.

Greer Mill (Greer, S.C.): W.W. Hanvey (coach), F.B. Jones (coach), Ader Hardin, Furman Taylor, Woodrow Taylor, Everett Pate, Fred Hemphill, Dewey Moore, Robert Brown, Wallace Taylor, James Burnett, Wyatt Copeland, Smith.

Orr Mill (Anderson, S.C.): Troy Kirby (coach), David Price (coach), Arnold Brown, Harman Gunnells, C.W. Blackwell, Ralph Sanders, C.H. Turner, Ben Day, John Perrin, J.R. Ashworth, W.N. Burriss, Milford Ellison.

Poe Mill (Greenville, S.C.): Paul Kinnett (coach), Dude Grastley (coach), Alvin McCall, Bill Williams, J.R. Westmoreland, William Bright, John Spencer, Forest Kinnett, Roy Morgan, James Pittman, James Rogers, Rufus Vaughan, Marion Dudley, Dudley.

Mills Mill (Greenville, S.C.): Thomas Putman (coach), J.B. McCall (coach), Cecil Lowery, Troy Laws, Earl Cooper, D.A. Lowery, Boyce Couch, R.D. Smith Jr., Charles Pearson, Ansel McAlister, Clark Henry.

Brandon Mill (Greenville, S.C.): James Carnes (mgr), Charles Foster (coach), John Barnett Jr., Robert Ingle, Barnell Morrow, J.B. Friar, Charles Ross, Furman Mahon, Earl Reeves, Roy Duncan, John Whitmire, Joe Anders.

American Spinning (Greenville, S.C.): Velt Nix (coach), Edgar Harbin (coach), Wallace Miller, James Bolt, Carl Summey, Norman McDaniel, Williard Bagwell, William Morgan, James McCullough, Ansel Hollingsworth, Thurman Morgan, Jack Fowler.

Equinox Mill (Anderson, S.C.): Allen Parnell (coach), J.B. Spearman (coach), Wade Sanders, James Simpson, Jack Smith, E.L. Harbin, John Cheek, William Meredith, Randy Gibbs, Jerry Goodson, Ernice Voyles, Hubert Vickery.

Camperdown Mill (Greenville, S.C.): C.E. Penland (coach), Louie McDonald (coach), Melvin Gunter, George Maddox, Alvin Burnett, Enoch Copeland, Harold Davis, Frank Goodwin, Dennis Whitaker, Haskell Goodwin, Fred Johnson, Mack Bruce.

Monaghan Mill (Greenville, S.C.): A.J. McMinn (coach), Thornwell Henson (coach), James Worley, Franklin Griffith, Palmer McAvoy, Marion Ross, Jack Campbell, Allen Keller, Carlos Thompson, Fred Bagwell, Robert Campbell, John Oglesby.

Slater Mill (Slater, S.C.): F.V. Weathers (coach), James Oglesby (coach), Charles Clark, Marion Cody, Ernest Ellis, W.M. Lybrand Jr., Gartnell McDuffie, James McMakin, Wade Puckett, Gilbert Rogers, Harold Taylor, William Cashion.

Victor Mill (Greer, S.C.): B.J. Nix (coach), Lloyd Compton (coach), George Painter, Junior Pruitt, Stanyarn Wilson, Jerome Smith Jr., Leon Bennett, William Myers, Proctor Wood, Charles Putman, Marion Tucker, Andrew Cabiness.

Judson Mill (Greenville, S.C.): Frank McDaniel (coach), Tap Pack (coach), William Grissop, Carvin Landreth, James Case, Bruce Davis, Roy Cobb, James Long, Paul Hazel, Narlan Duncan, David Greer, Furman Blakely.

Dunean Mill (Greenville, S.C.): C.M. Campbell (coach), William Gilmore, Fred Parks Jr., Fred Snoddy, W.G. Stroud Jr., Jess Putman, Aubrey Jones, Thomas Roddy Jr., Marion Donnan, William Johnson Jr., Lee Christopher Jr.

Abbeville Mill (Abbeville, S.C.): Rayford Carroll (coach), O.B. Duffie (coach), Ray Duffie, Oscar New, Gordon Campbell, William Woolbright, William Cox, George Powell, Alfred Woolbright, Lee Fossett, Ira Lewis, John Barton.

Woodside Mill (Greenville, S.C.): Ray Herbert (coach), Carlton Couch (coach), Clyde Richard, Douglas Smith, Alvin Chapman, Charlie Payne, Manly Sanders, Julian Pruitt, Veldee Hines, James Neece, Carlos Reeves, Charley Phillips.

Simpsonville Mill (Simpsonville, S.C.): E.M. Goodenough (coach), J.C. Hamby (coach), Willie Cox, Robert Cox, Earl Brashier, Charles Hamby, Horace McKay, Richard Terry, Bernice West, Charles Brashier, Odell Barbery, L.A. Coker.

CLASS A WOMEN

Chatham Mfg. (Elkin, N.C.), champions: Claudia Austin (coach), Russell Plaster (coach), Aldie Biddix, Cleo Dunn, Ann Lineback, Melba Poole, Mildred Poole, Hattie Robbins, Dorothy Samuels, Jessie Smith, Leva Smith, Jennie Sherrill, Jannie Sherrill, Katherine Whitener, Revis, Gordon.

Drayton Mill (Spartanburg, S.C.), runners-up: J.B. Powell (coach), Connie Harley, Sallie West, Virginia Lancaster, Ruby Adams, Pauline Smith, Ruth Bobo, Trudy English, Tamar Durham, Beulah Splawn, Alma Rogers, Rachel Durham, Mary Whitlock.

Pelzer Mill (Pelzer, S.C.), consolation winners: Wesley Tripp (coach), Leoda Jordan, Emma Davenport, Mildred Houston, Eva Saylors, Flora Addison, Inez Dixon, Pauline Waters, Margaret Mayfield, Virginia Dixon, Beatrice Davis, Kathryn Ramey, Avis Jordan.

Glen Lowery Mill (Whitmire, S.C.): Elma Pearson (coach), Thelma Puckett, Lena Evans, Agnes Bailey, Helen Black, Stella Bailey, Margaret McKain, Lillian Huckaby, Lois Erskine, Lois Eubanks, Margie Ray.

Judson Mill (Greenville, S.C.): Junius Kelly (coach), Lillie Westmoreland, Janet Cobb, Louise Calvert, Ruth Barr, Ruby Ward, Lois Sellers, Janie Putman, Frances von Holland, Sarah Ellis, Helen Ayers.

Dunean Mill (Greenville, S.C.): C.H. Thomas (coach), Mildred Carpenter, Mildred Williams, Margaret Donnan, Mary Gault, Thelma Mason, Olive Tinsley, Myrtle Turner, Josie Barr, Helen Quinn, Violet Bowman, Evelyn Putman, Annette Smith.

American Enka (Enka, N.C.): Louise Agee (coach), Beulah Brown, Geneva Burnett, Ella Corn, Gussie Couch, Mildred Crownover, Blanche Drake, Lois Greene, Mary Hensley, Mary Lyman, Jessie Mills, Alice Owensby, Mertis Prince.

Southern Worsted (Greenville, S.C.): John Whitt (coach), Argil Hogg, Byrtha Whitt, Sara West, Ethel Jackson, Mary Greene, Earleen Gosnell, Bartie Brown, Ruby Roe, Gladys Hogg, Dot West, Lottie Jackson.

Class B Women

Lanett Mill (Lanett, Ala.), champions: Fred Ballenger (coach), Louise Wood, Matilee Smith, Lula Looser, Jewell Bishop, Avis Cook, Florrie Lovelace, Cornell Hayes, Virginia Edwards, Agnes Wood, Sarah Bishop, Catherine Purcell, Webb.

Brandon Mill (Woodruff, S.C.), runners-up: Mrs. E.M. Leopard (coach), Polly Keesler, Martha Clem, Hazel Sumner, Rose Roebuck, Dorothy Padgett, Harriett Bruce, Mary Padgett, Eleanor Bryson, Dorothy Cox, Myrtle Fennell, Mary Lydia, Evelyn Long.

Draper Mill (Draper, N.C.), consolation winners: Dillard Stultz (coach), E.W. Mooney (coach), Gladys Hundley, Evelyn Barker, Drucilla Stein, Margaret Kendrick, Lois Gilland, Hazel Marlowe, Mildred Lindsay, Margaret Stultz, Madeline Hamrick, Tullah Rogers, Ruth Hodges, Eva Hensley.

Union Bleachery (Greenville, S.C.): J.D. Ivey (coach), Robert Price (coach), Helen Batson, Annie Evington, Carolme Evatt, Frances Harrison, Mary Ivey, Mary Robinson, Irene Ivey, Elizabeth Johns, Evelyn Myles, Vera McKinney, Mary Robertson, Hazel Willis.

Abbeville Mill (Abbeville, S.C.): O.B. Duffie (coach), Virginia Vaughn, Ruth Blum, Anne Campbell, Mary Young, Beatrice Blanchett, Lou McCurry, Sarah McConnell, Blanche Cox, Margie New, Florence Woolbright, Evelyn Campbell, Frances Henderson, McCall.

Monaghan Mill (Greenville, S.C.): Fred Ellis (coach), Ruth McCall, Dixie Thompson, Kathleen Gosnell, Elmyra Davis, Gladys Strange, Gladys Carson, Mary Bradley, Frances Blackstone, Millie Vehorn, Mildred Bishop, Hazel Sanders, Erminia Christopher.

Brandon Mill (Greenville, S.C.): F.H. Smith (coach), Elizabeth Mahon (coach), Mary Gwinn, Margaret Baker, Sarah Baker, Elizabeth Loftis, Margaret Sheriff, Lena Thomas, Joyce Rollins, Agnes McDonald, Frances McDonald, Billie Baker, Kathryn McDonald, Joyce Tannery.

Joanna Mill (Joanna, S.C.): A.B. Galloway (coach), Evelyn Garner, Marie Prater, Elizabeth Ross, Lavinia Ross, Tootsie O'Dell, Ruth Starnes, Sara Starnes, Ruby Harrelson, Elizabeth Willingham, Ruby Hawkins, Victoria Murrah, Nell Hamm.

Woodside Mill (Greenville, S.C.): C.W. Hodge (coach), C.E. Heath (coach), Nellie Ellison, Ruby Greene, Margaret Johnson, Vera Mann, Dellaree Bowen, Gladys Miller, Zelphia Miller, Thelma Whitlow, Mary Justus, Zelpha Heath, Julia Hickam, Edna Bedenbaugh.

1939

Officers: Leonard Howard (Greenville, S.C.), President; Horace Whitmire (Greenville, S.C.), Vice President; Ted Crain (Spartanburg, S.C.), Treasurer; Clarence Thomas (Greenville, S.C.).

Executive Committee: W.M. Grier (Greenville, S.C.), Fred Ballenger (Lanett, Ala.), Coker Candler (Enka, N.C.), C.F. Stancell (Greenville, S.C.), Lyles Alley (Greenville, S.C.), J.M. Bailey (Greenville, S.C.).

Class A Men

McCrary Hosiery Mill (Asheboro, N.C.), champions: Paul Cheek (coach), Wayne Harris, Carlos Holleman, Bill Wright, Murray Rogers, Henry Essick, James Copeland, Neil Cockerham, Jack Cox, Paul Roye, Clark, McClean, Monroe, Drumheller, Mann.

Southern Bleachery (Taylors, S.C.), runners-up: Lyles Alley (coach), Bert Hill, Connie Mack Berry, Bud Hendley, Ray Wilson, Ben Burnett, Mays Williams, Buddy Nau, George Blackwell, Sherb Wall, Ted Suddeth.

Union Bleachery (Greenville, S.C.), consolation winners: Charlie Brooks (coach), Ansel Bridwell, W.A. Bishop, Roy Brooks, McClure Epps, B.C. Hawkins, Walker Dilworth, William Nelson, William Harrison, Harold Green, Cecil Brooks.

Chicopee Mill (Gainesville, Ga.): J.A. Neighbors (coach), James Baker, Arthur Hudgins, Lewis Clark, Junius Boggs, Ralph Smith, Willis Bridges, Hayne DeLong, Robert Abercrombie, Hugh Dorsey, Charles Strickland, Hodges.

Monaghan Mill (Greenville, S.C.): J.G. Suttles (coach), Lee Coleman (coach), Dennis Elder, Ralph Snelson, Palmer McAvoy, Paul Case, Carlos Thompson, Franklin Griffith, Marvin Hopkins, Nathan Nichols, Millwood Stephens, Philip Stewart.

American Enka (Enka, N.C.): Coker Candler (coach), Sam Patton, Roy Patton, Owen Morgan, Mitchell Gaddy, Holly Hipps, Robert Stafford, Vincent Cooper, Charles Munday, Fred Allen, Dan Ball.

Muscogee Mfg. (Columbus, Ga.): C.L. Hall (coach), Henry Weaver, Sherard Wilson, Kenneth Smith, Harry Williamson, Ezekiel Robinson, Cleo Ray, Richard Parks, James Barnes, Woodfin Combs.

Piedmont Mill (Piedmont, S.C.): J.M. Terry (coach), Leroy Anderson (coach), Curtis Terry, Charles Poole, Edgar Patterson, Ford Waldrop, Robert Traynham, Ray Darnell, J.W. Rampey, J.D. Hunnicutt, Jerry Underwood, Wilton Smith.

Avondale Mill (Alexander City, Ala.): David Long (coach), Bill Evans, Wilbur Payne, Charles Hurst, William Hurst, Philip Avery, Troy Holley, Fred Boose, Roscoe Slagle, Long.

Greenwood Mill (Greenwood, S.C.): James Hall (coach), Thomas Gastley, Earl Morse, Henry Bland, Irby Raines, Charlie Girk, John Franklin, Dewey Southern, Ernest Godfrey, Carl Jenkins.

Dunean Mill (Greenville, S.C.): Clarence Thomas (coach), Sam Turner, Ralph Stroud, Robert Donnan, Roy Owens, Oscar Cox, William Riddle, Elmo Moody, Lewis McDonald.

Judson Mill (Greenville, S.C.): James Kelly (coach), Fred Pack (coach), James Trammell, Alvin Estes, J.D. McAlister, Charles Cobb, J.W. James, Arley Chapman, James Roddy, Fountain Williams, W.T. Tidwell, G.C. Scott.

Pelzer Mill (Pelzer, S.C.): James Carey (coach), John Byars, Ralph Cannon, Telford Harris, Curtis Walker, William Floyd, Horace Davenport, Willie Crymes, J.W. Jordan, Walker Bagwell, Jack Coker.

Walhalla Mill (Walhalla, S.C.): Lee Smith (coach), Coley Garrett (coach), John Galliard, Carl Rackley, William Robinson, John Smith, Carlos Williams, James McCall, William Gibson, Claud Galliard, Grady Pepper, Ballard, R. Smith.

Glen Lowery Mill (Whitmire, S.C.): J.C. Abrams (coach), William Bryce (coach), Fred Prather, Richard Kohn, Harry Summers, Mark Connor, Clyde Brank, Charles Gaffney, Caroll Hester, Ted Black.

Dixie Mercerizing (Lupton City, Tenn.): Harry Anderson (coach), Charles Cox, Fred Ballard, Bob Klein, Efford Norris, Louis Baxter, Melvin Seals, Leroy Mann, Lee Lawing, Don Spargo.

Brandon Mill (Woodruff, S.C.): William Padgett (coach), Harold Taylor, Dennis Loftis, Edward Kirby, Travis Wall, Lee Roy Taylor, Ulysses Sprouse, Louis Keesler, C.D. Padgett, James Tiller, Sam Kilgore.

Drayton Mill (Spartanburg, S.C.): L.R. Corbin (coach), J.D. Morgan, Paul Ellis, John Lacey, Leonard Hill, Ralph Gibbs, Charlie Seay, Joe Durham, Raymond Smith, Pete Laurens, Manning Bagwell.

Lonsdale Mill (Seneca, S.C.): Roy Leatherwood (coach), J.F. Mason (coach), Ralph James, Frank Galliard, Lasco Alsep, William Pruitt, George Morgan, Wilton Shaver, Frank Whitt, Dewey Stevenson, Ernest Dooley, Eddie Weathers.

Winnsboro Mill (Winnsboro, S.C.): Frank Gale (coach), Edward Ward, Brice Wages, Gary Brunnemer, Charles Mixon, George Osborne, Clarence Rushing, C.F. Cline, Charles Wyndham, Homer Sargent, Albert Molnar, Marvin Stevenson, Melvin Wales.

CLASS B MEN

Adams-Millis (High Point, N.C.), champions: J.W. Smotherly (coach), Ray Intrieri, John Sappenfield, Claude Wright Jr., Clayton Steele, Lelon Cooper, Enoch Cooper, C.W. Martin, Forrest Edwards, J.C. Spencer, Dolan Hendrick.

Converse Mill (Spartanburg, S.C.), runners-up: H.B. Davis (coach), Pete Fowler Jr., Paul Mathis, James Quinn, Sephas Green, Vance Powers, Theron Evans, Robert Thompson, Hugh Howard, Voyle Massey, James Mason.

Southern Franklin Processing (Greenville, S.C.), consolation winners: L.A. Burgess (coach), John Jones, Charles Sterling, James Perry, Jeriah McNeely, Charles Delk, Jones McNeely, Guy Davis, James Watson, Clyde Lollis Jr., Edwin Briggs.

Slater Mill (Slater, S.C.): Torrey Tyner (coach), James Oglesby (coach), F.W. Dawkins, Marion Dudley, Robert Ellis, Gartrell McDuffie, James McMakin, Gilbert Rogers, Harold Taylor, Clarence Wright.

Martha Mill (Thomaston, Ga.): Bert Gunter (coach), Clayton Watson, Irving Earls, Charles Sproull, Guy Lacy Jr., Carter Mitchell, Clarence Ard, John Lawhorne, Robert Matthews, Reno Blackstock, Arthur Perkins.

Abbeville Mill (Abbeville, S.C.): C.B. Duffie (coach), Preston Able, Ralph Simpson, Leslie Wilson, Ralph Wilson, Miller New, Oscar New, Gordon Campbell, Walter Fossett, Wallace Cox, George Powell.

Peerless Cotton Mill (Thomaston, Ga.):

Roy Salter (coach), Bartow Causey, James Cowart, Bandice West, Tarvie Lester, Worth Williams, Norman Faircloth, Charles Parker, Summer Wood, Elmo Daniel, Carl Lowery.

Judson Mill (Greenville, S.C.): Cleo Tumblin (coach), Frank McDaniel (coach), Paul Hazel, Ray Duffie, Carvin Landreth, William Grissop, John Cobb, James Case, David Greer, G.T. Crowe, James Long, Bruce Davis.

Hanes Hosiery Mill (Winston-Salem, N.C.): E.E. Wilson (coach), William Musten, Frank Dunn, Fred Dunn, Clyde Spears, Carl Snow, Joseph Sprinkle, Cecil Prim, Pete Futrell, Phil Poole, Charles Gough.

Poinsett Mill (Greenville, S.C.): Claude Campbell (coach), L.J. Fair (coach), Monroe Millwood, Paul Fair, James Townsend, Wilbur Long, Lee Roy Chapman, Arthur Hammett, James Millwood, Elbert Lavender, Luther Landers, Ray Wilson.

Dixie Mercerizing (Lupton City, Tenn.): Harry Anderson (coach), Ed Anglin, Julius Pickens, Fred Shirley, D.L. Durham, Alex Wilkey, Pete Tolbert, Charles Tolbert, Harry Bolden.

Joanna Mill (Joanna, S.C.): A.B. Galloway Jr. (coach), Earnest Spires, Edward Hunnicutt, Rudolph Prater, Cecil Farmer, Clisby Templeton, Willis Phillips, Olga Hair, Tillman Morse, Algie Abrams, Snow Prater.

Piedmont Mill (Piedmont, S.C.): Walter Madden (coach), A.G. Taylor, Sloan Terry, Ernest Henderson, Fred Clifford, Fred Collins, Gomer Evans, Clayton Boiter, Leroy Hunnicutt, Veldee Cooper, Frank Grover, Smith.

Cramerton Mill (Cramerton, N.C.): R.W. Dyer (coach), James Reece, Leroy Reece, Sol Brindle, W.B. Stover, Z.V. Brindle, B.A. Cunningham, T.L. Ware Jr., L.B. Keeler, T.P. Brindle, V.L. Reece.

Renfrew Bleachery (Travelers Rest, S.C.): Dudley Tollison (coach), Marvin England, William Quinn, Lyman Eddy, Leonard Brown, Norman Riddley, Charles Werner, James Vernon, William Johnson, Woodrow Wilson, William Bridges, Werner.

Woodside Mill (Greenville, S.C.): Jerry Jackson (coach), Dewey Bowen (coach), Ralph Harbin, Fred Bomar, Alvin Chapman, Douglas Smith, Charles Freeman, Monroe Ramsey, Joe Whitmire, Jack Harden, Harold McConnell, Andrew Manley.

McEwen Mill (Burlington, N.C.): Ralph Berryhill (coach), James Burnette, Fletcher Garner, John Gallimore, Thomas Webster, Clarence Vaughn, James Rabey, Joseph Cox, Edwin Ketner, William Slaughter.

Brandon Mill (Greenville, S.C.): J.L. Loftis (coach), Clarence Bentley (coach), Robert Fortune, Jesse Ross, Pete Huff, Harold Baldwin, James Thomas, Admiral Dewey Foster, Roland Wherry, James Sherrill, Lloyd Ingle, Howard Thackston.

Calhoun Falls Mill (Calhoun Falls, S.C.): Charles Verner (coach), Arthur Verner, Joe Martin, Lloyd Chasteen, Howard Thomas, Dean Thomas, Benford Burton, Earle Stone, Weaver Hilley, John Helms, R.L. Chrisley, Kenneth.

Mills Mill (Greenville, S.C.): Tom Ingle (coach), Carl Hawkins (coach), Charles Pearson, Frank Norris, Wilburn Trammell, Harold Abbott, Charlie Briggs, James Cothran, Odell Crisp, Paul Campbell, James Abbott, Albert Osborne, Corn.

Dunean Mill (Greenville, S.C.): C.H. Thomas (coach), Otis Putman, Clarence Odell, David Scott, Bissell Garran, Minor Christopher, Aubrey Jones, Marion Donnan, William Johnson, Tommy Roddy, Robert Snoddy, Owens.

Gluck Mill (Anderson, S.C.): E.E. Manley (coach), Jerome Ripley, Lester Hughes, Henry Ripley, James Herring, William Ivester, Wilton Hanna, Dick Perry, Ray Perry, Boots Perry, Lee Chitwood.

Southern Bleachery (Taylors, S.C.): Lyles Alley (coach), Clarence Smith, Wayman Edwards, Lloyd Edwards, Willie Bishop, Bernice Bowers, Warren Trammell, Rufus Nichols, James Epting, Jimmie Bull, Tom Batson.

Class C Men

Dunean Mill (Greenville, S.C.), champions: Clarence Thomas (coach), Raymond Putman, Charles Callahan, Roy Bogan, Julian Lollis, Edward Hale, William Putman, Max Foster, Ralph Johnson, Fred Parks, Fred Snoddy.

Monaghan Mill (Greenville, S.C.), runners-up: Thornwell Henson (coach), Fred Bagwell, Marion Ross, James Worthy, Clayton Langston, Bomar Keller, John Whelchel, Henry Ford, Jack Ballew, Martin Oglesby, Fred Rigdon, Wilson.

Brandon Mill (Greenville, S.C.), consolation winners: Floyd Smith (coach), Milford Carter (coach), Clarence Orr, Harold Limbaugh, Burnell Morrow, Charles Aiken, Maurice Morrow, Roy Duncan, Fred Mahon, Charles Ross, Buck Friar, Joe Anders.

Poe Mill (Greenville, S.C.): Lewis Grastie (coach), Carlos Grastie (coach), Roy Morgan, Edward Spencer, John Guest, Forest Kinnett, Jack Williams, Roy Wilson, Alvin McCall, Ben Doar, Everette Pittman, Ray Rodgers.

Woodside Mill (Greenville, S.C.): R.N. Ramsey (coach), Ray Herbert (coach), James Green, Doyle Phillips, Carl Reeves, Edwin Reeves, Manley Sanders, Jerry Jackson Jr., George Miller, J.B. Neese, Veldee Hines, Clyde Richards.

Mills Mill (Greenville, S.C.): R.R. Brock (coach), E.B. McAllister (coach), Douglas Amick, William Blair, Henry Dittmer, Benjamin Henry, Leroy Moon, R.D. Smith, Junior McAllister, Edwin Cooper, Roscoe Ball, Herbert Capps.

Lonsdale Mill (Seneca, S.C.): J.F. Mason (coach), Clyde Davis (coach), Ostell Shirley, Ralph Maxey, Garnett Latham, Martin Abbott, Thomas James, James Black, Horace Gaillard, Billy Gibson, Joe Mattison.

Simpsonville Mill (Simpsonville, S.C.): Spec Barbary (coach), Thomas Cox, Richard Terry, Donald Barbery, Robert Cox, James Garrett, Ed Sanders, Charles Hamby, Earl Brashier, Jack McGill, Jack Brashier, McCall.

Camperdown Mill (Greenville, S.C.): Charlie Penland (coach), Louie McDowell (coach), Melvin Gunter, Walter Goodwin, Jack Whitaker, Alvin Burnette, James Bruce, Dennis Whitaker, Jack Thompson, Odell Scott, Fred Johnson, Henry Goodwin.

Pelzer Mill (Pelzer, S.C.): H.G. Smith (coach), Harley Heath (coach), Jack Bannister, William Harris, Garvin Pridmore, Jarnette Floyd, Harold Ross, Cyral Haney, Billy Fowler, Clyde McKee, Bill Quinn, Hoyt Jordan, Haney.

Greer Mill (Greer, S.C.): W.W. Hanvey (coach), Crate Taylor (coach), Melvin Hardin, Dewey Moore, Wallace Taylor, Furman Taylor, Everette Pate, Billy Bishop, James Burnette, Robert Brown, A.D. Hardin, Wyatt Copeland, W. Turner.

Judson Mill (Greenville, S.C.): Robert Tallant (coach), Junius Kelley (coach), Ralph Tallant, J.T. Nimmons, Bill Hall, Douglas Pritchard, Gerald Crawford, Hubert Robinson, Gilbert Minor, W.A. Pridmore Jr., Albert Turner, L.C. Littlejohn.

Victor Mill (Greer, S.C.): B.J. Nix (coach), Wilbur Wilson (coach), S.V. Wilson Jr., Junior Pruitt, Charles Putnam, Brock Becks, Perry Lowe, Proctor Wood, Henry Tucker, Richard Simmons, Lewis Hughes, Belton Cabiness.

Draper Mill (Draper, N.C.): E.W. Mooney (coach), F.A. Stein (coach), Barney Carter, Monroe Grant, Jim Powell, Henry Gerringer, Dan Squires, Frank Henry, Moir Martin, Clifford Ball, Clyde Minter, Charles Aaron, Purcell, Garner.

Orr Mill (Anderson, S.C.): Troy Kirby (coach), David Hawkins, Roy Ashworth, Clyde Blackwell, Jack Buchanan, Fred Whitten, Roy Blackwell, James Herring, Ralph Sanders, Carl Hampton, Walter O'barr.

Ninety Six Mill (Ninety Six, S.C.): Fred Ross (coach), John Drummond, Calvin Drummond, Alvin Drummond, Harold Ivester, Walter Bryant, Jack Padgett, Glenn Harrison, Tittler Voiselle, Willis Stribbling, Victor Drummond, Fortner.

CLASS A WOMEN

Chatham Mfg. (Elkin, N.C.), champions: A.R. Plaster (coach), Mildred Poole, Aldie Biddix, Cleo Petree, Leva Smith, Jannie Sherrill, Jennie Sherrill, Melba Poole, Dorothy Samuels, Catherine Whitener, Annie Lineback, Maurice Gordon, Myrtie Reavis.

Lanett Mill (Lanett, Ala.), runners-up: Buell Warren (coach), Jewell Bishop, Louise Wood, Mary Mitchell, Verna Webb, Avis Cook, Ada Thaxton, Mary Rainey, Cornell Hays, Virginia Edwards, Marie Rice, Rosalie Looser, Mattilee Smith.

Glen Lowery Mill (Whitmire, S.C.), consolation winners: Elma Pearson (coach), Agnes Bailey, Louise Horton, Lois Erskine, Mamie Ray, Helen Black, Lois Eubanks, Sara King, Shady Huckaby, Margie Woods, Muriel Garrett.

Union Bleachery (Greenville, S.C.): Smith Batson (coach), Beulah Bozemore, Annie Evington, Frances Harrison, Irene Ivey, Mary Ivey, Elizabeth Johns, Bernice Keith, Mildred Keith, Evelyn Moles, Vera McKinney, Katherine Turner, Hazel Willis.

American Enka (Enka, N.C.): Betty Henry (coach), Mildred Hargrove, Edith Stamey, Ella Corn, Alice Owenby, Mertis Prince, Beulah Brown, Jessie Mills, Gussie Couch, Blanche Cooper, Geneva Burnette, Mary Hensley, Nannie Roane.

Pelzer Mill (Pelzer, S.C.): R.R. Hood

(coach), Virginia Dixon, Leoda Jordan, Edna Ford, Evelyn Jordan, Kathleen Roberts, Flora Addison, Clara Holliday, Montez Dixon, Mildred Jordan, Jacqueline Holliday, Emma Davenport, Mrs. H.E. Heath.

Drayton Mill (Spartanburg, S.C.): Smith Crow (coach), Wilma Whitlock, Beulah Splawn, Connie Harley, Della Clayton, Mayo Barnett, Rachel Durham, Alma Rogers, Trudie English, Melba Duckett, Nell Jackson, Elsie Skipper, Virginia Lancaster, Pennington.

CLASS B WOMEN

Hanes Hosiery Mill (Winston-Salem, N.C.), champions: E.E. Wilson (coach), Kate Scott, Gladys Reavis, Verniece Boyles, Viola Hester, Louise Newman, Lucille Snow, Ozelma Burwell, Louise Spainhour, Aleen Hutchins, Ruby Wilson, Lorene Linville, Ruhmel Wilson.

McEwen Mill (Burlington, N.C.), runners-up: Glenn Slaughter (coach), Grace McAdams, Inez Cannady, Isabell Pugh, Annie Pender, Elizabeth Scoggins, Idell Dixon, Margaret Long, Mary Dismuke, Thelma Roach, Louise Pender, Kathleen Efland, Polly Merritt.

Brandon Mill (Woodruff, S.C.), consolation winners: C.M. Padgett (coach), Mrs. E.M. Leopard (coach), Polly Keesler, Dorothy Padgett, Lavelle Sprouse, Helen Padgett, Rose Roebuck, Lena Jones, Louise West, Hazel Sumner, Margaret Clem, Evelyn Long, Vassie Lydia, Dorothy Cox.

Dunean Mill (Greenville, S.C.): C.H. Thomas (coach), Margaret Cox, Mary Moody, Earline Phillips, Lois Carpenter, Gladys Foster, Myrtie Mason, Eleanor Carpenter, Margaret Putman, Kathryn Morris, Margaret Donnan, Helen Lynn, Margie Lollis.

Gluck Mill (Anderson, S.C.): G.W. Weathers (coach), Grace Picklesimer, Hazel Allen, Evelyn Allen, Willie Stephens, Sara McCullough, Caroline McAllister, Inez Allen, Doris Warren, Ruth Allen, Catherine Allen, Helen Picklesimer, Irene Picklesimer.

Abbeville Mill (Abbeville, S.C.): Nell Cochran (coach), Ruth New, Lou McCurry, Eva Campbell, Mary Cox, Marjorie New, Florence Woolbright, Mary Young, Ethelyn Blanchett, Beatrice Blanchett, Frances Scott, Virginia Vaughn, Ann Campbell.

Slater Mill (Slater, S.C.): Mrs. Clarence Wright (coach), James Oglesby (coach), Kathryn Cleveland, Sarah Collins, Inez Hadden, Dot Hamilton, Virginia Knight, Gladys Means, Helen Means, Elise Means, Aileen Springfield, Ivah Springfield.

Piedmont Mill (Piedmont, S.C.): Mrs. Jerome Grover (coach), Jerome Grover (coach), Helen McCall, Evelyn Suber, Margaret Garrett, Alta Wilson, Annie Terry, Mary Davenport, Ressie Reeves, Hazel Trammel, Mary Boiter, Helen Trammel.

Dixie Mercerizing (Lupton City, Tenn.): Harry Anderson (coach), Opal Outlaw, Ina Cox, Ester Goodner, Inez Roberts, Marie Martin, Juanita Walker, Inez McGuire, Edith Higgins, Willia Street.

1940

Officers: Leonard Howard (Greenville, S.C.), President; Horace Whitmire (Greenville, S.C.), Secretary; Ted Crain (Spartanburg, S.C.), Treasurer; Clarence Thomas (Greenville, S.C.), Assistant Secretary.

Executive Committee: Harry Anderson (Lupton City, Tenn.), W.T. Kennedy Jr. (Taylors, S.C.), Fred Ballenger, (Lanett, Ala.), A.R. Plaster (Winston-Salem, N.C.), Ralph Bowie (Piedmont, S.C.), C.F. Stancell (Greenville, S.C.), W.M. Grier (Greenville, S.C.).

CLASS A MEN

Dixie Mercerizing (Lupton City, Tenn.), champions: Melvin Seals, Grayson Davis, L.D. Tolbert, Charles Tolbert, Efford Norris, Charles Cox, D.L. Durham, Harry Anderson, Lew Lawing, Fred Ballard, Shirley.

Southern Bleachery (Taylors, S.C.), runners-up: Wilbanks, Burnett, Ray Wilson, Suddeth, Wall, Hendley, Bert Hill, George Blackwell.

Winnsboro Mill (Winnsboro, S.C.), consolation winners: Wilmot Spires, D. Stevenson, Gary Brunnemer, McSwain, Rushing, Ward, Molner, M. Stevenson.

Chicopee Mill (Gainesville, Ga.): Clark, Taylor, Abercrombie, Hudgens, DeLong, Adams, Nix, Eberhart.

Calhoun Falls Mill (Calhoun Falls, S.C.): Charlie Verner, Hilley, Ford Waldrop, Bland, Jenkins, Stone, D. Thomas, Chastain, Boling, Stone, H. Thomas.

Dunean Mill (Greenville, S.C.): Robert Donnan, Willie Riddle, Owens, Stroud, Moody, O'Dell, Cooper.

Victor Mill (Greer, S.C.): Ted Cabiness,

Tom Pack, Traynham, Morgan, Emery, Hutchinson, Tucker, Durham, Jackson, Waters.

Adams-Millis (High Point, N.C.): Wright, L. Cooper, Moreland, E. Cooper, Sappenfield, Edwards, C. Cooper.

Woodside Mill (Greenville, S.C.): Charlie Couch, B. Couch, Tucker, Ramey, Canup, Foster, Justice, Bowen.

American Enka (Enka, N.C.): Hipps, Ray Patton, Sam Patton, Munday, Cooper, Campbell, Allen, Merrie, Lovingood.

Drayton Mill (Spartanburg, S.C.): Gibbs, Seay, Durham, Ellis, Morgan, Dodd, Condrey, Hill, Bagwell, Harrison.

Union Bleachery (Greenville, S.C.): Roy Brooks, Dilworth, Hawkins, Bishop, Ansel Bridwell, McClure Epps.

Judson Mill (Greenville, S.C.): Greer, Tidwell, McDaniel, Cobb, Trammell, James.

Piedmont Mill (Piedmont, S.C.): Hunnicutt, S. Terry, Patterson, Rampey, C. Terry, Grover, Henderson, Darnell.

Walhalla Mill (Walhalla, S.C.): Galliard, Whitt, J.Smith, Garrett, R. Smith, Shaver, McCall.

Monaghan Mill (Greenville, S.C.): Stephens, Allen, Elder, Case, Thompson, Griffith, McAvoy, Ross, Keller.

Oconee Mill (Westminster, S.C.): Robinson, Hawkins, Bagwell, Marvin Rackley, Seymour, Williams, Cobb, Cain.

Virginia Maid Hosiery (Pulaski, Va.): P. Rice, Studebaker, R. Rice, Darnell, Painter, Haskins, Burch.

McCrary Hosiery Mill (Asheboro, N.C.): Roy, Neal Cockerham, Monroe, Harris, McLean, Malcomb Drumheller, Wright, Copeland, Essick, Cheek.

Peerless Woolen Mill (Rossville, Ga.): Roark, Bailey, Clint Norman, Phillips, Rogers, Millsaps, Scott, Lykins.

Brandon Mill (Woodruff, S.C.): Loftis, Kirby, Padgett, H. Taylor, R. Taylor, Smith, Keesler, McBride, Sprouse.

Glen Lowery Mill (Whitmire, S.C.): Summers, Black, C. Gaffney, Branks, Connor, Prince, R. Gaffney, Estes.

Greer Mill (Greer, S.C.): F. Taylor, Hemphill, Copeland, R. Taylor, Burgin, Pate, W. Taylor.

Mills Mill (Greenville, S.C.): Osborne, Cothran, Smith, Pearson, G. McAllister, Trammell, A. McAllister.

Class B Men

Hanes Hosiery Mill (Winston-Salem, N.C.), champions: Clyde Speas, Phil Poole, Esca Carroll, Vestal Speas, Lehman Johnston, Weldon Johnston, Robert Slaydon, Lee Boddie, Dave Odom, Carl Snow.

Dunean Mill (Greenville, S.C.), runners-up: Fred Snoddy, Putman, Marion Donnan, Callahan, Parks, Christopher, Lollis, Johnson.

Peerless Cotton Mill (Thomaston, Ga.), consolation winners: Boss, Wilder, Reeves, West, J.W. Howard, Brown, Parker, Causey, Lester, Cowart.

Spartan Mill (Spartanburg, S.C.): J.F. Smith, Lancaster, C.R. Smith, Mahaffey, Burch, Lands, Edwards, Peake, Guy.

Southern Bleachery (Taylors, S.C.): Epting, Waymond Edwards, L. Edwards, Bowers, Warren Trammell, Clayton, Smith, Hayes.

Beacon Mill (Swannanoa, N.C.): Patton, Blankenship, William Horne, Davidson, C. Barnwell, Kitchens, Vallencourt, Brown, B. Barnwell.

Brandon Mill (Greenville, S.C.): Thackston, Cox, Buck Friar, Ray Wynn, Morrow, Ross, Ingle, Campbell.

Mills Mill (Greenville, S.C.): Trammell, Osborne, Smith, Pearson, Cothran, A. McAllister, C. McAllister.

Peerless Woolen Mill (Rossville, Ga.): Green, Cook, Brown, Settles, Bevis, Bailey, Crosslin, Rader, Davis.

Poinsett Mill (Greenville, S.C.): Millwood, Chapman, Lavender, Fair, Townsend, Hammett, Wilson.

Pacific Mill (Columbia, S.C.): D.Pursley, E. Herbert, Asa Herbert, Darby, McQuarters, Gordon, McDaniel, Martin, Jennings.

Clifton Mill (Clifton, S.C.): Massey, Greene, Howard, Powers, Evans, Reid, Fowler, Thompson.

Ninety Six Mill (Ninety Six, S.C.): Harrison, Cal Drummond, T. Voiselle, Wells, Bill Voiselle, V. Drummond.

Southern Franklin Processing (Greenville, S.C.): Jones McNeely, Sterling, J. McNeely, Bragg, Shuttleworth, Lollis, Jones.

Marshall Field Mill (Fieldville, Va.): Griggs, Mirriman, Hunter, Pickup, Dalrymple, Martin, Joyce, Hagan, Warwick.

Tennessee Eastman (Kingsport, Tenn.): Cantwell, Wright, Neufer, Grills, Stone, Germand.

Woodside Mill (Greenville, S.C.): Waldrop,

Harbin, Chapman, Freeman, Richards, Smith, Ramsey.

Columbus Mill (Columbus, Ga.): Carmack, Martin, Widgeon, Hurston, Richardson, Donahue.

Judson Mill (Greenville, S.C.): Long, Grissop, Cobb, Davis, Hazel, Tallent, Hall.

Poe Mill (Greenville, S.C.): Pittman, Wilson, Morgan, Grastie, Jack Williams, Spencer, McCall.

Renfrew Bleachery (Travelers Rest, S.C.): Johnson, Vernon, Pearson, Brown, Werner, Bledsoe.

Greer Mill (Greer, S.C.): Hemphill, F. Taylor, Copeland, Pate, Burnett, R. Taylor, W. Taylor.

CLASS C MEN

Lonsdale Mill (Seneca, S.C.), champions: J.F. Mason (coach), Clyde Davis (coach), Leroy Oxley, Martin Abbott, James Black, Ralph Maxie, Otis Latham, Garrett Latham, Jammie Shirley, Ostell Shirley, Conway Vickery.

Dunean Mill (Greenville, S.C.), runners-up: Clarence Thomas (coach), Angus Marshbanks, Harold Quinn, Guy Shook, Ralph Mann, Harold Johnson, Manning Garren, Harold Holbrook, Martin Oglesby, Curtis Carpenter, Clyde Simmons.

Victor Mill (Greer, S.C.), consolation winners: Grady Waters (coach), Clyde Simmons (coach), Brock Beeks, Perry Lowe, S.V. Wilson Jr., Lewis Hughes, Cecil Campbell, Charles Putman, Austin Wilson, Belton Cabiness, Harold Tucker, Charles Vehorn.

Monaghan Mill (Greenville, S.C.): C.D. Hughes (coach), Joseph Worthy (coach), Fred Bagwell, Preston Welchel, Harold Davis, Edward Ford, Raymond Christopher, Fred Rigdon, Vernon Moore, Jack Ballew, Bomar Keller.

Southern Worsted (Greenville, S.C.): W.P. Jackson (coach), George Alverson (coach), Jack Blanchett, Marion West, Robert Davis, Joe Hogg, Mitchell Howard, Furman Kay, Perry Bridwell, James Simpson, Howard Waldrop, Richard Waldrop.

Orr Mill (Anderson, S.C.): Milford Ellison (coach), J.W. Powers, J.R. Ashworth, W.J. Porter, C.T. Hampton, J.D. Jolly, J.A. Day, B.B. Vernon, J.E. Prince, Sammy Meeks, J.D. Pierce.

Slater Mill (Slater, S.C.): Clarence Wright (coach), James Oglesby (coach), Harold Taylor, Dacus Tucker, Charlie Vaughn, William Cody, Pearl Ledford, William Cashion, Pete Brown, Jack Cashion, Price Weaver, Wade Puckett.

Woodside Mill (Greenville, S.C.): Ray Herbert (coach), R.N. Ramsey (coach), James Green, Doyle Phillips, Veldee Hines, J.B. Kneece, Talmadge Tollison, Jerry Jackson, Ed Reeves, Carl Reeves, George Miller, George Pruitt.

Mills Mill (Greenville, S.C.): R.R. Brock (coach), A.J. Burns (coach), John Dittmar, Harold Goss, Leslie Henry, Charles Brock, Eddie Cooper, Wallace Brock, Roscoe Ball, James Smith, Ansel McJunkin, Edgar Goss.

Piedmont Mill (Piedmont, S.C.): R.W. Allen (coach), S.C. Hawkins (coach), Charles Anderson, Milford Howard, Charles Davis, George Brannon, Robert Porter, Bert McAdams, Edward Fowler, Harry Terry, W.Y. Poole, Willard Bishop.

Pelzer Mill (Pelzer, S.C.): Robert Geer (coach), Harley Heath (coach), Jarnett Floyd, Bill Fowler, Bill Quinn, Earl Wooten, Junior Ragsdale, Edgar Smith, Bill Harris, Garvin Pridmore, Harold Ross, Hoyt Jordan, Suddeth, Davis.

Brandon Mill (Greenville, S.C.): Dewey Foster (coach), James Carnes (coach), Fred Mahon, Joe Anders, Harry Foster, Doyle Clary, Clarence Orr, Elvin Morrow, Harold Limbaugh, James Orr, Joe Saunders, Roy Duncan.

Union Bleachery (Greenville, S.C.): Pat Patterson (coach), William Burns, Charles Batson, Aromus Belcher, Charles Epps, James Evington, Sherwood Green, Adger Jones, Paul Turner, Kenneth Robertson, J.W. Trammell.

Appleton Mill (Anderson, S.C.): King, Williams, Burris, Middleton, Carlton, Bailey, Mayfield, S. Spake, Hunter.

Central Mill (Central, S.C.): Suttles, Craig, Atkinson, Oates, Green, Elrod, Gambrell, Ackerson, Chambers.

Camperdown Mill (Greenville, S.C.): Goodwin, Neal, Gunter, Thompson, J. Whitaker, Scott, Cooper, Burnette.

CLASS A WOMEN

American Enka (Enka, N.C.), champions: Jane Branch, Beulah Brown, Geneva Burnett, Adalee Couch, Gussie Couch, Mildred Hargrove, Beryle Jackson, Alice Mallonee, Jessie Mills, Mildred Reynolds, Mertis Prince, Mildred Holbrook, Duckett.

Chatham Mfg. (Elkin, N.C.), runners-up: Claudia Austin (coach), A.R. Plaster (coach),

Melba Poole, Mildred Poole, Louise McGhee, Ann Lineback, Helen Doub, Pete Amburn, Maurice Gordon, Dorothy Samuel, Jennie Sherrill, Jannie Sherrill, Leva Smith, Katherine Whitener, Sawyer.
Hanes Hosiery Mill (Winston-Salem, N.C.), consolation winners: Chick Wilson (coach), Lorene Linville, Vernice Boyles, Kate Scott, Viola Reich, Rhumel Wilson, Myrtle Reavis, Gladys Reavis, Mary Masten, Doodle Brunner, Edith Smitherman, Margaret Landreth, Georgia Key.
Glen Lowery Mill (Whitmire, S.C.): Inez Kelly (coach), Sarah Huckaby, Mamie Ray, Erskine, Helen Black, Agnes Bales, Muriel Garrett, Rosa Hester, Dolly Chapman, Eva Black, Willie Dickert, Bailey, H. Bailey.
Drayton Mill (Spartanburg, S.C.): Smith Crow (coach), Wilma Whitlock, Eva Saylors, Mayo Burnett, Alva Rogers, Evelyn Rogers, Isabel Brown, English, Rachel Durham, Della Clayton, Wilma Cleveland, Merle Smith, Beulah Splawn.

Class B Women
Dixie Mercerizing (Lupton City, Tenn.), champions: Pepper Martin, Ina Cox, Edna Wagner, Jackie Henderson, Myrtle Dooley, Juanita Walker, Opal Outlaw, Marie Martin, Virginia Parris, Helen Waddell, Ruby Caver, Jackie Marlow, Roberts.
Grey Hosiery Mill (Hendersonville, N.C.), runners-up: Dorothy Nelson, Arledge, Lassie Dunn, Anders, McCrary, Orr, Fisher, Drake.
Dunean Mill (Greenville, S.C.), consolation winners: C.H. Thomas (coach), Lois Carpenter, Margaret Donnan, Catherine Morris, Margaret Putman, Katherine Cox, Margie Lollis, Viola Thompson, Billie Riddle, Evelyn Cox, Eleanor Carpenter, Edna Anderson.
Brandon Mill (Greenville, S.C.): Raymond Reid (coach), F.H. Smith (coach), Lenora Baker, Mildred Sheriff, Frances Gwinn, Joyce Rollins, Clinton Hutchinson, Sara Baker, Christine Rollins, Joyce Tannery, Mattie Sons, Nancy Thackston, Lena Thomas.
Lonsdale Mill (Seneca, S.C.): Winder Gary (coach), Frank Gaillard (coach), Elizabeth Young, Ruth Latham, Reginald Gaillard, Lizzie Black, Eunice Black, Junie James, Grace McKee, Martha Whitt, Dorothy Newton, Sara Ayers, McKee.
Joanna Mill (Joanna, S.C.): Ross, Starnes, Morse, Prater, Cooley, Garner, Hughes, Feltman.
Piedmont Mill (Piedmont, S.C.): Suber, Anderson, Davenport, Barter, Heaton, Trammell, Rampey, Ayers.
Converse Mill (Spartanburg, S.C.): Easler, T. Childers, Mabry, Crocker, Wells, M. Childers, Gault, Belcher.
Judson Mill (Greenville, S.C.): Dill, V. Owens, W. Hall, M. Owens, Hale, McDuffie, Hartsell.
Ninety Six Mill (Ninety Six, S.C.): Elizabeth Drummond, Elsie Collins, V. Drummond, T. Highsmith, McKinney, Wood, M. Campbell, O .Campbell.
Woodside Mill (Greenville, S.C.): Cole, Miller, Ruby Green, Price, Whitlow, O. Smith, L. Smith, McAllister, Mann, Bowen.
Brandon Mill (Woodruff, S.C.): Patty Keesler, Nell Abernathy, Sumner, Foster, Jones, Huff, West, Padgett, Long.
Inman Mill (Inman, S.C.): Lucy Rogers, Cartee, Fisher, Fox, Lovenich, M. Emory, C. Emory, Thrift.
Equinox Mill (Anderson, S.C.): M. Phillips, Crenshaw, R. Phillips, D. Phillips, Gibbs, Carlton, Goodson, Kates, Hicks.

1941

Officers: Horace C. Whitmire (Greenville, S.C.), President; Clarence Thomas (Greenville, S.C.), Secretary.
Executive Committee: Harry Anderson (Lupton City, Tenn.), Ralph Bowie (Piedmont, S.C.), Jesse D. Brown (Greenville, S.C.), Paul Cheek (Asheboro, N.C.), W.T. Kennedy, Jr. (Taylors, S.C.), A.R. Plaster (Winston-Salem, N.C.), Fred B. Pollard (Kingsport, Tenn.), Roy Salter (Thomaston, Ga.), J.W. James (Greenville, S.C.), Charles Freeman (Greenville, S.C.).

Class A Men
Dixie Mercerizing (Lupton City, Tenn.), champions: Harry Anderson (coach), Charles Cox, Charles Tolbert, Grayson Davis, Fred Shirley, D.I. Durham, Efford Norris, Lew Lawing, Fred Ballard, Neal Anderson, Melvin Seals, L.D. Tolbert.
Southern Bleachery (Taylors, S.C.), runners-up: O.W. Robinson (coach), Bert Hill, C.T. Suddeth, Ray Wilson, Ben Burnett, Andy

Hawthorne, Snow Kirby, Willie Wilbanks, George Blackwell.

Beacon Mill (Swannanoa, N.C.), consolation winners: J.O. Buchanan (coach), Milton Ellis, F. Blankenship, William Horne, Parks Poteat, Samuel Patton, Lester Branson, Roy Patton, Woodrow Patton, Claude Kitchen.

Judson Mill (Greenville, S.C.): Robert Pridmore (coach), Albert Nickles (coach), James Trammell, Frank McDaniel, J.W. James, John Cobb, Charles Cobb, Homer Compton, J.D. McAlister.

Union Bleachery (Greenville, S.C.): James Wood (coach), W.A. Bishop (coach), Roy Brooks, Ansel Bridwell, William Bishop, Charles Brooks, John Dilworth, James Ivey, James Rogers, James Trammell, Barney Hawkins, Adger Jones.

Pelzer Mill (Pelzer, S.C.): Dewey Quinn (coach), J.W. Jordan, Ralph Cannon, L.T. Harris, J.E. Henderson, Cyrial Haney, Garvin Pridmore, David Greer, Earl Byers, Horace Davenport, T.C. McKee.

Piedmont Mill (Piedmont, S.C.): Maurice Terry (coach), Harry Waldrop (coach), Frank Grover, J.D. Hunnicutt, Edgar Patterson, Lee Parker, Marvin Smith, Tom Pack, G.B. Buckheister, John Rampey, LeRoy Hunnicutt.

Calhoun Falls Mill (Calhoun Falls, S.C.): Charles Verner (coach), Henry Bland, Howard Thomas, Howard Thackston, Ford Waldrop, Joe Martin, Lloyd Chastain, Ray Darnell, Dean Thomas, Thomas Ripley.

American Enka (Enka, N.C.): Andy Brandl (coach), Russell Allen, William Allen, Don Campbell, Vincent Cooper, Mitchell Gaddy, Arthur Hazeltine, Holly Hipps, Arnold Holcombe, N.L. Lovingood, Charles Munday.

Hanes Hosiery Mill (Winston-Salem, N.C.): George Watson (coach), Hugh Hampton, Clyde Speas, Vestal Speas, Weldon Johnson, Reece McSwain, Carl Snow, Robert Slaydon, Phil Poole, Glen LeVan.

Dunean Mill (Greenville, S.C.): C.H. Thomas (coach), Fred Parks, James Roddy, James Gosnell, William Riddle, Fred Snoddy, Robert Donnan, Robert Cooper, Roy Owens, Paul Case, Otis Putnam.

Oconee Mill (Westminster, S.C.): Ben Sharp (coach), D.J. Hamilton (coach), W.D. Robinson, Marvin Rackley, Vernon McCrary, Carlos Williams, T.J. Canup, A.W. Bagwell, R.S. King, A.V. Seymour, F.A. Sharp, Robert Grogan, Crawford.

Chicopee Mill (Gainesville, Ga.): J.A. Neighbors (coach), Arthur Hudgins, Gerald Meeks, Edmond Bennett, John Weldon, Levis Clark, June Boggs, Ivan Buice, Jerry Weldon, Eugene Taylor, Charles Adams.

Monaghan Mill (Greenville, S.C.): Lee Coleman (coach), Thorn Henson (coach), Demus Elder, Harry Herring, Palmer McAvoy, Carlos Thompson, Franklin Griffith, Fred Bagwell, James Worthy, Phillip Stewart, Jack McCall, O.D. Gosnell.

Adams-Millis (High Point, N.C.): J.R. McCachern (coach), Lelon Cooper, Carl Cooper, Enoch Cooper, Eiland Farlow, Forrest Edwards, John Sappenfield, Nelson Blue, Claude Wright Jr., C.W. Martin.

Peerless Woolen Mill (Rossville, Ga.): Walter Lauter (coach), C.R. McIntosh, Jeff Roark, Bill Rogers, Jack Bailey, Ray Fritts, Louie Fitzgerald, John Peck, Sam Millsapps, Andy Curley.

Chatham Mfg. (Elkin, N.C.): Bill Mann (coach), Paul Badgett, Jim Merrill, Don Brock, Bill Dixon, Thomas Tuttle, Hassell Frye, E.D. Lane, Maurice Eddinger, Bernard Mock, Crater, Harris.

Ninety Six Mill (Ninety Six, S.C.): Fred Ross (coach), William Harris, Clarence Allen, Buna Wells, Jim Voiselle, Glenn Forrester, Bill Voiselle, Bennie Faulkner, Alvin Drummond, Roy May.

Drayton Mill (Spartanburg, S.C.): L.R. Corbin (coach), Garland Oshields, Charles Seay, William Dixon, Ralph Dodds, John Earnhart, Ralph Gibbs, Louie Davis, Manning Bagwell, Luther Corbin, J.D. Morgan.

Victor Mill (Greer, S.C.): S.V. Wilson (coach), Paul Moreland (coach), Sam Turner, S.V. Wilson Jr., Belton Cabaniss, Robert Traynham, Milton Maness, Donald Jackson, William Tidwell, Charles Putman, Willie Hutchinson.

Walhalla Mill (Walhalla, S.C.): Lee Smith (coach), Clyde Seigler (coach), J.A. Galliard, Willard Mills, Louis Elliott, Coley Garrett, John Smith, Joyce Burgess, Frank Whitt, Ralph James, Reuben Hartley, R. Smith.

McCrary Hosiery Mill (Asheboro, N.C.): Paul Cheek (coach), Paul Roy, Neal Cockerham, William Wright, Jack Hammond, Maurice Watts, Fred Tompkins, Wayne Harris, Earl Ruth, Julian McClean, Roy Boles.

Peerless Cotton Mill (Thomaston, Ga.): Roy Salter (coach), Tarvie Lester, Tom Collins,

Robert Williams, J.L. Wilder, James Cowart, C.R. McIntosh, Frank Boss, Joseph Howard, Charles Parker.

Brandon Mill (Woodruff, S.C.): Harold Taylor (coach), George Morgan, Dennis Loftis, C.D. Padgett, LeRoy Taylor, William Waters, Louis Keesler, Herbert Hundley, Ulysses Sprouse, R.C. Boyter, H. Taylor, Howley.

Calloway Mill (LaGrange, Ga.): J.B. Crawford (coach), Cleo Noles, James Burdette, John Huff, Amon Eady, James Reed, Tom Noles, Cecil Kelly, Delbert Heard, Edmund Fahl, W.J. Amason, T. Wales.

CLASS B MEN

Pacific Mill (Columbia, S.C.), champions: J.D. Pittman (coach), Lewis White (coach), Archie Pearson, Andrew Daniels, James Darby, W.S. Gordon, Dewey Pursley, Bill Simpson, Ed Herbert, Ace Herbert, Allen Martin, B.E. Davis, Shorty McQuarters, Mauldin, Hamm.

Tennessee Eastman (Kingsport, Tenn.), runners-up: Robert Cunningham (coach), Kent Neufer, Harry Garmand, W.K. Cantwell, James Neely, Claude Wright, Fred Stone, Paul Schneider, G.A. Wessinger, George Shipley, George Grills, Shetley.

Orr Mill (Anderson, S.C.), consolation winners: Troy Kirby (coach), Harry Davis (coach), W.N. Burris, Johnny Ashworth, James Orr, George Jolly, Fred Whitten, Clyde Blackwell, James Hawkins, William Strickland, Claude Turner, George Hammett.

Peerless Woolen Mill (Rossville, Ga.): Paul Ellis (coach), Jennings Green, Arthur Cook, Arthur Brown, Reba Wyatt, Peck Hansard, Charles Gifford, Cecil Fowler, Raines Bailey.

Dunean Mill "Owls" (Greenville, S.C.): Roy Moore (coach), Charles Mullinax (coach), T. Roddy, A. Jones, Bill Moore, Floyd Owens, Joe Hunter, David Scott, Ed Hale, Ralph Johnson, Tommy Carpenter, Earnest Millsap.

Dunean Mill (Greenville, S.C.): C.H. Thomas (coach), Louie Morgan, William Putman, Johnny Oglesby, William Lollis, Minor Christopher, Robert Snoddy, Charles Callahan, Raymond Putman, Marion Donnan, Robert Carpenter.

Cramerton Mill (Cramerton, N.C.): Ed Maxwell (coach), Cecil Bolix, Jay Rotan, G.V. Brendle, James Reese, Vernon Reese, James Rotan, Pat Ware, T.P. Brendle, Edward Van Pelt, Sol Brendle.

Renfrew Bleachery (Travelers Rest, S.C.): Dudley Tollison (coach), Boyce Greer, Ralph Johnson, Grady Bridwell, N.H. Forrest, Leslie Wood, William Johnson, Joel Roe, Leonard Brown, John Bledsoe, Woodrow Wilson.

Poe Mill (Greenville, S.C.): Wilson, Westmoreland, Williams, Spencer, Grastie, Guest, Pittman, Friddle, Bright.

Converse Mill (Spartanburg, S.C.): R. Calvert (coach), Wister Donald, Art Fowler, Yonnie Greene, Richard Evans, Robert Greene, Charles Reid, William Wooten, Elmer Burch, Walter Fowler, James King, A. Powell.

Camperdown Mill (Greenville, S.C.): J.W. McDowell (coach), Charles Penland (coach), Alvin Burnette, Jim Lollis, James Dill, Louie McDowell, John McDowell, Melvin Gunter, Frank Goodwin, Charles Whitaker, Mack Bruce, Dennis Whitaker.

Mills Mill (Greenville, S.C.): A.H. Wells (coach), F.H. Cunningham (coach), C.H. Smith, W.H. Shuttleworth, V.M. Norris, Charles Pearson, Frank Sexton, Welborn Trammell, William Henry, Edward Bridges, J.R. Cothran, A.J. Abbott, McJunkin.

Judson Mill (Greenville, S.C.): J.R. Forrest (coach), William Grissop, Jack Roddy, Ray Duffie, Paul Hazel, Alvin Kemp, Johnny Hall, Max Foster, Tony Long, Ralph Tallant, Robert Tallant.

Southern Worsted (Greenville, S.C.): W.H. Grant (coach), W.P. Jackson (coach), Marion West, Hoke Styles, James Simpson, Robert Davis, George Alverson, Thomas McCauley, William Vess, Mack Waldrop, Dupree Vess, Henry Brannon.

Laurens Mill (Laurens, S.C.): Walter Gosnell (coach), Francis Thompson (coach), Clyde Taylor, F.P. Thompson, Charles Kirby, Bruce Templeton, James Copeland, William Roberts, Samuel Gosnell, Raymond Spoon, Harold Taylor, Albert Campbell.

Poinsett Mill (Greenville, S.C.): Frank Millwood (coach), James Townsend (coach), Ray Wilson, Arthur Hammett, Paul Fair, Shaw Brannon, Leroy Chapman, Artis Bridwell, William Mardis, Horace Fair, Lawrence Landers, Elbert Lavender.

Joanna Mill (Joanna, S.C.): A.B. Galloway (coach), Cecil Farmer, Rudolph Prater, Willis Phillips, Earnest Spires, Olga Hair, Morton Hamm, Guy Prater, Horace Ridings, Charles Ross, Furman Mauldin.

McEwen Mill (Burlington, N.C.): Glenn Slaughter (coach), James Roach, Joe Cox, Sam

Southern Textile Basketball Tournament Rosters   Appendix 1   153

Gatlin, Dewey Melton, Edwin Walker, Howard Walker, Kenneth Hughes, Earl Cox, Cyrus Alphine.

Lonsdale Mill (Seneca, S.C.): J.F. Mason (coach), Clyde Davis (coach), Ottice Latham, James Black, Garnett Latham, Ostell Shirley, Ralph Maxey, Clarence Galliard, James Shirley, Conway Vickery, Ernest Dooley, Frank Loftis.

Rogers Hosiery Mill (Laurens, S.C.): William McDade (coach), John Putnam, W.E. Ballenger, Jack Adams, Richard Bell, Frank Waldrop, James Coleman, A.B. Campbell, Rossie Gahan.

Slater Mill (Slater, S.C.): Wade Puckett (coach), C.H. Wright (coach), Dacus Tucker, F.W. Dawkins, F.V. Weathers, Gilbert Rogers, James McMakin, Marion Dudley, William Cashion, Gartrell McDuffie, William Clark, Harold Taylor.

Greer Mill (Greer, S.C.): Woodrow Hanvey (coach), C.C. Taylor (coach), Roy Taylor, Furman Taylor, Wallace Taylor, Fred Hemphill, Wyatt Copeland, Everette Pate, Charlie Roper, A.D. Hardin.

Southern Bleachery (Taylors, S.C.): O.W. Robinson (coach), Bo Bowers, Warren Trammell, Lloyd Edwards, Basco Clayton, William Bishop, James McNamara, James Epting, C.L. Smith.

Columbus Mill (Columbus, Ga.): J.K. Davis (coach), Frederick Hurston, Fentress Richardson, Gordon Donahue, Edward Carmack, Robert Shelton, Elzy Widgeon, Thomas Noble, Hugh Hasty, Walter Grey, Lassiter.

Abbeville Mill (Abbeville, S.C.): Thomas Argo (coach), Ralph Simpson, Rufus Powell, W.H. Woolbright, Leslie Wilson, Walter Fossett, George Powell, Charles Chase, E.W. McCurry Jr., Oscar New, Jack Hughes.

Brandon Mill (Greenville, S.C.): J.A. Carnes Sr. (coach), J.A. Carnes Jr. (coach), James Limbaugh, Joe Anders, Robert Ingle, Buck Friar, Fred Mahon, Burnell Morrow, Marvin Duncan, Earl King, Norman Chapman, Ray Wynn.

Valdese Community Center (Valdese, N.C.): Jimmie Chambers (coach), Claude Owens, Henry Bounous, Howard Pruett, Edd Pitts, Edd Perrou, Charles Campbell, Louie Viney, Clarence Stassavich, Edd Flack, James DeBerry.

Goodyear Clearwater Mill (Rockmart, Ga.): Bob McGhee (coach), Harrison Anderson, Hugh Britt, Carl Cown, Jack Parham, John Purcell, Thomas McKeown, Lester Garrison, Howard Thomas, Russell.

Class C Men

Monaghan Mill (Greenville, S.C.), champions: M. Herring (coach), Bud Stephens (coach), Bomar Keller, Roy Link, John Blackston, Jack Ballew, Charles Staton, Raymond Christopher, Fred Ellis, Jack Ellis, Charles Summer, Clyde Christopher.

Pelzer Mill (Pelzer, S.C.), runners-up: Dewey Quinn (coach), Wilton Dickson, Charlie McConnell, Wallace Suddeth, James Davis, Henry Smith, Leon Kay, Bill Fowler, Dan Ragsdale, Jarnette Floyd, Earl Wooten, Ross.

Appleton Mill (Anderson, S.C.), consolation winners: A.E. Elrod (coach), Claude Spake (coach), Billy Middleton, Samuel Carlton, James Faulkner, Farris Bailey, Jim Massey, Harold Bailey, Harold Gunter, Lewis King, Welton Junkins, Gary Spake.

Camperdown Mill (Greenville, S.C.): Frank Brown (coach), C.T. Whitaker (coach), Jack Whitaker, William Dendy, Harold Cooper, Jack Mintz, James Cureton, Eugene Davis, Robert Marchbanks, Carl Chewning, Sydney Bruce Jr., Jack Coln.

Dunean Mill (Greenville, S.C.): C.H. Thomas (coach), R.W. Donnan, Angus Marchbanks, Harold Quinn, Frank Lollis, Joe Farris, Ralph Mann, Gaines Campbell, Roy Whitehead, Guy Shook, Garren, Lankford.

Judson Mill (Greenville, S.C.): James Dill (coach), James Harbin (coach), Gerald Crawford, L.S. Littlejohn, John Nimmons, Harold Pearce, George Davenport, Charles Davenport, K.C. Kuykendall, Vernon Treadway, Alton Grissop, Leon Mason.

Equinox Mill (Anderson, S.C.): Allen Parnell (coach), J.B. Spearman (coach), Sam Simpson, Jerry Goodman, Bo Adams, Carl Adams, Herman Simpson, Jake Smith, Harvey Brock, Howard Goodson, Doodle Smith, J.R. Dillingham, Dixon.

Orr Mill (Anderson, S.C.): Milford Ellison (coach), Henry Lindsay (coach), G.C. Stamps, Britt Vernon, Robert Hulme, James McCurry, John Pierce, Tom Cleveland, Marvin Meeks, Sammy Meeks, Eugene Porter, Donald Powers.

Piedmont Mill (Piedmont, S.C.): Ralph Allen (coach), S.C. Hawkins (coach), Charles Anderson, Harry Terry, Robert Porter, Willard Bishop, Edward Fowler, Robert Bryson, Fred

Shackleford, Thomas Trammell, Dillard Burrell, Billy White.

Dunean Scouts (Greenville, S.C.): C.H. Thomas (coach), Gaines Luther Jr., Charles Coleman, James Allen, Raymond Cox Jr., Joe Wood, Thomas Hughes, Harold Waldrop, Lewis Allison, Virgil Roddy.

Renfrew Bleachery (Travelers Rest, S.C.): Dudley Tollison (coach), Douglas Debrabant, James Blalock Jr., Lewis Lockaby, James Tribble, Alvin Batson, Charles Bridges, Roy Lockaby, William Donnelly, Ford Duncan.

Union Bleachery (Greenville, S.C.): Mrs. Nettie Patterson (coach), Alton Patterson (coach), Aronus Belcher, Elbert Brown, James Evington, Richard Evington, Warrie Green, Theodore Ivey, Vernon McJunken, Kenneth Robertson, Paul Turner, Bagwell, Bridwell.

Victor Mill (Greer, S.C.): Clyde Simmons (coach), Lloyd Campbell (coach), Louis Hughes, Harold Tucker, Dewey Elders, Cecil Campbell, Thomas Miller, Benford Fleming, Eugene Compton, Marion Wilson, Roy Vehorn, Earl Young.

Woodside Mill (Greenville, S.C.): Andrew Manley (coach), Ray Herbert (coach), Jerry Jackson, Talmadge Tollison, George Miller, Billy Wakefield, Curtis Beasley, Elbert Christopher, Walter Davis, S.N. McConnell, George Pruitt, Clarence Richard.

Brandon Mill (Greenville, S.C.): Charlie Rogers (coach), Doyle Clary (coach), W.P. Dilworth Jr., William Griffin, George Austin, James Orr, Harry Foster, Calvin Morrow, Carlyle Huff, Joe Huff, Jack Pitts, G.W. McAmish.

Class A Women

Chatham Mfg. (Elkin, N.C.), champions: Claudia Austin (coach), Melba Poole, Leva Smith, Anne Lineback, Dot Samuels, Jannie Sherrill, Jennie Sherrill, Maurice Gordan, Jennie Amburn, Katherine Whitener, Viola Norman, Hazel Howell, Helen Doub, Crater, Perkins.

American Enka (Enka, N.C.), runners-up: Dorothy Gaston (coach), Frances Bailey, Beulah Brown, Geneva Burnett, Ella Corn, Gussie Couch, Betty Henry, M.H. Holbrook, Alice Mallonee, Mertis Price, Hazel Reynolds, Mildred Reynolds, Edith Stamey.

Hanes Hosiery Mill (Winston-Salem, N.C.), consolation winners: George Watson (coach), Helen Hanes, Gwen Bruner, Ruhmel Cox, Ozelma Burwell, Verniece Boyles, Edith Smitherman, Myrtle Reavis, Gladys Reavis, Margaret Landreth, Aniece Shields, Mary Masten, Nancy Linville.

Drayton Mill (Spartanburg, S.C.): Smith Crow (coach), Wilma Whitlock, Rachel Durham, Isable Brown, Della Clayton, Elsie Skipper, Mayo Barnett, Nell Elder, Rosa Brown, Eva Saylors, Audrey Parris, Mildred Cope, Alma Rogers, Splawn.

Dixie Mercerizing (Lupton City, Tenn.): Melvin Seals (coach), Opal Outlaw, Ina Cox, Ressie Hunley, Essie Henderson, Inez Roberts, Edna Wagner, Nellie Keaton, Floy Jones, Virginia Paris, Willie Mae Street, Ellen Martin, Mildred Tallant, Marlowe.

Class B Women

Grey Hosiery Mill (Hendersonville, N.C.), champions: Dorothy Hamilton (coach), Margaret McCrary, Lassie Dunne, Bernice Anders, Mary Orr, Marjorie Huffman, Dorothy Orr, Ola Godfrey, Adleyn Ward, Della Sitton, Lucy Anders, Margaret Jones, Katherine Staton, Ila Nix.

McEwen Mill (Burlington, N.C.), runners-up: Glenn Slaughter (coach), Thelma Roach, Grace McAdams, Margaret McAdams, Lucille Clayton, Mae Rudd, Avon Dixon, Evelyne Jones, Harris Garrison, Louise Pender, Corine Moore, Lena Parker, Lillian Hedrick.

Lonsdale Mill (Seneca, S.C.), consolation winners: Winder Gary (coach), Frank Gaillard (coach), Ruth Latham, Martha Whitt, Grace McKee, Rachel Wyatt, Eunice Black, Reginald Gaillard, Lizzie Black, Dot Newton, Elizabeth Young, Kathlyn Owens, Junie James, Callahan.

Judson Mill (Greenville, S.C.): Johnny Stokes (coach), Sybil Hall, Gladys Means, Margaret Owens, Bobbie Hall, Elise Means, Dolly Stokes, E.M. Moreland, Odette Rhymer, Margaret Duffie, Kathleen Roberts, Nealy Hall, Ethel Trammell, J. Means.

Anderson Mill (Anderson, S.C.): Carlisle Thompson (coach), Ninetta Thompson, Fredda Thompson, Mildred James, Elize Bridges, D. Higgenbotham, Eloise Craft, Winona Chandler, Mildred Morris, Betty Boggs, Hazel Raynolds, Cornelia Timms, Sybil Stastny.

Dunean Mill (Greenville, S.C.): C.H. Thomas (coach), Billie Riddle, Betty Lollis, Margie Lollis, Geraldine Shook, Margaret Donnan, Evelyn Cox, Viola Thompson, Margaret Putnam, Margaret Cox, Lois Roddy, M. Cox.

Pickens Mill (Pickens, S.C.): Harold Adams (coach), Wilson Hunt (coach), Leander Hayes, M. Woodward, Effie Parker, Mary Powell, Josie Powell, Pauline Pace, Sophie Coleman, Fannie Moore, Mildred Holder, Velma Adams, Martha Harden, Anna Wilson.

Oconee Mill (Westminster, S.C.): Ben Sharp (coach), Louise Hamilton, Sarah Wilson, Reba Cain, Ruth Cain, Vozelle Martin, Lucille White, Evelyn Williams, Lucille Gilden, Margaret Freeman, Wilma King.

Converse Mill (Spartanburg, S.C.): DeFoix Calvert (coach), Teadie Childers, Beulah Burch, Ruth Burch, Millie Childers, Alta Crocker, Madge Wells, Helen Bozeman, Vivian Wooten, Lois Gault.

Rock Hill Bleachery (Rock Hill, S.C.): Wayne White (coach), Dorothy Robinson, Rebecca Robinson, Jean Moore, Frances Therrell, Cleon Tolbert, Jean Smith, Kitty Tucker, Wilma Bell.

Ninety Six Mill (Ninety Six, S.C.): Fred Ross (coach), Edna Jones, Emma Wood, Elsie Collins, E. Drummond, Thelma Highsmith, Helen Belue, Hazel Turner, Beatrice Cheek, Margie Campbell, Lesie Smith, Frances Wells, Betty Padgett.

--------- 1942 ---------

Officers: Horace Whitmire (Greenville, S.C.), President; J.D. Brown (Greenville, S.C.), Vice President; Clarence Thomas (Greenville, S.C.), Secretary; Ralph Bowie (Piedmont, S.C.), Treasurer.

Executive Committee: Harry Anderson (Lupton City, Tenn.), Paul Cheek (Asheboro, N.C.), A.R. Plaster (Winston-Salem, N.C.), Roy Salter (Thomaston, Ga.), J.W. James (Greenville, S.C.), Charles Freeman (Greenville, S.C.), A.B. Galloway (Goldville, S.C.), Lee Coleman (Greenville, S.C.), Bert Hill (Taylors, S.C.), L.R. Corbin (Spartanburg, S.C.).

Class A Men

Dixie Mercerizing (Lupton City, Tenn.), champions: Harry Anderson (coach), Clyde Mize (mgr), Efford Norris, Lee Lawing, Fred Ballard, Fred Shirley, Grayson Davis, Charles Tolbert, Bill Cordell, Reba Wyatt, Cox.

McCrary Hosiery Mill (Asheboro, N.C.), runners-up: Paul Cheek (coach), Paul Roye, Neal Cockerham, Bill Wright, Arthur Powers, Roy Patton, Frank Brower, Garland Routh, Julian McLean, Jim McCracken, Ruth.

Peerless Woolen Mill (Rossville, Ga.), consolation winners: Carl Crosslin (coach), Walter Lauter (coach), Louis Fitzgerald, Clint Norman, Clifford McIntosh, Bill Rogers, Dave Telford, Ray Fritts, Phil Thach, R.C. Williams, Raines Bailey, Arthur Brown.

Hanes Hosiery Mill (Winston-Salem, N.C.): B.C. Hall Jr. (coach), Carl Snow, William Greer, William Gardner, Hugh Hampton, Robert Slaydon, Walter Frye, Vestal Speas, Joe Sprinkle, Pete Futrell, Dunklee Dunlap.

Piedmont Mill (Piedmont, S.C.): Ralph Allen (coach), Mrs. Ford Waldrop (mgr), Tom Pack, Edgar Patterson, Ford Waldrop, A.C. Taylor, J.D. Hunnicutt, Charles Anderson, Robert Porter, Harry Terry, Doc Anderson, Reese Shirley.

Brandon Mill (Woodruff, S.C.): J.K. Taylor (coach), Harold Taylor (coach), C.D. Padgett, L.G. Morgan, Walter Lowe, Alvin Waters, Louis Keesler, Grady Stafford, Edward Padgett, Buck Cheek, J.C. Fleming, Harold Taylor.

Drayton Mill (Spartanburg, S.C.): L.R. Corbin (coach), J.D. Morgan, John Earnhart, Ralph Gibbs, Dennis Loftis, Joe Durham, Jack Bagwell, Charlie Seay, Garland Oshields, Harold Taylor, Perry Lyles.

Pelzer Mill (Pelzer, S.C.): E.J. O'Bannion (coach), William Harris, Elger Smith, Willie Crymes, James Davis, Ralph Cannon, Dan Ragsdale, Cyril Haney, Horace Davenport, J.W. Jordan, Telford Harris.

Ninety Six Mill (Ninety Six, S.C.): T.S. Bratcher (coach), Roy Drummond, Fred Ross, Clarence Allen, Robert Barbery, Jim Voiselle, Glenn Forrester, Bennie Faulkner, Roy May, Bill Voiselle.

American Enka (Enka, N.C.): Hilliard Arrowood (coach), Ray Lindsey, Charles Munday, Thomas Tweed, Carl McCain, Jennings Henson, Isaac Gaddy, Russell Allen, G.H. Turbefield, Harry Brooks.

Winnsboro Mill (Winnsboro, S.C.): J.W. Jelks (coach), Bill Porter, C.F. Rushing, Brice Wages, Dempsey Gunter, James Askew, Bill Spires, D.E. Stevenson, M.D. Spigner Jr., John Copeland, Furman Reynolds.

Southern Bleachery (Taylors, S.C.): Edward Kirby (coach), J.S. Kay (coach), Furman Taylor, Bernice Bowers, Lloyd Edwards, Willie

Wilbanks, Buck Friar, C.T. Suddeth Jr., John Harbin, Palmer McAvoy, Ray Watson, Everette Pate, Wilson.

Dunean Mill (Greenville, S.C.): Bill Byers (coach), Robert Donnan, Fred Parks, Fred Cox, C.H. Thomas, Raymond Putnam, Clarence Odell, William Riddle, Bailey Byers.

Oconee Mill (Westminster, S.C.): Ben Sharp (coach), Frank Sharp, William Robinson, John Smith, LeRoy Smith, Coley Garrett, Thurston Canup, Walker Bagwell, Roddy King, Lester Wilson, Marvin Rackley.

Goodyear Clearwater Mill (Rockmart, Ga.): Bob McGhee (coach), H.L. Anderson, Carl Cown, Charles Womack, Jack Parham, H.W. Hudspeth, Elbert Coalson, Garrison.

Class B Men

May-McEwen-Kaiser (Burlington, N.C.), champions: Howard Walker (coach), Earl Cox, John Burwell, James Roach, Frank Phillips, Glen Slaughter, Ira Crenshaw, John Reiber, Sam Gatlin, Joe Frasier, Howard Walker.

Brandon Mill (Greenville, S.C.), runners-up: James Carnes Jr. (coach), Carlisle Huff, Clarence Orr, Robert Ingle, James Limbaugh, Ray Wynn, Joe Anders, James Orr, Jack Pitts, Doyle Clary, Charlie Rogers.

Lonsdale Mill (Seneca, S.C.), consolation winners: J.F. Mason (coach), C. Davis (coach), Horace Galliard, Harley James, Ralph Maxie, Ottice Latham, E.O. Shirley, Hoyt Gibson, B.F. Taylor, Frank Harbin, James Shirley, Clarence Galliard, Garrison.

Gossett Mill (Anderson, S.C.): Chris Suber Jr. (coach), N.G. Hardie (coach), James Cobb, C.M. Hendrix, Fred Whitten, David Morgan, D.H. Hendrix, H.T. McClellan, C.C. Chavious, Stephen Jones, Thomas Hampton, G.E. Dickard.

Jackson Mill (Iva, S.C.): H.G. Baskin (mgr), Hurtgrove Baskin (coach), E.D. Alexander, Don Latham, B.P. Burdette, Roy Pryor, Harold Pryor, Joe Yeargin, Fent Latham, Hoyt Dixon, Clyde McAlister.

Poinsett Mill (Greenville, S.C.): James Townsend (coach), I.J. Fair (coach), Luke Landers, Ray Wilson, Paul Fair, B.C. Mardis, L.R. Chapman, S.E. Brannon, Claude Gilstrap, J.B. Templeton, E.A. Fair, R.F. Alexander.

Anderson Mill (Anderson, S.C.): W.H. Embler (coach), Chafer Honea, Samuel Kay, Marshall Hill, Jefferson Embler, Ezra Embler, Jimmie Embler, Waymon Moore, Luiaco Goodson, Roy Bridges, D. Embler.

Mills Mill (Greenville, S.C.): Boyd McCall (coach), Jimmy Reeves (coach), A.C. Crout, Charles Smith, Ted Ratenski, Rudy Cothran, Frank Norris, Paul Putnam, R.M. Hillhouse, H.C. Pearson, Myron Floyd, T.C. Putnam.

Dunean Mill (Greenville, S.C.): Bill Byers (coach), Floyd Owens, Robert Snoddy, Guy Shook, M.L. Christopher, William Putnam, Joe Hunter, Claude Long.

Joanna Mill (Joanna, S.C.): A.B. Galloway (coach), Guy Prater, Rudolph Prater, Joe Hunter, Cecil Farmer, L.W. Little, Morton Hamm, Voight Kunkle, E.T. Spires, Willis Phillips.

Poe Mill (Greenville, S.C.): Henry Williams (coach), Elmo Reese (coach), Jack Williams, John Guest, Joe Mostella, William Wilson, William Bishop, Everette Pittman, Roy Morgan, Ray Rogers, Alva Phillips, C.C. Thompson.

Monaghan Mill (Greenville, S.C.): Harry Herring (coach), Frank Griffith (coach), W.C. Johnson Jr., John Blackston, Charles Ross, B.R. Traynham, J.G. Hancock, Jack Ellis, Ernest Ellis, Ralph Johnson, Joe Hodgens, Harry McCall, Christopher.

Simpsonville Mill (Simpsonville, S.C.): Len Goodenough (coach), Joe Smith (coach), Robert Cox, Carl Hamby, Donald Barbery, Richard Terry, O'dell Barbery, Sam Sloan, R.J. Goodenough, George Burgess, Earl Brashier, E.M. Goodenough.

Lockhart Mill (Lockhart, S.C.): Byrdie Allgood (coach), Edward Eubanks (coach), James Burns, Walter Burns, Bill Broome, Edward Adams, Robert Cabiness, Ralph Howard, Cecil Candler, T.E. Broome, Cecil Carter, James Goode, Edwards.

Columbus Mill (Columbus, Ga.): D.W. Corzine (coach), Edward Carmack, F. Richardson, Frederick Hurston, Elzy Widgeon, Gordon Donahue, Buddy Hasty, Cecil Bailey, Walter Gray, Cliff Catchings, Billy Sizemore.

Class C Men

Pelzer Mill (Pelzer, S.C.), champions: Roy Taylor, Bill Quinn, Dewey Quinn, Earl Wooten, C.J. McConnell, Roy Whitlock, W.H. Dickson, J.W. McConnell, Hoyt Jordan, William Maness.

Dunean Mill (Greenville, S.C.), runners-up: Bill Byers (coach), Manning Garren,

Horace Turner, James Allen, Frank Lollis, R.W. Donnan Jr., Lewis Allison, Roy Whitehead, Raymond Cox, Patrick Sorgee, Milton Hughes.

Orr Mill (Anderson, S.C.), consolation winners: Henry Lindsay (coach), B.M. Gunnells (coach), Britt Vernon, Jim Meeks, Grover Stamps, Henry McCurry, Marvin Meeks, Eugene Porter, Beaty Pierce, William Powers, Tom Cleveland, Albert Powell.

Monarch Mill (Union, S.C.): Walter Trammell (coach), Bennie Bobo, T.D. Smith Jr., Milan Berry, L.M. Kirby Jr., James Wright, E.P. Russell, Mack Garner, S.S. Sanders.

Brandon Mill (Greenville, S.C.): Ralph McDonald (coach), Burnell Morrow (coach), E.M. Morrow, C.W. Morrow, M.H. Foster, L.E. Lanford, G.L. Austin, D.H. Henson, Joe Huff, James Wilson, William Dilworth, James Tribble.

Monaghan Mill (Greenville, S.C.): J.W. Ross Jr. (coach), Buck Waldrop (coach), Robert McAvoy, Richard Barbare, Furman Moman, C.F. Christopher, Harold Johnson, Charles Staton, Billy Griffith, Robert Foster, Harold Greene, Carl Whitten.

Calhoun Falls Mill (Calhoun Falls, S.C.): Ray Darnell (coach), Jessie Ayers, Thomas Ripley, L.G. Alexander, Morris Manley, W.E. Lovern, Billie Gilliam, Mickey Gray, William Thomas, Clarence Cox, Joe Owens.

Renfrew Bleachery (Travelers Rest, S.C.): Dudley Tollison (coach), L.T. Lockaby, Roy Lockaby, Charles Bridges, Edmund Poole, Doyle Belcher, Jimmy Balloch Jr., Ford Duncan, Roy Wood, Joe Cook.

Judson Mill (Greenville, S.C.): D.L. Lockee (coach), Bill Grissop (coach), C.G. Luther Jr., J.N. McFadden Jr., D.W. Garrett, C.W. Bishop, James Roberts, V.P. Treadway, John Nimmons, G.T. Crawford, C.H. Crews, H.T. Blackwell.

Camperdown Mill (Greenville, S.C.): C.E. Penland (coach), J.W. Dill (coach), Eugene Davis, Hubert Bishop, Wallace Huff, Bill Dendy, Jack Whitaker, Harold Cooper, Jack Mintz, Carlos Davidson, Robert Marchbanks, Earl Evett.

Dunean Mill Anchors (Greenville, S.C.): C.H. Thomas (coach), Bruce Marchbanks, Austin Owens, James Bell, James Osteen, Virgil Roddy, Maurice Lankford, Charles Coleman, Harold Waldrop, Joe Simmons, William Riddle, Campbell.

Appleton Mill (Anderson, S.C.): Austin Elrod (coach), Monk Spake (coach), Billy Middleton, Inman Roland, S.L. Carlton, Vernon Jarrett, James Faulkner, Welton Junkins, Lewis King, Farris Bailey, Harold Gunter, Clarence Free.

Victor Mill (Greer, S.C.): Ted Cabaniss (coach), S.V. Wilson Jr. (coach), Harold Tucker, Marion Wilson, Cecil Campbell, Robert Lamb, Walter Bruce, Curtiss McKain, Thomas Miller, Belton Cabaniss, Cody McKinley.

Woodside Mill (Greenville, S.C.): Jerry Jackson (coach), Ray Herbert (coach), George Miller, T.A. Tollison, Veldee Hines, George Pruitt, Curtis Beasley, W. Davis Jr., S.M. McConnell, Billie Wakefield, Robert King, John McKinney.

Mills Mill (Greenville, S.C.): R.R. Brock (coach), Henry Guiles (coach), Charles Brock, A.W. McJunkin, John Guess, Harry Friar, John King, Lloyd Pittman, Wade Bell, Robert Ross.

Brandon Mill (Woodruff, S.C.): C.M. Padgett (coach), R.C. Boyter (coach), John LeRoy, Robert Rogers, James Lucker, Paul Pressley, Phillip LeRoy, Floyd Hughes, Fred Skinner, Earl Stafford, Charles Huff, Floyd Taylor.

Greer Mill (Greer, S.C.): Charlie Taylor (coach), Troy McAllister (coach), Robert Campbell, W.R. Taylor, Thomas Duncan, Charles Clarke, Charles Brannon, James Campbell, Edgar Gowan, Theron Giles, Grady Harvey.

Union Bleachery (Greenville, S.C.): Pat Patterson (coach), Walker Dilworth (coach), R.T. Evington, N.M. Bridwell, Cornelius Evington, Clyde Robertson, W.H. Robertson, Aromus Belcher, Paul Turner Jr., K.H. Henderson.

CLASS A WOMEN

Chatham Mfg. (Elkin, N.C.), champions: Claudia Austin (coach), Bill Mann (coach), Dorothy Samuel, Viola Norman, Leva Smith, Jennie Sherrill, Jannie Sherrill, Maurice Gordon, Ann Lineback, C. Whitener, Helen Doub, Hazel Steelman, Pauline Martin, Violet Ring.

Hanes Hosiery Mill (Winston-Salem, N.C.), runners-up: B.C. Hall Jr. (coach), Helen Hanes, Bernice Petree, Aniece Shields, M.E. Landreth, Verniece Boyles, Gwendolyn Bruner, Myrtle Reavis, Mary Masten, Ruhmel Cox, E.M. Smitherman, N.S. Newsome, Gladys Reavis.

Drayton Mill (Spartanburg, S.C.), consolation winners: G.G. Simmons (coach), Wilma Whitlock, Mayo Barnett, Beulah Splawn, Elsie Skipper, Alma Rogers, Ailene Cudd, Audrey Parris, Beulah Elders, Jessie McIntyre, Margery Fagan, Della Clayton, Lillian Scarborough.

American Enka (Enka, N.C.): Dorothy Gaston (coach), G.L. Burnette, Jessie Mills, Beulah Brown, Gussie Couch, Mildred Reynolds, Mertis Prince, Mary Hensley, Edith Stamey, Hazel Reynolds, Hazel Davis, Raymond.

Grey Hosiery Mill (Hendersonville, N.C.): Dorothy Hamilton (coach), Dorothy Orr, Ila Nix, Margaret McCrary, Bernice Anders, Ola Godfrey, Adelyn Ward, Margaret Drake, Jessie Arledge, Marjorie Huffman, Ethel Osteen, Eva Staton, Ethel Perry.

Class B Women

May-McEwen-Kaiser (Burlington, N.C.), champions: Glenn Slaughter (coach), Grace McAdams, M.K. McAdams, Agnes Phillips, Vera Walker, Frances Walker, Dorthia Jones, Evelyn Jones, Lena Parker, Thelma Roach, Mae Rudd, Polly Merritt, Corene Sorrell.

Dunean Mill (Greenville, S.C.), runners-up: Mrs. Bill Byers (coach), Margaret Donnan, M.J. Putnam, Margie Lollis, Margaret Cox, Betty Lollis, Ninetta Thompson, Viola Thompson, Geraldine Shook, Billy Riddle, Willene Enloe, Evelyn Cox, Nellie Donnan.

Ninety Six Mill (Ninety Six, S.C.), consolation winners: Frances Allen (coach), Clarence Allen (coach), Edna Jones, Frances Wells, Elsie Collins, E.F. Drummond, Alice Hall, T.V. Highsmith, Gladys Garrett, Helen Barbery, Betty Padgett, Desaree Martin, West.

Brandon Mill (Greenville, S.C.): Charlie Rogers (coach), Douglas Hutchinson (coach), Mary Quinn, O.E. Buchanan, M.C. Hutchinson, Millie Pitts, Lenora Baker, Joyce Wynn, Evelyn Barr, Frances Nelson, Sara Baker, K.L. McDonald, F.E. McDonald, C.B. Rollins.

Lonsdale Mill (Seneca, S.C.): Winder Gary (coach), J.F. Galliard (coach), Ruth Latham, Frances Lee, Reginald Galliard, Rachael Wyatt, Martha Whitt, Dot Newton, Eunice Black, Alma Wilson, Reba Landers, Betty Latham, Kathlyn Owens, Gladys Foster.

Woodside Mill (Greenville, S.C.): C.B. Carter (coach), Dewey Bowen (coach), Ophelia Smith, Azalee Smith, Juanita Smith, Gladys Price, Annie Waldrop, Dellaree Bowen, Madge Cole, Evelyn Heath, Frances Carter, Anna Osborne, Audrey Nash, Evelyn Norris.

Orr Mill (Anderson, S.C.): Lee Whitten (coach), B.M. Gunnells (coach), Effie Broome, Lura Craft, Ruth King, Ruth Allen, Frances Hanna, Nadine Franks, Delma Porter, Dorothy Porter, Judy Bryant, Vivian Cooley, Ethel Thackston.

Southern Textile Basketball Tournament Suspended 1943-1945

--- 1946 ---

Officers: C.H. Thomas (Greenville, S.C.), President, Treasurer; Jack Reames (La Grange, Ga.), Vice President; J.D. Brown (Greenville, S.C.), Secretary.

Executive Committee: Harry Anderson (Lupton City, Tenn.), Charles Freeman (Greenville, S.C.), Hubert Nolin (Greenville, S.C.), Paul Cheek (Asheboro, N.C.), A.B. Galloway (Goldville, S.C.), A.R. Plaster (Winston-Salem, N.C.), Lee Coleman (Greenville, S.C.), Bert Hill (Taylors, S.C.), Roy Salter (Thomaston, Ga.), Webb Kennedy (Taylors, S.C.), L.R. Corbin (Spartanburg, S.C.), J.W. James (Greenville, S.C.), Aug W. Smith (Greenville, S.C.).

Class A Men

Hanes Hosiery Mill (Winston-Salem, N.C.), champions: B.C. Hall Jr. (coach), Danny Miller, Hugh Hampton, Coot Greer, Wayne Harris, Thomas Sewell, Joseph Sheets, Henry Jackson, Miles Carter Jr., Thurman Binkley, James Conrad, Carl Snow, Virgil Yow.

Peerless Woolen Mill (Rossville, Ga.), runners-up: Walter Lauter (coach), Louis Fitzgerald, Charles Hicks, Reba Wyatt, Charles Cox, Bill Crow, Wilson Bigger, Troy Gregg, Roy Lykins, Robert James, Charles Gifford, John Barger, Ellis.

Pelzer Mill (Pelzer, S.C.), consolation winners: Virgil Lavender (coach), Pete Harris, Earl Wooten, J.W. Jordan, Cyril Haney, Ralph Cannon, L.T. Harris, H.P. Jordan, Horace Davenport, Buck Harris, D.W. Quinn, Taylor, Suddeth.

Tennessee Eastman (Kingsport, Tenn.): Buck Thornton (coach), George Grills, Howard Duncan, Joe Greene, Ralph Williams, C.J.

Southern Textile Basketball Tournament Rosters   Appendix 1   159

Phillips, Kenneth Cantwell, Jack Showalter, Lawrence Thayer, Frank Smith, Neufer.

Woodside Mill (Greenville, S.C.): Jerry Jackson (coach), W.W. Hunter (coach), Ralph Harbin, Fred Bomar, Charles Freeman, Charles Couch, Carlton Couch, Monroe Ramsey, Leonard Canup, Andrew Manley, Julian Pruitt, Dewey Bowen.

Piedmont Mill (Piedmont, S.C.): J.M. Terry (coach), Leroy Anderson (coach), John Emory, J.W. Rampey, Charles Anderson, Sloan Terry, Tom Pack, Ford Waldrop, Curt Terry, Boyce Wynn, R.W. Allen, Ernest Henderson.

Cramerton Mill (Cramerton, N.C.): G.M. Matlack (coach), Arnold Reese, J.A. Cunningham, Cecil Bolick, Thomas Brendle, Vernon Reese, Zob Brendle, Jenks Brendle, A.B. Cunningham, Edward Maxwell, Alvin McKeown.

Ninety Six Mill (Ninety Six, S.C.): Fred Ross (coach), Charles Ross, Jim Voiselle, Glenn Forrester, Lewis Drummond, Calvin Drummond, Harold Ivester, Lloyd Ivester, Charles Byers, Bennie Faulkner.

Monaghan Mill (Greenville, S.C.): Dan Bagwell (coach), Bill Reece (coach), Harry Herring, William Johnson, Aaron Powers, Fred Bagwell, Frank Anderson, Frank Griffith, Lewis Elder, Palmer McAvoy, Paul Fair, James Worthy, J. Ellis, E. Ellis.

Dunean Mill (Greenville, S.C.): Ward Williams (coach), Carl Green, Naula Frix, William Riddle, James Gosnell, Clarence O'Dell, Roy Owens, Milton Hughes, Robert Stowe, Christopher, F. Cox.

Mills Mill #1 (Greenville, S.C.): S.E. Murdock (coach), Carthel Crout, Rudy Cothran, Charles Smith, Ted Ratenski, Charles Pearson, Lewis Abbott, Arthur Cummings, Walter McJunkin, Albert Osborne, James Trammell.

American Enka (Enka, N.C.): Zeno Wall Jr. (coach), Tom Tweed, James Rhea, Arnold Holcombe, George Turbeyville, Duane Morgan, Mitch Grady, Bill Allen, Newton Lovingood, R. Gudger, George Price, Holder, Wekkes.

Union Bleachery (Greenville, S.C.): Roy Brooks (coach), Cullen Turner (coach), James Evington, William Bishop, Aromus Belcher, John Dilworth, Andrew Epps, R.T. Evington, William Harrison, Harold Green, Charles Brooks.

Southern Bleachery (Taylors, S.C.): Fred Coleman (coach), Ray Wilson, Lloyd Edwards, Clarence Smith, Ernest Bridgman, K.C. Tankersley, J.B. Friar, Furman Taylor, Warren Trammell, James Wilson, R.R. Asbury Jr.

McCrary Hosiery Mill (Asheboro, N.C.): Paul Cheek (coach), Neal Cockerham, Weldon Johnson, Maurice Watts, Robert Slaydon, Hiott Morgan, Alton William, Charlie Barnes, Mack McGinn, Bob Wilkins, Bart Walker.

Drayton Mill (Spartanburg, S.C.): E.D. Coker (coach), M.G. Cox (coach), Lemuel Walker, Pete Laurens, Leonard Hill, Charlie Seay, Dennis Loftis, Manning Bagwell, Virgil Caton, W.E. Simmons, Harold Harrelson, Morgan.

CLASS B MEN

Anderson Mill (Anderson, S.C.), champions: C.T. Ripley (coach), Jerry Goodson, Ezra Embler, Marcus Dillard, Donald Hendrix, Chafer Honea, Marvin Spake, Jimmie Embler, Samuel Kay, Roy Bridges, Harold Madden, Good, Moore, Lewis Martin, Marshall Hill, Bill Embler, Delbert Pierce, Fred Whitten.

Woodside Mill (Greenville, S.C.), runners-up: Ralph Mann (coach), Otto Herbert (coach), Walter Davis Jr., Veldee Hines, Everett Waldrop, James Green, George Miller, James Nease, S.N. McConnell Jr., Ray Herbert, Winston Herbert, R.W. Ramey, Pruitt.

Camperdown Mill (Greenville, S.C.), consolation winners: J.W. McDowell (coach), Charlie Penland (coach), Louie McDowell, Melvin Gunter, Alvin Burnett, Harold Cooper, Jack Whitaker, Jamie Dill, Walter Goodwin, Jack Thompson, Kenneth Rollins, R.Y. Marchbanks, Center.

Appleton Mill (Anderson, S.C.): Claude Spake (coach), James Carlton, William Middleton, Farriss Bailey, Andrew King, Welton Junkins, James Morrison, William Shirley, James Williams, Henry Bailey, Henry Spake.

Pacolet Mill (Pacolet, S.C.): Browne Trent (coach), W.A. Dotherow (coach), Kansas Goforth, J.A. Mathis, Chandler Parker, Guy Parker, Walter Harrison, Sam Hogan, James Green, Bill Gardner, Bill Ligon, Arthur Goforth.

Dunean Mill (Greenville, S.C.): Ward Williams (coach), Paul Turner, Harold Quinn, John Garren, Bruce Long, Claude Long, Manning Garren, Vernon Walden, Maford Milsap, Raymond Cox, Lollis.

Brandon Mill (Greenville, S.C.): Charles Harper (coach), Ralph McDonald (coach), Norman Chapman, Eugene Batson, Harold

Limbaugh, Harry Foster, Fred Byrd, Joe Anders, Burnell Morrow, Roy Duncan, Lloyd Ingle, Maurice Morrow.

Mills Mill (Greenville, S.C.): L.C. Burgin (coach), Curtin Powell, Ansel McAlister, Alfred Sizemore, Jimmy Adkins, Ned Davis, Richard Dittmer, Coy Watson, Osborne Ballew, Cecil Lowery, Thomas Cox, Charlie Brock, Fred Dittman.

Orr Mill (Anderson, S.C.): J.O. Ellison (coach), Troy Kirby (coach), W.O. Jackson Jr., Fred Whitten, Ben Day, Baxter Gunnells, George Hammett, John Pierce, Joseph Jolly, Britt Vernon, Johnny Ashworth, Henry Buchanan.

Calhoun Falls Mill (Calhoun Falls, S.C.): C.M. Hendrix (coach), Billy Patton, John Helms, James Wilhite, Walter Lovern, Millias Helms, James Godfrey, James Chrisley, Jess Ayers, William Thomas, C.N. Hendrix.

Simpsonville Mill (Simpsonville, S.C.): D.L. Goodenough (coach), Jack Goodenough, Earl Brashier, Cecil Barbery, Richard Terry, Herman Campbell, Odell Barbery, Beecy Barbery, James Alexander, Nick Alexander, Harry Barbery, Smith.

Lonsdale Mill (Seneca, S.C.): Clyde Davis (coach), J.F. Gaillard (coach), James Black, Ralph Maxie, Rufus Black, Clarence Gaillard, Hoyt Gibson, Jamie Shirley, Harley James, Horace Gaillard, Martin Abbott.

New Holland Mill (Gainesville, Ga.): Bonnell Jarrard (coach), William Anglin, John Stoyles, Ernest Jenkins, Ausband Morgan, Ralph Chapman, M.E. Marchbanks, Jacob Miller, Charles Lay, R.W. Marchbanks, J.C. Hamilton.

Beacon Mill (Swannanoa, N.C.): J.D. Hardin (coach), L.E. Carroll (coach), Alger Rainwater, Jay Burgess, Richard Sides, Harold Patton, Clarence Suttles, Bill McMurray, Ned Straphler, Parks Poteat, James Davidson, J.D. Hardin.

Piedmont Mill (Piedmont, S.C.): Wilton Smith (coach), Judge Buckleister (coach), Billy Davis, Marvin Smith, Milford Howard, Gomer Evans, Ben Bowen, Harry Terry, J.C. Powell, J.R. Hooper, Kennett Pearson, Paul Rampey.

Renfrew Bleachery (Travelers Rest, S.C.): John McDowell (coach), Roy Lockaby, Boyce Greer, Gene Cunningham, James Ivey, Leonard Brown, Melvin Poole, Calvin Bryant, Mets Robertson, Charles Werner, Donnie Bridges.

Class C Men

Monaghan Mill (Greenville, S.C.), champions: Clyde Hudgens (coach), Robert Ward, Hanson Griffith, Norris Newton, Horace Wilson, James Glenn, William Keller, Kenneth Hudgens, Fred Powers, Ken Pittman, Harold Fuller.

Dunean Mill (Greenville, S.C.), runners-up: Ward Williams (coach), Larry Ashley, Gene Fuller, Mendel Stroud, William LaBoone, David Putnam, Joe Glenn, Don Cox, Mack Buckner, Dillard Wilbanks.

Brandon Mill (Greenville, S.C.), consolation winners: Bob Kay (coach), James Thomas (coach), Kent Massingale, John Buchanan, Johnny Arnold, James Williamson, Jack Taylor, Fred McAbee, Roy Frost, Rudolph Donahue, George Burnett, Lloyd McAbee.

Orr Mill (Anderson, S.C.): J.O. Ellison (coach), John Thomas, Winfred Farmer, Jeff Shifflett, John Lyons, Cecil Buchanan, James Shaw, Marvin Meeks, Wade Hampton, Herbert Cleveland, Bill Burnette.

Camperdown Mill (Greenville, S.C.): Charles Whitaker (coach), Dennis Whitaker (coach), Floyd Goodwin, Billy Gosnell, Roy Landreth, Cecil Rollins, Robert Penland, John Anderson, Arthur Holland, Noah Lowe.

Dunean Scouts (Greenville, S.C.): Ralph Compton (coach), Worth Carroll, Hugh Campbell, Charles Hudgens, Billy Huff, Gene Hill, Don Landreth, Cylea Hudson, Hugh Stephenson, Paul Lindsay, Ken Stroud.

Judson Mill (Greenville, S.C.): W.E. Holland (coach), James Landreth, Jack Clark, Walter Hamilton, Richard Powers, Floyd Loftis, Gene Bolin, James Hendricks, Stan Lee, Hawkins, P. Hendricks.

Victor Mill (Greer, S.C.): Tom Wilson (coach), T.W. McGaha, Robert Elders, Kenneth Godfrey, J.W. Brown Jr., Ray Jones, Edwin Wilson, Bobby Lynch, Joseph Lamb, William Lynch, Owens, Brown, Moss.

Union Bleachery (Greenville, S.C.): Roy Brooks (coach), Heber Evatt, Marion Robertson, Martin Robinson, George Dunn, Ben Robertson, Donald Jewell, Hugh Revis, William Cantrell, Harris Turner, Jewell.

Greer Mill (Greer, S.C.): L.C. Taylor (coach), Paul Moreland (coach), James Gowan, Robert Burnette, Theron Giles, William Durham Jr., Grady Harvey, Leroy Miller, Robert Campbell, John Henson, Doyle Stansell, William Christmas.

Southern Textile Basketball Tournament Rosters Appendix 1 161

Piedmont Shirt Co. (Greenville, S.C.): G.E. Warrell (coach), Paul Darnell, Leonard Riddle, Sam Pittman, Bill Nivens, O.O. Crowe, Billy Taylor, Willie Murphey, Charles Moore, James Conwell, Jimmie Thompson.

Woodside Mill (Greenville, S.C.): Benny Perry (coach), Lloyd Jones (coach), Everett Queen, Charles McConnell, David Cater, Kenneth Bowen, Charles Riggins, Charles Wakefield, Harmon Wood, Joe Farrow, Jack Dover, Jack Wilson.

CLASS A WOMEN

Chatham Mfg. (Elkin, N.C.), champions: Don Brock (coach), Anne Lineback, Leva Smith, Doris Shugart, Jennie Sherrill, Jannie Lackey, Polly Martin, Betty Cope, Ruth Reich, Maurice Gordon, Ada Thorpe, Ruth Thorpe, Betty Oliver, Ruby Clark, Carolyn Fletcher, Jannie Sherrill, Pearl Burge.

Hanes Hosiery Mill (Winston-Salem, N.C.), runners-up: B.C. Hall Jr. (coach), Vera Hester, Mae Idol, Frances Dunlap, Mary Linville, Hazel Starrett, Pauline Reich, Helen Greer, Jean Hill, Cornelia Lineberry, Blake Mock, Frances McBride, Ethel Griggs.

Drayton Mill (Spartanburg, S.C.), consolation winners: Mrs. J.J. Bruce (coach), Beulah Splawn, Alma Rogers, Lamar Pennington, Rachel Knight, Margaret Todd, Alice Cantrell, Wilma Whitlock, Ellen Toney, Ailene Scruggs, Hazel Wright, Martha Hayship, Mayo Condrey.

Pelzer Mill (Pelzer, S.C.): Aliene Houston, Leoda Turpin, Evelyn Jordan, Roberta Fowler, Jean Fowler, Mildred Jordan, Chaddean Stewart, Malveen Greer, Virginia Jackson.

American Enka (Enka, N.C.): Zeno Wall Jr. (coach), Edna Williams, Eloise West, Elizabeth Fullam, Gussie Couch, Alice Owensby, Jessie Mills, Mary Hensley, Hazel Reynolds, Mabel Randall, Betty Lindsey, Nathalie Glance, Hilda West, Phipps.

General Asbestos & Rubber Co. (Charleston, S.C.): Donald Thompson (coach), Barbara Oldham, Rose McLaughlin, Thelma Riddle, Elizabeth Hogg, Maleeta Hill, Cora Fort, Dorothy Cautrell, Bernice Smith, Lottie Cammer, Juanita Gooding, Daire Griffith, Winfred Witt.

CLASS B WOMEN

Dunean Mill (Greenville, S.C.), champions: Margaret Donnan (coach), Margaret Putman (coach), Mary Gosnell, Sadie Elliott, Patti Brown, Laura Pepper, Billie Epps, Ruth McDonald, Peggy Wood, Dorothy Wood, Doris Stairley, Kay Williams, Betty Lollis, Donnan.

Anderson Mill (Anderson, S.C.), runners-up: C.T. Ripley (coach), Viola Thompson (coach), Lena Alexander, Willie Embler, Dorothy Rainey, Mildred James, Mildred Jenkins, Fannie Mann, Beulah Edwards, Sybil Stastny, Fredda Acker, Ninetta Spearman, Peggy Picklesimer, Norma Ivester, Hanes.

Joanna Mill (Joanna, S.C.), consolation winners: A.B. Galloway (coach), Mrs. A.B. Galloway (coach), Ruth Phillips, Virginia Bolt, Ruth Hair, Inez Tinsley, Thelma Bridges, Christine Buchanan, Evelyn Templeton, Ruby Morse, Betty Prater, Mary Spires.

Woodside Mill (Greenville, S.C.): Homer Landreth (coach), Boyd Tollison (coach), Evelyn Heath, Margaret Vehorn, Gladys Alexander, Earline Manley, Gay Blankenship, Anna Farrow, Juanita Pitts, Carolyn Nash, Ruby Greene, Dellane Bowen, Juanita Smith, Madge Cole.

Piedmont Mill (Piedmont, S.C.): Allan Brannon (coach), Elizabeth Hickson, Dorothy Ferguson, Jean Pepper, Dorothy Nimmons, Mary Boiter, Alene Payne, Sybil Fletcher, Betty Garrett, Roxie Reeves, Margie Payne, Hazel Trammell, Lottie Liberty.

Renfrew Bleachery (Travelers Rest, S.C.): John McDowell (coach), Grace Werner, Evelyn Bridges, Helen England, Frances Duncan, Martha Trammell, Mary Mathis, Lucille Ivey, Doris Ivey, Doris McDaniel, Edna Brown, Frances Holtzclaw, Ruth Lockaby.

Union Bleachery (Greenville, S.C.): M. Dix, Trinieris, Stone, E. Bishop, F. Bishop, B. Rector, Turner.

Lonsdale Mill (Seneca, S.C.): Burton, Latham, Foster, Black, Gaillard, Nicholson, Freeman.

1947

Officers: Clarence Thomas (Greenville, S.C.), President; Horace Whitmire (La Grange, Ga.), Vice President; J.D. Brown (Greenville, S.C.), Secretary; Aug W. Smith (Greenville, S.C.), Treasurer; Ted Ratenski (Greenville, S.C.), Assistant Secretary.

Executive Committee: L.W. Meisenheimer

(Taylors, S.C.), Charles Freeman (Greenville, S.C.), A.R. Plaster (Elkin, N.C.), Jack Reames (Abbeville, S.C.), Lee Coleman (Greer, S.C.), Walter Lauter (Rossville, Ga.), Leroy Anderson (Piedmont, S.C.), Jim Westmoreland (Pelzer, S.C.), B.C. Hall Jr. (Winston-Salem, N.C.).

Class A Men

Hanes Hosiery Mill (Winston-Salem, N.C.), champions: B.C. Hall Jr. (coach), Virgil Yow (coach), Hugh Hampton, Coot Greer, Cedric Loftis, Don Anderson, Neal Cockerham, Carl Snow, Al Loftis, Simpson Nelson, Sid Carlton, Hedron Coble.

McCrary Hosiery Mill (Asheboro, N.C.), runners-up: Paul Cheek (coach), Bobby Wilkins, Furman Taylor, Abe Williams, Robert Slaydon, Hillard Nance, Max McGinn, Don Nance, Weldon Johnson, Walter Hobson, Hiott Morgan, Bartlette Walker, Alton Williams.

Brandon Mill (Greenville, S.C.), consolation winners: Charles Harper (coach), Raymond Wynn (coach), Ralph McDonald, James Thomas, Joe Anders, James Orr, J.B. Friar, Harold Limbaugh, James Carnes, Roy Hunter, Clarence Orr.

Union Bleachery (Greenville, S.C.): E.S. Tillinghast (coach), McClure Epps, Roy Brooks, W.A. Bishop Jr., Paul Turner, Aromus Belcher, Harold Green, Walker Dilworth, James Evington, Harry Dilworth, Cecil Brooks.

American Enka (Enka, N.C.): Andy Brandl (coach), George Price, Richard Gudger, James Rhea, Mitchell Gaddy, Thomas Graham, T.N. Holder Jr., Long.

Avondale Mill (Alexander City, Ala.): Robert Graves (coach), Preston Blankenship, John Turner, Joe Florine, Douglas McGill, Fred Boos, Wendell Boos, Marlin Holman, Jasper McCullough, F.C. Holman, Gaines Coker.

Goodyear Clearwater Mill #2 (Rockmart, Ga.): Robert McGhee (coach), Elbert Coalson, Hubert Harris, Charles Womack, Harrison Anderson, Jack Parham, Richard Davis, Carl Cown, Robert Blissett, James Watts, Souls.

Piedmont Mill (Piedmont, S.C.): Wilton Smith (coach), J.W. Rampey (coach), Clarence Emery, Gomer Evans, Marvin Smith, Robert Davenport, Charles Davis, John Powell, J.E. Pitts, Tom Pack, Ford Waldrop, Howard.

Ninety Six Mill (Ninety Six, S.C.): Ralph Spires (coach), Otis Porter (coach), Fred Ross, Lloyd Ivester, Buna Wells, Glenn Forrester, William Ross, Alvin Drummond, Douglas McCarthy, Clarence Allen, Bill Corley, Jim Voiselle.

Southern Bleachery (Taylors, S.C.): Fred Coleman (coach), James Wilson (coach), Preston Belcher, William Bishop, Sam Bridgman, Lloyd Edwards, William Forrest, Edward Kirby Jr., Robert Spencer, Clarence Smith, Odell Broadnax, Parker.

Dunean Mill (Greenville, S.C.): Willie Wilbanks (coach), Bob Stowe, Willie Riddle, Naula Frix, Paul Turner, Fred Cox Sr., Floyd Owens, Carl Greene, Clarence Odell, H. Turner, Bill Moody.

Drayton Mill (Spartanburg, S.C.): John O'Sullivan (coach), R.J. McClellan, Wallace Dean, Charles Seay, Dennis Loftis, Manning Bagwell, Samuel Bagwell, Leonard Hill, Ralph Gibbs, Maurice Cox, Danny McGraw, Harrell Walker, Croft.

Pelzer Mill (Pelzer, S.C.): Virgil Lavender (coach), Paul Edwards, J.W. Jordan, Earl Wooten, Ralph Cannon, Cyril Haney, Horace Davenport, Charles Hodge, Hoyt Jordan, Wilton Dickson.

Peerless Woolen Mill (Rossville, Ga.): Walter Lauter (coach), Glenn Michaels, William Crow, George Blakemore, Wilson Bigger, John Barger, Robert James, Bruce Goins, Jack Connelly, Reba Wyatt, Charles Geyer, Gaines.

Anderson Mill (Anderson, S.C.): W.H. Embler (coach), Chafer Honea, Luiaco Goodson, Jimmie Embler, Roy Bridges, Marshall Hill Jr., Fred Whitten, Ezra Embler, Melvin Burriss, Marvin Spake.

Oconee Mill (Westminster, S.C.): Henry Buchanan (coach), Martin Abbott, Frank Sharp, William Robinson, Lester Wilson, Robert Grogan, Elliott Sprouse, Marvin Rackley, A.V. Seymour, James Hamilton.

Tennessee Eastman (Kingsport, Tenn.): Buck Thornton (coach), Joseph Barr, Ben Booker, Andrew Warren, Jack Pectal, Lawrence Thayer, George Grills, Ralph Wilson, Frank Smith, Ralph Richards, Charles Phillips, Williams.

Class B Men

Dunean Mill (Greenville, S.C.), champions: Bob Stowe (coach), Bruce Long, Claude Long, John Langston, Mendel Stroud, Bill LaBoone, Raymond Cox, Ed Manley, Harold Quinn, William Moody, Guy Shook.

Ware Shoals Mill (Ware Shoals, S.C.), runners-up: Andy Hawthorne (coach), Olin Wells, George Abrams, O'dell Barbary, James McDuffie, Virgil Stallcup, Herbert Pitts, Wade Burton, Dick Hartman, Ray Couch.

Appleton Mill (Anderson, S.C.), consolation winners: Claud Spake (coach), Henry Spake (coach), Farris Bailey, Carter Gaines, Andrew King, James Carlton, William Middleton, James Morrison, William Bannister, William Gurley, Earl Smith, Welton Junkins.

Columbus Mill (Columbus, Ga.): David Corzine (coach), Hugh Hasty, James Wright, Howard Jackson, Roy Williams, James Smith, Elmer Durden, Cecil Bailey, Earl Cutchings, A.J. Widgeon.

American Enka (Enka, N.C.): Andy Brandl (mgr), Warren Bryant, Grover Fowler, Earl Clontz, German Miller, Donald McCabe, Kenneth Watts.

Orr Mill (Anderson, S.C.): George Jolley (coach), James McCurry, Clyde Blackwell, Pete Stamps, Ben Day, George Hammett, Britt Vernon, Joseph Jolley, Sammy Meeks, Johnny Ashworth, James Hawkins.

Laurens Mill (Laurens, S.C.): W.P. Sheppard (coach), Jack Adams, John Bolt, Henry Bowie, Clifford Cox, Jack Cox, William Mauldin, George Russell, Raymond Spoon, Clyde Werner.

New Holland Mill (Gainesville, Ga.): B.C. Jarrard (coach), Gordon Campbell (coach), Jacob Miller, William Chapman, Charles Lay, John Brown, Ausbond Morgan, Ernest Jenkins, H.L. Childress Jr., John Stoyles, William Jones.

Brandon Mill (Greenville, S.C.): Doyle Clary (coach), Raymond Wynn (coach), Rudolph Donahue, Joe Huff, Fred Byrd, Carvin Landreth, James Pierce, James Tribble, William Dilworth, Melvin Forrester, Elvin Morrow, Calvin Morrow.

Joanna Mill (Joanna, S.C.): A.B. Galloway (coach), George Frady, Guy Prater, Rudolph Prater, Hack Prater, Cecil Farmer, Julian Hunnicutt, Bill Tinsley, Morton Hamm, Verlyn Davenport, R.D. Frazier.

Slater Mill (Slater, S.C.): James Oglesby (coach), B.Y. Miller, William Hall, Wilburn Knox, James McMakin, William Cashion, William Cody, William Lybrand, Roy Lybrand, Harold Knight, Fred Cox.

Calhoun Falls Mill (Calhoun Falls, S.C.): Edward Dickard (coach), Morris Manley, Jesse Ayers, Wallace Powell, Garnett Hall, Eugene Wilhite, J.P. Parnell, Robert Chrisley, Everette Lovern, Hoyt Tilley, John Pearson.

Woodside Mill (Greenville, S.C.): Ray Herbert (coach), Dewey Bowen (coach), William Wakefield, Talmadge Tollison, Bert Wilson, George Miller, Curt Beasley, Leslie Nash, Fornie Huffman, Veldee Hines, James Green, George Pruitt.

Lyman Mill (Lyman, S.C.): Dudley Tollison (coach), W.A. Beasley Jr., Furman Cook, Larry Gresham, Lloyd Leonard, Vernon Medlock, Fred Mullinax, Luther Mullinax, Thurman Patton, Oliver Smart.

Monaghan Mill #1 (Greenville, S.C.): Thomas Henderson (coach), Douglas Campbell, Thomas Blackston, Harold Fuller, Morris Newton, Furman Moman, Kenneth Hudgens, Hanson Griffith, Fred Rigdon, Ralph McKinney, Charles Summers.

Pacolet Mill (Pacolet, S.C.): Arthur Goforth (coach), Robert Brown, John Brown, James Mathis, J.J. Osment, Robert Pierce, Robert Phillips, Walter Harrison, William Trent, Samuel Hogan, Gregg Scott.

Mills Mill #1 (Greenville, S.C.): James Trammell (coach), Harold Abbott (coach), Charlie Brock, Curtis Powell, Ralph Bell, Richard Dittmer, Myron Floyd, Cecil Lowery, George Patterson, Osborne Ballew, Thomas Cox.

Leakesville Mill (Leakesville, N.C.): J.T. White (coach), John Gallimore (coach), Odell Simmons, Homer Johnson, Howard Carter, Roy Davis Jr., Artis Carter, Valma White, Herman Perry, Hobart Hundley, Weldon Reynolds.

Poinsett Mill (Greenville, S.C.): Arthur Hammett (coach), Lee Chapman (coach), Bert Tate, Charlie Vaughn, Rudolph Crump, Jack Vaughn, William Taylor, Monroe Millwood, Benjamin Mardis, Robert Lavender.

Watts Mill (Laurens, S.C.): Rhoten Shetley (coach), A.R. Chapman (coach), John Coy, Horace Garrison, Paul Cavender, Francis Crane, James Stokes, Jack Cox, Horace Waddell, Stanley Johnson, David Waddell, Mac Weathers.

Camperdown Mill (Greenville, S.C.): Charles Penland (coach), Jack Mintz, Melvin Gunter, Louie McDowell, Frank Goodwin, Alvin Burnette, Harold Cooper, Mack Bruce, Jack Whitaker, Eugene Davis, Jamie Dill, Robert Marchbanks.

Clifton Mill #3 (Clifton, S.C.): Yonnie Greene (coach), Art Fowler, Jack Gossett, Walter Greene, Voyle Massey, Charles Reid, Robert

Greene, Edsel Sprouse, Wister Donald, James King, Clyde Hawkins.

Judson Mill (Greenville, S.C.): Frank Aiken (coach), Red Owens (coach), Gaines Luther, Doyle Garrett, James Kuykendall, James Davis, Mack Patton, Chisley Crews, Jack McGill, Robert McAway, Batson.

Simpsonville Mill (Simpsonville, S.C.): C.L. Land, Harold Bagwell, Robert Goodenough, Richard Terry, Fred Barbery, Wilton Chandler, William Gault, Buddy Hammond, Gary Henderson, Samuel Payne, Earl Brashier.

Beacon Mill (Swannanoa, N.C.): L.E. Correll (coach), J.D. Hardin (coach), Alger Rainwater, Kenneth Rudeen, Dwight Patterson, Richard Sides, Jay Burgess, Ned Stroehla, Hugh Penley, Brock Burgess, James Rice.

Southern Franklin Processing (Greenville, S.C.): E.A. Briggs (coach), John Holliday, J.W. McCullough, Robert Cater, John Cooper Jr., James Ayers, John Jones, Fred Forrester, John Stafford, Miles Grant, Joe Farress.

Greer Mill (Greer, S.C.): H.H. Burgin (coach), Woodrow Hanvey (coach), Fred Hemphill, Roy Taylor, Wilson Taylor, Charles Brannon, Grady Harvey, James Gowan, William Foster, Clint Greene, Claude Burgin, Landy Crisp, Wilson.

Monaghan Mill #2 (Greenville, S.C.): Dan Bagwell (coach), P.J. McAvoy (coach), Bomar Keller, Jack Busbee, Ken Pittman, John Blackston, H.J. McCall, Fred Powers, J.D. Bagwell.

Pelzer Mill (Pelzer, S.C.): R.B. Harris (coach), J.P. Floyd, Roy Whitlock, William Maness, Clayton Copeland, James Davis, Charlie McConnell, Carl Davis Jr., Robert Floyd, Taylor.

Sylacauga Mill (Sylacauga, Ala.): James Pasley (coach), Doug Powell, Clarence Hebson, Harold Moore, Virgil Adams, William Brooks, Ray Dean, Emory Sewell, Hulan Harris, Tip Canady, Parris.

Dan River Mill (Danville, Va.): W.L. Williams, Samuel Jenkins, John Smith, Frank Carter, Raleigh Hubbard, Carl Morton, Randolph Boaze, Harry Terrell, Herbert Ware, Wayne King.

Class C Men

Dunean Mill (Greenville, S.C.), champions: Rogers Stairley, Herman Hudson, Don Cox, David Putman, Larry Ashley, Charles Hudgens, Billy Granger, Fred Holder, Floyd Kay, Gene Fuller.

Woodside Mill (Greenville, S.C.), runners-up: Leonard Canup (coach), Everett Waldrop (coach), Jack Wilson, Roy Queen, Joe Farrow, Charles Wakefield, Roger McKinney, Dewey Morrow, Jack Dover, Jack Tollison, Kenneth Bowen, David Carter.

Monaghan Mill (Greenville, S.C.), consolation winners: Aaron Powers (coach), J.G. Suttles (coach), Robert Hudgens, Charles Wyatt, Danny Bagwell, Buddy Rogers, Gary Parker, Billy McKinney, Hoyt Davis, Joe Wyatt, Donald Newton.

Oconee Mill (Westminster, S.C.): Marvin Rackley (coach), William Jones, Johnny Jones, Joe Duvall, John Smith, Charles Smith, George Stansell, Lloyd Haley, Donnie Williams, Clarence Hawkins.

Appleton Mill (Anderson, S.C.): Clarence Free (coach), Henry Spake (coach), John Daniel, David Bowen, Boyd Moore, Bobby Leverette, Charles Williams, Douglas Wilson, Robert Speares, Donald Hanna, Horace Rhodes.

Drayton Mill (Spartanburg, S.C.): Clarence Powell (coach), Robert Gossett, Larry Edwards, Hugh Hill, James McGaha, David Lawrence, Melvin Wallace, Hollis Morris, Dennis Rogers, Jack Weaver, Alford Wood.

Ware Shoals Mill (Ware Shoals, S.C.): Leo Hancock (coach), Bill Ashley, Bobby Knight, James Gordon, Hoyt Trulove, William Woods, Hoyt Hembree, Lamar Smith, Jack Crawford.

Brandon Mill (Greenville, S.C.): Joe Melear (coach), Raymond Wynn (coach), George Burnette, Fred Huffman, James Williamson, Fred McAbee, John Arnold, Lloyd McAbee, Joe Taylor, Paul Moon.

Brandon Duck Mill (Greenville, S.C.): Joe Reid (coach), Harold Alexander (coach), Robert Moon, Troy Miller, Melvin Fletcher, Charles Holcombe, James Brooks, Roy Frost, Jack Parnell, Charles Taylor, Kentworth Massingale, Clayborn Sentell.

Camperdown Mill (Greenville, S.C.): J.W. McDowell (coach), Charles Whitaker (coach), Floyd Goodwin, John Anderson, Roy Landreth, Robert Penland, Cecil Rollins, Billy Gosnell, Noah Lowe, Bobby Batson, Carol Carver, James Erwin.

Victor Mill (Greer, S.C.): Charlie Taylor (coach), Carlos Garrett, Joseph Lamb, Charles Lister, Kenneth Godfrey, Dennis Heaton, Ray Jones, Jerry Moon, T.W. McGaha, Denny Owens, Frank Merck.

Union Bleachery (Greenville, S.C.): Pat

Patterson (coach), Charles Brooks (coach), Marion Robertson, Donald Jewell, Heber Evatt, Martin Robinson, Marlin Stroud, George Dunn, Herley Dix, Hugh Boswell, Henry Keith Jr., Hugh Revis.

Lonsdale Mill (Seneca, S.C.): Roy McCurry (coach), Clyde Davis (coach), R.S. Sosebee, James Reed, Jack Bates, Johnnie Bates, Furman Gibson, Edward Alexander, Thomas Poole, Jones Davis, Spencer Tinsley, William Wyatt.

Southern Bleachery (Taylors, S.C.): Fred Coleman (coach), Thomas Ridgeway (coach), Fred Bridgeman, David Brown Jr., Royce Cannada, George Derrick Jr., John Hammond, Walter Henson, Rudolph Hughes, Ned Phillips, Hugh Badger, Kenneth Tankersley.

Judson Mill (Greenville, S.C.): Dewey Foster (coach), C. Grissop (coach), Joseph Smith, Bobby Blackwell, Junis Campbell Jr., Gene Burroughs, John Haney, Richard Powers, Charles Garrett, Floyd Loftis, Bobby Porter, Billy Taylor.

CLASS A WOMEN

Chatham Mfg. (Elkin, N.C.), champions: Donald Brock (coach), Ruth Reich, Doris Shugart, Jennie Sherrill, Jannie Sherrill, Pauline Martin, Pearl Burge, Betty Cope, Maurice Gordon, Betty Melvin, Anne Lineback, Kathryn Smith, Ruth Vestal, Elizabeth Brinkema, Leola Shore, Lorene White, Frances McBride.

Hanes Hosiery Mill (Winston-Salem, N.C.), runners-up: B.C. Hall Jr. (coach), Helen Greer, Mary Lineberry, Pattie Johnston, Ruth Phelps, Jacqueline Swain, Irma Williard, Eunice Futch, Geneva Hicks, Melba Adkins, Wanda Pegram, Frances McBride.

Drayton Mill (Spartanburg, S.C.), consolation winners: A.J. Wallace (coach), Alma Wilson, Audrey Parris, Inez Turner, Ailene Scruggs, Helen Gosnell, Beulah Splawn, Wilma Whitlock, Helen Melton, Eva Grant, Thelma Arms, Martha Hayslip, Mayo Condrey, Collins, Garrett.

American Enka (Enka, N.C.): Andy Brandl (coach), Gussie Couch, Eloise West, Oberia Owen, Reya Leophard, Betty Lindsey, Edith Metcalf, Frances Finley, Dorothy Wheeler, Lillian Massie, Juanita Sparks, Sue Glance.

Pelzer Mill (Pelzer, S.C.): Audrie Edwards (coach), Jean Fowler, Beatrice Davis, Roberta Wooten, Montez Floyd, Chaddeen Stewart, Mildred Jordan, Joan Hunt, Willene Barnett, Sybil Gambrell, Evelyn Jordan.

CLASS B WOMEN

Judson Mill (Greenville, S.C.), champions: Ralph Harbin (coach), Ola James, Ruby Newman, Nealy Hall, Margaret Owens, Ruth Slay, Ruth Matthews, Mary Ayers, Gladys Means, Sue Means, Johnnie Means, Dorothy Luther, Leona Evans.

Oconee Mill (Westminster, S.C.), runners-up: A.V. Seymour (coach), Frances Turk, Josephine Greer, Lucille Jackson, Sarah Ledford, Katherine Gilliam, Mary Chrisley, Frances Chrisley, Rebecca Wilson, Ruth Cain, Christine Carver.

Calhoun Falls Mill (Calhoun Falls, S.C.), consolation winners: Edward Dickard (coach), Mary Nance, Gaynelle Bonds, Neva Martin, Mary Hall, Edna Jones, Velma Binns, Betty Bryant, Delma Cooper, Syble Cooper, Gladys Pettit, Muree Manning, Ruby Tucker.

Ware Shoals Mill (Ware Shoals, S.C.): Robert Barbery (coach), Martha Maybin, Katherine Davis, Evelyn Snyder, Beatrice Cheek, Mildred Snyder, Molly Davis, Bernice Ezell, Telar Powell, Eunice Powell, Helen Barbery, Doris Truelove.

Woodside Mill (Greenville, S.C.): Dellaree Bowen (coach), Fred Bomar (coach), Carolyn Nash, Alma Harris, Anna Farrow, Doris Brookshire, Gay Blankenship, Mildred Waldrop, Madge Cole, Juanita Smith, Virginia Campbell, Evelyn Heath, Juanita Pitts, Ruby Greene.

Anderson Mill (Anderson, S.C.): W.H. Embler (coach), Dot Lyles, Myra Alexander, Lena Alexander, Sybil Stastny, Jeannette Mann, Mary Thompson, Evelyn Hill, Mildred James, Edna Bowen, Mildred Morris, Mary Shearer, Delma Porter, McAllister.

Brandon Mill (Greenville, S.C.): Marie Kruckel (coach), Elizabeth Mahon, Joyce Wynn, Clarice Turner, Frances Hall, Margaret Morrow, Christine Rollins, Woodie Landreth, Mattie Sons, Margaret Powers, Frances Page, Betty Morgan, Lois Taylor.

Watts Mill (Laurens, S.C.): Betty Richards (coach), Betty Blakely (coach), Bonnie Lemmons, Dot Powers, Martha Johnson, Mildred King, Jeanne Garrett, Bobbie Taylor, Argil Hill, Trudelle Leopard, Omega Knight, Katherine Waldrop, Mary Long, Betty Barber.

Orr Mill (Anderson, S.C.): Stasney, Morris, Alexander, Thompson, James, Mann, Mann, McAllister, Hill, Bowen.

1948

Officers: Clarence Thomas (Greenville, S.C.), President; Horace Whitmire (Greenville, S.C.), Vice President; Ted Ratenski (Greenville, S.C.), Secretary; Aug W. Smith (Greenville, S.C.), Treasurer.

Executive Committee: L.W. Meisenheimer (Taylors, S.C.), Jesse Brown (Greenville, S.C.), A.R. Plaster (Elkin, N.C.), Jack Reames (Abbeville, S.C.), Lee Coleman (Greer, S.C.), Walter Lauter (Rossville, Ga.), Leroy Anderson (Piedmont, S.C.), Hugh Anderson (Greenville, S.C.), Jim Westmoreland (Pelzer, S.C.), B.C. Hall Jr. (Winston-Salem, N.C.), Albert Wallace (Spartanburg, S.C.), J.B. Owens (Easley, S.C.), Paul Cheek (Asheboro, N.C.).

CLASS A MEN

Hanes Hosiery Mill (Winston-Salem, N.C.), champions: B.C. Hall Jr. (coach), Virgil Yow (coach), Hugh Hampton, Carl Snow, Coot Greer, Donald Anderson, Cedric Loftis, Hilliard Nance, Arthur Sheek, Neal Cockerham, Benjamin Cagle, Lonnie Smith, Harvey Tedder, Simpson Nelson.

Chatham Mfg. (Elkin, N.C.), runners-up: Tige Harris (coach), Richard Stockton, Howard Vaughn, Paul Badgett, Wayne Harris, Gib Pardue, Veo Story, Neil Melvin, Greg Collins, Don Brock.

Huntsville Mfg. (Huntsville, Ala.), consolation winners: T.D. Moore (coach), Floyd Bryant (coach), Jack Kelly, James Remington, Harold Parks, J.B. Russell, Taylor Myers, Clifton McGinness, Howard Wallace, Earl Gossett, Paul Anderson, Gordon Garrison.

American Enka (Enka, N.C.): Sam Patton (coach), Bill Lindsey (coach), Warren Bryant, Richard Gudger, Arthur Hazeltine, Tom Holder, Edwin Long, George Price, James Rhea, Thomas Tweed, Kenneth Watts, Norman Wells.

Calloway Mill (LaGrange, Ga.): Paul Gauntt (coach), Ocky Walls, William Adcock, Joe McManus, Glynn Bailey, Calvin Brooks, Ralph Williams, Fred Anderson, Elbert Walls, Amisons.

Clifton Mill (Clifton, S.C.): W.A. Quinn (coach), Reubin Reid (coach), Walter Greene, Arthur Fowler, Charles Reid, Voyle Massey, Edsel Sprouse, Robert Greene, Wister Donald, Jack Gossett, Walter Fowler, Paul Groce Jr.

Oconee Mill (Westminster, S.C.): Henry Buchanan (coach), Marvin Rackley, Leslie Wilson, James Hamilton, G.L. Morgan, J.A. Smith, W.A. Robinson, A.E. Sprouse, Frank Sharp, A.V. Seymour.

Brandon Mill (Greenville, S.C.): Ray Wynn (coach), J.B. Friar, Carvin Landreth, James Orr, Joe Anders, John Harbin, James Carnes, Ralph McDonald, Douglas McCarthy, Roy Hunter.

Dunean Mill (Greenville, S.C.): Willie Wilbanks (coach), Bob Stowe, Carl Greene, William Moody, Horace Turner, Paul Turner, Claude Long, Bruce Long, Willie Riddle, Fred Cox.

Manchester Mill (Manchester, Ga.): J.E. Kierbow (coach), Royce Nipper, Rufus Brady, Ralph Sosebee Jr., Tillman White, Jack Clark, Horace Denny, Forrest Allen, LeRoy Boswell, Clifford McIntosh, Lee Edmondson.

McCrary Hosiery Mill (Asheboro, N.C.): Paul Cheek (coach), Warren Hawkins, Pete Messina, Max McGinn, Bob Stevenson, Abe Williams, Weldon Johnson, Robert Slaydon, Bob Wilkins, Don Nance, W.L. Hobson.

Pelzer Mill (Pelzer, S.C.): Bill Hopkins (coach), Paul Edwards (coach), Hoyt Jordan, Earl Wooten, John Jordan, Ralph Cannon, Wilton Dickson, Elmer Suddeth, James Harris, Charles Hodge, Robert Chapman.

Piedmont Mill (Piedmont, S.C.): J.W. Bailey (coach), Tom Pack, Milford Howard, Ray Darnell, Joe Nesbitt, Charles Davis, John Emery, Edgar Patterson, J.C. Powell, Gomer Evans, Marvin Smith.

Anderson Mill (Anderson, S.C.): William Embler (coach), Chafer Honea, Marvin Spake, Marshall Hill Jr., Jimmie Embler, Roy Bridges, Ezra Embler, Ray Bolick, Fred Whitten, William Spencer.

Southern Bleachery (Taylors, S.C.): Fred Bridgeman (coach), Edward Kirby, Lloyd Edwards, C.L. Smith, William Bishop, Harold Parker, Robert Stewart, Warren Trammell, Leon Bennett, Douglas Forrest, Robert Spencer.

Simpsonville Mill (Simpsonville, S.C.): Bill Chonko (coach), Richard Terry, Earl Brashier, Fred Barbery, Cutty Cox, Jack Goodenough, Jesse Kilpatrick, Herman Campbell.

Drayton Mill (Spartanburg, S.C.): G.G. Simmons (coach), Bill Jefford (coach), Maurice Cox, Jimmie Tollison, Ralph Gibbs, Dennis Loftis, Manning Bagwell, Leonard Hill, Joe O'Shields, Charles Seay, Harold Walker, Jack Bagwell.

Southern Textile Basketball Tournament Rosters   Appendix 1   167

Union Bleachery (Greenville, S.C.): E.S. Tillinghast (coach), Charles Brooks (coach), W.A. Bishop Jr., Walker Dilworth, Cornelius Evington, Roy Brooks, Beattie Epps, Clyde Robertson, Hagood Brown, Harry Dilworth, Richard Evington.

Ninety Six Mill (Ninety Six, S.C.): Ralph Spires (coach), Tobe Porter (coach), Dewey Quinn Jr., Clarence Allen, Jim Voiselle, James Henderson, Alvin Drummond, Roy May, Glenn Forrester, Fred Ross, Charles Ross, Buna Wells.

Peerless Woolen Mill (Rossville, Ga.): Walter Lauter (coach), Raymond Atkins (coach), Robert James, Bill Crowe, Glenn Michaels, Thomas Maynor, Lamar North, Howard Sompayrac, James Cooke, Charles Hicks, Claude Morris, Joe Dunagan.

Cramerton Mill (Cramerton, N.C.): Bennie Cunningham (coach), Hayes Homer (coach), Harry Jenkins, Edward Maxwell, James Cunningham, Jenks Brendle, Z.V. Brendle, Sam Brendle, Charles Cleveland, Russell Connard, Bill Fletcher.

Class B Men

Monaghan Mill #1 (Greenville, S.C.), champions: J.L. Summers (coach), Pete Henderson (coach), Fig Newton, Thomas Blackston, Bomar Keller, Jack Busbee, Ken Pittman, Herb Lindsay, Doug Campbell, Jack Pittman, James Keller, Glenn Hollis, Jack Earle.

Dunean Mill (Greenville, S.C.), runners-up: Willie Wilbanks (coach), Roy Whitehead, Don Cox, Billy Farrow, Andrew Stafford, Manning Garren, Douglas Stroud, David Putman, Larry Ashley, Billy Granger, Billy Poe.

Columbus Mill (Columbus, Ga.), consolation winners: David Corzine (coach), Joseph Wommack, James Wright, Earl Catchings, George Forrester, Morris Hyles, Chase Riddle, Cecil Bailey, Cliff Catchings, Henry Edwards, William Tinkler.

North Georgia Processing (Toccoa, Ga.): B.H. Barrett (coach), O.W. Thompson (coach), Ray Davis, Joe Stowe, Ray Stowe, Charles Davis, Mark Turner, Tom Lecroy, Grady Medlin, Freeman Payne, Leon Denman, Joe Carson.

Monaghan Mill #2 (Greenville, S.C.): Dan Bagwell (mgr), Garvin Suttles (coach), Robert Ward, Jack Watts, James Glenn, Earl Connor, James Turner, Charles Ross, John Blackstone, Kenneth Hudgens, Hansen Griffith.

New Holland Mill (Gainesville, Ga.): Clarence Brown (coach), Marchel Lord (coach), B.C. Jarrard (coach), Jacob Miller, William Chapman, Charles Lay, John Brown, Ausbond Morgan, Ernest Jenkins, John Stoyles, James Barnes, William Jones, Roy Riley.

Pelzer Mill (Pelzer, S.C.): Horace Davenport (coach), Carl Davis, Marion Smith, Earl Reeves, John Floyd, Thomas McKee, Robert Floyd, Clayton Copeland, Roy Whitlock, Charlie McConnell, James Thomason.

Appleton Mill (Anderson, S.C.): Henry Spake (coach), Claud Spake (coach), William Middleton, Henry Bailey, Andrew King, Carter Gaines, Farris Bailey, James Morrison, James Carlton, Wilton Junkins, Neil Stovall.

Laurens Mill (Laurens, S.C.): Clyde Simmons (coach), W.P. Sheppard (coach), Dan Kirby, Franklin Russell, Jack Cox, Albert Turner, Ralph Laughridge, Elmo Roberts, Grady Chumley, Wayne Mills, Clyde Werner, Henry Bowie.

Piedmont Mill (Piedmont, S.C.): V.J. Lipscombe (coach), Walter Finley, Ben Bowen, James Cooper, Tom Trammell, J.E. Pitts, Carroll Patterson, Bert Garrison, Judge Buckhister.

Pacolet Mill (Pacolet, S.C.): Arthur Goforth (coach), James Mathis, Kansas Goforth, John Brown, Robert Brown, Robert Phillips, Jimmy Howell, Samuel Hogan, Harold Brown, William Trent, Edward Toney, Chandler Parker, William Phillips.

Poinsett Mill (Greenville, S.C.): J.B. Templeton (coach), James Townsend (coach), Jack Long, Earl Fair, Rudolph Crump, Edgar Harbin Jr., Bobby Gray, Charles Alexander, Edward Landers, Ader Hardin, Bert Tate Jr., Robert Lavender.

Glendale Mill (Spartanburg, S.C.): Jerry Pruitt (coach), Billy White, Marvin Lindsay, Charles Warren, Jerome Millwood, Archie Pruitt, Bill McCreary, James Reeves, Jimmy Fisher, Victor Parker, Robert Sams.

Brandon Mill (Greenville, S.C.): Ray Wynn (coach), Doyle Clary (coach), Calvin Morrow, James Pierce, William Carter, Joe Huff, George Burnett, Carlisle Huff, Fornie Huff, William Beasley, Fred Byrd.

Greer Mill (Greer, S.C.): H.H. Burgin (coach), Furman Taylor (coach), Theron Giles, Charles Brannon, Robert Campbell, Wilson Taylor, Grady Harvey, Clint Green, Ralph Bramlett, James Gowan, James Campbell.

Woodside Mill (Greenville, S.C.): James

Collier Jr. (coach), Ray Herbert (coach), Talmadge Tollison, Lloyd Jones, James Wilson Jr., Jack Wilson, Billy Wakefield, Alvin Chapman, James Greene, Robert King, Leslie Nash, George Miller.

Lyman Mill (Lyman, S.C.): John Wahonick (coach), Dudley Tollison (coach), Thurman Patton, A.W. Beasley Jr., Fred Mullinax, Luther Mullinax, Francis Hendrix, Jack Anderson, Dewey Halford, Darrell Medlock, Larry Gresham, Paul Earle.

Renfrew Bleachery (Travelers Rest, S.C.): Perry Poole (coach), Elex Edwards, Doyle Belcher, James Balloch, Lewis Lockaby, Joel Roe Jr., Roy Wood, William Poole, Gene Cunningham, Boyce Green, Edmond Poole.

Leakesville Mill (Leakesville, N.C.): J.T. White (coach), John Gallimore (coach), Hobard Hundley, Howard Carter, Odell Simmons, Francis Buckner, Joe Tolbert, Irvin McBride, Marvin Pruitt, Melvin Pruitt, Dan Squires, Harold Squires, Horace Penn, Homer Johnson, Edwards.

Russell Manufacturing (Alexander City, Ala.): Herman Thomas (coach), Grady Gunn, Jim Forbes, Gene Gilbert, Rayford Duck, Edsell Riddle, Lee Collins, Harvel Johnson, Doyle McManus, William Carter.

American Enka (Enka, N.C.): Sam Patton (coach), Frank Beaty, Earl Clontz, William Clontz, James Dotson, Louis McKinney, Germain Miller, James Moody, John Pinkerton, Ebb Williams, Herman Williams.

Watts Mill (Laurens, S.C.): Stokes, Word, Paul Cavender, Brown, Weathers, Lyles, Cox, Johnson.

Chicopee Mill (Gainesville, Ga.): S.B. Jones (coach), Edward Reed, William Turk, Ray Godfrey, Owen Patton, Sylvia Clark, Charles Berryman, Ernest Wood, Otis McNeal, Andy Griffin, George Mize.

Southern Franklin Processing (Greenville, S.C.): Edwin Briggs (coach), J.W. McCullough, John Jones, Clarence Barr, John Cooper, James Ayers, Wallace Putman, Rudolph Craig, Charles Delk, Robert Carter.

Calhoun Falls Mill (Calhoun Falls, S.C.): G.E. Dickard (coach), William Hall, Thomas O'Shields, Robert Bailey, Lloyd Johnson, Hoyt Tilley, Russell Lyon, Robert Gann, Charles Parnell, Neil Chrisley, Delma Chandler.

Dan River Mill (Danville, Va.): Lee Pugh, Perry, Stillwell, Jones, Fitzgerald, Carter, Reynolds, Faille, Hudgens, Jenkins.

Beacon Mill (Swannanoa, N.C.): Tommy Vanover (coach), J.D. Hardin (coach), Alger Rainwater, Norman Gamache, Jay Burgess, Ted Folsom, Howard Edmonds, Fred Nichols Jr., Harold Patton, Hugh Penley, James Davidson.

Glen Lowery Mill (Whitmire, S.C.): Stephen Dubose (coach), Fred Prather (coach), Hubert Elrod, Carl Basden, Harmon Jennings, Clarence Bowers, Ralph Elrod, Jarrett Friar, Arthur Bradley, Arthur Branks, Robert Branks.

Mills Mill #1 (Greenville, S.C.): Coy Watson (coach), Rudy Cothran (coach), Ralph Bell, Curtis Powell, Ansel McAlister, Jake Floyd, Richard Dittmer, Roy Emery, Jack Williams, George Ballew, Cecil Lowery.

Judson Mill (Greenville, S.C.): Harry Clark (coach), Joe Rhodes, James Landreth, John Bowen, Lawrence Fisher, Floyd Loftis, Walter Hamilton, Claude Luther, Harold Holbrook, Maurice Lankford, McGill.

Camperdown Mill (Greenville, S.C.): Charlie Penland (coach), Harold Cooper, Mac Bruce, Kenneth Rollins, Jack Whitaker, Cecil Rollins, Leonard Riddle, Eugene Davis, Robert Penland, Thurmond Hudgens, Louie McDowell.

Class C Men

Brandon Mill (Greenville, S.C.), champions: John Buchanan (coach), Pete McAbee (coach), Ray Wynn (coach), James Williamson, Melvin Fletcher, John Arnold, Fred McAbee Jr., Kent Massingale, Charles Taylor, Troy Miller, Harold Martin, Robert Moon, John Rochester.

Monaghan Mill (Greenville, S.C.), runners-up: Bill Sandel (coach), Aaron Powers (coach), Tiny Wyatt, Robert Hudgens, Don Newton, Dan Bagwell, Bill McKinney, Wilbur Austin, Hoyt Davis, Buddy Rogers, Bill Fuller, Mickey Brazie.

Woodside Mill (Greenville, S.C.), consolation winners: Leonard Canup (coach), Benny Perry (coach), Charles Wakefield, Charles Garrett, Charles Barbare, Dewey Morrow, John Harris Jr., Joe McConnell, Bobby Nelson, Joe Sparks, Harmon Woods, Kenneth Bowen.

Camperdown Mill (Greenville, S.C.): Jamie Dill (coach), R.A. Lee (coach), Jimmy Irwin, John Anderson, Jimmy Johnson, Robert Batson, Charles Carter, Rick Lowe, Henry Wilburn, Billy Gosnell, Billy Gardner.

Greer Mill (Greer, S.C.): Woodrow Hanvey (coach), John Brewton (coach), Don Giles, Ponder Rollins, William Lindsay, Paul Hardin,

James Stepp, Harold Stansell, Donald Flynn, Dan Brewton, Marshall Clark.

Lonsdale Mill (Seneca, S.C.): Frank Gaillard (coach), George Morgan (coach), Jack Bates, Thomas Poole, Cliff Poole, Rudolph Thrasher, Edward Alexander, Edward Foster, James Reed, Jones Davis, Joe Hughes, Johnnie Bates.

Piedmont Mill (Piedmont, S.C.): Oliver Howard (coach), Lewis Howard, Carroll Gilreath, Clyde Davenport, Kenneth Friddle, Jerry Ayers, Charles Blackston, James Allen, Robert Fletcher, Billy Fletcher, Norman Chandler.

Glenwood Mill (Easley, S.C.): Jack Owens (coach), George Hagood (business mgr), J.F. Owens, Bobby Rankin, Joe Vaughn, Doyle Cannon, Bruce Stansell, Waymon Knox, Donald League, Jerry Rankin, Osscar Hudson Jr.

Oconee Mill (Westminster, S.C.): Bruce Lockaby (coach), Miles Chrisley, George Stansell, Johnny Jones, Charles Smith, Joe Duvall, Jack Chambers, John Smith, Donnie Williams.

Mills Mill #1 (Greenville, S.C.): James Trammell (coach), James McCall Jr., James Thompson, William Davis, Clyde Bell, Evon Green, Robert Putman, Paul Eubanks, Truman Ballew, Willard Meeks.

Appleton Mill (Anderson, S.C.): Henry Spake (coach), Curtiss Daniel (coach), Ansel Chapman, John Daniel, George Langston, Robert Spears, Harold Rhodes, Charles Williams, Frank Allen, Donald Hanna, William Carlton, Bobby Leverette.

Anderson Mill (Anderson, S.C.): Fred Whitten (coach), Theron Bowman, Bob Bowman, Ernest Childs, George Mize, Rufus Byce, Raymond Hopkins, Homer Ross, Clyde Childs, Coy Gray, Maurice Webb.

Southern Bleachery (Taylors, S.C.): Jimmy Gay (coach), Clifton Lister, Rudolph Hughes, Broadus Farr, Thomas Ridgeway, Walter Fayssoux, William Gay, Johnny Badger, James Stevens, Ned Phillips.

Victor Mill (Greer, S.C.): Golden Wilson (coach), Ray Jones, Joseph Lamb, Carlos Garrett, Billie Graydon, Denny Owens Jr., Jesse Morris, John Caldwell, Luther Wilson, Kenneth Godfrey.

Dunean Mill (Greenville, S.C.): Willie Wilbanks (coach), Joel Greene, Alan Cox, Bobby Grant, Jimmy Farrow, Walter Bowers, Earl Stroud, Paul Lindsey, Hugh Campbell, Charles Granger, James Reed.

Judson Mill (Greenville, S.C.): J.F. Hickling (coach), Virgil Hill, Billy Taylor, Lou Loftis, Joseph Smith, Mark Buckner, Robert Wyatt, William Aiken, Roy Queen, David Linder, Bobby Porter.

Renfrew Bleachery (Travelers Rest, S.C.): Perry Poole (coach), Charles Werner (coach), Harry Johnson, Luther Bridges, Donald Bridwell, William Edwards, James Crosby, John Vernon, Charles Hart, Ervin Poole, Johnnie Granger Jr., Fred McClure.

Union Bleachery (Greenville, S.C.): Harold Greene (coach), Cecil Connley (coach), Herley Dix, Henry Keith, Harris Turner, Donald Jewell, Billie Robertson, Martin Robertson, Heber Evatt, Kenneth Boswell, Wyman Harrison, Marilyn Stroud, Williams.

CLASS A WOMEN

Chatham Mfg. (Elkin, N.C.), champions: Donald Brock (coach), Ruth Reich, Frances McBride, Betty Cope, Jennie Sherrill, Jannie Sherrill, Maurice Gordon, Doris Norman, Elizabeth Brinkema, Anne Chatham, Leola Shore, Lorene White.

Hanes Hosiery Mill (Winston-Salem, N.C.), runners-up: B.C. Hall Jr. (coach), Jackie Swain, Helen Greer, Ruth Phelps, Eunice Futch, Cornelia Lineberry, Melba Atkins, Irma Williard, Martha Mason, Lois Herring, Margaret Selle, Hazel Starrett, Ruth Brim.

American Enka (Enka, N.C.), consolation winners: Sam Patton (coach), Gussie Couch, Geneva Herron, Betty Lindsey, Nathalie Lovingood, Edith Metcalf, Eleanor Price, Beatrice Rollins, Ethel Taylor, Aileen Vaughn, Virginia Walker, Eloise West, League.

Drayton Mill (Spartanburg, S.C.): G.G. Simmons (coach), Alma Wilson, Alene Cudd, Kathleen Collins, Margaret Todd, Wilma Whitlock, Helen Melton, Dorothy Faust, Judith Jordan, Thelma Arms, Eva Grant, Martha Hayslip, Mayo Condrey.

Judson Mill (Greenville, S.C.): Quinn James (coach), Mary Massey, Margaret Owens, Sue Means, Gladys Means, Johnnie Means, Ola James, Dorothy James, Margaret Cobb, Betty Dobson, Mildred Dobson, Mary Ayers, Jones.

CLASS B WOMEN

Ware Shoals Mill (Ware Shoals, S.C.), champions: J.E. Thompson (coach), Virgil Stallcup (coach), Doris Truelove, Elaine

Thompson, Kathryn Ashley, Molly Davis, Ruth Poore, Beatrice Cheek, Fay Powell, Jean Davenport, Beverly Mayer, Mildred Snyder, Doris Thompson, Joyce Ridgeway, Ruth Jenkins.

North Georgia Processing (Toccoa, Ga.), runners-up: B.H. Barrett (coach), O.W. Thompson (coach), Sarah Bailey, Frances Payne, Polly McAlister, Jane Thornton, Laverne Kesler, Marion Thornton, Lucile Patterson, Mary Cann, Kate Powers.

Oconee Mill (Westminster, S.C.), consolation winners: A.V. Seymour (coach), Sara Ledford, Frances Turk, Frances Yarborough, Jeannette Quarles, Christine Carver, Mary Chrisley, Frances Chrisley, Riline Cox, Ruth Cain, Bernice Tippet.

Glen Lowery Mill (Whitmire, S.C.): S.R. DuBose (coach), Ted Black (coach), Mary Pruitt, Dorothy Frier, Jett Gregory, Ruth Ray, Sara McCall, Lola Bostic, Billie Kirby, Ruth Glenn, Zula Bacot, Virginia Renwick, Rachel Jones, Eleanor Nance.

Laurens Mill (Laurens, S.C.): Mrs. Roy Cooper (coach), W.P. Sheppard (coach), Jean McGee, Eddie Wilson, Margaret Mills, Katherine Cooper, Margaret Cooper, Lois Simmons, Bobbie Mills, Virginia Cooper, Peggy Walker, Mary Hembree, Rebecca Tollison, Neal.

Piedmont Mill (Piedmont, S.C.): James Bailey (coach), Betty Simpson, Jean Davis, Dorothy Nimmons, Mary Boiter, Betty Garrett, Jewel Duke, Mary Hiott, Alice Rampey, Patsy Smith, Patsy Drennan, Sybil Fletcher, Betty Ford.

Brandon Mill (Greenville, S.C.): Harold Alexander (coach), Madge Beasley (coach), Clarice Turner, Bobbie Baker, Joyce Smith, Lou Anders, Bettie Pierce, Frances Hall, Barbara McCarthy, Margaret Morrow, Jeanette McCall, Ruth Phillips, Betty Morgan.

Dunean Mill (Greenville, S.C.): Willie Wilbanks (coach), Bobby Mayfield, Mary Mayfield, Mildred Taffer, Henrietta Forrester, Audrey Wyatt, Eloise Medlin, Gertrude Medlin, Gwendolyn Nelms, Nancy Pitts, Edith Nicholson, Sarah Connell, Lucille Wilbanks.

Lonsdale Mill (Seneca, S.C.): Wilton Shaver (coach), Edna James, LaRue Nicholson, Martha Dyer, Rita Wade, Janet Poole, Inez Poole, Betty Reeves, Betty Moss, Doris Reeves, Bobbie Wade, Elizabeth James, Imojean Adkins.

Woodside Mill (Greenville, S.C.): G.R. Bodie (coach), Otto Herbert (coach), Evelyn Heath, Gay Blankenship, Anna Farrow, Nancy Taylor, Alma Harris, Mildred Shirley, Gladys Landreth, Doris Brookshire, Virginia Campbell, Margaret Taylor, Margaret Vehorn.

Calhoun Falls Mill (Calhoun Falls, S.C.): G.E. Dickard (coach), Gladys Pettit, Mary Hall, Edna Gibson, Gaynell Bonds, Clarice Jordan, Willie Embler, Delma Cooper, Dorothy Manning, Sybil Cooper, Willie Holmes, Mary Martin, Peggy Martin.

1949

Officers: Horace Whitmire (Greenville, S.C.), President; Clarence Thomas (Greenville, S.C.), Vice President; Ted Ratenski (Greenville, S.C.), Secretary; Aug W. Smith (Greenville, S.C.), Treasurer.

Executive Committee: Jesse Brown (Greenville, S.C.), Gary Bodie (Greenville, S.C.), A.R. Plaster (Elkin, N.C.), Harry Clark (Greenville, S.C.), Hugh Anderson (Greenville, S.C.), Jack Reames (Abbeville, S.C.), Walter Lauter (Rossville, Ga.), Lee Coleman (Greer, S.C.), Jim Westmoreland (Pelzer, S.C.), B.C. Hall Jr. (Winston-Salem, N.C.), Albert Wallace (Spartanburg, S.C.), J.B. Owens (Simpsonville, S.C.), Paul Cheek (Asheboro, N.C.).

CLASS A MEN

Pelzer Mill (Pelzer, S.C.), champions: Paul Edwards (coach), Wilton Dickson, Gerald Becker, Ed Copeland, Ralph Cannon, J.W. Jordan, Hoyt Jordan, Pete Harris, Earl Wooten, Dewey Quinn.

Peerless Woolen Mill (Rossville, Ga.), runners-up: Charles Geyer (coach), Walter Lauter (coach), Dick Thomas, James Cook, Charles Cox, Lamar North, Glenn Michaels, Robert James, Joe Dunagan, Thomas Maynor.

Piedmont Mill (Piedmont, S.C.), consolation winners: Henry Sneed (coach), James Bailey, J.H. Nesbitt, John Rampey, Milford Howard, Clarence Emery, Charles Davis, J.D. Hunnicutt, Thomas Trammell, John Powell, Ernie Chambers, Shorty McCreary.

Anderson Mill (Anderson, S.C.): Ezra Embler (coach), William Embler, Jimmie Embler, Fred Whitten, Roy Bridges, Luiaco Goodman, Lewis Whitworth, Marshall Hill, Chafer Honea, Tommie Owens, Jerry Goodson.

American Enka (Enka, N.C.): Sam Patton (coach), Bruce Goforth (coach), Rex Randall, Veo Story, Deran Walters, Kenneth Watts, Ebb

Williams, William Allen, Warren Bryant, Claude Green, Richard Gudger, Patton.

Clifton Mill (Clifton, S.C.): W.A. Quinn (coach), Dick Evans (coach), Edsel Sprouse, James King, Walter Greene, Robert Greene, Walter Fowler, Art Fowler, Charles Reid, Donald Wister, Voyle Massey, Paul Groce.

Southern Bleachery (Taylors, S.C.): Eugene Hodgens (coach), T. Lister (coach), George Blackwell, Walter Henson, Thomas Ridgeway, Sidney Badger, O'dell Broadnax, Clarence Smith, William Bishop, Lloyd Edwards, Harold Parker, Howard Waldrop.

Drayton Mill (Spartanburg, S.C.): Bill Lewis (coach), Sammy Sewell (coach), Ralph Gibbs, Wally Dean, Albert Wallace Jr., Danny McCraw, Manning Bagwell, Earle Berry, Leonard Hill, Jimmy Tollison, Charlie Seay, Cal Rogers.

Victor Mill (Greer, S.C.): Fred Snoddy (coach), Bert Cabaniss, June Pruitt, W.W. Hathuson, Don Jackson, William Moody, Ted Cabiness, William Tidwell, Brown.

Cramerton Mill (Cramerton, N.C.): H.D. Smith (coach), Bill Fletcher, Jenks Brendle, Billy Rabb, Ed Maxwell, Don Fletcher, Ben Cunningham, Nig Cunningham, Harry Jenkins, Ed Robinson, Ted Reece.

Dunean Mill (Greenville, S.C.): Willie Wilbanks (coach), Fred Cox, Horace Turner, Milton Hughes, Robert Stowe, Claude Long, Paul Turner, Edward Manley, Mendel Stroud, Carl Greene.

Monaghan Mill (Greenville, S.C.): Thomas Henderson (coach), Palmer McAvoy, Morris Newton, Tommie Blackston, Herbert Lindsey, Herman Dill, Bomar Keller, Doug Campbell, Harold Fuller, Jack Busbee, Ken Pittman.

Mills Mill #1 (Greenville, S.C.): James Trammell (coach), S.E. Murdock (coach), Myron Floyd, Richard Dittmer, Charles Smith, Curtis Powell, Ted Ratenski, Ansel McAlister, James Cothran, George Ballew.

Class B Men

Lyman Mill (Lyman, S.C.), champions: Dudley Tollison (coach), R. Powell (coach), Lloyd Leonard (coach), Larry Gresham, William Gosnell, Fred Mullinax, Leon Moss, Eugene Mullinax, Thurman Patton, Travis Taylor, Woodford Beasley, Eurell Eubanks Jr., Dewey Halford.

Southern Franklin Processing (Greenville, S.C.), runners-up: Edwin Briggs (coach), Harold Simpson, John Stafford, James McCullough, James Simpson, Wallace Putman, James Ayers, James Green, James Landreth, Charles Brock, Robert Carter.

Judson Mill (Greenville, S.C.), consolation winners: Charles Lankford, Leslie Pugh Jr., John Bowen, Harold Poole, Lloyd Lomax, Harold Holbrook, Floyd Loftis, Christopher Roberts, Walt Hamilton, Charles Riggins, Patton.

Orr Mill (Anderson, S.C.): Troy Kirby (coach), Cecil Buchanan, Junior Bridges, Henry McCurry, T.D. Simmons, Brit Vernon, Johnny Lyons, Sammy Meeks, Nelson Henderson, Horace Rhodes, Columbus Shaw.

Martel Mill (Asheville, N.C.): J.T. Brown (coach), William Horne, Wallace Fox, Clarence Young, John Edmonds, Roy Fox, Henry Clontz, Leonard Dillingham, Crover Frisbee, Luther Robinson.

Erlanger Mill (Lexington, N.C.): Conrad Hinson (coach), William White, Shelburn Temple, William Haynes, Max McGinn, James Davenport, William Jenkins, John Temple, Claude Medlin, Judson Brooks, Don Koontz.

Beacon Mill (Swannanoa, N.C.): Tommy Jackson (coach), J.D. Hardin (coach), Norman Gamache, William Penley, Jim Davidson, Carl Poteat, Harold Patton, James McMahan, Brock Burgess, Charles Johnson, John Lee Jr., Quentin Enloe.

North Georgia Processing (Toccoa, Ga.): Tom Mosely (coach), Orval Thompson (coach), Charles Davis, Joe Stowe, Ray Stowe, Roy Hollifield, Joe Carson, Freeman Payne, Grady Medlin, Randall McClain, Leon Denman, Lee Deaton.

Chicopee Mill (Gainesville, Ga.): S.B. Jones (coach), Ray Godfrey, Grady Brownlow, Charles Berryman, George Mize, Arlen Berryman, James Godfrey, Sylvia Clark, Edward Reed, Clyde Turk.

Glen Lowery Mill (Whitmire, S.C.): Clyde Brank (coach), Carl Basden, Ralph Elrod, Boyce Garman, Robert Brank, Ernest Jennings, Jarrett Frier, Hubert Elrod, Arthur Bradley, Arthur Brank, Teddy Weaver.

Springs Mill (Lancaster, S.C.): C.F. Rushing (coach), Robert Anderson, Halstead Owens, Albert Gibson, Robert McCorkle, James Watts, Ernest Luna, Kenneth Torr, Frank Reeves, Arthur Hunter, Charles McManus, Barefoot, Poore.

Brandon Mill (Greenville, S.C.): Carvin

Landreth (coach), George Burnett, Douglas Desaussure, William Carter, Rudolph Donehue, Charles Taylor, James Pierce, Roy Frost, James Williamson, Robert Moon, Fred McAbee.

Dunean Mill (Greenville, S.C.): Billy Farrow, W.G. Stroud Jr., Willie Chastine, Billy Threet, Manning Garren, Billy Granger, Roy Whitehead, Charles Gilstrap, James Martin.

Joanna Mill (Joanna, S.C.): Johnny Moore (coach), Allen O'Shields, Harold Prater, George Frady, Paul Fants, Joe Stroud, Richard Willingham, William Tinsley, Marion Oxner, Cecil Farmer.

Monaghan Mill (Greenville, S.C.): Joe Worthy (coach), Hanson Griffith, Pete Watts, Don Newton, Skeet Ward, Ava Phillips, Kenneth Hudgens, Charles McIntosh, Hugh Glymph, Jimmy Lindsey, Kalure Meng, Thomas Chapelear.

Pelzer Mill (Pelzer, S.C.): R.K. Chapman (coach), Earl Wooten (coach), J.P. Floyd, Marion Smith, Clyde McKee, Roy Whitlock, Bob Glasby, Carl Davis, Harold Major, Mickey Burton, Dewey Ross, Carl Martin.

Slater Mill (Slater, S.C.): M.J. McMakin (coach), Harold Knight, Willis Veal, Roy Lybrand, Marion Dudley, Jack McGill, Henry Taylor, Fred Cox, Archie Smith, Wilburn Knox, Fred Cashion.

Renfrew Bleachery (Travelers Rest, S.C.): J.D. Ivey (coach), Jimmie Balloch, Lewis Lockaby, Melvin Poole, Harold McKinney, Lester McDowell, Joel Roe Jr., Roy Wood, Edmond Poole, Gene Cunningham, Doyle Belcher.

Lonsdale Mill (Seneca, S.C.): Joe Dalton (coach), Rhett Evatt (coach), James Black, Joe Hughes, Hines Hamilton, Harley James, A.C. James, James Shirley, Hoyt Gibson, Morris Whitt, Joyce Burgess, Edward Sosebee.

Greer Mill (Greer, S.C.): Hicks Burgin (coach), Furman Taylor (coach), Samuel Stack, Grady Harvey, John Henson, Ralph Bramlett, Clint Green, Charles Brannon, Robert Campbell, Wilson Taylor, James Gowan, James Campbell.

Victor Mill (Greer, S.C.): Bill Moody (coach), Thomas Tipton, Willie Woodward, Paul Garrett, Lewis Hughes, Roy Livingston, Thomas Miller, John Caldwell, Boyce Howard Jr., Thurman McGaha, Roy Vehorn.

Watts Mill (Laurens, S.C.): Lloyd Moore (coach), Harold Pearson, Kenneth Word, Clyde Werner, David Wardell, Marion Craine, Dean Lyles, John Cox, Paul Cavender, Harold Walther, Stanley Johnson, James Stokes.

Woodside Mill (Greenville, S.C.): Floyd Giebell (coach), Reuben Ramsey (coach), Robert King, Joe Farrow, Bert Wilson, Jack Wilson, James Farrow, Ray Herbert, Veldee Hines, James Greene, Dewey Morrow, William Wakefield.

Camperdown Mill (Greenville, S.C.): J.W. McDowell (coach), Charlie Penland (coach), Billy Gosnell, Pete Rollins, Jack Mintz, J.H. Bruce, J.H. Ruff, James Riddle, Paul Darnell, Roy Rollins, Bruce Moreland, Jack Anderson.

Easley Mill (Easley, S.C.): Jack Sandell (coach), Lloyd Smith, Ray Waldrop, Melvin Owens, E.W. Evans, Edward Putman, Jack Long, Randall Putman, James Henson, Verland McIntyre, James Rogers.

Firestone Textile Inc. (Gastonia, N.C.): Leonard Bumgardner (coach), Clyde Phillips, James Dobbins, Harold Robinson, Charles Lunsford, John Owens, Billy Green, Kenneth Deal, Jack Guffey, Fred Deal, William Padgett.

Piedmont Mill (Piedmont, S.C.): Dillard Burrell (coach), Calvin Parker, Carroll Patterson, Bert Garrison, Charles Burrell, James Cooper, Joseph Humphries, Carroll Gilreath, Charles Bowen, Browning.

Glendale Mill (Spartanburg, S.C.): F. Millwood, Warren, White, Key, McCrary, Reeves, Ammons, Fisher, Ogle, Waldrop.

CLASS C MEN

Dunean Mill (Greenville, S.C.), champions: Willie Wilbanks (coach), H. Turner (coach), Joe Granger, Junior Stowe, Alvin LaBoone, Joe Greene, Ed Holbrook, Bobby Grant, Pete Stroud, Gary Ashley, Alan Cox, Bud Granger.

Pelzer Mill (Pelzer, S.C.), runners-up: J.D. Whitt (coach), Paul Edwards (coach), Raymond Bair, Olin Davis, Joe Garrett, James Bryant, Gordon Davenport, Freeman Watt, Ernest O'Bannion, Jimmy Hedden, Harold Drennon, Clifford Thompson.

Appleton Mill (Anderson, S.C.), consolation winners: James Morrison (coach), Henry Spake (coach), Ted Smith, Milton White, Ansel Chapman, James Williams, Charles Ertzberger, Claude Hancock, Benny Spears, John Daniel, Howard Bowen, Bobby Leverette.

Camperdown Mill (Greenville, S.C.): Louie McDowell (coach), J.B. Irvin (coach), Norman Lowe, Thomas Jenkins, Bobby Batson, Henry

Wilburn, Jimmy Johnson, Charles Carter, Bill Sanders, William Davidson.

Anderson Mill (Anderson, S.C.): Ezra Embler (coach), Clyde Childs, Theron Bowen, Marshall Hopkins, Ernest Childs, Marshall McAllister, Artis Martin, Kenneth Ellis, Rufus Byce, Aubery Chasteen, Coy Gray.

Gluck Mill (Anderson, S.C.): Early Hanna (coach), Bobby Richards (coach), Thomas Cromer, Joe Stansell, David McGuffin, J.D. McCombs, Charles Brooks, William Ragsdale, William Lother, Robert Moody, Robert Hancock.

Brandon Mill (Greenville, S.C.): Louis Clary (coach), Pierce Powers, Ted McClellan, Bobby Powers, Edward Key, Thomas Hall, James Fortune, J.D. Williamson, William Pierce, Joe Jones, Clayton Gilstrap.

Orr Mill (Anderson, S.C.): Winfred Farmer (coach), Melzer Welborn, Billy Stamps, Billy Cleveland, Beverly Davis, Gene Stamps, Walter Holcombe, Tommy McLean, Herbert Meeks, Jack Sanders.

Union Bleachery (Greenville, S.C.): Hughes Boswell, Phil Knight, Marilyn Stroud, James Wynn, Donald Stroud, Bobby Bishop, Thomas Butler, Bobby Lazar, Billy Moody, Billy Robertson.

Glenwood Mill (Easley, S.C.): George Hagood (coach), Jerry Rankin, Waymon Knox, Clyde Hudson, Franklin Hudson, Charles Smith, Bobby Rankin, Doyle Cannon, Wallace Browning, Bruce Stansell, George Pitts Jr.

Oconee Mill (Westminster, S.C.): Henry Buchanan (coach), Robert Grogan (coach), George Stansell, Johnny Jones, Joe Duvall, Thomas Broome, Herman Smith, Jack Chambers, Charles Smith, Doris Houston, Miles Chrisley, John Smith.

Lonsdale Mill (Seneca, S.C.): C.W. Gaillard (coach), George Morgan (coach), Eugene Sosebee, Billy Cornell, Cliff Poole, Gibson, William Wyatt, Edward Alexander, Jack Bates, Rudolph Thrasher, Thomas Poole, Billy Cain, Roach.

Greer Mill (Greer, S.C.): C.W. Flynn (coach), James Brannon (coach), James Stepp, Robert Spencer, Thomas Oliver, Murphy Harvey, Lewis Knighton, Harold Stansell, Donald Flynn, Marshall Clark, William Lindsay, Paul Hardin.

Woodside Mill (Greenville, S.C.): Harold Limbaugh (coach), Tobe Herbert (coach), Charles Barbary, Eddie White, Clyde Spearman, Charles Wakefield, Billy Haney, Charles Baker, Thomas Taylor, Joe McConnell, Curtis Hickam, Bobby Nelson.

Slater Mill (Slater, S.C.): Snow Kirby (coach), Max Robinson, Bobby Cole, Robert Cashion, Billy Ramsey, Louie Henson, Maxin Waldrop, Ansel McMakin Jr., George Gossett, Gene Cox, Joe Cashion.

Monaghan Mill (Greenville, S.C.): Jack Ballew (coach), Johnny Atkins, Mutt Compton, Tommy Burgess, Bill Fuller, Columbus Medlin, Joe Wyatt, Charles Olson, Benny Brown, Danny Bagwell, Bill McKinney.

Renfrew Bleachery (Travelers Rest, S.C.): K.D. Crosby (coach), Leslie Wood (coach), Bucky Abbott, Donny Vernon, Larry Foster, Charles Hart, Randall Poole, Jim Crosby, Frank Edwards, Harry Johnson, Fred McClure.

Southern Bleachery (Taylors, S.C.): Herman Jackson (coach), Walker Dilworth (coach), William Gay, Walter Fayssoux, Broadus Farr, Roy Coker, Joseph Belcher, William Bramlett, Jack Carlton, Samuel Forrester, Rudolph Hughes, John Badger.

Southern Worsted (Greenville, S.C.): W.C. Vess (coach), J.B. Simpson (coach), Lee Ford, James Waldrop, Joe Grant, Charles Davis, Homer Hogg, James Hogg, Robert Mabry, Charles Mabry, James Pruitt.

Laurens Mill (Laurens, S.C.): W.P. Sheppard (coach), Albert Smith (coach), James Hawkins, Billy Snow, William Smith, Joe Edwards, Jack Burns, Donald Good, Donald Cothran, Tommy Reames, Bobby Clark.

Lyman Mill (Lyman, S.C.): D.K. Smith (coach), Johnny Wahonic (coach), Joe Mullinax, Lawrence Eubanks, Kenneth Williams, Choice Watson, J.C. Reed, Raymond Miller, Harold Eubanks, Joe Smith, Jerry Smith, William Oliver.

Victor Mill (Greer, S.C.): Fred Snoddy (coach), Ray Jones, Richard McCuen, Dan Wilson, Joe Lamb, Melvin Morris, Walter Bain, Kenneth Moss, Dennis Owens Jr., R.E. Southerland, Wayne Godfrey.

Judson Mill (Greenville, S.C.): L.P. Loftis Jr., Wallace Reid, Bobby Blackwell, Bobby Pierce, Joseph Smith Jr., Virgil Hill, Jimmie Durham, Calvin Ford, Terry Cline.

Easley Mill (Easley, S.C.): Edward Putman (coach), George Owens, Ben Fox, J.M. Ellison, Bobby Rogers, J. Barnes Jr., Bobby Bagwell, Charles Holliday, Hulet Holliday, Doyle Brooks, Rudolph Evett.

Piedmont Mill (Piedmont, S.C.): Herman

Merritt (coach), Joe Ayers, Kenneth Smith, Furman Foxx, Tommy Nelson, Billy Turpin, Lewis Howard, Robert Hooper, Gilbert Ivie, Thomas Powell, Bobby Bryson.

Simpsonville Mill (Simpsonville, S.C.): Herman Williams (coach), Roger Cannady, Billy Chandler, Joseph Payne, Jones Thackston, Bill Goodenough, Don Stokes, Glenn Knight, Bobby Jones, Billy Hanks, Joe Runyan, Hawkins.

Mills Mill #1 (Greenville, S.C.): Myron Floyd (coach), Jimmy McCall, Willard Meeks, Gene Bell, Paul Eubanks, William Davis, Robert Putman, Jerry Patterson, Evon Green, Rudolph Simmons, Walter Jackson.

CLASS A WOMEN

Chatham Mfg. (Elkin, N.C.), champions: Don Brock (coach), Ruth Brim, Ruth Reich, Alta McCann, Betty Cope, Ann Paradise, Betty Steadman, Liz Padgett, Frances Hall, Pat Carney, Jennie Sherrill, Jannie Sherrill, Gladys Watson.

Drayton Mill (Spartanburg, S.C.), runners-up: Wilma Whitlock (coach), Susie McGraw, Judith Jordan, Doris Gregory, Thelma Arms, Helen Melton, May Condrey, Maxine Garrett, Margaret Todd, Kathleen Collins, Pauline Collins, Shirley Wilson.

American Enka (Enka, N.C.), consolation winners: Sam Patton (coach), Dorothy Gaston (mgr), Jewel Goodwin, Wilma Morgan, Mabel Randall, Betty Lindsey, Virginia Walker, Mary Allison, Hattie Carland, Betty Cope, Frances Corn, Beatrice Robinson, Eloise Reagon, Betty Elpey.

Judson Mill (Greenville, S.C.): Gynn James (coach), Frances Wofford (coach), Betty Dobson, Mildred Dobson, Frances Walker, Catherine Stroups, Jewel Ayers, Margaret Strange, Johnnie Means, Gladys Means, Polly Bridwell, Babs Clark, Margaret Owens, Cobb.

CLASS B WOMEN

North Georgia Processing (Toccoa, Ga.), champions: Tom Moseley (coach), Orval Thompson (coach), Alline Hollifield, Maxine Hollifield, Drucilla Bailey, Janet Smith, Jannie McCain, Nannie McClain, Laverne Kesler, Vernell Turner, Sarah Edmonds, Frances Payne, Elene Harris, Edith Bailey, Crowder.

Ware Shoals Mill (Ware Shoals, S.C.), runners-up: O'Dell Barbary (coach), Doris Thompson, Beatrice Cheek, Ruth Poore, Peggy Moss, Mildred Snyder, Rubie Black, Mildred Martin, Lelar Powell, Dorothy Everette, Katherine Smith, Fay Davis, Nancy Kay.

Springs Mill (Lancaster, S.C.), consolation winners: C.F. Rushing (coach), Marjorie Buchanan, Mary Hendrix, Ruth Lancaster, Joy Edwards, Doris Shaw, Susie Head, Martha Watts, Lou Lucas, Betty Whaley, Jacqueline Adams, Alma Cooke, Mary Reeves.

Calhoun Falls Mill (Calhoun Falls, S.C.): C.E. Dickard (coach), Dorothy Manning, Mabel Cobb, Willie Embler, Velma Sanders, Clarice Jordan, Betty Latham, Peggy Martin, Faye Ayers, Betty May, Martha O'Shields, Paula Waldrop, Delma Cooper.

Glen Lowery Mill (Whitmire, S.C.): Ted Black (coach), Sara McCall, Julia Garman, Betty Dunean, Willie Brock, L. Mooneyhan, Jette Gregory, Dorothy Frier, Rachel Jones, Ruth Glenn, Grace Brock, Ruth Ray, M. Yarborough.

Avondale Mill (Alexander City, Ala.): Troy Holley (coach), Luna Brown, Maudine Sprayberry, Marguitte Coker, Mary Montgomery, Hilda Coker, Edith Florine, LaRue Hutcherson, Exell Taunton, Alice Cromer, Barbara Brown, Marie Burkhalter.

Brandon Mill (Greenville, S.C.): Ray Wynn (coach), Jeanette McCall, Betty Morgan, Shirley Jones, Patsy Johnson, Lou Anders, Peggy Pierce, Joyce Smith, Betty Pierce, Delores Smith, Ruth Phillips, Clarice Turner.

Dunean Mill (Greenville, S.C.): Willie Wilbanks (coach), Wyleen Abercrombie, Billy Jo Waldrop, Nancy Pitts, Joan Sisk, Edith Nicholson, Joan Kelley, Gwendolyn Nelms, Mildred Taffer, Evelyn McClure, Louella Tate, Bobbie Mayfield, Mary Mayfield.

Monaghan Mill (Greenville, S.C.): Glenn Hollis (coach), Lucile Hollis, Alada Major, Joanna Hudgens, Mozelle Gooch, Jean Powell, Sue Dobbs, Tina Rollins, Pat Pearson, Betty Mauldin, Juanita Campbell, Jewell Pittman, Laura Payne.

Orr Mill (Anderson, S.C.): Carl Thomason (coach), Lou Jaymes, Jo Parnell, Jenny Jennings, Lois Thackston, Texie Thackston, Doris Stone, Norma Thomason, Betty Grant, Florence McLane, Lelia Brown, Rachel Cleveland, Martha Dorn, Texie Thackston, Irene Brown.

Lonsdale Mill (Seneca, S.C.): Roy McCurry (coach), Wilton Shaver (coach), Larue Nicholson, Jeanette Poole, Betty Moss, Genell Rowland, Barbara Lewis, Ollie James, Bobbie

Wade, Doris Reeves, Rota Wade, Betty Reeves, Edna James, Ruth Reynolds.

Watts Mill (Laurens, S.C.): Mary Hudson (coach), Betty Blakely (coach), Trudy Leonard, Eunice Walther, Dorothy Culbertson, Mary McGaha, Juanita Tollison, O'Shields, Virginia Owens, Emily Coates, Hattie Davis, Omega Knight, Martha Johnson, Bobbie Taylor, Martin.

Victor Mill (Greer, S.C.): L.T. Puckett (coach), Margaret Ballenger, Loretta Heatherly, Drucilla Godfrey, Mae Snoddy, Sisie Forrester, Elizabeth Lane, Martha Lowe, Tillie Morgan, Madeline Williams, Joyce Willis, Frances Barker.

Woodside Mill (Greenville, S.C.): Squire Grogan (coach), Frances Webb (coach), Anna Farrow, Jo Rigdon, Norma Julian, Ann Bowen, Hazel Hyde, Frances Hall, Margaret Wilson, Gladys Landreth, Earlene Manley, Gay Blankenship, Vinazell Brady, Mary Gillespie.

Piedmont Mill (Piedmont, S.C.): Wilton Smith (coach), Roxie Reeves, Joan Davis, Elizabeth Fleming, Mary Hiott, Alice Rampey, Betty Garrett, Dorothy Nimmons, Margie Payne, Doris Stone, Mary Boiter, Peggy Wyrosdick, Sybil Fletcher.

Simpsonville Mill (Simpsonville, S.C.): Terry Rich (coach), Jack Cox (coach), Bobbie Tumblin, Agnes Barbery, Josephine Hill, J. Spillars, Edna Goodenough, Helen Singleton, Mary Hart, Alefa Kirby, Bobbie Hanks, Jeanette James, Jeanette Thackston, Joanetta Thackston.

Renfrew Bleachery (Travelers Rest, S.C.): Alec Edwards (coach), John McDowell (coach), Blanche Lenderman, Doris McDaniel, Evelyn Lenderman, Viola Ivey, Emma Ivey, Bobbie Ivey, Marcia Wynn, Helen Boswell, Betty Moody, Dora Murphy, Anna Murphy, Margaret Lockaby.

---------- 1950 ----------

Officers: Horace C. Whitmire (Greenville, S.C.), President; Hugh Anderson (Greenville, S.C.), Vice President; Harry Clark (Greenville, S.C.), Secretary; Bill Sandel (Greenville, S.C.), Treasurer.

Executive Committee: Jesse Brown (Greenville, S.C.), Gary Bodie (Greenville, S.C.), Fred Snoddy (Greer, S.C.), Don Brock (Winston-Salem, N.C.), Clarence Thomas (Greenville, S.C.), Jack Reames (Abbeville, S.C.), Walter Lauter (Rossville, Ga.), Willie Wilbanks (Greenville, S.C.), Jim Westmoreland (Pelzer, S.C.), B.C. Hall Jr. (Winston-Salem, N.C.), Albert Wallace (Spartanburg, S.C.), J.B. Owens (Simpsonville, S.C.), Paul Cheek (Asheboro, N.C.), Ted Ratenski (Greenville, S.C.).

CLASS A MEN

Dunean Mill (Greenville, S.C.), champions: Ward Williams (coach), Robert Stowe, Horace Turner, David Putman, Milton Hughes, Carl Green, Manning Garren, Bruce Long, Bud Granger, Fred Cox.

Peerless Woolen Mill (Rossville, Ga.), runners-up: Walter Lauter (coach), Robert James (coach), Thomas Maynor, Ray Griffith, Willard Lovelady, Donald Gaines, Brownell Bryant, Frank Drake, William Miller, James Cooke, John Barger, James Ellis.

Pelzer Mill (Pelzer, S.C.), consolation winners: J.P. Edwards (coach), Ralph Cannon, Earl Wooten, Clayton Copeland, Carl Davis, James Harris, Charles Hodge, J.W. Jordan, Hoyt Jordan, Kent Chapman, Ray Smith.

Lyman Mill (Lyman, S.C.): D.K. Smith (coach), Leon Moss (coach), Carvin Medlock, Fred Mullinax, Woodford Beasley, Eurell Eubanks Jr., William Gosnell, Hugh Rogers, Luther Mullinax, Thurman Patton, Furman Taylor, E.C. Cothran.

Anderson Mill (Anderson, S.C.): Ezra Embler (coach), Billy Hopkins, Perry Whitworth, Roy Bridges, William Embler, Jimmie Embler, Brent Breedin, Fred Whitten, James Walker, Arthur Hester.

Appleton Mill (Anderson, S.C.): Henry Spake (coach), Andrew King, William Middleton, Jack Carlton, Richard White, Curtiss Daniel, Henry Bailey, Louie Mayfield, Claud Spake, Marvin Gurley, J.A. Poole.

Columbus Mill (Columbus, Ga.): Charles Carmack (coach), Jack Guinn, Billy Tinkler, James Wright, Leonard Brown, Kenny Braxton, Charles Harris, Edwards Hurston, Dorsy Hasty, W.F. Richardson, Carval Hubbard.

Monaghan Mill (Greenville, S.C.): Pete Henderson (coach), Herman Dill (coach), Robert Chambers, Palmer McAvoy, Herbert Lindsay Jr., Douglas Campbell, William Pitman, James Wilson Jr., Bomar Keller, Dan Burkhardt, Morris Newton, Pert Griggin.

Piedmont Mill (Piedmont, S.C.): J.H. Nesbitt (coach), Tom Pack, Tom Trammell, Billy

Davis, Veo Storey, Milford Howard, Ernie Chambers, Ben Bowen, Glenn Michaels, Charles Burrell, Harry Waldrop.

Southern Bleachery (Taylors, S.C.): June Pruitt (coach), Clarence Smith, William Bishop, Lloyd Edwards, Howard Waldrop, John Dilworth, General Pruitt, Harold Parker, Walter Henson, Theron Stone, Sidney Badger.

Victor Mill (Greer, S.C.): Lowe, Dixon, Snoddy, Frix, Green, Hutchinson, Lamb.

CLASS B MEN

Springs Mill (Lancaster, S.C.), champions: R.H. King (coach), Charles Zimmerman (coach), Arthur Williamson, Roy Collins, Lee Collins, John Shannon, Curtis Beasley, Ernest Luna, Howard Faulkenberry, Arthur Hunter, Roland Barefoot, Cyril Havird.

Orr Mill (Anderson, S.C.), runners-up: Sammy Meeks (coach), Cecil Buchanan, Horace Rhodes, Johnny Lyons, Joe Fleming, Bob Nicora, Bo Williams, Junior Bridges, Tommy Stubblefield, Johnny Ashworth, Hooks.

Russell Manufacturing (Alexander City, Ala.), consolation winners: C.B. McEachern (coach), Edsel Riddle, Lee Collins, Grady Gunn, Marvin Brown, Charles Bailey, Murray Hammond, Rayford Duck, Eugene Gilbert, James Walden, Obie Forbus.

Victor Mill (Greer, S.C.): Marvin English (coach), Denny Owens, John Caldwell, Billy Mayfield, Lewis Hughes, Wallace McGaha, Bobby Porter, Joe Lamb, Carlos Garrett, Melvin Morris.

Glen Lowery Mill (Whitmire, S.C.): S.R. DuBose (coach), Carl Basden (coach), Hubert Elrod, Arthur Bradley, Arthur Brank, Terrel Fowler, Luke Hart, Richard Harrison, Luther Jones, John Miller, Melvin McCall.

Beacon Mill (Swannanoa, N.C.): J.D. Hardin (coach), Lefoia Thompson, Fred Nichols, Arvel Silvers, Charles Johnson, Bill McMahan, Brock Burgess, John Lee, Joe McIntosh, Norman Gamache, Bill Holcombe.

Brandon Mill (Greenville, S.C.): James Carnes Jr. (coach), John Buchanan, Ansel McCall, Robert Frost, Robert Moon, Fred McAbee Jr., Harry Foster, Calvin Morrow, James Williamson, Robert Burnett, Don Rich.

Camperdown Mill (Greenville, S.C.): J.B. Irvin (coach), John Guest (coach), Paul Darnell, Harold Davis, Eugene Davis, Harold Cooper, Billy Gosnell, Cecil Rollins, John Anderson, Vernon Rollins, Leonard Riddle, Koliure Meng.

Chicopee Mill (Gainesville, Ga.): S.B. Jones (coach), Ray Godfrey, Charles Berryman, Paul McDonald, Ted Ivey, Arlen Berryman, Clyde Turk, Blanton Griffin, Jackson Burrell, W.B. Gunter Jr., Billie Brocks.

Easley Mill (Easley, S.C.): Courtney Heath (coach), Joe Anders (coach), Verlon McEntyre, George Owens, Marvin Waldrop, James Campbell, William Holcombe, Calvin Bagwell, Roy Waldrop.

Firestone Textile Inc. (Gastonia, N.C.): Leonard Bumgardner (coach), Lynn Athinson, Charles Lunsford, Donald, Harold Robinson, Jack Guffey, Fred Deal, Spee Padgett, Billy Queen, J.M. Tate, E.T. Green, John Owens, Jolley.

Glendale Mill (Spartanburg, S.C.): Bob Cannon (coach), Charles Warren, Bob Cannon, Richard Ogle, Carl Mabry, Phil McCreary, Jerome Millwood, Harold Ammons, James Reaves.

Greer Mill (Greer, S.C.): Hicks Burgin (coach), Johnny Stack (coach), Doyle Stansell, Robert Campbell, Elford Campbell, Samuel Stack, Marshall Lindsey, Zeke Harvey, Robert Burdette, Arnold Campbell, Ralph Bramlett, J.T. Henson.

Joanna Mill (Joanna, S.C.): James Orr (coach), Richard Willingham, Johnny Moore, Bill Tinsley, George Frady, Pope Oxner, Cecil Farmer, Virlyn Davenport, Rudy McCarthy, Barron O'Shields, Paul Fouts.

Judson Mill (Greenville, S.C.): Ansel Bridwell (coach), Harold Holbrook, Maurice Lankford, Walter Hamilton, Floyd Loftis, Kenneth Linder, Bruce Stroup, Hoyt Smith, Charles Riggins, George Bobo, Cecil Pressley, Sprouse.

Laurens Mill (Laurens, S.C.): Otis Townsend (coach), Paul Cavender (coach), Francis Craine, Clifford Cox, Frank Dambeck, Vernon Taylor, Henry Bowie, Bobby Clarke, Franklin Russell.

Mills Mill (Greenville, S.C.): Myron Floyd (coach), Ralph Bell, Roy Emory, Bobby Fortune, Alvin LaBoone, Robert Putman, Leroy Smith, Jackie Williams.

Monaghan Mill (Greenville, S.C.): Bobby Foster (coach), J.D. Bagwell (coach), William McKinney, Jack Watts, Robert McAvoy, Charles Olson, James Turner, Oscar Gooch, Donald Dean, Don Newton, Fred Busbee, Gary Parker, Alva Phillips.

Southern Textile Basketball Tournament Rosters   Appendix 1   177

North Georgia Processing (Toccoa, Ga.): Thomas Moseley (coach), Jack Watson, Lee Deaton, Charles Davis, Fernando Payne, Jack Collier, Randall McClain, Joe Carson, Joe Stowe, Roy Hollifield, Mark Turner.

Southern Bleachery (Taylors, S.C.): June Pruitt (coach), Boyce Howard, Perry Howard, Rudolph Hughes, Bobby Belue, Charles Painter, Delma Hodgens, Albert Tucker, Samuel Forrester, John Hawkins, Charles Evington.

Union Bleachery (Greenville, S.C.): W.A. Bishop Jr. (coach), Roy Brooks (coach), Martin Robinson, Heber Evatt Jr., Walter Robertson, Richard Evington, Hugh Revis, James Gentry, Jesse Camp Jr., Donald Jewell, Roy Lockaby, Garland Revis Jr.

Ware Shoals Mill (Ware Shoals, S.C.): Willie Wilbanks (coach), Raymond Bowden, Lewis Bagwell, Richard Hartman, T.M. Wright, Lamar Smith, Odell Barbery, Herman Burrell, Wade Burton, Billy Poore, Hoyt Hembree.

Jackson Mill (Iva, S.C.): Berry Burdette (coach), Neil Stovall, Eugene Burdette, Harold Fleming, Alfred Jordan, Jack McMahan, Ralph Allen, Hiram Bruce, Ernest Alexander, Grier Brown, James Powell, Machen.

Woodside Mill (Greenville, S.C.): Dewey Bowen (coach), Floyd Giebell (coach), Jess Cumby, Ray Herbert, Dewey Morrow, Joe Farrow, Robert King, James Greene, Harman Wood, Charles Wakefield, Jack Wilson, Otto Herbert.

Dunean Mill (Greenville, S.C.): Alan Cox, Billy Farrow, Holmes Duncan, Bobby Grant, Junior Stowe, Joe Granger, Charles Gilstrap, Pete Stroud, Gordon Jones, Bill McWhite.

Slater Mill (Slater, S.C.): Snow Kirby (coach), Jack Long, Fred Cox, Roy Lybrand, Harold Taylor, Harold Knight, Gene Cox, William Knox, Jack Cashion.

Simpsonville Mill (Simpsonville, S.C.): Fred Barbery (coach), Carroll Chandler (coach), Bill Porter, Roger Cannady, J.R. Runyan, Nick Alexander, W.D. Smith, William McGill, Cliff Paxton, Cobb Landers, Jones Thackston, R.T. Williams, Fowler.

CLASS C MEN

Pelzer Mill (Pelzer, S.C.), champions: Joe Williams (coach), Joe Garrett, Jimmy Hedden, Gordon Davenport, Bobby Thomason, James Thomason, Bobby Southerland, Olin Davis, Richard Reeves, Randolph Whaley, Bobby Ross.

Camperdown Mill (Greenville, S.C.), runners-up: J.H. Bruce (coach), Louie McDowell (coach), Jimmy Irvin, Buddy Breazeale, Robert Batson Jr., Charles Davis, William Davidson, Henry Wilburn, Noah Lowe, Bobby Jones, Charles Carter, Jimmy Johnson.

Monaghan Mill (Greenville, S.C.), consolation winners: Lewis Cook (coach), Elizabeth Phillips (coach), Benny Brown, Winston Major, James Crain, Charles Crawford, Edward Burgess, Joe Wyatt, Bobby Cook, Johnny Atkins, Dan Bagwell.

Slater Mill (Slater, S.C.): Bill Hall (coach), Joe Cashion, Ansel McMakin, Maxie Waldrop, Alton White, James Payne, Gene Henson, Wallace Payne, Bobby Johnson, Bobby Cole, Max Robinson.

Anderson Mill (Anderson, S.C.): Ezra Embler (coach), Lewis McCollum, Charles Ertzberger, John McAllister, Rufus Byce, Clyde Childs, Newlan Sanders, Arlis Martin, Ronald Ripley, Lewis Kelly, Graeme Keith.

Appleton Mill (Anderson, S.C.): Henry Spake (coach), Benny Spears, DuBose Leverette, Milton White, David Bowen Jr., Charles Conwell, Junior McElrath, John Daniel, Billy Hanks, Gary Speares.

Brandon Mill (Greenville, S.C.): Louis Clary (coach), William Price, James Fortune, Thomas Hall, Joe Jones, Edward Key, Jack Waters, J.D. Williamson, Bobby Powers, Willie Murphy, Pierce.

Brandon Rayon Mill (Greenville, S.C.): Ray Wynn (coach), Richard Parnell, Jack Garren, Joseph Alexander, Alvin McClellan, Pierce Powers, Bobby Garren, Bobby Crawford, William Johnson.

Easley Mill (Easley, S.C.): Tommy James (coach), Ike Cannon (coach), James McCollum, Bobby Bagwell, Waymon Knox, Charles Bagwell, Claude Evatt, Ben Fox, Doyle Brooks, Randal Searcy, Doyce Surratt, Charles Garrett.

Glenwood Mill (Easley, S.C.): George Hagood (coach), Jack Parrish (coach), Bobby Rankin, Charles Smith, Gene West, Franklin Hudson, Wallace Browning, Jerry Rankin, Doyle Cannon, Charles Holcombe, Clarence Smith, James McQueen.

Greer Mill (Greer, S.C.): C.W. Flynn (coach), Johnny Stack (coach), Lewis Knighton, Charles Flynn, Dean Stansell, Thomas Oliver, Robert Spencer, Lewis Pinson,

Donald Flynn, Thurlough Gowan, Jerry Burgess, Marshall Clark.

Judson Mill (Greenville, S.C.): Ansel Bridwell (coach), Bobby Blackwell, Leonard Green, Wallace Reid, Bill Konduras, Richard Stephens, Pete Loftis, John Pierce, Terry Cline, Bill Massey.

Laurens Mill (Laurens, S.C.): C.B. Simmons (coach), Bobby Bishop (coach), Winston Roberts, Tommy Reames, Billy Snow, James Carlton, Wayne Campbell, Donald Cothran, James Hawkins, Jack Burns, Harold Mitchell, Richard Coker.

Orr Mill (Anderson, S.C.): Sammy Meeks (coach), Herbert Meeks, Leroy Parnell, Jack McLane, Walter Holcombe, Red Jameson, Ralph Smith, Doug Sanders, Jack Sanders, Gene Stamps, Melzer Welborn.

Lyman Mill (Lyman, S.C.): Warren Eubanks (coach), Eurell Eubanks Sr. (coach), Billy High, Benjamin Adkins, Kenneth Williams, Judson Reed, Harold Eubanks, Joseph Smith, Lawrence Eubanks, Kenneth Pettigrew, Odell Pace, Choice Watson.

Mills Mill (Greenville, S.C.): Harry Smith (coach), Francis Ballew, Clyde Bell, William Davis, Paul Eubanks, Charles Funk, Evon Green, David Lloyd, William Marler Jr., James McCall, William Simmons.

Poinsett Mill (Greenville, S.C.): Donald Gilstrap (coach), Luke Landers (coach), Ralph Durham, Jack Gray, Fred Freeman, Bobby Gray, Robert Burdett, Charlie Crowe, Wilford Crowe, Leonard Garrett, Jack Bridges, Jack Riddley, Campbell.

Southern Bleachery (Taylors, S.C.): June Pruitt (coach), Walter Fayssoux, Joseph Belcher, Joe Smith, William Gay, Broadus Farr, Roy Coker, John Badger, Bill Bramlett, Coleman Pace, Harold Wham.

Union Bleachery (Greenville, S.C.): Harold Green (coach), Rhodan Batson (coach), Billy Robertson, Hughes Boswell, Maryln Stroud, Jack League, Ronald Knight, Phil Knight, Billy Moody, Thomas Lazar, Roger Bishop, William Wyatt.

Lonsdale Mill (Seneca, S.C.): Hill Sosebee (coach), Leon Dooley, Alton Burgess, Lee Gilliard, Michael Gilliard, Gene Sosebee, Thomas Poole, Edward Alexander, Grady Poole, Cliff Poole, Thrasher.

Ware Shoals Mill (Ware Shoals, S.C.): Andy Hawthorne (coach), Wayne Richey, Joe Skinner, Lonnie Martin, Joe Teague, Irvin Pitts, Carol Heath, Stanley Hilley, William Parnell, Alton Harvey, Clyde Duckworth, Burton.

Woodside Mill (Greenville, S.C.): Earl Jones (coach), Jim Hendrix (coach), William Harbin, Joe McConnell, Eddie White, Milward Griffith, Bobby Nelson, Cartis Hickman, Clyde Spearman, Thomas Taylor, Jerry Baker, Woody Moore, Batson.

Gluck Mill (Anderson, S.C.): Earley Hanna (coach), Dick Perry (coach), Curtis Brooks, Dennis Slater, Ralph Nimmons, Thomas Wood, William Ragsdale, Curtis Wood, William Lother, Douglas Dyar, Ervin Fowler, John Swetenburg, Culbertson.

Oconee Mill (Westminster, S.C.): Robert Grogan (coach), Bruce Lockaby (coach), Thomas Broom, Jack Chambers, Eustus Ellis, Ted Gaines, William Hilley, Lloyd Houston, Daris Houston, Bobby Long, Mutt Smith, Franklin Smith.

Liberty Mill (Liberty, S.C.): Roberts, Shook, Cheek, B. Garrison, Smith, D. Garrison, Riggins, T. Garrison, Chandler, Wilburn.

Simpsonville Mill (Simpsonville, S.C.): Harmon Williams (coach), Don Jones (coach), Jack Brookshire, Clyde Bridwell, T.C. Abbott, Leroy Cole, Bobby Jones, Pat McCurry, Roy Gilliam, Preston Barbery, Billie Hanks, Don Stokes.

Dunean Mill (Greenville, S.C.): Billy Lollis, Jimmie Smith, Doyle Hall, Charles Carpenter, David McDonald, LaVern Williams, Durall Cheek, A.J. Sewell, Bobby Sexton, Buddy Gibson.

Victor Mill (Greer, S.C.): Fred Snoddy (coach), Kenneth Moss, Ray Jones, Robert Southerland, Douglas Garren, Millard Leonhardt, Walter Bain, Wayne Godfrey, Bobby Taylor, Billy Norris, Leon Gravely.

Renfrew Bleachery (Travelers Rest, S.C.): James Vernon (coach), John Vernon, Broadus Abbott, Harry Johnson, James Crosby, Ervin Poole, Ernest Bryson, William Edwards, James Lenderman, Larry Farmer, Larry Abbott.

CLASS B WOMEN

North Georgia Processing (Toccoa, Ga.), champions: O.W. Thompson (coach), Robert McAloney (coach), Vennie Reed, Vernell Turner, Frances Payne, Nonnie McClain, Drucilla Bailey, Maxine Hollifield, Alline Hollifield, Martha Carroll, Mary Carroll, Betty Payne, Jacquelyn Davis, Betty Epperson.

Springs Mill (Lancaster, S.C.), runners-up:

G.O. Jenkins (coach), Rushing (coach), Louise Floyd, Lou Lucas, LaNelle Bethea, Betty Whaley, Doris Shaw, Joyce Kennington, Elaine Adams, Josephine Gardner, Edna Collins, Bill Rogers, Ozell Hunter, Carroll Culp.

Ware Shoals Mill (Ware Shoals, S.C.), consolation winners: Odell Barbery (coach), Sylvia Massey, Corinne Coskrey, Ruth Poore, Elaine Burrell, Telor Powell, Dot Thompson, Fay Davis, Peggy Moss, Beatrice Cheek, Catherine Ashley, Mary Kay, Kathryn Smith.

Glen Lowery Mill (Whitmire, S.C.): S.R. DuBose (coach), Hazel Suber (coach), Mary Yarborough, Zula Bacot, Jette Gregory, Jessie Brock, Sara McCall, Willie Brock, Eleanor Nance, Norvelle Baskin, Mary Gaffney, Peggy Lominick, Ruth Glenn, Godfrey.

Brandon Mill (Greenville, S.C.): Ray Wynn (coach), Joyce Smith, Betty Pierce, Delores Smith, Betty Anders, Vivian Williamson, Guynell Smith, Shirley Jones, Elizabeth Reeves, Betty Friar, Shirley Townsend, Doris Reeves, Barbara Williams.

Calhoun Falls Mill (Calhoun Falls, S.C.): Edward Dickard (coach), Jimmie Embler (coach), Willie Embler, Beatrice Waldrop, Clarice Jordan, Ellen Chrisley, Delma Cooper, Gaynel Bonds, Nuree Dockery, Betty Lathan, Willie Holmes, Peggy Martin, Melbe Toms, Mable Cobb.

Easley Mill (Easley, S.C.): Barbara Garrett (coach), Joe Anders (coach), Reba Horton, Fay Gunter, Annie Gunter, Helen Surratt, Mary Woods, Ruth Jones, Gladys Ellenburg, Barbara Galloway, Christine Horton, Betty Prince, Doris Hunter, Mary Anderson.

Greer Mill (Greer, S.C.): E.H. McAlister (coach), Johnny Stack (coach), Shirley Hobart, Patricia Gowan, Mary Gowan, Betty Foster, Aileen Grubbs, Wilma Hood, Betty Burnette, Mary Stansell, Betty Ellenburg, Mary Nix, Edna Garrett, Dorothy Morgan.

Joanna Mill (Joanna, S.C.): Johnny Moore (coach), J. Orre (coach), Betty Sams, Thelma Bridges, Peggy Shands, Linda Childers, Shirleen Hannah, Clara Gosnell, Helen Bridges, Lillie Franklin, Faye Montjoy, Ruby Thomas, Christine Buchanan, Inez Tinsley.

Judson Mill (Greenville, S.C.): Johnnie Means (coach), Ansel Bridwell (mgr), Charlene Neal, JoAnn Sellers, Gwen James, Bertie Allison, Frances Wofford, Elva Upchurch, Aretha Sellers, Bobbie Black, Mary Taylor, Gladys Means, Mildred Dobson, Margaret Owens.

Monaghan Mill (Greenville, S.C.): Lucille Hollis (coach), Glenn Hollis (coach), Mozelle Gooch, Jewell Pittman, Barbara Odom, Nora Taylor, Patsy Pearson, Doris Fuller, Louise Tinsley, Christine Rollins, Joanna Hudgens, Alena Campbell, Lou George, Betty Dean.

Piedmont Mill (Piedmont, S.C.): Joe Fleming (coach), Kathryn Buckner, Ruth Allen, Alice Rampey, Elizabeth Fleming, Jean Davis, Peggy Simpson, Sybil Fletcher, Roxie Reeves, Margie Payne, Elsie Verner, Doris Stone, Dorothy Nimmons.

Lonsdale Mill (Seneca, S.C.): Roy McCurry (coach), Wilton Shaver (coach), Willa Addis, Mary Crenshaw, Doris Reeves, Bobbie Wade, Edna James, Ruth Reynolds, Betty Reeves, Orie Addis, Rita Wade, Kathryn Gilliam, Barbara Rowland, Ollie James.

Woodside Mill (Greenville, S.C.): Tater McConnell (coach), Bill Thomas (coach), Gladys Landreth, Mary Gillespie, Gay Blankenship, Earline Manley, Maxine Gillespie, Beatrice Cippard, Vinazell Brady, Drucilla McCracken, Joan Rigdon, Ann Bowen, Myrtle Wilson, Rebecca Ellison.

Dunean Mill (Greenville, S.C.): Lena Hancock (coach), Evelyn McClure, Sis Mayfield, Gwendolyn Nelms, Billy Waldrop, Jerry Stairley, Nancy Pitts, Patsy Barnett, Jerry Duncan, Barbara Campbell, Joyce Allen, Bobby Mayfield, Joan Kelly.

Renfrew Bleachery (Travelers Rest, S.C.): Hazel Moody (coach), John McDowell (coach), Doris McDaniel, Sarah Lenderman, Martha Roper, Marcia Wynn, Helen Belcher, Ann Murphy, Lura Turner, Dorothy Bridges, Betty Moody, Blanche Lenderman, Syble Barnette, Gladys McDaniel.

Victor Mill (Greer, S.C.): L.T. Puckett (coach), Margaret Ballenger, Martha Lowe, Frances Barker, Joyce Willis, Mildred Garrett, Jane Hemphill, Sue Forrester, Lib Lowe, Faye Russell, Barbara Monroe, Joyce Cameron, S. Willis, Center.

1951

Officers: Hugh Anderson (Greenville, S.C.), President; Paul Edwards (Pelzer, S.C.), Vice President; Harry Clark (Greenville, S.C.), Secretary; Horace C. Whitmire (Greenville, S.C.), Treasurer.

Executive Committee: Jesse Brown

(Greenville, S.C.), Gary Bodie (Greenville, S.C.), Fred Snoddy (Greer, S.C.), Orval Thompson (Toccoa, Ga.), Clarence Thomas (Greenville, S.C.), Jack Reames (Abbeville, S.C.), Walter Lauter (Rossville, Ga.), Willie Wilbanks (Greenville, S.C.), Jim Westmoreland (Pelzer, S.C.), S.R. DuBose (Whitmire, S.C.), C.Y. Havird (Lancaster, S.C.), J.B. Owens (Simpsonville, S.C.), Bruce Stroupe (Greenville, S.C.), Ted Ratenski (Greenville, S.C.).

Class A Men

Pelzer Mill (Pelzer, S.C.), champions: Ray Smith (coach), Paul Edwards (coach), Pete Harris, Clarence Lowery, Dewey Quinn, Earl Wooten, Gerald Becker, Jack Gentry, Truman Hill, Herman Dill, Jimmy Hedden.

Dunean Mill (Greenville, S.C.), runners-up: Charles Tidwell (coach), Bob Stowe, Melvin Bell, Larry Ashley, Horace Turner, Middy Hughes, Carl Green, Raymond Cox, Manning Garren, Ward Williams, David Putman.

Piedmont Mill (Piedmont, S.C.), consolation winners: Carroll Gilreath (coach), Curtis Terry (coach), Veo Story, Milford Howard, Frank Kelly, Billy Davis, Ernie Chambers, Hoss Nesbitt.

Anderson Mill (Anderson, S.C.): Ezra Embler (coach), Fred Whitten, Jimmie Embler, William Embler, John Smith, Wayne Ballard, Carlton Aldrich, Frank Navratil, E.C. White, Marvin Spake.

Monaghan Mill (Greenville, S.C.): D.W. Broadwell (coach), Harold Burns, Bill Kerr, Ken Pittman, Fig Newton, Herb Lindsay Jr., Walt Deal, Bert Wilson, Bomar Keller, Effie Evington, Doug Campbell.

Southern Bleachery (Taylors, S.C.): June Pruitt (coach), Willie Bishop, Clannie Smith, Theron Stone, Mack Waldrop, Lloyd Edwards, Walker Dilworth, Sidney Badger, George Blackwell, Furman Taylor.

Class B Men

Southern Franklin Processing (Greenville, S.C.), champions: Harold Lewis (coach), Clarence Porter (coach), John Stafford, James McCullough, Charles McCullough, Bobby Sexton, James Hartsell, Calvin Cooper, Gary Cooper, Charles King, Wallace Putman, Charles Watson.

North Georgia Processing (Toccoa, Ga.), runners-up: Tom Moseley (coach), O.W. Thompson (coach), Charles Davis, Jack Watson, Randall McClain, Roy Hollifield, Joe Carson, LeRoy Deaton, Joe Stowe, Leon Denman, Dwain Toney, Ray Keeling.

Russell Manufacturing (Alexander City, Ala.), consolation winners: Grady Gunn, Charles Bailey, Ed Watson, Gene Brown, Gene Gilbert, Obie Forbus, Dick Galloway, Bill Lynn, Tom Rainey, Dwight Bell, Delton Forbus.

Liberty Mill (Liberty, S.C.): Marion Butler Jr. (coach), Buddy Shook, Tot Garrison, Lee Grogan, O'Neil Roberts, Donnie Garrison, Gene Bryant, Dickie Ballew, Dick Hendley, Bailey.

Glen Lowery Mill (Whitmire, S.C.): S.R. DuBose (coach), Luke Hart (coach), Terrell Fowler Jr., Hubert Elrod, Ralph Elrod, Jarrett Frier, Arthur Bradley, Cecil Frier, Arthur Brank, Teddy Weaver, Gene Clark.

Beacon Mill (Swannanoa, N.C.): Tommie Jackson (coach), J.D. Hardin (coach), Robert Morgan, William Davis, Robert Stroupe, Gerald Briggs, Louis Joyner, Bob Richie, Grey Chandley, Joseph Van Roth, Vernon Mull, Bill Smith.

Belton Mill (Belton, S.C.): Luther Rentz (mgr), Jimmy Jones, Ray Stephens, Dick Stephens, Glenn Kennedy, J.C. Thompson, Bo Williams, Dean Cannon.

Brandon Mill (Greenville, S.C.): Ray Wynn (coach), James Carnes (coach), Donald Rich, William Upton, Willie Murphy, William Dilworth Jr., Robert Strange, Gerald Robinson, George Burnett, Fred McAbee Jr., Harry Foster, James Williamson.

Chicopee Mill (Gainesville, Ga.): S.B. Jones (coach), Arlen Berryman, Robert Cook, Ted Ivey, Lowell Turner, Ray Godfrey, Paul McDonald, Clyde Turk, William Jones, James Roberts, William Gunter Jr.

Clinton Mill (Clinton, S.C.): Claude Crocker (coach), George Frady, Calvin Cooper, Charles Tedder, Jimmy Hairston, Albert Rowe, Clyde Beaumont, William von Horten, Gregg Rowe, Brown.

Dunean Mill (Greenville, S.C.): Charles Tidwell (coach), Bobby Grant, Alvin LaBoone, Frank Lollis, Goulon Jones, Roy Whitehead, Charles Ashley, Donald Hartin, Herman Hudson, Newton Stowe, Joe Granger.

Easley Mill (Easley, S.C.): Courtney Heath (coach), Joe Anders (coach), George Owens,

James Smith, Melvin Owens, James Campbell, Calvin Bagwell, Vernon McEntyre, James Rogers, James Henson, Kenneth Thomas.

Firestone Textile Inc. (Gastonia, N.C.): Leonard Bumgardner (coach), Harold Robinson, Marshall Clary, Charles Lunsford, Doc Queen, Devant Purvis, Wilson Bolick, E.T. Green, W.N. Phillips, Bob Payne, Ted Gaston.

Judson Mill (Greenville, S.C.): Joe O'Shields (coach), Walter Hamilton, Harold Holbrook, Charles Lankford, Bruce Stroupe, Floyd Loftis, Pete Loftis, Bill Massey, Hoyt Smith, Sandy Howie, Kenneth Linder.

Laurens Mill (Laurens, S.C.): Harold Pearson (coach), Marshall Revis (coach), Bruce Taylor, Frank Dambeck, Marion Craine, Henry Bowie, Clifford Cox, Joe Edwards, William Smith, Richard Bowlin, Franklin Russell, Leslie Pugh.

Lyman Mill (Lyman, S.C.): Eurell Eubanks (coach), Walt Barbare (coach), Jackie Anderson, Derrell Medlock, James Ward, Allan Beach, Lawrence Eubanks, Joe Mullinax, Donald Smith, Fred Bird, Robert Satterfield, John Carter.

Monaghan Mill (Greenville, S.C.): Alva Phillips (coach), Dom Dean, Bennie Brown, Charles Ross, Charles McIntosh, Tom Fore, Charles Landreth, Don Newton, Hanson Griffith, Rudolph Simmons.

Mills Mill (Greenville, S.C.): Myron Floyd (coach), Walter Patton (coach), Ralph Bell, Carl Hanes, Paul Simpson, Robert Putnam, William Davis, Roy Emory, James McMahan, Charlie Brock, Hugh Glymph.

New Holland Mill (Gainesville, Ga.): James Smith (coach), B.C. Jarrard, Reginald Reynolds, John Brown, Charles Lay, Jake Miller, Pete Jenkins, Charley Cox, Ralph Chapman, Pete Morgan, Hoyt Hollifield.

Pelzer Mill (Pelzer, S.C.): Horace Davenport (coach), James Thomason, Marion Smith, Richard Reeves, Earl Reeves, Buddy Bear, Bobby Ross, Olin Davis, Joe Garrett, Paul Rogers, Harold Major.

Poinsett Mill (Greenville, S.C.): J.B. Templeton (coach), Jack Long, Larry Gray, Lewis Mardis, Johnny Gilliam, Robert Lavender, George Tucker, Billy Williams, Charles Scott, Bill Taylor, Lawrence Landers.

Renfrew Bleachery (Travelers Rest, S.C.): James Vernon (coach), Randall Poole (coach), Boyce Greer, Gene Cunningham, Roy Wood, Joel Rowe Jr., James Balloch Jr., Dyle Belcher, Fred McClure, Harry Johnson, William Poole, Lewis Lockaby.

Slater Mill (Slater, S.C.): Snow Kirby (coach), Charles Newsome, James Gowan, Fred Cox, Gene Cox, John Caldwell, Fred Bridgeman, Harold Knight.

Simpsonville Mill (Simpsonville, S.C.): Gary Henderson (coach), Bill Porter, Roy Gilliam, Charles Allen, William Finley, Roger Cannady, William Smith, Charles Johnson, Charles Hodge, Paul Moore.

Southern Bleachery (Taylors, S.C.): Raustus Hawkins (coach), Perry Howard, Boyce Howard, Rudolph Hughes, Broadus Farr, Delmas Hodges, Sam Forrester, Bill Waldrop, Johnnie Badger, Blaine Bramlett.

Victor Mill (Greer, S.C.): Fred Snoddy (coach), Rube Wilson (coach), Richard McCuen, Lewis Hughes, Paul Cavender, Wallace McGaha, Denny Owens Jr., Walter Bain.

Woodside Mill (Greenville, S.C.): Bill Thomas (coach), Floyd Giebell (coach), Veldee Hines, Billy Wakefield, Jess Cumby, Leslie Nash, Paul Hice, Ray Herbert, James Greene, Robert King, Charles Barbare, John Greene.

CLASS C MEN

Piedmont Mill #2 (Piedmont, S.C.), champions: J.H. Nesbitt (coach), Robert Hooper, James Smith, Carroll Stone, Troy Evans, Stanley Gilreath, Joe Ayers, Henry Picklesimer, Carroll Emery, Donald Roper, Lewis Howard, Joe Everett.

Camperdown Mill (Greenville, S.C.), runners-up: Louie McDowell (coach), J.B. Irvin (coach), Charles Bartram, William Wilburn, Charles Carter, Charles Davis, Bobby Jones, Jimmy Johnson, William Davidson, Robert Batson, Alvin DeLong.

Joanna Mill (Joanna, S.C.), consolation winners: Johnny Moore (coach), Buddy Thurston (coach), Richard Motes, L.M. Long, Harold Willingham, Kenneth Boyce, Jimmy Kirby, James Clark, Marshall Smith, Robert Hair, H.M. Elliott Jr., Darrell Johnson.

Lyman Mill (Lyman, S.C.): D. Leonard (coach), Lloyd Leonard (coach), Kenneth Williams, Don Satterfield, Harold Eubanks, Joe Smith, William White, Jack Eubanks, Harold Boyles, Kenneth Pettigrew, Rudolph High, Clayton Hensley.

Anderson Mill (Anderson, S.C.): Ezra Embler (coach), John Long, Billy Evans, Melvin Long, John McAllister, Bobby Fleming,

Cecil Radford, Gerald Fleming, Ronald Ripley, James Hopkins, Wayne Ballard.

American Spinning (Greenville, S.C.): Art Schiffer (coach), Jerry Chapman, Danny Fowler, Willard Fowler, Jack Giaradeau, Charles Hendrix, Jimmie Morgan, Bill Neely, Jimmie Painter, Larry Porter, Bill Smith.

Appleton Mill (Anderson, S.C.): Brown Glenn (coach), Henry Spake (coach), Benny Speares, Gary Speares, James Speares, Berry McElrath, Billy Hanks, Eugene Alford, Jimmy Smith, Calvin Daniel, Sam Moss, Joe Moss.

Belton Mill (Belton, S.C.): Luther Rentz (coach), Beauford Campbell, Theodore Shirley, Stokes Estes, Dale Owens, Billy Coker, Don Campbell, J.K. Meeks Jr., John Broome.

Brandon Mill (Greenville, S.C.): J.B. Friar (coach), Dewey Corbin, Charles Parnell, Jack Stegall, Jack Garren, Alvin McClellan, Fred Parker, Pierce Powers, William Rollins, Bobby Powers, J.D. Williamson.

Brandon Rayon Mill (Greenville, S.C.): Jack Parnell (coach), Tommy Abbott, James Harrison, Charles Browning, Alvin Smith, Robert Paris, George Williams, Truman Smith, Charles Williams, Milton Taylor, Hugh McKinney.

Dunean Mill (Greenville, S.C.): Charles Carpenter, LaVerne Williams, Herbert Dodson, Jack Tatham, James Smith, Doyle Hall, Harold Huff, Bobby Parker, Tracy Roddy, John Gibson.

Easley Mill (Easley, S.C.): Harold Simpson (coach), Bobby Rankin, Bobby Bagwell, Charles F. Bagwell, Ben Fox, Charles E. Bagwell, Randel Searcy, Rudy Evatt, Buddy Holiday, Kenneth Marshbanks, Jack Dalton.

Glenwood Mill (Easley, S.C.): George Hagood (coach), Jack Parrish (coach), Charles Smith, Sammie Owens, Kenneth Lesley, Franklin Hudson, Jerry Rankin, Dell Owens, Jack Nicholson, Lloyd Christopher, Charles Holcombe, Alvin Spearman.

Greer Mill (Greer, S.C.): H.H. Burgin (coach), Johnny Stack (coach), Raymond Pinson, Harold Stansell, Jerry Burgess, Lewis Knighton, Charles Flynn, Marshall Clark, Robert Spencer, Dan Brewton, Thomas Edwards, Roger Stepp.

Judson Mill (Greenville, S.C.): Joe O'Shields (coach), Richard Stephens, Robert Means, John Proffitt, Truman Shirley, Jack Roddy, Eugene Thomas, Joe Upchurch, Ted Drew, Paul Black, Terry Cline.

Laurens Mill (Laurens, S.C.): Donald Stover (coach), Bobby Bishop (coach), Winston Roberts, George Crocker, William Noffy, Donald Cothran, Jack Waldrop, Jack Burns, Tommy Reames, Jimmy Hawkins, Bill Jones, Buck Waldrop.

Mills Mill (Greenville, S.C.): Charles Smith (coach), Jimmie Garrett (ass't coach), Paul Eubanks, David Lloyd, Harold Bell, Evon Green, Clyde Bell, James Staton, Charles McMahan, James McCall Jr., Charles Funk Jr., William Marler Jr.

Monaghan Mill (Greenville, S.C.): Bert Wilson Jr. (coach), James Bagwell, Winston Major, Franklin Haney, Charles Crawford, Bobby Cook, Danny Bagwell, Bruce Galloway, Darrell Pearson, Tillman Capps, James Crain.

Orr Mill (Anderson, S.C.): Britt Vernon (coach), Douglas Sanders, Ralph Smith, Donald Rowell, Charles Fausek, Sherman McLane, Leroy Parnell, Gene Stamps, Jack McLane, Robert Wilson, Larry Cash.

Piedmont Mill (Piedmont, S.C.): Homer Powell (coach), James Sherman, LeRoy Ivey, Bruce Reeves, Kenneth Smith, Joe Long, Jerry Ayers, James Hughey, Furman Foxx, Harry Stamps, Bobby Bryson, Harris.

Poinsett Mill (Greenville, S.C.): Jack Long (coach), R.C. Campbell (coach), Fred Freeman, Jack Bridges, Jack Gray, Jack Riddley, Charles Crowe, Billy Monroe, Bryant Millwood, James McCall, David Solsbee, Pat Campbell.

Slater Mill (Slater, S.C.): Snow Kirby (coach), William Stephenson, Thomas Cox, Alton White, James Wylie, Bobby Johnson, Bobby Sprouse, Billy Garrett, Robert Cole, Jimmie Lell, Jimmie Hembree.

Simpsonville Mill (Simpsonville, S.C.): George Gregory (coach), Richard Terry (coach), Jimmie Abercrombie, Kirby Ballew, Dick Goodenough, Jimmy Hamby, Milton Cantrell, Carroll Norris, Preston Barbery, Jack Brookshire, Leroy Cole, T.C. Abbott.

Union Bleachery (Greenville, S.C.): Harold Greene (coach), P.C. Gregory (coach), Bill Moody (coach), David Smith, John Robertson, James Clevenger, Phil Knight, Rogers Bishop, Ronnie Knight, Jack League, Billy Robertson, Rhoden Batson, Marilyn Stroud.

Lonsdale Mill (Seneca, S.C.): Ed Alexander (coach), Tommy Poole (coach), Clifford Poole, Larry Hughes, Donald Gaillard, Rissell Moore, William Carson, Lee Gaillard, Leon Dooley, LeRoy Smith, Carey Taylor, Michael Gaillard.

Southern Textile Basketball Tournament Rosters Appendix 1 183

Gluck Mill (Anderson, S.C.): Earley Hanna (coach), J.F. Stansell (coach), Shirley Huitt, Callie Maddox, Charles Giles, John Bailey, William Lother, Douglas Dyer, Curtis Wood, David McGuffin, John Swetenburg, Dennis Slater.

Victor Mill (Greer, S.C.): Fred Snoddy (coach), Robert Southerland (coach), Douglass Garren, Millard Leonhardt, Leon Gravely, Joe Wyatt, Billy Morris, Bobby Taylor, Wayne Godfrey, Ronald Burnette, Jimmy Bennett.

Woodside Mill (Greenville, S.C.): Carl Grogan (coach), Tobe Herbert (coach), Eddie White, Curt Hickam, Thomas Taylor, Clyde Spearman, Dennis Brookshire, Mickey Griffith, Ray Howard, Joe Julian, Wallace Black, Harry Wells.

CLASS B WOMEN

Judson Mill (Greenville, S.C.), champions: Bruce Stroupe (coach), Jo Ann Hunter, Jo Ann Sellars, Evelyn McDowell, Gwen James, Frances Wofford, Betty Moody, Shirley Roberts, Lois Inman, Dot Walker, Betty Taylor.

North Georgia Processing (Toccoa, Ga.), runners-up: Tom Moseley (coach), O.W. Thompson (coach), Vennie Reed, Marion Stubbs, Helen Howe, Betty Newsome, Mary Carroll, Estelle Willis, Lucille Patterson, Frankie Kicklighter, Elise Donaldson, Ann Moorhead.

Calhoun Falls Mill (Calhoun Falls, S.C.), consolation winners: Densel Dockery (coach), Nuree Dockery, Delma Cooper, Irma Hilley, Georgia Wiles, Gaynell Bonds, Willie Holmes, Faye Ayers, Evelyn Robinson, Edith Lowe, Nadine Broadwell, Jo Ann Ross, Peggy Dickert, Barnes.

Glen Lowery Mill (Whitmire, S.C.), consolation winners: S.R. DuBose (coach), Hazel Suber (coach), Zula Bacot, Ruth Glenn, Jessie Brock, Peggy Lominick, Willie Brock, Rachel Brown, Betty Duncan, Sarah McCall, Emily Freeman, Dorothy Frier, Betty Evans.

Anderson Mill (Anderson, S.C.): Ezra Embler (coach), Willie Embler, Annie Stephens, Viola Thompson, Barbara Navrath, Fredda Acker, Grace Embler, Garthedon Embler, Doris Hiott, Mary James, June Buchanan, Joan Holbrooks.

Brandon Mill (Greenville, S.C.): Ray Wynn (coach), Shirley Townsend, Joyce Taylor, Frances Hall, Delores Donohue, Vivian Williamson, Betty Pierce, Betty Anders, Clarice Robinson, Shirley Jones, Helen Adams, Ruth Phillips.

Dunean Mill (Greenville, S.C.): Charles Tidwell (coach), Evelyn McClure, Nancy Pitts, Mary Mayfield, Gwendolyn Nelms, Billy Waldrop, Jerry Duncan, Patricia Barnette, Joyce Allen, Barbara Smith, Shirley Buckner.

Joanna Mill (Joanna, S.C.): Johnny Moore (coach), Hilda Oxner (coach), Clara Gosnell, Lillie Franklin, Thelma Bridges, Betty Sons, Inez Tinsley, Christine Buchanan, Stella Shealy, Betty Thomas, Evelyn Evans, Carolyn Thomas, Peggy Lambert, Annelle Shealy.

Monaghan Mill (Greenville, S.C.): Alva Phillips (coach), Doris Walker, Willodene Waldrop, Bootsie Anderson, Louise Tinsley, Betty Dean, Helen Fore, Nora Brown, Elizabeth Phillips, Doris Wilson, Tina Rollins, Joanna Hudgens, Ruth Gambrell, Doris Fuller.

Piedmont Mill (Piedmont, S.C.): Jack Turner (coach), Shorty Smith (coach), Sybil Fletcher, Betty Reeves, Mary Evans, Alice Rampey, Jean Davis, Elsie Verner, Virginia Burrell, Margie Payne, Doris Cothran, Betty Shirley, Patsy Drennon, Roxie Reeves.

Renfrew Bleachery (Travelers Rest, S.C.): John McDowell (coach), Aromus Belcher (coach), Marcia Wynn, Hazel Moody, Helen Belcher, Dorothy Bridges, Blanche Linderman, Ann Murphy, Bill Moody, Joyce Center, Dora Murphy, Margaret Lockaby, Gladys McDaniel, Lura Turner, Miller.

Simpsonville Mill (Simpsonville, S.C.): Mrs. George Gregory (coach), Mary Parrish, Mary Henderson, Margarite Forrester, Eschol Carlton, Juanita Godfrey, Joan Porter, Lora Terry, Jannette Thackston, Geneva Forrester, Mildred Todd, Spillers.

Lonsdale Mill (Seneca, S.C.): Roy McCurry (coach), Wilton Shaver (coach), Evelyn Reynolds, Carrie Dawkins, Ruth Reynolds, La Rue Hamilton, Sarah Lacy, Nell Dawkins, Barbara Stephens, Doris Willimon, Billie Lacy, Redinald Owens, Kathryn Chrisley, Ovenall Clark.

Victor Mill (Greer, S.C.): Leumas Puckett (coach), Joyce Willis, Martha Lowe, Margaret Ballenger, Pat Belue, Barbara Lynch, Ruth Garrett, Jo Anne Oliver, Millis Tooke, Sara Morrow, Dorothy Morgan, Jo Russell, Juanita Eubanks.

Ware Shoals Mill (Ware Shoals, S.C.): Odell Barbery (coach), Joyce Pitts, Vera Moon, Hattie Powell, Doris Thompson, Catherine Smith, Catherine Ashley, Mary Medlin, Ruby

Knox, Mildred Pruitt, Ruthann Poore, Ann Humbree, Betty Barbery.

Woodside Mill (Greenville, S.C.): Earl Jones (coach), Jo Ann Rigdon, Gay Blankenship, Jean Julian, Mary Tollison, Pete Gillespie, Margaret Wilson, Ann Bowen, Mary Gillespie, Madolyn Wilson, Juanita Pitts, Jo Ann Ware, Carol Fowler.

--- 1952 ---

Officers: Hugh Anderson (Greenville, S.C.), President; Fred Snoddy (Greenville, S.C.), Vice President; J.B. Owens (Greenville, S.C.), Secretary; Horace Whitmire (Greenville, S.C.), Treasurer.

Executive Committee: Jesse Brown (Greenville, S.C.), Gary Bodie (Greenville, S.C.), Paul Edwards (Pelzer, S.C.), Orval Thompson (Toccoa, Ga.), Clarence Thomas (Greenville, S.C.), Jack Reames (Abbeville, S.C.), Walter Lauter (Rossville, Ga.), Willie Wilbanks (Greenville, S.C.), D.K. Smith (Lyman, S.C.), S.R. DuBose (Whitmire, S.C.), Snow Kirby (Slater, S.C.), Bruce Stroupe (Greenville, S.C.), Ted Ratenski (Greenville, S.C.).

CLASS A MEN

Dunean Mill (Greenville, S.C.), champions: Ward Williams (coach), Larry Ashley, Tex Ritter, Melvin Bell, Horace Turner, Bob Stowe, Herman Dill, Fig Newton, Don Cox, Dave Putman.

Pelzer Mill (Pelzer, S.C.), runners-up: Harry Major (coach), J.W. Jordan, Elmer Suddeth, Dewey Quinn, James Hedden, Randy Whaley, Truman Hill, Earl Wooten, James Harris, Ed Copeland, Gerald Becker.

Peerless Woolen Mill (Rossville, Ga.), consolation winners: Walter Lauter (coach), Hal Hall (coach), Thomas Maynor, Paul Maynor, Frank Drake, Glenn Michaels, Willard Lovelady, Bob McCoy, Ray Griffith, John Barger, Joe Moore, Howard Sompayrac Jr., Cook, Cox.

Slater Mill (Slater, S.C.): Snow Kirby (coach), William Bagwell, James Gowan, Harold Knight, Fred Cox Jr., Marcus McMakin.

American Enka (Enka, N.C.): Sam Patton (coach), Fred Brendell, Gus Colagerakis, Richard Gudger, James Hales, Willard Kaylor, George Lancaster, Vernon Rhodes, Joe Volrath, Deran Walters.

Hanes Hosiery Mill (Winston-Salem, N.C.): B.C. Hall Jr. (coach), Hugh Hampton (coach), David Greer, Donald Anderson, Cedric Loftis, Robert Paxton, Tom Paladino, LeRoy Halpern, Roy Harris, Sam Smith, Jack Hartness.

Piedmont Mill (Piedmont, S.C.): Carroll Gilreath (coach), Veo Story (coach), Milford Howard, Ernie Chambers, Harold Cully, Thomas Bailey, Bill Spender, Lewis Howard, Jim Shalton.

Southern Bleachery (Taylors, S.C.): Phil Thornton (coach), Willie Bishop, Mack Waldrop, June Pruitt, Theron Stone, Walker Dilworth, Hoover Parker, Boyce Howard, Phil Clark, Lloyd Edwards, C.L. Smith.

Monaghan Mill (Greenville, S.C.): Doug Campbell (mgr), Effie Evington (coach), Eddie Edwards, Bill Kerr, Pert Griffith, Alva Phillips, Ansel Bridwell, Harold Burns, Francis Salerno, Bill Moody, Herb Lindsay.

CLASS B MEN

Chicopee Mill (Gainesville, Ga.), champions: S.B. Jones (coach), William Reed, Ben Martin, Sylvia Clark, J.D. Kennedy, Benjamin O'Dell, Paul McDonald, Clyde Turk, Bill Bryson, James Godfrey, Glenn Turk.

Woodside Mill (Greenville, S.C.), runners-up: Jim McDuffie (coach), Ray Herbert (coach), Charles Allen, Charles Wakefield, Jack Wilson, George Miller, Talmadge Tollison, Robert Nask, Jess Cumby, Carl Grogan, Edward White, John Haney.

Monaghan Mill (Greenville, S.C.), consolation winners: Aaron Powers (coach), Tiny Wyatt (coach), Charles McIntosh, Jim Turner, Charles Landreth, Ken Hudgens, John Atkins, Bill Fuller, Benny Brown, Bob Porter, Jim Bagwell, Don Dean.

Liberty Mill (Liberty, S.C.): Paul Bowie (coach), Marion Butler, Alan Cox, Lee Grogan, George Cantrell, Jimmy Gaines, Donnie Garrison, O'Neal Roberts, Fred Powers, Gene Bryant, Charles Edwards.

Glen Lowery Mill (Whitmire, S.C.): S.R. DuBose (coach), Earl Prince (coach), Hubert Elrod, Jarrett Frier, Baggott Frier, Thomas Frier, Ralph Wallen, Waymon Bostic, Arthur Brank, Arthur Bradley, Donald Basden, Dickard, Reed.

Brandon Mill (Greenville, S.C.): Ray Wynn

Southern Textile Basketball Tournament Rosters **Appendix 1** 185

(coach), Bobby Powers, Clyde Hodge, Charles Holcombe, Jack Parnell, Jimmie Mattos, Tom Hall, J.D. Williamson, Don Rich, William Dilworth, Bridges.

Dunean Mill (Greenville, S.C.): Bob Stowe (coach), Joel Greene, Alvin LaBoone, Junior Stowe, Gordon Jones, Robert Milsap, Gary Ashley, Charles Gilstrap, Cuyler Hudson, Pete Jamison, Frank Lollis.

Firestone Textile Inc. (Gastonia, N.C.): Ralph Johnson (coach), Bud Atkinson (coach), Harold Robinson (coach), Marshall Clary, Phil Clarke, Harry Lunsford, E.T. Green, Jerry Keisler, John Monteith, Bill Green, Jerry Rice, Charles Collins.

Greer Mill (Greer, S.C.): Hicks Burgin (mgr), Johnny Stack (coach), Robert Campbell, Wilson Taylor, James Campbell, Dan Brewton, Samuel Stack, John Henson, Doyle Stansell, Jerry Burgess, Dean Stansell, Marshal Linsdey, Huff.

Judson Mill (Greenville, S.C.): Joe O'Shields (coach), Bruce Stroupe, Charles Rogers, Earl Stroud, L.P. Loftis, Charles Simpson, Rudolph Smith, Bill Snelson, Mack Patton, Coy Watson.

New Holland Mill (Gainesville, Ga.): Ausbond Morgan (coach), Hoyt Hollifield, William Jones, Sammy Hudgins, Charles Smith, Clarence Canup, John Brown, Bobby Wiley.

Pelzer Mill (Pelzer, S.C.): Carl Davis Jr. (coach), Leonard Muth, Roy Taylor, A.C. Taylor, Dot Reeves, Harold Major, Bobby Thomason, Marion Smith, Roy Whitlock, Bo Williams.

Russell Manufacturing (Alexander City, Ala.): Grady Gunn (coach), Robert Machen, Bryan Yates, Reginald Spraggins, Delton Forbus, Edsel Riddle, Lenford McCreight Jr., C.W. Milam, Lee Collins, Charles Bailey, Doyt Alford.

Victor Mill (Greer, S.C.): Fred Snoddy (coach), Leon Gravely, Millard Leonhardt, William Owens, John Caldwell, Ray Jones, Walter Bain, Ansel Smith, Stephen Addyman, Robert Southerland, Kenneth Moss.

CLASS C MEN

Camperdown Mill (Greenville, S.C.), champions: Louie McDowell (coach), Doug Bartram, Toby Long, Charles Davis, Charles Carter, Ken Carter, Bobby Jones, Jimmy Johnson, Bill Wilburn, Bill Davidson, Dick Rollins.

Dunean Mill (Greenville, S.C.), runners-up: Don Ritter (coach), LaVerne Williams, William Roddy, Jack Kelly, Robert Henderson, Tracy Roddy, Robert Parker, Jim Smith, LaVerne Holder, Herbert Dodson, William Mathis.

Laurens Mill (Laurens, S.C.), consolation winners: Marion Craine (coach), Frank Dambeck (coach), William Bone, Marion Roberts, George Crocker, Lester Burns, William Owings, Frederick Waldrop, Natson Stewart, Thomas Reames, Donald Cothran, Harold Mitchell.

Woodside Mill (Greenville, S.C.): Carlton Couch (coach), Thomas Reeves (coach), Norman Poole, Dennis Brookshire, Clyde Spearman, Billy Hines, Joe Julian, Ray Howard, Milward Griffith, Harold Swofford, Woodrow Moore, Rodney Canup.

Anderson Mill (Anderson, S.C.): Ezra Embler (coach), Clyde Childs, John McAllister, David Watt, Bobby Fleming, Dennis Bannister, Walter Cooper, John Long, Ken Bannister, Bobby Radford, Melvin Long.

Appleton Mill (Anderson, S.C.): Henry Spake (coach), Bill Tidwell (coach), George Brown, Willie Alford, Gary Speares, Jackie Middleton, Jimmie Smith, Benny Speares, Charles Cornwell, Joe Moss, Larry Spears, Calvin Daniels.

American Spinning (Greenville, S.C.): Art Schiffer (coach), Willard Fowler, Danny Fowler, Larry Porter, William Neely, Jerry Chapman, Jimmie Painter, Bill Smith, Robert Miller, Charles Hendrix, Jack Gerendeu.

Brandon Mill (Greenville, S.C.): Lee Herman (coach), Robert Paris, Truman Smith, James Gilstrap, Tommy Abbott, Charles Browning, Robert Williamson, Jack Garren, Pierce Powers, William Pittman, Dewey Corbin.

Calhoun Falls Mill (Calhoun Falls, S.C.): Selma Manning (coach), Edward Dickard (coach), Arthur Burdette, Charles Carlisle, Bobby Chrisley, Claude Herndon, William Brown, Marvin Burton, Norman Dove, Ralph Parnell, William Powell, James Martin.

Easley Mill (Easley, S.C.): Courtney Heath (coach), Alvin Simpson (coach), Courtney Heath Jr., Larry Bagwell, Charles Bagwell, Bobby Chandler, Ray Owens, Joe Garrick, Edward James, Jack Dalton, Billy Evans, Ben Fox.

Equinox Mill (Anderson, S.C.): Clarence

Voyles (coach), Kenneth McAlister, Leroy Parks, Harold Coile, Sammy Chasteen, Billy Speer, Leslie McCraw, Wesley Welborn, Franklin Metz, D.C. Sanders, Harold Huntsinger.

Greer Mill (Greer, S.C.): Johnny Stack (coach), Arnold Campbell (coach), Donald Black, Donald Jones, Marion Woodward, William Taylor, Roger Stepp, Bobby Grubbs, Ray McMakin, Thurlough Gowan, Harold Huff, Ernie Ellenburg.

Poinsett Mill (Greenville, S.C.): Robert Lavender (coach), Richard Campbell, Jerry Monroe, Jack Gray, Charles Crowe, Maxie Garrett, Jack Riddley, James Gilliam, Eugene Tench, Champ Osteen, Theron Powell.

Joanna Mill (Joanna, S.C.): Johnny Moore (coach), S. Humphery (coach), Henry Elliott Jr., Charles Davenport, Marshall Smith, James Clark, Darnell Johnson, Robert Hair, Jimmy Kirby, Kenneth Boyce, Aubrey Turner, Lester Long.

Judson Mill (Greenville, S.C.): Ted Adams (coach), Jack Roddy, Floyd Sweet, Charles Shockley, Richard Stephens, Eugene Thomas, Bobby Pridmore, Paul Black, J.D. Sellers, Terry Cline, Franklin Harvey.

Mills Mill #1 (Greenville, S.C.): Tony Smith (coach), Charles Funk, Harold Bell, James Staton, James McCall Jr., Bill Marler, Melvin Thompson, Robert McCall, Tommy Putman, Harold Lowery, Johnny Thompson.

Monaghan Mill (Greenville, S.C.): Bobby Foster (mgr), Alva Phillips (coach), Bobby Cook, Winston Major, John Haney, Danny Bagwell, Charles Powers, Marilyn Stroud, Darrell Pearson, James Crain, Lewis Hardin, James Campbell, Gambrell.

Orr Mill (Anderson, S.C.): Gary Glenn (coach), J.H. McCurry (coach), Robert Hancock, Larry Smith, Larry Cash, Douglas McLane, Donald Rowell, Marvin Rowell, Leroy Parnell, Colyer Parnell, Jack McLane, Donald King.

Pelzer Mill (Pelzer, S.C.): Leonard Muth (coach), Grady Cooley, Wade Phillips, Ed Smith, Bill Taylor, Leroy Moody, Jimmy Smith, Ellis Coker, Ray Whaley, Eugene Auglin, Billy Chandler.

Piedmont Mill (Piedmont, S.C.): Curtis Terry (coach), Ray Darnell (coach), Jerry Hooper, Roger Weisner, J.D. Hunnicutt, James Evatt, Kenneth Smith, Ronald Davis, John Reeves, Tony Turpin, Troy Coker, Jimmy Nelson.

Slater Mill (Slater, S.C.): Snow Kiry (coach), Kenneth Cox, Alton White, Joe Smith, Weldon Daniel, Richard Payne, Billy Garrett, Thomas Cox, Bobby Sprouse, John Bowles, William Stephenson.

Southern Bleachery (Taylors, S.C.): Bill Barnett (coach), Coley Pace, Herman Jackson, Charles Miller, Kenneth Wham, Gene Derrick, Jimmy Barton, Bill Barbary, Buck Jones, Gary Hawkins, Reg Bumgardner, V. Barton.

Spartan Mill (Spartanburg, S.C.): Jack Blackwell (coach), Hershell Baytes, Jack Donald, Raymond Edwards, Ted Fowler, Charles Graham, Harold Hudson, Bobby Martin, Gayland McGinn, Floyd Orr.

Union Bleachery (Greenville, S.C.): Bill Moody (coach), Harold Green (coach), Rogers Bishop, Alvin Bayne, James Clevinger, Albert Knight, Jack League, Jerry Robertson, Dan Rhodes, David Smith, Randall Turner, Houston Turner.

Lonsdale Mill (Seneca, S.C.): Roy McCurry (coach), George Morgan (coach), Grady Poole, Michael Gaillard, Alton Burgess, Donald Gaillard, William Perry, Larry Hughes, Thomas McCurry, Joe Gibson, Cecil Taylor, Gerald Gaillard.

Victor Mill (Greer, S.C.): Fred Snoddy (mgr), William Gravley, Roland Lee, Kenneth Edge, Grady Greer, Kenneth Hawkins, James Smith, James Godfrey, Douglas Garren, Ronnie Burnette, Bobby Lemmons.

Gluck Mill (Anderson, S.C.): Bill Bostic (coach), Early Hanna (coach), Kenneth Jordan, Joe Slater, Curtis Wood, Charles Giles, Teddy Tabor, C.F. Maddox Jr., J.R. Swetenburg Jr., Marion Pickens, Shirley Pruitt, James Pruitt Jr.

Liberty Mill (Liberty, S.C.): Fred Powers (coach), David Garrison, Wallace Lyda, Billy Allgood, Jennings Farr, Jimmy Cantrell, Donnie Hill, Jimmy Garrison, Lawrence Isler, Quilin Finley, Billy Hardy.

Greenwood Mill (Greenwood, S.C.): H.W. Herring Jr., William Falls, Richard Burnette, Ronald Barnette, Richard Rowland, Marshall Weaver, Donnie Burnett, Sims Bowers, Ronald Aughtry, David Andrews.

Belton Mill (Belton, S.C.): Dale Owens, Billy Coker, Billy Lowe, Stokes Estes, Jerry Fleming, Donnie Campbell, Larry Smith, Murray Wright, Louie Croft, Broome.

Simpsonville Mill (Simpsonville, S.C.): Paul Landers (coach), Alvin Barbery, Milton

Cantrell, Ralph Brookshire, Ray Gilliam, Kirby Ballew, James Hamby, James Brooks, Preston Calvert, Billy Goodenough, Thomas Abbott.

Class B Women

Appleton Mill (Anderson, S.C.), champions: Lewis Acker (coach), Horace Thompson (coach), Fredda Acker, Bobbie Martin, Joyce Smith, Joyce Sheridan, Annie Stephens, Barbara Sanders, Opal Spears, Pat Leverette, Sue Greenway, Mary Broadwell, Viola Thompson, May Leverette.

Judson Mill (Greenville, S.C.), runners-up: Joe O'Shields (coach), Joann Hunter, Gwendolyn Tyler, Betty Moody, Dorothy Walker, Doris Cole, Ruth James, Frances Wofford, Norma Jones, Helen Raines, Evelyn McDowell.

Brandon Mill (Greenville, S.C.), consolation winners: Ray Wynn (coach), Shirley Jones, Frances Hall, Shirley Townsend, Betty Anders, Vivian Williamson, June Sauls, Ruth Phillips, Lora Marrett, Jean Sloan, Lila Hall, Nell Watson, Lena Ivester.

Joanna Mill (Joanna, S.C.): M. Frazen (coach), C.B. Cole (coach), Johnny Moore (coach), Doris Long, Gwendolyn Price, Patsy Rowe, Sara Hollingsworth, Helen Bridges, Carolyn Thomas, Louise Wise, Lillie Franklin, Diane Morse, Thelma Bridges, Buchanan.

Glen Lowery Mill (Whitmire, S.C.): S.R. DuBose (coach), Hazel Suber (coach), Betty Duncan, Dorothy Frier, Willie Brock, Grace Brock, Sara McCall, Peggy Lominick, Alma Gregory, Elsie Gilliam, Loretta Black, Jette Gregory.

Calhoun Falls Mill (Calhoun Falls, S.C.): Densel Dockery (coach), Delma Cooper (coach), Georgia Wiles, Irma Hilley, Evelyn Robinson, Doris Ross, Nadine Broadwell, Mary Helms, Gaynell Bonds, Lena Lowe, Willie Holmes, Nuree Dockery, Fay Ayers, Dorothy Sellers.

Dunean Mill (Greenville, S.C.): Ward Williams (coach), Charles Tidwell (coach), Sis Mayfield, Nancy Pitts, Miriam Poole, Jerry Duncan, Pat Barnette, Jo Smith, Shirley Buckner, Joan Ritter, Sandy Williams, Bobby Ashley, Meta Stowe.

Easley Mill (Easley, S.C.): Barbara Garrick (coach), Lois Galloway, Mary Brown, Gladys Ellenburg, Kathryn McCombs, Mary Garrett, Helen Surrett, Latrilla Henson, Barbara Galloway, Mary Anderson, Betty Prince.

Pelzer Mill (Pelzer, S.C.): Ed McCuen (coach), Lillie Vaughn, Jean Henderson, Merle Crane, Katherine Nelson, Mamie Whitt, Syble Gambrell, Patsy Gambrell, Carolyn Mahaffey, Margaret Smith, Fay Moody, Burline Reeves, Romona Whitt.

Piedmont Mill (Piedmont, S.C.): Jack Turner (coach), Tom Pack (coach), Sybil Fletcher, Margie Payne, Doris Cothran, Jennie Turner, Margie Whiteside, Elsie Verner, Alice Rampey, Betty Garrett, Jo Shelton, Janet Morrison, Peggy Nelson, Gail Leslie.

Victor Mill (Greer, S.C.): Lee Coleman (coach), Martha Lowe, Margaret Ballenger, Polly Mason, Molly Mason, Dorothy Morgan, Joyce Willis, Emma Lane, Eleanor Center, Faye Grant, Mae Grant, Barbara Heatherly.

Woodside Mill (Greenville, S.C.): Charles Couch (coach), Earl Jones (coach), Eunice Couch, Martha Bowen, Mary Gillespie, Maxine Gillespie, Nancy Byers, Sarah Farrow, Jo Rigdon, Jean Julian, Betty Hunter, Jo Ware, Mary Tollison, Sybil Wilson, Brown, Tollison.

Liberty Mill (Liberty, S.C.): Fred Powers (coach), Ossie Grogan, Bernice Edwards, Helen Simmons, Fannie Gaines, Margaret Butler, Leatrice Powers, Hazel Allgood, Frances Rowl, Earline Bowie, Linna Powers.

Simpsonville Mill (Simpsonville, S.C.): Ruth Thackston (coach), Edna Goodenough, Mary Barbery, Eschol Carlton, Nancy Brown, Mary Morris, Marguerite Forrester, Geneva Forrester, Mary Parrish, Mary Henderson, Lola Terry, Betty Barbery, Myrtle Coker.

1953

Officers: Hugh Anderson (Greenville, S.C.), President; Fred Snoddy (Greer, S.C.), Vice President; J.B. Owens (Greenville, S.C.), Executive Secretary; Mrs. W.B. Mulligan (Greenville, S.C.), Acting Secretary; Horace Whitmire (Greenville, S.C.), Treasurer.

Executive Committee: Bruce Stroupe (Greenville, S.C.), Charles Allen (Greenville, S.C.), Veo Storey (Piedmont, S.C.), Sam Patton (Enka, N.C.), Clarence Thomas (Greenville, S.C.), Jack Reames (Abbeville, S.C.), Walter Lauter (Rossville, Ga.), Willie Wilbanks (Greenville, S.C.), D.K. Smith (Lyman, S.C.), S.R. DuBose (Whitmire, S.C.), Snow Kirby (Slater, S.C.), Hugh Hampton (Winston-Salem, N.C.), Divver Hendrix (Greenville,

S.C.), Harry Clark (Greenville, S.C.), J.D. Brown (Greenville, S.C.).

Class A Men

Monaghan Mill (Greenville, S.C.), champions: Effie Evington (coach), Ken Pittman, Fig Newton, Brice Kirkpatrick, Warren Mullinax, William Kerr, Harold Burns, Herbert Lindsay, James Gowan, Roy Skinner.

Peerless Woolen Mill (Rossville, Ga.), runners-up: Walter Lauter (coach), Harold Hall (coach), Brownell Bryant, Ray Cox, James Cooke, John Barger, Ray Griffith, Joe Moore, Don Gainer, Gene White, Claude Morris, John Alonzo.

Dunean Mill (Greenville, S.C.), consolation winners: Ward Williams (coach), Larry Ashley, Don Ritter, Bob Stowe, Melvin Bell, Herman Dill, Bomar Keller, Don Cox, Dave Putman, Bud Granger.

Piedmont Mill (Piedmont, S.C.): Tom Pack (coach), Ernie Chambers, Bill Quinn, Judd Farr, Lewis Howard, Robert Hooper, Carroll Stone, Don Roper, Veo Storey, Carroll Gilreath.

American Enka (Enka, N.C.): Sam Patton (coach), Ed Brinkley, Alton Brooks, Joe Conner, Richard Gudger, Willard Kaylor, George Lancaster, Roy Pressley, Richard Sides, Deran Walters.

Chicopee Mill (Gainesville, Ga.): S.B. Jones (coach), Ben Martin, Howard Bridges, George Mize, Ross O'Dell, Ray Godfrey, Paul McDonald, Larry Baird, Clyde Turk.

Class B Men

Greer Mill (Greer, S.C.), champions: Hicks Burgin (coach), Bob Campbell (coach), John Henson, Marilyn Stroud, Harold Huey, Prock Ruff, Charles Brannon, Jerry Burgess, Chuck Spencer, Zeke Harvey, Pat Lindsey, Don Brewton.

Lyman Mill (Lyman, S.C.), runners-up: Lloyd Leonard (coach), Woodward Beasley (coach), Joe Smith, Don Satterfield, Darrell Medlock, Roy Beach, Harold Eubanks, Harold Mullinax, Douglas Pettigrew, Junior Henson, Gerald Moody, Edward Medlock.

Woodside Mill (Greenville, S.C.), consolation winners: Harold Limbaugh (coach), William Wakefield (coach), Mick Griffith, Joe Farrow, Dewey Morrow, C.H. Wakefield, James McDuffie, Edward White, David Carter, Carl Grogan, Buddy Gibson.

Dunean Mill (Greenville, S.C.): Bob Stowe (coach), Alvin LaBoone, Bill Davidson, Frank Lollis, Bobby Grant, Joel Greene, Marvin Grant, Robert Milsap, Pete Jamison, Charles Gilstrap, Kenneth Stroud.

Beacon Mill (Swannanoa, N.C.): George Thompson (mgr), J.D. Hardin (coach), Billy Allen, Johnny Shaver, Jim Johnson, Billy Smith, Bud Harper, Edward Reese, Grey Chandler, Marion Taylor, Floyd Waldrop, Kenneth Rudden.

Clinton Mill (Clinton, S.C.): Charles Leatherwood (coach), Calvin Cooper, Charles Oxner, Charles Foster, James Braswell, Alvin Hampton, Sam Owens, Charles Tedder, James Owens.

Camperdown Mill (Greenville, S.C.): Eugene Davis (coach), James Johnson, Charles Carter, Toby Long, Paul Darnell, Cecil Rollins, Richard Rollins, Ken Rollins, Bobby Jones, Louie McDowell, Billy Wilburn.

Easley Mill (Easley, S.C.): Joe Anders (coach), Ken Thomas, Early Bagwell, James Campbell, Verlon McEntyre, Roy Waldrop, James Rogers, Robert Hancock, Fred Owens, Ben Fox.

Joanna Mill (Joanna, S.C.): S. Humphrey (coach), Johnny Moore (coach), George Merchant, Henry Elliott, Kenneth Boyce, Darrell Johnson, Charles Davenport, Jimmy Kirby, Robert Hair, James Templeton, James Clark, Lester Long.

Liberty Mill (Liberty, S.C.): Fred Powers (coach), Ben Crosland, Billy O'Dell, Allen Cox, O'Neal Roberts, George Cantrell, Buddy Shook, Donnie Garrison, Charles Edwards, Ray Matthews.

Pelzer Mill (Pelzer, S.C.): Leonard Muth (coach), Marion Smith, James Thomason, Olin Davis, Ellis Coker, Roy Taylor, Bill Thomason, Earl Reeves, David Frady, E.J. Washington.

New Holland Mill (Gainesville, Ga.): Pete Morgan (coach), Charles Smith, Hoyt Hollifield, James Barnes, Sammy Hudgins, James Smith, W.A. Harris, Buddy Martin, Clemmie Tyner, Charles Riley, Eugene Winters.

Russell Manufacturing (Alexander City, Ala.): James Forbus (coach), Edsel Riddle, Charles Bailey, Ardath Robinson, Doyt Alford, B.G. Stephenson, Dean Aiken, James Yates, Reginald Spraggins, James Coger, Thomas Kennedy.

Simpsonville Mill (Simpsonville, S.C.): Rick Alexander (coach), Carl Henderson,

Southern Textile Basketball Tournament Rosters   Appendix 1

William Gault, Edwin Davis, William Smith, Roger Cannady, J.L. Abercrombie, Preston Barbary, William Porter, T.C. Abbott.

Slater Mill (Slater, S.C.): Bliss McCall (coach), John Blackstone, Bobby Williams, Bobby Johnson, William Knox, Paul Hazel, Gaines Campbell, Archie Smith, Thomas Cox, Horace James.

Lonsdale Mill (Seneca, S.C.): Roy McCurry (coach), Nig Griffith (coach), Clyde Davis (ass't coach), Tommy Poole, Hill Sosebee, James Black, Jim White, Frank White, Jamie Shirley, Harold Shirley, Ben Bleckley, Dan Williams, Bill Vickery.

Southern Bleachery (Taylors, S.C.): Walker Dilworth (coach), Bobby Belue, Gene Hodgens, Rudy Hughes, Kenneth Wham, Reggie Bumgardner, Bill Rainey, Ralph Moose, Frank Tucker, Arnold Pace.

Victor Mill (Greer, S.C.): Rudy Godfrey (coach), Kenneth Godfrey, William Lybrand, Bobby Lemmons, Douglas Garren, Walter Bain, William Smith, Ray Jones, Leon Gravley, Carlos Garrett, Wayne Godfrey.

Brandon Mill (Greenville, S.C.): Pete McAbee (coach), J.D. Williamson Jr., Thomas Hall, Melvin Hudson, Willie Murphy, John Buchanan, Charles Goss, Jimmy Mattos, Donald Rich.

Coats & Clark (Toccoa, Ga.): Charles Davis (coach), Tom Gailey (coach), LeRoy Deaton, Leon Denmon, Dwain Toney, Randall McClain, Marvin Whitworth, Fernando Payne, Jack Watson, Hoke Davis, Kenneth Herron.

Appleton Mill (Anderson, S.C.): Henry Spake (coach), Benny Speares, Bobby Holcombe, Thomas Carlton, Charles Williams, Horace Rhodes, John Acker, Jimmy Gilbert, Owen Bailey, James Morrison, Parson.

Monaghan Mill (Greenville, S.C.): Richard Evington (coach), Benny Brown, Charles Landreth, James Gambrell, Billy Fuller, Franklin Haney, Edward Wyatt, Donald Dean, T.J. Hudgens, Tom Fore, Dean Stancell.

Union Bleachery (Greenville, S.C.): Clyde Robertson (coach), Charles Brooks (coach), Roger Bishop, Herley Dix, Henry Keith, Walter Robertson, George Dunn, Charles Robertson, Kenneth Boswell, Heber Evatt, Bobby Lazar, Billy Moody, Stroud.

Judson Mill (Greenville, S.C.): Frank Russell (coach), Arthur Sides, Paul Black, Grant Sullivan, Melvin Keith, Hoyt Smith, Bruce Stroupe, George Russell, William Snelson, Franklin Harvell, Ted Adams.

CLASS C MEN

Union Bleachery (Greenville, S.C.), champions: Harold Green (coach), Billy Moody (coach), Jack League, Ronnie Knight, Bruce Turner, Houston Turner, Jerry Robertson, David Smith, Bruce Bayne, Dan Rhodes, Keavan Hester, Morris Evington.

Dunean Mill (Greenville, S.C.), runners-up: Donald Ritter (coach), Robert Henderson, Gene Henderson, Jimmy Smith, Bill Roddy, Tracy Roddy, Carol Byrd, Jack Kelly, Martin Holder, Bobby Parker, Ted Burgess.

Appleton Mill (Anderson, S.C.), consolation winners: Henry Spake (coach), Delwyn Whitton (coach), Calvin Daniel, Larry Speares, Charles Smith, Jimmy Smith, Buddy Conwell, Harold Brown, Eugene Alford, Billy Tidwell, Billy Hanks, Joe Moss.

Anderson Mill (Anderson, S.C.): Ezra Embler (coach), Walter Cooper, Kenneth Bannister, Donnie Hancock, Mack Fleming, Bobby Fleming, Hampton Hunter, John Long, William Evans, Dennis Bannister, David Hooper, Toney.

Apalache Mill (Greer, S.C.): Ralph Bogan (coach), Wilson Garrett, Larry Belue, Jack Fuller, Eddie Leopard, Larry Edge, Gerald Jones, Melvin Roper, John Wilson.

Belton Mill (Belton, S.C.): Luther Rentz (coach), John Broome, Jimmy Lowe, Jimmy Nelson, Stokes Estes, Dale Owens, Billy Coker, Louie Craft, Don Campbell.

Brandon Mill (Greenville, S.C.): Ray Wynn, Charles Browning, William Pittman, William Capps, Robert Paris, Robert Williamson, Jack Garren, Pierce Powers, Eugene Seay, Tommy Abbott, Robert Garren.

Easley Mill (Easley, S.C.): Courtney Heath (coach), Larry Bagwell, Bobby Chandler, Harold Waldrop, Leon Chandler, Courtney Heath Jr., Billy Garrick, Clarence Perry, Charles Bagwell, Joe Spearman, James Lankford.

Greer Mill (Greer, S.C.): Robert Campbell (coach), Donald Black, Harold Durham, Thomas Johnson, Ernie Ellenburg, Alton Jones, Mitchell Flynn, Ben Burnett, Bob Grubbs, Wilson Ellenburg, Pete Taylor.

Liberty Mill (Liberty, S.C.): Fred Powers (coach), David Garrison, Jimmy Cantrell, Donnie Hitt, Wallace Lyda, Jimmy Garrison,

Billy Allgood, Jennings Farr, Jimmy Harrison, Lawrence Isler, Dale Martin.

Mills Mill #1 (Greenville, S.C.): Harry Smith (coach), Harold Bell, Jimmy Garrett, Walter Garrett, Harold Lowery, Donald Kitchen, Michael Massey, Charles McMahan, James Thompson, Melvin Thompson, Buddy McCall.

Orr Mill (Anderson, S.C.): Mack Gunnells (coach), Joe Tilley, Gene Adams, Marshall Adams, Melvin Aiken, John Nixon, Kenneth Smith, Colyer Parnell, Leroy Parnell, Jack McLane, Larry Cash.

Greenwood Mill (Greenwood, S.C.): David Andrews, William Wilson, Richard Rowland, Aughtry, R. Burnette, Falls, D. Burnette, Pate, R. Burnette.

Pelzer Mill (Pelzer, S.C.): Leonard Muth (coach), Harold Roberts, Bill Rogers, Hubby Rogers, Randall Frady, LaFoy Moody, David Hollingsworth, Dickie Sanders, John Ross, Jimmy Smith.

Piedmont Mill (Piedmont, S.C.): Claud Picklesimer (coach), Joe Hiott, Charles Weisner, Thomas Bryant, Jerry Hooper, Carroll Emery, Ronald Davis, Johnny Richey, J.D. Hunnicutt Jr., Jack Bagwell, David Rampey.

Simpsonville Mill (Simpsonville, S.C.): O'dell Barbary (coach), Donald Jones, Dickie Goodenough, William Norris, Preston Calvert, Johnny Knight, Roy Gilliam, Troy Stokes, Jack Brookshire, Tom Moore, Roy Stokes.

Southern Bleachery (Taylors, S.C.): Phil Thornton (coach), Billy Barbary, Herman Jackson, Charles Miller, Donald Coker, Jesse Barton, Ronald Coker, James Barton, Don Dillard, Martin.

Lonsdale Mill (Seneca, S.C.): Junior Bibb (coach), Tommy Bailey (coach), Joel Perry (coach), Bill Perry, Donald Gaillard, Bobby Gibson, Gary Pruitt, Thomas Burgess, Thomas McCurry, Bill Carson, James Orr, Clarence Abbott, Robert Lacey.

Victor Mill (Greer, S.C.): Harold Owens (coach), Donald Elder, Donald Godfrey, D.G. Leonhardt, Thomas Watson, William Wilson, James Smith, M.D. Campbell, Grady Greer, R.D. Burnette, Leon McLemore.

Woodside Mill (Greenville, S.C.): Clyde Hodge (coach), Leonard Canup (coach), Billy Farmer, Dennis Brookshire, Joe Julian, Harold Grogan, Rodney Canup, Billy Ware, Harold Swafford, Billy Howell, Ray Kellett, Joe Aiken.

Monaghan Mill (Greenville, S.C.): Fig Newton (coach), Donald Haley, Louis Pittman, Billy Gambrell, Jimmy Crain, Charles Stillwell, Michael Ross, John Merck Jr., Winston Major, Bobby Foster, Darrell Pearson, Donald Maloy.

American Spinning (Greenville, S.C.): Art Schiffer (coach), Willard Fowler, Charles Hendrix, Joseph Bates, Bill Neely, Bill Smith, Larry Porter, Jerry Chapman, Johnny Hunnicutt, Jimmie Painter.

Judson Mill (Greenville, S.C.): Ted Adams (coach), J.D. Sellars, Richard Stephens, Gene Sweat, Charles Schockley, Jack Roddy, Jimmy Holden, Harold Morris, Furman Neal.

Class B Women

Appleton Mill (Anderson, S.C.), champions: Lewis Acker (coach), Joyce Spears, Joyce Sheridan, Fredda Acker, Bobbie Martin, Annie Allen, Mary Broadwell, Opal Spears, Doris Hiott, Sue Greenway, Edna Rhodes, Jo Billings, Barbara Sanders.

Judson Mill (Greenville, S.C.), runners-up: B.W. Stroupe (coach), Juanita Jones, Jo Hunter, Betty Moody, Doris Bryant, June Bryant, Catherine Upchurch, Frances Ballew, Carolyn Kelly, Willie Hale.

Easley Mill (Easley, S.C.), consolation winners: Joe Anders (coach), Patsy Heath, Latrilla Henson, Helen Surrett, Grace Galloway, Sybil Wilson, Margie Roper, Norma Hancock, Mary Hairston, Peggy Nalley, Mary Thompson, Barbara Howard.

Piedmont Mill (Piedmont, S.C.): M.L. Morgan (coach), Betty Joan Garrett, Sue Fletcher, Betty Jo Garrett, Doris Cothran, Patsy Drennon, Kathleen Nelson, Carolyn Mahaffey, Peggy Baskin, Shirley Farrow, Sara Hooper, Becky Ayers, Alice Rampey.

Calhoun Falls Mill (Calhoun Falls, S.C.): Edward Dickard (coach), Ann Helms, Billie Powell, Doris Ross, Bobbie Dower, Edith Martin, Evelyn Carlisle, Elizabeth Pruitt, Dorothy Sellars, Nuree Dockery, Patricia Burdette, Willie Holmes, Dorothy Chrisley.

Dunean Mill (Greenville, S.C.): Ward Williams (coach), Jerry Duncan, Miriam Poole, Thelma Girardeau, Shirley Buckner, Betty McClure, Sis Mayfield, Florine Pollard, Peggy Barnette, Syble Jones, Gail Allison, Broadwell.

Joanna Mill (Joanna, S.C.): H. Frazier (coach), Johnny Moore (coach), Baron O'Shields (ass't coach), Nadine Bridges, Thelma Bridges, Gwen Price, Sara Hollingsworth, Doris Long, Bobbie Franklin,

Bobbie Bridges, Evelyn Evans, Lillie Franklin, Louise Force, Dorothy Morris.

Mills Mill #1 (Greenville, S.C.): Henry Giles (coach), Glenda Abbott, Frances Bates, Mary Cowan, Ann Eubanks, Nellie Funk, Joyce Garrett, Alpha Henry, Carolyn Lowery, Bobbie Marler, Audrey McMahan, Edna Nix, Carolyn Staton.

Lonsdale Mill (Seneca, S.C.): Fay Poole (coach), Frank Gaillard (coach), T.H. Reynolds (ass't coach), Edna Lee, Janet Lee, Mary Foster, Billie Lacey, Hattie Powell, Delores Rickard, Ruth Reynolds, Barbara Stephens, Betty Newton, Jo Dawkins, Evelyn Reynolds, Mary Nix.

Woodside Mill (Greenville, S.C.): Ruth Canup (coach), Charles Couch (coach), Jean Julian, Betty Hunter, Katherine Gillespie, Ann Bowen, Evelyn Bowen, Jo Ware, Mary Tollison, Sarah Farrow, Mary Gillespie, Barbara Foster, Jo Rigdon, Eunice Couch.

Brandon Mill (Greenville, S.C.): J.D. Williamson Jr. (coach), Deda Duncan, Betty Anders, Ruth Phillips, Mary McConnell, Vivian Wilson, Joyce Wilson, Frances Sears, Mary Williamson, Clarice Robinson, June Sauls, Lora Merritt.

1954

Officers: Fred Snoddy (Greer, S.C.), President; J.B. Owens (Greenville, S.C.), Vice President; Milford Howard (Greer, S.C.), Executive Secretary; Mrs. W.B. Mulligan (Greenville, S.C.), Acting Secretary; Horace Whitmire (Greenville, S.C.), Treasurer.

Executive Committee: Bruce Stroupe (Greenville, S.C.), John Mullikin (Piedmont, S.C.), Sam Patton (Enka, N.C.), Clarence Thomas (Greenville, S.C.), Jack Reames (Abbeville, S.C.), Walter Lauter (Rossville, Ga.), Willie Wilbanks (Greenville, S.C.), S.R. DuBose (Whitmire, S.C.), Snow Kirby (Slater, S.C.), Hugh Hampton (Winston-Salem, N.C.), Divver Hendrix (Greenville, S.C.), J.D. Brown (Greenville, S.C.), Hugh Anderson (Greenville, S.C.).

Class A Men

Pelzer Mill (Pelzer, S.C.), champions: J.B. Baker (coach), Earl Wooten (coach), Frank Felts, Neild Gordon, Pete Harris, Truman Hill, Tommy McCullough, John McGraw, Bobby Roberts, Randy Whaley, Harry Major.

Dunean Mill (Greenville, S.C.), runners-up: Larry Bell (coach), Ward Williams (coach), Bomar Keller, Alvin LaBoone, Larry Ashley, Melvin Bell, Bud Granger, Bob Stowe, Don Ritter, Jim Slaughter, Carl Greene.

American Enka (Enka, N.C.), consolation winners: Sam Patton (coach), Gus Colagerakis, Joe Conner, Willard Kaylor, George Lancaster, Robert Lance, Smith Langdon, James Patton, Richard Sides, Ned Straehla, Deran Walters.

Monaghan Mill (Greenville, S.C.): Fig Newton (coach), Benny Brown, Jimmy Crain, Effie Evington, James Gowan, Brice Kirkpatrick, Don Newton, Ken Pittman, Curtis Ward.

Victor Mill (Greer, S.C.): Hal Huey (coach), Robert Campbell, Jerry Burgess, Marilyn Stroud, Milford Howard, George Luther, Harold Haynie, Eddie Freeman.

Peerless Woolen Mill (Rossville, Ga.): Walter Lauter (coach), Harold Hall (coach), John Alonso, John Barger, Brownell Bryant, Corkey Cooke, Ray Cox, Claude Morris, Ray Griffith, Joe McCullough, Bill Pass, Bud Sloan, Carl White.

Piedmont Mill (Piedmont, S.C.): Bobby Brown, Ernie Chambers, Bobb Hooper, Lewis Howard, Paul Nye, Don Roper, Ken Smith, Carroll Stone, Thomas Tober, Ronald Davis.

Woodside Mill (Greenville, S.C.): James Faircloth, Jack League, Harold Limbaugh, Herbert Lindsay, James McDuffie, William Moody, Fred Powers, Jack Robinson, William Yarborough.

Class B Men

Union Bleachery (Greenville, S.C.), champions: Bill Moody (coach), Charles Brooks (coach), Roger Bishop, John Robertson, Hurley Dix, Jerry Robertson, Bruce Turner, Houston Turner, Ronnie Knight, Donald Stroud, Bobby Lazar, Walter Robertson.

Beacon Mill (Swannanoa, N.C.), runners-up: George Thompson (coach), J.D. Hardin (coach), Bill Allen, Martin Hair, Eugene Harper, James Johnson, Richard Ramsey, Kenneth Rudeen, John Shaver, Billy Smith, Robert Stroup, Gerald Warren, Hudson.

LaFrance Mill (Anderson, S.C.), consolation winners: Neal Hunnicutt (coach), Blake Griffith, Olin Mullikin, Garnett Smith, Joe Stegall, Lamar Elrod, Douglas Padgett, William Holcombe, Robert Williams, Jack Wardlaw.

Oconee Mill (Westminster, S.C.): Dean

Taylor (coach), Gerald Dempsey, Jack Chambers, Herman Smith, Robert Smith, Doris Huston, Joe Duvall, Randall Broome, Richard James, Cecil Kirby.

American Spinning (Greenville, S.C.): Fred Johnson (coach), Willard Fowler (coach), Bill Smith, Junior Harbin, Charles Hendrix, Jimmy Morgan, Ralph Durham, Charles Finley, Jimmy Painter, Burriss Owens, Danny Fowler.

Apalache Mill (Greer, S.C.): Ralph Bogan (coach), Stephen Addyman, Maurice Belue, Billy Fuller, Richard Justice, Carl Tillotson, Martin Tooke Jr., Buddy Rogers.

Appleton Mill (Anderson, S.C.): Henry Spake (coach), Eugene Alford, Gerald Bailey, George Brown, Charles Conwell, Jack Carlton, Billy Middleton, William Morrison, Benny Speares, Robert Speares, Billy Tidwell.

Brandon Mill (Greenville, S.C.): Pete McAbee (coach), John Buchanan, Dewey Corbin, Thomas Hall, Charlie Johnson, Fred McAbee Jr., Jerrel McKinney, Jimmie Mattos, Willie Murphy, James Williamson.

Calhoun Falls Mill (Calhoun Falls, S.C.): Densel Dockery (coach), Bill Quinn (coach), William Brown, Marvin Burton, Charles Carlisle, Bobby Chrisley, William Evans, Claude Herndon, James Hester, Ralph Parnell, Bill Powell, Maxey Putman.

Camperdown Mill (Greenville, S.C.): Louie McDowell (coach), Charles Bartram, Charles Carter, Ken Carter, Paul Darnell, Walter Glenn Jr., Bobby Jones, Toby Long, James Johnson, Richard Rollins, Billy Wilburn.

Dunean Mill (Greenville, S.C.): Fred Marsh (coach), Herbert Dodson, Parker Fennell, Joe Granger, Richard Kay, Billy Lollis, Robert Millsap, Bobby Parker, James Reid, Tracy Roddy, Kenneth Stroud.

Easley Mill (Easley, S.C.): Joe Anders (coach), Charles Bagwell, Early Bagwell, James Campbell, Verlon McIntyre, James Lankford, Fred Owens, Gerry Rankin, Roy Waldrop.

Victor Mill (Greer, S.C.): Charles Hartwell (coach), Denny Owens, Kenneth Godfrey, Eugene Lybrand, Carlos Garrett, Millard Leonhardt, Munroe Gravley, Ronald Burnette, Leroy Wright, Wayman Godfrey, Douglas Garren, Leon Gravley.

Joanna Mill (Joanna, S.C.): Wadsworth Niver (coach), Johnny Moore (coach), James Clark, Charles Estes, Thomas Flow, Lawrence Jenkins, Darrell Johnson, Lester Long, Allen O'Shields, Marshall Smith, H.M. Willingham.

Judson Mill (Greenville, S.C.): Mack Patton (coach), Joe Bramlett, Kenneth Linder, William Davidson, William Konduras, Eugene Henderson, Coy Watson, Francis Brothers, Richard Stephens, James Smith.

Laurens Mill (Laurens, S.C.): Wayne Roberts (coach), Paul Cavender (coach), Jack Burns, Charles Bowlin, Marion Craine, George Crocker, Frank Dambeck, William Noffz, Tommy Reames, Billy Snow, Brice Taylor, Fredrick Waldrop.

Lonsdale Mill (Seneca, S.C.): Doug Kingsmore (coach), Nig Griffith (coach), Alton Burgess, Joe Brown, Bobby Dozier, John Leutwyler, Thomas Mitchell, Wyman Morris, James Orr, Thomas Poole, Luther Rhodes, Charles Stancil, Coker.

Monaghan Mill (Greenville, S.C.): Robert McAvoy (coach), Fig Newton (coach), L.C. Alexander, Jimmy Bagwell, Buddy Hudgens, Charles Landreth, Clyde McKinney, Jewell Major, John Merck, James Moss, Joe Wyatt, Bob Cook.

Pelzer Mill (Pelzer, S.C.): Leonard Muth (coach), Bobby Brown, Grady Cooley, Harold Drennon, Robert Dunlap, Gene Gosnell, Cecil Masters, Albert Pittman, William Reeves, Bill Thomason, Clifford Thomason.

CLASS C MEN

Dunean Mill (Greenville, S.C.), champions: Jim Slaughter (coach), Ronald Simpson, Donald Allen, David Norris, Jack Kelly, Bill Roddy, Bill Mathis, David Shook, James Parker, Ted Burgess, Phillip Henderson.

Appleton Mill (Anderson, S.C.), runners-up: Henry Spake (coach), David Bryson, Walter Craft, Calvin Daniel, Donnie Edmonds, Billy Hanks, Nelson Massey, Larry Speares, Larry Trotter, Jerry Vaughn.

Judson Mill (Greenville, S.C.), consolation winners: Mack Patton (coach), Martin Holden, Robert Henderson, Ronald Timms, Jimmy Brown, Jimmy Holden, Joe Sellers, Charles Shockley, Jack Roddy, Harold Morris.

Anderson Mill (Anderson, S.C.): Ezra Embler (coach), Dennis Bannister, Tony Bannister, Walter Cooper, Donald Hancock, Julian Bannister, Curtis Long, Charles Scott, Grady Sanders, James Smith, Charles Smith.

Laurens Mill (Laurens, S.C.): Dean Lyles (coach), Henry Bowie (coach), Bobby Branson,

Gary Byrd, Russell Moore, Lanyn Porter, Ernest Rice Jr., Lewis Russell, Keith Russell, Nayson Stewart, Arthur Taylor, Bill Waldrop.

Liberty Mill (Liberty, S.C.): Fred Powers (coach), Joel Allgood, Robert Bowman, David Garrison, Jimmy Garrison, Donnie Hitt, Wallace Lyda, Dale Martin, Robert Trammell.

Mills Mill #1 (Greenville, S.C.): Tony Smith (coach), Rudy Simmons (ass't mgr), James Ball, Walter Garrett, Harold Lowery, James McAllister, Robert McCall, Michael Massey, Darrel Thompson, Thomas Putman, Jimmy Thompson, Gary Underwood.

Monaghan Mill (Greenville, S.C.): Ken Pittman (coach), Charles Busbee, Johnny McIntosh, Charles McKinney, Donald Malloy, Darrell Pearson, Louis Pittman, Charles Powers, Michael Ross, Charles Thompson, Lewis Vanadore.

Orr Mill (Anderson, S.C.): Dwain Addison, Melvin Aiken, Larry Cash, Gerald Mackey, Floyd Makison, John Nixon, Colyer Parnell, Joe Tilley.

Pelzer Mill (Pelzer, S.C.): L.A. Muth (coach), Donald Bell, Bill Chandler, Joe Eaton, Frankie Garrett, Johnny McCall, LaFoy Moody, Alton Owens, George Thomas, James Vaughan, John Dickerson.

Piedmont Mill (Piedmont, S.C.): Jiggs Woodcock (coach), James Bryant, Carroll Emery, Billy Evans, Ray Foxx, Rolf Garrison, Joe Hiott, Jerry Hooper, John Lindley, John Richey, Charles Weisner.

Renfrew Bleachery (Travelers Rest, S.C.): Roy Foster (coach), John McDowell (coach), Don Abbott, Claude Batson, Larry Farmer, Larry Foster, Jack Hayes, Charles Ivey, Franklin Murphy, Bobby Poole, Joe Stewart, John Vernon.

Ware Shoals Mill (Ware Shoals, S.C.): Willie Wilbanks (coach), Erwin Bagwell, Erwin Crittenden, Sam Gambrell, Robert Harrelson, William Johnson, Kenneth Kay, Jimmy Nicholson, Robert Seawright, Jimmy Trulove, William Sonenshine.

Woodside Mill (Greenville, S.C.): Leonard Camp (coach), Joe Aiken, Rodney Canup, Billy Farmer, Harold Grogan, Billy Hines, Joe Julian, Ray Kellett, Joe McKinney, Charles Sizemore, Billy Ware.

Greenwood Mill (Greenwood, S.C.): Lonnie Lyle (coach), Sam Beasley Jr., David Masters, Charles Mathews, James Nixon, Clyde Owings, Wade Sanders, Paul Smith, James Spivey, Johnny Steele.

Greer Mill (Greer, S.C.): Jerry Burgess (coach), Maurice Atkins, Donald Black, Hugh Craine, Harold Durham, Mitchell Flynn, Donald Jones, Leon McLemore, Allen Moore, D. Atkins, Brown.

American Spinning (Greenville, S.C.): Hal Smith (coach), Johnny Hunnicutt, Willard Fowler, Bobby Owens, Mac Massingale, James Morgan, Bill Neely, Pleasant Norris, David Martin.

Apalache Mill (Greer, S.C.): Ralph Bogan (coach), Douglas Belue, Jesse Brown, Larry Edge, Jack Fuller, Wilson Garrett, Carol Groce, Eddie Leopard, Larry Lister, Melvin Roper.

Belton Mill (Belton, S.C.): Jack Lowe, King, Martin, Nelson, Loftis, J. Lowe, Snipes, Campbell.

Brandon Mill (Greenville, S.C.): Harold Martin (coach), Charles Browning, Henry Freeman, Kenneth Gardner, Jack Garren, Robert Garren, Orr Ledford, Robert Paris, Bill Pittman, Gene Seay, Joel Turner.

Victor Mill (Greer, S.C.): Milford Howard (coach), Grady Greer, Harold Owens, James Godfrey, Donald Elders, Richard Gravley, Robert Gravley, Darrell Leonhardt, James Smith, Bill Wilson.

Easley Mill (Easley, S.C.): Joe Anders (coach), Dennis Atkinson, Larry Bagwell, Joe Garrett, Bobby Chandler, Charles Marshbanks, James Lesley, Charles James, Julian Hiott, Joe Spearman, Joel Noblitt.

CLASS B WOMEN

Lonsdale Mill (Seneca, S.C.), champions: Roy McCurry (coach), Frank Gaillard (coach), Jo Dawkins, Mary Foster, DeEtte Kelly, Willie Lacey, Edna Lacy, Jeanette Lee, Margaret Adams, Betty Newton, Ova Poole, Ruth Reynolds, Betty Stancil, Norma Turner.

Judson Mill (Greenville, S.C.), runners-up: Margaret Todd (coach), June Bryant, Doris Bryant, Doris Bramlett, Patsy Allison, Jo Ann Kelly, Juanita Jones, Betty Moody, Nancy Pierce, Carolyn Kelly, Smith.

Joanna Mill (Joanna, S.C.), consolation winners: Buddy Kirby (mgr), Johnny Moore (coach), Betty Bridges, Bobbie Bridges, Thelma Bridges, Helen Bridges, Mary Bishop, Frances Davenport, Evelyn Evans, Louise Force, Lillie Franklin, Dorothy Morris, Vera Smith, Gwen Price.

Piedmont Mill (Piedmont, S.C.): Shorty

Smith (coach), Doris Aiken, Gail Allison, Jean Ayers, Margaret Dorn, Avenelle Emery, Joanna Gaines, Betty Garrett, Mary Ivester, Helen Moore, Janet Morrison, Dorothy Rhyne, Janet Sewell.

Appleton Mill (Anderson, S.C.): Lewis Acker (coach), Doris Hiott, Barbara Cash, Joyce Smith, Becky Bates, Claudia Evans, Nancy Norman, Mary Morrison, Edna Rhodes, Mary Harris, Wilma Broadwell.

Brandon Mill (Greenville, S.C.): Ray Wynn (coach), Betty Anders, Marcelle Cobb, Frances Hall, Betty Henderson, Shirley Jones, Janice McDonald, Lora Marrett, June Nash, Vivian Williamson, Joyce Wilson, Vivian Wilson.

Dunean Mill (Greenville, S.C.): Joe Turner (coach), Gail Allison, Peggy Barnette, Jerry Duncan, Nellie Grant, Barbara Marshbanks, Ethyl Pollard, Miriam Poole, Janette Sewell, Angell Shedd.

Easley Mill (Easley, S.C.): Joe Anders (coach), Mary Hariston, Patsy Heath, Edith James, Patsy Garrett, Grace Galloway, Barbara Howard, Margaret Howard, Mary Hudson, Brown.

Greer Mill (Greer, S.C.): Harold Huey (coach), Pat Belcher, Elizabeth Dunn, Mary Ellenburg, Pat Gowan, Mary Gowan, Montez Greene, Alline Grubbs, Barbara Long, Doris Wilson.

Pelzer Mill (Pelzer, S.C.): L.A. Muth (coach), Gwen Burgess, Molly Henderson, Barbara McCuen, Barbara Means, Faye Moody, Barbara Pittman, Bettina Revis, Patricia Revis, Shirley Revis, Jean Rogers, Coker, Roach.

Oconee Mill (Westminster, S.C.): Gerald Dempsey (coach), Betty Boggs, Mary Boggs, Barbara Carroll, Martha Carroll, Jane Chrisley, Christine McAllister, Cathryn McAllister, Frankie Isbell, Mary Massingale, Christine Rholetter.

Woodside Mill (Greenville, S.C.): Charles Couch (coach), Carlton Couch (coach), Mary Beasley, Lois Brookshire, Ruth Camp, Eunice Couch, Perrie Couch, Dora Dover, Barbara Foster, Maxine Hammett, Doris Holcombe, Jean Julian, Martha McLeod, Mary Tollison.

---———1955———---

Officers: Fred Snoddy (Greer, S.C.), President; Willie Wilbanks (Ware Shoals, S.C.), Vice President; Bruce Stroupe (Greenville, S.C.), Executive Secretary; Mrs. W.B. Mulligan (Greenville, S.C.), Acting Secretary; Horace Whitmire (Greenville, S.C.), Treasurer; Divver Hendrix (Greenville, S.C.), Assistant Treasurer.

Executive Committee: Ed Dickard (Greenville, S.C.), Milford Howard (Greer, S.C.), Sam Patton (Enka, N.C.), Clarence Thomas (Greenville, S.C.), Jack Reames (Abbeville, S.C.), Walter Lauter (Rossville, Ga.), Fred Johnson (Greenville, S.C.), S.R. DuBose (Whitmire, S.C.), Snow Kirby (Slater, S.C.), Jim Collier (Greenville, S.C.), J.D. Brown (Greenville, S.C.), Hugh Anderson (Greenville, S.C.), Leonard Muth (Pelzer, S.C.), W.A. Griffith (Seneca, S.C.).

CLASS A MEN

Pelzer Mill (Pelzer, S.C.), champions: Earl Wooten (coach), Randy Whaley, Bobby Roberts, Tom Scott, Bill Scott, Pete Harris, Frank Felts.

Monaghan Mill (Greenville, S.C.), runners-up: Ken Pittman (coach), Fig Newton, James Gowan, Bennie Brown, Neild Gordon, Everette Pigg, Willard Fowler, Bill Moody, Brice Kirkpatrick.

Piedmont Mill (Piedmont, S.C.), consolation winners: Curtis Terry (coach), Ernie Chambers, John Touhy, Truman Hill, Paul Nye, Lewis Howard, Kenneth Smith, Ben Rosenbloom, Douglas Stamps, Don Roper, Carroll Stone.

Peerless Woolen Mill (Rossville, Ga.): Walter Lauter (coach), Harold Hall (coach), John Alonso, Robert James, Joe McCullough, Pete Brown, Brownell Bryant, Ray Griffith, Bud Sloan, Robert Case, John Arney, Buddy Howell.

Dunean Mill (Greenville, S.C.): Ward Williams (coach), Bob Stowe, Don Ritter, Larry Ashley, Jim Slaughter, Alan Cox, Bomar Keller, Bobby Peek, Don Cox.

American Enka (Enka, N.C.): Claude Davis (coach), Sam Patton (coach), Edward Brinkley, Gus Colagerakis, Leroy Combs, Joe Conner, George Lancaster, James Neal, James Patton, Robert Saylor, Richard Sides, Deran Walters.

Union Bleachery (Greenville, S.C.): Charles Brooks (coach), Bill Moody (coach), Rodger Bishop, Charles Sizemore, Ronnie Knight, Thomas Lazar, Fred McClure, Jerry Robertson, Walter Robertson, David Smith, Houston Turner, Bruce Turner, Dix.

Victor Mill (Greer, S.C.): Hal Huey

(coach), Milford Howard, Leon Gravley, Carl Hust, Wayne Godfrey, Bob Campbell, Marvin Gregory, Emmett Patrick.

Class B Men

Beacon Mill (Swannanoa, N.C.), champions: George Thompson (coach), J.D. Hardin (coach), Ken Rudeen, Jim Johnson, Floyd Waldrop, Bud Harper, Ted Brown, Martin Hair, Dick Ramsey, Gerald Warren, Jack Brinkley, Larry Smith.

Brandon Mill (Greenville, S.C.), runners-up: Ray Wynn (coach), Fred McAbee Jr., George Buchanan, J.B. Friar, Lee Hall, Edward Key, Johnnie Arnold, Robert Paris, Eugene Seay, Pierce Powers.

Easley Mill (Easley, S.C.), consolation winners: Joe Anders (coach), Charles Bagwell, Courtney Heath, James Rogers, Harold Ensley, Joe Spearman, George McIntyre, James Campbell.

Calhoun Falls Mill (Calhoun Falls, S.C.): Densel Dockery (coach), Benny Spears (coach), Marvin Martin, William Ross, James Hilley, William Evans, Maxie Putman, Ralph Parnell, Marvin Burton, Charles Carlisle, Claude Herndon.

Anderson Mill (Anderson, S.C.): Ezra Embler (coach), Harold Brown, Fred Whitten, Bobby Fleming, Jimmie Smith, Thomas Bridges, Roy Bridges, Grady Sanders, Kenneth Bannister, Gerald Fleming.

Camperdown Mill (Greenville, S.C.): Charles Penland (coach), Charles Bartram, Charles Carter, James Johnson, Bobby Jones, Andy Long, Cecil Rollins, Jack Mintz, Kenneth Carter, Buddy Davidson, Mac Bruce.

Dunean Mill (Greenville, S.C.): Jim Slaughter (coach), LaVerne Holder, Billy Lollis, Ronnie Simpson, David Shook, Walter Bowers, Edward Manly, James Reid, Bill Roddy, Jack Kelley, Bill Mathis.

Joanna Mill (Joanna, S.C.): Johnny Moore (coach), Wayne Ginn (coach), George Merchant, James Clark, Charles Estes, Tommy Davis, Richard Moates, Homer Jacks, Darnell Johnson, Lester Long, Rudy McCarthy, Richard Willingham, Holder.

Julius Kayser & Co. (Liberty, S.C.): E.J. Grasso Sr. (coach), Johnny Raines, Samuel Payne, E.J. Grasso Jr., Jon Cook, J.C. Davis, Joe Baxter, Jimmy Campbell, Bobby Balcombe, Joe Jones, Ted Wood.

LaFrance Mill (Anderson, S.C.): Neal Hunnicutt (coach), Jack Leutwyler, Joe Stegall, Douglas Padgett, Bill Holcombe, Dallas Wilson, Cleo Martin, Olin Mullikin, Kenneth Smith, Furman Elrod.

Monaghan Mill (Greenville, S.C.): Fig Newton (coach), John Merck, Harold Fuller, Jimmy Bagwell, Jewel Major, James Gambrell, Harry Jones, Douglas Campbell, Charles Landreth, Griffith.

Pelzer Mill (Pelzer, S.C.): Leonard Muth (coach), Clifford Thomason, Bill Thomason, Johnny McCall, Bobby Southerland, Pete Edens, F.K. Yarborough, Bill Reaves, Carl Stegall, Harold Major, Bobby Ross.

Simpsonville Mill (Simpsonville, S.C.): Larry Coker Sr. (coach), Jack Long, Roger Cannady, William Smith, Odell Barbary, Gary Henderson, Dick Goodenough, Preston Barbary, Don Stokes, Tom Cabiness, Paul Hensley.

Southern Franklin Processing (Greenville, S.C.): Clarence Porter (coach), Gary Garrison, Tracy Roddy, Walter Moore, James McCullough, Bobby Fortune, James McCall, Richard Cooper, John Langston, Jimmy Garrett, Jerry Chapman.

Victor Mill (Greer, S.C.): Charles Hartsell (coach), Kenneth Godfrey, Leroy Wright, Millard Leonhardt, James Smith, Joe Lamb, Ray Jones, Andrew Cabiness, Ronald Burnett.

Class C Men

Piedmont Mill (Piedmont, S.C.), champions: Furman Foxx (coach), Curtis Terry (coach), Joe Hiott, Larry Patterson, Roger Dill, Jimmy Thompson, Charles Burden, John Lindley, Tommy Coker, Ray Fox, Milford Williams, Jerry Hooper.

Pelzer Mill #2 (Pelzer, S.C.), runners-up: J.B. Baker (coach), Marion Bannister, Michael Jordan, Jimmy Watson, Jackie Rogers, Thomas Lollis, Everette Cooper, Marshall Sargent, Douglas Harris, John Ross, Bill Wilson.

Easley Mill (Easley, S.C.), consolation winners: Joe Anders (coach), Ken Garrett, Billy Garrick, Keith Galloway, Julian Hiott, Harold Waldrop, Larry Bagwell, Larry Chandler, Joel Knoblitt, Eddie Ellison.

Belton Mill (Belton, S.C.): Leo Fisher (coach), Douglas Broome, Jody Snipes, Billy Dunlap, Zane King, Terry Martin, Frank Cason, Randolph Snipes, Jonathan Escoe, Jimmy Lowe, Furman Bannister.

American Spinning (Greenville, S.C.): Hoyt Smith (coach), Mack Massingale,

Michael Durham, Daniel Palmer, Bobby Owens, Fred Johnson, John Stacey, Jyles Phillips, James Gould, Glenn Durham, Leon Smith, Bill Neeley.

Apalache Mill (Greer, S.C.): Ralph Bogan (coach), Melvin Roper, Willie Brown, Larry Lister, Joseph Brisontine, Benny Atkins, Riley Beeks, James Garrett, Douglas Belue, Franklin Cox.

Brandon Mill (Greenville, S.C.): Pete McAbee (coach), Kenneth Gardner, Henry Freeman, Charles Morgan, Gary Hall, Luther Smith, Joel Turner, Jimmy Williams, Billy Howell, Ray Morgan, Jack Pierce, Corbin, Foster.

Camperdown Mill (Greenville, S.C.): Charles Whitaker (coach), Jack Anderson (coach), Edward DeLong, Bobby Hudson, Dallas Davis, Jimmy Amspacher, Roger Coln, Don Nelson, Newton Johnson, Jimmy Gresham, Jimmy Smith, Ted Brown.

Dunean Mill (Greenville, S.C.): Ward Williams (coach), Tommy Williams, James Brown, Harold Watson, Larry McClellan, Michael Long, Tommy Turner, Phil Henderson, Ronnie Russell, Jerry Compton, Jack Campbell, Brewer.

Greer Mill #1 (Greer, S.C.): Wayne Godfrey (coach), Ulysses Greene, Sheldon Roper, Fred Ellenburg, Douglas Greene, Wilson Ellenburg, Homer Rudisail, Allen Moore.

Judson Mill (Greenville, S.C.): M.S. Patton (coach), Baxton Boggs, Charles Wyke, Ronnie Irvin, Eddie Jester, Jimmy Kidd, Harold Morris, Eugene Shockley, Bobby Stewart, Coy Whitmire, Farmer.

Liberty Mill (Liberty, S.C.): Fred Powers (coach), Dale Martin, Wallace Lyda, David Garrison, Jimmy Garrison, Bob Herndon, Don Hitt, Billy Allgood, Bud Trammell, Paul Bowie III, Bowman.

Mills Mill (Greenville, S.C.): Harry Smith (coach), Fred Thompson (coach), James Ball, Lawrence Gray, Max Hoover, M.D. Thompson, Harold Lowery, Robert Skelton, Michael Massey, Charles Franks, Robert McCall.

Monaghan Mill (Greenville, S.C.): Thornwell Henson (coach), Ken Pittman (coach), Charles McKinney, Ervin Burdette, Jack Fuller, Ed Wilhoit, Charles Busbee, Larry Major, Gary Scism, Bill Evatt, Mike Ross, Louis Pittman.

Orr Mill (Anderson, S.C.): Robert Burriss (coach), Bobby Franks, Wayne Vassar, Melvin Aiken, Floyd Mackinson, Marshall Adams, Joe Tilley, Harold Smith, Gary Patterson, Kenneth Cantrell, Bennie Cox, Evatt.

Pelzer Mill #1 (Pelzer, S.C.): Leonard Muth (coach), Bill Chandler, David Waters, Donald Belt, Jerry Garner, Heyward Watson, Louie Davenport, Joe Ross, George Thomas, Roy Davenport, Bobby Mardis.

Renfrew Bleachery (Travelers Rest, S.C.): John McDowell (coach), Roy Foster (coach), Don Abbott, Franklin Murphy, Bobby Poole, Joe Steward, Jack Hayes, Charles Ivey, Lee Burns, Jerry Davis, Wayne Nix, Larry Foster.

Simpsonville Mill (Simpsonville, S.C.): Odell Barbary (coach), Donald James, William Cox, Preston Calvert, Troy Stokes, Jerry Thackston, John Marler, Larry Coker, John Alexander, Bruce Young, Wilton Brooks.

Union Bleachery (Greenville, S.C.): Wallace Turner (coach), John Robertson (coach), Jesse Brown, William Bryson, Anthony Hester, Jimmie Moore, Larry Robertson, Hugh Robertson, Calvin Rumler, Dennis Sides, Stanley Smith.

Lonsdale Mill (Seneca, S.C.): Jack Lindsay (coach), Tommy Reynolds, Donald Robinson, William Watson, Tommy Wade, Robert Lacey, Joel Perry, George Randlette, Gerald Gaillard, Larry Allsep, Buddy Land.

Victor Mill #1 (Greer, S.C.): Roy Livingston (coach), Donald Elders, Donald Owens, Robert Vaughn, Jack McKinney, James Coleman, Earl Cromer, Malcolm Stewart, Robert Gravley, Richard Gravley, Charlton Miller.

Victor Mill #2 (Greer, S.C.): Denny Owens (coach), Billy Allen, Steven Brown, Raymond Steadman, Donald Krause, Daniel Harvey, Marion Pittman, Joe Parrish, Billy Pittman.

Woodside Mill (Greenville, S.C.): James McDuffie (coach), Rodney Canup, Joe Julian, Joe Aiken, Michael Perry, Jerry Suddeth, Joe McLeod, James Solomon, Kenneth Swafford, Ralph Kay, Bobby Bryson.

Greenwood Mill (Greenwood, S.C.): Marshall Weaver Sr. (coach), R.A. Anderson, Jerry Bradberry, Walter Marshall Jr., George Schlock, Cecil Hagood, Ronald Barnette, Harry Herring, M.D. Weaver Jr., Donald Burnett, William Falls.

Glen Lowery Mill (Whitmire, S.C.): Jerry Roberts (mgr), June Raines, Gary Woods, Sherrill Dallas, Atlee Brown, Lou McMurray, Rolland Lackey, Rodney Jordan, Willie Johnson, Hugh Riser, Raymond Lawson, Brock.

Southern Textile Basketball Tournament Rosters — Appendix 1

CLASS A WOMEN

Pelzer Mill (Pelzer, S.C.), champions: Bobby Roberts (coach), Jean Rogers, Barbara Pittman, Bettina Revis, Harriett Hayes, Gwen Burgess, Sue Coker, Judith Coker, Betty Coker, Elaine Ellis, Barbara Rogers, Judy Davis, Patricia Revis, Grant.

Her Majesty (Mauldin, S.C.), runners-up: George Forrester (coach), Hattie Bagwell, Dottie Smith, Martha Corn, Doris Styles, Margaret Styles, Diamond Styles, Dorothy Darby, Ann Taylor, Doris Bramlett, Sara Watson, Charlotte Saxon, June Smith, Dolly Woods, Mullinax.

Easley Mill (Easley, S.C.), consolation winners: Joe Anders (coach), Sandra Stewart, Helen McGaha, Patsy Heath, Mary Hairston, Nellie Garrett, Patsy Garrett, Virginia Brown, Carolyn Hairston, Julia Poole.

Judson Mill (Greenville, S.C.): B.W. Stroupe (coach), Glenda Allison, Patsy Allison, Doris Bryant, Juanita Jones, Mary Kellett, Carolyn Kelly, Joanne Kelly, Ruth Laws, Jo Ann Shelton, Jackie Thomason, Catherine Upchurch, June Bryant.

Brandon Mill (Greenville, S.C.): Pete McAbee (coach), Janice McDonald, Clara Pittman, Doris Lawson, Patsy Pitts, Marcelle Cobb, June Nash, Willette Quinn, Joyce Wilson, Ann Murphy, Mary Medlin, Williams.

Dunean Mill (Greenville, S.C.): Ward Williams (coach), Nellie Grant, Alice Grant, Carol McMahan, Mary Shedd, Barbara Marshbanks, Ethel Pollard, Sybil Sewell, Janet Sewell, Tee Garrison, Dorothy Sewell, Reita Allison, Edwina Grant.

Monaghan Mill (Greenville, S.C.): Ken Pittman (coach), Louise Taylor, Euon Stansell, Frances Nixon, Sheila Scism, Gail Galloway, Pat Brazie, Patsy Harvell, Evelyn Bryant, Loretta Boone, Lois Barbare, Joyce Stancil.

Liberty Mill (Liberty, S.C.): W.A. Carr (coach), Roberta Bowman, Roberta Kitchin, Harriet Kitchin, Laura McWhorter, Margaret Davis, Carol Gilstrap, Barbara Crowe, Linda Gilstrap, Martha Gravley, Jean Wood, Pat Leatherwood, Jimmie LaBoone.

Lonsdale Mill (Seneca, S.C.): W.A. Griffith (coach), Jo Dawkins, Norma Turner, Ova Poole, Barbara Stephens, Ruth Reynolds, Betty Towe, Hattie Powell, Winona Addis, Brenda Addis, Sue Winchester, Katie Land, Becky Powell.

Woodside Mill (Greenville, S.C.): James McDuffie (coach), Perrie Couch, Margaret Wilson, Sandra Yeargin, Barbara Foster, Margaret Couch, Carolyn Yeargin, Barbara Black, Mary Tollison, Doris Holcombe, Lois Brookshire, Gail Couch, Mary Gillespie.

1956

Officers: Willie Wilbanks (Ware Shoals, S.C.), President; Horace Whitmire (Greenville, S.C.), Vice President, Ass't Treasurer; Bruce Stroupe (Greenville, S.C.), Executive Secretary; Mrs. W.B. Mulligan (Greenville, S.C.), Acting Secretary; Divver Hendrix (Greenville, S.C.), Treasurer.

Executive Committee: Ed Dickard (Greenville, S.C.), J.B. Owens (Easley, S.C.), Sam Patton (Enka, N.C.), Clarence Thomas (Greenville, S.C.), Jack Reames (Abbeville, S.C.), Walter Lauter (Rossville, Ga.), Fred Johnson (Greenville, S.C.), S.R. DuBose (Whitmire, S.C.), J.D. Hardin (Swannanoa, N.C.), Jim Collier (Greenville, S.C.), J.D. Brown (Greenville, S.C.), Hugh Anderson (Greenville, S.C.), Leonard Muth (Pelzer, S.C.), W.A. Griffith (Seneca, S.C.), Fred Snoddy (Greer, S.C.), Ward Williams (Greenville, S.C.), Ray Wynn (Greenville, S.C.).

OPEN DIVISION

Dunean Mill (Greenville, S.C.), champions: Ward Williams (coach), Larry Ashley, Tex Ritter, Bob Stowe, Jim Slaughter, Joe Smith, Alan Cox, Bomar Keller, Ralph Moore, Don Cox.

American Enka (Enka, N.C.), runners-up: Claude Davis (coach), Sam Patton (coach), Gus Colagerakis, Joe Conner, George Lancaster, Ellerbe Neal, Jim Patton, Ronald Rogers, Walter Saylor, Dick Sides, Joe Volrath, Deran Walters.

Monaghan Mill (Greenville, S.C.), consolation winners: Ken Pittman (coach), Morris Newton, James Gowan, Benny Brown, Jack League, Francis Brothers, Randy Whaley, Jack Robinson, Eddie Edwards, Willard Fowler, Bobby Roberts, Harry Jones.

Paty Lumber Co. (Johnson City, Tenn.): Jim Seward (coach), Jack Maxey, Bob Paynter, Joe Treadway, Carl Gouge, Harold Stout, Hobart Powell, John Shanks, John Seward, Willis Kimbro, Herb Weaver, Farrell Bowman.

Piedmont Mill (Piedmont, S.C.): Curtis Terry (coach), Earl Wooten, Paul Nye, Robert

Wilson, Ernie Chambers, Lewis Howard, Robert Burgess, James Smith, Robert Hooper, Jimmy Hedden, Don Roper.

Victor Mill (Greer, S.C.): Hal Huey (coach), Marvin Gregory, Wayne Godfrey, Harold Haynie, Carl Hust, Ken Tankersley, Leon Gravley, Bob Campbell, Buck Hallman, Marilyn Stroud.

CLASS B MEN

Anderson Mill (Anderson, S.C.), champions: Ronnie Davis (coach), Rufus Byce (coach), Pete Carlisle, Harold Brown, Jimmy Embler, Grady Sanders, Gerald Fleming, Kenneth Bannister, Bobby Fleming, Thomas Davis, Jimmy Smith, Ezra Embler.

American Spinning (Greenville, S.C.), runners-up: Hoyt Smith (coach), Joseph Bates, Ralph Durham, Charles Finley, Danny Fowler, Edgar Harbin Jr., Charles Hendricks, Johnny Hunnicutt, Bill Neely, Mack Massingale, Jack Morgan.

Easley Mill (Easley, S.C.), consolation winners: Joe Anders (coach), Hal Ensley, Courtney Heath, Larry Bagwell, Verlon McEntyre, James Rogers, Charles Bagwell, Ken Garrett, Ken Lesley, Waymon Knox.

Slater Mill (Slater, S.C.): Fred Cox Jr. (coach), James Payne, Bobby Williams, Raymond Payne, Richards Stephenson, William Lell, Bobby Johnson, Joe Smith, Thomas Cox, Edward Kirk Jr., William Stephenson.

Brandon Mill (Greenville, S.C.): James Loftis (coach), Eddie Cannon, Fred McAbee Jr., George Buchanan, Bobby Powers, Pierce Powers, J.D. Williamson Jr., Edward Key, Buddy Helton, Robert Paris, Eugene Seay.

Calhoun Falls Mill (Calhoun Falls, S.C.): Densel Dockery (coach), Joe Loftis (coach), William Evans, Maxie Putman, James Hilley, Arthur Burdette, Ralph Parnell, Eddie Cannon, Lloyd Sammons, Franklin McConnell, Ray Waters, Ford Waldrop.

Camperdown Mill (Greenville, S.C.): Sydney Bruce Jr. (coach), Charles Phillips (coach), Otto Long, James Johnson, Charles Davis, James Irvin, Henry Wilburn, Willard Batson, Cecil Rollins, Kenneth Carter, William Davidson, Zeb Roberts, Riddle.

Clinton Mill (Clinton, S.C.): Truman Owens (coach), Earl Satterfield, Charles Foster, Ransome Rauton, James Braswell, Charles Oxner, James Owens, Sam Owens, Alvin Hampton, Charles Leatherwood, Joe Lark, Satterfield.

Dunean Mill (Greenville, S.C.): Jim Slaughter (coach), Bobby Grant, Jimmy Brown, Charles Carpenter, LaVerne Holder, Frank Lollis, Billy Lollis, Jack Kelly, Bobby Parker, James Reid, Eddie Bridges, Alvin LaBoone, Simpson, Greene, Tracy Roddy.

Greer Mill (Greer, S.C.): Wayne Godfrey (coach), Lewis Knighton, Arnold Campbell, James Shockley, Roger Stepp, Hugh Crain, James McAbee, Donald Dean, Sammy Arledge, Ernie Ellenburg.

Joanna Mill (Joanna, S.C.): Johnny Moore (coach), Tommy O'Shields (coach), Richard Motes, Darrell Johnson, Gary Bodie, Robert Hair, James Clark, Jimmie Kirby, William Tinsley, Charles Estes, George Merchant, William Braswell.

LaFrance Mill (Anderson, S.C.): Neal Hunnicutt (coach), Cleo Martin, Richard Morgan, Olin Mullikin, Walter Holcombe Jr., Furman Elrod, William Holcombe, Dallas Wilson, Blake Griffith, Alvin Clark.

Liberty Mill (Liberty, S.C.): Fred Powers (coach), Clyde Bowman, Donnie Garrison, David Garrison, Jimmy Cantrell, Buddy Shook, George Cantrell, Wallace Lyda, Jimmy Garrison, Olin Moore.

Lyman Mill (Lyman, S.C.): M.E. Cagle (coach), Larry Gresham (coach), Derrell Medlock, Lawrence Eubanks, James Hughes, Leon Eubanks, Benjamin Davis, James Smith, Alan Beach, William Eubanks, Travis Taylor, Harold Eubanks.

Monaghan Mill (Greenville, S.C.): Fig Newton (coach), Hansen Griffith (coach), Franklin Haney, Edward Wilhoit, Dennis Brookshire, Oscar McCombs, Billy Evatt, John Merck, Harold Fuller, Douglas Campbell, Pittman, Gambrell.

Fiberglas (Anderson, S.C.): R.K. Coolbough (coach), William Lother, George Wilson, Alvin Blume, Harold Smith, Johnnie Wardlaw, Larry Moore, Alvin Parks, William Childs, Jimmie Simmons, William Brown.

Pelzer Mill (Pelzer, S.C.): Leonard Muth (coach), Bobby Ross, Dot Reeves, Grady Cooley, James Thomason, George Thomas, Bobby Southerland, Carl Stegall, Eddie Copeland, Joe Ross, Harold Major.

Piedmont Mill (Piedmont, S.C.): Jerry Ayers (coach), Harry Stamps, Charles Weisner, Larry Patterson, Roger Dill, Ray Foxx, Joe Hiott, Jerry Hooper, Carroll Emery, Charles Blackston.

Southern Textile Basketball Tournament Rosters Appendix 1 199

Southern Franklin Processing (Greenville, S.C.): Clarence Porter (coach), Bobby Sexton, Bobbie Fortune, Robert McCall, Tracy Roddy, Jimmy Garrett, Richard Cooper, Harold Moore, John Langston, Jerry McNeely.

Union Bleachery (Greenville, S.C.): W.A. Bishop Jr. (coach), James Clevenger, Donald Brookshire, Douglas Blackwell, Davis Smith, Robert Garren, Marlin Stroud, Jerry Robertson, Clyde Bridwell, John Robertson.

Victor Mill (Greer, S.C.): Fred Snoddy (coach), Joseph Lamb, Donald Elder, James Cox, John Caldwell, Douglas Garren, Kenneth Turner, Charles Crocker, Bobby Lemmons, Rudy Godfrey, Wilburn Owens Jr.

Poe Mill (Greenville, S.C.): Ansel Bridwell (coach), Thomas Foy, William Davis, Maxie Dill, Philip Hughes, Charles Bishop, Russell Westmoreland, Troy Reeves, Jack Vaughn, Joe Spearman.

Simpsonville Mill (Simpsonville, S.C.): Bill Moody (coach), Troy Stokes, Gary Henderson, W.T. Wooten, Ernest Goodenough, Jack Long, Odell Barbary, Preston Calvert, Roger Cannady, Wilton Brooks, Jerry Thackston.

CLASS C MEN

Easley Mill (Easley, S.C.), champions: Joe Anders (coach), Putnam (coach), Julian Hiott, Gary King, Boyce Brooks, Johnny Skinner, Marion Owens, Benny Galloway, Harold Waldrop, Rodney Brown.

Lonsdale Mill (Seneca, S.C.), runners-up: Roy McCurry (coach), Jack Lindsay (coach), Tommy Reynolds, Roger Tippett, Dubby Robinson, Larry Allsep, Joel Perry, Thomas Martin, Tony Elliott, Dewey Anderson, Mickey Donald.

Monaghan Mill (Greenville, S.C.), consolation winners: Thronwell Henson (coach), J.L. Sumner (coach), Joe Julian, Charles Busbee, Larry Major, Jimmy Holden, Ervin Burdette, Leland Evatt, Tommy Fulbright, Charles McKinney, Joe Hooper, Harold Morris.

Dunean Mill (Greenville, S.C.): Ward Williams (coach), Michael Long, Phillip Henderson, Tommy Williams, Jerry Compton, James Brewer, Tommy Turner, Gaines Smith, Jimmy Gentry, Thomas Stroud, Tommy Vickery.

Camperdown Mill (Greenville, S.C.): Charles Whitaker (coach), Dallas Davis, James Amspacher, Mac Johnson, Billy Holden, Bobby Hudson, Clifton Egan, Jimmy Gresham, Jimmy Smith, Michael Davis, Roger Coin, Willard Batson.

Greer Mill #1 (Greer, S.C.): Bob Campbell (coach), Wilson Ellenburg, Allen Moore, Homer Rudisail, Douglas Greene, Fred Ellenburg, Harold Durham, Mickey Flynn, Donald Black, Michael McCallister, Kenneth Littlefield.

Greer Mill #2 (Greer, S.C.): Wayne Godfrey (coach), Ray Brewton, Ulysses Greene, Gary Long, Keith Wilson, Billy Moore, Douglas Brown, Leslie Roper, Bruce Stepp, Raymond Steadman, Ronald McCallister.

Apalache Mill (Greer, S.C.): Ralph Bogan (coach), Melvin Roper, Riley Beeks, Darrell Blackwell, Michael Smith, Joe Brisontine, Benny Atkins.

Belton Mill (Belton, S.C.): Leo Fisher (coach), Billy Dunlap, Doug Broome, Joda Snipes, Doyle Martin, Gary Patterson, J.L. Lowe, Zane King, Furman Bannister, Bob Herd, Frank Cason.

Brandon Mill (Greenville, S.C.): Tom Hall (coach), Garrell Freeman, Charles Hooper, Luther Smith, Gary Hall, Jimmy Williams, Jack Corbin, Charles Foster, Walter Reeves Jr., Charles Morgan.

Judson Mill (Greenville, S.C.): Mack Patton (coach), Wilton Lee, Ronnie Irvin, James Dunn, Coy Whitmire, Charles Weems, Heyward Brissie, Baxton Boggs, Charles Page, Billy Gaines, Kidd, Rollins.

Liberty Mill (Liberty, S.C.): Fred Powers (coach), Donnie Hitt, Dale Martin, Bob Herndon, Bobby Bowman, Paul Bowie III, Phillip Crotwell, Mickey Hitt, George Goldsmith.

Pelzer Mill #1 (Pelzer, S.C.): Leonard Muth (coach), Jerry Garner, David Waters, Roy Davenport, Don Thomas, Dickie Sanders, Steve Geddens, William Prickett, Ray Abberson, Kenneth Cooley, Johnny Shaw.

Pelzer Mill #2 (Pelzer, S.C.): Bobby Roberts (coach), Inky Cooper, Mike Jordan, John Ross, Doug Harris, Tommy Lollis, Don Gilmer, Gary Geddens, Jimmy Boyce, Marion Bannister, Jackie Rogers, Donald Brady, Buddy Snipes.

Union Bleachery (Greenville, S.C.): Bill Moody (coach), Robert Crumley, Larry Robertson, Jess Brown, Dennis Sides, William Brooks, Anthony Hester, Freddie Rumler, Stanley Smith, Jimmie Moore, Morris Evington.

Victor Mill (Greer, S.C.): Donald Owens, Robert Vaughn, Jack McKinney, Donald Krause, Stephen Brown, Billy Pittman, Daniel

Harvey, Melvin Rice, Malcolm Stewart, Billy Allen.

Renfrew Bleachery (Travelers Rest, S.C.): Larry Foster, Clark, Nix, Abbott, Murphy, Poole, Burns, Tankersley, Johnson, Robertson.

Class A Women

Hanes Hosiery Mill (Winston-Salem, N.C.), champions: Eckie Jordan (coach), Cynthia Bowers, Maude Fulp, Pearl Gaither, Bonnie Hobson, Ulala Mitchell, Rosa Nichols, Louise Sink, Phyllis Snipes, Wanda Harrelson.

Pelzer Mill (Pelzer, S.C.), runners-up: Miss Huggans (coach), Elaine Ellis, Barbara Pittman, Bettina Revis, Patricia Revis, Barbara Rogers, Barbara Harris, Brenda Harris, Iris Greer, Vera Davis, Judith Coker, Jean Rogers, Sue Woodson.

Liberty Mill (Liberty, S.C.), consolation winners: Fred Powers (coach), Linda Gilstrap, Barbara Crowe, Martha Gravely, Roberta Bowman, Harriett Kitchen, Laura McWhorter, Jean Wood, Laura Sullins, Judy Smith, Roberta Kitchen, Marlene Gilstrap, Ladd.

Judson Mill (Greenville, S.C.): B.W. Stroupe (coach), Nora Jones, Gwen Tyler, Joanne Kelley, Judy Brown, Carolyn Kelly, Doris Bryant, Carol Bryant, Barbara Brown, Doris Holcombe, Ruth Wofford, Martha Elder.

Beacon Mill (Swannanoa, N.C.): J.D. Hardin (coach), Barbara Sircy, Peggy Hare, Elsie Griffin, Betty Stroupe, Alma Balleu, Edna Ambrose, Peggy Gantt, Patsy Brown, Judie Ellis, Hope Wilson, Carolyn Fox, Wanda Cody.

Greer Mill (Greer, S.C.): Wayne Godfrey (coach), Ellen Long, Kay Hartsell, Betty Wier, Sara Huff, Nancy Hitt, Montez Greene, Patsy Gowan, Jo Staddard, Frankie Barton, Barbara Blackwell, Laurice Pruitt, Martha Rollins.

Joanna Mill (Joanna, S.C.): Johnny Moore (coach), Charles Force (coach), Betty Bridges, Louise Force, Gwen Price, Bobbie Bridges, Lillie Franklin, Evelyn Motes, Frances Davenport, Ellen Epting, Joanne Flow, Judith Tucker, Shirley Merchant, Patricia Wise, Mildred Benson.

Fiberglas (Anderson, S.C.): R.K. Coolbough (coach), Claudene Massey, Sue Bonds, Ninnetta Spearman, Betty Barnes, Delma Bradshaw, Hazel Gable, Bobbie Sokol, Jimmie Richardson, Claudia Whitten, Bobbie Evans, Connie Vermillion, Curtis Clinkscales, Stamps.

Slater Mill (Slater, S.C.): Snow Kirby (coach), Mally Cooper, Judy Cox, Lucille Collins, Priscilla Wright, Bobby Shirley, Carolyeen Cole, Nora Nelson, Barbara Thornton, Mary Roper, Ann Cooper, Mary McMakin, Linda Pace.

Lonsdale Mill (Seneca, S.C.): Tommy Poole (coach), Jack Lindsay (coach), Marcia Kelly, Ova Poole, Johelen Dawkins, Sue Winchester, Edna Gibson, Barbara Wade, Brenda Addis, Winona Addis, Jeanette Lee, Norma Miller, Hattie Powell, Mary Davis.

1957

Officers: Willie Wilbanks (Ware Shoals, S.C.), President; Horace Whitmire (Greenville, S.C.), Vice President; Bruce Stroupe (Greenville, S.C.), Executive Secretary; Jim Collier (Greenville, S.C.), Ass't Executive Secretary; Mrs. W.B. Mulligan (Greenville, S.C.), Acting Secretary; Divver Hendrix (Greenville, S.C.), Treasurer.

Executive Committee: Ed Dickard (Greenville, S.C.), Sam Patton (Enka, N.C.), Clarence Thomas (Greenville, S.C.), Jack Reames (Abbeville, S.C.), Walter Lauter (Rossville, Ga.), Fred Johnson (Greenville, S.C.), S.R. DuBose (Whitmire, S.C.), J.D. Hardin (Swannanoa, N.C.), J.D. Brown (Greenville, S.C.), Leonard Muth (Pelzer, S.C.), Fred Snoddy (Greer, S.C.), Ward Williams (Greenville, S.C.), W.H. Embler (Anderson, S.C.), John Mullikin (Piedmont, S.C.), Jack Lindsay (Seneca, S.C.), Johnny Moore (Joanna, S.C.), Fred Powers (Liberty, S.C.), Lloyd McAbee (Greenville, S.C.).

Class A Men

American Enka (Enka, N.C.), champions: Sam Patton (coach), M.L. Beasley, Gus Colagerakis, Joe Conner, George Lancaster, Ellerbe Neal, Ronald Rogers, Richard Sides, Joe Ward.

Piedmont Mill (Piedmont, S.C.), runners-up: Pete Beasley (coach), Larry Patterson, Earl Wooten, Ken Smith, Bob Hooper, Ernie Chambers, Paul Nye, Lewis Howard, Don Roper, Carroll Stone, Jim Slaughter.

Greer Mill (Greer, S.C.), consolation winners: Roy Beach (coach), W.S. Huff (coach), Monroe Gravley, James Moore, Jerry Burgess, Harold Huey, Robert Campbell, Noble Vaughn, Wayne Godfrey.

Southern Textile Basketball Tournament Rosters   Appendix 1   201

Dunean Mill (Greenville, S.C.): Ward Williams (coach), Larry Ashley, Don Ritter, Bob Stowe, Bobby Grant, Bomar Keller, David Putman, Bill Roddy.

Monaghan Mill (Greenville, S.C.): Nathan Nichols (coach), Ken Pittman (coach), James Gowan, Hanson Griffith, Willard Fowler, Bennie Brown, Tracy Roddy, Fig Newton, James Gambrell, Mike Ross.

CLASS B MEN

Courtaulds Inc. (Mobile, Ala.), champions: Cecil Dickey (coach), James McAdams, Gene Allen, Edward Sheffield, Gary Mugnier, Billy Williams, Bill Robinson, Billy McCombs, Tommy Drake, Francis Lott.

Russell Manufacturing (Alexander City, Ala.), runners-up: Vercho Carter (coach), Charlet Baitey, Rex Ficquette, James Yates, Doyt Alford, Bobby Bailey, Emory Windsor, Robert Ray, Charles Lloyd, Donald Pritchard, Carlton Scott.

Judson Mill (Greenville, S.C.), consolation winners: Mack Patton (coach), Joe Sellers, Harold Morris, William Snelson, Jack Tollison, Bobby Pridmore, Bruce Stroupe, Harold Holbrook, Charlie Rogers.

Joanna Mill (Joanna, S.C.): Johnny Moore (coach), Charles Force (coach), Darrell Johnson, G.W. Merchant, Richard Motes, Bobby Hair, Martin Gwen, Jim Kirby, Sam Owens, Truman Owens, Jimmy Braswell, Jerry Armstrong.

Anderson Mill (Anderson, S.C.): Morris Embler (coach), Rufus Byce (coach), Ezra Embler, Grady Sanders, Newlan Sanders, Jimmy Smith, Bobby Fleming, Roy Bridges, Kenneth Bannister, T.E. Davis, Walter Cooper, Raymond Hopkins.

American Spinning (Greenville, S.C.): Leo Birnie (coach), Danny Fowler, Frank Haight, Bill Neely, Riley Cothran, Charles Hendrix, Charles Finley, Ed Harbin, Hoyt Smith, Jimmie Painter, Gary McGueen.

Apalache Mill (Greer, S.C.): Ralph Bogan (coach), Billy Fuller, Buddy Rogers, James Mills, Melvin Roper, Joe Brisontine, Claude Cartee, David Hill, Charles Cole, Ruchard Justice.

Brandon Mill (Greenville, S.C.): Louis Clary (coach), Eugene Seay, Bobby Powers, Fred McAbee, John Buchanan, Bobby Parris, Pierce Powers, Thomas Hall, Eddie Cannon, Buddy Helton, Bobby Helton.

Calhoun Falls Mill (Calhoun Falls, S.C.): Densel Dockery (coach), Bobby Chrisley (coach), Fred Ross, Arthur Burdette, Ralph Parnell, F.R. McConnell, Walter Hilley, William Evans, Marion Martin, Claude Thornton, Wilton Ross.

Dunean Mill (Greenville, S.C.): Frank Lollis (coach), Tommy Turner, Billy Lollis, Alvin LaBoone, Bobby Parker, Jack Kelly, Joe Granger, Herbert Dodson, Wayne Ragsdale, Carl Greene.

Easley Mill (Easley, S.C.): Joe Anders (coach), Courtney Heath, Larry Bagwell, Julian Hiott, William Garrick, Dennis Atkinson, Harold Ensley, Charles Bagwell, Benny Galloway, Ken Garrett, Verlorn McEntyre.

Fiberglas (Anderson, S.C.): Melvin Robinson (coach), Ray Blume, Clyde Childs, Jimmy Lowe, Larry Moore, Delbert Moorhead, Leroy Parnell, Luther Rhodes, Curtis Wilson, Ross Overman, Hugh Humphries, Hancock.

Greer Mill (Greer, S.C.): Hugh Crain, Lewis Knighton, Donald Black, Arnold Campbell, Samuel Arledge, Ernie Ellenburg, Wilson Ellenburg, Brown, Rudisail.

LaFrance Mill (Anderson, S.C.): Neal Hunnicutt (coach), Furman Elrod, Olin Mullikin, William Holcombe, Benny Cox, Cleo Martin, Blake Griffith, Alvin Clark, Donnie Garrison, Richard Morgan, Dallas Wilson.

Piedmont Mill (Piedmont, S.C.): David Rampey (coach), Ray Foxx, Jerry Weisner, Bud Evans, Doug Emery, Carroll Emery, Ronald Davis, J.D. Hunnicutt, Troy Evans, Bradley Wallace, Fred Pruitt.

Liberty Mill (Liberty, S.C.): Fred Powers (coach), David Garrison, Clyde Bowman, Bill Yarborough, James Lewis, Bobby Morris, Charles Burden, Furman Taylor, Donnie Hitt, Walter McJunkin.

Monaghan Mill (Greenville, S.C.): James Bagwell, Louis Pittman, Dennis Brookshire, Kenneth Hudgens, Johnny Haney, Jimmy Holden, Charles Busbee, Oscar McCombs, Doug Campbell, John Merck, Roddy.

Pelzer Mill (Pelzer, S.C.): Leonard Muth (coach), George Thomas, Bill Thomason, James Thomason, Jerry Garner, Doug Harris, Grady Cooley, Joe Garrett, Bobby Southerland, Harold Roper, Harold Major.

Poe Mill (Greenville, S.C.): Ansel Bridwell (coach), Thomas Foy, Wesley Wicker, Roger Dill, Charles Landreth, Russell Westmorland, Troy Reese, Jack Vaughn, Charles Bishop, Maxie Dill, Michael Burnett.

Slater Mill (Slater, S.C.): Snow Kirby (coach), Billy Farmer, Bruce Farmer, R.C. Stephenson, Kenneth Hester, Joe Smith, Thomas Cox, Bobby Williams, Jimmie Lell, Dennis Garrett, Edward Kirby Jr.

Southern Franklin Processing (Greenville, S.C.): Franklin Langston (coach), Jimmy Marler (ass't coach), Harold Moore, Bill Massey, Bobby Fortune, Jerry McNeely, Jimmy McCall, Buddy McCall, J.D. Landreth, Pete Rollins, Bobby Sexton, Charles Raines.

Union Bleachery (Greenville, S.C.): Booty Bishop (coach), Charles Carter, Bruce Turner, Cecil Hickman, James Needham, John Robertson, David Smith, Donald Brookshire, Thomas Tezar, Charles Sizemore, Anthony Hester, W. Robertson.

Lonsdale Mill (Seneca, S.C.): Roy McCurry (coach), Jack Lindsay (coach), Tommy Poole, Larry Allsep, Edward Alexander, George Randlett, J.R. Brown, Joel Perry, Tommy Reynolds, Dubby Robinson, Charles Stancil, Pat Williams.

Victor Mill (Greer, S.C.): Fred Snoddy (coach), Douglas Garren, John Caldwell, Millard Leonhardt, Marvin Crow, Dickey Gravley, Kenneth Turner, Kenneth Hawkins, Roland Lee, Bobby Gravley.

Woodside Mill (Greenville, S.C.): Jim McDuffie (coach), Carl Grogan, John Haney, Bobby Nelson, Billy Hines, Joe McConnell, Rodney Griffith, Milward Griffith, Harold Limbaugh, Eddie White.

CLASS C MEN

Dunean Mill (Greenville, S.C.), champions: Ward Williams (coach), Dean Harvell, Ronald Russell, Tommy McFarland, Jerry Compton, Ricky Duncan, Sammy Ramsey, Jimmy Gentry, Tommy Williams, Mickey Long, Mickey Massey.

Victor Mill (Greer, S.C.), runners-up: Fred Snoddy (coach), Billy Allen, Dan Harvey, Don Krouse, Steve Brown, Jack Lister, Jack McKinney, Melvin Rice, Tony Tipton, Charleton Miller.

Brandon Mill (Greenville, S.C.), consolation winner: Pete McAbee (coach), Jimmy Porterfield, Ronald Land, Luther Smith, Harold Smith, Gary Hall, Charles Foster, Michael McDonald.

Union Bleachery (Greenville, S.C.): John Robertson (coach), Harold Green (coach), Mickey Duncan, Tim Brown, Bill Brooks, Gray Bradley, Jimmy Moore, Dennie Sides, Bill Batson, Fred Rumler, Carlton Chandler.

American Spinning (Greenville, S.C.): Ralph Maga (coach), Leo Birnie (coach), Michael Durham, Giles Phillips, Dean Holtzclaw, Marion McCall, Allen Sprouse, Harold McGaha, Dan Moore, Freddy Johnson, Gordon Seay, Bill Langley.

LaFrance Mill (Anderson, S.C.): Donnie Garrison (coach), Robby Martin, Johnny Medlock, Jesse Medlock, Jimmy Kay, Roderick Terry, Tommy Garrison, Gareth Scott, Larry Nash, Preston Gentry, Clinton Morgan.

Belton Mill (Belton, S.C.): Leo Fisher (coach), Marvin Allred, David Escoe, Jordan Snipes, James Herd, Charles Haggard, James Lollis, Thurman Elgin, Charles Moore Jr., Stephen Foster, Clayton, McKown, Dickert.

Liberty Mill (Liberty, S.C.): Fred Powers (coach), Dale Martin, Paul Bowie III, Philip Crotwell, Joe Lesley, George Goldsmith, Calvin Bryant, Mickey Hitt.

Mills Mill (Greenville, S.C.): Henry Giles (coach), Michael Massey, Charles Franks, James Ball, Roy Garrett, Ronald McGarity, David Porter, Carol Waldrop, Gerald Walker, Allen Patterson, Richard Kohn.

Monaghan Mill (Greenville, S.C.): Thorn Henson (coach), Harold Green (coach), Ervin Burdette, Joe Hooper, Joe Land, Tommy Fulbright, Raymond Gosnell, James Gould, Gordon Brown, Warner Wyatt, Jimmy Tucker, William Black.

Renfrew Bleachery (Travelers Rest, S.C.): Charles Hart (coach), Franklin Murphy, Lee Burns, H. Tankersley Jr., Darvin Hood, Raymond Johnson, Gary Duncan, Bobby Poole, Wayne Nix, Gilreath, Batson.

Easley Mill (Easley, S.C.): Coon Hendrix (coach), Gary King, Johnny Skinner, Troy Suddeth, Robert Couch, Donnie McCoy, Boyce Brooks, Bing Day, Dennis Dalton, Mack Pace.

Slater Mill (Slater, S.C.): Snow Kirby (coach), Aubrey Kirby, Albert Camden, Alton Canham, David Sprouse, James Buchanan, James Wilson, Robert Capps, Jimmy Wilson, Robert Addington.

Greer Mill (Greer, S.C.): Leon Gravley (coach), U.M. Greene Jr., Melvin Redd, James Payne, M.H. McCallister, Douglas Brown, Bruce Stepp, Douglas Greene, Gerald Wilson, Fred Ellenburg, Mitchell Flynn, Brewton.

Judson Mill (Greenville, S.C.): Bill Snelson (coach), Ronnie Irvin, James Dunn, William

Lee, Don Abee, Billy Gaines, Eugene Shockley, Robert Wike, Harold Davis, Heyward Brissey, Jimmy Kidd.

Pelzer Mill (Pelzer, S.C.): Bobby Roberts (coach), Everette Cooper, Gary Geddens, Michael Jordan, Don Helms, Don Gilmer, Robert Brown, Earle Mimms, Dickie Chapman, Billy Prickett, Donald Brady.

Woodside Mill (Greenville, S.C.): Jim McDuffie (coach), James Ware, William Griffith, Kenneth Fowler, Charles Phillips, James Carter, Don Nelson, Lee Aiken, Robert Crimley, Jerry Wynn, Wilton Lee.

CLASS A WOMEN

Fiberglas (Anderson, S.C.), champions: Charles Storm (coach), Lewis Acker (coach), Betty Barnes, Net Spearman, Betty Rowland, Vera Stamps, Dot Mullinax, Fredda Acker, Doris Simpson, Barbara Gentry, Betty Bale, Norma Hancock, Patsy Latham, Shelley Pryor.

Joanna Mill (Joanna, S.C.), runners-up: Johnny Moore (coach), Frances Davenport, Gwen Price, Lil Franklin, Louise Force, Joan Flow, Gloria Pitts, Ellen Epting, Ann Workman, Evelyn Motes, Nancy Pitts, Thelma Crolley, Nadine Bridges, Shirley Merchant.

Lonsdale Mill (Seneca, S.C.), consolation winners: Roy McCurry (coach), Jack Lindsay (coach), Winona Addis, Hattie Powell, Beverly Dooley, Brenda Addis, Willa Sosebee, Jo Dawkins, Norma Miller, Doris Miller, Ruth McDaniels, LaRue Hamilton, Mary Foster, Ova Poole.

Slater Mill (Slater, S.C.): Doots Wright (coach), Nora Nelson, Mary Thacker, Priscilla Wright, Jackie Clary, Helen Tucker, Sara Epps, Ann Cooper, Mally Cooper, Judy Cox, Martha Robinson, Patsy Tilley, Barbara Thornton, Greer.

Beacon Mill (Swannanoa, N.C.): J.D. Hardin (coach), Peggy Hare, Glenda Clark, Elsie Norris, Patricia Israel, Peggy Gantt, Shelley Jones, Lenora Padgham, Johnsie Gibbs, Alma Ballew, Laura Smith, Myrna Barlett, Betty Camofield.

Judson Mill (Greenville, S.C.): B.W. Stroupe (coach), Doris Bryant, Anne McSweeney, Evangeline Elder, Margaret Kinney, Jacqueline Corbin, Priscilla Tyner, Vaughn De Tyner, Doris Holcombe, Marilyn Holcombe, Marie Greer, June Nash, June Johnson.

Easley Mill (Easley, S.C.): Alvin Simpson (coach), Laura Hayes, Patsy Rackley, Jackie Rogers, Irene James, Lucy McGaha, Ann Spearman, Myra Putman, Nellie Garrett, Carolyn Hairston, Mary Hudson, Linda Stewart, Thompson, Barnes.

Liberty Mill (Liberty, S.C.): Fred Powers (coach), Roberta Bowman, Harriett Kitchen, Leatrice Powers, Barbara Crowe, Martha Gravely, Laura Sullens, Judy Smith, Linda Gilstrap, Marlene Gilstrap, Carol Littleton, Geraldine Ladd, Laura McWhorter.

Greer Mill (Greer, S.C.): Leon Gravley (coach), Frankie Barton, Jo Stoddard, Doris Justice, Jerry Wood, Ellen Long, Lucille Pittman, Ethelyn Burnett, Donna Jones, Judith Cox, Montez Greene, Norma Lister, Margaret Rowland.

Pelzer Mill (Pelzer, S.C.): Miss Laws (coach), Barbara Harris, Judith Coker, Elaine Ellis, Cecile Wooten, Brenda Harris, Barbara Rogers, Iris Greer, Ellen Trotter, Wanda Watson, Mary Thompson, Lonita Taylor, Katie Jeanes.

Her Majesty (Mauldin, S.C.): Doris Bramlette, Carol King, Doris Styles, Hattie Bagwell, Charlotte Saxon, Sara Watson, Mildred Styles, Jane Barton, Virginia Bagwell, June Smith, Dolly Woods.

——— 1958 ———

Officers: Willie Wilbanks (Ware Shoals, S.C.), President; Divver Hendrix (Greenville, S.C.), Vice President, Treasurer; Bruce Stroupe (Greenville, S.C.), Executive Secretary; Jim Collier (Greenville, S.C.), Ass't Executive Secretary; Mrs. W.B. Mulligan (Greenville, S.C.), Secretary.

Executive Committee: Ed Dickard (Greenville, S.C.), Sam Patton (Enka, N.C.), Clarence Thomas (Greenville, S.C.), Jack Reames (Abbeville, S.C.), Walter Lauter (Rossville, Ga.), Fred Johnson (Greenville, S.C.), S.R. DuBose (Whitmire, S.C.), J.D. Hardin (Swannanoa, N.C.), J.D. Brown (Greenville, S.C.), Ward Williams (Greenville, S.C.), W.H. Embler (Anderson, S.C.), John Mullikin (Piedmont, S.C.), Jack Lindsay (Seneca, S.C.), Lloyd McAbee (Greenville, S.C.), Horace C. Whitmire (Greenville, S.C.), Cecil Dickey (Mobile, Ala.), Ken Pittman (Greenville, S.C.).

CLASS A MEN

Piedmont Mill (Piedmont, S.C.), champions: Pete Beasley (coach), Earl Wooten (coach), Ernie Chambers, Ronald Davis, Joe Hiott, Lewis Howard, Mack Isner, Paul Nye, Larry Patterson, Don Roper, Jim Slaughter.

Monaghan Mill (Greenville, S.C.), runners-up: Ken Pittman (coach), Benny Brown, Hanson Griffith, James Gowan, John Merck, Charles McKinney, Fig Newton, Michael Ross, Eugene Seay.

Liberty Mill (Liberty, S.C.), consolation winners: Bobby Roberts (coach), Grover Bowman, Jimmy Cantrell, Roger Dill, Jim Lewis, Bobby Morris, Gene Phillips, Fred Powers.

Victor Mill (Greer, S.C.): Ray Sanderson (coach), Willard Fowler (coach), John Caldwell, William Davidson, Douglas Garren, Wayne Godfrey, Kenneth Godfrey, Roland Lee.

American Enka (Enka, N.C.): Sam Patton (coach), William Coffey, Joe Conner, George Lancaster, Jackson Lovingood, J.L. Mashburn, James Neal, James Patton, Ronald Rogers, Robert Saylor, Richard Sides, Joe Ward Jr.

Greer Mill (Greer, S.C.): Marshall Hill (coach), Robert Campbell, Leon Gravley, Harold Huey, Charlton Miller Jr., James Moore, Roy Wright, Knighton.

CLASS B MEN

Slater Mill (Slater, S.C.), champions: Snow Kirby (coach), Lewis Camdon, Robert Capps, Thomas Cox, Bill Farmer, Richard Payne, Joe Smith, David Sprouse, Buddy Stephenson, Harold Wilson, Alton White.

Russell Manufacturing (Alexander City, Ala.), runners-up: Vercho Carter (coach), Doyt Alford, Bobby Bailey, Rex Ficquette, Gerald Grogan, John Newberry, Jack Peters, Robert Ray, Douglas Reynolds, Emory Windsor, James Yates.

Monaghan Mill (Greenville, S.C.), consolation winners: Ken Pittman (coach), Charles Busbee, Franklin Haney, Jimmy Holden, Oscar McCombs, Johnny McIntosh, Louis Pittman, Charles Powers, Conrad Shook, Jimmy Stillwell, Edward Wilhoit.

Fiberglas (Anderson, S.C.): Thomas Stubberfield (coach), Alvin Blume, Arthur Clancy Jr., Charles Cornwell, Robert Hancock, Larry Moore, Delbert Moorehead, Leroy Parnell, Luther Rhodes, Johnnie Wardlaw, Ray Weddle.

Anderson Mill (Anderson, S.C.): Thomas Bridges Jr. (coach), Kenneth Bannister, Walter Cooper, Ronnie Davis, Bobby Fleming, Mack Fleming, Grady Sanders, Newlan Sanders, Larry Speares, Joe Stansell, Jimmy Smith.

Apalache Mill (Greer, S.C.): Jim Cox (coach), Benny Atkins, Ralph Bogan, Joe Brisontine, Charles Cole, James Cox, Billy Fuller, Ben Jones, James Mills, Melvin Roper.

Brandon Mill (Greenville, S.C.): Lewis Clary (coach), Eddie Cannon, Charles Foster, Boby Helton, Douglas Morgan, Johnny McCombs, Robert Paris, Jack Pierce, Bobby Powers, Luther Smith, Jimmy Williams.

Courtaulds Inc. (Mobile, Ala.): Cecil Dickey (coach), Tom Drake, Eugene Allen, Billy Hawkins, Bill Robinson, Ronnie Cochran, Don McAdams, Billy Williams, Edward Sheffield, James Ollis, Gary Mugnier.

Dunean Mill (Greenville, S.C.): Bob Stowe (coach), Ted Burgess, Jerry Compton, Ralph Durham, Carl Greene, Martin Holder, Ralph Kay, Bill Roddy, Kenneth Stroud, William Vickery, John Williams.

Easley Mill (Easley, S.C.): Harold Ensley (coach), Joe Anders, Dennie Atkinson, Larry Bagwell, Roy Coker, Benny Galloway, William Garrick, Julian Hiott, Ensley.

Greer Mill (Greer, S.C.): Leon Gravley (coach), Billy Allen, Donald Black, Hugh Crain, John Durham, Wilson Ellenburg, Richard Gravley, Robert Gravley, Douglas Greene, Lewis Knighton, Butch Miller, McCallister.

Piedmont Mill (Piedmont, S.C.): Tom Nelson (coach), Norman Chandler, Douglas Emery, Ray Foxx, Robert Hooper, John Marshall, Don Reeder, Kenneth Smith, James Smith, Bradley Wallace, Charles Weisner.

Liberty Mill (Liberty, S.C.): Roy Strickland (coach), Paul Bowie III, Jimmy Garrison, Harold Gray, Donnie Hitt, Dale Martin, Walter McJunkin, Kenneth Lindler, Wallace Lyda.

Mills Mill (Greenville, S.C.): Henry Giles (coach), Thomas Turner (coach), James Ball, Roy Emory, Charles Frank, Roy Garrett, Harold Lowery, Michael Massey, Robert McCall, David Porter, Carroll Waldrop.

Stone Mfg. (Greenville, S.C.): Buster Wood (coach), Johnny Garrett, John Hall, Jerry Heaton, Clyde Hodge, John Kemp, Willard Merritt, James Reynolds, Richard Trott, Jimmy Tucker, Dick Bracken.

Southern Bleachery (Taylors, S.C.): Donnie Coker (coach), Johnnie Badger (coach), Bill Barbary, Joseph Bates, Bobby Belue, Ronnie Coker, Walker Dilworth, Buck Gay, Boyce

Howard Jr., Perry Howard, Coleman Pace, Mack Waldrop.

Pelzer Mill (Pelzer, S.C.): Herman Taylor (coach), Donald Belt, Jerry Garner, Don Gilmer, Jim Moody, Harold Roper, Lloyd Scroggs, Bobby Southerland, George Thomas, Bill Thomason, James Thomason.

Style Crafters (Greenville, S.C.): Bill Nivens (coach), Julian Ashley, Roger Colin, Wayne Evatt, Robert Head, Raymond Jones, Larry Long Jr., Willie Murphy, Don Nivens, Bobby Rabb, Bobby Smith.

LaFrance Mill (Anderson, S.C.): Neal Hunnicutt (coach), Alvin Clark, William Cooper, Furman Elrod, Cleo Martin, Johnny Medlock, Richard Morgan, Olin Mullikin, Franklin McGuire, Franklin Smith, Grant, K. Smith.

Union Bleachery (Greenville, S.C.): W.A. Bishop Jr. (coach), Willie Alford, Franklin Bishop, Charles Carter, Dean Crain, John Luther, James Moore, James Needman, David Smith, Talmadge Stroud, Houston Turner, Robertson.

Lonsdale Mill (Seneca, S.C.): Jack Lindsay (coach), Larry Allsep, Junior Brown, Wallace Hughes, Thomas McCurry, Thomas Reynolds, Charles Robinson, Larry Shaw, Charles Stancil, Tommy Wade, Pat Williams.

Woodside Mill (Greenville, S.C.): Jim McDuffie (coach), Edward White, James Cantrell, James Griffith, Roddy Griffith, Joe Aiken, Jack Kirby, Rodney Canup, Bobby Nelson, Wylie Harbin.

CLASS C MEN

Dunean Mill (Greenville, S.C.), champions: Ward Williams (coach), Dean Harvell, Ronnie Russell, Ricky Duncan, Sammy Ramsey, James Cox, Ronald Cross, Michael Glenn, Richard Pollard, Earl Whittington.

Brandon Mill (Greenville, S.C.), runners-up: Tom Hall (coach), Jimmy Porterfield, Ronald Land, Harold Smith, Gary Hall, Dickey Hunley, William Lee, Dan Moore, Norman Stone, Tommy Williams.

Pelzer Mill (Pelzer, S.C.), consolation winners: Herman Taylor (coach), Gary Geddens, Michael Jordan, Don Helms, Roy Davenport, Gerald Duckworth, Robert Floyd, Leon Greer, Joe Jenkins, Thomas Snipes, Harry Thompson.

Liberty Mill (Liberty, S.C.): Bobby Roberts (coach), Pat Bowie, Philip Crotwell, Calvin Bryant, Mickey Hitt, Jerry Benjamin, Kenneth Burgess, Bobby Dorsey, Wales Gilstrap, Jackie Taylor.

Victor Mill (Greer, S.C.): Willard Fowler (coach), Billy Allen, Dan Harvey, Don Krouse, Steve Brown, Melvin Rice, Jerry Edwards, Jimmy Howell, Harry Johnson, Billy Smith, Donnie Young.

Union Bleachery (Greenville, S.C.): Walter Robertson (coach), Mickey Duncan, Tim Brown, Bill Brooks, Gary Bradley, Fred Rumler, Carlton Chandler, James Aiken, Glenn Barbary, Martin Padgett, Larry Robertson, Marzie Robertson.

American Spinning (Greenville, S.C.): Danny Fowler (coach), Michael Durham, Dean Holtzclaw, Marion McCall, Allen Sprouse, Harold McGaha, Bill Langley, Lewis Cooper, Walter Dacus, Gary Durham, Joseph Worrell.

Belton Mill (Belton, S.C.): Leo Fisher (coach), Marvin Allred, Charles Haggard, James Lollis, Thurman Elgin, Charles Moore Jr., Roger Foster, William Clayton, James Dickert, David Hayne.

Monaghan Mill (Greenville, S.C.): Ken Pittman (coach), Charles Landreth (coach), Charles Burdette, Gilbert Hooper, Raymond Gosnell, Harold Batson, John Coleman, Dickie Hughes, James Odom, John Raines.

Renfrew Bleachery (Travelers Rest, S.C.): Charles Hart (coach), Lee Burns, Harvey Tankersley Jr., Darvin Hood, Raymond Johnson, Gary Duncan, Alvin Gilreath, Bobby Duncan, Edward Crain, George Poteat, Boyd McWhite, McAllister.

Easley Mill (Easley, S.C.): Joe Anders (coach), Gary King, Johnny Skinner, Donnie McCoy, Dennis Dalton, Gary Dunn, Charles Galloway, Jerold Holliday, Thomas Lankford, David Marshbank, Wayne Turner.

Greer Mill (Greer, S.C.): Butch Miller (coach), James Payne, Ronald McAllister, Douglas Brown, Bruce Stepp, Gerald Wilson, David Brewton, Ben Crawford Jr., Mitchell Lancaster, Gary Moore, Tony Tipton.

Judson Mill (Greenville, S.C.): Bill Snelson (coach), James Dunn, Billy Gaines, Heyward Brissey, James Chapman, Ronnie Chapman, Gary Collins, Douglas Cromer, Henry Moore, Tony Moody, Joe Phillips.

Woodside Mill (Greenville, S.C.): Jim McDuffie (coach), James Ware, William Griffith, Charles Phillips, James Carter, Robert Byers, Larry Campbell, Gerald Collins, James Gillespie, Stanley McCarson, Lee, Hall.

Appleton Mill (Anderson, S.C.): Henry Spake (coach), Dick Perry (coach), Dan Blackwell, Jimmy Edmonds, William Findley, Claude Fortner, Chevis Kinley, Charles Moore, Jerry Poole, James Rhodes, Gary Spake, Marvin Smith, Orr.

Calhoun Falls Mill (Calhoun Falls, S.C.): Densel Dockery (coach), Billy Brown (coach), Ronnie Burton, Russ Lyon, Franchot Parnell, James Powell, Robbie Tisdale, Damon Thompson, Darrell Waites, Bobby Waters, James Waters.

Joanna Mill (Joanna, S.C.): Johnny Moore (coach), Charles Force (coach), John Cooley, James Farmer, Larry King, James Lollis, James Long, Kenneth Murphy, Thomas O'Shields, Flynn Owens, Wayne Tollison.

Orr Mill (Anderson, S.C.): Robert Burgess (coach), Charles Aiken, Ronald Burriss, Roger Chastain, Thomas Craft, Harold Ellis, Donald Head, Jerry Makison, Harold Nation, Jerry Parnell, Louis Sullivan.

Southern Bleachery (Taylors, S.C.): Phil Thornton (coach), Johnny Copeland, Gerald Johnson, Thomas James, Larry Johnson, Gerald Jones, Horace Jones, Dicky Lanford, Larry Ross, Horace Strickland, James Turner.

Southern Weaving (Greenville, S.C.): Hoyt Davis (coach), Dickie Dietz, Paul Garrison, Harold Gilstrap, Joe Hand, Merrill Kilpatrick, Gary Miller, Tommy McLees, Don Nelson, Garland Whitlock, Warner Wyatt.

Simpsonville Mill (Simpsonville, S.C.): Odell Barbary (coach), David Adams, Derrell Brewer, Donald Brookshire, James Christopher, Edward Grasso, Donald James, Jack Marler, Robert Nelson, T.H. Todd, Leland Vaughn.

CLASS A WOMEN

Slater Mill (Slater, S.C.), champions: Doots Wright (coach), Jane Nelson, Mary Thacker, Priscilla Wright, Helen Tucker, Ann Burrell, Molly Cooper, Judy Cox, Lucille Robinson, Jean Bivens, Barbara Elder, Bobbie Ivey, Claudette Osborne.

Anderson Mill (Anderson, S.C.), runners-up: B.F. Hollingsworth (coach), Gloria Black, Patricia Black, Mary Bannister, Olivia Bannister, Vivian Bannister, Virginia Bass, Barbara Cash, Zelma Dunn, Peggy Fleming, M.E. Hollingsworth, N.S. Hollingsworth, Sally Hilley.

Liberty Mill (Liberty, S.C.), consolation winners: Bobby Roberts (coach), Roberta Bowman, Harriett Kitchen, Barbara Crowe, Martha Gravely, Laura Sullins, Judy Smith, Marlene Gilstrap, Laura McWhorter, Lynn Lewis, Jean Wood, Sullivan, L. Gilstrap.

Joanna Mill (Joanna, S.C.): Johnny Moore (coach), Charles Force (coach), Gwen Price, Louise Force, Evelyn Motes, Thelma Crolley, Nadine Bridges, Mary Barrett, Bobbie Bridges, Frances Cole, Evelyn Evans, Betty Headrick, Gale Morse, H. Bridges.

Fiberglas (Anderson, S.C.): Thomas Stubblefield (coach), Betty Barnes, Betty Rowland, Vera Stamps, Dot Mullinax, Norma Hancock, Lessie Anderson, Delma Bradshaw, Frances Edmonds, Hazel Gabb, Caroline McLees, Willie Sanders, Louise Stovall.

Greer Mill (Greer, S.C.): Leon Gravley (coach), Frankie Barton, Jo Stoddard, Jerry Wood, Donna Jones, Montez Greene, Johnsye Boling, Martha Boling, Brenda Garren, Brenda Hawkins, Ruby Loftis, Sara Sanders, Doris Wilson.

Pelzer Mill (Pelzer, S.C.): Herman Taylor (coach), Barbara Harris, Judith Coker, Elaine Ellis, Cecile Wooten, Brenda Harris, Iris Greer, Ellen Trotter, Judy Thompson, Ola Cooper, Jan Pascoe, Maxie Phillips, Cashion.

Poinsett Lumber Co. (Anderson, S.C.): Billy Coker (coach), Lewis Acker (coach), Fredda Acker, Jo Billings, Bobbie Bone, Bobbie Burris, Willie Cantrell, Carolina Harbin, Peggy Hopkins, Linda James, Joan Ray, Annie Tribble, Brenda Saylors.

Stone Mfg. (Greenville, S.C.): Buster Wood (coach), Ophelia Bridwell, Betty Crisp, Doris Darnell, Patricia Few, Julia Forrester, Iris Guest, Helen McCollum, Rosemary Osborne, Janet Rainey, Dot Sewell, Martha Tucker, Mildred Wood.

1959

Officers: Divver Hendrix (Greenville, S.C.), President; John Mullikin (Piedmont, S.C.), Vice President, Ass't Treasurer; Ken Pittman (Greenville, S.C.), Executive Secretary.

Executive Committee: Jim Collier (Greenville, S.C.), Ed Dickard (Greenville, S.C.), Sam Patton (Enka, N.C.), Clarence Thomas (Greenville, S.C.), Jack Reames (Abbeville, S.C.), Fred Johnson (Greenville,

Southern Textile Basketball Tournament Rosters   Appendix 1   207

S.C.), S.R. DuBose (Whitmire, S.C.), J.D. Hardin (Swannanoa, N.C.), Ward Williams (Greenville, S.C.), W.H. Embler (Anderson, S.C.), Jack Lindsay (Seneca, S.C.), Cecil Dickey (Mobile, Ala.), Willie Wilbanks (Ware Shoals, S.C.), Bruce Stroupe (Greenville, S.C.), Vercho Carter (Alexander City, Ala.), Curtis Terry (Piedmont, S.C.), Jim McDuffie (Greenville, S.C.).

OPEN DIVISION

Piedmont Mill (Piedmont, S.C.), champions: Curtis Terry (coach), Earl Wooten (coach), Ernie Chambers, Jim Lewis, Mack Isner, Paul Nye, Don Roper, Jim Slaughter, Doug Hoffman, Tommy Smith, Tommy Kearns, Jack Salee.

Monaghan Mill (Greenville, S.C.), runners-up: Fig Newton (coach), Benny Brown, James Gowan, Charles McKinney, Michael Ross, Eugene Seay, Tom Conard Jr., Dick Wright, Ken Pittman, Johnny Haney, Steve Ross.

Carolina Plating (Greenville, S.C.), consolation winners: Claude Thompson (coach), Bobby Farmer, Jim Gentry, Eugene Shockley, Tony Moody, Dickie Hunley, James Gullette, Gene Seay, Jack Mathews, Harold Davis, Buddy Grahl, Brothers.

Victor Mill (Greer, S.C.): Lewis Knighton (coach), Willard Fowler, William Davidson, Douglas Garren, Wayne Godfrey, Leon Gravley, Allen Moore, Hugh Crain, Harold Huey, Robert Campbell, Marshall Perkins.

American Enka (Enka, N.C.): Sam Patton (coach), Joe Conner, J.L. Mashburn, James Neal, Ronald Rogers, Richard Sides, Joe Ward, Floyd Pryor, Larry Davis, Scott Conner.

Texize Chemical (Greenville, S.C.): Pat Perry (coach), Alva Phillips (coach), Jack Robinson, Randall Coleman, Buddy McCall, Grady Wallace, Harry Jones, Jack League, Dickie Hemric, Kenneth Carter, William Moody, Dwane Morrison.

Maness Sporting Goods (Spartanburg, S.C.): Milt Maness (coach), Joel Robertson (coach), Bill Bradford, Bill Barbee, Johnny Howren, Wesley Burrell, Tom Keegan, Trap Hart, Carl Short, Dennis Mathis, Charles Fowler, Glen Nelson.

Pelzer Mill (Pelzer, S.C.): Leonard Muth (coach), Jerry Garner, Robert Southerland, James Moody, Joe Garrett, Earl Reeves, James Thomason, William Ross, Harold Roper, George Thomas.

CLASS B MEN

Piedmont Mill (Piedmont, S.C.), champions: Jerry Hooper (coach), Doug Emery, Ray Foxx, Bob Hooper, Don Reeder, Bradley Wallace, Jerry Weisner, Joe Parker, Doc Morgan, Joe Hiott, David Rampey, Vince Yockel.

Victor Mill (Greer, S.C.), runners-up: Leon Gravley (coach), Donald Black, Wilson Ellenburg, Richard Gravley, Robert Gravley, Douglas Greene, Steve Brown, Charlton Miller, Ronald Coker, Fred Ellenburg, Gary Moore.

Style Crafters (Greenville, S.C.), consolation winners: Bill Nivens (coach), Mike Ashley, Roger Coln, Raymond Jones, Bobby Smith, Jerry Williamson, Donald Nelson, Tommy McLees, Ray Whaley, James Johnson, Gene Anglian.

Southern Bleachery (Taylors, S.C.): Walker Dilworth (coach), C.L. Smith (coach), Bill Bramlett, Joe Bates, Bobby Belue, Donnie Coker, Buck Gay, Coley Pace, Bob Waldrop, William Chastain, Edwin Crain, D.L. Farr.

Slater Mill (Slater, S.C.): Snow Kirby (coach), Bill Farmer, Richard Payne, David Sprouse, Buddy Stephenson, Harold Wilson, Gary Roper, Jack Fowler, Robert Capps, Bobby Johnson, Louie Wallace.

Russell Manufacturing (Alexander City, Ala.): Vercho Carter (coach), Doyt Alford, Bobby Bailey, Douglas Reynolds, Bryant Yates, Neil Anderson, James Jones, Berkley Steele, H.L. Carter, Olin Wingard, Edsel Riddle, Patterson.

Monaghan Mill (Greenville, S.C.): Fred Rigdon (coach), Charles Busbee, Jimmy Holden, Oscar McCombs, Louis Pittman, Charles Powers, Edward Wilhoit, Sammy Ramsey, Jyles Phillips, Raymond Gosnell, Billy Swaynghame.

Fiberglas (Anderson, S.C.): Thomas Stubblefield (coach), Charles Conwell, Delbert Moorhead, Leroy Parnell, William Acker III, Melvin Aiken, Colyer Parnell, Gilbert Robinson, Larry Speares, Jerry Parnell, Jimmy Lowe.

Brandon Mill (Greenville, S.C.): Ray Morgan, Elzie Smith, Gardner, Cannon, Bobby Pearce, L. Smith, Powers, Hooper, Foster, Fred McAbee.

Apalache Mill (Greer, S.C.): Bill Fuller (coach), Ralph Bogan, Joe Brisontine, Jim Cox, Melvin Roper, Jack Fuller, David Beeks, James Herring.

Dunean Mill (Greenville, S.C.): Billy Lollis (coach), Jerry Compton, Tracy Roddy, William

Vickery, Robert Dellinger, Jimmy Kirby, John Popson, Ronnie Russell, Mickey Long, Mickey Massey, Harvell.

Stone Mfg. (Greenville, S.C.): Joe Shinta (coach), Johnny Garrett, John Hall, John Kemp, Richard Trott, John Luther, Jack Davis, Ray Shockley, Gerald Taylor, Jim Seeger, Jon Howard.

Union Bleachery (Greenville, S.C.): Jim Grogan (coach), James Moore, David Smith, Don Stroud, Ted Colcolough, Maurice Evington, Roy Lockaby, Bill Painter, Larry Robertson, John Robertson.

Lonsdale Mill (Seneca, S.C.): Roy McCurry (coach), Larry Allsep, Wallace Hughes, Thomas McCurry, Charles Robinson, Tommy Wade, Clint Vickery, Roger Tippett, William Moskow, Kenneth Worley.

Calhoun Falls Mill (Calhoun Falls, S.C.): Densel Dockery (coach), William Brown (coach), Ray Hall, Bobby Waters, Joe Hall, Walter Hilley, Darrell Waits, Franchot Parnell, Maxie Putnam, James Hester, William Brown.

Monsanto (Pensacola, Fla.): Jim Diamond (coach), Ken Raines, Cecil Franklin, Johnny Taylor, Jerry Glenn, Don Luker, Raymond Johnston, Bill Williams, Tommy Bridges, Ted White.

Clinton Mill (Clinton, S.C.): Bill Terry (coach), Truman Owens, Sam Owens, Jimmy Braswell, Billy Cauble, Bobby Thomas, Billy Crawford, Billy Watkins, Cecil Davenport, Joe Lark.

LaFrance Mill (Anderson, S.C.): Neal Hunnicutt (coach), Jimmy Kay, Tommy Garrison, Danny Ferguson, Rod Terry, Joe Stegall, Alvin Clark, Tommy Grant, Jim Hudson, Virgil Dillion.

Poinsett Lumber Co. (Anderson, S.C.): Don Coker (coach), Don Carnes, Gerald Gillespie, Dwayne Martin, Robby Martin, Robert Moore, Gary Patterson, Robert Sanders, Olin Saylors, H.R. Wilson, Clifton Speares.

Saco-Lowell (Easley, S.C.): Theo Krieg (coach), Charles Huff, Charles Bagwell, John Burgess, Charles Rogers, Jimmy Morgan, Willie Benette, Richard Estes, Gerald Townes, Dan Knight, Kreig.

Class C Men

Monaghan Mill #1 (Greenville, S.C.), champions: Pete Henderson (coach), Charles Burdette, John Coleman, Lee Capps, Joe Keller, Donnie Riggins, Joe Kilpatrick, Nathan Smith, Douglas McCrary.

Woodside Mill (Greenville, S.C.), runners-up: Jim McDuffie (coach), Jimmy Carter, Larry Campbell, James Gillespie, Tim Brown, M.G. Stewart, Tommy Williams, Zimmie Mason, John Hall, James Lackey, Kirk Jordan, Ken Beasley, Johnny Edwards, Phillips.

Quinn Machine Works (Greenville, S.C.), consolation winners: James Hunley (mgr), Jimmy Chapman, Ronnie Chapman, Johnny Massey, Curtis Wilborn, Joe Phillips, John Burgess, Gary Collins, Bruce Suggs, Alvin Hawkins, Wendell Case.

Greer Mill (Greer, S.C.): Butch Miller (coach), Douglas Brown, Tony Tipton, Walter Burch, John McWilliams, Wayne Brown, John Green, David Johnson, Jack Green, Pat Suddeth, Billy Smith, Hall.

Dunean Mill (Greenville, S.C.): Ward Williams (coach), Ricky Duncan, James Cox, Ronald Cross, Michael Glenn, Richard Pollard, Earl Whittington, Eddie Forrester, Herman Patterson, Truman McCarter, Jimmy McAtee, Coleman, Smith, Stroud.

Liberty Mill (Liberty, S.C.): Bobby Morris (coach), Pat Bowie, Calvin Bryant, Lamar Gilstrap, Doyle Roper, Gerald Lyda, Philip Human, Gary Whitlock, Joe Watson, Jerry Brock.

Victor Mill (Greer, S.C.): R.V. Sears (coach), Mack Allen, Jerry Edwards, Jimmy Howell, Harry Johnson, Steve Foster, Don Lister, Jerry Deese, Buddy Bowman, Jan Cline, Clyde Hill, Sloan.

Union Bleachery (Greenville, S.C.): Jim Grogan (coach), Mickey Duncan, Bill Brooks, Lawrence Aiken, George Barbary, Martin Padgett, Marzie Robertson, Donnie Hammett, Buddy Wallace, Smith.

Monaghan Mill #2 (Greenville, S.C.): H.B. Gosnell (coach), Douglas Burton, James Odom, Jimmy Couch, Clarence Raines, Harold Chapman, Dickie Hughes, Charles Harvell, Buddy Taylor, Holcombe.

Easley Mill (Easley, S.C.): Joe Anders (coach), Dennis Atkinson (coach), Johnny Skinner, Mike McCoy, Charles Galloway, Melvin Holliday, Thomas Lankford, Wayne Turner, Ronald Noblitt, Dennis Waldrop.

Simpsonville Mill (Simpsonville, S.C.): Odell Barbary (coach), Darrell Brewer, Donald Brookshire, Edward Grasso, Frank Kinard, Roger Thackston, Mike Garrett, Jerry Gray,

Marcus Poore, Roger Weaver, Ken Goodwin, Kinard.

Pacific Mill (Columbia, S.C.): Bobby Giles (coach), Ken Currie, Donald Dailey, Boogie Gambrell, Victor Jordan, Jency Kelly, William Loftis, W.L. Sullivan, Eddie Taylor, Charlie Walker, Bill Martin.

Piedmont Mill (Piedmont, S.C.): Curtis Terry (coach), John Mullikin, Marvin Bryson, Charles Hooper, Larry Holcombe, Bob Richey, Jerry Gambrell, Jack Hart, Jess Bell, Larry Taylor, David Merritt.

Ware Shoals Mill (Ware Shoals, S.C.): J.W. McDill (coach), William Cooper, Frank Davis, Charles Hill, Sonny Pitts, Jerry Sims, Jerry Smith, Douglas Strawhorn, William Wates, Willie Wilbanks Jr., Larry Ashley, Gamble, Brock.

Stone Mfg. (Greenville, S.C.): Gary Durham, Ronnie Duncan, Dickerson, Barton, Cannon, Osteen, Piegler, Jordan, Johnson, Sloan, Dixon, Cooper.

Class A Women

Lonsdale Mill (Seneca, S.C.), champions: Roy Foster (coach), Jack Lindsay (coach), Winona Foster, Brenda Addis, Beverly Dooley, Nell Lumpkin, Martha Brucke, Ester Kelley, Barbara Wade, Evelyn Black, Johelen Dawkins, Doris Miller, Mary Foster.

Slater Mill (Slater, S.C.), runners-up: Doots Wright (coach), Jane Nelson, Mary Thacker, Priscilla Wright, Ann Burrell, Molly Cooper, Judy Cox, Barbara Harris, Bobbie Ivey, Ann Spearman, Ann Richardson, Linda Cox, Betty Garren.

Anderson Mill (Anderson, S.C.), consolation winners: B.F. Hollingsworth (coach), Gloria Black, Mary Bannister, Olivia Bannister, Vivian Bannister, Barbara Cash, Peggy Fleming, M.E. Hollingsworth, Bobbie Burris, Helen Smith, Barbara Riddley, Sue Smith, W.P. Scarborough.

Ware Shoals Mill (Ware Shoals, S.C.): Willie Wilbanks (coach), Peggy Bishop, Mary Bishop, Mickey Davis, Barbara Freeman, Jonnie Freeman, Kathy Hartman, Janet Holliday, Margaret McDonald, Gayle Metts, Lyndall Tolly, Susan McElevee, Joyce League, Elizabeth Sullivan, Pitts, Culbertson, Southerland.

Joanna Mill (Joanna, S.C.): Johnny Moore (coach), Charles Force (mgr), Gwen Clark, Louise Force, Nadine Bridges, Bobbie Bridges, Evelyn Evans, Betty Headrick, Ann Hunnicutt, Linda Epting, Gladys Steading, Linda Brown, Lillie Franklin, Vera Bodie.

Fiberglas (Anderson, S.C.): Colyer Parnell (coach), Betty Barnes, Vera Stamps, Norma Hancock, Frances Edmonds, Hazel Gable, Caroline McLees, Faye Sanders, Jimmie Richardson, Lois Bridges, Elaine Ellis, Connie Simpson.

Greer Mill (Greer, S.C.): Jo Stoddard (coach), Jerry Wood, Brenda Garren, Sarah Sanders, Janice Lowe, Hilliard Anderson, Mary McCuen, Margaret Rowland, Gloria Riley, Gwen Burton, Carolyn Reeves, Ann Dobson, Linda Bowman.

Poinsett Lumber Co. (Anderson, S.C.): Joe Stegall (coach), Jo Billings, Caroline Harbin, Peggy Hopkins, Linda Bryson, Joan Ray, Annie Tribble, Brenda Saylors, Beverly Ayers, Sybil Powers, Betty Bolt, Margaret Bracket, Sally Hilley.

Stone Mfg. (Greenville, S.C.): Buster Wood (coach), Doris Clark, Iris Guest, Martha Tucker, Mildred Wood, Judy Buddin, Mary Greene, Sandra Smith, Brenda Anders, Barbara Walker, Margaret Landreth, Brenda Harris, Barbara Stewart, Connors.

Saco-Lowell (Easley, S.C.): Pete Carlisle (coach), Evelyn Carlisle, Carolyn Putman, Barbara Pittman, Nellie Grant, Alice Grant, Jane Carson, Linda Callahan, Ann von Hollen, Ened Hicks, Gloria Sweat.

Jackson Mill (Iva, S.C.): Curtis Wilson (coach), Patsy Wilson, Ann Milford, Brenda Gable, Rachel Moore, L.C. McCullough, Grace Lawton, Betty Lawton, Shelby Pryor, Jean Burns, Martha Taylor, Judy McGraw, Eleanor Bruce.

Wunda Weve Carpets (Greenville, S.C.): Lloyd Kelly (coach), Kitty Pearce, Vivian Barnett, Joanne Kelly, Jane Chrisley, Jackie Wham, Jeanne Cauley, Genny Knight, Virgil Childress, Pat Murphy, Fritzie Munford, Judy Hudgens, Ann James.

Carolina Plating (Greenville, S.C.): Alice Cash (coach), Judy Bowen, Shelva McSwain, Betty Bolin, Linda Pirkle, Carolyn Clayton, Eloise Moss, Sybil Miller, Tracy Robbins, Barbara Martin, Carol Hairston, Martha Suddeth, Wanda Lamb, Elder.

---------- 1960 ----------

Officers: Divver Hendrix (Greenville, S.C.), President, Treasurer; John Mullikin (Piedmont,

S.C.), Vice President, Ass't Treasurer; Ken Pittman (Greenville, S.C.), Executive Secretary; Fred Byrd (Greenville, S.C.), Secretary.

Executive Committee: Jim Collier (Greenville, S.C.), Ed Dickard (Greenville, S.C.), Sam Patton (Enka, N.C.), Clarence Thomas (Greenville, S.C.), Jack Reames (Abbeville, S.C.), Fred Johnson (Greenville, S.C.), S.R. DuBose (Whitmire, S.C.), Ward Williams (Greenville, S.C.), W.H. Embler (Anderson, S.C.), Jack Lindsay (Seneca, S.C.), Willie Wilbanks (Ware Shoals, S.C.), Bruce Stroupe (Greenville, S.C.), Vercho Carter (Alexander City, Ala.), Curtis Terry (Piedmont, S.C.), Jim McDuffie (Greenville, S.C.), Willard Fowler (Greer, S.C.), Don Garren (Liberty, S.C.), Fred Powers (Asheville, N.C.).

OPEN DIVISION

Dillard's Sporting Goods (Easley, S.C.), champions: Tommy Jenkins (coach), Pete Carlisle, Byron Pinson, Dick Wright, George Krajack, Walt Gibbons, Larry Dial, Jack Owens, Don Gish, Kelly Coleman, Charles Carlisle, Fleming.

Stevens Rockets (Greer, S.C.), runners-up: James Gowan (mgr), Willard Fowler, Leon Gravley, Walt Hudson, Bury Hudson, Mike Callahan, Jimmy Herring, June Raines, James Cox, Richard Prater, Bob Frantz.

LaFrance Mill (Anderson, S.C.), consolation winners: Bill Marsh (coach), Neil Hunnicutt, Ed Brinkley, Dave Nelson, Bruce Thompson, Carl Reamer, Donnie Garrison, Frank Clark, John Moore, George Williams, Doug Daignault.

Engineering Products (Greenville, S.C.): Melvin Babylon (coach), James Branham, Leo Socha, John Riley, William Pough, Stephen Palmer, Joe Elkins, Ervin Maynard, Thomas McDonohough, William Wilson, Thomas Belk.

Piedmont Mill (Piedmont, S.C.): Bill Evans (coach), Earl Wooten, Jim Lewis, Mack Isner, Don Roper, Jim Slaughter, Doug Hoffman, Vince Yockel, Don Carver, Dag Wilson, Joe Hiott.

Monaghan Mill (Greenville, S.C.): Ken Pittman (coach), Fig Newton, Charles McKinney, Eugene Seay, Jack League, Dickie Hunley, Buddy McCall, Dick Tyler, Bob Powers, Jim Whitfield, Terry Litchfield, Brown.

Carolina Plating (Greenville, S.C.): James Hunley (coach), James Gentry, Charles Wike, John Burgess, Thomas Cameron, Robert Crumley, Cleon Reece, Michael Burnette, Buddy Broome, Gary Geddons, Tim Brown, Gullette.

American Enka (Enka, N.C.): Sam Patton (coach), Ellerbe Neal, Ronald Rogers, Richard Sides, Joe Ward Jr., Floyd Pryor, Scott Conner, Jerry Breazeale, William DeBruhl, Laurence Ledford, Harold Gudger, Greenwood, Morgan.

Maness Sporting Goods (Spartanburg, S.C.): Milt Maness (coach), Bill Barbee, Trap Hart, Dennis Mathis, Charles Cluff, Glen Melton, Alan Seay, Boyce Berry, Bob Stratton, Dean Brown.

Pelzer Mill (Pelzer, S.C.): Bud Teaster (coach), Jerry Garner, James Moody, James Thomason, Harold Roper, Douglas Harris, Albert Belt, Louie Davenport, Donald Brady, Perry Teaster, Grady Cooley, Thompson.

Speed Queen (Chattanooga, Tenn.): Ralph Hooper (coach), Teddy Penney, Larry Card, Billy Perry, Jim Traylor, Joe Cash, Frank Cate, Ronald Campbell, Jerry Edmondson, Tommy Springfield, Ward Lockhart, Peeples, McDaniels, Dockery, Myers, Power.

Centre Electric (Greenville, S.C.): Willie Merritt (coach), Bobby Sexton, Randy Atkins, Larry Stoephel, Carroll Merritt, Wayne Merritt, Terry Merritt, Bob Stratton, Darrell Range, Joe Parker, Denzil Ratliff.

Pharr Worsted Mills (McAdenville, N.C.): Carol Eaker (coach), Mike Ross, Bob Stewart, Francis Clair, Jim Sparrow, Thad Malonowski, Pete Tagley, Jim Stewart, Jack Huggins, Ron Ragan, Morris Seavens.

Dixie Ford (Greenville, S.C.): Gene Anglin (coach), Tommy McLees, John Rhine, Steve Ross, Donald Nelson, Francis Brothers, Jerry Williamson, Roger Coln, William Davidson, Charles Gallager, Blackwell.

CLASS B MEN

Dunean Mill (Greenville, S.C.), champions: Bobby Grant (coach), Ronnie Russell, Mickey Long, Dean Harvell, Richard Pollard, Ralph Kay, Sammy Ramsey, Tommy Williams, Ricky Duncan, Michael Glenn, Jimmy Cox.

Monaghan Mill (Greenville, S.C.), runners-up: Fred Rigdon (mgr), Jimmy Holden, Oscar McCombs, Charles Powers, Edward Wilhoit, Raymond Gosnell, Billy Swaynghame, John Coleman, James Carter, Donald Krause, Thomas Turner.

Homelite (Greer, S.C.), consolation winners: Thomas Poole (coach), Robert Bowyer, Stephen Brown, Harvey Forrester, Harold Brown, Billy Gambrell, Don Lister, Richard Watson, John Lashway, Durward Hoffman, Ray Ward, T. Brown.

Union Bleachery (Greenville, S.C.): Jim Grogan (coach), James Moore, Ted Colcolough, Morris Evington, Bill Painter, Larry Robertson, Bill Brooks, Don Carter, Charles Compton, Charles Sizemore.

Greer Mill (Greer, S.C.): Bob Campbell (coach), Donald Black, Wilson Ellenburg, Richard Gravley, Robert Gravley, Douglas Greene, Charlton Miller, Fred Ellenburg, Gary Moore, Keith Wilson, Robert Vaughan, Donald Jones.

Southern Bleachery (Taylors, S.C.): Clannie Smith (coach), Bill Bramlett, Donnie Coker, Bob Waldrop, William Chastain, Edwin Crain, Ronald Coker, Veto Barton, Horace Jones Jr., Walker Dilworth, Franklin Warefield.

Slater Mill (Slater, S.C.): W.M. Lybrand (coach), Bill Farmer, Richard Payne, David Sprouse, Buddy Stephenson, Harold Wilson, Louie Wallace, James Watson, Raymond Payne, Snow Kirby, Joe Smith.

Russell Manufacturing (Alexander City, Ala.): Vercho Carter (coach), Bobby Bailey, Neil Anderson, James Jones, Olin Wingard, James Patterson, Robert Ray, Charles Robinson, Johnny Newbery, Jimmy Jones, Huell.

Fiberglas (Anderson, S.C.): Leroy Parnell (coach), Melvin Aiken, Colyer Parnell, Gilbert Robinson, Jerry Parnell, Jimmy Lowe, Jimmy Smith, Alvin Blume, Stanley Whitfield, W. Parnell, L. Parnell, Blume.

Stone Mfg. (Greenville, S.C.): William Wood (coach), John Kemp, Jerry Heaton, Jesse Rainey, Gilbert Hooper, James Duncan, Milton Cisson, Kendall Cothran, James Foster, David Hickum, P.R. Tomlinson Jr., Forrester.

Lonsdale Mill (Seneca, S.C.): Jack Lindsay (coach), Larry Allsep, Thomas McCurry, Tommy Wade, William Moskow, Kenneth Worley, George Randlett, Junior Brown, Leon Dooley, Robert Gibson.

Monsanto (Pensacola, Fla.): Jim Diamond (coach), Ken Raines, Johnny Taylor, Jerry Glenn, Bill Williams, Tommy Bridges, Don Gates, Joe Salter, Howard Snead, Johnny Tringas.

Clinton Mill (Clinton, S.C.): Bill Terry (coach), Truman Owens, Sam Owens, Jimmy Braswell, Billy Watkins, Cecil Davenport, Joe Lark, Donnie Stewart, Pat Lowe, Howard Lewis, Ellis Hufstetler, Howard.

Poinsett Lumber Co. (Anderson, S.C.): Lewis Acker (coach), Gerald Gillespie, Robby Martin, Robert Moore, Gary Patterson, Robert Sanders, Olin Mullikin, Joe Stegall, Nelson Massey, Furman Elrod, Donnie Edmonds, G. Sanders.

Saco-Lowell (Easley, S.C.): G.H. Forrister (coach), Charles Huff, Charles Rogers, Gerald Townes, William Edgar, Edward Cooley, Hudgens Thurman, Charles James, Lee Nicholson, Bing Day, Hobert Crowe, James Huff.

Diehl Mfg. (Pickens, S.C.): Pat Edens (coach), Parker Hendricks, Pat Hunter, Charles Hudson, Don Alexander, Jerry Smith, Bobby Bryson, David Brown, Charles Aiken, Donald Boggs, Brezeale.

Easley Mill (Easley, S.C.): Coon Hendricks (coach), Johnny Skinner, Courtney Heath Jr., Dennis Atkinson, James Chandler, Troy Suddeth, James Brandt, Bobby Chandler, Larry Bagwell, Benny Galloway, Jim Smith, L. Chandler.

Poinsett Mill (Greenville, S.C.): Frank Millwood (coach), Pat Campbell, Bill Mathis, Robert Lavender, Doyles Gray, Buddy Herring, Bobby Gray, John Martin, Larry Campbell, Bobby Evatt, James Slaton, J. Gray.

Gower Mfg. (Greenville, S.C.): Nig Griffith (coach), Charles Reece, Jerry Wynn, Robert Holcombe, William Tate, Charles Reid, Marion McCall, James Stephens, Ronnie Burdette, Allen Griffith, William Griffith, Justice, H. Fuller, J. Fuller.

Class C Men

Dunean Mill (Greenville, S.C.), champions: Ward Williams (coach), Ronald Cross, Earl Whittington, Eddie Forrester, Herman Patterson, Jimmy McAtee, Kenneth Smith, Elmer Madden, Donnie Sargent, Clay Coleman, Jimmy Chapman.

Slater Mill (Slater, S.C.), runners-up: Roger White (coach), Harvey Tankersley, Robert Kirby, William White, Larry Ledford, John Jarrard, Jimmy Wilson, William Lybrand, Thomas Adkins, Gary Cox, Larry Dudley.

Brandon Mill (Greenville, S.C.), consolation winners: J.R. Raines (coach), Ralph McDonald, Joseph Smith, Jimmy Elrod, Jimmy Riddle, David Ashworth, George Wilson,

Johnny Holtzclaw, Lewis Wood, Terrell Watts, Mike Reid.

Monaghan Mill (Greenville, S.C.): Joseph Newton (coach), Clarence Raines, Ronnie Chapman, Charles Harvell, Furman Capps, Joe Kilpatrick, M.G. Stewart, Douglas McCrary, Phillip Stewart, Jerry Madison, Joe Keller.

Greer Mill (Greer, S.C.): Butch Miller (coach), Wayne Brown, Jimmy Simmons, Billy Vaughan, Steve Gambrell, Fred Blackwell, Troy Robertson, Wayne Gambrell, Reginald Wilson, Shirley Hall, Jan Cline.

Liberty Mill (Liberty, S.C.): Bobby Morris (coach), Pat Bowie, Lamar Gilstrap, Doyle Roper, Gerald Lyda, Gary Whitlock, Joe Watson, Wayne Petit, Herbert Head, Glen Skinner, Lloyd Burgess.

Victor Mill (Greer, S.C.): Doug Garren (coach), Steve Foster, Buddy Bowman, Thomas Singleton, Tommy Wilkerson, Robert Gillespie, Jimmy Ayers, Ingle, Edwards, Corn, Owens.

Union Bleachery (Greenville, S.C.): Jim Grogan (coach), Richard Aiken, George Barbary, Buddy Wallace, Robert Blakely, Arthur Dix, Jimmy Green, Carroll Smith, Steve Smith, Wallace Waldrop, Charles Ward.

Easley Mill (Easley, S.C.): Joe Anders (coach), Mike McCoy, Melvin Holliday, Wayne Brown, Dennis Waldrop, Joe Garrett, Terry Gillespie, Charles Garrett, Brax Cutchin, Terrell Lankford, George Hagood, D. Garrett.

Simpsonville Mill (Simpsonville, S.C.): Ted Yak (coach), Frank Kinard, Roger Thackston, Mike Garrett, Marcus Poore, Jack Marler, Charlie Brooks, Joe Allen, Roy Tumbleston, Jim Baldwin.

Piedmont Mill (Piedmont, S.C.): J.M. Lewis (coach), John Mullikin, Gary Hooper, Larry Holcombe, Jerry Gambrell, Jess Bell, Doug Barwick, Mike Hughey, Jerry Smith, Gary Helms, Jimmy Cobb.

Southern Weaving (Greenville, S.C.): Joe Murray (coach), Bob Hall, Donnie Pridmore, Bill Porter, Sandy Scott, Ed Collins, Bill Bailey, Larry Bruce, Fred Cooper.

Excelsior Mill (Pendleton, S.C.): W.H. Bagwell (coach), Thomas Risher, Richard Senn, Charles Stuart, Robert Lovett, Ronnie Maravich, James Lever, James Southerland, H.P. Cooper Jr., McNeill, Cox, Pete Maravich.

Pickens Mill (Pickens, S.C.): F.D. Thornton (coach), Francis Alward, Henry Bivens, Joseph Bowers, William Connelly, Gerald Owens, Jimmy Payne, Jack Reece, Arvel Reeves, Mendel Stewart, David Youngblood, Evans, Crumpton.

Stone Mfg. (Greenville, S.C.): Jimmy Beard (coach), Dickie Dietz, Douglas Armstrong, Gary Durham, Myrle Bell, Ronnie Trotter, Jimmy Cox, James Beard, Jerry Jones, Danny Bruce, Ralph Leslie, Piegler.

LaFrance Mill (Anderson, S.C.): Dennie Garrison (coach), Danny Ferguson, Kenneth Powell, Larry Orr, Buddy Brothers, Larry Clark, Kenneth Wood, Walter McAbee, Robert Hammett, Jerry Rhodes, Jackie Bridges, Toby Atkins, Billy Sutherland.

Newry Mill (Newry, S.C.): Dallas Campbell (coach), Bobby Fleming (coach), Wayne Lacy, Bill Hawkins, Charles Palmer, Sam Batson Jr., Howard Hughes, Johnnie Jones, William Chase Jr., Dewey O'Kelly, Eugene Gaillard, Calhoun Cox Jr.

Class A Women

Slater Mill (Slater, S.C.), champions: Doots Wright (coach), Priscilla Wright, Ann Burrell, Linda Cox, Barbara Elders, Carolyn Clayton, Stephanie Pickett, Sarah McCall, Jane Smith, Jean Jackson, Sue Vickers, Mattie Shelton, Carol Hairston, Sue Cox.

Lonsdale Mill (Seneca, S.C.), runners-up: Jack Lindsay (coach), Brenda Addis, Beverly Dooley, Esther Kelley, Barbara Wade, Evelyn Black, Johelen Dawkins, Bertha Bryant, Shirley Black, Rachel Allsep, Madeline Riley, Katie Brown, Betty Allsep, Foster, J. Black.

Sangamo Electric Co. (Pickens, S.C.), consolation winners: Ann Boiter (coach), Patsy Allamon, Linda Cunningham, Jane Evans, Judy Few, Ann Hayes, Teresa Nealy, Jackie Roper, Jean Roper, Linda Turner, Jane Underwood, Phyllis Waldrop, Frances Welborn.

Anderson Mill (Anderson, S.C.): Roy Bridges (coach), Mary Bannister, Olivia Bannister, Vivian Bannister, Mary Hollingsworth, Edith Smith, Barbara Riddley, Betty Lawton, Ann Milford, Linda Donald, Virginia Burns, C. Bannister.

Joanna Mill (Joanna, S.C.): Johnny Moore (coach), Charles Force (coach), Gwen Clark, Nadine Bridges, Bobbie Bridges, Evelyn Evans, Judith Hunnicutt, Linda Brown, Gladys Steading, Lillie Franklin, Lana Price, Sheila Jacks, Janice Ruff, Valarie Morse.

Fiberglas (Anderson, S.C.): Jimmy Smith (coach), Betty Barnes, Vera Stamps, Norma

Hancock, Elaine Ellis, Claudia Prater, Sally Hilley, Jennie Holden, Frankie Gilreath, Jo Knecht, Barbara Cox, Linda Kay.

Greer Mill (Greer, S.C.): Arnold Campbell (coach), Jerry Wood, Brenda Garren, Mary McCuen, Margaret Rowland, Carolyn Reeves, Jo Stoddard, Lona Fulmer, Patsy Woods, Linda Sloan, Betty Alverson, Joan Stephens, Sonja Miller, Lowe, McCall.

Poinsett Lumber Co. (Anderson, S.C.): Lewis Acker (coach), Jo Campbell, Caroline Harbin, Peggy Anderson, Annie Tribble, Brenda Gable, Margaret Thompson, Fredda Acker, Bobbie Burris, Barbara Cash, Patsy Wilson, Betty Cox, Pearl Scarborough, Moltman, Filtman.

Stone Mfg. (Greenville, S.C.): Buster Wood (coach), Mildred Wood, Judy Buddin, Mary Green, Janet Rainey, Carolyn Broad, Betty Garren, Dorothy Sewell, Marlene King, Judy Bolding, Bobbie Ward, Patricia Capps, Patricia Edens.

Renfrew Bleachery (Travelers Rest, S.C.): Margie McMeekin (coach), Billie Lewis, Ernestine Willis, Sarah Coleman, Pat Murphy, Genny Knight, Barbara Ivey, Mary Grier, Betty Vernon, Joan Knight, Judy Hodgens, Joyce Johnson, Ann Dobson.

──────── 1961 ────────

Officers: Divver Hendrix (Greenville, S.C.), President, Treasurer; John Mullikin (Piedmont, S.C.), Vice President, Ass't Treasurer; Ken Pittman (Greenville, S.C.), Executive Secretary; Fred Byrd (Greenville, S.C.), Secretary.

Executive Committee: Jim Collier (Greenville, S.C.); Sam Patton (Enka, N.C.), Clarence Thomas (Greenville, S.C.), Jack Reames (Abbeville, S.C.), S.R. DuBose (Whitmire, S.C.), Ward Williams (Greenville, S.C.), W.H. Embler (Anderson, S.C.), Jack Lindsay (Seneca, S.C.), Willie Wilbanks (Ware Shoals, S.C.), Vercho Carter (Alexander City, Ala.), Curtis Terry (Piedmont, S.C.), Jim McDuffie (Greenville, S.C.), Willard Fowler (Greer, S.C.), Fred Powers (Asheville, N.C.), Jim Anderson (Greenville, S.C.), Dan Foster (Greenville, S.C.), Keener Garrett (Greenville, S.C.), Bud Teaster (Pelzer, S.C.).

OPEN DIVISION

Piedmont Mill (Piedmont, S.C.), champions: Earl Wooten (coach), Jim Slaughter, Vince Yockel, Don Carver, Dag Wilson, Joe Hiott, Rex Frederick, Pete Carlisle, Jim Warren, Earl Maxwell, Carl Short, Jack Sullivan, Dave Wallace, Bill Warren.

Monaghan Mill (Greenville, S.C.), runners-up: Ken Pittman (coach), Fig Newton, Eugene Seay, Jack League, Buddy McCall, Dick Tyler, Ellerbe Neal, Jimmy Holden, W.L. Gray, Benny Brown, Mickey Long.

Slater Mill (Slater, S.C.), consolation winners: Snow Kirby (coach), John Ladd, Russell Milton, Jerry Brinkley, Billy Barbary, James Lewis, Clarence Russell, Jack Duncan Jr., Ronald Coker, Walter Gibbons, Joe Smith, Halford.

Lonsdale Mill (Seneca, S.C.): Bruce Thompson, Dave Neilson, Connie Mac Berry Jr., Berry, Black, Yarborough, Tippett, D. Thompson, Byrd, Bonzulak, Robinson.

Dillard's Sporting Goods (Easley, S.C.): Tommy Jenkins (coach), Byron Pinson, George Krajack, Jack Owens, Tom Conrad, Roger Kaiser, Bob Nordmann, John Adcock, Bob Short, Mat Herndon, Tom Sease, Conard, Ed Krajack, Etnre.

Stevens Rockets (Greer, S.C.): Willard Fowler (coach), Leon Gravley, Jimmy Herring, June Raines, James Cox, Dick Wright, John Morris, Doug Garren, Leo Berni, Roy Beach, Steve Ross, Grady Wallace.

Pelzer Mill (Pelzer, S.C.): Bill Hopkins (coach), James Thomason, Harold Roper, Douglas Harris, Gary Geddens, George Thomas, William Ross, William Carr, Thomas Craft, William Ohlendorf, Jerry Wolff.

Chattanooga VFW (Chattanooga, Tenn.): Ralph Hooper (coach), Larry Card, Jim Traylor, Tommy Springville, Clyde Eads, Harry Sparks, Joe Gardner, Tom Chilton, Bill Coulter, Hershell Smith, Bill Wade, Cox Dean.

Wyandotte Mill (Conestee, S.C.): Gene Anglin (coach), Don Nelson, Roger Coln, Bobby Smith, Tommy McLeese, Willie Murphy, Bill White, Francis Brothers, Bobby Wike, Don Johnson.

Pharr Worsted Mill (McAdenville, N.C.): Tim Sparrow, Mike Ross, Lewis Pittman, Malonowski, Huggins, Johnston, Walker.

CLASS B MEN

Monsanto (Pensacola, Fla.), champions: Jack Lovett (coach), Jim Diamond, Ken Rains, John Taylor, Billy Williams, Don Gates, John

Tringas, Billy Smith, Bill Griffin, Cecil Franklin.

Greer Mill (Greer, S.C.), runners-up: June Raines (coach), Richard Gravley, Douglas Greene, Charlton Miller, Fred Ellenburg, Gary Moore, Robert Vaughan, Mike McCallister, Jan Cline, Jimmy Howell, Steve Brown, Lister.

Stone Mfg. (Greenville, S.C.), consolation winners: John Kemp (coach), Walker Duncan, Milton Cisson, Paul Tomlinson, James Moon, Fred Mattison, Charles Fleming, Harold Grey, Marvin Cannon, Roy Tumberston, Kenneth Jenkins.

Monaghan Mill (Greenville, S.C.): Fred Rigdon (coach), Raymond Gosnell, Billy Swaynghame, John Coleman, James Carter, Buddy Helton, Elzie Smith, Jyles Phillips, Ronnie Argo, Johnny Haney, Tommy Massey, Coswell.

Dunean Mill (Greenville, S.C.): Bobby Grant (coach), Laverne Holden, Kenneth Stroud, Jack Bagwell, Leon McWhite, Earl Whittington, Ronald Cross, David Norris, Marvin Grant, Doug Gailey, Jimmy Chapman, Bailey.

Homelite (Greer, S.C.): Jack Kay (coach), Harold T. Brown, Harvey Forrester, Harold D. Brown, Billy Gambrell, Ray Ward, D.L. Hunnicutt, Larry Ellison, Wayne Hartman, Walter Dacus, Charles Smith.

Union Bleachery (Greenville, S.C.): Charles Sizemore (coach), Jim Grogan, James Moore, Larry Robertson, Gary Leslie, Walter Reeves, Ernest Simmons, Bruce Turner, Harold Batson, David Smith, Charles Busbee.

Clinton Mill (Clinton, S.C.): Bill Terry (coach), Truman Owens, Sam Owens, Jimmy Braswell, Billy Watkins, Ellis Hufstetler, William Caudle, Kinard Littleton, Robert Thomas, Rudolph Hamrick, Harry Nettles, Golden.

Poinsett Lumber Co. (Anderson, S.C.): Olin Mullikin (coach), Robert Moore, Robert Sanders, Joe Stegall, Nelson Massey, Furman Elrod, Joe Greenwood, William Moore, Grady Sanders, Donald Carnes, Michael Dobbins, Wiles.

Saco-Lowell (Easley, S.C.): Harry Foster (coach), Charles Huff, Charles Rogers, Gerald Townes, Glenn Edgar, Bing Day, Danny Donovon, Julian Hiott, Joe Lesley, Ralph Palmer, Harold Waldrop.

Easley Mill (Easley, S.C.): Ralph Hendricks (coach), Johnny Skinner, Courtney Heath Jr., Dennis Atkinson, Leon Chandler, Troy Suddeth, Bobby Chandler, Larry Bagwell, Joe Garrett, Harold Ensley, Charles Bagwell, Verlon McEntyre.

Davis Mechanical (Greenville, S.C.): Jerry Alexander (coach), Jack Edwards, Douglass Martin, Jim Foster, Robert Alverson, Charles Styles, James Mullinax, John Connor, Frank Durham, Luke Wyatt, William Taylor, Watson, Hooper, Williams.

Lonsdale Mill (Seneca, S.C.): B.M. Fleming (coach), J.R. Brown, T.C. McCurry, C.L. Worley, K.E. Worley, W.L. Dooley, T.H. Wade, J.M. Perry, Gary Wood, K.L. Black, Luther Hightower.

Anderson Hosiery Mill (Whitmire, S.C.): Joe Rose (coach), James Dallas, Donald Ramsey, William Brank, William Johnson, Charles Brown, William Hill, Irby Raines Jr., Alford Spotts, Arthur Branks, Edward Bostic.

Joanna Mill (Joanna, S.C.): Johnny Moore (coach), C. Force (coach), Larry King, Dwight Tucker, Kenneth Frazier, Ralph Braswell, James Haupfear, Eddie Johnson, Lester Long, David Parrish, John Clark, John Wise, Humphries.

Monsanto (Greenwood, S.C.): J.B. Shepherd (coach), Harold Nation, William Wilson, Jesse Powell, Thomas Fant, Joe Hall, Carlton Funderburk, Earl Florence, Edward Durham Jr., Harris.

Steel Heddle (Greenville, S.C.): Andy Bell (coach), Henry Reeman, Jimmy Morgan, David Hickum, Mack Masingille, Robert Burns, Richard Justice, Wallace Reid, George Tate, Buddy Herring, Willis Bell Jr., Freeman.

Pelzer Mill (Pelzer, S.C.): W.H. Taylor (coach), Don Helms, Everett Cooper, Gerald Duckworth, James Jordan, Harry Thompson, Robert Floyd, Floyd Scroggs, Bobby Luther, William Thomason, Calvin Bryson.

Lyman Mill (Lyman, S.C.): M.E. Cagle (coach), Wayne Blackmon, Donald Black, Cody Forrester, Frank Cook, Melvin Pearson, Travis Taylor, Larry Stokes, Leon Eubanks, Ted Wingo, Charles Eubanks, Bill Eubanks.

CLASS C MEN

Cannon Mill (Central, S.C.), champions: Pete Carlisle (coach), Ronnie Maravich, Pete Maravich, Dickie Senn, Jim Lever, Jimmy Sutherland, Charles Stuart, Tommy Risher, Jimmy Howard, Frank Cox, Johnny Chapman, Tommy McNeil, Walter Cox.

Slater Mill (Slater, S.C.), runners-up: Snow

Kirby (coach), Harvey Tankersley, William White, Larry Ledford, John Jarrard, William Lybrand, Thomas Adkins, Gary Cox, Paul Pritchett, Joe Taylor, Bill Williams.

Lyman Mill (Lyman, S.C.), consolation winners: Jim Jack (coach), William Green, Ray Owens, Wayne Green, Louis Carlisle, Alfred Weeks, Jack Green Jr., Robert Sanders, Daniel Rogers, Thomas Turner, Wallace Woolbright.

Union Bleachery (Greenville, S.C.): Gary Leslie (coach), Richard Aiken, Arthur Dix, Jimmy Green, Carroll Smith, Steve Smith, Wallace Waldrop, William Shivers, James Gilliland, James Holden, Tony Robertson, James Smith.

Dunean Mill (Greenville, S.C.): Ward Williams (coach), Herman Patterson, Kenneth Smith, Donnie Sargent, Clay Coleman, Jimmy Galloway, Gerald Pollard, Keith Russell, Charles Peake, Billy Allen, Arthur Hammett.

Brandon Mill (Greenville, S.C.): Charles Landreth (coach), Joseph Smith, Jimmy Riddle, Eugene Ashworth, George Wilson, Dale Lawson, Gary Reeves, Donald Morgan, Jerry Coker, William Vaughan, Billy Adams, Jerry Cooper.

Monaghan Mill (Greenville, S.C.): Fig Newton (coach), Douglas McCrary, Russell Wham, David Blackwell, George White, Johnny Holtzclaw, Danny Bagwell, Steve Satterfield, Billy Porter, Miller Bogan, Tommy Mullinax.

Liberty Mill (Liberty, S.C.): Bobby Morris (coach), Lamar Gilstrap, Archie Hitt, Herbert Head, Al Jones, Bobby Chambers, Donnell Smith, Tommy Haines, Ben Goldsmith, Noel Pettit.

Greer Mill #1 (Greer, S.C.): Butch Miller (coach), Steve Gambrell, Wayne Gambrell, Shirley Hall, Stanley Barton, Jimmy Few, James Wall, Johnny Ross, Patrick Farmer, Thomas Ingle, George Coan, Bob Barton, Sonner.

Greer Mill #2 (Greer, S.C.): Butch Miller (coach), Fred Blackwell, Troy Robeson, Reginald Wilson, William Dillard, Charles Wall, Wallace Sumner, Stephen Howell, Joe Brunson, Bill Brannon.

Simpsonville Mill (Simpsonville, S.C.): Odell Barbary (coach), Frank Garrett, Roger Thackston, Mike Garrett, Marcus Poore, Danny Norris, Denny Toby, Victor Blue, Jerry Melton, Harry Sprouse, Jerry Baughman.

Newry Mill (Newry, S.C.): Reginald Oliver (coach), James Hughes, Thomas Shaver Jr., Calhoun Cox Jr., Johnny Jones, William Field, Danna Gaillard, Dewey O'Kelley, Sammy Batson, Wayne Lacey, William Chase, Hawkins.

Piedmont Mill (Piedmont, S.C.): Curtis Terry (coach), John Mullikin, Gary Hooper, Jess Bell, Doug Barwick, Mike Welborn, Jammie Oliver, Alvin Hulsey, Billy Hooper, Gene Merritt, Joe Cely.

J.A. Nealy & Co. (Pickens, S.C.): Mat Herndon (coach), Henry Bivens, Gerald Owens, Arvel Reeves, David Youngblood, Jim McCall, Eddie Holder, Gene Finley, Jerry Roper, Jamie Rackley, Paul O'Shields, Bowers.

Stone Mfg. (Greenville, S.C.): Jimmy Beard (coach), Ted Godfrey (coach), James Beard, Danny Bruce, George Burns, Bobby Carroll, Neil Duncan, Earnest Westmoreland, Grady Wyatt, Richard Guinn, Clarence Raines, Raymond Bishop.

Poinsett Mill (Greenville, S.C.): Gene Seay (coach), Ronnie Ringstaff, Roy Johnson, Tommy Estes, Wayne Batson, Terrell Henson, Robert Smith, Billy Turner, Benjamin Morgan, John Hall, Mason.

Carolina Plating (Greenville, S.C.): J.G. Mattos (coach), Don McCrary, Cary Martin, Gary Osteen, Billy Black, Johnny Day, Sammy Christopher, Mike McCarson, Ronald Hilliard, Al Roach, Joe Keller, Lay.

Brandon Mill (Woodruff, S.C.): Bobby Sexton (coach), Richard Lambert, Willie Waddell, Ray Lyda, Jerry Burdette, James Garrett, Keith Cox, Thomas Pack, David Lowery, Jackie Smith, Gordon Godfrey.

Pelzer Mill #1 (Pelzer, S.C.): Gary Geddens (coach), Donny Autry, Roger Harris, William Harris, Billy Smith, John McClellion, Kenneth Collins, Derrell Lindley, Keith Rogers, Curtis Woodson, Ronnie Williams.

Pelzer Mill #2 (Pelzer, S.C.): Marion Middleton (coach), Larry Holcombe, Gary Helms, Don Sanders, Michael Muth, Walter Trammell, Samuel Rogers, James Cobb, Ray McClellion, Benny Smith, Gary Gregory.

CLASS A WOMEN

Slater Mill (Slater, S.C.), champions: Margaret Wright (coach), Linda Brown, Barbara Elders, Carolyn Clayton, Sue Vickers, Carol Richardson, Judy Hodgens, Joan Knight, Lillian Looper, Priscilla Hunt, Barbara Ivey, Judy Buddin, Pat Murphy.

Lonsdale Mill (Seneca, S.C.), runners-up:

B.M. Fleming (coach), Brenda Addis, Beverly Dooley, Barbara Wade, Evelyn Black, Johelen Dawkins, Bertha Bryant, Wanda Hanvey, Ruth Foster, Nell Lumpkin, Ova Poole, Willa Sosebee, Norma Miller, Hawkins.

Poinsett Lumber Co. (Anderson, S.C.), consolation winners: James Anderson (coach), Caroline Harbin, Peggy Anderson, Annie Tribble, Brenda Gable, Bobbie Burris, Barbara Sanders, Patsy Sanders, Pearl Scarborough, Elaine Davis, Nancy McCollum, Glenda Herring, Joyce Richardson.

Littlejohn's (Greenville, S.C.): Hunter, M. Looper, S. Lambert, Garrick, Moon, Sweat, Powell, Kelley, P. Lambert, Sheriff, Bauns.

Greer Mill (Greer, S.C.): Butch Miller (coach), Linda Sloan, Joan Stevenson, Beverly Warren, Anita McCallister, Carol Broad, Frances Welborn, Janice Hawkins, Ann Blackwell, Linda Arledge, Spearman, Pruitt, Suddeth, Barnette.

Carolina Plating (Greenville, S.C.): Cotton Williamson (coach), Dewey Corbin (coach), June Nash, Vivian Williamson, Jacquiline Corbin, Peggy Duncan, Doris Holcombe, Carolyn Batson, Carol Moore, Cheryl Caldwell, Beverly Cox, Martha Mostella, Ellen Wood, Martha Cordell, Judy Justus, Brenda Perry, Philpot.

Pelzer Mill (Pelzer, S.C.): Buddy Ross (coach), Barbara Pittman, Judy Edens, Brenda Harris, Cecil Wooten, Marsha Ross, Kay McClellion, Milly King, Judy Thompson, Barbara Bell, Joan Harris, Janet Pasco, Patsy Jordan.

Monsanto (Pensacola, Fla.): Carol Dumas (coach), Peggy Baldwin, Sandra Davis, Claudette Dubbery, Mary Dumas, Ann Ellis, Carolyn Frederickson, Marian Fillingim, Loraine Gomillion, Rusty LeVasseur, Jo McCall, Bea Simmons, Wanda Stevens.

---------- 1962 ----------

Officers: John Mullikin (Piedmont, S.C.), President; Ward Williams (Greenville, S.C.), Vice President; Ken Pittman (Greenville, S.C.), Executive Secretary; Fred Byrd (Greenville, S.C.), Secretary; Joe Gilreath (Piedmont, S.C.), Assistant Secretary; Divver Hendrix (Greenville, S.C.), Treasurer; Whitey Kendall (Greenville), Supervisor of Officials.

Executive Committee: Clarence Thomas (Greenville, S.C.), S.R. DuBose (Whitmire, S.C.), Jack Lindsay (Seneca, S.C.), Willie Wilbanks (Ware Shoals, S.C.), Curtis Terry (Piedmont, S.C.), Jim McDuffie (Greenville, S.C.), Willard Fowler (Greer, S.C.), Fred Powers (Asheville, N.C.), Jim Anderson (Greenville, S.C.), Dan Foster (Greenville, S.C.), Keener Garrett (Greenville, S.C.), Harry Foster (Easley, S.C.), Jim Grogan (Greenville, S.C.), Paul Kaiser (Anderson, S.C.), Snow Kirby (Marietta, S.C.), Fig Newton (Greenville, S.C.), Dudley Tollison (Lyman, S.C.).

OPEN DIVISION

Todd-Moore (Columbia, S.C.), champions: Randy Coleman (coach), Art Whisnant, Bud Cronin, Russell Porter, Bob Frantz, Grady Wallace, Mike Callahan, Richie Hoffman, Dan Morgan, Bob Dietz, Jerry Redman, Larry Dial, Charlie Todd.

Sherrill Mfg. (Dallas, N.C.), runners-up: Mike Ross (coach), Carol Youngkin, Doug Kistler, Howard Hurt, Jack Huggins, Phil Carrigan, Johnny Jenkins, Larry Neal, Terry Whistnant, Morris Newton, Fowler.

Poinsetta Upholstering (Greenville, S.C.), consolation winners: Bill Morrow (coach), Thomas Cameron, James Waldrop, Charles Senger Jr., Russell Wham, Harold Wham, Fred Lentz Jr., Willie Gray, Richard Wright, Steve Ross, Austin Cunkle Jr., Morris.

Chattanooga VFW (Chattanooga, Tenn.): Ralph Hooper (coach), Clyde Eads, Joe Gardner, Herschel Smith, Bill Wade, Billy Bolding, Ralph Lester, Ron Peeples, Chester Ryesindorth, Keith Ammons, Pinkney Gilchrist, Marvin Gregory, Powers, P. Gardner.

Piedmont Mill (Piedmont, S.C.): J.C. Blackston (coach), Vince Yockel, Don Carver, Dag Wilson, Gene Seay, Ed Krajack, Tom Mahaffey, Bob Benson, Bill Tuttle, Bob Pinson, Butch Miller.

Dillard's Sporting Goods (Easley, S.C.): Stoney Williams (coach), Pete Carlisle, Curtis Wilson, Jack Wiles, Tic Simonelli, Gene Beard, Bruce Stroud, Stanley Ayers, Billy Ensley, Bill Lavam, Joe Shirley, Pat Hall, Jimmy Chastain, Talley.

Piedmont Paint (Greenville, S.C.): Jim McCall (coach), Buddy McCall, Jack League, Gary Daniels, Ronnie Russell, Jimmy Gentry, Tony Moody, Bobby Wike, Tommy Turner, Jimmy Holden, Ken Taylor.

Seneca All Stars (Seneca, S.C.): Dave Neilson (coach), Bruce Thompson (coach), Dave Thompson, Connie Berry, Lloyd Jackson, Dub Robinson, Larry Allsep, Jerry Burt, Frank Bishop, Bob Johnson, Bob Fleming, Al Boni, Mat Herndon, Johnny McGoff, Mike Black, Bruce Thompson, Fowler, McMoore.

Class A Men

Apalache Mill (Greer, S.C.), champions: Marion Jones (coach), Jim Cox (coach), June Raines, Steve Gambrell, Jimmy Herring, Joe Brisontine, Don Lister, Billy Fuller, Wayne Gambrell, Ray Clark, Charles Perry.

Pelzer Mill (Pelzer, S.C.), runners-up: Tom Nash (coach), Floyd Scroggs, William Thomason, James Thomason, Jerry Garner, Harold Roper, Doug Harris, Gary Geddens, Derrell Lindley, Leon Autry, J.W. Hopkins, Don Helms.

Slater Mill (Slater, S.C.), consolation winners: Snow Kirby (coach), Jerry Brinkley, Billy Barbary, James Lewis, Dacus Tucker, Billy Farmer, Kenneth Garrett, Bill Lybrand, Robert Kirby, Richard Stephenson.

Monsanto (Pensacola, Fla.): Ralph Nelson (coach), Ken Raines, Johnny Taylor, Bill Williams, Don Gates, Bill Griffin, Frank Watson, James Hardin, Dennis Wilson, Thomas Poe, Charles Livingston.

Poinsett Lumber Co. (Anderson, S.C.): Lewis Acker (coach), Olin Mullikin, Robert Moore, Nelson Massey, Furman Elrod, Joe Greenway, William Poore, Grady Sanders, Michael Dobbins, Benny Speares, Bill Moore.

Monsanto (Greenwood, S.C.): Carl Treadway (coach), Harold Nation, William Wilson, Jesse Powell, Thomas Fant, Joe Hall, Jerry Johnson, Bobby Cox, Jim Diamond, Bennie Ross, William Marsh, A. Cox.

Piedmont Mill (Piedmont, S.C.): Harry Waldrop (coach), Earl Wooten, Joe Hiott, Earl Maxwell, Paul Nye, Ernie Chambers, Jim Slaughter, Don Roper, John Mullikin, Doug Emery, Ray Foxx.

Class B Men

Saco-Lowell (Easley, S.C.), champions: Bob Edgar (coach), Glen Forister (coach), Charles Rogers, Gerald Townes, Glenn Edgar, Bing Day, Joe Lesley, Ralph Palmer, Harold Waldrop, James Wilbanks, Jimmy Chapman, Holbert Crowe.

Pelzer Mill (Pelzer, S.C.), runners-up: Bill Hopkins (coach), Everett Cooper, Mike Jordan, Harry Thompson, William Harris, James Cobb, Herman Evatt, Tommy Brown, Ray Roach, Ronnie Williams, Don Helms, Lindley.

Davis Mechanical (Greenville, S.C.), consolation winners: J.D. Rudder (coach), Robert Alverson, Frank Durham, James Gillespie, Ralph Durham, Murray Hall, Thomas Welborn, Gary Moore, Douglas Greene, David Welborn, Jerry Alexander.

Union Bleachery (Greenville, S.C.): Lewis Redd (coach), James Moore, Larry Robertson, Ernest Simmons, Harold Batson, Stanley Smith, Everette Dix, James Green, William Sanders, Richard Ayers.

Stone Mfg. (Greenville, S.C.): John Kemp (coach), Charles Coleman, Harold Westbrooks, Joe Keller, Jesse Raines, James Ball, Walter Duke, Richard Shaw, James Ansel, Donald Howell, Jimmy Christopher.

Homelite (Greer, S.C.): Tom Poole (coach), Harold T. Brown, Harvey Forrester, D.L. Hunnicutt, Wayne Hartman, Steve Dacus, Darrell Toby, Melvin Roper, Jack Kay, Geddis Tucker, Dominie Mussori.

Easley Mill (Easley, S.C.): Larry Bagwell (coach), Johnny Skinner, Bobby Chandler, Troy Suddeth, Charles Garrett, Terry Gillespie, Ronald Brandt, Roy Coker, Micky Holiday, Julian Hiott, D. Garrett, J. Garrett.

Anderson Hosiery Mill (Whitmire, S.C.): Joe Rose (coach), James Dallas, Donald Ramsey, William Johnson, Charles Brown, Irby Raines, Alfred Spotts, Jerry Wilbanks, Billy Johnson, Philip Spotts, Kenneth Frazier.

Steel Heddle (Greenville, S.C.): Andy Bell (coach), Henry Freeman (coach), David Hickum, Mack Masingille, Richard Justice, Willis Bell Jr., Gary Durham, G.R. Gallemore, T.D. Holtzclaw, Richard Oliver, Ken Pittman, Gobel Reed.

Lyman Mill (Lyman, S.C.): M.E. Cagle (coach), Wayne Blackmon, Cody Forrester, Travis Taylor, Leon Eubanks, Horace Craig, James Sargent, Jack Fuller, James Shytle, Wayne Greene, Donald Godfrey.

Diehl Mfg. (Pickens, S.C.): Don Alexander (coach), David Breazeale, Don Alexander, Rex Corbitt, Kent Suddeth, Benny Hunter, Lee Welling, David Youngblood, Jamie Rackley, Alex Gettys Jr., Jerry Smith.

Greenville Airport (Greenville, S.C.): Ralph Warren (coach), Bill Gosnell, James Graydon, Amos Jarman, Charles Harrell, Joseph Martin,

Ronnie Ringstaff, Robert Stoner, Charles Todd, John Cooper, Roy Johnson.

Dunean Mill (Greenville, S.C.): Bobby Grant (coach), Kenneth Smith, Ralph Davis, Marion Hammond, Kenneth Stroud, Douglas Gailey, Truman McCarter, Ronald Cross, Donnie Sargent, Leon McWhite, Earl Whittington, Pollard.

Berkeley Mill (Balfour, N.C.): Norman Greene (coach), Paul Nickel, Lonnie Graham, Dwight Leroy, Frank Drake, Wayne Fletcher, Noah Goode, Charles Weisner, Charles Pace, Voyle Massey.

Poinsett Mill (Greenville, S.C.): Frank Millwood (coach), Pat Campbell, Bill Roach, Larry Campbell, Curtis Campbell, Mays Cooper, Jerry Autry, Wayne Evatt, Benjamin Morgan, Fredric Millwood, Roger Durham.

Belton Mill (Belton, S.C.): Jimmy Lowe (coach), Bill Dunlap, James Dickert, Jerry Dunlap, Terry Martin, Douglas Broome, Jerry Snipes, Joe Martin, David Shaw.

Sangamo Electric Co. (Pickens, S.C.): Joel Allgood (coach), Garland Rigdon, Frank Smith, Tommy McCue, Gerald Bice, Olin Smith, Charles Grant, Ray Fowler, William Garren, David Rogers, James Fortson, D. Smith.

Class C Men

Pelzer Mill (Pelzer, S.C.), champions: Lee Terry (coach), Marion Middleton (coach), Larry Holcombe, Gary Helms, Don Sanders, Mike Muth, Walter Trammell, Sammy Rogers, Ray McClellion, Benny Smith, Joe Ellenburg, Paul Proffitt.

Greer Mill (Greer, S.C.), runners-up: Benny Burrell (coach), Lewis Phillips (coach), Wayne Gambrell, Patrick Farmer, Thomas Ingle, Mike Fair, Robert Harley, William Payne, Mike Rogers, Billy Stewart, Benny Upton, Stephen Moore.

Liberty Mill (Liberty, S.C.), consolation winners: Bobby Morris (coach), Lamar Gilstrap, Noel Petit, Archie Hitt, Al Jones, Donnell Smith, Tommy Haines, Mike Burgess, Jimmy Pettit, Wilburn Dodson.

Lonsdale Mill (Seneca, S.C.): Bobby Fleming (coach), James Lever, Samuel Stowe, Ronald Knoerr, James Lawless, Bennie Sosebee, Wallace Peebles, William Field Jr., Richard Senn, Carol Kirby, Troy Lacey.

Cannon Mill (Central, S.C.): Don Carver (coach), Pete Maravich, Charles Lever, Jimmy Sutherland, Frank Cox, Calvin Evatt, Bobby Harrison, Gerald McMahon, Avery Nelson, Walter Sherman, Bruce Wofford.

Slater Mill (Slater, S.C.): Lloyd Kelly (coach), William White, Thomas Adkins, Gary Cox, Paul Pritchett, Joe Taylor, Roger White, Wayne Moon, Johnny Laws, Franklin Hall, Joel Burgess, D. White.

Monaghan Mill (Greenville, S.C.): Fig Newton (coach), Frank White, Danny Bagwell, Steve Satterfield, Miller Bogan, Vernon Stewart, Jerry McAtee, Donald Harkins, Teddy Hester, Ken Childress, Robert Griffin.

Simpsonville Mill (Simpsonville, S.C.): Red Barbary (coach), Frank Garrett, Marcus Poore, Victor Blue, Jerry Baughman, Tommy Crowe, Eddie Barbary, Edward Blakely, Donald Savage, Dean Willis, Thomas Keesley, Brooks.

Piedmont Mill (Piedmont, S.C.): Pat Patterson (coach), Billy Hooper, Jess Bell, Mike Welborn, Gene Merritt, David Riddle, Terry Smith, Truman Bates, Winfred Gambrell, Billy Harris, Truitt Tollison, Oliver, Bowie, G. Gambrell, D. Cooper.

Glenwood Mill (Easley, S.C.): Jerry McCarter (coach), Mackie Nichols, Roy Smith, James Wilson, Michael Donovan, Donald Hughes, David Stephens, John Cutchins, Daniel Garrison, Sydney McDaniel, James LeFevre.

Belton Mill (Belton, S.C.): Jimmy Lowe (coach), Joe Chandler, Calvin McCombs, George Chandler, Frank Snipes, Gary Dernhardt, Louis Blake, Steve Griffin, Micky Meeks, Joe Hawkins, C. Chandler.

Southern Weaving (Greenville, S.C.): Joe Murray (coach), Jack Miller (coach), Danny Williamson, Bob Bayne, William Perry, Robert Hall, William Porter, Larry Cox, Carroll.

McCrary Mechanical (Travelers Rest, S.C.): Thornwell Henson (coach), Richard Aiken, Grady Wyatt, Jerry Bagwell, William McCrary, Jake Christopher, Charles Roach, George Hilliard, Roger Hayes, Paul Grier, Johnny Day.

Woodside Mill (Greenville, S.C.): Jim McDuffie (coach), William Vaughan, Doyle Lawson Jr., Billy Whitman, Johnny Holtzclaw, Jimmy Griffin, Terry Najim, Jerry Coker, Charles Hall, James Galloway, William Burns.

American Spinning (Greenville, S.C.): Neil Duncan, Rando Clark, Jimmy Clark, Danny Williams, Bill Morgan, Ben Morgan, Kent Campbell, Wallace Evans, J.D. Norris, Charles Emery, Duncan.

Southern Textile Basketball Tournament Rosters Appendix 1 219

Saco-Lowell (Easley, S.C.): Cletis Perkins (coach), Marshall Scott, Ronald Wilson, Dennis Waldrop, Boyce Waldrop, James Benjamin, Gerry Lankford, Jim McCall, Nickey Gantt, Dean Holder, Kenny Harrison.

Class A Women
Slater Mill (Slater, S.C.), champions: Carolyn Clayton (coach), Margaret Wright, Linda Brown, Barbara Elders, Sue Vickers, Carol Richardson, Doris Clark, Joan Kirby, Priscilla Hunt, Beverly Cox, Margaret Tomlinson, Annie Tribble, Priscilla Coker, Doris Capps, Elizabeth Picklesimer.

Simpsonville Mill (Simpsonville, S.C.), runners-up: Red Barbary (coach), Mickey Brookshire, Linda Green, Patsy Hendrix, JoAnn Calvert, Charlotte Thackston, Sharon Tanner, Patricia Stone, Marian Styles, Dorothy Stone, Dolly Henderson, Pat Hudson, Mickey Davis, Judy Buddin, Morgan.

Carolina Plating (Greenville, S.C.), consolation winners: Broadus Miller (coach), Carolyn Heaton, Carol Broad, Ellie Worling, Brenda Lawson, Peggy Lambert, Sarah Lambert, Sandra Hunter, Linda Moon, Sue Lindsay, Carolyn Fant, Pat Grimball, Bonnie Hidd, Boone.

Pelzer Mill (Pelzer, S.C.): Betty Crain (coach), Brenda Rainey, Iris Thompson, Patsy Rogers, Delores Rogers, Betty Creamer, Jo Burton, Ann Fricks, Jeane Bowen, Fredia Smith, Margaret Kelly, Judith Thompson, Sandra Kinsey, Bunton, P. Rogers.

Monsanto (Pensacola, Fla.): Bob (coach), Claudette Duberly, Bea Simmons, Carolyn Williams, Marian Fillingim, Hayrul LeVasseur, Jo McCall, Nell Simmons, Wanda Stevens, Phyllis White, Irene Lahey, Drelia King, C.Y. Frederickson.

Overnite (Greenville, S.C.): Jim McDuffie (coach), Linda Sloan, Glenda Herring, Elizabeth Arant, Juanita Seay, Judy Justus, Mary Pruitt, Jane Welborn, Ann Spearman, Brenda Perry, Jo Padworski, Barbara McDuffie, Evelyn Burr, Foster, Addis, Wade.

Dunean Mill (Greenville, S.C.): Larry Ashley (coach), Nellie Grant, Sandra Turner, Gladys Norris, Doris Justice, Edwina Grant, Alice Grant, Gwyn Balcombe, Betty Johnson, Gail Kirby, Authia Paige, Delores Stewart, Bobbie Philpot.

Textile Plating (Greenville, S.C.): Grogan, S. Gilstrap, James, Churchwell, M. Gilstrap, Harvey, Stephens, Ukena, Brock, Jamison, Atkins, Danielson.

―――――― 1963 ――――――

Officers: John Mullikin (Piedmont, S.C.), President; Ward Williams (Greenville, S.C.), Vice President; Ken Pittman (Greenville, S.C.), Executive Secretary; Fred Byrd (Greenville, S.C.), Secretary; Joe Gilreath (Piedmont, S.C.), Assistant Secretary; Divver Hendrix (Greenville, S.C.), Treasurer; Whitey Kendall (Greenville), Supervisor of Officials.

Executive Committee: Clarence Thomas (Greenville, S.C.), S.R. DuBose (Whitmire, S.C.), Willie Wilbanks (Ware Shoals, S.C.), Curtis Terry (Piedmont, S.C.), Jim McDuffie (Greenville, S.C.), Willard Fowler (Greer, S.C.), Fred Powers (Asheville, N.C.), Jim Anderson (Greenville, S.C.), Dan Foster (Greenville, S.C.), Harry Foster (Easley, S.C.), Jim Grogan (Greenville, S.C.), Paul Kaiser (Anderson, S.C.), Snow Kirby (Marietta, S.C.), Fig Newton (Greenville, S.C.), Dudley Tollison (Lyman, S.C.), Bill Hopkins (Pelzer, S.C.), Summers Jarrett (Pensacola, Fla.).

Open Division
Pharr Worsted Mill (McAdenville, N.C.), champions: David Weideman, Johnny Walker, Louis Pittman, Doug Moe, Jack Huggins, Terry Brennan, Jerry Clemmer, Bob Woollard, Mike Ross, Lenny Rosenbluth, Joe McDermott, Danny Lotz, Brine Bermann, Blair Walker.

Murrell Brothers Sand (Greenville, S.C.), runners-up: W.C. Murrell (coach), Jimmy Holden, Buddy McCall, Bobby Wike, Charles Jennings, Don Seaver, Jimmy Herring, Bob Skells, Bob Sly, Jimmy Gentry, Jerry Smith, Gerald Glur, Ray Siminski, Carver, John Vickers, Wilkie, Angle.

Stanly Mill (Oakboro, N.C.), consolation winners: Riley Skidmore (coach), Richard Whitis, William Ficke, Bernard Brennan, Henry Steincke, Tom Burton, Kermit Williams, Jerry Wells, Jim Wiles, William Jarman, Charles Kelton, John Ladd, James Herring.

Sangamo Electric Co. (West Union, S.C.): Dave Neilson (coach), Bruce Thompson, Connie Berry, Mac Lemmons, John Jackson, Bill Gillespie, Leon McLemore, Mike Black, Pee

Wee Wade, Tom Shaver, Sam Smith, Saul Richardson, Jim Benson, Wayne Lacey, Larry Seitz, Camp, McCorkle, Gobel.

Todd-Moore (Columbia, S.C.): Cecil Woolbright (coach), Art Whisnant, Russell Porter, Grady Wallace, Mike Callahan, Dan Morgan, Scott Ward, Jim Podell, Bill Cary, Mel Patterson, Choo Choo Newman, Hank Martin, Paul Goode, Haney.

Brooks & Sons Textile Parts (Dallas, N.C.): Kenneth Bogle (coach), Jack Huggins, Larry Brown, Mike Ross, Jerry Wells, Tommy Burton, James Wiles, Joe McDermott, Fred Schmidt, Dave Wiedeman, Bob Woollard, Louis Pittman.

Dillard's Sporting Goods (Easley, S.C.): Leo Oney (coach), William Henson, William Carter, William Pugh, Jack Fitzgerald, Vernon Vance, James Solomon, Ammons, Buddy Cubitt, Bill Wade, Morris, Gardner, Belk, Nakum.

Bill Delany's Sporting Goods (Greenville, S.C.): Leo Berni (coach), W.L. Gray, Steve Ross, Dick Wright, Joe Cooper, Earl Maxwell Jr., June Raines, Butch Miller, Steve Gambrell, Hanes Herndon, George Krajack, Carl Hodge, Bill Mathis, Bob Waldrop, W. Gambrell.

Clark-Schwebel (Anderson, S.C.): Dag Wilson, Leroy Parnell, Phillips, Poole, Shain, Stevenson, Brooks, Ensley.

Class A Men

Piedmont Mill (Piedmont, S.C.), champions: Earl Wooten (coach), Joe Hiott, Ray Foxx, Larry Holcombe, Gene Seay, Vince Yockel, Billy Hooper, Larry Patterson, Clyde Bryson, Gambrell.

Pelzer Mill (Pelzer, S.C.), runners-up: Tom Nash (coach), James Thomason, Harold Roper, Doug Harris, Gary Geddens, J.W. Hopkins, James Harris, Everett Cooper, Wayne Thompson, Don Helms, Jimmy Cobb, Ben Roper, P. Harris, B. Harris.

Monsanto (Pensacola, Fla.), consolation winners: George Thomas Jr.(coach), Ken Raines, Johnny Taylor, Bill Farrish, Don Gates, Bill Griffin, Jim Hardin, Dennis Wilson, Jerry Gordon, Rof Fohl, Lester Baldwin, James Henley, Harkins.

Cranston Print Works (Fletcher, N.C.): Tom Hardee (coach), Norman Greene, Jerald Ramsey, Cloyd Pryor, Ronald Miller, David Orr, Floyd Pryor, Norman Youngblood, Frank Creasman, James Matthews, Yogi Poteet.

Slater Mill (Slater, S.C.): Snow Kirby (coach), Jerry Brinkley, Billy Barbary, James Lewis, Dacus Tucker, Billy Farmer, Kenneth Garrett, Robert Kirby, Richard Stephenson, William White, Harvey Tankersley, Ed Brinkley, Ted Tucker.

Poinsett Lumber Co. (Anderson, S.C.): James Morrison (coach), Olin Mullikin, Robert Moore, Nelson Massey, Furman Elrod, Joe Stegall, Grady Sanders, Michael Dobbins, Jack Wiles Sr., Jimmy Edmonds, Robby Martin, Acker.

Monsanto (Greenwood, S.C.): Carl Treadway (coach), Garrett Nation, Alvin Wilson, Jerry Johnson, Jim Diamond, Pete Carlisle, Herb Edmonds, Stick Wilson, Kiebler James, Herndon McElmurray.

Class B Men

Lyman Mill (Lyman, S.C.), champions: Virgil Pruitt (coach), Wayne Blackmon, Steve Brown, Fred Cariens, Leon Eubanks, Bill Eubanks, Cody Forrester, Johnny Johnson, James Shytle, Larry Stokes, Trig Taylor, Jerry Green, Bill Green.

Anderson Hosiery Mill (Whitmire, S.C.), runners-up: Joe Rose (coach), Eddie Walker, Wallace Alexander, Earl Hendrix, Alfred Spotts, James Dallas, Bill Johnson, Leonard Price, Billy Black, Phil Spotts, Larry Boswell.

Steel Heddle (Greenville, S.C.), consolation winners: Andy Bell (coach), Mack Lemmons, Mike Davis, Grover Owings, Ken Pittman, Richard Gallemore, David Hickum, Dean Holtzclaw, Gobel Reed, Donald Hill, Douglas Spooner.

Davis Mechanical (Greenville, S.C.): Jerry Alexander (coach), R.B. Durham (coach), Robert Alverson, Murray Hall, Thomas Welborn, Dewey Corbin, Allen Patterson, James Johnson, Eddie Forrester, Darrell Toby, Joel Phillips, Roy Johnson.

Saco-Lowell (Easley, S.C.): T.J. Hudgens, Charles Crowe, Joe Roper, Ray Palmer, James Wilbanks, Fredric Millwood, Russell Wham, Jerry Whaley, Terry Caldwell, Donald Foster, Harold Wham, Ray Whaley, B. Wham, Williams.

Union Bleachery (Greenville, S.C.): Charles Sizemore (coach), Ernest Simmons, Stanley Smith, Arthur Dix, William Sanders, Richard Aiken, Calvin Rumler, Thomas Bolton, Tommy Stevenson, James Smith, Moore, Sims, Redol.

Stone Mfg. (Greenville, S.C.): Gary Smith (coach), Harold Westbrook, Gary Smith, Phil Brown, Randy Smith, Robert Scoggins, Jake Tollison, Ronald Usery, Bobby Parks, Wendell Lee, Doug Smith.

Homelite (Greer, S.C.): Wayne Hartman (coach), Harold T. Brown, Harvey Forrester, D.L. Hunnicutt, Steve Dacus, Melvin Roper, Jack Kay, Howard Clayton, Willie Brown, Patrick Farmer, Edward Nelson.

Easley Mill (Easley, S.C.): Coon Hendrix (coach), Johnny Skinner, Bobby Chandler, Charles Garrett, Terry Gillespie, Roy Coker, Joe Garrett, James Campbell, Mike McCoy, Thomas Lankford.

Diehl Mfg. (Pickens, S.C.): Rex Corbitt (coach), David Breazeale, Don Alexander, Benny Hunter, Jamie Rackley, Alex Gettys Jr., David Garrison, Joseph Adams, Jim McCall, Wayne Nicholson, Ronald Freeman.

Dunean Mill (Greenville, S.C.): Douglas Gailey (coach), Kenneth Smith, Truman McCarter, Ronald Cross, Donnie Sargent, Leon McWhite, Earl Whittington, James Galloway, Jerry Camp, Jimmy Gossett, Gerald Pollard.

Sangamo Electric Co. (Pickens, S.C.): Joel Allgood (coach), Eugene Smith, Tommy McCue, Gerald Bice, Chester Smith, Bill Fowler, James Suddeth, W.K. Swaynghame, Robert Porter, Allen Adams, Frank Smith.

Torrington Co. (Clinton, S.C.): Jack Cox (coach), Jack Templeton (coach), James Smith, Robert Thomas, Donald Cauble, Melvin Bailey, Claude Hartline, William Fuller, Larry Walker, Russell Emerson, William Hopkins, Clisby Templeton.

Gluck Mill (Anderson, S.C.): Early Hanna (coach), Tommy Mahaffey, Gary Whitlock, Joe Stansell, Larry Whitten, Johnny Mauldin, Farrell Giles, Neil Whitfield, Glenn Smith, Curtis Wood.

Joanna Mill (Joanna, S.C.): Johnny Moore (coach), John Thomas, James Lollis, Joe Foster, Kenneth Frazier, Earl Rushton, Robert Tinsley, Larry King, Rudy Hamrick, Dwight Tucker, Richard Long.

Fiberglas (Anderson, S.C.): Roy Bridges (coach), Phil Robertson (coach), Melvin Aiken, Paul Scheuerle, Jerry Parnell, John Robertson, Michael Mitcham, Robert Passerello, Larry Moore, Robert Hancock, Charles Aiken, Jerry Wright.

Landrum Mill (Landrum, S.C.): Curt Beasley (coach), Gerald Collins, Bobby Fagan, Joe Horton, Robert Maulgram, Ray McIntyre, Keith Ritchey, Donald Smith, Dean Smith, Allen Smith, Wayne Thompson.

Poinsett Mill (Greenville, S.C.): Frank Millwood (coach), Curtis Campbell, Pat Campbell, Robert Lavender, Marshall Hall, Benny Morgan, Larry Campbell, Mays Cooper, Ronald Peebles, Leon Smith, Roger Durham.

CLASS C MEN

Cannon Mill (Central, S.C.), champions: Don Carver (coach), Pete Maravich, Jim Sutherland, Frank Cox, Jack Stallworth, Alex Brannon, Jack Federline, Jamie Gaillard, Kent Lawrence, John Benson, Barry Peck, Fred Stallworth, George Brannon.

Greer Mill (Greer, S.C.), runners-up: Butch Miller (coach), Larry Gambrell, Thomas Ingle, Robert Harley, William Payne, Mike Rogers, Billy Stewart, Steve Moore, Clint Turner, Arthur Craig, Clay Bradburn, Frank Rogers, G. Gambrell, C. Gambrell.

Fairforest Finishing (Clevedale, S.C.), consolation winners: R.D. Cannon (coach), Lloyd Hayes, Donald Jones, L.B. Ellefson, James Cobb, Bob Solesbee, Mickey White, Stephen Green, William Varner, James Ferguson, Anthony Everette, Ellison.

Sangamo Electric Co. (Pickens, S.C.): Larry Bagwell (coach), Bob Cochran, Gene Finley, Dean Holder, Alex Gettys, Paul O'Shields, Jamie Rackley, David House, David Hardin, Charles Taylor, Johnny Rhodes, Wilson.

Pelzer Mill (Pelzer, S.C.): W.H. Taylor (coach), Mike Muth, Bill Harris, Dicky McClellion, Steve Autry, Gary Gregory, Joe Ellenburg, Marty Crawford, Mike Kellett, Lee Terry, Terry Smith, James Darby, Evatt.

Lyman Mill (Lyman, S.C.): Jim Jack (coach), Arthur Craig, Forest Kinnett Jr., Louis Carlisle Jr., John Owens Jr., Warren Nicholson, Gary Hix, John Mullinax, Larry McFadden, Thomas Mullinax, Jerry Good.

Liberty Mill (Liberty, S.C.): Bobby Morris (coach), Donnell Smith, Tommy Haines, Mike Burgess, Jimmy Pettit, Wilburn Dodson, Dolan Ricketts, Hovey Roper, Kenneth Adcox, Don Kelly, Joe Hunter, Owens.

Lonsdale Mill (Seneca, S.C.): Bobby Fleming (coach), James Crooks, Samuel Stowe, James Lawless, Mickey Sosebee, Wallace Peebles, Gene Kirby, Jim Chase, Nicky Chapman, Wayne Shirley, Bill Smith, Lane Vickey, Glenn Hart.

Monaghan Mill (Greenville, S.C.): Charles Jennings (coach), James Bagwell, Vernon Stewart, Jerry Bagwell, Donald Harkins, Gary Hester, Philip Quinn, Leo Sutton, Danny Williamson, Mike Fair, Steve Connelly.

Piedmont Mill (Piedmont, S.C.): Earl Wooten (coach), David Riddle, Terry Smith, Truman Bates, Danny Gambrell, Truitt Tollison, Duke Pressley, Tommy Hart, Stanley Brown, Cleveland Richards, Donnie Porter.

McCrary Mechanical (Travelers Rest, S.C.): Paul Goebel (coach), Grady Wyatt, Jake Christopher, Charles Roach, Johnny Day, Tommy Brown, Chuck Werner, Charles Breazeale, Wayne Ward, Charles Hall, Mike McCarson, Hayes.

Woodside Mill (Greenville, S.C.): Jim McDuffie (coach), Jimmy Griffin, Donnie Lewis, Ronnie Hawkins, Harry Trammell, Tony Waldrop, Allen Turner, Earl Stewart, Larry Grice, Steve Allison, Dobbie Caldwell.

Easley Mill (Easley, S.C.): J.W. Waldrop (coach), Coon Hendrix (coach), Harvey Galloway, Richard Stewart, Eugene Waldrop, Marion Garrett, Roy Smith, James Fortescue, Dan Rampey, Deryl Stokes, Leon Suddeth.

Monarch Mill (Union, S.C.): Warren Humphries (coach), Frederick Baldwin, Robert Baldwin, Ralph Brown, William Gault, Kenneth Grady, Joe Humphries, Neal Linder, Derril Morris, Charles Moss, Thomas Sanders, Charles Moss, Thomas Sanders, S. Baldwin.

Glen Lowery Mill (Whitmire, S.C.): Ken Coleman (coach), Eddie Gaffney, James Abrams, Clay Hipp, Carey Ramsey, Kenneth Bruce, Ray Sharpe, Olin Raines, Ronald Erskine, James Smith.

Newry Mill (Newry, S.C.): Dave Neilson (coach), Wayne Lacy, Dana Gaillard, Charlie Holstead, John Chase, Sam Barfield, Henry Laye, Webb Daniel, Donnie Hall, Elwood Mays, Jim Dupre, Steele, Foster, Riley, Davis.

Brandon Mill (Greenville, S.C.): Charles Landreth (coach), James Caldwell, Doyle Clary, Joe Anders, James Orr, Billy Whitman, Dale Cannon, Dennis Stone, Billy Adams, James Cox, Kent Campbell.

Williams Gin (Dacusville, S.C.): Jim Johnson (coach), Barry Bynum, Henry Ballard, Jerry Stone, Donald Williams, Troy Davis, Danny Cox, Jimmy White, Wayne Holcombe, Bill McConnell, Joe McConnell.

CLASS A WOMEN

Slater Mill (Slater, S.C.), champions: Margaret Wright (coach), Sue Vickers, Doris Capps, Joan Kirby, Priscilla Hunt, Judy Clark, Leila Harvin, Darlene Wood, Peggy Chumley, Sandra Ingram, Joan Nelson, Diane Smith, Ann Thornton.

Poinsett Lumber Co. (Anderson, S.C.), runners-up: James Anderson (coach), Annie Tribble, Barbara Sanders, Julia Erwin, Sandra Lawton, Lynette Bryant, Janice Feltman, Melba Yeargin, Betty Brown, Joyce Richardson, Brenda Wiles, Peggy Anderson, Bobbie Burriss, Iris Blackwell, Beth Picklesimer, Newton, Ashley, Smith.

Carolina Plating (Greenville, S.C.), consolation winners: Broadus Miller (coach), Carolyn Heaton, Carol Broad, Ellie Worling, Brenda Lawson, Peggy Lambert, Sue Lindsay, Carolyn Friend, Pauline Grimball, Helen Rister, Antha Paige, Ann Criswell, Elizabeth Price, Dorothy Lindsay, Emily Hamm, Barbara Wallenzing, Brenda Wallenzing, Merritt, Marett, C. Rister, Harum, L. Rister.

Glen Lowery Mill (Whitmire, S.C.): Mrs. Lou Collins (coach), Bonnie Collins, Patricia Dallas, Dorothy DuBose, Martha DuBose, Nancy Gilliam, Kathy Gilliam, Ann Kibler, Kay Leaman, Margaret Miller, Bonita Mitchell, Delores Puckett, Joyce Sinclair, Owings, Dollar.

Monsanto (Pensacola, Fla.): Tom Murdock (coach), Bea Simmons, Nell Simmons, Phyllis White, Orelia King, Caroline Frederickson, Teddy Dubberly, Sandra Davis, Patricia Wynn, L. Gomillion, Jean Ayers, Rusty Gardner, Betty Woods.

Bahan Textile (Greenville, S.C.): Rita Funderburk (coach), Betty Alverson (coach), Libby Arant, Glenda Herring, Barbara Ferrell, Alice Cash, Ann Stone, Marie Montieth, Janice Ross, Juanita Seay, Barbara Clampitt, Beth Boyd, Jackie Lewter, Joan Byars.

Saco-Lowell (Easley, S.C.): Glen Forister (coach), Faye Ray, Judity Ray, Bonnie Williams, Sharon Boggs, Ann Massey, Gloria Davenport, Marlene Gilstrap, Evelyn Clayton, Mary Crowe, Barbara Turner, Elaine Bryant, Sally Brooks.

Stone Mfg. (Greenville, S.C.): Jimmy Christopher (coach), Linda Duncan, Joyce

Vermillion, Freddie Reid, Marie Greer, Norma McNew, Beverly Cox, Sandra Holden, Bertie Fowler, Sherry Spence, Janice Brown, Dorte Ignee, Flannagan.

Sangamo Electric Co. (Pickens, S.C.): Rose Barnes (coach), Pat Aultman, Freddie Grant, Jean Roper, Judy Sheriff, Deda Duncan, Betty Chambers, Wilma Ross, Martha Brewer, Frances Welborn.

Murrell Brothers Sand (Greenville, S.C.): B.J. Bell, Mickey Davis, Caroline Pharr, Stewart, Calvert, Payne, Weaver, Justus, Hunt.

1964

Officers: Ward Williams (Greenville, S.C.), President; Ken Pittman (Greenville, S.C.), Vice President and Executive Secretary; Fred Byrd (Greenville, S.C.), Secretary; Joe Gilreath (Piedmont, S.C.), Assistant Secretary; Divver Hendrix (Greenville, S.C.), Treasurer; Whitey Kendall (Greenville), Supervisor of Officials; Lt. J.T. Merck, Security Officer.

Executive Committee: Clarence Thomas (Greenville, S.C.), S.R. DuBose (Whitmire, S.C.), Willie Wilbanks (Ware Shoals, S.C.), Curtis Terry (Piedmont, S.C.), Jim McDuffie (Greenville, S.C.), Willard Fowler (Greer, S.C.), Fred Powers (Asheville, N.C.), Jim Anderson (Greenville, S.C.), Dan Foster (Greenville, S.C.), Harry Foster (Easley, S.C.), Jim Grogan (Greenville, S.C.), Paul Kaiser (Anderson, S.C.), Snow Kirby (Marietta, S.C.), Bill Hopkins (Pelzer, S.C.), Summers Jarrett (Pensacola, Fla.), R.E. Patrick (Greenwood, S.C.), D.K. Smith (Lyman, S.C.).

OPEN DIVISION

Murrell Brothers Sand (Greenville, S.C.), champions: W.C. Murrell (coach), Charles Jennings, Don Frye, Gerald Glur, Leroy Peacock, Jim Brennan, Donnie Mahaffey, Woody Morgan, Gary Burnisky, Mike Bonahak, Nick Milasnovich, Gene Anglin, Bill Wade, Ken Pittman.

Mikro (Charlotte, N.C.), runners-up: Doug Moe, Terry Holland, Bill Morningstar, Jim Miller, Joe McDermott, Lennie Rosenbluth, Joe Ladd, Jesse Branson, Mike Ross, Chick Kelton, Charles Shaffer, Linn Hollowell, Stone, Phil Branson.

Texize Chemical (Greenville, S.C.), consolation winners: Jerry Brock (coach), Tom Fuller, Willie Gray, Jack Halford, Bobby Wike, Jimmy Holden, Steve Gambrell, Earle Maxwell, Harvey Tankersley, Wright, Lacey, Phillips.

Brown-Rogers Sporting Goods (Winston-Salem, N.C.): Dan Hackney (coach), Glen Anderson, Clifford Dwyer, Robert Clodfelter, C.G. Holland Jr., Eddie Teague, Jerry Moss, Tex Flippin, Danny Sewell, Lowell Davis, Edward Mandy, Richard Budd, William Dixon, Highsmith.

Williamston All Stars (Williamston, S.C.): W.H. Taylor (coach), Mike Jordan, Dale Martin, Dag Wilson, Lee Ellis, David Murrell, Jimmy Cobb, Bob Douthet, Bill Walthers, Gary Boldry, Joe Santamis, Clark, Crook, Geddens.

Davidson Heating & Air (Greenville, S.C.): Dean Davidson (coach), James Crain, James Styles, Bobby Harrison, Charles Carter, Robert Burgess, Richard Wright, Connie Davis, Donald McCorkle, Douglas Hoffman, Joseph Smith, Bill Davidson, Lyon, Crabtree, Hayes, Talley, Lemmons.

Miller Tire (Columbia, S.C.): Grady Wallace (coach), Scotti Ward, Bob Haney, Art Whisenant, Ronnie Collins, Bill Yarborough, Jimmy Collins, Mike Callahan, Jim Podel, Ed Krajack, Dial.

Chattanooga VFW (Chattanooga, Tenn.): Charles Watkins (coach), Ralph Hooper (coach), Ronald Peeples, Eddie Test, Joe Gardner, Ralph Lister, Bill Nelson, Tom Wright, Orb Boweling, Wayne Standifer, Joe Pollock, Bill Woolsey, Donny Schultz.

CLASS A MEN

Monsanto (Greenwood, S.C.), champions: Carl Treadway (coach), Garrett Nation, Bill Wilson, Jerry Johnson, Jim Diamond, Pete Carlisle, Herb Edmonds, Kiebler James, Don Carver, John Roberts, Jerry Duncan.

Piedmont Mill (Piedmont, S.C.), runners-up: Earl Wooten (coach), Joe Hiott, Ray Foxx, Larry Holcombe, Gene Seay, Vince Yockel, Clyde Bryson, Danny Gambrell, Tommy Hart, Don Roper.

Monsanto (Pensacola, Fla.), consolation winners: John Tringas (coach), Ken Raines, Johnny Taylor, Jim Hardin, Jerry Gordon, Robert Fohl, Don Carver, David Patrick, Donald Livingston, Jerry Glenn, Thomas Murdock.

Russell Manufacturing (Alexander City, Ala.): Vercho Carter (coach), James Yates, Perry Anderson, Dewey Sanders, James Fuller,

Michael Hearn, Charles Gunn, Charles Robinson, Howard Byers, Charles Scott, Olin Wingard.

Pelzer Mill (Pelzer, S.C.): Tom Nash (coach), James Thomason, Douglas Harris, Gary Geddens, Bill Hopkins, Bill Harris, Everett Cooper, Don Helms, Don Sanders, Jerry Garner, John Scroggs.

Cranston Print Works (Fletcher, N.C.): David Orr (coach), Norman Greene, Jerald Ramsey, Ronald Miller, Floyd Pryor, Norman Youngblood, Frank Creasman, James Baker, Jim Murray.

Slater Mill (Slater, S.C.): J.M. Johnson (coach), Jerry Brinkley, Billy Barbary, James Lewis, Dacus Tucker, Billy Farmer, Robert Kirby, Richard Stephenson, William White, Johnny Laws, Larry Dudley, Ed Brinkley, Adkins, Burdette, Moon.

Lyman Mill (Lyman, S.C.): Virgil Pruitte (coach), Steve Brown, William Eubanks, Thomas Eubanks, Clarence Russell, Barry Bolding, Donald Black, William Green, Benny Upton, James Mullinax, Lloyd Leonard, Leon Eubanks, Ronnie Russell.

Singer Mfg. (Anderson, S.C.): Lewis Acker (coach), Nelson Massey, Danny Brooks, Curtis Wilson, Bill Hall, Furman Elrod, Eugene Patterson, Bobby Martin, Jon Acker, Benny Speares, Grady Sanders.

CLASS B MEN

Union Bleachery (Greenville, S.C.), champions: Larry Robertson (coach), Ernest Simmons, Steve Smith, Ed Sanders, Richard Aiken, Calvin Rumler, Tom Bolton, Tim Brown, Leon McWhite, Jimmy Smith, David Smith, Jesse Brown, Bill Sanders, K. Smith, Simmons.

Anderson Hosiery Mill (Whitmire, S.C.), runners-up: Joe Rose (coach), James Dallas, William Johnson, Kenneth Frazier, William Sample, Larry Boswell, Eddie Walker, Philip Spotts, Alfred Spotts, Bill Black, Leonard Price.

Saco-Lowell (Easley, S.C.), consolation winners: T.W. Krieg (coach), H. Waldrop (coach), Joe Roper, Ray Whaley, Harold Wham, Jerry Whaley, Donald Foster, Donnie Sargent, Dennis Waldrop, Doyce Waldrop, Charles Hall, A. Waldrop.

Singer Mfg. (Anderson, S.C.): Alexander, Rackley, Adams, Evatt, Crumpton, Hunter, Nicholson, Breazeale, Gettys.

Lyman Mill (Lyman, S.C.): Cody Forrester (coach), John Crain, Daniel Watson, Stanley Tapp, Johnny Mullinax, Lewis Carlisle Jr., Clint Turner, Neil Pettigrew, Micky Stepp, Jerry Vaughn, Horace Craig Jr.

Davis Mechanical (Greenville, S.C.): R.B. Durham (coach), Robert Welborn, Joseph Heaton, Douglass Martin, Joe Cooper, Russell Wham, Kenneth Smith, Arthur Dix, Bobby Alverson, Gerald Matteson, D.L. Hunnicutt, D. Welborn.

Stone Mfg. (Greenville, S.C.): Charles McConnell (coach), Harold Westbrook, Daniel Smith, Robert Scoggins, Jake Tollison, Kenneth Childress, Timothy McConnell, Kenneth Coleman, Cliff King, John McConnell, Michael Price, Jay Westbrook.

Homelite (Greer, S.C.): Steve Dacus (coach), Jack Kay, Edward Nelson, Kenneth Massey, Tony Tipton, Lollie Bryant, Nathan Jones, Robbie Lister, Jerry Gosnell, Robert Sanders, Don Krause.

Easley Mill (Easley, S.C.): Coon Hendrix (coach), Johnny Skinner, Leon Chandler, Terry Gillespie, James Campbell, Mike McCoy, Thomas Lankford, George McEntyre, Deryl Stokes, Ronald Brandt, Harold Ensley, Garrett.

Dunean Mill (Greenville, S.C.): Billy Lollis (coach), Ronald Cross, James Galloway, Gerald Pollard, Doug Gailey, Tony Campbell, John Gibson, William Vickery, Jimmie Riddle, William Blakely, Dean Cross.

Sangamo Electric Co. (Pickens, S.C.): Joel Allgood (coach), Olen Smith, Tommy McCue, Gerald Bice, Chester Smith, Bill Fowler, Robert Porter, Thomas Meier, Robert Cochran, Dean Holder, Gene Finley, Jesse Bice, F. Smith.

Gluck Mill (Anderson, S.C.): Early Hanna (coach), Tommy Mahaffey, Gary Whitlock, Joe Stansell, Larry Whitten, Farrell Giles, Neil Whitfield, Glenn Smith, Johnny Whitfield, Stanley Whitfield, M. Whitfield.

Monsanto (Blacksburg, S.C.): Bill Fisher (coach), Gary Clarke, Vincent Tharpe, Jimmy Bolin, Billy Pounders, Charles Mullinax, Marion Brown, Reginald Wylie, James Allen, James Moseley, James Norman.

Liberty Mill (Liberty, S.C.): Bobby Morris (coach), Donnell Smith, Lamar Gilstrap, Archie Hitt, Jack Taylor, Pat Bowie, Charles Bagwell, Dolan Ricketts, Louis Thomas, Powell, Paul Bowie, Jackson.

Landrum Mill (Landrum, S.C.): Curt

Beasley (coach), Wayne Thompson, Donald Smith, Bobby Fagan, William Beasley, William Bridges, Arnold Smith, Gerald Collins, Keith Ritchey, William McKinney, Wade Coley, Dean Smith.

Singer Mfg. (Pickens, S.C.): Eugene Hooper (coach), Don Alexander, Jamie Rackley, David Breazeale, Doc Evatt, Joe Adams, John Crumpton, Pat Hunter, Gary Anderson, Wayne Nicholson, Alex Gettys Jr.

Conso (Union, S.C.): Frank Mullinax (coach), Herbert Edwards (coach), Ray Mann, Carl Crocker, Frank Cody, Chalmers Lawson, Bobby Hyatt, William Pegram, Hubert Pegram, Ralph Brown, John Galloway, Donnie Kizer.

Southern Weaving (Greenville, S.C.): Jack Miller (coach), Jerry McNeely, James Solomon, Milford Stewart, James Cash, Earl Stewart, Jerry LaCount, Jackson Burnett III, Leon McCoig, Duncan.

Simpsonville Mill (Simpsonville, S.C.): Ed Coker (coach), Harold Gray, Danny Norris, Donnie Hitt, Ulysses Hinton, Bobby Chandler, Julian Hiott, Ken Matthews, Micky Creach, Jim Pridmore, Butch Tucker.

Pelzer Mill (Pelzer, S.C.): Jimmy Cobb (coach), Herman Evatt, David Major, Jerry Floyd, Ray McClellion, Steve Fricks, Joe Ellenburg, Ray Whitt, Ed White, William Thompson, Tom Nash, Keller, Smith.

CLASS C MEN

Monaghan Mill #1 (Greenville, S.C.), champions: Danny Bagwell (coach), Jerry Bagwell, Mark Stewart, Leo Sutton, Mike Fair, Steve Connelly, Grady Wyatt, Jackie Fricks, Donnie Lewis, Harry Trammell, David Glenn, Steve Lamb, Wilson, Sutton.

Saco-Lowell (Easley, S.C.), runners-up: Larry Bagwell (coach), Jimmy Campbell, Toby Westmoreland, Larry Ashley, Stanley Wilson, Hubert Bishop, Terry Chandler, Jimmy Wilson, Don Clark, Tommy Krieg, Douglas Bagwell.

Dunean Mill (Greenville, S.C.), consolation winners: Fred Cox (coach), Russell Holbrook, Tommy Gaston, James Locklair, Gary Duncan, Robert McDowell, Jerry Stowe, Steve Allison, James Brooks, Harvey Seuter, Andrew Ballard, Stone, Senter.

Pelzer Mill (Pelzer, S.C.): Bill Hopkins (coach), Steve Autry, Marty Crawford, Terry Smith, Jimmy Yates, Sammy Heller, Jimmy Crawford, Hiram Belt, Jimmy Hopkins, Sonny Saxon, Richard Floyd, Jackie Creel, Bobby Taylor, Lollis, Cooper, Bolt.

Liberty Mill (Liberty, S.C.): Flint Latham (coach), Hovey Roper, Kenneth Adcox, Joe Hunter, John Beeson, Henry Crotwell, Earl Skinner, Frank McKinney, Jimmy Ellenburg, Samuel Moore, Gilstrap, Grogan, Owens, Collins.

Lonsdale Mill (Seneca, S.C.): Bobby Fleming (coach), Johnny Crooks, Samuel Stowe, James Lawless, Nicky Chapman, Wayne Shirley, Bill Smith, Lane Vickey, Lester Clark, George Dupre, Doug Holden, Hall.

Monaghan Mill #2 (Greenville, S.C.): Danny Bagwell (coach), Keith Alexander, Hank Johnson, Dennis Holden, Dwight Swaynghame, Tommy Williams, Doug Tatham, Jimmy Bagwell, Bruce McIntyre, Dean Campbell, Jack Pace.

Piedmont Mill (Piedmont, S.C.): Curt Terry (coach), Cleveland Richards, Donnie Bell, David Hughey, Earl Foxx, Mike Potter, Dennis Allen, Steve Lindley, Wayne McClain, Jerry Cooper, Bob Merritt, White.

McCrary Mechanical (Travelers Rest, S.C.): John Coleman (coach), Charles Werner, Tommy Brown, Charles Poole, Wayne Ward, Hoyt Hudson, Johnny Foster, Hugh Daniel, Lyndell Fowler, Jerry Timmons, Pete Buchanan, Thomas Brown, Earnest Ward.

Woodside Mill (Greenville, S.C.): John Montieth (coach), Jimmy White, Allen Turner, Earl Stewart, Robbie Caldwell, Rusty Floyd, Ricky Strickland, Buddy Lofge, Chuck Poole, Art Pitman, Robert Vermillion, LaForge, Grice, Wyatt.

Easley Mill (Easley, S.C.): Joe Anders (coach), Harvey Galloway, Richard Stewart, Eugene Waldrop, Marion Garrett, Roy Smith, Sammie Eads, Joe Cassell, Larry Mason, Joe Smith.

Monarch Mill (Union, S.C.): Warren Humphries (coach), Harry Arthur Sr. (coach), Robert Betenbaugh, William Gault Jr., Charles Moss, Joe Teague, Gary Pegram, Rolfe Hughes III, Glenn Adcock, Newell Harrison Jr., Robert Thornton, William Fowler.

Brandon Mill (Greenville, S.C.): Charles Landreth (coach), James Caldwell, Doyle Clardy, Larry Bishop, Sammy Saxon, Grady Allen, Doug Rucker, Donald Smith, Michael Tate, Jerry Oliver, Johnny Echols, Clary.

American Spinning (Greenville, S.C.):

James Hester (coach), Cullen Turner, Buddy Bolt, David Baird, Don Baird, Richard Elrod, Wayne Nix, Donald Cleveland, Raymond Wyatt, Harbin.

Carolina Supply (Greenville, S.C.): Ron Cross (coach), Freddy Kelly, Reid Watson, William Bruce, Reid Guill, Jimmy Vissage, Don Childs, Harold Waldrop, Johnny Hendrix, Tom Mardre, Sammy Rouse, Roddy.

Maxon Shirt Co. (Greenville, S.C.): Jerry Williamson (coach), Joe Klein (coach), Buddy Moore, Lester Erwin, Charles Forrester, Adolph Klein, Jack Williamson, Don Evatt, Tommy Hitt, Jimmy Rickey, Charles Alford.

CLASS A WOMEN

Singer Mfg. (Anderson, S.C.), champions: James Anderson (coach), Fredda Acker (coach), Gloria Black, Iris Blackwell, Betty Brown, Bobbie Burriss, Carolyn Clayton, Margaret Dillard, Martha Jameson, Elizabeth Picklesimer, Barbara Sanders, Annie Tribble, Pat Wilson, Melba Yeargin, Linda Wilson, Linda Linn, Brenda Wiles.

Slater Mill (Slater, S.C.), runners-up: Margaret Wright (coach), Doris Capps, Joan Kirby, Priscilla Hunt, Judy Cox, Leila Harvin, Peggy Chumley, Joan Nelson, Jane Smith, Ann Coker, Mickey Davis, Lynn Lewis, S. Chumley.

Sangamo Electric Co. (Pickens, S.C.), consolation winners: Tater Garrett (coach), Jean Stone, Jackie McJunkin, Frances Welborn, Brenda Garren, Jean Ross, Martha Thompson, Gail Hunter, Deta Duncan, Sybil Wade, Ruthie Welborn, Carol Finley, Gladys Steddins, Elrod.

Carolina Plating (Greenville, S.C.): Fran Wood (coach), Dot Lindsay, Helen Rister, Miriam Burns, Sarah Brandt, Eva Sams, Elizabeth Fant, Judy Payne, June Brown, Vickie Linder, Mary Pruitt, Linda Rister, Emily Hamm, Broad, McCravy.

Monsanto (Pensacola, Fla.): Reynolds Johnston (coach), Bea Simmons, Nell Simmons, Phyllis White, Orelia King, Teddy Dubberly, Loraine Gomillion, Jo McCall, Ola Josey, Irene Lahey, Pat Rand.

Bahan Textile (Greenville, S.C.): Betty Alverson (coach), Pat Stone, Barbara Clampitt, Jolent Sparks, Marilyn Green, Carolyn Watkins, Judy Still, Kella Hall, Mary Cox, Barbara McDuffie, Betty Phillips, Sandra Stoudemayer, Dorothy Johnson.

Liberty Mill (Liberty, S.C.): Bobby Morris (coach), Roberta James, Sandra Brock, Jan Jones, Kathryn Moore, Judy Marett, Harriet Kitchens, Dot Stevens, Kay Tate, Laura Norris, Giles, Russ, Mauldin.

Lonsdale Mill (Seneca, S.C.): Wayne Lacey (coach), Brenda Kelly, Linda Worley, Barbara Wade, Brenda Gaillard, Beverly Dooley, Willie Cox, Jo Dawkins, Janice Grant, Beth Anderson, Wynona Foster, Glenda Herring.

Walhalla Mill (Walhalla, S.C.): Claude Wells (coach), Deanna Crenshaw, Pat Grant, Helen Smith, Cynthia Deal, Thelma Powell, Linda Derrick, Gayle Harvey, Jane Sanders, Mary Marett, Arlene Wood, Ann Darby, Becky Derrick.

Adams Oil (Fair Play, S.C.): Thurman Crooks (coach), Sandy Childs, Sharon Greer, Glenda Crooks, Ann Blakely, Barbara Glenn, Barbara Blakey, Willie Cox, Janice Grant, Ann Greer, Judy Childs, Mary Nix, E. Green, A. Green.

1965

Officers: Ward Williams (Greenville, S.C.), President; Ken Pittman (Greenville, S.C.), Vice President and Executive Secretary; Fred Byrd (Greenville, S.C.), Secretary; Joe Gilreath (Piedmont, S.C.), Assistant Secretary; Divver Hendrix (Greenville, S.C.), Treasurer; Harry Foster (Greenville, S.C.), Assistant Treasurer; Whitey Kendall (Greenville), Supervisor of Officials; Lt. J.T. Merck, Security Officer.

Executive Committee: Clarence Thomas (Greenville, S.C.), S.R. DuBose (Whitmire, S.C.), Willie Wilbanks (Ware Shoals, S.C.), Curtis Terry (Piedmont, S.C.), Jim McDuffie (Greenville, S.C.), Willard Fowler (Greer, S.C.), Fred Powers (Asheville, N.C.), Jim Anderson (Greenville, S.C.), Dan Foster (Greenville, S.C.), Jim Grogan (Greenville, S.C.), Snow Kirby (Marietta, S.C.), Bill Hopkins (Pelzer, S.C.), Summers Jarrett (Pensacola, Fla.), R.E. Patrick (Greenwood, S.C.), D.K. Smith (Lyman, S.C.), W.H. Embler (Anderson, S.C.), Lloyd McAbee (Greenville, S.C.).

OPEN DIVISION

Mikro (Charlotte, N.C.), champions: Mike Ross (coach), Doug Moe, Terry Holland, Bill Cunningham, Jesse Branson, Ronnie Watts, George Lyons, Louis Pittman, Bill Morningstar, Robert Sorrell, Jim Huddock.

Southern Textile Basketball Tournament Rosters   Appendix 1

Murrell Brothers Sand (Greenville, S.C.), runners-up: W.C. Murrell (coach), Charles Jennings, Don Frye, Gerald Glur, Gary Burnisky, Les Heicher, Norman Schaffer, Dave Selvey, Bane Sarrett, Hingleton, McCullough, Pike, Bob McCullough.

Hanes Dye & Finishing (Winston-Salem, N.C.), consolation winners: Jay Dilworth (coach), Cliff Dwyer, Jay Beal, C.G. Holland, Glen Anderson, Al Lozier, Bob Woollard, Howard Pardue, Jack Moffat, Dick Wherry, Peter Rowe, Bill Bell, Stone, Ladd.

Washington Mill (Winston-Salem, N.C.): Dan Hackney (coach), Whitey Bell, Danny Sewell, Bill McDermott, Al Trombetta, John Atkinson, Arvil Steelman, Harold Stephens Jr., Odell Powell, Robert Sessoms, John Garrison, Tex Flippin.

Greenville Old Pros (Greenville, S.C.): Jerry Brock (coach), Jimmy Holden, Earle Maxwell, Harvey Tankersley, Wayne Lacey, Buddy Hayes, Fred Hetzel, Barry Teague, Bill Wade, Hogan Hancock, Gene Seay, Don Davidson, Charles Marion.

Wilson Lewith Machinery (Charlotte, N.C.): Don Thomas (coach), Jippy Carter, Mel Gibson, Pete Campbell, Jack Fitch, John Kilgo, Bob Benson, Bill Watson, Ray Cox, Dwight Rea, Lee Marshall, Williams, Robinson.

Sunshine Cleaners (Columbia, S.C.): Bee Harper (coach), Scotti Ward, Jimmy Collins, Bob Haney, Everette Newman, Jim Fox, Jim Podell, Mike Callahan, Art Whisenant, Grady Wallace, Bill Gustafson, Bill Simpson.

Peerless Community Center (Rossville, Ga.): Walter Lauter (coach), Malvin Roberts, Bill Storm, Stan Brinker, Joe Gardner, Leon Ammerman, Hershel Smith, Rollin Stapp, Ron Peeples, Barnett.

Class A Men

Monsanto (Greenwood, S.C.): Carl Treadway (coach), Garrett Nation, Bill Wilson, Jim Diamond, Pete Carlisle, Herb Edmonds, Kiebler James, Don Carver, Woody Morgan, Butch Mattison, Walter Stone, Vance Boggs, James.

Lyman Mill (Lyman, S.C.), runners-up: Virgil Pruitte (coach), Steve Brown, William Eubanks, Thomas Eubanks, Clarence Russell, Donald Black, Bill Green, Benny Upton, Michael Page, Billy Stewart, Wayne Blackmon, Leon Eubanks, Vaughn, Ronald Russell.

Slater Mill (Slater, S.C.), consolation winners: Leroy Peacock (coach), Jerry Brinkley, James Lewis, Robert Kirby, Richard Stephenson, Roger White, Leroy Peacock III, Jack Halford, Thomas Adkins, Alfred Moon, Steve Burnett.

Monsanto (Pensacola, Fla.): John Tringas (coach), Ken Raines, Johnny Taylor, Jerry Gordon, Robert Fohl, Donald Livingston, Ronald Gates, Dennis Wilson, Mike Gussett, Gerald Bragg, Houston McCormick.

Russell Manufacturing (Alexander City, Ala.): Vercho Carter (coach), Perry Anderson, Dewey Sanders, Michael Hearn, Charles Gunn, Charles Scott, Calvin Futural, James Randall, John Stevenson, Willie Caldwell, Homer Keel, Wingard.

Singer Mfg. (Anderson, S.C.): Lewis Acker (coach), Curtis Wilson, Mickey Dobbins, William Hall, Jack Wiles, Eddy Massey, Grady Sanders, Eugene Patterson, Furman Elrod, Jon Acker, Jack Webb.

Class B Men

Saco-Lowell (Easley, S.C.), champions: Harold Waldrop (coach), Harry Foster (coach), Jerry Whaley, Harold Wham, Don Foster, Jimmy Carter, Earl Whittington, Thomas Ingle, Mike McCoy, Roy Smith, Steve Autrey, Joe Pierce, Ken Byrd.

Liberty Mill (Liberty, S.C.), runners-up: Bobby Morris (coach), Donnell Smith, Lamar Gilstrap, Archie Hill, Pat Bowie, Donnie Hill, Butch Parrish, Jimmy Wilson, Welborn Dobson, Doyle Roper, Hitt.

Dunean Mill (Greenville, S.C.), consolation winners: Buddy Gibson (coach), Gerald Pollard, Doug Gailey, Tony Campbell, William Vickery, Jimmie Riddle, Arthur Hammett, Robert Hughes, David Vickery, Gary Godfrey, Jack Wilson.

Poinsett Mill (Greenville, S.C.): Robert Lavender (coach), Pat Campbell, Bennie Morgan, Curtis Campbell, Larry Campbell, Marshall Hall, Mickey Campbell, Steve Hodge, Donnie Davis, Estes.

Lyman Mill (Lyman, S.C.): Lloyd Leonard (coach), John Crain, Daniel Watson, Stanley Tapp, Micky Stepp, Horace Craig Jr., William Payne, Kenneth Anderson, Wayne Greene, John Richards, Harold Brown, Upton.

Davis Mechanical (Greenville, S.C.): R.B. Durham (coach), Thomas Welborn, Joseph Heaton, Kenneth Smith, Arthur Dix, Ron Cross, Tommy Crump, Joe Phillips, Fredric

Millwood, Willie Mickel, Jerry Alexander, Cash.

Homelite #1 (Greer, S.C.): Bartie Brown (coach), Lollie Bryant, Robbie Lister, Robert Sanders, Harold Brown, Willie Brown, James Brown, Jerry Cooper, Johnny Johnson Jr., Harvey Forrester, Lonnie Harley, E. Brown.

Sangamo Electric Co. (Pickens, S.C.): Joel Allgood (coach), Gerald Bice, Chester Smith, Bill Fowler, Robert Porter, Dean Holder, Jerry Roper, Garland Rigdon, Randall Parson, Kenneth Suddeth, Bobby Kensley, Joel Allgood, Finley, Houston.

Monsanto (Blacksburg, S.C.): Gary Clarke (coach), Vincent Tharpe, Billy Pounders, Charles Mullinax, Reginald Wylie, James Allen, Kenneth Branch, Bill Moore, Jack Rice, John O'Brien, James Jones.

Singer Mfg. (Pickens, S.C.): Eugene Hooper (coach), Jamie Rackley, David Breazeale, Doc Evatt, Joe Adams, John Crumpton, Pat Hunter, Wayne Nicholson, James Looper, Jim McCall, Mason Taylor.

Milliken (Spartanburg, S.C.): Donald Gale (coach), Manuel Thomas, John Brown, John Etters, Larry Bruce, Joseph Carver, Duane Turner, Norman Scott Jr., Dennis Durham, James Brock, Robert Melton.

Homelite #2 (Greer, S.C.): Joe Ross (coach), F. Holscher (coach), George Vaughn, Patrick Farmer, Walter Dacus, William Dowis, Ted Brown, Howard Clayton, Donald Krause, Glenn Lowe, Earl Turner, Robert Harley.

Pelzer Mill (Pelzer, S.C.): W.H. Taylor (coach), Ronnie Davenport, David Magor, Lee Terry, Sammy Heller, Herman Evatt, Steve Frick, Dickie Sandau, Joe Ellenburg, Larry Coker, Jimmy Yates.

Anderson Hosiery Mill (Whitmire, S.C.): Joe Rose (coach), Larry Boswell, Billy Semple, Philip Spotts, Samuel Ramsey, Gordon Adam, Eddie Walker, Leonard Price, Eddie Raines, Richie Quillen, David Turner.

Bigelow-Sanford (Landrum, S.C.): Curt Beasley (coach), Wayne Thompson, Allen Smith, Bobby Fagan, William Beasley, Gerald Collins, William McKinney, Wade Coley, Russell Bradley, Jimmy Bradshaw, Jim Hill.

Class C Men

Saco-Lowell (Easley, S.C.), champions: Larry Bagwell (coach), Jimmy Campbell, Toby Westmoreland, Stanley Wilson, Terry Chandler, Tommy Krieg, Doug Bagwell, Jerry Cox, Earl Gilstrap, John Strickland, Woody Hopkins.

Monaghan Mill (Greenville, S.C.), runners-up: Charlie Jennings, (coach), Mike Fair, George Fricks, Donnie Lewis, William Alexander, Tommy Williams, Dwight Swaynghame, Dennis Holden, Stanley Nix, Robert Bagwell, Bruce McIntyre, J. Nix.

Maxon Shirt Co. (Greenville, S.C.), consolation winners: Johnny Ross (coach), John Graves, James Graves, Mike Morris, Robert Laforge, Frank Poole, Jacob Stewart, Carroll Pittman, Raymond Laforge, Fulton Pyle, Harling Sponseller, A. Pittman, L. Laforge.

Microtron (Greenville, S.C.): Henry Spake (coach), John Corn, Ronnie Bailey, James Bray, Buddy Vandier, Alan Hawkins, Boyce Sanders, Ronald Yates, Cecil Hall, Jerry Bailey, Freddy Free, Weldon, Brannon.

Simpsonville Mill (Simpsonville, S.C.): Red Barbary (coach), Tommy Mullinax, David Wilson, Jerry Good, Waymon Leroy, Jimmy Littlefield, Ken Price, James Thackston, Dickie Nelson, Fred McGill, Grove Riddle.

Dunean Mill (Greenville, S.C.): Fred Cox (coach), Russell Holbrook, Robert McDowell, Jerry Stone, Andrew Ballard, Joel Cisson, Neal Bradberry, William Goodlett, Ben Swindle, Stanley Roddy, Mike Henderson, Simms.

Pelzer Mill (Pelzer, S.C.): H.D. Adams (coach), Marty Crawford, Hiram Belt, Jimmy Hopkins, Sonny Saxon, Jackie Creel, Jimmy McKer, Steve Davenport, Kenny Ross, Jimmy Bair, Tim Galloway.

Liberty Mill (Liberty, S.C.): Flint Latham (coach), John Beeson, Earl Skinner, Frank McKinney, Jimmy Ellenburg, Don Grogan, Johnny Gilstrap, Ted Owens, Kenneth McWhorter, Steve Brooks, Moore, Bowie.

McCrary Mechanical (Travelers Rest, S.C.): Joe Small (coach), Charles Werner, Tommy Brown, Hoyt Hudson, Johnny Foster, Hugh Daniel, Jerry Timmons, Jack Anderson, Robert Hester, Joe Mathis, Ronald Shelton.

Woodside Mill (Greenville, S.C.): Allen Turner (coach), Earl Stewart, Robbie Caldwell, Maxie Krause, Jeff Green, Gary Bradwell, Eric Abraham, Duck Stewart, Steve Berry, John Stewart, Cary Durham, Duncan, Garren, Krause.

Brandon Mill (Greenville, S.C.): Ezra Embler (coach), Doyle Clardy, Larry Bishop, Sammy Huffman, Johnny Echols, Joel

McCombs, Gary Pace, Charles Taylor, Robert Trammell, Thomas Shockley, Roger Alexander.

American Spinning (Greenville, S.C.): James Hester (coach), Cullen Turner, Wayne Nix, Wayne McGaha, John Guest, Robert Ellis, Larry McFadden, Eddie White, Roddy McCarson, Hanky Harbin, Thomas Boone, Wyatt.

Poe Hardware (Greenville, S.C.): Broadus Miller (coach), Larry Erwin, Tommy Miller, Ben Reed, Henry Moore, Tecumseh Hooper, Michael Powell, Michael McCall.

Bigelow-Sanford (Landrum, S.C.): Cecil Younce (coach), Richard Landrum, Garrison Culbrett, William Ford, Maurice Staton, Douglas Nodine, Truman Bostic, Ronald Johnson, James Smith, James Byrd, Douglas Ayers.

Union Bleachery (Greenville, S.C.): Tim Brown (coach), Frank Reid, Jerry Rumler, James Rumler, Perrion Dix, Michael Aiken, Ronald Turner, Dewayne Evington, Paul Stewart, Tommy Stroud, David Epps, Jimmy Evatt, T. Rumler, E. Stewart.

Brandon Dryer Felt (Greenville, S.C.): Lloyd Kelly (coach), Larry Wynn, Donald Evans, Freddie Brown, Douglas McKinney, Terry Campbell, Donald Brown, Don Ferrell, Ronald Cobb, Roger White, Kenneth Penland.

CLASS A WOMEN

Slater Mill (Slater, S.C.), champions: Margaret Wright (coach), Doris Capps, Judy Clark, Leila Harvin, Peggy Chumley, Mickey Davis, Nadine Jeffords, Mae Hill, Susan Chumley, Carol Richardson, Toni Sellars, Nancy Oldham, Linda Weaver, Ouida Williams, Sandy Burgess.

Singer Mfg. (Anderson, S.C.), runners-up: James Anderson (coach), Gloria Black, Bobbie Burriss, Carolyn Clayton, Elizabeth Picklesimer, Annie Tribble, Patsy Wilson, Linda Lynn, Mildred Watt, Joyce Speares, Sandra Scott, Judy Charping, Judy Bryant, Claudia Garrett, Strickland.

Monsanto (Pensacola, Fla.), consolation winners: Reynolds Johnston (coach), Nell Simmons, Jo McCall, Ola Josey, Irene Lahey, Pat Rand, Jean Ayers, Patricia Wynn, Betty Wood, Marcia McCroan, Betsy Langley, Brenda Holley, Fredrickson.

Murrell Brothers Sand (Greenville, S.C.): W.C. Murrell (coach), Sybil Wade, Judy Johnson, Judy Cross, Carol Jones, Fran Wood, Linda Pirkle, Barbara Pridmore, Brenda Garren, Gail Hunter, Pat Hendrix, Judy Payne, Murrell, McGravey.

Carolina Plating (Greenville, S.C.): Broadus Miller (coach), Christeen Rister, Miriam Burns, Sarah Brandt, Lyn Sams, Dubose Fant, June Brown, Vickie Linder, Linda Rister, Gloria McKeown, Anita Miller, Patricia Epps, Betty Kellett, Babb, Putnam.

Microtron (Greenville, S.C.): Johnnie Turner (coach), Harold Limbaugh (coach), Becky Turner, Jolene Sparks, Ann Stone, Sandra Gaillard, Vicky Limbaugh, Nancy Blackstock, Tommie Stephens, Sherry McCall, Pat Rampey, Pat McWhorter, Peggy Brown, Barbara McDuffie, Taylor, Libshramy, Powell, Ledford.

Pelzer Mill (Pelzer, S.C.): Cecil Hopkins (coach), Vicki Chapman, Carolyn Adams, Marilyn Hinson, Kathy Bagwell, Patsy Chapman, Gale Chapman, Teddie Hampton, Judy Roberson, Brenda Ford, Linda Waters, Donna Gaillard, Debbie Sims, Coe.

1966

Officers: Ken Pittman (Greenville, S.C.), President and Executive Secretary; Ward Williams (Greenville, S.C.), 1st Vice President; R.E. Patrick (Greenwood, S.C.), 2nd Vice President; Fred Byrd (Greenville, S.C.), Ass't Executive Secretary; Joe Gilreath (Piedmont, S.C.), Assistant Secretary; Divver Hendrix (Greenville, S.C.), Treasurer; Harry Foster (Greenville, S.C.), Assistant Treasurer; Whitey Kendall (Greenville), Supervisor of Officials; Lt. J.T. Merck, Security Officer.

Executive Committee: Clarence Thomas (Greenville, S.C.), S.R. DuBose (Whitmire, S.C.), Willie Wilbanks (Ware Shoals, S.C.), Curtis Terry (Piedmont, S.C.), Jim McDuffie (Greenville, S.C.), Willard Fowler (Greer, S.C.), Fred Powers (Asheville, N.C.), Jim Anderson (Greenville, S.C.), Dan Foster (Greenville, S.C.), Snow Kirby (Marietta, S.C.), Bill Hopkins (Pelzer, S.C.), Summers Jarrett (Pensacola, Fla.), D.K. Smith (Lyman, S.C.), Lewis Acker (Anderson, S.C.), Lloyd McAbee (Greenville, S.C.), Tim Brown (Greenville, S.C.), Bobby Morris (Liberty, S.C.), Joe Newton (Greenville, S.C.), Henry Spake (Anderson, S.C.).

OPEN DIVISION

Sunshine Cleaners (Columbia, S.C.), champions: Grady Wallace (coach), Jimmy Collins, Jim Podell, Mike Callahan, Art Whisnant, Bill

Gustafson, Bill Simpson, John Shroeder, Don Whitehead, Ronnie Collins, Henry Logan, Terry Lucansky.

Greenville Old Pros (Greenville, S.C.), runners-up: Jerry Brock (coach), Buddy Hayes, Phil Squire, Phil Murrell, Tom Fuller, Gary Helms, Red Robbins, Dick Snyder, Brennan, Johnson, Lacey, Gambrell.

Charlotte All Stars (Charlotte, N.C.), consolation winners: Tom Wynn, Ronnie Stone, Pete Campbell, Bob Benson, Frank Clarke, Stone, Wiles.

Washington Mill (Winston-Salem, N.C.): Dan Hackney (coach), Whitey Bell, Danny Sewell, Harold Hayes, Jerry Moss, Glen Moss, Jay Beal, Alley Hart, Pat Moriarty, Larry Yates, Kirk Stewart, Wayne Duncan, Neil Mc-Geachey, Lindsay, Anderson, Flynt.

Chattanooga VFW (Chattanooga, Tenn.): Ralph Hooper (coach), Lee Defore, Clyde Lee, Bob Grace, Roger Verkoff, Bobby Murr, Harold Cordin, Harry Culbertson, Larry Barnett, Vic Arrowood, Ammerman, Helton, Goolsby, Breazeale.

Mikro (Charlotte, N.C.): Peacock, Mattocks, Dwight Durante, Gibson, Woolard, Goedeck, Lyons, Jennings, Schaffer, Les Heicher.

CLASS A MEN

Monsanto (Greenwood, S.C.), champions: Carl Treadway (coach), Garrett Nation, Jim Diamond, Herb Edmonds, Don Carver, Butch Mattison, Bill Stone, Johnny Taylor, Bobby Etheridge, Harold Echols, Jerry Johnson.

Monsanto (Pensacola, Fla.), runners-up: Dean Barnard (coach), Ken Raines, Johnny Taylor, Jerry Gordon, Robert Fohl, Donald Livingston, Donald Gates, Dennis Wilson, Gerald Bragg, Bill Williams, Jim Hardin.

A. Schottland Inc. (Rocky Mount, N.C.), consolation winners: Billy Winstead (coach), Wayne Davis, Troy Miller, Norman Pridgen, Bill Beacham, Bennie Harrell, Jimmy Winstead, Larry Stallings, Gerald Abrams, Paul Vick.

Saco-Lowell (Easley, S.C.): T.J. Hudgens (coach), James Carter, James Chapman, J.W. Clark, James Finley, Donnie Foster, Joe Lesley, Mike McCoy, Tony Moody, Charles Rogers, Harold Wham.

Russell Manufacturing (Alexander City, Ala.): Vercho Carter (coach), Perry Anderson, Michael Hearn, Charles Scott, Lamar Kennedy, James Leonard, James Scroggins, Don Ballard, Ray Chambers, Wayne Rape, George Long, Carter.

Singer Mfg. (Anderson, S.C.): Eddy Massey (coach), Curtis Wilson, Jack Wiles, Lamar Elrod, Jon Acker, Nelson Massey, Danny Brooks, Wardell Sims, James Dill, Bill Ellis, James Adams.

Davis Mechanical (Greenville, S.C.): Jim Johnson (coach), James Gillespie, Douglas Harris, Kenneth Smith, Francis Brothers, Wayne Thompson, Joel Phillips, Fred Autrey, Tommy Crump, Roger Coln, Joel Heaton, Dix.

Piedmont Mill (Piedmont, S.C.): Earl Wooten (coach), Billy Hooper, Tommy Hart, Gene Seay, Larry Holcombe, Jimmy Cobb, Troy Fowler, Ray Foxx, Joe Hiott.

CLASS B MEN

Lyman Mill (Lyman, S.C.), champions: Bill Eubanks (coach), Wayne Greene, Wayne Fagan, Rick Carlisle, John Crain, William Payne, Danny Watson, Horace Craig Jr., John Mullinax, Tommy Mullinax, Terry Sloan.

Monaghan Mill (Greenville, S.C.), runners-up: Benny Brown (coach), Billy Swaynghame, Larry Blakely, Vernon Stewart, Danny Bagwell, Dean Holtzclaw, Jyles Phillips, Dwight Swaynghame, Dennis Holden, Doyle Lawson Jr., Bennie Morgan.

Gluck Mill (Anderson, S.C.), consolation winners: Earley Hanna (coach), Gary Whitlock, Boyce Sanders, Michael Nelson, Roger Smith, Mike Thrasher, Tom Mahaffey, Johnny Mauldin, Joe Stansell Jr., Jerry Bostic, Ethan Embler.

Dunean Mill (Greenville, S.C.): Buddy Gibson (coach), Tony Campbell, Jimmie Riddle, Arthur Hammett, Robert Hughes, Ronald Turner, Charles Hudson, Joel Cisson, William Turner, Jerry Simpson, Daniel Ray.

Saco-Lowell (Easley, S.C.): Mike McCoy (coach), Douglas Roach, Grover Owings, Marvin Taylor, Charles Hall, Stanley Wilson, James Lackey, Joe Garrett, Tommy Krieg, Joe McCoy, Kenneth Payne.

Liberty Mill (Liberty, S.C.): Bobby Morris (coach), Wales Gilstrap, Archie Hitt, Pat Bowie, Donnie Hitt, Welborn Dobson, Calvin Bryant, Frank McKinney, Glenn Skinner, Homer Owens.

Homelite (Greer, S.C.): Steve Gambrell (coach), Robert Sanders, Charles Fleming,

Southern Textile Basketball Tournament Rosters Appendix 1

Eugene Benson, Alfred Weeks, Eddie Drummond, Clint Turner, Johnny Gregory, James Griffin, Glenn Lowe, Patrick Farmer.

Sangamo Electric Co. (Pickens, S.C.): Joel Allgood (coach), Grady Fowler, Jerry Roper, Garland Rigdon, Jimmy Roberts, Kerry Severson, Bill Rausenbach, Bobby Garren, Jimmy Arledge, Don Finley, Heyward Byers, Anderson.

Monsanto (Pensacola, Fla.): L.C. Collins (coach), Jerry Secrist, Milton Harden, James Forehand, Robert Edgecombe, Jerry Yelverton, Ken Blanton, Ron Bruce, Jim Lowe, Terry Scruggs, Cecil Salter.

Milliken (Spartanburg, S.C.): Donald Gale (coach), Joseph Carver, Dennis Durham, Randell Moxley, Buddy Wells, Lawrence Easley, James McAndrew, James Ledford, Orville Crabtree, Bill Workman.

Pelzer Mill (Pelzer, S.C.): Cecil Hopkins (coach), Sammy Heller, Herman Evatt, Larry Duncan, Jimmy Yates, Roger Harris, Hiram Belt, Jimmy Hopkins, Tommy Kearns, Jimmy McKee, James Bagwell, Walter Davis, Keller, Thomason.

Bigelow-Sanford (Calhoun Falls, S.C.): Frankie Nixon (coach), Thomas Edwards, Michael Burton, Robert Powell, Larry Alewine, F.R. McConnell, Claude Powell, Allen Heard, Nixon.

Fiber Industries (Greenville, S.C.): Dan Cash (coach), Wade Coley, Alvin Crisp, Jack Gilmore, Troy Godwin, Robert Harley, Carl Kirchner, Eugene McBride, Stanley Tapp, James Roper, Mike Bender.

Parker Mill (Greenville, S.C.): Willard Fowler (coach), Eugene Ballentine, Curtis Campbell, Mike Fair, Michael Campbell, Allen Dean, Ronald Bridges, Dewey Welborn, Donald Lewis, McIntyre, Cannon.

Martin Mfg. (Williamston, S.C.): Joe Lollis (coach), David Sanders, Andrew Pahokas, David Major, David Terry, Donald Brady, Barney Roper, Pals.

Class C Men

Saco-Lowell (Easley, S.C.), champions: Larry Bagwell (coach), Jimmy Campbell, Terry Strickland, Jerry Cox, Earl Gilstrap, John Strickland, John Coakley, Randy Bray, Elliott Eskew, Bob Wiggins, Steve Duncan.

Woodside Mill (Greenville, S.C.), runners-up: Mike Sanderson, Turner, Dean, Jack Anderson, Mathis, McCarson, Johnson, Tollison, Bell, White, Andrews.

Maxon Shirt Co. (Greenville, S.C.), consolation winners: Johnny Ross (coach), John Graves, James Graves, Robert LaForge, Lawrence Pyle, Thomas Wilson, Roger Bower, Dick Ploof, Kenneth Durham, Holmes Jones, Lou Williams, Johns, Jones, Morris.

Dacox (Seneca, S.C.): Don Hall (coach), Bill Moore, Merl Cooe, Charles Holstead, Ronnie Crooks, James Lewis, Freddie Patterson, James Hopkins, William Smith, Jones.

Monaghan Mill (Greenville, S.C.): Danny Bagwell (coach), William Alexander, Tommy Boone, Pat Swaynghame, Stanley Nix, Robert Bagwell, Allan Landreth, Donny Gossett, Donnie Bridges, Hanky Harbin, Joe Nix, Hooper.

Microtron (Greenville, S.C.): Larry Jones (coach), Freddie Coan, Tommy Gaul, Heath Dobson, Jeff Garren, John Stewart, Jerry Funderburk, Gregg Johnson, Reggie Kelley, Larry Walker, Lee Taylor.

Simpsonville Mill (Simpsonville, S.C.): Odell Barbary (coach), Dickie Nelson, Frank Garrison, Gordon Ballew, Tim Jenkins, Richard Kinard, Mike Jenkins, Larry Snipes, William Ballew, David Sharperson, John Smith, Bobby Pridmore, L. Jenkins.

Dunean Mill (Greenville, S.C.): Billy Lollis (coach), Ralph Pannell, Gary Powell, Ronald Jones, Gary Owensby, Ronald Bolds, John Guest, Hayes Stancell, Howard Clark, Bobby Cobb, Donnie Surrett, Terry Campbell.

Pelzer Mill (Pelzer, S.C.): W.H. Taylor (coach), Phil Hopkins, Sonny Saxon, Steve Horne, Kenny Ross, Jimmy Bair, Tim Galloway, Bill Hayes, James Williams, Jerry Bagwell, Don Wooten, Richie Medlin, McKee, Cooper.

Liberty Mill (Liberty, S.C.): Quillen Finley (coach), Don Grogan, Johnny Gilstrap, Ted Owens, James Messer, Roy Gillespie, Robert Kelly, Steve Sweezy, Chester Medlin, Jerry Dillenger, Stanley Sargent, Randy Bagwell, Robert Black.

Brandon Mill (Greenville, S.C.): Ezra Embler (coach), Sammy Huffman, Joel McCombs, Gary Pace, Roger Alexander, Marvin Clary, Richard Kelby, Matthew Williams, Clifton Landreth, Kenneth Oliver, Walter McCombs, T. McCombs.

Poe Hardware (Greenville, S.C.): Larry Miller (coach), Tommy Miller, Ben Reed, Sammy Eskew, William Rogers, Ronald Whitworth, Charles Timmons, Phillip Donnan, Mark Holmes, Capers Bouton.

Union Bleachery (Greenville, S.C.): Jack Williams (coach), Ronald Turner, Tommy Stroud, Jimmy Evatt, Clyde Cobb, Larry Holder, Joel Green, Steve Robertson, Paul Turner, L. Turner, G. Turner, C. Turner.

Salem Garment Co. (Salem, S.C.): Bobby Smith (coach), David Byers, Frank Collins, C.E. Ellenburg, James Gentry, Clyde Herron, Roger Lamb, Arthur Mason, Roderick Smith, Roy Strickland Jr., Randy Talley, John Dillard.

Appleton Mill (Anderson, S.C.): Henry Spake (coach), Donnie Adams, Gerald Bailey, Johnny Corn, David Edmonds, Alan Hawkins, Christopher Rash, Donnie Williams, James Yates, Allen.

Piedmont Mill (Piedmont, S.C.): Don Roper (coach), Ernie Chambers Jr., Roger Jones, James Bagwell, Ronnie Bagwell, Ronnie Smith, Steve Henderson, Terry Blackston, George Watson, Ernie Rice, Cotton Evans, Bell.

Print Shop (Greenville, S.C.): Pat Campbell (coach), Steve Vaughn, Thomas Ward, Richard Galloway, Henry Hunt, Jimmy Pittman, Len Turner, Wayne Nix, Alex Cawthon, Louis Mahaffey, Mike Merrill.

Dill's Warehouse (Greenville, S.C.): Ivester, Brown, Styles, Childress, Wynn, McKinney, Crews, Vest, Smith, Long.

Class A Women

Atlanta Tomboys (Atlanta, Ga.), champions: John Moon (coach), Mickey Davis, Vivian Maslen, Edwina Bryan, Vera Garrett, Annette Hammock, Linda Crook, Delores Owens, Martha Carmichal, D.L. Maslan, Sue Keith, Wilson, Bryson.

Singer Mfg. (Anderson, S.C.), runners-up: Caroline Brown, Clayton, Carolyn Garrett, Jamison, Phillips, Sara Strickland, Wilson, Lynn, Scott, Spearman, King, Watt.

Slater Mill (Slater, S.C.), consolation winners: Kirby, Chumley, J. Smith, Burgess, C. Smith, Weaver, Southerland, Merritt, Brown, Callahan, McCall, Andrews.

Poe Hardware (Greenville, S.C.): Easton Rice (coach), Lynn Sams, Kaye Burns, DuBose Fant, Ann Watson, Barbara Kress, Mary Lee, Jessie Ivie, Sandy Ross, Cheryl Bolton, Barbara Ridgeway, Lee Watson, Cross.

Murrell Brothers Sand (Greenville, S.C.): Frances Welborn (coach), Judy Cross, Carol Jones, Fran Wood, Judy Payne, Carolyn Pharr, Doris Nabors, Ann Lyons, Thelma DeVine, Sybil Murrell, Debbie Dill, Maxene Bishop, Mary Spearman, Chapman, Brooks.

Bigelow-Sanford (Calhoun Falls, S.C.): Ray McConnell (coach), Sandra Davis, Julia Bryant, Patsy Wilson, Carol Putnam, Carolyn Hilley, Brenda Wiles, Carolyn Bowman, Connie Lewis, Brenda Waters, Carol Jackson, June Payton, Joyce Bowman.

Lyman Mill (Lyman, S.C.): Virgil Pruitte (coach), Edna Holden, Geraldine Anderson, Frances Boxter, Vicky Sellars, Celia Boyter, Patricia Pike, Tuby Tipton, Sandra Gale, Mary Quinn, Dorothy Stone, Sandra Poole, Carolyn Poole, Smith, F. Boyter, M. Boyter, Parsons.

Sangamo Electric Co. (Pickens, S.C.): Jerry Roper (coach), Jean Stone, Jackie McJunkin, Brenda Cater, Brenda Grant, Mary Foster, Deda Duncan, Darlene Boozer, Donna Duncan, Katherine Gibson, Melba Krieg, Barbara Stone, McDaniel, L. Carter, Bingham, Hooper, Atone, Brigham, B. Carter, Daniels.

Piedmont Mill (Piedmont, S.C.): Curtis Terry (coach), Susie Garrett, Carolyn Spearman, Margaret Orr, Linda Porter, Shirley Merritt, Judy Parker, Alrilda Propes, Dianna Limbaugh, Anne Cely, Jessalene Jones, Jo King, Connie Ward, Garrett, Elrod, J. Porter, A. Merritt.

Oconee Gas (Westminster, S.C.): Buddy Herring (coach), Sandy Childs, Glenda Crooks, Peggy Glenn, Judy Stancil, Martha Price, Regina Greer, Avon Herring, Emily Bearden, Willie Cox, Jane Greer, Judy Ivester, Margaret Massey, Brooks, Lynn.

1967

Officers: Ken Pittman (Greenville, S.C.), President and Executive Secretary; Ward Williams (Greenville, S.C.), 1st Vice President; R.E. Patrick (Greenwood, S.C.), 2nd Vice President; Fred Byrd (Greenville, S.C.), Ass't Executive Secretary; Divver Hendrix (Greenville, S.C.), Treasurer; Harry Foster (Greenville, S.C.), Assistant Treasurer; Whitey Kendall (Greenville), Supervisor of Officials; Lt. J.T. Merck, Security Officer.

Executive Committee: Clarence Thomas (Greenville, S.C.), Willie Wilbanks (Ware Shoals, S.C.), Curtis Terry (Piedmont, S.C.), Jim McDuffie (Greenville, S.C.), Willard

Fowler (Greer, S.C.), Fred Powers (Asheville, N.C.), Jim Anderson (Greenville, S.C.), Dan Foster (Greenville, S.C.), Snow Kirby (Marietta, S.C.), Bill Hopkins (Pelzer, S.C.), Summers Jarrett (Pensacola, Fla.), D.K. Smith (Lyman, S.C.), Lewis Acker (Anderson, S.C.), Lloyd McAbee (Greenville, S.C.), Bobby Morris (Liberty, S.C.), Joe Newton (Greenville, S.C.), Henry Spake (Anderson, S.C.), Charlton Miller (Greer, S.C.), Grady Wallace (Columbia, S.C.).

OPEN DIVISION

Guthrie Motors (Williamston, S.C.), champions: Earl Wooten (coach), Don Helms, Gary Helms, Gene Seay, Joe Hiott, Jim Wiles, Tom Corcoran, Willie Pegram, Buddy Benedict, Ronald Sharmon, Harold Roper, Norman Shaffer, James Thomason, Roper Seward, Oneal Seward, Shiner.

Mikro (Charlotte, N.C.), runners-up: Jesse Branson, Dwight Durante, Holtzclaw, Sullivan, Kendall, Mike Ross, Bowes, Pridgen.

Washington Mill (Winston-Salem, N.C.), consolation winners: Whitey Bell (coach), Cliff Dwyer, Glenn Anderson, Bill Tomlinson, Ray Whitley, Jay Beal, Jim Boshart, Paul Long, Chris Lindsay, Bill McDermott, Harold Hayes, Brad Brooks, C. Bell.

Perkins Auto (Charlotte, N.C.): Joe Ladd (coach), Jim Kilby, Neal McGaha, Dennis Bagley, Tommy Burton, R.D. Carson, Paul Long, Jim Boshart, Jesse Branson, Stan Smith, Aubrey Cochran, LeMoreaux, Taylor, Miller, Duren.

Sunshine Cleaners (Columbia, S.C.): Grady Wallace (coach), Jimmy Collins, Mike Callahan, Art Whisnant, Bill Simpson, John Shroeder, Don Whitehead, Henry Logan, Terry Lucansky, Lyn Buckholder, Earl Lovelace, Al Salvadori.

Hinton's All Stars (Greenville, S.C.): Sam Picken (coach), Les Heicher, Dan Goolsby, Charlie Betchel, Steve Lawrence, Bane Sarrett, Norm Schaffer, Jerry Smith, Don Frye, Boyce Frederick, Terry Holland, Bob Haney, Charlie Jennings, Wike.

A. Schottland Inc. (Rocky Mount, N.C.): Bill Beacham (coach), Albert Batchelor, David Vick, James Reid, Charlie Lander, Gene Worthington, Harold Earnhardt, Billy Winstead, Troy Miller, Lee Schafer, Reid, N. Winstead.

CLASS A MEN

Monsanto (Greenwood, S.C.), champions: Jim Diamond (coach), Garrett Nation, Herb Edmonds, Don Carver, Bill Stone, Johnny Taylor, Bobby Etheredge, Bill Wilson, Jerry Gordon, Ray Lark, Jim Brown, Joe Martin.

Homelite (Greer, S.C.), runners-up: Edward Halley (coach), Steve Gambrell, Robert Sanders, Wayne Anderson, Earl Turner, Edward Nelson, George Weeks, Eddie Drummond, Willie Jones, Kenneth Price, Jerry Dowis.

Lyman Mill (Lyman, S.C.), consolation winners: Morris Cagle (coach), Daniel Watson, William Eubanks, Jerry Good, Wayne Blackmon, Stephen Brown, Mike Page, Cody Forrester, Sam Oliver, William Green, Thomas Mullinax, Carlisle.

Kendall Mill (Seneca, S.C.): John Williams (coach), Marshall Kirby, Jim Kay, Roger Tippett, Gary Rogers, Wayne Poore, Mike Black, Michael Donald, Thomas McBride, Robert Wilder, Troy Lacey.

Monsanto (Pensacola, Fla.): Dean Barnard (coach), Ken Raines, Johnny Taylor, Robert Fohl, Donald Livingston, Donald Gates, Dennis Wilson, Ronald Morton, Coy Carter.

Saco-Lowell (Easley, S.C.): Glenn Edgar (coach), James Carter, Donnie Foster, Joe Lesley, Mike McCoy, Charles Rogers, Harold Wham, Ira Black, Dennis Waldrop, Joe Bandy, Harold Waldrop.

Russell Manufacturing (Alexander City, Ala.): Vercho Carter (coach), Perry Anderson, Michael Hearn, Charles Scott, Ray Chambers, Wayne Rape, George Long, William Carter, Ronald Bradford, James Randall, Jimmy Childers, Sanders.

Singer Mfg. (Pickens, S.C.): Eddy Massey (coach), Elmer Elrod Jr., Nelson Massey, Wardell Sims, James Adams, John Nixon, Joseph Tucker, Andrew Crosby, William Hall, Ulysses West, Curt Wilson.

Slater Mill (Slater, S.C.): Snow Kirby (coach), Jack Halford, Robert Kirby, Jerry Brinkley, Thomas Adkins, Ted Tucker, Joe Smith, William White, Bill Farmer, Kenneth Smart, Carol Thornton.

CLASS B MEN

Saco-Lowell (Easley, S.C.), champions: Harold Waldrop (coach), Hershell Leatherwood (coach), Douglas Roach, Grover Owings, Stanley Wilson, Joe Garrett, Tommy Krieg, Joe McCoy, Jimmy Campbell, Cecil Clark, Jimmy Wilson, Roy Leatherwood.

Pelzer Mill (Pelzer, S.C.), runners-up: H.D. Adams (coach), Herman Evatt, Larry Duncan, Bill Harris, Jimmy Hopkins, James Bagwell, Ronnie Davenport, Raymond Rochester, Mike Welborn, Mike Clayton, Bill Barnett, John Scruggs, Adolph Young, Roach.

Dunean Mill (Greenville, S.C.), consolation winners: Buddy Gibson (coach), Jimmie Riddle, Arthur Hammett, Charles Hudson, Jerry Simpson, Maxie Burns, Andrew Ballard, Jeff Ware, Homer Robinson Jr., Robert Morrow, Sammie Young.

Monaghan Mill (Greenville, S.C.): Fred Rigdon (coach), Billy Swaynghame, Vernon Stewart, Danny Bagwell, James Bagwell, Alan Landreth, Elize Smith, Donald Bridges, Keith Alexander, Donnie Lewis, Terry Fowler.

Lyman Mill (Lyman, S.C.): Rick Carlisle (coach), Phil Hix, Carey Johnson, Rick Dunagan, John Owens, Paul Pace, Gussie Ballenger, Charles Hart, Fred Coan, Kenneth Pike, James Tapp.

Gluck Mill (Anderson, S.C.): Earley Hanna (coach), Gary Whitlock, Donald Smith, Mike Thrasher, Joe Stansell Jr., Ethan Embler, Grover Stewart, Jackie Poore, James Yates, Neil Whitfield, Thomas Christian, Ashworth, Nelson.

Liberty Mill (Liberty, S.C.): Bobby Morris (coach), Archie Hitt, Pat Bowie, Welborn Dobson, Glenn Skinner, Clyde Owens, Seth Sargent, Stanley Rosemond, Luther Austin, Charles Chamber, Dollan Ricketts.

Sangamo Electric Co. (Pickens, S.C.): Ted Krieg (coach), Jerry Roper, Garland Rigdon, Jimmy Duncan, Don Finley, David Byers, Doug Bagwell, Jess Brooks, Jim McCall, James Perry, Ronald Brank.

Monsanto (Pensacola, Fla.): Jack Gibson (coach), James Forehand, Robert Edgecombe, Jerry Yelverton, Jim Lowe, R.G. Cunnningham, Darryl Dawe, Edward Dixon, Donald Justice, Werner.

Milliken (Spartanburg, S.C.): Donald Gale (coach), Joseph Carver, Dennis Durham, Orville Crabtree, John Workman, Roy Phillips, Eugene Willimon, Ray Parris, Duane Turner.

Piedmont Mill (Piedmont, S.C.): J. Bagwell, K. Bagwell, F. Foxx, E. Foxx, Spearman, Stowe, Woodson, Cooper, McKinney, Garraux, Henry.

Greer Mill (Greer, S.C.): Robertson, Moody, Moore, Richardson, Brown, Barton, Stepp, Wolf, Mayfield, Jones.

Bigelow-Sanford (Calhoun Falls, S.C.): Archie Nixon (coach), Terry Chrisley, George Waters, Roscoe Powell, Frankie Nixon, Larry Alewine, William McMahan, Bobby McMahan, Frank McConnell, C. McMahan.

Fiber Industries (Greenville, S.C.): Dean Huskey (coach), Alvin Crisp, Stanley Tapp, Henry Sizemore, Vernon McMakin, Donald Simmons, James Yates, Claude Barnette, Paul Pritchett, Kenneth Edwards, Jack Kelley, Beach.

Martin Mfg. (Williamston, S.C.): Joe Lollis (coach), Dickie Sanders, David Major, David Terry, Donald Brady, Sam Drake, Ray McClellion, Benny Smith, Ervin Ligdon, Tony Boseman.

Union Bleachery (Greenville, S.C.): Jimmy Holder (coach), Cullen Turner, Tommy Stroud, Tommy Ward, Ronnie Turner, Steve Robertson, Kenneth Holder, James Evatt, Johnny Holtzclaw, L. TuRner, G. TuRner.

Pratt-Read (Central, S.C.): Kelley DuBose (coach), Luther Blackwell, Billy White, Garvin Pilgrim, Randolph Black, Charles Gillespie, Ronnie Hughes, Carl Kelly, Luther Pearson, Joseph Holcombe, Jesse Simmons.

Clark-Schwebel (Anderson, S.C.): W.E. Stephenson (coach), Raymond Bostic, James Day, William Macomso, Daniel Jackson, Jerry Partain, Ronald Gilstrap, Roy Jordan, Guy Meador Jr., Nance.

LTV ElectroSystems (Greenville, S.C.): Fred Snoddy (coach), Michael Miros, Joe Hayes, Lee Madrazo, Gerald Smith, Jerry Swanger, John Hughes, Larry Brownlee, Robert Smith, Ronald Williams, David Stephens, Buehring.

American Monorail (Simpsonville, S.C.): John Deter (coach), E.B. Millwood, Alex Murphy, G.M. Duckworth, O'Louis McCullough, Cleveland Moore, Roger Scott, Yancy Coxeton, Monore Williams, Robert Williams, Harold Gray, Cureton, Anderson.

Class C Men

Microtron (Greenville, S.C.), champions: Johnny Lamb (coach), Roddy McCarson, Mike Sanderson, Steve Henderson, Ernie Chambers, Ronnie Shelton, Stanley Hopkins, Jimmy Pittman, Gray Cheek, Willie Belton, Steve Lamb.

Slater Mill (Slater, S.C.), runners-up: Doots Wright (coach), David Byers, Floyd Burnette, Bill Cashion, Tommy Senn, Bill Poole, Ronald Cobb, Harold Aiken Jr., Lewis Talley, John Dillard, Jerry Farr, Darby.

Dunean Mill (Greenville, S.C.), consolation

Southern Textile Basketball Tournament Rosters

winners: Billy Lollis (coach), Tony Pannell, Gary Powell, Ronald Burns, Ronald Bolds, Hayes Stancell, Gene Morgan, Danny Watson, Dean Powell, Butch Dean, Jerry Dean, L. Powell.

Pelzer Mill #1 (Pelzer, S.C.): Jimmy Hopkins (coach), Sonny Saxon, Steve Horne, Kenny Ashley, Stanley Horton, Jerome Gambrell, Charles Lister, Larry Stone, William Adams, Gary Cooley, Jerry Bagwell, Cobb.

Brandon Mill (Greenville, S.C.): L. Phillips, Alexander, Bell, Campbell, Echols, McCombs, Williams, R. Phillips, Sorgee.

Pelzer Mill #2 (Pelzer, S.C.): W.H. Taylor (coach), Larry Hester, Roger Lollis, David Spurill, Tim Galloway, Doug Barnett, Mitchell McKee, Phil Hopkins, Frank Acker, Mike Copeland, Mosley, Mattress, Horne, Sewell.

Saco-Lowell (Easley, S.C.): James Carter (coach), Terry Strickland, Earl Gilstrap, Steve Duncan, Steven Crowe, R.G. McDaniel, Richard Gilstrap, Jerry Chapman, James Cleveland, Skip Acker, John Roper.

Monaghan Mill (Greenville, S.C.): Danny Bagwell (coach), Joe Nix, Joe Hancock, Roddy Turner, Bud Hooper, Steve Pace, Ted Ramsey, David Bishop, Terry Taylor, Massey, Landreth, Owens.

Poe Hardware (Greenville, S.C.): Broadus Miller (coach), Ben Reed, Sammy Eskew, Bill Rogers, Ronald Whitworth, Charles Timmons, Phillip Donnan, Capers Bouton, Chip Price, Ricky Snipes, Turner.

Appleton Mill (Anderson, S.C.): Henry Spake (coach), Donnie Adams, Ronnie Bailey, Johnny Corn, Alan Hawkins, Lacy Fuller, Doug Payton, Curtis Bowen, Johnny Edmonds, Andy Wooten, Arnold.

Piedmont Mill #1 (Piedmont, S.C.): Curtis Terry (coach), Ronnie Bagwell, Ronnie Smith, Steve Henderson, Terry Blackston, Mike McNeely, Tom Morgan, Wendell Merritt, Mike James, Arthur Anders, Dennis Grooms.

Piedmont Mill #2 (Piedmont, S.C.): Don Roper (coach), W.A. Gilliam, J.E. Rice, G.M. Lindley, B.L. Bell, H.A. Stewart, E.L. Albritton, D.O. Sutton, J.M. Crawford, J.A. Henderson, A.M. Knight Jr.

Piedmont Mill #3 (Piedmont, S.C.): Earl Wooten (coach), Allen Stevens, Bunyon McClain, Bobby Stover, Mark McClain, Charles Garrison, Steve Hughey, Troy Taylor, Bobby League, Bobby Higgins, Tommy Rice, White, Barbare.

Belton Mill (Belton, S.C.): Larry Lowe (coach), Gregory Jones, Randy Wright, John Campbell, Lanny Taylor, Mike Whitfield, Jack Ross III, Douglas Kelly, Mike Rowland, Harold Chandler, Jamie Allen, Cook.

Metro-Atlantic (Greenville, S.C.): Larry Jones (coach), Tommy Gaul, Reggie Kelley, Billy Harrill, John Stewart, John Bartone, Barry Toney, Tam Boggs, Terry Hughes, Steve Berry, Joel Odom, Kuhn, Hayes, Kay, Dobson.

John Perkins Industries (Greenville, S.C.): Jerry Knight (coach), R.R. Bouton, R.L. Bridwell, M.S. Carter, T.B. Carter, M.M. Clyatt, M.R. Holmes, J.P. Howard, J.O. Kelley, W.M. Norris, J.R. Brooks, Timmons.

Pacolet Mill (Pacolet, S.C.): Bill Allen (coach), Dale Mulwee, Wayne Kirby, Bill Courtney, Bobby Guyton, Ronnie Parris, Billy Smith, Rod Wells, Ray Harris, Donnie Hodge, Mike Padgett, Smith.

CLASS A WOMEN

IMMS (Greenville, S.C.), champions: John Mickler (coach), Doris Nabors, Patsy Neal, Tommie Greene, Vicki Chapman, Willoughby Jarrell, Debbie Dill, Carolyn Jones, Judy Cross, Carolyn Pharr, Judy Payne, Frances Wood, Frances Welborn.

Slater Mill (Slater, S.C.), runners-up: Margaret Wright (coach), Joan Kirby, Jane Smith, Cheryl Smith, Minnie Andrews, Jeannie Callahan, Sandra Burgess, Marsha Marrett, June Brown, Marion Koon, Peggy Chumley, Sue Chumley, Sherry McCall, Thackston, Murphy, Gossett, Day, Lauren Murphy.

Sangamo Electric Co. (Pickens, S.C.), consolation winners: Melba Krieg (coach), Jean Stone, Jackie McJunkin, Brenda Cater, Deda Duncan, Donna Duncan, Catherine Gibson, Janet Keener, Gail Hunter, Eleanor Pace, Linda Cater, Linda Houston, Sybil Murrell.

Piedmont Mill (Piedmont, S.C.): Sam Campbell (coach), D.J. Fitts, Kaye Roper, B.J. Edwards, J.B. Gilreath, D.A. Thompson, C.R. Campbell, B.A. Hughes, D.V. Schwiers, D.C. White, F. Davis, J.L. Chasteen, J.H. Chapman.

Lyman Mill (Lyman, S.C.): Virgil Pruitte (coach), Edna Holden, Geraldine Anderson, Patricia Davis, Sandra Gale, Carolyn Poole, Linda Pike, Margaret Wolf, Linda Belle, Paula Barbare, Nancy Eubanks, Ann Jackson, Patsy Jackson, Huckabee, Glenton.

Union Bleachery (Greenville, S.C.): Lan

Turner (coach), Ruth Williams, Jan Sutherland, Linda Nelson, Paula Williams, Lucille Rothell, Betty Watson, Frances Brooks, Christine Jones, Candy James.

Fiber Industries (Greenville, S.C.): Mike Bender (coach), Delores Cobb, Becky Strange, Mildred Smith, Betty Monroe, Aliene Creel, Edna Carter, Mary Pruitt, Pearlie Gray, Carol Stephenson, Ann Dobson, Betty Folds, Diane Solesbee, Stephens.

1968

Officers: R.E. Patrick (Greenwood, S.C.), President; Harry Foster (Greenville, S.C.), 1st Vice President and Ass't Treasurer; Ken Pittman (Greenville, S.C.), 2nd Vice President; Fred Byrd (Greenville, S.C.), Executive Secretary; Divver Hendrix (Greenville, S.C.), Treasurer; Fred Powers (Asheville, N.C.), Ass't Executive Secretary; Whitey Kendall (Greenville), Supervisor of Officials; Lt. J.T. Merck, Security Officer; Frank Ballenger (Greenville, S.C.), Director of Publicity.

Executive Committee: Clarence Thomas (Greenville, S.C.), Willie Wilbanks (Ware Shoals, S.C.), Curtis Terry (Piedmont, S.C.), Jim McDuffie (Greenville, S.C.), Willard Fowler (Greer, S.C.), Jim Anderson (Greenville, S.C.), Dan Foster (Greenville, S.C.), Snow Kirby (Marietta, S.C.), Bill Hopkins (Pelzer, S.C.), D.K. Smith (Lyman, S.C.), Lewis Acker (Anderson, S.C.), Lloyd McAbee (Greenville, S.C.), Bobby Morris (Liberty, S.C.), Joe Newton (Greenville, S.C.), Henry Spake (Anderson, S.C.), Charlton Miller (Greer, S.C.), Grady Wallace (Columbia, S.C.), Ward Williams (Greenville, S.C.), Bill Belcher (Pensacola, Fla.), T.C. Hooper (Greenville, S.C.), Dean Huskey (Greenville, S.C.).

OPEN DIVISION

Mikro (Charlotte, N.C.), champions: Mike Ross (coach), Ed Biedenbach, Bill Kretzer, Dwight Durante, Garland Davis, Bill English, Eugene Smiley, Tom Boerwinkle, John Hendrix, Lee Davis, Johnny Watkins, Jackie Wilson, Dave Wyscarver, Reggie Randolph, Paul Wolfcale, Weiskoph, Wiles, Weeks, David.

Guthrie Motors (Williamston, S.C.), runners-up: Earl Wooten (coach), Don Helms, Gary Helms, Willie Pegram, Jim Wiles, Buddy Benedict, Harold Roper, Norman Shaffer, Oneal Seward, Joe Ayoub, Mike Jenkins, Hank Channell, Walt Ayers, Chasteen, Kerns, Adkins, Jenkins.

Hinton's All Stars (Greenville, S.C.): Les Heicher (coach), Jerry Smith, Don Frye, Charlie Jennings, Gerald Glur, Art Beatty, Ray Ruhling, Jim Sutherland, Will Lucas, Don Webster, Les Heicher, Hortey, Halford, Wyke, Bechtel.

Spaulding Fibers (Spartanburg, S.C.): J.W. Deter (coach), Dean Sheetz, Richard Wright, Leroy Greggs, Jerry Smith, Tom Burton, Robert Fleming, Tom Neilson, Jim Mazoyen, Johnny Motes, David Sharperson, Jerry Lattimore, Bobby Lewis, Art Whisnant, Theodore Chapman.

Transit Homes (Greenville, S.C.): Ruppert Elliott (coach), Eugene Seay, Eugene Holtzclaw, Len Turner, Ricky Duncan, Jimmy Chapman, Buddy Moore, Leon McClinton, Thomas Caughman, William Kenny, Bo Wyenandt, Bob Warren.

Elkay Industries (Camden, S.C.): Carol Truesdale (coach), Bill Edison, Jim Hidy, Mike Callahan, Ron Smith, Joe Laird, Bobby Robinson, Roy Quinn, Collins, Mike Edison, Heidy, McCall.

K.G. Carpet (Atlanta, Ga.): Ken Griffith, Ken Rohloff, Bob Mance, Tony Cerknevik, Jerry Shipp, Phil Wagner, Greg Robinson, Jack Waters, Larry Barnett, Doug Alexander, James Brown, Ray Jeffords, Don Wix, Dave Denton, Walker, Stewart, Thorton, Patton, Harris.

Hunt Machinery (Columbia, S.C.): Skip Harlicka, Jack Thompson, Frank Standard, Gary Gregor, Lynn Burkholder, Henry Logan, Womack, Hudock.

CLASS A MEN

Russell Manufacturing (Alexander City, Ala.), champions: Vercho Carter (coach), Perry Anderson, Mike Hearn, Charles Scott, Wayne Rape, Jim Childers, Jerry Sanders, Larry Evans, Mike Sanders, Herman Watts, Charles Gunn, Neil Anderson.

Saco-Lowell (Easley, S.C.), runners-up: Glenn Edgar (coach), James Carter, Donnie Foster, Joe Lesley, Harold Waldrop, Jimmy Wilson, Stanley Wilson, Don Carver, Grover Owings, Cecil Clark, Douglas Roach.

Kendall Mill (Seneca, S.C.), consolation winners: Troy Reese (coach), Marshall Kirby, Roger Tippett, Gary Rogers, Wayne Poore, Mike Black, Michael Donald, Thomas

McBride, Billy Moore, Clyde Herron, Larry Winchester, Williams.

Homelite (Greer, S.C.): Ben Henderson (coach), Robert Sanders, Kenneth Massey, Eddie Drummond, Patrick Farmer, James Griffith, Jackie Cox, Calvin Cohens, Eugene Benson.

Monsanto (Greenwood, S.C.): Jim Diamond (coach), Garrett Nation, Johnny Taylor, Jerry Gordon, Joe Martin, Fred Schlock, Leon James Jr., Jack Spady, James Johnson.

Monsanto (Pensacola, Fla.): John Taylor (coach), Don Carver (coach), Ken Raines, Donald Livingston, Donald Gates, Dennis Wilson, Jerald Grant, Ken Blanton, Jim Lowe, David Patrick, Buddy Zukowski, Jim Chersire, Raws.

Singer Mfg. (Pickens, S.C.): Eddy Massey (coach), Nelson Massey, Wardell Sims, James Adams, Andrew Crosby, William Hall, Truman Evans, Lummie Young Jr., Michael Raines, Larry Smith, Marsh.

Fiber Industries (Greenville, S.C.): Dick Battle (coach), Earl Whittington, Bill Payne, Stan Tapp, Ronnie Lawson, Carl Kirchner, Jerry McNeely, Ron Foltz, Mike Neal, Ken Childers, Don Simmons.

PPG Industries (Shelby, N.C.): Eddie Duncan (coach), Troy Wallick, Richard Clary, Thomas Whitaker, Ralph Haynes, Jack Waters, Jerry Wease, Bobby Canipe, Don Wright, James Ledford, Jerry Floyd.

Class B Men

Madison Throwing Co. (Madison, N.C.), champions: Pete Bryant (coach), Semi Mintz, Orell Stovall, Bobby Mabe, Chuck Mullins, Glenn Ogburn, Harold Parker, Tim Smothers, Dennis Ellis, Winford Boles, Heyward Scales.

Fiber Industries (Greenville, S.C.), runners-up: Jack Kelly (coach), Alvin Crisp, Vernon McMakin, Donald Harkins, Paul Pritchett, Kenneth Edwards, Mickey Stepp, Robert Harley, Dennis Hicks, James Godwin, Donald Hughes, Hawkins.

Monaghan Mill (Greenville, S.C.), consolation winners: Jyles Phillips (coach), Danny Bagwell, James Allman, Alan Landreth, Keith Alexander, Terry Fowler, Jimmy Major, James McAtee, Johnny Stevens, B. Bagwell, Turner.

Union Bleachery (Greenville, S.C.): Thomas Bolton (coach), Tommy Stroud, Willie Thomas, Jake Williams, John Terrell, Ralph Bowen, Ernest Makins, James Workman, Jerome Dickey, James Smith.

Pelzer Mill (Pelzer, S.C.): Bill Hopkins (coach), Larry Duncan, Jimmy Hopkins, James Bagwell, Ronnie Davenport, Irvin Ligion, Tony Lollis, Lee Terry, Sammy Heller, John Price, Dickie Sandan, Tim Galloway, Rochester, Sanders, Ashley.

Dunean Mill (Greenville, S.C.): Buddy Gibson (coach), Grover Riddle, Arthur Hammett, Charles Hudson, Maxie Burns, Ralph McClain, Terry Campbell, Dean Harvell, Clifton Collins, James Galloway, Ronald Sims.

Lyman Mill (Lyman, S.C.): Virgil Pruitt (coach), Phil Hix, Carey Johnson, Gussie Ballenger, Dan Randall, John Walker Jr., Carl Crocker, Philip Childress, Ernest Murray, Marion Knuckles, Carol Kelly, Gresham, Garrett.

Gluck Mill (Anderson, S.C.): Earley Hanna (coach), Gary Whitlock, Donald Smith, Mike Thrasher, Grover Stewart, Jackie Poore, James Yates, Neil Whitfield, Thomas Christian, Steve Partain, Roger Smith, G. Smith, Sanders.

Sangamo Electric Co. (Pickens, S.C.): David Byers, Doug Bagwell, Jess Brooks, Jim McCall, Ronald Shoeman, W.W. Nicholson, James Kelsey, Randy Talley, Gary Goodman.

Bigelow-Sanford (Calhoun Falls, S.C.): Archie Nixon (coach), Terry Chrisley, George Waters, Frankie Nixon, Larry Alewine, Bobby McMahan, Bill Lewis, Jimmie Blackburn, Clarence Davis, Danny Johnson.

Pratt-Read (Central, S.C.): Kelley DuBose (coach), Luther Pearson, Billy White, Garvin Pilgrim, Randolph Black, Ronnie Hughes, Joseph Holcombe, Bobby Land, F.H. Burkette, W.A. Charping, Thomas Lusk.

Clark-Schwebel (Anderson, S.C.): Buddy Stephenson (coach), Raymond Bostic, James Day, William Macomson, Jerry Partain, Ronald Gilstrap, Roy Jordan, Lieri Willford, Johnny Corn, Mack Nance, Baskin.

LTV ElectroSystems (Greenville, S.C.): Clyde Smith (coach), Michael Miros, Lee Madrazo, Jerry Smith, John Hughes, William Harris, Melvin Longshore, Jimmy Weeks, Daniel Avery, Gerald Bice, Tommy Brown, M. Smith.

Phillips Fibers (Spartanburg, S.C.): William Jones (coach), John Painter, Ralph Brown, John Weaver Jr., John Mathias, Jack Turner, Curtis Sprouse, Luther Wilkins, Cother Miller, Perry Johnson, John Conley.

Greer Mill (Greer, S.C.): Bob Campbell

(coach), Bruce Stepp, Clarence Moody, Steven Moore, Gordon Barton, Verdell Richardson, Lawrence Williams, David Jones, Donell Moody, James Wolfe, Lee Cox.

Singer Mfg. (Pickens, S.C.): J.D. Brock (coach), Don Nicholson, Joe Adams, Calvin Evatt, Joseph Bowers, Joe Thompson, Grant Chappell, David Brezeale, John Crumpton, Brock.

CLASS C MEN

Poe Hardware (Greenville, S.C.), champions: Broadus Miller (coach), Sammy Eskew, Willie Rogers, Capers Bouton, Chip Price, Randy Miller, Mark Holmes, Billy Carpenter, Ray Venderwerff, Mike Jones.

Monaghan Mill (Greenville, S.C.), runners-up: Jimmy Holden (coach), David Massey, Charles Phillips, Ren Bell, Gary Pittman, Charles McIntyre, Mike McKinney, Gregory Barnette, Jimmy Bowen, Jack Gallamore, Irby.

Southern Filters (Greenville, S.C.), consolation winners: John Lamp (coach), Willie Neal, Johnny Harbin, Marvin Clary, Roddy McCarson, Roy Gillespie, Lewis McCullough, Stanley Hopkins, David Farnham, Ronald Vest, Styles, Belton.

John Perkins Industries (Greenville, S.C.): Jerry Knight (coach), Ronnie Bridwell, Bill Norris, Jimmy Brooks, Billy Hollis, R. Harrison, Skip Francis, Bosco McAbee, David Cleveland, Meadors Tanner, Ronnie Noe, Bouton.

Slater Mill (Slater, S.C.): Bill Farmer (coach), Jimmy Burnette, Harold Aikens, Johnny Dillard, Lonnie Turbeville, Samuel Parnell, Taby Burnette, B.L. Landreth, Jimmy Crain, Harold Kelly, James Davis, Bruce Rodman, Johnson, Grant, Williams.

Pelzer Mill (Pelzer, S.C.): Bill Hopkins (coach), Leland Saxon Jr., Stanley Horton, Jerome Gambrell, William Adams, Jerry Riddle, Doug Barnett, Mitchell McKee, Frank Acker, Buster Wooten, Tommy Richardson, Wesley Sloan.

Saco-Lowell (Easley, S.C.): Charles Crowe (coach), Earl Gilstrap, Steven Crowe, Bob McDaniel, Richard Gilstrap, Skip Acker, John Roper, Grey Mull, Mike Owen, Brad Williams, Tommy Krieg, Stevens.

Appleton Mill (Anderson, S.C.): Henry Spake (coach), Donnie Adams, Ronnie Bailey, Alan Hawkins, Curtis Bowen, Gary Grant, Andy Wooten, Terrell Suit, Randy Adams, Steve Couch, Ronnie Mosley, Kellam.

Piedmont Mill #1 (Piedmont, S.C.): Earl Wooten (coach), Stanley Bagwell, Mike McNeely, Leslie Morgan, Arthur Anders, Dennis Grooms, Butch Morton, Jerry Lollis, Allan Hudgens, Carl Chambers, Jackie Clevinger, James Turmon, Lamar Hudgens.

Piedmont Mill #2 (Piedmont, S.C.): Milford Howard (coach), W.A. Gilliam, J.M. Crawford, J.A. Henderson, Mac Knight, Ernest Smith Jr., J.D. Garrison, Louis Saylor Jr., B.G. Abrams, Steve Chandler, M.O. Howard, Sayles, Bagwell, Morgan, Turman, Grooms, Chambers, Lollis, Morton.

Piedmont Mill #3 (Piedmont, S.C.): Leonard Waldrop (coach), Bunyon McClain, Bobby Stover, Mark McClain, Bobby League, Ernie Rice, Mike Gilreath, Mike Lindley, Jerry Earls, Curtis Gautier, Terry Blackston, Anderson.

Metro-Atlantic (Greenville, S.C.): Larry Jones (coach), John Kay, Barry Toney, Tam Boggs, Steve Wade, Leon Hayes, Ricky Dobson, Howard Bean, Danny Yarborough, Calvin Hayslip, Donnie Kuhn, Kay.

Pacolet Mill (Pacolet, S.C.): Bill Allen (coach), Dale Mulwee, Wayne Kirby, Bill Courtney, Bobby Guyton, Ray Harris, Donnie Hodge, Wayne McSwain, Tommy Garner, Russell Spencer.

Ross Tire (Greenville, S.C.): Allen Turner (coach), Gary Turner, Waldo Watts, Mike Jones, Harold Babb, Lawyer Taylor, Michael Booker, Clarence Whittenburg, Gary Massey, Joe Styles, David Morrow, Painter, Gamble.

Equinox Mill (Anderson, S.C.): Clarence Voyles (coach), Mike McGuire, James Green, Terry Powell, Roy Heaton, Daniel Gray, James Brock, James Chapman, Terry Martin, Jimmy Martin, Barry Jenkins, Allen, Spiney, Block.

Dunean Mill (Greenville, S.C.): Dean, Bishop, Watts, Burns, Cole, Wynn, Wyatt, Thigpen, Heaton.

Singer Mfg. (Pickens, S.C.): David Breazeale (coach), Robert Roll, B.L. Landreth, James Summey, Robert Bolding, Fred Collins, Jerry Pace, Larry Davis, William Looper, Ronald Lewis, A.L. Hendricks, Skelton, Herron, Lamb.

Jackson Mill (Iva, S.C.): Alan Charney (coach), M.G. Epstein, Gary Gilmer, Michael Ashley, S.D. Alexander, M.R. Moseley, Jackie Moore, A.G. Jordan, Danny Arnold, C.R. Moseley, James Beard, Richey.

Southern Textile Basketball Tournament Rosters Appendix 1   239

CLASS A WOMEN

Slater Mill (Slater, S.C.), champions: Margaret Wright (coach), Bobby Kirby (coach), Joan Kirby, Cheryl Smith, Jeannie Callahan, Sandra Childs, Sherry McCall, Jane Smith, Linda Edwards, Judy Kelley, Kathy Willis, Dotty Kirby, Donna McGee, Kitty Brunette, Melinda Baucom, Sharon Morgan, Margaret Freeman, Diane Walker, Laura Freeman, Pat Morgan, Ann Simmons.

IMMS (Greenville, S.C.), runners-up: John Mickler (coach), Doris Fisher, Patsy Neal, Vicki Chapman, Debbie Dill, Judy Cross, Frances Welborn, Dolly Crouch, Dede Owens, Lucy Walters, Jean Bryant, Virginia Greer, Ann Lyons.

Spartan Express (Greer, S.C.), consolation winners: Roger Tippett (coach), Brenda Gaillard, Barbara Wade, Beverly Dooley, Winona Foster, Louise Mimms, Brenda Cobb, Brenda Laucey, Emily Bearden, Eugenia Greer, Jane Greer, Betty Whitmire, Murphree, Sandra Greer.

Pratt-Read (Central, S.C.): Kelly DuBose (coach), Linda Black, Glennis Fowler, Mott Brown, Vickie Kimbrell, Roberta James, Joy Whitaker, Wanda Worley, Judy Wardlaw, Mary Carter, Jan Sharp, Carolyn Williams, Edith Bowen, Alred, Winstead.

Sangamo Electric Co. (Pickens, S.C.): Jerry Roper (coach), Jean Stone, Jackie McJunkin, Brenda Garren, Deda Duncan, Sybil Murrell, Carol Pharr, Fran Brooks, Judy Payne, Jan Southerland, Sharon Scott, Vickie Edens, Judy Sherriff, Danielson.

Piedmont Mill #1 (Piedmont, S.C.): Curtis Terry (coach), Judy Elrod, Dorothy Barnes, Dianne Limbaugh, Becky Jones, Connie Ward, Aluida Propes, Judy Porter, Beth Mahathey, Connie Brown, Janet McCoy, Dianne Porter, Elizabeth Pickelsimer, Janet Jones, Linn, Watson.

Piedmont Mill #2 (Piedmont, S.C.): Don Roper (coach), Patricia Thompson, Carolyn Campbell, Debbie Schwiers, Marsha Davis, Janet Chasteen, Pam Harris, Jean Chapman, Debbie Crawford, Katie McClain, Sandra Hooper, Faye King, Ann Thompson, Harren.

Lyman Mill (Lyman, S.C.): Paula Barbare (coach), Patricia Davis, Linda Bell, Ann Jackson, Linda Henderson, Brenda DeYoung, Vennie Rogers, Becky Huckabee, Diane Walker, Martha Bagwell, Diane Holbert, Mary Vernon, Jenny Fowler, Bishop, Caldwell, Montgomery, Smith, Gosnell, Brady.

Fiber Industries (Greenville, S.C.): Stan Tapp (coach), Mildred Smith, Aliene Creel, Edna Carter, Pearlie Gray, Carol Stephens, Betty Jackson, Diane Solesbee, Gayle Frazier, Sandra Shelton, Pat Peden, Mary Pruitt, Clara Wharton.

Dunean Mill (Greenville, S.C.): Larry Ashley (coach), Debbie Wyatt, Bobbie Stevens, Brenda Stevens, Linda Allen, Sherry Jennings, June Brown, Marsha Marrett, Doris Bailey, Janice Rodgers, Karen Brown, Sharon Patterson, Lauren Murphy, Bayne, Wyatt.

───────── 1969 ─────────

Officers: R.E. Patrick (Greenwood, S.C.), President; Harry Foster (Greenville, S.C.), 1st Vice President and Ass't Treasurer; Ken Pittman (Greenville, S.C.), 2nd Vice President; Fred Byrd (Greenville, S.C.), Executive Secretary; Divver Hendrix (Greenville, S.C.), Treasurer; Fred Powers (Charlotte, N.C.), Ass't Executive Secretary; Whitey Kendall (Greenville), Supervisor of Officials; Lt. F.R. Hawkins, Security Officer; Frank Ballenger (Greenville, S.C.), Director of Publicity.

Executive Committee: Clarence Thomas (Greenville, S.C.), Willie Wilbanks (Ware Shoals, S.C.), Curtis Terry (Piedmont, S.C.), Willard Fowler (Greer, S.C.), Dan Foster (Greenville, S.C.), Snow Kirby (Marietta, S.C.), Bill Hopkins (Pelzer, S.C.), Lewis Acker (Anderson, S.C.), Lloyd McAbee (Greenville, S.C.), Bobby Morris (Liberty, S.C.), Joe Newton (Greenville, S.C.), Henry Spake (Anderson, S.C.), Charlton Miller (Greer, S.C.), Grady Wallace (Columbia, S.C.), Ward Williams (Greenville, S.C.), T.C. Hooper (Greenville, S.C.), Earl Wooten (Piedmont, S.C.), Vercho Carter (Alexander City, Ala.), Jim Anderson (Greenville, S.C.), Bill Belcher (Pensacola, Fla.), D.K. Smith (Lyman, S.C.).

OPEN DIVISION

K.G. Carpet (Atlanta, Ga.), champions: Johnny Moon (coach), Larry Cart, Rodney Knowles, Ken Rohloff, Tom Norwood, Mike Rickard, Larry Bagby, James Brown, Doug Alexander, Gary Williams, Larry Barnett, David Brookins, Allen Johnson, Rudy Taylor, Jim Nuckolls, Chuck Adamek.

Mikro (Charlotte, N.C.), runners-up: Dwight Durante, Lonnie Kluttz, Davis, Greg Patton, Cole, Johnson, Jones, English, Ring, Zinke.

Spaulding Fibers (Spartanburg, S.C.), consolation winners: Dick Esleeck, Les Heicher, Waller, Lawrence, Becthel, Moore, Greggs, Boche, Lattimore.

Guthrie Motors (Williamston, S.C.): Earl Wooten (coach), Gary Helms, Norman Shaffer, Mike Jenkins, Don Helms, Garland Davis, Buddy Benedict, Allen Goforth, Don Wheaton, Jimmy Wilson, Jerry Whaley, Harold Roper, Willie Peagram, Webster, McCarson.

Transit Homes (Greenville, S.C.): Rupert Elliott (coach), Eugene Seay, Jimmy Chapman, Steve Brown, Jimmy Herring, Johnny Holtzclaw, Rick Duncan, Buddy Moore, Mark Stewart, Graves, McClinton, Elliott.

Tolbert's (North Charleston, S.C.): Jim Brabham (coach), Charlie Gallagher, James Hooks, Tom Cochran, Dave Corless, H.F. Dunning Jr., Marion Salerni, Francis Petit III, Eric Lessmeister, Joe Allen, Tommy Lavelle, Mel Gibson, Jim Gardener.

King Oil (Anderson, S.C.): Joe Hammond (coach), James Dill, Jackie Arnold, Nat Hammond, Allen Mattison, Henry Hammond, Waddell Sims, Thomas Hammond, Robert Lee, John Moore, Flester West, Bobby Mattress, Bill Floyd.

Inman & Associates (Columbia, S.C.): Jimmy James (coach), Skip Kieky, Jimmy Jackson, Mike Callahan, Don Whitehead, Art Whisnant, Jack Thompson, Bill Edison, Darrell Murray, Nathaniel Dukes, Rick Grish, Ken Lester, Collins, Goley, Yates, Cheeseboro.

CLASS A MEN

Dunean Mill (Greenville, S.C.), champions: Buddy Gibson (coach), Ray Gosnell, Terry Campbell, Jimmy Riddle, James Galloway, Andrew Ballard, Ronnie Sims, Carroll Burns, Skeeter Hammett, Ronald Burns, Larry Ashley, Dean Harvell.

Monsanto (Pensacola, Fla.), runners-up: Wilson, Donald Gates, Henry Reid, Jerry Secrist, Holly, Ron Ellison, Eddie Carter, Taylor, Blanton, Raines.

Rohm-Haas (Fayetteville, N.C.), consolation winners: S.K. James (coach), Larry Bass, Charles Goff, Gayley Hester, Fred Vinson, Paul Bunce, Steven James, Morris Shepherd, Charles Carlisle, Jerry Brock, Richard Esslinger.

Fiber Industries (Greenville, S.C.): George Clay (coach), Earl Whittington, Ken Childers, Jimmy Yates, Stan Tadd, Donald Simmons, Ronnie Lawson, Ronald Foltz, Clarence Burdette, Robert Hargett, Gary Wardlaw, Tapp.

Monsanto (Greenwood, S.C.): Jim Diamond (coach), Johnny Taylor, Jerry Gordon, Joel Martin, Leon James Jr., James Johnson, Edward Hartman, William Wilson, Samuel Dukes, Don Livingston, Herbert Edmonds.

Russell Manufacturing (Alexander City, Ala.): Vercho Carter (coach), Mike Hearn, Wayne Rape, Jim Childers, Jerry Sanders, James Leonard, James Deason, Herman Watts, Mitchell Caldwell, Perry Anderson, Charles Scott.

Saco-Lowell (Easley, S.C.): Glenn Edgar (coach), James Carter, Joe Lesley, Stanley Wilson, Don Carver, Grover Owings, Douglas Roach, Doug Simpson, Roy Smith, Joel Garrett, Charles Rogers.

Kendall Mill (Seneca, S.C.): Troy Reese (coach), Roger Tippett, Mike Black, Michael Donald, Thomas McBride, Clyde Herron, Larry Allsep, John James, Clarence Gaillard, Charles Hopkins, Hershel Pearson.

Homelite (Greer, S.C.): Ben Henderson (coach), Robert Sanders, Eddie Drummond, Patrick Farmer, Eugene Benson, James Jennings, Dalton Wilbanks, Philip Case, Lollie Bryant, Earl Turner, Herbert Garren, Massengale.

Taylors Mill (Taylors, S.C.): J.W. Gentry (coach), Leon Gravely, Gene Ballentine, Hubie Prince Jr., Curtis Campbell, Thomas Dawkins, Kenneth Linder, Johnny Gregory, Donald Todd, Steven Moore, Ronald Coker, Roberson, Littlefield.

Madison Throwing Co. (Madison, N.C.): Pete Bryant (coach), Semi Mintz, Bobby Mabe, Glenn Ogburn, Harold Parker, Tim Smothers, Roger Carter, O'Neal Joyce, Michael Heekin, Billy Corns, Benjamin Gay.

Reeves Brothers (Rutherfordton, N.C.): David Wyscarver (coach), Bill Conner, Jackie Rowe, Laurence Davis, Ronald Hardin, James Burns, Charles Luckadoo.

CLASS B MEN

Phillips Fibers (Spartanburg, S.C.), champions: Nathaniel McSwain (coach), Ed Nesser (coach), Ralph Brown, Jack Turner, Luther Wilkins, Perry Johnson, George Sparks, Mike

Southern Textile Basketball Tournament Rosters   Appendix 1   241

Hewitt, Lawrence Collins, Claude Johnson, Perry Johnson, Greg Anderson, Montgomery.

Monsanto (Pensacola, Fla.), runners-up: Jerry Glenn (coach), Dennis Durant, Billy Kimbrough, Willie Broughton, Earl Terrell, Herbert Brewton, Royce Cunningham, Donald Justice, James Forehand, Milton Hardin, Enoch Tharpe, Lee.

Monaghan Mill (Greenville, S.C.), consolation winners: Bill Swaynghame (coach), Danny Bagwell, Alan Landreth, Terry Fowler, Johnny Stevens, Jerome Johnson, Al Roach, Roddy Turner, Mike McKinney, Jyles Phillips, C. McEntyre, W. McEntyre.

Pelzer Mill (Pelzer, S.C.): James Thomason (coach), Jimmy Hopkins, Ronnie Davenport, Tony Lollis, Sonny Saxon, Roger Scott, Mitchell McKee, Don Sanders, Jimmy McKee, Raymond Rochester, Phil Hopkins, Heller, Bozman.

Fiber Industries (Greenville, S.C.): Jack Kelly (coach), Alvin Crisp, Vernon McMakin, Donald Harkins, Paul Pritchett, Kenneth Edwards, Mickey Stepp, Troy Godwin, Gary Caldwell, Charles Breazeale, John Fisher.

Lyman Mill (Lyman, S.C.): Carey Johnson, John Walker Jr., Philip Childress, Ernest Murray, Marion Knuckles, Thomas Gresham, Larry Arms, John Owens, James Graham, O'neal.

Bigelow-Sanford (Calhoun Falls, S.C.): Frankie Nixon (coach), Terry Chrisley, Larry Alewine, Bill Lewis, Elmer Dowell, James Hodges, Charles Burden, Joe Loftis, Michael Burton, Powell.

LTV ElectroSystems (Greenville, S.C.): Jesse Byce (coach), Michael Smith, Jerry Smith, Melvin Longshore, Jimmie Weeks, Tommy Brown, Fred McGill, Garry McKinney, Elford Wilder, Doug Bagwell, Madrazzo, G. Smith.

Ware Shoals Mill (Ware Shoals, S.C.): George Abrams (coach), Melvin Miller, Raymond Kelly, Joe Freeman, Calvin Ryan, Phil Bush, Roosevelt Smith, Mike Abrams, Jerry Sims, John Lee, Jim Reeves, Anderson.

Southern Weaving (Greenville, S.C.): Johnny Turner (coach), Earl Phillips, James Smith, Steve Echols, Leon Ferguson, Jack Miller, John Leslie, Allen Turner, Tommy Boone, Earl Stewart, James Chapple.

Parker Mill (Greenville, S.C.): Leroy Pace (coach), Artis Stewart, Bill Ware, Edward Stewart, Ronald Bridges, Charles Morgan, John McKinney, James Dunn, William Garraux, Grady Gilliard, Michael Campbell.

Easley Mill (Easley, S.C.): Johnny Skinner (coach), Harvey Galloway, Roy Holloway, James Lackey, Monte Neese, Dewey Peace, Eugene Waldrop, Cecil Owens, Charles Robinson, Curtis Stewart, Charles Austin.

Texize Chemical (Greenville, S.C.): Ted Hillhouse (coach), Edward Mixon, Don Franklin, William Hendrix, Booker Johnson, Willie Moon, Robert Hughey, Hobart Smith Jr., Lyndon Manheim, James Knighton, Emanuel Sullivan.

Class C Men

Carter & Crawley (Greenville, S.C.), champions: Bryant Millwood (coach), Leroy Gregs (coach), Clyde Wooten, Clyde Mayes, Freddie Donald, Benny Adams, Leroy Copeland, Harold Babb, Louis McCullough, Willie Neal, Michael Booker, Marvin Drummond, Leonard Hill.

John Perkins Industries (Greenville, S.C.), runners-up: Jerry Knight (coach), Billy Hollis, Roosevelt Harrison, Joe Francis, David Cleveland, Larry Lollis, Edward Nabers, Howard Hines, Charles Hildebrand, Clarence Mitchell, Ben Leppard.

Monaghan Mill (Greenville, S.C.), consolation winners: Danny Bagwell (coach), Ralph Bell, Gary Pittman, Charles McIntyre, Donald Davis, Ronnie Ware, Ricky Elrod, Wayne Payne, Harbin, Douglas, Ward, Mitchell, Ross, Williams.

Southern Filters (Greenville, S.C.): John Simkins (coach), John Crapps, Dennis Collins, Walter Cottingham, C.E. Whittenberg, Charles Phillips, Robert Poole, David Lyles, Jack Batson, James Burns, Anderson, James, Brice.

Poe Hardware (Greenville, S.C.): Broadus Miller (coach), Charlie Bouton, Randy Miller, Billy Carpenter, Ray Venderwerff, Mike Smith, Skip Francis, Billy Hollis, Clyde Agnew, David Cleveland, Hunt, Ashmore, Payne, Pettus.

Slater Mill (Slater, S.C.): Doots Wright (coach), Toby Burnette, Johnny Dillard, Samuel Parnell, Butch Taylor, Ed Taylor, Larry Grant, Gene Williams, Phillip Hanback, Gary Reeves, Lamar Garrett, Campbell, Black, Mills, Custer, Parnell, Lister.

Pelzer Mill (Pelzer, S.C.): H.D. Adams (coach), Jerry Riddle, Doug Barnett, Buster Wooten, Phil Hopkins, Gary Cooley, Kenny Ashley, Robin Campbell, C.E. Saylors Jr., Charles Hall, Ben Garrett.

Saco-Lowell (Easley, S.C.): Stanley Wilson

(coach), Danny Gilstrap, Steven Crowe, Bob McDaniel, Brad Williams, Tim Krieg, Terry Smith, Tronnie Webb, Phil Williams, Gary Stephens, Johnny Chandler, Mull.

Appleton Mill (Anderson, S.C.): Henry Spake (coach), Terrell Suit, Jim Craine, Marshall Hobson, Raymond Bryson, Michael Cinelli, William Watt, Gregg Magers, George Butler, John Ross, Barry Jenkins.

Piedmont Mill #1 (Piedmont, S.C.): Ray Foxx (coach), Allen Gilliam, Danny Garrison, Langston Abrams, Steve Chandler, Mo Howard, Mike Chandler, Ben Abrams, Steve Anderson, Jack Ballew, Leonard Pollard, G. Abrams, Green, Burns, Jewell.

Piedmont Mill #2 (Piedmont, S.C.): Earl Wooten (coach), Stanley Bagwell, Leslie Morgan, Richard Anders, Beecher Morton, Carl Chambers, Jackie Clevinger, James Turmon, Lamar Hudgens, Larry McCall, T. Morgan, Garrison.

Metro-Atlantic (Greenville, S.C.): Billy Allen (coach), John Kay, Ricky Dobson, Howard Bean, David Dobson, Charles Crawford, Eric Mullinax, Richard Heatly, Bill Clayton, Ronnie Morris, Lynn Greenlee.

Jackson Mill (Iva, S.C.): Alan Charney (coach), Kenny Arnold, Johnny Wilson, Robert Wilson, Tommy Rutledge, Dwight Sullivan, Jerome King, Lester Robinson, Ronnie Cureton, Ralph Holloway, Tommy Richardson, Jordan, Beard, Brand.

CLASS A WOMEN

K.G. Carpet (Atlanta, Ga.), champions: Johnny Moon (coach), Dolores Owens, Charlotte Elchinger, Vera Garrett, Cathy Flanagan, Brenda Walker, Jean Dowell, Annette Hammock, Vivian Maslen, Shirley White, Alice Smith, Ethel Lister, Lila Brasher.

Ware Shoals Mill (Ware Shoals, S.C.), runners-up: Bob Fleming (coach), Diaz Cain, Kathy Willis, Debbie Skinner, Joyce Munns, Debbie Jackson, Dianne Davenport, Susan Anderson, Becky Ezell, Lynn Boland, Margaret Freeman, Ann Simmons, Beverly Latimer, Mickey Davis.

Slater Mill (Slater, S.C.), consolation winners: Margaret Wright (coach), Joan Kirby, Jane Smith, Linda Rikard, Judy Murray, Sharon Morgan, Diane Walker, Pat Morgan, Linda Edwards, Marion Brewer, Eileen Anderson, Sue Thompson, Malinda Balcomb, Ayers, Cashwell.

Piedmont Mill #2 (Piedmont, S.C.): Brown, Elizabeth Pickelsimer, Jameson, Limbaugh, Thrasher, Branham, McCoy, Gibbony, Wilson, Watson, Mahaffey.

Piedmont Mill #1 (Piedmont, S.C.): Don Roper (coach), Patricia Thompson, Debbie Cauble, Debbie Crawford, Sandra Hooper, Faye King, Marsha Davis, Essie Thoreson, Barbara Thoreson, Gail Porter, Gretta Mitchell, Donna Roper, Sheila Reeves, Chasteen, Treadway.

IMMS (Greenville, S.C.): John Mickler (coach), Doris Fisher, Patsy Neal, Debbie Dill, Judy Cross, Frances Welborn, Lucy Walters, Ann Lyons, Gail Anderson, Sandra Shelton, Carolyn Pharr, Betty Foster, Judy Payne.

Sangamo Electric Co. (Pickens, S.C.): Jerry Roper (coach), Jean Stone, Jackie McJunkin, Brenda Simmons, Deda Duncan, Fran Wood, Judy Sheriff, Kathy Williams, Donna Duncan, Eleanor Lewis, Dixie Duncan, Singleton.

Fiber Industries (Greenville, S.C.): Jerry Roper (coach), Aliene Creel, Edna Carter, Clara Whorter, Deani Solesbee, Joyce Brooks, Bobby Goldsmith, Nancy Brooks, Faye Parrish, Linda Bell, Linda Brooks, Harrison, Terrell.

Dunean Mill (Greenville, S.C.): Larry Ashley (coach), Debbie Wyatt, Bobbie Stevens, Brenda Stevens, Linda Allen, Sherry Jennings, June Brown, Marsha Marrett, Charlene Porter, Kaye Bayne, Kaye Ashley, Robin Stowe, Linda Stewart, Roddy.

LTV ElectroSystems (Greenville, S.C.): Jimmie Weeks (coach), Becky Cothran, Sybil Murrell, Linda Jackson, Betty Jackson, Connie Duff, Candy Ridgley, Jan Godsey, Jane Wilder, Patricia Tate, Pam Cothran, Margaret Lark, Ola Smith.

Westvaco (Charleston, S.C.): J.W. Stevens (coach), Delores Rogers, Teresa Graham, Peggy Coleman, Velda Runny, Ann Wiggins, Linda Brown, Carolyn Spragley, Brenda Carter, Jenene Batten, Betty Graham, Cecilia Oquinn, Rosalee Monzon.

Wunda Weve Carpets (Greenville, S.C.): Marion Lowe (coach), Harvey Forrester (coach), Reva Lowe, Lawanda Smith, Dottie Hill, Ann Jenkins, Yvonne Burnette, Joyce Thackston, Susan Calvert, Carol Waters, Linda Dillard, Faye Duncan, Jessie Ivey, Alice Cash.

Monaghan Mill (Greenville, S.C.): James Bagwell (coach), Mrs. James Bagwell (coach), Fran Brooks, Paula Westfall, Lucille Ware, Louise White, Carol Brockman, Marsha Farr, Zandra Watson, Vickie Busbee, Doris Porter,

Southern Textile Basketball Tournament Rosters   Appendix 1   243

Diane Elliott, Candy James, Linda Brown, Turner.

Texize Chemical (Greenville, S.C.): W.E. McCain (coach), Betty Pittman, Betty Green, Evelyn Spillers, Gail Hendrix, Pat Hendrix, Dolly Henderson, Libby Gray, Pat James, Frances Hillhouse, Barbara Pridmore, Mickey Brookshire, Martha Hendrix, Forrester, Pepper.

---------- 1970 ----------

Officers: Harry Foster (Greenville, S.C.), President; Ken Pittman (Greenville, S.C.), 1st Vice President; R.E. Patrick (Greenwood, S.C.), 2nd Vice President; D.K. Smith (Lyman, S.C.), 3rd Vice President; Fred Byrd (Greenville, S.C.), Executive Secretary; Divver Hendrix (Greenville, S.C.), Treasurer; Fred Powers (Charlotte, N.C.), Ass't Executive Secretary; Whitey Kendall (Greenville), Supervisor of Officials; Lt. F.R. Hawkins, Security Officer; Frank Ballenger (Greenville, S.C.), Director of Publicity.

Executive Committee: Clarence Thomas (Greenville, S.C.), Willie Wilbanks (Ware Shoals, S.C.), Curtis Terry (Piedmont, S.C.), Willard Fowler (Greer, S.C.), Dan Foster (Greenville, S.C.), Snow Kirby (Marietta, S.C.), Bill Hopkins (Pelzer, S.C.), Lewis Acker (Anderson, S.C.), Lloyd McAbee (Greenville, S.C.), Bobby Morris (Liberty, S.C.), Joe Newton (Greenville, S.C.), Henry Spake (Anderson, S.C.), Broadus Miller (Greenville, S.C.), Grady Wallace (Columbia, S.C.), Ward Williams (Greenville, S.C.), T.C. Hooper (Greenville, S.C.), Earl Wooten (Piedmont, S.C.), Vercho Carter (Alexander City, Ala.), Reynolds Johnston (Pensacola, Fla.), James Morrow (Greenville, S.C.).

OPEN DIVISION

Texize Chemical (Greenville, S.C.), champions: John Deter (coach), Les Heicher, Dick Esleeck, Joe Brunson, Jerry Waller, Don Webster, Bob Lenheardt, Harold Fox, Ron Schaffer, Dick Wright, John Boesche, Ricky Duncan, Jim Brennan, Art Polk, Terry Scott, Joe Daly.

Guthrie Motors (Williamston, S.C.), runners-up: Don Carver (coach), Gary Helms, Norman Shaffer, Mike Jenkins, Richie Mahaffey, Ronnie Yates, Butch Zatezlo, Jim Bradford, Earl Maxwell, Tyrone Jackson.

Transit Homes (Greenville, S.C.): Rupert Elliott (coach), Eugene Seay, Jimmy Chapman, Steve Hobson, Jimmy Herring, Leonard Black, Jerry Smith, Larry Patterson, Mike Barb, Tommy Meadows, Steve Hollingsworth, McCarson, Stewart.

General Fireproofing (Forest City, N.C.): Ken Napier, Jimmy Powell, Mike Kretzer, Larry Davis, Phil Luckadoo, Roland Bell.

Saturley's (Greenville, S.C.): Chuck Sullivan, Mike Reidy, Koph, Dinker, Zinke, Golding.

Tolbert's (North Charleston, S.C.): Jim Brabham, Charlie Gallagher, Tom Cochran, Dave Corliss, Marion Salerni, Tommy Lavelle, Mel Gibson, Jim Hanson, Tripp Jones, Sam Kenlaw, Roger White, Luther Poole, Mauldin, Dunning, Brown.

Pelzer Mill (Pelzer, S.C.): Jim Wiles (coach), Gary Key, Chuck Habelck, Anthony Brown, Gerald McCall, Willie Lewis, Derwood Dunlap, Stanley Horton, Hank Mickleson, Hugh McMurray, Stan Riddle, Hablutzel.

Kenro (Atlanta, Ga.): John Moon (coach), Ken Griffith (coach), Mike Dahl, Sonny Epps, Pat Moriarty, Chuck Adamek, Gary Williams, Larry Barnett, Doug Alexander, Ron Jackson, Allan Johnson, Ernie Crain, Larry Bagby, Cochran, Poug, Johnson.

Newberry All Stars (Newberry, S.C.): Buddy Moore, Martin, Gilroy, Howard, Neal, Joe Styles.

Mikro (Charlotte, N.C.): Greg Patton, Kluttz, Lathem, Adams, Gibson, Turner, Williams, Davis.

CLASS A MEN

Russell Manufacturing (Alexander City, Ala.), champions: Vercho Carter (coach), Mike Hearn, Wayne Rape, Jim Childers, Jerry Sanders, James Leonard, William Stevens, L.M. Hunter, Walter Green, Lamar Kennedy, Arthur Hicks, Neil Anderson, Roger Green.

Dunean Mill (Greenville, S.C.), runners-up: Buddy Gibson (coach), Jimmy Riddle, Skeeter Hammett, Maxie Burns, Terry Campbell, Dean Harvell, James Galloway, Ray Gosnell, Mack Holloway, Doug Gailey, James Bagwell.

Monsanto (Pensacola, Fla.), consolation winners: Harry Reid, Rains, Wilson, John Secrist, Ellison, Holley, Durant, Underwood, Brewton, Broughton Fisk, Bo Tharpe.

Monsanto (Greenwood, S.C.): Herb Edmonds (coach), Robert Williams, Charles

Stevens, Alfred Bell, Joe Stephens, Gerald Shurts, John Ridlehoover, Don Livingston, Jerry Gordon, Jim Diamond.

Rohm-Haas (Fayetteville, N.C.): Pete Carlisle (coach), Larry Bass, Steven James, Charles Carlisle, John Dixon, Doyle Owen, Michael Adams, Ronald Dickinson.

Fiber Industries (Greenville, S.C.): George Clay (coach), Earl Whittington, Stan Tadd, Ken Childers, Don Simmons, Jim Giambrowe, Steve Burnette, Robert Hargett, Robert Bagwell, Wayne Ward, Joe Pearson, Yates.

Saco-Lowell (Easley, S.C.): Don Finley (coach), James Carter, Stanley Wilson, Grover Owings, Joe Garrett, Ira Black, Cecil Clark, Horace McAlister, Michael Dononvan, Harold Wham, Dennis Waldrop.

Madison Throwing Co. (Madison, N.C.): Semi Mintz (coach), Bobby Dalton, Glenn Ogburn, Harold Parker, Tim Smothers, Michael Heekin, Benjamin Gay, Steve Spencer, Ronnie Tucker, Archie Hylton.

Phillips Fibers (Spartanburg, S.C.): Nathaniel McSwain (coach), Alonzo Briggs, Washington Parks, Claude Johnson Jr., Luther Wilkins, Jack Turner, Wilbur McHam, Greg Anderson, C.W. Coley, Henderson, Moore, Marrow.

Monaghan Mill (Greenville, S.C.): Mike Ross (coach), Terry Fowler, Jim Holden, Charles McIntyre, Bill Fuller, Tommy Williams, Bud Hooper, Bill Swaynghame, Dan Bagwell, Don Lewis, Alexander.

Taylors Mill (Taylors, S.C.): Leon Gravely (coach), Troy Roberson, Lawrence Poole, Harold Smith, Ray Pickett, Ronald Coker, Steven Moore, Thomas Dawkins, Curtis Campbell, Maxie Krause, Allen.

CLASS B MEN

Pelzer Mill (Pelzer, S.C.), champions: Bill Hopkins (coach), Jimmy Hopkins (coach), Sonny Saxon, Raymond Rochester, Phil Hopkins, Dwight Sullivan, Tommy Richardson, Jerry Riddle, William Adams, Kenny Ashley, Benny Garrett, Dave Major, Richard Keir, Keith Campbell, Tony Bozman.

Parker Mill (Greenville, S.C.), runners-up: Mickey Campbell (coach), Artis Stewart, Bill Ware, Edward Stewart, John McKinney, William Garraux, Bobby Mattress, Johnny Arnold, Robert Moses, Eddie Adams, Nix.

Ware Shoals Mill (Ware Shoals, S.C.), consolation winners: Bob Fleming (coach), Joe Freeman, Joe Smith, Mike Abrams, Jerry Sims, John Lee, Dennis Babb, Doug Knight, Scott Hughes, James Whatley, James Frazier.

Piedmont Mill (Piedmont, S.C.): Earl Wooten (coach), Dwight Thurmond, Lewis Sales, Ernie Chambers, Buster Wooten, Bob Stover, Bob League, Don Todd, Sylvester Donald, Willie Taylor, Jerome Chapman, Rice.

Monsanto (Greenwood, S.C.): Charles Crawford (coach), Jerald Burden, Sammy Randall, Porter Morton, William Young, Ricky Frix, Dale Jones, James Hackett, David Gunnells, Stan McElrath, Calvin Carson, Childs.

Monaghan Mill (Greenville, S.C.): Danny Bagwell (coach), Alan Landreth, Mike McKinney, Pat Swaynghame, Steve Sumner, William McIntyre, Paul Thomas, Gene Morgan, Doyle Lawson, Ricky Elrod, Wardlaw, Gazaway.

Fiber Industries (Greenville, S.C.): Jack Kelly (coach), Vernon McMakin, Paul Pritchett, Troy Godwin, Gary Caldwell, Robert Harley, Heyward Leake, Gary Wardlaw, Steve Hodge, Melvin Ewell, Gobel Reed.

Lyman Mill (Lyman, S.C.): Virgil Pruitte (coach), John Walker Jr., Phil Childers, Ernest Murray, John Owens, James Graham, Gary Hix, Mike Fulmer, Madison Meadows, Gussie Ballenger, Charles Robinson, Phil Hix, Ronnie Nolan.

Bigelow-Sanford (Calhoun Falls, S.C.): Jack Eskew (coach), Douglas Sheriff, John Earl, James Earl, Walter Duke, Jerry Spake, Eland Workman, Donald Nelson, Olin Willis, Norman Kelley, Walter Webb, Nichols, Wilkes.

LTV ElectroSystems (Greenville, S.C.): Gerald Byce (coach), Melvin Smith, Jerry Smith, Tommy Brown, Elford Wilder, Freddie Brown, Joseph Hartley, Robert Lemmons, Harvey Foxx, Leonard Black, Phillip Vassey, Davis.

Southern Weaving (Greenville, S.C.): Johnny Turner (coach), Earl Phillips, Steve Echols, Jack Miller, Allen Turner, Tommy Boone, Earl Stewart, Mark Davis, Carver.

Sally Mill (Greenville, S.C.): John Buchanan (coach), Bennie Sorgee, Alvin Smith, Henry Page, Anthony Kay, Mike Blackwell, Joe Smith, Elzie Smith, Luther Smith, Douglas McKinney, Danny Gray.

Hoechst Celanese (Greer, S.C.): J.B. Easlic (coach), William Belcher, Jimmy Bradshaw, Don Smith, James Holcombe, Roger Wilson, Ronald Brown, Thomas Roberts, Keith Dodson, Sam Inman, Zane Metcalf.

Southern Textile Basketball Tournament Rosters Appendix 1

Clark-Schwebel (Anderson, S.C.): Alex Cawthon (coach), Gary Hart, James Day, Jay Agnew, James Majeski, Johnny Corn, Erwin Chitwood, Ronald Gilstrap, Raymond Bostic, Roy Jordan, Payton, Taylor, Davis.

Sangamo Electric Co. (Pickens, S.C.): Gene Holliday (coach), Roy Holliday, Wayne Nicholson, Wayne Chappell, Dwayne Chappell, Tommy Crumpton, Tim Krieg, Joel Parsons, Joel Allgood, Gary Whitlock, Dale Findley, Pat Kelsey, Terry Odom.

Singer Mfg. (Pickens, S.C.): Tater Garrett (coach), Charles Burgess, Stan Williams, Kenneth Robinson, Joe Adams, Wayne Wagner, Tommy Bowen, Charles Taylor, Tim Looper, Wesley Bolding, Jerry Pace, Davis, Summey.

Poe Mill (Greenville, S.C.): Charles Landreth (coach), Alexander Colt, Joe McComb, Rando Clark, Wade Simpson Jr., John Harrison, Charles Phillips, Ray Crisp, Wayne Jones, Vernon Sellers, Lawrence Lewis, McAtee, Lindsay.

Dunean Mill (Greenville, S.C.): Larry Ashley (coach), George King, Ronnie Scarborough, Homer Robinson, Butch Dean, Charles Roddy, Robert Walker, Tommy Cobb, Marshall Wilson, Ricky Nelson, Danny Ballew.

CLASS C MEN

Crown-Metro (Greenville, S.C.), champions: Billy Allen (coach), Dick Dobson, Charles Crawford, Larry Rizzo, Ed Taylor, Butch Taylor, Don Wing, Norman McDonald, Doug Lowe, Joe Pickett, Glenn Goodwin, Billy Massingill, Randy McCullen.

Martin's (Anderson, S.C.), runners-up: Terrell Suit, Jackie Johnson, Daniel Martin, Rice, Barry Isom, Charles, Gantt, Elrod, Charles Lesley.

Jackson Mill (Iva, S.C.), consolation winners: Epstein, Al Jordan, Beard, Ike Sullivan, Mike Perkins, Billy Gray, Holloway, Ron Cureton.

Poe Hardware (Greenville, S.C.): Broadus Miller (coach), Charlie Bouton, Randy Miller, Mike Smith, Clyde Agnew, Larry Williams, Sammy Reese, Nixon Allen, William Yeargin, McCullough, Bobatis.

Carter & Crawley (Greenville, S.C.): Bryant Millwood (coach), Clyde Mayes, Freddie Donald, Benny Adams, Michael Booker, Leonard Hill, Lamar Hudgens, Gregory Knuckles, Horace Anderson, Lavanda Sweeney, Eugene Allen.

John Perkins Industries (Greenville, S.C.): Jerry Knight (coach), Ben Leppard, Robert Estes, James Davis, George Poe, James Johnson, H.C. Jennings, Michael Jewell, Hugh Brigham, Moates, Bell, Foy.

Monaghan Mill (Greenville, S.C.): Danny Bagwell (coach), Gary Pittman, Donald Davis, Wayne Payne, Terry Russell, Kenny Hardin, William Dilworth, Randy Harrison, John Ward, Mike Dean, Lamb.

Southern Filters (Greenville, S.C.): John Simpkins (coach), John Crapps, Dennis Collins, Walter Cottingham, Charles Phillips, Robert Poole, James Burns, Horace Anderson, Steve Mathis, William Brice, James Morgan.

Ross Tire (Greenville, S.C.): Allen Turner (coach), Earl Phillips (coach), Harold Babb, Mo Howard, Carl Chambers, Ricky Elrod, Stanley Bagwell, Steve Renoir, David Smith, Laverne Lattimore, Lamar.

Precise Machine Works (Simpsonville, S.C.): Jimmy Sullivan, Richard Henry, Minnon Berry, Milford Bryson, Harvard Dill, James Chandler, Mitchell Burns, Thomas Brown, Calvin Milam, Jerry Wharton.

Piedmont Mill (Piedmont, S.C.): Walt Harrison, Tommy Joy, Bill Turmon, Morton, McCall, Jewell, Henderson, Anderson, Jackson.

Saco-Lowell (Easley, S.C.): Lee Dukes, Bruce Stephens, John Allison, Danny Gilstrap, Terry Julian, Forte, Goudelock, Holcombe, Ross.

CLASS A WOMEN

Kenro (Atlanta, Ga.), champions: Johnny Moon (coach), Delores Owen, Vera Garrett, Cathy Flannagan, Brenda Walker, Annette Hammock, Shirley White, Alice Smith, Lila Brasher, Sara Sims, Linda Crook, Lane Shelton, Edwina Bryan, July Vickers, Childers.

Texize Chemical (Greenville, S.C.), runners-up: Ted Hillhouse (coach), Betty Pittman, Pat Hendrix, Dolly Crouch, Bonnie Ritter, Judy Murray, Paula Monroe, Marian Brewer, Ann Lyons, Judy Thomas, Patsy Neal, Emma Howard, Lucy Walters.

Homestead Terrace (Greenville, S.C.), consolation winners: Virginia Robinson (coach), Loucinda Allgood, Caroline Brown, Sissie Donaldson, Alice Godwin, Trisha Hunt, Kitty Parrott, Elaine McAlister, Sally Shaver, Frankie Shelly, Jody Unser, Candy Clarke, Sue Ellis, Godwin, Vaughn.

Wunda Weve Carpets (Greenville, S.C.):

Joyce Forrester (coach), Harvey Forrester (coach), Dot Sisk, Yvonne Burnette, Linda Dillard, Sherrie Jennings, Karen Brown, Joanne Kelly, Connie Strickland, Price, Tate, Briley, Fortesque, Waters, Duncan, Hooper.

Slater Mill (Slater, S.C.): Bobby Kirby (coach), Joan Kirby, Jane Smith, Linda Rikard, Judy Murray, Sharon Morgan, Diane Walker, Pat Morgan, Linda Edwards, Marion Brewer, Eileen Anderson, Sue Thompson, Malinda Balcomb, Reynolds, Dotty Kirby, Clark, Youngblood, Ezell, McCall, Ann Simmons, Sanders, Brooks, Griffin.

Piedmont Mill (Piedmont, S.C.): Don Roper (coach), Patricia Thompson, Debbie Eskew, Debbie Crawford, Sandra Hooper, Faye King, Donna Roper, Diane Henderson, Jeannie Bennett, Shirley McDaniel, Lunita Washington, Sheryl Robinson, Shelby Cooley, Southern.

IMMS (Greenville, S.C.): Bill Gebert (coach), Doris Fisher, Debbie Nichols, Judy Cross, Frances Welborn, Sandra Shelton, Carolyn Pharr, Betty Foster, Judy Payne, Reba Lowe, Vicki Lindner, Bess Chandler, Marcie Homonai, Lindner.

Sangamo Electric Co. (Pickens, S.C.): Jerry Roper (coach), Jan Stone, Jackie McJunkin, Deda Duncan, Kathy Williams, Donna Duncan, Dixie Duncan, Marty Russell, Linda Reid, Peggy Hardin, Rita McNealy, Rita Edens, Debra Anderson, Dodson.

Dunean Mill (Greenville, S.C.): Larry Ashley (coach), Debbie Wyatt, Bobbie Galloway, Brenda Stevens, Sherry Jennings, June Brown, Marsha Marrett, Charlene Porter, Kaye Bayne, Kaye Ashley, Vicky Busbee, Fay Duncan, Sandra Watson, Clary.

LTV ElectroSystems (Greenville, S.C.): Gerald Steen (coach), Sybil Murrell, Linda Turner, Betty Jackson, Connie Duff, Candy Ridgley, Jane Wilder, Margaret Lark, Mary Hanner, Lucy Hazel, Tanya Riordan, Carole Petty, Marlene Smith.

Westvaco (Charleston, S.C.): Bill Stevens (coach), Velda Runny, Ann Wiggins, Carolyn Spragley, Brenda Carter, Jenene Batten, Betty Graham, Cecilia Oquinn, Rosalee Mouzon, Patricia Kenlaw, Barbara Maddox, Pat Kohl, Conda Deas, Evans.

Beaunit (Fountain Inn, S.C.): Danny Kimbrough (coach), Vicki Baughcome, Wanda Trotter, Rosie Buice, Linda Arledge, Ann Jenkins, Martha Craine, Lynn Johnson, Martha Hendrix, Linda Roberson, Deborah Haney, Joyce Thackston, Dottie Marler, Pepple, Cromer, Marler.

Lyman Mill (Lyman, S.C.): Wayne Blackmon (coach), Sandra Clary, Judy Cooper, Linda Bell, Vennie Rogers, Brenda DeYoung, Gardenia Rogers, Beth Bishop, Michele Springman, Rose Maybin, Paula Westfall, Lauren Murphy, Janet Oliver, Brenda Sloan, Marion Satterfield, Hadden, Janet Cooper.

1971

Officers: Harry Foster (Greenville, S.C.), President; Ken Pittman (Greenville, S.C.), 1st Vice President; R.E. Patrick (Greenwood, S.C.), 2nd Vice President; D.K. Smith (Lyman, S.C.), 3rd Vice President; Fred Byrd (Greenville, S.C.), Executive Secretary; Divver Hendrix (Greenville, S.C.), Treasurer; Fred Powers (Charlotte, N.C.), Ass't Executive Secretary; Whitey Kendall (Greenville), Supervisor of Officials; Lt. F.R. Hawkins, Security Officer; Frank Ballenger (Greenville, S.C.), Director of Publicity.

Executive Committee: Clarence Thomas (Greenville, S.C.), Willie Wilbanks (Ware Shoals, S.C.), Curtis Terry (Piedmont, S.C.), Willard Fowler (Greer, S.C.), Dan Foster (Greenville, S.C.), Snow Kirby (Marietta, S.C.), Bill Hopkins (Pelzer, S.C.), Lewis Acker (Anderson, S.C.), Lloyd McAbee (Greenville, S.C.), Bobby Morris (Liberty, S.C.), Joe Newton (Greenville, S.C.), Henry Spake (Anderson, S.C.), Broadus Miller (Greenville, S.C.), Grady Wallace (Columbia, S.C.), Ward Williams (Greenville, S.C.), T.C. Hooper (Greenville, S.C.), Earl Wooten (Piedmont, S.C.), Vercho Carter (Alexander City, Ala.), Reynolds Johnston (Pensacola, Fla.), James Morrow (Greenville, S.C.).

OPEN DIVISION

Texize Chemical (Greenville, S.C.), champions: John Deter (coach), Haywood Hill, Ken Riley, Tom Brown, Joe Brunson, Glymph Childress, Booker Brown, Elrod, Graves, Long, Chicoress, Skip Goley, Esleeck, Boesch.

Kenro (Atlanta, Ga.), runners-up: Ken Griffith (coach), Pat Moriarty, Larry Barnett, Doug Alexander, Ernie Crain, Larry Bagby, Bob McCresdy, Joe Pollock, Roy Roberts, Billy

Southern Textile Basketball Tournament Rosters   **Appendix 1**   247

Carter, Roger McDowell, Richie Mahaffey, Sheets.

Transit Homes (Greenville, S.C.): Rupert Elliott (coach), Eugene Seay, Steve Hollingsworth, Jerry Martin, Mike Barb, Tommy Meadows, Charles Selvy, Marvin Selvy, Lisco Thomas, David Whitner, Joe Styles, Swygert, Barry Cohen, Mack Crenshaw, Brennan, Gimpel, Neal, Gilroy.

Southern Bank (Greenville, S.C.): Wayne Kruer, Lloyd King, Les Heicher, Don Webster, Gerald Glur, Marion Selvy, Goolsby, Wright, Keir, Stone, Litz, Schaffer.

Electric Services (Charleston, S.C.): Jim Brabham (coach), Marion Salerni, Ray Loucks, Mel Gibson, Dan Franz, Buddy Petit, Jim Hansen, Luther Poole, Roger White, Tom Cochran, Jim Chapman, Trip Jones, Banner, Duncan, Spencer.

Carolina Engineers (Greenville, S.C.): Earl Wooten (coach), Lanny Taylor, Tom Higdon, Jeff Reisinger, Neel, Yates, McMurray, Angel, Davis, Wooten.

Atlanta Satellites (Atlanta, Ga.): Earl Harris (coach), James Haines, William Hillary, Robert Pritchett, Skip Thomas, Charles Geer, McCaskill, Cheesboro, Lippett, Frye.

S.C. All Stars (Columbia, S.C.): Bobby Cremins, Skip Harlicka, Linn Burkholder, Eddie Powell, Skip Kickey, Carnevale, Dennis.

Class A Men

Russell Manufacturing (Alexander City, Ala.), champions: Vercho Carter (coach), Mike Hearn, Wayne Rape, Dewey Sanders, James Leonard, L.M. Hunter, Arthur Hicks, Perry Anderson, Jack Nelson, Felix Holley, Calvin Allen, Owen Butts.

Lyman Mill (Lyman, S.C.), runners-up: Virgil Pruitt (coach), John Walker, Troy Roberson Jr., Leonard Price, Gary Hix, Philip Childers, Howard Watson, Charles Robinson, James Graham, Michael Fulmer, Ralph Murphy, W. Roberson.

Monaghan Mill (Greenville, S.C.), consolation winners: Jyles Phillips (coach), Terry Fowler, Jim Holden, Charles McIntyre, Bill Phillips, Bill Swaynghame, Charles Coleman Jr., Gary Pittman, Michael McKinney, Levi Mitchell, Doyle Lawson, Alexander.

Taylors Mill (Taylors, S.C.): Leon Gravley (coach), Steven Moore, Billy Allen, Curtis Campbell, Maxie Krause, James Davidson Jr., George Copeland Jr., Marion Durham, M. Gravley.

Monsanto (Greenwood, S.C.): Herb Edmonds (coach), Jerry Gordon, Don Livingston, Garrett Nation, Jerry Shurts, Charles Stevens, Joe Stephens, Stick Wilson, Eddie Childs, Robert Williams.

Rohm-Haas (Fayetteville, N.C.): Pete Carlisle (coach), Larry Bass, Charles Carlisle, Doyle Owens, Michael Adams, Ronald Dickinson, Thomas Mains, Eddie Mason, Calvin Graham, Dennis Kinlaw, Robert Scott.

Fiber Industries (Greenville, S.C.): Jack Kelley (coach), Earl Whittington, Stan Tapp, Ken Childers, Steve Burnette, Robert Harley, David Pritchett, Mickey Stepp, Robert Hargett, Herman Evatt, Glenn Lowe.

Madison Throwing Co. (Madison, N.C.): Glenn Ogburn (coach), Harold Parker, Tim Smothers, Michael Heekin, Steve Spencer, Billy Corns, Brian Manuel, Glenn Ogburn Jr., Robert Lowe, Robert Pickard, Michael Stovall.

Pelzer Mill (Pelzer, S.C.): H.D. Adams (coach), Bill Harris, Raymond Rochester, William Adams, Benny Garrett, Jerry Riddle, Jerry Garner, James Thomason, Phil Hopkins, Jimmy Hopkins, Don Gilmer, Little.

LTV ElectroSystems (Greenville, S.C.): Robert Todd (coach), Fred Brown, Billy Tarrant, Robert Simmons, Robert Moyers, Leonard Black, Jesse Bice, Gerald Smith, Clarence Fricks.

Class B Men

Singer Mfg. (Pickens, S.C.), champions: Dave Breazeale (coach), Charles Taylor, Tommy Bowen, Tim Looper, Wesley Bolding, Steve Simmons, Ted Owen, Mike Holcombe, Joe Stephens, Hamp Summey, David Byers, Jimmy Funderburke, Tom Carver,

Victor Mill (Greer, S.C.), runners-up: Doug Garren (coach), Robert Vaughn, Anthony Bennett, Lewis Goldsmith, Ronald Bailey, Conrad Cline, Lawrence Williams, Verdell Richardson, Leroy Whiteside, Eugene Daniels, Allen Moore, Moody.

Fiber Industries (Greenville, S.C.), consolation winners: Earl Whittington (coach), Heyward Leake, Steve Barton, Broadus Durante Jr., Calvin Carter, Donald Hughes, Steve Richard, Larry Hill, Steven Hodge, Claude Barnett, Randy Booker.

Parker Mill (Greenville, S.C.): Paul Fair (coach), Artis Stewart, Bill Garraux, Edward

Stewart, John McKinney, Bobby Mattress, Marion Marchbanks, James Gaines, William Bruce, Charles Morgan, Mickey Campbell, Phillips.

Pelzer Mill (Pelzer, S.C.): Jimmy Hopkins (coach), Keith Jordan, Bill Thomason, James Duncan, Mike Stainer, Eddie Saylor, Henry Ledford, John Walker, Larry Hester, Sammy Duncan, Larry Duncan, McKee, Andrews, Bryant, Williams, Leverette.

Ware Shoals Mill (Ware Shoals, S.C.): Jim Drake (coach), Joe Pitt, Joe Smith, Mike Abrams, John Lee, James Whatley, James Frazier, Perry Whatley, Jimmy Freeley, Wayman Hannah, Donald Jones.

Monsanto (Greenwood, S.C.): Jerry Gordon (coach), Sammy Randall, William Young, Ricky Frix, Dale Jones, James Hackett, David Gunnells, Stan McElrath, Dean Goss, Sam Corley, Willie Wright, Bell, Heaton, Goss, Haltiwanger, Childs.

Hoechst Celanese (Greer, S.C.): J.B. Easlic (coach), Jimmy Bradshaw, Don Smith, James Holcombe, Roger Wilson, Ronald Brown, Sam Inman, Zane Metcalf, George Carver, James Curtis.

Clark-Schwebel (Anderson, S.C.): Alex Cawthon (coach), Gary Hart, James Day, Jay Agnew, Johnny Corn, Ronald Gilstrap, Arnold Cawthon, Harold Long, Johnny Rousey, Douglas Payton.

Sangamo Electric Co. (Pickens, S.C.): Gene Holliday (coach), Roy Holliday, Wayne Nicholson, Tim Krieg, Joel Allgood, Pat Kelsey, Terry Odom, Sammy Nix, Tommy Porter, Bobby Hiott, Jimmy Roberts, Skip Nix, Durham.

Dunean Mill (Greenville, S.C.): Doug Gailey (coach), George King, Ronnie Scarborough, Homer Robinson, Charles Roddy, Tommy Atkinson, Danny Ballew, Larry Cummings, Emerson Carter, Iler Lollis, Calvin Hill.

Taylors Mill (Taylors, S.C.): M.C. Butler (coach), Paul Few, Charles Fleming, John Frazier, James Gentry, Brian Herndon, Norman Howard, Michael Miller, Randall Ponder, Harold Widle, David Wilhoit.

Pratt-Read (Central, S.C.): G.E. Dickard (coach), Gary Nix, Ronnie Hughes, Frank Dyar, Leslie Porter, Melvin Jackson, Willie Norris, Louis Gambrell, William Ligon, Billy Busha, Tom Sparacino.

Cryovac (Simpsonville, S.C.): Husky Turner (coach), James Wilson, Robert Massingale, Jimmy Porterfield, John Boudoucies, James Sullivan, Archie Armstrong, Jimmy Bell, Robert Phelps, Lewis Whitmire, Kenneth Johnson.

Texize Chemical (Greenville, S.C.): Booker Johnson (coach), Minton Berry, L.V. Sullivan, Albert Sullivan, Henry Barksdale, Tommy Henderson, Donnie Noggle, Emanuel Sullivan, Joe Campbell, Marcus Poole.

Froehling-Robertson (Greenville, S.C.): C.T. Huff (coach), Earl Phillips, Phillip McCollum Jr., Jerry Hollingsworth, Gary Turner, Allen Turner, Earl Stewart, Terry Huff, D.M. Trusty, Patton Woodward, Willie Kirkser Jr.

General Electric (Greenville, S.C.): M.D. Miros (coach), Anthony Irby, William Boyd, James Gamble, Charles Fowler, Charley Wallace, Jefferson Ware, Charles Breazeale, James Brown, George Vaughn, Robert Brown, Cox, Ashe, Richardson.

Precise Machine Works (Simpsonville, S.C.): Larry Thackston (coach), Douglas Thackston, Bobby Chandler, Eddie Huff, Tip Thackston, Mike Garrett, Preston Calvert, Wayne Swinger, Ballew.

Sally Mill (Greenville, S.C.): John Buchanan (coach), Douglas McKinney, Robert Fennell, Jimmy Aiken, Richard Goldsmith, Joseph Smith, Danny Gray, Barry Dilworth, Fred Dilworth, Luther Smith, Robert Peden.

Conso (Union, S.C.): Warren Humphries (coach), Samuel Williford, John Gault, Ronald Kirby, Richard Sweatt, Frederick Baldwin, Cecil Brown Jr., Eugene McCullough, Jackie Parks, Tommy Broome, Jerry Farr, Vaughn, Teague, Wilbanks, J. Teague.

Stone Mfg. (Greenville, S.C.): John Kemp (coach), Harold Westbrook (coach), Lawrence Campbell, Jerry Hawkins, David Miller, Charles Stevens, Larry Ross, John Henderson, John Kemp, Donald Masters, James Beeks, David Dennis.

Easley Mill (Easley, S.C.): Johnny Skinner (coach), James Lackey, Jerry Brock, Terry Smith, Charles Williams, Pete Ladd, Charles Austin, M.C. Austin, Charles Hennessee, James Pridmore, William Rogers.

CLASS C MEN

Poe Hardware (Greenville, S.C.), champions: Phil Donnan (coach), Randy Miller, Mike Smith, Clyde Agnew, David Dean, Marion Valentine, Harry Bobotis, Marion Miller, Wayne Croft.

Southern Textile Basketball Tournament Rosters   Appendix 1   249

Crown-Metro (Greenville, S.C.), runners-up: Billy Allen (coach), David Dobson, Norman McDonald, Doug Lowe, Carl Chambers, Randy McCullen, Mark Davis, Forrest Jeffries, Stepp, Anderson.

Carter & Crawley (Greenville, S.C.), consolation winners: Leroy Greggs (coach), Bryant Millwood (coach), Clyde Mayes, Leonard Hill, Nixon Allen, Jack Taylor, Kenny Harbin, Phil Montieth, Danny Ballard, Preston Moore, Ricky Loftis, Calvin Edwards, Dover.

Carolina Supply (Greenville, S.C.): David Watson (coach), Will McNamara, Charles McClosky, Anthony Smith, William Goodwin, Tommy Lowden, Mark Collier, Steve Farrow, Ronnie Murray, Anthony Clark, Gambrell, Bobby Estes.

John Perkins Industries (Greenville, S.C.): Jerry Knight (coach), James Davis, James Parham, Michael Bell, Buck Farrow, Don Arledge, Donnie Linn, Frankie Marion, Jeff Ring, Gaines Huguley, Edwin Haskell, Boules.

Southern Filters (Greenville, S.C.): Fred Reed (coach), John Reed, Tikies Phillips, David Ballenger, Roger Newell, David Pruitt, Barry Pruitt, Jeff Rish, George Cheros, Jeff Baty.

Home Real Estate (Abbeville, S.C.): Donny Southard (coach), Phillip Southard, William Woolbright, Wyatt Smith, Larry Ray, James Martin, Barry Stone, Brent Smith, Isom.

The Tire Exchange (Greer, S.C.): Tommy Hughes (coach), Barry Beeks, Vincent Sweet, Jack Kay, Anthony Burnette, Larry Mills, Harold Crawford, David Carpenter, Phil Davis, James Anderson, Michael Brannon, B. Kay.

Piedmont Mill (Piedmont, S.C.): Ray Foxx (coach), James Foxx Jr., Ronnie Gunn, Ricky Moore, Lawrence Abrams, Milford Howard Jr., James Hartsell, Lewis Sweatman, Michael Sasser, Tommy Godfrey, David Haskell, Ballard, Cobb.

Saco-Lowell (Easley, S.C.): Jim Carter (coach), Charlie Crowe (coach), Dale Tant, Terry Julian, Stanley Morgan, John Leslie, Carl Forte, Ricky Gettys, Bruce Stephens, Odis Rhodes, Thomas Dukes, George Ellison.

Jackson Mill (Iva, S.C.): Alan Rainey (coach), Ronnie Cureton, James Sullivan, Mervin Epstein, Ralph Holloway, Tommy Rutledge, Aldred Jordan, William Gray Jr., Kenneth Gambrell, Chester Garrett, Robert Milligan, Harrison, McCauley.

Appleton Mill (Anderson, S.C.): Henry Spake (coach), Curtis Bowen, Wentford Gaines, Freddie Albertson, Donald Walls, Thomas Jones, Cecil Lee, Charles Lesley, Leroy Cherry, James Rice, Daniel Martin, Hardy.

Gluck Mill (Anderson, S.C.): Jim Roberts (coach), Earley Hanna (coach), Alfred Alexander, Stephen Whitfield, Rudolph Gray, Wayne Alexander, Jimmy Linker, Ernest Warren, Steven Allen, Roger Mullins, Rodney Thomas, Wayne Wells, Hull.

Southern Industrial Mechanical (Greenville, S.C.): Jackie Queen (coach), Joseph Boyter, Roy Brown, Steven Burns, Dennis Collins, John Cottingham, Cornell King, Steven Mathis, Frank Millwood, Robert Poole, Jerome Williams.

Darlington (Darlington, S.C.): D. Neilson (coach), Keith Ritter, Danny Sansbury, Eddie Lloyd, Gene Dargan, Tom Greer, Tommy King, John Holmes, Darrel Gettys, Billy Evans, Terry Gettys, Norwood, Britt, Benjamin.

CLASS A WOMEN

Texize Chemical (Greenville, S.C.), champions: Ted Hillhouse (coach), Judy Murray, Marian Brewer, Ann Lyons, Patsy Neal, Emma Howard, Lucy Walters, Reba Lowe, Marty Vaughan, Doris Plemmons, Barbara Jones, Susan Moss, Frances Hillhouse, Joyce Forrester, Zandra Watson, Paula Monroe.

Kenro (Atlanta, Ga.), runners-up: Johnny Moon (coach), Dolores Owen, Vera Garrett, Cathy Flannagan, Brenda Walker, Annette Hammock, Alice Smith, Lila Brasher, Edwina Bryan, Judy Bickers, Bonnie Ritter, Sandra Crozier, Bonnie Scott, Lee, Halton, Stinchcomb.

Dunean Mill (Greenville, S.C.), consolation winners: Larry Ashley (coach), Debbie Parker, Bobbie Galloway, Brenda Stevens, June Brown, Kaye Bayne, Rubin Stowe, Dot Sisk, Karen Brown, Debra Sisk, Penny Cooper, Janice Rogers, Rita Mantooth, Pat Morgan, Shell, Jessie Wilson.

Sangamo Electric Co. (Pickens, S.C.): Jerry Roper (coach), Clint Owens (coach), Jackie Krutzenzer, Deda Duncan, Donna Duncan, Dixie Duncan, Marty Russell, Linda Cox, Peggy Hardin, Debra Anderson, Jackie McJunkin, Janice Chapman, Barbara Lewis, Charlene Abercrombie, Sandra Simmons, Roberta James, Eleanor Lewis, M. Jones, N. Jones, M. Chapman, Murrell.

Homestead Terrace (Greenville, S.C.): Virginia Robinson (coach), Loucinda Allgood, Caroline Brown, Sissie Donaldson, Trisha Hunt, Kitty Parrott, Candy Clarke, Sue Ellis, Judy Clarke, Joyce McCarroll, Betsy Stricklin, Leah Alexander, Laurie Padker, Priscilla Wilcox, Kathy Myers, Jan Hopkins.

Wunda Weve Carpets (Greenville, S.C.): Ruey Evans (coach), George Waters (coach), Linda Dillard, Linda Brown, Vicki Clary, Edna Farmer, Carol Waters, Joyce Evans, Martha Stewart, Micky Maw, Mary Benton, Judy Hartin, Doris Reynolds, Monirah Taylor, Candis Ridgley, Mabel Sullivan, Dottie Hill.

Slater Mill (Slater, S.C.): Bobby Kirby (coach), Steve Burnett (coach), Joan Kirby, Linda White, Judy Clark, Sharon Brooks, Diane Walker, Dotty Kirby, Sherry McCall, June Brown, Laura Freeman, Ann Simmons, Becky Ezell, Susan Moon, Yvonne Griffin, Judy Young, Marsha Marrett, Bobbie Whitmire, Nichols, Quinn, Campbell.

Piedmont Mill (Piedmont, S.C.): Don Roper (coach), Edister Thompson, Debbie Eskew, Debbie Crawford, Susan Henderson, Shirley McDaniel, Lunita Washington, Sheryl Robinson, Shelby Cooley, Marsha Davis, Doretta King, Barbara Sullivan, Mary Thurman, Sylvia Henderson, Dorothy Rosemond, Linda White, Porter, Wilson, L. Clifford, Merritt, J. Clifford, Bennett, Vernon.

IMMS (Greenville, S.C.): John Mickler (coach), Doris Fisher, Debbie Haney, Judy Cross, Frances Welborn, Betty Foster, Vickie Lindner, Marcie Homonai, Ann Jenkins, Beth Verdin, Martha Craine, Pauline Callahan, Joyce Wrenn, Connie Brown, Dot Sick, Diane Brown, Clayton.

Westvaco (Charleston, S.C.): Bill Stevens (coach), Velda Runny, Ann Wiggins, Carolyn Cumbee, Jeanene Batten, Cecilia O'quinn, Rosalee Mouzon, Barbara Maddox, Pat Kolb, Jane George, Barbara Olson, Ann Corcoran, Jean Beatson, Ginny Martin, Ellen Evans, Cissy Missell, Jackson.

Lyman Mill (Lyman, S.C.): Wayne Blackmon (coach), Sandra Clary, Linda Bell, Vennie Rogers, Brenda DeYoung, Gardenia Rogers, Rose Maybin, Lauren Murphy, Alice Moore, Linda Roberson, Vicki Bradley, Christine Robinson, Patricia Porter, Marlene Vinson, Sandra Vinson, Vickie Vinson, Smith, J. Smith, Cobb, Winchester.

Pelzer Mill (Pelzer, S.C.): Cecil Hopkins (coach), Barbara Bell, Vickie Saxon, Marsha Coe, Frances Creamer, Judy Robertson, Diane Starnes, Danette Powell, Joan Waters, Molly King, Ellen Gidden, Brenda Gwinn, Diane Gaillard, Sue Ford, Marsha Ross, Joan Thomason, J. Hawkins, D. Hawkins, Leigion, Judy Apyne, Owens, McConnell, Hiott.

Singer Mfg. (Anderson, S.C.): Annie Tribble (coach), Dianne Limbaugh, Sherry Jennings, Martha Hendrix, Wanda Campbell, Denise Norris, Marsha McElveen, Dianne Elliott, Mary Hill, Gloria Curry, Nancy Evans, Joy Marcus, Dianne McConnell, Sallie Greneker, Connie Garrett, Suzanne Stephens.

Stone Mfg. (Greenville, S.C.): Barbara Pridmore (coach), Jackie Brazel, Fran Brooks, Sharon Chisom, Carol Davis, Charlene Dunn, Ruth Harper, Vickie Jennings, Carol Pharr, Emile Sanders, Patty Shaw, Jean Williams, Susan Smith, Grace Newton, Libby Mullinax, McCall.

Precise Machine Works (Simpsonville, S.C.): Kenneth Huff (coach), Lyn Johnson, Wanda Trotter, Evelyn Goldsmith, Jane Huff, Marie Huff, Connie Gibson, Jackie Best, Janet Hendrix, Teresa Wamack, Mary Henderson, Becky Chandler, Dolly Henderson, Susan Waldrop, Babb, Cook, Woods, Stephens.

───────── **1972** ─────────

Officers: D.K. Smith (Lyman, S.C.), President; Ken Pittman (Greenville, S.C.), 1st Vice President; Harry Foster (Greenville, S.C.), 2nd Vice President; James Morrow (Greenville, S.C.), 3rd Vice President; Fred Byrd (Greenville, S.C.), Executive Secretary; Divver Hendrix (Greenville, S.C.), Treasurer; Fred Powers (Charlotte, N.C.), Ass't Executive Secretary; Whitey Kendall (Greenville), Supervisor of Officials; Lt. F.R. Hawkins, Security Officer; Frank Ballenger (Greenville, S.C.), Director of Publicity.

Executive Committee: Clarence Thomas (Greenville, S.C.), Willie Wilbanks (Ware Shoals, S.C.), Curtis Terry (Piedmont, S.C.), Willard Fowler (Greer, S.C.), Dan Foster (Greenville, S.C.), Snow Kirby (Marietta, S.C.), Bill Hopkins (Pelzer, S.C.), Lloyd McAbee (Greenville, S.C.), Joe Newton (Greenville, S.C.), Henry Spake (Anderson, S.C.), Broadus Miller (Greenville, S.C.), Ward Williams (Greenville, S.C.), Earl Wooten (Piedmont, S.C.), Vercho Carter (Alexander

City, Ala.), Reynolds Johnston (Pensacola, Fla.), R.E. Patrick (Greenwood, S.C.), Phil Clark (Greer, S.C.), Ken Dockins (Greenville, S.C.), Patsy Neal (Brevard, N.C.).

OPEN DIVISION

Texize Chemical (Greenville, S.C.), champions: Dan Pike (coach), Joe Brunson, Don Jackson, Harold Fox, Ernie Fleming, Bernard Collier, Lindsay Orr, Heyward Hill, Gerald Glur, Les Heicher, Bill Moore, Will Robinson, Goley, Mazarol.

Transit Homes (Greenville, S.C.), runners-up: Rupert Elliott (coach), Steve Hirschorn, Ron Arnholt, Al Leapheart, Stan Elrod, Joe Styles, Steve Hobson, Seay, Wilborn, Dan Boe, Henry Harris.

Kenro (Atlanta, Ga.): Pat Moriarty, Larry Barnett, Doug Alexander, Bob McCready, Joe Pollock, Roy Roberts, Jimmy Pitts, Allan Johnson, Mike Dahl, William Sheats, Rupert Breedlove, Ken Griffith.

Pittman's Textile Machinery (Greenville, S.C.): Reisinger, Gregg, Childress, Davis, Jim Clark, Larry Taylor, Jack Ross, Mike Wrenn.

Brabham's TV (Charleston, S.C.): Jim Brabham (coach), Marion Salerni, Mel Gibson, Dan Franz, Jim Below, Roger White, Nate White, Norris Townsend, Donnie Sheppard, John Sutor, Don Holcombe, Gustafson, Buddy Petit, Spencer, Bo Jameson.

Mikro (Charlotte, N.C.): Mike Ross (coach), Danny Dixon, John Thornton, Bob Thurston, Robert Poole, Artis.

Atlanta Satellites (Atlanta, Ga.): James Haines (coach), William Hillary, Robert Pritchett, Ernest Thomas, Charles Geer, Ralph Long, Charles O'Kelly, James Doctor, Larry Cofield, Ken Burden, James Green, Early Cheesborough, L.D. Strozier, Lowe, Stockes, Haines.

Decorative Components (Forest City, N.C.): Howard White (coach), George Adams, Richard Thomas, David Smith, Rick Campbell, Wilson Scott, Greg Whitman, Dennis Childress, Bob Peterson, David Wyscarver, Don Bowler, Harry Boyd, Richards, Hamilton, Wesley.

ACME Distributors (Spartanburg, S.C.): Don Nelson (coach), Joe Bradson, D. Montgomery, J.C. Humphries, David Vaughn, Mac Lemmons, James Jenkins, Butch Zatazelo, Doug Brackett, Lee Miller, Leroy Smith, Lynburg Moody, Ulysses Dawkins.

Chattanooga VFW (Chattanooga, Tenn.): Leroy Alexander (coach), Ralph Hooper (coach), Richard Fuqua, Richard Stone, Jimmy Dillard, Harold Hicks, Fred McDode, George Autry, Jeffrey Poole, Mark Howard, Walt Biggs, Larry Baker.

CLASS A MEN

Russell Manufacturing (Alexander City, Ala.), champions: Vercho Carter (coach), Mike Hearn, Dewey Sanders, Arthur Hicks, Jack Nelson, Felix Holley, Thomas Boyd, Charles Scott, Owen Butts, Alonzo Ferguson, Marshall Robbins.

Rohm-Haas (Fayetteville, N.C.), runners-up: Pete Carlisle (coach), Larry Bass, Charles Carlisle, Michael Adams, Kenneth Hoffman, Michael Brown, Malachi Avery, Harold Melvin, James McKinnon, Lambert Johnson, Lawrence Dawson.

Singer Mfg. (Anderson, S.C.), consolation winners: Summey, Sims, Clinkscales, Taylor, Breazeale, Crumpton, Bowen, Bolding, Looper.

Taylors Mill (Taylors, S.C.): Steve Brown (coach), Steven Moore, Curtis Campbell, Maxie Krause, Michael Gravley, Leon Gravely, Ricky Fuller, William Thomas.

Lyman Mill (Lyman, S.C.): Wayne Blackmon (coach), John Walker, Gary Hix, Philip Childress, Charles Robinson, Ernest Murray, Rick Dunagan, John Mullinax, Clarence Moody, Charles West, Sam Simpson.

Monaghan Mill (Greenville, S.C.): Jyles Phillips (coach), Terry Fowler, Jim Holden, Charles McIntyre, Bill Phillips, Bill Swaynghame, Gary Pittman, Levi Mitchell, Ronald Ward, Barry Alexander.

Fiber Industries (Greenville, S.C.): Jack Kelley (coach), Wendell Lawson (coach), Robert Kirby, David Pritchett, Mickey Stepp, Robert Hargett, Herman Evatt, James Bagwell, Troy Godwin, Vernon McMakin, Julius Sizemore, Ernest Ward.

Pelzer Mill (Pelzer, S.C.): James Thomason (coach), Bill Harris, Raymond Rochester, William Adams, Benny Garrett, Phil Hopkins, Jimmy Hopkins, Cecil Williams, Tommy Richardson, Eddie Saylor, Keith Jordan, Tommy Stewart.

LTV ElectroSystems (Greenville, S.C.): J.W. Hunter (coach), Fred Brown, Gerald Bice, Elford Wilder, Samuel Fannin, James Jarrell Jr., James Starnes, Brodie Templeton, James Williams, Joe Hayes, Ben Plumbee.

General Electric (Greenville, S.C.): Mike Miros (coach), Donnie Foster (coach), Ray Brewer, Skeeter Hammett, Charles Breazeale, Charles Wallace, William Payne, Wayne Gamble, Lewis Ashe, Jerry Richardson, Joe Aiken.

Class B Men

Fiber Industries (Greenville, S.C.), champions: Ken Childers (coach), Phil Harley (coach), Steve Barton, Randy Booker, Walter Bubley Jr., Colvin Carter, Timothy Howell, Donald Hughes, Heyward Leake, O'Louis McCullough, Ronald Putman, Steve Richard.

Ware Shoals Mill (Ware Shoals, S.C.), runners-up: Bobby Fleming (coach), Joe Pitts, Joe Smith, Mike Abrams, John Lee, Perry Whatley, David Hannah, Jerry Sims, Willie Smith, Kenneth Black, Mike Ashley.

Cryovac (Simpsonville, S.C.), consolation winners: Mike Henderson (coach), James Wilson, Robert Massingill, James Sullivan, Robert Phelps, Freddie Goldsmith, David Buchanan, Michael Brock, Lewis Armfield, Larry Coker, Michael Styles.

Sangamo Electric Co. (Pickens, S.C.): Joel Allgood (coach), Doyle Nicholson, Tim Krieg, Sammy Nix, Tommy Porter, Lewis Monroe, Robert Dixon, Wayne Chappell, Floyd Nix, Ben Cannon, Frank Kelly, Gerald Foster, Roberts.

Victor Mill (Greer, S.C.): Doug Garren (coach), Gary Vaughn, Anthony Bennett, Lewis Goldsmith, Ronald Bailey, Verdell Richardson, Leroy Whiteside, Marvin Drummond, John Caldwell, Donnell Moody, Douglas Reed, Marion Jones.

Parker Mill (Greenville, S.C.): Mickey Campbell (coach), Edward Stewart, John McKinney, Bobby Mattress, James Clayton, Charles Morgan, Dwight Bolden, Danny Hall, Roger Donald, Theodore Pinson, Jerry Jackson.

Monsanto (Greenwood, S.C.): John Roberts (coach), Sammy Leamon, William Young, Dale Jones, David Gunnells, Bobby Chiles, Robert Bell, Doug Brown, James Hackett, Richard Timmerman, Alonzo Chappelle, A. Bell.

Hoechst Celanese (Greer, S.C.): J.B. Easlic (coach), Jimmy Bradshaw, Don Smith, James Holcombe, Roger Wilson, Zane Metcalf, Steve Merchant, Steve Howard, Mike Hopper, Andrew Hucek, Tom Young, Carver.

Sullivan Hardware (Anderson, S.C.): Furman Gray, Joel Cisson, Hughes, Payne, Few, Smith, Brown.

Clark-Schwebel (Anderson, S.C.): Gary Hart (coach), James Day, Jay Agnew, Johnny Corn, Ronald Gilstrap, Douglas McRumsey, Tyson Payton, Charles Humphries, Jordan, Eddie Bryant, Boynton, Rice.

Dunean Mill #1 (Greenville, S.C.): Doug Gailey (coach), George King, Larry Cummings, John Sullivan, Joe Marion, Ray Gosnell, Mike Henderson, Jimmy Downes, James Wardlaw, Bob King, Ken Stroud.

Dunean Mill #2 (Greenville, S.C.): Jim Riddle (coach), Bobby Morris (coach), Charles Hudson, Bobby Calhoun, Chilie Williams, Patrick Newman, Dennis Bolds, Pringle Clemons, Mike Morris, Bobby Mangrum, Clifton Collins, William Townes, Holloway.

Taylors Mill (Taylors, S.C.): J.W. Gentry (coach), Charles Fleming, John Frazor, Norman Howard, Michael Miller, Randall Ponder, James Wilde, David Wilhoit, Randy Coker, Thomas Holford, Frank Williams, Daniels.

Pratt-Read (Central, S.C.): G.E. Dickard (coach), Gary Nix, Ronnie Hughes, Leslie Porter, Melvin Jackson, Charles Gillespie, Lynn Greenlee, Elliot Eskew, James Tucker, Randall Johnson, Young Thomas, Pilgrim.

Precise Machine Works (Simpsonville, S.C.): Larry Thackston (coach), Tip Thackston, Spunky Chandler, Eddie Huff, Preston Barbary, Steve Mahon, Chuck Ballew, Calvin Milam, Robert Burns.

Sally Mill (Greenville, S.C.): John Buchanan (coach), Michael Goldsmith, Joseph Smith, Danny Gray, William Dilworth, Luther Smith, Anthony Kay, Leroy Arnold, Richard Elrod, Ken Chandler, William Bayne, Terrell Watts, J. Gray, Danny Gray.

Conso (Union, S.C.): Warren Humphries (coach), John Gault, Richard Sweatt, Jackie Parks, Larry Inman, Paul Vaughn Jr., Rupert Sizemore, Donald Bobo, Harold Jenkins, Doyle Crocker, Michael Vandeford, Carl Oates.

Stone Mfg. (Greenville, S.C.): Don Masters (coach), Harold Westbrook (coach), Jerry Hawkins, Charles Edens, Larry Ross, John Henderson, John Kemp, James Beeks, Lee Beeks, Cecil Runion, Jerry Moses.

Easley Mill (Easley, S.C.): Johnny Skinner (coach), James Lackey, Jerry Brock, Terry Smith, Charles Chambers, Ricky Sloan, Calvin Hendricks, James Breazeale, Gary Simpson, Roscoe Smith, Willie Mansell, Austin, McCall.

Saco-Lowell (Easley, S.C.): Jim Carter (coach), Larry Young, Roger Spearman, Johnny

Chandler, Charles Hall, Thomas Rogers, Gary Stephens, Herbert Bowen, Rudolph Murphy, James Bowens, Steve Gravley, Sloan.

J.W. Vaughn Co. (Greenville, S.C.): Gerard Leo (coach), Ronnie Scarborough, Jimmy Sellers, Bill Whitman, Robert Johnson, Thomas McCroskey, Ralph Bell, George Bussey, Leo.

Tele. Sec. (Greenville, S.C.): Jesse Brooks (coach), Phil Williams, James Kinard, David Simpson, Randy Talley, James Adams, Fred Collins, Douglas Bagwell, Barry Kirk.

Dow Badische (Anderson, S.C.): Doug Mazyck (coach), Albert Davis, Harry Reed, Nathaniel Leverette, Lester Garrison, Lawrence Green, Douglas Martins, Hugh Shearhouse, Sylvester Reed, Oscar Davis, Sims, Love.

Indian Head Yarn (Greenville, S.C.): Danny Hartsell (coach), James Hartsell, Harold Alexander, Joe Anderson, Roger Dove, Bobby Cobb, James Baird, Thelt Hiette, Jimmy Mattison.

Cryovac (Duncan, S.C.): Marvin Taylor (coach), Fred Dobbins, Steve Smith, William Friddle, Stan Stankus, Everett Turner, VanderPloeg, Preston Calvert, Warren Nicholson.

J.P. Stevens Distribution (Greenville, S.C.): Ray Foxx (coach), Herman McCullough, James Alexander, William Stewart, William Alexander, James McGee, Robert Stewart, Buddy McQueen, Milford Howard, William Chambers, Carl Chambers, Rollins.

Class C Men

Pelzer Mill #2 (Pelzer, S.C.), champions: Jimmy Hopkins (coach), Leroy Cherry, Thomas Jones, Tommy Rutledge, Ronnie Cureton, Edward Crawford, Cecil Lee, Charles Lesley, James Martin, Larry Ray, Willie Holloway, Frankie Major.

Crown-Metro (Greenville, S.C.), runners-up: Billy Allen (coach), Randy McCullen, Forrest Jeffries, George Dodkin, Ronnie Henderson, Mike Wood, Ralph Hanna, Mike Meadows, Lane Estes, Collie Feemster, Littlejohn.

Carter & Crawley (Greenville, S.C.), consolation winners: Allen, Valentine, Yeargin, Tim Helton, Daryl Wilder, Williams, McCullough, Choice, Martin.

The Tire Exchange (Greer, S.C.): Tommy Hughes (coach), Jack Taylor, Larry Mills, Harold Crawford, Phil Davis, James Brooks, Michael Brannon, Ricky Loftis, Preston Moore, Bobby Estes, Billy Tooley, Tony Chibarro, Abrams, McKinney.

Carolina Supply (Greenville, S.C.): David Watson (coach), Doug Evans, Carrol Couch, Frank Cole, Thomas Hunter, Gregory Grainer, David Stone, Jimmy Parham, David Sullivan, Keith Merck, Buddy Asbury.

John Perkins Industries (Greenville, S.C.): Jerry Knight (coach), Gaines Huguley, Mark Collier, Roger Gilbert, Tim Lindler, Bobby Carpenter, Sammy Reese, Tim Buchanan, Stan Sloeftoll, Reynolds, Francis, Forrester.

Home Real Estate (Abbeville, S.C.): Donny Southard (coach), William Woolbright, Reese Smith, Larry Ray, James Martin, Barry Stone, Brent Smith, Barry Isom, Mack Elrod, Cleveland Spencer, O'dell McClendon.

Piedmont Mill (Piedmont, S.C.): Ray Foxx (coach), James Foxx Jr., Ronnie Nunn, Ricky Moore, David Simpson, Mike McCauley, Walter Harrison, Robert Gilreath, Stanley Gilreath, Benjamin Sweatman, Donnie Nunn, Candler, Morton.

Saco-Lowell (Easley, S.C.): Jim Carter (coach), Terry Julian, Stanley Morgan, John Leslie, Odis Rhodes, Thomas Dukes, Marcus Rosemond, Roger Haskett, Dennis Brewer, Kenneth Gaskill, Owens, Dan Hendricks, Larry White, Green, Valentine, Don Hendricks, Williams, Gregg.

Jackson Mill (Iva, S.C.): Alan Charney (coach), Mervin Epstein, Willie Hunter, Eddie Wansley, Roy Anderson, Eddie McDonald, Wallace Richardson, Cornelius Hull, Smith.

Veeder-Root (Greenville, S.C.): Pete Huff (coach), Roger Blair, Mike Hawkins, Andy Dill, Mike Allen, Mike Sullivan, Gary Huff, Gary Blackston, Randy Holder.

Precise Machine Works (Simpsonville, S.C.): Charles Huff Jr. (coach), Rex Abercrombie, James Bolton, Michael Davis, Willie Harris, Richard Henry, Clarence Lewers, John Samuels, Clarence Sullivan, Willie Teague, Leon Westmoreland, Crowe, Fleming, Scott.

Pelzer Mill #1 (Pelzer, S.C.): Bill Thomas (coach), Billy Burns, Harold Thomason, Ronnie Cooley, Frank Woodcock, Tommy Hopkins, Steve Robinson, Jimmy Wooten, Carol Cooley, Phil Smith, Doug Austin, Jimmy Harrison, Talmon Harrison, Stewart, Cobb, Bob Andrews.

Pittman's Textile Machinery (Greenville, S.C.): Billy Phillips (coach), Phillip Sandlin, Phil Monteith, Richard Lawhorn, William Rowland, Robert Rice, Randy Harrison, Harry Hightower, Terry Emerson, W. Harrison.

Simmons Machinery Co. (Greenville, S.C.): Charles Theodore (coach), David Ballenger, David Pruitt, Barry Pruitt, Ben Hayes, Mike Daisley, Chuck Evans, Eddie Smith, Doug Cobb, George Cheros, Harry Bobotis.

Class A Women

Texize Chemical (Greenville, S.C.), champions: Ted Hillhouse (coach), Frances Hillhouse (coach), Judy Murray, Marian Brewer, Ann Lyons, Patsy Neal, Emma Howard, Lucy Walters, Reba Lowe, Marty Vaughan, Doris Plemmons, Barbara Jones, Joyce Forrester, Debbie Rogers, Janie Ingle, Janie Long, Jeanie Norris.

Lyman Mill (Lyman, S.C.), runners-up: Paul Culbreth (coach), Sandra Clary, Linda Roberson, Vennie Rogers, Brenda DeYoung, Lauren Murphy, Bonnie Moore, Vicki Utter, Diane Ayers, Elizabeth Bishop, Debbie Smith, Glenda Bullard, Diane Ruff, Kay Hillsdale, Debbie House, Gail Burgess, Robinson.

Westvaco (Charleston, S.C.), consolation winners: Bill Stevens (coach), Velda Runey, Ann Turner, Carolyn Cumbee, Jeanene Batten, Cecilia O'Quinn, Rosalee Mouzon, Barbara O'Quinn, Jean Beatson, Ellen Evans, Deborah Berry, June Easterwood, Linda White, Bruton Ballard, Lillian Pitts, Sally Hurley.

IMMS (Greenville, S.C.): Tom Bohlinger (coach), Judy Cross, Frances Welborn, Vickie Lindner, Pauline Callahan, Dianne Cronch, Carolyn Pharr, Barbara Lewis, Barbara Westray, Pat Bohlinger, Patricia Theodore, Valerie Vurnakes, Jean Callahan, Sandra Boyret, Sandra Leary, McCullough, Fisher, Porter, Ludwig.

Kenro (Atlanta, Ga.): Johnny Moon (coach), Dolores Owen, Vera Garrett, Brenda Walker, Annette Hammock, Edwina Bryan, Judy Bickers, Sandra Crozier, Bonnie Gibson, Janet Cox, Linda Shi, Sheila Stinchcomb, Bee Littlefield, Dale Baker, Cynthia Pue, Jean O'Neal, Wells, Branch, Thompson.

Dunean Mill (Greenville, S.C.): Larry Ashley (coach), Bobbie Galloway, Brenda Stevens, June Jones, Ruby Perry, Dot Smith, Debra Sisk, Peggy Owens, Rita Mantooth, Debby Vaughn, Vicki Sizemore, B.J. Shell, Jessi Wilson, Brown, Reid, Caraway, Merritt.

Sangamo Electric Co. (Pickens, S.C.): Jerry Roper (coach), Jackie McJunkin, Deda Duncan, Dixie Duncan, Janice Chapman, Roberta James, Eleanor Lewis, Martha Smith, Kat Laye, Jean Stone, Candy Ridgeley, Margaret Jones, Nancy James, Jan Holder, Dianne Mansell, Sara Roper, Walsh, Merrill.

Slater Mill (Slater, S.C.): Bobby Kirby (coach), Joan Kirby, Judy Clark, Sharon Wilson, Dotty Pierce, Sherry McCall, Ann Simmons, Becky Bowman, Susan Moon, Emily Sanders, Nena Simmons, Regina Gilstrap, Kathy Fowler, Corina Jackson, Paula Davenport, Jennie Campbell, Janie Hare, Burton, Adams, Daniel, Lyerly, Sandifer, Ramey.

Pelzer Mill (Pelzer, S.C.): Cecil Hopkins (coach), Barbara Bell, Marsha Ross, Danette Hanks, Joan Waters, Molly King, Ellen Geddens, Jane Hawkins, Cheryl Martin, Alice Clement, Jackie Williams, Joyce Ligon, Mary Thurman.

Singer Mfg. (Anderson, S.C.): Annie Tribble (coach), Dianne Limbaugh, Sherry Jennings, Martha Hendricks, Wanda Campbell, Denise Norris, Dianne Elliott, Gloria Curry, Sallie Greneker, Wanda Trotter, Jane Jones, Susan Gruber, Linda Bolick, Ren Windham, Vicki Cothran, Beth Yarborough.

Stone Mfg. (Greenville, S.C.): Barbara Pridmore (coach), Mervin Hamilton (coach), Jackie Davis, Fran Brooks, Carolyn Griffin, Charlene Dunn, Ruth Bobb, Vickie Jennings, Susan Jennings, Libby Mullinax, Tandra Watson, Kay Holder, Debbie Traynham, Ginger Holder, Mary Rogers, Brenda Washpon, Deloria Irby, Pridmore.

Precise Machine Works (Simpsonville, S.C.): Eddie Huff (coach), Steve Mahon (coach), Marie Huff, Jackie Gray, Janet Hendrix, Teresa Wamack, Beverly Cook, Debbie Woods, Terry Taylor, Shelby Wham, Charlene Wham, Gail Taylor.

Custom Printing (Greenville, S.C.): George Waters (coach), Joyce Wrenn, Jane Thackston, Ann Jenkins, Marilyn Wilkerson, Melle Barrow, Ann Bridges, Carol Waters, Susan Waldrop, Linda Dillard, Wanda Youmans, Vanise Poynter, Neeley.

Jackson Mill (Iva, S.C.): Yvonne McGee (coach), Sharon McGee, Dawn Gailey, Sonja McGee, Faith Bannister, Venda Young, Kathy Speares, Denise Bannister, Elaine Daniels, Hope Bannister, Bunny McGee, Diane Powell, Barbara Warren, McCullough, McMullin, Campbell, Jones, Bostic, Bryant,

Hanahan Park & Playground (Hanahan, S.C.): Bobby Turner (coach), Pam Bryson, Candy Crocker, Jean Clark, Ellen Evans, Pattie Gainey, Shyleen Jarell, Joyce Mathew, M.L.

McDonaugh, Dianne Robinson, Mandy Thibodeaux, Melissa Turner, Jacques.

Wholesale Fence Co. (Winston-Salem, N.C.): Jenny Holt (coach), Nancye Formo, Linda Ketner, Candy Newsom, Patsy Sebastian, Patsy Hartman, Carole Hutchins, Brenda Wooten, Ann Hester, Nancy Lawhern, Velma Bentley, Cothran.

Saco-Lowell (Easley, S.C.): Tom Arant (coach), Lisa Basinger, Karen Brown, Ann White, Kay Thompson, Janet White, Bobbi Whitmire, Susan Neal, Debbie Crenshaw, Janie Lee, Bonnie Whelan, Jenny Hillsman, Jenny DuBose, Janet Rampey, Andrea Smith, Sandra Thompson, Dennis.

DAYCO (Greenville, S.C.): Bill Turner (coach), Wallace Merck (coach), Kay Adams, Faye Anderson, Marilee Austell, Linda Corcoran, Tena Ginn, Peggy Gray, Mary Jameson, Annette Merritt, Pat Moore, Mavis Norville, Kathy Robinson, Pat Slay, Gay Willis.

Ware Shoals Mill (Ware Shoals, S.C.): Scott Hughes (coach), Larry Traynham (coach), Dianne Davenport, Becky Ezell, Beverly Allen, Lynn Boland, Ann Vinson, Nena Simmons, Jenny White, Zell Skinner, Mot Henderson, Sara Crocker, Faye Crawford, Susan Riley, Susan Anderson, Linda Griffin, Brownlee.

1973

Officers: D.K. Smith (Lyman, S.C.), President; Ken Pittman (Greenville, S.C.), 1st Vice President; Harry Foster (Greenville, S.C.), 2nd Vice President; James Morrow (Greenville, S.C.), 3rd Vice President; Fred Byrd (Greenville, S.C.), Executive Secretary; Divver Hendrix (Greenville, S.C.), Treasurer; Fred Powers (Charlotte, N.C.), Ass't Executive Secretary; Whitey Kendall (Greenville), Supervisor of Officials; Lt. F.R. Hawkins, Security Officer; Robert Ungerricht (Greenville, S.C.), Director of Publicity.

Executive Committee: Clarence Thomas (Greenville, S.C.), Willie Wilbanks (Ware Shoals, S.C.), Curtis Terry (Piedmont, S.C.), Willard Fowler (Greer, S.C.), Dan Foster (Greenville, S.C.), Snow Kirby (Marietta, S.C.), Bill Hopkins (Pelzer, S.C.), Lloyd McAbee (Greenville, S.C.), Joe Newton (Greenville, S.C.), Henry Spake (Anderson, S.C.), Broadus Miller (Greenville, S.C.), Ward Williams (Greenville, S.C.), Earl Wooten (Piedmont, S.C.), Vercho Carter (Alexander City, Ala.), Phil Clark (Greer, S.C.), Ken Dockins (Greenville, S.C.), Patsy Neal (Brevard, N.C.), Frank Ballenger (Shelby, N.C.).

OPEN DIVISION

Transit Homes (Greenville, S.C.), champions: Rupert Elliott (coach), Mike Barb, Stan Elrod, Gary Pittman, Clyde Agnew, Moses King, Joe Styles, Gene Seay, Steve Turner, Ray Maddux, Cris Schweer, Tom Arnholt, Mike Edwards, T. Sizemore, Dan Boe.

Texize Chemical (Greenville, S.C.), runners-up: Dan Pike (coach), Joe Brunson, Don Jackson, Lindsay Orr, Russ Hunt, Roy Simpson, Steve Dougherty, Derrick Dickey, Richard Fugua, Dwight Jones, Greg Ashorn, Allen Hornyak, Raymond Lewis, Will Robinson, Drummond, Greene, Lionel Harris.

Kenro (Atlanta, Ga.): Johnny Moon (coach), Pat Moriarty, Larry Barnett, Doug Alexander, Roy Roberts, Jimmy Pitts, Mike Dahl, William Sheats, Ken Griffith, Roger McDowell, Richie Mahaffey, John Fraley, White, Shufelt.

Atlanta Satellites (Atlanta, Ga.): James Haines (coach), Pritchett, Doctor, Strafler, Hillary, Haines, Thomas, Cofield.

Decorative Components (Forest City, N.C.): Howard White (coach), David Whitener, Wilson Scott, David Wyscarver, Al Graves, Ken Napier, Mike McDowell, John Drew, Billy Willis, Alex Hamilton, Randy Wesley, Harris, Wooland.

S.C. All Stars (Columbia, S.C.): Bobby Cremins (coach), Skip Harlicka, Corky Carnevale, Bobby Carver, Rick Adylett, Skip Kickey, Lynn Burkholder, Bill Walsh, Orr, Powell, Kickey, Clark, Weston.

Young-Love Fabrics (Charlotte, N.C.): Jerry Brock (coach), David Angel, Bo Hawkins, Anthony Brown, Buddy Martin, Mel Francisco, Danny Miller, Ray Loucks, Doug Lowe, Steve Crowe, Fred Melson, Horton, E. Gilstrap, R. Gilstrap, Bray.

Veeder-Root (Greenville, S.C.): Brian Dickens (coach), Barry Isom, Ric Butner, Charles Hughston, Rex Gregg, Joseph Bethea, James Clark, Jackie Boyd, Donald Davis, Goley, Gustafson.

CLASS A MEN

Russell Manufacturing (Alexander City, Ala.), champions: Vercho Carter (coach), Chester Parks (coach), Mike Hearn, Dewey

Sanders, Arthur Hicks, Thomas Boyd, Owen Butts, Calvin Tuck, Jimmy Boleware, Randy Adair, Freddie Martin, A.J. Jones, C. Tuck.

Rohm-Haas (Fayetteville, N.C.), runners-up: Pete Carlisle (coach), Larry Bass, Charles Carlisle, Michael Brown, Kenneth Hoffman, James Kelly, Cleo Dawson, Bernard Richardson, Calvin Graham, Charlie Williams, Wendell Brady.

Madison Throwing Co. (Madison, N.C.), consolation winners: Glenn Ogburn (coach), Harold Parker, Robert Lowe, Doug Pickard, Eddie Adams, James Moore, Jeff Loftis, Donnie Ellis, Brian Manuel, Robert Hughes.

Borden Mill (Kingsport, Tenn.): Mack Isner (coach), Dutter Wallen, Gary Alvis, Lewis Walters, Larry Page, J.W. Carpenter, Michael Luster, Mark Jones, John Barker, Christopher Crews, Calhoun.

Monaghan Mill (Greenville, S.C.): Bill Swaynghame (coach), Terry Fowler, Jim Holden, Bill Phillips, Barry Alexander, Horace Anderson, Jeff Bishop, Eddie Keeler, Eddie Leamon, Hugh Hurley, Dean Holtzclaw, Watson.

Taylors Mill (Taylors, S.C.): Steve Brown (coach), Steven Moore, Michael Gravley, Leon Gravley, Steve Autrey, Elbert Coker, James Davidson Jr., Norman Howard, James Mahaffey, Randall Ponder, Troy Roberson, Jimmy Williams.

Fiber Industries (Greenville, S.C.): Ken Childers (coach), Paul Pritchett, Robert Hargett, Herman Evatt, Vernon McMakin, Steve Barton, Walter Bubley Jr., Calvin Carter, Timothy Howell, Donald Hughes, Ronald Putman.

Fiber Processing (Greenville, S.C.): Lee Brown, J.L. Looper, Lewis, Burnette, Nathaniel Makin, Humbert, Dennis Hicks, Joel Williams.

Pelzer Mill (Pelzer, S.C.): James Thomason (coach), Bill Harris, Raymond Rochester, William Adams, Benny Garrett, Jimmy Hopkins, Tommy Reeder, Eddie Saylors, Phil Hopkins, Buster Wooten, James Duncan, Charlie Adams, Ellenburg.

General Electric (Greenville, S.C.): Donnie Foster (coach), Ray Brewer, Skeeter Hammett, Charles Breazeale, Charles Wallace, William Payne, Donnie Foster, Jim Chapman, Jeff Ware, Donald Smith, Gerald Gambrell.

Southern Bell (Greenville, S.C.): William Cartee (coach), E. Cheek (coach), Richard Strickland, Donald Bridges, Clifton Baxter, Donald Evans, Tommy Keesley, John Strickland, Charles Frazier, Herman Roberts Jr., Jimmy Wilson, Stanley Wilson.

E-Systems Inc. (Greenville, S.C.): J.A. Ellenburg (coach), Joe Haynes, Johnny Ehrlich, Johnny Hunter, Jimmy Lollis, Jerry Davis, Russell Whitley, Charles Ashworth, Williams, Todd.

Phillips Fibers (Spartanburg, S.C.): Nathaniel McSwain (coach), Alonzo Briggs, Wade Corley, Charles Cuff, Maxie Elliott, Raymond Gist, Tony Henderson, Lewis Jeter, Larry Parham, James Porter, Joe Walker, Dennis White, Luther Wilkins.

Clark-Schwebel (Anderson, S.C.): Johnny Corn (coach), Henry Richardson, Joe Richardson, Eddie Bryant, Doug Rumsey, James Day, Mike Raines, E.F. Patterson, Gary Grant, Douglas Huchin, John Corn, Willingham.

Singer Mfg. (Pickens, S.C.): David Breazeale (coach), Timothy Looper, Larry Davis, James Kelsey, Mason Taylor, John Bolding, Daniel Byers, David Byers, Robert Bolding, Michael McCoy.

Dunean Mill (Greenville, S.C.): Doug Gailey (coach), James McDonald, Ray Gosnell, Emzie Smith, Furman Gatewood, Larry Cummings, Joe Marion, James Bagwell, Robert Mangrum, Charles Caldwell, Roger Muckenfuss.

Daniel Construction Co. (Greenville, S.C.): Wayne Gambrell (coach), David Gambrell, William Gambrell, Danny Gambrell, Steve Brown, Ronnie Long, Robert Wagner, Frankie Williams, Howard Bryant, David Lewis, Massingale, Roddy.

Class B Men

Pelzer Mill (Pelzer, S.C.), champions: Bill Hopkins (coach), Keith Jordan, Bob Andrews, Ronnie Cobb, Edward Crawford, Ronnie Cureton, Tommy Rutledge, Butch Morton, Jimmy Wooten, Steve Horne, A. Cobb, D. Sullivan.

Sally Mill (Greenville, S.C.), runners-up: Luke Smith (coach), Joseph Smith, Danny Gray, Billy Dilworth, Jessie Smith, Anthony Kay, Leroy Arnold, Lloyd McAbee Jr., James Dilworth, Dairen Gazaway, Jerry Gray, Orr.

Dow Badische (Anderson, S.C.), consolation winners: John Warner (coach), Albert Davis, Douglas Martin, Rodney Shearouse, Sylvester Reed, Robert Waller, Richard Counts, Jamie Saville, Donald Johnson, John Warner, Don Brant.

Cryovac (Duncan, S.C.): Charles Turner

(coach), Fred Dobbins, Steve Smith, Preston Calvert, Warren Nicholson, Van VanderPloeg, Felton Walker Jr., Raymond Usilton, Richard Quinn, Mark Thornton, Jeff McConnell Jr., John Whitesides.

Fiber Industries (Greenville, S.C.): Burt Wilson (coach), Herman Alewine, Frank Armfield, Harold Boyce, David Johnson, Jerry Pritchett, Mike Reynolds, Tommie Summers, Dwight Thurman, John Williams, Robert Wilson.

Ware Shoals Mill (Ware Shoals, S.C.): Mike Abrams (coach), Joe Pitt, Joe Smith, Thomas Whatley, Kenneth Black, Bobby Ligon, Marion Lomax, Raymond Kelley, Stevie Griffith, Robert Zellars, Charles Parker.

Hoechst Celanese (Greer, S.C.): Don Smith (coach), Jimmy Bradshaw, James Holcombe, Roger Wilson, Steve Howard, Mike Hopper, Tom Young, Phillip Turner, Jerry Mansell, James Curtis, Lawrence Williams.

Sangamo Electric Co. (Pickens, S.C.): Joel Allgood (coach), Wayne Nicholson, Sammy Nix, Lewis Monroe, Floyd Nix, Frank Kelly, Cecil Smith, Stanley Grant, Gary Clark, Basil Trotter, Jim McCall, Bagwell, Lappin.

Pratt-Read (Central, S.C.): Ronnie Hughes (coach), Woody Comstock (coach), Charles Gillespie, Lynn Greenlee, Gene Johnson, Mickey Owens, Randy Fowler, John Sullivan, Donald Brown, Tom Sparacino, Charles Freeman, Norris, J. Gillespie.

Precise Machine Works (Simpsonville, S.C.): Larry Thackston (coach), Eddie Huff, Steve Mahon, Calvin Milam, Mitchell Burns, Matthew Milam, Theodore Pinson, Steve Maness, James Sullivan, Bobby Phelps, David King.

Easley Mill (Easley, S.C.): Johnny Skinner (coach), James Lackey, Jerry Brock, Charles Chambers, Michael Hiles, Melvin Holliday, Milton Garrison, Larry Aiken, Stanley Bagwell, Kenneth Nichols, Larry Pegg.

Saco-Lowell (Easley, S.C.): Joe Garrett (coach), Jim Carter (ass't coach), Charles Hall, Herbert Bowen, Rudolph Murphy, James Bowens, Benny Richardson, Billy Campbell, Mac Trotter, William Hoisington, Robert Hoisington, Clark.

Indian Head Yarn (Greenville, S.C.): Danny Hartsell (coach), James Hartsell, Joe Anderson, Roger Dove, Bobby Cobb, James Baird, Charles Wynn, Robert Sullivan, Robert Moore, William Cooke, Stanley McKinney.

J.P. Stevens Distribution (Greenville, S.C.): Ray Foxx (coach), Herman McCullough, James Alexander, William Alexander, James McGee, Bill McKee, Ron Amrine, Harold Alexander, Ricky Bagwell, Ricky Johnson, Lewis Richardson, Ronald Nunn, Rollins.

L.S. Green (Mauldin, S.C.): Jim Smith (coach), John Henry, Sam Green, James Hill, Welford Anderson, Gary Turner, John Turner, Bobby Canada, John Revis, Don Tucker, Jerry Balcombe, Mitchell.

Homelite (Greer, S.C.): Pat Farmer (coach), James Griffin, Doyle Howard, Willie Gibbs, Thomas McCrary, Gregory Knuckles, Lee Cox, Larry Anderson, William Horton, Jimmie Bruton, Robert Sanders.

Sullivan Hardware (Anderson, S.C.): Jimmy Brown (coach), Johnny Hughes, Jackie Henderson, Tim McCarson, Roger Evans, James Keith, James Smith, Steven Griffin, Barry Bridges, James Davis, Joel Cisson.

Slater Mill (Slater, S.C.): Richard Payne (coach), Scott Adkins, Marvin Suddeth, J.H. Bowles, James Wood, Terry Hightower, Jerry Hightower, Jimmy Cruell, Teddy Cashion, Wylie Hadaway, Keith Lyerly, R. Williams, Hawkins, Parnell, Mackey, M. Williams.

Brookline Carpets (Greenville, S.C.): Rich Cooper (coach), Robert Staley, Dal McGill, Leslie Williams, Michael Fowler, Gary Fowler, Jim Pridmore, Thomas Sherrard, Curtis Cofield, Robert Ferguson, Mack Barber.

CLASS C MEN

Pelzer Mill #1 (Pelzer, S.C.), champions: Bill Hopkins (coach), Jimmy Hopkins (coach), Leroy Cherry, Charles Leslie, Henry Caldwell, Tim Turner, Kenneth Davis, Herbert Ertzminger, Nate Davis, Wilbur Corley, P.J. Baker, Alvin Holland, Rickey Lacey, Robert Henderson.

Carotell (Taylors, S.C.), runners-up: Billy Allen (coach), Jack Taylor, Tony Chibarro, Mike Yeargin, James Robinson, George Spearman, Chris Littlejohn, Doug Calvert, John Cottingham, J. Williams, Whitesides, Forrester, Cheeks, T. Williams, Sanders.

Jackson Mill (Iva, S.C.), consolation winners: Alan Charney (coach), Steve Epstein, Willie Hunter, Ernest Wansley, Roy Anderson, Wallace Richardson, John Campbell, Willie Holloway, Ralph Martin, Phil Oakes, Jeffrey Charney, Hull, Jones.

Martin Printing Co. (Greenville, S.C.):

Harvey Forrester (coach), Joyce Forrester (coach), Butch Forrester, Gary Wooten, Wayne Wooten, Randy Batson, Daniel Carroll, Sid Major, Walter Harrison, Randall Harrison, William Campbell, Ted Allen, Brown, Laws, Alberts.

John Perkins Industries (Greenville, S.C.): Jerry Knight (coach), Tim Raines, David Stone, David Smith, Sandy Boyd, Stan Shetfall, Robbie Bell, Tim Buchanan, Beach Foster, Jeff Baty, Tim Lindler, Gilbert, Erwin.

The Tire Exchange (Greer, S.C.): Tommy Hughes (coach), Terry Moore, James Gay, Rodney Austin, George Spearman, Anthony Crossland, Greg Dobson, Heyward Duncan, Tommy Kay, Steve Gibbs.

Piedmont Mill (Piedmont, S.C.): David Fowler (coach), Mike Daisley, Eddie Smith, Barry Pruitt, Steve Francis, Garry Arnold, Powers Hunt, Joseph Berkowitz, Edward Stall, Charles Cook, Brent Cathcart, Cobb.

Saco-Lowell (Easley, S.C.): David Watson (coach), Jimmy Parham, Robert Riegel, Glenn Chavis, James Jones, Thomas Hunter, Kevin Malcolm, Reuben Asbury, Jerry Blair, Walter Parham, Greg Greiner, Kitterman, Freeman, Riegel.

Piedmont Industries (Greenville, S.C.): Kerry Edmonds, Mike Miller, Ayers, Powers, Harry McQuage, Morrow, Jennings, Impson, Summer, Teague.

Lebanon (Pendleton, S.C.): Cartee, Malone, Gambrell, P. Williams, C. Williams, Martin, Davis, Smith, Whitfield, Poore.

Precise Machine Works (Simpsonville, S.C.): Charles Huff Jr. (coach), Michael Davis, Willie Harris, Richard Henry, Albert Goldsmith, Walker Harris, Waymon Simpson, David Bayel, Matthew Gray, Bob Kenny, Terry Bugrschutt, Boyd, Pinson, Anderson, Sullivan.

Pelzer Mill #2 (Pelzer, S.C.): (coach), Billy Burns, Harold Thomason, Ronnie Cooley, Frank Woodcock, Tommy Hopkins, Steve Robinson, Jimmy Harrison, Phil Smith, Doug Austin, Talmon Harrison, Danny Fennell, Chunk Burns, Bobby Reeves, Donnie Thomason, Ragsdale.

Southern Filters (Greenville, S.C.): George Harrison (coach), Terry Stokes, Marshall Mattress, Kenneth Gaskill, Cedric Williams, Damon McCauley, Alvin Holland, Ricky Lacy, Fred Gregg, Rick Owen, Odis Rhodes, Greene, Ellenburg, Langston, Harrison.

Ross Tire (Greenville, S.C.): Wayne Evatt (coach), Mark Eoute, James Eoute, William Dogan, James Shields, Robert Burton, Robert Tolbert, John Byrd, Anthony Rucker, Richard Harris, Joey Franklin, Turner, Geyer, Youngblood.

Sally Mill (Greenville, S.C.): John Buchanan (coach), Robert Buchanan, John Buchanan Jr., Ricky Foster, Larry Arnold, Freddie McAbee, David Childs, James Moore, Charles Turner, Mike Nix, Steve Adams, Paul Watts Jr., Kenneth Chandler, Montieth.

Jet Brew (Greenville, S.C.): Lamar Chester (coach), Barry Bowling, Joe Gaines, Ronnie Grant, Tim Kasther, David Leonard, Ricky Lowry, Jerry Phillips, Mike Sullivan, Mike van Gieson, Mike Watts, Pepper, Hamby.

Carter & Crawley (Greenville, S.C.): F.B. Millwood (coach), David Helton, Jim Camden, Jim Riddlehover, Rick Eichelberger, Mike Yeargin, Bruce Martin, D. Hailstock, T. Campbell, Brother Choice, Marcus Rosemond, Wakefield, Doug Dukes, Valentine.

CLASS A WOMEN

Appleton Mill (Anderson, S.C.), champions: Annie Tribble (coach), Linda Bolick, Jackie Brady, Sherry Bridges, Sherry Caldwell, Susan Gruber, Jane Jones, Donna Kay, Janie Lee, Susan Milford, Brenda Paulk, Betty Shell, Mary Tindal, Doll Eadson, Vickie Burton, Janie Hare, Beth Yarborough.

Ware Shoals Mill (Ware Shoals, S.C.), runners-up: Ann Simmons, Nena Simmons, Vinson, Sirt, Jenny White, Diane Davenport, Ezell, Henderson, Riley, Long.

Slater Mill (Slater, S.C.), consolation winners: Bobby Kirby (coach), Joan Kirby, Dotty Pierce, Susan Moon, Regina Gilstrap, Loretta Daniel, Teresa Farmer, Debbie Garrett, Jennie Lyerly, Debbie Daniel, Karen Dalton, Debbie Oliver, Grace Lyle, Gayle Hull, Pam Adams, Nanney, Cook, Brown.

Discount Fence Co. (Winston-Salem, N.C.): Jerry Holt (coach), Nancy Formo, Linda Smith, Candy Newsome, Patsy Sebastian, Carole Hutchins, Brenda Wooten, Ann Hester, Sue Frye, Debbie Kiger, Issy Gardner, Ann Willis, Gina Hill, Faye Sapp, Jean Westmoreland, Tuelsome, Chastain, Nelson, Hold.

Texize Chemical (Greenville, S.C.): Ted Hillhouse (coach), Frances Hillhouse, Judy Murray, Marian Brewer, Patsy Neal, Emma Howard, Lucy Walters, Reba Lowe, Marty Vaughan, Doris Plemmons, Debbie Rogers,

Janie Ingle, Jennie Norris, Lelia Vaughn, Cathy Hayes, Nan Archibald, Lowe, Cothran.

Lyman Mill (Lyman, S.C.): Paul Culbreth (coach), Linda Roberson, Vennie Rogers, Brenda DeYoung, Lauren Murphy, Bonnie Moore, Diane Ayers, Debbie Smith, Glenda Bullard, Lisa Campbell, Marian Satterfield, Marcia Horne, Cheryl Fowler, Beth Bishop, Gardinia Rogers, Brenda Pearson, Cathy Walker.

Kenro (Atlanta, Ga.): Johnny Moon (coach), Dolores Owen, Vera Garrett, Annette Hammock, Edwina Bryan, Judy Bickers, Bonnie Gibson, Linda Shi, Sheila Stinchcomb, Cynthia Pue, Blunt Meadows, Barbara Perry, Nancy Fox, Jill Wolleath, Cathy Davis, Lewis.

Dunean Mill (Greenville, S.C.): Larry Ashley (coach), Bobbie Galloway, Brenda Fowler, June Jones, Peggy Owens, Rita Mantooth, Debby Vaughn, Betty Shell, Jessie Wilson, Kaye Bayne, Karen Brown, Robbie Reid, Robin Stowe, Terry Barr, N. Wilson, Roper, DeKoning.

Sangamo Electric Co. (Pickens, S.C.): Jerry Roper (coach), Deda Duncan (coach), Jackie McJunkin, Dixie Duncan, Janice Chapman, Roberta James, Eleanor Lewis, Kat Laye, Jean Stone, Margaret Jones, Nancy Jones, Brenda Garren, Teresa Rhone, Karen Perry, Reva Watts, Linda Clark, Mary Gillespie, Frances Bostic, Pace, Kelly, Robbins, Gantt, Warren.

Adams Real Estate (North Charleston, S.C.): Bobby Turner (coach), Velda Runey, Ann Turner, Jeanene Batten, Barbara O'Quinn, Jeannette Berry, Kay Bennett, Maureen Cobb, Pattie Gainey, Charlotte McDaniel, Elaine McMahon, Sharon Marlowe, Joyce Matthews, Karen Stokes, Candy Turner, Beth Wiggins.

Pelzer Mill (Pelzer, S.C.): Bill Hopkins (coach), Barbara Bell, Marsha Ross, Joann Waters, Jane Hawkins, Cheryl Martin, Kathy Graham, Betty Fite, Kitsy Curnou, Debbie Bowers, Nancy Baxter, Linda Ford, Barbara Ledford, Lynn Rogers, Reba Woodson, Bonnie West.

Baxter-Kelly-Faust Co. (Anderson, S.C.): Carl Patterson (coach), Sherry Edmonds, Rachelle Propp, Sarah Wilson, Susan Penn, Diane Brock, Pam Konduras, Lynn Armstrong, Bess Watson, Elizabeth Gable, Cile Cromer, Penelope Scott, Mary Hanvey, Jeanie Mandrell, Sherry Patterson, Jackie Keasler, Cothran, Trotter, Brock.

Saco-Lowell (Easley, S.C.): Whelan, Kim Basinger, Crenshaw, Hooper, Smith, Byrd, Rampey, Wallen, Kay, Ramsey, Findley, Thompson, McKnight.

Greenville Tec (Greenville, S.C.): Randy LaFoy (coach), Peggy Davenport, Bonnie Tuten, Karen Evans, Bobo Theodore, Frances Brooks, Debbie Traynham, Teresa Ludwig, Martha Porter, Laura Carhway, Teresa Owens, Howard, Smith, Few.

Fiber Industries (Greenville, S.C.): Vicki Byers (coach), Evelyn Goldsmith, Barbara Goldsmith, Margaret Simmons, Diane Simmons, Sharon Hicks, Margaret Ray, Jan Marbert, Eliza Harris, Linda Brooks, Joyce Brooks, Diane Solesbee, McCarroll, Allgood, Hunt, Jenkins, Watson.

———— 1974 ————

Officers: Fred Powers (Charlotte, N.C.), President; Ken Pittman (Greenville, S.C.), 1st Vice President; D.K. Smith (Lyman, S.C.), 2nd Vice President; James Morrow (Greenville, S.C.), 3rd Vice President; Harry Foster (Greenville, S.C.), Treasurer; Fred Byrd (Greenville, S.C.), Executive Secretary; Frances Welborn, Ass't Executive Secretary; Whitey Kendall (Greenville), Supervisor of Officials; Lt. F.R. Hawkins, Security Officer.

Executive Committee: Clarence Thomas (Greenville, S.C.), Willie Wilbanks (Greenwood, S.C.), Curtis Terry (Piedmont, S.C.), Willard Fowler (Greenville, S.C.), Dan Foster (Greenville, S.C.), Snow Kirby (Marietta, S.C.), Bill Hopkins (Pelzer, S.C.), Lloyd McAbee (Greenville, S.C.), Joe Newton (Greenville, S.C.), Henry Spake (Anderson, S.C.), Ward Williams (Greenville, S.C.), Earl Wooten (Piedmont, S.C.), Vercho Carter (Alexander City, Ala.), Phil Clark (Greer, S.C.), Patsy Neal (Brevard, N.C.), Divver Hendrix (Greenville, S.C.), Ruppert Elliott (Greenville, S.C.), Phil Harley (Greenville, S.C.), Larry Ashley (Greenville, S.C.), Charles Rogers (Salem, S.C.).

OPEN DIVISION

Transit Homes (Greenville, S.C.), champions: Ruppert Elliott (coach), Stan Elrod, Gene Seay, Tom Arnholt, Terry Compton, Bill Ligon, Lee Fowler, Bob Chess, R. Rucker, E. Kelly, G. Clark, B. Bierly, L. Doyle, Davis, Armentrout, Capps.

Pittman's Textile Machinery (Greenville, S.C.), runners-up: Broadus Miller (coach), Tommy Whitten, Gary Pittman, Clyde Agnew, Moses King, Mark Tracy, Danny Ballard, Randy Dickens, Randy Miller, Tommy Neal, Larry Weaver, Jiff Boyce, George Hester, Charles Crawford.

Young-Love Fabrics (Charlotte, N.C.): Jerry Brock (coach), Steve Crowe, Fred Melson, Joe Bridges, Jeff Reisinger, Terrell Suitt, Jive Brown, Butch Zatazelo, Randy Bray, Earl Gilstrap, Rick Gilstrap, Isom.

Varinit (Greenville, S.C.): Smith Danielson, Robert Smith, Nixon Allen, Brooks, Ballenger, Jones, Pruitt, Evans, Scales, M. Smith.

Piedmont Sheet Metal (Winston-Salem, N.C.): Jerry Holt (coach), Larry Hobegger, Rich Hobegger, Bill Cobb, John Lewkowicz, Gore Nelson, Mike Dickie, Jack Ballanger, Tommy Halley, Larry Richardson, Perea.

Castings Inc. (Greenville, S.C.): David Wyscarver (coach), Larry Davis, Jerry Shoenfelt, Billy Willis, Dennis Childress, Bob Willard, Jerry Barnett, Alex Booker, Lee.

Drummond Oil Co. (Greenwood, S.C.): Bill Scurry (coach), Terry Adkins, Ralph Logan, Jeff May, Cleo Morris, Robert White, Richard Todd, Greg Robinson, Edward White, Arthur Kemp, Buddy Nelson.

Jackson Five (Columbia, S.C.): Jim Jackson (coach), Larry Jacobs (coach), Danny Traylor, Sam Goodwin, Charlie Powell, Charlie Weston, Dick Penrod, Larry Martin, Jimmy Collins, John Kirkland, George Glymph, Wise, Joe Brunson.

Class A Men

Rohm-Haas (Fayetteville, N.C.), champions: Pete Carlisle (coach), Larry Bass, Mike Brown, Kenneth Hoffman, Bernard Richardson, Wendell Brady, Ivey Bryant, Lucius Daye, Willie Bethea, Terrence Murchinson.

Lyman Mill (Lyman, S.C.), runners-up: Sammy Simpson (coach), James Graham, Ralph Murphy, Charles Robinson, Clarence Moody Jr., Raymond Glenn, Henry Baker, Johnny Miller, Willie Jones, Calvin McGee, Michael Meadows.

Daniel Construction Co. (Greenville, S.C.), consolation winners: Wayne Gambrell (coach), David Gambrell, William Gambrell, Danny Gambrell, Steve Brown, Ronnie Long, James Freeman, Terry Allen, Ricky Harris, Roger Massengale.

Borden Mill (Kingsport, Tenn.): J.W. Carpenter (coach), J.G. Collier III (coach), Duffer Wallen, Gary Alvis, Lewis Walters, Larry Page, Michael Luster, Johnny Clark, Butch Perry, Tim Grant, Keith Ervin, Danny Hammonds, Dukes, J. Bryant, Locke.

Monaghan Mill (Greenville, S.C.): Bill Swaynghame (coach), Terry Fowler, Bill Phillips, Barry Alexander, Horace Anderson, Eddie Keeler, Eddie Leamon, Eugene Jackson Jr., Billy Chapman, Danny Curtis, John Ward, Gibson.

Taylors Mill (Taylors, S.C.): Leon Gravley (coach), Steven Moore, Luther Autrey, Troy Roberson, Bill Garraux, Jacob Smith, Donald McCarter, Bobby Mattress, Howard Sturgill, Donald Fuller.

Fiber Industries (Greenville, S.C.): Ken Childers (coach), Phil Harley (ass't coach), Robert Hargett, Herman Evatt, Paul Pritchett, Vernon McMakin, Steve Barton, Calvin Carter, Timothy Howell, Donald Hughes, Heyward Leake, Mickey Stepp.

Pelzer Mill (Pelzer, S.C.): Bill Harris (coach), Jimmy Wooten, Tommy Rutledge, Buster Wooten, James Duncan, Mitchell McKee, Edward Crawford, Keith Jordan, Ronnie Cureton, Ronnie Cobb, Steve Horne, Bubba Holloway, Jerry Riddle, Adams, Sullivan, Rochester.

General Electric (Greenville, S.C.): Donnie Foster (coach), Skeeter Hammett, Charles Breazeale, Charles Wallace, Jeff Ware, Gerald Harvey, John Alexander, Calvin Johnson, Kevin Casey, Tim McGrath, John Clinkscales.

Clark-Schwebel (Anderson, S.C.): Johnny Corn (coach), Joe Richardson, James Day, Mike Raines, William Gray Jr., Douglas McRumsey, Ronald Gilstrap, Dorsey, Hanks.

Singer Mfg. (Pickens, S.C.): Pat Kelsey (coach), Timothy Looper, Larry Davis, James Kelsey, Mason Taylor, Wesley Bolding, David Day, James Sumney, Stanley Williams, Russell Roper, Joseph Kelly.

Hoechst Celanese (Greer, S.C.): Don Smith (coach), Lawrence Williams, Verdell Richardson, Michael Hopper, Roger Wilson, Jimmy Bradshaw, Don Smith, James Holcombe, Grover Anderson, Marvin Drummond, Ronnie Murray.

Southern Bell (Greenville, S.C.): Bridges, J. Wilson, S. Wilson, Roberts, Evans, Baxter, Strickland, R. Strickland, Earl, Campbell.

Greenville County (Greenville, S.C.): Bagwell, Edwards, Smith, Arms, Sullivan, Carter, V. Williams, Jenkins, T. Williams, Davis.

Class B Men

Cryovac (Simpsonville, S.C.), champions: Larry Thackston (coach), Jim Holcombe (coach), James Sullivan, Fred Hill, Harold Wright, Bobby Phelps, Andy Roberson, Jimmy Wright, Calvin Milam, Jim Floyd, David Buchanan, Matthew Milam, Rex Abercrombie, Lewis Whitmire.

Brookline Carpets (Greenville, S.C.), runners-up: Steve Dougherty (coach), Robert Staley, Dal McGill, Leslie Williams, Michael Fowler, Gary Fowler, Thomas Sherrard, Robert Ferguson, Wilbert Robinson, David McKinney, Gene Ballentine, Charles Edens, Carlton Fisher.

Dow Badische #1 (Anderson, S.C.), consolation winners: Jimmy Belton (coach), Douglas Martin, Sylvester Reed, Jamie Saville, Clark Lee, Jay Agnew, Wallace Richardson, James Gray, Emerson Cooley, Lester Garrison, Robertson, Hardee.

Sally Mill (Greenville, S.C.): Luke Smith (coach), William Dilworth, Anthony Kay, Leroy Arnold, Lloyd McAbee Jr., James Dilworth, Michael Brown, Billy Bailey, David Childs, Johnny Buchanan, Fred Dilworth, Turner.

Pelzer Mill (Pelzer, S.C.): James Thomason (coach), Ronnie Cooley, Tommy Hopkins, Steve Robinson, Doug Austin, James Rucker, Roger Scott, Billy Burns, Harold Thomason, Allen Hendrix, McKee, Duncan.

Fiber Industries (Greenville, S.C.): J.C. Starkes (coach), Herman Alewine, Frank Armfield, David Johnson, Jerry Pritchett, Dwight Thurman, John Edmonds, Bernard Dawkins, Larry Dogan, James Hailstock, Joseph Phelps.

Ware Shoals Mill (Ware Shoals, S.C.): Mike Abrams (coach), Joe Pitt, Willie Smith, Thomas Whatley, Bobby Ligon, Marion Lomax, Steve Griffith, Charles Parker, James Whatley, Roy Whatley, Douglas Knight.

Hoechst Celanese (Greer, S.C.): Don Smith (coach), James Curtis, Richard Justice Jr., Thurmond Blackwell, James Thurmond, William Ballenger, Willie Gibbs, Larry Barnes, Andrew Houck, William Koon, Steve Merchant, Brock.

Sangamo Electric Co. (Pickens, S.C.): Joel Allgood (coach), Sammy Nix, Floyd Nix, Cecil Smith, Billy Looper, Johnny Chandler, David Watson, Steve Anderson, Robert Porter, Larry Stewart, Robert Cannon, Lowery.

Pratt-Read (Central, S.C.): Charles Gillespie (coach), Randall Johnson, Mickey Owens, Bobby Fowler, John Williams, Willie Norris, William Fowler, Patrick O'Dell, Lee, Jarrell, Hiawatha Hudson, Lonnie Gillespie.

Easley Mill (Easley, S.C.): Ronnie Lackey (coach), James Hallums, Jerry Lockaby, Mickey Holliday, Milton Garrison, Robert Pearson, Billy Cureton, Terry Stokes, Walter Bolden, John Williams, Franklin Turner.

Saco-Lowell (Easley, S.C.): Mack Trotter (coach), Charles Gillespie, Herbert Bowen, James Allen, William Hoisington, Dan Benfield, Calvin Clarke, Johnny Coleman, Ricky Cuddy, Edward Dobbins, Johnny White.

Dow Badische #2 (Anderson, S.C.): Jimmy Blanding (coach), Calvin Hunter, Jerome Blackwell, Freddy Banks, William Smith, Lawrence Green, Harry Reed, Charlie Lowe, Donald Brant, Jay Cooley, Frank Sims.

Indian Head Yarn (Greenville, S.C.): Danny Hartsell (coach), James Hartsell, Roger Dove, James Baird, Charles Wynn, Robert Moore, William Cooke, Governor Chancellor, James Chappelle, Luther McNeil, Jimmy Mattison, Cobb.

Cryovac (Duncan, S.C.): Van VanderPloeg (coach), Fred Dobbins, Steve Smith, Preston Calvert, Warren Nicholson, Felton Walker Jr., Mark Thornton, John Whitesides, Len Byrne, Bill Friddle, Charles Baine, Fred Stephens, Terry Taylor, Springle.

J.P. Stevens Distribution (Greenville, S.C.): Bill Alexander (coach), Herman McCullough, James Alexander, William Alexander, James Thomason, Harold Alexander, Michael Hendrickson, Edward Williams, Charles Riser, Clyde Herron, George Abercrombie.

Sullivan Hardware (Anderson, S.C.): Johnny Hughes (coach), Roger Evans, Keith Griffin, James Benoit, Scotty Cisson, Johnny Hughes, Ronnie Smith, William Gault, Tom Owens, Alan Calloway, Johnell Byars.

Bigelow-Sanford (Calhoun Falls, S.C.): John Earl (coach), Thomas Earl, John Smith, Clarence Sullivan, James Bryson, John Earl Jr., Richard Henry, Willie Teague, Robert Smith, Michael Banks, Donnie Anders.

Castings Inc. (Greenville, S.C.): Tony Robertson (coach), James Bell Jr., John Stephens, Darren Gazaway, Jackie Chambers,

Dennis Jones, Stanley Edwards, Willie Leonard, Jerrel Bolt, Anthony Bolt, Melvin Bolt.

Slater Mill (Slater, S.C.): Richard Payne (coach), James Wood, Steve Parnell, Marvin Suddeth, Teddy Cashion, Jimmy Cruell, J.H. Bowles, Raymond Williams, Butch Cox, Eddie Askew, J. Hightower, T. Hightower, C. Parnell, Shivers, M. Williams, T. Parnell.

Appleton Mill (Anderson, S.C.): James Savage, Phillip Holcombe, Gary Grant, Jesse Robinson, Andy Wooten, Terry Bailey, G.C. Stewart, John Barker, Farris Bailey, Tommy Gillespie, Ligon, Brock.

Galloway Upholstery (Piedmont, S.C.): Wayne Merritt (coach), Frank Merritt, Joe Mitchell, Robert Gravley, Robert Gilreath, Ricky Galloway, Bryan Culbertson, Chuck Lollis, Roger Hudgens, Al Impson, Keith Morton, Moore, White.

Dunean Mill (Greenville, S.C.): Doug Gailey (coach), James Wardlaw, Charles Brown, Dale Owens, Frank Holcombe, Ernest Kinard, John Jones, Dan Donald, Gene Elledge, Stan Cook, J.D. Jones.

CLASS C MEN

Pelzer Mill #2 (Pelzer, S.C.), champions: Jimmy Hopkins (coach), Rickey Lacey, Robert Henderson, Mark Shafir, Colon Abraham, Goley Augustus, Gregory Arceneaux, Whitt Plyer, Phil Oates, Gregory Jett, Ed Greer, Ray Holliday, George Watts, Willie Crumpton, Steve Ashe, Donnie Thompson, Donnie Tyler.

Saco-Lowell (Easley, S.C.), runners-up: Jack Brooks (coach), Arthur Ellenburg, Danny Jackson, George Harrison, Odis Rhodes, Marhall Mattress, Cedric Williams, Wayne Gaskill, Ricky Foster, Terry Gettys, Maurice Snipes, William Graham, Todd, Green.

Fairhaven Mill (Pickens, S.C.), consolation winners: Terry Hallums, Marcus Rosemond, Garland Dukes, Dannie Hendricks, Odis Rhodes, Reggie Cox, John Hendricks, Ronnie Anderson, Zion McKinney, Carl Valentine, D.D. Hendricks.

Pelzer Mill #3 (Pelzer, S.C.): Bill Hopkins (coach), Richard Reid, Grover Slade, Jeffrey Tate, George E. Turman, George W. Turman, Joe Hagood Jr., Randy Benton, Russell Jewell, William McNeely, Turner, Evans, Williams.

Carotell (Taylors, S.C.): Billy Allen (coach), Jack Taylor, Tony Chibarro, Mike Yeargin, David Sullivan, Prince Phelps, Greg Dobson, Jerome Williams, Oliver, Mooney, Mabry.

Piedmont Mill (Piedmont, S.C.): Charles Davis (coach), Andy Anderson, Al Bannister, John Pack, Paul Cagle, Terry Chastain, Doug Brown, Norman Wynn, Clifford Anders, Chuck Davis, Impson, Hudgens.

Pelzer Mill #1 (Pelzer, S.C.): Dan Ragsdale (coach), David Burns, Ronnie Creamer, Jimmy Harrison, Phil Smith, Doug Smith, Ray Holliday, Keith Ragsdale, Donnie Creamer, Buddy Kirby, Tony Tice, Jackie Lunsford.

Martin Printing Co. (Greenville, S.C.): Harvey Forrester (coach), Frank Cole (coach), Butch Forrester, William Campbell, Gregory Greiner, Mike Chibarro, James Kammer, James Wilkie Jr., Gil Gaillard, R.C. Bransford, Randy Benton, John Estes, Gilstrap.

Ross Tire (Greenville, S.C.): Wayne Evatt (coach), Mark Eoute, William Dogan, James Perkins, Robert Burton, John Byrd, Anthony Rucker, Reggie Harris, Richard Dubose, Lee Kennedy, Doyle Green, Eddie Young, Mansfield Golden, Harris.

Saco-Lowell #2 (Easley, S.C.): David Watson (coach), Glenn Chavis, James Christopher, John Hall, Robert Henderson, Jerry Hunt, Thomas Hunter, Timothy Jones, Louie King, Stephen Kitterman, Kevin Malcolm, Mike Daisley, Parham.

O'Kelley Textile Machine (Greenville, S.C.): Fred McAbee (coach), Rick Robertson, Charles Lipscomb, Charles Pinson, Melborn Redick, John Lay, Jimmie Marion, Dale Nash, Mike Jordan, McAbee.

Fisk-Carter (Greenville, S.C.): John Raines (coach), Barry Wilder, Rusty Dimsdale, Wayne White, Randy Batson, Daniel Carroll, Sid Major, Terry Raines, Greg Hensley, Wayne Wooten, Edward Morgan, Douglas Henson, Burns, Terry Freeman.

Dill's Warehouse (Greenville, S.C.): Curt Davis (coach), Olin Laws, Daryl Wilder, Michael Sullivan, James Camden, William Dendy, L.S. Ridlehoover, Hugh Dill, William Wakefield, Terry Wilder, Tony Lanford.

Varinit (Greenville, S.C.): Jerry Knight (coach), Barry Pruitt, David Stone, Don Shirley, Tim Lindler, David Miles, Glenn Mosely, Doug Shaw, Tim Raines, Pollock, Couch, Gilbert, Evans.

Duncan Pontiac (Greenville, S.C.): Garren Hughes (coach), Ronnie Garren, Anthony Crossland, Heyward Duncan, George Spear-

Southern Textile Basketball Tournament Rosters Appendix 1 263

man, Gary Harris, Curtis Jones, Leroy Lane, Rodney Austin, Mark Thornton, Rayburn, Brannon.

Beaunit (Fountain Inn, S.C.): Donny Bolton (coach), Steve Mahon (coach), Walker Harris, Willie Harris, Albert Goldsmith, Roger Sullivan, Bob Kenney, Avery Smith, Vernon Johnson, Haskel Huff, Sylvester Dennis, Tony Madden.

Bethlehem Center (Spartanburg, S.C.): James Greer (coach), George Lynch, Richard Lann, Thomas Nash, Grover Salters, Ralph Legg, Raymond Pitts, Terry Free, Lonnie Brannon, Terry Brannon, Draper.

Pete's Drive-In (Greenville, S.C.): Charles Roddy (coach), Richard Lowery, Barry Bowling, Melvin Coley, William Pitts, Joseph Turner, Robert Gaines, Ted Pittman, Charles Leaman, Door, Jones, Payne.

Jiffie Jonnie (Greenville, S.C.): Gus Rubio, Jerome Williams, Charles Pulaine, Barry Dorr, Edward Robinson, Benjamin Griffin, Douglas Jones, Larry Hall, Roy Brewer, V.K. McTeer, Steven Rodberg, Roger Crecall, Brown, Whitfield, Vernon.

Piedmont Industries (Greenville, S.C.): Arch Fowler (coach), Henry McQuage, Doug Jennings, Freddie Powers, Mike Miller, Fred Sullivan, Ansel Gilbreath, Dill Gause, Louie King, Kerry Edmonds, Rick Knight.

Carter & Crawley (Greenville, S.C.): Bob Raymond, Sutryk, Butter, Hobbs, Terry Freeman, Johnson, Burnette, Saunders, White, Gordon, McGowan.

Impson's (Greenville, S.C.): Lark, Andrew, Slice, Parker, Tarant, Curtis, Ballew, Monroe, Manley.

Lebanon (Pendleton, S.C.): Brue Martin, Smith, Morton, Cartee, Gambrell, Wentsky, Davis, Vernon, Burnette, Poore, Whitfield, Moore.

CLASS A WOMEN

Slater Mill (Slater, S.C.), champions: Bobby Kirby (coach), Joan Kirby, Dotty Pierce, Regina Gilstrap, Loretta Daniel, Debbie Crenshaw, Jennie Lyerly, Debbie Daniel, Karen Brown, Pam Adams, Marty Vaughn, Marian Brewer, Bonnie Whelan, Jan Rampey, Dot Clippard.

Ware Shoals Mill (Ware Shoals, S.C.), runners-up: Perry Rowland (coach), Becky Ezell, Ann Bailes, Ann Gambrell, Linda Griffin, Charlene Abercrombie, Dianne Davenport, Susan Riley, Donna Duncan, Frances Simmons, Nina Simmons, Ann Vinson, Jenny White, Boots Turner, Beth Turner, Kim Strawhorne.

Pelzer Mill (Pelzer, S.C.), consolation winners: Bill Hopkins (coach), Barbara Bell, Marsha Ross, Joann Waters, Jane Hawkins, Kathy Graham, Betty Fite, Kitsy Curnou, Debbie Bowers, Caroline Brown, Helen Williams, Mary Wooten, Amy Austin, Teresa Mays, Lee Thomason, Debbie Whitt, West, Hanks.

Greenville Tec (Greenville, S.C.): Randy LaFoy (coach), Randy Holt (coach), Peggy Jones, Bobo Theodore, Frances Brooks, Debbie Traynham, Teresa Ludwig, Laura Clark, Clare O'Connell, Brenda Marlowe, Clyo Wilson, Cindy Crenshaw, Pat Smith, Ruth Williams, Ahsmore, Irby.

Texize Chemical (Greenville, S.C.): Annie Tribble (coach), Susan Neal, Brenda Paulk, B.J. Shell, Janie Lee, Vickie Burton, Grace Lyle, Doll Eadon, Laura Lawton, Libby Mullinax, Marilyn Felkel, Dale Campbell, Sherry Caldwell, Vivian Humphries, Donna Kay, Pam Watkins.

Lyman Mill (Lyman, S.C.): Phil Childress (coach), Linda Roberson, Brenda DeYoung, Lauren Murphy, Diane Ayers, Debbie Smith, Glenda Bullard, Marcia Hains, Cheryl Fowler, Beth Bishop, Brenda Southern, Kathy Fowler, Elizabeth Nickles, Debbie Lahr, Rhonda Slatton.

Atlanta Tomboys (Atlanta, Ga.): Johnny Moon (coach), Dolores Owen, Vera Garrett, Annette Hammock, Edwina Bryan, Judy Bickers, Bonnie Gibson, Sheila Stinchcomb, Cynthia Henry, Blondine Woodard, Ann Clark, Mary Hobbs, Debbie Smith, Gwen Marlowe, Daniel, Murrell, Forrester, Pritchett, Head.

Dunean Mill (Greenville, S.C.): Larry Ashley (coach), Bobbie Galloway, Brenda Fowler, June Jones, Peggy Owens, Rita Mantooth, Debby Wyatt, Jessie Wilson, Libbie Reid, Nancy Wilson, Dot Smith, Pat Morgan, Debra Sisk, Barbie Flaspoehler, Kym Ashley, Blanton, Durham, McWhite.

Discount Fence Co. (Winston-Salem, N.C.): Jerry Holt (coach), Linda Smith, Candy Newsom, Carole Hutchins, Brenda Gaugh, Ann Hester, Issy Gardner, Brenda Wooten, Becky Williams, Martha Warner, Marty Clodfelter, Judy Davis, Judy Lockhart, Formo, Lavender.

Hanvey Construction (Anderson, S.C.): Carl Patterson (coach), Sherry Edmonds,

Rachelle Propp, Susan Penn, Pam Konduras, Lynn Armstrong, Bess Watson, Jane Hanvey, Sherry Mengis, Lynn Ivester, Lou Childress, Beverly Baker, Kathy Troutman, Sussy Proctor, April Baker, Gable.

Fiber Industries (Greenville, S.C.): David Tollison (coach), Barbara Sullivan, Margaret McAlister, Sharon Hicks, Joyce Gray, Van Booker, Sandy Duncan, Ann Ellerbe, Bonnie Hawkins, Nannie Hill, Debbie Jenkins, Barbara Johnson, Barbara Lyles, Sara Scarborough, Cathy Dowis, Ann Wood, Sutton.

Smith Brothers (Greenville, S.C.): John Deter (coach), Sharon Autrey, Becki Bagwell, Gail Blackston, Lethea Bracken, Debra Eskew, Sue Horn, Marsha Kellett, Constance Massey, Doris Mattison, Annette Merritt, Debbie Smith, Tina Toole, Tracey Tripp, Lenita Washington, Diane Limbaugh.

IMMS (Greenville, S.C.): Judy Cross (coach), Vicki Lindner, Mary Thurman, Susan Henderson, Barbara Sullivan, Cathy Dowis, Patsy Brannon, Connie McClain, Barbara Lewis, Jane Bradford, Pam Chiles, Cynthia Morant, Lois Leeson, Julie Huffstetler, Betty Sloan, Linda Walker.

Blackwell & Son Real Estate (Hanahan, S.C.): Bobby Turner (coach), Bill Stevens (coach), Ann Turner, Pattie Gainey, Sharon Marlowe, Vaidel Runey, Maureen Cobb, Cindy Hanenburger, Nancy Wilson, Nacey Payne, Dianne Wooten, Charlotte McDaniels, Smith.

Brookline Carpets (Greenville, S.C.): Ruby Jones (coach), Rosa Fowler, Debra Davis, Lucy Arnold, Cora Dickey, Betty Bearden, Andrea Callahan, J.A. Latimore, Chorice Barber, Mary O'Connell.

Community Superette (Etowah, N.C.): Patsy Neal, Judy Murray, Doris Plemmons, Lelia Vaughn, Diane Roberts, Kim Basinger, Debbie Rogers, Lisa Cochran, Pam Bostain, Cathy Daniels, Nina Timmons, Janie Hair, Sharon Boeing, Elaine Lewis, Humphrey.

Spartan Leasing (Spartanburg, S.C.): Margaret Suber, Peggy Hardin, Denise Nanney, Charlene Dubose, Porter, Carter, Wiggins, Allgood.

---------1975---------

Officers: Fred Powers (Charlotte, N.C.), President; Ken Pittman (Greenville, S.C.), 1st Vice President; James Morrow (Greenville, S.C.), 2nd Vice President; Lloyd McAbee (Greenville, S.C.), 3rd Vice President; Harry Foster (Greenville, S.C.), Treasurer; Fred Byrd (Greenville, S.C.), Executive Secretary; Frances Welborn, Ass't Executive Secretary; Whitey Kendall (Greenville), Supervisor of Officials; Lt. F.R. Hawkins, Security Officer.

Executive Committee: Clarence Thomas (Greenville, S.C.), Willie Wilbanks (Greenwood, S.C.), Curtis Terry (Piedmont, S.C.), Willard Fowler (Greenville, S.C.), Dan Foster (Greenville, S.C.), Snow Kirby (Marietta, S.C.), Bill Hopkins (Pelzer, S.C.), Joe Newton (Greenville, S.C.), Henry Spake (Anderson, S.C.), Ward Williams (Greenville, S.C.), Earl Wooten (Piedmont, S.C.), Vercho Carter (Alexander City, Ala.), Phil Clark (Greer, S.C.), Patsy Neal (Brevard, N.C.), Divver Hendrix (Greenville, S.C.), Ruppert Elliott (Greenville, S.C.), Phil Harley (Greenville, S.C.), Larry Ashley (Greenville, S.C.), Charles Rogers (Salem, S.C.), D.K. Smith (Lyman, S.C.), Lewis Golden (Greenville, S.C.).

OPEN DIVISION

Defender Chemical (Anderson, S.C.), champions: Cliff Malpass (coach), Terrill Suitt, Jeff Reisinger, Mel Francisco, Wayne Croft, Van Gregg, Marty Patterson, Gordy Bengel, Marty Jenkins, Jo Jo Bethea, John Ross, Jim Crain, Jack McGill.

Pittman's Textile Machinery (Greenville, S.C.), runners-up: Broadus Miller (coach), Tommy Whitten, Clyde Agnew, Moses King, Randy Dickens, Randy Miller, George Hester, Marion Miller, Charles Crawford, Adams, Bobby Griffin, Colie Feemster.

Drummond Oil Co. (Greenwood, S.C.): Robert White (coach), Ralph Logan, Jeff May, Robert White, William Robinson, Joe Drake, Buddy Nelson, Clinton Holloway, Carrol Timmerman, James Cowens, Oliver Pope, Roy Sander, Paul Gary, Rhodes, Taft, Shaft McMinns, Henderson.

Jackson Five (Columbia, S.C.): Jim Jackson (coach), Sam Goodwin, Charlie Powell, Larry Womack, John Kirkland, George Glymph, James Byrd, Lynn Burkholder, Gary Gregor, Skip Kickey, Skip Harlicka, Marty Woolbright, Frank Wise, Fred Melson, Mike Jacobs, Ron DeGray.

Love Joy Inc. (Greenville, S.C.): Clarence Cotton (coach), Dan Dillard, Ron Webb, Willie Anderson, Marion Reeves, Jackie Boyd,

T.C. Mattress, Charles Geer, Thomas Michael, William Moody, Ronald Harris, Louis Ashley, Dennis Cannon, Clyde Mayes, Don Jackson, Butler, Holland, Hill, Carnival.

Carolina Handling (Piedmont, S.C.): Bob Shell (coach), Lanny Taylor, Peter Reynolds, Ben Reed, Ernest Wansley, Ed Gholson, Dan McCarthy, Fred Powers, Charles Elvington, Steve Whittington, Woods, Strickland, Karlton, Hilton.

Green Creek Ruritan (Rutherfordton, N.C.): Tom Warrick (coach), Theodore Vernon, Linder Jackson, Terry Free, Cheyene Jones, Don Brahan, Charles Porter, Marshall Meadows, Glenn Williams, Jim Blanks, Ken Napier, Brooks, Dale Meadows.

Fleet Supply (Winston-Salem, N.C.): Larry Habegger (coach), Jerry Holt (coach), Bill Cobb, Rich Habegger, Mike Parrish, Eddie Payne, Tim Stare, Charlie Davis, Gil McGregor, Willie Griffin, James Williams, Jerry Gillespie, Roger Webb.

Gerald Glur Real Estate (Greenville, S.C.): Les Heicher (coach), Danny Ross, Richard Brown, Armand Curtis, Lucy Fowler, Fred Haley, Al Velchek, Tee Hooper, Richard Keir, Steve Crowe, Russ Hunt, Baron Hill, Gerald Glur, Goley.

CLASS A MEN

Daniel Construction Co. (Greenville, S.C.), champions: Gene Freeman (coach), E.A. Braham (coach), S.A. Brown, David Gambrell, Wayne Gambrell, Danny Gambrell, Larry Gambrell, Steve Brown, Steve Gambrell, Clint Turner, David Dobson, Ed Goode, Jim Greer, D. Jones, B. Watson.

Norwich Pharmacal (Greenville, S.C.), runners-up: Charles Levine (coach), Waddy Miller (ass't coach), Freddie Donalds, Jessie McCullough, James Chandler, Sam Gilliam, Tommy Rutledge, Charles Levine, Calvin Jones, Robert Murphy.

Hoechst Celanese (Greer, S.C.), consolation winners: R.M. Barras (coach), Lawrence Williams, Verdell Richardson, Roger Wilson, James Thurman, Grover Anderson, Marvin Drummond, Ronnie Murray, Gil Howarth, William Ballenger, Larry Barnes, Willie Gibbs, Bennie Foster, Bradshaw.

Lyman Mill (Lyman, S.C.): Sammy Simpson (coach), James Graham, Ralph Murphy, Charles Robinson, Clarence Moody Jr., Raymond Glenn, Johnny Miller, Willie Jones, Calvin McGee, Ernest Murray, Robert Williams.

Rohm-Haas (Fayetteville, N.C.): Pete Carlisle (coach), Larry Bass, Michael Brown, Kenneth Hoffman, Bernard Richardson, Terrence Murchinson, Clarence Rice, Milton Blue, Charles Gilmore, Kenneth McNair, Gifford Babb, Curtis Hughes.

Monaghan Mill (Greenville, S.C.): Bob Gibson (coach), Terry Fowler, Barry Alexander, Horace Anderson, Eddie Keeler, Eddie Leamon, Billy Chapman, Ronnie Ward, Edward Wilhoit, Ronnie Brown, Charles Leamon, James Ray, Phillips.

Taylors Mill (Taylors, S.C.): Leon Gravley (coach), Steven Moore, Troy Robinson, Harold Smith, Howard Sturgill, Donald Fuller, Jerry Jackson, James Meekin, Lewis Goldsmith, Evans.

Fiber Industries (Greenville, S.C.): Ken Childers (coach), Phil Harley (ass't coach), Robert Hargett, Herman Evatt, Paul Pritchett, Vernon McMakin, Steve Barton, Colvin Carter, Donald Hughes, Heyward Leake, Mickey Stepp, Roger Burton, Ronald Putman, Steve Richard, Howell.

Pelzer Mill (Pelzer, S.C.): Horace Davenport (coach), Buster Wooten, James Thomason, Edward Crawford, Keith Jordan, Ronnie Cureton, Ronnie Cobb, Bubba Holloway, Albert Hendricks, Billy Harris, Charlie Adams, Raymond Rochester.

Borden Mill (Kingsport, Tenn.): Michael Locke (coach), Duffer Warren, Larry Page, Michael Luster, Butch Perry, Keith Ervin, Danny Hammonds, Jimmy Dykes, Dwight Calhoun.

Cryovac (Simpsonville, S.C.): Jim Holcombe (coach), James Sullivan, Fred Hill, Harold Wright, Bobby Phelps, Jimmy Wright, Calvin Milam, Andy Roberson, Jim Floyd, Rex Abercrombie, John Boudoucies, Mike Styles, Mike Jenkins.

Sangamo Electric Co. (Pickens, S.C.): Hamp Summey (coach), Robert Cannon, Kenneth Tankersley, James Summey, William Fowler, Robert Davis, Doug Bagwell, Robert Parker, Peter Haley, Dwight Kelley, Frank Kelley.

CLASS B MEN

Sirrine Co. #1 (Greenville, S.C.), champions: Clark Templeton Jr. (coach), L. Yeargin (coach), Ralph Bouton, John Cooper, Mike

Yeargin, George Smith, Tom Freeland, Shelly Holiday, William Yeargin, Russell Karr, Phil Mitchell, David Martin, Bruce Martin, William Oliver, T. Templeton.

Ware Shoals Mill (Ware Shoals, S.C.), runners-up: Roosevelt Smith (coach), Willie Smith, Eddie Whatley, Bobby Ligon, Charles Parker, James Whatley, Roy Whatley, Douglas Knight, Luther Hawthorne, Willie Stewart, Willie Mathis, Darrough Aiken, Raymond Kelley, Nathaniel Lewis.

Parke-Davis (Greenwood, S.C.), consolation winners: Wilbert Harris (coach), Len White, Larry Cooper, Sammy Cooper, Curtis Cannon, Thomas Jackson, Marvin Williams, Alfred Warren, Darryl Williams, Mitchell Tolbert.

Dunean Mill #2 (Greenville, S.C.): Jimmy Riddle (coach), Andrew Carson, Wayne Robinson, David Young, Chris Taylor, Isaiah Walker Jr., Jimmy Sullivan, Charles Hudson, Howard Maddox, George Renrick, James Stewart, Richard Smith, J.D. Jones, Elledge.

Cryovac (Simpsonville, S.C.): Jim Holcombe (coach), Matthew Milam, William Ballew, Jerry Thomason, Robert Massingale, Joe Freeman, Eddie Stenhouse, David Stenhouse, Robert Gravley, Johnny Watts, Rodger Terry, James Mabry, Talmon Harrison, Crowley.

Brookline Carpets (Greenville, S.C.): Steve Dougherty (coach), Robert Staley, Leslie Williams, Michael Fowler, Gary Fowler, Thomas Sherrard, Wilbert Robinson, David McKinney, Charles Edens, Herman McCullough, Luther Johnson, Johnny Abercrombie, Roosevelt Mansell, Staton.

Pelzer Mill (Pelzer, S.C.): J.D. Whitt (coach), Ronnie Cooley, Tommy Hopkins, Steve Roberson, Doug Austin, James Duncan, Charles Burns, Harold Thomason, Donnie Bryant, Carroll Cooley, Keith Ragsdale, Rucker.

Fiber Industries (Greenville, S.C.): John Gaines (coach), Ron Putman (coach), Frank Armfield, David Johnson, Jerry Pritchett, Dwight Thurman, John Edmonds, Joseph Phelps, Wendell Baker, Charles Gray, Jimmy Gray, David Humphrey, George Martin, Jasper Martin, Taylor, Dogan, Hallstock.

Sangamo Electric Co. (Pickens, S.C.): Joel Allgood (coach), Floyd Nix, Billy Looper, David Watson, Steve Anderson, Ronald Lewis, Leonard Russell, James Griffin, Phil Griffin, James Hendricks, Al Clark, Dale Aiken, Lee Day, Grant.

Pratt-Read (Central, S.C.): Charles Gillespie (coach), Mickey Owens, Bobby Fowler, William Fowler, Patrick O'Dell, Chip Sulser, Anthony Dowdy, Timothy Putnam, David Porter, Phillip Vassey, Charles Breazeale, Donald Case, Dennis McCall, Hughes.

Saco-Lowell (Easley, S.C.): Mack Trotter (coach), Jim Carter (coach), Charles Gillespie, Herbert Bowen, James Allen, Dan Benfield, Calvin Clarke, Johnny Coleman, Edward Dobbins, Sam McCrary, Mickey Rogers, Rex Smith, Stephen Fulton, J. Bowen.

Dow Badische (Anderson, S.C.): Earl Green (coach), Jamie Saville, Emerson Cooley, Lester Garrison, William Smith, Lawrence Green, Charlie Gallivan, Donald Johnson, Frank Sims, Jay Agnew, Boyce Sanders, Bobby Mattress, George Harrison.

Cryovac (Duncan, S.C.): Van VanderPloeg (coach), Fred Dobbins, Robert Smith, Warren Nicholson, Felton Walker Jr., Fred Stephens, Richard Perdue, Paul Audet, E.W. Hardy, Hiram Springle, Dennis Wine, Donald Hutchinson.

Bigelow-Sanford (Calhoun Falls, S.C.): John Earl (coach), Glenn Sullivan, James Bryson, Willie Thurman, Walter Bailey, Charles Hopkins, James Custer, Tim Sullivan, Dean Willis, J. Earl.

Slater Mill (Slater, S.C.): Richard Payne (coach), James Wood, Marvin Suddeth, Teddy Cashion, Randall Cruell, J.H. Bowles, Michael Williams, Norwood Cox, Gary Askew, Jerry Hightower, Terry Hightower, Joe Hill, Rick Hamilton.

Appleton Mill (Anderson, S.C.): Henry Spake (coach), James Savage, Phillip Holcombe, Gary Grant, Terry Bailey, G.C. Stewart, Bobby Mattison, James Ligon, Donald Witcher, Steve Bowen, James Brock, Roger Rhodes, Douglas Hutchins, Dewey.

Dunean Mill #1 (Greenville, S.C.): Doug Gailey (coach), Dale Owens, Dan Donald, Lynn Thigpin, Dan Mason, Steve Gailey, Jake Darnell, Ray Gosnell, Jaylan Robinson, Ernest Kinard, David Hawkins, Thomas Owens, Don Gossett.

Ashworth Brothers (Greenville, S.C.): Bill Dendy (coach), Bill Williams (coach), Walter Fowler, Bud Kennedy, Stanley Matthews, Carlton Reeves, John Weathers, Bob Ashworth, Mike Blackwell, James Stark, Bruce Taylor, Robert Johnson, Marion Breazeale, Withington.

Southern Textile Basketball Tournament Rosters Appendix 1

Norris Mill (Norris, S.C.): C.F. Chandler (coach), Steve Lesley (coach), Johnny Chandler, Harold Snow, Earl Reynolds, Morris Henderson, Bill Anders, Al Baker, Gary Youngblood, Valley Simmons, Pat Kelly, Terry Chandler.

Butte Knitting Mill (Spartanburg, S.C.): Josephus Wells (coach), Madison Meadows, Willie Robinson, Curtis Williams, Clarence Brackett, Rufus Thomas, Lonnie Simpson, Benjamin Lyles, Jimmy Young, Grayson Gurley, Grover Salters, Robert Jones, Charles Wilson.

Sirrine Co. #2 (Greenville, S.C.): Bob Runk (coach), Ken Johnson, Bill Peake, Reggie Smith, John Mickler, Jim Uz, Jim Brooks, Earl Daniel, Dennis Hare, Curtis Dixon, Paul Turner, Robby Compton, Jim Craig.

Carolina Material Handling (Mauldin, S.C.): John Raines (coach), Jack Gallamore, Hugh Alexander, Ralph Raines, Barry Raines, Michael Collins, Marshall Chasteen, Charles Shockley, Terry Raines, Bennie Adams, David Morrow.

CLASS C MEN

Pelzer Mill #1 (Pelzer, S.C.), champions: Jimmy Hopkins (coach), M. Brewton, Everne Carr, Ronnie Creamer, Alonzo Harrison, Donnie Creamer, Carl Heyward, George Turman, F. Williams, Thomas Walker, James Hill, E. Dennis, Nathaniel Simpkins.

Dunean Cafe (Greenville, S.C.), runners-up: Charles Roddy (coach), William Dimsdale, William Wakefield, Claude Barnette, Olin Laws, Tony Lanford, Barry Bowling, Ted Pittman, Tommy Brown, Ronald White, P. Brown.

Ross Tire (Greenville, S.C.), consolation winners: Tom Carlton (coach), William Dogan, James Perkins, Anthony Rucker, Melvin Harris, Richard Dubose, Mansfield Golden, Ben Houston, Eddie Mars, Terry Wilder, Steve Riddlehoover, Willie Suber, Ronnie Wilson, Feskings.

Jiffie Jonnie #2 (Greenville, S.C.): Joe Shell (coach), Billy Young, Kenneth Johnson, Craig Greene, Larry Lewis, Tim Williams, Jimmy Williams, Roger Cox, Phil Brown, Tommy McCombs, Dale Stegall, Gregg Coleman, Wesley O'Neal, Carson, Shultz.

Saco-Lowell (Easley, S.C.): Arthur Ellenburg, Danny Jackson, Ricky Foster, Terry Davis, John Todd, Dale Crowe, Barry Grier, Brad Caldwell, Brian Kilby, De Wayne Gardner, Steve Looper, George Davis, Shaw, Hunt, Rosemond.

Pelzer Mill #2 (Pelzer, S.C.): Smith, Murphy, Mahaffey, Burns, Tate, Thomason, Jimmy Harrison, George Turman, Holliday, Eskew, Powell.

Martin Printing Co. (Greenville, S.C.): Harvey Forrester (coach), Butch Forrester, Mike Chibarro, James Kammer, James Wilkie Jr., Gil Gaillard, John Estes, Brian Kelley, Mike Washington, Ricky Aldridge, Benton, Gilstrap.

Jiffie Jonnie #1 (Greenville, S.C.): Gary Scism (coach), Charles Pulcine, Benjamin Griffin, Perry Vernon, James Whitfield, Ted Mann, Bryan Roper, Ronald Gary, Donald Gary, McBruce Young, Wayne Kinard, Roger Cruell, Wesley O'Neal.

Smith Inc. (Greenville, S.C.): Ricky Smith (coach), Travis Dove, Ricky Dove, Mike Galloway, Gary Bible, Robby Riley, Mark Rackley, Greene, Childress.

Transit Homes (Greenville, S.C.): Ruppert Elliott, Danny Bayne, Curt Taylor, Ricky Morris, Barry Dorr, Tony Campbell, Chuck Orr, Eugene Seay Jr., Gary Anthony, Mike Ware, Randy Elliott, Jimmy Bell, Mark Seay, Medlock.

Precise Machine Works (Simpsonville, S.C.): Donny Bolton (coach), Eddie Huff (coach), Ken Vilcheck, Cliff Vilcheck, Waymen Simpson, Sylvester Dennis, David Woolle, Albert Goldsmith, Chris Ryan, Johnny Pressley, Vernon Johnson, Tony Madden, Beeson, Brown, Applebee, Johnson.

Little Pigs Bar-B-Que (Anderson, S.C.): Tommy Dunn (coach), Joel Taylor, Paul Wolfe, Charles Craft, Donald Allen, Ricky Price, Marshall Meadors, Brent Rogers, Gilbert Rogers, Herbert Phillips, Eddie Martin, Kent Saad, Tony Leopard, Roberts.

Fred Fraley Tru Ride (Spartanburg, S.C.): Fred Fraley (coach), Paul Fraley, Charles Bagwell, Roger Cohen, Mike Humphries, Steve Fuller, Rick McKinney, Mark Hinson, L.A. Hill, Dee Williams, Gregg Wade, Alford Dawkins Jr., John Richardson, Mark Richardson, Loy Jeffords, John Nesbitt, Thompson.

Lebanon (Pendleton, S.C.): Ray Thompson (coach), Steve Malone, Alan Carter, Grady Gambrell, Larry Whitfield, Billy Martin, Ronnie Poore, Eddie Wentsky, Dan Gentry, Ben Evatt, Steve Sears, Billy Reed, Ronnie Gossett.

Simpsonville Mill (Simpsonville, S.C.):

Jamison, Yeargin, Benson, Boyd, R. Sullivan, Anderson, J. Sullivan, Satterwhite, Vance, Pinson, Wright.

CLASS A WOMEN

Appleton Mill (Anderson, S.C.), champions: Annie Tribble (coach), Vicky Burton, Laura Lawton, Doll Eadon, Susan Neal, Gladys Elmore, Karen Brown, Shirley McAdams, Mary Thurman, Sally Black, Grace Lyle, Debbie Holcombe, Donna Forrester, Dale Campbell, Donna Kay, Katrine Anderson.

Slater Mill (Slater, S.C.), runners-up: Bobby Kirby (coach), Joan Kirby, Regina Gilstrap, Debbie Crenshaw, Jennie Lyerly, Debbie Daniel, Pam Adams, Marty Vaughn, Marian Brewer, Bonnie Whelan, Jan Rampey, Dot Smith, Tracy Burch, Kim Basinger, Reid.

Monroe & Co. (Winnsboro, S.C.): Wanda Cromer (coach), Paul Monroe (coach), Becky Sirt, Sandy Sirt, Janet Sirt, Kay Monroe, Paula Monroe, LaRue Fields, Linda Robertson, Gracie Lyles, Susan Boulware, Hightower, McGriff, Vivian Humphrey, Freeman, Jones, Floyd.

Discount Fence Co. (Winston-Salem, N.C.): Jerry Holt (coach), Linda Smith, Issy Gardner, Brenda Wooten, Becky Williams, Jo Haubenreiser, Kim Goodson, Marcie Hellard, Linda Cottrell, Lynn Milner, Betty Harsh, Susan Lloyd, Charman Coffer, Beeding.

Atlanta Tomboys (Atlanta, Ga.): Johnny Moon (coach), Dolores Owen, Annette Hammock, Edwina Bryan, Judy Bickers, Bonnie Gibson, Sheila Stinchcomb, Cynthia Henry, Blondine Woodard, Debbie Smith, Tywantha Head, Elinor Ferry, Davis, Meadows, Collins.

Pelzer Mill (Pelzer, S.C.): Bill Hopkins (coach), Dan Kennett (coach), Barbara Bell, Marsha Kellett, Jane Jackson, Betsy Hopkins, Debbie Lollis, Amy Austin, Debbie Whitt, Lynn Rogers, Lois Hanks, Janet Hopkins, Janet Owens, Brenda Bell.

Blackwell & Son Real Estate (Hanahan, S.C.): Bobby Turner (coach), Bill Stevens (coach), Pattie Gainey, Sharon Marlowe, Cindy Hanenburger, Nacey Wilson, Dianne Wooten, Christie Smith, Luanne Gillis, Debbie Boatnight, Tresie Sheena, Grace Glispia, Janie Lee, Hunter, Moss, Wall.

Brookline Carpets (Greenville, S.C.): Ruby Jones (coach), Cora Dickey, Betty Bearden, Jenny Callahan, Chorice Barber, Miriam Wingate, Janet Latta, Ruth Williams, Annie Cannon, Mary Copeland, Vonda Watson, Yates.

Hampton Industries (Kinston, N.C.): Fred Powers (coach), B.J. Shell, Diane Limbaugh, Sherry Carter, Karen Ashley, Janie Lee, Larua Lawton, Vicki Burton, Donna Forrester, Kay Bayne, Stephanie Vurnakes, Ann Welborn, Metts, Hall.

Pittman's Textile Machinery (Greenville, S.C.): LaFoy Theodore (coach), Pat Theodore (coach), Peggy Davenport, Fran Brooks, Cindy Crenshaw, Denise Blakely, Theresa Ludwig, Cheryl Marsh, Laura Clark, Hood, Pat Smith.

Belton Mill (Belton, S.C.): Pat Silva (coach), Rita Rice, Kathy Graham, Caroline Marshall, Betty Fite, Debbie Bowers, Caroline Brown, Kitsy Curnou, Julie Thompson, Brenda Miller, Kathy Little, Johnson.

Bobby's Shell (Ware Shoals, S.C.): Joe Pitt (coach), Ann Vinson, Dixie Duncan, Dianne Davenport, Cindy Collins, Ann Dean, Nina Simmons, Susan Riley, Beverly Allen, Linda Griffin, Beth Turner, Jenny White, D. Turner.

Select Distributors (Taylors, S.C.): Leon Gravley (coach), Patsy Howell, Ann Shelton, Sandra Lister, Annamay Stockman, Nancy Moore, Kathy Matthews, Debbie Center, Jane Harley, Vickie Howard, Tracy Burch, Few, Fowler, Smith.

South Carolina Book Store (Columbia, S.C.): Mr. Brady (coach), Denise Nanney, Martha Suber, Peggy Harden, Cissie Jones, Eire Griffith, Beth Wiggins, Brenda Paulk, Diane Elliott, Van McCloud, Maureen McCauley, Way, Yaghlan, Covington, Workman, Hughes.

Enro Shirt Co. (Woodruff, S.C.): Stanley Waldrep (coach), Kay Stribble, Gail Phillips, Betty McAbee, Lois Jennings, Brenda Sloan, Lauren Murphy, Joy Moore, Marlene Stephens, Joye Meadows, Rene Smith, Starr Wood, Jane Foster, Liz Nickle, Doris Cox, Owens, Knight.

1976

Officers: James Morrow (Greenville, S.C.), President; Ken Pittman (Greenville, S.C.), 1st Vice President; Fred Powers (Charlotte, N.C.), 2nd Vice President; Lloyd McAbee (Greenville, S.C.), 3rd Vice President; Harry Foster (Greenville, S.C.), Treasurer; Fred Byrd (Greenville, S.C.), Executive Secretary; Frances

Welborn, Ass't Executive Secretary; Whitey Kendall (Greenville), Supervisor of Officials; Lt. F.R. Hawkins, Security Officer.

Executive Committee: Clarence Thomas (Greenville, S.C.), Willie Wilbanks (Greenwood, S.C.), Curtis Terry (Piedmont, S.C.), Willard Fowler (Greenville, S.C.), Dan Foster (Greenville, S.C.), Snow Kirby (Marietta, S.C.), Bill Hopkins (Pelzer, S.C.), Joe Newton (Greenville, S.C.), Henry Spake (Anderson, S.C.), Ward Williams (Greenville, S.C.), Earl Wooten (Piedmont, S.C.), Vercho Carter (Alexander City, Ala.), Phil Clark (Greer, S.C.), Divver Hendrix (Greenville, S.C.), Ruppert Elliott (Greenville, S.C.), Phil Harley (Greenville, S.C.), Larry Ashley (Greenville, S.C.), Charles Rogers (Salem, S.C.), D.K. Smith (Lyman, S.C.), Lewis Golden (Greenville, S.C.).

OPEN DIVISION

Lexington Co. Recreation (Lexington, S.C.), champions: Melvin Young (coach), William Hutto (coach), Robert Jeter, Cres Clayruth, Wilbur Corley, Ben Taylor, James Taylor, Steve Ashe, Donald Golston, Jive Brown, Monte Noble, Jerome Brown, Willie Crumpton, Eddie Robinson, Nate Davis, Robert Moore, Purvis McDaniels, Johnny Burrett, Bobby Goldman, A. Brown, C. Brown, Alex English.

Non-Fluid Oil (Greenville, S.C.), runners-up: Eugene Seay (coach), Stan Elrod, Billy Smith, Ben Skipper, Bill Ligon, Tom Arnholt, Charlie Fishback, Jimmy Powell, Tim Sisneros, Mike Moore, Steve Peele, Pratt.

Pittman's Textile Machinery (Greenville, S.C.): Broadus Miller (coach), Clyde Agnew, Moses King, Randy Dickens, Randy Miller, Charles Crawford, Sammy Adams, Scott Conaut, Robert Edwards, Bobby Griffin, Tony Chibarra, Rick Horton, Colie Feemster, White, Pittman, Baty, Hall, H. Griffin, Klondernicke, Klernknecht.

Jackson Five (Columbia, S.C.): Jim Jackson (coach), Sam Goodwin, Charlie Powell, Larry Womack, John Kirkland, George Glymph, James Byrd, Gary Gregor, Frank Wise, Fred Melson, Mike Jacobs, Allen Searson.

Arnold Palmer Cadillac (Charlotte, N.C.): Charles Richards (coach), Gar Laux (ass't coach), Tony Byers, George Jackson, George Adams, Irwin Hill, Chuck Richards, David Moser, Herbert Davis, Harry Davis, Billy Early, Ben Basinger, Richard Dean, Eppa Rixey.

A & M Mobile Homes (Spartanburg, S.C.): Tom Warrick (coach), Mike McAdams, Ducie Robinson, Cheysee Jones, Bobby Livingston, Forrest Jeffries, Lloyd Taylor, Corn, MEadows, Turner, Seawright, Smith, Henderson, Mallory, Brooks.

TMR Inc. (Fairforest, S.C.): Frank Durham (coach), Mel Francisco, Wayne Croft, Jeff Reisinger, Van Gregg, Terrell Suit, Jo Jo Bethea, Eddie Payne, Bruce Harman, Charlie Rogers.

Daniel Construction Co. (Jenkinsville, S.C.): Fred Pearson (coach), Jackie Boyd, Curtis Carter, Virgil O'Neal, Michael Davis, Colie Feemster, Henry Smith, James Moore, Stanley Kennedy, David Seibles, Howard Smith, Henry Boyd, Alvin Holland, Pearson, Henry Holmes, Backford.

Able Supply (Spartanburg, S.C.): Ronald Fisher (coach), Donny Walker (coach), Bobby Sheffield, Ted Fisher, Joe Bates, Richard Todd, Willie Byrd, Earnest Brock, Glenn Williams, Marion Miller, Curtis Byrd, Dexter Robinson, E. Byrd.

J & S Garage (Orangeburg, S.C.): Jimmy Owens (coach), P. Phelps, Joe Bronson, David Sharperson, Bennie Adams, D. Pinson, D.J. Jackson, F. Oliver, Willie Harris, Joe Thompson, Lee McKennedy, Wayne Clarke, G. Blanding, Ronnie Murray, Durant, "Bear" Knuckles, Taylor.

Young-Love Fabrics (Charlotte, N.C.): Jack McGill, Jim Clark, Steve Crowe, Skip Goley, Don Davis, Russ Hunt, George Adams, Ken Gufstafson, Sam Meade, Bray Smith.

Drummond Oil Co. (Greenwood, S.C.): Spencer, McMinns, White, Brooks, King, Nelson, Cowan, Pope, Henderson, Sanders.

CLASS A MEN

Brookline Carpets (Greenville, S.C.), champions: Phil Chapman (coach), Mike Yeargin, Gary Fowler, Bill Yeargin, Luther Johnson, Charles Eden, Nixon Allen, Robert Staley, Wilbert Robinson, Rick Williams, Robert Burton, Johnny Abercrombie, Amos Herbert, Odell Sherrard, Leslie Williams.

Sangamo Electric Co. (Pickens, S.C.), runners-up: Joel Allgood (coach), Robert Cannon, Ken Tankersley, Doug Bagwell, Peter Haley, Sammy Nix, Al Clark, Tommy Porter, Ronald Lewis, Samuel Hughes, Jim Medlin, Billy

Looper, Roger Garrett, Dennis Arnold, Griffin, Carroll.

Barley Plumbing (Greenville, S.C.), consolation winners: John Turner (coach), Gary Turner, Larry Wooten, Pete Anderson, David Massey, James Camden, Jerry Sloan, Mike Parkins, Mike McGill, Bruce Zschokke, A. Turner.

Parker Mill (Greenville, S.C.): C.T. Phillips (coach), Norman Norris (coach), Alexander Brockman, Clifford Chapman, John Childress, Albert Donald, Jerry Jackson, Marshall Mattress, Robert McDowell, Bill McGowan, John McKinney, Jimmie Robinson, Bill Turmon, Willie Tutt, Kenneth.

Daniel Construction Co. (Greenville, S.C.): Howard Killen (coach), Gene Freeman (coach), David Gambrell, Wayne Gambrell, Danny Gambrell, Larry Gambrell, Steve Brown, Steve Gambrell, Clint Turner, David Dobson, Larry Plemmons, Randy Miller, Steve Roberson, Jones.

Singer Mfg. (Anderson, S.C.): Lattimer, Williford, Leverette, Mark, Simms, Walker, Johnson, Rainey, Gray, Mattison, Colbert.

Norwich Pharmacal (Greenville, S.C.): Waddy Miller (coach), Freddie Donald, Jesse McCullough, Dennis Grooms, Freddie Smith, Robert Murphy, Robert Gilreath, Richard Smith, Samuel Gilliam, James Chandler, Charles Levine.

Lyman Mill (Lyman, S.C.): Sonny Moody (coach), Ralph Murphy, Charles Robinson, Clarence Moody, Raymond Glenn, Johnny Miller, Willie Jones, Lewis Jennings, Lawrence Benson, Billy Fowler, Frederick Anderson, Gary Harris, Michael Durch, Mosley.

Monaghan Mill (Greenville, S.C.): Bill Swaynghame (coach), Terry Fowler, Eddie Keeler, Billy Chapman, Edward Wilhoit, Ronnie Brown, Charles Catoe, Terry Christy, Donald Craig, Fred Dilworth, Eugene Jackson, Kenneth McAlister, Alan Landreth, Ward, J. Dilworth.

Taylors Mill (Taylors, S.C.): David Morgan (coach), Steven Moore, Harold Smith, Howard Sturgill, Donald McCarter, Lewis Goldsmith, Mickey Campbell, Luther Autrey, Mark Lemmons, Kenneth Duncan, David Morgan, Dean.

Fiber Industries (Greenville, S.C.): David Pritchett (coach), Phil Harley (coach), Herman Evatt, Robert Hargett, Steve Barton, Colvin Carter, Heyward Leake, Steve Richard, Frank Armfield, Tim Howell, David Johnson, Glenn Lowe, Jasper Martin, Dwight Thurman.

Borden Mill (Kingsport, Tenn.): Michael Locke (coach), Larry Page, Michael Luster, Butch Perry, Keith Ervin, Danny Hammonds, Jimmy Dykes, Steve Calhoun, Carl Chambers, Wayne Carr, Maxwell, Harkerson, McPherson.

Hoechst Celanese (Greer, S.C.): Roger Wilson (coach), Richard Barras (coach), Lawrence Williams, James Thurman, Grover Anderson, Marvin Drummond, Gil Howarth, William Ballenger, Steve Arms, Raeford Wideman, Ernest Merck, Calvin Durham, Kenneth Taylor, Wilson.

Cryovac (Simpsonville, S.C.): Jim Holcombe (coach), James Sullivan, Fred Hill, Harold Wright, Bobby Phelps, Jimmy Wright, Calvin Milam, Rex Abercrombie, Joe Freeman, Robert Massingill, Mathew Milam, Barksdale.

Sirrine Co. (Greenville, S.C.): Sandy Templeton (coach), Ralph Bouton, William Oliver, Shelly Holiday, Harry Moats, John Templeton, James Brooks, Phillip Mitchell, John Cooper, Thomas Keith Jr., James Uzell, Bruce Martin, James Johnson, Smith.

Singer Mfg. (Pickens, S.C.): Hamp Summey (coach), Michael Galloway, James Griffin, Glenn Thrift, Charles Taylor, Joe Kelley, Doug Dukes, Larry Davis, Eddie Allgood, David Norris, Anthony Carver, Telford King, Timothy Looper, Seymore, Gilbert, McCoy, Robinson.

Dunean Mill (Greenville, S.C.): Doug Gailey (coach), David Hawkins, Jimmy Riddle, Charles Hudson, Ernest Kinard, Jaylan Robinson, Dale Owens, Gary McDowell, Dan Mason, Charles Roddy, Ray Gosnell, Carol Burns.

General Electric (Greenville, S.C.): James Gamble (coach), Kevin Casey, Donald Smith, Ralph Morton, Charles McNeil, James Dawkins, Walter Moseley, Charles Breazeale, Raymond Dean, Preston McKinney, Robert Wilson, Calvin Johnson, Martin, Simpson.

CLASS B MEN

Alice Mfg. (Easley, S.C.), champions: Terry Smith (coach), Mendel Masters (coach), Roy Aiken, Jackie Anderson, Freddie Turmon, Johnny White, Carl Valentine, Harry Blake, Avery Anders, Linus Blake, Kenneth Galloway, Ross Bowen, Kenneth Roper.

Renfrew Bleachery (Travelers Rest, S.C.), runners-up: Ron Howell (coach), William

Southern Textile Basketball Tournament Rosters   Appendix 1   271

Ford, Nave Thomas, Dennis Walker, Kyle Turner, William Brooks, John Turner, Earnest Griffith, Jerome Williams, Darren Gazaway, Fred McGill, William Dilworth, James Bell.

S.C.N Bank (Greenville, S.C.), consolation winners: Charles Eldridge (coach), William Carpenter, Frank Wrenn, Stephen Brown, Larry Miller, Jackson Mizell, William Ariail, Michael Jordan, Cole, Ward.

Woodside Mill (Greenville, S.C.): Gary Woods (coach), Agie Green, Larry McCall, Larry Bryant, Dennis Cordell, Billy Jones, Tommy Baldwin, George Abercrombie, Jimmy Chappelle, John Jenkins, James Hunter, Willie Blandin, Johnny Blandin.

Sirrine Co. (Greenville, S.C.): B.D. Ray (coach), Reggie Smith, Billy Chandler, Robert Compton, James Craig, Charles Dalton, Horace Jones, David Kirk, DeWitt Patterson, Bill Peake, Dennis Poole, Frederick Schroder, James Thomas.

Ware Shoals Mill (Ware Shoals, S.C.): Roosevelt Smith (coach), Willie Smith, Eddie Whatley, Thomas Whatley, Roy Whatley, Willie Anderson, Willie Mathis, Darrough Aiken, Raymond Kelley, Mitchell Lewis, Don Wright, Alvin Smith, Jerry Butler.

Cryovac (Simpsonville, S.C.): Jim Holcombe (coach), Eddie Stenhouse, David Stenhouse, Robert Gravley, Johnny Watts, Roger Sullivan, Talmon Harrison, Barry Wright, Johnny Barksdale, Ralph Sullivan, Billy Byrd, Robert Alexander, J. Wright.

Pelzer Mill (Pelzer, S.C.): Bill Hopkins (coach), Tommy Tice, Doug Austin, Billy Burns, Donnie Creamer, Ronnie Creamer, Vic Albusen, David Burns, Lyndon Mahaffey.

Fiber Industries (Greenville, S.C.): John Gaines (coach), Ken Childers (coach), Dwight Thurman (coach), Jerry Pritchett, Joseph Phelps, Charles Gray, Jimmy Gray, George Martin, Wayne Clark, Larry Dogan, Kenneth Durham, James Hailstock, Claude Halstead, Clifton Ladd, Tommie Summers.

Pratt-Read (Central, S.C.): Charles Gillespie (coach), Mickey Owens, Bobby Fowler, William Fowler, Timothy Putnam, Phillip Vassey, David Breazeale, Dennis McCall, Chip Sulser, Ronnie Hughes, William Moody.

Saco-Lowell (Easley, S.C.): Mack Trotter (coach), Charles Gillespie, Herbert Bowen, Mike Allen, Dan Benfield, Calvin Clarke, Randy Coleman, Jesse Bowen, Bill Pitts, Jimmy Bowen, Fred Richardson.

Slater Mill (Slater, S.C.): Cruell, Cashion, Hill, Williams, M. Young, McCall, McKenzie, J. Simpson, Joe Simpson, D. Young, Cox.

Dow Badische (Anderson, S.C.): LeRoy Boseman (coach), Jamie Saville, Emerson Cooley, John Smith, George Harrison, Jimmy Blanding, James Brenson, Robert Berg, Jay Cooley, Dennis Philyaw, Robert Wright, James Jones, Sylvester Brown.

Cryovac (Duncan, S.C.): Hezzie Simmons (coach), Fred Dobbins, Van VanderPloeg, Steve Smith, Warren Nicholson, Fred Stephens, Richard Dixon, Paul Audet, E.W. Hardy, Hiram Springle, Glenn Taylor, Charles Stapleton.

Bigelow-Sanford (Calhoun Falls, S.C.): John Earl (coach), James Bryson, Willie Thurman, Tim Sullivan, Dean Willis, Jones Pardlow, Sam Woods, Steve Holcombe, Larry Jordan, Al Gossett, Keith Ormand, Greg DiBacco, Pardon, Waring, Ritz, Gordon.

Dunean Mill (Greenville, S.C.): Doug Gailey (coach), Jimmy Riddle (coach), Steve Gailey, Ernest Kinard, David Hawkins, Andrew Carson, Chris Taylor, Isaiah Walker Jr., Jimmy Sullivan, James Wardlaw, Bill Powell, Mitchell Brewer, Ronnie Garnett, Philip Terry.

Ashworth Brothers (Greenville, S.C.): Bill Dendy (coach), Walter Fowler, Carlton Reeves, Mike Blackwell, Robert Johnson, Marion Breazeale, David Whitlock, Mike Lamb, William B. Dendy, William N. Dendy III, Taylor.

Carolina Material Handling (Mauldin, S.C.): John Raines (coach), Jack Gallamore, Hugh Alexander, Ralph Raines, Barry Raines, Michael Collins, Marshall Chasteen, Terry Raines, Bennie Adams, Sid Majors, William Dimsdale, Darrell Smith, Dan Carroll, Hensley.

Parke-Davis (Greenwood, S.C.): Wilbert Harris (coach), Len White, Larry Cooper, Sammy Cooper, Curtis Cannon, Thomas Jackson, Melvin Stibbling, Arthur Caldwell, Donald White, Terry Lathren, Mike Traynham, J. Cooper.

J.P. Stevens Distribution (Greenville, S.C.): Richard Witt (coach), Herman McCullough, James Johnson, Randy Lesley, Charles Riser, John Mayes, David Scarborough, Larry Franks, David Jones, James McGee, Larry Essick.

Phillips Fibers (Spartanburg, S.C.): Luther Wilkins (coach), Gergory Anderson, Alonzo Briggs, Calvin Byrd, Dessie Canty, Charles

Cuff, Mike Fuller, Darius Miller, Earl Moring, James Pearson, Brewton.

Class C Men

Pelzer Mill #1 (Pelzer, S.C.), champions: Jimmy Hopkins (coach), Carl Heyward, Heyward Graves, Jonathan Moore, Jack Beckett, Jerome Anderson, Zam Frederick, Alonzo Harrison, James Hill, George Turmon, Bernard Horton, Randy Boggs, Harry Rutledge, Barry Howell, Hampton.

Dunean Cafe (Greenville, S.C.), runners-up: Charles Roddy (coach), William Wakefield, Ted Pittman, Ronald White, Joseph Short, Paul Brown, Russell Phillips, Vilcheck, Cleveland, Holden, Pressley.

Neely's Inc. (Greenville, S.C.), consolation winners: Ken Pittman (coach), Wes Neely (coach), Joel Walker, Robert Hudson, Charles Mitchell, Randy Tillery, Jeffrey Neely, Ken Gilstrap, Paul Shaw, Doug Schmieding, Allen Cooper, Michael Beeson, Frankie Spurgeon, Bobby Gillespie.

S-M Norgetown (Marietta, S.C.): Gary Scism (coach), Joel Patterson, Tommy McCombs, Henry Carson, Wesley O'Neal, Craig Greene, Billy Young, Kenneth Johnson, Dennis Thompson, Mike Arms, Billy Campbell, Garrett.

Pelzer Mill #2 (Pelzer, S.C.): J.D. Whitt (coach), Larry Jones, Sylvester Burns, Jimmy Harrison, Ray Holliday, Tommy Waters, Johnny Robinson, David Eskew, Jimmie Babb, Danny Scroggs, Truman, Howell, Williams, Tate, Hagood, Turmon.

Saco-Lowell (Easley, S.C.): Randy Bray (coach), Terry Davis, John Todd, Dale Crowe, Barry Grier, Ray Hooper, George Davis, Dean Sorgenfrei, Clyde Hunt, Steve Anders, Ken Murphy, Mike Chandler, Jackson, Shaw, Withington.

Martin Printing Co. (Greenville, S.C.): Harvey Forrester (coach), Butch Forrester, Mike Chibarro, James Kammer, Jimmy Wilkie, Brian Kelley, Jimmy Foster, Craig Sahms, Philip Wise, Robin Smiley, John Bowden, Gra Wagner, Walls.

Ross Tire (Greenville, S.C.): Wayne Evatt (coach), Anthony Rucker, Melvin Harris, Richard Dubose, Mansfield Golden, Ben Houston, Eddie Mars, Julius Golden, James Murray, Jerry Scurry, Calvin Shumate, Richard Wakester, Gentry, Cruell, Wilson.

Jiffie Jonnie (Greenville, S.C.): Gary Scism (coach), Charles Pulcine, Benjamin Griffin, Ronald Gary, Donald Gary, Melvin Young, Wayne Kinard, Roger Cox, Barry Dorr, Larry Lewis, Gregg Coleman.

Transit Homes (Greenville, S.C.): Rupert Elliott (coach), Curt Taylor, Ricky Morris, Chuck Orr, Gene Seay, Gary Anthony, Randy Elliott, Jimmy Bell, Mark Seay, Gary Medlock, Donald Ellis, John McMahan, Eric Smith, Robert Shell.

Precise Machine Works (Simpsonville, S.C.): Donny Bolton (coach), Jerry Heightower (coach), Cliff Vielcheck, Sylvester Dennis, David Miller, Rick McKinney, L.A. Hill, Mark Hinson, Randy Harling, Steve Durham, Mike Cohen, Don Kershaw, Avery Smith, Randall Smith, McCarroll, Rice, Anderson, Yeargin, Reddmond, Davis.

Vaughn Woodwork (Duncan, S.C.): Larry Westmoreland (coach), Johnny Sanders (ass't coach), Robert Rhodes, Barry Hadden, Ronald Payne, Michael Bridwell, Eddie James, Miler Dimery, Anthony Seay, Monty Sanders, Martin Dimery, William Loftis, Patrick Cagle, John Pennell.

PBM (Anderson, S.C.): Eugene Patterson (coach), Darrel Brown, Warren White, Ronnie Payton, Larry Clinkscales, Jerry Hanks II, Larry Nance, Danny McAlister, Terence Roberts, Donnie Barrett, Dennis Lee, Danny Humphries, Ronney Davis, Gambrell, Cobb, Galloway.

Jackson Mill (Iva, S.C.): Al Charney (coach), Phil Oakes, Wayne Thomas, Marshall Hunter, Anthony Blackwell, Charles Reed, Bernard Horton, Randy Boggs, Harry Rutledge, Barry Howell, Jimmy Harrison, Jeffrey Charney, Neal Chambers, T. Oaks, Scotland, McBride.

Carotell (Taylors, S.C.): Leon Gravley (coach), Robert Gravley, William Aughtry, John Kuntz III, William DeLoache III, Warren Kimmons, Greg Dobson, Rickey Watts, Hardy, Brown.

Class A Women

Slater Mill (Slater, S.C.), champions: Bobby Kirby (coach), Joan Kirby, Regina Gilstrap, Debbie Crenshaw, Jennie Lyerly, Marty Vaughn, Marian Brewer, Bonnie Whelan, Jan Rampey, Dot Smith, Pam Adams, Terri Reid, Kim Basinger, Vivian Humphries, Mary Kinard, Sheila Morgan.

Discount Fence Co. (Winston-Salem,

N.C.), runners-up: Jerry Holt (coach), Brenda Wooten, Jo Haubenreiser, Linda Cantrell, Dianne Limbaugh, Janice Markland, Patricia Chaffin, Sherry Carter, Georgene Hightower, Sheila Starchcomb, Lucy Carmichael, Sherry Burford, Angela Crenatzer.

Darrell Floyd's Sandwich Shop (Greenville, S.C.), consolation winners: Darrell Floyd (coach), Susan Blair, Nancy Floyd, Karen Noland, Susie Johnson, Diane Floyd, Sharon Morrell, Janet Cone, Susan Sullivan, Barbara Berry, Susan Reynolds, Rita Mantooth, Ann Horton, Brooks.

Jackson Mill (Iva, S.C.): John Neiswender (coach), Tommie Langston, Frances Bostic, Betty Fite, Mary Devlin, Dale Campbell, Brenda Cooper, Kathleen Little, Grace Lyle, Barbara Warren, Stacy Hall, Patricia Metz, Kathy Spears, June Hyder, Wall.

Pelzer Mill (Pelzer, S.C.): Bill Hopkins (coach), Barbara Bell, Marsha Kellett, Jane Jackson, Betsy Hopkins, Debbie Hawkins, Debbie Whitt, Janet Hopkins, Vicki Cummings, Linda Garland, Alice Kuntz, Fay George, Sybil Murrell, Debbie Sumers, Karen McCullough, Karen Ashley, Samero.

Brookline Carpets (Greenville, S.C.): Doris Simpson (coach), Jenny Callaham, Janet Latta, Ruth Williams, Annie Allen, Carrie Garrison, Leila Vaughan, Cleona Harrison, Judy Murray, Margaret Looper, Jean Irby, Arleen Looper, Sullivan, Simpson.

Duncan Pharmacy (Duncan, S.C.): Robert Sanders (coach), Lee Gilreath, Sandra Bruce, Kathy Matthews, Annamay Stockman, Dorothy Parks, Glenda Bullard, Jane Harley, Lauren Murphy, Tracy Burch, Priscilla Graham, Marian Brewer, Patsy Howell.

Mayfair Mill (Pickens, S.C.): Pat Grant (coach), Peggy Anthony, Karen Perry, Cathy Mansell, Patti Bobo, Dede Cartee, Dale Forest, Ann Vinson, Hazel Anderson, Connie Morrow, Venise Nanney, Pat Haskett, Duncan, McJunkin.

Lynn's Superette (Greenville, S.C.): Brandy Lafoy (coach), Pat Theodore (coach), Thersa Ludwig, Laura Clark, Dora Thompson, Ruth Ellis, Cindy Crenshaw, Judy Munser, Vicky Rice, Nancy Joy, Cheryl Mason, Carol Higbuen, Marsh, Matthew, Gilreath, Harley, Becker, DeKonig, Davis, Bayne.

---1977---

Officers: James Morrow (Greenville, S.C.), President; Ken Pittman (Greenville, S.C.), 1st Vice President; Fred Powers (Charlotte, N.C.), 2nd Vice President; Lloyd McAbee (Greenville, S.C.), 3rd Vice President; Harry Foster (Greenville, S.C.), Treasurer; Fred Byrd (Greenville, S.C.), Executive Secretary; Frances Welborn, Ass't Executive Secretary; Whitey Kendall (Greenville), Supervisor of Officials; Lt. F.R. Hawkins, Security Officer.

Executive Committee: Clarence Thomas (Greenville, S.C.), Willie Wilbanks (Greenwood, S.C.), Curtis Terry (Piedmont, S.C.), Willard Fowler (Greenville, S.C.), Dan Foster (Greenville, S.C.), Snow Kirby (Marietta, S.C.), Bill Hopkins (Pelzer, S.C.), Joe Newton (Greenville, S.C.), Henry Spake (Anderson, S.C.), Ward Williams (Greenville, S.C.), Earl Wooten (Piedmont, S.C.), Vercho Carter (Alexander City, Ala.), Phil Clark (Greer, S.C.), Divver Hendrix (Greenville, S.C.), Ruppert Elliott (Greenville, S.C.), Phil Harley (Greenville, S.C.), Larry Ashley (Greenville, S.C.), William Dendy Jr. (Greenville, S.C.), D.K. Smith (Lyman, S.C.), Lewis Golden (Greenville, S.C.), Jerry Holt (Winston-Salem, N.C.), Richard Stowe (Greenwood, S.C.).

OPEN DIVISION

Non-Fluid Oil (Greenville, S.C.), champions: Jim Phillips (coach), Jerry Compton (coach), Bruce Harmon (coach), John Franklin, Dave Brown, Tree Rollins, Clyde Agnew, John Cottingham, Wayne Croft, Jo Jo Bethea, Stan Elrod, Eddie Payne.

Chick-Fil-A (Greenville, S.C.), runners-up: Tom Warrick (coach), Art Landrum (coach), Ken Napier, Tony Byers, Rocky Costa, George Adams, John Seawright, Lester Stinson, Forrest Tome, McLeod, G. Byers, Julian Miller, Dave Borman.

Lexington Co. Recreation (Lexington, S.C.): Melvin Young (coach), William Hutto (coach), Robert Geter, Steve Ashe, Ben Taylor, Willie Crumpton, Nate Davis, Craig Cayruth, Mike Cayruth, Ronnie Bass, McDaniels, Dona, Gaston.

D & L Advertising (Greenville, S.C.): Joe Lynch (coach), Bob Davis, Michael Hall, Jay Spain, Aiken, Willie Teague, Dallas, McKimmon, Donald, Jackson, Craig Lynch.

Albany Felt Co. (St. Stephens, S.C.): Benjamin Tue (coach), Franklin Jefferson, Donald Green, Ernell Wright, Sidney Austin, Robert

Gadsden, Wayne Jefferson, William Manigault, Leonard King, Henry Stewart, McCutcheon.

Daniel Construction Co. (Jenkinsville, S.C.): Fred Pearson (coach), Henry Boyd, Jackie Boyd, Alvin Holland, Henry Holmes, Charles Marshall, Curtis Carter, Rhine, Virgil O'Neal, Heyward Smith, Frank Pearson.

Jackson Five (Columbia, S.C.): Jim Jackson (coach), Charlie Powell, Howard White, Fred Melson, Sam Goodwin, Allen Searson, James Byrd, Glymph Childress, Steve Singletary, John Kirkland.

Sullivan Pontiac (Anderson, S.C.): Jim Wiles (coach), John Campbell, Thomas Wimbush, Al Daniel, Ronald White, Dale Crowe, Reggie Small, Jon Dupre, Ken Vilcheck, George Turman.

Class A Men

Athletic Attic (Anderson, S.C.), champions: Dave Lasswell (coach), Jim Clark, Don Davis, Darrell Taunton, Keith Ballew, Jim Phillips, Tom McIntyre, Robin Ellenburg.

Brookline Carpets (Greenville, S.C.), runners-up: Phil Chapman (coach), Jack Taylor, Robert Staley, Wilbert Robinson, Lee Kennedy, Lavanda Sweeney, Robert Burton, Agee, Nixon Allen, Leslie Williams, Johnny Abercrombie, Luther Johnson, Doyle Green.

Cryovac (Simpsonville, S.C.), consolation winners: Lewis Whitmire (coach), Rex Abercrombie, Bobby Phelps, Robert Massingill, James Sullivan, Calvin Milan, Fred Hill, Paul Wharton, Jimmy Wright, Roger Sullivan, Barry Wright, Joe Freeman, Matthew Milan.

Homelite (Greer, S.C.): Stevie Upton, Coker, Charles Crawford, Gerald Edwards, Ashby, Benson, Farmer, Bobby Griffin, Cohen, Meadows, Thornton, Scott, Cox.

Ware Shoals Mill (Ware Shoals, S.C.): Roosevelt Smith (coach), Mitchell Lewis, Joe Smith, Willie Smith, Darrough Aiken, John Johnson, Willie Wright, John Carroll, Roy Hicks, Lurman Hawthorne.

Alice Mfg. (Easley, S.C.): Terry Smith (coach), Carl Valentine, Kenneth Galloway, Ken Murphy, Linus Blake, Billy Curenton, Rick Corn, Jackie Anderson, Dan McCreight, Freddie Turmon, James McGowan, Kenneth Roper.

Golden Strip Motors (Mauldin, S.C.): Dullah Forrest (coach), Carroll Long, Mike McGill, James Camden, David Helton, Kenneth Harbin, Clyde Wooten, Barry Dilworth, John Guest, David Burns.

Saco-Lowell (Easley, S.C.): Mack Trotter (coach), James Bowens, Herb Bowens, Jim Carter, Larry Davis, Joe Garrett, Ron Lewis, Jim Roberts, Edward Pitts, Mack Trotter, Hall, Mike Satterfield.

Southern Bell (Greenville, S.C.): Louis Morgan (coach), Herman Roberts, Jerry Cheek, Donny Bridges, David Baxter, D.D. Evans, Madison Meadows, Jerry Earl, Gillespie, Jerry Daigle, Steve Lomax, Atkinson, Graham.

Singer Mfg. (Anderson, S.C.): Walker, Madison, Smith, Willford, Leslie, Latimer, Simms, Leverette, Johnson, Mack,

Daniel Construction Co. (Greer, S.C.): Steve Brown (coach), Danny Gambrell, Earl Turner, Mark Thornton, Terry Medlin, David Gambrell, Steve Gambrell, Steve Lamb, Ronnie Reeves, Larry Plemmons, Malcolm Blankenship.

Lyman Mill (Lyman, S.C.): Sonny Moody (coach), Charles Staler, Charles Robinson, Willie Jones, Ralph Murphy, Lewis Jennings, Raymond Glenn, Lawrence Benson, Michael Durrch, Sonny Moody, Starks.

Monaghan Mill (Greenville, S.C.): Bill Swaynghame (coach), Horace Anderson, Jimmy Leamon, Charles Leamon, Donald Craig, Eddie Keeler, Alan Landreth, Joseph Holden, Daniel Rose, Frank Dye, Mitchell Goodson, Eddie Leamon, Pittman.

Taylors Mill (Taylors, S.C.): David Morgan (coach), Howard Sturgill, Kenneth Duncan, Steven Moore, Marshall Bouton, Willie Smith, Ricky Dean, Donald McCarter, Harold Smith, Rick Mansour, Lewis Goldsmith.

Fiber Industries (Greenville, S.C.): Phil Harley (coach), Ken Childers (coach), Paul Pritchett, Colvin Carter, Jerry Pritchett, Dwight Thurman, Steve Barton, Herman Evatt, Frank Armfield, Heyward Leake, Jasper Martin, Jimmy Smith, Steve Richard.

Borden Mill (Kingsport, Tenn.): Michael Locke (coach), Butch Perry, Steve Addington, Keith Ervin, Mike Christian, Carl Chambers, Mike Luster, Duffer Wallen, Danny Hammonds, Wayne Carr, Larry Page.

Hoechst Celanese (Greer, S.C.): K.O. Taylor (coach), Gil Howarth (coach), Dick Barras (coach), Sonny Anderson, Steve Arms, Lawrence Williams, Ronnie Murray, Marvin Drummond, Vincent Herron, Raeford Wideman, Kenneth Taylor, Bill Ballenger, Bennie Foster, Calvin Durham.

3M (Greenville, S.C.): Allen Turner (coach), John Turner, Gary Turner, James Galloway, Charles Crawford, Donald Scott, Marvin Arnold, Sells, Billy Davis, Steve Garner, Douglas Owens.

Sirrine Co. (Greenville, S.C.): Sandy Templeton (coach), David Martin, Bruce Martin, Thomas Keith, George Smith, Shelly Holiday, Ken Johnson, Phillip Mitchell, John Cooper, James Brooks, William Oliver, James Uz, Ralph Bouton.

Singer Mfg. (Pickens, S.C.): Sammy Nix (coach), David Norris (coach), Richard Spann, Terry Hallums, Joe Kelly, Wesley Bolding, William Anthony, Floyd Nix, Jerry Golden, Glenn Thrift, David Harper, Garland Dukes.

Greenville Law Enforcement (Greenville, S.C.): S. Smith (coach), Anthony Morton, James Perry, Bobby Smith, Barry Cook, Fred Carter, Fred Cooper, Harry Clyburn, William Wilford, Henry Harbin.

Parker Mill (Greenville, S.C.): C.T. Phillips (coach), Jimmie Robinson, Marshall Mattress, Bennett, McGowan, Clifford Chapman, Jerry Jackson, Jack McGill, McKinney.

Dunean Mill (Greenville, S.C.): Doug Gailey (coach), Gary McDowell, Dale Owens, Phil Terry, Dan Mason, Bobby Mangrum, Carroll Burns, Ray Gosnell, Randy Wardlaw, Charles Emory, Fred Sullivan.

General Electric (Greenville, S.C.): James Gamble (coach), Paul Graham, Donald Smith, Calvin Johnson, Ralph Morton, Hendricks, James Dawkins, Gaines, Thompson.

CLASS B MEN

Slater Mill (Slater, S.C.), champions: Bobby Johnson (coach), James Bowers (coach), Randy Cruell, Jody Cox, McBruce Young, Joe Hill, Jerome Williams, J. Simpson, Tony Simpson, Harold Allmond, Donnie Young.

Sally Mill (Greenville, S.C.), runners-up: P.J. Smith (coach), Ricky Foster, Pete McAbee, David Childs, Terry Roberts, Larry Megenhardt, Edwin Childs, James Moore, Marty Smith, Richard Smith, Gary Murrell, Richard Ellison.

Simpsonville Mill (Simpsonville, S.C.), consolation winners: Madden, Willie Williams, Earnest Westmoreland, Ray Wright, Webb, Thackston, Meise, Sullivan, Tumblin.

J.P. Stevens Distribution (Greenville, S.C.): Ricky Johnson (coach), James McGee, Dickie Witt, Kevin Hawkins, John Mayes, Charles Riser, David Jones, Ken Chapman, Ron Mayes, Gibson.

Singer Mfg. (Anderson, S.C.): Henry Hammond, Gordon, Jack Kelly, Scott, Daniel, Keaton, Mike Barrett, Smith, D. Hammond, A. Jones, S. Jones, Walker.

Fiberglas (Anderson, S.C.): James Chastain, Roy Jordan, Banks, Hill, Garrison, Ronald Davis, Moseley, Gambrell, Terry Boseman.

3M (Greenville, S.C.): Guthrie, Sam Horne, Michael Robertson, Gregory, Mahaffey, Tony Tice, Burrell, McNeeley, West.

American Monorail (Simpsonville, S.C.): Eason, Wiggins, Wayne Wooten, Gary Wooten, Suber, Bradshaw, B. Wooten, Fortner, Lollis.

Alice Mfg. (Easley, S.C.): Terry Smith (coach), Masters, Terry Smith, Ken Ross, Harry Sutton, Jackson, Sloan, Goodline, Harry Blake, Poole, Ledbetter, Austin, Boulder.

Renfrew Bleachery (Travelers Rest, S.C.): Ron Howell (coach), John Turner (coach), Robert Poole, Ernest Griffin, Gene Harris, Joe Mathis, Nelson Gilreath, Ansel Gilreath, Kyle Turner, Steve Mathis, Stewart Clark.

Sirrine Co. (Greenville, S.C.): B.D. Ray (coach), James Craig, Horace Jones, Charles Dalton, Dennis Haire, Youngblood, King, Clippard, Reggie Smith, Campbell, Hubbard, Carson.

Pelzer Mill (Pelzer, S.C.): Bill Hopkins (coach), Douglas Austin, Pressley, Buster Wooten, Billy Burns, Vic Alberson, James Harrison, Coleman, Sloan.

Fiber Industries (Greenville, S.C.): John Gaines (coach), Ken Childers (coach), Alewine, Larry Dogan, Clifton Ladd, Wayne Clark, Ken Durham, Baker, Joseph Phelps, Jimmy Gray, Harrison, C. Gray, Smith, Summers.

Saco-Lowell (Easley, S.C.): Mack Trotter (coach), Dan Benfield, Eddie Dobbins, James Allen, Randy Coleman, William Hoisington, Jesse Bowens, Langston.

Dow Badische (Anderson, S.C.): LeRoy Boseman (coach), Greene, Agnew, George Harris, Donnie Philyaw, Sherard, Bryant, John Smith, Jay Cooley, Myzack, Mattress.

Cryovac (Duncan, S.C.): Hezzie Simmons (coach), Steve Smith, Fred Stevens, Richard Dixon, E.W. Hardy, Paul Audet, Glenn Taylor, Greg Hall, Lester Long.

Bigelow-Sanford (Calhoun Falls, S.C.):

John Earl (coach), Mike Thompson, Willie Thurman, Manning, Al Gossett, Reed, Crain, Kennedy, James Bryson, Lance Sullivan, Potson, Greg DiBacco, Weller.

Dunean Mill (Greenville, S.C.): Doug Gailey (coach), Isaiah Walker, Jim Marion, Chris Taylor, Golden, Richard Dubose, Thigpen, McKinney, Hamilton.

Ashworth Brothers (Greenville, S.C.): Bill Dendy (coach), William Dendy III, Robert Johnson, William Roberson, Michael Blackwell, Carlton Reeves, David Whitlock, Albert Goldsmith, Merritt, Fowler.

Carolina Material Handling (Mauldin, S.C.): John Raines (coach), Terry Raines, Michael Collins, Benny Adams, Barry Raines, Darrell Smith, Ralph Raines, McDonald, Rocker, Owens, David McKinney, James Adams.

Parke-Davis (Greenwood, S.C.): Wilbert Harris (coach), Leonard White, Terry Evans, Donald White, Sammy Cooper, Larry Cooper, Arthur Caldwell, Jackson, Cannon, Calvin White.

S.C.N Bank (Greenville, S.C.): Charles Eldridge (coach), Larry Miller, Ledford, Meekin, William Ariail, Frank Wrenn, Livesay, Mullins, Ellison, Jackson Mizell.

Michelin Blue (Greenville, S.C.): Gray, Scarborough, Dennis Kelley, Robert Walker, Jackie Chambers, Harris, Larry Jackson, Brown, Robinson, Votaw, Mike Jewell.

Appleton Mill (Anderson, S.C.): Joe Geer, Don Pressley, R. Harrison, M. Wicker, Walter White, Ligon, Donnie Banks, Joseph Harrison.

Michelin Gold (Greenville, S.C.): Archie Henderson, Halstead, Reginald Neeley, Crawford, Winston, Renoir, Roger McGowan, M. Williams, Beaty, A. Williams.

Southern Weaving (Greenville, S.C.): T. Elliott, Thomas, S. Langston, Dolphus Phillips, Collins, Cole, Oglesby, Mantigoult, Wright.

Woodside Mill (Greenville, S.C.): Gary Woods (coach), Lockaby, James Hallums, Terry Stokes, W. Bolden, Washington, E. Bolden, Robinson, Rangers, Anders, Thackston,

Class C Men

American Can (Darlington, S.C.), champions: Al Eads Jr. (coach), Wilbert Singleton, Horace Wyatt, Wade Moore, Ray Bridgeman, Terry Kinard, Alfred Taylor, Al Eads.

Neely's Inc. (Greenville, S.C.), runners-up: Ken Pittman (coach), Dick Wright (coach), Randy Tillery, Schmidt, Brian Gilbertson, Britt Hudson, Doug Schmelding, Jimmy Foster, Bridges, McMahan, Jeff Neely, Vilcheck.

Dogwood Hills Mfg. (Walhalla, S.C.), consolation winners: Jim DuPre (coach), Larry Brown, Ronnie DuPre, Faron Daniels, Chuck Starks, David Parker, Keith Abercrombie, Tony Foster, Michael Parker, Jack Cochran.

Huskey Construction (Greenville, S.C.): Stan Huskey (coach), Charles Wimphrie, Mike Harris, David Mills, Bubba Whittington, Ken Billy, Charles Nevitt, Ray Lattimore, Reed, Victor Huskey, Phillip Thompson, Gradden Frezell.

Bob Jones Co. (Greenville, S.C.): Hasselbring (coach), Cox (coach), Bruce McCrary, Mike Houston, Bobby Bailey, Robbie Williamson, Charles Johnson, Greg Walls, Raymond Thomas, Brook Cely.

Akron Corp. (Greenville, S.C.): Jim Porterfield (coach), Mike Anthony (coach), Perry Craig, Robert Porterfield, William Short, Ricky Wyatt, Randy Wynn, Paul Brown, Robbie Smiley, John Collins, McGrady.

Able Sanitation (Greenville, S.C.): Gary Scism (coach), Jerry Lell (coach), Bryan Freeman, Scott Styles, Mark Carson, Brown, Joey Batson, Joel Pritchett, Eric Singleton, Joey Patterson.

PBM (Anderson, S.C.): Eugene Patterson (coach), Ronnie Payton, Dennis Lee, Steve Adams, Larry Nance, Larry Clinkscales, Brown, Carson, Evans.

Bethlehem Center (Spartanburg, S.C.): Butch Greer (coach), Anthony Thompson, Jimmy Salters, George Talley, Anthony Sanders, David Miller, Willie Barber, Reginald Larr, Joseph Long, Edward Thompson, B. Thompson.

Port City All Stars (Charleston, S.C.): Doots Wright (coach), John Mathis, Larry Nesmith, Keith Miller, John Bates, James Blake, Edward Stead, Smith, Gary Grant, James Williams, Dwayne Nelson.

Spartan All Stars (Spartanburg, S.C.): Bob Pinson (coach), Dennis Good, Joseph Page, Roy Hunnicutt, Harrison Foster, David Heatly, John Martin, Greg Simmons, William Jeffords, Jerome Richardson, Ted Williams.

Non-Fluid Oil (Greenville, S.C.): Earl Wooten (coach), Jerry Compton (ass't coach), Marc Seay, Don Ellis, Carl Feemster, Willie Scott, Simpson, Shaw, Randy Wise, Chibarro, Greg Huguley.

Southern Textile Basketball Tournament Rosters   Appendix 1   277

Sam's Drive-In (Fountain Inn, S.C.): Donny Bolton (coach), Sam Baughman (coach), Steve Durham, David Kershaw, Frankie Spurgeon, James Ferguson, Waddy Talley, Randall Smith, Fred Gilliam, James Murray, Randy Lollis, Oren Gilmore.

Pelzer Mill #2 (Pelzer, S.C.): Harold Thomason (coach), Billy Austin, Tommy Waters, Eugene Davis, Ray Holliday, Timmy Robinson, Mike Thomason, Donnie Thomason, Franklin, Steve Davis, Ronald Breazeale.

Pelzer Mill #1 (Pelzer, S.C.): Jimmy Hopkins (coach), Zam Frederick, Milen Daniels, Jerome Anderson, David Bradley, Carl Heyward, Randy Boggs, Mike Hackett, Jon Springs.

Dill's Warehouse (Greenville, S.C.): Charles Roddy (coach), Jeff McLeskey, Johnny Burgess, William Shain, Travis Cleveland, Charles Ferguson, Steve Mullinax, Michael Parker, Bill Hunt, Wilder, Tommy Brown.

Shannon Forest (Greenville, S.C.): Roger Allen (coach), George Hopson (coach), Stacy Hicks, Mike Downing, Scott George, Randy Sturgis, Jimmy Christian, Ricky Sturgis, Alan Deck, Jeff Coleman.

Jiffie Jonnie (Greenville, S.C.): Jimmy Pritchett (coach), Henry Carson, Cruell, Craig Greene, Doug McBee, Salzman, Howard, Wilson, William Short, Putman, Patterson.

Transit Homes (Greenville, S.C.): Rupert Elliott (coach), Chuck Orr, Gary Medlock, Gary Anthony, Mark Seay, Gerard, Ken Taylor, Robert Shell, Ricky Morris, Bell.

Carotell (Taylors, S.C.): Leon Gravley (coach), Robert Gravley, James Simpson, Perry, Billy DeLoche, Morgan, Cagle, Sanders, Hollis, Bratton, Morris, Talley, William Aughtry.

S-M Norgetown (Marietta, S.C.): Gary Scism (coach), Marvin Tate (coach), Melvin Young, Daryl Young, Frank Mansell, Paul Gambrell, Clinton Cobb, Wesley O'Neal, Bob Garrett, Billy Young, Porterfield, Morgan.

Parker Mill (Greenville, S.C.): Holiday, Robinson, P. Davis, Franklin, Breazeale, M. Thompson.

Class A Women

Darrell Floyd's Sandwich Shop (Greenville, S.C.), champions: Darrell Floyd (coach), Miller Perdue (coach), Bobbie Mims, Ruth Ellis, Laura Clark, Ann Horton, Kathy Wilson, Sharon Rice, Susan Reynolds, Barbara Langford, Jackie Scovel, Susan Blair, Abby Kennedy.

Discount Fence Co. (Winston-Salem, N.C.), runners-up: Jerry Holt (coach), Diane Limbaugh, Delphine Williams, Denise Rodman, Jo Haubenreiser, Gwyn Brockman, Thornton, Jan Markland, Barbara Buffet, Diane Smith.

Slater Mill (Slater, S.C.), consolation winners: Bobby Kirby (coach), Jenny Lyerly, George, Marty Vaughn, Vivian Humphries, Joan Kirby, Gadsen, Kinard, Kasper.

Duncan Pharmacy (Duncan, S.C.): Robert Sanders (coach), Lauren Murphy, Marian Brewer, Patsy Howell, Janice Morrow, Carolyn Pegram, Cheryl Fowler, Mary Henderson, Tracy Burch, Jane Harley, Thurman.

Pelzer Mill (Pelzer, S.C.): Bill Hopkins (coach), Barbara Bell, Marsha Kellett, Boggs, Golden, Massey, T. Bell, Linda Williams, Helen Williams, Andy Ashmore, S. Williams.

American Auto Parts (Hodges, S.C.): Stephen Griffith (coach), Martha Vinson, Patti Metz, Karen Brown, Jenny White, Susan Riley, Beth Turner, Dottie Turner, Cathy Speares.

Laurens Glass Co. (Laurens, S.C.): Bob LeRoy (coach), Kay Monroe, Paula Monroe, Jo Lundy, Pamela Player, McDonald, Frances Dean, Maureen McCauley, Judy Stroud, Victoria Horne, Shelia Foster, Elizabeth Ramage, Diane Ayers.

Beacon Mill (Westminster, S.C.): Roy Ward (coach), Bobby Smith (coach), Kim Marcengill, Debra Smith, Karen Hare, Karen Dalton, Susan Bradley, Vickie Burton, Gretchen Becker, Margie Everett, Pat Gasque.

Lexington Co. Recreation (Lexington, S.C.): William Hutto (coach), Westley Cullier (coach), Gerry Booker, Linda Cayruth, Rosa Henegan, Lewis, Darlene Brown, Peggy Tucker, Joyce Cunningham.

Brown's Woodworks (Greer, S.C.): Charles Kent (coach), Ann Shelton, Pam Meeler, Annamay Stockman, Terri Reid, Novalena Smith, Gault, Kathy Matthews, Carla Buchanan, Nancy Moore, Francis Young, Connie Workman, Marsha Pruitt.

Brookline Carpets (Greenville, S.C.): Doris Simpson (coach), Margaret Looper, Smith, Pam McCullough, Lelia Vaughn, Denise Warren, Calleyman, Deborah Sullivan, Walters, Latta.

1978

Officers: Lloyd McAbee (Greenville, S.C.), President; Ken Pittman (Greenville, S.C.), 1st

Vice President; Fred Powers (Charlotte, N.C.), 2nd Vice President; Bill Hopkins (Pelzer, S.C.), 3rd Vice President; Harry Foster (Greenville, S.C.), Treasurer; Phil Harley (Greenville, S.C.), Ass't Treasurer; Fred Byrd (Greenville, S.C.), Executive Secretary; Frances Welborn, Ass't Executive Secretary; Whitey Kendall (Greenville), Supervisor of Officials; Lt. F.R. Hawkins, Security Officer.

Executive Committee: Clarence Thomas (Greenville, S.C.), Willie Wilbanks (Greenwood, S.C.), Curtis Terry (Piedmont, S.C.), Willard Fowler (Greenville, S.C.), Dan Foster (Greenville, S.C.), Snow Kirby (Marietta, S.C.), Henry Spake (Anderson, S.C.), Ward Williams (Greenville, S.C.), Vercho Carter (Alexander City, Ala.), Phil Clark (Greer, S.C.), Divver Hendrix (Greenville, S.C.), Ruppert Elliott (Greenville, S.C.), Larry Ashley (Greenville, S.C.), William Dendy Jr. (Greenville, S.C.), Lewis Golden (Greenville, S.C.), Jerry Holt (Winston-Salem, N.C.), Richard Stowe (Greenwood, S.C.), James Morrow (Greenville, S.C.), James Collier III (Kingsport, Tenn.), Darrell Floyd (Greenville, S.C.).

OPEN DIVISION

Non-Fluid Oil (Greenville, S.C.), champions: Jim Phillips (coach), Dave Brown, Stan Elrod, Eddie Payne, Robin Ellenburg, Dave Hampton, Colon Abraham, Stan Rome, Jim Howell, Bobby Porter, Ronnie Creamer, Donnie Creamer, Scott Conate, Mike Massey, Lucius Pitts, Pitts.

Chick-Fil-A (Greenville, S.C.), runners-up: Tom Warrick (coach), Tony Byers, George Adams, John Seawright, Forrest Toms, Willie Joplin, Herbert Entzminzer, Mormon Mukes, Carl Martin, Rodney Young, Napier, Harrell, Jackson.

Lexington Co. Recreation (Lexington, S.C.): Taylor, Crompton, Xavier McDaniel, Corley, Cayruth, Ashe.

D & L Advertising (Greenville, S.C.): Joe Lynch (coach), Jay Spain, Willie Teague, Craig Lynch, Ron Smith, Don Harris, Wayman Oliver, Chuck Orr, Carl Mabry, Clark, Young, Bruce Grimm, Williams.

Albany Felt Co. (St. Stephens, S.C.): Henry Stewart (coach), Benjamin Tue (coach), Franklin Jefferson, Ernell Wright, Sidney Austin, Robert Gadsden, Wayne Jefferson, William Manigault, Hezekiah King, L.T. Jefferson, Bill Wright, J.L. Summers, Ronnie Jordan, Larry Bursy.

Daniel Construction Co. (Jenkinsville, S.C.): Fred Pearson (coach), Henry Boyd, Jackie Boyd, Alvin Holland, Henry Holmes, Virgil O'Neal, Heyward Smith, Melvin Williams, Stanley Kennedy, James Thompson, Rhodes, David Gambrell, Steve Gambrell, Medlin, Danny Gambrell, Plemmons, Krause.

Tri Dip Inc. (Columbia, S.C.): Anthony Brown (coach), James Brown, James Sanders, Joe Rice, Melvin Jones, David Sanders, Irvin Earle, Mike Harris, Rudolph Walker, Leroy Isaac, Donald Harris, Ken Pralour, Harold Rice, Jim Brown.

Brevard (Brevard, N.C.): Lyndon Clayton (coach), Charles Owenby (coach), Denny Griffin, Derek Thomas, Carlos Showers, Rodney Johnson, Dale Griffin, Arnold Nicholson, Larry Grant, Roy Williams, Mark Manuel, Marty Griffin, Taylor.

Arnold Palmer Cadillac (Charlotte, N.C.): Edward Wells (coach), Glenn Scott (coach), George Jackson, Mickey Bell, Charles Richards, Robert Lewis, Irwin Hill, Robert Carver, Herbert Davis, Gregg Whitman, Harry Davis, Larry Horwitz, Gerald Basinger, Rich Mazoyer, Littles.

Union Bleachery (Greenville, S.C.): Jerome Dickey (coach), Robert Poole, Jerome Williams, Clifton Scott, Doug Belt, Ricky Morris, Ricky Watts, Melvin Coley, Jack Beckett, Brando Manigo, Marion Phelps, Ernest Griffin, Robert Shell, Larry Louis, Ricky Martin, Donald, White, Dotson.

Rhymer & Littlejohn (Spartanburg, S.C.): Jim Mullen (coach), Edward Cohen, Robert Cross, William DeLoache, Scott Gould, Ronnie Harris, Robert Heil, Francis Herndon, Robert Moorer, Jeffrey Tedder, Brian Crowder, Hamlin Withington.

Keyboards (Columbia, S.C.): Jim Jackson (coach), Howard White, Charlie Powell, George Glymph, Allen Searson, Fred Melson, Rodney Bass, James Byrd, Frank Wise, John Kirkland, Glymph Childress, Mike Jacobs, Whitten.

Coca Cola (Asheville, N.C.): Jerry Green (coach), George Gilbert, Gary Grace, Ben Harper, Bamford Jones, Eddie Latta, Philip Oakes, Carl Redd, David Stickel, Ogden Braxton, Tony Bumphus, Jacob Jordan, Craig Brewer.

J & J Nursery (Winston-Salem, N.C.): Jerry

Southern Textile Basketball Tournament Rosters Appendix 1

Holt (coach), Lou Dorn, John Lentz, Donny Traylor, Hal White, Rick Barron, Neal McGochez, Bily Simpson, Don Mullinx, Rodney Young, George Brown, Mike Goshens, Wilson Parker, Bob Smith, Dunn, King, Pittman, Dobson.

CLASS A MEN

Alice Mfg. (Easley, S.C.), champions: Terry Smith (coach), Matt Valentine, Ken Galloway, Ken Murphy, Linus Blake, Billy Curenton, Jackie Anderson, Dan McCreight, Curt McGowans, Danny Hunter, John Todd, Avery Anders.

Duke Power (Greenville, S.C.), runners-up: James Earl (coach), Alexander McElrath, Gary Arnold, John Snyder, Willie Harris, David Sharperson, Ken Lister, Eddie White, Chris Anderson, James Bowen, Henry Duck, Jimmy Arnold, Ben Galloway, Jerry Shelinger, Bowden.

Monaghan Mill (Greenville, S.C.), consolation winners: Bill Swaynghame (coach), Horace Anderson, Charles Leamon, Donald Craig, Alan Landreth, Joseph Holden, Daniel Rose, Eddie Leamon, Jimmy Green, Leroy Mason, John Ward, Fred Dilworth, Bobby Jones.

Hoechst Celanese (Greer, S.C.): Ken Taylor (coach), Bill Koon (coach), Sonny Anderson, Steve Arms, Lawrence Williams, Ronnie Murray, Marvin Drummond, Raeford Wideman, Bill Ballenger, Lee Williams, Larry Arms, David Hawkins, Gilbert Howarth, Verdell Richardson.

Brookline Carpets (Greenville, S.C.): Phil Chapman (coach), Robert Staley, Wilbert Robinson, Lee Kennedy, Lavanda Sweeney, Robert Burton, Nixon Allen, Leslie Williams, Doyle Green, Robert Ellis, Tom Davis, Bruce Bufford, Elliott Owens, David McKinney, Ray Mason.

Homelite (Greer, S.C.): Pat Farmer (coach), Lee Cox (coach), Charles Crawford, Gerald Edwards, James Griffin, Luther Cohen, Robert Meadows, William Horton, Douglas Scott, Donnell Rosemond, Ricky Pickett, Theron Evans, Andrew Wright, Williams.

Ware Shoals Mill (Ware Shoals, S.C.): Roosevelt Smith (coach), Mitchell Lewis, Joe Smith, Willie Smith, Darrough Aiken, John Johnson, John Anty, Roy Hicks, Laurman Hawthorne, Stephen Griffith, David Wilson, Doug Knight, Serge Holmes.

Saco-Lowell (Easley, S.C.): Mack Trotter (coach), Larry Davis, Ron Lewis, Edward Pitts, Charles Alexander, Charles Gillespie, Roger Hilton, Russell Perdue, Kevin Reardon, Douglas Roach, Jeffrey Robbins, Larry Young, Mickey Rogers, Hendrix.

Singer Mfg. #1 (Anderson, S.C.): Kenneth Williford (coach), Cecil Mattison, Fred Smith, Wardell Sims, Richard Leverette, Calvin Wansley, James Ligon, Willie Estrick, Sam Jones.

Singer Mfg. #2 (Anderson, S.C.): Doug Rumsey (coach), Tom Stubblefield (coach), Walter Johnston, Waymon Hood, Clyde Clemmons, Clifford Leslie, Earl Walker, Thomas Greene, Jackie Kelley, J.D. Hunt, F. Smith, D. Hart, Glenn.

Daniel Construction Co. (Greer, S.C.): Darrell Jones (coach), Danny Gambrell, Mark Thornton, David Gambrell, Steve Gambrell, Larry Plemmons, Maxie Krause, Wayne Gambrell, Lawrence Watson, Medlin.

Lyman Mill (Lyman, S.C.): Sonny Moody (coach), Charles Stagger, Charles Robinson, Willie Jones, Ralph Murphy, Lewis Jennings, Raymond Glenn, Lawrence Benson, Alvin Smith, Al Murphy.

Taylors Mill (Taylors, S.C.): Ricky Dean (coach), Willie Smith, Donald McCarter, Jacob Smith, Lewis Goldsmith, Donnell Moody, Randy Neely, Wesley Ball, Jones, L. Smith.

Fiber Industries (Greenville, S.C.): Phil Harley (coach), Ken Childers (coach), Paul Pritchett, Colvin Carter, Jerry Pritchett, Steve Barton, Frank Armfield, Jasper Martin, Steve Richard, Timothy Howell, Robert Hargett, Clifford Harrison, Donald Hughes, William McKinney.

Cryovac (Simpsonville, S.C.): Lewis Whitmire (coach), Floyd Lancaster (coach), Rex Abercrombie, Bobby Phelps, Robert Massingill, James Sullivan, Calvin Milan, Fred Hill, Jimmy Wright, Roger Sullivan, Barry Wright, Joe Freeman, Matthew Milan, Albert Goldsmith.

3M (Greenville, S.C.): Allen Turner (coach), John Turner, James Galloway, Marvin Arnold, Billy Davis, Steve Garner, James Mahaffey, Lewis Styles Jr., William Junkins, John Robinson, James Counts, Lyle Stanley, John Gest, Dan Ritchie, Gravley.

Sirrine Co. (Greenville, S.C.): Sandy Templeton (coach), David Martin, Bruce Martin, Thomas Keith, George Smith, Shelly Holliday, Phillip Mitchell, John Cooper, James Uz, Ralph Bouton, Lee Clippard, Ted Templeton.

Singer Mfg. (Pickens, S.C.): Sammy Nix (coach), David Day, Terry Hallums, Joe Kelly, Wesley Bolding, William Anthony, Garland Dukes, Bill Beasley, Jerry Thomas, Tim Looper, James Adams, Sammy Baker.

Greenville Law Enforcement (Greenville, S.C.): Steve Smith (coach), Keith Morton, Bobby Smith, Steve Henry, Chip Price, Ernie Hamilton, Don Peden, Steve Smith, Ezelle Sullivan, David Helton, Kellum Allan, Mac McCrary.

Parker Mill (Greenville, S.C.): C.T. Phillips (coach), Barry Littlefield (coach), Jimmie Robinson, Marshall Mattress, Eldridge Bennett, William McGowan, Jerry Jackson, John McKinney, Fred Williams, Robert McDowell, Jimmy McDaniels, Tony Bowen, Jerry Griggs, Walter Harrison.

General Electric (Greenville, S.C.): Preston McKinney (coach), James Gamble, Donald Smith, Calvin Johnson, Ralph Morton, Charles Hendricks, James Dawkins, David Thomason, Robert Wilson, Wilbert Evans, Charles Joy, Ray Dean, James Murphy, Dickenson.

Edgecomb Metals (Greenville, S.C.): Charles Dallas (coach), William Ariail, Doug Bagwell, Rhea Bowden, Thomas Brennan, Terry Chasteen, Marvin Clary Jr., Arne Dacus, James Moore, Dennis Stone, William Vaughn, Robert Williams, Matthew Williams.

Berkeley Mill (Balfour, N.C.): Maurice Jones (coach), Michael Corn, Michael Hill, John Williams, Alton Williams, John Case, Billy Williams, Jackie Corn, Robert Haynes, Johnny Barnett, Russell Lyda, Harold Pryor.

Pelzer Mill (Pelzer, S.C.): H.D. Adams (coach), Bobby Robinson, Jackie Robinson, Leon Rochester, Leonard Williams, Jimmy Wooten, Eugene Coley, Ronnie Cureton, Ronnie Creamer, Blanding, Sullivan.

Greenville Valve (Greenville, S.C.): Gene Crook (coach), Ken Lynn, Doyle Pruitt, Ivey Stewart, Steve Crowl, Billy Hollis, Neely, Owens.

Bahan Textile (Greenville, S.C.): Ronald Sloan (coach), James Camden, Melvin Thompson, John Turner, William Bradley, Roy Burns, Donald Pressley, Michael Pressley, Douglas Pressley, Roy Johnson, Terry Hightower, Ricky Gosnell, Angelo Ferguson, S. Pressley, Christopher, D. Burns.

Slater Mill (Slater, S.C.): Snow Kirby (coach), Bobby Johnson (ass't coach), Ansel Hill, Harold Allmond, McBruce Young, Ricky Cruell, Joe Hill, Roger Cox, Alvin Cox, Keith Lyerly, John Simpson, Richard Hamilton, Donald Burnside, J. Cox, Parnell.

CLASS B MEN

Slater Mill (Slater, S.C.), champions: Mike Whitfield (coach), Jerry Hightower, John Grobelewski, Jim Bennett, Toby Burnett, Hugh McMillan, Jim Meek, Preston Smith, Charles Carter, Bob Hackle, Robert McGowens.

Michelin Gold (Greenville, S.C.), runners-up: Archie Henderson, Reginald Neeley, Winston, Renoir, Roger McGowan, M. Williams, Beaty, A. Williams, Ricky Foster, Randy Cannon, Bennon, Battle, Rollinson, Jackie Chambers.

Michelin Blue (Greenville, S.C.), consolation winners: Gray, Scarborough, Dennis Kelley, Robert Walker, Harris, Larry Jackson, Brown, Robinson, Votaw, Mike Jewell, M. Chandler, Morgan, Lollis, Kastner, Childs, Crawford, Halstead.

Sirrine Co. (Greenville, S.C.): Bob Ray (coach), James Craig, Horace Jones, Dennis Haire, William King, Reggie Smith, Carlyle Campbell, Kenneth Hubbard, Michael Brewster, Ronald Greer, James Wimbrow, Ellis Styles, Green.

Singer Mfg. (Anderson, S.C.): Doug Rumsey (coach), Henry Hammond, Charles Daniel, Donald Keaton, Mike Barrett, David Hammond, Aaron Jones, Larry Greenlee, Thomas Hammond, Ken Garrison, Scott.

Fiberglas (Anderson, S.C.): Tony Boseman (coach), David Crockett (coach), Furman Banks, William Harrison, Ronald Davis, Rufus Gambrell, Mike Meek, Larry Johns, Byrd Hennessee, Floyd Sullivan, Carl Freeman, Albert Thompson, Randy Murphy, Donald Witcher, Kenneth Groves, James McAlister.

3M (Greenville, S.C.): David Bostic (coach), Sam Horne, Tony Tice, Robert Burrell, William McNeeley, Billy Junkins, Darnell Flemmings, Terry Davis, James Brookie, Williams, Byrd.

Alice Mfg. (Easley, S.C.): Mendel Masters (coach), Sammy Smith, Ken Ross, Harry Sutton, Earl Jackson, Bradford Blake, George Ellison, John Langston, Terry McGowens, William Downs, Tommy Anderson, John Ashmore, James Blandin.

Pelzer Mill (Pelzer, S.C.): Bill Hopkins (coach), Douglas Austin, Eddie Pressley, Billy Burns, Vic Alverson, James Harrison, Ceapher

Coleman, David Burns, Sylvester Burns, Jack Golden, O. Burns.

Fiber Industries (Greenville, S.C.): Phil Harley (coach), Ken Childers (coach), Larry Dogan, Wayne Clark, Ken Durham, Joseph Phelps, Jimmy Gray, Charles Gray, Michael Brockman, Calvin Edwards, Victor Gardner, Donald Hargette, Johnny Housley, Martin Ketterer, C. Gardner.

Saco-Lowell (Easley, S.C.): Mack Trotter (coach), Dan Benfield, Eddie Dobbins, James Allen, Randy Coleman, William Hoisington, Jesse Bowens, Langston, Turman, Anderson, Sherrill, Sisk, Young, Hooper, Tucker.

Dow Badische (Anderson, S.C.): LeRoy Boseman (coach), Greene, Agnew, George Harris, Donnie Philyaw, Sherard, Bryant, John Smith, Jay Cooley, Myzack, Mattress, Rucker, Harrison, Blackwell, Seville, Webb, Broner.

Southeastern-Kusan (Greenville, S.C.): McAlister, Ashmore, Thompson, Bruster, Chandler.

Cryovac (Duncan, S.C.): Hezzie Simmons (coach), Steve Smith, Fred Stevens, Richard Dixon, E.W. Hardy, Paul Audet, Glenn Taylor, Greg Hall, Lester Long, Keonig, Edwards, R. Smith, Russell, Byrne, Calvert, Hagins, A. Edwins, Vanderploge, Dobbins, Johnson, Holcombe.

Bigelow-Sanford (Calhoun Falls, S.C.): John Earl (coach), Mike Thompson, Willie Thurman, Manning, Al Gossett, Reed, Crain, Kennedy, James Bryson, Lance Sullivan, Potson, Greg DiBacco, Weller.

Dunean Mill (Greenville, S.C.): Doug Gailey (coach), Isaiah Walker, Jim Marion, Chris Taylor, Golden, Richard Dubose, Thigpen, McKinney, Hamilton, Powell, Goodwin, Harris, Carson.

Ashworth Brothers (Greenville, S.C.): Bill Dendy (coach), William Dendy III, Robert Johnson, William Roberson, Michael Blackwell, Carlton Reeves, David Whitlock, Albert Goldsmith, Merritt, Fowler, C. Withington, J. Withington, Anders.

Carolina Material Handling (Mauldin, S.C.): John Raines (coach), Terry Raines, Michael Collins, Benny Adams, Barry Raines, Darrell Smith, Ralph Raines, McDonald, Rocker, Owens, David McKinney, James Adams.

Parke-Davis (Greenwood, S.C.): Wilbert Harris (coach), Leonard White, Terry Evans, Donald White, Sammy Cooper, Larry Cooper, Arthur Caldwell, Jackson, Cannon, Calvin White, Smiley, Jaffe, Strong.

S.C.N Bank (Greenville, S.C.): Charles Eldridge (coach), Larry Miller, Ledford, Meekin, William Ariail, Frank Wrenn, Livesay, Mullins, Ellison, Jackson Mizell.

Appleton Mill (Anderson, S.C.): Joe Geer, Don Pressley, R. Harrison, M. Wicker, Walter White, Ligon, Donnie Banks, Joseph Harrison, Allen, Jones, Gaines, Brock, Ashworth, Dendy, C. Whittington, Johnson, J. Whittington, Reeves, Blackwell, Aiken, Robinson, Calhoun, D. Greer.

Southern Weaving (Greenville, S.C.): T. Elliott, Thomas, S. Langston, Dolphus Phillips, Collins, Cole, Oglesby, Mantigoult, Wright, Griffin, Westmoreland, Chambers, S.P. Collins, McKinney, Mann, Watts.

Woodside Mill (Greenville, S.C.): Gary Woods (coach), Lockaby, James Hallums, Terry Stokes, W. Bolden, Washington, E. Bolden, Robinson, Rangers, Anders, Thackston, Bryant, Jenkins, Sims, Jones, Evans, Freeman, McCombs, McCall, Tucket.

Jet Rest Furniture (Greer, S.C.): Wilson, Smith, Goodman, Wright, Cohen, Merck, Goodlett, Bud McClinton.

F.W. Woolworth (Greenville, S.C.): Donald, Franks, Bolton, Sullivan, Chandler, Steele, Ducey, Brownlee.

Victor Mill #2 (Greer, S.C.): Nance, Jones, Mitchell, Gilliam, Everette, Foster, Garren, J. Graydon, D. Graydon, Savala.

Singer Mfg. (Pickens, S.C.): Hopkins, Sobil, Golden, Burgess, Parker, Glover, Kirk, Baker, Millwood, Putnam, Holcombe.

Cryovac (Simpsonville, S.C.): Dendy, Stenhouse, Valentine, Satterwhite, Johnson, Wright, Sims, Sullivan.

Sharon Corp. (Greenville, S.C.): Gallamore, K. McCullough, M. McCullough, Millwood, Leopard, McKinney, Street, Howell, Silvers, Raines, Scruggs.

Victor Mill #1 (Greer, S.C.): Mills, C. Davis, W. Davis, Compton, E. Smith, Gilliam, L. Davis, Grant, Dennis.

Sally Mill (Greenville, S.C.): Megenhardt, R. Smith, Williams, Roberts, Ellison, Ra. Smith, M. Smith, Standard.

Greenville County Recreation (Greenville, S.C.): Belk, Mack, Dersch, McCullough, Henson, Jones, Chappelle, Dreher, Wilson, McKeown, Sleigh, Porter.

Reliance Electric (Greenville, S.C.):

Carithers, Mauldin, Dallaire, Merritt, Jones, Thompson, Barbery.

Class C Men

Pelzer Mill #1 (Pelzer, S.C.), champions: Bill Hopkins (coach), Jimmy Hopkins (coach), Zam Frederick, Jerome Anderson, David Bradley, Carl Heyward, Randy Boggs, Mike Hackett, John Springs, Ronnie Carr, Jimmy Foster, Darrell Fowler, John Williams, Monty Crocker, Terrence Roberts, Raymond Jones, Terry Haney, Mel Daniel, Harper.

Neely's Inc. (Greenville, S.C.), runners-up: Ken Pittman (coach), Dick Wright (coach), Randy Tillery, Schmidt, Brian Gilbertson, Britt Hudson, Doug Schmieding, Bridges, McMahan, Jeff Neely, Vilcheck, Ed Young, Ricky Wyatt, Shaw, Thompson, Morgan, Sneed, Cohen, Gilmore.

Huskey Construction (Greenville, S.C.), consolation winners: Stan Huskey (coach), Charles Wimphrie, Mike Harris, David Mills, Bubba Whittington, Ken Billy, Charles Nevitt, Ray Lattimore, Reed, Victor Huskey, Phillip Thompson, Gradden Frezell, Meadows, Page, Hunnicutt, Massey, Hymen, Henderson, Williams, Pearson, Gillespie.

Dill's Warehouse (Greenville, S.C.): Charles Roddy (coach), Jeff McLeskey, Johnny Burgess, William Shain, Travis Cleveland, Charles Ferguson, Steve Mullinax, Michael Parker, Bill Hunt, Wilder, Tommy Brown, Chuck Starks, Mills, Harris, Porter, Grier, Hawthorne, Sams, Tony Foster.

Dogwood Hills Mfg. (Walhalla, S.C.): Jim DuPre (coach), Larry Brown, Ronnie DuPre, Faron Daniels, David Parker, Keith Abercrombie, Jack Cochran.

American Can (Darlington, S.C.): Al Eads (coach), Wilbert Singleton, Horace Wyatt, Wade Moore, Ray Bridgeman, Terry Kinard, Alfred Taylor.

Bob Jones Co. (Greenville, S.C.): Hasselbring (coach), Cox (coach), Bruce McCrary, Mike Houston, Bobby Bailey, Robbie Williamson, Charles Johnson, Greg Walls, Raymond Thomas, Brook Cely.

Lance (Greenville, S.C.): Jim Porterfield (coach), Mike Anthony (coach), Craig Perry, Robert Porterfield, William Short, Ricky Wyatt, Randy Wynn, Paul Brown, Robbie Smiley, John Collins, McGrady, Wardlaw, Sullivan, Ball, Shuford, Ely, Thomas.

Able Sanitation (Greenville, S.C.): Gary Scism (coach), Jerry Lell (coach), Bryan Freeman, Scott Styles, Mark Carson, Brown, Joey Batson, Joel Pritchett, Eric Singleton, Joey Patterson.

PBM (Anderson, S.C.): Eugene Patterson (coach), Ronnie Payton, Dennis Lee, Steve Adams, Larry Nance, Larry Clinkscales, Brown, Carson, Evans.

Bethlehem Center (Spartanburg, S.C.): Butch Greer (coach), Anthony Thompson, Jimmy Salters, George Talley, Anthony Sanders, David Miller, Willie Barber, Reginald Larr, Joseph Long, Edward Thompson, B. Thompson.

Port City All Stars (Charleston, S.C.): Doots Wright (coach), John Mathis, Larry Nesmith, Keith Miller, John Bates, James Blake, Edward Stead, Smith, Gary Grant, James Williams, Dwayne Nelson.

Spartan All Stars (Spartanburg, S.C.): Bob Pinson (coach), Dennis Good, Joseph Page, Roy Hunnicutt, Harrison Foster, David Heatly, John Martin, Greg Simmons, William Jeffords, Jerome Richardson, Ted Williams.

Non-Fluid Oil (Greenville, S.C.): Earl Wooten (coach), Jerry Compton (coach), Marc Seay, Don Ellis, Carl Feemster, Willie Scott, Simpson, Shaw, Randy Wise, Chibarro, Greg Huguley, Ours, Gibson, Hudson, Schmelding, McAfee, Harvey, McHugh.

Sam's Drive-In (Fountain Inn, S.C.): Donny Bolton (coach), Sam Baughman (coach), Steve Durham, David Kershaw, Frankie Spurgeon, James Ferguson, Waddy Talley, Randall Smith, Fred Gilliam, James Murray, Randy Lollis, Oren Gilmore.

Pelzer Mill #2 (Pelzer, S.C.): Harold Thomason (coach), Billy Austin, Tommy Waters, Eugene Davis, Ray Holliday, Timmy Robinson, Mike Thomason, Donnie Thomason, Franklin, Steve Davis, Ronald Breazeale, R. Smith, T. Smith, Eskew, Knight, Jameson, Hall, Brady, Looper.

Shannon Forest (Greenville, S.C.): Roger Allen (coach), George Hopson (coach), Stacy Hicks, Mike Downing, Scott George, Randy Sturgis, Jimmy Christian, Ricky Sturgis, Alan Deck, Jeff Coleman.

Jiffie Jonnie (Greenville, S.C.): Jimmy Pritchett (coach), Henry Carson, Cruell, Craig Greene, Doug McBee, Salzman, Howard, Wilson, William Short, Putman, Patterson, Pendergrass, Thompson, Garrett, Fincher, Freeman, Snyder.

Southern Textile Basketball Tournament Rosters — Appendix 1

Transit Homes (Greenville, S.C.): Rupert Elliott (coach), Chuck Orr, Gary Medlock, Gary Anthony, Mark Seay, Gerard, Ken Taylor, Robert Shell, Ricky Morris, Bell.

Carotell (Taylors, S.C.): Leon Gravley (coach), Robert Gravley, James Simpson, Perry, Billy DeLoche, Morgan, Cagle, Sanders, Hollis, Bratton, Morris, Talley, William Aughtry, Mayfield, Arthur, Smith, Huguley, Collins, Moorer.

S-M Norgetown (Marietta, S.C.): Gary Scism (coach), Marvin Tate (coach), Melvin Young, Daryl Young, Paul Gambrell, Clinton Cobb, Wesley O'Neal, Bob Garrett, Billy Young, Morgan.

Parker Mill (Greenville, S.C.): Holiday, Robinson, P. Davis, Franklin, Breazeale, M. Thompson.

Grady's Sports (Anderson, S.C.): Marshall, Morton, Carson, Rhodes, Skelton, Adams, Lomax, Norris, Clinkscales, Barrett.

Ashworth Brothers (Greenville, S.C.): Ashworth, Sullivan, Williams, Elias, Grimmett, Wilder, Jochimson, D. Ashworth, R. Norris, G. Norris, Parry.

Blankenship Electric (Greenville, S.C.): S. Mullinax, Blankenship, Bowers, Steel, Jackson, R. Mullinax, Guest, Wright, Wilder, Merritt, Medlock.

Dean Hill Cars (Greenville, S.C.): T. Duncan, Tolbert, B. Duncan, P. Duncan, Schwartz, McAbee, Culpepper, Marshall, M. Marshall, Carroway.

Hardee's (Spartanburg, S.C.): Streater, Hopkins, Gilliam, Edmonds, Franklin, Craig, Redmond, Pinson, Reed, Frank Mansell, Mitchell, DeShields.

Athletic Attic (Anderson, S.C.): Scruggs, Pace, Ferguson, Duncan, Simpson, Browning, Helderman.

Courtesy Mechanical (Greenville, S.C.): C. Butler, Mullinax, Patterson, Stapleton, Ridley, Thompson, D. Butler, Webb.

Old Mill Stream (Greenville, S.C.): Thomas, Boyd, Durham, B. Cox, Steading, McDonald, Neely, R. Cox, Griffin, J. Cox, Bayne.

CLASS A WOMEN

Pelzer Mill (Pelzer, S.C.), champions: Bill Hopkins (coach), Doots Wright (coach), B.J. Bell, Marsha Kellett, Tammy Boggs, Golden, Massey, T. Bell, Linda Williams, Helen Williams, Andy Ashmore, S. Williams, Trish Roberts, Sister Green, Sybil Blalock, Pearl Moore, Lisa Garrett, Neet Cooper, Susan Fuller, Sadie Sellers, Shuford.

Slater Mill (Slater, S.C.), runners-up: Bobby Kirby (coach), Jenny Lyerly, George, Marty Vaughn, Vivian Humphries, Joan Kirby, Gadsen, Kinard, Kasper, Burgin, Ramsey, Reid, Gilstrap, Adams.

Griggs Electric (N/A), consolation winners: Leatherman, Bishop, Mickle, Robinson, Scott, Bonnett, Long, McLorin.

Brookline Carpets (Greenville, S.C.): Doris Simpson (coach), Margaret Looper, Smith, Pam McCullough, Lelia Vaughn, Denise Warren, Calleyman, Deborah Sullivan, Walters, Latta, Fleming, Kinard, Thompson, Durham, Callahan, Winegate, Blackman, Diane Sullivan.

Darrell Floyd's Sandwich Shop (Greenville, S.C.): Darrell Floyd (coach), Miller Perdue (coach), Bobbie Mims, Ruth Ellis, Laura Clark, Horton, Kathy Wilson, Susan Reynolds, Barbara Langford, Jackie Scovel, Susan Blair, Abbey Kennedy, Forester, Kim Basinger, Becker, Jennings, N. Floyd, Debra Buford, Greer.

Discount Fence Co. (Winston-Salem, N.C.), runners-up: Jerry Holt (coach), Diane Limbaugh, Delphine Williams, Denise Rodman, Jo Haubenreiser, Gwyn Brockman, Thornton, Jan Markland, Barbara Buffet, Diane Smith.

Duncan Pharmacy (Duncan, S.C.): Robert Sanders (coach), Lauren Murphy, Marian Brewer, Patsy Howell, Janice Morrow, Carolyn Pegram, Cheryl Fowler, Mary Henderson, Tracy Burch, Jane Harley, Thurman, Skelton, Annamay Stockman, Sharon Rice, Osborne, Ray, Murphy, Bullard, Lawter, Jackson.

American Auto Parts (Hodges, S.C.): Stephen Griffith (coach), Martha Vinson, Patti Metz, Karen Brown, Jenny White, Susan Riley, Beth Turner, Dottie Turner, Cathy Speares, Looney, Whelan, Williamson, Basket, McAlister.

Laurens Glass Co. (Laurens, S.C.): Bob LeRoy (coach), Kay Monroe, Paula Monroe, Jo Lundy, Pamela Player, McDonald, Frances Dean, Maureen McCauley, Judith Stroud, Victoria Horne, Elizabeth Ramage, Diane Ayers, Pridgeon, LaForge, Fowler, Campbell, Pyles, Wentzky.

Beacon Mill (Westminster, S.C.): Roy Ward (coach), Bobby Smith (coach), Kim Marcengill, Debra Smith, Karen Hare, Karen Dalton,

Susan Bradley, Vickie Burton, Gretchen Becker, Margie Everett, Pat Gasque, Lee, Halley, Abbott, Stone.

Lexington Co. Recreation (Lexington, S.C.): William Hutto (coach), Westley Cullier (coach), Gerry Booker, Linda Cayruth, Rosa Henegan, Lewis, Darlene Brown, Peggy Tucker, Joyce Cunningham.

Brown's Woodworks (Greer, S.C.): Charles Kent (coach), Ann Shelton, Pam Meeler, Novalena Smith, Gault, Carla Buchanan, Nancy Moore, Francis Young, Connie Workman, Marsha Pruitt, Terri Reid.

Gould Associates (Taylors, S.C.): Gould, Hogue, Holland, Nicks, Dickard, Buchanan, Spear, Traynham, Hudson, McKinney.

Bennett Oil (Spartanburg, S.C.): Culbreath, Jones, Reid, Stroud, Sheila Foster, McCrary, Albright.

Hoechst Celanese (Greer, S.C.): Creasman, Bennett, W. Dogan, Kathy Matthews, S. Dogan, Mullinax, Turner.

Atlanta Cards (Atlanta, Ga.): Owen, Bryan, Garrison, Gibson, Hodges, Montgomery, Rankins.

Saco-Lowell (Easley, S.C.): Fant, Ricken, Wright, Meals, Cartee, Allen, Smith, Knight.

Georgia Electric (N/A): M. Everette, Stoddard, Reid, George, Bostic, J. Everette, Geddens, Harris, Burden, Hanks.

Athletic Attic (Anderson, S.C.): Scovell, Beth Couture, Langston, Chambers, Clinkscales, Allen, Hanks, Black.

1979

Officers: Lloyd McAbee (Greenville, S.C.), President; Ken Pittman (Greenville, S.C.), 1st Vice President; Fred Powers (Charlotte, N.C.), 2nd Vice President; Bill Hopkins (Pelzer, S.C.), 3rd Vice President; Harry Foster (Greenville, S.C.), Treasurer; Phil Harley (Greenville, S.C.), Ass't Treasurer; Fred Byrd (Greenville, S.C.), Executive Secretary; Ruppert Elliott (Greenville, S.C.), Ass't Executive Secretary; Whitey Kendall (Greenville), Supervisor of Officials; Lt. F.R. Hawkins, Security Officer.

Executive Committee: Clarence Thomas (Greenville, S.C.), (Greenwood, S.C.), Curtis Terry (Piedmont, S.C.), Willard Fowler (Greenville, S.C.), Dan Foster (Greenville, S.C.), Snow Kirby (Marietta, S.C.), Henry Spake (Anderson, S.C.), Ward Williams (Greenville, S.C.), Vercho Carter (Alexander City, Ala.), Phil Clark (Greer, S.C.), Divver Hendrix (Greenville, S.C.), Lewis Golden (Greenville, S.C.), Jerry Holt (Winston-Salem, N.C.), James Morrow (Greenville, S.C.), Darrell Floyd (Greenville, S.C.), David Bailey (Greenville, S.C.), Jyles Phillips (Greenville, S.C.).

OPEN DIVISION

Non-Fluid Oil (Greenville, S.C.), champions: Jim Phillips (coach), Stan Elrod (coach), Johnson, Coles, Dickerson, Wells, Zane, Hampton, Donnie Creamer, Ronnie Creamer, B. Griffin, Pitts.

Chick-Fil-A (Greenville, S.C.), runners-up: Tom Warrick (coach), Terry Shelton (coach), Tony Byers, George Adams, John Seawright, Lew Young, Phil Cox, Mike Meadows, Daryl Robinson, Mel Hubbard, Colon Abraham, Franklin, Jones, Napier, Nesbitt, Miller.

Daniel Construction Co. (Jenkinsville, S.C.): Fred Pearson (coach), Henry Boyd, Jackie Boyd, Alvin Holland, Virgil O'Neal, Heyward Smith, Stanley Kennedy, Fred Pearson Jr., Ernest Owens, Costello Boyd, Otis Rhodes, Curtis Carter, David Seibles, V. Pearson, F. O'Neal, Glenn.

Tri Dip Inc. (Columbia, S.C.): Anthony Brown (coach), James Brown, Larry Sanders, Joe Rice, Melvin Jones, Irvin Earle, Mike Harris, Rudolph Walker, Wade Jenkins, Robert Geter, Tommy Portee, Jim Brown.

Keyboards (Columbia, S.C.): Woody Sharpe (coach), Howard White, George Glymph, Allen Searson, Fred Melson, James Byrd, John Kirkland, Glymph Childress, Mike Grenier, Scott Conant, Tommy Whitten.

Wofford College (Spartanburg, S.C.): Jim Mullen (coach), Charles Bagwell, Mark Bruce, Scott Gould, Ronnie Harris, Robert Heil, Francis Herndon, James Moody, Robert Moorer, Michael O'Driscoll, Michael Upchurch, Michael Howard.

Sam Wyche Sports World (Greenville, S.C.): Charles Thompson (coach), Al Daniel, John Gerdy, Bobby Porter, Jim Clark, Bobby Griffin, Collie Feemster, Gus Rubio, Alonzo Harrison, Tracey Oxendine, William Teague, Matt Simpkins, Larry Gibson, Isom, Mabry, Hayes, Strickland.

Albany Felt Co. (St. Stephens, S.C.): Henry Stewart (coach), Ernell Wright, Hezekiah King, Louis Jefferson, Larry Bursey, Sidney Alston,

Ernest Mallard, Wayne Jefferson, William Manigault, Donald McCutcheon, Bill Wright, James Summers, Franklin Jefferson Jr., Hawkins, Dingle.

Greenwood Jazz (Greenwood, S.C.): Donny Southard (coach), Wayne Southard, Harry Godley, David Havird, Charles Marshall, Larry Ray, Sammy Belcher, Bobby Shaw, Barry Isom, Greg Robinson, Daniels, Brownlee, Goodby, Stalnaker, Stone.

Time Out (Greenville, S.C.): Heil, Harris, Moody, Moorer, Bagwell, Boone, Herndon, Driscoll, Howard, Blair.

CLASS A MEN

Dunean Mill (Greenville, S.C.), champions: Randy Wardlaw (coach), Charles Hudson (coach), Isaiah Walker, Richard DuBose, Christopher Taylor, Jimmy Marion, Clyde Agnew, James McGee, James Harris, Timothy Blackmon, Andrew Carson, Mark Mangrum.

Michelin (Sandy Springs, S.C.), runners-up: Mike Thrasher (coach), Roscoe Powell, Roger Rhodes, James Lesley, Charles Johnson, Jackie Clement, Jimmy Johnson, Larry Hall, Gregory Franklin, Charles Lesley, Henry Leverette Jr., William Sanders, James Yates, S. Lesley.

Homelite (Greer, S.C.), consolation winners: Calvin Cohen (coach), Charles Crawford, Gerald Edwards, James Griffin, Robert Meadows, Donnell Rosemond, Ricky Pickett, Andrew Wright, Ricky Bruton, Jesse Flemings, Ricky Wilson, Brown, Horton.

Applied Engineering (Orangeburg, S.C.): Charles Clark (coach), Dan Carver (coach), Chris Carver, Harry Shuler, David Prince, David Paul, Sam Richardson, Ronald Huggins, Charles Clark Jr., Jacob Smith, Tim Gadson, Tommy Frazier, Richard Rivers.

Brookline Carpets (Greenville, S.C.): Phil Chapman (coach), Charles Robinson, Lavanda Sweeney, Robert Burton, Nixon Allen, Leslie Williams, Bruce Bufford, Elliott Owens, Henry Phelps, Ben Houston, Ronald White.

Ware Shoals Mill (Ware Shoals, S.C.): Roosevelt Smith (coach), Joe Smith, Willie Smith, Serge Holmes, Clarence Brownlee, William Brownlee, Michael Epps, Raymond Kelly, Tim Stewart, Eddie Whatley, Alvin Jackson.

Duke Power (Greenville, S.C.): Earle, Bowden, Arnold, Snyder, Williams, Britton, Laws, Blakely.

Alice Mfg. (Easley, S.C.): Terry Smith (coach), Matt Valentine, Kenneth Galloway, Ken Murphy, Linus Blake, Billy Curenton, Jackie Anderson, Dan McCreight, Curt McGowans, George Davis, William Jackson, Bobby Smith, Langston.

Saco-Lowell (Easley, S.C.): Mack Trotter (coach), Larry Davis, Charles Gillespie, Russell Perdue, James Allen, Bret Bishop, James Bowens, Jimmy Bowens, David Clark, Eddie Dobbins, Mike Hughes, Gregory Pepper, David Smith, M. Allen.

Edgecomb Metals (Greenville, S.C.): Chasteen, Bagwell, Arial, Bowden, Brennan, Williams, McDonald, Dacus, Clary.

Singer Mfg. (Anderson, S.C.): Wardell Sims (coach), Fred Smith, Willie Estrick, Earl Walker, Thomas Hammond, Clyde Clemons, Clifford Leslie, Henry Hammond, Waymon Hood, David Hammond, Kenneth Garrison, Walter Johnson, A. Hammond, Sims.

Lyman Mill (Lyman, S.C.): Sonny Moody (coach), Charles Stagger, Charles Robinson, Willie Wright, Lewis Jennings, Raymond Glenn, Lawrence Benson, Bobby Jackson, Thomas Aiken, Clarence Moody, Douglas Hemphill, Clarence Carson, Cohen, Johnson, Leslie.

Monaghan Mill (Greenville, S.C.): Bill Swaynghame (coach), Horace Anderson, Charles Leamon, Alan Landreth, Eddie Leamon, John Ward, Fred Dilworth, Bobby Jones, Marcus Dowdy, Edward Wilhoit, Lewis McCoy Jr., Maxie Burns, Ted Pittman.

Fiber Industries (Greenville, S.C.): Phil Harley (coach), Ken Childers (coach), Colvin Carter, Steve Barton, Frank Armfield, Jasper Martin, Steve Richard, Timothy Howell, Robert Hargett, Ronald Hughes, William McKinney, Claude Barnett, Heyward Leake, Richard, Harley.

Hoechst Celanese (Greer, S.C.): Verdell Richardson (coach), Roy Wideman (coach), Sonny Anderson, Steve Arms, Lawrence Williams, Marvin Drummond, Lee Williams, David McKinney, Gilbert Howarth, James Williams, Marvin Hawkins, Kenneth Duncan, Ray Davis, Kenneth Taylor, B. Williams.

Cryovac (Simpsonville, S.C.): Lewis Whitmire (coach), James Sullivan (coach), Rex Abercrombie, Bobby Phelps, Robert Massingill, Calvin Milan, Fred Hill, James Sullivan, Barry Wright, Matthew Milan, Albert Goldsmith, Benny Baldwin, Barry Church, Clarence Whittenburg.

3M (Greenville, S.C.): Barry Cook (coach),

John Williams, James Galloway, Marvin Arnold, Steve Garner, James Mahaffey, Louis Sayles Jr., William Collins, John Robinson, James Gwinn, Jesse Looper, Gravley.

Sirrine Co. (Greenville, S.C.): Ken Johnson (coach), Ted Templeton, Bruce Martin, Thomas Keith, George Smith, Phillip Mitchell, John Cooper, James Uz, Ralph Bouton, James Perkins, Harry Moats.

Singer Mfg. (Pickens, S.C.): Sammy Nix (coach), David Norris (coach), Terry Stokes, Joe Kelly, Wesley Bolding, William Anthony, Tim Dukes, Bill Beasley, John Adams, Sammy Baker, John Burgess, Marty Hopkins, Wade Collins, Stone, Looper.

Greenville Law Enforcement (Greenville, S.C.): L. Greggs (coach), Steve Smith, Henry Harbin, Chip Price, Don Peden, Steve Smith, David Helton, Jim Perry, Dan Ballard, Wayne Clark, Harold Jennings, Johnnie Talbert, James Meekins, Robert Dorrah, Rice, Morris.

Parker Mill (Greenville, S.C.): C.T. Phillips (coach), Barry Littlefield (coach), Marshall Mattress, William McGowan, Jerry Jackson, John McKinney, Jerome Williams, Walter Harrison, Dwayne Wilder, Robert Pepper, Michael Sullivan, Alexander Brockman, Clifford Chapman, Donald.

General Electric (Greenville, S.C.): Gary Smith (coach), Bobby Hart (coach), Donald Smith, Calvin Johnson, Ralph Morton, Rick Hendricks, James Murphy, Robert Wilson, Gary Ravan, Thomas Hallums, Michael Jones, Edward McGowens, Steve Martin.

Pelzer Mill (Pelzer, S.C.): Horace Davenport (coach), Bobby Robinson, Jackie Robinson, Leonard Williams, Eugene Coley, Ronnie Curenton, Willie Evans, Jesse Blanding, Wesley Sloan, Gary Burts, Jimmy Harrison, Elrod, Clardy, Willimon, Airline.

Slater Mill (Slater, S.C.): Snow Kirby (coach), McBruce Young, Ricky Cruell, Joe Hill, Roger McCall, Keith Lyerly, John Simpson, Richard Hamilton, Terry Harbin, James Wood, William Parnell, Bruce Hume, Ricky Laws.

Michelin (Spartanburg, S.C.): Steve Brown (coach), Ronnie Rice, Charles Rogers, Bryant Wallace, Ronald McClain, Eddie Battle, Lynn Brown, Alan King, Stan Jones, David Bibb, James Lindsay.

Marietta Substation II (Marietta, S.C.): Mike Whitfield (coach), Floyd Burnett, Randy Burns, Charles Carter, John Groblewski, Robert Hackle, Garry Helms, Terry Hightower, James Meek, Robert McGowens, Preston Smith, Tom Clark.

Mayfair Mill (Pickens, S.C.): Ted Shehan (coach), Roger Cater, Rocky Cater, John Howard, Ronnie Rosemond, Dan Desrocher, James Rosemond, Doug Dukes, Jessie Thomas, Lewis Monroe, Bobby Kirksey, John Ashmore.

American Enka (Central, S.C.): Larry Bowens (coach), Gary Nix (coach), Les Porter, Mike Hagood, William Peppers, Carl Valentine, Morris Henderson, Dannie Cannon Jr., Alvin Holland, Danny Rogers, Larry Kopp, Howard McDowell, Mike Church, Bagwell.

CLASS B MEN

Michelin Gold (Greenville, S.C.), champions: J.C. Starkes (coach), Archie Henderson, Francis Halstead, Harold Crawford, Melvin Williams, Donnie Chambers, Steve Rollinson, Ricky Foster, Mike Winston, Johnny Smith, Bernard Tompkins, Danny Gilreath, Robert Austin.

Whitten Village (Clinton, S.C.), runners-up: Alex Rogers (coach), Thomas Rogers, Francis Robbins, Glenn Bledsoe, Julian Bryan, John Woodside, Samuel McCrary, Edgar Acree, Dan Lanford, Donnie Kidd, George Saunders, Grady Suber.

Ashworth Brothers (Greenville, S.C.), consolation winners: Bill Williams (coach), William Dendy III, Carlton Reeves, Steve Goldsmith, Joe Bayne, Gerald Pitts, Jimmy Withington, David Whitlock, Steve Kataveck, Craig Grimmett, Richard McAlhaney, Ashworth, Johnson.

Jet Rest Furniture (Greer, S.C.): Bobby Corn (coach), James Smith, Thomas Goodlett, David Anderson, Charles Miller, John Ward, Elliott Everett, Curtis Hardy, Willie Nesbitt, David Williams, Chris Sanal, Cohen, Wilson, Davis, Wilson, Alexander.

Fiberglas (Anderson, S.C.): Tony Boseman (coach), Bill White (coach), Ronald Davis, Rufus Gambrell, George Thompson, Donald Witcher, Kenneth Groves, Clinton Crosby, Wayne Kelley, Banks Furman, Gary Mattison, Thomas Graves, Kevin Clayburn, Boseman.

3M (Greenville, S.C.): Bill Davis (coach), Randy Bridges (coach), Thomas Tice, Robert Burrell, William McNeeley, Darnell Flemming, Terry Davis, James Brookie, Dennis Blakely, Michael Bryant, Hiram Davis, James Austin, Stanley Sullivan, Willie Madden.

Southern Textile Basketball Tournament Rosters Appendix 1

Alice Mfg. (Easley, S.C.): Benny Sloan (coach), Sammy Smith, Ken Ross, John Langston, Terry McGowens, William Downs, Tommy Anderson, James Bowens, Benny Sloan, Gerald Gambrell.

Sirrine Co. (Greenville, S.C.): Bob Ray (coach), James Craig, Horace Jones, Dennis Poole, Kenneth Hubbard, Michael Brewster, James Wimbrow, Larry Dalton, Ray Drummond, Clay Aldebol, Kline.

Pelzer Mill (Pelzer, S.C.): Jack Golden (coach), Eddie Pressley, Billy Burns, Vic Alverson, James Harrison, Ceaphes Coleman, David Burns, Sylvester Burns, Bobby Burns, Todd Hall, Danny Scroggs, Turner, J. Burns.

Fiber Industries (Greenville, S.C.): Phil Harley (coach), Ken Childers (coach), Larry Dogan, Ken Durham, Jimmy Gray, Charles Gray, Michael Brockman, Donald Hargette, Johnny Housley, Martin Ketterer, Clifton Bloise, Luther Floyd III, Thaddeus Franklin, Franklin Lewis, Gregory Wilson, Wright, Dirton, Harrison.

Saco-Lowell (Easley, S.C.): Herbert Bowen (coach), Dan Benfield, Randy Coleman, Reginald Anderson, Steve Sisk, Gregg Corbin, George Turmon, Scott Brown, William Anderson, Eddie Ballew, Dale Gillespie, Mike Youngblood, Wes Hunter.

Cryovac #1 (Duncan, S.C.): Hezekiah Simmons (coach), Paul Audet, Fred Dobbins, Fred Stephens, Richard Dixon, Van VanderPloeg, E.W. Hardy, Arthur Edwards, Grady Gaston, Michael Shuck, Leonard Byrne, Robert Smith, Robinson.

Cryovac #2 (Duncan, S.C.): Joseph Browder (coach), Hugh Bunn, Edward Holcombe, Steve Johnson, Greg Hall, Edward Davis Jr., Timothy Gleason, Milan Williams, John Martin, Will Rogers, Steve Smith, Browder.

Parke-Davis (Greenwood, S.C.): Bobby Wideman (coach), Leonard White, Sammy Cooper, Larry Cooper, Arthur Caldwell, Curtis Cannon, Calvin White, James Strong, James Rush, Randolph Dendy, I. White, J. Cooper.

Michelin Blue (Greenville, S.C.): Ron Scarborough (coach), Dennis Kelley, Jackie Chambers, Larry Jackson, Mike Jewell, David Childs, Jim Morgan, Jack Lollis, Michael Chandler, Reginald Nealey, Ricky Starkes, Joel Starkes Jr, Sewell, J. Chandler, Bayne.

Appleton Mill (Anderson, S.C.): Henry Spake (coach), Joe Geer, Don Pressley, Joseph Harrison, Rodney Allen, Ernest Brock, Roy Calhoun, Judson Gaines, David Geer, Mack Nance, Leroy Cherry, Ricky Craft.

Southern Weaving (Greenville, S.C.): James Chappell (coach), Verlon McEntyre (coach), Earl Phillips, Sid Collins, Rory Griffin, Donny Westmoreland, Anthony Chamber, Wilbur McGowan, David Mann, Charles Watts, Robert Moran, Clifford McKinney, James Clark, Franklin Collins, Kevin White.

Woodside Mill (Greenville, S.C.): Troy Stanley (coach), Jack Tucker, Larry McCall, Barry McCombs, Billy Jones, John Jenkins, Alan Sims, Tom Edens, Vernard Heyward, Terry Landis, Sammy Jones, Cornell Young.

Southeastern-Kusan (Greenville, S.C.): Steve McAlister (coach), Mark Thompson, Ernest Ashmore, Fred Bailey, Luther Burgess, Les Martin, Anthony Miller, Doug Ginn, Demetrius Jones.

F.W. Woolworth (Greenville, S.C.): Don Bolton (coach), Bill Brownlee (coach), James Bolton, Roger Donald, Governor Chandler, Glenn Langrehr, Kevin Hawkins, Robert Dicey, David Robinson, Louis Steel, Randall Smith, Larry Frank, Bernard Dawkins, Bobby Dendy, Governor Chancellor, J. Roberson, Austin.

Sharon Corp. (Greenville, S.C.): Michael McCullough (coach), James Millwood, Jack Gallamore, Keith McCullough, Danny McKinney, Mike Wilson, Gary Anthony, Leon Garrett, Wayne White, Mike Seay, Lewis White, Jackie Joy, Barry Dilworth, Danny Mason.

Victor Mill #2 (Greer, S.C.): Perry Dennis (coach), M.D. Redd (coach), Stanley Compton, Calvin Davis, Walter Davis, Jeffrey Gilliam, Ralph Mills, Paul Foster Jr., David Jones, Joe Nance, Wilbert Wright, Willie Grayson, John Durham, Donald White.

Mayfair Mill (Arcadia, S.C.): Dean Hayes (coach), Tommy Sarratt (coach), Mike Moss, Edward Thompson Jr., David Posey, James Pearson, Russell Bransford, James Meadows, Stanley Briggs, Larry Gilliam, Doc Brannon, Martin.

Orders Tile Co. (Greenville, S.C.): James Orders III (coach), Charles Garrison, Greg Russ, David Orders, John Orders, Stewart Clark, Charles Atkins, James Kelley, David Hannon, Bobby Pridmore, Charles Smith, Mark Little, Blake Kelley.

Cryovac (Simpsonville, S.C.): Floyd Lancaster (coach), Harold Wright (coach), Johnny

Wright, Robert Shell, Danny Sullivan, Johnny Jackson, Vernon Johnson, Paul Satterwhite, Anthony Ling, William Dendy, Willie Wright, Jerry Thompson, G. Milam.

Bostik-South (Greenville, S.C.): Jim Bennett (coach), Lennie Scovel, Ronnie German, Randall Warren, Larry Blakely, Bob Waterfield, Jerry Brown, Randall McClure, Johnny Hackett, Glenn German, Warner.

South Boston Mill (South Boston, Va.): George Whitted Jr. (coach), Bradford Ballou, Willie Womack, Cecil Hogue, Ernest Hogue, Claude Womack, Edward Martin, James Smith, Moses Foster Jr., Larry Burrell.

Union Carbide (Simpsonville, S.C.): William Hucks (coach), Dennis Rain (coach), Waddy Talley, Anthony Copeland, Henry Hucks, Stephen Rabe, Edward Lee, John Lipgens, Jerry Lollis, William Robinson, Stephen Culpepper, Jimmy Sullivan, Bill Gosnell, Jim Spearman.

Class C Men

Non-Fluid Oil (Greenville, S.C.), champions: Jerry Compton (coach), Rick Duncan (coach), Mike Massey, Ken Blankenship, Jo Jo Hartsfield, Jeff Malone, Dale Ellis, Mike Hunt, Alvin Grey, Gary McDonald.

Pelzer Mill #1 (Pelzer, S.C.), runners-up: Jimmy Hopkins (coach), Jimmy Foster, Raymond Jones, Monte Crocker, Ronnie Carr, John Williams, Russell Todd, Terry Smith, Fred Gilliam, Robert Elrod, Willie Stewart, Curt Garner, Steve Shaw, Lamar Heard, Pat Jolley, Floyd, Edwards, Bynum.

Grady's Sports (Anderson, S.C.), consolation winners: Doug Rumsey (coach), Steve Adams, Grady Lomax, David Edwards, Randy Morris, Wes Ballard, Jackie Walker, Jerry Webb, Bubba Galloway, George Parks, Jimmy Thick, Garry Grier, Gene Holland, Davis.

Snyder's Auto (Greenville, S.C.): John Robertson (coach), Larry Roddy (coach), Richard King, Terry Lynn, Mack Vanatta, Philip Snyder, Bruce Friddle, Tom Walters, Leigh Smith, Jeffrey Mudge, David Decarlis, Gerald Head, Joseph Johnson, Robertson.

Pelzer Mill #2 (Pelzer, S.C.): J.G. Hopkins (coach), Bruce Scroggs, Tony Bannister, Wayne Eskew, Johnny Robinson, Bobby Bearden, Jeff Taylor, Dale Darby, Johnny Lollis, Billy Miller, R. Ballard, Cohen, Cole.

Jiffie Jonnie (Greenville, S.C.): Gary Scism (coach), Henry Carson, Doug McBee, Floyd Williams, Derrick Pendergrass, Anthony Jackson, Mark Thomason, Ricky Swindell, Mark Cox, Darren Adams, Fuller, Withington, Belcher, Freeman, Hudgens.

Carotell (Taylors, S.C.): Leon Gravley (coach), Ray Smith, Grier Huguley, Dempsey Cohen, Lamar Flatt, Kenny Tremeill, Rodney Williams, John Collins, Kris Nastapolous, Westbury, Burnette, Gist, Drummond.

Blankenship Electric (Greenville, S.C.): Danny Ballew (coach), Mike Parker (coach), Tim Sullivan, Rick Mullinax, Randy Jackson, Capers Easterby, John Sterling, James Hartness, Mark Bostic, Keith Wilder, Derrick Pendergrass, J.C. Miller, Robert Bouton, Tim Parker, Shaw.

Associated Insulation (Slater, S.C.): Bobby Kirby (coach), Sam Shields, Jimmy Gray, Robert Caldwell, Glenn Ferguson, Pete Holbert, Jeff Malone, Mike Hunt, Dale Ellis, Melvin Turpin, Thurl Bailey, Chris Cox, Mark Fothergill, Blakely, Kearney, Bolds, Aiken.

Bryant & Lell Tire (Travelers Rest, S.C.): David Bridwell (coach), Scott Foster, Robert Solomonic, Kenneth Johnson, Albert Hudgens, Craig Bailey, Shawn McCall, Anthony Carr, Mark Seay, Sammy Belcher, Valentine, Eppes, Carson, Swindell, Jackson.

Pelzer Mill #3 (Pelzer, S.C.): Donald Brady (coach), Ray Holliday, Ronald Breazeale, Victor Haigler, Steve Simmons, Greg Abrams, Ricky Mosley, Ballard, DeShields, Guest.

Belton Recreation (Belton, S.C.): Leroy Martin (coach), Wallace Clinkscales, Richard Martin, Ray Putnam, Greg Rochester, Robert White, Willie Pruitt, David Brenson, Troy Rucker, Willie Scott, Tommy Henry, Halwak.

Travel Inn (Greenville, S.C.): Charles Roddy (coach), Tim Owens, Eddie Cox, Jimmy Greer, Ken Donald, Dale Turner, Perry Craig, Jeff Cox, Lattimore, Talbert, Boyd, Durham.

Class A Women

Darrell Floyd's Sandwich Shop (Greenville, S.C.), champions: Darrell Floyd (coach), Miller Perdue (coach), Kathy Wilson, Susan Fuller, Barbara Langford, Nancy Floyd, Drema Greer, Linda Shelton, Judy Stroud, Deborah Buford, Sheila Foster, Rosita Fields, Katrina Anderson, Nessie Harris, Jackie Scovel, Pearl Moore, Diane Floyd.

Slater Mill (Slater, S.C.), runners-up: Bobby Kirby (coach), Jenny Lyerly, Marty

Vaughn, Vivian Humphries, Joan Kirby, Regina Gilstrap, Pam Adams, Bonnie Whelan, Ingle Nivson, Angela Cotman, Sally Reid, Cindy Brogdon, Jones, Taylor, K. Kirby, T. Reid.

West Greenville Community Center (Greenville, S.C.), consolation winners: Douglas Belk (coach), Ray Kirksey (coach), Linda Simpson, Ingrid White, Octavia Sullivan, Elaine Chambers, Beverly David, Janice Simpson, Jan Moore, Renee Bolden, Jackie Gillespie, Paula Perkins, Anita Davis, Dorothea Belk, Flemming, M. Smith.

Phyllis Wheatley Association (Greenville, S.C.): Joseph Floyd (coach), Pam McCullough, Johnnie Yeargin, Margaret Looper, Helen Thompson, Chrystel Bennett, Deloris Kelley, Linda Bennett, Ruth Williams, Pat Smith, Barbara Hill, Myra Wilson, Alice Harrill, Cain.

Laurens Glass Co. (Laurens, S.C.): Arvin Kruse (coach), Kay Monroe, Jo Lundy, Ann Glover, Lynn Woods, Luanne Wentzky, Mary Campbell, Lynn Hope, Ruth LaForge, Sandy Kruse, Jan McDonald, Denise Dayberry, Alfreda Raye, Hall, Elmore.

Athletic Attic (Anderson, S.C.): Ron Scarborough (coach), Ronnie Scovel, Beth Couture, Kim Chambers, Teresa Allen, Patricia Hanks, Lorretta Clinkscales, Kim Langston, Kim Eskew, Linda Crawford, Cindy Sims, Angie McCullough, Dee McClure, Adger.

Atlanta Cards (Atlanta, Ga.): Lisa Leonard, Libby Rodden, Lisa Alexander, Susan Shanblin, Karen Nicotra, Wanda Bishop, Debi Bendock, Debbie Tucker, Cathy Davis, Donna Stevenson, Karen Cunningham, Hazel Hall, Lineberger, Kay.

Saco-Lowell (Easley, S.C.): Mike Youngblood (coach), Peggy Bolding (coach), Sherri Smith, Kay Allen, Sally Atkins, Ann McKnight, Lisa Knight, Denise Mills, Susan Ricken, DeDe Cartee, Cindi Owens, Elaine Martin, Cecilia Chamberlain, Kathy Preston.

Gould Associates (Taylors, S.C.): Jim Wilson (coach), Nancy Gould, Kelly Traynham, Elisabeth Holland, Laurie Nix, Lou Beckham, Pam Dickard, Sharon Barbrey, Susie Black, Moss, Hughes, Loonie, Garrett.

F.W. Woolworth (Greenville, S.C.): Kevin Hawkins (coach), Bob Dicey (coach), Phyllis Bates, Donna Hartong, Liz Foreman, Annie Sullivan, Doris Holbrook, Bobbie Galloway, Dorothy Miller, Dorothy Donald, Tracie Meredith, Sally Pielou, Brenda Fowler, Debbie Vaughn, Shirley Davis, Faress, Lord, Edwards.

——— 1980 ———

Executive Officers: Divver Hendrix, James Morrow, Ken Pittman, Fred Powers, Clarence Thomas, Willie Wilbanks, Ward Williams.

Officers: Bill Hopkins (Pelzer, S.C.), President; Ruppert Elliott (Greenville, S.C.), 1st Vice President; Lloyd McAbee (Greenville, S.C.), 1st Vice President; Harry Foster (Greenville, S.C.), Treasurer; David Bailey (Greenville, S.C.), Ass't Treasurer; Fred Byrd (Greenville, S.C.), Executive Secretary; Mendel Masters (Greenville, S.C.), Ass't Executive Secretary; Whitey Kendall (Greenville), Supervisor of Officials; Lt. F.R. Hawkins, Security Officer.

Executive Committee: Willard Fowler (Greenville, S.C.), Dan Foster (Greenville, S.C.), Henry Spake (Anderson, S.C.), Vercho Carter (Alexander City, Ala.), Phil Clark (Greer, S.C.), Lewis Golden (Greenville, S.C.), Darrell Floyd (Greenville, S.C.), Jyles Phillips (Greenville, S.C.), Don Ball (Greenville, S.C.), Steve Brown (Greer, S.C.), Jerry Compton (Greenville, S.C.), Phil Harley (Greenville, S.C.), Terry Harbin (Slater, S.C.), Jim Phillips (Greenville, S.C.).

OPEN DIVISION

Chick-Fil-A (Greenville, S.C.), champions: Terry Shelton (coach), Tom Warrick (coach), Al Daniel, Reggie Smith, Ronald White, Dale Crowe, Rick McKinney, Tommy Wimbush, Earl Nesbitt, Jonathan Moore, Clyde Mayes, Small, Kershaw.

Non-Fluid Oil (Greenville, S.C.) runners-up: Chubby Wells, Billy Williams, Dickerson, Marc Campbell, Pitts, Conrad, Coles, Hampton, Fuzy, Creamer, Elrod.

Daniel Construction Co. (Jenkinsville, S.C.): Fred Pearson Jr. (coach), Henry Boyd, Jackie Boyd, Alvin Holland, Virgil O'Neal, Stanley Kennedy, Fred Pearson, Curtis Carter, Dwayne Mack, Vincent Pearson, Thomas Vinegar, Donnie Crosby, Finley O'Neal, Bostic, Marsh.

Tri Dip Inc. (Columbia, S.C.): Anthony Brown (coach), James Brown, James Sanders, Joe Rice, Melvin Jones, Irvin Earle, Wade Jenkins, Tommy Mack, Brownie Johnson, Doug Myers, Bobby McDuffie, Willis McKichen, Ricky Fulton.

Keyboards (Columbia, S.C.): Jim Swan (coach), Allen Searson, Fred Melson, John Drafts, Glymph Childress, Mark Grenier,

Tommy Whitten, Tom Dennard, Joe Thompson, Bryan Drafts, Dave Koesters, Woody Sharpe, Doyle, Hordges, Griffin.

Krispy Kreme (Spartanburg, S.C.): Bob Cross (coach), Mark Bruce, Robert Heil, James Blair, Michael O'Driscoll, Michael Howard, Harold Jackson, Brian Lynch, Barry Rhodes, Dan Price, Randy McMillan, Beard.

Sam Wyche Sports World (Greenville, S.C.): Phillip Brown (coach), John Hindler, Alonzo Harrison, Danny Jackson, Mike Owens, Garland Jefferson, Chuck Orr, Lenny Horton, Levon Mercer, Walter Anderson, Terry Stockland, Reggie Johnson, Mel Hubbard, Strickland, Mabry, Hayes, Gus Rubio, T. Pinson, C. Pinson, Teague, Wyatt, Sullivan.

CLASS A MEN

Singer Mfg. (Pickens, S.C.), champions: Sammy Nix (coach), David Norris (coach), Jo Jo Kelley, Charlie Anthony, Tom Looper, Steve Beasley, John Rogers, Marty Hopkins, Wade Collins, Sammy Baker, Rocky Cater, Bobby Rice, Benny Byrd, Ken Robinson, Glenn Thrift, Rock Cater.

Dunean Mill (Greenville, S.C.), runners-up: Randy Wardlaw (coach), Charles Hudson (coach), Isaiah Walker, Richard DuBose, Christopher Taylor, Jimmy Marion, Clyde Agnew, James McGee, Mark Mangrum, Olin Wright, William McGee, Anthony Rolls, Rhodes, Gailey.

American Enka (Central, S.C.), consolation winners: Larry Bowens (coach), Gary Nix (coach), Les Porter, William Peppers, Carl Valentine, Morris Henderson, Dannie Cannon Jr., Danny Rogers, Howard McDowell, Mike Church, James Bagwell, Odis Rhodes, John van Sordam, John Todd.

Sirrine Co. (Greenville, S.C.): Bruce Martin (coach), Ted Templeton, Thomas Rucker, John Cooper, Harry Moats, Glenn McCoy, Bruce Martin, John Satterfield, Alex Tomanovich.

Michelin #1 (Sandy Springs, S.C.): Randy Alexander (coach), James Lesley, Nate Leverette, Chuck Johnson, Tony Rochester, Jackie Clement, Frank Prater, David Burns, Sammy Norris, Charles Lesley, Dale Rhodes, David Sanders, James Yates, Gene Angle, Barker Stone, Richard Lynn.

Michelin #2 (Sandy Springs, S.C.): Mike Thrasher (coach), Jimmy Johnson, Larry Hall, Gregory Franklin, Walter Yates, Tim Putnam, Steve Skelton, John Baker, Marshall Isom, Calvin Scott, Ron Perkins, Harold Williams, David Skelton, Ricky Dickson, Mike Price, Joe Ervin.

Homelite (Greer, S.C.): Calvin Cohen (coach), James Griffin, Robert Casey, Donnell Rosemond, Ricky Pickett, Ricky Bruton, Jesse Flemings, Paul Brown, Dean Martin, Carlos Hardy, Jimmy Williams, Harvey Davis.

Michelin (Greenville, S.C.): Rasnake, Holstead, Henderson, Crawford, Foster, Chambers, Winston, Turner, Bane, Lollis.

Gene A. Smith (Lexington, S.C.): Gene Smith (coach), Rick Fulton, Steve Ashes, Henry Noble, Jim Strickland, Robert Myers, Gregory Mebane, Mike Bland, Reggie Noble, Maurice Kitt, Robert Geter, Cedrick Hovoues, Steve Graze, Calvin Davis, Golie Augustus, Reavis.

Ambassadors for Christ (Greenville, S.C.): Melvin Montgomery (coach), Arthur Robinson, Samuel Shelton, John Saxton, Michael Watson, Michael Ages, Bobby Little, Anthony Gibson, James Parker, John Montgomery, Dexter Hooks, Alston, Williams, Gamble, Jordan.

Skip's All Stars (Pelzer, S.C.): Roundtree, Wells, Harrison, Davis, Thomas, Foster, Cobb, Moore, Wilson.

Ware Shoals Mill (Ware Shoals, S.C.): Roosevelt Smith (coach), Joe Smith, Willie Smith, Clarence Brownlee, Willie Wright, Michael Epps, Raymond Kelly, Tim Stewart, Roy Whatley, Sammy Williams, Roger Cyrus, Darrough Aikens, Henry Robinson.

Alice Mfg. (Easley, S.C.): Terry Smith (coach), Matt Valentine, Kenneth Galloway, Ken Murphy, Linus Blake, Billy Curenton, Dan McCreight, Terry Smith, Ross Bowens, James Pitts, Kevin Smith, Leonard Jameson.

Saco-Lowell (Easley, S.C.): Lanny Taylor (coach), Ken Chapman (coach), Larry Davis, Russell Perdue, James Allen, Jimmy Bowens, James H. Bowens, Eddie Dobbins, Randy Coleman, Dan Benfield, Gwinn, Blake, Hunter.

Singer Mfg. (Anderson, S.C.): Thomas Hammonds (coach), Earl Walker, Henry Hammond, Clifford Leslie, Henry Hammond, Waymon Hood, Walter Johnson, Oscar Means, Cecil Mattison, Aaron Jones, Garrison, Williams.

Monaghan Mill (Greenville, S.C.): Bill Swaynghame (coach), Horace Anderson,

Southern Textile Basketball Tournament Rosters   Appendix 1   291

Charles Leamon, Alan Landreth, Eddie Leamon, John Ward, Fred Dilworth, Bobby Jones, Marcus Dowdy, Lewis McCoy Jr., Larry Brown, Terry Sullivan, Tony Blakely, Ray Anders.

Fiber Industries (Greenville, S.C.): Phil Harley (coach), Wayne Hargette (coach), Steve Richard, Frank Armfield, Timothy Howell, Claude Barnett, Kenneth Childers, Curtis Evans, Larry Dogan, Pritchard, Martin, McMakin, McKinney.

Hoechst Celanese (Greer, S.C.): Sonny Moody (coach), Donny McCarter (coach), Sonny Anderson, Steve Arms, Lawrence Williams, Marvin Drummond, Lee Williams, David McKinney, Kenneth Duncan, David Hawkins, James Wells, Bennie Foster, Charles Crawford, Gary Medlock.

Cryovac (Simpsonville, S.C.): James Sullivan (coach), Rex Abercrombie, Bobby Phelps, Calvin Milam, Barry Wright, Matthew Milam, Bobby Church, Vernon Johnson, Anthony Alexander, Marcus Sims, Elliott Owens, Massingale.

3M (Greenville, S.C.): Booker Johnson (coach), Chuck Holcombe (coach), John Williams, James Gwinn, Louis Sayles Jr., William Gamble, John Robinson, Jesse Looper, Larry Crosby, David Rose, Richard Reid, Kenny Arnold, Billy Davis, Mahaffey.

Parker Mill (Greenville, S.C.): Steve Johnson (coach), Barry Littlefield (coach), William McGowan, Jerry Jackson, John McKinney, Robert Pepper, Michael Sullivan, Clifford Chapman, Albert Donald, Jimmie Robinson, Roy Smith, Jerry Nix Jr., Irvin Bowens, Alvarez Chiles.

Pelzer Mill (Pelzer, S.C.): Horace Davenport (coach), Ronnie Cureton, Willie Evans, Wesley Sloan, Joe Elrod, William Adams, Cephas Coleman, Sylvester Burns, Jerry Arnold, Eugene Coley, Billy Burns, J. Burns.

Slater Mill (Slater, S.C.): J.F. Roberts (coach), Richard Hamilton (coach), McBruce Young, Ricky Cruell, Joe Hill, Roger McCall, Keith Lyerly, John Askew, William Parnell, Ricky Laws, Toll Plumley Jr., Mark Lybrand, Anthony Williams, Randy Bowles, Banks, Roberts.

Michelin (Spartanburg, S.C.): Steve Brown (coach), Stan Jones, David Bibb, George McCarroll, Michael Cherry, Lynn Brown, Eddie Battle, Terry Moore, Alonzo Briggs, Jerry Sanders, Patrick Still, William Stacey, Lindsey, Jervey, S. Brown.

Marietta Substation II (Marietta, S.C.): Earl Keaton (coach), Roger Barnhart (coach), Floyd Burnett, Randy Burns, Charles Carter, Robert Hackle, Garry Helms, Terry Hightower, Robert McGowens, Preston Smith, Rick Swine, Mike Whitfield, John McElheny, Richard Brown, Swing.

Mayfair Mill (Pickens, S.C.): Gilbert Benson (coach), Gregory Coles, Joe Hagood, Thurman Ramsey, Ted Ledbetter, Willis Robinson, Kevin Smith, Ricky Sloan, James Benson, Alfred Jones.

Applied Engineering (Orangeburg, S.C.): Harry Shuler (coach), Chris Carver, David Prince, David Paul, Ronald Huggins, Jacob Smith, Tim Gadson, Tommy Frazier, Richard Rivers, Walter Runager, Ed Bryant, Shuler.

Eldeco (Greenville, S.C.): Harry Poole (coach), John Dill (coach), Malcolm Mason, William Hawkins, Jon Barkman, Eddie Campbell, Richard Lipscomb, Roger Carlton, Charles Poole, Tommy Bishop, Hugh Howard, Jack Wilson, Edwin Mosley, Dill, C. Hawkins, K. Hawkins.

F.W. Woolworth (Greenville, S.C.): W.J. Brownlee (coach), Randall Smith, Marshall Mattress, Roger Donald, Butch Snipes, Steve Martin, David Sullivan, Governor Chancellor, Jerry Robinson, Bernard Dawkins, Robert Thompson, Jerry Lattimore, Larry Franks.

CLASS B MEN

Union Carbide (Simpsonville, S.C.), champions: William Hucks (coach), Mike Butler (coach), Waddy Talley, Anthony Copeland, Steve Rabe, John Lipgens, Jerry Lollis, Ron Suber, Jimmy Sullivan, Jim Spearman, Don Young, Mike Miller, Richard Rickenbach, Mike Cleveland.

Cryovac (Simpsonville, S.C.), runners-up: Jackie Scroggins (coach), Johnny Wright, Robert Shell, Danny Sullivan, Paul Satterwhite, Jerry Boyd, Calvin Barksdale, Thornton Pulley, Clarence Sweeney, Preston Calvert, Frankie Bryson, George Jones, Donald Frazier.

Piedmont Mill (Piedmont, S.C.), consolation winners: Earl Wooten (coach), Al Banister, Terry Elrod, Paul Johnson, Michael Roseman, B.R. McClain, Ray Simmons, Aaron Crowe, Calvin Donaldson, John Anderson, Tony Nash, Sylvester Lee, Stewart Vaughn.

Wangner Systems (Greenville, S.C.): P.J. Smith (coach), Mark Ellison, Robert Hoover, David Shank, Gary Roberts, Larry Williams,

Joseph Smith, Robert Buchanan, George Pendergrass, Terry Roberts, John Smith, Larry Magemhardt, Larry Johnson, M. Smith, R. Smith.

Cryovac (Duncan, S.C.): Arthur Cleveland (coach), Steve Johnson, John Martin, E.W. Hardy, Bruce Hagins, Michael Shuck, Frank Bauer, David Richardson, Robert Roten, Grady Gaston, Arthur Edwards, Joseph Browder.

3M (Greenville, S.C.): Bill Davis (coach), Thomas Tice, William McNeeley, Darnell Flemming, Terry Davis, James Brookie, Michael Zellner, James Austin, Eddie Madden, Ernest Goodis, Ray Holliday, Charles Williams.

Alice Mfg. (Easley, S.C.): Benny Sloan (coach), Sammy Smith, Ken Ross, John Langston, Terry McGowens, Tommy Anderson, James Bowens, Ricky McGowens, Gregory Garrett.

Sirrine Co. (Greenville, S.C.): Bob Ray (coach), James Craig, Horace Jones, Michael Brewster, James Wimbrow, Ray Drummond, Regan Klein, Ellis Styles, David Owens, Reggie Smith, Franks.

Pelzer Mill (Pelzer, S.C.): Jack Golden (coach), Billy Burns, Vic Alverson, David Burns, Bobby Partain, Todd Hall, Johnny Robinson, Scotty Jamerson, Scotty Keels, Harry Smith, Mike McConnell, Phil Smith.

Fiber Industries #1 (Greenville, S.C.): Wayne Hargette (coach), Ken Durham, Jimmy Gray, Donald Hargette, Martin Ketterer, Tom Davis, J.W. Wright, Jimmy Brown, Steve Garland, Mike Brockman, Craig Dirton, McConnell, Booker, Ashburn, Johnny Pinson.

Saco-Lowell (Easley, S.C.): Doug Roach (coach), Ron Thomas (coach), Randy Tucker, Steve Sisk, Gregg Corbin, George Turmon, Scott Brown, Ted Anderson, Dale Gillespie, Mike Youngblood, Mike Gravley, Mike Reynolds, Wayne O'Shields.

Grace Distribution (Duncan, S.C.): Mike Williams (coach), Edward Davis, Greg Hall, Ken Whiteside, Michael Quinn, Michael Dorrian, Deyrell Farmer, Timothy Gleason, Dan Burrell, Ken Bessent, Gary Cort, Don Lusk, Milan Williams.

Ashworth Brothers (Greenville, S.C.): Bill Williams (coach), William Dendy, Carlton Reeves, Jimmy Withington, David Whitlock, Craig Grimmett, Fred Moon, Wade Brown, Charles Ashworth, Willie Calwile, Billy Williams, Robert Johnson, David Ashworth.

Michelin Blue (Greenville, S.C.): Ron Scarborough (coach), Mike Kelley, Jackie Chambers, Mike Jewell, David Childs, Jim Morgan, Michael Chandler, Reginald Nealey, Lynn Dunn, L. Brown, K. Brown.

Appleton Mill (Anderson, S.C.): Henry Spake (coach), Joe Geer, Don Pressley, Joseph Harrison, Rodney Allen, David Geer, Roy Calhoun, Mack Nance, Ricky Craft, David Vickery, Thomas Webb, Harvey Thompson, Danny Colbert.

Southern Weaving (Greenville, S.C.): James Chappell (coach), Verlon McEntyre (coach), Sid Collins, Rory Griffin, Donny Westmoreland, Anthony Chambers, Ted Mann, Clifford McKinney, Kevin White, Curtis Blakely, Ronald McKinney, Wyatt.

Woodside Mill (Greenville, S.C.): Thomas Baldwin (coach), Jack Tucker, Barry McCombs, John Lloyd, John Sims, Marion Reeves, Jimmy Chappelle, George Wilson, James Hunter, James Sullivan, Seaborg.

Southeastern-Kusan (Greenville, S.C.): Steve McAlister (coach), Mark Thompson, Ernest Ashmore, Fred Bailey, Anthony Miller, Robert Fields, J.W. Williams, Leroy Burgess, Tyronne Robinson, Loudenslager.

F.W. Woolworth (Greenville, S.C.): James Bolton (coach), John Watts (coach), Glenn Langrehr, Kevin Hawkins, Robert Dicey, David Hill, Louis Still, Randall Sheppard, John Pack, Keith Peary, Sam Huffling, Thomas Goodjione, Jimmy Ward, John Vail.

Jet Rest Furniture (Greer, S.C.): Bobby Cohen (coach), Thomas Goodlett, Charles Miller, Bobby Williams, Charles Bennon, Douglas Scott, Michael Wilson, Ken Jones, Bill Foster, Dwayne Edwards, Dodd.

Victor Mill (Greer, S.C.): Perry Dennis (coach), Benny Coggins (coach), Doug Garren (coach), Stanley Compton, Calvin Davis, Walter Davis, Jeffrey Gilliam, Ralph Mills, Paul Foster Jr., David Jones, Joe Nance, Donald White, Thomas Smith, Eddie Smith, Thomas Pearson.

Orders Tile Co. (Greenville, S.C.): Ed Shell (coach), David Harrell, Charles Atkins, David Hannon, Bobby Pridmore, Michael Smith, Mark Little, Bryan Kelley, Wiley Johnson, Ralph Michael, Bryan Deitke, Randy Gidaro, Larry Pittman.

Apalache Mill (Greer, S.C.): Ben Jones (coach), O. Harris (coach), Ralph Grant, Frankie Sterling, Ricky Wilson, Stanley Woodruff, Carl Chambers, Greg Vaughn, Mike

Watson, Gary Austin, Calvin Redding, Richard Gravely.

Greenville County Recreation (Greenville, S.C.): Charlie Hall (coach), Ray Smerdon, Chris Teague, Rickey Morris, Claude Smith, Tim Smerdon, James Meekins, Rickey Watts, Garrison, Waddell, Reid, Callahan, Hughes.

Kerr Finishing (Travelers Rest, S.C.): Anthony Gary (coach), Charles Burgess (coach), Billy Young, Samuel Cruell, Larry Simmons, Tommy Thompson, Robert McBee, Ralph Cox, Pleas Lewis, G.A. Satterfield, Anthony Jordan, Ernest Griffin.

A & C Warehouse (Clinton, S.C.): Gary Wilbanks (coach), Sam Jones, James Suber, Thomas Rogers, Robert Stapleton, David Robbins, Sam Lake, Randy Thompson, Glenn Bledsoe, Bob Brian, Shields.

Singer Mfg. (Pickens, S.C.): David Norris (coach), Sammy Nix (coach), Thomas Whitner, Anthony Carver, Johnny Millwood, Avery Bagwell, Jerry Golden, Ronald Alexander, Mike Holcombe, Freddie Hagood, Russell Chapman, Glenn Thrift, James Alexander, Wendell Lusk, Sargent.

City of Greenville (Greenville, S.C.): Bob Capps (coach), Ronnie McKeown, Robert Dersch, Douglas Henson, Alan Sweet, James Morgan, Melvin Harris, Kenny Jackson, Johnny Jones, Roy Mack, Douglas Belk, Vaughn Wicker.

Fiber Industries #2 (Greenville, S.C.): Steve Richard (coach), Dennis McConville, Gregory Neely, Victor Gardner, James Rusak, Phillip Arnold, Lewis, Bloise, Pogan, Satterfield, Wilson.

U.S. Post Office (Greenville, S.C.): Newell Tucker (coach), James Mayes, Willie Thurman, Donnie Scovel, Stephen Toliver, William Crawford, John Miller, Ronald Mahon, James Holder, Thomas Brown, Richard Robertson, Tucker.

Haynesworth Mill (Anderson, S.C.): Doug Rumsey (coach), Stevie Adams, James Hunter, Billy Wansley, Jesse Thomas, Harry Jones, Howard Goodwin, Snipes Martin, Luther Walker, Charlie Bowen, Charles Jones, Robert Richardson, Winfred Green, James McDowell.

Easley Mill (Easley, S.C.): Ronnie Lackey (coach), William Kellam, Carey Beard, Edward Bolden, Stanley Lance, Stephen Capps, Michael Hiles, William Knupp, Walter Bolden, Jack Anderson, Harold Hoke, John Taylor, Wayne Robinson, Black, McDowell, Crowe.

American Hardware (Greenville, S.C.): W. Brockman (coach), Jeffrey James, Milas Officer, Steve Rollinson, Richard Moore, Mac Stevens, Blake Curry, Joe Mitchell, Charles Lake, Thad Franklin, Robert Sullivan, Don Wooten, Billy Storey, Bernard Johnson, Annison, Stray, Brockman.

CLASS C MEN

Pelzer Mill #1 (Pelzer, S.C.), champions: Jimmy Hopkins (coach), Bill Hopkins (coach), Jimmy Foster, Raymond Jones, Terry Smith, Eldorado Valentine, Ken Haygood, Don Brady, Eddie Burton, Don Walton, Randy Jackson, Robbie Brannon, James Gist, Lance Snyder, Skip Hopkins.

Dalton's Furniture (Pickens, S.C.), runners-up: Steve Graveley (coach), Al Rogers, Steve Sams, Anthony Jenkins, Donnie Pearson, Marc Campbell, Dewayne Grace, Ikie Scipio, Reggie Meadows, Russell Foster, Buzz Peterson, Cozell McQueen, Richey Taylor, Crowe, Pendergrass.

Fashion First (Greer, S.C.), consolation winners: Ronnie Garren (coach), Allen Lewis, Billy Rucker, Kevin Heaton, Robert Solomonic, Craig Smith, Wendell Jordan, Stanley Dubose, Scott Lane, Wilkins, Pittard, Mattox, Vaughn.

Chick-Fil-A (Greenville, S.C.): Miller, Graham, Maddox, Page, Lane, Washington, Simmons, Massey, Landrum, Jones, Palmer.

Jiffie Jonnie (Greenville, S.C.): Gary Scism (coach), Henry Carson, Anthony Carr, Bryan Freeman, Horace Davis, Michael Jones, Scott Styles, Sammy Belcher, Skip Johnson, Darren Adams, Westbury, Adams, Bailey, Bouton, A. Carson.

Pelzer Mill #2 (Pelzer, S.C.): J.G. Hopkins (coach), Tony Belt, Tony Bannister, Jeff Taylor, Johnny Harrison, Billy Miller, Johnny Lollis, Dale Darby, Tim Henderson, Wayne Eskew, Jerry Wilson, Reid, Allen, Robinson.

Blankenship Electric (Greenville, S.C.): Danny Ballew (coach), Don Davis (coach), Rick Mullinax, James Anderson, Dan Nunnery, James Roberts, Fred Young, Jimmy Booker, C.E. Rhodes, Steven Mullinax, Larry Freeman, Whaley, Ellison.

Bryant & Lell Tire (Travelers Rest, S.C.): Scott Foster, Shawn McCall, Darryl Young, James Jones, Chev Boozer, Nelson Talley, Tyrone Smith, Doug McBee, Todd Garrett, John Young, Weaver, Davis.

Southeastern Products (Greenville, S.C.): Jim Porterfield (coach), Lee Stegall, Wesley Ballard, Gary Bannister, Jeff Sumner, Brian Freeman, Tracy Langrehr, Todd Porterfield, Tino Sullivan, J.W. Miller, Todd Mattos, Sammy Belcher, Perry.

Alford Real Estate (Greenville, S.C.): Warren Rollins (coach), Nelson Giles, Joseph Britt, Richard Rollins, John Brissey, Elbert Parks, Steve Posey, Larry Posey, Hall, Hagood, Anderson, Means, B. Britt.

D.B. Carter Used Cars (Greenville, S.C.): Ricky Ingram (coach), Gary Barlow (coach), Shane Moody, Terry Owens, Tim May, Mike Brown, Mark Davis, Mark Thomasson, Kim Owens, Greg McDonnell.

CLASS A WOMEN

Hanna-Sides (Pelzer, S.C.), champions: Jane Fontaine (coach), Lenora Freeman, Charlotte Nicholson, Emma Mumphrey, Risa Turton, Vivian Humphreys, Sunnie O'Neal, Jane Fontaine.

Darrell Floyd's Sandwich Shop (Greenville, S.C.), runners-up: Darrell Floyd (coach), Susan Fuller, Barbara Williams, Nancy Floyd, Linda Shelton, Judy Stroud, Deborah Buford, Rosita Fields, Sheila Morgan, Teresa Allen, Mary Connelly, Jan Rampey, Cynthia Austin, S. Morgan, Brooks, Cowart, Dukes, Lloyd.

Slater Mill (Slater, S.C.), consolation winners: Bobby Kirby (coach), Jenny Lyerly, Marty Vaughn, Vivian Humphries, Regina Gilstrap, Pam Adams, Inge Nilssen, Nancy Lieberman, Sally Reid, Donna Reed, Teresa Braswell, Debbie Raper, Genea Beasley, Jones, Kirby, Clark, T. Reid.

Tramps Inc. (Greenville, S.C.): Randy LaFoy (coach), Tricia Theodore, Cheryl Marsh, Denise Blakley, Mia Marianos, Teresa Ludwig, Cindy Crenshaw, Karen Marianos, Joey Brown, Farmer, Kindley, Rice, Black.

Athletic Attic (Anderson, S.C.): Ronnie Scarborough (coach), Beth Couture, Lorretta Clinkscales, Linda Crawford, Cindy Sims, Rosalind Jennings, Lynn George, Pam Moore, Alfreda Ray, Everette, Keanoy, Kennedy, Crenshaw.

Saco-Lowell (Easley, S.C.): Cecil Chamberlain (coach), Peggy Bolding (coach), Ann McKnight, Lisa Knight, Denise Mills, Susan Rickens, DeDe Cartee, Kathy Preston, Carol Stephens, Libby Mullinax, Louise Aldman, Marcia Cartee, Debbie Stegall, Carol Harrison, O'Shields, Moody.

Gould Associates (Taylors, S.C.): Jim Wilson (coach), Nancy Gould, Laurie Nix, Pam Moss, Sharon Barbrey, Mary Brooks, Sandy Kruse, Cindy Williams, Looney, Puckette.

Phyllis Wheatley Association (Greenville, S.C.): Leroy Greggs (coach), Furman Hill (coach), Johnnie Yeargin, Helen Thompson, Linda Bennett, Ruth Williams, Pat Smith, Cynthia Davis, Sharon Jones, Frankie Whiteside, Van Cohen, Maggie Smith, Janet Latta, Looper.

West Greenville Community Center (Greenville, S.C.): Douglas Belk (coach), Linda Simpson, Ingrid White, Elaine Chambers, Jackie Moore, Paula Perkins, Wanda Flemming, Barbara Hill, Maggie Smith, Lillie Young, Thompson, Evans, Sullivan.

Michelin (Greenville, S.C.): Jack Hart (coach), Joan Cole, Donna Cates, Holly Dixon, Janice Zack, Linda Garland, Vicki Daniels, Elizabeth Goode, Mary Tevyaw, Cathy Swicegood, Pittman, Shelton, Howell, Stockman, Lowery.

Greenwood Stars (Greenwood, S.C.): Tim Walker (coach), Roger Bagwell (coach), Luanne Wentzky, Darryl McClure, Sheila Foster, Karen Brown, Sally Campbell, Patricia Hanks, Cathy Ladson, Evelyn Johnson, Melinda Hall, Kay Monroe, Mary Campbell, Gladden, Turner, Jackson, Basket, D. Turner.

Mayo (Mayo, S.C.): Marsha Horne, Sheryl McClure, Beth Bell, Glenda Bullard, Lori Foster, Kathy Booker, Deanna Lynch, Kay Blackwell, Laureen Murphy, Cheryl Fowler, Andi Ashmore, Janice Allen, Pruitt, Hunt, Smith, Allison, Wallace, Farmer.

Old Keg Party Shop (Greenville, S.C.): Jim Bennett (coach), Donnie Scovel (coach), Beth Couture, Jenny Mills, Angie McCulloch, Lillie Young, Mary Scovel, Jackie Scovel, Kim Horny, Pam Moss, Park, Cowan, Biediger.

Dunean Mill (Greenville, S.C.): Doug Gailey, (coach), Kathy Tate, Rhonda Staton, Wilma Strange, Deborah Robbins, Melanie Phillips, Tammy Cureton, Annie Blackmon, Dottie James, Frances Gailey, Diane Crowe, Brightwell, Kinard.

Sam Wyche Sports World (Greenville, S.C.): William Teague (coach), Lily Young, Susan Black, Cheryl Gudalock, Angie Dixon,

Sheila Foster, Suzanne Woolston, Debbie Fulton, B. Harris, Cheryl Autry, Evelyn Johnson, Rita Johnson.

Piney Mountain T.A.P.S. (Greenville, S.C.): Leon Ferguson (coach), William Moultrie (coach), Amy Booker, Ruth Dodson, Jo Allman, Sherbar Moultrie, Brenda McAbee, Frances Young, Shirley Taylor, Darlene Morgan, Louis Allman, Ernestine Cromer, Ora Booker.

Pelzer Byrd's (Pelzer, S.C.): Donnelly, Williamson, Jones, Leatherman, Ansley, Sellars, Turner.

Atlanta Tomboys (Atlanta, Ga.): Hoden, Leonard, Osborne, Hines, Hammock, Grainger, Salmon.

--- 1981 ---

Executive Officers: Divver Hendrix, James Morrow, Ken Pittman, Vercho Carter, Fred Powers, Clarence Thomas, Willie Wilbanks, Ward Williams.

Officers: Bill Hopkins (Pelzer, S.C.), President; Ruppert Elliott (Greenville, S.C.), 1st Vice President; Lloyd McAbee (Greenville, S.C.), 1st Vice President; Harry Foster (Greenville, S.C.), Treasurer; David Bailey (Greenville, S.C.), Ass't Treasurer; Fred Byrd (Greenville, S.C.), Executive Secretary; Mendel Masters (Greenville, S.C.), Ass't Executive Secretary; Whitey Kendall, Greenville, Supervisor of Officials; Lt. F.R. Hawkins, Security Officer.

Executive Committee: Willard Fowler (Greenville, S.C.), Dan Foster (Greenville, S.C.), Henry Spake (Anderson, S.C.), Phil Clark (Greer, S.C.), Lewis Golden (Greenville, S.C.), Darrell Floyd (Greenville, S.C.), Jyles Phillips (Greenville, S.C.), Don Ball (Greenville, S.C.), Steve Brown (Greer, S.C.), Phil Harley (Greenville, S.C.), Jim Phillips (Greenville, S.C.).

OPEN DIVISION

Chick-Fil-A (Greenville, S.C.), champions: Terry Shelton (coach), Tom Warrick (coach), Al Daniel, Reggie Small, Ron White, Rick McKinney, Tom Wimbush, Jonathan Moore, Clyde Mayes, Zam Fredrick, Charles Brunson, Larry Nance, Mickey Fleming, Lucius Pitts, Mike Doyle, Don Ball, Ricky Camp, Keith Cauis, James Ball.

Tri Dip Inc. (Columbia, S.C.), runners-up: Anthony Brown (coach), James Brown, James Sanders, Irvin Earle, Wade Jenkins, Tommy Mack, Doug Myers, Bobby Jackson, Ricky Fulton, Howard White, Ronnie Hamm, Strickland, Jones.

Sam Wyche Sports World (Greenville, S.C.): William Teague (coach), Jones Sullivan (coach), Chuck Dahms, Lenny Horton, Frank Johnson, Horace Yeargin, Winfred King, Larry Linney, Charles Brunson, Wilbert Singleton, Kenney Dennard, Pat Jolly, Barry Isom.

Sonics (Abbeville, S.C.): Archibald Letman (coach), Hellie Martin, Greg Wright, Reggie Williams, Morris Jackson, Jesse Roundtree, Donald Young, Jimmy Bell, Courtney Abrams, Kenneth Watson, Clinton Cobb, Charles Wimphire, Carroll Wells, Harrison.

Daniel Construction Co. (Jenkinsville, S.C.): Fred Pearson (coach), Virgil O'Neal, Ernest Owens, Alvin Holland, Vincent Pearson, Wayne Pearson, Jackie Boyd, Henry Boyd, Costello Boyd, Charles Marshall, Curtis Carter, Finley O'Neal, Colie Feemster, Vinegar.

Jet Rest Furniture (Greer, S.C.): Bobby Cohen (coach), Keith Cohen, Sonny Moody, Michael Wilson, Larry Rice, Karon Jones, Roy Williams, Mark Cohen, Donald Young, Bo Hardy, Ricord Davis, Kenneth Sterling, Dean Martin, Spurgeon, Taylor, Burnette.

CLASS A MEN

Dunean Mill (Greenville, S.C.), champions: Randy Wardlaw (coach), Charles Hudson (coach), Isaiah Walker, Richard DuBose, Chris Taylor, Jimmy Marion, Clyde Agnew, James McGee, Mark Mangrum, Olin Wright, William McGee, Horace Anderson, Joseph Holden, Jeff McLeskey.

Alice Mfg. (Easley, S.C.), runners-up: Terry Smith (coach), Kenneth Galloway, Ken Murphy, Linus Blake, Billy Curenton, Eddie Williams, Ken Murphy, Rick Wyatt, Terry McGowens, George Davis, Douglas Adams, Ray Womack, Crumpton.

American Enka (Central, S.C.), consolation winners: Larry Bowens (coach), Les Porter, William Peppers, Carl Valentine, Morris Henderson, Dannie Cannon Jr., Howard McDowell, Mike Church, Odis Rhodes, Randy van Surdam, John Williams, Clayton Wideman, Vince Earl, Stan Hamilton.

Saco-Lowell (Easley, S.C.): Victor Gwinn (coach), Russell Perdue, Mike Allen, Eddie Dobbins, Randy Coleman, Dan Benfield, Mike

Gravley, Ted Anderson, William Pitts, Roger Furr, Mac Trotter, George Turmon, Mike Reynolds, Charlie Hall, Gwinn.

Singer Mfg. (Pickens, S.C.): Sammy Nix (coach), Jo Jo Kelley, Bill Anthony, John Todd, Marty Hopkins, Sammy Baker, Kenneth Robinson, Bryan Roper, Walter Helms, James Alexander, Keith Scoggins, Danny Hunter, Boyd Lusk.

Michelin #1 (Sandy Springs, S.C.): Wayne Yates (coach), Charles Lesley, Tony Robertson, Chuck Johnson, Jackie Clement, David Sanders, James Yates, Dale Rhodes, Lou Spear, Greg Franklin, Mike Haygood.

Michelin #2 (Sandy Springs, S.C.): Wayne Yates (coach), Jimmy Johnson, Harold Williams, David Skelton, Mike Price, Joe Ervin, Tony Hutchinson, Early Adger, Steve Shelton, Ronald Perkins, Barker Stone, Nate Leverette, James Adams, Ted Murrah, Hunter.

Homelite (Greer, S.C.): Calvin Cohen (coach), James Griffin, Casey Jones, Donnell Rosemond, Ricky Pickett, Ricky Burton, Paul Brown, Eric Martin, Jimmy Williams, Herman Wright, Marty Knighton, William Simpson, Greg Carson.

Ware Shoals Mill (Ware Shoals, S.C.): Roosevelt Smith (coach), Joe Smith, Willie Smith, William Brownlee, Raymond Kelly, Tim Stewart, Sammy Williams, Roger Cyrus, Albert Smith, Doug Hill, Otis Simpson, Johnny Anty, Bernard Latimer.

Singer Mfg. (Anderson, S.C.): Ken Williford (coach), Thomas Hammond, Earl Walker, Henry Hammond, Clifford Leslie, Waymon Hood, Walter Johnson, Michael Barrett, Kenneth Garrison, Timmy Williams, Dan Daniel, Raymond Gray, George Gantt.

Monaghan Mill (Greenville, S.C.): Bill Swaynghame (coach), Ted Anderson, Charles Leamon, Eddie Leamon, Bobby Jones, Marcus Dawdy, Lewis McCoy Jr., Tony Brown, Terry Sullivan, Tony Blakely, Tommy Brown, Charles Walker, David Grant Jr.

Fiber Industries (Greenville, S.C.): Herman Evat (coach), Steve Richard, Frank Armfield, Timothy Howell, Kenneth Childress, Larry Dogan, Jasper Martin, Dick Hughes, Bob Hargett, Vernon McMakin, Steve Barton, David Pritchett, Cecil King, Phil Harley, McKinney.

Hoechst Celanese (Greer, S.C.): Sonny Moody (coach), Sonny Anderson, Larry Arms, Lawrence Williams, Marvin Drummond, Leroy Williams, David Hawkins, James Wells, Edward Crawford, Joel Gilliam, Ted Morton, Ricky Whitmore, Steinor Murray, Verdell Richardson, Brown.

Cryovac (Simpsonville, S.C.): James A. Sullivan (coach), Rex Abercrombie, Bobby Phelps, Calvin Milam, Matthew Milam, Bobby Church, Anthony Alexander, Elliott Owens, Gus Rubio, Lee Barksdale, James Sullivan, Cleveland Beaufort, Melvin Baptista.

3M (Greenville, S.C.): James Gwinn (coach), Louis Sayles Jr., William Davis, John Robinson, Jesse Looper, Larry Crosby, Kenny Arnold, John Williams, Bruce Middleton, Doug Austin, Mike Bridwell, Charles Hall, Dennis Blakely, Quinn, Gravley.

Sirrine Co. (Greenville, S.C.): Clark Templeton Jr. (coach), Bruce Martin, Tom Templeton, Thomas Rucker, John Cooper, Harry Moats, Glenn McCoy, Mark Satterfield, Ron Templeton, Jeff Ray, David Martin, Holiday, Bouton.

Pelzer Mill (Pelzer, S.C.): Ken McInnis (coach), Ronnie Cureton, Cephas Coleman, David Burns, Jerry Arnold, Ernest Cooley, Charles Pinson, John Henry, Scott Keels, Dwight Sullivan, Bobby Robinson, Leonard Williams, Bob Cloutier.

Slater Mill (Slater, S.C.): J.F. Roberts (coach), McBruce Young, Ricky Cruell, Joe Hill, John Askew, William Parnell, Anthony Williams, Randy Bowles, Brian Lewis, Jimmy Roberts Jr., Ray Cruell, Gary Wallace, Toll Plumley, Lybrand.

Michelin (Spartanburg, S.C.): Eddie Battle (coach), Steve Brown, David Owens, George McCarroll, Michael Cherry, Lynn Brown, Terry Moore, Alonzo Briggs, Patrick Still, William Stacey, Dean Dawkins, Danny Dalton, Milton Smith, James Lindsay, Barry Brown, Wilkin Walker.

Gayley Mill (Marietta, S.C.): Rusty Keaton (coach), Earl Keaton, Charles Carter, Robert Hackle, Garry Helms, Terry Hightower, Robert Keasler, Preston Smith, Rick Swing, Mike Whitfield, Butch McElheny, Jeff Price, Otis Smith.

Applied Engineering (Orangeburg, S.C.): Harry Shuler (coach), David Prince, David Paul, Ronald Huggins, Jacob Smith, Tim Gadson, Tommy Frazier, Richard Rivers, Ed Bryant, Joe Davis, James Benjamin, Carey Wade, Jr.

Greenville Valve (Greenville, S.C.): Steve Crowe (coach), Gene Crook, Robin Ellenburg,

Southern Textile Basketball Tournament Rosters   Appendix 1   297

William Hollis Jr., Bill Neely, Larry Joyner, Bill Tarver, Duncan Harvin.

Michelin (Greenville, S.C.): J.C. Starkes (coach), Larry Garvin, Roger Allen, Jeff Medford, Bernard Moore, Rufus Wilson, Mike Winston, Nixon Allen, Frankie Halstead, Irvin Johnson, Kerry Rasnake, Joel Henderson, Danny Bayne, Melvin Williams, Crawford.

Bahan Textile (Greenville, S.C.): David Burns (coach), Jim Camden, Ricky Eichelberger, Doug Pressley, Ron Taffer, Stanley Young, Marvin Cox, Ray Surett, Stanley Pressley, Ronald White, Scott McHugh, John Burns, Henry Pickney.

Emb-Tex (Travelers Rest, S.C.): Phillip Owens (coach), Henry Robertson (coach), Jim Rice, Robert Poole, Dennis Thompson, Melvin Young, Zernie Morgan, Roy Brown, Larry Brinkley, William McBee, Mark Vaughn, Raymond Williams, Robert McBee.

Parker Mill (Greenville, S.C.): Barry Littlefield (coach), Albert Donald, John Williams, Ernest Fuller Jr., Jimmy Robinson, John McKinney, Charles White, James Donald, Robert Pepper, Jerry Jackson, William McGowan, James Anderson Jr., Jerry Nix Jr., Renee Dawson.

American Federal (Greenville, S.C.): David Watson (coach), Leroy Abercrombie, Vance Cline Jr., Michael Dean, Charles Hardaway, Russell Hunt, Wayne McKinney, Chuck Werner, Douglas Baird, Charles Cornish, Keih Greene, Gary Jordan, Ronald Looper, David Nugent, William Weede, John Musgrove.

F.W. Woolworth (Greenville, S.C.): William Brownlee (coach), Randall Smith, Roger Donald, Willie Lewis, Jerry Robinson, David Sullivan, Robert Thompson, Albert Goldsmith, Marshall Mattress, Bernard Dawkins, Governor Chancellor, John Lollis, Steve Martin, Thomas O'Daniel.

Union Carbide (Simpsonville, S.C.): Steve Horne (coach), James Spearman, William Roberson, Steve Ladson, John Lipgens, Michael Cleveland, Waddy Talley, Jerry Lollis, Michael Miller, Willie Suber, James Andrews, Anthony Copeland, Steve Rabe, Michael Butler, Lawless.

Daniel Construction Co. (Greenville, S.C.): Terry Medlin (coach), Michael Burn, Donald Maxwell, Zachary Johnson, Paul Little, Michael Beerson, Terry W. Medlin, William Stephens, James Perkins, Alan Greer, James Shaw, Christopher Means, Roscoe Watson, Mike Stephens.

Class B Men

Black's Mechanical (Greenville, S.C.), champions: John Turner (coach), Jerry Evatt, Ken Johnson, Kent Sargent, Joe Evatt, Roger Carlton, James Choice, Kyle Turner, Mark Dickerson, Dennis Black, Gary Southern, Daris Childress.

Arcadia Mill (Spartanburg, S.C.), runners-up: Johnny Whiteside (coach), James Meadows, Kenneth Watt, Michael Moss, Clarence Anderson, Russell Bransford, James Pearson, Willie Anderson, Stanley Compton, Gilliam.

F.W. Woolworth (Greenville, S.C.), consolation winners: J.W. Richardson Jr. (coach), Kevin Hawkins, Robert Dicey, Louis Still, Randall Sheppard, John Pack, Thomas Goodjione, Rory Griffin, Vernon Freeman, Jerry Moses, Terry Duncan, Horace Gaines, David Turner.

Wangner Systems (Greenville, S.C.): Don Geenen (coach), Robert Hoover, Gary Roberts, Larry Williams, Rusty Smith, Robert Buchanan, George Pendergrass, Terry Roberts, John Johnson, Larry Abrams, Tim Carlton, Anthony Evans, Wiggins.

Cryovac (Duncan, S.C.): Wyn Hardy (coach), Steve Johnson, John Boudoucies, Bruce Hagins, Michael Shuck, Joseph Russell, Bruce Holliday, Mark Boudoucies, Donald Harrison, Warren Elliott, James Mize, Steve Smith, Roger Lee, Bauer.

3M (Greenville, S.C.): Jim Ross (coach), William McNeeley, Darnell Flemming, Terry Davis, Ernest Goodis, Ray Holliday, Mike Williams, Henry Byrd Jr., Eldarado Valentine, Jimmy Tucker, Randy Lollis, George Caldwell, Bill Davis, Brookie, Pendergrass, Madden, Bryant, Garrett.

Alice Mfg. (Easley, S.C.): Benny Sloan (coach), Greg Langston, Ricky McGowens, Tommy Anderson, Gregory Garrett, John Langston, Keith Moore, Terry Rosemond, Ricky Evans, Leroy Craig, Sid Collins.

Sirrine Co. (Greenville, S.C.): Bob Ray (coach), Michael Brewster, James Wimbrow, Donald Drummond, Regan Klein, Ellis Styles, Reggie Smith, James Neal Jr., William Tumblin Jr., Don Adams, Robert McClain.

Pelzer Mill (Pelzer, S.C.): William Adams (coach), Bobby Partain, Johnny Robinson, Marvin Bonds, Bobby Henderson, Darrell Tate, Tony Bannister, Tim Henderson, Bruner, Howard, Blanding, Shirley.

Fiber Industries (Greenville, S.C.): Gene

Evatt (coach), Ken Durham, Jimmy Gray, Wayne Hargette, Martin Ketterer, Jimmy Rusak, Steve Garland, Dennis McConville, Mike Brockman, Frank Lewis, Dick Reid, Clifton Bloise, Cliff Harrison, Furman Dirton, Jack Clubb.

Saco-Lowell (Easley, S.C.): Mike Youngblood (coach), Randy Tucker, Steve Corn, Gregg Corbin, Wayne O'Shields, Mickey Rogers, Sammy Baker, Bruce Taylor, Don Roper, Roger Finley, Eddie Chapman, Randy Durham, Ed Ballew, Lanny Taylor.

Grace Distribution (Duncan, S.C.): Greg Hall (coach), Michael Quinn, Michael Dorrian, Timothy Gleason, Dan Burrell, Ken Bessent, Gary Cort, Don Lusk, Bo Farmer, Cliff Ratgen.

Michelin (Greenville, S.C.): Steve Roberson (coach), Jim Morgan, Thomas Hopkins, Kevin Brown, Leon Brown, Chester Garrett, Alfred Williams, James Wright, Larry Jackson, Rufus Pressley, Barry McAbee, Eldridge Bennett.

Appleton Mill (Anderson, S.C.): Henry Spake (coach), Joe Geer, Don Pressley, Joseph Harrison, Rodney Allen, David Geer, Roy Calhoun, Ricky Craft, Thomas Webb, Ricky Vernon, Andy Wooten, Sammy Price, Tommy Vickery, Jimmy White.

Dunean Mill (Greenville, S.C.): Nash, Johnson, Vaughn, Smith, Donaldson, Rhodes, Evans, Anderson.

Woodside Mill (Greenville, S.C.): Gary Woods (coach), Barry McCombs, Allen Sims, Marion Reeves, George Wilson, Bobby Stevens, Don Anderson, David Rhinehart, Larry McCall, Oneal Tyler, Michael Seaborn, Donald Owens, David Ebert.

Southeastern Freight (Greenville, S.C.): Larry Holden, Billy Griffith, Glen Pritchard, Curt Gautier, Billy McDavid, Ronnie Bagwell, Darren Gazaway, Billy Murphy, David Duerling, Richard Tyson, Ron Howell.

Orders Tile Co. (Greenville, S.C.): Ed Shell (coach), Charles Atkins, David Hannon, Bobby Pridmore, Michael Smith, Mark Little, Bryan Deitke, Wiley Johnson, Randy Gidaro, Martin Miller, Jerry Garraux, Capers Owens, Calvin Williams, Jim Kelley, Gary.

Cryovac (Simpsonville, S.C.): Barry Wright (coach), Johnny Wright, Danny Sullivan, Paul Satterwhite, Jerry Boyd, Calvin Barksdale, Clarence Dawkins, Robert Barksdale, Fred Dean, Greg Sweeney, Harold Thompson, Jack Goodenough, Willie Gray, Willie Wright.

A & C Warehouse (Clinton, S.C.): Gary Wilbanks (coach), Sam Jones, Thomas Rogers, Robert Stapleton, Everett Robbins, Sam Lake, Randy Thompson, Glenn Bledsoe, Alan Roebuck, Mike Stapleton, MacArthur Duberry, Ben Pits.

Greenville Law Enforcement (Greenville, S.C.): Keeter McCullough (coach), Alan Sweet, Wayne Clark, Terrance Brooks, Steve Johnson, Michael Sweeney, Paul Guy, Chuck Butler, Troup, Bryan.

U.S. Post Office (Greenville, S.C.): Newell Tucker (coach), James Mayes, Donnie Scovel, Stephen Toliver, William Crawford, John Miller, James Holder, Thomas Brown, Richard Robertson, John Overbeck, Newell Tucker Jr, Rogers, Gambrell.

Piedmont Landscaping (Piedmont, S.C.): Ronnie Ayers (coach), Al Banister, Terry Elrod, Charles Davis Jr., Jerry Ayers, Thomas Rogers, Barry Kelly, Wayne Watson, Starnes.

Haynesworth Mill (Anderson, S.C.): Bill Wansley (coach), James Hunter, Jesse Thomas, Luther Walker, Max McDowell, Cedric Patterson, Ronnie Miller, C.J. McDonald, Robert Blunt, Seymour Brock, Bo Rousey, Tony Saylors, Meeks, Brown.

American Hardware (Greenville, S.C.): W.L. Brockman (coach), Milas Officer, Mac Stevens, Joe Taylor, Charles Lake, Robert Sullivan, Don Wooten, Billy Storey, Bernard Johnson, Tony DeYoung, Willie Shaw, Anderson.

Neptune Measurement (Greenwood, S.C.): Sam Arnold (coach), Jerry Boone, Buddy Nelson, Mitchell Adams, Bill Dillon, Robert Carroll, Mike Williams, James Gray, Marion Johnson, Richard Edmonds, Mark Riopko.

Bigelow-Sanford (Calhoun Falls, S.C.): Bill Brown (coach), Horace Thomas (coach), Elbert Turman Jr., Clarence McIntosh, Charles Wideman, Sam McDuffie, Charles Jones, Walter Hilley, Ernest Turman, John Glover, Jimmie Tinch, Clarence Robinson, Mike Evans, Charlie Henry.

Reliance Electric (Greenville, S.C.): Jim Riddle (coach), Jeff Foster, Jimmy Klugh, Larry Blakely, Donnie Byrd, Tim Wall, Ricky Norris, Charles Hancock, Robert Nash, O'Dell Gamble, Charles Lipscomb, Wayne Merritt, Johnny Buchanan, Whatley, Lindstrom.

Belk Simpson (Greenville, S.C.): Bayard Lindell (coach), Greg Morrison, Sydney Smith, Rodney Garrett, James Stewart, Charles Mattox, Mark Pardue, Tim O'Berry, Richard Lancianese, James Ledbetter, David Turner, Roy Hulehan, David Kirkland, Ward.

Winn Dixie (Greenville, S.C.): Joe Mathis (coach), Aaron Abrams, Charles Madden, Bill Holmes, Tex Young, Brown Miller, Eddie Prevette Jr., Neal Abrams, Phillip Smith, Tim Kelly, Harold Silvers, Richards.

Clinton Mill (Clinton, S.C.): Sam Owens (coach), Mike Owens, Jimmy Miller, Matt King, Doug Ward, Butch Roberson, Brian Shealy, Sammy Lanford, Harry Sullivan, Billy Watkins, Roger Higgins, Bill Stanton, Smith.

Class C Men

Fast Fare (Hartwell, Ga.), champions: Ron Garren (coach), Rob Gravley (coach), Dee Hunter (coach), Joe Ward, Scott Lane, Gerald Wilkins, Rick Kinney, Rudy Hill, Sammy Echols, Buzz Peterson, Mike Smith, Scott Harrison, Michael Partridge, Reggie Johnson, Maurice Colbert, James Wilson, Wilkins, Darren Gravley, Gerald Williams.

Dalton's Furniture (Pickens, S.C.), runners-up: Steve Gravley (coach), Charles Rogers, Dewayne Grace, Ikie Scipio, Buzz Peterson, Colzell McQueen, Dan Nunnery, Kevin Bryant, Mike Crowe, Warren Wallace, Jerome Williams, Albert Hudgens, Webb, Williams.

Southeastern Products (Greenville, S.C.), consolation winners: Jim Porterfield (coach), Lee Stegall, Wesley Ballard, Gary Bannister, Jeff Sumner, Todd Porterfield, Tino Sullivan, Todd Mattos, Sammy Belcher, Kevin Bryant, Joey Fowler, Eddie Franklin, Bailey, B. Sullivan, Smith.

Pelzer Mill #2 (Pelzer, S.C.): Don Belt (coach), Tony Belt, Billy Styles, Johnny Lollis, Billy Miller, Edward Nash, Joey Stewart, Don Walton, Mattison, Doug Breazeale, Owens, Cooley.

Pelzer Mill #1 (Pelzer, S.C.): Horace Davenport (coach), Don Brady, David Reid, Jerry Wilson, Eric Robinson, Hudgens, Allen, Lynch, Billy Styles.

Emery Air (Greenville, S.C.): Dillard, Al Deck, Gibson, McDowell, Byers, Stephens, Groce, Avery Deck, Smith.

Blankenship Electric (Greenville, S.C.): Danny Ballew (coach), Rick Mullinax, Reggie Thompson, Bob Bouton, Tim Easter, Scott Gardner, Darryl Rowley, Hank Harbin, Brian Pope, Noel Gilliard, Steve Fricks, Searles, Brown, Beasley, Bowen, Mirros.

Alford Real Estate (Greenville, S.C.): Warren Rollins (coach), Nelson Giles, Joseph Britt, Richard Rollins, Elbert Parks, James Simmons, Thomas Britt, Brian Lattimore, Bryan Britt, Jackson, Hagood, Thompson, Mosley, Cox, Taylor.

Chick-Fil-A (Greenville, S.C.): Mike Massey (coach), Hal Martin, Tyrone Corbin, Donnie Pearson, Darnell Jones, Mike Crowe, Noel Gilliard, Kevin McDavid, Anthony Jenkins, Alan Washington, David Shealy, Xavier McDaniel.

Carper Real Estate (Greenville, S.C.): Pat Eidson (coach), Tom Carlton (coach), Greg Slagle, Kevin Coffey, Jonathan Grubbs, Mike Brown, Steve Silva, John Weaver, Eddie Burton, David Suddeth, Steve Ware, Brian Evans, Calvin Duncan, Mark Letson, Tinsley, Stamey.

Pete's Market (Pelzer, S.C.): Don Bolton (coach), Chris Leonard (coach), Noel Gilliard, Joe Parker, Greg Mack, Ricky McDowell, Robbie Schultz, Bill Simms, Kevin Bryant, Steve Reece, Andrea Hills, Reggie Thompson, Danny Pearson, Irwin McCullough, Mullinax.

Boys' Club (Greenville, S.C.): Billy Hughes (coach), Norman Eoute (coach), Charles Booker, Anthony Chambers, Kenneth Coleman, David DeCarlis, Oren Gilmore, Lee Phelps, Darrell Washington, Mike Burdine, Calvin Chriswell, James Freeman, Kevin Mayes, John Sligh, Vernon.

Class A Women

Slater Mill (Slater, S.C.), champions: Bobby Kirby (coach), Jenny Lyerly, Vivian Humphries, Sally Reid, Debbie Raper, Debra Buford, Brantley Southers, Carolyn Thomas, Joan Kirby, Barbara Kennedy, Lisa O'Connor, Marsie McAlister, Vickie Andrews, Deborah Lloyd, Temple Elmore, Jackson, Kay Kirby, Ray Clappord.

Pelzer Byrd's (Pelzer, S.C.), runners-up: Angie Jones, Sadie Sellers, Martha Williamson, Harris, Ansley, Leatherman.

Sam Chapman Karate (Greenville, S.C.), consolation winners: Randy LaFoy (coach), Tricia Theodore, Cheryl Marsh, Teresa Ludwig, Cindy Cash, Karen Marianos, Kim Kindley, Jan Chappelle, Laura Galloway, Kristie Kerns, Toni Edwards, Lydia McElrath, McCullough, Young, Parks, Roper.

Piney Mountain T.A.P.S. (Greenville, S.C.): Jerome Dickey (coach), Jo Allman, Brenda Winfield, Hy Evans, Jana Duncan, Belinda Howard, Effie Lyles, Terri Meade, Jeanette

Thompson, Sonya Henderson, Frances Young, Vanessa Lanier, Gwen Bailey, Durham, Yeargin, Thurman, Jenkins, P. Davis, S. Davis, Williams, Dunn.

Pelzer Mill #1 (Pelzer, S.C.): B.J. Bell (coach), Karen Kelly, Karen Neely, Tammy Boggs, Jane Jackson, Lynn Starnes, Robin Neely, Eunice Campbell, Holly Bland, Anne Osteen, Beverly Davenport, Grover, Crenshaw, George, Thompson, McDonald.

Gould Associates (Taylors, S.C.): Jim Wilson (coach), Nancy Gould, Laurie Jerome, Paula Kirkland, Allyn Hogue, Jan Rampey, Susanne Wright, B.C. Barbary, Looney, Weatherford, Batson, Jordan.

Dunean Mill (Greenville, S.C.): Doug Gailey, (coach), Tammy Cureton, Lois Ashworth, Sandra Gossett, Vickie Moates, Tes Dreher, Doris Bigby, Rietta Hill, Beth Ashworth, Nira Moates, Beverly Pressley, Wella Williams, Uneta Chandler, Huffman, Baxter.

Fountain Inn Lumber (Fountain Inn, S.C.): Barry Smith (coach), Roger Terry (coach), Kim Eskew, Terri Meetz, Cynthia Stoddard, Lynn Thomason, Boo Crawford, Katie Welborn, Jan McDonald, Robin Adger, Donna Cannon, Clara Bruton, Debra Jackson, Cathy Locke.

Black's Mechanical (Greenville, S.C.): Angela Black, Cindy Mattos, Laurie Nix, Sonja Smith, Sharon Dickerson, Kim Holbrooks, Toni Edwards, Cindy Williams, Dendy, Simpson, Simmons, Wharton, R. Williams.

Revis Trucking (Spartanburg, S.C.): Danny Hall (coach), Frank Revis (coach), Annamay Stockman, Terri Reid, Catherine Cruell, Donna Vaughn, Judy Clark, Brenda DuBose, Pat Ward, Susan Jones, Regina Gilstrap, Pam Adams, Tammy Winchester, Marty Vaughn, Darlena Morgan, Cindy Ashton, Reid, Kindley.

Parker Mill (Greenville, S.C.): Jimmie Robinson (coach), Loretta Gatewood, Dorothy Byrd, Sheila Morris, Brenda Jones, Gail Gaines, Loretta McKinney, Frances McGowan, Brenda Summers, Teresa Evans, Linda Tutt, Brenda Walker, Kim Brock.

Non-Fluid Oil (Greenville, S.C.): Beth Couture, Ida Clinkscales, Sandy Kruse, Crenshaw, Hanson, Pittman, Roberts, Glover, Franklin.

---1982---

Executive Officers: Divver Hendrix, James Morrow, Vercho Carter, Fred Powers, Clarence Thomas, Willie Wilbanks, Ward Williams.

Officers: Ruppert Elliott (Greenville, S.C.), President; David Bailey (Greenville, S.C.), 1st Vice President & Ass't Treasurer; Bill Hopkins (Pelzer, S.C.), 2nd Vice President; Harry Foster (Greenville, S.C.), Treasurer; Fred Byrd (Greenville, S.C.), Executive Secretary; Lloyd McAbee (Greenville, S.C.), Ass't Executive Secretary; Whitey Kendall (Greenville, S.C.), Supervisor of Officials; Lt. F.R. Hawkins, Security Officer.

Executive Committee: Dan Foster (Greenville, S.C.), Henry Spake (Anderson, S.C.), Phil Clark (Greer, S.C.), Lewis Golden (Greenville, S.C.), Darrell Floyd (Greenville, S.C.), Jyles Phillips (Greenville, S.C.), Don Ball (Greenville, S.C.), Steve Brown (Greer, S.C.), Phil Harley (Greenville, S.C.), Jim Phillips (Greenville, S.C.), Mendel Masters (Greenville, S.C.), Fred McAbee (Greenville, S.C.).

OPEN DIVISION

Chick-Fil-A (Greenville, S.C.), champions: Terry Shelton (coach), James Ball, Wendell Gibson, Horace Wyatt, K. Laws, Reggie Small, Al Daniel, M. Doyle, Chubby Wells, J. Holland, Mel Daniel, W. Hanks, Dale Crowe, W. Gibson.

Sonics (Abbeville, S.C.), runners-up: Archibald Letman (coach), Greg Wright, Reggie Williams, Morris Jackson, Jesse Roundtree, Clinton Cobb, Alonzo Harrison, Curtis Harkness, Larry Ray, David Graham, Scot Taylor, Carroll Wells, Charles Jones, Dawson.

Cole's Barber Shop (Columbia, S.C.): Anthony Brown (coach), James Brown, Thomas Sanders, Irvin Earle, Wade Jenkins, Ricky Fulton, Ronnie Hamm, Kenny Reynolds, Tom Wimbush, Roosevelt Hingleton, Joe Rice, Billy Ingram, Mack, Frank Streeter, Cayruth.

Daniel Construction Co. (Jenkinsville, S.C.): Fred Pearson (coach), Virgil O'Neal, Alvin Holland, Vincent Pearson, Wayne Pearson, Henry Boyd, Charles Marshall, Curtis Carter, Finley O'Neal, Tom Vinegar, Jackie Boyd, Colie Feemster, Bouknight.

Pulliam Investment Co. (Spartanburg, S.C.): Shed Jolly (coach), James Blair, Kevin Gainey, Rooney Brockwell, Keith Dorsey, Mark Hoffman, William Tinder, Harold Jackson, Dennis Belcher, Fred Johnson Jr., Dwayne Harris, Scott Lane, Robert Mickle Jr.

Southern Textile Basketball Tournament Rosters

Quinby IGA (Florence, S.C.): Ashby Gregg (coach), Mike Meadows, Kermit Moore, Arthur Wanler, Julius Henderson, David Brown, Marvin Hamlin, Angelo Kelley, Greg Wright, Albert Washington, Dennis Sullen, Ervin Douglas.

Washington City Association (Greenville, S.C.): James Meekins (coach), James Jones, Joe Hancock, Muyon Cheeks, Michael Donald, Rickey Morris, James Garrison, James Cunningham, Artie Knight, Jay Spann, McAuther Brock, John Bird, Anthony Chamber, R. Smith, Jackson, John Perry, J. Smith, Hardy, Byers, Miller.

CLASS A MEN

Ware Shoals Mill (Ware Shoals, S.C.), champions: Roosevelt Smith (coach), Larry Traynham (coach), Joe Smith, Albert Smith, Bill Brownlee, Sammy Williams, Roger Cyrus, Doug Hill, Otis Simpson, Robert Fuller, Clarence Searles, Hollie Martin.

Bahan Textile (Greenville, S.C.), runners-up: David Burns (coach), Jim Camden, Ricky Eichelberger, Doug Pressley, Stanley Pressley, Ronald White, John Richardson, Henry Pickney, Nathaniel Washington, Chris Langley, Phillip Heyward, Roy Burns, Allen Johnson.

Duke Power (Greenville, S.C.), consolation winners: James Earl (coach), Mark Seay, Maurice Hawkins, James Bowens, Gregg Morton, Mike Williams, Jeff James, Gary Arnold, Terry Mansell, Willie Harris, Larry Bowens, David Earl, Ricky McDonald, Spott, Penny, Wade.

Black's Mechanical (Greenville, S.C.): John Turner (coach), Dennis Black (coach), Kyle Turner, Jerry Evatt, Roger Carlton, Donnie Rhodes, Charles Bridwell, Calvin Christwell, Ken Johnson, Charles Choice, James Copeland, Kent Sargent, Mitch Barron, Rick Mullinax.

Dunean Mill (Greenville, S.C.): Charles Hudson (coach), Isaiah Walker, Richard DuBose, Jimmy Marion, Clyde Agnew, Olin Wright, William McGee, Horace Anderson, Joseph Holden, Jeff McLeskey, Dale Owens, Mosley.

Singer Mfg. (Pickens, S.C.): Sammy Baker (coach), Jo Jo Kelley, Marty Hopkins, Ken Robinson, Walter Helms, Keith Scoggins, Glen Thrift, Neal Jetton, Ed Parris, Doc Evatt, Reggie Womack, Joey Stancell, Tim Looper, Anthony.

Michelin A (Sandy Springs, S.C.): Wayne Yates (coach), Charles Shiflet, David Skelton, Anthony Hutchinson, Lou Spear, Michael Hagood, John Geer, Ricky Dickson, Michael Card, Richard Vance, Barry King, Ronald Allen.

Michelin B (Sandy Springs, S.C.): Wayne Yates (coach), Harry Skelton, Johnny Hunter, James Adams, Marty Chapman, Roger Gilbert, James Yates, Lymunel Stowers, Charles Johnson, Glenn Davis, Nate Leverette, Walter Yates.

Alice Mfg. (Easley, S.C.): Terry Smith (coach), Kenneth Galloway, Ken Murphy, Linus Blake, Billy Cureton, Terry McGowens, George Davis, Douglas Adams, Ray Womack, Jackie Anderson, Ronnie Austin,

Monaghan Mill (Greenville, S.C.): Ted Anderson, Eddie Leamon, Bobby Jones, Marcus Dowdy, Lewis McCoy Jr., Tony Blakely, Ronnie Brown, Donnie Burpo, James Ferguson, Fred Dilworth, Ronnie Ward, Taylor.

Fiber Industries (Greenville, S.C.): Phil Harley (coach), Herman Evatt, Steve Richard, Frank Armfield, Timothy Howell, George Martin, Don Hughes, Bob Hargette, David Pritchett, Wayne Hargette, Bob Anderson, Tommy Summers, David Thomas.

Hoechst Celanese (Greer, S.C.): Grover Anderson, Steve Arms, Lawrence Williams, Marvin Drummond, Charles Crawford, Joel Gilliam, Ted Morton, Steinor Murray, Verdell Richardson, Gary Medlock, Steve Gambrell, Tim Easter, Calvin Durham, Pete Rollins, Fulton, Easter.

Cryovac (Simpsonville, S.C.): James A. Sullivan (coach), Lewis Whitmire (coach), Rex Abercrombie, Bobby Phelps, Calvin Barksdale, Matthew Milam, Bobby Church, Anthony Alexander, Elliott Owens, Gus Rubio, Lee Barksdale, James Sullivan, Jimmy Wright, Paul Satterwhite, Jerry Boyd, Ellis Meredith.

3M (Greenville, S.C.): Booker Johnson (coach), Louis Sayles Jr., William Davis, John Robinson, Jesse Looper, Larry Crosby, Kenny Arnold, Doug Austin, Charles Hall, Lyndon Mahaffey, Eddie Gwinn, Jimmy Tucker.

Sirrine Co. (Greenville, S.C.): Shelly Holliday (coach), Bruce Martin, Thomas Rucker, John Cooper, Mark Satterfield, Ron Templeton, David Martin, Charles Isham, Lawrence Kaminsky, James Uz, Ralph Bouton, Chandler, Holliday.

Pelzer Mill (Pelzer, S.C.): Ken McInnis (coach), Ronnie Cureton, David Burns, Charles Pinson, Scott Keels, Dwight Sullivan,

Bob Cloutier, Charles Mattison, Billy Burns, Charlie Adams, David Jenkins, Calvin Evans.

Slater Mill (Slater, S.C.): James Roberts (coach), J.F. Bowles (coach), Darryl Young, Ricky Cruell, Joe Hill, William Parnell, Randy Boyles, Brian Lewis, Bobby Allmond, Alfred Allmond, Jerry Sullivan, Lybrand.

Michelin (Spartanburg, S.C.): Eddie Battle (coach), David Owens, Fred McCarroll, Michael Williams, Terry Moore, Alonzo Briggs, William Stacey, Dean Martin, James Lindsay, Rodney Sullivan, Willie Hardy, Terry Free, Tom Davis, Still.

American Enka (Central, S.C.): Morris Henderson (coach), William Pepper (coach), Les Porter, Carl Valentine, Dannie Cannon Jr., Mike Church, Odis Rhodes, Randy van Surdam, John Williams, Clayton Wideman, Vince Earl, Stan Hamilton, Russell Fair, Ron Smith.

Greenville Valve (Greenville, S.C.): Steve Crowe (coach), Gene Crook, Robin Ellenburg, William Hollis Jr., Bill Tarver, Duncan Harvin, Mike Temby.

Michelin (Greenville, S.C.): Ed Collins (coach), Nixon Allen, Kerry Rasnake, Joel Henderson, Danny Bayne, Alfred Williams, Ricky Foster, C.L. Turner Jr., Jack Pearson, Jackie Chambers, Reggie Nealy, James Hartsell, Eldridge Bennett, Jackie Lollis, Benot.

Emb-Tex (Travelers Rest, S.C.): Henry Robertson (coach), Jim Rice, Robert Poole, Dennis Thompson, Melvin Young, Zernie Morgan, Roy Brown, Larry Brinkley, William McBee, Mark Cox, Robert Barker, Jimmy Hallums, James Rochester.

Parker Mill (Greenville, S.C.): Barry Littlefield (coach), Kenneth Waldrop (coach), Albert Donald, John Williams, Ernest Fuller Jr., Jimmy Robinson, Dwight Donald, Leon Pepper, Jerry Waldrop, William McGowan, James Anderson Jr., Albert Johnson, David Reid, Gill McDonald.

F.W. Woolworth (Greenville, S.C.): William Brownlee (coach), Roger Donald, Jerry Robinson, Robert Thompson, Albert Goldsmith, Marshall Mattress, Bernard Dawkins, Governor Chancellor, Steve Martin, Thomas O'Daniel, Michael Austin, Sandy Proffitt, Don Potter.

Union Carbide (Simpsonville, S.C.): Steve Horne (coach), Michael Butler (coach), Bill Coofer (coach), James Andrews, William Roberson, Steve Ladson, John Lipgens, Michael Cleveland, Waddy Talley, Michael Miller, Willie Suber, Anthony Copeland, Donald Young, Carl Schuff, Ricky Chapplear, Anderson.

Daniel Construction Co. (Greenville, S.C.): Terry Medlin (coach), Michael Burns, Zachary Johnson, Michael Beeson, William Stephens, James Perkins, Alan Greer, Christopher Means, Glenn Sullivan.

Belk Simpson (Greenville, S.C.): Bruce Howard (coach), Carl Chambers, Donald Peek, Murial Wilson, Rick Bailey, R.L. Harris, Rusty Wilson, Paul Shealy, Joel Richardson, Douglas Hall, Donald Holler, Roddy Jackson, Mike Johnson.

Stevens Beechcraft (Greer, S.C.): James Williams (coach), Mark Harvey, Randy Knowlton, Wally Burton, Danny Nelson, Christopher Longwill, William Smith, Johnny Crain, Terry Hawkins, Nelson Gilreath, Bob Sommers, Jim Keller.

Greenville Co. Sheriff's Dept. (Greenville, S.C.): Bobby Smith (coach), Alan Sweet, Wayne Clark, Steve Johnson, Michael Sweeney, Paul Guy, Chuck Butler, Hank Harbin, Mike Jolly, David Helton, Harris Clark, Fred Carter.

Class B Men

PPG Industries (Shelby, N.C.), champions: Eaker Campbell (coach), Nelson Webber, Paul Gash, Greg Beam, Larry Lynch, Darrell Hines, Kevin Willis, Don Gash, Terry Hunt, James Howell, Roger Shade, J.C. Cannon Jr, C. Prayor.

Appleton Mill (Anderson, S.C.), runners-up: Henry Spake (coach), Joe Geer, Don Pressley, Joseph Harrison, Rodney Allen, David Geer, Roy Calhoun, David Craft, Tommy Vickery, Willie Strobhart, Dewitt Johnson, Walter Jones, Mack Nance.

George Coleman Ford (Travelers Rest, S.C.), consolation winners: Gregg Coleman (coach), Moses Goodine, Ronnie Poole, Frankie Evans, Bobby Tinsley, Spencer Brown, Sonny Yeargin, Eddie Smith, Richard Davis, Doug Parris, Ronald Davis.

3M (Greenville, S.C.): Ernie Goodis (coach), Darrell Flemming, Hiram Davis, Ray Holliday, Henry Byrd Jr., Eldorado Valentine, Jim Brookie, George Caldwell, Scott Kay, Tony McNeely, Willie Madden, Phillip Arnold, Mike Madden, Mitch Madden, Goodis.

Cryovac (Duncan, S.C.): Wyn Hardy (coach), Steve Johnson, John Beckroge, Michael Shuck, Donald Harrison, Steve Smith,

David Sonday, Terry Dailey, Fred Dobbins, Arthur Edwards, Robert Smith, Frank Edwards, Steve Garland, Barr.

Alice Mfg. (Easley, S.C.): Benny Sloan (coach), Gregg Garrett, Ricky McGowens, John Massingale, Keith Moore, Terry Rosemond, Sid Collins, Carl Gambrell Jr., Tony McGowens, Benny Sloan, Michael Sargent, Clayton Rhodes, David Smith, Langston.

Sirrine Co. (Greenville, S.C.): Bob Ray (coach), Michael Bruster, James Wimbrow, Donald Drummond, Regan Klein, Reggie Anderson, James Neal Jr., William Tumblin Jr., Don Adams, Andrew Wilson, James Craig Jr.

Saco-Lowell (Easley, S.C.): Mike Youngblood (coach), Mike Allen (coach), Gregg Corbin, Eddie Ballew, Johnny Millwood, Eugene Galloway, Mike Gilstrap, David Smith, Tim Winchester.

Michelin Blue (Greenville, S.C.): Kevin Brown (coach), Jim Morgan, Thomas Hopkins, Chester Garrett, Alfred Burgess, Tommy Wright, Larry Jackson, Michael Jewell, Ted Barmore, Michael Sullivan, Willie Davis.

Woodside Mill (Greenville, S.C.): James Chappelle (coach), Donnie Wilson, Oneal Tyler, Michael Adams, Glen Gordon Jr., Richard Stenhouse, Willie Griffin, Jimmy Ponder, Nathaniel Blakely, Ron Harris, Willie Amos, Mayes.

Southeastern Freight (Greenville, S.C.): Darren Gazaway (coach), Larry Holden, Billy Griffith, Glen Pritchard, Curt Gautier, Billy Murphy, James Rooks, Lemon Collins, Melvin Raines, Spencer Collins Jr., Roy Collins, Ray Whaley.

F.W. Woolworth (Greenville, S.C.): Johnny Watts (coach), Kevin Hawkins, Robert Dicey, Lewis Still, Randy Sheppard, John Pack, Thomas Goodjione, Rory Griffin, Vernon Freeman, Horace Gaines, David Turner.

Orders Tile Co. (Greenville, S.C.): Bob Pridmore (coach), Jim Ray (coach), Ed Shell (coach), Randy Atkins, Michael Smith, Wiley Johnson, Martin Miller, Calvin Williams, Larry Duncan, T.M. Moore, Chris Wilson, Craig Bridges, Steve McCarthy.

Cryovac (Simpsonville, S.C.): Jerry Thompson (coach), Vernon Johnson (coach), Johnny Wright, Robert Barksdale, Fred Dean, Greg Sweeney, Richard Thompson, Willie Gray, Barnabus McFalls, Cody Porter Jr., Thomas Harris III, J.W. Wright, Jerry Simpson, Randy Wharton, Dawkins.

Abbeville Mill (Abbeville, S.C.): Coleman, T. Smith, Sutton, Reid, W. Smith, Campbell, Telfoy.

A & C Warehouse (Clinton, S.C.): Gary Wilbanks (coach), Sam Jones, Thomas Rogers, Robert Stapleton, Everett Robbins, Sam Lake, Randy Thompson, Glenn Bledsoe, Alan Roebuck, Mike Stapleton, Robert Lake, Bobby Shields.

U.S. Post Office (Greenville, S.C.): Paul Hill Jr. (coach), James Mayes, Stephen Toliver, John Miller, Thomas Brown, Mike Parkins, Chuck Taylor, Claude Mattison, Lyle Watson, Windell Rodgers, Franco Jackson, Willie Thompson, Ed Rogers, Bryson, Revis, Dowell.

Piedmont Landscaping (Piedmont, S.C.): Larry Ayers (coach), Terry Seawright, Charles Davis Jr., Jerry Ayers, Greg Ayers, Harold Monroe, Doug Brown, Carl Chambers, Jay Smith, Gary Burts, Ronnie Ayers, Al Bannister, Rogers, Owens.

American Hardware (Greenville, S.C.): William Brockman (coach), Milas Officer, Mark Stephens, Billy Taylor, Charles Lake, Robert Sullivan, Don Wooten, Billy Storey, Bernard Johnson, Rudolph Norris, Charlie McConnell.

Bigelow-Sanford (Calhoun Falls, S.C.): Bill Brown (coach), Horace Thomas (coach), Clarence McIntosh, Charles Wideman, Charles Jones, Ernest Turman, Clarence Robinson, E.T. Turman, Charlie Henry, James Lyons, Michael Bowie, Clarence Reid, Keith Williams, Osbey Turman, Glover, Johnson.

Reliance Electric (Greenville, S.C.): Bobby Milliam (coach), Jimmy Klugh, Larry Blakely, Donnie Byrd, Danny Norris, Charles Hancock, Robert Nash, O'Dell Gamble, Charles Lipscomb, Mark Christopher, Randall Ross, Billy Hovis, Steve Simmons.

Belk Simpson (Greenville, S.C.): Bayard Lindell (coach), Sydney Smith, James Stewart, Charles Mattox, Tom O'Berry, Richard Lancianese, James Ledbetter, David Turner, Roy Hulehan, Paul Murphree, Eric Lethco, Steve Ward.

Winn Dixie (Greenville, S.C.): Joe Mathis (coach), Charles Madden, Brown Miller, Phillip Smith, Van Brooks, Dennis Swafford, Kanada Roach, Tony Tucker, George Thompson, Ronnie Hammett, John Puette, Louis Mann, Finley, Waldrop, Guest.

Clinton Mill (Clinton, S.C.): Sam Owens (coach), Jimmy Miller, Matt King, Scott

Roberson, Billy Osborne, Roger Higgins, Bill Smith, Tom Davenport, Joe Bramlett, Aaron Simpson, Jay Swetenburg, Terry King, Jesse Brewster, Cromer.

U.S. Post Office (Seneca, S.C.): Randy Holder (coach), Gary Huff (coach), Charles Fleming, Windell Rodgers, Bill Crawford, Mike Curran, Tommy Difresco, John Overbeck Jr., Richard Robertson, Donnie Scovel, Robert Fowler, Newell Tucker, Ulysses Gambrell, Clemons.

Simpsonville Mill (Simpsonville, S.C.): Bennie Pinson (coach), Edward Sullivan, Allen Henry, Ernest Westmoreland, Joe Madden, Larry Norris, Carey Sullivan, Stanley Webb, Robert Bailey, Willie Williams, Jerry Norris.

Spartan Foods (Spartanburg, S.C.): Frank Talley (coach), Skip Corn, Claude Crocker, Allen Johnston, Carey Johnson, B.J. Luther, Bill Mitchell, Dub Hammett, Vince Sanders, Rick McGuire, Ezell, Gowan.

Southern Bank (Greenville, S.C.): Steve Berry (coach), Robert Long, Fred Aldeason, Jeffrey Thomason, Richard Galloway, Marshall Prince, Buddy Turner, Randolph Smith, John Johns, Jr., Culclasure.

Michelin (Greenville, S.C.): Ron Scarborough (coach), Ed Collins (coach), Mike Brown, Jim Morgan, Jackie Chambers, James Bryson, Darrell McCarson, Mike Kelley, Mike Jewell, Randy Tarrett, Bill Wooten, Chandler.

Greenville Fire Dept. (Greenville, S.C.): Bob Capps (coach), H.L. Harrison (coach), Doug Henson, Robert Dersch, Kenny Jackson, Don Craig, Melvin Harris, Billy Seay, Dwight Durrah, Ronnie McKeown, Roy Mack, Eddie Keeler, Jimmy Harris.

Capsugel (Greenwood, S.C.): Carl Chiles (coach), David Whitaker, Jerry Fortune, Ricky Backus, John Oliver, Seth Caldwell, Dale Chrisley, James Strong, John Brooks, Jerry Lawton, James Hawkins, Charlie Martin.

Class C Men

Chick-Fil-A (Greenville, S.C.), champions: Mickey Massey (coach), D. Wright (coach), William Mills, G. Elliott, Allen Washington, K. Laws, Gerald Perry, Daryl Bedford, George Adams, Mickey Massey Jr., J. Sadler, D. Haley, J. Wyatt, Lee Sartor, H. Dillard.

Dalton's Furniture (Pickens, S.C.), runners-up: Steve Graveley (coach), Charles Rogers, Dewayne Grace, Kevin Teustch, Vincent McQueen, James Earle, Anthony Crooks, Doug Breazeale, Vance Wyatt, Chad Dalton, John Walker, Albert Mattison, Roy Collins, Smith, Holland.

Alford Real Estate (Greenville, S.C.), consolation winners: Warren Rollins (coach), Nelson Giles, Eric Rollins, James Ellenburg, Thomas Coan III, Kenneth Waddell, John Brissey II, Mark Scott, Davis, Shaw, Anderson, Styles.

Andrews Vending Co. (Greenville, S.C.): Keith Alexander (coach), Bryan Cox, Kevin Phillips, Lamonte Oliver, Silas Gray, Don Tesner, Santos Sullivan, Mark McCall, Jimmy Mosley, Jensen, Young.

Pelzer Mill #2 (Pelzer, S.C.): William Adams (coach), Marvin Blanding, David Henry, Joey Stewart, Kyle Rollins, John Mize, Dee Dee Crompton, Louis Shirley, Dale Darby, Darren Darby, Greg Bell, Mike Shirley, Williford, Robinson, Dockman.

Pelzer Mill #1 (Pelzer, S.C.): Don Belt (coach), Billy Miller, Johnny Lollis, Jerry Wilson, Doug Breazeale, Albert Mattison, Mark Vaughn, Andrew Thompson, David Simmons, Jennings, Matt Gibson, Woods.

Blankenship Electric (Greenville, S.C.): Danny Ballew (coach), Reggie Thompson, Darrell Bowens, Brian Pope, Steve Frick, Edward Chandler, Joe Young, Jimmy Thick, Lamount Williams, Keith Johnson, Richardson, Florini, Singleton, Dawson.

Southeastern Products (Greenville, S.C.): Jim Porterfield (coach), Gary Bannister, Jeff Sumner, Bobby Sullivan, Todd Mattos, Sammy Belcher, John Bailey, Terrum Smith, Kenyon Roberson, Greg Suddeth, Donnie Mann, Tim Thick, Williams, Hunt, Vance, Lloyd, Terry Cobb, Wallace.

Carper Real Estate (Greenville, S.C.): Tom Carlton (coach), Mike Brown, John Stamey, Brian Pitts, Mark Lawson, Danny Edwards, Skip Mull, Andy Black, Ken McCann, Kelvin Jackson, Franz Smith, Suddeth, Cummings, Seezy, Furiate, Patterson, Waldrop.

Pete's Market (Pelzer, S.C.): Don Bolton (coach), Rick Owens (coach), Greg Leckie, Robbie Schultz, Bill Simms, Danny Pearson, Irwin McCullough, Glenn McCants, Brian Pope, James Allen, Jerry Wilson, Barron Boyd, Thompson, Walton.

Travel Inn (Greenville, S.C.): Bob Bailey (coach), J. Bailey, M. Whitman, B. Cox, R. Foster, E. Cox, B. McCall, S. Johnson, Lander, Musser, Lewis, Levi, Serles, Pace, Kelly.

CLASS A WOMEN

Pittman's Textile Machinery (Greenville, S.C.), champions: Ray Clippard (coach), Bobby Kirby (coach), Jennie Lyerly, Brantley Southers, Debra Lloyd, Lisa O'Connor, Sharon Gilmore, Melinda Hall, Marsie McAlister, Sally Reid, Vickie Andrews, Joan Kirby, Marty Vaughn, Mary Cubelic, Brenda Hill, Amy McAlister.

Non-Fluid Oil (Greenville, S.C.), runners-up: Ron Scarborough (coach), Beth Couture, Linda Crawford, Debra Buford, Barbara Kennedy, Janene Crenshaw, Melinda Hall, Ronda Chanson, Loretta Clinkscales, Peggy Caple, Cynthia Austin, Jackie Jones, Karen Jenkins.

Revis Trucking (Spartanburg, S.C.), consolation winners: Frank Revis (coach), Anna Mae Stockman, Terri Reid, Judy Clark, Susan Jones, Regina Smith, Pam Adams, Kim Kindley, Grace Lyle, Mary Kinard, Amy Booker, Lynn Auint, Nellie Boman, Stroble, James, Johnson.

Black's Mechanical (Greenville, S.C.): Buck Hooper (coach), James Odom (coach), Angela Black, Cindy Chapman, Laurie Nix, Kim Holbrook, Janice Simpson, Rene Williams, Denise Blakely, Sandtrice McDavid, Ingrid White, Jane Chappelle, Kathy Simmons, Dunlop, Reid, Womack.

Sam Chapman Karate (Greenville, S.C.): Randy LaFoy (coach), Cheryl Marsh, Cindy Cash, Kristie Kerns, Sandy Cash, Brenda Miller, Missy Parks, Patsy Johnson, Renee Foster, Tracy Trantham, Karen Weisner, Cheryl Gilmore, Beth Crisp, Gwen Whiteside, Valerie Whiteside, Moore, Morris.

Fountain Inn Lumber (Fountain Inn, S.C.): Barry Smith (coach), Kim Eskew, Lynn Thomason, Boot Crawford, Donna Canady, Clara Bruton, Debra Jackson, Cindy Williams, Kim Horner, Janice Allen, Darlene Morgan, Tracy Dennis, Frances Young, Stone, Slater.

Parker Mill (Greenville, S.C.): Loretta Brock, Dorothy Miller, Sheila Morris, Brenda Jones, Frances McGowan, Brenda Hawkins, Nina Moates, Dianne Turmon, Nancy Johnson, Charlene Cleveland, Shirl Makins, Nellie Bowens, Vickie Moates, Jeanette Jackson, Ann Allen, Melinda Hall, McKinney, Furman, Kelly, Reid.

Old Keg Party Shop (Greenville, S.C.): Charlie Bishop (coach), Tommy Lollis (coach), Judy Munson, Debbie Jenkins, Roonie Scovell, Deb Osborne, Jane Arledge, Brenda Wrak, Helen Wallace, Jackie Scovel, Donna McKinney, Alfreda Ray, Elizabeth Tankersley, Bowens, Reynolds, Glenn, Dunn.

Mac's All Stars (Greenville, S.C.): Archie McArthur (coach), R.G. Witters (coach), Johnnie Yeargin, Lillie Young, Maggie Smith, Margaret Looper, Dora Thompson, Patricia Rivers, Cheryl Elder, Connie Fleming, Mary Thurman, Cynthia Durham, Jeanette Dingle, Jackie Moore, Frances Young, Sandra Price, Jimmie Gatlin, Pat Smith.

1983

Executive Officers: Divver Hendrix, James Morrow, Vercho Carter, Fred Powers, Clarence Thomas, Willie Wilbanks, Ward Williams.

Officers: Ruppert Elliott (Greenville, S.C.), President; David Bailey (Greenville, S.C.), 1st Vice President & Ass't Treasurer; Bill Hopkins (Pelzer, S.C.), 2nd Vice President; Harry Foster (Greenville, S.C.), Treasurer; Fred Byrd (Greenville, S.C.), Executive Secretary; Lloyd McAbee (Greenville, S.C.), Ass't Executive Secretary; Whitey Kendall, Greenville, Supervisor of Officials; Lt. F.R. Hawkins, Security Officer.

Executive Committee: Dan Foster (Greenville, S.C.), Phil Clark (Greer, S.C.), Lewis Golden (Greenville, S.C.), Darrell Floyd (Greenville, S.C.), Jyles Phillips (Greenville, S.C.), Don Ball (Greenville, S.C.), Phil Harley (Greenville, S.C.), Jim Phillips (Greenville, S.C.), Jimmy Hopkins (Pelzer, S.C.), Fred McAbee (Greenville, S.C.), Ted Pittman (Greenville, S.C.), Charles Roddy (Greenville, S.C.).

OPEN DIVISION

Chick-Fil-A (Greenville, S.C.), champions: G. Mack, Mel Daniel, K. Laws, J. Helleman, Reggie Small, Jim Cleamons, Al Daniel, T. Shelton, B. Lewis, Gerald Peacock, T. Small, J. Ball, S. Wilson, Doyle Carr, Bryant.

Goin' Jesse's Restaurant (Columbia, S.C.), runners-up: Anthony Brown (coach), James Brown, Thomas Sanders, Irvin Earle, Wade Jenkins, Ricky Fulton, Tommy Mack, Roosevelt Hingleton, Joe Rice, Billy Ingram, Maurice Kitt, Moses Brown, Melvin Jones, Henry Hamilton, Craig Cayruth, Tom Wimbush.

Sonics (Abbeville, S.C.): Archibald Letman (coach), Reggie Williams, Jesse Roundtree, Clinton Cobb, Alonzo Harrison, Curtis Harkness, Scott Taylor, Kenny Holmes, Johnny

Edwards, Charles Jones, Carroll Wells, Nellie Martin, Winfred King, Tolbert, Wright.

Spartanburg YMCA (Spartanburg, S.C.): Tom Vinegar Jr. (coach), James Brown, Russell Edwards, Colie Feemster, Bill Humphries, Terry Smith, Marty Varne, Tim Burrell, Carl Feemster, Mike Galloway, Vincent Sanders, Mike Trexler, Thomas W. Vinegar.

Bow Tie Grand (Columbia, S.C.): James Meekins (coach), Tom Davis (coach), Joe Hancock, Mike Crow, Artie Knight, David Darby, Mike Todd, Kenneth Sterling, John Perry, Wyatt Milton, Raymond Lawson, Milton, Burnett, Bowen, Miller, Camp, Spurgeon.

Maintenance Supply Co. (Greenville, S.C.): Mike Howard (coach), Dennis Belcher, Brad Eppley, Mike Beardsley, David Nelson, James Blair, Kevin Gainey, Craig Burgess, Fred Johnson, Robert Mickle, Jay Davis, Cam Johnson, Harold Jackson, Howard Coe, Gray, Harris, Lynn.

Black Diamond (Greenville, S.C.): Tommy Hughes (coach), Sonny Moody (coach), George Short, David Kershaw, Carlos Hardy, J.W. Miller, Tyrone Sellers, Mike Miller, James Garrison, Ray Smith, Marvin Drummond, Mitch Anderson, J. Miller, Cohen, Dendy.

Class A Men

Emb-Tex (Travelers Rest, S.C.), champions: Dennis Walker (coach), Tommy Johnson (coach), Dennis Thompson, Melvin Young, Zernie Morgan, Larry Brinkley, Robert McBee, Mark Cox, Henry Carson, Doug McBee, Cecil Duck, Mike Williams, Henry Robinson.

Parker Mill (Greenville, S.C.), runners-up: Barry Littlefield (coach), Kenneth Waldrop (coach), Albert Donald, Ernest Fuller Jr., Jimmy Robinson, Dwight Donald, Leon Pepper, William McGowan, David Simmons, Gill McDonald, Paul Johnson, Marshall Mattress, O'dell Harrison, Kelvin Riley.

Bahan Textile (Greenville, S.C.), consolation winners: Harold Pressley (coach), Jim Camden, Stanley Woodruff, Ronald White, John Richardson, Henry Pickney, Roy Burns, Michael Pressley, Carlos Hardy, Robert Irby, Charlie Turner Jr., Sammy Edwards, Fowler, Ross.

Cryovac (Simpsonville, S.C.): Lewis Whitmire (coach), Rex Abercrombie, Bobby Phelps, Calvin Barksdale, Matthew Milam, Bobby Church, Anthony Alexander, Elliott Owens, James Sullivan, Paul Satterwhite, Jerry Boyd, Vernon Johnson, Barry Wright, Yates, A. Abercrombie, Chiles.

Duke Power (Greenville, S.C.): James Earl (coach), Ricky McDonald (coach), Mark Seay, Maurice Hawkins, James Bowens, Gary Arnold, Terry Mansell, Willie Harris, David Earl, Michael Wade, Keith Holcombe, Larry Woolums, Brian Jones, Marvin Burnette, Peahuff, Bishop, L. Bowens, K. Wade.

Singer Mfg. (Pickens, S.C.): Kenneth Williford (coach), Keith Lollis, Earl Walker, Waymon Hood, Raymond Gray, Elijah Kemp, Ronald Watkins, Calvin Wansley, George Gantt, Cecil Mattison, Cornell Gantt.

Michelin #1 (Greenville, S.C.): Brian Pearson (coach), Jack Pearson, Jackie Chambers, Charles Turner Jr., Stephen Butler, Billy Glasby, Rufus Pressley, Wayne Freeman, Henry McGowan, Reggie Nealey, James Bryson, Michael Jordan, Ricky Smith, Kevin Brown.

Michelin (Spartanburg, S.C.): Battle, Free, Moore, Martin, Williams, Lindsay, McCarroll, Elmore, Conner, Hanley, Owens.

Alice Mfg. (Easley, S.C.): Terry Smith (coach), Linus Blake, Billy Cureton, Terry McGowens, George Davis, Ray Womack, Spencer Collins, Mike Chandler, John Langston, Sid Collins, Ricky McGowens, Clayton Rhodes, Tony McGowens, James Langston.

Fiber Industries (Greenville, S.C.): Hargett, Childers, G. Martin, Howell, Phelps, Anderson, Armfield, Summers, Richards, J. Martin.

Ware Shoals Mill (Ware Shoals, S.C.): Kelly, Fuller, Quarles, Cyrus, Warren McGrier, Jones, Smith, Powell, Brownlee, Lewis, Johnson, Anly.

American Enka (Enka, N.C.): Church, Cannon, Valentine, Van Surdam, Rhodes, Hamilton, Fair, Pepper, Wideman, Williams.

Monaghan Mill (Greenville, S.C.): Bill Swaynghame (coach), Ted Anderson, Bobby Jones, Lewis McCoy Jr., Tony Blakely, Ronnie Brown, Donnie Burpo, Mike Riley, Anthony Ward, Wayne Jones, Anthony Talley, Dale White, Taylor.

Hoechst Celanese (Greer, S.C.): Richard Barras (coach), Lawrence Williams, Marvin Drummond, Charles Crawford, Steiner Murray, Gary Medlock, Tim Easter, Sonny Anderson, Ray Martin, Donnie McCarter, Mike Brooks, Pat Smith, Gerald Williams, Arms.

Sirrine Co. (Greenville, S.C.): Shelly Holliday (coach), Bruce Martin, John Cooper, Mark Satterfield, Theodore Templeton, David Martin, Charles Isham, Lawrence Kaminsky, James Uz, Lee Clippard, Denis Zeigler.

Slater Mill (Slater, S.C.): James Roberts (coach), McBruce Young, Ricky Cruell, Joe Hill, William Parnell, Randy Bowles, Scott Harbin, Mark Lybrand, Anthony Williams, Leonard Monroe, James Roberts, Suddeth, Waldrop.

Michelin #2 (Greenville, S.C.): J.C. Starnes (coach), Nixon Allen, Kerry Rasnake, Joel Henderson, Alfred Williams, Donnie Chambers, Kevin Brown, Leslie Williams, John Furmanski, Frank Halstead, Matthew Ryan, Rodney Sullivan.

Union Carbide (Simpsonville, S.C.): Jim Spearman (coach), Bob Andrews, Andy Roberson, Steve Rabe, John Lipgens, Waddy Talley, Anthony Copeland, William Hucks, Jerry Lollis, Bill Gosnell, Mauldin, Bryson.

Stevens Beechcraft (Greer, S.C.): Randy Knowlton (coach), Mark Harvey, Danny Nelson, William Smith, Terry Hawkins, Nelson Gilreath, Bob Sommers, Jim Williams, Greg Hairston.

PPG Industries (Shelby, N.C.): Eaker Campbell (coach), Nelson Webber, Paul Gash, Greg Beam, Larry Lynch, Darrell Hines, Kevin Willis, Donald Gash, Terry Hunt, James Howell, Roger Shade, J.C. Cannon Jr, C. Prayor.

Dunean Mill (Greenville, S.C.): DuBose, Walker, Marion, Thomason, Holden, Owens, McGee, Watson, Carson, Thurman.

CLASS B MEN

Southeastern Freight (Greenville, S.C.), champions: Darren Gazaway (coach), Spencer Collins (coach), Curt Gautier (coach), Larry Holden, Glen Pritchard, Lemon Collins, Wayne Raines, Roy Collins, Phillip Teague, Alvin Pritchard, William Cassels, David Duerling, Mark Nations, Rick Mullinax, Donnie Westmoreland, Perry Craig, Rory Griffin, Patrick, Bill Gazaway.

Appleton Mill (Anderson, S.C.), runners-up: Robert Clinkscales (coach), Joe Geer, Don Pressley, Rodney Allen, David Geer, Roy Calhoun, David Vickery, Dewitt Johnson, Walter Jones, Bernard Hill, Thomas Webb.

Sirrine Co. (Greenville, S.C.), consolation winners: Bob Ray (coach), James Wimbrow, Donald Drummond, Regan Klein, Reggie Anderson, James Neal Jr., William Tumblin Jr., Don Adams, Andrew Wilson, James Craig Jr.

Cryovac (Simpsonville, S.C.): Jimmy Wright (coach), Harold Wright (coach), Johnny Wright, Robert Barksdale, Fred Dean, Greg Sweeney, Willie Gray, Barnabus McFalls, Cody Porter Jr., J.W. Wright, Jerry Simpson, Otis Williams, Daniel Sullivan, Al Chiles, McGill, Dawkins, Harris.

Wangner Systems (Greenville, S.C.): Evans, Edwards, Huff, Williams, Grant, McDonald, Roberts, Hoover.

George Coleman Ford (Travelers Rest, S.C.): George Coleman Jr. (coach), Moses Goodine, Ronnie Poole, Eddie Smith, Gregg Coleman, Michael McGrady, Mitchell Barron, Levis Gilstrap Jr., Vernon Wade, Tinsley.

Cryovac (Duncan, S.C.): Wyn Hardy (coach), Steve Johnson, Michael Shuck, Donald Harrison, Steve Smith, Terry Dailey, Fred Dobbins, Robert Smith, Frank Edwards, Steve Fuller, Chris Robinson, Brannon.

3M (Greenville, S.C.): Tony McNeely (coach), Henry Byrd Jr., Eldorado Valentine, Jim Brookin, George Caldwell, Scott Kay, Willie Madden, William McNeely, Derrick Pendergrass, Mike Williams, Ernie Goodis, Ernie Goodis Jr., Dwayne Henderson, Frankie Melton, Flemmings.

Michelin Blue (Greenville, S.C.): Kevin Brown (coach), Larry Jackson, Michael Brown, William Wooten, Ron Scarborough, Billy Manley, Donnie Rhone, Eddy Tyner, Rick Morley, Ed Collins, Bill Bogen, Mark Chandler, Kelly, Freeman, Dirton, Tyner, Freeman.

A & C Warehouse (Clinton, S.C.): Gary Wilbanks (coach), Sam Jones, Thomas Rogers, Robert Stapleton, Sam Lake, Randy Thompson, Glenn Bledsoe, Alan Roebuck, Mike Stapleton, Robert Lake, Bobby Shields, George Watson.

U.S. Post Office #1 (Greenville, S.C.): Donnie Scovel (coach), John Miller, Ed Rogers, Richard Robertson, William Crawford, Newell Tucker, Gary Huff, Charles Fleming, James Holder, Michael Curran, Terry Hudson.

U.S. Post Office #2 (Greenville, S.C.): Windell Rodgers (coach), Stephen Tolliver, Thomas Brown, Chuck Taylor, Franco Jackson, Willie Thompson, Gregory Fielder, Robert Fowler, U. Gambrell, Mitchell Bryson, Prince Brock, Julius Revis, Taylor.

American Hardware (Greenville, S.C.): William Brockman (coach), Milas Office, Mark Stephens, Billy Taylor, Charles Lake, Robert Sullivan, Don Wooten, Billy Storey, Bernard

Johnson, Tony Ellenburg, David Bernsteil, Lawrence DeYoung, Mitch Reeves.

Bigelow-Sanford (Calhoun Falls, S.C.): Bill Brown (coach), Horace Thomas (coach), Clarence McIntosh, Charles Wideman, Charles Jones, Ernest Turman, Clarence Robinson, Elbert Turman, Charlie Turman, Keith Williams, John Glover, Alfonso Tucker, Robert Lyons.

Piedmont Landscaping (Piedmont, S.C.): Davis, Impson, Brown, J. Ayers, G. Ayers, McAbee, Smith, Jones, Perkins, Page, Gilliam.

Winn Dixie #1 (Greenville, S.C.): Joe Mathis (coach), Van Brooks, Canada Roach, Tony Gilliard, Tim Stephens, Roosevelt Brooks, Jim Young, Curt Farmer, Steve White, Benny Mauldin, Mike Price, Finley.

Clinton Mill (Clinton, S.C.): Joe Bramlett (coach), Sam Owens, Jimmy Miller, Matt King, Scott Roberson, Billy Osborne, Bill Smith, Tom Davenport, Aaron Simmons, Terry King, Jesse Brewster, Brawley Pitts, Ben Johnson, Bryan Shealy, William Mims.

Capsugel (Greenwood, S.C.): Carl Chiles (coach), Jerry Fortune, John Oliver, Seth Caldwell, James Strong, John Brooks, James Hawkins, Phil Martin, Eugene Day, Gary Norman, Tony Sleister, Herbert Foster.

St. Francis Hospital (Greenville, S.C.): Bobby Garrison (coach), Lloyd Kelly (coach), Forest Thomas, Bobby Reynolds, Rusty Brown, Robert Church, Anthony Simpson, Joe Flemming, Barron Padgett, Bernard Edwards, James Boynton Jr., Bob Craig, Emanuel Taylor, Douglas Keir, Gibson.

Professional Medical Products (Greenwood, S.C.): Bobby Wideman (coach), Calvin White, Curtis Cannon, Clinton Holloway, Larry Cooper, Kenneth Goodwin, Leonard White, Randy Dendy, Sammy Cooper, William Norman.

T & S Brass & Bronze Works (Greenville, S.C.): Dale Foster (coach), Eugene Pam, Jeff Duncan, Dwight Ferguson, John Burgess, Emmanuel Luin, Bronston Horton, Larry Cox, Tommy Murray, R. Burgess.

Winn Dixie #2 (Greenville, S.C.): Gerald Waldrep, Randy Zercher, Sonny Manheim, Fred Robinson, Alan Silvers, Bill Springfield, Louis Mann, William Lathem, Phillip Smith, Tom Rabon, George Thompson, Gary Murrell.

Pelzer Mill (Pelzer, S.C.): David Burns (coach), Dan Scroggs, Darren Darby, Wayne Eskew, Dale Darby, Bruce Scroggs, Vic Alverson, Mike Epps, Randall Darby, Mize.

Class C Men

Chick-Fil-A (Greenville, S.C.), champions: Mickey Massey (coach), Patrick Callaway, C. Newell, D. Goodwin, D. Jensen, H. Sims, C. Brown, S. Wilson, R. Brogden, K. Laws, James Ball, Gary Martin, G. Salters, Gerald Perry, Mike Massey, D. Robinson.

Pelzer Mill (Pelzer, S.C.), runners-up: Ernie Todd (coach), David Lee, John Harrison, Louie Henry, Greg Bruce, Mike Thomas, Johnny Lollis, Mark Acker, Frankie Simmons, Richard Lee, Eric Robinson, Vincent Webb, Derrick Galloway.

Alford Real Estate (Greenville, S.C.), consolation winners: Warren Rollins (coach), James Ellenburg, John Brissey, Spencer Black, John Jones, Bruce Davis, Vincent Anderson, Conrad Crews Jr., Clifton Rush, John Dawson, Bailey, Kimball, Shaw, Rollins, Leonard, Inabinet, Phillips.

Carper Real Estate (Greenville, S.C.): Larry Carper (coach), J. Smith, T. Smith, Bridges, Greg Merritt, Wicker, Crooks, Patterson, Frazier, Salley, Willis, Luke, Jackson.

Pete's Market (Pelzer, S.C.): Bill Sims, Leon Jones, Anthony Daniels, B. Boyd, Anderson, K. Boyd, W. Boyd, Hale, Ramey, Reames.

Travel Inn (Greenville, S.C.): Bob Bailey (coach), Jay Bailey, Mike Whitman, Bryan Cox, Linden Musser, Keith Lewis, Robert Bailey, Darin Pace, Barron Searls, William Levi, Chris Jones, Joe Holbert, Thomas.

The Athlete's Foot (Greenville, S.C.): Sherrall Jenkins (coach), Danny McAfee, Silas Gray, Patrick Byers, Timothy Guin, James King, Anthony Carr, Kenneth Hunt, Hayes, Burnette, Lloyd.

Cooper's Super Market (Greenville, S.C.): Jackie Arnold (coach), Mike Arnold (coach), Curtis Hightower, Donald Tucker, Henry Helmsley, Dale Page, William Arnold, Gary Burgess, Jeff Hodge, Garrett.

Class A Women

Chem-Size (Travelers Rest), champions: Ron Scarborough (coach), Jack Hart (coach), Traci Waits, Linda Crawford, Ronda Chanson, Lilly Young, Debra Buford, Laura Reed, Karen Jenkins, Toni Edwards, Davis, Powers, Freeman, Durham.

Pittman's Textile Machinery (Greenville, S.C.), runners-up: Bobby Kirby (coach), Jennie Lyerly, Brantley Southers, Debra Lloyd, Sharon Gilmore, Marsie McAlister, Sally Reid, Vickie

Andrews, Kay Kirby, Marty Vaughn, Brenda Hill, Amy McAlister, Becky Jackson, Dawn Raab, Bishop, Dunn, Carlton, Jennings, Laurie Nix, Lincoln, Sheila Hodge, Flatten.

Black's Mechanical (Greenville, S.C.), consolation winners: Buck Hooper (coach), James Odom (coach), Angela Black, Kim Holbrook, Rene Williams, Kathy Simmons, Karen Weisner, Sandra Rice, Donna Glenn, Cam Langston, Alecia Coaxun, Carrol Dunn, Beverly Staton, Barnita Bowens, Jennette Jones, Marcie Davis, Cristy Koyle, Martin.

Sam Chapman Karate (Greenville, S.C.): Randy LaFoy (coach), Cheryl Marsh, Tracy Korbutt, Deborah Kelly, Shirl Greer, Audrey Watson, Barbara Walker, Valerie Whiteside, Michelle Hendrix, Bridgette Martin, Jennette Watson.

D.J.'s (Greenville, S.C.): Beth Couture, Rosalind Jennings, Arledge, Ray, Osborne, Scovel, Yeargin, McKinney, Wallace, Brady, Fenish.

1984

Executive Officers: Divver Hendrix, Vercho Carter, Fred Powers, Clarence Thomas, Willie Wilbanks.

Officers: Bill Hopkins (Pelzer, S.C.), President; Jyles Phillips (Greenville, S.C.), 1st Vice President; Ruppert Elliott (Greenville, S.C.), 2nd Vice President; Harry Foster (Greenville, S.C.), Treasurer; Fred Byrd (Greenville, S.C.), Executive Secretary; B.J. Bell (Pelzer, S.C.), Ass't Executive Secretary; Janet Hopkins (Pelzer, S.C.), Ass't Executive Secretary; Lt. F.R. Hawkins, Security Officer.

Executive Committee: Dan Foster (Greenville, S.C.), Phil Clark (Greer, S.C.), Lewis Golden (Greenville, S.C.), Don Ball (Greenville, S.C.), Phil Harley (Greenville, S.C.), Jim Phillips (Greenville, S.C.), Jimmy Hopkins (Pelzer, S.C.), Fred McAbee (Greenville, S.C.), Ted Pittman (Greenville, S.C.), Charles Roddy (Greenville, S.C.), James Ball (Greenville, S.C.), Frank Ballenger (Shelby, N.C.), A.C. Jones (Ware Shoals, S.C.).

OPEN DIVISION

Black Diamond (Greenville, S.C.), champions: Tommy Hughes (coach), Tom Davis (coach), Joey Short, David Kershaw, Carlos Hardy, J.W. Miller, Monroe Garrison, Ray Smith, Wyatt Minton, Charles Dendy, Demsey Cohen, Raymond Lawson, John Perry.

Hobart Mfg. (Blythewood, S.C.), runners-up: Jacob Pearson (coach), David Poole, Bobby Cunningham, Roger Carr, Anthony Kelly, Calvin Davis, Anthony Flager, Curtis Boyd, Reggie Nova, Ronnie Ham, Howard White, Willie Crumpton, Brian Robinson, Golie Augustus, Tim Cheesboro, Vincent Pearson, Bernard Bell, East, Kelly.

Sonics (Abbeville, S.C.): Archibald Letman (coach), Reggie Williams (coach), Alonzo Harrison, Scott Taylor, Kenny Holmes, Charles Jones, Hollie Martin, Leon Harrison, Shun Davis, Jimmy Lott, Kenneth Thomas, Calvin Dorn, David Graham, Gary Gatewood, Robinson, Sullivan, Nanney, Millen, Cobb, McClarey, Harkness.

Spartanburg YMCA (Spartanburg, S.C.): Tom Vinegar Jr. (coach), James Brown, Russell Edwards, Colie Feemster, Bill Humphries, Marty Varne, Tim Burrell, Carl Feemster, Mike Vick, Vincent Sanders, Mike Trexler, Miller.

V.A. Jets (Columbia, S.C.): Primus, Kirkland, Hicks, Nipson, L. Wilson, Jackson.

Rug Doctor (Spartanburg, S.C.): Richard Heatly (coach), Mike Howard, Dennis Toms, Mike Meadows, David Heatly, James Blair, Robert Parker, Jim Garland, James Holland, Phillip McAbee, Wendel Gibson, John Toms, Chuck Toms, Gray, Sartor, Harris, Drummond.

Mt. Zion (Lexington, S.C.): James Young (coach), Robert Jeter, Kenneth Leaphart, Doug Thompson, Ben Taylor, Roscoe Wilson, Nate Davis, Steve Ashe, Wayne Leaphart, Craig Cayruth, Willie Crumpton, Reggie Noble, Anthony Flager, Grier, Beck, Wright.

Vince Perone's Restaurant (Greenville, S.C.): Joe McCrary (coach), Mark Campbell, Murray Jarman, Steve Crowe, Floyd Creed, Tim Roper, Joey McCrary, Chubby Wells, George Singleton, Fred Gilliam, Gary Bannister, Mel Daniel, Al Daniel.

Cross Stitch Originals (Cliffside, N.C.): Dalmar Shirley (coach), Richard Kenney, Eddie Walker, Dean Johnson, Norman Aiken, Ronald Hargrave, Vincent Jackson, Terry Camp, Richard Davis, Wilkins, Bridges.

CLASS A MEN

Singer Mfg. (Anderson, S.C.), champions: Kenneth Williford (coach), Earl Walker, Waymon Hood, Raymond Gray, Charles Dacus,

Nelson Heard, Joe Geer, Steve Adams, Ed Parris, Ken Spears, Julius Clinkscales, Richard Kelly, George Gantt, Hood.

Monaghan Mill (Greenville, S.C.), runners-up: Bill Swaynghame (coach), Bobby Jones, Lewis McCoy Jr., Tony Blakely, Anthony Taylor, Wayne Jones, Elvis Gordon, Frank Fuller, Nathaniel Sligh, James Ferguson, James Jones, Grant, Keton.

Ware Shoals Mill (Ware Shoals, S.C.), consolation winners: Larry Traynham (coach), Gerald Anderson, Otis Simpson, Larry Brownlee, Cleveland Walker, Edward Quarles, Willie Smith, Tommy Lewis, Roger Cyrus, Robert Fuller, Clarence Brownlee, Jeff Jones, Joe Smith, Kelly, Dial, Stewart.

Parker Mill (Greenville, S.C.): Barry Littlefield (coach), Albert Donald, Ernest Fuller Jr., James Donald, Robert Pepper, William McGowan, David Simmons, Gil McDonald, O'dell Harrison, Kelvin Riley, David Reid, Jerry Jackson, James Adams, Williams, Robinson.

Emb-Tex (Travelers Rest, S.C.): Dennis Walker (coach), Tommy Johnson, Dennis Thompson, Zernie Morgan, Larry Brinkley, Robert McBee, Mark Cox, Henry Carson, Bill McBee, Cecil Duck, Mike Williams, Richard Davis, Roy Brown.

Bahan Textile (Greenville, S.C.): Harold Pressley (coach), Jim Camden, Stanley Woodruff, Ronald White, Henry Pickney, David Burns, Mark Pressley, Stanley Pressley, Ricky Eichelberger, Doug Pressley, Gary Fowler, Mark Durham, Ricky Prince.

Michelin (Spartanburg, S.C.): Eddie Battle (coach), Michael Williams, Alonzo Briggs, James Lindsey, Donnie Alexander, Irvin Player, Terry Moore, Jimmy Williams, Greg Elmore, Terry Free, Eric Martin, Willie Hardy, Shawn Wager.

Alice Mfg. #1 (Easley, S.C.): Terry Smith (coach), Terry McGowens, George Davis, Ray Womack, John Langston, Clayton Rhodes, Ronnie Austin, Matthew Valentine, Douglas Smith, Ken Galloway, Ken Ross, Fred Valentine, Owens, T. Smith, Anderson.

Alice Mfg. #2 (Easley, S.C.): Michael Chandler (coach), Jackie Anderson, Randolph Raines, Brian Lewis, Alan Parsons, Sid Collins, Randy Porter, Ken Murphy, Terry Smith.

Hoechst Celanese (Greer, S.C.): Richard Barrows (coach), Lawrence Williams, Marvin Drummond, Charles Crawford, Steiner Murray, Gary Medlock, Sonny Anderson, Ray Martin, Pat Smith, Gerald Williams, Ted Morton, Joel Gilliam, David Hawkins, Gambrell.

Cryovac (Simpsonville, S.C.): James Sullivan (coach), Rex Abercrombie, Bobby Phelps, Calvin Barksdale, Matthew Milam, James C. Sullivan, Paul Satterwhite, Jerry Boyd, Vernon Johnson, Clarence Dawkins Jr., Alvarez Chiles, Lewis Whitmire, Fred Dean Jr., Robert Massingill.

Slater Mill (Slater, S.C.): James Roberts (coach), McBruce Young, Ricky Cruell, Joe Hill, William Parnell, Randy Bowles, Mark Lybrand, Anthony Williams, Alfred Allmond, Gary Wallace, Randy Waldrop, Monroe.

Michelin (Greenville, S.C.): J.C. Starkes (coach), Nixon Allen, Kerry Rasnake, Joel Henderson, Ricky Williams, Donnie Chambers, Melvin Williams, John Furmanski, Frank Halstead, Rodney Sullivan, Curtis Hood, David Lewis.

Union Carbide (Simpsonville, S.C.): John Lipgens (coach), Bob Andrews, Waddy Talley, Jerry Lollis, Hal Perkins, Jim Spearman, Jeff Spearman, Jerry Powell, Daniel Cohen, Bob Willoughby, Mark Payne, Calvin Pinson, Marcus Farrenkopf, Carl Schuff, Bob Boysen.

Stevens Beechcraft (Greer, S.C.): Randy Knowlton (coach), Danny Nelson, William Smith, Bob Sommers, Jim Williams, David Dudley, Sam Browne, Chris Miller, Nelson Gilreath.

PPG Industries (Shelby, N.C.): Eaker Campbell (coach), Nelson Webber, Paul Gash, Greg Beam, Larry Lynch, Donald Gash, J.C. Cannon Jr., Elijah Brown, Larry Wilson, Donnie Thurman, Sidney Smith, Dennis Johnson, Bobby Surratt.

Monsanto (Spartanburg, S.C.): Steve Longfield (coach), Donald Young, James Thomas, Wolffe Bagby, Donald Thompson, Keith Hunter, Kelvin Gainey, Kenny Duncan, Chris Moore, Milton Hunter, Barry Brown.

Fiber Industries (Greenville, S.C.): George Martin, Steve Richard, Joe Phelps, Jasper Martin, Bob Anderson, Tommie Summers, Tim Howell, Frank Armfield, Wayne Hargette, Vernon McMakin, Ketterer, Rusak.

Dunean Mill (Greenville, S.C.): Walker, Holden, Anderson, Marion, McGee, McLesky, Wilson, Evans, Watson.

Michelin #2 (Spartanburg, S.C.): Steve Brown (coach), Butch Rogers, Johnny Swofford, Lynn Brown, George McCarroll,

Southern Textile Basketball Tournament Rosters Appendix 1 311

Alonzo Briggs, Wayne McKinney, Ken Duncan, Danny Dalton, Ronnie Sims, Pat Still, Fred McCarroll.

Saco-Lowell (Easley, S.C.): Herbert Bowen (coach), Reginald Anderson, James Bowens, Monte Hudson, Dale Gillespie, Mike Youngblood, Steve Gracely, Charles Miller, Michael Gilstrap, Gregg Corbin, Mike Allen, Mike Gravely, Jeff Cooper, Pitts.

Black's Mechanical (Greenville, S.C.): Dennis Black (coach), Glenn Tate, William Black, Charles Bridwell, Doug Renner, William Cummings, Michael Williams, Kenneth Johnson, Billy Ledford, Paul Clendenon, Brian Erickson, Vernon Thompson.

Pelzer Mill #1 (Pelzer, S.C.): Ronnie Cureton (coach), Charles Pinson, Greg Rochester, Calvin Evans, Charles Dean, Rudolph Moseley, Dwight Sullivan, David Jenkins, Scotty Keels, Charles Mattison, Eugene Corley, Cephus Coleman, Blanding.

Pelzer Mill #2 (Pelzer, S.C.): David Burns (coach), Danny Scroggs, Wayne Eskew, Bruce Scroggs, Vic Alverson, Billy Burns, Johnny Robinson, Bobby Henderson, Dale Darby, Mike Epps, Ray Holliday, Gene Roberts.

CLASS B MEN

George Coleman Ford (Travelers Rest, S.C.), champions: Dennis Black (coach), Ronnie Poole, Greg Coleman, Chip Gilstrap, Jeff Holstein, Joe LeNoir, David Owens, Rick Houghton, Chuck Kelley, Milton Smith.

Greenwood Mill (Greenwood, S.C.), runners-up: Mark Friedrich (coach), Ken D. Frazier, Guy Bridges, Darryl Cromer, Bailey Harris, Wayne Conway, Tony Kinard, Mike Stoddard, Ken T. Frazier, Steve Conway, Derrick Cromer, Allen Petty, Dan Orr, Kevin Prater, Billy Martin.

Givens Youth Center (Fountain Inn, S.C.), consolation winners: Butch Clark (coach), Brian Nesbitt, James Kirksey, Stephen Walton, Ronnie Martin, George Abercrombie, Richard Bruce, Ray Thompson, Rodney Morris, Jim Hardy, James Murphy, James O'Neal.

US Post Office #2 (Greenville, S.C.): Paul Hill Jr. (coach), Windell Rodgers, Chuck Taylor, Franco Jackson, Willie Thompson, Mitchell Bryson, Prince Brock, Julius Revis, Stanley Stegall, Wade Martin, Carol Hill, James Dowell, Taylor, Brown, Zimmerman.

Sirrine Co. (Greenville, S.C.): John Currin (coach), Donald Drummond, Regan Klein, James Neal Jr., William Tumblin Jr., Don Adams, Andrew Wilson, John Boulos, Robert Tinsley, Donald Gillespie, Bobby Ray, Craig.

Cryovac #1 (Simpsonville, S.C.): Terry Dailey (coach), Don Harrison (coach), Steve Johnson, Steve Smith, Fred Dobbins, Robert Smith, Frank Edwards, Steve Fuller, Ralph Sizemore, Gus Rubio, Barry King, John Boudoucies, Dailey.

3M (Greenville, S.C.): William McNeely (coach), Henry Byrd Jr., Eldorado Valentine, Willie Madden, Mike Williams, Ernie Goodis, Dwayne Henderson, Darnell Fleming, Charles Hall, Michael Stewart, Kenny Arnold, Lyndon Mahaffey, Mike Madden, Jesse Looper, Doug Austin, Mitch Madden.

Michelin Blue (Greenville, S.C.): Ed Collins (coach), Larry Jackson, Michael Brown, William Wooten, Ron Scarborough, Greg Chandler, Dennis Kelley, Joel Tyner, Wayne Freeman, Bruce Taylor, Melvin Dirton, James Wilson, Beaty.

Cryovac #2 (Simpsonville, S.C.): Jimmy Wright (coach), Harold Wright (coach), Johnny Wright, Robert Barksdale, Greg Sweeney, Willie Gray, Barnabus McFalls, Cody Porter Jr., J.W. Wright, Michael Brockman, Aaron Thompson, Willie Wright.

U.S. Post Office #1 (Greenville, S.C.): Newell Tucker Jr. (coach), Donnie Scovel, John Miller, Ed Rogers, Richard Robertson, William Crawford, Charles Fleming, Michael Curran, Mike Hawkins.

American Hardware (Greenville, S.C.): William Brockman (coach), Milas Officer, Mark Stephens, Charles Lake, Robert Sullivan, Don Wooten, Billy Storey, Bernard Johnson, David Bernsteil, Doc Reeves, Rudy Norris, Moore.

Southern Bank (Greenville, S.C.): Joe Stack (coach), William Parrish, Glymph Childress, Jimmy Gulledge, Steve Berry, Stan Vaughn, Ben Hagood, Richard Galloway, Glenn Poole, Shane Taylor, Fred Culclasure, Bill Foster, Ben Satcher, Curtis Carter, Tom Dark.

Avco Lycoming (Greer, S.C.): Mickey Stepp (coach), David Pritchett (coach), Steve Addyman, Terry Blanton, Jeff Meadows, Michael Bomar, Richard Brown, Bobby Lyles, Russell Blanton, Jeffrey Jennewine, David Drummond, Jonathan Freeman, Lawrence Vessels.

Multimedia (Greenville, S.C.): David Wade (coach), David Wade Jr., Joel Cobb, Richard Gentry, Scott Regan, Stewart Lawrence, Van

McClenaghan, Louis Redmond, Rick Good, Andy Warfield, Chris Burritt, Meadors Tanner.

Wangner Systems (Greenville, S.C.): Larry Williams, Robbie Hoover, Chuck Riley, Robert Edwards, Carl McDonald, Lewis Still, David Grant, Anthony Evans, Ronnie Allen, Gary Roberts, Bobby Huff, Slatton.

CLASS C MEN

Industrial Packaging (Greenville, S.C.), champions: Mike Gay (coach), Tommy Howe, Mike Henderson, Brandt Williams, Carone Ferguson, Steven Gay, Derrick Robinson, Davis Gaines, Todd Lindsay, Kirby Henderson, Boogie Duckett, Kenny Woods, John Whitehead, Brandt Williams.

Alford Real Estate (Greenville, S.C.), runners-up: Warren Rollins (coach), Kevin Fowler, Mike Garrison, Keith Rollins, Brad Winsor, Bernard Leonard, Kris Kimball, Michael Dogan, Cox, Kearns, Lynch, Bennett, Oglesby, Martin, Rogers, Oliver.

May Napper (Greenville, S.C.), consolation winners: Tidwell, Lyles, Ray, Richard Owens, Jones, Tierney, Graves, Hughes.

C. Dan Joyner (Greenville, S.C.): Mac Johnson (coach), James Johnson Jr. (coach), Yancey Johnson, Willie Johnson, Barry Lankford, Walter Sanders, Stephon Leonard, Clarey Joyner Jr., Joseph Jackson, Timothy Young, David Jensen, David DuPre, Himes, De Bruhl.

Pelzer Mill #2 (Pelzer, S.C.): Earle Ford (coach), Johnny Lollis, Marcus Scott, Frankie Hopshall, Richard Jones, John Hudson, Chris Jones, Wilson Odom, Patrick Hunter, Lee Ozmint, Robert Whitner.

Florence Boy's Club (Florence, S.C.): Tony Shaw, David Brown, Moses, Taylor, C. Brown, Calvin, Selks, Wise, Johnson, Burns, Heldon, King.

Carper Real Estate (Greenville, S.C.): Larry Carper (coach), Robert Cantrell, Milt Blakely, Eric Skeen, Andy Ronan, Raymond Brown, Andre Wicker, Roy Browne, Larry Jenkins, Reynold Bailey, Paris Dennis, Hinton, Williams, Nance, Anderson.

Pelzer Mill #1 (Pelzer, S.C.): Michael Shirley (coach), Anthony Wilson, Joey Stewart, Leon Stallings, Rockney Rector, Mike Stone, Brad West, Robert Gaffney, Darren Darby, Robert Bruce, Robert Davis, Anthony Caffrey, Skip Hopkins, Thompson, Watson.

Dunean Mill (Greenville, S.C.): Ken Hunt, Rodney Harrison, Ben Mayfield, Billy Williams, Bill Henderson, Norman Floyd, Ed Young, Coan, D. Tesner, Phillips, Smith, Byers, Christie, Suber, R. Tesner.

CLASS A WOMEN

Bennett Oil (Spartanburg, S.C.), champions: Pat Kirk (coach), Vickie Daniel (coach), Pearl Moore (coach), Paula Kirkland, Connie Culbreth, Pam Adams, Gwen Miller, Lillie Young, Yvette Moore, Lynn Avant, Susan Jones, Sandra Wallace, Anne Long, Lisa Washington, Troye Matthews.

Gilstrap Real Estate (Greenville, S.C.), runners-up: Jan McDonald, Darlene Morgan, Beth Couture, Angie McCullough, Sheila Morgan, Lyle, Arledge, Nix, Ludwig, Crenshaw, Williams.

Athletic Dept. (Greenville, S.C.), consolation winners: Channson, Jenkins, Hood, Davis, Young, Debra Buford, Yeargin, Scovil, C. Davis.

Pelzer Mill (Pelzer, S.C.): Tracy Korbutt, Rhonda Chambers, Ellenburg, Bradley, Karen Kelley, Makins, Marsh, Clinkscales, Glover, Peele, Johnson.

C. Dan Joyner (Greenville, S.C.): Kay Kirby, Dawn Raab, Angela Dunn, Karla Horton, Sally Bradshaw, Carolyn Dehn-Duhr, Jenny Lyerly, Bennie Lincoln, Rosie Carlton, Kathy Flaten, Anita Kidd, Susan Jones, Schweers, Barbara Schmauch, Barbery, Cubelic, McSwain, Riddle, Henderson, Eyerman.

---1985---

Executive Officers: Divver Hendrix, Ward Williams, Fred Powers, Clarence Thomas, Willie Wilbanks.

Officers: Jyles Phillips (Greenville, S.C.), President; Charles Roddy (Greenville, S.C.), 1st Vice President; Bill Hopkins (Pelzer, S.C.), 2nd Vice President; Harry Foster (Greenville, S.C.), Treasurer; Phil Harley (Greenville, S.C.), Ass't Treasurer; Fred Byrd (Greenville, S.C.), Executive Secretary; B.J. Bell (Pelzer, S.C.), Ass't Executive Secretary; Janet Hopkins (Pelzer, S.C.), Ass't Executive Secretary; Lt. F.R. Hawkins, Security Officer.

Executive Committee: Phil Clark (Greer, S.C.), Lewis Golden (Greenville, S.C.), Jimmy Hopkins (Greenville, S.C.), Fred McAbee (Greenville, S.C.), Ted Pittman (Greenville,

S.C.), Ronnie Scarborough (Greenville, S.C.), A.C. Jones (Ware Shoals, S.C.).

OPEN DIVISION

Southeastern Electric (Greenville, S.C.), champions: Bill Patterson (coach), Scott Little, Mike Smith, James Holland, Mark Townsend, Mike Quick, Roy Wright, Robert Campbell, Ed Patterson, Mel Daniel, Marc Campbell, Jimmy Favotto, Steve May, Gillson.

Black Diamond (Greenville, S.C.), runners-up: Joey Short, Carlos Hardy, J.W. Miller, Monroe Garrison, Charles Dendy, Demsey Cohen, Raymond Lawson, John Perry, Mike Hunt, Gary Fowler, Curt Harkness, Ronald White, Terry.

V.A. Jets (Columbia, S.C.): Barry Wilson (coach), Frank Wise, Marcelleons Primus, Larry Wilson, Joe Rice, Larry James, Roger Carr, David Jones, John Kirkland, Howard White, Charles Kirkland, Ronald DeGray, Isaac Nipson, Wendel Nolan, Stephone Darby, Todd Wilson, Brown.

Sixers (Columbia, S.C.): Jacob Pearson (coach), Roger Carr, Anthony Kelly, Richard Cannon, David Alston, John Sharpe, Vincent Pearson, David Poole, Curtis Dunbar, Willie Bynum, Ronald DeGray, Robert Geter, Wyatt Minton, Norris Ashford, Nate Mitchell.

Rug Doctor (Spartanburg, S.C.): Sartor, Garland, Perry, Smith, Clowney, Thompson, Parker.

CLASS A MEN

Michelin Gold (Greenville, S.C.), champions: J.C. Starkes (coach), Nixon Allen, Kerry Rasnake, Joel Henderson, Ricky Williams, Donnie Chambers, Melvin Williams, John Furmanski, Frank Halstead, Rodney Sullivan, Alfred Williams, Anthony Chambers, Mike Winston, Dave Mahoney.

PPG Industries (Shelby, N.C.), runners-up: Larry Lynch (coach), Nelson Webber, Paul Gash, Greg Beam, Donald Gash, J.C. Cannon Jr., Larry Ross, Donnie Thurman, Sidney Smith, Bobby Surratt, Steve Cannon, Michael Kelly, Kirby Allen, Darrell Hines, Garnett Hunt, Elton Cannedy, Hayes.

Union Carbide (Simpsonville, S.C.), consolation winners: John Lipgens (coach), Bob Andrews, Bob Bumgarner, Hal Perkins, Robert Willoby, Calvin Penson, Jim Bolt, Tony Copeland, James Spearman, Waddy Talley, Mark Payne, Michael Hurley, West, B. Payne.

Greenville Fire Dept. (Greenville, S.C.): Allen Quinn (coach), Richard Roach, Henry Stanton, Roy Mack, Rodney McCauley, Alfred McElrath, Doug Henson, Don Craig, Vincent Means, Preston Lindsay, Jimmy Harris, Kenneth Spivey, Kenneth Sterling, Mullinax.

Monaghan Mill (Greenville, S.C.): C.D. Roach (coach), Bobby Jones, Tony Blakely, Anthony Taylor, Wayne Jones, Keith Jones, Timothy Mayes, Ted Anderson, Dale White, Larry Ballew, Bryan Boyd, Anthony Nesitt, George Jones, Anthony Talley, William Johnson, Wilson.

Emb-Tex (Travelers Rest, S.C.): Henry Robertson (coach), Dennis Thompson, Zernie Morgan, Larry Brinkley, Mark Cox, Bill McAbee, Mike Williams, Richard Davis, Roy Brown, Adrian Miller, Fredrick Carr, Anthony Carr, Dennis Walker.

Parker Mill (Greenville, S.C.): Jimmie Robinson (coach), Albert Donald, Ernest Fuller Jr., James Anderson, Robert Pepper, William McGowan, David Simmons, Jerry Jackson, James Jones, Andrew Thompson, Paul Johnson, Darwin Moore, Vincent Dirton, George Turman.

Michelin (Spartanburg, S.C.): Eddie Battle (coach), Michael Williams, James Lindsey, Donnie Alexander, Terry Moore, Joseph Williams, Greg Elmore, Terry Free, Eric Martin, Willie Hardy, Mark Casey, Eddie Conner, Ed Major, Dean Dawkins.

Alice Mfg. #1 (Easley, S.C.): Terry A. Smith (coach), Terry McGowens, George Davis, John Langston, Clayton Rhodes, Matthew Valentine, Douglas Adams, Michael Chandler, Jackie Anderson, Terry B. Smith, Tony McGowens, Melvin Dukes, Blake.

Hoechst Celanese (Greer, S.C.): Richard Barras (coach), Marvin Drummond, Charles Crawford, Steiner Murray, Sonny Anderson, Pat Smith, Joel Gilliam, Steve Arms, Mark Peahuff, Tim Powell, Danny Parker, Ken Lynn, Ricky Whitmire, Morton, Ayers.

Cryovac (Simpsonville, S.C.): Matthew Milam (coach), Rex Abercrombie, Bobby Phelps, Calvin Barksdale, James Sullivan, Paul Satterwhite, Jerry Boyd, Vernon Johnson, Clarence Dawkins Jr., Fred Dean Jr., Bolden, Church.

Slater Mill (Slater, S.C.): James Roberts (coach), McBruce Young, Ricky Cruell, Joe Hill, William Parnell, Randy Bowles, Alfred

Allmond, Randy Waldrop, Marion Price, James Roberts Jr.

Singer Mfg. (Pickens, S.C.): Johnson, Scoggins, Austin, Looper, Williams, Looper, Thrift.

Michelin #2 (Spartanburg, S.C.): Steve Brown (coach), Lynn Brown, Alonzo Briggs, Wayne McKinney, Ken Duncan, Ronnie Rice, Pat Still, James Lindsay, Eddie Conner, Wayne Rice, Eugene McKinney, Jones, Sterling, McCarroll.

Pelzer Mill #1 (Pelzer, S.C.): Tommy Jackson (coach), Charles Pinson, Greg Rochester, Calvin Evans, Charles Mattison, Dwight Sullivan, David Jenkins, Scotty Keels, Bobby Blanding, Ronnie Cureton, Tommy Johnson, Tony Jordan, David Burns.

Pelzer Mill #2 (Pelzer, S.C.): Danny Scroggs, Wayne Eskew, Greg Bruce, Vic Alverson, Johnny Robinson, Bobby Henderson, Mike Epps, Danny Poe, Chris Knight, Steve Gagong.

Mayfair Mill (Easley, S.C.): Roosevelt Brown (coach), Gilbert Blackwell (coach), Tim Sutton, Douglas Sutton, Anthony Blake, Billy Cureton, Willis Robinson, June Ramsey, Alvin Sutton, Joe Hagood, Dale Bishop, Todd McAlister, Ben Long, Keith Moore.

Stouffer's (Greer, S.C.): Phil Neill (coach), Frank Woodruff (coach), Jay Dewart, Maurice Phillips, William Ford, Albert Ford, Robert Marion, Arvin Corry, Kennedy Drummond, Lynn Dawkins, Ron Best, Ray Otey, Thomas Batchler, Terry Haney.

Greenville Valve (Greenville, S.C.): Steve Crowe (coach), Steve Smith, Robin Ellenburg, Scot Nunnery, Gene Crook, Gary Long, David Crook.

Dunean Mill (Greenville, S.C.): Jaylon Robinson (coach), Jimmy Marion, Tony Watson, William McGee, Mike Lowery, Donald Sullivan, Kevin Phillips, Horace Anderson, Isaiah Walker Jr., Wayne Toney, Paul Hill, Nathaniel Shumate.

CLASS B MEN

Avco Lycoming (Greer, S.C.), champions: Mickey Stepp (coach), Bobby Milam (coach), David Pritchett, Jeff Meadows, Michael Bomar, Rick Brown, Russell Blanton, David Drummond, Jack Wilson, Jimmy Brown, Ray Johnson, James McClam, William Drummond, Henry Davis Jr.

Southern Bank (Greenville, S.C.), runners-up: Joe Stack (coach), William Parrish, Glymph Childress, Jimmy Gulledge, Steve Berry, Glenn Poole, Fred Culclasure, Bill Foster, Curtis Carter, Tom Darr, Kevin Sims, Rob Reeves, Frank Wrenn, Bob Decker, Tim Thigpen, Larry Lee.

Cryovac (Duncan, S.C.), consolation winners: John Boudoucies (coach), Clarence Whittenburg (coach), Steve Johnson, Steve Smith, Fred Dobbins, Frank Edwards, Ralph Sizemore, Gus Rubio, Barry King, Terry Dailey, Mike Tolson, Max Shanks, Walter Thurman.

Multimedia (Greenville, S.C.): David Wade (coach), David Wade Jr., Scott Regan, Van McClenaghan, Rick Good, Andy Warfield, Meadors Tanner, Ron Green, John Fontana, Witzke, Peterson.

United Insurance (Greenville, S.C.): B. Griffin, R. Griffin, W. Griffin, Johnson, Westmoreland, Mike Beeler, Re. Griffin.

Givens Youth Center (Fountain Inn, S.C.): Jeffrey Anders (coach), James Berry (coach), James Kirksey, Ray Morrison, Rodney Morris, Curtis Moore, Robert Faulk, Kim Lyles, Glenn Smith, Tommy Vance, Donnie McGriff, Michael Williams, Reginald Long, Jay Autry, Abercrombie.

Sirrine Co. (Greenville, S.C.): Bob Ray (coach), Regan Klein, James Neal Jr., William Tumblin Jr., Don Adams, Andrew Wilson, Robert Tinsley, Donald Gillespie, Charles Stewart, Robert Miller, William Utt.

3M (Greenville, S.C.): William McNeely (coach), Henry Byrd Jr., Eldorado Valentine, Willie Madden, Mike Stewart, Ernie Goodis, Darell Fleming, Kenny Arnold, Lyndon Mahaffey, Jesse Looper, William McNeely, Henderson, Bayne, McGowan.

U.S. Post Office (Greenville, S.C.): Newell Tucker Jr., Donnie Scovel, Ed Rogers, Richard Robertson, William Crawford, Charles Fleming, Michael Curran, Mike Parkins, Chuck Taylor, Willie Thompson, Mitchell Bryson, Dennis Zimmerman, Freeman.

American Hardware (Greenville, S.C.): Milas Office (coach), Mack Stephens, Charles Lake, Robert Sullivan, Don Wooten, Billy Storey, Bernard Johnson, David Bernsteil, Mitch Reeves, Rick Morse, Tony Ellenburg, Joe Mitchell, Jimmy Williams, Michael Gowan.

Reliance Electric (Greenville, S.C.): Jim Riddle (coach), Charles Lipscomb, Donnie Byrd, Clay Jones, Tommy Tice, Charles Niver, O'Dell Gamble, Steve Simmons, Joe Malorino,

Danny Norris, Mark Christopher, Jimmy Klugh, Tony Ruscetta.
Belk Simpson (Greenville, S.C.): Carl Chambers, Joseph Barton, Russell Wilson, Bo Brown, Gary Turner, Stanley Coker, Jeff Bright, Tripp Childers.
Cryovac (Simpsonville, S.C.): Brockman, Gray, Sweeney, J. Wright, J.W. Wright, Group, Barksdale.
Michelin (Greenville, S.C.): Jackson, Stacey, Wooten, Scarborough, Nash, Duncan, Childs, Chambers.
Bi-Lo (Greenville, S.C.): Smith, Williams, Mason, Phillips, Lykes, Clark, Schaffer, Jackson, Burton.
General Nutrition (Greenville, S.C.): Golden, Henderson, Owens, Jackson, Sligh, Bailey, Burton, Foster.

Class C Men

Central Savannah River Area All Stars (Augusta, Ga.), champions, Mike Roberts (coach), Donnie Holland (coach), Steve Grogan (coach), Dave Dickerson, Rodney Estes, D.J. Harrison, Tim Gaffney, Eric Bush, Kevin Wright, Anthony Rice, James Johnson, James Muncyn, Buck Robinson, Dave Holloway, Brent Hughes, Rodney Geter.
Chick-Fil-A (Greenville, S.C.), runners-up: Kelsey Weems, Chris Duncan, Tony Benton, Leonard, Jones, Hammond, Gambrell, Burdette.
B.J. Music (Greenville, S.C.), consolation winners: Ricky Jones, Holmes, Blasingame, Kaminski, Hunter, Tierney, Coleman.
C. Dan Joyner (Greenville, S.C.): Jones, Selvy, Cline, Rich, Murray, Danny Joyner, Johnson, Johnson, Scott Dupree, Current.
A. C. H. Wildcats (Greenville, S.C.): C. Dacus, S. Dacus, Stone, Dogan, Epps, Brock, Fant, Hunt, Thomas, Enlow.
All Stars (Greenville, S.C.): Dodd, Howell, Sizemore, Garrison, S. Williams, Herring, Hill, Dixon, Lewis, Cureton, Christie.
Monaghan Mill (Greenville, S.C.): Elrod, McKinney, Shockley, Wade, McCoy.
Brady's Barber Shop (Greenville, S.C.): Stewart, Darby, Davis, Geddens, Johnson, Rector, Stalling, Mackey.
Gault's Cleaners (Greenville, S.C.): Ellis Williams, Everick Sullivan, Thompson, David Nance, Carlos Yeargin, Hal Henderson, Hall, Jackson.
Pelzer Mill (Pelzer, S.C.): Hudson, Grove, Ozmint, Jones, Breil, Merck, Fant, Shera.
Industrial Packaging (Greenville, S.C.): Henderson, Cudd, Suber, Richardson, Simmons, Smith.
Home Plate Restaurant (Greenville, S.C.): Ross, Leach, Carter, McClure, Newton, Beaty. Armstrong.

Class A Women

Bennett Oil (Spartanburg, S.C.), champions: Lynn Avant, Stephanie Garner, Pearl Moore, Paula Kirkland, Elizabeth Walker, Sandy Bishop, Beverly Hawkins, Susan Jones, Connie Culbreth, Nessie Harris.
Gilstrap Real Estate (Greenville, S.C.), runners-up: Beth Couture, Sheila Morgan, Lyle, George, Jan McDonald, Cole, Arledge, Cheryl Makins, Smoak, Smith.
Home Plate Restaurant (Greenville, S.C.), consolation winners: Karen Jenkins, Jenny Lyerly, Barbara Kennedy, Lauren Reid, Peggy Caple, Tate, Susan Woolston, Edwards, Jennings, Cynthia Austin, Mary Cubelic, Lillie Young, Debra Buford, Sandy Bishop.
Howell's Cleaners (Greenville, S.C.): Ron Scarborough (coach), Susan Smith, Pat Johnson, Linda Crawford, Tan Barton, Kim Shockley, Debra Kelley, Lisa Bradley, Cynthia Durham, Davis, Jackie Moore, Yeargin, Heyward.
C. Dan Joyner (Greenville, S.C.): Bobby Kirby (coach), Joan Kirby, Sandy Holcombe, Donna Oliver, Tori Quick, Vivian King, Marty Vaughn, Monica Henderson, Elizabeth Tankersley, Tina Drutonis, Tonya Hamilton, Mickey Garrett, Shelly Wilson.
Dunean Mill (Greenville, S.C.): Alan Turner (coach), Gisela Veltman, Amiee Turner, Beverly Hawkins, Sabrina Stockman, Leslie Jennings, Kristie Kerns, Kelly Garrett, Diane Farrington, Alice Wingo, Julie McCarver, Allison Waters, Stacey Ford, Rumsey, Hamel.
Pest Control (Greenville, S.C.): Bobby Kirby (coach), Kay Kirby, Martha Parker, Teresa Eyerman, Sally Bradshaw, Beth Hunt, Amanda Scheen, Marsi McAlister, Becky Barbary, Susan Jewell, Gina McNeilage, Jena Barnett, Vickie Orr, Adrienne Singleton, Andria Singleton, Sandy Holcombe.

--- 1986 ---

Executive Officers: Divver Hendrix, Ward Williams, Ruppert Elliott, Fred Powers, Clarence Thomas, Willie Wilbanks.

Officers: Jyles Phillips (Greenville, S.C.), President; Charles Roddy (Greenville, S.C.), 1st Vice President; Bill Hopkins (Pelzer, S.C.), 2nd Vice President; Harry Foster (Greenville, S.C.), Treasurer; Phil Harley (Greenville, S.C.), Ass't Treasurer; Fred Byrd (Greenville, S.C.), Executive Secretary; B.J. Bell (Pelzer, S.C.), Ass't Executive Secretary; Janet Hopkins (Pelzer, S.C.), Ass't Executive Secretary; Lt. F.R. Hawkins, Security Officer.

Executive Committee: Phil Clark (Greer, S.C.), Lewis Golden (Greenville, S.C.), Jimmy Hopkins (Pelzer, S.C.), Fred McAbee (Greenville, S.C.), Ted Pittman (Greenville, S.C.), Ronnie Scarborough (Greenville, S.C.), Ray Adams (Greer, S.C.), Paul Ellis (Greenville, S.C.), Johnny Foster (Marietta, S.C.), John Greene (Greenville, S.C.), Gary Pittman (Greenville, S.C.).

Open Division

V.A. Jets (Columbia, S.C.), champions: Barry Wilson (coach), Choco Namittose (coach), Tommy Watts, Howard White, Kenny Reynolds, Roger Cam, William Snok, Joe Rice, Charles Kirkland, Troy Mikell, Fred Wise, William Irick, Roger Carr, Hammond.

Bridges' Lounge (Greenville, S.C.), runners-up: Alvin Dodd (coach), Tom Davis (coach), Dempsey Cohen, Junior Box, Buck Jackson, Bo Hardtt, Rex Smith, George Carter, James Garrison, John Perry, Raymond Lawson, Jerry Wilson, J.C. Miller, Rod Wedds, Young, T. Hardy, Johnson, O. Hardy, Goodson.

Sixers (Columbia, S.C.): Jacob Pearson (coach), Roger Carr, Anthony Flager, Richard Cannon, Vincent Pearson, David Poole, Willie Bynum, Howard White, Greg Wright, Timothy McLeod, James Brown, Marcellous Primus, Tommy Mack, James Sanders.

Sonics (Abbeville, S.C.): Archibald Letman (coach), Reggie Williams (coach), Hollie Martin, David Graham, Calvin Dorn, Curtis Harkness, Earl Chandler, Kenny Holmes, Bradley Leak, Jesse Roundtree, Kenneth Robinson, Johnny Tolbert, Donnie Pearson, Jesse Scruggs.

Henderson Plumbing (Greenville, S.C.): David Henderson (coach), Joel Henderson, Sammy Karr, Ben Davis, Jay Bowsher, Stephon Leonard, John Haskins, Clay Dorn, Stan Easterling, Sonny Vinson, DeMorris Black, Curtis Harkness.

The Pitts (Greenville, S.C.): Ronnie Pitts (coach), Ronald White, Gary Fowler, Roderick Terry, Greer Hugeley, Michael Hunt, Odis Rhodes, Reggie Copeland, Reggie Small, Rick Aldridge.

Brown's Bombers (Greenville, S.C.): Tom Davis (coach), Monroe Garrison, John Perry, Raymond Lawson, J.W. Miller, George Carter, Lawrence Lawson, Larry Grove, Kelvin Fowler, Rico Williams, Reggie Thompson, Jerry Wilson, Chubby Wells, Campbell, Morris.

Class A Men

PPG Industries (Shelby, N.C.), champions: Larry Lynch (coach), David Banks (coach), Roger Shade (coach), Paul Gash, Greg Beam, Donald Gash, J.C. Cannon Jr., Larry Ross, Donnie Thurman, Sidney Smith, Steve Cannon, Mike Kelly, Kirby Allen, Darrell Hines, Elton Cannedy, Terry Camp, Leonard Flack, Rodney Whittenburg, Greg Ramsey, Freddie Jones, David Hector.

Emb-Tex (Travelers Rest, S.C.), runners-up: Larry Brinkley (coach), Dennis Thompson, Zernie Morgan, Mark Cox, Bill McBee, Mike Williams, Richard Dalli, George Brown, Adrian Miller, Henry Robertson, Michael Robinson, Robert Poole, Nelson Talley, Phillip Owens, Davis.

Alice Mfg. (Easley, S.C.), consolation winners: Terry A. Smith (coach), Terry McGowens, George Davis, John Langston, Clayton Rhodes, Douglas Smith, Terry B. Smith, Tony McGowens, Melvin Dukes, Ricky Adams, Ken Galloway, Roy Collins, Hollins.

American Federal (Greenville, S.C.): Charles Ferguson (coach), Donald Davis, Keith Westbury, Blake Curry, Garcia Gilmore, Douglas Young, Donald Beamon, Bob Hoffman, Stuart Ellison, Michael Dean, Bill Weade.

Michelin Gold (Greenville, S.C.): J.C. Starkes (coach), Nixon Allen, Kerry Rasnake, Joel Henderson, John Furmanski, Rodney Sullivan, Anthony Chambers, Alan Foxx, Kenneth Carter, Halstead.

Parker Mill (Greenville, S.C.): David Simmons (coach), Leon Pepper, William McGowan, James Jones, Andrew Thompson, Paul Johnson, Vincent Dirton, Jimmie Robinson, John Williams, David Reid, Edgar Brock, Sullivan.

Michelin (Spartanburg, S.C.): Mike Ungar (coach), Michael Williams, James Lindsey, Donnie Alexander, Terry Moore, Greg Elmore, Terry Free, Eric Martin, Willie Hardy, Mark Casey, Fred Anderson, Fred McCarroll, Jackie Gillespie.

Hoechst Celanese (Greer, S.C.): Nerdell Richardson (coach), Marvin Drummond, Charles Crawford, Steiner Murray, Sonny Anderson, Pat Smith, Joel Gilliam, Steve Aruse, Mark Peahuff, Lawrence Williams, Ray Martin, Leroy Williams, Gerald Williams, Eddie Johnson, E. Drummond, Richardson.

Cryovac (Simpsonville, S.C.): Matthew Milam (coach), Rex Abercrombie, Bobby Phelps, Calvin Barksdale, James Sullivan, Paul Satterwhite, Jerry Boyd, Vernon Johnson, Clarence Dawkins Jr., Fred Dean Jr, Greg Sweeney, Willie Calwile.

Union Carbide (Simpsonville, S.C.): Andrews, Pinson, Jim Spearman, Perkins, Talley, Chandler, West, Jeff Spearman, Young.

Slater Mill (Slater, S.C.): James Roberts (coach), McBruce Young, Ricky Cruell, Joe Hill, Randy Bowles, Alfred Allmond, James Roberts, Jimmy Barbare, Steve Parnell.

Emb-Tex (Travelers Rest, S.C.): Cox, Morgan, Williams, Thompson, McBee, Robinson, Brown.

Pelzer Mill #1 (Pelzer, S.C.): Tommy Johnson (coach), Charles Pinson, Dwight Sullivan, Scotty Keels, Ronnie Cureton, Tony Jordan, Billy Burns, Walter Smith, Johnny Robinson, Danny Scroggs, Robert Henderson, Ernest Carley, Preston.

Greenville Fire Dept. (Greenville, S.C.): Allen Quinn (coach), Roy Mack, Rodney McCauley, Alfred McElrath, Vincent Means, Jimmy Harris, Kenneth Spivey, Kenneth Sterling, Rick Mullinax, Bobby Dersch, Dwight Greg, Gray.

High Techs (Greenville, S.C.): Waddy Talley (coach), Bob Andrews, Hal Perkins, Calvin Penson, Tony Copeland, James Spearman, John Lipgens, Clarence West, Jeff Spearman.

Greenville Valve (Greenville, S.C.): Steve Crowe (coach), Steve Smith, Robin Ellenburg, Gene Crook, Gary Long, David Crook, Fred Nelson, Alvin Hilliard.

Southern Bank (Greenville, S.C.): Tim Lee (coach), Steve Whitaker, Tim Thigpen, Mel Daniel, Jimmy Guledge, Roy Childress, Russell Rogers, Kevin Sims, David King, Tom Darr, Frank Wrenn, Glenn Poole.

Singer Mfg. (Pickens, S.C.): Doc Evatt (coach), Lawrence Crenshaw (coach), Chris Austin, Ken Robinson, Rodney Wakefield, Glenn Thrift, W.C. Helms, Tim Looper, Corey Keith, Leroy Williams, Reggie Womack, Bucky Webb, Keith Scoggins, Skippy Nix.

St. Francis Hospital (Greenville, S.C.): Allen Young (coach), Michael Barksdale, Willie Hampton, George Harrison, Bobby Harper, Jimmy Ponder, Bentley Gibson, Melvin Phelps, Mark Barksdale, Charles Black, J. Harper, S. Harper.

Class B Men

M & L Construction (Greenville, S.C.), champions: Chuck Waldron (coach), Charles Waldron Jr., Kevin Prather, Columbus Copeland, Alan Roebuck, David Graham, Bruce Thompson, Conway, Freeze, Langford.

Clinton Mill (Clinton, S.C.), runners-up: Brian Shealy (coach), William Mims, Billy Smith, Ricky Martin, Henry Blalock, Aaron Simmons, John Dixon, Rick Page, Rusty Iusti, L. Mims, Roberson.

Cleveland Memorial Hospital (Shelby, N.C.), consolation winners: Richard Jones (coach), Maurice Campbell, Marcus Wells, Matthew Campbell, Terry Cannon, Wayne Davis, Floyd Bridges, Jerry Webber, Terrence Petty, Matt Hornsby, Warrick Ross, Johnny McCormick, Johnny Johnson, Brown, Bowen.

Cryovac (Duncan, S.C.): Frank Edwards (coach), Steve Smith, Gus Fernandez-Rubio, Terry Dailey, Max Shanks, Walter Thurman, Donald Moore, William King, Bobby Church.

Cryovac (Simpsonville, S.C.): Russell Evans (coach), Rici Thompson, Walter Webb, Willie Gray, Tommy Hood, Greg Drummond, Michael Brockman, Joseph Pirkle, Johnny Wright, Aaron Thomas, Daniel Sullivan, Dickerson, Black, Danny, J.W. Wright.

Givens Youth Center (Fountain Inn, S.C.): Jeffrey Anders (coach), James Berry, Robert Faulk, Calvin Criswell, Roderick Little, Lawrence Golden, Calvin Pettigrew, Marvin Leaman, Johnny McManus, Jimmy Anderson, Calvin Smith, Marc Driver, Eddie Clark, Kenneth Parks, Oglesby.

Sirrine Co. (Greenville, S.C.): Bob Ray (coach), James Neal Jr., William Tumblin Jr., Don Adams, Andrew Pickens, Robert Tinsley, Charles Stewart, Robert Miller, J.M. Satterfield, James Craig, Charles Isham, Charles Wallace, Brock.

3M (Greenville, S.C.): Tony McNeely (coach), Eldorado Valentine, Mike Stewart, Ernie Goodis, Kenny Arnold, Lyndon Mahaffey, William McNeely, Doug Austin, Billy Grover, John Watts, Michael Saylors, Henderson, Flemson.

U.S. Post Office #1 (Greenville, S.C.): Newell Tucker Jr. (coach), Donnie Scovel, Ed Rogers, Richard Robertson, William Crawford, Charles Fleming, Michael Curran, Mike Parkins, Mitchell Bryson, Tommy Halley, J.C. Revis, Bill Dalton, John Miller Jr., Bonnie Crawford, Stiles.

U.S. Post Office #2 (Greenville, S.C.): Paul Hill Jr. (coach), Willie Thompson, Frankie Jackson, Thomas Brown, Dennis Zimmerman, Joel Pritchett, Prince Brock, Dwight Donald, Dwaine Malphrus, James Bell.

American Hardware (Greenville, S.C.): Gil Garrett (coach), Milas Officer, Mack Stephens, Charles Lake, Robert Sullivan, Don Wooten, Billy Storey, Bernard Johnson, David Bernsteil, Rick Moore, Joe Mitchell, Michael Gowan, Robert Cowans, Gary VanPatten, Ron Flack.

General Nutrition (Greenville, S.C.): Stanley Jackson (coach), Henry Whitner, Brian Carithers, Kim Owens, Clarence Wright, James Henderson, Jeff Sligt, Mark Ellis, Brian Adams, James Burton, Gilbert Ware, Ronnie Todd, Rodd, Henson.

Stevens Aviation (Greenville, S.C.): Randy Knowlton (coach), Jim Williams, Billy Smith, Nelson Gilreath, Clint Harvey, Tim Robson, Bob Somers, Steven Westside, Jeff Flack.

Lowenstein (Anderson, S.C.): Charles Staggs (coach), William Wright, Charles Staggs, Greg Kruse, Charles Robinson, Clarence Moody Jr., Willie Jones, Teddie Williams, Ronald Bomar, Frank Williams, Donnie Alexander, Lewis Jenning, Edwin Davis, Rodney Shipman, Wade Kershaw.

Leigh Fibers (Spartanburg, S.C.): Alfred Ballenger (coach), Keith Taylor, James Ray, Oree Mack, Bobby Jones, James Brewton, Paul Foster, Rodney Austin, David Young, Roger Cohen, Paul Pace, Timothy Miller, Bob Tennyson.

Westinghouse (Greenville, S.C.): Larry Smith (coach), David Lowery, Frank Larry Jr., L.H. McDowell, Kevin Owens, William Peppers, Greg Isom, Jim Youngblood, David Saleeby, Daryl Snipes, Frankie Austin, Doug Sober.

Saco-Lowell (Easley, S.C.): Mike Gilstrap (coach), Mike Allen, James Bowen, Mike Reynolds, Danny Benfield, David Smith, Ed Ballew, Dale Gillespie, Danny Capps, Richard Pitts, Gravley, Winchester, James, Owens.

Class C Men

Corporate Benefits (Greenville, S.C.), champions: George Funderburk (coach), Rod Mitchell, Kenny Dixon, John Sellers, Everick Sullivan, Jerry Crosby, Dean Smith, Tommy Hammer, Bennett Jackson, H. Henderson, Rick David, Darby Rick.

Chick-Fil-A (Greenville, S.C.), runners-up: Mickey Massey (coach), Terry Shelton (coach), Hardy, Black, Jones, Green, Keys, Thompson, Larrie, Manning, Cudd, Rhett, Lawless.

Pelzer Mill (Pelzer, S.C.), consolation winners: Earle Ford (coach), Anthony Moses, Stanley Roberts, Kevin Fuller, Chuck Scotland, Tracy Garrick, James Brunson, David Lesesne, Randy Howard, Tony Wilson, Anthony Bracey, Stephen Blanding, Acoy, Sanders, Cox, Means.

Dunean Mill (Greenville, S.C.): Taylor Robinson (coach), Derrick Harrison (coach), David Young, Marc Watts, Reggie Epps, Thomas Brock, Sidney Smith, Greg Bruce, Ricky Tesner, Kelly Walker, Scruggs, Harlin, Thompson, Evans, Jose, Wallace.

Central Savannah River Area All Stars (Augusta, Ga.): Donnie Holland (coach), Eric Bush, James Munlyn, Dave Holloway, Keith Tripp, Tyrone Boykin, Eric Perry, Ernest Phelps, Stanley Roberts, Tracy Garrick, Joe Rhett, Barry Manning, Curry, McRay, Shroppshire, Walker, Williams.

Alford Real Estate (Greenville, S.C.): Warren Rollins (coach), Keith Rollins, Trenny Dawkins, Barry Littlefield, Darby Rich, Tim Hightower, Lee Ferguson, Steve Lineburger, Michael Dogan, Rogers, Davis, Chapman, Moore, Greer, Gray.

Harris Sporting Goods (Anderson, S.C.): Eddie Perry (coach), Jimmy DuPre, Don Parker, Tony Williams, Mack Smith, Tim Blassingame, Michael Hardy, Bill Fath, James Brown, Land.

Carper Real Estate (Greenville, S.C.): Larry Carper (coach), Dale McClough, Lawrence Jones, Tony Rice, Kenneth Moore, Tommy Brown, Tim Waters, Derrick Dennison, Lemuel Howard, David Young, Sims, Smith, Kincaid, Goss, Shifley.

Class A Women

Four Star Sports (Spartanburg, S.C.), champions: Pearl Moore (coach), Paula Kirkland, Beverly Hawkins, Susan Jones, Nessie Harris, Mindy Belue, Sharon Gilmore, Brantley

Southers, Marlene Jeter, Gwen Canty, Jeannette Alston, Annette Alston, Kim Slawson.

The Hot Shots (Greenville, S.C.), runners-up: Ronnnie Scarborough (coach), Barbara Kennedy, Peggy Caple, Sandy Bishop, Beth Couture, Renee Williams, Wendy Anderson, Janet Knight, Melinda Ashworth, Grace Lyle, Morine Fox, Aleasha Tate, Teresa Ludwig, Jenny Lylery.

Chick-Fil-A (Greenville, S.C.), consolation winners: Allen Turner (coach), Amy Mason, Amiee Turner, Kelli Garrett, Melissa Robinson, Kim Farrell, Vangie Smith, Melinda Jeter, Marlene Jeter, Johnson, Bradley, Drakeford, Blassingame, Chester, Gordon.

C. Dan Joyner (Greenville, S.C.): Bobby Kirby (coach), Donna Oliver, Tori Quick, Monica Henderson, Elizabeth Tankersley, Marsi McAlister, Brantley Southers, Sharon Gilmore, Susan Jewell, Becky Barbary, Adrian Singleton, Jane Arledge, Jan McDonald, Holcombe, Adams, Hunt.

Kosta's Restaurant (Greenville, S.C.): Ranoy Lafoy (coach), Lindy Williams, Rose Pele, Cheryl Marsh, Phyllis Garrett, Renee Sublette, Karen Jackson, Karen Hennen, Karla Grambell, Teresa Garrison, Tabatha Peleras, Sharon Barbary, Roper, Hennison, Phillips, Border, Gambrell.

Mac's All Stars (Greenville, S.C.): Archie McArthur (coach), Lenora Hood, Jennifer Yeargin, Sharon Mack, Mary Truman, Loretta Clinkscales, Jackie Moore, Jake Simpson, Tonie Edwards, Lilly Young, Sheila Morgan, Connie Rush, Sharon Clinkscales, Tammy Dendy, Dingle.

William's Enterprise (Greenville, S.C.): Porter Simmons (coach), Paulette Hawthorn, Paula Hawthorn, JoJo Jackson, Sam Mansell, Shelly Mitchell, Tara Youngblood, Terena Starks, Veronica Jenkins, Blondie Harrison, Annett Anderson, Phyllis Smith, Monica Inabinet.

Foothills Real Estate (Greenville, S.C.): Shelton, Poole, Fahrenkrug.

---1987---

Executive Officers: Divver Hendrix, Ward Williams, Ruppert Elliott, Jyles Phillips, Fred Powers, Clarence Thomas, Bill Hopkins.

Officers: Charles Roddy (Greenville, S.C.), President; Fred McAbee (Greenville, S.C.), 1st Vice President; Ted Pittman (Greenville, S.C.), 2nd Vice President; Phil Harley (Greenville, S.C.), Treasurer; Gary Pittman (Greenville, S.C.), Ass't Treasurer; B.J. Bell (Pelzer, S.C.), Ass't Executive Secretary; Janet Hopkins (Pelzer, S.C.), Ass't Executive Secretary; Lt. F.R. Hawkins, Security Officer.

Executive Committee: Phil Clark (Greer, S.C.), Lewis Golden (Greenville, S.C.), Jimmy Hopkins (Pelzer, S.C.), Ronnie Scarborough (Greenville, S.C.), Warren Rollins (Greenville, S.C.), Johnny Foster (Marietta, S.C.), Bob Brown (Greenville, S.C.), Pearl Moore (Spartanburg, S.C.).

OPEN DIVISION

Snyder's Auto (Greenville, S.C.), champions: Head Hunter (coach), Toogie Robinson (coach), Kevin Bryant, Mike Milling, Ray Gromlowich, John Perry, Frankie McGowan, Eric Moore, Mel Daniel, Rod Terry, Kent Washington, Raymond Lawson, Jim Weinzetter.

Olympic Gym (Columbia, S.C.), runners-up: Bob Brown (coach), Marc Campbell, Murray Jarman, Fred Gilliam, Chubby Wells, Larry Middleton, Ray Jones, Vince Hamilton, Horace Grant, Anthony Jenkins, Michael Tait, Jeff Holstein, McCants.

V.A. Jets (Columbia, S.C.): Barry Wilson (coach), Howard White, Kenny Reynolds, William Irick, Charles Kirkland, Troy Mikell, Golie Augustus, Harold Martin, Marcellous Primus, Donald Golson, Henry Hamilton, David Crumlin, Frank Wise, Davis.

Sixers (Columbia, S.C.): Jacob Pearson (coach), Kenny Cook (coach), Roger Carr, Anthony Flager, Willie Bynum, Greg Wright, James Brown, Tommy Mack, James Doby, Jimmy Davis, Nate Ellis, Steven Johnson, Curtis Dunbar, Joe Rice.

Sonics (Abbeville, S.C.): Archibald Letman (coach), Reggie Williams (coach), Hollie Martin, Calvin Doan, Curtis Harkness, Kenneth Robinson, Reggie Thompson, Derrick Galloway, Clay Doan, Dale Fleming, Sammy Karr, Columbus Copeland, Terry Bryant, Ellerbe.

Dick Brooks Honda (Columbia, S.C.): Scott Forrester (coach), Terry Lea (coach), Larry Walker, Spankey Goodjames, Chris McLemore, Jeff Harris, Stephon Leonard, Bernard Leonard, Steve Garnett, Robert Garnett, Danny Fields, Cokame Davis, Todd Gambrell, Kaminski.

Tri Dip Inc. (Columbia, S.C.): Tony Brown (coach), Wade Jenkins, James Sanders, Joe Rice, Rich Fulton, Frank Streeter, Ken Pralour, Willie Fairnot, Ricky Hamilton, James Brown, Billy Ingram, Melvin Jones, Earl, Cornelius Lindsay.

Greenwood Mill (Greenwood, S.C.): James Harkness (coach), Steve Gay, Wesley Stroman, Terry Bryan, William Bingham, George Carter, Brandt Williams, Wiley Adams, Vest, Thompson.

Lowenstein (Anderson, S.C.): Willie Wright (coach), Michael Tew, Mike McKinney, Ray Gist, Shell Haywood, Buck Jackson, Reggie Meadows, Amp Maybrey, Dexter Oneal, Wade Kershaw, Watson, Young.

Carolina Fine Foods (Greenville, S.C.): Melvin Young (coach), John Turner (coach), Wesley Oneal, Michael Williams, Bryan Britt, Eric Williams, Monroe Garrison, Lee Washington, Ronald White, Calvin Criswell, Kelvin Fowler, Gerrard Donald, Randy Odom, Art Johnson, J. Williams, Gordon.

CLASS A MEN

PPG Industries (Shelby, N.C.), champions: Larry Lynch (coach), Roger Shade (coach), Greg Beam, J.C. Cannon Jr., Larry Ross, Lopez Smith, Steve Cannon, Mike Kelly, Kirby Allen, Darrell Hines, Elton Cannedy, Terry Camp, Rodney Whittenburg, Steve Bean, Benji Camp, Freddie Jones, Clarence Whitworth, David Hector, David Banks.

Michelin US-1 (Greenville, S.C.), runners-up: J.C. Starkes (coach), Joel Henderson, John Furmanski, Rodney Sullivan, Anthony Chambers, Alan Foxx, Kenneth Carter, Luther Johnson, Clayton Rhodes, Mark Cox, Thompson, Gosnell, M. Williams, R. Williams, Cox.

Cryovac (Simpsonville, S.C.), consolation winners: Matthew Milam (coach), Rex Abercrombie, Bobby Phelps, Calvin Barksdale, James Sullivan, Paul Satterwhite, Jerry Boyd, Vernon Johnson, Clarence Dawkins Jr., Greg Sweeney, Alvarez Chiles, Brockman, Porter, Charles, Dean, Wright, Carwile, Wright.

Singer Mfg. (Pickens, S.C.): Terry Chandler (coach), Chris Austin, Ken Robinson, Glenn Thrift, Tim Looper, Leroy Williams, Tyrone Webb, Keith Scoggins, Jimmy Arledge, Randy Hayes, Tommy Slave, Tony Carver.

Emb-Tex (Travelers Rest, S.C.): Larry Brinkley (coach), Dennis Thompson, Zernie Morgan, Bill McBee, Mike Williams, Henry Robertson, Michael Robinson, Nelson Talley, Gill McDonald, Roger Robinson, Mitchell Davis, Troy Beaty, Lanny Lewis.

Alice Mfg. (Easley, S.C.): George Davis (coach), Terry McGowens, John Langston, Douglas Adams, Terry B. Smith, Tony McGowens, Melvin Dukes, Roy Collins, Ted Anderson, Matthew Valentine, Curtis Rosemond, Roy Owens, Smith, A. Anderson, B. Anderson, Chandler, Smith.

Michelin A (Spartanburg, S.C.): James Lindsay (coach), Michael Williams, Donnie Alexander, Terry Moore, Greg Elmore, Terry Free, Eric Martin, Fred Anderson, Fred McCarroll, Javon Drummond Jr., Butch Rodgers, George McCarroll, Doug Karmel, Westfield.

Slater Mill (Slater, S.C.): James Roberts (coach), McBruce Young, Joe Hill, Jimmy Barbare, Steve Parnell, Stacy Adams, Jimmy Allen, Kenneth Johnson, Leonard Monroe, Carl Poole, Greg Moore, Roberts, Bowles.

Pelzer Mill #1 (Pelzer, S.C.): Tommy Johnson (coach), Walter Smith, Johnny Robinson, Danny Scroggs, Victor Alverson, Mark Creamer, Jerry Rutledge, Timothy Kelly, Maurice Lewis, Terry Smith, Donald Clardy.

Pelzer Mill #2 (Pelzer, S.C.): Ronnie Cureton (coach), Alvin Sullivan (coach), Charles Pinson, Dwight Sullivan, Scotty Kech, Billy Burns, Robert Henderson, Ernest Corley, Greg Rawlins, David Burns, Charles Dean, Clardy.

Greenville Fire Dept. (Greenville, S.C.): Allen Quinn (coach), Rodney McCauley, Alfred McElrath, Vincent Means, Jimmy Harris, Kenneth Spivey, Kenneth Sterling, Rick Mullinax, Dwight Gray, Ronnie McKeown, Sam Stubbs, Dempsey Cohen, Stubbs.

Greenville Valve (Greenville, S.C.): Steve Crowe (coach), Steve Smith, Robin Ellenburg, Gary Long, Fred Melson, Tony Lanford, Mike Crowe, Henry.

St. Francis Hospital (Greenville, S.C.): Michael Barksdale (coach), Bobby Harper (coach), Willie Hampton, Jimmy Ponder, Mark Barksdale, John Little, Jeffrey Harper, Donald Binns, Tyrone Sherman, Stan Whittenberg, Maurice Thomason, Baker, S. Harper, Thompson.

Michelin B (Spartanburg, S.C.): Willie Hardy (coach), Mike Ungar (coach), Charlie Proctor, Ronnie Mulkey, Willie Ferguson, Mark Jackson, Bobby Jackson, William Casey, Johnny Williams, Jerome Miller, Stacey Fowler, Kelvin Brown.

Michelin US-2 (Greenville, S.C.): Chris Matten (coach), Ron Perkins, Dale Rhodes, Chuck Johnson, Eddie Corley, David Sanders, Jerry Minyard, Reno Allen, Whit Plyler, Tony Rochester, Robert Adger, Nat Leverette, Mike Price, Chester, Rhodes, Circle.

Clinton Mill (Clinton, S.C.): Brian Shealy (coach), William Mims, Billy Smith, Ricky Martin, Henry Blalock, Lewis Mims, George McMorris, Kenyon Robertson, Steve Coleman, Sammy Moses, Junius Boyd, Carlton Watts.

CLASS B MEN

Cleveland Memorial Hospital (Shelby, N.C.), champions: Richard Jones (coach), Matthew Campbell (coach), Maurice Campbell, Terry Cannon, Wayne Davis, Floyd Bridges, Terrence Petty, Warrick Ross, Johnny McCombs, Johnny Johnson, Rodney Ross, Dennis Laborn, Ronnie Ussery, Jeff Flowers.

Givens Youth Center (Fountain Inn, S.C.), runners-up: Jeffrey Anders (coach), Calvin Smith, Marvin Williams, Kenneth Parks, Daniel Callahan, Jerome Hughes, Oscar Hunter, Albert Jones, Michael Richardson, Arthur Smith Jr., Harold Stevenson, Keith Robinson, Ronnie Martin, Donley, Martin, Porter, Butler, Edwards.

O'Neal Engineering (Greenville, S.C.), consolation winners: Ralph Bouton (coach), Andy Wilson (coach), Mark Boudoucies, Tim Miller, Michael Burn, Howard Smith, Phil Smith, Billy Chandler, Chris Clark, Benton, T. Smith.

Sangamo Electric Co. (Pickens, S.C.): Clyde Herron (coach), Chris Guenthner (coach), Grady Gains, Aaron Goldsmith, Henry Jenkins, Eugene Jordan, Chuck McAtee, Eric Moss, Bill Nathan, Mac Raedy, Mark Salsbury, Leroy Wideman, Duane Wilson, Dwight Wilkes.

Cryovac (Simpsonville, S.C.): Jimmy Wright (coach), Rici Thompson, Walter Webb, Willie Gray, Tommy Hood, Michael Brockman, Johnny Wright, Aaron Thomason, Daniel Sullivan, Douglas Whitson, J.W. Wright, Willie Calvich, Cody Porter, R. Wright.

Sirrine Co. (Greenville, S.C.): Bob Ray (coach), James Neal Jr., William Tumblin Jr., Don Adams, Andrew Pickens, Charles Stewart, Robert Miller, James Ur, Ted Clark, Richard Hammond, Michael Cooper.

U.S. Post Office Gold (Greenville, S.C.): Donnie Scovel (coach), Newell Tucker Jr., William Crawford, Michael Curran, Mitchell Bryson, Bill Dalton, Scott Johnson, Ricky Robertson, Scovel, DiFresco.

U.S. Post Office #2 (Greenville, S.C.): Paul Hill Jr. (coach), Frankie Jackson, Dennis Zimmerman, Joel Pritchett, Prince Brock, James Donald, James Bell, Chuck Taylor, Scott Johnson, Stanley Griffin, Ben Sweeney.

American Hardware (Greenville, S.C.): Milas Officer (coach), David Bernsteil (coach), Mack Stephens, Charles Lake, Robert Sullivan, Bernard Johnson, Eric Bruster, Bryan Whiteside, Tony DeYoung, Tony King, Michael Murphy, Douglas Russ.

General Nutrition (Greenville, S.C.): Roger Kelly (coach), Clarence McDonald (coach), Clarence McDonald, James Henderson, Jeff Sligh, James Burton, Wayne Wood, Victor Austin Jr., Ron Kirby, Michael Patterson, Stephen Sullivan, Curtis Golden, Kelly, Roger.

Westinghouse (Greenville, S.C.): Larry Smith (coach), David Lowery, William Peppers, Greg Isom, Jim Youngblood, David Saleeby, Frankie Austin, Johnny Scotland, James Norman, Donnie Pressley, John Williams, Butch Bowling.

Video Express (Greenville, S.C.): Scott Freeman (coach), Chuck Thompson, Mark Townsend, Allan Holston, Eddie Bowens, Jamie Livingston, Brian Barnette, Todd Reynolds, Craig Scott.

Roadway (Greenville, S.C.): Marvin Adams (coach), Curtis Taylor, Jimmy Eoute, Ronald Wallace, Andrew Moss, Curtis Blakely, Terry Chandler, John Lollis, Joey Holden, Herbert Goodjoin, Craig Williams, Bradley.

United Insurance (Greenville, S.C.): J.R. Eirley (coach), Ronald Johnson, Ronald Griffin, Reggie Griffin, Stephan Westfield, Wayne Griffin, Butch Griffin, Donnell Rosemond.

Naron (Greenville, S.C.): Jim Bruce (coach), Billy Young, Tim Catoe, Marvin Anderson, Doug McBurney, Jerry Metcalf, Mark Wilson, Bill Dunlap, Mike Ferguson, Buice, Young, Wood, Allison.

Finley Revis Hanes (Greenville, S.C.): Gregg Finley (coach), Scott Brown, Greg Smith, Bob Rush, Chris Holiday, Allen Duncan, Tim Revis, Bryan Golden, Kenny Watts, Carroll Hembree.

Belton Industries (Belton, S.C.): David Pace (coach), Darrell Crocker, James Pace, Robert Kay, Lynn Stallings, Larry Curry, Maxie Brock, Marion Burkett, James Davis, David Brown, Phillip Ellington, James Burdette, Terry.

Class C Men

Chick-Fil-A (Greenville, S.C.), champions: George Glymph (coach), Marty McGraw, Joe Gilliam, Jo Jo English, Anton Brown, Barry Manning, Pete Foster, John Curry, Tracy Garrick, William Goodwin, Joe Rhett, Mike Glover, Sanders Means.

Alford Real Estate (Greenville, S.C.), runners-up: Warren Rollins (coach), Keith Rollins, Barry Littlefield, Darby Rich, Tim Hightower, Lee Ferguson, Thomas Gray, Shawn Golden, Marion Brown, Troy Dillard, Deon Irby, Harden, Johnson, Tennyson, Sproyce.

North Georgia #1 (Toccoa, Ga.), consolation winners: Jim Ganey (coach), Arlande Bennett, Perrell Goss, Marshall Wilson, Bruce Brown, Kenny Cooper, James Wilburn, Will Wood, Shane Maxwell, Dale Davis, Tony Sorrells, Larry Hamrick, Marvin Nash.

Limestone Mill (Gaffney, S.C.): Phillips, Leigh, Drennon, Moore, Weathers, Littlefield, Eaves.

Carper Real Estate (Greenville, S.C.): Tom Davis (coach), David Young, Harold Tomkins, Sean Lattimore, Derek Alvin, Chris Ingram, Mack Smith, Cleve Cox, Calvin Ward, Holloway, Berry, D. Holloway, Acock.

North Georgia #2 (Toccoa, Ga.): Jim Ganey (coach), Jerry Sadler, Donnie Clinkscale, Chad Beasley, Tyrone Oglesby, Keith Gantt, Byron Major, Jarvis Brown, Clarence Sorrells, Robert Renfroe, Larry Sparks, Chris Bailey, Steve Rayton, Stowers, Dunn, Nash, Garrett.

Blankenship Electric (Greenville, S.C.): Mark Huff (coach), John Starks, Tim Weathers, Stephen Houston, Mike Beckett, Lincoln Brock, Willie Goolsby, Mac Johnson, Hall, Tanner, Robinson, Parrott.

Dunean Mill (Greenville, S.C.): Reginald Epps, Watts, Corey Dugan, Evans, Stephen Houston, Patrick McCullough, Sullivan, Barton, Evans, Ellison.

Class A Women

Four Star Sports (Spartanburg, S.C.), champions: Pearl Moore (coach), Beverly Hawkins, Susan Jones, Nessie Harris, Mindy Belue, Marlene Jeter, Jennette Alston, Annette Alston, Kim Slawson, Melissa Robinson, Stacey Ford, Trudy Lacey, Chris Moye.

Foothills Real Estate (Greenville, S.C.), runners-up: Ronnie Scarborough (coach), Don Waldrop (coach), Peggy Caple, Beth Couture, Janet Knight, Melinda Ashworth, Grace Lyle, Sherri Oldevak, Kim Smith, Jennie Lyerly, Cynthia Austin, Laurie Morton, Julie Larson, Niki Lynch, Brickley.

Mac's All Stars (Greenville, S.C.), consolation winners: Archie McArthur (coach), Lenora Hood, Jennifer Yeargin, Loretta Clinkscales, Jackie Moore, Tonie Edwards, Sheila Morgan, Tammy Dendy, Jo Jo Jackson, Jeanette Dingle.

C. Dan Joyner (Greenville, S.C.): Bobby Kirby (coach), Donna Oliver, Marsi Kenyon, Sandy Holcombe, Pam Adams, Chris MacMurdo, Temple Elmore, Kay Kirby, Marty Vaughn, Marie Bolt, Amy McAlister, Sally Campbell, Kim Shockley.

1988

Executive Officers: Divver Hendrix, Ward Williams, Ruppert Elliott, Fred Byrd, Jyles Phillips, Fred Powers, Clarence Thomas, Bill Hopkins, Pete McAbee.

Officers: Charles Roddy (Greenville, S.C.), President; Fred McAbee (Greenville, S.C.), 1st Vice President; Ted Pittman (Greenville, S.C.), 2nd Vice President; Phil Harley (Greenville, S.C.), Treasurer; Gary Pittman (Greenville, S.C.), Ass't Treasurer; B.J. Bell (Pelzer, S.C.), Ass't Executive Secretary; Janet Hopkins (Pelzer, S.C.), Ass't Executive Secretary.

Executive Committee: Phil Clark (Greer, S.C.), Lewis Golden (Greenville, S.C.), Jimmy Hopkins (Pelzer, S.C.), Ronnie Scarborough (Greenville, S.C.), Warren Rollins (Greenville, S.C.), Johnny Foster (Marietta, S.C.), Bob Brown (Greenville, S.C.), Pearl Moore (Spartanburg, S.C.), Dan Pike (Greenville, S.C.), James Ball (Greenville, S.C.), Jim Johnson (Greenville, S.C.).

Open Division

Dillard's Sporting Goods (Easley, S.C.), champions: Terry Gould, Steven Gay, Marc Campbell, Mike Massey, James Scott, Wylie Adams, Chubby Wells, Tony Shaw, Kelvin Montegue.

Snyder's Auto (Greenville, S.C.), runners-up: Toogie Robertson (coach), Mike Milling, John Perry, Mel Daniel, Rod Terry, Lee Washington, Raymond Lawson, John Castille, Curtis Harkness, Albert Mattison, Mark Robertson, John Sterling, Herman Simms, Gromlowicz.

Sonics (Abbeville, S.C.): Reggie Williams

Southern Textile Basketball Tournament Rosters   Appendix 1   323

(coach), Hollie Martin, Kenneth Gillerson, Philip Thomas, Carl Seades, Raymond Briggs, Warren Franklin, Richard Ramey, Jeff Wilderson, Albert Smith, Jeff Sheppard, Mike Robinson, Ken Simmons, Jones, Ray, Goodjoines.

Carolina Fine Foods (Greenville, S.C.): Melvin Young (coach), Sonya Young (coach), Wesley Oneal, Michael Williams, Eric Williams, Monroe Garrison, Lee Washington, Art Johnson, Billy Young, Lionel Collins, James Anderson, Henry Carson, Shawn Reid, Mark Cox.

Bausch & Lomb (Greenville, S.C.): Hayden Vernon (coach), Jerry Wilson, Jeff Hoffler, Derrick Pendergrass, Barron Searles, Dave Altman, Artie Knight, Tim Young, Rodney Smith, Dondi McGowan, Chuck Orr Jr.

Hopewell (Greenville, S.C.): Willie Wright (coach), M. Peach (coach), James Grayson, Tyrone Meadows, Joey Moore, Joe Smith, Rick Harris, Wade Kershage, Michael McKinney, Buck Jackson, Anipe Maybre, Hardy, Gist.

Cobras (Greenville, S.C.): Jackie Anderson (coach), Sid Collins (coach), Ed Young III, Aaron Johnson, Dion Holmes, Lemon Collins, Mike Chandler, Rodney Clowney, Scott Smith, Calvin Criswell, Dwayne Long, Junior Anderson, Terry Smith, Tony Holiday.

Poinsett Grocery (Greenville, S.C.): Steve Jones (coach), Steve Brown (coach), Dempsey Cohen, Todd Gambrell, Derrick Robinson, Roy Wright, Terry Stewart, Rodney Mayers, John Kaminski, Ray Smith, Gerald Williams, Harris, Anderson, Johnson, Woodruff.

CLASS A MEN

Michelin US-1 (Greenville, S.C.), champions: J.C. Starkes (coach), Melvin Williams (coach), Joel Henderson, John Furmanski, Rodney Sullivan, Anthony Chambers, Alan Foxx, Kenneth Carter, Luther Johnson, Clayton Rhodes, Mark Cox, Andrew Thompson, Greg Cummings, Mark Williams, Kenny Rasnake.

Greenville Fire Dept. (Greenville, S.C.), runners-up: Allen Quinn (coach), Rodney McCauley, Alfred McElrath, Jimmy Harris, Kenneth Spivey, Ken Sterling, Rick Mullinax, Dempsey Cohen, D. Parham, R. Sitton, B. Hyatt, R. Anderson.

PPG Industries #1 (Shelby, N.C.), consolation winners: Larry Lynch (coach), Greg Beam, J.C. Cannon Jr., Larry Ross, Lopez Smith, Michael Kelly, Kirby Allen, Darrell Hines, Terry Camp, Steve Beam, Andra Miller, Paul Gash, Reginald Schenck, Hacks, Brown.

PPG Industries #2 (Shelby, N.C.): Larry Lynch (coach), Freddie Jones, Darryl Warren, Leonard Flack, Roger Shade, David Hector.

Michelin (Sandy Springs, S.C.): Chris Mattern (coach), Chuck Johnson, Robert Adger, Brian Kelly, David Lee, Ron Perkins, Reno Allen, Chris Cullen, David Sanders, Mark Mize, Mike Price, Barker Stone, Jeff Cooper, Stowe.

Cryovac (Simpsonville, S.C.): Matthew Milam (coach), Rex Abercrombie, Calvin Barksdale, James Sullivan, Paul Satterwhite, Jerry Boyd, Vernon Johnson, Clarence Dawkins Jr., Alvarez Chiles, Barry Wright.

Emb-Tex (Travelers Rest, S.C.): Larry Brinkley (coach), Dennis Thompson, Zernie Morgan, Bill McBee, Michael Robinson, Nelson Talley, Gill McDonald, Roger Robinson, Larry Lewis, Robert Poole.

Alice Mfg. (Easley, S.C.): Terry A. Smith (coach), Terry McGowens, Douglas Adams, Terry B. Smith, Tony McGowens, Roy Collins, Ted Anderson, Matthew Valentine, George Davis, Randy Smith, Ray Womack, Randy Raines, Jackie Anderson.

Slater Mill (Slater, S.C.): James Roberts (coach), McBruce Young, Joe Hill, Jimmy Roberts, Leonard Monroe, Greg Moore, William Parnell, Ricky Cruell, Johnson.

Greenville Valve (Greenville, S.C.): Steve Crowe (coach), Steve Smith, Robin Ellenburg, Gary Long, Fred Melson, Dale Crowe, Glymph Childress.

Singer Mfg. (Pickens, S.C.): Terry Chandler (coach), Chris Austin, Ken Robinson, Tim Looper, Leroy Williams, Tyrone Webb, Keith Scoggins, Jimmy Arledge, Randy Hayes, Tommy Burgess, Billy Tutt, Ted Webb, Mike Owens, Cooper.

St. Francis Hospital (Greenville, S.C.): Michael Barksdale (coach), John Little (coach), Willie Hampton, Jeffrey Harper, Bobby Harper, Corey Kirksey, Melvin Cureton, Chuck Mullen, James McNaughten, Terry Warnex, Kevin Lassen, Mike Kelly, Mike Neeley.

Cleveland Memorial Hospital (Shelby, N.C.): Richard Jones (coach), Matthew Campbell (coach), Maurice Campbell, Terry Cannon, Floyd Bridges, Terrence Petty, Warrick Ross, Johnny Johnson, Rodney Abrams, Ronnie Ussery, Jeff Gillespie, Charles Littlejohn, Donnie Peeler, Gingles.

Monaghan Mill (Greenville, S.C.): Eddie Leamon (coach), Bobby Jones, Alfred Sadler, Thomas Whitner, Anthony Grayson, George Wilson, Anthony Taylor, Michael Evans, George Crossman, Roy Richey, Lavon Phelps, Patrick Brooks, Andrew Green, Chuck McFarlin.

Pelzer Mill (Pelzer, S.C.): Robinson, Charles Pinson, Vic Alverson, Ronnie Cureton, Billy Burns.

CLASS B MEN

Saco-Lowell (Easley, S.C.), champions: Herbert Bowens (coach), Marion Breazeale (coach), Dale Gillespie, Mark Smith, Bryant Bowens, David Simmons, Ed Ballew, John Hodge, William Pitts, Mike Allen, Wallace Moore, Mike Reynolds, Mike Gilstrap, Benfield.

US Post Office (Greenville, S.C.), runners-up: Donnie Scovel (coach), Newell Tucker Jr., William Crawford, Mitchell Bryson, Bill Dalton, Ricky Robertson, James Bell, Dwight Donald, Stanley Griffin, Ken Dukes, Jack Hamilton.

Roadway (Greenville, S.C.), consolation winners: John Lollis (coach), Curtis Taylor, Jimmy Eoute, Ronald Wallace, Curtis Blakely, Marvin Adams, Ron Cracker, Lloyd Creed, Fred Glynn, Gary Bradley, William Wolff, Stephen Beitz, Lawless, Young, Hardy, Bell, Bridges.

Givens Youth Center (Fountain Inn, S.C.): Jeffrey Anders (coach), Michael Williams, Keith Parks, Harold Stevenson, Wilford Brooks, Bernard Austin, Franklin Fuller, Cleveland Bryant, Willie Dawkins, Joel Garrett, Barrett Harris, Billy Johnson, Jacob Patton, Jefferson, Sullivan, McKinney.

O'Neal Engineering (Greenville, S.C.): Ralph Bouton (coach), Andy Wilson, Mark Boudoucies, Tim Miller, Billy Chandler, Scott Wilson, Ron McPeters, Charles Stewart, Charles Brendle.

Clinton Mill (Clinton, S.C.): Brian Shealy (coach), William Mims, George McMorris, Kenyon Robertson, Carlton Watts, William Booker, John Williams, Walter, Robinson, Coleman.

Sirrine Co. (Greenville, S.C.): Bobby Mills (coach), James Neal Jr., William Tumblin Jr., Don Adams, Andrew Pickens, Robert Miller, Ted Clark, Bob Coffey, Reggie Anderson.

Finley Revis Hanes (Greenville, S.C.): Gregg Finley (coach), Scott Brown, Greg Smith, Chris Holliday, Tim Revis, Billy Finley, Alvin Sutton, Charles Edison, Pete Doneel, Derrick Thomas.

Sangamo Electric Co. (Pickens, S.C.): Chris Guenthner (coach), Aaron Goldsmith, Eugene Jordan, Chuck McAfee, Robert Nathan, Leroy Wideman, Dwight Wilkes, Marion Tuten, Dennis Barry.

Belton Industries (Belton, S.C.): Charles O'Conner (coach), Robert Kay, Lynn Stallings, Larry Curry, Phillip Ellington, Rex Pruitt, Undray Smith, Doug Breazeal, Wayne Brown, Timothy Rice, Charles O'Cain.

Touring Sports BMW (Greenville, S.C.): Ed Cota (coach), Fred Johnson, Anthony Johnson, Joseph Frasher, Samuel Oates, Chip Gilstrap, Jack Frasher, Al Banister, Dion Holmes, Jerome Williams, Billy Stormy, Gay, Hill, Lonine.

Shedd's (Greenville, S.C.): Terry Aiken (coach), James Jones, Bruce Adams, Henry Cheeks, Danny Collins, Terry King, John Jackson, Joe Abercrombie, Randall Wright, Bennie Parks, Johnnie Parks, Willie Brownlee, Sullivan.

F.W. Woolworth (Greenville, S.C.): Lewis Daniels (coach), Timothy Hines, James Robinson, Bernard Dawkins, Thomas Goodjione, Randall Smith, Richard Beeks, Roger L. Donald, Michael Elrod, Governor Chancellor, Steven Martin, Benjamin Glouse, Roger C. Donald.

3M (Greenville, S.C.): Jesse Looper (coach), Thomas Stance (coach), Kenny Arnold, Rick Calmile, Eldorado Valentine, Lyndon Mahaffey, Thomas Dixon, Eddie Gwynne, Louis Sayles, Willie Madden, Steve Eskew, Tony McNeely.

Michelin (Greenville, S.C.): Ronnie Scarborough (coach), Frankie Halstead, Keith Young, Bryant Dean, Fred Wilson, Kenneth Dean, Donnie Chambers, Jackie Chambers, Williams.

American Federal (Greenville, S.C.): Mike Dean (coach), Bill Weede, Tom Coan, Don Davis, Don Beamon, Keith Westbury, David Thomkins, Barry Starling, Chuck Werner, Charles Ferguson.

TIC (Greenville, S.C.): Richard Herd (coach), Joseph Finley, Daniel Morris, Bradford Johnson, Lynn Brown, Kenny Powell, Robert Henderson, Van Brannon, Robin Johnson, Barry Littlefield, Douglas Brown.

James River (Simpsonville, S.C.): Bob Bandholz (coach), Robert Hyslop, Craig Sahms, Tom Davis, James Parks, Melvin Allen,

Southern Textile Basketball Tournament Rosters   Appendix 1

Paul Graham, Mike McGrady, Bob Papes, Brian Czaplicki, Mike Morris, David Meyers, Bedford Bruno, Dogan.

Michelin A (Greenville, S.C.): Donnie Alexander (coach), Terry Free, Roland Dawkins, Gregory Elmore, Fred McCarroll, Ronnie Mulkey, Terry Moore, Michael Williams, Eric Martin, Alonso Briggs, George McCarroll, Harold Max, P. Free, Ferguson, F. Free, McFadden.

Cryovac (Duncan, S.C.): Jackie Scroggins (coach), Tommy Hood, Joel Eady, Walter Webb, J.W. Wright, Lester Smith, Johnny Wright, Aaron Thomason, Michael Brockman, Aaron Gamble, Richard Thompson, Darrell Lancaster, Cody Porter, Ray Calhoun, Hood.

CLASS C MEN

Chick-Fil-A (Greenville, S.C.), champions: George Funderburk (coach), Dag Wilson (coach), David Stavey, Cleve Cox, Hal Henderson, Clint Satterfield, John Lilly, Chris Lesco, Shawn Golden, Everick Sullivan, Bruce Evans, Amey, Burton.

Dillard's Sporting Goods (Easley, S.C.), runners-up: Sidney Thomas, Mike Beckett, Bennington, Schumpert, Johnson, Jones, Cofer, Bonds, Zellner, C. Jones.

North West Astros (Greenville, S.C.), consolation winners: Donald Dollar (coach), Chad Dollar, Gerald Houston, Clayton Driver, Richard Winfrey, Tommy Anderson, Chris Harvest, Bryan Brown, Kevin Chamberlain, Marguis Hicks.

Alford Real Estate (Greenville, S.C.): Warren Rollins (coach), Thomas Gray, Shawn Golden, Jimmy Thompson, Sherman Pride, Willie Murdaugh, John Hardin, J.R. McIlwaine, Mac Johnson, Mike Whatley, L.C. Zeller, James Whatley, Tito Smith, Brannon, Berry, Robinson.

Bumpers Car Wash (Greenville, S.C.): Jaylon Robinson (coach), Mark Watts, Currie Dogan, Reggie Epps, Tyrone Brock, Adrian Barton, T. Gaines, R. Blassigame, Pat McCullough, Wynn, Gaston, Sales, Bryant, Blakes, Robinson.

Budget Rent-A-Car (Greenville, S.C.): Sydney Smith (coach), Floyd Rohm (coach), Thomas Gray, G. Freeman, Vernon Redmond, Marco Brown, Chris Hall, James Long, Scott Cox, Tito Ballenger.

Systems & Service (Greenville, S.C.): Butler, Latimore, Goolsby, Parrott, Aikens, Knotts, Steinbacher, Tankersley, Pepper, Johnson.

Carper Real Estate (Greenville, S.C.): Davis, Barton, Epps, Sims, Hambrick, Acox, Young, Burroughs.

CLASS A WOMEN

Gould's Surveyors (Greenville, S.C.), champions: Ronnie Scarborough (coach), Renee Williams, Cheryl Nix, Melinda Ashworth, Niki Lynch, Peggy Caple, Lucy Dunn, Miriam Walker, Toni Edwards, Wendy Anderson, Helen Blakley, Ruby Bird, Marie Stuckey.

Foothills Real Estate (Greenville, S.C.), runners-up: Ron Scarborough (coach), Don Waldrop (coach), Beth Couture, Grace Lyles, Sherrie Oldevak, Jennie Lyerly, Cynthia Durham, Tonya Williams, Tracy Korbit, Amy Austin, Mary Kinnard, Liz Tankersley, Moore, Davis, Thomas.

Four Star Sports (Spartanburg, S.C.), consolation winners: Pearl Moore (coach), Kim Hawkins, Susan Jones, Mindy Belue, Marlene Jeter, Jennette Alston, Annette Alston, Melissa Robinson, Trudy Lacey, Connie Culbreth, Tracey Tillman, E. Jones, Slawson.

C. Dan Joyner (Greenville, S.C.): Bobby Kirby (coach), Marsi McAlister-Kenyon, Sandy Scott, Kay Kirby, Amy McAlister, Sally Campbell, Joy Brown, Shannon Holland, Barbara Nelson, Brock Goodwin, L. Glass, P. Glass, Laura Rowe.

Chick-Fil-A (Greenville, S.C.): Allen Turner (coach), Amiee Turner, April Hatcher, Pam Deanhardt, Killi Garrett, Millette Drakeford, Dorothy Whimphrey, Toni Steed, Tina Drutonis, Andrea Riddick, Emily Davis, Helen Williams, Ashley Turner, Johnson, Blassingame, Thomas.

Haynesworth Mill (Anderson, S.C.): Webb, Morton, Dinge, Hood.

1989

Executive Officers: Divver Hendrix, Ward Williams, Ruppert Elliott, Fred Byrd, Jyles Phillips, Fred Powers, Clarence Thomas, Bill Hopkins, Pete McAbee.

Officers: Fred McAbee (Greenville, S.C.), President; Ted Pittman (Greenville, S.C.), 1st Vice President; Charles Roddy (Greenville, S.C.), 2nd Vice President; Phil Harley (Greenville, S.C.), Treasurer; Gary Pittman (Greenville, S.C.), Ass't Treasurer; B.J. Bell (Pelzer,

S.C.), Ass't Executive Secretary; Janet Hopkins (Pelzer, S.C.), Ass't Executive Secretary.

Executive Committee: Phil Clark (Greer, S.C.), Lewis Golden (Greenville, S.C.), Jimmy Hopkins (Pelzer, S.C.), Ronnie Scarborough (Greenville, S.C.), Warren Rollins (Greenville, S.C.), Pearl Moore (Spartanburg, S.C.), Dan Pike (Greenville, S.C.), James Ball (Greenville, S.C.), Jim Johnson (Greenville, S.C.), Donald Davis (Greenville, S.C.).

OPEN DIVISION

Jimmy's Disco (Greenville, S.C.), champions: Jimmy Green (coach), J.W. Miller, J.C. Miller, Ed Young, Mark Still, Art Davis, Robert Simpson, Steve Garnett, Aaron Johnson, Ray Lawson, John Perry, Calvin Criswell, Amp Brown, Lee Washington.

Charleston Flyers (Charleston, S.C.), runners-up: Ralph Miller, Mike Gillison, Thomas, Wright, Dease, Pierce, Lowe, Hawkins, Rodney, Stewart.

Sonics (Abbeville, S.C.): Reggie Williams (coach), Hollie Martin, Kenneth Simmons, Phillip Thomas, Raymond Briggs, Warren Franklin, Richard Murphy, Douglas Belcher, John Davis, Gerald Dawkins, Randall James, Chuckie Scotland.

Poinsett Grocery (Greenville, S.C.): Todd Gambrell, Ray Smith, J. Hardin, Murdaugh, Thomas, Pride, McFadden, Martin, Kirkland, Nelson, Selvy, Gibson.

Carper Real Estate (Greenville, S.C.): Jerry Wilson, Kenny Wood, Derrick Robinson, Tom Chase, Monroe Garrison, George Carter, Rod Terry.

Sixers (Columbia, S.C.): Roger Carr, James Brown, Robert Fulton, Melvin Jones, James Sanders, Arthur Snipe, Henry Hamilton, Marcus Ecter, Willis Holliday, Doug Myers, Curtis Dunbar, Tony Shaw, Joe Rice, Williams Irick.

Carolina Fine Foods (Greenville, S.C.): Sims, Washington, Williams, Collins, O'Neal, Champion, Young, Hartness, Wright.

V.A. Jets (Columbia, S.C.): Walker, Hughey, Kirkland, Freeman, Jones, White, Brown.

CLASS A MEN

Michelin US-1 (Greenville, S.C.), champions: J.C. Starkes (coach), Andrew Thompson, Greg Cummings, Rodney Sullivan, Anthony Chambers, Mark Cox, Joel Henderson, Clayton Rhodes, Melvin Williams.

PPG Industries (Shelby, N.C.), runners-up: Greg Beam, J.C. Cannon Jr., Larry Ross, Kirby Allen, Donald Gash, Reginald Schenck, Chris Degree, Sidney Smith, Kevin Whitworth, Frank Spikes, Donnie Thurman, Vincent Haynes.

Emb-Tex (Travelers Rest, S.C.), consolation winners: Dennis Thompson, Zernie Morgan, Doug McBee, Michael Williams, Nelson Talley, Gill McDonald, Roger Robinson, Robert Poole, Wally Smith, Keith Breazeale.

Cryovac (Simpsonville, S.C.): Matthew Milam, Rex Abercrombie, Calvin Barksdale, James Sullivan, Paul Satterwhite, Jerry Boyd, Vernon Johnson, Clarence Dawkins Jr., Alvarez Chiles, Davy Wright, Bobby Phelps, Thomas Barry, Hood.

Alice Mfg. (Easley, S.C.): Dale Rosemond, Terry Smith, David Gilstrap, Matthew Valentine, Terry McGowens, Leon Bowens, Steven Burgess, Victor Sherman, Roy Owens, Keith Williams, Evans, Smith, Byrd, M. Owens.

Greenville Fire Dept. (Greenville, S.C.): Alfred McElrath, Jimmy Harris, Kenneth Spivey, Kenneth Sterling, Rick Mullinax, Dempsey Cohen, R. Sitton, B. Hyatt, R. Anderson, R.D. Ellison, V.L. Means, L.R. Gaines.

Saco-Lowell (Easley, S.C.): Roy Collins, Ramone Anderson, David Simmons, Bryant Bowen, Wallace Moore, Mike Allen, Mike Reynolds, Mike Gilstrap, David Kelley, Chip Cantrell, Anthony Whitner, Tony Talley.

Slater Mill (Slater, S.C.): Joe Hill, Jimmy Roberts, Leonard Monroe, William Parnell, Ricky Cruell, Jimmie Barbare, James Mann, Anthony Williams, Johnson.

Cleveland Memorial Hospital (Shelby, N.C.): Matthew Campbell, Maurice Campbell, Floyd Bridges, Terrence Petty, Johnny Johnson, Rodney Abrams, Ronnie Ussery, Jeff Gillespie, Charles Littlejohn, Dennis Laborn, Alan Ledbetter.

Pelzer Mill (Pelzer, S.C.): Greg Rochester, Myles Crawford, Johnny Robinson, Charles Mattison, David Burns, Billy Burns, Danny Scroggs, Daren Kay, Vic Alverson, Ronnie Cureton, Charles Pinson.

Hoechst Celanese (Greer, S.C.): Medlock, Anderson, Smith, Murray, Hawkins, Peahuff, Gust, Crawford, Drummond.

CLASS B MEN

Shedd's (Greenville, S.C.), champions: Anthony King (coach), Jimmy Rogers, Bruce Adams, Danny Collins, Randall Wright, James

Jones, Dion King, Johnny Parks, Henry Cheeks, Frank McDowell, Joe Abercrombie, "Root Beer" Johnson, Kell Brownlee, David Johnson.

Digital (Greenville, S.C.), runners-up: Peter Boykins, Gregory Rhodes, Gregory Gambrell, Keith Caldwell, Michael Hunt, Eric Fuller, Peter Mangrum, Joe Young, Andrew Sherman, Mark Donovan, David Mitchell, Donnie Byrd, Alan Bush.

Kemet (Simpsonville, S.C.), consolation winners: Ellis Williams III, David Taylor, Jim Spearman, Ken Sims, Waddy Talley, Anthony Copeland, Delano Carter, John Southern, Robert Willoughby, James Andrews, Phil Sargent, Rick Rickebach, B. Smith, S. Smith, Polly, Costes.

Oconee Nuclear (Seneca, S.C.): Scott Townsend, David Rathbone, Roy Foster, Frederick Gregg, Alvah Martin, Guy Sherwood, Richard Winchester, Harry Downam, Harry Hunter, Tony Foster.

Roadway (Greenville, S.C.): John Lollis, Curtis Taylor, Jimmy Eoute, Ronald Wallace, Marvin Adams, William Wolff, Stephen Beitz, Gene Reeder, James Lowe, David Williams, Burdine.

O'Neal Engineering (Greenville, S.C.): Ralph Bouton, Andy Wilson, Tim Miller, Randy Chandler, Scott Campbell, Charles Stewart, Chad Brendle, Mark Levesque, Scott Wilson, Jeffrey Griffith, Jeffrey Hull, Armstrong.

Clinton Mill (Clinton, S.C.): Brian Shealy, William Mims, George McMorris, Kenyon Robertson, Curtis Williams, Steve Coleman, Willard Hester, David Speaks, Olin Robertson, Leroy McGee, Byrd.

Sirrine Co. (Greenville, S.C.): James Neal Jr., William Tumblin Jr., Don Adams, Robert Miller, Ted Clark, Bob Coffey, Ray Holliday, James Wright, Doug Karmel.

F.W. Woolworth (Greenville, S.C.): James Robinson, Bernard Dawkins, Thomas Goodjione, Randall Smith, Roger Donald, Governor Chancellor, Steven Martin, Benjamin Glouse, Joe Martin, Donald.

Michelin US-1 (Greenville, S.C.); Free, Moore, Dean, Casey, Williams, Elmore, Alexander, McCarroll.

Michelin US-2 (Greenville, S.C.): Ron Perkins, David Lee, Nelson Heard, Brian Kelly, Barker Stone, Mike Price, Martin Stills, David Sanders, Chuck Johnson, Robert Adger, Whit Plyer, Tony Rochester, Shelton, Cullen.

James River (Simpsonville, S.C.): Robert Hyslop, Craig Sahms, Tom Davis, James Parks, Larry Simons, Stanley Byrd, William Teague, Larry Dogan, Gary Sanders, Mark McKinney, Jack Jolly, Mark Dease, Waddy Brown, Allen.

St. Francis Hospital (Greenville, S.C.): Bentley Gibson, Bobby Harper, Mike Barksdale, Barry Kiser, Roger Mauney, Jeff Skelton, Jeffrey Harper, Willie Hampton, Bernard Cureton, Joe Golob, Larry Vaughn, Bobbie MacNaughton, Warner, Robinson.

Sangamo Electric Co. (Pickens, S.C.): Marion Tuten, Dennis Barry, Robert Nathan Jr., Randy Seay, Barry Bryant, Chuck McAtee, Marty Hopkins, Eugene Jordan, Aaron Goldsmith, Leroy Wideman, Terry Bryant, Tyrone Hunter, Matthews.

Givens Youth Center (Fountain Inn, S.C.): Wilford Brooks, John Blander, Billy Johnson, Keith Parks, Michael Williams, Robert Wells, Luther Farley, Hinzell Gambrell, James Maddox, Marin Bonds, Tony Clark, Claude Henry.

Roll Technology (Greenville, S.C.): Connors, Chandler, Riddle, Owens, McAllister, Casey, Gilstrap.

Monaghan Mill (Greenville, S.C.): Sadler, Jones, Wilson, Henderson, Crossman, Taylors, Brooks, Phelps.

Print Machine (Greenville, S.C.): Lee Moore, Jeff Finley, Greg Kays, Leonard Hill, Steven Suttles, Al Banister, Mike Link, Bruce Harris, Shane Enloe.

Cryovac (Simpsonville, S.C.): Robert Barker, Michael Brockman, Reginald Lomax, Richard Montgomery, Gerald Sims, Aaron Gamble, J.W. Wright, Johnny Wright, Lester Smith, J. Eudy, J.D. Stewart, Fredere.

Dow Brands (Mauldin, S.C.): Phillip Baldwin, Nathaniel Hawthorne, Jimmy Hardy, Keith Wilson, Derrick Braddock, David Hill, Joey Freeman, Fred Spurgeon, Johnny Abercrombie, Kelvin Knight, Donald Harrison, D.M. Wozniak, Sullivan, Sitton, Boyd, Childress.

Easley Housing Center (Easley, S.C.): Scott Brown, Greg Smith, Tim Revis, Gregg Finley, Mike Anderson, Billy Finley, Scott Frye, Kevin Jackson, Alvin Sutton, Steve Frye.

Bay Brokerage (Greenville, S.C.): Robert Dean, Keith Rollins, John Hannon, Andrew Carter, Jeff Johnson, Doug Barmore, George Walker, Kenny Powell, Brad Johnson, Berry, Knight, Brannon, Davidson.

Wangner Systems (Greenville, S.C.): Larry

Williams, Robert Edwards, Steve Greggs, Charles Gamble, Cliff Archie, Samuel Cantrell, Kerry Edmunds, Mark Landrum, Lewis Still, Irwin McCullough, Paul Hill, Renoir Allen, Gray, Howard.

Williams, Williams & Knight (Greenville, S.C.): Richard Williams, Darrell Knight, John Ross, Dale Knight, Scott Trentham, John Krueger, Steve Wilham, Keith Burton, David Williams, Rick Smith, David Hurley.

CLASS C MEN

Chick-Fil-A (Greenville, S.C.), champions: Marion Busby (coach), Dan O'Shaughnessey (coach), Coley O'Shaughnessey, Vett Kilgore, Lincoln Simmons, Demetric Johnson, Steve Harris, George Funderburk, Charlie Edmond, Josh Hawkins, Chris Leso, Terry Bynum, John Smith, Sidney Thomas, C. Thomas.

Carper Real Estate (Greenville, S.C.), runners-up: Donnie Clinkscales, Tyrone Oglesby, Bruce Oglesby, Spezio Stowers, Tim Weathers, Jason Scott, Tino Ballenger, Donnell King, Jackie Robinson, Jay Booth, Chuck Graham, Marvin Nash.

Northwestern (Greenville, S.C.), consolation winners: Donald Dollar, Tommy McGee, Chris Williams, Marquis Hicks, Dathan Brown, Conara Hill, Brian Thompson, Michael Jones, Sean Jones, Lorenzo Varner, Derek Caine, Andre Stephens.

Krispy Kreme (Spartanburg, S.C.): G. Reese, D. Reese, Wofford, N. Bagwell, G. Bagwell, Riggins, Powell, Parton, Brooks, Finkelstein, Querin.

Bumpers Car Wash (Greenville, S.C.): Barley Robinson, Tyrone Brock, Michael Blassigame, Shawn McCullough, Steve Harris, Eugene Williams, Angelo Sales, Horatio Butler, Larry Brown, Giovanni Freeman, Kevin Wynn, Barton, Doungers.

Sterling (Greenville, S.C.): Ben Whitehurst, Johnny Spurgeon, Martin Arnold, Terry Gaston, Percy Moultrie, Willie Thompson, Jack Smith, Cedric Lawrence, Charles Brown, Deshun Gray, Simmons, Sitton, Irby.

CLASS A WOMEN

Boston Beanery (Greenville, S.C.), champions: Bobby Kirby (coach), Tammy Dendy, Tonya Williams, Jackie Moore, Jennie Lyerly, Toni Edwards, Melissa Robinson, Rushia Brown, LaToya Armstrong, Dia Haynes.

Comfort Inn (Greenville, S.C.), runners-up: Renee Williams, Kelli Garrett, Cheryl Nix, Bryant, Oldevak, Anderson, Crocket, Ashworth.

D & D Specialties (Greenville, S.C.), consolation winners: Pearl Moore, Kim Hawkins, Marlene Jeter, Elnora Jeter, Shayla Wilkins, Kim Booker, Tammy Harvey, Sharon Gilmore, Jessica Barr, Sharon Rivers, Sheila Foster, Brantley Southers, Alston, Cain, Montague, Haygood.

Alford Real Estate (Greenville, S.C.): Sally Campbell, Regina Brown, Shannon Holland, Temple Elmore, Lisa Washington, Kelly Finch, Kim Choice, Lisa Crosby.

1990

Executive Officers: Divver Hendrix, Ward Williams, Ruppert Elliott, Fred Byrd, Jyles Phillips, Fred Powers, Clarence Thomas, Bill Hopkins, Pete McAbee.

Officers: Ted Pittman (Greenville, S.C.), President; Gary Pittman (Greenville, S.C.), 1st Vice President; Fred McAbee (Greenville, S.C.), 2nd Vice President; Don Davis (Greenville, S.C.), Treasurer; Charles Roddy (Greenville, S.C.), Ass't Treasurer; B.J. Bell (Pelzer, S.C.), Ass't Executive Secretary; Janet Hopkins (Pelzer, S.C.), Ass't Executive Secretary.

Executive Committee: Phil Clark (Greer, S.C.), Lewis Golden (Greenville, S.C.), Phil Harley (Greer, S.C.), Ronnie Scarborough (Greenville, S.C.), Warren Rollins (Greenville, S.C.), Pearl Moore (Spartanburg, S.C.), Dan Pike (Greenville, S.C.), Jim Ball (Greenville, S.C.), Jim Johnson (Greenville, S.C.), Steve Brown (Greer, S.C.).

OPEN DIVISION

Poinsett Grocery (Greenville, S.C.), champions: Steve Jones (coach), Jimmy Brown, Eric Marable, Tim Moody, Carl Smith, Roger Massengale, Todd Wray, Todd Gambrell, Thomas Gray, Roy Wright, Brooks.

Charleston Flyers (Charleston, S.C.), runners-up: D. Thomas, Mike Gillison, Miller, Jordan, Tyler, T. Thomas, Edwards, Lowe, Gregg, Wright, Keith Freyer.

Top Gun (Greenville, S.C.): John Perry, Miller, Ed Young, Calvin Criswell, Howard, Raymond Lawson, Arthur Davis, Lee Washington.

Sixers (Columbia, S.C.): Roger Carr, Kincaid, James Brown, Young, Haskins, Williams Irick, Freeman, Robert Fulton, Curtis Dunbar, Hill, Melvin Jones, Arthur Snipe.

Sam Wyche Sports World (Greenville, S.C.): Jones, Atkinson, Perry, Brewster, Culp, Bailey, Pew, Faulkner.

McCrary Sprinkler (Greenville, S.C.): Campbell, Brown, Champion, Wells, Daniel, Hartness, Haynes.

S&M Sports (Shelby, N.C.): Littlejohn, Cannon, Crank, Degree, Thomas, Hines, Camp, Todd Wray, Ross, Lawrence, Wray.

Central (Central, S.C.): Wimphire, Goolsby, Bowen, Riley, Peckham, Mendenhall, Lattimore, Davis, Lawson, Rooks.

Z Control (Greenville, S.C.): Walker, Garnett, Sales, Durham, Grayson, Wallace, Wilson.

V.A. Jets (Columbia, S.C.): White, Rice, Kirkland, Goldson, J. Brown, Primus, C. Brown, A. Brown.

Other Teams: Sonics (Abbeville, S.C.)

CLASS A MEN

Michelin US-1 (Greenville, S.C.), champions: J.C. Starkes (coach), Andrew Thompson, Greg Cummings, Rodney Sullivan, Mark Cox, Joel Henderson, Clayton Rhodes, Bobby Williams, Kenneth Carter, Barron Searles, Ken Knapp, Chambers.

Greenville Fire Dept. (Greenville, S.C.), runners-up: Dempsey Cohen, B. Hyatt, Ken Sterling, R. Sitton, Jimmy Harris, R. Anderson, V.L. Means.

Saco-Lowell (Easley, S.C.), consolation winners: Bryant Bowen, David Simmons, Anthony Whitner, Roy Collins, Mike Allen.

Emb-Tex (Travelers Rest, S.C.): Dennis Thompson, Doug McBee, Gill McDonald, Zernie Morgan, Bowen, Michael Williams, Robert Poole, Keith Breazeale.

PPG Industries (Shelby, N.C.): Kevin Whitworth, Sidney Smith, Kirby Allen, Kelly, Vincent Haynes, Woods, Milkin, Greg Beam, Kimball, Hines.

Cryovac (Simpsonville, S.C.): Clarence Dawkins Jr., Calvin Barksdale, Vernon Johnson, Rex Abercrombie, Hood, Jerry Boyd, Davy Wright, Paul Satterwhite, Alvarez Chiles.

Alice Mfg. (Easley, S.C.): Terry B. Smith, Holloway, Dale Rosemond, Davis, M. Owens, Webb, Leon Bowens, Roy Owens, Terry A. Smith.

Pelzer Mill (Pelzer, S.C.): Ronnie Cureton, Charles Pinson, David Burns, Scott.

Other Teams: Cleveland Memorial Hospital (Shelby, N.C.).

CLASS B MEN

Shaw Properties (Greenville, S.C.), champions: Glenn Shaw, Ron Shaw, Keith Nance, Pat McCullough, Joel Anderson, Joseph Young, White.

Greenville Valve (Greenville, S.C.), runners-up: Grove, Steve Smith, Hunt, Nunnery, Steve Crowe, Long, M. Crowe, D. Crowe.

Kemet (Simpsonville, S.C.), consolation winners: Waddy Talley, E. Miller, B. Smith, David Taylor, S. Williams, James Andrews, G. Miller, Lanford, Lollis.

Monaghan Mill (Greenville, S.C.): Sadler, Jones, Wilson, Taylors, Brooks, Phelps, Evans, Phillips, Johnson, Stellar, Wells.

O'Neal Engineering (Greenville, S.C.): Andy Wilson, Ralph Bouton, Randy Chandler, Chad Brendle, Charles Stewart, Jeffrey Hull.

Digital (Greenville, S.C.): Keith Caldwell, Mark Donovan, T. Sherman, Peter Mangrum, Lindsay, Eric Fuller, Alan Bush, Bloise, Michael Hunt, Andrew Sherman.

Oconee Nuclear (Seneca, S.C.): Scott Townsend, David Rathbone, Roy Foster, Frederick Gregg, Alvah Martin, Richard Winchester, Robinson.

Clinton Mill (Clinton, S.C.): William Mims, George McMorris, Kenyon Robertson, Curtis Williams, Willard Hester, Olin Robertson, Mobley.

Sirrine Co. (Greenville, S.C.): Robert Miller, Ray Holliday, James Wright, Doug Karmel, Backmon, Adams.

James River (Simpsonville, S.C.): Tom Davis, William Teague, Larry Dogan, Waddy Brown, Allen, Baldwin.

St. Francis Hospital (Greenville, S.C.): Bobby Harper, Mike Barksdale, Roger Mauney, Jeffrey Harper, Willie Hampton, Joe Golob, Bobbie MacNaughton, Warner, Flores, Neeley, Vernon.

Roll Tech (Greenville, S.C.): Chandler, McAllister, Emory, M. Seay, W. Seay, Tilley, Mullinax.

Cryovac (Simpsonville, S.C.): Michael Brockman, Richard Montgomery, Gerald Sims, Aaron Gamble, Johnny Wright, J. Eudy, Fredere, Hanley.

Wangner Systems (Greenville, S.C.): Robert

Edwards, Steve Greggs, Charles Gamble, Cliff Archie, Kerry Edmunds, Irwin McCullough, Renoir Allen, Edwards, Brewer.

General Nutrition (Greenville, S.C.): Campbell, Suber, Williams, Martin, Inabinet.

Torrington (Clinton, S.C.): Martin, Creamer, Creamer, Boyce, Hellum, Sanders, Bobb, Goggins, Stanley.

Vanden Bergh (Greenville, S.C.): King, Abercrombie, Wright, Jones, Brownlee, Huff, Robinson.

Stevens Aviation (Greenville, S.C.): Miller, Harvey, Arms, Knowlton, Brandon.

Southeastern Freight (Greenville, S.C.): Madden, Richardson, Seay, Hyatt, Pickel, Price.

Schlumberger (Greenwood, S.C.): Barry, Hunter, T. Bryant, McAtee, B. Bryant, Jordan, Tuten, Goldsmith.

Jacob's Jazz (Fountain Inn): Burton, Merck, Miller, Jackson, Terry, Baker, Yates, Grimes.

3M (Greenville, S.C.): Valentine, Wyatt, Goodis, Arnold, McNeely, Dixon, Calwile.

CLASS C MEN

Chick-Fil-A (Greenville, S.C.), champions: George Funderburk (coach), Steve Harris, John Smith, David Stubblefield, Andre Bovain, Marion Busby, Dee Dee Hook, Greg James, Robbie Schultz, Darren Moore, Jay Hagood, Derrick Carroll, Brian Franklin, Bynum.

Carper Real Estate (Greenville, S.C.), runners-up: Bruce Oglesby, Jason Scott, Mincey, Blackwell, Hal McManus, Tony Sorrells, Maxwell, Bell, Fowler, Greg Minor.

Carolina Upstate (Greenville, S.C.): Pruitt, Ballenger, Bruster, Brad Ledford, Brady Ledford, Blassingame, Bowens, Lynn.

Dunean Mill (Greenville, S.C.): Cedric Brockman, Trell Robinson, Tony Robinson, Lamont Jones, Adrian Barton, Tron Brock, Ashmore, Foster, Carr.

Miller Oil (Greenville, S.C.): Shell, Berry, Williams, Burnett, Boucher, Berry, Timmons, Hertwig.

Rottweilers (Greenville, S.C.): T. Simmons, Smith, R. Simmons, Knuckles, Jones, Williams, Sitton, White, Cureton.

Washington City (Greenville, S.C.): Evans, Michael Thorsland, Oglesby, Jacque Rogers, McKnight, O'Shaughnessy, Penson, Thompson, Stallard, Sullivan, Bowden.

Original Concepts (Greenville, S.C.): Moss, Grant, Armstrong, Burton, Johnson, Bryan, Watts, Lattimore, Hoag.

CLASS A WOMEN

None.

---------- 1991 ----------

Executive Officers: Ward Williams, Ruppert Elliott, Fred Byrd, Fred McAbee, Jyles Phillips, Fred Powers, Clarence Thomas, Bill Hopkins, Pete McAbee.

Officers: Don Davis (Greenville, S.C.), President; Ted Pittman (Greenville, S.C.), 1st Vice President; Gary Pittman (Greenville, S.C.), 2nd Vice President; Charles Roddy (Greenville, S.C.), Treasurer; Warren Rollins (Greenville, S.C.), Executive Secretary; Dave Estes (Greenville, S.C.), Executive Secretary.

Executive Committee: Phil Clark (Greer, S.C.), Lewis Golden (Greenville, S.C.), Phil Harley (Greer, S.C.), Pam McCain (Greenville, S.C.), Darren Gazaway (Greenville, S.C.), Pearl Moore (Spartanburg, S.C.), Dan Pike (Greenville, S.C.), Jim Ball (Greenville, S.C.), Jim Johnson (Greenville, S.C.), Steve Brown (Greer, S.C.), David Banks (Shelby, N.C.), Randy LaFoy (Greenville, S.C.).

OPEN DIVISION

Poinsett Grocery (Greenville, S.C.), champions: Steve Brown (coach), Steve Jones (coach), Roger Massengale (coach), Jimmy Brown, Carl Smith, Todd Wray, Todd Gambrell, Jeff Williams, Ellis, Brooks.

Spirit Express (Memphis, Tenn.), runners-up: Quinton Lytle, Bill Jackman,

Top Gun (Greenville, S.C.): R. Simpson, John Perry, Ed Young, K. Howard, J.W. Miller, Terry, Patterson.

Sixers (Columbia, S.C.): McKinley, Hill, Shaw, Mack, Geter, Jones, Young, Irick.

S&M Sports (Shelby, N.C.): Benji Camp, Larry Ross, Robinson, David Dickerson, Miller, Sanders, Blese Young.

Orangemen (Columbia, S.C.): Gilliam, Mack, Richardson, Moody, Dawkins, Adams, Barton.

Sharkheads (Columbia, S.C.): Barry Kincaid, J. Darby, R. Carr, Martin, J. Dooley, Melson, Everhart, Freeman.

Excalibur (Greenville, S.C.): Criswell, Ellis, Terry, Johnson, White, Leonard, Copeland, Kerns.

Sincerely Yours (Greenville, S.C.): Albert Mattison, James Davidson, Reggie Thompson,

Scott Smith, Bernard Hampton, McCullough, Rooks.

Over the Hill (Greenville, S.C.): Rand Peterson, Earnhardt, Mike Smith, Warnock, Hodge.

Other Teams: Lynch Mob (Columbia, S.C.); Steak & Waffle (Seneca, S.C.); Soul Patrol (Spartanburg, S.C.).

CLASS A MEN

Michelin US-1 (Greenville, S.C.), champions: Melvin Williams (coach), Andrew Thompson, Mark Cox, Joel Henderson, Clayton Rhodes, Bobby Williams, Paul Johnson, Eric Hunter, Rodney Sullivan.

PPG Industries (Shelby, N.C.), runners-up: Terry Camp, Eric Marable, Kirby Allen, Kevin Whitworth, Miller, Robbs, Mike Kelly, Beam.

Alice Mfg. (Easley, S.C.), consolation winners: Owens, Rosemond, Williams, Webb, T.B. Smith, T. McGowens, G. Davis, T.A. Smith.

Greenville Fire Dept. (Greenville, S.C.): Sitton, Cohen, Hyatt, Watson, Harris, R. Anderson, Gray, Spivey, Mullinax, M. Anderson.

Emb-Tex (Travelers Rest, S.C.): Dennis Thompson, Gil McDonald, Zack Bowens, Doug McBee, Travis Bowens, Robinson, Williams.

Cryovac (Simpsonville, S.C.): C. Dawkins, Barksdale, Johnson, Abercrombie, Boyd, Harrison, J.W. Wright, Gambrell, J. Wright.

Pelzer Mill (Pelzer, S.C.): Ronnie Cureton, Burns, Keels, Henry, D. Burns, Smith, Hunter, Talley, Hunt.

Michelin US-3 (Greenville, S.C.): T. Free, McKinney, Dean, T. Foster, Rice, McCarroll, P. Free, Williams.

CLASS B MEN

American Amusement (Greenville, S.C.), champions: Tim Elliott (coach), Andy Carter, Jeff Lollis, Rodney McCauley, Clay Carter, Greg Travis, Yancey Johnson, Randy Rice, John Williams.

St. Francis Hospital (Greenville, S.C.), runners-up: Bobby Harper, Jeffrey Harper, Hampton, Vernon, McNaughton, Houston, Gibson, Roger Mauney, Julius Thompson, Tyrone Brock, Jackson.

Cryovac (Simpsonville, S.C.), consolation winners: G. Sims, Chiles, Montgomery, Ellis, Fredere, Lomax, Brockman, Booker, Smith.

Textron (Greenville, S.C.): Lehman, K. Smith, Roseman, Mitchell, S. Smith, E. Robinson, Blanton, Scott, Donald, Carey.

Greenville Valve (Greenville, S.C.): Steve Crowe, Smith, Nunnery, Long, Francis, Hart, Ellenburg.

O'Neal Engineering (Greenville, S.C.): Hall, Wilson, Ralph Bouton, Randy Chandler, Brendle, Miller, Wood.

Clinton Mill (Clinton, S.C.): Tim Davis, Curtis Wilson, William Mims, George McMorris, K. Robertson, Curtis Watson, Young, Booker, Carter, Hester, Coleman.

Sirrine Co. (Greenville, S.C.): Holloway, Miller, Wright, Karmel, Michols, Adams, Neal, Marsicek.

Southeastern Freight (Greenville, S.C.): Robert Pickle, Hyatt, Richardson, Buddy Williams, Cureton, Bailey, Hensley, Cook, Little.

Jacob's Mfg. (Greenville, S.C.): Burton, Merck, Thompson, Good, Yates.

3M (Greenville, S.C.): Alexander, Lollis, Arnold, Carwile, Harder, Wyatt, Looper.

Fiberweb (Greenville, S.C.): John Bennett, Larry Simmons, Brown, Davis, Scott Copper, Baldwin, Bruno, Peterson.

Futuras (Greenville, S.C.): John Spratling, Allen, Mark Simmons, Cunningham, Baker.

Saco-Lowell (Easley, S.C.): Don Benfield, Mike Allen, Chip Cantrell, Carter, Gilstrap, Powell, Krenik, Capps, Ballew, Reynolds.

Michelin US-1 (Greenville, S.C.): Stewart, Watson, Williams, Young, Jordan, Bryson, Rasnake, Halstead, Deshields, Brown, Wilson.

Mike Davis Landscaping (Piedmont, S.C.): Henderson, Lister, Morris, Gay, James Brown, Brannon, Wilson, Gravley.

93.7 Bombardiers (Greenville, S.C.): Tanner, Logan, Gibbs, McCarry, McClain.

American Federal (Greenville, S.C.): Dean, Schmitt, Keith Westbury, Estes, Tom Britt, Robinson, Griffin, Welborn, Brian Eliason, Starling.

Michelin US-3 (Greenville, S.C.): Jones, B. Jackson, M. Jackson, F. Williams, J.T. Williams, L. Wallace, Hardy, Coulter, Watson, Davidson.

Roadway Express (Duncan, S.C.): Dotson, Taylor, Lollis, Wallace, MAdden, Benfield, Adams.

Wunda Weve (Greenville, S.C.): Jimmy Rogers, Mack Burnside, Jerry Chapman, Davenport, Willis Abercrombie, James, Frank Mansell.

Other Team: Schlumberger (Greenwood, S.C.).

Class C Men
Beach Ball All Stars (Myrtle Beach, S.C.), champions: Robbie Johnson, Jackie Simmons, Jermaine Alston, Desi McQueen, Laron Toney, Wendel Brown, Alfonso Grissett, Jermaine Scott, Ricky Daniels, Chuck Robinson, Mike Blasingame, Sammy Haley, Simeon Haley.

Metro (Greenville, S.C.), runners-up: Nick Griffin, Kenny Jackson, Kevin Irby, Tarrance Albert, Virgil Lynch, Hagood, Cruell, Breazeale, Kevin Benson, Nolan.

Alford Real Estate (Greenville, S.C.), consolation winners: Michael Timmons, Michael Brown, Shell, Barbary, Wilson, Horn, Whitworth, Peters, Picklesimer.

Dunean Mill (Greenville, S.C.): McKinney, Hill, Charles Young, John Irby, Trell Robinson, White, Giles, Kelada, Ashmore, Bell, Moore.

Carolina Upstate (Greenville, S.C.): Burt, Brady Ledford, Brad Ledford, Jeff Evans, Rogers, Young, Oliver, O'Shaughnessy, Marcus Penson, Jones, Allen, Talley, Shawn Robinson.

Dave's Restaurant (Greenville, S.C.): Jamie Hedgepath, Kevin Kerr, Waters, Stevens, Kay, Givens.

8 O'Clock Supers (Greenville, S.C.): Bill Harder, Merl Code, Duck, Meekins, Jamie Rhome, Bowen, Wakefield, Robinson, Evans, Hobbs, Kent Stallard.

Class A Women
T-Shirts Plus (Greenville, S.C.), champions: Pearl Moore, Denise Johnson, Laura Byrd, Kim Booker, Dorothy Bowers, Branda Cain, Quisha Lawson, Nessie Harris.

St. Francis Hospital (Greenville, S.C.), runners-up: Pam McCain, Toni Edwards, Sandra Vicoury, Tripp, Beth Couture.

Other Teams: Central CWC (Central, S.C.); Hot Shots (Clemson, S.C.).

1992

Executive Officers: Ward Williams, Ruppert Elliott, Fred Byrd, Fred McAbee, Charles Roddy, Ted Pittman, Jyles Phillips, Fred Powers, Clarence Thomas, Bill Hopkins, Pete McAbee.

Officers: Don Davis (Greenville, S.C.), President; Gary Pittman (Greenville, S.C.), 1st Vice President; Warren Rollins (Greenville, S.C.), 2nd Vice President; Dave Estes (Greenville, S.C.), Treasurer.

Executive Committee: Phil Clark (Greer, S.C.), Lewis Golden (Greenville, S.C.), Phil Harley (Greer, S.C.), Pam McCain (Greenville, S.C.), Darren Gazaway (Greenville, S.C.), Pearl Moore (Spartanburg, S.C.), Dan Pike (Greenville, S.C.), Jim Ball (Greenville, S.C.), James Meekins (Greenville, S.C.), Steve Brown (Greer, S.C.), David Banks (Shelby, N.C.), Randy LaFoy (Greenville, S.C.), Ronnie Hunter (Greenville, S.C.), Tom Davis (Greenville, S.C.), Mike Gravley (Greer, S.C.).

Open Division
Southeastern Products (Greenville, S.C.), champions: Bruce Evans, David Stamey, Tracey Garrick, David Brown, Castill, Barry Manning, Jo Jo English, Brooks, Tom O'Donnell, Crosby.

S&M Sports (Shelby, N.C.), runners-up: Benji Camp, Larry Ross, Dewayne Long, Harvey Macomson, Moore, Littlejohn, Purdy, Good, David Lawrence.

Poinsett Grocery (Greenville, S.C.): Jimmy Brown, Carl Smith, Todd Wray, Yancey Johnson, James Thomas, Bill Henderson, Roy Wright, D. Henderson.

Top Gun (Greenville, S.C.): John Perry, Ed Young, K. Howard, J.W. Miller, Reggie Terry, Adrian Barton, Washington, Davis, A. Terry.

Sixers (Columbia, S.C.): William Irick, Howard White, Marion Haynes, Henry Hamilton, Wayne Sims, Brooks.

Lynch Mob (Columbia, S.C.): Sales, Paul Davis, King, Ulysses Hackett, Ray Durham, David Young, Bryan, Walker, Ellison, Marion Brown.

Sharkheads (Columbia, S.C.): Barry Kincaid, James Darby, Roger Carr, Daryl Martin, Eric Bradford, Glover, Brown, Haskins.

Steak & Waffle (Seneca, S.C.): Chris Hamilton, Gambrell, Raymond Lawson, James Davidson, Ty Mendenhall, Al Mattison, Bryan, Foster.

Auto Tech (Greenville, S.C.): Moore, Pat McCullough, Ellis Williams, Jerry Wilson, Williams, W. Franklin, T. Franklin, Whitnel.

Other Teams: Spirit Express (Memphis, Tenn.), Orangemen (Columbia, S.C.), USA Wet (Greenville, S.C.).

Southern Textile Basketball Tournament Rosters

CLASS A MEN

Alice Mfg. (Easley, S.C.), champions: Roy Collins, Dale Rosemond, Tracey Williams, Ricky Webb, Terry B. Smith, Terry McGowens, George Davis, Scott Smith, Ronald Garrett, Donald Garrett, Randy Raines, Matthew Valentine.

Greenville Fire Dept. (Greenville, S.C.), runners-up: Sitton, Dempsey Cohen, Hyatt, Watson, Harris, R. Anderson, Mitch Anderson.

Michelin US-1 (Greenville, S.C.), consolation winners: Andrew Thompson, Mark Cox, Joel Henderson, Clayton Rhodes, Bobby Williams, Paul Johnson, Rodney Sullivan, Cunningham, Searles.

Michelin (Spartanburg, S.C.): P. Free, Jackson, Ron Coulter, Mike Williams, T. Foster, T. Free.

Cryovac (Simpsonville, S.C.): Johnson, Abercrombie, J.W. Wright, Gambrell, J. Wright, Brockman, Reid, Satterwhite, Hood.

CLASS B MEN

American Federal (Greenville, S.C.), champions: Keith Westburg, Stan Griffin, David Welborn, Brian Eliasson, Jim Weinzettel, Jeff Waddell, Mel Daniel, Tom Coan.

Vernon Heating & Air (Greenville, S.C.), runners-up: Ben Cox, Cleve Cox, Kelly Hall, Willie Goolsby, Lawson, Cline, Steve Rooks.

Clinton Mill (Clinton, S.C.), consolation winners: William Mims, George McMorris, Kenyon Robertson, Curtis Watson, Carter, Willard Hester, Leroy McGee, Tony Mobley, Mills.

Westinghouse (Duncan, S.C.): Morris, Church, Todd Finkley, Reggie Nance, Roy Hunter, Donnie Pressley, Maurice Woods, Peppers, Dill.

St. Francis Hospital (Greenville, S.C.): Bobby Harper, Jeffrey Harper, Hampton, Leonard Vernon, Houston, Gibson, Julius Thompson, Tyrone Brock, Montgomery, Brockman, Vest.

Cryovac (Simpsonville, S.C.): Chiles, Richard Montgomery, Frank Fredere, Lomax, Richard Booker, Patterson, Jerry Boyd, Hall, Cureton.

Textron (Greenville, S.C.): Lehman, Kenny Smith, Donnell Rosemond, Mitchell, S. Smith, Eric Robinson, Blanton, Andria Spurgeon.

Greenville Valve (Greenville, S.C.): Steve Crowe, Steve Smith, Nunnery, Skip Francis, Mike Crowe, Mortimer, Chad Montgomery, Shaw.

Sirrine Co. (Greenville, S.C.): Doug Karmel, Jim Merck, Merlina, Driggers, Seaborn, Richard Moseley, Coffee, Hoyle.

Southeastern Freight (Greenville, S.C.): Robert Pickel, Hyatt, Fred Richardson, Revis, Hawthorne, Charles Butler, Landson, Sullivan, Griffin.

3M (Greenville, S.C.): Rick Carwile, Byrd, McNeely, Eldorado Valentine, Caldwell.

Fiberweb (Greenville, S.C.): John Bennett, Larry Simmons, William Brown, Davis, Buff Brula, Dogan, Waddy Brown.

Saco-Lowell (Easley, S.C.): Don Benfield, Mike Allen, Chip Cantrell, Johnny Kelly, Cureton.

Michelin US-1 (Greenville, S.C.): Williams, Kerry Rasnake, Dellagrotte, Wilson, Jackson, Knapp.

Mike Davis Landscaping (Piedmont, S.C.): Bobby Henderson, Chad Lister, Steven Gay, James Brown, Travis Brannon, Wilson, James Grayson, Gravley.

Wunda Weve (Greenville, S.C.): Mack Burnside, Jerry Chapman, Joseph Davenport, Willis Abercrombie, Frank Mansell, Rogers, Troy Davenport.

Ace Sports (Greenville, S.C.): Hedgepath, Hamilton, Kevin Broderick, Joel Powell, Timothy Campbell, John Wilson, Brent Wilson.

Duke Power (Greenville, S.C.): Rathbone, Roy Foster, Hunter, Winchester, Townsend, F. Gregg, Doug Davis, T. Foster, Robinson, Garrett.

Northside Correctional Center (Greenville, S.C.): Mark Vaughn, Allen Boyd, Frank Carter, Step Murray, Barry Turner, Allen, Jones, Parker, Richardson.

Palmetto Enterprises (Greenville, S.C.): John Willis, Parker, Brian Brown, Chuck Thompson, C. Brown, King, Stock, Chuck Orr, Kid Haley, Dale Knight.

Roll Tech (Greenville, S.C.): Ronnie McAllister, Tim Lee, Brooks, Mitch Bryson, Brad Williams, Jimmy Mullinax, Elliott.

Sara Lee Bakery (Greenville, S.C.): Kelvin Riley, John Williams, Brian Smith, McMorris, Tim Wardlaw, Todd Collins, Deck, Holland, Black.

Meyer's Bakery (Greenville, S.C.): J. Suber, Owens, Greer, Bennett, Cox, Noah Suber, Wright, Scott, Floyd Jackson, Bradley.

C&S Bank (Greenville, S.C.): Mike Kelly, Chapman, Sarvis, Art Seaver, Silander.

Mt. Vernon Mill (Williamston, S.C.): Gary Williams, Kurt Pindron, Cochrane, David Wade, Hollis Mann, Taylor, Little.

Class C Men

Carper Real Estate (Greenville, S.C.), champions: Maurice Ramsey, Derrick Hammonds, Whitt, B. McGowans, Clarence Turnage, Manjue Sampson, Frye, Robinson, Anthony Jackson, Padgett, Anton Hatchett.

Metro (Greenville, S.C.), runners-up: Kevin Irby, Vincent Lynch, Breazeale, Kevin Benson, Williams, Jamie Rhome, Shawn Robinson, Jeff Evans, Glenn.

Palmetto Expo (Greenville, S.C.), consolation winners: Layne Fowler, Mike Jett, Bo Sims, Chad Waddell, Smith, Jake Cox, Gillespie, David Gulley.

Boyd's Spinners (Greenville, S.C.): Henry Bailey, William Coleman, Billy Davis, T. Davis, Omar Houston, Alex Thurmond, White, Beagle, Eddie Donald, Hackens, Brown.

Southeastern Products (Greenville, S.C.): Hobbs, Timmons, Mike Fair, Bill Harder, Cody Porter, Hough, Linton, Tazari Green, Pittario, Lamann Cruell, Rollins, Roddy, Adair.

TFBC (Greenville, S.C.): Royal, Kay, Blackwell, Sepko, Beebe, Terry, Bradenbury.

Dice & Associates (Greenville, S.C.): Corey Collins, Shell, Brown, Horn, Darryl Murray, Clayton, Derrick Miller, Burnside, Lee, Gray, Bledsoe, Tapp.

Chick-Fil-A (Greenville, S.C.): Michael Hamilton, Sidney Moore, Shoomond Williams, Eldrick Leamon, Jeff Maness, Ralph Roundtree, Ricky Robertson, Freeman.

LYF-TYM Products (Greenville, S.C.): Glenn Wates, Kevin Kerr, Stevens, Eudy, Davidson.

Washington City (Greenville, S.C.): Code, Meekins, Stallard, Wakefield, Chapman, Bowens, Albert, Duck.

Class A Women

Triple Play (Greenville, S.C.), champions: Melinda Hall, Renee Williams, Sherry Oldevak, Michelle Bryant, Natalie Kleckley, Roselyn Jennings, Saudia Roundtree, Lillie Young.

TKO (Greenville, S.C.), runners-up: Pearl Moore, Brenda Cain, Quisha Lawson, Nessie Harris, Lisa Diaz, Sherry Davis, Annette Alston, Morgan, Anderson.

St. Francis Hospital (Greenville, S.C.), consolation winners: Pam McCain, Toni Edwards, Sandra Vicary, Curry, Simpson, Gotshall, Jenkins, Kelley, Madre, Cox, Catina Freeman, Barton.

C. Dan Joyner (Greenville, S.C.): Simmons, Lyle, Hughes, Karen Neely, Cornish, Holcombe, S. Wilson, Rentz.

Skocdopole & Co. (Travelers Rest): Paulette Hawthorne, Jenkins, Rachel Graham, Cox, Vaughn, Tonya Williams, Lisa Davis, Holland, Buckner, Jones.

R&G (Greenville, S.C.): Jenny Lyerly, Tracy Rucker, Dawa Raab, Carla Campbell, Creech Cox, Freeman, Marsh.

Class C Women

Buncombe St. #1 (Greenville, S.C.): Maxwell, Breckenridge, Littlepage, Anderson.

Buncombe St. #2 (Greenville, S.C.): Smith, Banner.

1993

Executive Officers: Ward Williams, Ruppert Elliott, Fred Byrd, Fred McAbee, Charles Roddy, Jyles Phillips, Fred Powers, Clarence Thomas, Bill Hopkins, Pete McAbee, Ted Pittman.

Officers: Don Davis (Greenville, S.C.), President; Gary Pittman (Greenville, S.C.), 1st Vice President; Warren Rollins (Greenville, S.C.), 2nd Vice President; Dave Estes (Greenville, S.C.), Treasurer.

Executive Committee: Phil Clark (Greer, S.C.), Lewis Golden (Greenville, S.C.), Phil Harley (Greer, S.C.), Pam McCain (Greenville, S.C.), Darren Gazaway (Greenville, S.C.), Pearl Moore (Spartanburg, S.C.), Dan Pike (Greenville, S.C.), Jim Ball (Greenville, S.C.), James Meekins (Greenville, S.C.), Steve Brown (Greer, S.C.), David Banks (Shelby, N.C.), Randy LaFoy (Greenville, S.C.), Ronnie Hunter (Greenville, S.C.), Tom Davis (Greenville, S.C.), Mike Gravley (Greer, S.C.).

Open Division

Southeastern Products (Greenville, S.C.), champions: David Stamey, Tracey Garrick, David Brown, Barry Manning, Shawn Golden,

Southern Textile Basketball Tournament Rosters

Chris Leso, Joe Rhett, Edmond Wilson, Troy McKoy, Pete Faust.
  Sincerely Yours (Greenville, S.C.), runners-up: John Perry, Albert Mattison, Raymond Lawson, Melvin Patterson, Thompson, Hartness, Steven Rooks, Howard, Young, Lawson.
  S&M Sports (Shelby, N.C.): David Lawrence, John Reeves, Charlie Herbert, Pearson, Eric Coates, Metts.
  Orangemen (Columbia, S.C.): Tim Moody, Kelvin Richardson, Dawkins, Nige Ramage, Mack, Eric Bradford, Epps, Corey Dogan, Franklin.
  Dream Team (Shelby, N.C.): Harvey Macobson, Dewayne Long, Tyshawn Staggs, Donnell King, Tyrone Meadows, George Adams, Richard Hollis, Tim Montgomery.
  Fiber Processing (Greenville, S.C.): Gay Elmore, Jeff Phillips, Tegtmeyer, Stanley, Alsop, Jeff Brown, Benson.
  Other Teams: Poinsett Grocery (Greenville, S.C.), Chester's Chicken (Greenville, S.C.), Shaw's Boys (Greenville, S.C.).

CLASS A MEN

Greenville Fire Dept. (Greenville, S.C.), champions: Robert Sitton, Dempsey Cohen, Bryant Hyatt, Jeff Watson, Alan Anderson, Houghton, Nick Gaines, Scotty Freeman, Cedric Bennett, Ricky Anderson.
  Alice Mfg. (Easley, S.C.), runners-up: Roy Collins, Williams, Terry A. Smith, Terry McGowens, G. Davis, Scott Smith, R. Garrett, Donald Garrett, Valentine, Owens, Terry B. Smith.
  American Federal (Greenville, S.C.), consolation winners: Dean, Waddell, Eliasson, Welborn, Keith Westbury, Tom Coan, Joel Eudy, Mel Daniel.
  Michelin (Spartanburg, S.C.): Phillip Free, Terry Free, Wallace, Free, Moore, Blackledge, McCarroll.
  Michelin US-1 (Greenville, S.C.): Mark Cox, Joel Henderson, Clayton Rhodes, Bobby Williams, Rodney Sullivan, Cunningham, Bo Chambers.
  Cryovac (Simpsonville, S.C.): Johnson, Abercrombie, J.W. Wright, Gambrell, J. Wright, Brockman, Reid, Satterwhite, Hood.

CLASS B MEN

Clinton Mill (Clinton, S.C.), champions: William Mims, George McMorris, Curtis Watson, Willard Hester, Tony Mobley, Derrick Booker, Steve Coleman, Tim Davis, Bobby Hall, Norman Irby, Thomas Gary, David Satterfield, Sedric Hollard.
  Parker Mill (Greenville, S.C.), runners-up: Adams, Knox, David Simmons, Jan Berrea, Bobby Harris, John Williams, Geer, Joel Brooks, Reggie Teasley, Pleasant.
  Palmetto Expo (Greenville, S.C.), consolation winners: Cleve Cox, Hall, Bennett Cox, Cline, Yacu, Steve Rooks, S. Smith, Todd Collins, Vernon.
  SMC (Spartanburg, S.C.): Pete Rozzle, Kilisa Williams, Eddie Chapman, Gillespie, Antoine Huff, Shawn Colt, Brian Smith, Mitchell, Lamar Riley, Huggins, Eric Bright.
  St. Francis Hospital (Greenville, S.C.): Bobby Harper, Jeffrey Harper, Hampton, Leonard Vernon, Tyrone Brock, Brockman, Warner, Durham.
  Cryovac (Simpsonville, S.C.): Richard Montgomery, Frank Fredere, Lomax, Sims, Thomas, Alexander, Aaron Gamble, J.W. Wright.
  Greenville Valve (Greenville, S.C.): Steve Crowe, Steve Smith, Nunnery, Skip Francis, Mike Crowe, Shaw, Steve Crane, Johnson.
  Southeastern Freight (Greenville, S.C.): Robert Pickel, Hyatt, Hawthorne, Charles Butler, Williams, Kenneth Nelson, Boggs.
  Fiberweb (Greenville, S.C.): John Bennett, William Brown, Tom Davis, Griffin, Berry, William Pressley, Scott Cooper, Earl Gray.
  Saco-Lowell (Easley, S.C.): Don Benfield, Mike Allen, Chip Cantrell, Tim Powell, Trull, Nabors, Leo Strick.
  Davis-Morris Landscaping (Piedmont, S.C.): Chad Lister, Steven Gay, James Brown, Van Brannon, James Grayson, Robert.
  Wunda Weve (Greenville, S.C.): Jerry Chapman, Joe Abercrombie, Frank Mansell, Jimmy Rogers, Tracey Shrader, Kenny Bridwell, Holt.
  Ace Sports (Greenville, S.C.): James Hedgepath, M. Hamilton, Burgess, Brown, R. Hamilton, Wates.
  Northside Correctional Center (Greenville, S.C.): Mark Vaughn, Frank Carter, Kenneth Coleman, Eichelberger, Epps, Frazier, Benny Adams, Dion Irby, Jeff Anders, Kevin White, Zinga Devine.
  Mt. Vernon Mill (Williamston, S.C.): Gary Williams, Kurt Pindron, David Wade, Taylor, Little, Brush, Fox, Coffee.

Bi-Lo (Greenville, S.C.): Mann, Sherman, Milam, Harris, Bloise.

Rick's Landscaping (Greenville, S.C.): Marty Hopkins, Rick Tuck, Gray, Scott Townsend, Brian Lusk, Payne, Chris Hamilton, McSwain, Garrett.

GE (Greenville, S.C.): Gillespie, Foster, Woods, A. White, Haas, Lehman, Waddy.

Employee Benefits (Greenville, S.C.): Gravley, Steve Grant, Barry Lynch, John Wofford, Dave Ellison, Barton, Wagner, Todd Steryons, Cavin, Valkonis, Eric Hash, Sam Louis.

Alice Mfg. (Easley, S.C.): Alder, Bostic, Hawkins, Moss, Riddle, Robinson, A. Smith, J. Smith, Womack.

Other Teams: Northwestern Mutual (Greenville, S.C.), Bausch & Lomb (Greenville, S.C.).

Class C Men

Carper Real Estate (Greenville, S.C.), champions: Earl McPherson, Glenn Young, Jeff McInnis, Tavaris Johnson, Maktar Ndiaye, Deon Carson, Williams, Heywood Smith, Aveion Jones, Redd Davis.

Metro I (Greenville, S.C.), runners-up: Breazeale, Shammond Williams, Jeff Evans, Mike Minnifield, McGowan, Matthews, Tarrance Albert, Eldrick Leamon, Anthony Flanagan.

Dice & Associates (Greenville, S.C.), consolation winners: Horn, Kensey Adair, Erik Rothwell, Tommy Johnstone, Jett, Jamie Kelley, Matthew Rollins, Washington, Snyder.

Southeastern Freight (Greenville, S.C.): Antro Ferguson, Che Freeman, Brown, Travis Henderson, Mims.

Southeastern Products (Greenville, S.C.): Steve Norton, Patrick Garner, Mark Himes, Lamont Boozer, Nikki Davis, Ryan Streetman, Harper, Geoff Bentzel, Garner, Williams.

Dunean Mill (Greenville, S.C.): Shawn Robinson, Rimm, King, Rice, Tarrance, Topp.

Metro II (Greenville, S.C.): Chad Davis, Fortson, Caldwell, Robinson, Lindsay, Trey Staley, Dashun Cureton, McDavid, McGowens, Haynes.

Plan Home Health Care (Greenville, S.C.): Kevin Garnett, Graham, Hill, Aaron Shelton, Rice Booker, Derrick Drummond, Germany Thompson, Ivery, Hagen Rouse.

Carver Builders (Greenville, S.C.): Addis, Dean, David Thompson, Rush, Strange, Groves, Matt Nestburg.

St. Giles (Greenville, S.C.): Vowels, Dice, Sinclair, Clayton, Coker, Wilson, Thompson.

Sullivan's Sonics (Greenville, S.C.): Tony Boyd, Tyrone Dennis, Joshua Dowling, Kpoouwa Wharton, Jackson, Shennie McDaniel.

Poinsett Grocery (Greenville, S.C.): Fowler, Peake, Waddell, Titus Shelton, Shane McCravey, Mike Robbs, Chad Wilson, Fath, Moss.

Robbins Brothers (Simpsonville, S.C.): Sutton, Gibbons, Bo Bullock, Wilson, Sloan.

Brown's Bombers (Greenville, S.C.): Busby, Antonio Hargrove, Lagroon, McWilliams, Vance, Cobb, Sullivan.

Class A Women

M. Vick (Spartanburg, S.C.), champions: Pearl Moore, Elnora Jones, Jolette Law, Monique Pompili, Brenda Cain, Kim Booker, Lisa Diaz, Nessie Harris, Cheryl Nix, Marsha Williams, Lori Joyner, Law.

Triple Play (Greenville, S.C.), runners-up: Melinda Campbell, Renee Williams, Sherry Oldevak, Michelle Bryant, Young, Miller, Moore, Rhynehardt.

R&G (Greenville, S.C.), consolation winners: Catina Freeman, Jennifer Cox, Spearman, Karen Neeley, Gotshall, Hudson, Flournay, Lee Haley.

Greenville City Recreation (Greenville, S.C.): Katie Holden, Rooker, Jenkins, Simpson, Kelly.

NCR (Easley, S.C.): Dupre, Leatherwood, Lightsey, Nelson, Owens, Smith, Thorsland, Lin Williams, Garrett.

Gateway Balloons (Greenville, S.C.): Shannon Holland, Davis, Tracy Ricker, Cox, Williams, Vaughn, Beth Couture, Dawn Rabb.

--- 1994 ---

Executive Officers: Ward Williams, Ruppert Elliott, Fred Byrd, Charles Roddy, Ted Pittman, Jyles Phillips, Clarence Thomas, Bill Hopkins, Pete McAbee.

Officers: Don Davis (Greenville, S.C.), President; Gary Pittman (Greenville, S.C.), 1st Vice President; Warren Rollins (Greenville, S.C.), 2nd Vice President; Dave Estes (Greenville, S.C.), Treasurer; Ronnie Hunter (Greenville, S.C.), Secretary.

Executive Committee: Phil Clark (Greer,

S.C.), Lewis Golden (Greenville, S.C.), Darren Gazaway (Greenville, S.C.), Pearl Moore (Spartanburg, S.C.), Dan Pike (Greenville, S.C.), Jim Ball (Greenville, S.C.), James Meekins (Greenville, S.C.), Steve Brown (Greer, S.C.), David Banks (Shelby, N.C.), Randy LaFoy (Greenville, S.C.), Tom Davis (Greenville, S.C.), Mike Gravley (Greer, S.C.), Geary Dice, Eddie Moore, Terry Smith, Miller Bogan.

OPEN DIVISION

Southeastern Products (Greenville, S.C.), champions: Barry Manning, Joe Rhett, Pete Faust, Hal Henderson, Sammy Liberatore, Jamie Watson, Terry Acox.

Carolina Magic (Greenville, S.C.), runners-up: Kelvin Richardson, Thomas Mack, Nige Ramage, Warren Franklin, Paul Davis, Harvey Macobson, Kelly, Tim Moody.

S&M Sports (Shelby, N.C.): David Lawrence, Moore, Bolen, Joe Badgett, Brett Badgett, Bragg, Hutchins, Ervin, Bannister.

Chester's Chicken (Greenville, S.C.): Adams, Adrian Barton, Kris Burton, Thomas Gray, Griffin, Goolsby, Brock.

USCS (Spartanburg, S.C.): Parham, Miller, Coleman, Shane Hensley, Chaplin, Williams, Jamono Johnson, Allen, Vernon Redman, Walker, John Shell, Carr.

Panthers (Chicago, IL.): Brian Weathers, Dale Louis, R. Beaty, M. Beaty, Wally Willard, Merrill, Brown.

Sixers (Columbia, S.C.): Marion Haney, Eric Braford, Pearson, McGraw, Junior Laurie, Brook, Robinson.

CLASS A MEN

Greenville Fire Dept. (Greenville, S.C.), champions: Robert Sitton, Dempsey Cohen, Bryant Hyatt, Jeff Watson, Mitch Anderson, Scotty Freeman, Ricky Anderson, Nick Gaines, Cedric Bennett, David Houghton, Kenneth Spivey,

American Federal (Greenville, S.C.), runners-up: Dean, Jeff Waddell, Tom Coan, Mel Daniel, Stroud, Lynn, Burner, Sartin, Brown, Vorhees.

Alice Mfg. (Easley, S.C.): Tracy Williams, Terry Smith, Scott Smith, Ronald Garrett, Donald Garrett, Roy Owens, Bost.

Michelin (Spartanburg, S.C.): Terry Free, Moore, Blackledge, Casey, Davidson, Robinson.

Clinton Mill (Clinton, S.C.), consolation winners: McGee, Tim Williams, Boola, Hester, Robertson, Watson, Miller.

Other Teams: PPG Industries (Shelby, N.C.).

CLASS B MEN

Parker Mill (Greenville, S.C.), champions: David Simmons, Jan Berrio, David Geer, Joey Brooks, Bryant Bowen, Richard Pleasant, Wade Chappell, Spencer Black, Leo Turner, Fredrick Styles, Patrick McCullough, Jimmie Robinson.

Cryovac (Simpsonville, S.C.), runners-up: Frank Fredere, Lomax, Gerald Sims, Aaron Gamble, J.W. Wright, Tommy Hood, George Calhoun, Mike Chandler, Hardy, All, Johnson, Ellis.

Wunda Weve (Greenville, S.C.), consolation winners: Jerry Chapman, Willie Abercrombie, Kenny Bridwell, Joe Davenport, Lee Washington, Norris, Gilmore.

Roll Tech (Greenville, S.C.): Elliott, Mullinax, Ronnie McAlister, Brown, Hayworth, Darren Bayne, Atkinson.

Clinton Mill (Clinton, S.C.): George McMorris, Steve Coleman, David Satterfield, Thompson, Tim Gilliam, Steve Conway, Todd Alexander, Moses.

St. Francis Hospital (Greenville, S.C.): Bobby Harper, Jeffrey Harper, Leonard Vernon, Reginald Neal, Princell, Kumpel, Jackson.

Greenville Valve (Greenville, S.C.): Steve Crowe, Steve Smith, Shaw, Chad Campbell, Jordan, Cedric Mansell, Ellenburg.

Southeastern Freight (Greenville, S.C.): Robert Pickel, Hyatt, Charles Butler, Williams, Seth Wylie, Mike Adams, Travis Butler, Travis Henderson.

Fiberweb (Greenville, S.C.): John Bennett, William Brown, Cannon, Tim Allen, Rice, Berry Henderson, Tim Bennett, Dogan.

Saco-Lowell (Easley, S.C.): Don Benfield, Mike Allen, Tim Powell, Trull, Leo Strick, Jay Littleton, Gilstrap, Ballew.

Rick's Landscaping (Greenville, S.C.): Adam Hopkins, Rick Tuck, Scott Townsend, Chris Hamilton, Keith Abercrombie, McCall.

GE (Greenville, S.C.): Foster, Woods, Mike Haas, Chris Thompson, Terry Pepper, Sutton, Whitener, Sloan.

Employee Benefits (Greenville, S.C.): Gravley, Lister, T. Brannon, James Grayson, Brown, B. Henderson, Bo Henderson, D. Henderson, Gay.

Aneda Clock #1 (Greenville, S.C.): McRay,

Taylor, Christophyllis, Taylor, K. Petrokes, Spence.
Aneda Clock #2 (Greenville, S.C.): George Grumbles, Kiryshos, Diema Psychos, Nick Skinteros, Reagan Kline, Manios.
Dunean Mill (Greenville, S.C.): Straub, Mangrum, Rogers, Chapman, Grant, Isaiah Walker, Kip Haley, Todd Ellison, Phelps.
Enterprise All Stars (Greenville, S.C.): Tate, Lynn, Brian Lane, Gibson, Macey, Norman, Greg Thompson, Jay Cox, Hurley, Alan McNeer.
AMP-AKZO (Greenville, S.C.): J. Young, Ed Young, David Young, Little, Harrison, Oliver, Fowler, Caldwell, R. Young, Serald, Pinson.
Greenville Fire Dept. (Greenville, S.C.): J.C. Booker, Mike Vance, McKinney, Marcus Ledson, Leamon, Michael Sullivan, Kelley.
Jacob's Mfg. (Greenville, S.C.): Burton, Williams, Brooks, Nathan, Barton, Nicholson, Tony Mosley, McWhorter, Johnson, Romero.

Class C Men
Southeastern Products (Greenville, S.C.), champions: Ryan Streetman, Kevin Garnett, Derrick Drummond, Will Gallman, Hagen Rouse, Damous Anderson, Germany Thompson, Tim Heskett, Carlos Brown, Marcus Bryson.
Upperstate I (Chattanooga, Tenn.), runners-up: Tank Montgomery, Anthony Flanagan, Ryan Lookabill, Robert Fears, Tawambi Settles, Atlba Daniels, Tony Fortson, Larry Penn.
Dice & Associates (Greenville, S.C.), consolation winners: Tommy Johnstone, Matthew Rollins, Prince, Sarratt, Givens, McMorris, Derrick Earl, Rodney Spain, McKinney.
Carper Real Estate (Greenville, S.C.): Williams, Orr, Rafer Alston, Clifford Harrison, Blyden, Cedric Webber, Ward, Corey Wright, Franklin.
Metro (Greenville, S.C.): Chris McGowan, Tarrance Albert, C.C. Ivery, Griffin, Onta Hallstock, Cureton, Red McDavid, Smith, Head.
Sullivan's Sonics (Greenville, S.C.): Tyrone Dennis, Kpoouwa Wharton, B. Griffin, Antonio Hargrove, Lamont Vance, Durham, Alexander.
Poinsett Grocery (Greenville, S.C.): Titus Shelton, Shane McCravey, Reccus Nix, Geoff Bentzel, Patrick Garner, Erik Rothwell, Stan Simmons, Jermaine Gaines, Dowling.

Brown's Bombers (Greenville, S.C.): Busby, Darius Lagroon, Johnny Mitchell, Christopher Brashier, Jackson, Teague, Jason Boyd.
Sterling (Greenville, S.C.): David Nelson, Derrick Boyd, Tywan Harris, Peterson, Bennett, Quaveen Barber, Sullivan, Freeman, Shackleford, Pearson, Gordon, Fowler.
Peden (Greenville, S.C.): Chip Woodruff, Pauls, Smith, Jake Cox, McGowan, Matt Mashburn, Jeff Brown.
Subway (Greenville, S.C.): Beamon, Aaron Shelton, Josh Mills, Thompson, Carlos Washington, Eldrick Leamon, Ferguson, Graham.
Sonics (Abbeville, S.C.): Meadows, Spanky Hammonds, McClesky, Wilson, Gamble, Sutton, Bogains.
Washington City (Greenville, S.C.): Autorle Bowens, Dennie Cannon, Joe Owens, Mark Joseph, Yahnick Martin, Bob Green, Rory Hargrove, Jay West, Reginald Tarrance.
Upperstate II (Chattanooga, Tenn.): Antonio Carroll, Doug Beaty, Terrance Gist, Goodjoine, McGee, Ramon Robinson, Kinard, Kenneth Sims, Trey Staley.

Class A Women
Triple Play (Greenville, S.C.), champions: Melinda Campbell, Sherry Oldevak, Michelle Bryant, Karen Jenkins, Jackie Mattress, Rushia Brown, Jennifer Jones, Kathy Warner, Renee Williams, Michelle Gregoire,
T-Shirts Plus (Greenville, S.C.), runners-up: Pearl Moore, Monique Pompili, Lisa Diaz, Elnora Jones, Mary Jackson, Caine, Harvey.
Charleston Naval Base (Charleston, S.C.), consolation winners: Audrey Watson, Garrett, Hammond, Cooper, Currin, Felder.
Greenville All Stars (Greenville, S.C.): Jackie Moore, Sharon Davis, Carter, Cassidy, Williams, Beverly Dewberry, Simpson, Kelley, Tracy Ricker, Young.
Mauldin Video (Mauldin, S.C.): Boyd, Curtis, Bryson, Hill, Coleman, Chappell, Singleton, Byrd, Williams.

Class C Women
R&G (Greenville, S.C.), champions: Niki Meser, Kellie Edwards, Shannon Harde, Anicia Rimm, Lea Haley, Cullen Gutshall, Rachel Sloan, Kelly Moorhead, Holly Flournoy, Leshell Hughes, Lisa Langley.
Pizza Hut Spinners (Greenville, S.C.), runners-up: Blake, Carter, Sherell Harrison,

Southern Textile Basketball Tournament Rosters   Appendix 1   339

Nicole Jackson, Wilson, Griffin, Long, McKinney, McNeil, Rolanda Jackson,

Western 3A All Stars (Simpsonville, S.C.): Thompson, Butler, Nikki Blassingame, Cooley, Nelson, Kirksey, Wansley, Genia Webb, Garrison.

Triple Play (Greenville, S.C.): O'Shaughnessey, Hyde, King, McCoy, Rucker, Quinta Harris, Motler.

1995

Executive Officers: Ward Williams, Ruppert Elliott, Charles Roddy, Ted Pittman, Jyles Phillips, Pete McAbee, Don Davis.

Officers: Warren Rollins (Greenville, S.C.), President; Gary Pittman (Greenville, S.C.), 1st Vice President; Ronnie Hunter (Greenville, S.C.), 2nd Vice President; Dave Estes (Greenville, S.C.), Treasurer; Steve Brown (Greer, S.C.), Secretary.

Executive Committee: Phil Clark (Greer, S.C.), Lewis Golden (Greenville, S.C.), Darren Gazaway (Greenville, S.C.), Pearl Moore (Spartanburg, S.C.), Dan Pike (Greenville, S.C.), Jim Ball (Greenville, S.C.), James Meekins (Greenville, S.C.), David Banks (Shelby, N.C.), Randy LaFoy (Greenville, S.C.), Tom Davis (Greenville, S.C.), Mike Gravley (Greer, S.C.), Geary Dice, Eddie Moore, Terry Smith, Miller Bogan, Carlton Greene, Carol Riley, Shane Moody, Robbie Gravley, Ricky Batson, Ronnie Scarborough, Charles Breazeale.

OPEN DIVISION

Fat Friday's (Clemson, S.C.), champions: Patrick McCullar, David Young, Devin Gray, Milton Williams, Andre Bocain, Eldorado Valentine, Willie Goolsby, Tony Perkins, Thomas Gray, Charles Claxton, Ricky Jones, Bruce, Adrian Barton.

Sharkheads (Columbia, S.C.), runners-up: Roger Carr, Barry Kincaid, Kevin Burroughs, Steve McTeer, Adams, Mike Hoskins, Marion Haney.

S&M Sports (Shelby, N.C.): David Lawrence, Woodrow Bolen, Joe Badgett, Ervin, Bannister, Duante Johnson, Eru Coates, Henson, Hubert.

USCS (Spartanburg, S.C.): Parham, Rice Miller, Walker, Greg Rounds, Dwayne Prioleau, Lance Jude, James Roddy.

Showtime (Greenville, S.C.): Willie Battle, Harry Jeter, Robert Hutchinson, Scruggs, Thomas, Trent Boyle, James Griffin, T. Griggs, J. Griggs.

Anderson Shockers (Anderson, S.C.): E. Rodriquez, H. Rodriquez, Brad Watson, Reterford, Michael Proctor, Moore, Black, Aull.

S&R Auto (Shelby, N.C.): Christopher Michael, Benji Camp, Ram Huskey, Jack Degree, Jamie Miller, Kevin Makerson, Larry Ross, B. Miller.

MEN'S CLOSED DIVISION

PPG Industries (Shelby, N.C.), champions: David Hector (coach), Todd Wray, Wayne Wray, Vincent Haynes, Dennis Mintz, Mike Kelly, Donnie Harmon, Jeffrey Shade, Undra Miller, Antonio Washington, Kirby Allen, George Washington.

Carolina Circuit (Greenville, S.C.), runners-up: Ed Young, Vince Oliver, Caldwell, Paul Pinson, Sherman, Bobby Owens, Joe Young, Rodney Harrison.

Cryovac I (Simpsonville, S.C.), consolation winners: Lomax, Tommy Hood, George Calhoun, Mike Chandler, Michael Hardy, Johnson, All, Cureton, Satterwhite, Montgomery, Ed Baudu.

Meyer's Bakery (Greenville, S.C.): Suber, Mike Garrison, James Green, Scott, Shamley, Antonio Taylor, Wallace, Jackson.

City of Greenville (Greenville, S.C.): Mike Vance, J.C. Booker, Michael Sullivan, Leamon, Hall, McKinney, Corey Grossett, David Ferrell, William, Marcus Ledson.

Alice Mfg. #1 (Easley, S.C.): Scott Smith, Ronald Garrett, Donald Garrett, Roy Owens, Raines, Dale Rosemond, Cannon, K. Owens.

Alice Mfg. #2 (Easley, S.C.): Dee Curenton, Jacob Alder, Charles Crawford, Chapman, Bird, Vodanovich, George Davis.

Clinton Horsemen (Clinton, S.C.): Willard Hester, Kenyon Robertson, Carlton Watts, Babbs, Conway, B. Coleman, Ken Caldwell, Forrest Werts, Boyd.

Clinton Mill (Clinton, S.C.): Stanley McMorris, Price, Robertson, Danny Kinard, Franks, Todd Alexander, G. McMorris, Leake, Stevenson.

Cryovac II (Simpsonville, S.C.): Gerald Sims, Chris Williams, Berg, Cheeks, Gamble.

St. Francis Hospital (Greenville, S.C.): Bobby Harper, Jeffrey Harper, Charlie Park, Barone, Gibson, Brooks Stanton, Kelvin Washington, Perry, Trushing, Whitehurst.

Greenville Valve (Greenville, S.C.): Steve Crowe, Steve Smith, Tate, Chad Campbell.

Southeastern Freight (Greenville, S.C.): Robert Pickel, Hyatt, Charles Butler, Seth Wylie, Mike Adams, Cathcart, Cook.

Fiberweb (Greenville, S.C.): John Bennett, Brent Williams, Rice, Ken Sterling, Joe Robinson, T. Davis, R. Davis, Boule.

GE (Greenville, S.C.): Welton, Gillespie, Waddy, C. Thompson, Whitier.

Dunean Mill (Greenville, S.C.): Straub, James Mangrum, Kip Haley, Todd Ellis, Butler, Byron Arnold, Turner.

Enterprise All Stars (Greenville, S.C.): Wallace Tate, Gibson, Macey, Norman, Chris Owell, Cooper, Barnett.

Greenville Fire Dept. (Greenville, S.C.): Bryant Hyatt, Dempsey Cohen, Robert Sitton, Mitch Anderson, David Houghton, Jeff Watson.

Nissan (Greenville, S.C.): McCauley, Stewart, John Shell, Tim Campbell, Jerry Wilson, Miller.

YMCA (Greenville, S.C.): John Williams, Kendrick Meekins, Amory, O'dell, Walker, Eric Thompson, Stevens, Morgan, Bagwell, Larry Seyley.

Michelin US-1 (Greenville, S.C.): Cunningham, Dougherty, Bobby Williams, Mark Cox, Rasnake, Clayton Rhodes, Andrew Thompson, Joel Henderson, Chambers.

Sara Lee Bakery (Greenville, S.C.): Dirton, Kelvin Riley, Tim Wardlaw, Deck, McMorris, Wes Champion, Brian Smith.

Whitney Auto Auction (Greer, S.C.): Woody Eubanks, John Hooks, Perry, Jamie Kelly, D. Tapp, Brannon, Water.

Pizza Inn (Greenville, S.C.): Matt Cannon, Woods, David Baird, Jamie Palmer, Long, Chris Touchstone, Jason Durham, Bennett.

MCP (Clemson, S.C.): Marty Hopkins, Scott Townsend, Winchester, Rathbone, McSwain, Bob McCall, Gregg, Chris Hamilton.

CLASS C MEN

Southeastern Products (Greenville, S.C.), champions: Ryan Streetman, Derrick Drummond, Will Gallman, Hagen Rouse, Damous Anderson, Germany Thompson, Shawn Ellis, Chris McGowens, Darren Gazaway, Charlie Breazeale, Robert Pickel.

Carper Real Estate (Greenville, S.C.), runners-up: Seco Camero, Rob Turner, Kevin Carroll, Joe Aiken, Bernard Wheeler, James Hunter, Josh Gibson, Eric Burrow, Sadler, Scott.

Western Carolina V (Simpsonville, S.C.), consolation winners: Carlton Greene, Joe Brice, Tywan Harris, Bobo, Ron Bruton, Hargrove, Bailey, Carrington, Trangmar, Weatherall, Bob Greene.

Spain & Prince Sonics (Greenville, S.C.): Cedric Spain, McKinney, Antonio McGowan, Paul Givens, Matt Rollins, Stewart, Timothy Nesbitt, Gibson, Johnny Mitchell, Milbourne.

Upperstate I (Chattanooga, Tenn.): Goodjoine, Dixon, Williams, Wharton, Antonio Hargrove, Tony Boyd, Dennis, Carlos Ramage, Cook.

Metro I (Greenville, S.C.): C. Williams, Brewster, Fleming, Berry, Lewers, Williams, Gray, Antonio Davis, Chuck Gamble, Chapman, Kelly.

Metro II (Greenville, S.C.): James Griffin, Red McDavid, Hallstock, C.C. Ivery, Dennis Cannon, Hammonds, Bowens, Fisher, Byers, Bobb, Franklin.

Poinsett Grocery (Greenville, S.C.): Shane McCravey, Geoff Bentzel, Patrick Garner, Stan Simmons, Mark Trust, Trickett, Downs, Jamison, David Ivey.

Upperstate II (Chattanooga, Tenn.): Fortson, Moore, Ternae Ashley, Milner, Woodruff, McColley, Michael Jones, Robert Feas, Reno Earls, Jason Stewart.

Christ Church (Greenville, S.C.): Montague Laffitte, Will Holk, Brown, Colour, Kieron Walker, Hamrick, Rollins.

UCBA (Greenville, S.C.): Tarmaine Hall, Jamie Lewis, Alex Hawthorne, Ty Shine, Dante Bowman, Yusef Jenkins, Clark, Duncan.

Sullivan's Sonics (Greenville, S.C.): Kenyatta Campbell, Jaykest Davis, Dogan, Hamilton, Jackson, Hunt, Manley, Nate McDaniel, Perry Ridgeway, Revera, Harris.

Walmart (Greenville, S.C.): Joey Kelly, Chorballen, Erkins, Joshua Witt, Sparks, Martin.

Western Carolina (Simpsonville, S.C.): Tim Heskett, Lamont Vance, Davis, Steve Surratt, Clark, Lagroon, Linder.

Hillcrest (Simpsonville, S.C.): Corey Busbee, Dowling, Durham, Jeremy Ellison, Gray, Griffin, Jackson, Kpaduwa, Kelvin Robinson, Stolz, Webb.

Class A Women

Sissy's Furniture (Columbia, S.C.), champions: Joey Holman (coach), Carolyn Brown, Lisa Diaz, Shalia King, Lisha Morant, Patricia Houser, Iris Pearson, Latasha Anderson, Shayla Wilkins, Renee Suber, Harrison.

Triple Play (Greenville, S.C.), runners-up: Sherry Oldevak, Karen Jenkins, Jackie Mattress, Renee Williams, Michelle Gregoire, Karen Stanley, Shandy Bryan, Miller, Kramer.

T-Shirts Plus (Greenville, S.C.), consolation winners: Pearl Moore, Monique Pompili, Caine, Jones, Libby Carry, Dewberry, Satchell, Harris, Rosie Hall, Garner.

USCS (Spartanburg, S.C.): Shanita Scott, Johnson, Michele Graham, Stephanie Dacus, Lewis, Paula Blackwell.

Classy Ladies (Columbia, S.C.): Webb, Aiken, Norman, Tywanna Duck, Smith.

Sportsman Shop (Charleston, S.C.): Garrett, Stanton, Steed, Perry, Tara Currin, Evans, Washington.

1996

Board of Directors: Don Davis (Chairman); Ronnie Hunter, Ted Pittman, Gary Pittman, Dave Estes, Ruppert Elliott, Darren Gazaway, Charles Roddy, Steve Brown, Pete McAbee, Geary Dice, Carol Riley, Randy LaFoy, Warren Rollins, Jyles Phillips.

Executive Committee: Lewis Golden, Pearl Moore, Jim Ball, Dan Pike, Carlton Greene, Charles Breazeale, Terry Smith, Robbie Gravley, Ricky Batson, Mike Gravley, Ronnie Scarborough.

Open Division

Fiber Processing (Va.), champions: Gary Thompson, Steve Berger, Tim Dagostine, Dave Walker, Roger Alsup, Scott Yahike, Dwayne Price, Jim Shanley, Mark Craft, Gay Elmore.

Sharkheads (Columbia, S.C.), runners-up: Barry Kincaid, Cary Rich, Joe Rhett, Mike Wolfe, Smith, Jones, Wilson.

UNV (Greenville, S.C.): Scott Patterson, Henry Bailey, Durham, Chris Brashier, J. Dowling, Zach Dowling, Dondray Burton, Houston.

Represent (Greenville, S.C.): W. Coleman, Cook, N. Gardner, Ward, A. Smith, Staley, Wakefield, Burton, Turbo Moore, Moody, Gambrell.

Other Teams: Fat Friday's (Clemson, S.C.), Dream Team (Shelby, N.C.), Charleston Sportsman (Charleston, S.C.).

Men's Closed Division

Michelin US-1 (Greenville, S.C.), champions: Kelly Cunningham, Mark Cox, Clayton Rhodes, Andrew Thompson, Joel Henderson, Anthony Chambers, Dewey Roof, Doug McBee, Eric Tuggle.

PPG Industries (Shelby, N.C.), runners-up: Todd Wray, Wayne Wray, Vincent Haynes, Mike Kelly, Antonio Washington, Kirby Allen, T.L. Boyce, James Harbison, Shell.

AMP-AKZO (Greenville, S.C.), consolation winners: Lewis, Vince Oliver, Ed Young, Rodney Harrison, Sherman, Tracy Williams, Rick Moore.

Parker Mill (Greenville, S.C.): David Simmons, Greer, Blake Sizemore, Richards, Donnie Westmoreland, Brooks, Henderson, Martin, Bryant Bowers.

Cryovac (Simpsonville, S.C.): Lomax, Tommy Hood, Satterwhite, Sims.

St. Francis Hospital (Greenville, S.C.): Bobby Harper, Jeffrey Harper, Simmons, Durham, Cox, Ballenger.

Southeastern Freight (Greenville, S.C.): Robert Pickel, Hyatt, Seth Wylie, Mike Adams, Bruster, Bagwell, Griffin.

Fiberweb (Greenville, S.C.): John Bennett, Brent Williams, Rice, S. Davis, Clyde Davis, Wright, Foster, Tim Allen, Bailey.

GE (Greenville, S.C.): Whitner, Foster, Wood, Pepper, Shaw, Sloan, Mile.

Dunean Mill (Greenville, S.C.): Straub, James Mangrum, Kip Haley, Byron Arnold, Tankersley, Walker, Chapman, Humbert.

YMCA (Greenville, S.C.): John Williams, Kendrick Meekins, Walker, Eric Thompson, Morgan, Henderson, Huskey, Spain, Boyette.

MCP (Clemson, S.C.): Marty Hopkins, Scott Townsend, Bob McCall, Gregg, Chris Hamilton, Martin, Davis, Foster.

Alice Mfg. (Easley, S.C.): Raines, Chapman, Pullen, Valentine, Holcombe, Moore, Scott Smith.

Class C Men

Dick James (Greenville, S.C.), champions: Travis Smith, Dustin Childress, Lamont Vance, Mac Harper, Jarvis Davis, Steve Surratt, Shawn Ellis, Charles Wright, Simon Moore, Lamont Babb.

Poinsett Grocery (Greenville, S.C.), runners-up: Downs, Quincy Haywood, Brooks, Yahnik Martin, Andy Wilson, Adam Ziemer, Joesph Brice, Baker.

Carper Real Estate (Greenville, S.C.), consolation winners: Scotty Scott, Kokic, Edison, High, Stewart, Boyd, Curt Small, Karreda McCray.

Spain & Prince Sonics (Greenville, S.C.): Cedric Spain, McKinney, Paul Givens, Prince, Gamble, Durand, Booker, Hughes.

Upperstate (Chattanooga, Tenn.): Jackie Williams, Cook, Andre Bobo, Nubeia, Onta Hallstock, Moss, Kethcover.

Metro I (Greenville, S.C.): Kelly, Ivery, White, Lewers, Phelps, Antron Burton, Finley, Stehle, Byrd, Bailey, Sloan.

Brown's Bombers (Greenville, S.C.): Warren, Patrick, Stoltz, Gray, Ryan, Griffin, Sullivan.

SC Bulls (Greenville, S.C.): Rouse, James Griffin, Dennis Cannon, Marcus Bryson, Bailey, Leamon, Rhodes, Carter, Clark.

Cavalier Warriors (Greenville, S.C.): Jennings, Laffitte, Hamrick, Sullivan, Meadows, Monroe, Jackson, Austin.

Skywalkers (Piedmont, S.C.): Webb, Franklin, Youngblood, Ledbetter, Campbell, Scott, Howard, Spear, Rhodes.

Alford Real Estate (Greenville, S.C.): White, Craft, Williams, Gracley, Wilson.

Other Teams: Metro II (Greenville, S.C.), UCBA Jr. (Greenville, S.C.), UCBA Sr. (Greenville, S.C.), Sullivan's Sonics (Greenville, S.C.), Hillcrest (Simpsonville, S.C.), Washington City (Greenville, S.C.), Suns (Greenville, S.C.), Berea (Greenville, S.C.).

CLASS A WOMEN

WCCP (Clemson, S.C.), champions: Renee Williams, Melinda Campbell, Dana Puckett, Michelle Gregoire, Jackie Roberts, Shandy Bryan, Angie Crosby, Melisa Mandenhall.

King Valley (Columbia, S.C.), runners-up: Tasha Anderson, Morant, Morgan, Wilkins, Shannon Johnson, Goodwin, DeLoche, Carolyn Brown.

Low Country All Stars (Charleston, S.C.), consolation winners: Evans, Sneed, Maria Williams, Kelli Garrett, Perry, Joy Clifford, Brenda Washington.

Lady Hornets (Greenville, S.C.): Moore, Willis, Thorne, Hammonds, Lincoln, Byrd.

CLASS C WOMEN

Upstate Lady Sonics (Greenville, S.C.), champions: Janet Vicks, Ashleigh Fuller, Krystal Scott, Maya Grady, Sarah Rowan, Heather Crowe, Crishina Hill, Eboni Littlejohn, Caltresha McKinney, April Mitchell.

Roll Tech (Greenville, S.C.), runners-up: Huffman, Terri Rucker, Owens, Shorelle Harrison, Blake, Clayton, Dopplehuer, Lynn, Lang, Nolan.

Marquee (Greenville, S.C.), consolation winners: Jackson, Wyatt, Shelby, Woody, Cissy Hunter, Parris, Ross, White, Monica Davis, Bennett, Rachel Sloan.

R&G (Greenville, S.C.): S. Brown, Gailey, Mathis, Poteat, Tulley, Neal, Tracey Brown, Coplin.

--- 1997 ---

Board of Directors: Charles Roddy (Chairman); Ronnie Hunter, Ted Pittman, Dave Estes, Ruppert Elliott, Darren Gazaway, Steve Brown, Don Davis, Pete McAbee, Carol Riley, Randy LaFoy, Warren Rollins, Jyles Phillips.

Executive Committee: Lewis Golden, Jim Ball, Dan Pike, Carlton Greene, Charles Breazeale, Joe Stewart, Terry Smith, Ronnie Scarborough, Geary Dice, John Gilstrap.

MEN'S CLOSED DIVISION

Parker Mill (Greenville, S.C.), champions: David Simmons, Dan Greer, Joey Brooks, Ken Henderson, Joey Tedford, Terry Cobb, Tim Young, Bryant Bowens.

YMCA (Greenville, S.C.), runners-up: Eric Thompson, Danny Morgan, Chris Huskey, Randy Boyette, Tim Moody, Paul Givens, Armory O'Dell, Jay Spain, Cedric Spain, Lloyd, Darren Tooley.

Cryovac (Simpsonville, S.C.): Reginald Lomax, Paul Satterwhite, Gerald Sims, Brian Crowe, Rodney McKinney, Richard Montgomery, Randy Raines, Kevin Henderson, Rami El-Boyard.

GE (Greenville, S.C.): Stanley Sloan, Thomas Wood, Albert Gillespie, Bill Foster.

MCP (Clemson, S.C.): Marty Hopkins, Scott Townsend, Bob McCall, Chris Hamilton, Doug Davis, Tony Foster, Rick Tuck, Fred Gregg.

Alice Mfg. (Easley, S.C.): Terry Gowens, Jody Collins, Roy Owens, Dwayne Gilbert,

Southern Textile Basketball Tournament Rosters   Appendix 1   343

Roosevelt Chapman, Matthew Valentine, Jerron Lawrence.

U.S. Post Office (Greenville, S.C.): James Bell, Darrell Washington, Andre Jenkins, Santos Sullivan, James Donald, David Cooper, Donald Pollian, Garry Nash.

AMP-AKZO (Greenville, S.C.): Andrew Sherman, Rodney Harrison, Ed Young, Vince Oliver, Keith Williams, Joe Young, Stanley Dirton, Keith Caldwell, Ed Carroll.

Northern Sports Officials (Greenville, S.C.): Mike McMorris, Kelvin Riley, John Williams, Brian Smith, Avery Deck, Don Johnson, T.C. Gray, Tim Wardlaw.

O'Neal Inc. (Greenville, S.C.): Billy Dunlap, Jay Cox, Brad Dunn, Andrew Wilson, Walter Henson, Michael Bones, Scott Sherwin.

Allied Signal (Greer, S.C.): Donnell Rosemond, Kenny Smith, Russell Blanton, Reggie Terrance, Jason Smith, Ray Johnson, Mark Joesph, Michael Fisher.

Kemet (Pickens, S.C.): Aaron Whitmire, Chris Oliver, Anthony Shands, William Miller, Ray Owens, Homanda Thompson, Chris Kimbrell, Chad Brannon, Shane Phelps, O.J. Tompkins, Chris Edwards, Chris McDonald, K. Suit, D. Fowler, B. Andrew, Michael Crawley.

City of Greenville (Greenville, S.C.): Tommy Norman, Dreco Leamon, Mike Baker, Mike Vance, J.C. Booker, David Farrow, Mike Sullivan, Quentin Thompson, Artis Johnson.

CLASS C MEN

Carper Real Estate (Greenville, S.C.), champions: Chuck Edison, Will Tucker, Jonathon Neely, Dan Tollens, Cortland Freeman, Shaun Wade, Chet King, Alex Fair, Clinton Brown, Mark Henderson.

Anderson Shockers (Anderson, S.C.), runners-up: Clay Huggins, James Dawson, Antwon Jones, Will Hellaums, Eric Meekins, Fermico Little, Rasheed West, Kevin Reed.

Spain & Prince Sonics (Greenville, S.C.): Marc Gamble, Marcus Monroe, Travis Smith, Lamont Vance, Corey Boggains, Chris Fuller, Trey Meadows, Rytorin Gary, Shaun Spain.

Upperstate Youth (Greenville, S.C.): Andre Bobo, Antonio Davis, Demetrius Fleming, Cliff Holsenberg, Adam Styles, Mike Thomas, John Warren, Rashad Harrison.

Upstate Jrs. (Chattanooga, Tenn.): Andrea Goodman, Travis Wilson, Bruce Craig, Josh Linder, Thomas Young, Matt Childress, Mike Wallace, Charles Sullivan, J.R. Byrd, Kendrick Spearman.

Upstate Srs. (Chattanooga, Tenn.): Rodney Gilliam, Derrick Burton, Keith Stringer, Sal Smith, Carlos Copeland, D.J. Humphries, Daniel Miller, Marcus Bryson, Derrick Jackson, Darant Jackson.

SC Bulls (Greenville, S.C.): Wayne Clark, John Houston, Kenyatta Campbell, Joe Hamilton, Lamont Speaks, Rhdala Sojo, Steve Carter, Richard Vernon.

Who's Who (Greenville, S.C.): Calvin Austin, Keith Cooley, Willie Brown, Dominique Clarke, B.J. Jackson, Andre Brantley, Calvin Norris, Anthony Henderson, Dana Jones, Andre Igaroon, Marco Apustron.

Southeastern Products (Greenville, S.C.): Matt Rollins, Tyler Burgess, Jonathan Williams, Demetrius Harris, Bradd Reed, Tory Atkins, Brett Myers, Alex Goare, Aaron Levett.

Laurens AAU (Laurens, S.C.): Ryan Grayson, Jwan Robinson, Travis Evans, Ron Smith, Willie Brown, Archie Grant, Josh Lee, Marcus Whitmore.

Christ Church (Greenville, S.C.): H. Cleveland, David Ryan, Hal Shaw, Rusty Hamrick, Jimmy Ryan.

Interstate-Johnson-Lane (Greenville, S.C.): Davey Breazeale, Charles Wright, D.J. Hughes, Collins Rouse, James Griffin, Dennis Cannon, Shawn Bailey, Pete Newbia.

Greer AAU (Greer, S.C.): Kenny Ruby, Lee Rains, Hasson Smith, Jimmy Gravley, Shad Harvey, Burt Epting, Matt Vickery, Brandon Howard.

Southern Oaks (Piedmont, S.C.): Kevin Campbell, Kevin Sanders, Will Merritt, Josh Lankford, Derrell Jackson, Derek Watson, Caron Davis, Corey.

Golden Strip (Mauldin, S.C.): Dustin Willis, Matthew Manley, Jonathon Taylor, Blake Holmes, Nathaniel Perry, Freddie Williams, Kevin Farmer, Bramlette Litinbu, Adams Lloyd, David Akins.

CLASS A WOMEN

King Valley (Columbia, S.C.), champions: Carolyn Brown, Lisa Diaz, Michelle Murray, Patricia Houser, Petrinia Houser, Keshia Hickman, Cynthia Little, Angela Dickey, Melody Davis, Christeen Hagood, Maeretta Luallen, Shayla Wilkens.

Low Country All Stars (Charleston, S.C.), runners-up: Andrea Evans, Maria Williams,

Kelli Garrett, Mary Perry, Tammy Hammonds, Annette Alston, LaTeese Irving, O. Cooper.

WPJM (Greer, S.C.), consolation winners: Beverly Dewberry, Mary Simpson, Karen Jenkins, Sherry Payton, Valerie Scott, Dedra Howard, Tina Fleeman, Sharon Davis, Porsche Bennett.

WCCP (Clemson, S.C.): Renee Williams, D. Kidd, J. Stinson, A. Rhoad, S. Ridgeway, L. Cottrell, R. Miller, A. Schuler, S. Butler, Ade, A. Kwange.

I&T Connection (Lexington, S.C.): Iris Pearson, Latasha Anderson, Lisa Marant, Rita Whitmire, Brenda Williams, Jessica Barr, Tara Hopkins, KeShawn Jacobs, Latina Jeter, Trina Lattery, Sandra Dickerson.

St. Francis Hospital (Greenville, S.C.): Kathy Burns, Jenny Lylerly, Pam Putman, Kena Kelly, Nancy Gould, Deridge Hixson, Allison Waters, Kathy Hopkins, Joy Shuck.

Class C Women

R&G (Greenville, S.C.), champions: Rachel Sloan, Laura Robinson, Katinea Neal, Amanda Fancher, Shannon Tulley, Kenya Young, Monica Choplin, LaShonda Maxwell, Jamie Johnson, Katherine Gailey, Summer Woods.

Laurens AAU (Laurens, S.C.), runners-up: Christy Blackwell, Yoneko Allen, Chrisoula Floyd, Jevorah Whitfield, Latreses Davis, Nardia Moore, Chrissa Cross, Chicara Patterson, Valerio Evans.

Upstate Lady Sonics (Greenville, S.C.), consolation winners: Maya Grady, Krystal Scott, Trece McKinney, Eboni Littlejohn, Ashleigh Fuller, Crishina Hill, Heather Crowe, Tasha Hemphill.

Berea (Greenville, S.C.): Felicia Hellams, Terri Rucker, Tyesha Leamon, Constance Byrd, Camile Brown.

Appendix 2

All Southern (All Tournament) Teams

Denotes Class B players chosen All Southern in the Tournament's early years and placed on the Class A squad.

1924

CLASS A MEN
Walter Henson, Woodside Mill (Greenville, S.C.)
Hubert Nolin, Monaghan Mill (Greenville, S.C.)
____ Bunting, New Holland Mill (Gainesville, Ga.)
Arthur Bedenbaugh, Pacific Mill (Columbia, S.C.)
Jim Oeland, Converse Mill (Spartanburg, S.C.)

1925

CLASS A MEN
Bob Ingram, Pacific Mill (Columbia, S.C.)
Hubert Nolin, Monaghan Mill (Greenville, S.C.)
Paul Barbare, Judson Mill (Greenville, S.C.)
Buddy Martin, Pacific Mill (Columbia, S.C.)
Jim Oeland, Converse Mill (Spartanburg, S.C.)

1926

CLASS A MEN
Dave Sanders, Dunean Mill (Greenville, S.C.)
C.B. Mooneyham, Spartan Mill (Spartanburg, S.C.)
Paul Barbare, Lyman Mill (Lyman, S.C.)
Britt Bryson, Piedmont Mill (Piedmont, S.C.)
Lawrence Pruitt, Lyman Mill (Lyman, S.C.)

1927

CLASS A MEN
Dick Wilson, Victor Mill (Greer, S.C.)
Johnny Beasley, Piedmont Mill (Piedmont, S.C.)
Paul Barbare, Lyman Mill (Lyman, S.C.)
Clyde Gilreath, Piedmont Mill (Piedmont, S.C.)
D.K. Smith, Lyman Mill (Lyman, S.C.)

1928

CLASS AA MEN
D.K. Smith, Lyman Mill (Lyman, S.C.)
Dick Wilson, Victor Mill (Greer, S.C.)
Fred Emerson, Lyman Mill (Lyman, S.C.)
Fletcher Heath, Victor Mill (Greer, S.C.)
Lawrence Pruitt, Lyman Mill (Lyman, S.C.)

CLASS A MEN
Clarence Higginbotham, Calloway Mill (LaGrange, Ga.)
Ansel Kay, Judson Mill (Greenville, S.C.)
Irwin Spence, Calloway Mill (LaGrange, Ga.)
Glen Simpson, Calloway Mill (LaGrange, Ga.)
*Felton Leverette, Lanett Mill (Lanett, Ala.)

CLASS A WOMEN
____ Silvers, Beacon Mill (Swannanoa, N.C.)
Lucille Foster, Monaghan Mill (Greenville, S.C.)

Madge Doggett, Piedmont Mill (Piedmont, S.C.)
Carlie Penley, Beacon Mill (Swannanoa, N.C.)
Thelma Boiter, Piedmont Mill (Piedmont, S.C.)
Katherine Shope, Beacon Mill (Swannanoa, N.C.)

―――― 1929 ――――

Class A Men
James Sargent, Pelzer Mill (Pelzer, S.C.)
Walter Bozeman, Avondale Mill (Alexander City, Ala.)
*Odell Roberts, Avondale Mill (Alexander City, Ala.)
Felton Leverette, Lanett Mill (Lanett, Ala.)
*Edwin Price, Avondale Mill (Alexander City, Ala.)

Class A Women
Oveida Henderson, Monaghan Mill (Greenville, S.C.)
*Sara Kennett, Orr Mill (Anderson, S.C.)
Katherine Shope, Beacon Mill (Swannanoa, N.C.)
Inez Brown, Monaghan Mill (Greenville, S.C.)
Elvie Osteen, Piedmont Mill (Piedmont, S.C.)
Reavelle Penley, Beacon Mill (Swannanoa, N.C.)

―――― 1930 ――――

Class A Men
Esco Leopard, Lonsdale Mill (Seneca, S.C.)
*Albert Bullington, Spartan Mill (Spartanburg, S.C.)
*Leon Dill, Victor Mill (Greer, S.C.)
Courtney Heath, Lonsdale Mill (Seneca, S.C.)
*Homer Kelly, Dunean Mill (Greenville, S.C.)

Class A Women
Lucille Foster, Monaghan Mill (Greenville, S.C.)
Virginia Kennett, Orr Mill (Anderson, S.C.)
Willie McMahan, Beacon Mill (Swannanoa, N.C.)
Madge Turner, Dunean Mill (Greenville, S.C.)
Kathleen Cooper, Orr Mill (Anderson, S.C.)
Minnie Pack, Piedmont Mill (Piedmont, S.C.)

―――― 1931 ――――

Class A Men
Walter Bozeman, Avondale Mill (Alexander City, Ala.)
Esco Leopard, Lonsdale Mill (Seneca, S.C.)
Odell Roberts, Avondale Mill (Alexander City, Ala.)
Fletcher Heath, Lonsdale Mill (Seneca, S.C.)
Elliott Eubanks, Lyman Mill (Lyman, S.C.)

Class A Women
Lucille Foster, Monaghan Mill (Greenville, S.C.)
Sarah Jordan, Pelzer Mill (Pelzer, S.C.)
Jenny Cathey, American Enka (Enka, N.C.)
Charlotte Smith, American Enka (Enka, N.C.)
Virginia Langston, Monaghan Mill (Greenville, S.C.)
Vera Blackwell, Dunean Mill (Greenville, S.C.)

―――― 1932 ――――

Class A Men
Esco Leopard, Lonsdale Mill (Seneca, S.C.)
Leon Dill, Victor Mill (Greer, S.C.)
William Pruitt, Lonsdale Mill (Seneca, S.C.)
Marvin Stevenson, Lonsdale Mill (Seneca, S.C.)
Sam Fayonsky, Winnsboro Mill (Winnsboro, S.C.)

Class A Women
Lucille Foster Thomas, Monaghan Mill (Greenville, S.C.)
Sarah Jordan, Pelzer Mill (Pelzer, S.C.)
Willie Justus, American Enka (Enka, N.C.)
Virginia Langston, Monaghan Mill (Greenville, S.C.)
Charlotte Justus, American Enka (Enka, N.C.)
Faye Herron, American Enka (Enka, N.C.)

―――― 1933 ――――

Class A Men
James Suddeth, Victor Mill (Greer, S.C.)
Joe Gibson, Lyman Mill (Lyman, S.C.)
Connie Mack Berry, Monaghan Mill (Greenville, S.C.)
Fletcher Heath, Monaghan Mill (Greenville, S.C.)
Alvin Waters, Victor Mill (Greer, S.C.)

All Southern (All Tournament) Teams Appendix 2 347

Class A Women
Helen Shuford, American Enka (Enka, N.C.)
Dessie Pettigru, Lyman Mill (Lyman, S.C.)
Oveida Henderson, Monaghan Mill (Greenville, S.C.)
Gena Bright, Lyman Mill (Lyman, S.C.)
Charlotte Justus, American Enka (Enka, N.C.)
Helen Black, Glen Lowery Mill (Whitmire, S.C.)

1934

Class A Men
Ray Wilson, Winnsboro Mill (Winnsboro, S.C.)
John Emery, Pelzer Mill (Pelzer, S.C.)
Connie Mack Berry, Monaghan Mill (Greenville, S.C.)
Jack Ohlsen, Winnsboro Mill (Winnsboro, S.C.)
Nick Elder, Monaghan Mill (Greenville, S.C.)

Class A Women
Sarah Jordan, Pelzer Mill (Pelzer, S.C.)
Mary Byrd, American Enka (Enka, N.C.)
Dessie Pettigru, Lyman Mill (Lyman, S.C.)
Lillie Ballard, Pelzer Mill (Pelzer, S.C.)
Nina Barry, Lyman Mill (Lyman, S.C.)
Helen Kelly, Pelzer Mill (Pelzer, S.C.)

1935

Class A Men
Willie Riddle, Dunean Mill (Greenville, S.C.)
Ted Cabiness, Victor Mill (Greer, S.C.)
Frank McDaniel, Judson Mill (Greenville, S.C.)
Sam Turner, Dunean Mill (Greenville, S.C.)
Bert Hill, Poe Mill (Greenville, S.C.)

Class A Women
Mary Byrd, American Enka (Enka, N.C.)
Sarah Jordan, Pelzer Mill (Pelzer, S.C.)
Mary Clark, American Enka (Enka, N.C.)
Terrell Hollifield, American Enka (Enka, N.C.)
Grace Garrison, Stanly Mill (Oakboro, N.C.)
Virginia Dickson, Pelzer Mill (Pelzer, S.C.)

1936

Class A Men
John Emery, Piedmont Mill (Piedmont, S.C.)
Hoyt Hambright, Chatham Mfg. (Elkin, N.C.)
Don Campbell, Chatham Mfg. (Elkin, N.C.)
Ed Maxwell, Chatham Mfg. (Elkin, N.C.)
James Suddeth, Dunean Mill (Greenville, S.C.)

Class A Women
Eva Saylors, Pelzer Mill (Pelzer, S.C.)
Mary Clark, American Enka (Enka, N.C.)
Mary Byrd, American Enka (Enka, N.C.)
Blanche Medford, American Enka (Enka, N.C.)
Lois Allen, American Enka (Enka, N.C.)
Nina Barry, Lyman Mill (Lyman, S.C.)

1937

Class A Men
John Emery, Piedmont Mill (Piedmont, S.C.)
Bud Kinard, Spartan Mill (Spartanburg, S.C.)
Ford Waldrop, Piedmont Mill (Piedmont, S.C.)
Bert Hill, Southern Bleachery (Taylors, S.C.)
Clarence Rushing, Southern Bleachery (Taylors, S.C.)

Class A Women
Melba Poole, Chatham Mfg. (Elkin, N.C.)
Mary Clark, American Enka (Enka, N.C.)
Louise Wood, Lanett Mill (Lanett, Ala.)
Kathryn Whitner, Chatham Mfg. (Elkin, N.C.)
Blanche Medford, American Enka (Enka, N.C.)
Nina Barry, Lyman Mill (Lyman, S.C.)

1938

Class A Men
John Emery, Piedmont Mill (Piedmont, S.C.)
Charles Suddeth, Southern Bleachery (Taylors, S.C.)
Carlos Halleman, McCrary Hosiery Mill (Asheboro, N.C.)
Bert Hill, Southern Bleachery (Taylors, S.C.)
Mays Williams, Judson Mill (Greenville, S.C.)

Class A Women
Connie Harley, Drayton Mill (Spartanburg, S.C.)
Melba Poole, Chatham Mfg. (Elkin, N.C.)
Ella Corn, American Enka (Enka, N.C.)
Cleo Dunn, Chatham Mfg. (Elkin, N.C.)
Beulah Splawn, Drayton Mill (Spartanburg, S.C.)
Dorothy Samuels, Chatham Mfg. (Elkin, N.C.)

---------- 1939 ----------

Class A Men
Neil Cockerham, McCrary Hosiery Mill (Asheboro, N.C.)
Paul Roy, McCrary Hosiery Mill (Asheboro, N.C.)
Connie Mack Berry, Southern Bleachery (Taylors, S.C.)
Bert Hill, Southern Bleachery (Taylors, S.C.)
Bob Klein, Dixie Mercerizing (Lupton City, Tenn.)

Class A Women
Louise Wood, Lanett Mill (Lanett, Ala.)
Jewell Bishop, Lanett Mill (Lanett, Ala.)
Connie Harley, Drayton Mill (Spartanburg, S.C.)
Melba Poole, Chatham Mfg. (Elkin, N.C.)
Jennie Sherrill, Chatham Mfg. (Elkin, N.C.)
Dorothy Samuels, Chatham Mfg. (Elkin, N.C.)

---------- 1940 ----------

Class A Men
Harry Anderson, Dixie Mercerizing (Lupton City, Tenn.)
Ray Wilson, Southern Bleachery (Taylors, S.C.)
Clint Norman, Peerless Woolen Mill (Rossville, Ga.)
Grayson Davis, Dixie Mercerizing (Lupton City, Tenn.)
Bert Hill, Southern Bleachery (Taylors, S.C.)

Class A Women
Wilma Whitlock, Drayton Mill (Spartanburg, S.C.)
Beulah Brown, American Enka (Enka, N.C.)
Ann Lineback, Chatham Mfg. (Elkin, N.C.)
Melba Poole, Chatham Mfg. (Elkin, N.C.)
Jennie Sherrill, Chatham Mfg. (Elkin, N.C.)
Mildred Reynolds, American Enka (Enka, N.C.)

---------- 1941 ----------

Class A Men
Bert Hill, Southern Bleachery (Taylors, S.C.)
Harry Anderson, Dixie Mercerizing (Lupton City, Tenn.)
Hugh Hampton, Hanes Hosiery Mill (Winston-Salem, N.C.)
C.R. McIntosh, Peerless Woolen Mill (Rossville, Ga.)
Grayson Davis, Dixie Mercerizing (Lupton City, Tenn.)

Class A Women
Leva Smith, Chatham Mfg. (Elkin, N.C.)
Beulah Brown, American Enka (Enka, N.C.)
Melba Poole, Chatham Mfg. (Elkin, N.C.)
Gussie Couch, American Enka (Enka, N.C.)
Jennie Sherrill, Chatham Mfg. (Elkin, N.C.)
Nellie Keaton, Dixie Mercerizing (Lupton City, Tenn.)

---------- 1942 ----------

Class A Men
Louis Fitzgerald, Peerless Woolen Mill (Rossville, Ga.)
Neal Cockerham, McCrary Hosiery Mill (Asheboro, N.C.)
Harry Anderson, Dixie Mercerizing (Lupton City, Tenn.)
Willie Wilbanks, Southern Bleachery (Taylors, S.C.)
Hugh Hampton, Hanes Hosiery Mill (Winston-Salem, N.C.)

Class A Women
Ann Lineback, Chatham Mfg. (Elkin, N.C.)
Wilma Whitlock, Drayton Mill (Spartanburg, S.C.)
Mary Masten, Hanes Hosiery Mill (Winston-Salem, N.C.)
Aniece Shields, Hanes Hosiery Mill (Winston-Salem, N.C.)
Jannie Sherrill, Chatham Mfg. (Elkin, N.C.)
Leva Smith, Chatham Mfg. (Elkin, N.C.)

All Southern (All Tournament) Teams   Appendix 2   349

1946

Class A Men
Hugh Hampton, Hanes Hosiery Mill (Winston-Salem, N.C.)
Ward Williams, Dunean Mill (Greenville, S.C.)
Louis Fitzgerald, Peerless Woolen Mill (Rossville, Ga.)
Coot Greer, Hanes Hosiery Mill (Winston-Salem, N.C.)
John Barger, Peerless Woolen Mill (Rossville, Ga.)

Class A Women
Ann Lineback, Chatham Mfg. (Elkin, N.C.)
Jannie Lackey, Chatham Mfg. (Elkin, N.C.)
Vera Hester, Hanes Hosiery Mill (Winston-Salem, N.C.)
Jennie Sherrill, Chatham Mfg. (Elkin, N.C.)
Mary Linville, Hanes Hosiery Mill (Winston-Salem, N.C.)
Beulah Splawn, Drayton Mill (Spartanburg, S.C.)

1947

Class A Men
Earl Wooten, Pelzer Mill (Pelzer, S.C.)
Cedric Loftis, Hanes Hosiery Mill (Winston-Salem, N.C.)
Hugh Hampton, Hanes Hosiery Mill (Winston-Salem, N.C.)
Bob Stowe, Dunean Mill (Greenville, S.C.)
Hillard Nance, McCrary Hosiery Mill (Asheboro, N.C.)

Class A Women
Jacqueline Swain, Hanes Hosiery Mill (Winston-Salem, N.C.)
Doris Shugart, Chatham Mfg. (Elkin, N.C.)
Ann Lineback, Chatham Mfg. (Elkin, N.C.)
Ruth Phelps, Hanes Hosiery Mill (Winston-Salem, N.C.)
Alma Wilson, Drayton Mill (Spartanburg, S.C.)
Jennie Sherrill, Chatham Mfg. (Elkin, N.C.)

1948

Class A Men
Earl Wooten, Pelzer Mill (Pelzer, S.C.)
Don Brock, Chatham Mfg. (Elkin, N.C.)
Hugh Hampton, Hanes Hosiery Mill (Winston-Salem, N.C.)
Bob Stowe, Dunean Mill (Greenville, S.C.)
Hillard Nance, Hanes Hosiery Mill (Winston-Salem, N.C.)

Class B Men
Larry Ashley, Dunean Mill (Greenville, S.C.)
Ken Pittman, Monaghan Mill (Greenville, S.C.)
Jake Floyd, Mills Mill (Greenville, S.C.)
Billy Wakefield, Woodside Mill (Greenville, S.C.)
Fig Newton, Monaghan Mill (Greenville, S.C.)

Class C Men
Charles Carter, Camperdown Mill (Greenville, S.C.)
James Williamson, Brandon Mill (Greenville, S.C.)
Jack Chambers, Oconee Mill (Westminster, S.C.)
James Thompson, Mills Mill (Greenville, S.C.)
Don Newton, Monaghan Mill (Greenville, S.C.)

Class A Women
Doris Norman, Chatham Mfg. (Elkin, N.C.)
Ruth Reich, Chatham Mfg. (Elkin, N.C.)
Jackie Swain, Hanes Hosiery Mill (Winston-Salem, N.C.)
Jennie Sherrill, Chatham Mfg. (Elkin, N.C.)
Eunice Futch, Hanes Hosiery Mill (Winston-Salem, N.C.)
Frances McBride, Chatham Mfg. (Elkin, N.C.)

Class B Women
Doris Trulove, Ware Shoals Mill (Ware Shoals, S.C.)
Dorothy Nimmons, Piedmont Mill (Piedmont, S.C.)
Peggy Martin, Calhoun Falls Mill (Calhoun Falls, S.C.)
Ruth Cain, Oconee Mill (Westminster, S.C.)
Ruth Jenkins, Ware Shoals Mill (Ware Shoals, S.C.)
Frances Payne, North Georgia Processing (Toccoa, Ga.)

1949

Class A Men
Earl Wooten, Pelzer Mill (Pelzer, S.C.)
Glenn Michaels, Peerless Woolen Mill (Rossville, Ga.)

Gerald Becker, Pelzer Mill (Pelzer, S.C.)
James Cook, Peerless Woolen Mill (Rossville, Ga.)
Deran Walters, American Enka (Enka, N.C.)

Class B Men
Woodford Beasley, Lyman Mill (Lyman, S.C.)
Eurell Eubanks, Lyman Mill (Lyman, S.C.)
Brock Burgess, Beacon Mill (Swannanoa, N.C.)
William Horne, Martell Mill (Asheville, N.C.)
James Landreth, Southern Franklin Processing (Greenville, S.C.)

Class C Men
Bud Granger, Dunean Mill (Greenville, S.C.)
Alan Cox, Dunean Mill (Greenville, S.C.)
Harold Brennon, Pelzer Mill (Pelzer, S.C.)
Joe Wyatt, Monaghan Mill (Greenville, S.C.)
Danny Bagwell, Monaghan Mill (Greenville, S.C.)

Class A Women
Ann Paradise, Chatham Mfg. (Elkin, N.C.)
Liz Padgett, Chatham Mfg. (Elkin, N.C.)
May Condray, Drayton Mill (Spartanburg, S.C.)
Helen Melton, Drayton Mill (Spartanburg, S.C.)
Jannie Sherrill, Chatham Mfg. (Elkin, N.C.)
Betty Cope, Chatham Mfg. (Elkin, N.C.)

Class B Women
Dorothy Nimmons, Piedmont Mill (Piedmont, S.C.)
Peggy Martin, Calhoun Falls Mill (Calhoun Falls, S.C.)
Doris Thompson, Ware Shoals Mill (Ware Shoals, S.C.)
Maxine Hollifield, North Georgia Processing (Toccoa, Ga.)
Ruth Poore, Ware Shoals Mill (Ware Shoals, S.C.)
Frances Payne, North Georgia Processing (Toccoa, Ga.)

1950

Class A Men
Earl Wooten, Pelzer Mill (Pelzer, S.C.)
Ward Williams, Dunean Mill (Greenville, S.C.)
Horace Turner, Dunean Mill (Greenville, S.C.)
Brownell Bryant, Peerless Woolen Mill (Rossville, Ga.)
William Miller, Peerless Woolen Mill (Rossville, Ga.)

Class B Women
Louise Floyd, Springs Mill (Lancaster, S.C.)
Ruth Poore, Ware Shoals Mill (Ware Shoals, S.C.)
Vennie Reid, North Georgia Processing (Toccoa, Ga.)
Maxine Hollifield, North Georgia Processing (Toccoa, Ga.)
Betty Moody, Renfrew Bleachery (Travelers Rest, S.C.)
Wille Embler, Calhoun Falls Mill (Calhoun Falls, S.C.)

1951

Class A Men
Effie Evington, Monaghan Mill (Greenville, S.C.)
Gerald Becker, Pelzer Mill (Pelzer, S.C.)
Ward Williams, Dunean Mill (Greenville, S.C.)
Melvin Bell, Dunean Mill (Greenville, S.C.)
Earl Wooten, Pelzer Mill (Pelzer, S.C.)

Class B Women
Ruth Glenn, Glen Lowery Mill (Whitmire, S.C.)
Annie Stephens, Anderson Mill (Anderson, S.C.)
Georgia Wiles, Calhoun Falls Mill (Calhoun Falls, S.C.)
Gwen James, Judson Mill (Greenville, S.C.)
Ann Moorehead, North Georgia Processing (Toccoa, Ga.)
Betty Moody, Judson Mill (Greenville, S.C.)

1952

Class A Men
Ward Williams, Dunean Mill (Greenville, S.C.)
Bob Stowe, Dunean Mill (Greenville, S.C.)
Gerald Becker, Pelzer Mill (Pelzer, S.C.)
Effie Evington, Monaghan Mill (Greenville, S.C.)
Earl Wooten, Pelzer Mill (Pelzer, S.C.)
Hugh Hampton, Hanes Hosiery Mill (Winston-Salem, N.C.)
Truman Hill, Pelzer Mill (Pelzer, S.C.)

All Southern (All Tournament) Teams   Appendix 2

CLASS B WOMEN
Frances Wofford, Judson Mill (Greenville, S.C.)
Gwendolyn Tyler, Judson Mill (Greenville, S.C.)
Annie Stephens, Appleton Mill (Anderson, S.C.)
Bobbie Martin, Appleton Mill (Anderson, S.C.)
June Sauls, Brandon Mill (Greenville, S.C.)
Georgia Wiles, Calhoun Falls Mill (Calhoun Falls, S.C.)

—— 1953 ——

CLASS A MEN
James Cooke, Peerless Woolen Mill (Rossville, Ga.)
Effie Evington, Monaghan Mill (Greenville, S.C.)
Ken Pittman, Monaghan Mill (Greenville, S.C.)
Ward Williams, Dunean Mill (Greenville, S.C.)
Brice Kirkpatrick, Monaghan Mill (Greenville, S.C.)

CLASS B WOMEN
Edna Lee, Lonsdale Mill (Seneca, S.C.)
Bobbie Martin, Appleton Mill (Anderson, S.C.)
Barbara Sanders, Appleton Mill (Anderson, S.C.)
Juanita Jones, Judson Mill (Greenville, S.C.)
Sue Fletcher, Piedmont Mill (Piedmont, S.C.)
Norma Hancock, Easley Mill (Easley, S.C.)

—— 1954 ——

CLASS A MEN
Jim Slaughter, Dunean Mill (Greenville, S.C.)
Earl Wooten, Pelzer Mill (Pelzer, S.C.)
Neild Gordon, Pelzer Mill (Pelzer, S.C.)
Bob Stowe, Dunean Mill (Greenville, S.C.)
Deran Walters, American Enka (Enka, N.C.)
Smith Langdon, American Enka (Enka, N.C.)
Fig Newton, Monaghan Mill (Greenville, S.C.)
Effie Evington, Monaghan Mill (Greenville, S.C.)

CLASS B MEN
Ronnie Knight, Union Bleachery (Greenville, S.C.)
Leon Gravley, Victor Mill (Greer, S.C.)
Bruce Turner, Union Bleachery (Greenville, S.C.)
Charles Carlisle, Calhoun Falls Mill (Calhoun Falls, S.C.)
Martin Hair, Beacon Mill (Swannanoa, N.C.)

CLASS C MEN
Larry Speares, Appleton Mill (Anderson, S.C.)
Calvin Daniel, Appleton Mill (Anderson, S.C.)
Bill Roddy, Dunean Mill (Greenville, S.C.)
Jack Kelly, Dunean Mill (Greenville, S.C.)
Charles Powers, Monaghan Mill (Greenville, S.C.)

CLASS B WOMEN
Edna Lee, Lonsdale Mill (Seneca, S.C.)
Ova Poole, Lonsdale Mill (Seneca, S.C.)
Gwen Price, Joanna Mill (Joanna, S.C.)
Juanita Jones, Judson Mill (Greenville, S.C.)
Jo Ann Kelly, Judson Mill (Greenville, S.C.)
Avenell Emery, Piedmont Mill (Piedmont, S.C.)

—— 1955 ——

CLASS A MEN
Earl Wooten, Pelzer Mill (Pelzer, S.C.)
Tom Scott, Pelzer Mill (Pelzer, S.C.)
Neild Gordon, Monaghan Mill (Greenville, S.C.)
Fig Newton, Monaghan Mill (Greenville, S.C.)
Bob Stowe, Dunean Mill (Greenville, S.C.)

CLASS B MEN
Gary Henderson, Simpsonville Mill (Simpsonville, S.C.)
Ray Wynn, Brandon Mill (Greenville, S.C.)
Harold Brown, Anderson Mill (Anderson, S.C.)
Martin Hair, Beacon Mill (Swannanoa, N.C.)
Jack Brinkley, Beacon Mill (Swannanoa, N.C.)

CLASS C MEN
Roger Dill, Piedmont Mill (Piedmont, S.C.)
Marion Bannister, Pelzer Mill (Pelzer, S.C.)
Bill Wilson, Pelzer Mill (Pelzer, S.C.)
Charles Busbee, Monaghan Mill (Greenville, S.C.)
Larry Patterson, Piedmont Mill (Piedmont, S.C.)

Class A Women
Gwen Burgess, Pelzer Mill (Pelzer, S.C.)
Judith Coker, Pelzer Mill (Pelzer, S.C.)
Dolly Woods, Her Majesty (Mauldin, S.C.)
Reita Allison, Dunean Mill (Greenville, S.C.)
Mary Hairston, Easley Mill (Easley, S.C.)
Barbara Pittman, Pelzer Mill (Pelzer, S.C.)

1956

Open Division
Earl Wooten, Piedmont Mill (Piedmont, S.C.)
Wayne Godfrey, Victor Mill (Greer, S.C.)
Tex Ritter, Dunean Mill (Greenville, S.C.)
Ward Williams, Dunean Mill (Greenville, S.C.)
Ellerbe Neal, American Enka (Enka, S.C.)

Class B Men
Alan Beach, Lyman Mill (Lyman, S.C.)
Charles Carlisle, Anderson Mill (Anderson, S.C.)
Ezra Embler, Anderson Mill (Anderson, S.C.)
Bill Neely, American Spinning (Greenville, S.C.)
Tracy Roddy, Southern Franklin Processing (Greenville, S.C.)

Class C Men
Harold Waldrop, Easley Mill (Easley, S.C.)
Gary King, Easley Mill (Easley, S.C.)
Tommy Reynolds, Lonsdale Mill (Seneca, S.C.)
Dubby Robinson, Lonsdale Mill (Seneca, S.C.)
Joe Julian, Monaghan Mill (Greenville, S.C.)

Class A Women
Phyllis Snipes, Hanes Hosiery Mill (Winston-Salem, N.C.)
Roberta Bowman, Liberty Mill (Liberty, S.C.)
Winona Addis, Lonsdale Mill (Seneca, S.C.)
Elsie Griffin, Beacon Mill (Swannanoa, N.C.)
Eckie Jordan, Hanes Hosiery Mill (Winston-Salem, N.C.)
Johelen Dawkins, Lonsdale Mill (Seneca, S.C.)

1957

Class A Men
Earl Wooten, Piedmont Mill (Piedmont, S.C.)
Paul Nye, Piedmont Mill (Piedmont, S.C.)
Ellerbe Neal, American Enka (Enka, N.C.)
Willard Fowler, Monaghan Mill (Greenville, S.C.)
Harold Huey, Greer Mill (Greer, S.C.)
Ernie Chambers, Piedmont Mill (Piedmont, S.C.)
Ronald Rogers, American Enka (Enka, N.C.)

Class B Men
Bill Yarborough, Liberty Mill (Liberty, S.C.)
James Yates, Russell Manufacturing (Alexander City, Ala.)
Bobby Bailey, Russell Manufacturing (Alexander City, Ala.)
Edward Sheffield, Courtaulds (Mobile, Ala.)
Bill Robinson, Courtaulds (Mobile, Ala.)

Class C Men
Ricky Duncan, Dunean Mill (Greenville, S.C.)
Ronald Russell, Dunean Mill (Greenville, S.C.)
James Carter, Woodside Mill (Greenville, S.C.)
Charlton Miller, Victor Mill (Greer, S.C.)
Jack McKinney, Victor Mill (Greer, S.C.)

Class A Women
Winona Addis, Lonsdale Mill (Seneca, S.C.)
Shelly Pryor, Fiberglas (Anderson, S.C.)
Gwen Price, Joanna Mill (Joanna, S.C.)
Peggy Hare, Beacon Mill (Swannanoa, N.C.)
Roberta Bowman, Liberty Mill (Liberty, S.C.)
Betty Rowland, Fiberglas (Anderson, S.C.)

1958

Class A Men
Earl Wooten, Piedmont Mill (Piedmont, S.C.)
Ken Pittman, Monaghan Mill (Greenville, S.C.)
Mack Isner, Piedmont Mill (Piedmont, S.C.)
Ernie Chambers, Piedmont Mill (Piedmont, S.C.)
Fig Newton, Monaghan Mill (Greenville, S.C.)

Class B Men
Bill Robinson, Courtaulds (Mobile, Ala.)
James Yates, Russell Manufacturing (Alexander City, Ala.)
David Sprouse, Slater Mill (Slater, S.C.)
Buddy Stephenson, Slater Mill (Slater, S.C.)
Gerald Grogan, Russell Manufacturing (Alexander City, Ala.)

Class C Men
Tommy Williams, Brandon Mill (Greenville, S.C.)
Ricky Duncan, Dunean Mill (Greenville, S.C.)

All Southern (All Tournament) Teams   Appendix 2   353

Tim Brown, Union Bleachery (Greenville, S.C.)
Sammy Ramsey, Dunean Mill (Greenville, S.C.)
Jimmy Porterfield, Brandon Mill (Greenville, S.C.)

Class A Women
Lucille Robinson, Slater Mill (Slater, S.C.)
Jane Nelson, Slater Mill (Slater, S.C.)
Harriett Kitchen, Liberty Mill (Liberty, S.C.)
Barbara Harris, Pelzer Mill (Pelzer, S.C.)
Barbara Cash, Anderson Mill (Anderson, S.C.)
Peggy Fleming, Anderson Mill (Anderson, S.C.)

1959

Open Division
Tommy Kearns, Piedmont Mill (Piedmont, S.C.)
Jack Salee, Piedmont Mill (Piedmont, S.C.)
Tom Conard, Monaghan Mill (Greenville, S.C.)
Dick Wright, Monaghan Mill (Greenville, S.C.)
Buddy McCall, Texize Chemical (Greenville, S.C.)

Class B Men
Vince Yockel, Piedmont Mill (Piedmont, S.C.)
Joe Hiott, Piedmont Mill (Piedmont, S.C.)
Charleton Miller, Victor Mill (Greer, S.C.)
Jim Diamond, Monsanto (Pensacola, Fla.)
Jimmy Holden, Monaghan Mill (Greenville, S.C.)

Class C Men
Nathan Smith, Monaghan Mill (Greenville, S.C.)
Jimmy Carter, Woodside Mill (Greenville, S.C.)
Douglas McCrary, Monaghan Mill (Greenville, S.C.)
Pat Bowie, Liberty Mill (Liberty, S.C.)
Larry Campbell, Woodside Mill (Greenville, S.C.)

Class A Women
Winona Foster, Lonsdale Mill (Seneca, S.C.)
Johelen Dawkins, Lonsdale Mill (Seneca, S.C.)
Jane Nelson, Slater Mill (Slater, S.C.)
Barbara Harris, Slater Mill (Slater, S.C.)
Bobbie Burriss, Anderson Mill (Anderson, S.C.)
Gwen Clark, Joanna Mill (Joanna, S.C.)

1960

Open Division
Jim Slaughter, Piedmont Mill (Piedmont, S.C.)
Dick Tyler, Monaghan Mill (Greenville, S.C.)
George Krajack, Dillard's Sporting Goods (Easley, S.C.)
Mike Callahan, Victor Mill (Greer, S.C.)
Dick Wright, Dillard's Sporting Goods (Easley, S.C.)

Class B Men
Mickey Long, Dunean Mill (Greenville, S.C.)
Ronnie Russell, Dunean Mill (Greenville, S.C.)
Jim Diamond, Monsanto (Pensacola, Fla.)
Jimmy Holden, Monaghan Mill (Greenville, S.C.)
James Jones, Russell Manufacturing (Alexander City, Ala.)

Class C Men
Jimmy Chapman, Dunean Mill (Greenville, S.C.)
Jerry Gambrell, Piedmont Mill (Piedmont, S.C.)
Harvey Tankersly, Slater Mill (Slater, S.C.)
Earl Whittington, Dunean Mill (Greenville, S.C.)
Ronnie Maravich, Excelsior Mill (Pendleton, S.C.)

Class A Women
Sue Vickers, Slater Mill (Slater, S.C.)
Frances Welborn, Sangamo Electric Co. (Pickens, S.C.)
Johelen Dawkins, Lonsdale Mill (Seneca, S.C.)
Brenda Addis, Lonsdale Mill (Seneca, S.C.)
Stephanie Pickett, Slater Mill (Slater, S.C.)
Brenda Gable, Poinsett Lumber (Anderson, S.C.)

1961

Open Division
Rex Frederick, Piedmont Mill (Piedmont, S.C.)
Vince Yockel, Piedmont Mill (Piedmont, S.C.)
Ellerbe Neal, Monaghan Mill (Greenville, S.C.)
Dick Tyler, Monaghan Mill (Greenville, S.C.)

Joe Gardner, Chattanooga VFW (Chattanooga, Tenn.)

CLASS B MEN
William Moore, Poinsett Lumber (Anderson, S.C.)
Steve Brown, Greer Mill (Greer, S.C.)
Jim Diamond, Monsanto (Pensacola, Fla.)
Don Gates, Monsanto (Pensacola, Fla.)
Earl Whittington, Dunean Mill (Greenville, S.C.)

CLASS C MEN
Harvey Tankersley, Slater Mill (Slater, S.C.)
Ronnie Maravich, Cannon Mills (Central, S.C.)
Wayne Lacey, Newry Mill (Seneca, S.C.)
Gary Helms, Pelzer Mill (Pelzer, S.C.)
Pete Maravich, Cannon Mills (Central, S.C.)

CLASS A WOMEN
Sue Vickers, Slater Mill (Slater, S.C.)
Pat Murphy, Slater Mill (Slater, S.C.)
Brenda Addis, Lonsdale Mill (Seneca, S.C.)
Johelen Dawkins, Lonsdale Mill (Seneca, S.C.)
Annie Tribble, Poinsett Lumber (Anderson, S.C.)
Loraine Gomillion, Monsanto (Pensacola, Fla.)

———— 1962 ————

OPEN DIVISION
Art Whisnant, Todd-Moore (Columbia, S.C.)
Grady Wallace, Todd-Moore (Columbia, S.C.)
Carol Youngkin, Sherrill Mfg. (Gastonia, N.C.)
Howard Hurt, Sherrill Mfg. (Gastonia, N.C.)
Doug Kistler, Sherrill Mfg. (Gastonia, N.C.)

CLASS A MEN
Don Helms, Pelzer Mill (Pelzer, S.C.)
Doug Harris, Pelzer Mill (Pelzer, S.C.)
Jimmy Herring, Apalache Mill (Greer, S.C.)
Don Lister, Apalache Mill (Greer, S.C.)
Earl Maxwell, Piedmont Mill (Piedmont, S.C.)

CLASS B MEN
Alfred Spotts, Anderson Hosiery Mill (Whitmire, S.C.)
Charles Rogers, Saco-Lowell (Easley, S.C.)
Jimmy Chapman, Saco-Lowell (Easley, S.C.)
Mike Jordan, Pelzer Mill (Pelzer, S.C.)
Everett Cooper, Pelzer Mill (Pelzer, S.C.)

CLASS C MEN
Mike Muth, Pelzer Mill (Pelzer, S.C.)
Gary Helms, Pelzer Mill (Pelzer, S.C.)
Mike Rogers, Greer Mill (Greer, S.C.)
Frank Garrett, Simpsonville Mill (Simpsonville, S.C.)
Mackey Nichols, Glenwood Mill (Easley, S.C.)

CLASS A WOMEN
Sue Vickers, Slater Mill (Slater, S.C.)
Mickey Davis, Simpsonville Mill (Simpsonville, S.C.)
Annie Tribble, Slater Mill (Slater, S.C.)
Carolyn Clayton, Slater Mill (Slater, S.C.)
Judy Buddin, Simpsonville Mill (Simpsonville, S.C.)
Sarah Lambert, Carolina Plating (Greenville, S.C.)

———— 1963 ————

OPEN DIVISION
Dave Weideman, Pharr Worsted Mill (McAdenville, N.C.)
Gerald Glur, Murrell Brothers Sand (Greenville, S.C.)
Bob Woollard, Pharr Worsted Mill (McAdenville, N.C.)
Art Whisnant, Todd-Moore (Columbia, S.C.)
Joe McDermott, Pharr Worsted Mill (McAdenville, N.C.)

CLASS A MEN
Don Helms, Pelzer Mill (Pelzer, S.C.)
Doug Harris, Pelzer Mill (Pelzer, S.C.)
Pete Carlisle, Monsanto (Greenwood, S.C.)
Earl Wooten, Piedmont Mill (Piedmont, S.C.)
Larry Patterson, Piedmont Mill (Piedmont, S.C.)

CLASS B MEN
Leon Eubanks, Lyman Mill (Lyman, S.C.)
Steve Brown, Lyman Mill (Lyman, S.C.)
Donnie Sargent, Dunean Mill (Greenville, S.C.)
Calvin Rumler, Union Bleachery (Greenville, S.C.)
Eddie Walker, Anderson Hosiery Mill (Whitmire, S.C.)

CLASS C MEN
Mike Muth, Pelzer Mill (Pelzer, S.C.)
Charles Breazeale, McCrary Mechanical (Travelers Rest, S.C.)

All Southern (All Tournament) Teams

Mike Fair, Monaghan Mill (Greenville, S.C.)
Jim Sutherland, Cannon Mills (Central, S.C.)
Steve Moore, Greer Mill (Greer, S.C.)

Class A Women
Joan Kirby, Slater Mill (Slater, S.C.)
Sue Vickers, Slater Mill (Slater, S.C.)
Annie Tribble, Poinsett Lumber (Anderson, S.C.)
Phyllis White, Monsanto (Pensacola, Fla.)
Carol Broad, Carolina Plating (Greenville, S.C.)
Iris Blackwell, Poinsett Lumber (Anderson, S.C.)

1964

Open Division
Jesse Branson, Mikro (Charlotte, N.C.)
Doug Moe, Mikro (Charlotte, N.C.)
Nick Milasnovich, Murrell Brothers Sand (Greenville, S.C.)
Gary Burnisky, Murrell Brothers Sand (Greenville, S.C.)
Gerald Glur, Murrell Brothers Sand (Greenville, S.C.)

Class A Men
Don Carver, Monsanto (Greenwood, S.C.)
Pete Carlisle, Monsanto (Greenwood, S.C.)
Vince Yockel, Piedmont Mill (Piedmont, S.C.)
Gene Seay, Piedmont Mill (Piedmont, S.C.)
Steve Brown, Lyman Mill (Lyman, S.C.)

Class B Men
Richard Aiken, Union Bleachery (Greenville, S.C.)
Calvin Rumler, Union Bleachery (Greenville, S.C.)
Al Spotts, Anderson Hosiery Mill (Whitmire, S.C.)
Bill Black, Anderson Hosiery Mill (Whitmire, S.C.)
Donnie Sargent, Saco-Lowell (Easley, S.C.)

Class C Men
Jimmy Wilson, Saco-Lowell (Easley, S.C.)
Mark Stewart, Monaghan Mill (Greenville, S.C.)
Donnie Lewis, Monaghan Mill (Greenville, S.C.)
Douglas Blackwell, Saco-Lowell (Easley, S.C.)
Mike Fair, Monaghan Mill (Greenville, S.C.)

Class A Women
Pat Wilson, Singer Mfg. (Anderson, S.C.)
Joan Nelson, Slater Mill (Slater, S.C.)
Frances Welborn, Sangamo Electric Co. (Pickens, S.C.)
Mickey Davis, Slater Mill (Slater, S.C.)
Marilyn Green, Bahan Textile (Greenville, S.C.)
Carolyn Clayton, Singer Mfg. (Anderson, S.C.)

1965

Open Division
Doug Moe, Mikro (Charlotte, N.C.)
Jesse Branson, Mikro (Charlotte, N.C.)
Billy Cunningham, Mikro (Charlotte, N.C.)
Gerald Glur, Murrell Brothers Sand (Greenville, S.C.)
Bob McCullough, Murrell Brothers Sand (Greenville, S.C.)

Class A Men
Pete Carlisle, Monsanto (Greenwood, S.C.)
Don Carver, Monsanto (Greenwood, S.C.)
Steve Brown, Lyman Mill (Lyman, S.C.)
Bill Green, Lyman Mill (Lyman, S.C.)
Leroy Peacock, Slater Mill (Slater, S.C.)

Class B Men
Earl Whittington, Saco-Lowell (Easley, S.C.)
Mike McCoy, Saco-Lowell (Easley, S.C.)
Pat Bowie, Liberty Mill (Liberty, S.C.)
Tommy Crump, Davis Mechanical (Greenville, S.C.)
Kenneth Anderson, Lyman Mill (Lyman, S.C.)

Class C Men
Mike Fair, Monaghan Mill (Greenville, S.C.)
Donnie Lewis, Monaghan Mill (Greenville, S.C.)
Jimmy Littlefield, Simpsonville Mill (Simpsonville, S.C.)
Stanley Wilson, Saco-Lowell (Easley, S.C.)
Tommy Krieg, Saco-Lowell (Easley, S.C.)

Class A Women
Mickey Davis, Slater Mill (Slater, S.C.)
Linda Weaver, Slater Mill (Slater, S.C.)
Claudia Garrett, Singer Mfg. (Anderson, S.C.)
Carolyn Clayton, Singer Mfg. (Anderson, S.C.)
Jo McCall, Monsanto (Pensacola, Fla.)
Betty Wood, Monsanto (Pensacola, Fla.)

1966

OPEN DIVISION
Henry Logan, Sunshine Cleaners (Columbia, S.C.)
Red Robbins, Greenville Old Pros (Greenville, S.C.)
John Shroeder, Sunshine Cleaners (Columbia, S.C.)
Phil Murrell, Greenville Old Pros (Greenville, S.C.)
Grady Wallace, Sunshine Cleaners (Columbia, S.C.)

CLASS A MEN
Don Carver, Monsanto (Greenwood, S.C.)
Donald Gates, Monsanto (Pensacola, Fla.)
Michael Hearn, Russell Manufacturing (Alexander City, Ala.)
Garrett Nation, Monsanto (Greenwood, S.C.)
Gerald Abrams, A. Schottland Inc. (Hickory, N.C.)

CLASS B MEN
Horace Craig, Jr., Lyman Mill (Lyman, S.C.)
William Payne, Lyman Mill (Lyman, S.C.)
Vernon Stewart, Monaghan Mill (Greenville, S.C.)
Bennie Morgan, Monaghan Mill (Greenville, S.C.)
Clint Turner, Homelite (Greer, S.C.)

CLASS C MEN
Jack Anderson, Woodside Mill (Greenville, S.C.)
John Coakley, Saco-Lowell (Easley, S.C.)
Mike Sanderson, Woodside Mill (Greenville, S.C.)
Randy Bray, Saco-Lowell (Easley, S.C.)
Ernie Chambers, Jr., Piedmont Mill (Piedmont, S.C.)

CLASS A WOMEN
Linda Porter, Piedmont Mill (Piedmont, S.C.)
Caroline Brown, Singer Mfg. (Anderson, S.C.)
Mickey Davis, Atlanta Tomboys (Atlanta, Ga.)
Delores Owens, Atlanta Tomboys (Atlanta, Ga.)
Sara Strickland, Singer Mfg. (Anderson, S.C.)

1967

OPEN DIVISION
Jesse Branson, Mikro (Charlotte, N.C.)
Dwight Durante, Mikro (Charlotte, N.C.)
Willie Pegram, Guthrie Motors (Williamston, S.C.)
Gary Helms, Guthrie Motors (Williamston, S.C.)
Jerry Smith, Hinton's All Stars (Greenville, S.C.)

CLASS A MEN
Jimmy Childers, Russell Manufacturing (Alexander City, Ala.)
Wayne Anderson, Homelite (Greer, S.C.)
Don Carver, Monsanto (Greenwood, S.C.)
Donald Gates, Monsanto (Pensacola, Fla.)
Johnny Taylor, Monsanto (Greenwood, S.C.)

CLASS B MEN
Doug Bagwell, Sangamo Electric Co. (Pickens, S.C.)
Joe Garrett, Saco-Lowell (Easley, S.C.)
Grover Owings, Saco-Lowell (Easley, S.C.)
Jimmy Wilson, Saco-Lowell (Easley, S.C.)
James Bagwell, Pelzer Mill (Pelzer, S.C.)

CLASS C MEN
Lanny Taylor, Belton Mill (Belton, S.C.)
Willie Belton, Microtron (Greenville, S.C.)
John Dillard, Slater Mill (Slater, S.C.)
Mike Sanderson, Microtron (Greenville, S.C.)
Louis McCullough, Microtron (Greenville, S.C.)

CLASS A WOMEN
Joan Kirby, Slater Mill (Slater, S.C.)
Patsy Neal, IMMS (Greenville, S.C.)
Carolyn Pharr, IMMS (Greenville, S.C.)
Judy Payne, IMMS (Greenville, S.C.)
Frances Brooks, Union Bleachery (Greenville, S.C.)
Lauren Murphy, Slater Mill (Slater, S.C.)

1968

OPEN DIVISION
Dwight Durante, Mikro (Charlotte, N.C.)
Willie Pegram, Guthrie Motors (Williamston, S.C.)
Garland Davis, Mikro (Charlotte, N.C.)
Lee Davis, Mikro (Charlotte, N.C.)

All Southern (All Tournament) Teams Appendix 2   357

Mike Jenkins, Guthrie Motors (Williamston, S.C.)

CLASS A MEN
Jim Childers, Russell Manufacturing (Alexander City, Ala.)
Wayne Rape, Russell Manufacturing (Alexander City, Ala.)
Donnie Foster, Saco-Lowell (Easley, S.C.)
Don Carver, Saco-Lowell (Easley, S.C.)
Donald Gates, Monsanto (Pensacola, Fla.)

CLASS B MEN
Chuck Bullins, Madison Throwing Co. (Madison, N.C.)
Tim Smothers, Madison Throwing Co. (Madison, N.C.)
Paul Pritchett, Fiber Industries (Greenville, S.C.)
Robert Harley, Fiber Industries (Greenville, S.C.)
James Yates, Gluck Mill (Anderson, S.C.)

CLASS C MEN
Willie Rogers, Poe Hardware (Greenville, S.C.)
Chip Price, Poe Hardware (Greenville, S.C.)
Gregory Barnette, Monaghan Mill (Greenville, S.C.)
Jimmy Bowen, Monaghan Mill (Greenville, S.C.)
David Morrow, Ross Tire (Greenville, S.C.)

CLASS A WOMEN
Dianne Walker, Slater Mill (Slater, S.C.)
Joan Kirby, Slater Mill (Slater, S.C.)
Patsy Neal, IMMS (Greenville, S.C.)
Dede Owens, IMMS (Greenville, S.C.)
Dianne Limbaugh, Piedmont Mill (Piedmont, S.C.)

——— 1969 ———

OPEN DIVISION
Greg Patton, Mikro (Charlotte, N.C.)
Lonnie Kluttz, Mikro (Charlotte, N.C.)
Doug Alexander, K.G. Carpet (Atlanta, Ga.)
Dick Esleeck, Spaulding Fibers (Spartanburg, S.C.)
Allen Johnson, K.G. Carpet (Atlanta, Ga.)

CLASS A MEN
Skeeter Hammett, Dunean Mill (Greenville, S.C.)
Eddie Carter, Monsanto (Pensacola, Fla.)
Wayne Rape, Russell Manufacturing (Alexander City, Ala.)
Terry Campbell, Dunean Mill (Greenville, S.C.)
Henry Reid, Monsanto (Pensacola, Fla.)

CLASS B MEN
Enoch Tharpe, Monsanto (Pensacola, Fla.)
Perry Johnson, Phillips Fibers (Spartanburg, S.C.)
Herbert Brewton, Monsanto (Pensacola, Fla.)
Ralph Brown, Phillips Fibers (Spartanburg, S.C.)
Mike McKinney, Monaghan Mill (Greenville, S.C.)

CLASS C MEN
Lewis McCullough, Carter & Crawley (Greenville, S.C.)
Willie Neal, Carter & Crawley (Greenville, S.C.)
Clyde Mayes, Carter & Crawley (Greenville, S.C.)
Joe Francis, John Perkins Industries (Greenville, S.C.)
Billy Hollis, John Perkins Industries (Greenville, S.C.)

CLASS A WOMEN
Jean Dowell, K.G. Carpet (Atlanta, Ga.)
Mickey Davis, Ware Shoals Mill (Ware Shoals, S.C.)
Shirley White, K.G. Carpet (Atlanta, Ga.)
Ann Simmons, Ware Shoals Mill (Ware Shoals, S.C.)
Brenda Walker, K.G. Carpet (Atlanta, Ga.)
Margaret Freeman, Ware Shoals Mill (Ware Shoals, S.C.)

——— 1970 ———

OPEN DIVISION
Doug Alexander, Kenro (Atlanta, Ga.)
Ronnie Yates, Guthrie Motors (Williamston, S.C.)
Art Polk, Texize Chemical (Greenville, S.C.)
Terry Scott, Texize Chemical (Greenville, S.C.)
Joe Brunson, Texize Chemical (Greenville, S.C.)

Class A Men
Jim Childers, Russell Manufacturing (Alexander City, Ala.)
Arthur Hicks, Russell Manufacturing (Alexander City, Ala.)
Skeeter Hammett, Dunean Mill (Greenville, S.C.)
L.M. Hunter, Russell Manufacturing (Alexander City, Ala.)
Michael Adams, Rohm-Haas (Fayetteville, N.C.)

Class B Men
Richard Keir, Pelzer Mill (Pelzer, S.C.)
Tommy Richardson, Pelzer Mill (Pelzer, S.C.)
Raymond Rochester, Pelzer Mill (Pelzer, S.C.)
Bobby Mattress, Parker Mill (Greenville, S.C.)
Eddie Adams, Parker Mill (Greenville, S.C.)

Class C Men
Ricky Dobson, Crown-Metro (Greenville, S.C.)
Doug Lowe, Crown-Metro (Greenville, S.C.)
Terrell Suit, Martin's (Anderson, S.C.)
Daniel Martin, Martin's (Anderson, S.C.)
Butch Taylor, Crown-Metro (Greenville, S.C.)

Class A Women
Edwina Bryan, Kenro (Atlanta, Ga.)
Alice Smith, Kenro (Atlanta, Ga.)
Emma Howard, Texize Chemical (Greenville, S.C.)
Paula Monroe, Texize Chemical (Greenville, S.C.)
Annette Hammock, Kenro (Atlanta, Ga.)
Caroline Brown, Homestead Terrace (Greenville, S.C.)

1971

Open Division
Haywood Hill, Texize Chemical (Greenville, S.C.)
Pat Morarity, Kenro (Atlanta, Ga.)
Lloyd King, Southern Bank (Greenville, S.C.)
Ken Riley, Texize Chemical (Greenville, S.C.)
Doug Alexander, Kenro (Atlanta, Ga.)

Class A Men
Arthur Hicks, Russell Manufacturing (Alexander City, Ala.)
L.M. Hunter, Russell Manufacturing (Alexander City, Ala.)
Dewey Sanders, Russell Manufacturing (Alexander City, Ala.)
Philip Childers, Lyman Mill (Lyman, S.C.)
Harold Parker, Madison Throwing Co. (Madison, N.C.)

Class B Men
Joe Smith, Ware Shoals Mill (Ware Shoals, S.C.)
David Byers, Singer Mfg. (Anderson, S.C.)
Anthony Bennett, Victor Mill (Greer, S.C.)
Terry Smith, Easley Mill (Easley, S.C.)
Wesley Bolding, Singer Mfg. (Anderson, S.C.)

Class C Men
Randy Miller, Poe Hardware (Greenville, S.C.)
Clyde Agnew, Poe Hardware (Greenville, S.C.)
Marion Valentine, Poe Hardware (Greenville, S.C.)
Doug Lowe, Crown-Metro (Greenville, S.C.)
David Dobson, Crown-Metro (Greenville, S.C.)

Class A Women
Marty Vaughn, Texize Chemical (Greenville, S.C.)
Patsy Neal, Texize Chemical (Greenville, S.C.)
Edwina Bryan, Kenro (Atlanta, Ga.)
Lauren Murphy, Lyman Mill (Lyman, S.C.)
Roberta James, Sangamo Electric Co. (Pickens, S.C.)
Dianne Limbaugh, Singer Mfg. (Anderson, S.C.)

1972

Open Division
Dan Boe, Transit Homes (Greenville, S.C.)
Al Leapheart, Transit Homes (Greenville, S.C.)
Henry Harris, Transit Homes (Greenville, S.C.)
Will Robinson, Texize Chemical (Greenville, S.C.)
Bill Moore, Texize Chemical (Greenville, S.C.)

Class A Men
Arthur Hicks, Russell Manufacturing (Alexander City, Ala.)
Dewey Sanders, Russell Manufacturing (Alexander City, Ala.)
Alonza Ferguson, Russell Manufacturing (Alexander City, Ala.)
Charles Carlisle, Rohm-Haas (Greenville, S.C.)

All Southern (All Tournament) Teams Appendix 2 359

Skeeter Hammett, General Electric (Greenville, S.C.)

Class B Men
O'Louis McCullough, Fiber Industries (Greenville, S.C.)
Steve Barton, Fiber Industries (Greenville, S.C.)
Joe Smith, Ware Shoals Mill (Ware Shoals, S.C.)
Joe Pitts, Ware Shoals Mill (Ware Shoals, S.C.)
Lewis Armfield, Cryovac (Simpsonville, S.C.)

Class C Men
Ronnie Henderson, Crown-Metro (Greenville, S.C.)
Randy McCullen, Crown-Metro (Greenville, S.C.)
Larry Ray, Pelzer Mill (Pelzer, S.C.)
Cecil Lee, Pelzer Mill (Pelzer, S.C.)
Cleveland Spencer, Home Real Estate (Abbeville, S.C.)

Class A Women
Patsy Neal, Texize Chemical (Greenville, S.C.)
Lauren Murphy, Lyman Mill (Lyman, S.C.)
Marty Vaughn, Texize Chemical (Greenville, S.C.)
Diane Ayers, Lyman Mill (Lyman, S.C.)
Judy Murray, Texize Chemical (Greenville, S.C.)
Cee Cee O'Quinn, Westvaco (Charleston, S.C.)

─────────── 1973 ───────────

Open Division
Tom Arnholt, Transit Homes (Greenville, S.C.)
Clyde Agnew, Transit Homes (Greenville, S.C.)
Cris Schweer, Transit Homes (Greenville, S.C.)
Derrick Dickey, Texize Chemical (Greenville, S.C.)
Will Robinson, Texize Chemical (Greenville, S.C.)

Class A Men
Dewey Sanders, Russell Manufacturing (Alexander City, Ala.)
Owen Butts, Russell Manufacturing (Alexander City, Ala.)
Arthur Hicks, Russell Manufacturing (Alexander City, Ala.)

Bernard Richardson, Rohm-Haas (Fayetteville, N.C.)
Skeeter Hammett, General Electric (Greenville, S.C.)

Class B Men
Ronnie Cureton, Pelzer Mill (Pelzer, S.C.)
Edward Crawford, Pelzer Mill (Pelzer, S.C.)
Tommy Rutledge, Pelzer Mill (Pelzer, S.C.)
Leroy Arnold, Sally Mill (Greenville, S.C.)
Barry Dilworth, Sally Mill (Greenville, S.C.)

Class C Men
Henry Caldwell, Pelzer Mill (Pelzer, S.C.)
Charles Leslie, Pelzer Mill (Pelzer, S.C.)
Tim Turner, Pelzer Mill (Pelzer, S.C.)
Mike Yeargin, Carotell (Taylors, S.C.)
Tony Chibarro, Carotell (Taylors, S.C.)

Class A Women
Janie Lee, Appleton Mill (Anderson, S.C.)
Vicky Burton, Appleton Mill (Anderson, S.C.)
Nena Simmons, Ware Shoals Mill (Ware Shoals, S.C.)
Diane Davenport, Ware Shoals Mill (Ware Shoals, S.C.)
Regina Gilstrap, Slater Mill (Slater, S.C.)

─────────── 1974 ───────────

Open Division
Tom Arnholt, Transit Homes (Greenville, S.C.)
Lee Fowler, Transit Homes (Greenville, S.C.)
Bill Ligon, Transit Homes (Greenville, S.C.)
Clyde Agnew, Pittman's Textile Machinery (Greenville, S.C.)
George Hester, Pittman's Textile Machinery (Greenville, S.C.)

Class A Men
Pete Carlisle, Rohm-Haas (Fayetteville, N.C.)
Bernard Richardson, Rohm-Haas (Fayetteville, N.C.)
Ivey Bryant, Rohm-Haas (Fayetteville, N.C.)
Clarence Moody, Lyman Mill (Lyman, S.C.)
Michael Meadows, Lyman Mill (Lyman, S.C.)

Class B Men
Calvin Milam, Cryovac (Simpsonville, S.C.)
Bobby Phelps, Cryovac (Simpsonville, S.C.)
Rex Abercrombie, Cryovac (Simpsonville, S.C.)
David McKinney, Brookline Carpets (Greenville, S.C.)

Leslie Williams, Brookline Carpets (Greenville, S.C.)

CLASS C MEN
Terry Freeman, Fisk-Carter (Greenville, S.C.)
William Graham, Saco-Lowell (Easley, S.C.)
Wayne Gaskill, Saco-Lowell (Easley, S.C.)
Donnie Tyler, Pelzer Mill (Pelzer, S.C.)
Colon Abraham, Pelzer Mill (Pelzer, S.C.)

CLASS A WOMEN
Marty Vaughn, Slater Mill (Slater, S.C.)
Bonnie Whelan, Slater Mill (Slater, S.C.)
Jan Rampey, Slater Mill (Slater, S.C.)
Nena Simmons, Ware Shoals Mill (Ware Shoals, S.C.)
B.J. Shell, Texize Chemical (Greenville, S.C.)

1975

OPEN DIVISION
Jo Jo Bethea, Defender Chemical (Anderson, S.C.)
Wayne Croft, Defender Chemical (Anderson, S.C.)
Clyde Agnew, Pittman's Textile Machinery (Greenville, S.C.)
Marion Miller, Pittman's Textile Machinery (Greenville, S.C.)
Gil McGregor, Fleet Supply (Winston-Salem, N.C.)

CLASS A MEN
Steve Brown, Daniel Construction Co. (Greenville, S.C.)
David Dobson, Daniel Construction Co. (Greenville, S.C.)
Tommy Rutledge, Norwich Pharmacal (Greenville, S.C.)
Freddie Donalds, Norwich Pharmacal (Greenville, S.C.)
Marvin Drummond, Celanese (Greer, S.C.)

CLASS B MEN
Mike Yeargin, Sirrine Co. (Greenville, S.C.)
Bruce Martin, Sirrine Co. (Greenville, S.C.)
Mickey Rogers, Saco-Lowell (Easley, S.C.)
Nathaniel Lewis, Ware Shoals Mill (Ware Shoals, S.C.)
Len White, Parke-Davis (Greenwood, S.C.)

CLASS C MEN
William Wakefield, Dunean Cafe (Greenville, S.C.)
Tony Lanford, Dunean Cafe (Greenville, S.C.)
Nathaniel Simpkins, Pelzer Mill (Pelzer, S.C.)
Thomas Walker, Pelzer Mill (Pelzer, S.C.)
Carl Heyward, Pelzer Mill (Pelzer, S.C.)

CLASS A WOMEN
Vivian Humphrey, Monroe & Co. (Winnsboro, S.C.)
Donna Forrester, Appleton Mill (Anderson, S.C.)
Susan Neal, Appleton Mill (Anderson, S.C.)
Pam Adams, Slater Mill (Slater, S.C.)
Kim Basinger, Slater Mill (Slater, S.C.)

1976

OPEN DIVISION
Robert Jeter, Lexington County Recreation (Lexington, S.C.)
Willie Crumpton, Lexington County Recreation (Lexington, S.C.)
Wilbur Corley, Lexington County Recreation (Lexington, S.C.)
Tim Sisneros, Non-Fluid Oil (Greenville, S.C.)
Tom Arnholt, Non-Fluid Oil (Greenville, S.C.)

CLASS A MEN
Leslie Williams, Brookline Carpets (Greenville, S.C.)
Nixon Allen, Brookline Carpets (Greenville, S.C.)
Doug Bagwell, Sangamo Electric Co. (Pickens, S.C.)
Dennis Arnold, Sangamo Electric Co. (Pickens, S.C.)
David Dobson, Daniel Construction Co. (Greenville, S.C.)

CLASS B MEN
Terry Smith, Alice Mfg. (Easley, S.C.)
Johnny White, Alice Mfg. (Easley, S.C.)
Jerome Williams, Renfrew Bleachery (Travelers Rest, S.C.)
Benny Adams, Carolina Material Handling (Mauldin, S.C.)
Charles Eldridge, SCN Bank (Greenville, S.C.)

CLASS C MEN
Jonathan Moore, Pelzer Mill (Pelzer, S.C.)
Carl Heyward, Pelzer Mill (Pelzer, S.C.)

All Southern (All Tournament) Teams   Appendix 2   361

Ronald White, Dunean Cafe (Greenville, S.C.)
William Wakefield, Dunean Cafe (Greenville, S.C.)
Warren Kimmons, Carotell (Taylors, S.C.)

Class A Women
Regina Gilstrap, Slater Mill (Slater, S.C.)
Vivan Humphries, Slater Mill (Slater, S.C.)
Dianne Limbaugh, Discount Fence (Winston-Salem, N.C.)
Georgene Hightower, Discount Fence (Winston-Salem, N.C.)
Rita Mantooth, Darrell Floyd's Sandwich Shop (Greenville, S.C.)

1977

Open Division
Tree Rollins, Non-Fluid Oil (Greenville, S.C.)
Dave Brown, Non-Fluid Oil (Greenville, S.C.)
Tony Byers, Chick-Fil-A (Greenville, S.C.)
Dave Borman, Chick-Fil-A (Greenville, S.C.)
Alvin Holland, Daniel Construction Co. (Jenkinsville, S.C.)

Class A Men
Jim Clark, Athletic Attic (Anderson, S.C.)
Donald Davis, Athletic Attic (Anderson, S.C.)
Robin Ellenburg, Athletic Attic (Anderson, S.C.)
Nixon Allen, Brookline Carpets (Greenville, S.C.)
Jack Taylor, Brookline Carpets (Greenville, S.C.)

Class B Men
Jerome Williams, Slater Mill (Slater, S.C.)
McBruce Young, Slater Mill (Slater, S.C.)
Ricky Foster, Sally Mill (Greenville, S.C.)
Leonard White, Parke Davis (Greenwood, S.C.)
Joe Geer, Appleton Mill (Anderson, S.C.)

Class C Men
Jimmy Foster, Neely's Inc. (Taylors, S.C.)
Doug Schmelding, Neely's Inc. (Taylors, S.C.)
Wilbert Singleton, American Can (Darlington, S.C.)
Horace Wyatt, American Can (Darlington, S.C.)
Zam Fredrick, Pelzer Mill (Pelzer, S.C.)

Class A Women
Bobbie Mims, Darrell Floyd's Sandwich Shop (Greenville, S.C.)
Kathy Wilson, Darrell Floyd's Sandwich Shop (Greenville, S.C.)
Diane Limbaugh, Discount Fence (Winston-Salem, N.C.)
Delphine Williams, Discount Fence (Winston-Salem, N.C.)
Judy Stroud, Laurens Glass (Laurens, S.C.)

1978

Open Division
Stan Rome, Non-Fluid Oil (Greenville, S.C.)
Tony Byers, Chick-Fil-A (Greenville, S.C.)
Horace Porter, Non-Fluid Oil (Greenville, S.C.)
Rodney Young, Chick-Fil-A (Greenville, S.C.)
Colon Abraham, Non-Fluid Oil (Greenville, S.C.)

Class A Men
Terry Smith, Alice Mfg. (Easley, S.C.)
Willie Harris, Duke Power (Greenville, S.C.)
John Todd, Alice Mfg. (Easley, S.C.)
James Earl, Duke Power (Greenville, S.C.)
Matt Valentine, Alice Mfg. (Easley, S.C.)

Class B Men
Jerry Hightower, Slater Mill (Slater, S.C.)
Ricky Foster, Michelin (Greenville, S.C.)
John Grobelewski, Slater Mill (Slater, S.C.)
Archie Henderson, Michelin (Greenville, S.C.)
Joe Geer, Appleton Mill (Anderson, S.C.)

Class C Men
Jimmy Foster, Pelzer Mill (Pelzer, S.C.)
Ed Young, Neely's Inc. (Taylors, S.C.)
Ronnie Carr, Pelzer Mill (Pelzer, S.C.)
Ricky Wyatt, Neely's Inc. (Taylors, S.C.)
Mike Hackett, Pelzer Mill (Pelzer, S.C.)

Class A Women
Sybil Blalock, Pelzer Mill (Pelzer, S.C.)
Jennie Lyerly, Slater Mill (Slater, S.C.)
Sister Green, Pelzer Mill (Pelzer, S.C.)
Sandra Bishop, Griggs Enterprises (Hartsville, S.C.)
Trish Roberts, Pelzer Mill (Pelzer, S.C.)

1979

No record of selections available.

1980

Open Division
Ronald White, Chick-Fil-A (Greenville, S.C.)
Jonathan Moore, Chick-Fil-A (Greenville, S.C.)
Al Daniel, Chick-Fil-A (Greenville, S.C.)
Chubby Wells, Non-Fluid Oil (Greenville, S.C.)
Billy Williams, Non-Fluid Oil (Greenville, S.C.)

Class A Men
Isaiah Walker Jr., Dunean Mill (Greenville, S.C.)
Richard Dubose, Dunean Mill (Greenville, S.C.)
Marty Hopkins, Singer Mfg. (Pickens, S.C.)
Charlie Anthony, Singer Mfg. (Pickens, S.C.)
Terry Smith, Alice Mfg. (Easley, S.C.)

Class B Men
Mike Miller, Union Carbide (Simpsonville, S.C.)
Waddy Talley, Union Carbide (Simpsonville, S.C.)
Paul Satterwhite, Cryovac (Simpsonville, S.C.)
Johnny Wright, Cryovac (Simpsonville, S.C.)
Tony Nash, Piedmont Mill (Piedmont, S.C.)

Class C Men
Scott Lane, Fashion First (Greer, S.C.)
Richey Taylor, Dalton's Furniture (Pickens, S.C.)
Cozell McQueen, Dalton's Furniture (Pickens, S.C.)
Jimmy Foster, Pelzer Mill (Pelzer, S.C.)
Eldorado Valentine, Pelzer Mill (Pelzer, S.C.)

Class A Women
Rosalind Jennings, Athletic Attic (Anderson, S.C.)
Sheila Morgan, Darrell Floyd's Sandwich Shop (Greenville, S.C.)
Teresa Allen, Darrell Floyd's Sandwich Shop (Greenville, S.C.)
Jane Fontaine, Pelzer Mill (Pelzer, S.C.)
Vivian Humphries, Slater Mill (Slater, S.C.)

1981

Open Division
James Brown, Tri-Dip Inc. (Columbia, S.C.)
Ricky Fulton, Tri-Dip Inc. (Columbia, S.C.)
Zam Fredrick, Chick-Fil-A (Greenville, S.C.)
Larry Nance, Chick-Fil-A (Greenville, S.C.)
Al Daniel, Chick-Fil-A (Greenville, S.C.)

Class A Men
Terry Smith, Alice Mfg. (Easley, S.C.)
Ken Murphy, Alice Mfg. (Easley, S.C.)
Isaiah Walker Jr., Dunean Mill (Greenville, S.C.)
Horace Anderson Jr., Dunean Mill (Greenville, S.C.)
Albert Smith, Ware Shoals Mill (Ware Shoals, S.C.)

Class B Men
James Meadows, Arcadia Mill (Spartanburg, S.C.)
Michael Moss, Arcadia Mill (Spartanburg, S.C.)
James Choice, Black's Mechanical (Greenville, S.C.)
Mark Dickerson, Black's Mechanical (Greenville, S.C.)
Kenneth Johnson, Black's Mechanical (Greenville, S.C.)

Class C Men
Joe Ward, Fast Fare (Hartwell, Ga.)
Gerald Wilkins, Fast Fare (Hartwell, Ga.)
DeWayne Grace, Dalton's Furniture (Pickens, S.C.)
Jerome Williams, Dalton's Furniture (Pickens, S.C.)
Andrea Hills, Pete's Market (Pelzer, S.C.)

Class A Women
Sadie Sellars, Pelzer Byrd's (Pelzer, S.C.)
Angie Jones, Pelzer Byrd's (Pelzer, S.C.)
Brantley Southers, Slater Mill (Slater, S.C.)
Marsie McAlister, Slater Mill (Slater, S.C.)
Pam Adams, Revis Trucking (Spartanburg, S.C.)

1982

Open Division
Mel Daniel, Chick-Fil-A (Greenville, S.C.)
Al Daniel, Chick-Fil-A (Greenville, S.C.)

All Southern (All Tournament) Teams   Appendix 2   363

Horace Wyatt, Chick-Fil-A (Greenville, S.C.)
Carrol Wells, Sonics (Abbeville, S.C.)
Charles Jones, Sonics (Abbeville, S.C.)

Class A Men
Ronald White, Bahan Textile (Greenville, S.C.)
Ricky Eichelberger, Bahan Textile (Greenville, S.C.)
Hollie Martin, Ware Shoals Mill (Ware Shoals, S.C.)
Roger Cyrus, Ware Shoals Mill (Ware Shoals, S.C.)
Albert Smith, Ware Shoals Mill (Ware Shoals, S.C.)

Class B Men
Joe Geer, Appleton Mill (Anderson, S.C.)
Willie Strabhart, Appleton Mill (Anderson, S.C.)
Terry Hunt, PPG Industries (Shelby, N.C.)
Don Gash, PPG Industries (Shelby, N.C.)
Richard Davis, George Coleman Ford (Travelers Rest, S.C.)

Class C Men
Charles Rogers, Dalton's Furniture (Pickens, S.C.)
Dewayne Grace, Dalton's Furniture (Pickens, S.C.)
George Adams, Chick-Fil-A (Greenville, S.C.)
William Mills, Chick-Fil-A (Greenville, S.C.)
Daryl Bedford, Chick-Fil-A (Greenville, S.C.)

Class A Women
Debra Buford, Non-Fluid Oil (Greenville, S.C.)
Jackie Jones, Non-Fluid Oil (Greenville, S.C.)
Brantley Southers, Pittman's Textile Machinery (Greenville, S.C.)
Marsie McAlister, Pittman's Textile Machinery (Greenville, S.C.)
Pam Adams, Revis Trucking (Spartanburg, S.C.)

1983

Open Division
Ray Smith, Black Diamond (Greenville, S.C.)
Mel Daniel, Chick-Fil-A (Greenville, S.C.)
Jim Cleamons, Chick-Fil-A (Greenville, S.C.)
Tom Wimbush, Goin' Jesse's Restaurant (Columbia, S.C.)
Thomas Sanders, Goin' Jesse's Restaurant (Columbia, S.C.)

Class A Men
Gill McDonald, Parker Mill (Greenville, S.C.)
Ernest Fuller Jr., Parker Mill (Greenville, S.C.)
Zernie Morgan, Emb-Tex (Travelers Rest, S.C.)
Mark Cox, Emb-Tex (Travelers Rest, S.C.)
Ronald White, Bahan Textile (Greenville, S.C.)

Class B Men
Joe Geer, Appleton Mill (Anderson, S.C.)
Bernard Hill, Appleton Mill (Anderson, S.C.)
Rick Mullinax, Southeastern Freight (Mauldin, S.C.)
Perry Craig, Southeastern Freight (Mauldin, S.C.)
Reggie Anderson, Sirrine Co. (Greenville, S.C.)

Class C Men
Derrick Galloway, Pelzer Mill (Pelzer, S.C.)
Vincent Webb, Pelzer Mill (Pelzer, S.C.)
Mike Massey, Chick-Fil-A (Greenville, S.C.)
Gary Martin, Chick-Fil-A (Greenville, S.C.)
Vincent Anderson, Alford Real Estate (Greenville, S.C.)

Class A Women
Jennie Lyerly, Pittman's Textile Machinery (Greenville, S.C.)
Dawn Raab, Pittman's Textile Machinery (Greenville, S.C.)
Toni Edwards, Chem-Size (Travelers Rest, S.C.)
Debra Buford, Chem-Size (Travelers Rest, S.C.)
Lilly Young, Chem-Size (Travelers Rest, S.C.)

1984

Open Division
George Singleton, Vince Perone's Restaurant (Greenville, S.C.)
Howard White, Hobart Mfg. (Blythewood, S.C.)
Calvin Davis, Hobart Mfg. (Blythewood, S.C.)
Ray Smith, Black Diamond (Greenville, S.C.)
Monroe Garrison, Black Diamond (Greenville, S.C.)

Class A Men
Charles Dacus, Singer Mfg. (Anderson, S.C.)
Steve Adams, Singer Mfg. (Anderson, S.C.)

James Ferguson, Monaghan Mill (Greenville, S.C.)
Anthony Taylor, Monaghan Mill (Greenville, S.C.)
Robert Fuller, Ware Shoals Mill (Ware Shoals, S.C.)

Class B Men
Brian Nesbitt, Givens Youth Center (Fountain Inn, S.C.)
Mitchell Bryson, Greenville Post Office (Greenville, S.C.)
Steve Conway, Greenwood Mill (Greenwood, S.C.)
Gregg Coleman, George Coleman Ford (Travelers Rest, S.C.)
Chip Gilstrap, George Coleman Ford (Travelers Rest, S.C.)

Class C Men
Tony Shaw, Florence Boy's Club (Florence, S.C.)
Kevin Fowler, Alford Real Estate (Greenville, S.C.)
Mike Garrison, Alford Real Estate (Greenville, S.C.)
Kenny Woods, Industrial Packing (Greenville, S.C.)
Brandt Williams, Industrial Packing (Greenville, S.C.)

Class A Women
Jan McDonald, Gilstrap Real Estate (Greenville, S.C.)
Darlene Morgan, Gilstrap Real Estate (Greenville, S.C.)
Connie Culbreth, Bennett Oil (Spartanburg, S.C.)
Pearl Moore, Bennett Oil (Spartanburg, S.C.)
Lisa Washington, Bennett Oil (Spartanburg, S.C.)

1985

Open Division
Ronald White, Black Diamond (Greenville, S.C.)
Monroe Garrison, Black Diamond (Greenville, S.C.)
Scott Little, Southeastern Electric (Greenville, S.C.)
Mel Daniel, Southeastern Electric (Greenville, S.C.)
Marc Campbell, Southeastern Electric (Greenville, S.C.)

Class A Men
Steve Crowe, Greenville Valve (Greenville, S.C.)
Larry Ross, PPG Industries (Shelby, N.C.)
Greg Beam, PPG Industries (Shelby, N.C.)
Joel Henderson, Michelin (Greenville, S.C.)
John Furmanski, Michelin (Greenville, S.C.)

Class B Men
Gus Rubio, Cryovac (Simpsonville, S.C.)
Glymph Childress, Southern Bank (Greenville, S.C.)
Glenn Poole, Southern Bank (Greenville, S.C.)
Richard Brown, Avco Lycoming (Greer, S.C.)
David Drummond, Avco Lycoming (Greer, S.C.)

Class C Men
Kelsey Weems, Chick-Fil-A (Greenville, S.C.)
Chris Duncan, Chick-Fil-A (Greenville, S.C.)
Rodney Geter, C.S.R.A. All Stars (Augusta, Ga.)
Dave Dickerson, C.S.R.A. All Stars (Augusta, Ga.)
D.J. Harrison, C.S.R.A. All Stars (Augusta, Ga.)

Class A Women
Karen Jenkins, Home Plate Restaurant (Greenville, S.C.)
Beth Couture, Gilstrap Real Estate (Greenville, S.C.)
Sheila Morgan, Gilstrap Real Estate (Greenville, S.C.)
Pearl Moore, Bennett Oil (Spartanburg, S.C.)
Sandy Bishop, Bennett Oil (Spartanburg, S.C.)

1986

No records of selections available.

1987

Open Division
Wylie Adams, Greenwood Mills (Greenwood, S.C.)
Mel Daniel, Snyder's Auto (Greenville, S.C.)
Raymond Lawson, Snyder's Auto (Greenville, S.C.)

All Southern (All Tournament) Teams Appendix 2   365

Larry Middleton, Olympic Gym (Columbia, S.C.)
Anthony Jenkins, Olympic Gym (Columbia, S.C.)

Class A Men
Dempsey Cohen, Greenville Fire Dept. (Greenville, S.C.)
Clayton Rhodes, Michelin US-1 (Greenville, S.C.)
Mark Cox, Michelin US-1 (Greenville, S.C.)
Larry Ross, PPG Industries (Shelby, N.C.)
Benji Camp, PPG Industries (Shelby, N.C.)

Class B Men
Mark Boudoucies, O'Neal Engineering (Greenville, S.C.)
Ronnie Martin, Givens Youth Center (Fountain Inn, S.C.)
Michael Richardson, Givens Youth Center (Fountain Inn, S.C.)
Terrence Petty, Cleveland Memorial Hospital (Shelby, N.C.)
Floyd Bridges, Cleveland Memorial Hospital (Shelby, N.C.)

Class C Men
Marvin Nash, North Georgia #1 (Toccoa, Ga.)
Darby Rich, Alford Real Estate (Greenville, S.C.)
Barry Manning, Chick-Fil-A (Greenville, S.C.)
Joe Rhett, Chick-Fil-A (Greenville, S.C.)
Mike Glover, Chick-Fil-A (Greenville, S.C.)

Class A Women
Toni Edwards, Mac's All Stars (Greenville, S.C.)
Sherrie Oldavak, Foothills Real Estate (Greenville, S.C.)
Beth Couture, Foothills Real Estate (Greenville, S.C.)
Pearl Moore, Four Star Sports (Spartanburg, S.C.)
Nessie Harris, Four Star Sports (Spartanburg, S.C.)

---1988---

Open Division
Tony Shaw, Dillard's Sporting Goods (Easley, S.C.)
Chubby Wells, Dillard's Sporting Goods (Easley, S.C.)
Terry Gould, Dillard's Sporting Goods (Easley, S.C.)
Rod Terry, Snyder's Auto (Greenville, S.C.)
Raymond Lawson, Snyder's Auto (Greenville, S.C.)

Class A Men
Ken Sterling, Greenville Fire Dept. (Greenville, S.C.)
Dempsey Cohen, Greenville Fire Dept. (Greenville, S.C.)
Mark Cox, Michelin US-1 (Greenville, S.C.)
Clayton Rhodes, Michelin US-1 (Greenville, S.C.)
Andrew Thompson, Michelin US-1 (Greenville, S.C.)

Class B Men
John Lollis, Roadway (Greenville, S.C.)
Mitchell Bryson, Greenville Post Office (Greenville, S.C.)
David Simmons, Saco-Lowell (Easley, S.C.)
Bryant Bowen, Saco-Lowell (Easley, S.C.)
Dale Gillespie, Saco-Lowell (Easley, S.C.)

Class C Men
Sidney Thomas, Dillard's Sporting Goods (Easley, S.C.)
Mike Beckett, Dillard's Sporting Goods (Easley, S.C.)
Shawn Golden, Chick-Fil-A (Greenville, S.C.)
Bruce Evans, Chick-Fil-A (Greenville, S.C.)
Hal Henderson, Chick-Fil-A (Greenville, S.C.)

Class A Women
Sherie Oldevak, Foothills Real Estate (Greenville, S.C.)
Beth Couture, Foothills Real Estate (Greenville, S.C.)
Rene Williams, Gould's Surveyors (Greenville, S.C.)
Toni Edwards, Gould's Surveyors (Greenville, S.C.)
Cheryl Nix, Gould's Surveyors (Greenville, S.C.)

---1989---

Open Division
John Perry, Jimmy's Disco (Greenville, S.C.)
Raymond Lawson, Jimmy's Disco (Greenville, S.C.)

Calvin Criswell, Jimmy's Disco (Greenville, S.C.)
Ralph Miller, Charleston Flyers (Charleston, S.C.)
Mike Gillison, Charleston Flyers (Charleston, S.C.)

Class A Men
Larry Ross, PPG Industries (Shelby, N.C.)
Reginald Schenck, PPG Industries (Shelby, N.C.)
Clayton Rhodes, Michelin US-1 (Greenville, S.C.)
Joel Henderson, Michelin US-1 (Greenville, S.C.)
Andrew Thompson, Michelin US-1 (Greenville, S.C.)

Class B Men
Tony Foster, Oconee Nuclear (Seneca, S.C.)
Joe Young, Digital (Greenville, S.C.)
Michael Hunt, Digital (Greenville, S.C.)
David Johnson, Shedd's (Greenville, S.C.)
Joe Abercrombie, Shedd's (Greenville, S.C.)

Class C Men
Marvin Nash, Carper Real Estate (Greenville, S.C.)
Bruce Oglesby, Carper Real Estate (Greenville, S.C.)
Terry Bynum, Chick-Fil-A (Greenville, S.C.)
Steve Harris, Chick-Fil-A (Greenville, S.C.)
Sidney Thomas, Chick-Fil-A (Greenville, S.C.)

Class A Women
Kelli Garrett, Comfort Inn (Greenville, S.C.)
Renee Williams, Comfort Inn (Greenville, S.C.)
Toni Edwards, Boston Beanery (Greenville, S.C.)
LaToya Armstrong, Boston Beanery (Greenville, S.C.)
Jackie Moore, Boston Beanery (Greenville, S.C.)

1990

Open Division
Jimmy Brown, Poinsett Grocery (Greenville, S.C.)
Carl Smith, Poinsett Grocery (Greenville, S.C.)
Roy Wright, Poinsett Grocery (Greenville, S.C.)
Mike Gillison, Charleston Flyers (Charleston, S.C.)
Kevin Freyer, Charleston Flyers (Charleston, S.C.)

Class A Men
Ken Sterling, Greenville Fire Dept. (Greenville, S.C.)
Dempsey Cohen, Greenville Fire Dept. (Greenville, S.C.)
Clayton Rhodes, Michelin US-1 (Greenville, S.C.)
Mark Cox, Michelin US-1 (Greenville, S.C.)
Andrew Thompson, Michelin US-1 (Greenville, S.C.)

Class B Men
Waddy Talley, Kemet (Simpsonville, S.C.)
Pat McCullough, Shaw Properties (Greenville, S.C.)
Keith Nance, Shaw Properties (Greenville, S.C.)
Steve Smith, Greenville Valve (Greenville, S.C.)
Steve Crowe, Greenville Valve (Greenville, S.C.)

Class C Men
Marion Busby, Chick-Fil-A (Greenville, S.C.)
Steve Harris, Chick-Fil-A (Greenville, S.C.)
Brian Franklin, Chick-Fil-A (Greenville, S.C.)
Greg Minor, Carper Real Estate (Greenville, S.C.)
Hal McManus, Carper Real Estate (Greenville, S.C.)

Class A Women
None

1991

Open Division
Jimmy Brown, Poinsett Grocery (Greenville, S.C.)
Carl Smith, Poinsett Grocery (Greenville, S.C.)
Todd Wray, Poinsett Grocery (Greenville, S.C.)
Quinton Lytle, Spirit Express (Memphis, Tenn.)
Bill Jackson, Spirit Express (Memphis, Tenn.)

Class A Men
Clayton Rhodes, Michelin US-1 (Greenville, S.C.)
Mark Cox, Michelin US-1 (Greenville, S.C.)

All Southern (All Tournament) Teams Appendix 2 367

Joel Henderson, Michelin US-1 (Greenville, S.C.)
Terry Camp, PPG (Shelby, N.C.)
Eric Marable, PPG (Shelby, N.C.)

CLASS B MEN
Yancey Johnson, American Amusement (Greenville, S.C.)
John Williams, American Amusement (Greenville, S.C.)
Clay Carter, American Amusement (Greenville, S.C.)
Bobby Harper, St. Francis Hospital (Greenville, S.C.)
Jeff Harper, St. Francis Hospital (Greenville, S.C.)

CLASS C MEN
Nick Griffin, Metro (Greenville, S.C.)
Kenny Jackson, Metro (Greenville, S.C.)
Chuck Robinson, Beach Ball All Stars (Myrtle Beach, S.C.)
Mike Blassingame, Beach Ball All Stars (Myrtle Beach, S.C.)
Ricky Daniels, Beach Ball All Stars (Myrtle Beach, S.C.)

CLASS A WOMEN
Beth Couture, St. Francis Hospital (Greenville, S.C.)
Toni Edwards, St. Francis Hospital (Greenville, S.C.)
Nessie Harris, T-Shirts Plus (Greenville, S.C.)
Laurie Byrd, T-Shirts Plus (Greenville, S.C.)
Pearl Moore, T-Shirts Plus (Greenville, S.C.)

1992

OPEN DIVISION
David Stamey, Southeastern Products (Greenville, S.C.)
Bruce Evans, Southeastern Products (Greenville, S.C.)
Barry Manning, Southeastern Products (Greenville, S.C.)
David Lawrence, S&M Sports (Shelby, N.C.)
Larry Ross, S&M Sports (Shelby, N.C.)

CLASS A MEN
Dempsey Cohen, Greenville Fire Dept. (Greenville, S.C.)
Mitch Anderson, Greenville Fire Dept. (Greenville, S.C.)

Ricky Webb, Alice Mfg. (Easley, S.C.)
Scott Smith, Alice Mfg. (Easley, S.C.)
Roy Collins, Alice Mfg. (Easley, S.C.)

CLASS B MEN
Mel Daniel, American Federal (Greenville, S.C.)
Tom Coan, American Federal (Greenville, S.C.)
Keith Westburg, American Federal (Greenville, S.C.)
Cleve Cox, Vernon Heating & Air (Greenville, S.C.)
Steve Rooks, Vernon Heating & Air (Greenville, S.C.)

CLASS C MEN
Anton Hatchett, Carper Real Estate (Greenville, S.C.)
Anthony Jackson, Carper Real Estate (Greenville, S.C.)
Derrick Hammonds, Carper Real Estate (Greenville, S.C.)
Kevin Benson, Metro (Greenville, S.C.)
Jamie Rhome, Metro (Greenville, S.C.)

CLASS A WOMEN
Annette Alston, TKO (Greenville, S.C.)
Pearl Moore, TKO (Greenville, S.C.)
Melinda Hall, Triple Play (Greenville, S.C.)
Sherry Oldevak, Triple Play (Greenville, S.C.)
Natalie Kleckley, Triple Play (Greenville, S.C.)

1993

OPEN DIVISION
David Stamey, Southeastern Products (Greenville, S.C.)
Edmond Wilson, Southeastern Products (Greenville, S.C.)
Troy McKoy, Southeastern Products (Greenville, S.C.)
Raymond Lawson, Sincerely Yours (Greenville, S.C.)
John Perry, Sincerely Yours (Greenville, S.C.)

CLASS A MEN
Dempsey Cohen, Greenville Fire Dept. (Greenville, S.C.)
Alan Anderson, Greenville Fire Dept. (Greenville, S.C.)
Jeff Watson, Greenville Fire Dept. (Greenville, S.C.)

Scott Smith, Alice Mfg. (Easley, S.C.)
Terry B. Smith, Alice Mfg. (Easley, S.C.)

Class B Men
Joey Brooks, Parker Mill (Greenville, S.C.)
John Williams, Parker Mill (Greenville, S.C.)
Curtis Watson, Clinton Mill (Clinton, S.C.)
George McMorris, Clinton Mill (Clinton, S.C.)
Pete Rozell, SMC (Spartanburg, S.C.)

Class C Men
Jeff McInnis, Carper Real Estate (Greenville, S.C.)
Tavaris Johnson, Carper Real Estate (Greenville, S.C.)
Kensey Adair, Dice & Associates (Greenville, S.C.)
Mike Minnifield, Metro I (Greenville, S.C.)
Tarrance Albert, Metro I (Greenville, S.C.)

Class A Women
Elnora Jones, M. Vick (Spartanburg, S.C.)
Lisa Diaz, M. Vick (Spartanburg, S.C.)
Pearl Moore, M. Vick (Spartanburg, S.C.)
Melinda Campbell, Triple Play (Greenville, S.C.)
Michelle Bryant, Triple Play (Greenville, S.C.)

1994

Open Division
Barry Manning, Southeastern Products (Greenville, S.C.)
Joe Rhett, Southeastern Products (Greenville, S.C.)
Jamie Watson, Southeastern Products (Greenville, S.C.)
Paul Davis, Carolina Magic (Greenville, S.C.)
Nige Ramage, Carolina Magic (Greenville, S.C.)

Class A Men
Dempsey Cohen, Greenville Fire Dept. (Greenville, S.C.)
Mitch Anderson, Greenville Fire Dept. (Greenville, S.C.)
Jeff Watson, Greenville Fire Dept. (Greenville, S.C.)
Mel Daniel, American Federal (Greenville, S.C.)
Tom Coan, American Federal (Greenville, S.C.)

Class B Men
Joey Brooks, Parker Mill (Greenville, S.C.)
Patrick McCullough, Parker Mill (Greenville, S.C.)
David Simmons, Parker Mill (Greenville, S.C.)
Mike Chandler, Cryovac (Simpsonville, S.C.)
Tommy Hood, Cryovac (Simpsonville, S.C.)

Class C Men
Will Gallman, Southeastern Products (Greenville, S.C.)
Kevin Garnett, Southeastern Products (Greenville, S.C.)
Derrick Drummond, Southeastern Products (Greenville, S.C.)
Ryan Lookabill, Upperstate I (Chattanooga, Tenn.)
Larry Penn, Upperstate I (Chattanooga, Tenn.)

Class A Women
Elnora Jones, T-Shirts Plus (Greenville, S.C.)
Lisa Diaz, T-Shirts Plus (Greenville, S.C.)
Sherry Oldevak, Triple Play (Greenville, S.C.)
Rushia Brown, Triple Play (Greenville, S.C.)
Michelle Bryant, Triple Play (Greenville, S.C.)

Class C Women
Cullen Gutshall, R&G (Greenville, S.C.)
Holly Flournoy, R&G (Greenville, S.C.)
Shannon Harde, R&G (Greenville, S.C.)
Shorell Harrison, Pizza Hut Spinners (Greenville, S.C.)
Nicole Jackson, Pizza Hut Spinners (Greenville, S.C.)

1995

Open Division
Patrick McCullar, Fat Friday's (Clemson, S.C.)
David Young, Fat Friday's (Clemson, S.C.)
Devin Gray, Fat Friday's (Clemson, S.C.)
Barry Kincaid, Sharkheads (Columbia, S.C.)
Roger Carr, Sharkheads (Columbia, S.C.)

Closed Division Men
Todd Wray, PPG Industries (Shelby, N.C.)
Wayne Wray, PPG Industries (Shelby, N.C.)
Vincent Haynes, PPG Industries (Shelby, N.C.)
Ed Young, Carolina Circuit (Greenville, S.C.)
Vincent Oliver, Carolina Circuit (Greenville, S.C.)

All Southern (All Tournament) Teams   Appendix 2

CLASS C MEN
Will Gallman, Southeastern Products (Greenville, S.C.)
Shawn Ellis, Southeastern Products (Greenville, S.C.)
Derrick Drummond, Southeastern Products (Greenville, S.C.)
Seco Camero, Carper Real Estate (Greenville, S.C.)
Rob Turner, Carper Real Estate (Greenville, S.C.)

CLASS A WOMEN
Lisa Diaz, Sissy's Furniture (Columbia, S.C.)
Carolyn Brown, Sissy's Furniture (Columbia, S.C.)
Shalia King, Sissy's Furniture (Columbia, S.C.)
Renee Williams, Triple Play (Greenville, S.C.)
Karen Stanley, Triple Play (Greenville, S.C.)

1996

OPEN DIVISION
Dwayne Price, Fiber Processing (Virginia)
Gay Elmore, Fiber Processing (Virginia)
Scott Yahike, Fiber Processing (Virginia)
Joe Rhett, Sharkheads (Columbia, S.C.)
Cary Rich, Sharkheads (Columbia, S.C.)

CLOSED DIVISION MEN
Todd Wray, PPG Industries (Shelby, N.C.)
Antonio Washington, PPG Industries (Shelby, N.C.)
Clayton Rhodes, Michelin US-1 (Greenville, S.C.)
Mark Cox, Michelin US-1 (Greenville, S.C.)
Andrew Thompson, Michelin US-1 (Greenville, S.C.)

CLASS C MEN
Steve Surratt, Dick James (Greenville, S.C.)
Shawn Ellis, Dick James (Greenville, S.C.)
Charles Wright, Dick James (Greenville, S.C.)
Quincy Haywood, Poinsett Grocery (Greenville, S.C.)
Yahnik Martin, Poinsett Grocery (Greenville, S.C.)

CLASS A WOMEN
Renee Williams, WCCP (Clemson, S.C.)
Melinda Campbell, WCCP (Clemson, S.C.)
Michelle Gregoire, WCCP (Clemson, S.C.)
Shannon Johnson, King Valley (Columbia, S.C.)
Tasha Anderson, King Valley (Columbia, S.C.)

CLASS C WOMEN
Krystal Scott, Upstate Lady Sonics (Greenville, S.C.)
Ashleigh Fuller, Upstate Lady Sonics (Greenville, S.C.)
Crishina Hill, Upstate Lady Sonics (Greenville, S.C.)
Shorelle Harrison, Roll Tech (Greenville, S.C.)
Terri Rucker, Roll Tech (Greenville, S.C.)

1997

CLOSED DIVISION MEN
Joey Brooks, Parker Mill (Greenville, S.C.)
David Simmons, Parker Mill (Greenville, S.C.)
Tim Young, Parker Mill (Greenville, S.C.)
Tim Moody, YMCA (Greenville, S.C.)
Armory O'Dell, YMCA (Greenville, S.C.)

CLASS C MEN
Chet King, Carper Real Estate (Greenville, S.C.)
Will Tucker, Carper Real Estate (Greenville, S.C.)
Chuck Edison, Carper Real Estate (Greenville, S.C.)
Will Hellaums, Anderson Shockers (Anderson, S.C.)
Fermico Little, Anderson Shockers (Anderson, S.C.)

CLASS A WOMEN
Carolyn Brown, King Valley (Columbia, S.C.)
Michelle Murray, King Valley (Columbia, S.C.)
Lisa Diaz, King Valley (Columbia, S.C.)
Kelli Garrett, Low Country (Charleston, S.C.)
Tammy Hammonds, Low Country (Charleston, S.C.)

CLASS C WOMEN
Rachel Sloan, R&G (Greenville, S.C.)
Laura Robinson, R&G (Greenville, S.C.)
Katinea Neal, R&G (Greenville, S.C.)
Christy Blackwell, Laurens AAU (Laurens, S.C.)
Yoneko Allen, Laurens AAU (Laurens, S.C.)

Appendix 3

War-Time Tournament Rosters

1943 Greater Greenville Basketball Tournament

CLASS A MEN

Mills Mill (Greenville, S.C.), champions: Spot Trammell, Earl Wooten, Harris, Cannon, Jordan, Pearson, Ted Ratenski.

Dunean Mill (Greenville, S.C.), runners-up: Willie Riddle, Owens, Gumbo Odell, Willie Wilbanks, Fred Cox, Snoddy, Stowe.

Monaghan Mill (Greenville, S.C.), consolation winners: Bomar Keller, Raymond Christopher, Johnny Blackston, Johnson, Stewart, McCall, Turner.

349th Service Squardron (Grenville, S.C.): Mississippi Hinton, Buynak, Boyle, Kelszak, Simmons, Smith, Walton, Holley, Lamers, Billberry.

70th Service Squadron (Greenville, S.C.): Sherrington, Purkheiser, Russell, Martin, Evans, Goeghas, Kennard, Nuckles, Atkinson, Gatano, Lombardy, Atchinson.

Slater Mill (Slater, S.C.): Tucker, Hall, Cashion, Price, Pinson, McCall, Knight, Ward, Hembree.

470th Bombardment Squadron (Greenville, S.C.): Durant, Atkinson, Boynton, Plagman, Cohen, Boyle, Reese, Chinaese, Arney.

Woodside Mill (Greenville, S.C.): Ceedy Couch, Tollison, Chapman, Tucker, Canup, J. Couch, Talmadge.

Brandon Mill (Greenville, S.C.): Morrow, Carnes, Orr, Wynn, McDonald, Rogers, Henson.

25th Service Squadron (Greenville, S.C.): Kemp.

CLASS B MEN

Woodside Mill (Greenville, S.C.), champions: Mickey Ellis, Bill Wakefield, George Pruitt, Beasley, Davis, Nash, King.

Dunean Mill (Greenville, S.C.), runners-up: Horace Turner, Bob Stowe, Raymond Cox, Reynolds, Allen, McJunkin, Wood, Osteen, Campbell, B. Turner.

Renfrew Bleachery (Travelers Rest, S.C.), consolation winners: Harry Foster, L. Lockaby, E. Poole, R. Lockaby, Balloch, Cunningham.

Slater Mill (Slater, S.C.): H. Knight, Lynch, Barnett, Cox, McGill, Knox, Snelgrove.

Union Bleachery (Greenville, S.C.): Effie Evington, C. Turner, C. Robertson, C. Evington, W. Robertson, Revis, M. Turner.

Brandon Mill (Greenville, S.C.): Gwinn, Batson, Dilworth, Calvin Morrow, Fred Byrd, Wilson, Huff, Tribble.

Monaghan Mill (Greenville, S.C.): Campbell, Busbee, Mooreman, Griffith, Murray, Cook, Wood, Bill Moody.

St. Albans High School (Greenville, S.C.): Loftis, Holcombe, Owens, Talley, Banks, Kellett.

Camperdown Mill (Greenville, S.C.): Mintz.

Poe Mill (Greenville, S.C.): Elliott, Pittman, Guest, Mostella, Gilliard, Burns, Styles.

1944 Piedmont Area Basketball Tournament

Class A Men

Dunean Mill (Greenville, S.C.), champions: Willie Riddle, Frix, Floyd Owens, Snow Kirby, Willie Wilbanks, Turner, O'Dell.

Monaghan Mill (Greenville, S.C.), runners-up: Palmer McAvoy, Johnny Blackston, George Blackwell, Bomar Keller, Stewart, Morgan, Thompson, Mintz, Wilson.

471st Bomb Squadron (Greenville, S.C.), consolation winners: Eldridge, Hoffman, Martin, Mitchell, Demarest, Maris, Dauer, Thompson, Holmes.

Mills Mill (Greenville, S.C.): Moody, Norris Abbott, McAlister, Lollis, Phillips.

Ninety Six Mill (Ninety Six, S.C.): Drummond, L. Ross, Voiselle, C. Ross, Forrester, Ivester.

Ramblers (Greenville, S.C.): Wilson, Burns, J. Stroud, Lancaster, R. Stroud, Fuller, D. Burns, Boland.

Pelzer Mill (Pelzer, S.C.): Earl Wooten, Floyd, H. Jordan, Rushing, J. Jordan, Pete Harris, Tripp, B. Harris.

Woodside Mill (Greenville, S.C.): Justus, Ramsey, Harden, Canup, Foster, Perry, League.

Drayton Mill (Spartanburg, S.C.): O'Shields.

Class B Men

Beacon Mill (Swannanoa, N.C.), champions: Patton, Johnson, Folson, Jenkins, Mills, Patterson.

Dunean Mill (Greenville, S.C.), runners-up: Long, Morrow, Moody, Bob Stowe, Hughes, Green, Langston, Manley, Robertson, Smith.

Union Bleachery (Greenville, S.C.): Fred Byrd, Batson, Wilson, Effie Evington, Turner, Ward, Wyatt, Dunn, Christmas, Revis.

Greer High School (Greer, S.C.): Tooke, Stancil, Lamb Taylor, Howell, Mullinax, Williams, Hipdell, Durham, Jones.

Wellford-Lyman-Tucapau High School (Spartanburg, S.C.): Humphries, A. Bolin, Medlock, Austin, Mullinax, Fisher.

Woodside Mill (Greenville, S.C.): Elexious Riddle, Melvin Bell, S. McConnell, Billy Wakefield, C. McConnell, Mathis, Huffman, Taylors, Pittman.

Camperdown Mill (Greenville, S.C.): Landreth, Penland, Riddle, Hudgens, Moreland, Marchbanks, Robbins, Huff.

Monaghan Mill (Greenville, S.C.): Ken Pittman, B. Griffin, McAvoy, Pearson, Barbare, J. Pittman.

Red Shield (Greenville, S.C.): Pearson, Darnell, Street, Pittman, Nivens, Moore, Conwell, Craig, Roper.

American Spinning (Greenville, S.C.): Mostello, Turner, Bagwell, Porter, Smith, Vaughn.

Taylors High School (Taylors, S.C.: Henson, Belcher, Parker, Jordan, Tankersley.

Mills Mill (Greenville, S.C.): Bell, Ditmar, Putman, Carmon, Webb, Goodenough, Powell, Gaines, Ballew.

Anderson Mill (Anderson, S.C.): Whitlock, Perry, Stubblefield, English, Spake, Allen, Whitworth.

Class A Women

Asheville Victory (Asheville, N.C.), champions: Hensley, M. Reynolds, Holcombe, Couch, Mills, H. Reynolds, Owensby, White.

Dunean Mill (Greenville, S.C.), runners-up: Elliott, Jordan, Donnan, Putnam, Roberts, Hinton, Stewart, Riddle.

Asheville Victory Juniors (Asheville, N.C.), consolation winners: Elizabeth Fullam, Doris Lauce, Mabel Reynolds, Jean Thornburg, Rogers, Sara Boyd, Zethia Orr, Virginia Ingle, Polly Bagwell.

Anderson Mill (Anderson, S.C.): D. Porter, Stastny, Alexander, Penland, A. Porter, Loftis, James, Long, Embler.

Mills Mill (Greenville, S.C.): F. Thompson, D. Howard, Viola Thompson, Mahon, Long, Johnson, Miles, Moody, Trammell, Howard.

Drayton Mill (Spartanburg, S.C.): Splawn, Galger, Whitlock, Rogers, Sitton, Owens, Nabors, Taylor, R. Sitton, Goins.

1945 Piedmont Area Basketball Tournament

Class A Men

Drayton Mill (Spartanburg, S.C.), champions: Loftis, Hilton, Salmans, Morgan, Lancaster, Ted Petosky, Moffett.

Dunean Mill (Greenville, S.C.), runners-up: Turner, Willie Riddle, Fricks, Middie Hughes, Willie Wilbanks, O'dell, Snow Kirby, Orr.

Pelzer Mill (Pelzer, S.C.), consolation

winners: B. Harris, Tripp, Pete Harris, Allen, Earl Wooten, Hadden.

Campobello All Stars (Campobello, S.C.): Weaver, D. Gosnell, Wright, G. Gosnell, Rodgers.

J Bomber Squadron (Greenville, S.C.): Munce, Shook, Boynton, Oakleaf, Court, Bane, Gallagher, Smith, Van Atta, J. Bowen.

Monaghan Mill (Greenville, S.C.): Dilworth, Brooks, Phillips, Thompson, Palmer McAvoy, Lollis, Mintz, Stewart.

Holly Springs All Stars (Greenville, S.C.): Bryant, A. Jackson, Cooper, Gaines, Tidwell, Lydia, J. Jackson, Johnson.

Ecusta (Brevard, N.C.): M. Taylor, O. Taylor, Case, Coan, Sterling, Suttles, Simpson, Nelson.

Lonsdale Mill (Seneca, S.C.): Gibson, Morgan, Pruitt, Gilliard, Allsep, Shaver, McDonald.

Mills Mill (Greenville, S.C.): Snoddy, Cox, Barbary, Abbott, Powell, Smith, Norris, McAlister, Trammell.

Class B Men

Brandon Mill (Greenville, S.C.), champions: Byrd, Ward, Evington, Stowe, Goodenough, Carter, Willimon, Buchanan.

Woodside Mill (Greenville, S.C.), runners-up: McConnell, Billy Wakefield, Gwinn, Bert Wilson, Willie Mathis, H. Wilson, Farrow, J. Wilson, Taylor.

Beacon Mill (Swannanoa, N.C.), consolation winners: Carson, Davis, Patton, Marlow, Rudeen, Pittillo, Sides, Edmunds, Mills.

Monaghan Mill (Greenville, S.C.): Powers, McAvoy, Pittman, Pearson, Busbee, Griffith.

Anderson Mill (Anderson, S.C.): Spake, Whitworth, Hill, Morris, Bridges, McCombs.

Greenville High School (Greenville, S.C.): Carter, Bobby Roberts, Chiles, Garrett, Robertson, Taylor, Burdette, Wilkie, Loftis, Boling.

Red Shield (Greenville, S.C.): Darnell, Pittman, Hudgens, D. Nivens, B. Nivens, Moore, Conwell.

Greer High School (Greer, S.C.): Stancil, Henson, Lamb, Hemphill, Greer, Durham, Christmas.

Dunean Mill (Greenville, S.C.): Greene, Manley, LaBoone, Moody, Long, Langston, Walden, Fortune, Putnam.

San Souci (Greenville, S.C.): Locke.

Other Teams: Optimist (Greenville, S.C.), Slater Mill (Slater, S.C.), West Gantt (Greenville, S.C.).

Class A Women

Pelzer Mill (Pelzer, S.C.), champions: E. Jordan, J. Fowler, Turpin, Stewart, Hunt, R. Fowler, M. Jordan, Davis.

Gradegg (Asheville, N.C.), runners-up: Owenby, Reynolds, Holcombe, Couch, Mills, Corn, Randall, Chambers, Lindsay.

Anderson Mill (Anderson, S.C.), consolation winners: Burton, Alexander, Stastny, Embler, Pendleton, A. James, Jenkins, Thompson, James.

Monaghan Mill (Greenville, S.C.), Snelgrove, Hall, Shelton, L. Pepper, Major, Mull, Powell, Burrell, D. Pepper.

Lonsdale Mill (Seneca, S.C.): Wyatt, Foster, Alexander, Gilliard, Reeves, McClellan, Black, Shirley.

Dunean Mill (Greenville, S.C.): Donnan, Putnam, M. Lollis, Riddle, Bolt, Roberts, B. Lollis, Cox, Holcombe.

Taylors (Taylors, S.C.): Ward, Mauney, Jackson, E. Turner, Smith, Odum, C. Turner, Ballard.

Ecusta (Brevard, N.C.): Merrill, Watkins, W. Prince, Sisk, Smith, Taylor, Pangle, M. Prince.

Appendix 4

War-Time All Tournament Selections

1943 Greater Greenville Basketball Tournament

CLASS A MEN
Willie Wilbanks, Dunean Mill (Greenville, S.C.)
Earl Wooten, Mills Mill (Greenville, S.C.)
____ Cannon, Mills Mill (Greenville, S.C.)
Mississippi Hinton, 349th Service Squadron (Greenville, S.C.)
Spot Trammell, Mills Mill (Greenville, S.C.)

CLASS B MEN
Horace Turner, Dunean Mill (Greenville, S.C.)
Bob Stowe, Dunean Mill (Greenville, S.C.)
George Pruitt, Woodside Mill (Greenville, S.C.)
George Beasley, Woodside Mill (Greenville, S.C.)
Mickey Ellis, Woodside Mill (Greenville, S.C.)

1944 Piedmont Area Basketball Tournament

CLASS A MEN
____ Demarest, 471st Bomber Squadron (Greenville, S.C.)
Earl Wooten, Pelzer Mill (Pelzer, S.C.)
____ O'Shields, Drayton Mill (Spartanburg, S.C.)
Palmer McAvoy, Monaghan Mill (Greenville, S.C.)
Willie Wilbanks, Dunean Mill (Greenville, S.C.)

CLASS A WOMEN
____ Holcombe, Asheville Victory (Asheville, N.C.)
Viola Thompson, Mills Mill (Greenville, S.C.)
____ Putnam, Dunean Mill (Greenville, S.C.)
____ Jordan, Dunean Mill (Greenville, S.C.)
Mabel Reynolds, Asheville Victory Juniors (Asheville, N.C.)
____ Mills, Asheville Victory (Asheville, N.C.)

1945 Piedmont Area Basketball Tournament

CLASS A MEN
Middie Hughes, Dunean Mill (Greenville, S.C.)
Earl Wooten, Pelzer Mill (Pelzer, S.C.)
____ Salmans, Drayton Mill (Spartanburg, S.C.)
Palmer McAvoy, Monaghan Mill (Greenville, S.C.)
____ Lancaster, Drayton Mill (Spartanburg, S.C.)

CLASS A WOMEN
____ Holcombe, Gradegg (Asheville, N.C.)
Eckie Jordan, Pelzer Mill (Pelzer, S.C.)
W. Prince, Ecusta (Brevard, N.C.)
____ Corn, Gradegg (Asheville, N.C.)
____ Smith, Ecusta (Brevard, N.C.)
____ Stewart, Pelzer Mill (Pelzer, S.C.)

Appendix 5

Southern Textile Athletic Association Hall of Fame
(by Year Elected)

1961

(Charter Members)
Dr. L.P. Hollis (Greenville, S.C.); founder, past president.
Clarence Thomas (Greenville, S.C.); past president.

1962

C.V. Verner (Piedmont, S.C.); past president.
Horace Whitmire (Greenwood, S.C.); past president.

1963

Jesse Brown, Union Bleachery (Greenville, S.C.); past president.
Willie Riddle, Dunean Mill (Greenville, S.C.); All Southern.

1964

Harley Heath, Pelzer Mill (Pelzer, S.C.); coach, past president.
Sara Jordan Ellis, Pelzer Mill (Pelzer, S.C.); All Southern.

1965

Bert Hill, Southern Bleachery (Taylors, S.C.), All Southern.
Lucille Foster Thomas, Monaghan Mill (Greenville, S.C.); All Southern.

1966

Willie Wilbanks, Southern Bleachery (Taylors, S.C.), Dunean Mill (Greenville, S.C.); past president, All Southern.
Earl Wooten, Pelzer Mill (Pelzer, S.C.), Piedmont Mill (Piedmont, S.C.); coach, All Southern, All Time Scoring Leader (Men).

1967

Esco Leopard, Lonsdale Mill (Seneca, S.C.); All Southern.
John Emery, Piedmont Mill (Piedmont, S.C.); All Southern.

1968

Jack Reames (Abbeville, S.C.); past vice-president, past executive director.
Ward Williams, Dunean Mill (Greenville, S.C.); All Southern, coach, past president.

STAA Hall of Fame Appendix 5

---1969---

J.L. Gourley (Marion, N.C.).
G.L. Doggett (Piedmont, S.C.).

---1970---

Sam Patton, American Enka (Enka, N.C.); All Southern, coach.
Divver Hendrix (Greenville, S.C.); past president, past treasurer.

---1971---

Dick Wilson, Victor Mill (Greer, S.C.); All Southern.
Vercho Carter, Russell Manufacturing (Alexander City, Ala.); All Southern, coach.

---1972---

Hubert Nolin, Monaghan Mill (Greenville, S.C.); All Southern.
Ken Pittman, Monaghan Mill (Greenville, S.C.); All Southern, past president.

---1973---

Fred Byrd (Greenville, S.C.); past executive secretary.
Mickey Davis, Ware Shoals Mill (Ware Shoals, S.C.), Slater Mill (Marietta, S.C.); All Southern

---1974---

Sue Vickers, Slater Mill (Slater, S.C.); All Southern, All Time Scoring Leader (Women).
Whitey Kendall (Greenville, S.C.); referee and Superintendent of Officials.

---1975---

Effie Evington, Monaghan Mill (Greenville, S.C.); All Southern.
D.K. Smith, Lyman Mill (Lyman, S.C.); All Southern, past president.

---1976---

Bob Stowe, Dunean Mill (Greenville, S.C.); All Southern.
Snow Kirby, Southern Bleachery (Taylors, S.C.), Dunean Mill (Greenville, S.C.); player, coach, executive committee member.

---1977---

Lyles Alley, Southern Bleachery (Taylors, S.C.); player, coach.

---1978---

None elected.

---1979---

Fred Snoddy, Dunean Mill (Greenville, S.C.); player, coach, referee, past president, past executive committee member.

---1980---

Harry Foster, Brandon Mill (Greenville, S.C.); player, coach, past president, past treasurer, past executive committee member.

---1981---

None elected.

---1982---

Bill Hopkins, Pelzer Mill (Pelzer, S.C.); player, coach, past president, past vice-president, past executive committee member.
Fred Powers (Greenville, S.C.); player, coach, past president, past vice-president, past executive committee member.

---1983---

Frank Ballenger (Greenville, S.C.); sportswriter.

Barbara Jean Bell, Pelzer Mill (Pelzer, S.C.); All Southern, past executive committee member.

1984

Jimmy Hopkins, Pelzer Mill (Pelzer, S.C.); player, coach, past executive committee member.

Lt. F.R. Hawkins (Greenville, S.C.); security chief.

1985

Don Carver, Monsanto (Greenwood, S.C.); player, coach.

1986

Fred McAbee, Brandon Mill (Greenville, S.C.); player, coach, past executive committee member.

Lloyd McAbee, Brandon Mill (Greenville, S.C.); player, coach, past executive committee member.

1987

None elected.

1988

Bobby Roberts, Pelzer Mill (Pelzer, S.C.); player, coach, later coach for Clemson University.

Jyles Phillips, American Spinning (Greenville, S.C.); player, coach, past president, past executive committee member.

1989

Ruppert Elliott (Greenville, S.C.); player, coach, past executive committee member.

Charles Roddy, Dunean Mill (Greenville, S.C.); player, coach, referee, past president, past executive committee member.

1990

Leon Gravley (Greer, S.C.); coach, referee.

1991

Jim Ball, Mills Mill (Greenville, S.C.); player, team sponsor.

1992

Chip Gray (Greenville, S.C.); team sponsor.
Donald Roddy (Greenville, S.C.).

1993

Gene Seay, Piedmont Mill (Piedmont, S.C.); player.

1994

Steve Brown (Greer, S.C.); player, coach, past executive committee member.

Appendix 6

Southern Textile Basketball Tournament Timeline

February 12, 1926— Piedmont defeated Dunean in Class B women's semifinal action; 37 fouls were called.

February 10, 1927— In a Class B women's game, Lonsdale Mill defeated Apalache 37–10 behind Padgett's 27 points.

February 10, 1927— In the Class A men's division, Lyman defeated Lonsdale Mill 70–26, led by Paul Barbare's 20.

February 10, 1927— In Class A men's action, Piedmont defeated Manchester Mill 62–36 behind Beasley's 24 points.

February 12, 1927— Three thousand spectators saw the championship games.

February 16, 1928— In the opening Class C men's game, Camperdown defeated Calloway Mill 19–18 on a last second shot by John McDowell.

February 16, 1928— In Class AA men's action, Lyman defeated Piedmont 37–33 before 2,000 spectators.

February 17, 1928— In the Class C men's semifinals, Draper defeated Monaghan 11–10.

February 14, 1929— J.C. Davis of Dunean's C men was handicapped by poor eyesight, which explains his plaudits as a "wizard on short shots."

February 14, 1929— In Class B men's action, Simpsonville defeated Columbus Mill 38–37 in four overtimes.

February 15, 1929— In the Class B men's semifinals, Avondale routed Saxon 47–16 as Roberts' 18 outpaced the loser's point total.

February 16, 1929— In the Class B women's championship, Orr defeated Monaghan 26–9 as Virginia Kinnett scored 20.

February 19, 1931— Victor Mill flew past Anderson Mill 61–4 in Class C men's action.

February 20, 1931— Ware Shoals Mill defeated Abbeville 26–3 in Class B women's semifinal action. Abbeville scored no field goals.

February 26, 1932— Lonsdale Mill defeated Victor Mill in Class A men's action, freezing the ball the last seven-and-a-half minutes of the game. Victor never regained possession.

February 28, 1932— The Spartan Mill Class B women pummeled Kenneth Mill 26–5 to capture the consolation prize. Spartan's Wilma Whitlock was said to be "mannish" in her scoring.

February 15, 1934— Lonsdale's Class A men defeated Spindale Mill 51–26, and the winners were led by Pruitt's 25 points.

February 20, 1935— Beulah Brewton scored all but one of her team's points, but she could not stave off defeat as Drayton's Class B women defeated Greer Mill 27–22.

February 20, 1935— Judson Mill's Class A men, led by Dan Matthews' 25 points, swamped Glen Lowery Mill 63–24.

February 19, 1936— In Class B men's action, Equinox Mill's Thomas Ray scored 35 in a 64–21 win over Brandon.

377

March 3, 1937—Peerless Woolen Mill's Class B men powered through Mills Mill 60–5, holding the losers without a field goal.

March 4, 1937—The Class A men from Lyman Mill crushed Glen Lowery 76–28, and the winners were led by Cabiness's 39 points.

March 2, 1938—The Chatham Mfg. Class A women completed the regular season with a record of 38–2.

March 3, 1938—McCrary Hosiery Mill doubled Winnsboro Mill 70–35 in a Class A men's game. Paul Roye's 35 powered the winners.

March 1, 1939—In Class B women's action, Slater Mill defeated Abbeville 11–7.

March 4, 1939—In the Class A women's finals, Lanett Mill's star center, Louise Wood, fouled out with *four* personals, and the Alabama team lost to Chatham Mfg. 24–20.

March 6, 1940—The Class B women of Grey Hosiery Mill defeated Judson 66–18 as Lassie Dunn scored 38.

March 7, 1940—Brandon Mill's Class B women crushed Converse 47–8, and they were led by Christine Rollins' 24 points.

March 7, 1940—In Class B women's action, Dixie Mercerizing blasted Woodside Mill 60–8. Myrtle Dooley's 25 led the winners.

March 5, 1941—The Class B women of Grey Hosiery Mill nailed Converse 64–3. Lassie Dunn's 34 led the winners.

March 5, 1942—Earl Wooten's 32-point effort led the Class C Pelzer men over Dunean 47–33.

February 26, 1947—It was reported that electric clocks had been added to facilitate accurate timekeeping.

February 26, 1947—The Class A men from Peerless Woolen blew away Piedmont Mill 104–64, and the winners were led by John Barger's 30.

February 27, 1947—Brandon defeated Drayton Mill 63–34 in Class A men's action as James Orr's 24 led the victors.

March 2, 1950—In the Class B men's consolation bracket, Russell Manufacturing blew away Glendale Mill, placing five men in double figures.

March 4, 1953—The C men from Dunean routed Greer Mill 78–18.

March 5, 1953—Judson Mill upset Calhoun Falls 33–26 in Class B women's action. Forty-three fouls were called.

March 3, 1954—Gene Seay scored 59, leading Brandon Mill to a 94–37 crushing of Apalache in a Class C men's consolation game.

March 2, 1955—Wayne Godfrey scored 30 for Victor Mill, but Monaghan still defeated the Greer team 90–79 in Class A men's action.

March 2, 1955—In a Class C men's game, Cecil Hagood scored 32 as Greenwood Mill edged Simpsonville Mill, 64–63.

March 3, 1955—Gary Henderson's 33 led his Simpsonville Class B squad over Monaghan Mill, 61–57.

March 4, 1955—Piedmont defeated Glen Lowery 79–52 in Class C men's action, led by Roger Dill's 37 points.

March 4, 1955—Earl Wooten's 37 led Pelzer's A men past American Enka, 99–77.

March 4, 1955—Orr Mill's Melvin Aiken scored 30 to lead his mates to a 69–44 win over Apalache Mill in the Class C men's consolation bracket.

March 4, 1955—Peerless Woolen won the Class A men's semifinal consolation matchup, 87–32 over Union Bleachery. Pete Brown, former football All-American at Georgia Tech, had 27 points for the winners.

February 29, 1956—In Class A women's action, Joanna beat Greer 51–24 as Frances Davenport's 33 led the winners.

March 6, 1957—Fiberglas crushed Joanna Mill 102–62 in Class B men's action, led by Leroy Parnell's 41 points.

March 6, 1957—The Class B men from Monaghan defeated Poe Mill 82–66 behind Jimmy Holden's 33 points.

March 6, 1957—Courtaulds' B men popped Fiberglas 85–56, led by James McAdams' 31 points.

March 12, 1958—Leon Gravley, coach of the Class A Greer men, scored 42 to pace his team to a 106–80 win over the Pirates of Victor Mill.

March 13, 1958—Monaghan Mill's Class A men defeated Greer Mill 104–93, led by Willard Fowler's 36 points.

March 11, 1959—Jimmy Holden had 37 as Monaghan Mill defeated Stone Mfg. 84–54 in Class B men's action.

March 11, 1959—Apalache's Class B men, led by Jimmy Herring's 34 points, bested Lonsdale Mill 76–57.

March 11, 1959—The Class A women of Carolina Plating bested Stone Mfg. 50–28, behind the 26 points of Judy Bowen.

March 12, 1959—Dunean Mill pounded Poinsett Lumber 57–36 as Mickey Long's 28 led his Class B team to the win.

March 12, 1959—Monaghan edged Fiberglas 70–63 in a Class B men's game; the winners were paced by Jimmy Holden's 32 points.

March 12, 1959—In a Class B men's consolation game, Bob Waldrop scored 35 as Southern Bleachery reversed Calhoun Falls 64–46.

March 13, 1959—Monaghan defeated American Enka 94–79 in Open Division play. The winners were led by Dick Wright (31 points), the losers by Daddy Neal (25) and Ron Rogers (25).

March 14, 1959—In Open Division consolation play, Carolina Plating slipped by Victor Mill 79–75, despite Hal Huey's 31 points for Victor.

March 14, 1959—Roger Coln's 32 points moved Style Crafters past Southern Bleachery 78–68 in a Class B men's consolation game.

March 9, 1960—Dunean destroyed Diehl 88–39 in Class B men's action. Ricky Duncan and Ronnie Russell (both of North Greenville Junior College) had 32 and 28 points, respectively.

March 9, 1960—Russell Manufacturing crushed Union Bleachery 119–64 in Class B men's action, placing five in double figures: Jimmy Jones (20), Bobby Bailey (20), Olin Wingard (19), Charles Robinson (17), Huell (11).

March 9, 1960—Monaghan defeated Southern Bleachery 88–73 in a Class B men's game behind Jimmy Holden's 34 points.

March 11, 1960—Defending Class A women's champions Lonsdale held on for a 50–46 win over Greer Mill. Brenda Addis led the winners with 31 points.

March 12, 1960—In the Class C men's championship, Dunean defeated Slater 70–55 as all five starters hit for double figures: Kenneth Smith (17), Jimmy Chapman (16), Earl Whittington (13), Eddie Forrester (12), Herman Patterson (10).

March 7, 1961—Earl Whittington scored 36 to lead Dunean past Monsanto (Greenwood) 84–58 in a Class B men's game. Garrett Nation's 25 led the losers.

March 7, 1961—Newry rallied in the fourth period to beat Lyman 58–52 in Class C men's action, sparked by Wayne Lacey's 30 points.

March 7, 1961—Donnie Sargent had 36 to lead Dunean over Union Bleachery 70–49 in a Class C men's game.

March 9, 1961—In a Class B men's consolation matchup, Monsanto (Greenwood) defeated Davis Mechanical 79–55 behind Harold Nation's 43-point performance.

March 10, 1961—Monsanto (Pensacola, Fla.) bested Poinsett Lumber 85–69 in a Class B men's game. Former Auburn University star Jim Diamond had 27 for the winners, Bill Moore 35 for the Lumbermen.

March 10, 1961—Jim Lewis's 38 led the Slater Mill Class B men's team over Wyandotte Mill 97–67; teammate John Ladd had 26.

March 6, 1962—Lonsdale's Class C men ran past Piedmont Mill 89–61 behind Wayne Lacey's 37 points.

March 7, 1962—In Class B men's action, Leon Eubanks scored 30 to move Lyman past Steel Heddle, 77–64.

March 7, 1962—In the Open Division, Wofford College's Ronnie Russell had 30 to lead Piedmont Paint past the Seneca All Stars, 94–71.

March 8, 1962—Slater Mill prevailed 95–85 in a Class A men's win over Poinsett Mill despite Mickey Dobbins' fine 30-point effort in a losing cause.

March 8, 1962—Glen Lowery Mill stopped Dunean 77–62 in Class B men's play behind the fine 35-point performance of Alfred Spotts.

March 9, 1962—Apalache Mill's Class A men defeated Monsanto (Pensacola, Fla.) 87–59, as Don Lister scored 33.

March 10, 1962—Saco-Lowell edged Pelzer 74–71 for the Class B men's title. Michael Jordan had 32 points in the Bears' losing effort.

March 4, 1963—Charles Aiken scored 31 for Fiberglas, but he and his teammates could not overcome Poinsett, 73–70, in a Class B men's tilt.

March 6, 1963—Pharr Worsted raced past Clark-Schwebel 83–61 in Open Division play, led by Joe McDermott's 30 points.

March 6, 1963—Class A men's action saw Monsanto (Greenwood) defeat Cranston, 95–72. "Pistol Pete" Carlisle, former Furman University player, had 40 for the winners.

March 6, 1963—Monaghan walloped Newry 74–34 in Class C men's action; they were led by Mike Fair's 31 points.

March 7, 1963—In Open Division play, Todd-Moore edged Sangamo 102-95. Art Whisnant (41 points) paced Todd-Moore, and Larry Seltz's 30 led Sangamo.

March 9, 1963—Steel Heddle won the Class B men's consolation trophy with an 81–56 win over Davis Mechanical. Mike Davis had 34 for the winners.

March 10, 1964—Clemson University's Vince Yockel scored 36 to move Piedmont past Cranston 97–78 in Class A men's play.

March 10, 1964—Glenda Crooks's 27 led Adams Oil over Walhalla Mill 51–27 in Class A women's play.

March 11, 1964—All Lyman starters were in double figures in a 100–88 Class A men's win over Russell Manufacturing: Steve Brown (36), Ronnie Russell (26), Leon Eubanks (15), William Green (12), and Bill Eubanks (10).

March 12, 1964—Belton High School coach Carolyn Clayton scored all five points in overtime in Singer's 47–44 win over Monsanto (Pensacola, Fla.) in Class A women's play.

March 9, 1965—Kenneth Anderson scored 33 and the Class A men of Lyman defeated Singer (Pickens), 73–62.

March 10, 1965—Davis Mechanical defeated Homelite #1, 76–61, in Class B men's play; Tommy Crump's 30 led the way.

March 10, 1965—Jack Wilson's 30 paced Dunean over Monsanto (Blacksburg) 66–62 in Class B men's action.

March 10, 1965—Slater's Nancy Oldham scored 25 as her team bested Microtron 50–39 in Class A women's action.

March 11, 1965—Herman Evatt scored 34 but Lyman defeated his Pelzer Class B teammates, 92–73.

March 12, 1965—In Class C men's play, Donnie Lewis's 32 led Monaghan over Simpsonville, 72–62.

March 12, 1965—In Open Division action, Bob McCullough scored 30 for Murrell Brothers Sand in a 105–90 win over Sunshine Cleaners.

March 13, 1965—In the Class A men's consolation finals, Slater rode Leroy Peacock's stellar 40-point effort to an 82–57 win over Monsanto (Pensacola, Fla.).

March 15, 1966—Monsanto (Greenwood) blew past Davis Mechanical 106–69 in a Class A men's game. Don Carver, former Clemson University player, had 36 for the winners.

March 16, 1966—Piedmont defeated Saco-Lowell 107–73 in Class A men's action. Joe Hiott (31 points), Gene Seay (22 points and the leading rebounder), and Larry Holcombe (20 points) paced the win.

March 17, 1966—In the Class B men's division, Lyman edged Monsanto (Pensacola, Fla.) 71–64 as Dan Watson scored 30 (20 in the first half).

March 17, 1966—Mike Fair (40) and Mike Campbell (29) moved Parker Mill past Milliken 104–72 in Class B men's consolation play.

March 17, 1966—Skeeter Hammett's 38 points led Dunean over Fiber Industries 70–65 in Class B men's consolation play.

March 18, 1966—Dunean defeated Sangamo 100–65 in a Class B men's consolation game as three players scored more than 20 points: Charles Hudson (28), Skeeter Hammett (26), and Jimmy Riddle (21). Garland Rigdon had 30 for Sangamo.

March 19, 1966—In Open Division consolation play, the Charlotte All Stars beat Washington Mill, 99–89. Tom Wynn (42 points) led Charlotte; Jay Beal (40) paced Washington.

March 7, 1967—Russell Manufacturing's Class A men ran past Slater 101–86 behind Jimmy Childers' 33 points.

March 7, 1967—Greer squeaked past Dunean 83–82 in Class B action despite Skeeter Hammett's 30 points for Dunean.

March 7, 1967—Saco-Lowell, led by Wardell Sims' 40 points, defeated Singer's Class A men, 100–82.

March 7, 1967—Donnie Adams' 33 led Appleton's Class C men over Piedmont #2, 71–57.

March 8, 1967—Skeeter Hammett's 33 points helped ease Dunean's Class B men past Gluck Mill, 68–62.

March 10, 1967—Mikro rallied for an 89–87 Open Divison win over Hinton's All Stars. Jesse Branson (28) and Dwight Durante (21) led the way.

March 11, 1967—Lyman captured the Class A men's consolation title with an 85–56 win over Kendall (Seneca). They were paced by Jerry Green's 33-point effort.

Southern Textile Barketball Tournament Timeline Appendix 6 381

March 13, 1968 — Bigelow-Sanford defeated Union Bleachery 77–54 in a Class B contest behind Terry Chrisley's 39 points.

March 14, 1968 — In Open Division play, K.G. Carpet raced by Elkay Industries, 115–81. Don Wix (29 points, 20 in the second half) and Dave Denton (25 points) led the win.

March 14, 1968 — Maxie Burns' 34 moved Dunean past Greer 82–72 in Class B men's play.

March 15, 1968 — Russell Manufacturing's Class A men blasted Monsanto (Pensacola, Fla.) 93–61 as Wayne Rape scored 32.

March 16, 1968 — Kendall (Seneca) captured the Class A men's title with a 95–72 win over Homelite; Mike Black's 38 points led Kendall.

March 11, 1969 — Gary Helms scored 31 to lead Guthrie Motors over Transit Homes 101–85 in Open Division play.

March 11, 1969 — In Class B men's play, Terry Chrisley scored 31 and Bigelow-Sanford defeated Parker, 66–50.

March 13, 1969 — Charles McIntyre's 38 helped move Monaghan past Easley 96–61 in a Class B men's consolation game.

March 13, 1969 — Mitch Caldwell's 31 points led Russell Manufacturing's 120–56 pounding of Rohm-Haas in Class A men's action.

March 14, 1969 — Phillips Fibers, behind Ralph Brown's 30 points, edged Lyman 82–77 in Class B men's action.

March 14, 1969 — Slater ran away from LTV 77–30 in Class A women's play. Four reached double figures for the winners: Linda Rikard (21), Judy Murray (21), Joan Kirby (18), and Linda Edwards (13)

March 10, 1970 — Richard Keir scored 36 and Pelzer's Class B men defeated Bigelow-Sanford, 79–63.

March 10, 1970 — In a Class C men's game, Clyde Agnew's 31 lifted Poe Hardware over Precise Machine Works, 81–77.

March 11, 1970 — Taylors Mill's Class A men blew away Phillips Fibers 83–43 behind Steve Moore's 37 points.

March 12, 1970 — The Class A Dunean men defeated Madison Throwing Co. 85–74, led by Skeeter Davis's 40.

March 12, 1970 — Doug Lowe's 31 points moved Crown-Metro's Class C men past Ross Tires, 79–64.

March 13, 1970 — Jimmy Childers scored 36 as Class A Russell Manufacturing defeated Taylors Mill, 98–72.

March 13, 1970 — Richard Keir's 32 propelled the Class B men from Pelzer over Monaghan, 77–61.

March 9, 1971 — In Class A women's play, Judy Murray had 26 to lead Texize over Piedmont, 70–18.

March 11, 1971 — The B men from Precise Machine Works defeated Taylors Mill 63–37 as Doug Thackston scored 40 points.

March 29, 1972 — In Class B men's play, Victor Mill defeated Hoechst Celanese behind the 33 points of Ron Bailey.

March 29, 1972 — Pelzer #2 edged Simmons Machinery Co. 63–56 in Class C men's action. Larry Ray scored 35 for the winners.

March 29, 1972 — Piedmont's Mike McCauley had 37 to lead the his Class C squad past John Perkins Industries, 52–41.

March 30, 1972 — In Open Division play, Will Robinson had 34 to pace Texize over Decorative Components, 114–84.

March 21, 1973 — The Class A men from Fiber Processing defeated Borden Mill 77–66 behind Lee Brown's 38 (26 in the first half).

March 25, 1975 — In Class B men's play, Mickey Rogers' 31 led Saco-Lowell by Cryovac (Simpsonville), 60–56.

March 27, 1975 — Carolina Material Handling slipped by Sangamo Electric Co. 73–69 in overtime. Leonard Russell's 34 took game high honors for the losers in this Class B men's game.

March 27, 1975 — Saco-Lowell's Class B men edged Butte Knitting Mill 65–62 in overtime as Mickey Rogers scored 33 for the winners.

March 29, 1975 — In Class B men's consolation action, Len White had 35 to lead Parke-Davis by Dunean Mill, 73–72.

March 23, 1976 — Marvin Drummond's 32 led Hoechst Celanese over Dunean, 84–59, in Class A men's play.

March 24, 1976 — Renfrew Bleachery's Class B men defeated Saco-Lowell 68–54; the winners were led by Jerome Williams' 38 (26 in the first half).

March 25, 1976 — Sangamo's Class A men ran past Lyman Mill 87–63 behind Robert Cannon's 33 points.

March 25, 1976 — In Class B men's action, Alice Mfg. blasted Fiber Industries 101–77, led by the duo of Terry Smith (38) and Johnny White (33).

March 27, 1976— James Camden had 31 to lead Barley Plumbing over Parker Mill 57–52 and the Class A men's consolation cup.

March 22, 1977— Parker Mill's Class A men claimed a 68–67 win over Homelite, overcoming a 32-point effort by the losers' Charles Crawford.

March 23, 1977— Monaghan bested Parker Mill in Class A men's play, led by Chuck Leamon's 31 points.

March 23, 1977— Lyman Mill had five players in double figures, topped by Lewis Jennings' 31 points, and blasted Dunean 108–61 in Class A men's action.

March 23, 1977— Athletic Attic's Class A men crushed General Electric 100–57 behind the 31-point performance of Donald Davis.

March 23, 1977— For the Class B men of Simpsonville Mill, Ernest Westmoreland scored 35 to key an 86–54 win over American Monorail.

March 24, 1977— Athletic Attic's Class A men rode James Clark's 39 to a 95–88 win over Lyman Mill.

March 24, 1977— Marvin Drummond's 37 led Hoechst Celanese past Alice Mfg., 84–72, in Class A men's play.

March 21, 1978— Cryovac (Simpsonville) defeated Saco-Lowell 96–58 in Class A men's play, despite a 33-point effort by the losers' Larry Davis.

March 17, 1980—Collis Hardy scored 41 as Homelite defeated Slater 88–75 in Class A men's action.

March 20, 1980— Mike Miller's 37 points led Union Carbide to a 77–63 Class B men's win over A & C Warehouse.

March 18, 1981— Non-Fluid Oil blasted Parker Mill 74-8 in women's action.

March 20, 1981— Alice Mfg. edged Ware Shoals Mill 92–90 in a Class A men's game. Albert Smith had 46 in a losing cause.

March 27, 1982— Pam Adams' 31 points led Revis Trucking to a 60–47 victory over Black's Mechanical in the Class A women's consolation bracket.

March 27, 1984— Monsanto defeated Dunean 81–54 in a Class A men's game, led by Barry Brown's 37 points.

March 22, 1985— PPG's Larry Ross scored 30 to lead his team past Alice Mfg. 84–83 in a Class A men's game.

March 22, 1985— Steve Smith of Greenville Valve had 33, but Michelin prevailed 62–51 in Class A men's action.

March 26, 1986— In a Class A men's tilt, Marvin Drummond's 32 moved Hoechst Celanese past Michelin, 80–64.

March 27, 1987— Pearl Moore scored 19 and Four Star Sports defeated Mac's All Stars 61–50 in women's semifinal action.

March 27, 1987— Terry Camp scored 31, and PPG defeated Emb-Tex 83–67 in a Class A men's game.

March 29, 1988— Bennie Parks scored 40 to lead Shedd's to a men's Class B win, 72–54, over Sangamo Electric Co.

March 24, 1989— PPG defeated Saco-Lowell 78–73 in Class A men's action behind the 38 points of Larry Ross.

March 26, 1990— Hoskin's 30 led the Sixers over Sam Wyche Sports World 119–69 in men's Open action.

March 28, 1990— Steve Crowe scored 35 to move Greenville Valve past Clinton Mill 73–71 in Class B men's action.

March 30, 1990— Steve Smith had 39 as Greenville Valve defeated Cryovac 63–56 in a Class B men's game.

March 30, 1990— Mike Gillison had 41 as the Charleston Flyers defeated S&M Sports 123–117 in the men's Open division. David Lawrence had 43 for S&M.

March 30, 1990— Carl Smith (36) and Jimmy Brown (31) powered Poinsett Grocery past the Sixers 119–113 in a men's Open division semifinal game.

March 26, 1991— John Perry scored 40 as Top Gun outlasted the Orangemen 80–77 in men's Open action.

March 29, 1991— For the Class B men, American Amusements beat Mike Davis Landscaping 85–69 as six players reached in double figures: John Williams (25), Rodney McCauley (12), Clay Carter (12), Andy Carter (12), Greg Travis (10), and Jeff Lollis (10).

March 30, 1991— T-Shirts Plus swamped St. Francis Hospital 72–44 for the Class A women's title behind the play of Laura Byrd (22), Dorothy Bowers (16), Nessie Harris (13), and Pearl Moore (12).

March 16, 1992— Mike Kelly scored 30, but American Federal still defeated his Class B C&S Bank team, 81–60.

March 18, 1992— Greenville Valve used the

scoring of Steve Smith (36) to edge Wunda Weve 79–72 in Class B men's action.

March 21, 1992—In the women's Class A consolation finals, Toni Edwards' 30 moved St. Francis Hospital over C. Dan Joyner, 48–42.

March 15, 1993—NCR blasted Greenville City Recreation 49–10 in a Class A women's game. Katie Holden scored all the points for the losers.

March 16, 1993—John Bennett's 33 allowed Fiberweb to edge Employee Benefits 63–61 in Class B men's action.

March 17, 1993—Curtis Watson scored 37 and the Class B Clinton Mill men defeated Northside Correctional, 95–77.

March 19, 1993—Pete Rozell had 32 and SMC won over Employee Benefits 81–70 in a Class B men's consolation game.

March 20, 1993—Todd Collins scored 31 as his Palmetto Expos defeated SMC 81–73 for the Class B men's consolation title.

March 23, 1994—David Lawrence's 32 moved S&M Sports past Chester's Chicken 86–61 in men's Open Division play.

March 25, 1994—Upperstate I had six in double figures to crush Sullivan's Sonics 85–59 in Class C men's play: Ryan Lookabill (16), Tawambi Settles (13), Atlba Daniels (13), Tank Montgomery (12), Anthony Flanagan (12), and Larry Penn (10).

March 21, 1995—Geoff Bentzel's 31 powered Poinsett Grocery over Walmart 99–36 in Class C men's action.

March 22, 1995—Christopher Michael's 34 led S&R Auto over the Anderson Shockers 94–59 in a men's Open Division game.

March 29, 1997—Carolyn Brown scored 30 as King Valley defeated the Low Country All Stars for the Class A women's championship.

Appendix 7

Player Profiles

Pete Rollins and Frank Norris

If blood runs thicker than water, then for the Rollins and Norris clans add the sweat of the gym coursing through their veins. For them, the Southern Textile Basketball Tournament is a family affair.

Pete Rollins was born on the Judson Mill village, and had a second home at the YMCA there. "We played ball, either at home, where my brothers and I put a goal up in the back yard, or at the 'Y,' where we were encouraged in our play by director John H. Garraux, long a familiar presence in the tournament," he said.

Rollins joined his brothers Robert, Ray, Dick, Vernon and Phil to field a solid team, not at Judson but at Camperdown, where his family had moved. "In 1946 we all played Class C ball, and three years later we moved up to Class B," Pete recalled. "Heck, Vernon would get leave from the Navy and suit up with us like he'd never been away. We scrimmaged teams from Simpsonville to Piedmont, and competed against some fine players, but I really had the greatest respect for Monaghan's Fig Newton. He was a competitor and a gentleman."

A big thrill for Rollins occurred in 1948, when his West Gantt High team played for the state championship. "Bennettsville High beat us by eight." A bigger thrill was going to Gardner-Webb College as their 6'3" center. "John Roberts, recently retired editor of the *Baptist Courier*, and his wife drove me up there for my initial tryout. They gave me lots of encouragement." The biggest thrills, though, were reserved for the Southern Textile Basketball Tournament.

Rollins prowled the courts of old Textile Hall for seven years. "It was always such a festive occasion, the original March Madness," he said. "Charlie Pendleton, our coach at Camperdown, lived for that time of year. He would come on our jobs at the mill and talk with us about how we needed to play that night." Competing against the likes of Bouncing Bob Smith and Bobby Fortune was something Rollins relished.

Tempers occasionally flared. "Woodside and Brandon were always big rivals, but the wildest game I ever remember involved Dunean. One of their players hit the referee during a heated contest, and two of the official's brothers leaped out of the balcony and onto the floor to help. The awfullest fight you ever saw proceeded to break out, and it took quite a while to restore order."

Rollins is quick to relate that his greatest enjoyment came not from playing but from coaching. "Working with the kids from Grace Road Baptist Church in their Sunday School League always meant a lot to me. Shoot, basketball had given me so much, so many good memories, and if I can give just a little bit of that back to these youngsters, that will suit me just fine." A nice way to keep the textile sports tradition going, too.

Frank Norris's association with textile athletics began in 1931 at Mills Mill, a quick sprint down Church Street from Camperdown. "I played ball in the tournament from 1932 to 1942, but family ties go back to the very beginning in 1921," he said. "My uncle, John Freeman, played with Woodside Mill on their championship team in that inaugural event. The Norris folks have been around for quite a while, as you can see.

"My favorite memory of the Southern Textile Basketball Tournament had to be 1938, when Mills Mill went up against Union Bleachery for the Class B championship. They beat us, but I took three shots from half court, made two of 'em, and the third hit the rim and bounced off. Of course, that feat may not be as good as it sounds, since I recall that the courts in old Textile Hall were only about two-thirds the size of a regulation court. There were big crowds then, and for me it was truly the best of times."

Norris left the mill life in 1942 to work for the railroad, a career move he has never regretted. Still, he has not missed a tournament since his playing days began in 1931. "In December of 1984, I had gangrene and lost sixty pounds, but come March I was in my accustomed seat at Memorial Auditorium. I most enjoyed watching Earl Wooten play, but there were a lot of good athletes who have been here. Billy Cunningham, Henry Logan, Tree Rollins, Ward Williams, Eckie Jordan, Patsy Neal, and so many more brought a lot of enjoyment to the fans."

Changes, he believes, have not been kind to the tournament. As folks in the mill village started to buy automobiles, as mill owners sold the mill houses and the sense of community died, and as television became more popular, the games suffered greatly. Norris, though, keeps coming back every year.

"I've just always loved to watch the tournament games. Seems like I always knew someone who was competing, and I'd pull for their team. Last year [1995], my great-grandson played on the team that won the Eight and Under championship, and he was high scorer for the league during the season. And shoot, if I don't know anybody, I'll take a deep breath and yell like crazy for the underdog. Might sound odd for somebody my age, but I just love the game. Always have. Always will."

Kathlyn Kelley Owens

She was a young lady led to a particular place in history by her athletic ability. She touched that special moment, moved ahead unafraid, and got on with the business of living. Many of us would fear slipping into insignificance after such an encounter, but not Kathlyn Kelley Owens.

"Mama was always her own person, and never tried to impress anyone," says daughter Carolyn Owens. "She believed 'God made me to be me' and didn't ever want to be anyone but herself." The pieces of the puzzle have a way of fitting together, just as intended, when life is viewed in such a way.

"Sports like basketball, softball, baseball, I enjoyed them all, but it was running and jumping that I truly loved," notes Kathlyn. Daughter Carolyn adds that there were other sports, such as roller skating and ice skating, in which her mom excelled. "As far as athletics go, there really wasn't very much Mama couldn't do." It was Keowee School, and later Seneca High School (where she graduated in 1935), which bore a mere regional witness to her skills, but there were forces in motion which would change all that.

Her coach was principal Julian Davis, who saw something special in the 5'11" lass and convinced her to try out for sports, with an emphasis in track and field. During one of their meets, Kathlyn jumped 5'1½" using the standard scissors kick—going over the bar in an upright position, and first kicking the front, and then the back leg, over. "High jumping just came natural to me," Owens said, "but Mr. Davis sure got excited about that one effort."

And with good reason. A little checking established that the women's world record was held by the legend herself, Babe Didrickson Zaharias, at 5'3¼", so Davis thought it imperative to publicize young Owens' achievement. Her photo was sent to "Scoop" Latimer, sports editor of the Greenville *News*, who agreed with Davis that such talent should not be restricted to the local climate. And so began the push to the Olympics, scheduled for Berlin in 1936.

"Mr. Davis took me to Clemson to meet Frank Howard and Jess Neely, and they agreed to have the track coaches work with me. That was a big deal, because up until then I had had no formal coaching in any track or field events. For me, success was the combination of three things: talent, a desire to excel, and a good coach. The Good Lord put the first two in me, and wonderful gentlemen like Mr. Davis, Coach Howard, Coach Neely and the other track coaches at Clemson provided that last ingredient." Momentum continued to build toward the Olympic trials, scheduled for Brown University in Providence, Rhode Island.

The trip was made in a 1935 V-8 Ford. "It was Mr. Davis, his wife Lucille, my mom and me, and I guess I was pretty excited," remembered Owens. She was excited and pumped up enough to finish tied for third in the trials. In the "jump off," she actually jumped higher than the second-place finisher, and received a bronze medal for the accomplishment. The youngster had made the Olympic team, but there was still another hurdle to clear.

It had been common practice for the United States Olympic Committee to sponsor all the athletes who made the team, but for these games, every team member had to come up with $500 to fund the trip—no small amount when the Depression was still very real. Enter Julian Davis one more time.

"He was able to get in touch with Harry Hughes, state senator from Oconee County," said Lucille Davis. "Hughes called upon the South Carolina Legislature to appropriate the money, which was done." Nothing but a few incidentals and a boat ride stood between the 16-year-old and Germany's capital city.

There was a stop in Washington, D.C., on the way back to New York. "I was taken on a shopping spree so that I'd be properly outfitted for the trip, and that was special," Owens said. Another moment to remember occurred in the Big Apple. "At a dinner for the team, I was at the same table with Jean Schally, who had won the gold medal in the women's high jump during the 1932 Olympics in Los Angeles. Another very special moment." It was finally time, and the team boarded the *Manhattan*, second largest U.S. passenger steamship, heading first to Le Havre, France. A few hundred more miles, and Berlin loomed straight ahead.

"It was one of the cleanest places I had ever seen, and of course we were all excited." She performed well—not a medal-winning performance, but good enough to place seventh among the world's best. More importantly, there were the impressions of her teammates, and for the second youngest member of the squad, such memories overshadowed the fleeting glory of athletic performance.

"Jesse Owens was such a great man, quiet and dignified, and everyone liked and admired him. Marjorie Gestering was only thirteen, but won a gold medal in diving. Our flag bearer was sixteen-year-old Alfred Joachim, and during the opening ceremonies he did not dip the flag when we marched past Adolf Hitler. Not one member of the American contingent saluted, either. I don't think any of it was planned quite that way, but as it turned out we were right in what we did.

"Later, I shook hands with Hitler. He even arranged for members of his body guard—I don't know if they were SS or not—to escort the dozen or so members of the U.S. women's team around the city. The gentlemen spoke fluent English, and we had a pleasant enough time, but with everything that would soon happen ... I've never forgotten those moments."

After leaving the games, the Americans traveled to Dusseldorf and Paris before returning home. New York City Mayor Fiorella La Guardia presented all of them with medals from a proud city and nation, and then it was time to say farewell to her teammates.

"We did get together in September of 1946 for the fiftieth anniversary of the modern Olympics. The USOC brought the former competitors together at the Pennsylvania Hotel in New York, and we got to meet some of the folks who kicked everything off in Athens back in 1896. That was a fun evening."

Back in South Carolina, Owens was offered a track scholarship to Greenville Women's College, later incorporated into Furman University, and attended one year. She wed Jim Owens in December of 1938, and was summarily dismissed from school, "an established policy at that time, as hard as it is to believe now." Her track career over, it was now time to have a little fun with basketball.

"Frank Gilliard was the coach at Lonsdale Mill in Seneca, and he recruited me to play with the women's team there. The Southern

Textile Basketball Tournament was fun, and I think we had a pretty good team in 1941," she noted. In the women's Class B consolation finals that year, she poured in 20 points and led her team to a 29–11 win over Judson Mill. "The Lonsdale Mill Brass Band accompanied us over to Greenville and provided a lot of support, just like they did at textile baseball games. Folks around the mill hill took their athletics seriously!"

Nineteen forty-two would be her last year in the roundball competition, though. "I was pregnant, and our daughter was born in July of 1942, and with the war and all, I just didn't play anymore."

More than an Olympic adventure, her young life was spent waltzing in time as the destiny of the world was played out. "I've been active and enjoyed life, and am fortunate to have few regrets to lament."

Eckie Jordan and Eunice Futch

Theirs were distinct and separate paths, destined to converge at some point and run parallel for a lifetime. Evelyn "Eckie" Jordan called the small textile community of Pelzer, South Carolina, home, while Eunice Futch was comfortable in the big city of Jacksonville, Florida. Jordan was the diminutive playmaker, a slick catalyst for the offense; Futch, nearly a foot taller, controlled the defensive side of the court.

"I loved the time and place I grew up, because Pelzer was such a unique mill village. And I never knew what it was like not to be involved in sports. Heck, I teethed on a basketball," laughs Jordan. "From the fifth grade on, our team was together, and we were undefeated and won the state championship for Pelzer High in 1942. Of course, the best player, man or woman at that time, was Earl Wooten, and we were just like brother and sister. We'd stay after school and shoot baskets, then go home and shoot some more. Basketball was wonderful.

"You know, there would be a family member—and that included in-laws, of course—who would play in the Southern Textile Basketball Tournament from 1926 to 1957. My aunt, Mrs. Leroy Ashley, was there in 1936 and probably would have played for thirty years if they hadn't changed the uniform style. When they went away from the black bloomers to the shorts, she retired gracefully! Aunt Sarah Jordan Wilson was All-Southern four years in the nineteen thirties, and she was the mainstay on Pelzer's first women's championship team in 1930.

"Lord, the places basketball took me. It was great being part of the textile tournament, sitting in the front row with my uncle [and Pelzer coach] Harley Heath and Aunt Leoda, watching players and teams. Seeing the great women's teams from American Enka, Drayton Mill and Chatham Manufacturing was wonderful, and then finally competing against the likes of Ann Lineback [Chatham] was exciting."

And the best she ever saw? "Well, *I* was pretty good! But the best I ever played against was Alline Banks, a star with the Nashville (Tenn.) Business team and the Atlanta Blues. Every bit as good as Hugh Hampton when he played with Hanes Hosiery, you understand, and I saw both of them play for many years."

In 1948 it was on to Winston-Salem, North Carolina, and a rather extended stay with Hanes Hosiery, where she finally retired. "Those years with Hanes were great, and we'd make the trip back to Greenville every season for the tournament, so I got to stay in touch with the folks at home. Then in 1955 I was chosen to participate in the Pan American Games, played in Mexico City, where we were 8-0 and won the gold medal.

"We toured South America afterwards, and had some interesting games. In one place, the referee gave the ball to the local team *thirteen* times before we could finally get the ball past half court. They really wanted to win, but we finally did notch a victory. In another town we played on a makeshift court constructed over ice, since an Ice Capades or something followed our game. We won 19–16, and the score was so low because water seeped up onto the floor and you'd fall down after taking two steps! Neat memories, huh?" Her Pan American Games uniform, complete with name on the back, is in the Smithsonian, flanked by the uniforms of Boston Celtics star Bob Cousy and Minneapolis Lakers legend George Mikan.

Regrets? "How can you have regrets when you're able to do what you love best for your whole life? I was an athlete, and had the opportunity to be in athletics. Playing ball brought me to a company, Hanes Hosiery, where I worked my whole life and loved the people I was around. No one could ever have asked for more."

"There was no interscholastic girls' competition in Florida," recalls Futch, "and that was a tough pill to swallow for someone who grew up with a basketball in one hand and a softball in the other. So I latched on to the Pepsi Cola team, not all that difficult since I was six-two and a good defensive ballplayer. We came north to play Hanes Hosiery in 1946, and lost the game by two points. I must have had a pretty good outing, because they invited me to come to Winston-Salem and play for them. Took them up on it in January of '47."

Futch always figured on going back home after a year or so, but it just never seemed to work out. Things got busy with the Southern Textile Basketball Tournament in 1947 and '48, but then she suffered what every hardwood player dreads — the knee injury. "I tore it up big time in 1949, and missed the whole year. Then they put me on the company plane and flew me to Raleigh, North Carolina, where the best doctor of all, Lennox Baker, did the surgery. I came back in 1950 and limped through a long season, working twice as hard to hold my own.

"Bad as it was, there were positive things that came from that injury. First, I learned to use my head more as a one-legged basketball player; had to use my court smarts to make up for a lack of mobility. And second, I truly learned to enjoy teamwork, and appreciate it more than individual effort. And playing ball with Eckie put an exclamation point next to teamwork. We had a great time."

Futch hung up the sneakers in 1956, but played four more years of softball. A fine pitcher, she participated in three world tournaments, and her finest memories involved the pure enjoyment of the competition. It brought to mind another story she and Jordan could share.

"We were playing in a golf tournament, but not all that well. Heck, we were spraying the ball so badly that we didn't see each other until we reached the green," she laughs. "But we hung on to take first place honors, and I think the prize was a pair of golf shoes. Why, we felt like we'd won the Ryder Cup! Those rich girls could never understand our enthusiasm, but we were athletes, and enjoyed the game for the sake of the game."

That one-year stint she had planned turned into a 44-year career with Hanes, and allowed her to enjoy University of North Carolina athletics as a die-hard fan, especially during the days of Charlie "Choo Choo" Justice. "You know, if I had my life to live over, I'd do the exact same thing, except for the knee injury."

Together Jordan and Futch became sports legends, leading the women of Hanes Hosiery to the Amateur Athletic Union national title from 1951–1953; they lost in the semifinals in 1954. Those teams once put together a streak of 102 straight wins, and as Futch remembered, "It was Wayland Baptist College [Texas] that finally brought that streak to an end, but then they gave us fits every time we played."

How closely their careers paralleled is amazing. Both are in the North Carolina Softball Hall of Fame and the North Carolina Sports Hall of Fame. Both were selected for the AAU Hall of Fame in Jackson, Tennessee, and Jordan is sending along her Pan American Games warm-up jacket to be put on display. Both also won the Teague Award, given annually to the best male and female athletes in North and South Carolina. Jordan was selected along with Dick Groat, standout performer at Duke University and with the Pittsburgh Pirates, and Futch was paired with Frank Selvy of Furman University and the Minneapolis Lakers.

"When we walk through the mall here in Winston-Salem, people still recognize us and stop to talk basketball for a bit," says Jordan. Futch adds, "We still get interviews, though some of those games were played fifty years ago. Can you believe that?"

Don Roper

He is the keeper of the flame, athlete turned historian to preserve, not just his, but all the moments of textile sports. In this comfortable role, Don Roper moves easily across all the decades touched by mill-sponsored baseball and basketball. His wife, Evelyn, offers testimony to his passion.

"We bought the mobile home and lot next door to rent, and provide a little extra income as our retirement years approached. Of course, now Don has all his scorebooks, scrapbooks, and boxes of who-knows-what!" she laughs, offering a wink. "But he loves it so much, and folks are always calling for this or that tidbit of textile lore. He always has time to look it up, though I still don't know how he finds it in all those mountains of paper!"

To a kid growing up on the mill hill, it was The Tournament. No one had to be more specific than that. Roper was a sixth grader at Beattie Memorial Grammar School when he was first introduced to the Southern Textile Basketball Tournament. "Back then, the mill sponsored every level of teams, from midgets all the way to Class A men and women. From the moment kids found out they could dribble a basketball, it was their dream to play in the tournament."

Servicemen returning from World War II to take up their old jobs at Piedmont Mill and play baseball used the event as a preseason training camp. Most of the veterans had been home through that first winter after the war, 1945-46, and had not kept themselves in shape. They got together, worked hard and entered the 1946 tournament. "I don't remember how they did," Don said, "but in baseball that year they had the greatest season a Piedmont team ever had, winning the pennant and playoff championship of the Western Carolina League."

Nineteen fifty-one was a fun year for the Piedmont boys. Many of the players from the high school's Blue Devils, the 1950 state championship team, entered as a Class C team in the tournament, had a close semifinal game with Dunean Mill (predominantly Parker High players), and then edged Camperdown Mill (boasting almost the entire Greenville High team).

How hotly contested was that Camperdown game? "I remember local sports columnist 'Scoop' Latimer saying that each team should have been equipped with boxing gloves. Guess who was one of the first players to be banished?" laughs Roper. "You know, it was a tradition to put the photos of the winning team in next year's program. So 1952 rolls around, and darned if Camperdown isn't shown as champs in the Class C Division. Talk about not being able to win for losing! And I don't think that mistake has ever been corrected."

A few of Roper's great memories bear special mention. The Class A bracket had only five teams in 1953. A powerful Dunean team drew a first-round bye, and then was upset in the last Friday night game by Monaghan. The contest ended long after midnight, and Dunean was forced to play at 9:00 A.M. Saturday. A win placed them in the consolation finals against Piedmont, their third game in 15 hours. Because of this strenuous schedule, it was decided to play eight-minute quarters rather than the traditional 20-minute halves. Dunean's Bob Stowe set a single game record, popping in 55 points. "He had eight in the first quarter," remembers Don, "and since that seemed like a lot, teammate Ernie Chambers wanted a crack at him. I still remind Ernie that four times eight would only have equalled thirty-two points!"

Piedmont won the consolation championship two years later, 102–84 over Peerless Woolen Mill. "But they had a guy named Pete Brown who was a linebacker for the San Francisco Forty-Niners. Going for rebounds, I'd usually be blasted in one direction while he and the ball went the other."

In the 1957 competition, Earl Wooten led Piedmont to the Class A Men's championship finals against Enka. Scoring at a tremendous clip, he had 34 points at the half, and Piedmont led 44–29. After intermission he scored a couple more baskets, and Southern Textile Basketball Tournament president Divver Hendrix stopped the game to present the Blond Blizzard the ball for scoring his 1,000th point in tournament play. "I wished he'd never done that," said Roper, as Wooten scored only 12 the rest of the way.

Enka's Ron Rogers got hot and poured in 41 (Wooten had 50) to lead the North Carolina boys back to a seven-point victory. "My most disappointing basketball moment occurred in the game. With the score tied at eighty-nine, I went up over six-eleven 'Big Daddy' Neal and got a rebound, but he clobbered me good when I tried to put the miss back in." sighed Roper. "Of course, I missed both free throws, and they went down and scored two of their final eight straight points. My career high fourteen tallies didn't do much to fill up the emptiness inside."

Piedmont won the Class A championship of

the last Southern Textile tournament held in old Textile Hall (1958), and the first one ever played in the new Memorial Auditorium (1959).

Nineteen fifty-eight was special, because for years we had been adding one piece of the puzzle at a time to complete our version of the Dream Team. First it was Earl Wooten, perhaps the best who ever graced the tournament; then Ernie Chambers, "Big Jim" Slaughter, Paul Nye and Larry "Choppy" Patterson. The last to be added was Mack Isner, University of West Virginia graduate who had played against the Rangers in 1957 while in the army and stationed at Fort Jackson. Our personnel director, John Mullikin, arranged for him to come to Piedmont. Big Mack's rebounding and inside strength was a perfect complement to the shooting of Wooten, the ballhandling ability of Nye, the all-around play of Chambers, and the inside play of Slaughter. It was good to take the big trophy home and let
it reside in the old awards case at Beattie Hall.

In 1959, though, something was different, and it was more than just moving across town to play the tournament games. The Open Division became the real focal point, and teams went out and recruited college talent in a really big way. Mr. Mullikin, now president of the Southern Textile Athletic Association, didn't let the Rangers go wanting. He picked up Doug Hoffman and Jim Lewis from Clemson, but his last two recruits astounded us all.

Tommy Kearns, a starter on the 1957 University of North Carolina team which beat Kansas and Wilt Chamberlain for the national title that year, was stationed at Fort Jackson. He came up and played with us on Friday and Saturday nights. Mr. Mullikin also landed Jack Sallee, a former All-American from Dayton University. He came into the dressing room just before our opening game with Pelzer, shook hands all around, put on his uniform, and sat out the first couple of minutes. When Jack took the court, it was magic: twelve points in five minutes, thirty-two for the game in an easy win. He had thirty-two again in the Saturday championship game against Monaghan, and Kearns added fifteen. Wooten, who couldn't resist being a part of all that talent, contributed fourteen.

Nineteen sixty-two was Roper's last year as a player, though he did some coaching for the Class C Men and the women's teams. Something had happened to his beloved tradition, and slowly his interest waned. It reached a point when he no longer bothered to go to the auditorium. "Many of the mills quit sponsoring teams, and those that continued picked up players just to participate in the tournament." There was outstanding representation in the Open Division, and the Class C men's division was ablaze with the finest regional high school talent, but it just was not the same.

Then, about eight years ago, Roper and a bunch of old-timers started an annual reunion on the Friday night of the tournament schedule. The keeper of the flame was bringing his many scrapbooks for folks to peruse, enjoy and relive those moments cherished for so long. And as "Saluda Sam," mild mannered reporter for the daily community newspaper, he began to chronicle the stories which made textile sports such a rich tradition. He is the man with the keys to the memories.

"Doing this reunion, getting together with the folks who made industrial basketball great, has given us back our enjoyment of the Southern Textile Basketball Tournament. We'll keep it up, because none of us wants to lose that love again."

John Burgess

"My memories of growing up in a textile community are far better than what athletic ability I possessed!" Make no mistake, John Burgess is a good athlete. It is just that his memories run deep and strong, like the river in Northern Ireland from which the mill village of Dunean takes its name.

Legends come forth, like R.H. Howell hooking a vicious foul ball past the third base coach in a close game with Monaghan Mill in the 1920s. The ball smashed a liquor bottle in the hip pocket of a slightly inebriated fan, who, as the liquid oozed down his leg, was convinced he was bleeding to death. Or perhaps it is Ollie B. Springfield cutting from first to third base on a single when the lone umpire in the game was not looking. Old Ollie once was involved in a fight at home plate after a collision with the catcher, and he proceeded to bite the fellow in the butt when things got out of hand. Joe Perry used to serve hot dogs to the folks on the mill hill, and his tasty treats were proclaimed the best in the world. Ted Prince delivered ice to folks in those days when an "ice box" in the home was exactly that, and the people loved him for providing that convenience.

"My folks lived across the tracks between Dunean and Judson mills, so there was a choice of which village I'd cast my loyalty to, said Burgess." Chose Dunean because they had streetlights and provided uniforms to their athletic teams. In 1950 I was playing basketball in the Grey Y League, and we'd have games at Parker High School every Saturday morning. All of us kids felt like a million bucks wearing those uniforms and fighting for the glory of dear old Dunean. I went on through midget and Class C ball, and loved every minute of it."

That participation led first to a job as official scorekeeper for the Dynamo teams from 1951–1954, and then to at least one story involving local legend Bob Stowe.

"Bob was a character. At one game, I forgot to adequately publicize a double he hit, though I raved about his excellent pitching. Forgot how sensitive pitchers can be about their hitting, I guess, and he let me have it. 'Damn, Bob,' I remember saying, 'they pay me seventy-five cents a game for this, and that's not enough to listen to your bellyaching,' and he simmered down a little after that. It was my pleasure to be chosen to induct such a wonderful athlete and gentleman into the Dunean Hall of Fame."

There is a memory that burns brighter than all of these, sainted though they may be. "I got to know Shoeless Joe Jackson," Burgess says quietly. "You know, he drove a blue forty-nine Packard, probably the only one in Greenville in those years, and sometimes stopped on his way home from work to watch a bunch of rag-tag kids playing baseball in a vacant lot next to my house. He'd take his coat off, loosen his tie, roll up the sleeves of that white shirt he always wore, come out to pitch for both sides, and then give some pointers after the game was over. He was a gentle man, with big hands and a bigger heart, and he would tell us stories about Ty Cobb, Walter Johnson, the Babe, and we'd soak it all up like sponges. No wonder us mill kids thought we lived in the greatest place in all the world."

And when they all congregated for the Southern Textile Basketball Tournament each year? "Playing in it offered some of the best times I'd ever know. One year we finished runner-up to Victor Mill, losing fifty-one to fifty, but it was the way we lost that I remember. Dunean was ahead with very little time left, and we had the ball out of bounds. One of our guys threw the inbounds pass, hit the backboard, and the ball went over to Victor. They of course scored, and we of course lost. And I can recall when the Open Division started. The Dunean team, a bunch of kids really, lost fifty-nine to fifty-three to a team led by Ellerbe 'Big Daddy' Neal, a basketball legend in this area." Sometimes the hard lessons set the stage for later victories.

Team spirit, "we" rather than "me," determination, responsibility — rare qualities today. "But these are the very things basketball, and my whole life on the mill village, taught me," said Burgess. "Best of all, they never left. As I started my own business, all those lessons served me well."

Burgess gives back to the tournament and the community. Whether sponsoring Southeastern Products teams in local sporting events, giving to local schools and charities, providing funds so that mill village reunions can take place, or giving to those in need, he is there to help. He speaks reluctantly about any recognition he has ever received, except for one very special instance.

"Some friends took me out to lunch one day, supposedly to talk about a project or something, and after our meal they placed before me a trophy making me an honorary member of the Dunean Hall of Fame. That was the first time in a long while that I had tears in my eyes. It was such a wonderful thing for them to do."

What has he grown to love so much about the Southern Textile Basketball Tournament? "The neatest thing is the resurgence of the kids' teams, boys and girls having a chance to enjoy the game like I did. Hey, let's let this old tournament go right on making memories for a whole new generation." A few more to place beside Shoeless Joe, Ollie B. Springfield and Joe Perry would suit Burgess just fine.

Doug Kingsmore

Doug Kingsmore attended public schools in Buffalo, South Carolina, and graduated from Clemson University in 1955 with a bachelor of science degree in business administration. He was a three sport athlete at Union High School, lettering in baseball (four years), football (three years) and basketball (two years). "Basketball didn't interest me until my sophomore year, and it was good, strenuous activity during the winter months," remembered Kingsmore. "And I enjoyed traveling on the bus to the games with the girls team.

"Playing in the Southern Textile Basketball Tournament was always a thrill, though I only played Class C ball with Lonsdale Mill one year and Class B ball with Excelsior Mill for two. It's funny," he said, "but my best memory doesn't involve a game I played in. One night, though, I watched Pelzer Mill play Furman University. Pelzer had Earl Wooten and Gee Becker, and Furman countered with Frank Selvy and Darrell Floyd. The outside shooting in that game was unparalleled in its day. Wooten was always my pick for the best offensive player I ever saw, while Clemson's Marvin Robinson took the honor as best defensive player.

"The old tournament," Kingsmore maintains, "was truly the king of the hill. Those who participated were a mixture of great veteran players, emerging college stars, and developing high school standouts. And we got to see some exciting matchups over the years. In the nineteen forties and nineteen fifties, there was greater participation than in later years, and the structured divisional play most always kept the games competitive. It was wonderful to be a young athlete during the tournament's heyday."

"Sports were always a big part of my life," explained Kingsmore, who spent three years in the Baltimore Orioles baseball organization, "but the tournament meant more than that to me. It gave me a great appreciation for tradition, for sportsmanship, and for the values of participation and competition. Just to be associated with the Southern Textile Basketball Tournament was a thrill I can never forget."

Effie Evington and Steve Brown

Effie Evington and Steve Brown were products of different times, one the child of a country emerging from a depression, the other witnessing postwar affluence. What they shared was stronger than their differences, these boys of the mill village who grew into men of integrity. They shared sports, especially basketball, and all that was learned from competition.

"My family lived at Union Bleachery, and I started playing in 1937 on the hundred and ten pound team," said Evington. "All the boys jumped in, played basketball, and we had a great time."

Brown said it was much the same at Victor Mill. "At the age of eight or nine, I was on the midget team, and I guess the ball was near as big as I was," he chuckled. Both moved through the ranks of the Southern Textile Basketball Tournament, excelling wherever they competed.

For Evington, it was Class C and B ball at Union Bleachery, then Class A at Monaghan Mill. Somewhere in all this came his college years at Furman University (1946–1949), where he was an all-around athlete, starring on the football field as a linebacker. "Fellas on the other teams said I hit pretty hard, and they were right," he said. How good was he? Parker High School elected him to its Hall of Fame, and Furman followed suit. The Southern Textile Athletic Hall of Fame bestowed the honor as well, since a mill kid should be honored by his own.

Brown played 24 years in the tournament, moving from midget ball on through classes C, B, A and the Open Division for Victor, Greer and Lyman mills. He was inducted into the Southern Textile Athletic Hall of Fame in 1994, one of his biggest thrills. "Maybe the biggest was getting to play against Earl Wooten his last year in the tournament," he said. "I scored thirty-eight that night, but all I can remember was thinking about being on the court with the greatest player ever to grace this competition. Our team started with ten players, but only had four on the floor when the game was over. Heck of a night."

They speak with great respect of the men they played against all those years. Both agreed that Pelzer's Earl Wooten was the finest offensive performer, but differed on their choice for the defensive honor. "Bob Stowe, without a doubt," Evington remembered. Brown's choice is his former Lyman teammate, Jerry Green, now head coach at Oregon University. "In '63 and '64, it was a pleasure to watch him harass ballhandlers all over the court. A fine talent."

Evington's favorite tournament moment was Monaghan's win over Dunean for the 1953 Class A championship. Former teammate Brice Kirkpatrick, however, would rather focus on how Evington livened up everything.

"For the life of me, I don't remember where the nickname 'Effie' came from, but he fit in well with our Parker High School team. We had folks like 'Dooby' Hamby, 'Toddle' Robinson, 'Fig' Newton, 'Blackie' Durham, and 'Shag' Bagwell. And anyway, 'Effie' sounds better than Richard.

"He was a great defensive player, and could steal the ball away from the best guards. He also made an offense go with his playmaking skills. I have no problem putting him in the same league with Bob Stowe and Earl Wooten, the greatest I ever saw in this tournament. Effie was a winner, and you had to love the guy."

Each man witnessed many changes in the old tournament. "We were more competitive," Evington remembered. "And there are no real rivalries today since there's not as much textile company competition. Our Class A players could probably have beaten these guys playing today, but the Open, B and C players, no, they're much better now than back then."

Brown noted "the attendance is down, and fans don't really seem to be interested any more. That's a shame, because these guys playing now are so much bigger and quicker than we were. We did have more love for the game, though."

Regrets? Very, very few, both agreed. "It was my life when I was young," Evington said. "I'd be there from nine A.M. until they ran us out that night, and all the kids on the mill village looked forward to that week every year. You know, I'd have to get a note from my mother to miss school, but she understood my love for the game. Loved it so much my only regret are the years I couldn't play when I was at Furman."

Brown remembered "lots of good friends, both when I played and when I served on the executive committee. Nothing but fond memories; one of the greatest times in my life. I missed a couple of years, and still regret that. But now it's fun to watch my daughter carry on the family tradition, and she's probably better than her old dad, having made All-Southern the last two years."

So it goes, generation to generation, passing down the best of the values that made the Southern Textile Basketball Tournament an unforgettable attraction. Evington and Brown, each quite a talent, molded and shaped by competition into better men. Records and game accounts become unimportant, even cumbersome, and thankfully slip away from us. But not the mark of a person's character. That stays close, the only thing necessary to make the memories special.

Ellerbe Neal

Ellerbe "Big Daddy" Neal was a small-town kid, a high school hero, a college star, and a professional player, but more than anything he was a hometown boy made good.

He got his start at a poetic sounding little place — Silverstreet. The "Silverstreet Sensation" was a big kid, 6'8" or so, introduced to basketball by his sister. It was the only big sport at the school, so he scored 447 points his senior year.

Neal was not a one-sided individual. For instance, as a high school senior he was voted Most Athletic, Tallest, Most Curious, Noisiest, and Biggest Brag. He was also president of the Tennysonian Literary Society and played the lead role of Andrew Browne in the senior play *Antics of Andrew*. There is one glaring miscalculation, however, in the class prophecy: "Ellerbe Neal, after going to Clemson, has become a professional football player, and plays the position of fullback." That did not happen, of course. He wound up at Wofford College, playing basketball.

With Neil coming out of such a small school like Silverstreet High, some wondered if he could pass muster in the college game. Let's check for Neal's name in the record book:

1. Best single game scoring records: 57 points vs. Erskine in the 1952-53 season; 52 vs. the College of Charleston in 1952-53; 45 vs. Piedmont College in 1951-52.

2. Most rebounds in a game: 40 (since tied) vs. Piedmont College in 1952-53.

3. Most points in a season: 750 in 23 games, 32.6 points per game, in 1952-53. Had 681 (29.6 ppg) in 1951-52.

4. Most field goals in a single season: 263 in both 1951-52 and 1952-53.

5. Best single season rebound averages: 26.5 rebounds per game in 1952-53 (best in the nation); 21.5 in 1951-52; 18.0 in 1950-51.

6. Most rebounds in a career: 1,521 from 1949-53 for a 22.0 per game average.

7. Career scoring: 2,078 points from 1949-53 for a 23.3 per game average, number 4 all-time at Wofford.

His number 17 jersey was retired by the school. In 1952-53 when Frank Selvy of Furman led the NCAA in scoring with a 29.6 points per game average, Neal led the NAIA with 32.6 and was the Small College Player of the Year.

Neal was good enough to be recruited right out of high school for the Southern Textile Basketball Tournament. In 1954-55, he was a solid performer with the old Syracuse Nationals and Baltimore Bullets of the NBA.

Neal participated in the tournament from 1956–63, (with American Enka and Monaghan), and was slated to play in 1954, but his participation in pro ball made him ineligible.

"I loved the big crowds, playing against fine players on so many different teams," said Neal. It was wild, with two games going on, side by side, at the same time.

"It was fun to compete against the likes of Bob Cousy and Dolf Shays in the NBA, and Earl Wooten in the tournament. All of them played me pretty tough, and I got double teamed a lot. At six-eleven, you kind of expected that.

"I used to look forward to the tournament, and Greenville was the center of basketball because of the excellent textile teams."

On March 2, 1956, Neal scored 35 as Enka topped Victor Mill 100–85 in the Open semifinals. The next night he had 49, but Dunean outdistanced Enka 119–105 in a classic battle for the first ever Open crown. He passed on his love of life and of the game to both a son and a daughter who played in the tournament.

Ward Williams

It is a place to go and share hot coffee and good fellowship on a cold winter morning. Or order up some bacon and eggs for a fine breakfast. Or stop in for a lunch of french fries, one really fine hamburger, and a guaranteed frosty soft drink. Whether you sit on the stools at the counter, spinning around to take in the sights and sounds, or lounge in a booth and talk quietly of things as they once were, you are welcomed here. The Cafe is tucked away in the old Dunean mill village, part of a time when textiles dominated this hard working city of Greenville, when cotton mill people, "lintheads" all, sweated and worked and fought the other villages for the honor of their homeplace.

The service is friendly, assured by the owner, Mrs. Jo Hughes. It is guaranteed, too, by the tall, quiet gentleman who moves from behind the counter to circulate among the tables. Orders are filled, new ones taken, tables straightened up and wiped clean. Ward Williams can stop to chat then, in the midst of this magic place, filled with remembrances of things past.

"A few years ago, we tried to fix the place up so the men and women who used to live and work here could come back and enjoy the memories," said Williams. "And they could bring their own kids back to share that special family heritage." Williams points to the glass trophy cases mounted on the wall behind the booths, housing treasures of long ago conquests. Photographs of the old warriors line up in all available spaces, and some stare up from under the glass covering the tables. He and Hughes are proud of this mill hill Hall of Fame.

Williams came to the area in 1942, entering service at the Greenville Army Air Base as a bombardier on a B-25. A product of the basketball-crazy state of Indiana, he played on the base team and competed against several mill teams, notably Monaghan, Dunean and Pelzer. There was something, though, special about Dunean.

"The first time I ever played here with the base team, we came over early to watch the ten to twelve year old village kids play a preliminary game. I was astonished," he laughs softly, shaking his head, "because they were the most fundamentally disciplined group of young players I'd ever seen. And remember, my home was the premier basketball location in the United States at that time, but we were neither as fundamentally sound nor as well coached as those boys. Mostly what we did back home was scrape away snow and shoot at baskets hung up on the barn, since we couldn't get into the local high school gym. And here, why they had a gym and really nice uniforms. That impressed me."

Much like its baseball counterpart, textile league basketball became a mill village sport and paralleled the emergence of the big time college game in the South. Everett Case left Frankfurt (Ind.) High School and accepted the head coaching position at North Carolina State University. Many of Indiana's fine players followed him, including Norm Sloan (who later succeeded Case at N.C. State) and Vic Bubas (head man at Duke University several years later). "And Sloan was only good enough to be a reserve," Williams chuckled. "But that bunch pretty much controlled the old Southern Conference."

After World War II, Williams stayed around to play basketball and baseball with Dunean, eventually signing on as athletic director. In that role, he became curator of the past awards won by the mill teams, and some of the trophies are now displayed in the Cafe. "We lost so many memories several years ago when the old Dunean gym burned," he says quietly. Some of the patrons' favorites include trophies won by the 1922 Piedmont Textile Baseball League championship team, the 1926 Parker Textile Baseball B League winners, the 1929 B Women's Southern Textile Basketball Tournament consolation winner, and the 1940 regular season Men's Southern Textile Basketball Championship quintet.

"We have others, too, like the 1952 champs of the Dixie League Basketball Tournament," Williams said. "You can just about take your pick of basketball and baseball memories of the old Dunean Mill teams, and we probably have something here tied to it."

His own, most special memory "was a game when we were playing arch-rival Pelzer in the finals of the 1952 Southern Textile Basketball Tournament over in old Textile Hall. Remember, they had Earl Wooten, probably the greatest all-around athlete I ever saw. You know he played major league baseball, and that wasn't even his best sport! At one of our old-timers' gatherings here at Dunean, we presented Earl with the *Thorn In The Side* award, since couldn't any of us hold him down, not even this old Indiana import," he laughs easily.

"In that particular game, we fought back and trailed by one. With seconds to go, one of our guys, Dave Putman, found himself with the ball after a great steal. Now, he was a fine defensive player, but not the man you wanted to be taking the last shot. All of us were yelling 'Shoot! Shoot!' because it looked like he would hold the ball until the horn sounded! Finally, after what seemed an eternity, he tossed the ball in the air, it went in, and Dunean won the game.

"Earl was playing baseball for the Chattanooga Lookouts then, I think. He had his car loaded up, and was ready to leave the next morning for spring training in Florida. After the game, though, Wooten was so mad he showered, changed clothes, found his wife in the stands, and left right then. Thelma was driving as they reached the lower part of Georgia, and Earl, jostled awake as they went through a small town, drowsily asked where they were. On as cheery a note as possible at that gosh awful early hour, she answered, 'Putman, Georgia.'

"'Great, just great,' Wooten muttered as he nestled down in the back seat. 'Driving for six hours, and I still can't get away from Dunean.' We've had a good laugh about that one for a long time now."

Honors came the way of this fiery athlete who managed so well the balance between competitor and gentleman. Voted All-Southern several times in the Southern Textile Basketball Tournament, coach of many Dunean championship teams, president and executive committee member of that same tournament on various occasions, Williams received his most treasured tribute in October of 1992.

"Indiana University invited me back, and with several former teammates I was honored on the fiftieth anniversary of receiving my first Block 'I' varsity letter. Standing on that football field at halftime, there were a whole lot of memories running through my mind, and you know, I was just thankful for all the great things basketball had given to me." He looked once more around the Dunean Cafe, put his big hands on the counter top, leaned forward and smiled. "Couldn't anybody be much luckier."

He turned to greet another old friend taking a seat, ready to order up some breakfast, with an extra helping of good conversation about the old times.

Earl Wooten

In 1921, the Kingdom came to be. The Southern Textile Basketball Tournament was born in South Carolina and was played in the old Textile Hall for 38 years, giving way finally to the more modern Greenville Memorial Auditorium. For 20 years people witnessed the annual event with interest: there were good games and good players, but the Kingdom knew no monarch, no man to take the helm and lay claim to the stardom offered. And no one appeared for two long decades, not until 1941, when the Earl held court for the first time at the age of 17.

When he was learning to play basketball, Wooten nailed a goal to a tree in his yard, minus the backboard. He credits that shortage of equipment with helping to develop his shooting eye. Wooten still has that goal, with part of the tree trunk that grew around it.

Under many titles—"The Earl of Pelzer," "Wonder Boy," "The Mystic Marvel," "Mr. Automatic," "The Blonde Blizzard," "Mr. Basketball"—Earl Wooten dominated the game. At 5'10", he was adept at playing either guard or forward. From the start of his career, he knew no equal. From the set shot to the unstoppable "left hand driving out" hook, he could do it all. Fantastic shooting, awesome outside accuracy, quick moves and incredible playmaking were part of his arsenal on the court. But it was his astounding sense of where the ball would go, what teammates and opponents alike would do when it got there, and his all-around hustle to make certain he was in the midst of the resulting action, that made Wooten the favorite of the fans wherever he played. The textile communities of Pelzer and Piedmont, where he spent his career, became familiar bywords in the annals of the Southern Textile Basketball Tournament.

The rule was a continuous one, lasting 23 years. The laurels given to the victorious Earl were many, and his achievements withstood all challenges. In one game he was 21-of-21 from the free-throw line. He totaled 100 or more points in five different tournaments (1947, 1949, 1950, 1954, 1956). "The Scoring Machine," "The Man of a Hundred Shots" secured his Kingdom, though many would come to test his abilities and attempt to seize the Earl's honors and glory for themselves. Mill teams recruited players to represent them in their quest for the Southern Textile Basketball championship. From the Big Ten came Ward Williams and Tex Ritter, from Furman University stormed Frank Selvy and Neild Gordon (a teammate of Wooten's and later a coach of Newberry College and Winthrop College), and from Clemson University charged Bobby Roberts (also a teammate and later a coach at his alma mater). None could best "The Earl of Pelzer." His Kingdom, the hardwood at Textile Hall, was inviolate.

Knowledgeable basketball men offered praise. Selvy stated simply, "Sure, I remember him. About five-nine or so, with about a hundred different kinds of shots. A heck of a shooter." Perhaps Selvy recalled one particular game between Pelzer and Furman, when he totaled 17 points and Wooten 45 as Pelzer won 97–72. Press Maravich, while coach at Clemson, added to the legend. "I'm telling you, I saw the greatest player I've ever seen the other night, the greatest in the game today—better than Bob Cousy. A couple of weeks ago I watched this wiry little blonde guy score forty points and never break a sweat; he wasn't even trying. Three straight games not too long ago he scored sixty, fifty-two and forty points, and he only played through three quarters. And he doesn't even have a jump shot!"

The comparisons between Wooten and the best of pro basketball, the Celtics' Cousy and the Minneapolis Lakers' George Mikan, were inevitable. After the Earl scored 63 points in a game, veteran coach "Rock" Norman of Clemson noted that "if I hadn't seen the game, I'd have figured Wooten just shot every time he got his hands on the ball, but that just wasn't so. He worked hard for practically every shot he took, and must have hit six of every ten. If Wooten isn't in Cousy's class, then Cousy isn't human. I've seen enough basketball in the past forty years to know a great player when I see one. And Wooten is one. He can do anything with a basketball."

Fred Campbell, coach of the professional Detroit Vagabond Kings, commented after his team had played the Bears of Pelzer Mill. "I've been all over the country, and Pelzer has a wonderful player. I'd take him against any I've seen. If he had the height that George Mikan had, Mikan wouldn't be in his class."

The words meant little to the Earl of Pelzer, for he just enjoyed playing the game. No one could step onto the court and compete with him. And yet, it was this remarkable ability that would prevent his achieving an even greater glory. The conflict of Wooten's two great loves in athletics — basketball and baseball — would inevitably occur.

The two games at which Wooten excelled existed side-by-side in peaceful harmony for many years. When basketball ended, it was the most natural thing in the world for him to begin practice on the diamond. "Back then, all we did was play basketball and baseball. I enjoyed playing, and there was nothing else to do. In the winter I would play basketball and in the summer I'd switch to baseball."

He was just as good, if not better, on the diamond. Good enough to play with the Chattanooga Lookouts and the Atlanta Crackers of the Southern League, and with the old Washington Senators of the American League. Throughout his professional baseball career, Wooten continued to play the game he loved most of all during the winter months, exciting the crowds at the Southern Textile Basketball Tournament every year, and claiming record upon record for his own. But the two loves were finally to clash and, as Wooten said, "I probably made my biggest mistake in 1948," when he ignored a stipulation in a Senators contract and played basketball in the off-season. The game at which Wooten was so magnificent caused him to miss his calling in the major leagues.

He had played in 86 games with the Senators in 1948 as an outfielder, first baseman, and pitcher. He was listed as the third string catcher, even though he was left-handed. Wooten had signed a 1949 contract calling for a raise, but Senators president Clark Griffith and Wooten had reached an agreement regarding his off-season occupation. Without a doubt the most colorful player in the mill leagues, Wooten was to abandon the Pelzer Bears during the winter of 1948-49 (and all subsequent seasons) and instead work to stay in shape for the big leagues. Too much running during the winter months continued to take a lot out of his legs and caused him to start slowly on the baseball diamond in the spring and early summer. In return for following the wishes of Griffith, disregarding basketball and the countless loyal fans at home, Wooten was to receive a payment each month from the Washington team. Wooten accepted the money graciously, but he also played basketball as much as ever, often under an alias. He even said it was his brother pouring in all the points in those textile league games. When Griffith was informed of what was going on, he did not even bother to contact Wooten again, except to inform him that his contract had been sold to Chattanooga. Earl Wooten never got another shot at the major leagues.

Though an additional field of conquest had been forfeited, the Earl of Pelzer continued to dominate the game of basketball in the Piedmont area, and his presence on the hardcourt was the topic of conversation among sports enthusiasts throughout the South. His loyal following watched as "The Blonde Blizzard" scored 70 points against Champion "Y" of Canton, North Carolina, on December 12, 1954, and pronounced him the greatest player alive. Even in the midst of his pro baseball career, the Washington Capitols, 1948 runners-up for the National Professional Basketball Championship, offered him a handsome salary to play for them. Wooten did not accept, choosing to play his game before people he knew and loved.

The honors continued to mount, and record after record fell before the onslaught of the little blonde guy from the mill town. When he finally called an end to his playing days in 1964, Wooten held seven of nine Southern Textile Basketball Tournament records in the men's division. Those likely to remain unbroken are most years played (21), most points scored (1,262 in 45 games for a 28 points per game average), and most times All-Southern (12–9 for Pelzer, 3 for Piedmont). In 1962, Wooten's home state bestowed upon its native son perhaps the greatest honor of his long career — induction into the South Carolina Sports Hall of Fame.

Legends are destined to surround individuals who dominate a sport as completely as Earl Wooten did in the semi-pro basketball ranks of the South. There is the story that he would not attend classes in high school, so the principal locked him in the gym and made the young man shoot hoops for hours on end. Whether true or not, he did lead Pelzer High to the Class B state championship in 1940-41. Certainly not a one-sport star, he also lettered in baseball and football.

And yet, all the stories, all the records pale before the reality of Earl Wooten. Records did not matter to him. Quite simply, he was the local boy who made good, the hero who stayed home to entertain the fans he knew and loved with unmatched skill on the basketball court. In these days of high-priced sports figures, perhaps the nicknames have been overworked. But even if there were no mention of "The Earl of Pelzer," "Wonder Boy," "The Mystic Marvel," "Mr. Automatic," "The Blonde Blizzard," or "Mr. Basketball," Earl Wooten would still remain "The Man."

Patsy Neal

Leo Durocher was wrong. A Georgia girl turned world citizen counters the "nice guys finish last" slam with a worthy alternative. "I have always been a firm believer that if you live long enough, good things will catch up with you," Patsy Neal said, but that also assumes there is something deep inside a person which will attract that good. A study of this sojourner proves the point.

As a youngster, Neal practiced day by day on the basketball courts in Elberton, Georgia, honing God-given talents, but to what end? "The Amateur Athletic Union was the *only* organization offering anything for women on the national or international level back then, " she remembers. "I saw a two sentence paragraph in some publication that the Wayland Baptist College women's team, way off in Plainview, Texas, had just won the AAU championship." A letter to the coach led to introductions and eventually a four-year scholarship.

To say that Neal took the campus by storm would be an understatement. As a freshman, she was the national free throw champion, but it was team records which astounded even a casual observer. An undefeated 29–0 and national champs in 1956-57; 28–1 and third nationally in 1957-58; 34–2 and national champs in 1958-59; and 20–4 and runners-up in 1959-60. For good measure, she was elected the first woman president of the Student Government Association her junior year, and still found time to be Homecoming Queen. But amid all these honors, it was a lesson she learned from Coach Harley Redin which she came to cherish.

"Our AAU team had won a hundred and thirty-one straight games, and we came up against a powerful bunch from Nashville [Tenn.] Business College. It was a tight, winner-take-all affair, with the victors going on to tour Russia and play against their top teams. With only a few seconds left in the game, we were down by four and knew our streak was at an end. During the last time out coach quietly told us to accept defeat with the same dignity we had shown in victory. You don't forget that kind of class."

Class, coupled with her strong Christian faith and God-given physical skills, combined to make Neal a much demanded participant in several hardwood adventures. An AAU All-American in 1959, 1960, and 1965, she played in the 1959 Pan American Games, and was selected to play with the U.S. All Stars against the Russian women's team on a tour of the States during the winter of 1959-60. In 1964, she captained the U.S. team during the World Basketball Tournament in Peru, South America, and a year later was selected to the American women's all stars as they toured Russia, France, and Germany, competing against those national teams. For good measure, she coached and played with the AAU Utah Lakers of Salt Lake City from 1962–66.

While an associate professor at Brevard (N.C.) College, she heard about the Southern Textile Basketball Tournament. "I was teaching and coaching there [including the men's tennis team], but when I got word of the competition down in Greenville, I just couldn't resist." Tours of duty with IMMS and Texize Chemical occupied her winter schedule for the next eight years. "The talent was excellent, and that's why I played. There were a lot of memories, from winning championships to throwing a pass away that cost our team a crucial game, but the greatest pleasure I had was meeting a lot of very wonderful people. No one could regret such an experience as that." Neal also became the first woman to serve as a member of the tournament's executive committee (1972–75), just one more groundbreaking exercise for a talented lady.

Athletic achievements are but one part of this Renaissance spirit, whose talents move through many fields of endeavor. A freelance writer, Neal authored five books, and her first, *Basketball Techniques for Women,* has served as a definitive text for the sport. Others, which bear witness to her intense love of the game, include

Coaching Girls and Women: Psychological Perspectives, So Run Your Race, Sport and Identity, and *Coaching Methods for Women.* Articles have found their way to *Newsweek, Prevention, The Olympian,* and *The Christian Athlete,* and her essays have netted four Freedom Foundation awards.

Neal was a panelist, with Brent Musburger, Diana Nyad and others, for a "Women in Sport" program; was a speaker for "Direction '75," with Jim McKay, Roone Arledge and Calvin Hill; and was selected as the only woman to attend the 1973 "Multidisciplinary Symposium on Sport and the Means of Elevating International Understanding," held at the State Department in Washington, D.C. She has been listed in *Outstanding Educators of America, Outstanding Young Women of America, Dictionary of International Biography, World's Who's Who of Women,* and *Contemporary Authors.*

Neal was inducted into both the National Association of Sports and Physical Education Hall of Fame (1981) and the National Amateur Athletic Association Women's Basketball Hall of Fame (1993). She received the 1993 Josten's Service Award, given by the Women's Basketball Coaches Association for lifelong commitment and service to the game. Coming full circle, she was presented the 1995 Distinguished Leadership Alumni Award by her alma mater.

As a ballplayer, Neal once said, "It would be the greatest tragedy if an athlete could not find God on a playing field. God knows all the rules of every game. He knows the difference between right and wrong, between fair and unfair." She has succeeded in living this philosophy.

Leo Durocher was wrong. And Patsy Neal can prove it.

Henry Logan

The 1960s — a time of change, sometimes violent, almost always difficult. Henry Logan was there, himself an agent of that change, a great athlete whose very ability was subject to being overshadowed by his courage.

"My mother and grandmother raised me, and they taught me to see the world for what it could be. I don't ever remember my life being shaped by negative racial perceptions," Logan said. But it was definitely transformed by his athletic ability.

"When I was eight years old, I saw the big guys playing basketball, and just fell in love with the game. My first real honor was being selected Most Valuable Player when our eighth grade class beat the ninth graders in the annual showdown, and I realized then that I could play the game well."

But it was football at which he excelled, getting scholarship offers from several schools. "I was all state as a quarterback, and played some defensive back, but those guys were just too big," he laughed. "They beat up on me more than I liked."

So it would be basketball, and that courage fostered in a loving home, which would soon make the world sit up and take notice. He was the first African American to be recruited, and to play, intercollegiate athletics at a predominantly white institution in the Southeast. Logan handled the pressure with his quiet pride. "There was a lot of love on that Western Carolina University team," he recalled, "and we all got through those changing times together."

It was pretty much a spartan life in the hamlet of Cullowhee, North Carolina, with little or no social life. "We'd go into Asheville, then come back to campus, and there would be racial slurs painted on my door. And on the road, some folks would be yelling for the black boy to go home, saying I didn't belong at their school. Once we went to a tournament in Louisiana, and there was a state law that said blacks couldn't participate in games sponsored by the host college. I had to go back to the hotel and sit. It was tough."

The anger fused with the pride and the courage to form an incredible determination, and collegiate basketball was never the same. He once scored eight points in the final ten seconds to steal a win from High Point College in a Carolinas Conference tournament game. Six times he scored more than 50 points (tops was 60 versus Atlantic Christian during the 1966-67 season), and in 14 more he ripped through 40-plus. To put that into perspective, there have been only nine other 40-plus point performances in Western Carolina University history.

Logan only got better. His scoring average moved from 26.7 (1964-65), to 29.1 (1965-66), to 30.2 (1966–67) and topped out at 36.2 (1967–68); his senior totals were good enough to lead the entire nation. He jumped center on the opening tip, routinely outdueling opponents nearly a foot taller. Logan's abilities were enough to awe even veteran coaches who thought they had seen it all.

"I've played college basketball, pro basketball, and coached, and he is the greatest I have ever seen," said Elon College coach Bill Miller. "In the pros I played with Bob Cousy, and talent-wise Logan is as good as him." Such talent could not be sequestered for long high up in the Blue Ridge Mountains, and Henry was asked by Grady Wallace, former University of South Carolina All-American, to be part of the powerful Sunshine Cleaners team for some postseason play. The Southern Textile Basketball Tournament was another world waiting to be conquered.

Some observers called Logan the best player ever in the tournament, as he hit outside jumpers, dunked the ball with ease, and goaltended by pinning the ball against the backboard. He was greeted by a marquee outside Memorial Auditorium that read "Henry Logan and the Sunshine Cleaners." "My mother just wouldn't believe this," he said.

The Sunshine Boys swept into the Open Division finals behind the play of their superstar, but that game against the Greenville Old Pros quickly became a blood-and-guts game. Down by 15 in the first half, the Columbia team rallied behind Logan's 28 points and claimed a 90–82 win and the division title.

"People sometimes ask how I was treated, being in that first group of black players in the Southern Textile Basketball Tournament. As an athlete, I was worrying about competing, not about race. Hey, all of us, black and white, concentrated on basketball, not on color. There was still some name calling by a few fans, but that didn't bother me. We were all playing a wonderful game at a very high level of competition.

"Being part of the tournament helped me a lot. With so many great college athletes there, it upped my game and better prepared me for the pros. Going head-to-head against the likes of Dwight Durante and Gene Little alerted you real fast that you had better be ready to play. It was a great time."

Then it was on to the pros, and a dream come true. For a while, at least. A bonus baby with Oakland of the American Basketball Association, he teamed with Rick Barry, Larry Brown and Warren Jabali to lead the Oaks to the 1969 title; Logan averaged 21 minutes and 14 points per game. With financial trouble battering the fledgling league, the Oakland franchise moved to Washington the next year and became the Capitals. Logan was averaging 20 points a game when he blew out his knee in December. The Caps moved again and became the Virginia Squires in 1971-72 in an effort to survive, much as Logan was trying to do.

But rehabilitation and a 1972 comeback only resulted in his sixth and final knee operation. This time, the kneecap had to be removed. "It made me angry that folks never got to see what Henry Logan could do in that league," he recalls. "But I didn't have the discipline to keep myself in top shape for an eighty-four game schedule, so much of the blame rests with me." Thoughts of what might have been only resulted in a deepening bitterness.

Life without basketball became an eight year descent into hell. "I began to drink heavily, lost some decent jobs because of my alcoholism, and tried to commit suicide." But a miracle found its way to a broken man, alone and out of options.

"A preacher from Black Mountain, North Carolina, called on the phone and asked me to run the gym his church had just built. Soon I was part of his congregation, and found my way back home. In Jesus Christ I discovered a reason for living, and all the emptiness went away. Without Him, I would not have survived."

Logan now works at Rockwell Axles in Asheville, and sometimes wonders if he came along too soon. "I watch Michael Jordan and those other NBA guys palm and walk with the ball. Shoot, if I could have gotten away with that, wouldn't old Henry have been something! And with the three-pointer, it would have been easy to up my scoring average." But then he grew quiet, reflective.

"No. No regrets. My life turned out just the way it should have, and if I've accomplished anything at all, the credit belongs to Jesus Christ." Not the awesome talent on the basketball court, not even the courage to be a leader in a time of social upheaval, defines his life. It all came full circle, back to the little boy who learned from his mother and grandmother that he is special simply because he is a child of God. And in that knowledge, there is peace for Henry Logan.

Mickey Davis

Mickey Davis's childhood revolved around the activities provided by the Ware Shoals Mill, especially sports. "My dad, Jake Davis, was the catcher on the mill baseball team, and one of his best friends there was Lou Brissie, who would go on to be a war hero and a major league pitcher. So my love of sports was a birthright." Her father once poled a home run out of Poe Mill Park, nearly hitting the train rolling by a good hundred feet beyond the fence.

Other things, though, were more important to her parents. "Mom and Dad would come home dead tired after working in the mill all day, but they made sure my sister and I did our homework before anything else, which in my case was either heading out to play tackle football with the boys on my street, or going to the gym to play basketball. That discipline, and basketball, made it possible for me to go on to college.

"We were taught right from wrong, and learned to accept responsibility for our actions. But that didn't make us saints. I can remember cutting class to go up to the cafe by the company store, enjoying a great hot dog and Coca-Cola, when in walks the principal. We were hauled right back to school, of course." Mill kids learned early on that you had 20 or so sets of parents on the village, and that being out of sight of your own mom and dad was no license to misbehave. Folks looked out for one another, and it made for a strong sense of family among all the citizens of the mill hill.

"Shoot, I remember being called a 'linthead,' but I thought it was a compliment that my hair was pretty and fluffy. I didn't know people were trying to make fun of me by saying that the cotton from the mill stuck in my mom's and dad's hair. But you know, it really was a compliment. We were a hardworking bunch."

Athletes at Ware Shoals started their careers early, and by the third grade Davis was being coached by textile sports great Willie Wilbanks, whose talents were good enough to land him a job in the National Football League as a respected official. Two evenings a week entailed fundamentals on top of fundamentals, dribbling around chairs, switching hands and coming back again. But Saturday mornings meant league play and real competition.

"Do you remember the T-shirts with the felt numbers ironed on? Oh, I can still smell those! We loved to play, and we were encouraged to be competitive." After the scheduled practices, there was still time to shoot baskets in the Caughmans' backyard. If you missed, though, the ball rolled down into the Seawrights' garden. Mr. and Mrs. Seawright would good-naturedly return the ball, after keeping it overnight.

"Willie Wilbanks would get Bob Johnson to come over from Erskine College, and he taught us how to fake, calling it mustard on the hot dog. He spent hours with us, teaching ball control skills, always driving us, making us better. Coach Ramsey was another of Willie's friends who shared his basketball knowledge with us, and his speciality was conditioning. Drill after drill, running and cutting, and coming back to do it again. We *wanted* to get better, and we could outlast anyone we played." Then back to the Caughmans for extra practice after supper until the dreaded, "Maxine, it's time to come home now."

"When Mom called me Maxine, there was no reason to argue, but I still tried the standard 'just a little bit longer, please?' I never expected it to work, and it never did!"

All the practice and hard work paid off, as Wilbanks took his young charges to the Southern Textile Basketball Tournament to compete in the midget divisions. There was the day at Woodside Mill gym when sunlight streamed through the windows, forming mosaics on the polished wooden floor, and Davis swore she was in basketball heaven. "Later in the game, one of the Woodside girls broke her leg, and I sat down and cried because we had lost that moment of perfection."

The hard work continued, dreams chased during windsprints and daily scrimmages. Basketball was the only sport available to the high school girls, but one practice a day just did not satisfy the hunger. "Bobbie Freeman was a senior when I was in the ninth grade," Davis remembers, "and we'd finish girls' practice, then hang around and practice with the boys' team. We learned to be aggressive and play hard."

With the Ware Shoals women up against the powerhouse Slater team in the 1959 tournament, Davis had 15 in a 38–24 loss. Veteran Sue Vickers impressed her that night, enough so that Davis now calls her "the best competitor I ever saw." In the consolation bracket the next night, Davis increased her point total, but 20 was not enough to overcome the Anderson Mill ladies, and Ware Shoals lost again, 55–47. "Winning and losing mattered, of course, but you gave it your all and loved the game for what it was — a game. Folks said I was a good sport, and that meant a lot. I always felt it was worthless to have any kind of contest if you couldn't have the fairest, fiercest competition."

The kid came to play, and it was on to Winthrop for four years of intercollegiate competition. "While I was in school, one of the mills, J.P. Stevens, I think, sent a limousine to pick me up and carry me to Greenville for the tournament. Not bad transportation for a girl with no car!" But it would be another sporting event that would open bigger doors.

In Davis's senior year, her team went to North Greenville Junior College for a track and field meet. She entered the softball throw and got off a *long* throw ("probably had five chocolate bars beforehand!"), and the team made a very strong showing overall. The Associated Press picked up the story, and before long Davis received a letter from Johnny Moon, coach of the powerful Atlanta Tomboys. "He asked if I wanted to play for him and work in the Atlanta area. So small town girl goes to the big city for an interview, likes the set-up, and stays."

John Oliver, owner of some prime real estate in Georgia's capital city, offered her a summer job in one of his banks, and gave her a special present. "My very first pair of cleats! I was still playing softball barefoot, and I guess it was dangerous, but I was faster without shoes. I thanked him, wore the things for awhile, but took them off and played the way I was used to. It was more comfortable, and I could do without the blisters.

"Nera White, a great athlete with Nashville Business College, hung the nickname 'Daisy Mae' on me during one of those softball games." And like Shoeless Joe Jackson, the moniker stuck. "She was the greatest basketball player I ever saw. We played them once in Lebanon, Tennessee, the gym was absolutely pulsating, and I think we lost by four points. During the action, I stole the ball from her and drove hard and fast to lay the ball in. And do you know she came from three steps back to block the shot. She could play defense, shoot with either hand, and even dunk the ball. Nera would be my pick for the female Michael Jordan, and she inspired me to improve. Because of her, I learned to train myself to be better than my opponent's *strength*. Such a goal always leaves you room to pursue excellence. Just a great, great player and person."

Two other favorite memories, however, are associated with the Southern Textile Basketball Tournament. "One year with Atlanta, I hurt my knee — had to put a brace on it to keep the thing from bending both ways — but I only missed a minute or so of action. Just after getting back in, I caught an in-bounds pass at half court, turned and fired a lead pass to a teammate breaking for the basket. Some lead pass," Davis laughed, "the darned thing swished through the net. The magic that filled the old Woodside gym so many years before was *still* a part of the game, and I truly counted my blessings.

"The second special moment happened when I ran into Earl Wooten at a golf tournament. We talked for a bit and I finally got to express my profound respect for him as an athlete. Inch for inch and pound for pound, there was no one better. No one, period."

For Mickey Davis, there were lots of reasons to smile. She played the game she loved so much with an enthusiasm that swept over teammates, opponents and fans. The game led her from the mill village in Ware Shoals to Long Beach (Ca.) City College, where she serves as athletic director.

"The greatest thing in life is to give back a bit of that joy to those who supported you during all the years of competition. And for those people we influence, when they can learn to say 'we' and 'our' instead of 'I' and 'mine,' then you've succeeded in passing along the best human nature has to offer.

"You know, I never second guess how I was raised and what I was taught, and I still go back to those roots when I have big decisions to make. The love Mom and Dad gave, the support of the folks on the mill hill, the code of conduct we were expected to live up to — they're more precious with each passing year."

The lady could play, make no mistake, but to define her only as a player would be to sell her short. Start to finish, she is a class act, and that is what matters.

Mel and Al Daniel

Their paths through life have run both parallel and divergent. Finally, one a banker, the other a coach. They are bound by athletics, yes, but far more for Mel and Al Daniel. They are bound by love and respect, and that is the measure of their greatness.

Al is the older by two short years. From Saluda High School he moved to Anderson Junior College on a basketball scholarship, playing a solid forward, and then on to Furman. He helped lead the Paladins to the 1978 Southern Conference Tournament championship and to a near upset of Indiana University in the opening round of the NCAA show. A second team All-Conference pick that year, he garnered first team honors as a senior, and was drafted by the San Antonio Spurs.

Mel followed the path of his older brother, striving to match the excellence now expected of the Daniel clan. A fine point guard who probably did not shoot enough, he was a three time All-Conference selection while at Furman (1980–82) and twice an All-American Honorable Mention (1981 and 1982). Mel played in the World University Games in Bucharest, Romania (1981), and like his brother was drafted into the NBA, by the New Jersey Nets.

The honors did not cease to parallel as college drew to a close. Both went on to play in the Southern Textile Basketball Tournament, each being selected for All-Southern honors four times in the Open Division. "The level of play was good, especially those Open teams loaded with top quality college players," said Al. "Around here, the college players, both men and women, were kind of expected to play in the tournament. That familiarity made for some fine rivalries. And it was always good when a team of Furman guys could upset one filled with Clemson folks."

"I started in high school," remembered Mel, "playing with Ronnie Carr on the C team sponsored by Pelzer Mill. Most of those guys were good enough to go on and play college ball, and we brought home some titles during those years." He played in C, A, and Open divisions, making five championship appearances, and the one constant was always the high level of play.

"Competition was always good, and some of the teams, especially those made up of all stars, were on par with some NCAA teams I played against." And like Al, the Clemson teams presented a special challenge. "Those teams Chubby Wells played on were solid and well organized. He played hard all the time, and so did the other guys on the court with him."

With so much similarity in their athletic careers, you have to wonder how they must have been as kids. "We were close, always playing basketball and doing things together. We were taught by our parents to do the right things, and they not only taught it, they lived it," Al said proudly.

Mel agreed. "We were brought up by great parents, and everyone in the family was close. Mom and Dad emphasized God, education and athletics, and made sure we kept the order straight. I don't think anyone could have asked for more than we had, thanks to our parents."

From favorite stories to fondest wishes, both are equally adept at expressing their deep feelings of affection. For Al, Mel "just wants him to be happy, to achieve his highest aspirations, and I think that would probably be a head coaching position at a major university." Al has served as assistant coach at Furman and North Carolina State University, and was interviewed for a like position by Louisville and Washington State.

"If I could grant Mel anything," says Al, "it would be that he and Holly [Mel's wife] would be the kind of parents like ours, teaching their children the same values that he and I learned from Mom and Dad. That would be a wonderful gift to pass on."

And what would they like to accomplish? For Mel, "to be the best parent that I can be, and to teach my children with the same patience and love like Dad did with Al and me." And Al? "To be happy and lead an exemplary life. You know, there's no need to have everything you want in order to be happy. Giving back to the world, like our folks taught us, that would fill my life with meaning."

Records fade quickly, newspaper clippings turn yellow and grow brittle. And the world cares little what was accomplished yesterday, or how much someone might cherish those memories. What Mel and Al Daniel possess cannot be taken from them. From their parents they inherited a mutual and abiding love, a desire to leave the world better than they found it, and a quiet and unshakable confidence. Theirs is a legacy worthy enough to endure.

Bibliography

Greenville *News*, 1921–1990.
Interview: Anders, Joe; March 1995.
Interview: Burgess, John; March 1995.
Interview: Burton, Wade; April 1995.
Interview: Cunningham, Billy; April 1996.
Interview: Daniel, Al; May 1996.
Interview: Daniel, Mel; May 1996.
Interview: Davis, Mickey; June 1995.
Interview: Davis, Walter; March 1995.
Interview: Evatt, Herman; March 1995.
Interview: Evington, Effie; March 1995.
Interview: Futch, Eunice; June 1995.
Interview: Hilley, Stan; April 1995.
Interview: Honea, Chafer; May 1995.
Interview: Howard, "Punchy"; March 1995.
Interview: Jordan, Eckie; June 1995.
Interview: Kingsmore, Doug; April 1995.
Interview: Logan, Henry; November 1995.
Interview: McCurry, Hinkie; June 1995.
Interview: Moe, Doug; April 1996.
Interview: Moore, Allan; March 1995.
Interview: Neal, Ellerbe; March 1995.
Interview: Neal, Patsy; April 1996.
Interview: Norris, Frank; March 1995.
Interview: Owens, Kathleen Kelley; March 1996.
Interview: Parris, Jerry; March 1995.
Interview: Perry, Thomas; June 1995.
Interview: Pittman, Ted; March 1995.
Interview: Rollins, Pete; March 1995.
Interview: Rollins, Wayne; June 1996.
Interview: Roper, Don; March 1995.
Interview: Seawright, Bob; February 1995.
Interview: Sims, Jerry; April 1995.
Interview: Stansell, "Frog"; April 1995.
Interview: Walters, Deran; March 1995.
Interview: White, Alton; April 1995.
Interview: Williams, Ward; February 1995.
Interview: Wooten, Earl; April 1982.
Southern Textile Basketball Tournament Programs, 1921–1997.

Index

A & C Warehouse (Clinton, SC) Class B men 84, 293, 298, 303, 307, 382
A & M Mobile Homes (Spartanburg, SC) Open Division men 76, 269
A.C.H. Wildcats (Greenville, SC) Class C men 315
A. Schottland Inc. (Rocky Mount, NC): Class A men 230; Open Division men 63, 233
Abbeville Mill (Abbeville, SC): Class B men 106, 107, 113, 116, 136, 140, 144, 153, 303; Class B women 118, 143, 147, 377, 378; Class C men 107, 142
Abercrombie, Joe 91
Abernathy, Woodrow 19
Able Sanitation (Greenville, SC) Class C men 276, 282
Able Supply (Spartanburg, SC) Open Division men 76, 269
Ace Sports (Greenville, SC) Class B men 333, 335
Acker, Fredda 32
Acker, Lewis 229, 233, 236, 239, 243, 246
ACME Distributors (Spartanburg, SC) Open Division men 251
Adair, Kenisey 95
Adams, Donnie 380
Adams, George 76, 77, 95
Adams, Mike 70, 96
Adams, Pam 382
Adams, Ray 316
Adams, Wiley 89
Adams-Millis (High Point, NC) Class A men 148, 151; Class B men 43, 144
Adams Oil (Fair Play, SC) Class A women 226, 380

Adams Real Estate (North Charleston, SC) Class A women 259
Adcock, John 52
Addis, Brenda 46, 50, 52
Agee, Louise 131, 135, 139
Agnew, Clyde 73, 74, 76, 381
Aiken, Charles 379
Aiken, Melvin 378
Aiken County Economic Development Board 392
Aiken Mill (Bath, SC) Class B women 130
Aiken Rotary Club 392
Akron Corp. (Greenville, SC) Class C men 276
Albany Felt Co. (St. Stephens, SC) Open Division men 273, 278, 284
Albert, Tarrance 93
Alexander, Chuck 67
Alexander, Doug 67, 68, 70, 73
Alford Real Estate (Greenville, SC): Class A women 328; Class B men 312; Class C men 86, 89, 294, 299, 304, 308, 318, 322, 325, 332, 342
Alice Mfg. (Easley, SC) Class A men 78, 82, 84, 94, 95, 96, 274, 279, 285, 290, 295, 301, 306, 310, 313, 316, 320, 323, 326, 329, 331, 333, 335, 337, 382; Class B men 77, 84, 85, 270, 275, 280, 287, 292, 297, 303, 336, 381; Closed Division men 339, 341, 342
All American Girls Professional Baseball League 29
All Southern 9, 12, 16, 18, 20, 27, 36, 41, 42, 45, 55, 56, 58, 62, 345, 387, 393, 395, 397, 403

All Stars (Greenville, SC) Class C men 315
Allen, Charles 187
Allen, Nixon 78, 88
Allen University 85
Alley, Lyles 20, 54, 143
Allied Signal (Greer, SC) Closed Division men 343
Alston, Annette 94
Amateur Athletic Association Hall of Fame 399
Amateur Athletic Union 41, 62, 388, 398; Hall of Fame 388; National Tournament 31
Ambassadors for Christ (Greenville, SC) Class A men 290
American Amusements (Greenville, SC) Class B men 331, 382
American Auto Parts (Hodges, SC) Class A women 78, 79, 277, 283
American Basketball Association 76, 77, 400
American Can (Darlington, SC) Class C men 78, 276, 282
American Enka (Central, SC): Class A men 286, 291, 295, 302; Class A women 290
American Enka (Enka, NC) 394; Class A men 18, 28, 33, 34, 37, 38, 41, 42, 44, 126, 131, 135, 140, 143, 148, 151, 155, 159, 162, 166, 170, 184, 188, 191, 194, 200, 204, 306, 378, 389, 394; Class A women 18, 19, 25, 120, 122, 125, 129, 134, 138, 142, 146, 149, 154, 158, 161, 165, 169, 174, 387; Class B men 121, 124, 128, 163, 168; Class B women 118, 120, 123, 125, 130;

Class C men 129; Open Division men 39, 45, 197, 207, 210, 379, 394
American Federal (Greenville, SC) Class A men 96, 297, 316, 335, 337; Class B men 94, 324, 331, 333, 382
American Hardware (Greenville, SC) Class A men 86; Class B men 293, 298, 303, 307, 311, 314, 318, 321
American League 41, 397
American Monorail (Simpsonville, SC) Class B men 234, 275, 382
American Spinning (Greenville, SC) 12; Class A men 121; Class A women 12, 14, 104–107, 112, 113, 115, 118, 120, 123, 129; Class B men 14, 106, 108, 111, 112, 114, 116, 119, 132, 137, 192, 198, 201, 371; Class B women 11, 105, 109, 110; Class C men 107, 108, 110, 111, 113, 114, 122, 125, 129, 138, 141, 182, 185, 190, 193, 195, 202, 205, 218, 225, 229
American Textile Manufacturers Institute 392
AMP-AKZO (Greenville, SC): Class B men 95, 338; Closed Division men 97, 341, 343
Anders, Joe 22, 29
Anderson, Damous 95, 96
Anderson, Donald 29
Anderson, Harry 42, 43, 147, 150, 155, 158
Anderson, Hugh 166, 170, 175, 179, 184, 187, 191, 194, 197
Anderson, Jack 61
Anderson, Jim 36, 42, 213, 216, 219, 223, 226, 229, 233, 236, 239
Anderson, Kenneth 380
Anderson, Leroy 162, 166
Anderson, Waddy 26
Anderson Girls' High School 12
Anderson Hosiery Mill (Whitmire, SC) Class B men 57, 59, 214, 217, 220, 224, 228
Anderson Junior College 73, 74, 84, 86, 403
Anderson Mill (Anderson, SC): Class A men 32, 162, 166, 170, 175, 180; Class A women 27, 47, 120, 123, 206, 209, 212, 371, 372, 402; Class B men 18, 28, 43, 48, 119, 121, 124, 128, 137, 156, 159, 195, 198, 201, 204, 371, 372; Class B women 32, 116, 118, 154,
161, 165, 183; Class C men 27, 117, 133, 138, 169, 173, 177, 181, 185, 189, 192, 377
Anderson Shockers (Anderson, SC): Class C men 343; Open Division men 339, 383
Andrews Vending Co. (Greenville, SC) Class C men 304
Aneda Clock (Greenville, SC) Class B men 96, 337, 338
Apalache Mill (Greer, SC): Class A men 8, 10, 54, 106, 108, 109, 217, 379; Class A women 8, 105; Class B men 7, 103–107, 114, 192, 201, 204, 207, 292, 378; Class B women 110, 377; Class C men 39, 111, 113, 189, 193, 196, 199, 378; Open Division men 50
Appleton Mill (Anderson, SC): Class A men 175; Class A women 73, 258, 268; Class B men 78, 128, 132, 159, 163, 167, 189, 192, 262, 266, 276, 281, 287, 292, 298, 302, 307; Class B women 34, 187, 190, 194; Class C men 63, 149, 153, 157, 164, 169, 172, 177, 182, 185, 189, 192, 206, 232, 235, 238, 242, 249, 380
Applied Engineering (Orangeburg, SC) Class A men 285, 291, 296
Arab Oil Embargo 73, 74
Arcadia Mill (Spartanburg, SC) Class B men 297
Arledge, Roone 399
Arnholt, Tom 72–74
Arnold Palmer Cadillac (Charlotte, NC) Open Division men 76, 269, 278
Asheville Victory (Asheville, NC) Class A women 27, 371
Asheville Victory Juniors (Asheville, NC) Class A women 27, 371
Ashley, Larry 33, 34, 259, 264, 269, 273, 278
Ashley, Mrs. Leroy 387
Ashmore, Johnny 25
Ashworth Brothers (Greenville, SC): Class B men 74, 266, 271, 276, 281, 286, 292; Class C men 283
Associated Insulation (Slater, SC) Class C men 288
Associated Press 402
The Athlete's Foot (Greenville, SC) Class C men 308
Athletic Attic (Anderson, SC):
Class A men 78, 274, 382; Class A women 80, 284, 289, 294; Class C men 283
Athletic Dept. (Greenville, SC) Class A women 312
Atlanta Blues 387
Atlanta Cards (Atlanta, GA) Class A women 284, 289
Atlanta Crackers 397
Atlanta Hawks 76
Atlanta Satellites (Atlanta, GA) Open Division men 72, 247, 251, 255
Atlanta Tomboys (Atlanta, GA) Class A women 62, 84, 90, 232, 263, 268, 295, 402
Atlantic Christian College 399
Atlantic Coast Conference 59, 62, 65
Auburn University 47
Auschwitz 22
Auto Tech (Greenville, SC) Open Division men 332
Avco Lycoming (Greer, SC) Class B men 86, 88, 311, 314
Avondale Mill (Alexander City, AL): Class A men 15, 16, 18, 41, 114, 116, 118, 120, 126, 144, 162; Class B men 112, 124, 377; Class B women 174; Class C men 122
Avondale Mills 392
Aydlett, Rick 73

B.J. Music (Greenville, SC) Class C men 88, 315
Bacon Mill (Lenoir City, TN) Class B men 124, 127
Badders, Hurley 34
Bagwell, Danny 64, 393
Bagwell, Doug 62, 74, 77
Bagwell, Manning 18
Bahan Textile (Greenville, SC): Class A men 84–86, 280, 297, 301, 306, 310; Class A women 55, 222, 226
Bailey, David 284, 289, 295, 300, 305
Bailey, Henry 97
Bailey, J.M. 143
Bailey, Ron 381
Baker, Lennox 388
Ball, Don 289, 295, 300, 305, 309
Ball, Jim 309, 322, 326, 328, 330, 332, 334, 337, 339, 341, 342
Ballenger, Frank 236, 239, 243, 246, 250, 255, 309
Ballenger, Fred 143, 147
Ballenger, Margaret 31

Baltimore Bullets 394
Baltimore Orioles 392
Banks, Alline 387
Banks, David 330, 332, 334, 337, 339
Bannister, Furman 39
Baptist College 74
Baptist Courier 384
Barbare, Paul 10, 42, 377
Barbare, Walt 4, 7, 8, 21, 51
Barbary, Bill 43
Barbery, O'dell 29
Barger, John 378
Barley Plumbing (Greenville, SC) Class A men 270, 382
Barnett, Larry 68
Barnum, P.T. 20
Barry, Rick 400
Barton, Adrian 92, 96
Barton, Bob 52
Basinger, Kim 79
Bataan 22
Batson, Ricky 339, 341
Bausch & Lomb (Greenville, SC): Class B men 336; Open Division men 323
Baxter-Kelly-Faust Co. (Anderson, SC) Class A women 259
Bay Brokerage (Greenville, SC) Class B men 327
Baylor, Elgin 41
Beach Ball All Stars (Myrtle Beach, SC) Class C men 93, 332
Beacon Mill (Swannanoa, NC): Class A men 124, 151; Class A women 12, 14, 44, 111, 113, 115, 125, 200, 203; Class B men 27, 37, 112, 114, 148, 160, 164, 168, 171, 176, 180, 188, 191, 195, 371, 372
Beacon Mill (Westminster, SC) Class A women 277, 283
Beal, Jay 63, 380
Beasley 377
Beattie Memorial Grammar School 389
Beaunit (Fountain Inn, SC): Class A women 246; Class C men 263
Beck, Zinn 36
Becker, Gerald 34, 42, 392
Bedenbaugh, Arthur 9
Belcher, Bill 236, 239
Belk, G.W. 106
Belk Simpson (Greenville, SC): Class A men 302; Class B men 298, 303, 315
Bell, B.J. 309, 312, 316, 319, 322, 325, 328
Belmont Abbey College 72

Belton High School 380
Belton Industries (Belton, SC) Class B men 321, 324
Belton Mill (Belton, SC): Class A women 268; Class B men 127, 180, 218; Class C men 39, 44, 63, 64, 133, 182, 186, 189, 193, 195, 199, 202, 205, 218, 235
Belton Recreation (Belton, SC) Class C men 288
Belue, Jean 18
Benedict College 58
Bennett, John 383
Bennett Oil (Spartanburg, SC) Class A women 86–88, 284, 312, 315
Bennettsville High School 384
Benson, Bob 53
Benson, Kevin 93
Bentzel, Geoff 95, 383
Berea (Greenville, SC): Class C men 342; Class C women 98, 344
Berkeley Mill (Balfour, NC): Class A men 280; Class B men 53, 218; Class C men 113, 115
Berry, Connie Mac 42, 43
Bethea, Jo Jo 76, 79
Bethlehem Center (Spartanburg, SC) Class C men 263, 276, 282
Bi-Lo (Greenville, SC) Class B men 315, 336
Bi-Lo Center 96
Biedenbach, Eddie 66
Big Ten Conference 396
Bigelow-Sanford (Calhoun Falls, SC): Class A women 61, 232; Class B men 62, 63, 66, 67, 74, 231, 234, 237, 241, 244, 261, 266, 271, 275, 281, 298, 303, 308, 381
Bigelow-Sanford (Landrum, SC): Class B men 228; Class C men 229
Bill Delany's Sporting Goods (Greenville, SC) Open Division men 220
Binghamton, NY 21
Bishop, Dean 123
Bishop, Willie 56
Black, Mike 381
Black Diamond (Greenville, SC) Open Division men 86–88, 306, 309, 313
Black's Mechanical (Greenville, SC): Class A men 84, 301, 311; Class A women 300, 305, 309, 382; Class B men 297

Blackston, Johnny 26
Blackwell, George 18, 23, 43
Blackwell & Son Real Estate (Hanahan, SC) Class A women 73, 264, 268
Blalock, Sybil 80
Blankenship Electric (Greenville, SC) Class C men 283, 288, 293, 299, 304, 322
Blanton, Ken 66
Blassingame, Michael 93
Blenheim High School 89
Blue Jackets Class A men 103
Board of Directors 341, 342
Bob Jones Co. (Greenville, SC) Class C men 276, 282
Bobby's Shell (Ware Shoals, SC) Class A women 268
Bodie, Gary 170, 175, 180, 184
Bogan, Miller 337, 339
Bohanak, Mike 56
Boiling Springs High School 78
Boiter, Thelma 12
Boling, Charles 105, 106
Borden Mill (Kingsport, TN) Class A men 256, 260, 265, 270, 274, 381
Bostik-South (Greenville, SC) Class B men 288
Boston Beanery (Greenville, SC) Class A women 91, 328
Boston Braves 51
Boston Celtics 387, 396
Boston Red Sox 22
Bow Tie Grand (Columbia, SC) Open Division men 85, 306
Bowen, Judy 379
Bowers, Dorothy 382
Bowie, Ralph 147, 150, 155
Bowman, Roberta 39, 47, 50
Boyd's Spinners (Greenville, SC) Class C men 334
Boys' Club (Greenville, SC) Class C men 299
Bozeman, Walter 16, 17
Brabham's TV (Charleston, SC) Open Division men 251
Brady's Barber Shop (Greenville, SC) Class C men 88, 315
Bragg, F.C. 103
Brandon Dryer Felt (Greenville, SC) Class C men 229
Brandon Duck Mill (Greenville, SC) Class C men 164
Brandon Mill (Greenville, SC) 384; Class A men 29, 131, 135, 162, 166, 370, 378; Class A women 197; Class B men 22, 25, 27, 36, 43, 44, 127, 132, 137, 141, 145, 148, 153, 156, 159, 163, 167, 171, 176, 180,

184, 189, 192, 195, 198, 201, 204, 207, 370, 372, 377; Class B women 29, 32, 118, 123, 125, 130, 135, 143, 150, 158, 165, 170, 174, 179, 183, 187, 191, 194, 378; Class C men 22, 43, 115, 117, 122, 125, 129, 133, 141, 145, 149, 154, 157, 160, 164, 168, 173, 177, 182, 185, 189, 193, 196, 199, 202, 205, 211, 215, 222, 225, 228, 231, 235, 378
Brandon Mill (Woodruff, SC): Class A men 131, 135, 140, 144, 148, 152, 155; Class B men 127; Class B women 143, 147, 150; Class C men 157, 215
Brandon Rayon Mill (Greenville, SC) Class C men 177, 182
Branson, Jesse 59, 63, 380
Brashier, Chris 97
Breazeale, Charles 69, 70, 339, 341, 342
Brennan, Jim 56
Brevard (Brevard, NC) Open Division men 79, 278
Brevard Junior College 65, 398
Brewton 377
Brewton, Beulah 377
Bridgeman, Ralph 62
Bridges' Lounge (Greenville, SC) Open Division men 89, 316
Bridwell 11
Brinkley, Ed 50
Brissie, Lou 401
Brock, Don 31, 175
Brock, Tron 92
Brockman, Cedric 92
Brookline Carpets (Greenville, SC): Class A men 77, 78, 269, 274, 279, 285; Class A women 74, 76, 264, 268, 273, 277, 283; Class B men 257, 261, 266
Brooklyn Dodgers 22, 29
Brooklyn (Football) Dodgers 29
Brooks, Charles 20
Brooks, Joey 97
Brooks & Sons Textile Parts (Dallas, NC) Open Division men 220
Broome, Bill 43
Broome, Doug 39
Brown, Anthony 82
Brown, Barry 382
Brown, Bob 319, 322
Brown, Bobby 30
Brown, Booker 72

Brown, Carolyn 61, 96, 383
Brown, David 78, 93
Brown, J.D. 110, 112, 113, 116, 118, 155, 158, 161, 188, 191, 194, 197, 200, 203
Brown, J.W. 118
Brown, James 67, 92
Brown, Jesse 116, 120, 123, 126, 131, 150, 166, 170, 175, 179, 184
Brown, Jimmy 92, 382
Brown, Larry 400
Brown, Lee 381
Brown, Linda 52
Brown, Pete 378, 389
Brown, Ralph 56, 381
Brown, Steve 52, 56, 58, 73, 76, 289, 295, 300, 328, 330, 332, 334, 337, 339, 341, 342, 380, 392, 393
Brown, Tim 229
Brown, Wendell 93
Brown-Rogers Sporting Goods (Winston-Salem, NC) Open Division men 223
Brown University 386
Browning, Sandra 52
Brownlee, Kell 91
Brown's Bombers (Greenville, SC): Class C men 95, 336, 338, 342; Open Division men 89, 316; Class A women 78, 277, 284
Bryan, Edwina 62, 70
Bryan, Shandy 96
Bryant, Michelle 94, 96
Bryant & Lell Tire (Travelers Rest, SC) Class C men 288, 293
Bubas, Vic 395
Buchanan, Jess 8, 43
Buchanan, John 43
Budget Rent-A-Car (Greenville, SC) Class C men 325
Buford, Debra 80, 86
Bullington, Albert 14
Bumpers Car Wash (Greenville, SC) Class C men 325, 328
Buncombe St. #1 (Greenville, SC) Class C women 334
Buncombe St. #2 (Greenville, SC) Class C women 334
Bunting 8, 9
Burgess, John 390, 391
Burham 11
Burkholder, Lynn 64
Burnett, Ben 20
Burnette, Steve 70
Burnisky, Gary 56
Burns, Bobbie 47
Burns, Maxie 381

Burroughs, Kevin 96
Burton, Derrick 98
Burton, Dondray 97
Burton, Tom 54
Burton, Vicki 73
Burton, Wade 30
Burwell 25
Butler, Charles 96
Butler, Travis 96
Butler, PA 21
Butte Knitting Mill (Spartanburg, SC) Class B men 267, 381
Butts, Owen 72, 73
Byers, David 61
Byrd, Fred 88, 210, 213, 216, 219, 223, 226, 229, 232, 236, 239, 243, 246, 250, 255, 259, 264, 268, 273, 278, 284, 289, 295, 300, 305, 309, 312, 316, 322, 325, 328, 330, 332, 334, 336
Byrd, Laura 382
Byrnes, James F. 32
Byrnes High School 61, 65

C&S Bank (Greenville, SC) Class B men 334, 382
C. Dan Joyner (Greenville, SC): Class A women 86, 90, 312, 315, 319, 322, 325, 334, 383; Class C men 312, 315
Cabiness 378
Cabiness, Ted 43
Cain, Brenda 94
Caldwell, Mitch 381
Calhoun Falls Mill (Calhoun Falls, SC): Class A men 147, 151; Class A women 139; Class B men 37, 41, 145, 160, 163, 168, 192, 195, 198, 201, 208, 379; Class B women 32, 165, 170, 174, 179, 183, 187, 190, 378; Class C men 157, 185, 206
Callahan, Mike 50, 54
Calloway Mill (LaGrange, GA): Class A men 12, 111, 124, 126, 152, 166; Class B men 105, 109; Class C men 111, 377
Camden, James 382
Camero, Seco 96
Camp, Terry 382
Campbell, Arnold 62
Campbell, Fred 396
Campbell, Jimmy 62
Campbell, John 63, 64
Campbell, June 51
Campbell, Kenyatta 98
Campbell, Marc 89
Campbell, Melinda 97

Campbell, Mike 380
Campbell, Mrs. Dee 112, 113
Camperdown Mill (Greenville, SC) 385; Class B men 27, 39, 112, 121, 152, 159, 163, 168, 172, 176, 188, 192, 195, 198, 370, 371, 384; Class C men 110, 111, 133, 137, 142, 146, 149, 153, 157, 160, 164, 168, 172, 177, 181, 185, 196, 199, 377, 389
Campobello All Stars (Campobello, SC) Class A men 372
Candler, Coker 143
Cannon, Robert 74, 381
Cannon Mill (Central, SC) Class C men 52, 54, 214, 218, 221
Cannon Mills 392
Cantalfio, Joe 95
Capsugel (Greenwood, SC) Class B men 304, 308
Carlisle, Charles 73
Carlisle, Pete 43, 52, 57, 379
Caroleen Mill (Caroleen, NC): Class B men 125; Class C men 110
Carolina Circuit (Greenville, SC) Closed Division men 339
Carolina Conference 67
Carolina Engineers (Greenville, SC) Open Division men 70, 247
Carolina Fine Foods (Greenville, SC) Open Division men 320, 323, 326
Carolina Handling (Piedmont, SC) Open Division men 265
Carolina Magic (Greenville, SC) Open Division men 96, 337
Carolina Material Handling (Mauldin, SC) Class B men 78, 267, 271, 276, 281, 381
Carolina Plating (Greenville, SC): Class A women 46, 52, 54, 55, 209, 216, 219, 222, 226, 229, 378; Class C men 215; Open Division men 48, 49, 207, 210, 379
Carolina Supply (Greenville, SC) Class C men 226, 249, 253
Carolina Upstate (Greenville, SC) Class C men 93, 330, 332
Carolinas Conference 399
Carotell (Taylors, SC) Class C men 77, 257, 262, 272, 277, 283, 288
Carper, Larry 93
Carper Real Estate (Greenville, SC): Class C men 86, 89, 91–93, 95, 96, 299, 304, 308, 312, 318, 322, 325, 328, 330, 334, 336, 338, 340, 342, 343; Class C women 97; Open Division men 326
Carr, Roger 89, 93, 96
Carr, Ronnie 403
Carson, R.D. 62
Carter, Andy 382
Carter, Clay 382
Carter, Eddie 67
Carter, Vercho 73, 207, 210, 213, 239, 243, 246, 250, 255, 259, 264, 269, 273, 278, 284, 289, 295, 300, 305, 309
Carter & Crawley (Greenville, SC) Class C men 241, 245, 249, 253, 258, 263
Carver, Bobby 73
Carver, Don 53, 57, 380
Carver Builders (Greenville, SC) Class C men 94, 336
Case, Everett 395
Castings Inc. (Greenville, SC): Class B men 261; Open Division men 74, 260
Castro, Fidel 29
Catawba College 63, 67
Cathcart, Eleanor 120
Cavalier Warriors (Greenville, SC) Class C men 342
Central (Central, SC) Open Division men 329
Central CWC (Central, SC) Class A women 332
Central Mill (Central, SC) Class C men 149
Central Savannah River Area All Stars (Augusta, GA) Class C men 88, 89, 315, 318
Central Wesleyan College 89, 90
Centre Electric (Greenville, SC) Open Division men 210
Chamberlain, Wilt 390
Chambers, Ernie 34, 44, 389, 390
Champion "Y" (Canton, NC) 397
Chapman, Jimmy 52
Chapman, Vickie 58
Charles, Jim 85
Charleston Flyers (Charleston, SC) Open Division men 90, 92, 326, 328, 382
Charleston Naval Base (Charleston, SC) Class A women 338
Charleston Sportsman (Charleston, SC) Open Division men 341
Charlotte (NC) YMCA 4
Charlotte All Stars (Charlotte, NC) Open Division men 230, 380
Chatham Mfg. (Elkin, NC): Class A men 31, 37, 41, 127, 131, 151, 166; Class A women 25, 29, 138, 142, 146, 149, 154, 157, 161, 165, 169, 174, 378, 387; Class B women 135
Chattanooga Lookouts 36, 395, 397
Chattanooga VFW (Chattanooga, TN) Open Division men 52, 54, 213, 216, 223, 230, 251
Cheek, Paul 150, 155, 158, 166, 170, 175
Chem-Size (Travelers Rest, SC) Class A women 86, 308
Chesnee Mill (Chesnee, SC): Class B men 106; Class B women 105
Chester High School 95
Chester's Chicken (Greenville, SC) Open Division men 335, 337, 383
Chick-Fil-A (Greenville, SC): Class A women 90, 319, 325; Class C men 84, 88–94, 293, 299, 304, 308, 315, 318, 322, 325, 328, 330, 334; Open Division men 77, 79, 81, 82, 85, 86, 273, 278, 284, 289, 295, 300, 305
Chicopee Mill (Gainesville, GA): Class A men 36, 116, 118, 136, 140, 143, 147, 151, 188; Class B men 112, 114, 127, 132, 168, 171, 176, 180, 184; Class C men 125
Childers, Jimmy 66, 380, 381
Chilton, Tom 52
Chiquola Mill (Honea Path, SC): Class B men 19, 128, 132; Class C men 125
Chrisley, Terry 381
Christ Church (Greenville, SC) Class C men 340, 343
Christopher, Raymond 26
Cincinnati Reds 23, 29, 32
Cinderella 18
The Citadel 8
City of Greenville (SC): Class B men 293; Closed Division men 96, 97, 339, 343
City View 8
Civil Rights movement 62
Claflin College 90
Clark, Harry 30, 170, 175, 179, 188
Clark, James 78, 382

Clark, Phil 77, 251, 255, 259, 264, 269, 273, 278, 284, 289, 295, 300, 305, 309, 312, 316, 319, 322, 326, 328, 330, 332, 334, 336, 339
Clark-Schwebel (Anderson, SC): Class A men 256, 260; Class B men 69, 234, 237, 245, 248, 252; Open Division men 220, 379
Classy Ladies (Columbia, SC) Class A women 341
Clayton, Carolyn 46, 380
Cleamons, Jim 86
Clemson University 20, 32, 37, 43, 47, 50, 52, 53, 56, 62, 66, 68, 76, 78, 80, 81, 84–86, 89, 90, 95, 380, 386, 390, 392, 393, 396, 403; Athletic Hall of Fame 392; Board of Trustees 392
Cleveland Memorial Hospital (Shelby, NC) Class A men 323, 326, 329; Class B men 317, 321
Clifford, Joy 97
Clifton Mill (Clifton, SC): Class A men 166, 171; Class B men 148, 163
Clifton Mill (Spartanburg, SC) Class B men 29
Clinchfield Mill (Marion, NC): Class B men 107, 108; Class C men 12
Clinton Mill (Clinton, SC): Class A men 321, 337, 382; Class B men 180, 188, 198, 208, 211, 214, 299, 303, 308, 317, 324, 327, 329, 331, 333, 335, 337, 382, 383; Closed Division men 96, 339
Clover Mill (Clover, SC) Class B men 106, 107
Coan, Fred 63
Coan, George 52
Coats & Clark (Toccoa, GA) Class B men 189
Cobb, Doc 4
Cobb, Ronnie 64
Cobb, Ty 391
Coble, Jimmy 54
Cobras (Greenville, SC) Open Division men 323
Coca-Cola 18, 20
Coca-Cola (Asheville, NC) Open Division men 278
Cohen, Dempsey 92, 95
Coleman, Lee 155, 158, 162, 166, 170
Coleman, W. 97
Coles, Greg 81

Cole's Barber Shop (Columbia, SC) Open Division men 300
College of Charleston 393
Collier, James III 278
Collier, Jim 194, 197, 200, 203, 206, 210, 213
Collins, Todd 383
Collins & Aikman (Roxboro, NC) Class B men 119, 127
Coln, Roger 379
Columbus Mill (Columbus, GA): Class A men 136, 140, 175; Class B men 113, 127, 132, 149, 153, 156, 163, 167, 377
Comfort Inn (Greenville, SC) Class A women 91, 328
Community Superette (Etowah, NC) Class A women 264
Compton, Jerry 289
Conard, Tom 47
Connell, Billy 54
Conso (Union, SC) Class B men 56, 70, 225, 248, 252
Converse Mill (Spartanburg, SC): Class A men 9, 106, 108; Class B men 15, 23, 117, 121, 141, 144, 152; Class B women 22, 150, 155, 378; Class C men 138
Conway, Steve 86
Cooper's Super Market (Greenville, SC) Class C men 308
Copeland, Carlos 98
Corbin, L.R. 155, 158
Corbin, Tyrone 84
Corn Products Company 20
Corn Trophy 20, 25, 31, 39, 62, 73
Corporate Benefits (Greenville, SC) Class C men 89, 318
Corwin, F.R. 5, 104
Cottingham, A.H. 5
Couch, C. 18
Couch, Ceedy 25
Courtaulds Inc. (Mobile, AL) Class B men 44, 201, 204, 378
Courtesy Mechanical (Greenville, SC) Class C men 283
Cousy, Bob 387, 394, 396, 400
Couture, Beth 86, 90
Cox, _____ 22
Cox, Cleve 94, 95
Cox, Don 30
Cox, Fred 25
Cox, Jennifer 95
Crain, Ernie 68
Crain, Ted 139, 143, 147
Cramerton Mill (Cramerton,

NC): Class A men 159, 167, 171; Class B men 132, 145, 152
Cranston Print Works (Fletcher, NC) Class A men 220, 224, 379, 380
Crawford, Charles 382
Creamer, Ronnie 81
Cremins, Bobby 70, 73
Crescent High School 46
Croft, Wayne 78
Crooks, Glenda 380
Crosley Broadcasting 13
Cross, Ronnie 52
Cross Stitch Originals (Cliffside, NC) Open Division men 309
Crowe, Heather 98
Crowe, Steve 74, 79, 84, 88, 92, 382
Crown-Metro (Greenville, SC) Class C men 69, 70, 72, 245, 249, 253, 381
Crump, Tommy 380
Cryovac (Duncan, SC) Class B men 253, 256, 261, 266, 271, 275, 281, 287, 292, 297, 302, 307, 314, 317, 325
Cryovac (Simpsonville, SC): Class A men 79, 265, 270, 274, 279, 285, 291, 296, 301, 306, 310, 313, 317, 320, 323, 326, 329, 331, 333, 335, 382; Class B men 82, 86, 248, 252, 261, 266, 271, 281, 287, 291, 298, 303, 307, 311, 315, 317, 321, 327, 329, 331, 333, 335, 337, 381, 382; Closed Division men 96, 97, 339, 341, 342
Cunningham, Billy 55, 57, 59, 69, 385
Cureton, Ronnie 69, 79, 86
Custom Printing (Greenville, SC) Class A women 254
Czechoslovakia 22

D & D Specialties (Greenville, SC) Class A women 328
D & L Advertising (Greenville, SC) Open Division men 78, 79, 273, 278
D.B. Carter Used Cars (Greenville, SC) Class C men 294
D.J.'s (Greenville, SC) Class A women 309
Dacox (Seneca, SC) Class C men 231
Dacus, Charles 87
Dacus, Steve 53
Dahl, Mike 68
Dalton's Furniture (Pickens, SC)

Class C men 82, 84, 85, 293, 299, 304
Dan River Mill (Danville VA) Class B men 164, 168
Daniel, Al 82, 86, 403
Daniel, Holly 403
Daniel, Mel 85, 86, 88, 89, 96, 403
Daniel Construction Co. (Greenville, SC): Class A men 73, 76, 256, 260, 265, 270, 297, 302; Open Division men 76
Daniel Construction Co. (Greer, SC) Class A men 274, 279
Daniel Construction Co. (Jenkinsville, SC) Open Division men 78, 80, 269, 274, 278, 284, 289, 295, 300
Daniel High School 61
Daniels, Atlba 383
Daniels, Ricky 93
Darby, Bill 64
Darlington (Darlington, SC) Class C men 249
Darrell Floyd's Sandwich Shop (Greenville, SC) Class A women 78–80, 273, 277, 283, 288, 294, 394
Davenport, Frances 378
Dave's Restaurant (Greenville, SC) Class C men 332
Davidson, Buddy 39, 43
Davidson, Don 58, 59
Davidson College 58, 59, 62, 63
Davidson Heating & Air (Greenville, SC) Open Division men 223
Davis, Chad 94
Davis, Charlie 76
Davis, Don 328, 330, 332, 334, 336, 339, 341, 342
Davis, Donald 68, 79, 326, 382
Davis, J.C. 377
Davis, Jake 401
Davis, Julian 385, 386
Davis, Larry 382
Davis, Lee 66
Davis, Lucille 386
Davis, Mickey 54, 59, 62, 401, 402
Davis, Mike 380
Davis, Robert 74
Davis, Sherry 94
Davis, Skeeter 381
Davis, Tom 332, 334, 337, 339
Davis, Walter 23
Davis Landscaping (Piedmont, SC) Class B men 382
Davis Mechanical (Greenville, SC): Class A men 230, 380; Class B men 53, 214, 217, 220, 224, 227, 380
Davis-Morris Landscaping (Piedmont, SC) Class B men 335
Dawson, Cleo 73
DAYCO (Greenville, SC) Class A women 255
Dayton University 46, 390
Dean, Don 62
Dean Hill Cars (Greenville, SC) Class C men 283
Decorative Components (Forest City, NC) Open Division men 73, 251, 255, 381
Defender Chemical (Anderson, SC) Open Division men 76, 264
Del Ray, Ron 76
Democratic National Convention 64
Dendy, William Jr. 273, 278
Denton, Dave 381
Detroit Tigers 378
Detroit Vagabond Kings 396
Diamond, Jim 47, 57
Diaz, Lisa 94, 96
Dice, Geary 337, 339, 341, 342
Dice & Associates (Greenville, SC) Class C men 94, 95, 334, 336, 338
Dick Brooks Honda (Columbia, SC) Open Division men 89, 319
Dick James (Greenville, SC) Class C men 97, 341
Dickard, Ed 194, 197, 200, 203, 206, 210
Dickerson, David 88
Dickey, Cecil 203, 207
Diehl Mfg. (Pickens, SC) Class B men 211, 217, 221
Dietz, Dickie 49
Digital (Greenville, SC): Class A men 327; Class B men 92, 329
Dill, Roger 378
Dillard, Don 36
Dillard, John 61
Dillard, Johnny 64
Dillard's Sporting Goods (Easley, SC): Class C men 325; Open Division men 48, 52–54, 90, 210, 213, 216, 220, 322
Dill's Warehouse (Greenville, SC) Class C men 61, 232, 262, 277, 282
Direction '75 399
Discount Fence Co. (Winston-Salem, NC) Class A women 78, 258, 263, 268, 272, 277, 283
Dixie Ford (Greenville, SC) Open Division men 48, 50, 210
Dixie League Basketball Tournament 395
Dixie Mercerizing (Lupton City, TN): Class A men 22, 25, 37, 42, 131, 135, 144, 147, 150, 155; Class A women 154; Class B men 145; Class B women 22, 147, 150, 378
"Dixie's Own World Series" 18
Dixon, Danny 72
Doar, J.B. 126, 131
Dobbins, Mickey 379
Dobson, Ann 63
Dobson, David 76
Dockins, Ken 251, 255
Doggett, Carlisle 5
Doggett, G.L. 5, 20, 21, 30, 116, 118, 120, 123, 126, 131, 135, 139
Doggett, Madge 12
Dogwood Hills Mfg. (Walhalla, SC) Class C men 79, 276, 282
Donald, Lena 11
Donnan, Bob 25
Dooley, Beverly 44, 52
Dooley, Myrtle 22, 378
Douglas, G.N. 5
Douglas, George M. 8
Dow Badische (Anderson, SC) Class B men 253, 256, 261, 266, 271, 275, 281
Dow Brands (Mauldin, SC) Class B men 327
Dowling, Zack 97
Draper Mill (Draper, NC): Class A men 106, 118; Class B men 109, 111, 117, 136; Class B women 11, 109, 110, 143; Class C men 108, 111, 146, 377
Drayton Mill (Spartanburg, SC): Class A men 27, 135, 140, 144, 148, 151, 155, 159, 162, 166, 171, 371, 378; Class A women 27, 139, 142, 147, 150, 154, 158, 161, 165, 169, 174, 371; Class B men 18, 104, 127, 132; Class B women 20, 130, 134, 377, 387; Class C men 164
Dream Team (Shelby, NC) Open Division men 95, 335, 341
Driesell, Lefty 62, 63
Drummond, David 88
Drummond, Derrick 95, 96
Drummond, Lewis 28

Drummond, Marvin 381, 382
Drummond Oil Co. (Greenwood, SC) Open Division men 76, 260, 264, 269
Dubose, Dorothy 55
DuBose, S.R. 180, 184, 187, 191, 194, 197, 200, 203, 207, 210, 213, 216, 219, 223, 226, 229
Duke Power (Greenville, SC): Class A men 279, 285, 301, 306; Class B men 333
Duke University 20, 29, 30, 39, 41, 43, 58, 388, 395
Dukes, Garland 79
Dunagin, Rick 63
Duncan, Chris 88
Duncan, Ricky 50
Duncan, V.O. 106
Duncan Pharmacy (Duncan, SC) Class A women 273, 277, 283
Duncan Pontiac (Greenville, SC) Class C men 262
Dunean Cafe (Greenville, SC) 394, 395; Class C men 76, 77, 267, 272
Dunean Mill (Greenville, SC) 17, 25, 384, 390, 391, 394, 395; Class A men 10, 18, 19, 23, 25–30, 33, 34, 36, 37, 41–44, 48, 67, 68, 82, 84, 105, 106, 108, 118, 121, 124, 126, 131, 136, 140, 144, 147, 151, 156, 159, 162, 164, 166, 171, 175, 180, 184, 188, 191, 194, 201, 240, 243, 256, 270, 275, 285, 290, 295, 301, 307, 310, 314, 370, 371, 381, 382, 389, 393–395; Class A women 18, 20, 53, 66, 107, 110, 115, 118, 122, 125, 129, 134, 139, 142, 197, 219, 239, 242, 246, 249, 254, 259, 263, 294, 300, 315, 371, 372; Class B men 15, 26, 30, 34, 43, 50, 52, 66, 69, 77, 104, 106–109, 114, 116, 132, 136, 145, 148, 152, 156, 159, 162, 167, 172, 177, 180, 185, 188, 192, 195, 198, 201, 204, 207, 210, 214, 218, 221, 224, 227, 230, 234, 237, 245, 248, 252, 262, 266, 271, 276, 281, 298, 338, 370–372, 378–381; Class B women 109, 113, 147, 150, 154, 158, 161, 170, 174, 179, 183, 187, 190, 194, 377, 395; Class C men 30, 43, 44, 86, 92, 108, 111, 113, 115, 117, 119, 125, 129, 133, 138, 142, 145, 149, 153, 154, 156, 157, 160, 169, 172, 178, 182, 185, 189, 192, 196, 199, 202, 205, 208, 211, 215, 225, 228, 231, 234, 238, 312, 318, 322, 330, 332, 336, 377, 378, 389, 391; Closed Division men 340, 341; Hall of Fame 391; Open Division men 39, 197, 391, 394
Dunn, Lassie 378
Durante, Dwight 63, 66, 67, 380, 400
Durham, Ralph 393
Durocher, Leo 398, 399
Dwyer, Cliff 58

E-Systems Inc. (Greenville, SC) Class A men 73, 256
Eads, Clyde 52
Easley High School 74
Easley Housing Center (Easley, SC) Class B men 327
Easley Mill (Easley, SC): Class A women 39, 43, 197, 203; Class B men 43, 70, 172, 176, 180, 188, 192, 195, 198, 201, 204, 211, 214, 217, 221, 224, 241, 248, 252, 257, 261, 293, 381; Class B women 179, 187, 190, 194; Class C men 53, 173, 177, 182, 185, 189, 193, 195, 199, 202, 205, 208, 212, 222, 225
East Tennessee State University 39, 52, 95
Eastside High School 97
Eau Claire High School 89
"Echoes of Sports" 17
Ecusta (Brevard, NC): Class A men 372; Class A women 372
Eddy, C.L. 131, 135, 139
Edgecomb Metals (Greenville, SC) Class A men 280, 285
Edmonds, Herb 57
Edwards, Linda 381
Edwards, Paul 179, 184
Edwards, Toni 91, 383
8 O'Clock Supers (Greenville, SC) Class C men 93, 332
Eldeco (Greenville, SC) Class A men 291
Electric Services (Charleston, SC) Open Division men 70, 247
Elizabeth James Mill (Marion, NC) Class B men 121
Elkay Industries (Camden, SC) Open Division men 236, 381
Ellenburg, C.E. 61
Ellenburg, Mary 86
Ellenburg, Robin 84
Elliott, Ruppert 72, 90, 259, 264, 269, 273, 278, 284, 289, 295, 300, 305, 309, 315, 319, 322, 325, 328, 330, 332, 334, 336, 339, 341, 342
Ellis, Fred 51
Ellis, Mickey 25
Ellis, Paul 316
Ellis, Shawn 96
Elon College 59, 63, 400
Emb-Tex (Travelers Rest, SC) Class A men 85, 297, 302, 306, 310, 313, 316, 317, 320, 323, 326, 329, 331, 382
Embler, Ethan 62
Embler, Ezra 28
Embler, Jimmy 28
Embler, W.H. 200, 203, 207, 210, 213, 226
Emery, Arnelle 36
Emery, Carroll 36
Emery, Douglas 36
Emery, John 36, 42, 43
Emery Air (Greenville, SC) Class C men 299
Employee Benefits (Greenville, SC) Class B men 336, 337, 383
Engineering Products (Greenville, SC) Open Division men 210
English, Alex 76
English, Jo Jo 93
Enro Shirt Co. (Woodruff, SC) Class A women 268
Enterprise All Stars (Greenville, SC): Class B men 338; Closed Division men 96, 340
Equinox Mill (Anderson, SC): Class A men 136; Class B men 132, 137, 377; Class B women 150; Class C men 133, 138, 142, 153, 185, 238
Erlanger Mill (Lexington, NC): Class A men 124, 126; Class B men 121, 137, 171
Erskine College 52, 66, 72, 86, 90, 393, 401
Erwin Mill (Erwin, TN): Class A men 131; Class B men 125, 128
Eskew, Sammy 66
Estes, Dave 330, 332, 334, 336, 339, 341, 342
Eubanks, Bill 380
Eubanks, Leon 52, 380
Evans, Bruce 90, 93
Evatt, Herman 55, 380
Evington, Effie 25–27, 32, 42, 43, 392, 393
Excalibur (Greenville, SC) Open Division men 93, 330
Excelsior Mill (Pendleton, SC):

Class B men 34, 392; Class C men 212
Executive Committee 341, 342
Executive Officers 289, 295, 300, 305, 309, 312, 315, 319, 322, 325, 328, 330, 332, 334, 336, 339

F.W. Woolworth (Greenville, SC): Class A men 291, 297, 302; Class A women 289; Class B men 281, 287, 292, 297, 303, 324, 327
Fair, Mike 57, 380
Fairfax Mill (Fairfax, AL) Class B men 132, 136
Fairforest Finishing (Clevedale, SC) Class C men 221
Fairhaven Mill (Pickens, SC) Class C men 262
Fashion First (Greer, SC) Class C men 293
Fast Fare (Hartwell, GA) Class C men 84, 299
Fat Friday's (Clemson, SC) Open Division men 96, 339, 341
Fiber Industries (Greenville, SC): Class A men 70, 73, 237, 240, 244, 247, 251, 256, 260, 265, 270, 274, 279, 285, 291, 296, 301, 306, 310; Class A women 63, 74, 236, 239, 242, 259, 264; Class B men 55, 66, 67, 72, 231, 234, 237, 241, 244, 247, 252, 257, 261, 266, 271, 275, 281, 287, 292, 293, 297, 380, 381
Fiber Processing (Greenville, SC): Class A men 256, 381; Open Division men 335
Fiber Processing (Virginia) Open Division men 341
Fiberglas (Anderson, SC): Class A women 44, 200, 203, 206, 209, 212; Class B men 49, 198, 201, 204, 207, 211, 221, 275, 280, 286, 378, 379
Fiberweb (Greenville, SC): Class B men 94, 331, 333, 335, 337, 383; Closed Division men 96, 340, 341
Finley Revis Hanes (Greenville, SC) Class B men 321, 324
Firestone Textile Inc. (Gastonia, NC) Class B men 34, 172, 176, 181, 185
Fisk-Carter (Greenville, SC) Class C men 262
Fitzgerald's University Club Orchestra 18

Flanagan, Anthony 383
Fleet Supply (Winston-Salem, NC) Open Division men 76, 265
Fleming, Bobby 48
Florence Boy's Club (Florence, SC) Class C men 312
Florida State University 52
Floyd, Darrell 80, 278, 284, 289, 295, 300, 305, 392
Floyd, Diane 80
Floyd, Libby 80
Floyd, Nancy 80
Flynn, Mickey 43
Fogler, Eddie 95
Foothills Real Estate (Greenville, SC) Class A women 90, 319, 322, 325
Forrest, Nettie 8
Fort Jackson 390
Fortune, Bobby 384
Foster, Charles 36, 43
Foster, Charles Jr. 43
Foster, Dan 213, 216, 219, 223, 226, 229, 233, 236, 239, 243, 246, 250, 255, 259, 264, 269, 273, 278, 284, 289, 295, 300, 305, 309
Foster, Dewey 36
Foster, Fred 36
Foster, Harry 36, 68, 69, 89, 216, 219, 223, 226, 229, 232, 236, 239, 243, 246, 250, 255, 259, 264, 268, 273, 278, 284, 289, 295, 300, 305, 309, 312, 316
Foster, Jimmy 78
Foster, Johnny 316, 319, 322
Foster, Roy 36
Foster, Sheila 78
Foster, Winona 46, 47
Fountain Inn Lumber (Fountain Inn, SC) Class A women 300, 305
470th Bombardment Squadron (Greenville, SC) Class A men 370
471st Bomb Squadron (Greenville, SC) Class A men 371
Four Star Sports (Spartanburg, SC) Class A women 88, 90, 318, 322, 325, 382
Fowler, Art 23
Fowler, Jean 28
Fowler, Kevin 86
Fowler, Lee 74
Fowler, Pete 17
Fowler, Pete Jr. 17
Fowler, Roberta 28
Fowler, Wayne 43

Fowler, Willard 50, 210, 213, 216, 219, 223, 226, 229, 236, 239, 243, 246, 250, 255, 259, 264, 269, 273, 278, 284, 289, 295, 378
Fox Movietone 32
Francis Marion College 84, 88
Frankfurt (IN) High School 395
Frantz, Bob 50
Fred Fraley Tru Ride (Spartanburg, SC) Class C men 76, 267
Frederick, Rex 52
Fredrick, Zam 78, 84
Freedom Foundation 399
Freeman, Bobbie 401
Freeman, Catina 94, 95
Freeman, Charles 150, 155, 158, 162
Freeman, John 385
Freyer, Keith 92
Friar, Buck 22
Froehling-Robertson (Greenville, SC) Class B men 248
Frye, Don 56
Fuller, Harold 62
Furman University 4, 8, 20, 29, 36, 43, 47, 52, 54, 56, 62, 65, 66, 70, 79, 80, 82, 84–86, 88, 89, 93, 95, 98, 379, 386, 388, 392–394, 396, 403
Furmanski, John 88
Futch, Eunice 387, 388
Futuras (Greenville, SC) Class B men 331

Gaffney, Jimmy 95
Gaines, Jermaine 95
Gallman, Will 95, 96
Galloway, A.B. 155, 158
Galloway, Chick 21, 41
Galloway Upholstery (Piedmont, SC) Class B men 262
Gambrell, Carla 94
Gambrell, Steve 52, 54
Gambrell, Todd 92
Gambrell, Wayne 52, 54
Gardner, _____ 25
Gardner, Joe 52
Gardner, N. 97
Gardner-Webb College 384
Garner, F.C. 123, 126
Garner, Jerry 39, 46
Garner, Patrick 95
Garner, Stephanie 88
Garnett, Kevin 94, 95
Garraux, John H. 19, 20, 112, 113, 116, 118, 120, 123, 126, 130, 135, 139, 384
Garren, Don 210
Garrett, Carolyn 61

Garrett, Christine 18
Garrett, Claudia 58
Garrett, Joe 62
Garrett, Keener 213, 216
Garrett, Kelli 96, 97
Garrick, Tracy 89
Garrison, Ford 21, 22
Garrison, Mike 86
Gash, Paul 85
Gates, Don 66, 67
Gateway Balloons (Greenville, SC) Class A women 336
Gator Bowl Tournament 62
Gault's Cleaners (Greenville, SC) Class C men 315
Gay, James 20
Gayley Mill (Marietta, SC) Class A men 296
Gazaway, Darren 330, 332, 334, 337, 339, 341, 342
GE (Greenville, SC): Class B men 336, 337; Closed Division men 340–342
Geer, Joe 78
Gene A. Smith (Lexington, SC) Class A men 290
General Asbestos & Rubber Co. (Charleston, SC) Class A women 161
General Electric (Greenville, SC): Class A men 252, 256, 260, 270, 275, 280, 286, 382; Class B men 69, 70, 248
General Fireproofing (Forest City, NC) Open Division men 68, 243
General Nutrition (Greenville, SC) Class B men 315, 318, 321, 330
George Coleman Ford (Travelers Rest, SC) Class B men 84, 86, 302, 307, 311
Georgia Electric Class A women 284
Georgia Tech 378
Gerald Glur Real Estate (Greenville, SC) Open Division men 76, 265
Gestering, Marjorie 386
Gibson, Mel 68
Giebell, Floyd 378
Gilliard, Frank 386
Gillison, Mike 90, 92, 382
Gilreath, Joe 216, 219, 223, 226, 229
Gilstrap Real Estate (Greenville, SC) Class A women 86–88, 312, 315
Gilstrap, John 342
Gilstrap, Regina 74, 76
Givens Youth Center (Fountain Inn, SC) Class B men 88, 311, 314, 317, 321, 324, 327
Glen Lowery Mill (Whitmire, SC): Class A men 103, 120, 124, 126, 136, 140, 144, 148, 377, 378; Class A women 55, 104, 122, 125, 130, 139, 142, 146, 150, 222; Class B men 30, 105–107, 116, 119, 168, 171, 176, 180, 184, 379; Class B women 32, 105, 118, 120, 170, 174, 179, 183, 187; Class C men 38, 39, 110, 129, 196, 222, 378
Glendale Mill (Spartanburg, SC) Class B men 167, 172, 176, 378
Glenwood Mill (Easley, SC): Class B men 114, 117; Class C men 113, 169, 173, 177, 182, 218
Gluck Mill (Anderson, SC) 27; Class B men 28, 43, 62, 66, 145, 221, 224, 230, 234, 237, 380; Class B women 147; Class C men 173, 178, 183, 186, 249
Glur, Gerald 56
Glymph, George 89
Godfrey, Wayne 43, 378
Goin' Jesse's Restaurant (Columbia, SC) Open Division men 86, 305
Golden, Lewis 264, 269, 273, 278, 284, 289, 295, 300, 305, 309, 312, 316, 319, 322, 326, 328, 330, 332, 334, 337, 339, 341, 342
Golden, Shawn 95
Golden Strip (Mauldin, SC) Class C men 343
Golden Strip Motors (Mauldin, SC) Class A men 78, 274
Goley, Skip 72
Goodwin, Sam 76
Goodwin, William 89
Goodyear Clearwater Mill (Rockmart, GA): Class A men 156, 162; Class B men 153
Gordon, Neild 36, 38, 62, 87, 396
Gordon, W.D. 5
Gossett Mill (Anderson, SC) Class B men 121, 124, 156
Gould Associates (Taylors, SC) Class A women 284, 289, 294, 300
Gould's Surveyors (Greenville, SC) Class A women 90, 325
Gourley, J.L. 5, 82, 103, 104
Gower Mfg. (Greenville, SC) Class B men 211
Grace Distribution (Duncan, SC) Class B men 292, 298
Grace Road Baptist Church 384
Gradegg (Asheville, NC) Class A women 27, 372
Grady, Maya 97
Grady's Sports (Anderson, SC) Class C men 283, 288
Graniteville Company 392
Grant, Gerald 66
Gravley, Leon 50, 56, 62, 378
Gravley, Mike 332, 334, 337, 339, 341
Gravley, Robbie 339, 341
Gray, Devin 96
Gray, Thomas 96
Grayson, Gerald 44
Great Depression 14, 22, 386
Greater Greenville Basketball Tournament 25, 370
"The Greatest Athletic Meet in the World" 18
Green, Carl 28
Green, E.T. 34
Green, Jerry 380, 393
Green, Jimmy 7
Green, William 380
Green Creek Ruritan (Rutherfordton, NC) Open Division men 76, 265
Greene, Carlton 339, 341, 342
Greene, John 316
Greene, Norman 53
Greene, Wayne 58
Greenville Airport (Greenville, SC) Class B men 217
Greenville All Stars (Greenville, SC) Class A women 338
Greenville Army Air Base 394
Greenville City Recreation (Greenville, SC) Class A women 95, 336, 383
Greenville County (Greenville, SC) Class A men 260
Greenville County Recreation (Greenville, SC) Class B men 82, 281, 293
Greenville County Sheriff's Dept. (Greenville, SC) Class A men 302
Greenville Fire Dept. (Greenville, SC): Class A men 92, 94, 95, 313, 317, 320, 323, 326, 329, 331, 333, 335, 337; Class B men 304, 338; Closed Division men 340
Greenville General Hospital 31
Greenville High School

(Greenville, SC) 18, 61, 65, 97, 389; Class B men 372
Greenville Junior Chamber of Commerce 5
Greenville Law Enforcement (Greenville, SC): Class A men 275, 280, 286; Class B men 298
Greenville Memorial Hospital 81
Greenville Old Pros (Greenville, SC) Open Division men 58, 59, 62, 227, 230, 400
Greenville Spinners 29
Greenville Tec (Greenville, SC) Class A women 259, 263
Greenville Valve (Greenville, SC): Class A men 79, 84, 88, 280, 296, 302, 314, 317, 320, 323, 382; Class B men 92, 94, 95, 329, 331, 333, 335, 337, 382; Closed Division men 96, 340
Greenville Women's College 386
Greenwood Jazz (Greenwood, SC) Open Division men 285
Greenwood Mill (Greenwood, SC): Class A men 144; Class B men 86, 311; Class C men 186, 190, 193, 196, 378; Open Division men 89, 320
Greenwood Stars (Greenwood, SC) Class A women 294
Greer, Coot 25
Greer AAU (Greer, SC) Class C men 343
Greer High School (Greer, SC) 20, 61, 65; Class B men 371, 372
Greer Mill (Greer, SC) 392; Class A men 7, 21, 42, 109, 111, 112, 135, 140, 148, 200, 204, 378; Class A women 39, 52, 105, 112, 200, 203, 206, 209, 213, 216, 378; Class B men 7, 44, 47, 49, 52, 104–109, 112, 127, 132, 149, 153, 164, 167, 172, 176, 185, 188, 198, 201, 204, 211, 214, 234, 237, 380, 381; Class B women 105, 108, 109, 116, 130, 179, 194, 377; Class C men 32, 43, 52, 105–108, 111, 113, 115, 122, 125, 128, 134, 137, 141, 146, 157, 160, 168, 173, 177, 182, 186, 189, 193, 196, 199, 202, 205, 208, 212, 215, 218, 221, 378; Open Division men 36, 39, 50
Gregoire, Michelle 96, 97
Gregor, Gary 64, 76
Greiner, Mike 80

Grey Hosiery Mill (Hendersonville, NC): Class A women 158; Class B women 22, 150, 154, 378
Grey Y League 391
Grier, John G. 110
Grier, W.M. 5, 9, 12, 104, 106, 113, 116, 120, 123, 143, 147
Griffin, Bobby 81
Griffin, Nick 93
Griffin, Willie 76
Griffith, Clark 397
Griffith, W.A. 194, 197
Griggs Electric Class A women 283
Grimm, Bruce 79
Groat, Dick 388
Grogan, Jim 216, 219, 223, 226
Guilford College 70
Guthrie Motors (Williamston, SC) Open Division men 62, 64, 66–69, 233, 236, 240, 243, 381
Guy, Paul 84

Hagood, Cecil 378
Haines, James 72
Haley, Lee 95
Haley, Sammy 93
Haley, Simeon 93
Hall, B.C. Jr. 162, 166, 170, 175
Hall, Melinda 94
Hall, Nealy 30
Hambright, Hoyt 29
Hamby, Earl 393
Hamilton, Joe 98
Hamilton, Michael 94
Hammett, Skeeter 67, 68, 380
Hammonds, Derrick 93
Hampton, Hugh 25, 43, 187, 191, 387
Hampton Industries (Kinston, NC) Class A women 76, 268
Hamrick, W.P. 8
Hanahan Park & Playground (Hanahan, SC) Class A women 254
Hanenburger, Cindy 73
Hanes Dye & Finishing (Winston-Salem, NC) Open Division men 227
Hanes Hosiery Mill (Winston-Salem, NC) 387, 388; Class A men 25, 29–31, 33, 43, 151, 155, 158, 162, 166, 184, 387; Class A women 31, 150, 154, 157, 161, 165, 169, 200, 388; Class B men 145, 148; Class B women 147; Open Division men 58

Hanna-Sides (Pelzer, SC) Class A women 82, 294
Hanvey Construction (Anderson, SC) Class A women 263
Harbin, Edgar 14
Harbin, Ken 68, 78
Harbin, Ralph 17, 21
Harbin, Terry 289
Hardee's (Spartanburg, SC) Class C men 283
Hardin, J.D. 197, 200, 203, 207
Harding, Warren G. 5
Hardy, Collis 382
Harlem Globetrotters 63, 67
Harley, Phil 88, 259, 264, 269, 273, 278, 284, 289, 295, 300, 305, 309, 312, 316, 319, 322, 325, 328, 330, 332, 334
Harlicka, Skip 64, 73, 76
Harper, Jeffrey 92
Harris, Barbara 44
Harris, Doug 54
Harris, Nessie 382
Harris Sporting Goods (Anderson, SC) Class C men 318
Harrison, D.J. 88
Harrison, John L. 4, 5, 7
Harrison, Mrs. J.L. 106, 108, 116, 118
Harrison, Shorelle 97
Hart County High School 89
Hatchett, Anton 93
Havana (Cuba) 29
Havird, C.Y. 180
Hawkins, F.R. 239, 243, 246, 250, 255, 259, 264, 269, 273, 278, 284, 289, 295, 300, 305, 309, 312, 316, 319
Haynesworth Mill (Anderson, SC): Class A women 90, 325; Class B men 293, 298
Haywood, Quincy 97
Hearn, Mike 72, 73
Heath, Buddy 43
Heath, Courtenay 43
Heath, Fletcher 42, 43
Heath, Harley 108, 123, 126, 130, 135, 139, 387
Heath, Minnie 8
Hedrick, Dolen 43
Helms, Don 54
Helms, Gary 62, 64, 66, 68, 381
Henderson Plumbing (Greenville, SC) Open Division men 316
Henderson, C.V. 9
Henderson, Gary 39, 378
Henderson, Joel 88
Henderson, Oveida 8
Hendley, Bud 20
Hendrix, Divver 187, 191, 194,

197, 200, 203, 206, 209, 213, 216, 219, 223, 226, 229, 232, 236, 239, 243, 246, 250, 255, 259, 264, 269, 273, 278, 284, 289, 295, 300, 305, 309, 312, 315, 319, 322, 325, 328, 389
Henson, Martin 4, 5, 7
Henson, Walter 9
Her Majesty (Mauldin, SC) Class A women 38, 39, 197, 203
Herbert, Charlie 95
Herrin, Hubert 377
Herring, Jimmy 50, 54, 378
Hester, George 74
Hetzel, Fred 58, 59, 69
Hicks, Arthur 72, 73
Higgenbotham, Clarence 12
High Point College 399
High Techs (Greenville, SC) Class A men 317
Highland Park Mill (Charlotte, NC): Class A men 104–106; Class A women 9, 106, 107; Class B men 107; Class B women 105; Class C men 107
Hill, Bert 18, 20, 43, 58, 155, 158
Hill, Calvin 399
Hill, Crishina 97, 98
Hill, Haywood 70
Hill, Joe 78
Hillcrest High School 61
Hillcrest (Simpsonville, SC) Class C men 340, 342
Hilley, Stan 31
Hinton, Mississippi 26
Hinton's All Stars (Greenville, SC) Open Division men 63, 66, 233, 236, 380
Hiott, Joe 43, 380
Hitler, Adolf 386
Hobart Mfg. (Blythewood, SC) Open Division men 87, 309
Hodge, Sheila 86
Hodgens, Judy 52
Hoechst Celanese (Greer, SC): Class A men 78, 260, 265, 270, 274, 279, 285, 291, 296, 301, 306, 310, 313, 317, 326, 381, 382; Class A women 284; Class B men 244, 248, 252, 257, 261, 381
Hoffman, Doug 390
Hoffman, Ken 73
Holcombe, Larry 380
Holden, Jimmy 44, 52, 378, 379
Holden, Katie 383
Hollings, Fritz 54
Hollis, L.P. 4, 5, 10, 32, 38, 44, 49, 51, 52, 73, 80–82, 84, 98, 103–105, 108, 109
Holloway, David 88
Holly Springs All Stars (Greenville, SC) Class A men 372
Holmes, Henry 86
Holmes, Kenny 85
Holt, Jerry 273, 278, 284
Home Plate Restaurant (Greenville, SC): Class A women 315; Class C men 88, 315
Home Real Estate (Abbeville, SC) Class C men 72, 249, 253
Homelite (Greer, SC): Class A men 64, 233, 237, 240, 274, 279, 285, 290, 296, 381, 382; Class B men 53, 211, 214, 217, 221, 224, 228, 230, 257, 380
Homestead Terrace (Greenville, SC) Class A women 68, 245, 250
Honea, Chafer 28
Hooper, Fred 7
Hooper, T.C. 236, 239, 243, 246
Hopewell (Greenville, SC) Open Division men 323
Hopkins, Bill 219, 223, 226, 229, 233, 236, 239, 243, 246, 250, 255, 259, 264, 269, 273, 278, 284, 289, 295, 300, 305, 309, 312, 316, 319, 322, 325, 328, 330, 332, 334, 336
Hopkins, Janet 309, 312, 316, 319, 322, 326, 328
Hopkins, Jimmy 305, 309, 312, 316, 319, 322, 326
Hopkins, Marty 82
Hot Shots (Clemson, SC) Class A women 332
The Hot Shots (Greenville, SC) Class A Women 319
Hotel Imperial 7
Houston, Allene 28
Houston, Dave 32
Howard, Boyce Jr. 62
Howard, Emma 68, 72
Howard, Frank 50, 386
Howard, Leonard 110, 112, 113, 116, 118, 135, 139, 143, 147
Howard, Mike 86
Howard, Milford 191, 194
Howard, Punchy 29
Howell, R.H. 390
Howell's Cleaners (Greenville, SC) Class A women 315
Huddock, Jim 59
Hudson, Charles 380
Hudson, Walt 50
Huey, Hal 379
Hughes, Harry 386
Hughes, Jo 394
Hughes, Ronnie 62
Humphries, Vivian 76, 82
Hunnicutt, Osborn 4
Hunt Machinery (Columbia, SC) Open Division men 64, 66, 236
Hunter, James 96
Hunter, Johnny 43
Hunter, L.M. 72
Hunter, Ronnie 332, 334, 336, 339, 341, 342
Huntington, Robert S. 5
Huntsville Mfg. (Huntsville, AL) Class A men 109, 166
Huskey, Dean 236
Huskey Construction (Greenville, SC) Class C men 276, 282
Hyatt, B. 92

I&T Connection (Lexington, SC) Class A women 344
IMMS (Greenville, SC) Class A women 64–67, 235, 239, 242, 246, 250, 254, 264, 398
Impson's (Greenville, SC) Class C men 263
Indian Head Yarn (Greenville, SC) Class B men 253, 257, 261
Indiana University 395, 403
Industrial Packaging (Greenville, SC) Class C men 86, 312, 315
Ingle, T.J. 52
Inman & Associates (Columbia, SC) Open Division men 67, 240
Inman Mill (Inman, SC): Class A men 136; Class A women 139; Class B men 19, 124, 128, 132; Class B women 130, 135, 150; Class C men 134, 138
Interstate-Johnson-Lane (Greenville, SC) Class C men 343
Irby, Kevin 93
Irick, William 89
Isner, Mack 44, 390
Isom, Barry 72
Iwo Jima 22

J & J Nursery (Winston-Salem, NC) Open Division men 278
J & S Garage (Orangeburg, SC) Open Division men 269
J Bomber Squadron (Greenville, SC) Class A men 372
J.A. Nealy & Co. (Pickens, SC) Class C men 215
J.L. Mann High School 61, 94

Index 419

J.P. Stevens Distribution (Greenville, SC) Class B men 253, 257, 261, 271, 275
J.W. Vaughn Co. (Greenville, SC) Class B men 253
Jabali, Warren 400
Jackson Five (Columbia, SC) Open Division men 76, 260, 264, 269, 274
Jackson Mill (Iva, SC): Class A women 46, 72, 209, 254, 273; Class B men 156, 177; Class C men 68, 69, 238, 242, 245, 249, 253, 257, 272
Jackson, Anthony 93
Jackson, Bennett 89
Jackson, James 88
Jackson, Kenny 93
Jackson, Shoeless Joe 391, 402
Jacobs, William P. 22
Jacob's Blocking Trophy 29
Jacob's Jazz (Fountain Inn, SC) Class B men 330
Jacob's Mfg. (Greenville, SC) Class B men 331, 338
James, J.W. 150, 155, 158
James River (Simpsonville, SC) Class B men 324, 327, 329
Jarman, Murray 89
Jarrett, Summers 219, 223, 226, 229, 233
Jenkins, Anthony 89
Jenkins, Mike 66
Jennings, Charlie 56
Jennings, Lewis 382
Jennings, Rosalyn 94
Jet Brew (Greenville, SC) Class C men 258
Jet Rest Furniture (Greer, SC): Class B men 281, 286, 292; Open Division men 84, 295
Jets, Rodney 88
Jiffie Jonnie (Greenville, SC) Class C men 79, 263, 267, 272, 277, 282, 288, 293
Jimmy's Disco (Greenville, SC) Open Division men 90, 326
Joachim, Alfred 386
Joanna Mill (Joanna, SC): Class A men 18, 127, 132; Class A women 47, 49, 200, 203, 206, 209, 212, 378; Class B men 42, 44, 119, 124, 145, 152, 156, 163, 172, 176, 188, 192, 195, 198, 201, 214, 221, 378; Class B women 143, 150, 161, 179, 183, 187, 190, 193; Class C men 138, 141, 181, 186, 206
John Perkins Industries (Greenville, SC) Class C men 63, 235, 238, 241, 245, 249, 253, 258, 381
Johnson, Allen 67, 68
Johnson, Bill 97
Johnson, Bob 401
Johnson, Derrick 81
Johnson, Etrulia 18
Johnson, Fred 194, 197, 200, 203, 206, 210
Johnson, Jim 322, 326, 328, 330
Johnson, Root Beer 91
Johnson, Tavaris 95
Johnson, Walter 391
Johnston, Olin D. 20
Johnston, Reynolds 243, 246, 251
Johnston, Tommy 95
Jolley, Frances 14
Jones, A.C. 309, 313
Jones, Angie 84
Jones, Elnora 95
Jones, Harry B. 110, 112, 113, 118, 120, 123, 126
Jones, Lamont 92
Jones, Melvin 82
Jones, Mike 66
Jones, Nathaniel 92
Jones, Rachel 97
Jones, Ricky 96
Jordan, Eckie 27, 28, 385, 387, 388
Jordan, Leoda 387
Jordan, Michael 53, 379, 402
Jordan, Michael (Chicago Bulls) 400
Jordan, Mildred 28
Jordan, Sarah 387
Jordan, Vic 46
Josten's Service Award 399
Judson Mill (Greenville, SC) 30, 384, 391; Class A men 6, 9, 19, 41, 42, 103, 105, 106, 108, 109, 111, 112, 120, 123, 126, 131, 135, 140, 144, 148, 151, 377; Class A women 11, 20, 39, 104–106, 108, 110, 139, 142, 169, 174, 197, 200, 203; Class B men 21, 27, 34, 41, 42, 104–109, 119, 132, 137, 145, 149, 152, 164, 168, 171, 176, 181, 185, 189, 192, 201, 372; Class B women 8, 23, 30, 105, 126, 130, 134, 150, 154, 165, 179, 183, 187, 190, 193, 378, 387; Class C men 12, 105–107, 111, 113, 114, 117, 119, 122, 125, 128, 133, 137, 142, 146, 153, 157, 160, 165, 169, 173, 178, 182, 186, 190, 192, 196, 199, 202, 205; Class C women 108
Judson Mill YMCA (Greenville, SC) 384
Julius Kayser & Co. (Liberty, SC) Class B men 195
Justice, Charlie 388

K.G. Carpet (Atlanta, GA): Class A women 67, 242; Open Division men 66, 67, 236, 239, 381
Kaiser, Paul 216, 219, 223
Kearns, Tommy 47, 390
Keir, Richard 381
Keller, Bomar 26
Kelly, James 73
Kelly, Jamie 95
Kelly, Dr. Mike 90
Kelly, Mike 382
Kemet (Pickens, SC) Closed Division men 343
Kemet (Simpsonville, SC) Class B men 327, 329
Kendall, Whitey 62, 216, 219, 223, 226, 229, 232, 236, 239, 243, 246, 250, 255, 259, 264, 269, 273, 278, 284, 289, 295, 300, 305
Kendall Mill (Seneca, SC) Class A men 67, 233, 236, 240, 380, 381
Kennedy, Robert 64
Kennedy, W.T. Jr. 147, 150
Kennedy, Webb 158
Kenneth Mill (Walhalla, SC) Class B women 120, 123, 377
Kenro (Atlanta, GA): Class A women 70, 72, 73, 245, 249, 254, 259; Open Division men 68, 70, 72, 73, 243, 246, 251, 255
Kentucky-Tennessee Interstate Game 72
Keowee School 385
Kerr Finishing (Travelers Rest, SC) Class B men 293
Keyboards (Columbia, SC) Open Division men 80, 81, 278, 284, 289
Keys, Susan 18
Kinard, Terry 78
Kincaid, Barry 92, 93, 96
King, Dion 91
King, Lloyd 70
King, Martin Luther 64
King Oil (Anderson, SC) Open Division men 240
King Valley (Columbia, SC) Class A women 97, 342, 343, 383
Kingsmore, Doug 392
Kinnett, Virginia 14, 377

Kirby, Joan 381
Kirby, Snow 184, 187, 191, 194, 216, 219, 223, 226, 229, 233, 236, 239, 243, 246, 250, 255, 259, 264, 269, 273, 278, 284
Kirkpatrick, Brice 36, 393
Kitchen, Harriett 44
Kleckley, Natalie 94
Knight, Joan 52
Kosta's Restaurant (Greenville, SC) Class A women 319
Krajack, Ed 52
Krieg, Tommy 62
Krispy Kreme (Spartanburg, SC): Class C men 328; Open Division men 290
Kruer, Wayne 70

L.S. Green (Mauldin, SC) Class B men 257
La Guardia, Fiorella 386
Lady Hornets (Greenville, SC) Class A women 97, 342
LaFoy, Randy 97, 330, 332, 334, 337, 339, 341, 342
LaFrance Mill (Anderson, SC) Class B men 39, 191, 195, 198, 201, 205, 208; Class C men 202, 212; Open Division men 49, 210
Lance (Greenville, SC) Class C men 282
Landrum Mill (Landrum, SC) Class B men 221, 224
Lanett Mill (Lanett, AL): Class A men 106, 112; Class A women 20, 139, 146, 378; Class B men 111; Class B women 21, 113, 143
Langford, Barbara 80
Latimer, Scoop 7, 9, 18, 20, 22, 25, 30, 31, 385, 389
Laurens AAU (Laurens, SC): Class C men 343; Class C women 344
Laurens Glass Co. (Laurens, SC) Class A women 78, 277, 283, 289
Laurens Mill (Laurens, SC): Class B men 152, 163, 167, 176, 181, 192; Class B women 170; Class C men 173, 178, 182, 185, 192
Laurinburg Institute (Laurinburg, NC) 86
Lauter, Walter 162, 166, 170, 175, 180, 184, 187, 191, 194, 197, 200, 203
Law, John A. 9
Law, Jolette 95
Law Enforcement Center (Greenville, SC) Class B men 84
Lawrence, David 59, 94, 95, 382, 383
Lawson, Raymond 89, 90
League, Jack 48, 51
Leakesville Mill (Leakesville, NC): Class A women 11, 106–108, 110; Class B men 114, 117, 163, 168
Leamon, Chuck 382
Leamon, Eldrick 94
Leatherwood, Peck 7
Lebanon (Pendleton, SC) Class C men 258, 263, 267
Ledford, Brady 93
Lee, Hob 43
Lee, Jamie 73
Lee, Janice 76
Lee, Wendell 54
LeForce, Alan 95
Leigh Fibers (Spartanburg, SC) Class B men 318
Lemmons, Mac 54
Leopard, Esco 42
Lesley, Charles 72
Leso, Chris 95
Lewis, Bobby 65
Lewis, Don 62
Lewis, Donnie 380
Lewis, Jim 390
Lexington Co. Recreation (Lexington, SC): Class A women 277, 284; Open Division men 76, 269, 273, 278
Liberty Mill (Liberty, SC): Class A men 87, 204; Class A women 39, 44, 197, 200, 203, 206, 226; Class B men 36, 43, 59, 180, 184, 188, 198, 201, 204, 224, 227, 230, 234; Class B women 187; Class C men 46, 52, 178, 186, 189, 193, 196, 199, 202, 205, 208, 212, 215, 218, 221, 225, 228, 231
Limbaugh, Diane 78
Limestone Mill (Gaffney, SC) Class C men 322
Lindsay, Jack 200, 203, 207, 210, 213, 216
Lineback, Ann 387
Linn, Linda 57
Lister, Don 54, 379
Little, Gene 400
Little, Scott 88
Little Pigs Bar-B-Que (Anderson, SC) Class C men 267
Littlejohn, Eboni 98
Littlejohn's (Greenville, SC) Class A women 216
Livingston, Don 66
Lockhart Mill (Lockhart, SC) Class B men 25, 156
Loftis, Cedric 29
Logan, Henry 62, 66, 67, 385, 399, 400
Lollis, Jeff 382
Long, Dewayne 95
Long, Jack 39
Long, Mickey 43, 50, 379
Long Beach City College 402
Lonsdale Mill (Seneca, SC): Class A men 15, 16, 27, 42, 109, 113, 116, 118, 124, 136, 144, 372, 377; Class A women 9, 38, 44, 46, 47, 50, 52, 105, 107, 112, 197, 200, 203, 209, 212, 215, 226, 372; Class AA men 12, 110; Class B men 22, 28, 44, 48, 104, 107, 108, 132, 153, 156, 160, 172, 189, 192, 202, 205, 208, 211, 214, 378; Class B women 23, 105, 106, 109, 110, 150, 154, 158, 161, 170, 174, 179, 183, 191, 193, 377, 386; Class C men 53, 105, 106, 115, 117, 119, 122, 125, 129, 141, 146, 149, 165, 169, 173, 178, 182, 186, 190, 196, 199, 218, 221, 225, 392; Class C women 108; Open Division men 52, 213
Lonsdale Mill Brass Band (Seneca, SC) 387
Lonsdale Mill YMCA (Seneca, SC) 30
Lookabill, Ryan 383
Louisville University 403
Love Joy Inc. (Greenville, SC) Open Division men 264
Low Country All Stars (Charleston, SC) Class A women 97, 342, 343, 383
Lowe, Doug 69, 70, 381
Lowe, J.L. 39
Lowe, Larry 49
Lowe, Reba 67, 72
Lowenstein (Anderson, SC): Class B men 318; Open Division men 89, 320
Lower Richland High School 89
LTV ElectroSystems (Greenville, SC): Class A men 70, 247, 251; Class A women 242, 246, 381; Class B men 63, 234, 237, 241, 244
Lyerly, Jenny 76, 85, 94
LYF-TYM Products (Greenville, SC) Class C men 334
Lyman Mill (Lyman, SC) 392, 393; Class A men 10, 32, 56,

58, 63, 72, 74, 106, 108, 109, 111, 116, 120, 124, 126, 136, 175, 224, 227, 233, 247, 251, 260, 265, 270, 274, 279, 285, 377, 378, 380–382; Class A women 73, 107, 108, 110, 112, 118, 120, 122, 125, 129, 134, 139, 232, 235, 239, 246, 250, 254, 259, 263; Class AA men 110, 377; Class B men 36, 52, 59, 63, 66, 68, 108, 109, 121, 124, 137, 163, 168, 171, 181, 188, 198, 214, 217, 220, 224, 227, 230, 234, 237, 241, 244, 380, 381; Class B women 109; Class C men 110, 117, 119, 129, 173, 178, 181, 215, 221
Lynch, Vincent 93
Lynch Mob (Columbia, SC) Open Division men 94, 331, 332
Lynchburg Mill (Lynchburg VA) Class B men 125
Lynn's Superette (Greenville, SC) Class A women 273
Lyons, George 58
Lyons, Joe 135

M & L Construction (Greenville, SC) Class B men 317
M. Vick (Spartanburg, SC) Class A women 95, 336
Mack, Connie 41
Mack, Tommy 82
Macobson, Harvey 95
Mac's All Stars (Greenville, SC) Class A women 305, 319, 322, 382
Madison Throwing Co. (Madison, NC): Class A men 240, 244, 247, 256, 381; Class B men 66, 237
Mahaffey, Don 56
Mahon, Brown 106
Mahon, Elizabeth 29
Mahoney, Dave 88
Maintenance Supply Co. (Greenville, SC) Open Division men 306
Major, Frances 12
Manchester Mill (Manchester, GA) Class A men 106, 109, 124, 126, 166, 377
Maness, Howard 20
Maness, Jeff 94
Maness Sporting Goods (Spartanburg, SC) Open Division men 46, 207, 210
Mann, A.G. 15
Manning, Barry 89, 93, 95, 96
Marable, Eric 92

Maravich, Pete 52, 54, 55, 59
Maravich, Press 32, 52, 54, 59, 396
Maravich, Ronnie 51, 52
Marietta Substation II (Marietta, SC) Class A men 286, 291
Marion Mfg. (Marion, NC): Class B men 124, 133; Class B women 120, 126, 130, 134; Class C men 119, 122
Marlowe, Jackie 22
Marquee (Greenville, SC) Class C women 97, 342
Marshall Field Mill (Fieldville VA) Class B men 148
Martel Mill (Asheville, NC) Class B men 171
Martha Mill (Thomaston, GA) Class B men 136, 144
Martin, W.V. 5, 103, 104
Martin, Yahnik 97
Martin Mfg. (Williamston, SC) Class B men 62, 231, 234
Martin Printing Co. (Greenville, SC) Class C men 257, 262, 267, 272
Martin's (Anderson, SC) Class C men 245
Marwick, A.E. 103
Maslen, Vivian 62, 67
Mason, J.F. 126, 131
Massey, Tip 53
Masters, Mendel 289, 295, 300
Matthews, Dan 377
Mauldin High School 38, 94
Mauldin Video (Mauldin, SC) Class A women 338
Maxon Shirt Co. (Greenville, SC) Class C men 61, 226, 228, 231
Maxwell, Earl 52
May-McEwen-Kaiser (Burlington, NC): Class B men 156; Class B women 158
May Napper (Greenville, SC) Class C men 312
Mayes, Clyde 82
Mayfair Mill (Arcadia, SC) Class B men 287
Mayfair Mill (Easley, SC) Class A men 314
Mayfair Mill (Pickens, SC): Class A men 286, 291; Class A women 273
Mayo (Mayo, SC) Class A women 294
McAbee, Fred 43, 90, 93, 98, 300, 305, 309, 312, 316, 319, 322, 325, 328, 330, 332, 334
McAbee, Lloyd 200, 203, 226, 229, 233, 236, 239, 243, 246,

250, 255, 259, 264, 268, 273, 277, 284, 289, 295, 300, 305
McAbee, Pete 322, 325, 328, 330, 332, 334, 336, 339, 341, 342
McAdams, James 378
McAlister, Marsie 84, 90
McAvoy, Palmer 25
McCain, Pam 330, 332, 334
McCall, Buddy 48
McCallister, Ronnie 43
McCarter 8
McCartney, H.R. 5, 103, 104
McCauley, Mike 381
McCauley, Rodney 382
McCrary Hosiery Mill (Asheboro, NC) Class A men 25, 29, 140, 143, 148, 151, 155, 159, 162, 166, 378
McCrary Mechanical (Travelers Rest, SC) Class C men 218, 222, 225, 228
McCrary Sprinkler (Greenville, SC) Open Division men 329
McCravy, Shane 95
McCullough, Bob 58, 380
McCullough, O'Louis 72
McCurry, Hinkie 25
McDaniel, Ruth 44
McDaniel, Xavier 84
McDermott, Joe 379
McDonald, Michael 43
McDonald, Whitey 43
McDonald's High School All American 94
McDowell, Jean 67
McDuffie, Jim 207, 210, 213, 216, 219, 223, 226, 229, 232, 236
McEntyre, Tony 52
McEwen Mill (Burlington, NC): Class A women 139; Class B men 25, 137, 145, 152; Class B women 147, 154
McGowens, Chris 96
McGuire, Al 72
McGuire, Frank 64, 73
McInnis, Jeff 95
McIntyre, Charles 381
McKay, Jim 399
McKinley, Jewel 14
McMahon, Willie 12
McMinns, Shaft 76
McNaughton, Dr. James 90
MCP (Clemson, SC) Closed Division men 97, 340–342
McPherson, Earl 95
McQueen, Desi 93
McWhite, Leon 52
Meadors Manufacturing Company 26

Means, V.L. 92
Meekins, James 332, 334, 337, 339
Meeks, Sammy 25, 29, 32
Meisenheimer, L.S. 20
Meisenheimer, L.W. 161, 166
Melson, Fred 80
Memorial Auditorium 45, 46, 96, 385, 390, 396, 400
Merck, J.T. 223, 226, 229, 232, 236
Metro-Atlantic (Greenville, SC) Class C men 63, 65, 93–95, 235, 238, 242, 332, 334, 336, 338, 340, 342
Mexico City 387
Meyer's Bakery (Greenville, SC): Class B men 333; Closed Division men 339
Michael, Christopher 383
Michelin (Greenville, SC): Class A men 88, 90, 94, 290, 297, 302, 306, 307, 310, 313, 316, 320, 321, 323, 326, 329, 331, 333, 335, 382; Class A women 294; Class B men 80, 276, 280, 286, 287, 292, 298, 303, 304, 307, 311, 315, 324, 325, 327, 331, 333; Closed Division men 96, 340, 341
Michelin (Sandy Springs, SC) Class A men 285, 290, 296, 301, 323
Michelin (Spartanburg, SC) Class A men 82, 94, 96, 286, 291, 296, 302, 306, 310, 313, 314, 316, 320, 333, 335, 337, 382
Microtron (Greenville, SC): Class A women 229, 380; Class C men 61, 228, 231, 234
Middle Tennessee State University 72, 76
Middleton, Larry 89
Mikan, George 387, 396
Mike Davis Landscaping (Piedmont, SC) Class B men 331, 333
Mikro (Charlotte, NC) Open Division men 57–59, 62–64, 66, 67, 72, 223, 226, 230, 233, 236, 240, 243, 251, 380
Milasnovich, Nick 56, 57
Miller, Bill 400
Miller, Broadus 243, 246, 250, 255
Miller, Butch 44
Miller, Charlton 233, 236, 239
Miller, J.W. 90
Miller, Marion 72, 76
Miller, Mike 382

Miller Oil (Greenville, SC) Class C men 92, 330
Miller Tire (Columbia, SC) Open Division men 223
Milliken (Spartanburg, SC) Class B men 228, 231, 234, 380
Mills, William 85
Mills Mill (Greenville, SC) 25, 385; Class A men 25, 26, 28, 120, 124, 148, 159, 171, 370–372; Class A women 27, 44, 371; Class B men 22, 104, 117, 119, 137, 140, 145, 148, 152, 156, 160, 163, 168, 176, 181, 204, 371, 378, 385; Class B women 191; Class C men 38, 111, 113, 115, 122, 125, 128, 134, 138, 141, 146, 149, 157, 169, 174, 178, 182, 186, 190, 193, 196, 202
Minneapolis Lakers 387, 388, 396
Mintz, Colin 66
Mississippi State University 20
Moe, Doug 55, 57, 59
Mollohon Mill (Newberry, SC) Class B women 130
Monaghan Mill (Greenville, SC) 4, 98, 390; Class A men 5, 7, 9, 15, 21, 26, 27, 31, 32, 36, 38, 41–44, 68, 73, 78, 79, 87, 103–106, 112, 114, 116, 119, 120, 123, 126, 131, 136, 140, 143, 148, 151, 159, 171, 175, 180, 184, 188, 191, 194, 201, 204, 244, 247, 251, 256, 260, 265, 270, 274, 279, 285, 290, 296, 301, 306, 310, 313, 324, 370–372, 378, 382, 389, 390, 392–394; Class A women 7–10, 12, 14, 58, 67, 104–107, 109, 110, 112, 113, 115, 117, 120, 123, 197, 242, 372; Class B men 7, 25, 29, 44, 50, 51, 63, 67, 103–109, 111, 112, 114, 121, 124, 156, 163, 164, 167, 172, 176, 181, 184, 189, 192, 195, 198, 201, 204, 207, 210, 214, 230, 234, 237, 241, 244, 327, 329, 370, 372, 378, 379, 381, 384; Class B women 21, 105, 113, 126, 130, 134, 143, 174, 179, 183, 377; Class C men 45, 46, 53, 57, 65–68, 105–108, 110, 111, 113, 115, 117, 119, 122, 129, 134, 138, 142, 145, 149, 153, 157, 160, 164, 168, 173, 177, 182, 186, 190, 193, 196, 199, 202, 205, 208, 212, 215, 218, 222, 225, 228,

231, 235, 238, 241, 245, 315, 377, 380; Open Division men 39, 47, 48, 51, 52, 197, 207, 210, 213, 379, 394
Monaghan Mill YMCA (Kannapolis, NC) 82
Monarch Mill (Union, SC): Class B men 107, 108; Class C men 157, 222, 225
Monroe & Co. (Winnsboro, SC) Class A women 268
Monsanto (Blacksburg, SC) Class B men 224, 228, 380
Monsanto (Greenwood, SC): Class A men 57, 63, 64, 66, 217, 220, 223, 227, 230, 233, 237, 240, 243, 247, 379, 380; Class B men 62, 214, 244, 248, 252
Monsanto (Pensacola FL): Class A men 66, 67, 217, 220, 223, 227, 230, 233, 237, 240, 243, 379–381; Class A women 54, 216, 219, 222, 226, 229, 380; Class B men 47, 48, 62, 63, 208, 211, 213, 231, 234, 241, 380
Monsanto (Spartanburg, SC) Class A men 310, 382
Montgomery, Dewayne 67
Montgomery, Tank 383
Montgomery, Walter S. 29
Moody, Bill 25, 29
Moody, Sammy 74
Moody, Shane 339
Moody, Tim 97
Moon, Johnny 402
Moore, Allan 36
Moore, Eddie 337, 339
Moore, Jackie 91
Moore, Johnny 200
Moore, Jonathan 83
Moore, Pearl 88, 95, 319, 322, 326, 328, 330, 332, 334, 337, 339, 341, 382
Moore, Sidney 94
Moore, Steve 70, 381
Moore, Turbo 97
Morgan, Sharon 66
Moriarity, Pat 68, 70
Morman, Liz 5
Morningstar, Bill 59
Morris, Bobby 229, 233, 236, 239, 243, 246
Morrison, Fred 25
Morrow 22
Morrow, Calvin 25
Morrow, David 66
Morrow, James 243, 246, 250, 255, 259, 264, 268, 273, 278, 284, 295, 300, 305

Morrow, Ken 289
Mt. Vernon Mill (Williamston, SC) Class B men 94, 334, 335
Mt. Zion (Lexington, SC) Open Division men 309
Mulligan, Mrs. W.B. 187, 191, 194, 197, 200, 203
Mullikin, John 191, 200, 203, 206, 209, 213, 216, 219, 390
Multimedia (Greenville, SC) Class B men 311, 314
Munlyn, James 88, 89
Murphy, Pat 46, 52
Murray, Judy 72, 381
Murrell Brothers Sand (Greenville, SC): Class A women 54, 223, 229, 232; Open Division men 55, 57–59, 219, 223, 227, 380
Musburger, Brent 399
Muscogee Mfg. (Columbus, GA) Class A men 144
Muth, Leonard 194, 197, 200
Myers, Red 53, 54

Naismith, James A. 3, 4
Nance, Hilliard 31
Nance, Larry 78, 84
Naron (Greenville, SC) Class B men 321
Nashville Business College 387, 398, 402
Nation, Garrett 57
National Amateur Athletic Association women's Tournament 31
National Association of Sports and Physical Education Hall of Fame 399
National Association of Intercollegiate Athletics 76, 89, 90, 394
National Basketball Association 41, 78, 86, 95, 394, 400, 403
National Collegiate Athletic Association 84, 394, 403
National Football League 78, 401
National Junior College Tournament 43, 73
National Professional Basketball Championship 397
NCR (Easley, SC) Class A women 95, 336, 383
Ndiaye, Maktor 95
Neal, Ellerbe 33, 37, 39, 41, 42, 44, 51, 52, 379, 389, 391, 393, 394
Neal, Patsy 64–67, 72, 251, 255, 259, 264, 385, 398, 399

Neely, Jess 386
Neely, Karen 95
Neely's Inc. (Greenville, SC) Class C men 78, 80, 272, 276, 282
Neptune Measurement (Greenwood, SC) Class B men 298
New Holland Mill (Gainesville, GA) 4; Class A men 8, 9, 104–106, 108, 109, 111, 112, 114; Class B men 132, 137, 160, 163, 167, 181, 185, 188
New Jersey Nets 403
New York (Baseball) Giants 43
New York Giants 23
New York Yankees 21
Newberry All Stars (Newberry, SC) Open Division men 48, 243
Newberry College 16, 37, 62, 73, 74, 76, 80, 81, 87, 396
Newry Mill (Newry, SC) Class C men 48, 212, 215, 222, 380
Newton, Fig 43, 49, 51, 52, 216, 219, 384, 393
Newton, Joe 229, 233, 236, 239, 243, 246, 250, 255, 259, 264, 269, 273
Nichols, Mackie 53
Nimmons, Dorothy 32
1973 Multidisciplinary Symposium on Sport 399
Ninety Six Mill (Ninety Six, SC): Class A men 25, 27, 28, 151, 155, 159, 162, 167, 371; Class B men 23, 137, 148; Class B women 150, 155, 158; Class C men 137, 146
93.7 Bombardiers (Greenville, SC) Class B men 331
Nissan (Greenville, SC) Closed Division men 96, 340
Nix, Cheryl 90
Nix, Reccus 95
Nolin, Hubert 9, 45, 79, 158
Non-Fluid Oil (Greenville, SC): Class A women 85, 300, 305, 382; Class C men 78, 276, 282, 288; Open Division men 76, 78, 79, 81, 82, 269, 273, 278, 284, 289
Norman, Rock 396
Normandy 22
Norris, Frank 88, 384, 385
Norris Mill (Norris, SC) Class B men 267
North Carolina Softball Hall of Fame 388
North Carolina Sports Hall of Fame 388

North Carolina State University 51, 54, 58, 66, 395, 403
North Georgia (Toccoa, GA) Class C men 322
North Georgia Processing (Toccoa, GA): Class B men 167, 171, 177, 180; Class B women 170, 174, 178, 183; Class C men 322
North Greenville Junior College 39, 43, 50, 54, 402
North West Astros (Greenville, SC) Class C men 325
Northern Ireland 390
Northern Sports Officials (Greenville, SC) Closed Division men 343
Northside Correctional Center (Greenville, SC) Class B men 333, 335, 383
Northwestern (Greenville, SC) Class C men 328
Northwestern Mutual (Greenville, SC) Class B men 336
Norwich Pharmacal (Greenville, SC) Class A men 76, 265, 270
Nyad, Diana 399
Nye, Paul 44, 390

Oakland Oaks 400
Oconee Gas (Westminster, SC) Class A women 61, 232
Oconee Mill (Westminster, SC): Class A men 29, 148, 151, 156, 162, 166; Class B men 191; Class B women 155, 165, 170, 194; Class C men 22, 29, 32, 164, 169, 173, 178
Oconee Nuclear (Seneca, SC) Class B men 327, 329
O'Dell, Billy 36
Oeland, Jim 9
Officers 103–106, 108–110, 112, 113, 116, 118, 120, 123, 126, 130, 135, 139, 143, 147, 150, 155, 158, 161, 166, 170, 175, 179, 184, 187, 191, 194, 197, 200, 203, 206, 209, 213, 216, 219, 223, 226, 229, 232, 236, 239, 243, 246, 250, 255, 259, 264, 268, 273, 277, 284, 289, 300, 305, 309, 312, 316, 319, 322, 325, 328, 330, 332, 334, 336, 339
Official Women's Basketball Guide (1934) 18
Oglethorpe College 67, 70
Ohio State University 86
Ohio Valley Conference 68
O'Kelley Textile Machine

(Greenville, SC) Class C men 262
Old Keg Party Shop (Greenville, SC) Class A women 294, 305
Old Mill Stream (Greenville, SC) Class C men 283
Oldevak, Sherry 94, 96
Oldham, Nancy 380
Oliver, John 402
Olympic Gym (Columbia, SC) Open Division men 89, 319
Olympics 23, 80, 386, 387
O'Neal Engineering (Greenville, SC) Class B men 321, 324, 327, 329, 331
O'Neal Inc. (Greenville, SC) Closed Division men 343
O'Neal-Williams Sporting Goods 377
Optimist (Greenville, SC) Class B men 372
Orangemen (Columbia, SC) Open Division men 95, 330, 332, 335, 382
Orders Tile Co. (Greenville, SC) Class B men 84, 287, 292, 298, 303
Oregon University 393
Original Concepts (Greenville, SC) Class C men 330
Original rules of play 3
Orr Mill (Anderson, SC): Class A men 119; Class A women 14, 15, 115, 117, 125; Class B men 25, 28, 29, 32, 114, 117, 152, 160, 163, 171, 176; Class B women 29, 113, 158, 165, 174, 377; Class C men 119, 128, 133, 138, 141, 146, 149, 153, 157, 160, 173, 178, 182, 186, 190, 193, 196, 206, 378
Orr, James 378
Ottaray Hotel 7
Ottaray Mill (Union, SC) Class B men 104–107, 109
Outlaw, Opal 22
Over the Hill (Greenville, SC) Open Division men 93, 331
Overnite (Greenville, SC) Class A women 219
Owens, Carolyn 385
Owens, Floyd 27
Owens, J.B. 166, 170, 175, 180, 184, 187, 191, 197
Owens, Jesse 386
Owens, Jim 386
Owens, Kathlyn Kelley 23, 385, 386

P & N Warehouse 4
Pacific Mill (Columbia, SC) 8; Class A men 8–10, 103–106; Class B men 20, 105–107, 132, 141, 148, 152; Class B women 107; Class C men 46, 107, 108, 209
Pacolet Mill (Pacolet, SC): Class B men 30, 159, 163, 167; Class C men 235, 238
Padgett 377
Palmetto Enterprises (Greenville, SC) Class B men 333
Palmetto Expo (Greenville, SC): Class B men 95, 335, 383; Class C men 93, 334
Palmetto High School 44
Pan American Games 387, 388, 398
Panthers (Chicago IL) Open Division men 337
Parke-Davis (Greenwood, SC) Class B men 78, 266, 271, 276, 281, 287, 381
Parker High School 9, 17, 25, 40, 389, 391–393
Parker Mill (Greenville, SC): Class A men 88, 270, 275, 280, 286, 291, 297, 302, 306, 310, 313, 316, 382; Class A women 300, 305, 382; Class B men 62, 69, 231, 241, 244, 247, 252, 335, 337, 380, 381; Class C men 277, 283; Closed Division men 97, 341, 342
Parker Textile Baseball 'B' League 395
Parks, Bennie 382
Parks, Fred 25
Parnell, Jerry 49
Parnell, Leroy 49, 378
Parris, Jerry 59
Parrish, Mike 76
Parson, Marcus 93
Patrick, R.E. 223, 226, 229, 232, 236, 239, 243, 246, 251
Patterson, Larry 55, 390
Patterson, Scott 97
Patton, Sam 45, 187, 191, 194, 197, 200, 203, 206, 210, 213
Paty Lumber Co. (Johnson City, TN) Open Division men 39, 197
Paulk, Brenda 73
Payne, Eddie 76
PBM (Anderson, SC) Class C men 78, 272, 276, 282
Peacock, Leroy 56, 58, 380
Pearl Harbor 22
Peden (Greenville, SC) Class C men 338
Peerless Community Center (Rossville, GA) Open Division men 58, 227
Peerless Cotton Mill (Thomaston, GA): Class A men 151; Class B men 144, 148
Peerless Woolen Mill (Rossville, GA): Class A men 22, 23, 29–31, 34, 140, 148, 151, 155, 158, 162, 167, 170, 175, 184, 188, 191, 194, 378, 389; Class B men 136, 148, 152, 378; Class C men 21, 138, 141
Pegram, Willie 66
Pelzer Byrd's (Pelzer, SC) Class A women 82, 295, 299
Pelzer High School (Pelzer, SC) 387, 397
Pelzer Mill (Pelzer, SC) 10, 396; Class A men 12, 23, 25, 27, 29, 31–34, 36, 38, 39, 42, 43, 54, 55, 79, 80, 86, 109, 111, 112, 124, 126, 131, 136, 140, 144, 151, 155, 158, 162, 166, 170, 175, 180, 184, 191, 194, 217, 220, 224, 247, 251, 256, 260, 265, 280, 286, 291, 296, 301, 311, 314, 317, 320, 324, 326, 329, 331, 371, 378, 390, 392–397; Class A women 27, 28, 44, 58, 73, 78, 80, 84, 86, 117, 120, 122, 125, 129, 134, 139, 142, 146, 161, 165, 197, 200, 203, 206, 216, 219, 229, 250, 254, 259, 263, 268, 273, 277, 283, 300, 312, 372; Class B men 37, 38, 41, 53, 55, 63, 64, 66, 104–108, 112, 114, 121, 164, 167, 172, 181, 185, 188, 192, 195, 198, 201, 205, 214, 217, 225, 228, 231, 234, 237, 241, 244, 248, 256, 261, 266, 271, 275, 280, 287, 292, 297, 308, 379–381; Class B women 115, 187, 194, 387; Class C men 39, 44, 54, 67, 72, 76–78, 82, 86, 106–108, 110, 111, 115, 117, 119, 122, 128, 133, 138, 141, 146, 149, 153, 156, 172, 177, 186, 190, 193, 195, 196, 199, 203, 205, 215, 218, 221, 225, 228, 231, 235, 238, 241, 253, 257, 258, 262, 267, 272, 277, 282, 288, 293, 299, 304, 308, 312, 315, 318, 378, 381, 403; Open Division men 46, 52, 207, 210, 213, 243
Pendleton, Charlie 384
Penley, Carley 12
Penley, Pauline 12
Penn, Larry 383
Penn, Moss 5

Pennsylvania Hotel 386
People's State Bank 16
Pepsi Cola 388
Perkins Auto (Charlotte, NC) Open Division men 62, 233
Perry, Joe 391
Perry, John 90, 92, 93, 95, 382
Perry, Thomas 27, 28
Pest Control (Greenville, SC) Class A women 88, 315
Pete's Drive-In (Greenville, SC) Class C men 263
Pete's Market (Pelzer, SC) Class C men 83, 84, 299, 304, 308
Pharr, Carolyn 65, 67
Pharr Worsted Mill (McAdenville, NC) Open Division men 210, 213, 219, 379
Philadelphia Athletics 41
Philadelphia 76ers 63
Phillips, Jim 289, 295, 300, 305, 309
Phillips, Jyles 88, 284, 289, 295, 300, 305, 309, 312, 316, 319, 322, 325, 328, 330, 332, 334, 336, 339, 341, 342
Phillips Fibers (Spartanburg, SC): Class A men 244, 256, 381; Class B men 67, 237, 240, 271, 381
Phyllis Wheatley Association (Greenville, SC) Class A women 289, 294
Pickel, Robert 96
Pickens Mill (Pickens, SC): Class B women 155; Class C men 212
Picklesimer, James 16, 17
Piedmont Area Basketball Tournament 26, 27, 371
Piedmont College 393, 394
Piedmont High School 389
Piedmont Industries (Greenville, SC) Class C men 258, 263
Piedmont Landscaping (Piedmont, SC) Class B men 298, 303, 308
Piedmont Mill (Piedmont, SC) 29, 389, 396; Class A men 16, 17, 25, 33, 34, 36, 41–44, 55–57, 103, 108, 109, 112, 113, 116, 118, 120, 123, 131, 136, 144, 148, 151, 155, 159, 162, 166, 170, 175, 180, 184, 188, 191, 194, 200, 203, 217, 220, 223, 230, 377, 378, 380, 389, 390, 397; Class A women 10–12, 18, 61, 62, 65, 67, 104, 105, 109–111, 113, 115, 118, 122, 125, 139, 232, 235, 239, 242, 246, 250, 381; Class AA men 12, 110, 377; Class B men 43, 47, 63, 104–108, 111, 112, 124, 127, 133, 137, 140, 145, 160, 167, 172, 198, 201, 204, 207, 234, 244, 291; Class B women 32, 36, 105, 109, 123, 147, 150, 161, 170, 175, 179, 183, 187, 190, 193, 377; Class C men 36, 41, 52, 54, 61, 65, 105, 107, 108, 110, 115, 117, 119, 121, 128, 133, 149, 153, 169, 173, 181, 182, 186, 190, 193, 195, 209, 212, 215, 218, 222, 225, 232, 235, 238, 242, 245, 249, 253, 258, 262, 378, 380, 381, 389; Open Division men 39, 43, 46, 47, 50, 52, 53, 197, 207, 210, 213, 216
Piedmont Mill Band 15
Piedmont Paint (Greenville, SC) Open Division men 216
Piedmont Sheet Metal (Winston-Salem, NC) Open Division men 74, 260
Piedmont Shirt Co. (Greenville, SC) Class C men 161
Piedmont Textile Baseball League 395
Pike, Dan 322, 326, 328, 330, 332, 334, 337, 339, 341, 342
Pilot Mill (Valdese, NC): Class A women 139; Class B men 127, 132; Class B women 134
Piney Mountain T.A.P.S. (Greenville, SC) Class A women 84, 295, 299
Pinson, Bryan 52
Pirkle, B.J. 116
Pittman, Connie 87
Pittman, Gary 68, 87, 316, 319, 322, 325, 328, 330, 332, 334, 336, 339, 341
Pittman, Ken 84, 85, 87, 203, 206, 210, 213, 216, 219, 223, 226, 229, 232, 236, 239, 243, 246, 250, 255, 259, 264, 268, 273, 277, 284, 289, 295
Pittman, Ted 87, 88, 98, 305, 309, 312, 316, 319, 322, 325, 328, 330, 332, 334, 336, 339, 341, 342
Pittman's Textile Machinery (Greenville, SC): Class A women 84–86, 268, 305, 308; Class C men 253; Open Division men 74, 76, 251, 260, 264, 269
Pitts, Lucius 81
The Pitts (Greenville, SC) Open Division Men 316
Pittsburgh Pirates 4, 388
Pizza Hut (Greenville, SC): Class C women 338; Closed Division men 340
Plan Home Health Care (Greenville, SC) Class C men 94, 336
Plaster, A.R. 147, 150, 155, 158, 162, 166, 170
Poe Hardware (Greenville, SC): Class A women 62, 232; Class C men 61, 63, 65, 66, 69, 72, 229, 231, 235, 238, 241, 245, 248, 381
Poe Mill (Greenville, SC): Class A men 18, 43, 58, 126; Class B men 26, 128, 149, 152, 156, 199, 201, 245, 370, 378; Class B women 126, 130, 135; Class C men 125, 129, 133, 138, 141, 146
Poe Mill Park 401
Poinsett Grocery (Greenville, SC): Class C men 95, 97, 336, 338, 340, 342, 383; Open Division men 90, 92–94, 323, 326, 328, 330, 332, 335, 382
Poinsett Hotel 17
Poinsett Lumber Co. (Anderson, SC): Class A men 217, 220; Class A women 43, 50, 55, 206, 209, 213, 216, 222; Class B men 208, 211, 214, 379
Poinsett Mill (Greenville, SC): Class A men 379; Class B men 49, 140, 145, 148, 152, 156, 163, 167, 181, 211, 218, 221, 227, 379; Class C men 178, 182, 186, 215
Poinsetta Upholstering (Greenville, SC) Open Division men 216
Polk, Art 68
Pollard, Fred 150
Pompili, Monique 95
Port City All Stars (Charleston, SC) Class C men 276, 282
Porter, Linda 61
Potwin, Marjorie 5
Powell, Jimmy 76
Powers, Fred 43, 200, 210, 213, 216, 219, 223, 226, 229, 233, 236, 239, 243, 246, 250, 255, 259, 264, 268, 273, 278, 284, 289, 295, 300, 305, 309, 315, 319, 322, 325, 328, 330, 332, 334
Powers, Ward 312
PPG Industries (Shelby, NC): Class A men 66, 88, 90, 237, 307, 310, 313, 316, 320, 323,

326, 329, 331, 337, 382; Class B men 85, 302; Closed Division men 96, 339, 341
Pratt-Read (Central, SC): Class A women 239; Class B men 62, 63, 234, 237, 248, 252, 257, 261, 266, 271
Precise Machine Works (Simpsonville, SC): Class A women 250, 254; Class B men 248, 252, 257, 381; Class C men 245, 253, 258, 267, 272, 381
Presbyterian College 21, 22, 41, 50, 74, 79, 89
Prince, Ted 391
Print Machine (Greenville, SC) Class B men 327
Print Shop (Greenville, SC) Class C men 232
Professional Medical Products (Greenwood, SC) Class B men 86, 308
Proximity Mill (Greensboro, NC): Class A men 105, 123, 131; Class B men 119, 121
Pruitt 377
Pryor, Shelby 46
Pulliam Investment Co. (Spartanburg, SC) Open Division men 300
Putman, Dave 34, 395
Putman, R. 17
Putman, Scoop 43

Queen of the Tournament 18
Quinby IGA (Florence, SC) Open Division men 301
Quinn Machine Works (Greenville, SC) Class C men 208

R&G (Greenville, SC): Class A women 94, 95, 334, 336; Class C women 97, 338, 342, 344
Raab, Dawn 94
Rackley, Marvin 22, 29
Rackley, Patsy 43
Railway Express 48
Raines, June 38, 54
Ramblers (Greenville, SC) Class A men 371
Ramey, L.A. 108
Ramey, Richard 90
Rampey, Jan 74, 76
Rape, Wayne 72, 381
Ratenski, Ted 161, 166, 170, 175, 180, 184
Ray, Larry 381
Ray, Thomas 377
Reames, Jack 17, 40, 158, 162, 166, 170, 175, 180, 184, 187, 191, 194, 197, 200, 203, 206, 210, 213
Red Shield (Greenville, SC) Class B men 371, 372
Redin, Harley 398
Reeves Brothers (Rutherfordton, NC) Class A men 240
Reiber 25
Reisinger, Jeff 76
Reliance Electric (Greenville, SC) Class B men 88, 281, 298, 303, 314
Renfrew Bleachery (Travelers Rest, SC): Class A men 119, 120, 124; Class A women 134, 213; Class B men 77, 145, 149, 152, 160, 168, 172, 181, 270, 275, 370, 381; Class B women 20, 125, 130, 161, 175, 179, 183; Class C men 154, 157, 169, 173, 178, 193, 196, 200, 202, 205
Represent (Greenville, SC) Open Division men 97, 341
Revis Trucking (Spartanburg, SC) Class A women 300, 305, 382
Rex Mill (Gastonia, NC) 29
Rhett, Joe 89, 95
Rhodes, Clayton 84, 85, 90, 94, 96
Rhymer & Littlejohn (Spartanburg, SC) Open Division men 278
Rice, Anthony 88
Richardson, Bernard 73, 74
Rick's Landscaping (Greenville, SC) Class B men 336, 337
Riddle, Jerry 67
Riddle, Jimmy 68, 380
Riddle, Willie 18, 23, 25–27, 41
Riegel Textile Corporation 392
Riegels, Roy 34
Rigdon, Garland 380
Rikard, Linda 381
Riley, Carol 339, 341, 342
Ritter, Tex 29, 33, 34, 36, 39, 396
Riverdale Mill (Riverdale, AL) Class B men 111, 117
Roach 25
Roadway (Greenville, SC) Class B men 321, 324, 327
Roadway Express (Duncan, SC) Class B men 331
Robbins Brothers (Simpsonville, SC) Class C men 336
Roberts, _____ 377
Roberts, Bobby 37, 39, 43, 44, 53, 54, 396
Roberts, John 384
Roberts, Stanley 89
Roberts, Trish 80
Robertson, Ricky 94
Robinson, Charlie 74
Robinson, Chuck 93
Robinson, Marion 393
Robinson, Marvin 392
Robinson, Wilbert 78
Robinson, Will 381
Roche, John 70
Rock Hill Bleachery (Rock Hill, SC): Class B men 104, 105; Class B women 155
Roddy, Charles 90, 91, 305, 309, 312, 316, 319, 322, 325, 328, 330, 332, 334, 336, 339, 341, 342
Rogers, Charles 259, 264, 269
Rogers, Debbie 72
Rogers, Mickey 381
Rogers, Ron 42, 379, 389
Rogers, Sam 54
Rogers, Willie 66
Rogers Hosiery Mill (Laurens, SC) Class B men 153
Rohm-Haas (Fayetteville, NC) Class A men 70, 73, 74, 76, 240, 244, 247, 251, 256, 260, 265, 381
Roll Tech (Greenville, SC): Class B men 329, 333, 337; Class C women 97, 342
Roll Technology (Greenville, SC) Class B men 327
Rollins, Christine 378
Rollins, Dick 384
Rollins, Matthew 95
Rollins, Pete 384, 385
Rollins, Phil 384
Rollins, Ray 384
Rollins, Robert 384
Rollins, Vernon 384
Rollins, Warren 319, 322, 326, 328, 330, 332, 334, 336, 339, 341, 342
Rollins, Wayne 78, 385
Roosevelt, Franklin D. 32
Roper, Don 388–390
Roper, Evelyn 389
Rose Bowl 34
Rosenbluth, Lenny 55
Ross, Jack 63
Ross, Larry 382
Ross, Mike 66, 72
Ross Tire (Greenville, SC): Class A men 381; Class C men 66, 76, 238, 245, 258, 262, 267, 272
Rothwell, Erik 95
Rottweilers (Greenville, SC) Class C men 330

Roundtree, Ralph 94
Rouse, Hagen 95
Roye, Paul 378
Rozell, Pete 383
Rucker, Terri 98
Rucker, Tracy 94
Rug Doctor (Spartanburg, SC) Open Division men 86, 309, 313
Rushing, Clarence 20
Russell, Clarence 58
Russell, Leonard 381
Russell, Ronnie 50, 380
Russell Manufacturing (Alexander City, AL): Class A men 66, 68, 72–74, 223, 227, 230, 233, 236, 240, 243, 247, 251, 255, 380, 381; Class B men 32, 41, 44, 48, 127, 168, 176, 180, 185, 188, 201, 204, 207, 211, 378
Ruth, Babe 391
Rutherfordton-Spindale Central High School 89
Rutledge, Tommy 76
Ryder Cup 388

S&M Sports (Shelby, NC) Open Division men 93–96, 329, 330, 332, 335, 337, 339, 382, 383
S&R Auto (Shelby, NC) Open Division men 96, 339, 383
S-M Norgetown (Marietta, SC) Class C men 272, 277, 283
Saco-Lowell (Easley, SC): Class A men 65, 66, 86, 92, 230, 233, 236, 240, 244, 274, 279, 285, 290, 295, 311, 326, 329, 380, 382; Class A women 46, 55, 72, 209, 222, 255, 259, 284, 289, 294; Class B men 56, 62–64, 74, 208, 211, 214, 217, 220, 224, 227, 230, 233, 252, 257, 261, 266, 271, 275, 281, 287, 292, 298, 303, 318, 324, 331, 333, 335, 337, 379, 381; Class C men 61, 219, 225, 228, 231, 235, 238, 241, 245, 249, 253, 258, 262, 267, 272
St. Albans High School (Greenville, SC) 26; Class B men 370
St. Francis Hospital (Greenville, SC) 90; Class A men 317, 320, 323; Class A women 94, 332, 334, 344, 382, 383; Class B men 92, 95, 308, 327, 329, 331, 333, 335, 337; Closed Division men 339, 341

St. Giles (Greenville, SC) Class C men 336
St. Louis Cardinals 17
St. Mary's School 17, 18
Salem Garment Co. (Salem, SC) Class C men 61, 232
Salerni, Mike 70
Sallee, Jack 46, 47, 390
Sally Mill (Greenville, SC): Class B men 72, 244, 248, 252, 256, 261, 275, 281; Class C men 258
Salmans 27
Salter, Roy 150, 155, 158
Saluda High School 403
"Saluda Sam" 390
Sam Chapman Karate (Greenville, SC) Class A women 84, 299, 305, 309
Sam Wyche Sports World (Greenville, SC): Class A women 294; Open Division men 82, 284, 290, 295, 329, 382
Sam's Drive-In (Fountain Inn, SC) Class C men 277, 282
San Antonio Spurs 403
San Diego Conquistadors 76
San Francisco Forty Niners 389
San Souci (Greenville, SC) Class B men 372
Sandel, Bill 175
Sanders, Boyd 62
Sanders, Dave 10
Sanders, Dewey 72
Sanders, James 82
Sanders, Jerry 73
Sangamo Electric Co. (Pickens, SC): Class A men 65, 74, 77, 265, 269, 381; Class A women 63, 65, 67, 212, 223, 226, 232, 235, 239, 242, 246, 249, 254, 259; Class B men 62, 63, 66, 218, 221, 224, 228, 231, 234, 237, 245, 248, 252, 257, 261, 266, 321, 324, 327, 380–382; Class C men 221; Open Division men 380
Sangamo Electric Co. (West Union, SC): Class A women 54; Open Division men 219
Sara Lee Bakery (Greenville, SC): Class B men 333; Closed Division men 340
Saturley's (Greenville, SC) Open Division men 243
Saxon, Charlotte 38
Saxon Mill (Spartanburg, SC) 9; Class A women 105; Class B men 104–107, 109, 113, 377;

Class B women 107; Class C men 107, 108
Sayles Biltmore Bleachery (Biltmore, NC) Class B men 124, 132
SC All Stars (Columbia, SC) Open Division men 70, 73, 247, 255
SC Bulls (Greenville, SC) Class C men 97, 342, 343
Scarborough, O.S. 123, 126, 130, 135, 139
Scarborough, Ronnie 313, 316, 319, 322, 326, 328, 339, 341, 342
Schally, Jean 386
Schlumberger (Greenwood, SC) Class B men 330, 332
Schoolfield Mill (Danville VA) 7, 8; Class A men 5, 7, 8, 103–105; Class A women 8, 105, 106; Class B men 8, 104–106; Class B women 105, 106; Class C men 106
SCN Bank (Greenville, SC) Class B men 271, 276, 281
Scott, Jermaine 93
Scott, Krystal 97, 98
Scott, Willie 78
Seattle Supersonics 86
Seay, Gene 43, 48, 51–53, 378, 380
Secrist, Jerry 67
Select Distributors (Taylors, SC) Class A women 268
Sellers, Doyle 42
Sellers, Sadie 84
Seltz, Larry 380
Selvy, Frank 62, 388, 392, 394, 396
Seneca All Stars (Seneca, SC) Open Division men 216
Seneca High School 385
Settles, Tawambi 383
70th Service Squadron 25
70th Service Squadron (Greenville, SC) Class A men 26, 370
Seward, Jimmy 39
Seward, John 39
Shannon Forest (Greenville, SC) Class C men 277, 282
Sharkheads (Columbia, SC) Open Division men 93, 96, 330, 332, 339, 341
Sharon Corp. (Greenville, SC) Class B men 281, 287
Shaw Properties (Greenville, SC) Class B men 92, 329
Shaw's Boys (Greenville, SC) Open Division men 335

Shays, Dolf 394
Shedd's (Greenville, SC) Class B men 91, 324, 326, 382
Shell, John 96
Shelton, Terry 84
Shelton, Titus 95
Sherrill Mfg. (Dallas, NC) Open Division men 216
Shetley, Rhoten 29
Shockley, Hugh T. 6
Shope, Katherine 12
Showtime (Greenville, SC) Open Division men 96, 339
Shugart, Doris 29
Silvers 12
Silverstreet High School 393
Simmons, Stan 95
Simmons Machinery Co. (Greenville, SC) Class C men 254, 381
Simpsonville Mill (Simpsonville, SC): Class A men 166; Class A women 54, 219; Class B men 14, 39, 113, 114, 121, 128, 156, 160, 164, 177, 181, 188, 195, 199, 225, 275, 304, 377, 378, 382; Class B women 109, 130, 175, 183, 187; Class C men 61, 108, 110, 111, 115, 133, 142, 146, 174, 178, 182, 186, 190, 196, 206, 208, 212, 215, 218, 228, 231, 267, 378, 380
Sims, Jerry 65
Sims, Wardell 380
Sincerely Yours (Greenville, SC) Open Division men 95, 330, 335
Singer Mfg. (Anderson, SC): Class A men 87, 224, 227, 230, 251, 270, 274, 279, 285, 290, 296, 309; Class A women 57-59, 61, 226, 229, 232, 250, 254, 380; Class B men 224, 275, 280
Singer Mfg. (Pickens, SC): Class A men 76, 78, 79, 82, 233, 237, 256, 260, 270, 275, 280, 286, 290, 296, 301, 306, 314, 317, 320, 323, 380; Class B men 225, 228, 238, 245, 247, 281, 293; Class C men 66, 238
Singleton, George 86
Sirrine Co. (Greenville, SC): Class A men 77, 270, 275, 279, 286, 290, 296, 301, 306, 394; Class B men 92, 265, 267, 271, 275, 280, 287, 292, 297, 303, 307, 311, 314, 317, 321, 324, 327, 329, 331, 333
Sirrine Foundation 392

Sisneros, Tim 76
Sissy's Furniture (Columbia, SC) Class A women 96, 341
Sitton, R. 92
Sixers (Columbia, SC) Open Division men 92, 93, 313, 316, 319, 326, 329, 330, 332, 337, 382
Skip's All Stars (Pelzer, SC) Class A men 290
Skocdopole & Co. (Travelers Rest, SC): Class A women 94; Class A women 334
Skywalkers (Piedmont, SC) Class C men 342
Slater-Marietta High School 53
Slater Mill (Slater, SC): Class A men 34, 54, 58, 79, 184, 217, 220, 224, 227, 233, 280, 286, 291, 296, 302, 307, 310, 313, 317, 320, 323, 326, 370, 380, 382; Class A women 47, 49, 50, 52-55, 57, 59, 64, 66, 67, 70, 72, 74, 76, 80, 200, 203, 206, 209, 212, 215, 219, 222, 226, 229, 232, 235, 239, 242, 246, 250, 254, 258, 263, 268, 272, 277, 283, 288, 294, 299, 380, 381, 401; Class B men 37, 44, 74, 78, 80, 128, 137, 144, 153, 163, 172, 177, 181, 189, 198, 202, 204, 207, 211, 257, 262, 266, 271, 275, 280, 370, 372; Class B women 130, 134, 147, 378; Class C men 37, 49, 52, 53, 64, 66, 138, 142, 149, 173, 177, 182, 186, 202, 211, 214, 218, 234, 238, 241; Open Division men 52, 213
Slaughter, Jim 36, 39, 44, 390
Sloan, Norm 395
Small, Curt 97
SMC (Spartanburg, SC) Class B men 335, 383
Smith, A. 97
Smith, Albert 382
Smith, Aug W. 158, 161, 166, 170
Smith, Bob 384
Smith, Carl 92, 93, 382
Smith, Charles 120, 123
Smith, D.K. 184, 187, 223, 226, 229, 233, 236, 239, 243, 246, 250, 255, 259, 264, 269, 273
Smith, Daisy 8
Smith, Dean 59
Smith, Denny 21
Smith, Ellison Durant 20
Smith, Jerry 63, 66
Smith, Jimmy 49, 62
Smith, Joe 36

Smith, Lawrence 118, 120
Smith, Lee 79
Smith, Milton G. 5
Smith, Preston 80
Smith, Ray 86
Smith, Ron 86
Smith, Sara 14
Smith, Steve 96, 382, 383
Smith, Terry 70, 77, 82, 337, 339, 341, 342, 382
Smith, Tom 21
Smith, Travis 97
Smith Brothers (Greenville, SC) Class A women 264
Smith Inc. (Greenville, SC) Class C men 267
Smithsonian Institution 387
Snipe, Arthur 92
Snipes, Ricky 63
Snoddy, Fred 62, 175, 180, 184, 187, 191, 194, 197, 200
Snyder's Auto (Greenville, SC): Class C men 288; Open Division men 89, 90, 319, 322
Sojo, Rhdala 98
Sonics (Abbeville, SC): Class C men 95, 338; Open Division men 85, 86, 90, 295, 300, 305, 309, 316, 319, 322, 326, 329
Sorrell, Robert 59, 67
Soul Patrol (Spartanburg, SC) Open Division men 331
South Aiken High School 89
South Boston Mill (South Boston VA) Class B men 288
South Carolina Book Store (Columbia, SC) Class A women 268
South Carolina Cotton Manufacturer's Association 22
South Carolina Hall of Fame 397
South Carolina Secretary of State 17
South Carolina State University 65, 72
Southeastern Conference 62
Southeastern Electric (Greenville, SC) Open Division men 88, 313
Southeastern Freight (Greenville, SC): Class B men 96, 298, 303, 307, 330, 331, 333, 335, 337; Class C men 95, 336; Closed Division men 96, 340, 341
Southeastern-Kusan (Greenville, SC) Class B men 281, 287, 292
Southeastern Products (Green-

ville, SC) 391; Class B men 85; Class C men 83, 84, 94–96, 294, 299, 304, 334, 336, 338, 340, 343; Open Division men 93–96, 332, 334, 337
Southern Bank (Greenville, SC): Class A men 317; Class B men 88, 304, 311, 314; Open Division men 70, 247
Southern Baptists 30
Southern Bell (Greenville, SC) Class A men 256, 260, 274
Southern Bleachery (Taylors, SC): Class A men 18, 20, 22, 23, 25, 29, 42, 43, 56, 58, 120, 124, 126, 132, 135, 139, 143, 147, 150, 155, 159, 162, 166, 171, 176, 180, 184; Class B men 21, 43, 107, 116, 119, 133, 140, 145, 148, 153, 177, 181, 189, 204, 207, 211, 379; Class C men 21, 36, 107, 108, 113, 114, 125, 129, 141, 165, 169, 173, 178, 186, 190, 206
Southern Conference 29, 39, 43, 59, 63, 395, 403
Southern Depot 48
Southern Filters (Greenville, SC) Class C men 69, 238, 241, 245, 249, 258
Southern Franklin Processing (Greenville, SC) Class B men 141, 144, 148, 164, 168, 171, 180, 195, 199, 202
Southern Industrial Mechanical (Greenville, SC) Class C men 70, 249
Southern League 397
Southern Oaks (Piedmont, SC) Class C men 343
Southern Professional Basketball League 31
Southern Textile Athletic Association 9, 10, 12, 13, 15–18, 32, 39, 42, 56, 69, 77, 82, 88, 90, 390; Hall of Fame 52, 58, 90, 374, 392
Southern Weaving (Greenville, SC): Class B men 225, 241, 244, 276, 281, 287, 292; Class C men 206, 212, 218
Southern Worsted (Greenville, SC): Class A women 21, 125, 129, 142; Class B men 114, 117, 119, 121, 124, 141, 152; Class B women 120, 123; Class C men 115, 149, 173
Southers, Brantley 84
Spain & Prince Sonics (Greenville, SC) Class C men 340, 342, 343
Spake, Henry 229, 233, 236, 239, 243, 246, 250, 255, 259, 264, 269, 273, 278, 284, 289, 295, 300
Spartan All Stars (Spartanburg, SC) Class C men 276, 282
Spartan Express (Greer, SC) Class A women 239
Spartan Foods (Spartanburg, SC) Class B men 85, 304
Spartan Leasing (Spartanburg, SC) Class A women 73, 74, 264
Spartan Mill (Spartanburg, SC) 29; Class A men 108, 109, 119, 135; Class B men 14, 106, 107, 114, 116, 127, 133, 148; Class B women 120, 377; Class C men 111, 113, 119, 122, 125, 138, 141, 186
Spartanburg Junior College 43
Spartanburg YMCA (Spartanburg, SC) Open Division men 306, 309
Spaulding Fibers (Spartanburg, SC) Open Division men 64, 236, 240
Speaks, Lamont 98
Speed Queen (Chattanooga, TN) Open Division men 48, 49, 210
Spindale Mill (Spindale, NC): Class A men 123, 377; Class B men 121; Class C men 133
Spirit Express (Memphis, TN) Open Division men 330, 332
Sportsman Shop (Charleston, SC) Class A women 96, 341
Spotts, Alfred 379
Spray Mill (Spray, NC): Class A men 106; Class B men 137
Springfield, Ollie B. 390, 391
Springfield College 3, 4
Springs, Holmes B. 7
Springs Mill (Lancaster, SC): Class B men 171, 176; Class B women 174, 178
Staggs, Tyshawn 95
Stallard, Kent 93
Stallcup, Virgil 29
Stalworth, H.C. 108
Stamey, David 93, 95
Stancell, C.F. 143, 147
Stanly Mill (Oakboro, NC): Class A women 19, 129, 134, 139; Class B women 123, 125; Open Division men 54, 219
Stansell, Frog 43
Stark Mill (Hogansville, GA) Class B men 124, 127
Steading, Ralph 14
Steak & Waffle (Seneca, SC) Open Division men 94, 331, 332
Steel Heddle (Greenville, SC) Class B men 54, 214, 217, 220, 380
Steele, Dr. 4, 98
Sterling, Ken 92
Sterling (Greenville, SC) Class C men 95, 328, 338
Stevens Aviation (Greenville, SC) Class B men 318, 330
Stevens Beechcraft (Greer, SC) Class A men 302, 307, 310
Stevens Rockets (Greer, SC) Open Division men 50, 210, 213
Stewart, Joe 342
Stewart, Terry 90
Stewart's Apparel Shop 18
Stoddard, Frank 64
Stone Mfg. (Greenville, SC): Class A women 206, 209, 213, 222, 250, 254, 379; Class B men 54, 204, 208, 211, 214, 217, 221, 224, 248, 252, 378; Class C men 49, 209, 212, 215
Storey, Veo 187
Stouffer's (Greer, SC) Class A men 314
Stowe, Bob 26, 27, 33, 42, 43, 97, 389, 391, 393
Stowe, Richard 273, 278
Stribbling, J.W. 106
Stringer, Keith 98
Stroud, Judy 78
Stroupe, Bruce 180, 184, 187, 191, 194, 197, 200, 203, 207, 210
Style Crafters (Greenville, SC) Class B men 205, 207, 379
Subway (Greenville, SC) Class C men 338
Suddeth, Charles 20
Suddeth, Rags 43
Sullivan, Everick 90
Sullivan, Rodney 88
Sullivan Hardware (Anderson, SC) Class B men 252, 257, 261
Sullivan Pontiac (Anderson, SC) Open Division men 274
Sullivan's Sonics (Greenville, SC) Class C men 336, 338, 340, 342, 383
Sumner, Jeff 83
Suns (Greenville, SC) Class C men 342
Sunshine Cleaners (Columbia, SC) Open Division men 62, 64, 227, 229, 233, 380, 400

Sutherland, Jim 54
Suttles, G.C. 106, 110, 112, 113
Sycamore Mill (Sycamore, AL) Class B men 125, 128
Sylacauga Mill (Sylacauga, AL): Class A men 124, 127; Class B men 164
Syracuse Nationals 394
Systems & Service (Greenville, SC) Class C men 325

T & S Brass & Bronze Works (Greenville, SC) Class B men 308
T-Shirts Plus (Greenville, SC) Class A women 96, 332, 338, 341, 382
Talley, Lewis 64
Talley, Randy 61
Taylor, Lanny 63, 64
Taylor, Larry 70
Taylors (Taylors, SC) Class A women 372
Taylors High School (Taylors, SC) 21; Class B men 371
Taylors Mill (Taylors, SC): Class A men 70, 79, 240, 244, 247, 251, 256, 260, 265, 270, 274, 279, 381; Class B men 248, 252, 381
Teague Award 388
Teaster, Bud 213
Tele. Sec. (Greenville, SC) Class B men 72, 253
Tennessee Eastman (Kingsport, TN): Class A men 158, 162; Class B men 148, 152
Terry, Curtis 207, 210, 213, 216, 219, 223, 226, 229, 232, 236, 239, 243, 246, 250, 255, 259, 264, 269, 273, 278, 284
Texize Chemical (Greenville, SC): Class A women 68, 72–74, 243, 245, 249, 254, 258, 263, 381, 398; Class B men 241, 248; Open Division men 47, 68–70, 72, 73, 207, 223, 243, 246, 251, 255, 381
Textile Hall 5, 7–10, 17–19, 22, 31, 37, 41, 45, 47, 73, 87, 93, 384, 385, 390, 395, 396
Textile Industrial Institute (Spartanburg, SC) Class B men 104
Textile League baseball 5
Textile Plating (Greenville, SC) Class A women 219
Textron (Greenville, SC) Class B men 331, 333
TFBC (Greenville, SC) Class C men 334

Thackston, _____ 22
Thackston, Doug 381
Thomas, Clarence 26, 52, 143, 147, 150, 155, 158, 161, 166, 170, 175, 180, 184, 187, 191, 194, 197, 200, 203, 206, 210, 213, 216, 219, 223, 226, 229, 232, 236, 239, 243, 246, 250, 255, 259, 264, 269, 273, 278, 284, 289, 295, 300, 305, 309, 312, 315, 319, 322, 325, 328, 330, 332, 334, 336
Thomas, D. 92
Thomas, Lucille 7, 12, 58, 123, 126, 131
Thomason, Bill 38
Thomason, James 54
Thompson, Jack 64
Thompson, Jimmie 18, 126, 131, 135
Thompson, Orval 180, 184
Thompson, Viola 29
Thorn in the Side Award 395
Thornton, Eual 15
Thornton, John 72
Threads Inc. (Gastonia, NC) Class B men 137
349th Service Squadron (Greenville, SC) Class A men 25, 26, 370
3M (Greenville, SC): Class A men 82, 275, 279, 285, 291, 296, 301 Class B men 86, 94, 275, 280, 286, 292, 297, 302, 307, 311, 314, 317, 324, 330, 331, 333
TIC (Greenville, SC) Class B men 324
Tillinghast, Dave 17
Time Out (Greenville, SC) Open Division men 285
Timmerman, George Bell 36
The Tire Exchange (Greer, SC) Class C men 249, 253, 258
TKO (Greenville, SC) Class A women 94, 334
TMR Inc. (Fairforest, SC) Open Division men 76, 269
Todd-Moore (Columbia, SC) Open Division men 53, 216, 220, 380
Tolbert's (North Charleston, SC) Open Division men 68, 240, 243
Tollison, Dudley 216, 219
Top Gun (Greenville, SC) Open Division men 92, 93, 328, 330, 332, 382
Torrington Co. (Clinton, SC) Class B men 221, 330

Touring Sports BMW (Greenville, SC) Class B men 324
Tramps Inc. (Greenville, SC) Class A women 294
Transit Homes (Greenville, SC): Class C men 267, 272, 277, 283; Open Division men 68, 72–74, 236, 240, 243, 247, 251, 255, 259, 381
Travel Inn (Greenville, SC) Class C men 288, 304, 308
Travelers Rest High School 74
Travis, Greg 382
Treadway, Joe 39
Tri Dip Inc. (Columbia, SC) Open Division men 82, 278, 284, 289, 295, 320
Tribble, Annie 43, 73
Tribble's Trotters 73
Triple Play (Greenville, SC): Class A women 94, 96, 334, 336, 338, 341; Class C women 339
Troutman, Paul 112, 113
Trussell 11
Tryon Mill (Tryon, GA) Class B men 127
Tryon Mill (Tryon, NC) Class B men 105
Turner, Rob 96
Turpin, Leoda 28
25th Service Group (Greenville, SC) Class A men 25
25th Service Squadron (Greenville, SC) Class A men 370
Tyler, Dick 49, 51, 52

UCBA (Greenville, SC) Class C men 96, 340
UCBA Jr. (Greenville, SC) Class C men 342
UCBA Sr. (Greenville, SC) Class C men 342
Ungerricht, Robert 255
Union Bleachery (Greenville, SC) 392; Class A men 30, 143, 148, 151, 159, 162, 167, 194, 371, 378; Class A women 146, 235; Class B men 25–27, 32, 37, 39, 48, 57, 62, 116, 119, 128, 137, 140, 177, 189, 191, 199, 202, 205, 208, 211, 214, 217, 220, 224, 234, 237, 370, 381, 385, 392; Class B women 130, 134, 143, 161; Class C men 22, 44, 61, 110, 115, 119, 122, 133, 138, 149, 154, 157, 160, 164, 169, 173, 178, 182, 186, 189, 196, 199, 202, 205, 208, 212, 215, 229, 232; Open Division men 278

Union Carbide (Simpsonville, SC): Class A men 297, 302, 307, 310, 313, 317; Class B men 288, 291, 382
Union High School (Union, SC) 392
United Insurance (Greenville, SC) Class B men 314, 321
United States Olympic Committee 386
University of Alabama 8
University of Georgia 67, 70, 95
University of Kansas 390
University of Massachusetts 93
University of Miami (FL) 52
University of North Carolina 29, 33, 47, 57, 59, 388, 390
University of South Carolina 4, 20, 29, 36, 38, 41, 43, 50, 54, 62, 64, 65, 74, 76, 78, 80, 84, 90, 93, 95, 96, 400
University of South Carolina–Spartanburg 81, 88, 90
University of Tennessee 39, 80
University of Texas 79
University of West Virginia 390
UNV (Greenville, SC) Open Division men 97, 341
Upperstate (Chattanooga, TN) Class C men 95, 97, 338, 340, 342, 343, 383
Upstate Jrs. (Chattanooga, TN) Class C men 343
Upstate Lady Sonics (Greenville, SC) Class C women 97, 98, 342, 344
Upstate Srs. (Chattanooga, TN) Class C men 97, 343
US Post Office (Greenville, SC): Class B men 84, 88, 293, 298, 303, 307, 311, 314, 318, 321, 324; Closed Division men 343
US Post Office (Seneca, SC) Class A men 304
USA Wet (Greenville, SC) Open Division men 332
USCS (Spartanburg, SC): Class A women 341; Open Division men 337, 339
USCS Club (Spartanburg, SC) Open Division men 96
Utah Lakers 398

V.A. Jets (Columbia, SC) Open Division men 89, 92, 309, 313, 316, 319, 326, 329
V-E Day 27
V-J Day 27
Valdese Community Center (Valdese, NC) Class B men 153
Vanden Bergh (Greenville, SC) Class B men 330
Vanderbilt University 72, 73
Varinit (Greenville, SC): Class C men 262; Open Division men 260
Varner, Charles 38
Vaughn, Marty 72–74, 76
Vaughn Woodwork (Duncan, SC) Class C men 272
Veeder-Root (Greenville, SC): Class C men 253; Open Division men 255
Verner, C.V. 108, 110, 112, 113, 116, 118, 120, 123, 126, 130, 135
Verner Springs Water Company 20
Vernon Heating & Air (Greenville, SC) Class B men 94, 333
Vickers, Sue 49, 50, 52–55, 401
Victor Mill (Greer, SC) 392; Class A men 7, 19, 29, 36, 41, 42, 103–106, 108, 109, 118, 120, 124, 126, 131, 135, 147, 151, 171, 176, 191, 194, 204, 377, 378; Class A women 104, 105, 112; Class AA men 110; Class B men 41, 43, 104, 105, 113, 114, 128, 172, 176, 181, 185, 189, 192, 195, 199, 202, 207, 247, 252, 281, 287, 292, 381; Class B women 31, 108, 109, 130, 175, 179, 183, 187; Class C men 105–108, 110, 111, 115, 117, 121, 125, 129, 133, 137, 142, 146, 149, 154, 157, 160, 164, 169, 173, 178, 183, 186, 190, 193, 196, 199, 202, 205, 208, 212, 377, 391; Open Division men 50, 198, 207, 379, 394
Victor Mill YMCA (Greer, SC) 82
Video Express (Greenville, SC) Class B men 321
Vietnam War 64
Vince Perone's Restaurant (Greenville, SC) Open Division men 86, 309
Virginia Maid Hosiery (Pulaski, VA) Class A men 148
Virginia Squires 400
Virginia Tech University 70
Voiselle, Bill 23

Wade, Bill 56
Wade Hampton High School 61
Wake Forest University 30, 33, 76
Wakefield, Billy 25
Waldrop, Bob 379
Waldrop, Ford 41
Walhalla Mill (Walhalla, SC): Class A men 112, 116, 119, 121, 124, 126, 131, 135, 140, 144, 148, 151; Class A women 107, 226, 380; Class B men 111; Class B women 105, 110; Class C men 105, 107, 108, 110, 117
Walker, _____ 25
Walker, Miriam 90
Walker, Nathaniel 76
Wall, Herbert 20
Wall, Jim 52
The Wall Street Transcript 392
Wallace, A.J. 10
Wallace, Albert 166, 170, 175
Wallace, Grady 41, 54, 55, 62, 64, 233, 236, 239, 243, 246, 400
Wallace Mill (Union, SC): Class B men 104, 105; Class B women 105
Walmart (Greenville, SC) Class C men 340, 383
Walsh, Billy 73
Walters, Deran 33
Wangner Systems (Greenville, SC) Class B men 92, 291, 297, 307, 312, 327, 329
Ward, Joe 84
Ware, Billy 69
Ware Shoals High School 67
Ware Shoals Mill (Ware Shoals, SC) 401, 402; Class A men 85, 104, 116, 121, 124, 127, 131, 274, 279, 285, 290, 296, 301, 306, 310, 382; Class A women 47, 67, 73, 74, 209, 242, 255, 258, 263, 401, 402; Class B men 29, 30, 47, 65, 72, 109, 111, 113, 162, 177, 241, 244, 248, 252, 257, 261, 266, 271; Class B women 115, 118, 165, 169, 174, 179, 183, 377; Class C men 31, 46, 138, 164, 178, 193, 209
Washington, Brenda 97
Washington, Lisa 86
Washington Bullets 37
Washington Capitals 400
Washington Capitols 397
Washington City (Greenville, SC) Class C men 93, 330, 334, 338, 342
Washington City Association (Greenville, SC) Open Division men 85, 301

432   Index

Washington Mill (Winston-Salem, NC) Open Division men 58, 62, 63, 227, 230, 233, 380
Washington Senators 29, 397
Washington State University 403
Watson, Curtis 383
Watson, Dan 380
Watts Mill (Laurens, SC) 29; Class B men 163, 168, 172; Class B women 165, 175
WAXA-TV 90
Wayland Baptist College 388, 398
WCCP (Clemson, SC) Class A women 97, 342, 344
Weems, Kelsey 88
Weimer, Carl 15
Welborn, Frances 259, 264, 273, 278
Wellford-Lyman-Tucapau High School (Spartanburg, SC) 27; Class B men 371
Wells, Chubby 81, 86, 89, 95, 403
West Gantt (Greenville, SC) Class B men 372
West Gantt High School 384
West Greenville Community Center (Greenville, SC) Class A women 289, 294
Western Carolina (Simpsonville, SC) Class C men 340
Western Carolina League 389
Western Carolina University 62, 66, 68, 399
Western Carolina V (Simpsonville, SC) Class C men 96, 340
Western Kentucky University 68
Western 3A All Stars (Simpsonville, SC) Class C women 339
Westinghouse (Duncan, SC) Class B men 333
Westinghouse (Greenville, SC) Class B men 318, 321
Westmoreland, Ernest 382
Westmoreland, Jim 162, 166, 170, 175, 180
Westvaco (Charleston, SC) Class A women 68, 242, 246, 250, 254
WFBC Radio 18, 20
Whaley, Randy 39
Whisnant, Art 54, 65, 380
White, Alton 37
White, Howard 80
White, Johnny 74, 77, 382
White, Len 381
White, Leonard 78
White, Nera 402
White, Ronald 76, 77, 82, 84–86
Whitfield, Jim 49
Whitis, Dick 54
Whitlock, Gary 62
Whitlock, Wilma 20, 27, 377
Whitmire, Horace 32, 135, 139, 143, 147, 150, 155, 161, 166, 170, 175, 179, 184, 187, 191, 194, 197, 200, 203
Whitney Auto Auction (Greer, SC) Closed Division men 340
Whitney Mill (Spartanburg, SC): Class A men 108; Class B men 104–107; Class B women 105, 107, 109
Whitten, Fred 25, 28
Whitten Village (Clinton, SC) Class B men 286
Whittington, Earl 44, 52
Wholesale Fence Co. (Winston-Salem, NC) Class A women 255
Who's Who (Greenville, SC) Class C men 343
Wilbanks, Willie 25, 26, 37, 39, 65, 89, 175, 180, 184, 187, 191, 194, 197, 200, 203, 207, 210, 213, 216, 219, 223, 226, 229, 232, 236, 239, 243, 246, 250, 255, 259, 264, 269, 273, 278, 284, 289, 295, 300, 305, 309, 312, 315, 401
Wiles, Jim 54
Williams, James 78
Williams, Jerome 381
Williams, Joel 73
Williams, John 382
Williams, Maria 97
Williams, Renee 97
Williams, Shoomond 94
Williams, Ward 28, 29, 33, 36, 42–44, 56, 197, 200, 203, 207, 210, 213, 216, 219, 223, 226, 229, 232, 236, 239, 243, 246, 250, 255, 259, 264, 269, 273, 278, 284, 289, 295, 300, 305, 312, 315, 319, 322, 325, 328, 330, 332, 334, 336, 339, 385, 394–396
William's Enterprise (Greenville, SC) Class A women 319
Williams Gin (Dacusville, SC) Class C men 222
Williams, Williams & Knight (Greenville, SC) Class B men 328
Williamston All Stars (Williamston, SC) Open Division men 56, 223
Wilson, Dag 43, 52, 53
Wilson, Dennis 66
Wilson, Jack 380
Wilson, Jackie 66
Wilson, James 45
Wilson, Jimmy 62
Wilson, Kathy 80, 81
Wilson, Stanley 62
Wilson Lewith Machinery (Charlotte, NC) Open Division men 227
Winck, W.V. 8
Wingate College 54
Winn Dixie (Greenville, SC) Class B men 299, 303, 308
Winnsboro Mill (Winnsboro, SC): Class A men 16, 118, 121, 123, 127, 131, 139, 144, 147, 155, 378; Class A women 20, 125, 139; Class B men 14, 114, 117, 136; Class B women 116, 118, 120, 123; Class C men 134
Winthrop College 37, 81, 396
Winthrop University 402
Wix, Don 381
WLW Radio 13
Wofford College (Spartanburg, SC) 16, 20, 43, 58, 86, 393, 394; Open Division men 284
Women's Basketball Coaches Association 399
Wood, J.W. 110
Wood, Louise 20, 378
Wood, Lucille 21
Wooden, John 97
Woods, Dolly 38
Woodside Mill (Fountain Inn, SC) Class B men 127, 133
Woodside Mill (Greenville, SC) 4, 12, 384, 401, 402; Class A men 5, 7–9, 25, 27, 44, 103–106, 108, 109, 112, 114, 131, 135, 148, 159, 191, 370, 371, 385; Class A women 9, 107, 197; Class B men 8, 18, 21, 25–29, 43, 104–107, 109, 111, 113, 124, 128, 137, 141, 145, 148, 159, 163, 167, 172, 177, 181, 184, 188, 202, 205, 271, 276, 281, 287, 292, 298, 303, 370–372, 378; Class B women 12, 31, 106, 110, 116, 143, 150, 158, 161, 165, 170, 175, 179, 184, 187, 191, 194, 378; Class C men 37, 45, 46, 53, 61, 105–108, 110, 111, 113, 115, 119, 122, 129, 133, 137, 142, 146, 149, 154, 157, 161, 164, 168, 173, 178, 183, 185,

190, 193, 196, 203, 205, 208, 218, 222, 225, 228, 231; Class C women 108
Woodside Mill YMCA (Greenville, SC) 23
Woodward, J.L. 108
Wooten, Earl 23, 25–27, 29–34, 36, 38, 39, 41–44, 48, 55, 59, 97, 239, 243, 246, 250, 255, 259, 264, 269, 273, 378, 385, 387, 389, 390, 392–398, 402
Wooten, Sara 38
Wooten, Thelma 395
World Basketball Tournament 398
World Series 17
World University Games 403
WPJM (Greer, SC) Class A women 344
Wray, Todd 96
Wray, Wayne 96
Wren High School 61
Wright, Dick 47, 65, 379
Wright, Roy 92
Wunda Weve (Greenville, SC) Class B men 331, 333, 335, 337, 383
Wunda Weve Carpets (Greenville, SC) Class A women 46, 67, 209, 242, 245, 250
Wyandotte Mill (Conestee, SC) Open Division men 51, 213
Wyatt, Horace 78
Wyatt, Reba 23
Wylie, Seth 96
Wynn, Ray 22, 197
Wynn, Tom 380

Yates, Jim 66
YMCA (Greenville, SC) Closed Division men 96, 97, 340–342
Yockel, Vince 47, 52, 53, 56, 57, 380
Young, David 96
Young, Ed 90
Young, Glen 95
Young, McBruce 78, 79
Young, Tim 97
Young Harris College 52
Young-Love Fabrics (Charlotte, NC) Open Division men 74, 76, 255, 260, 269

Z Control (Greenville, SC) Open Division men 92, 329
Zaharias, Babe Didrickson 385
Zatezalo, Butch 68, 69